Fourth Amendment
Supreme Court Decisions

Edited by Robert Dittmer

Note on the text: most italics and bold has been removed.

Acknowledgements

Websites (in no particular order):

www.law.cornell.edu
supreme.justia.com
caselaw.findlaw.com
Public.Resource.Org
Openjurist.org
scholar.google.com
en.wikipedia.org

Table of Contents

Contents

Introduction

From the Virginia Declaration of Rights, principal author George Mason (1776):

SEC. 10. That general warrants, whereby an officer or messenger may be commanded to search suspected places without evidence of a fact committed, or to seize any person or persons not named, or whose offense is not particularly described and supported by evidence, are grievous and oppressive and ought not to be granted."

From the Maryland Declaration of Rights (1776):

"XXIII. That all warrants, without oath or affirmation, to search suspected places, or to seize any person or property, are grievous and oppressive; and all general warrants-to search suspected places, or to apprehend suspected persons, without naming or describing the place, or the person in special-are illegal, and ought not to be granted.

XXIV. That there ought to be no forfeiture of any part of the estate of any person, for any crime except murder, or treason against the State, and then only on conviction and attainder."

From A Declaration of the Rights of the Inhabitants of the Commonwealth of Massachusetts, principal author John Adams (1780):

"Art. XIV. Every subject has a right to be secure from all unreasonable searches and seizures of his person, his houses, his papers, and all his possessions. All warrants, therefore, are contrary to this right, if the cause or foundation of them be not previously supported by oath or affirmation, and if the order in the warrant to a civil officer, to make search in suspected places, or to arrest one or more suspected persons, or to seize their property, be not accompanied with a special designation of the persons or objects of search,

arrest, or seizure; and no warrant ought to be issued but in cases, and with the formalities, prescribed by the laws."

From the Pennsylvania Dissent (Dec 12, 1787):

"5. That warrants unsupported by evidence, whereby any officer or messenger may be commanded or required to search suspected places, or to seize any person or persons, his or their property, not particularly described, are grievous and oppressive, and shall not be granted either by the magistrates of the federal government or others."

From Virginia Ratification Convention (June 27, 1788):

"Fourteenth, That every freeman has a right to be secure from all unreasonable searches and seizures of his person, his papers, and property; all warrants, therefore, to search suspected places, or seize any freeman, his papers, or property, without information on oath (or affirmation of a person religiously scrupulous of taking an oath) of legal and sufficient cause, are grievous and oppressive; and all general warrants to search suspected places, or to apprehend any suspected person, without specially naming or describing the place or person, are dangerous, and ought not to be granted."

From James Madison's speech offering the amendments (June 8, 1789):

"The rights of the people to be secured in their persons; their houses, their papers, and their other property, from all unreasonable searches and seizures, shall not be violated by warrants issued without probable cause, supported by oath or affirmation, or not particularly describing the places to be searched, or the persons or things to be seized."

From Rhode Island Ratifying Convention (1790):

"XIV. That every person has a right to be secure from all unreasonable searches and seizures of his person his papers, or his property; and therefore, that all warrants to search suspected places, to seize any person, his papers, or his property, without information upon oath or affirmation of sufficient cause, are grievous and oppressive; and that all general warrants (or such in which the place or person suspected are not particularly designated) are dangerous, and ought not to be granted."

From Amendments to the United States Constitution (1791):

"4. The right of the people to be secure in their persons, houses, papers, and effects, against unreasonable searches and seizures, shall not be violated, and no Warrants shall issue, but upon probable cause, supported by Oath or affirmation, and particularly describing the place to be searched, and the persons or things to be seized."

Boyd v. US (Feb 1, 1886) [Notes omitted]

MR. JUSTICE BRADLEY delivered the opinion of the court.

This was an information filed by the District Attorney of the United States in the District Court for the Southern District of New York, in July, 1884, in a cause of seizure and forfeiture of property, against thirty-five cases of plate glass, seized by the collector as forfeited to the United States, under § 12 of the "Act to amend the customs revenue laws, and to repeal moieties," passed June 22, 1874, 18 Stat. 186.

It is declared by that section that any owner, importer, consignee, &c., who shall, with intent to defraud the revenue, make, or attempt to make, any entry of imported merchandise by means of any fraudulent or false invoice, affidavit, letter or paper, or by means of any false statement, written or verbal, or who shall be guilty of any willful act or omission by means whereof the United States shall be deprived of the lawful duties, or any portion thereof, accruing upon the merchandise, or any portion thereof, embraced or referred to in such invoice, affidavit, letter, paper, or statement, or affected by such act or omission, shall for each offence be fined in any sum not exceeding $5,000 nor less than $50, or be imprisoned for any time not exceeding two years, or both; and, in addition to such fine, such merchandise shall be forfeited.

The charge was that the goods in question were imported into the United States to the port of New York, subject to the payment of duties, and that the owners or agents of said merchandise, or other person unknown, committed the alleged fraud, which was described in the words of the statute. The plaintiffs in error entered a claim for the goods, and pleaded that they did not become forfeited in manner and form as alleged. On the trial of the cause, it became important to show the quantity and value of the glass contained in twenty-nine cases previously imported. To do this, the district attorney offered in evidence an order made by the District Judge under § 5 of the same act of June 2, 1874, directing notice under seal of the court to be given to the claimants, requiring them to produce the invoice of the twenty-nine cases. The claimants, in obedience to the notice, but objecting to its validity and to the constitutionality of the law, produced the invoice, and. when it was offered in evidence by the district attorney. they objected to its reception on the ground that, in a suit for forfeiture, no evidence can be compelled from the claimants themselves, and also that the statute, so far as it compels production of evidence to be used against the claimants, is unconstitutional and void.

The evidence being received, and the trial closed, the jury found a verdict for the United

States, condemning the thirty-five cases of glass which were seized, and judgment of forfeiture was given. This judgment was affirmed by the Circuit Court, and the decision of that court is now here for review.

As the question raised upon the order for the production by the claimants of the invoice of the twenty-nine cases of glass, and the proceedings had thereon, is not only an important one in the determination of the present case, but is a very grave question of constitutional law, involving the personal security, and privileges and immunities of the citizen, we will set forth the order at large. After the title of the court and term, it reads as follows, to-wit:

"The United States of America"

"against"

"E. A. B., 1-35, Thirty-five Vases of Plate Glass."

"Whereas the attorney of the United States for the Southern District of New York has filed in this court a written motion in the above-entitled action, showing that said action is a suit or proceeding other than criminal, arising under the customs revenue laws of the United States, and not for penalties, now pending undetermined in this court, and that, in his belief, a certain invoice or paper belonging to and under the control of the claimants herein will tend to prove certain allegations set forth in said written motion, hereto annexed, made by him on behalf of the United States in said action, to-wit, the invoice from the Union Plate Glass Company or its agents, covering the twenty-nine cases of plate glass marked G.H.B., imported from Liverpool, England into the port of New York in the vessel Baltic, and entered by E. A. Boyd & Sons at the office of the collector of customs of the port and collection district aforesaid on April 7th, 1884, on entry No. 47,108:"

"Now, therefore, by virtue of the power in the said court vested by section 5 of the act of June 22, 1874, entitled 'An act to amend the customs-revenue laws and to repeal moieties,' it is ordered that a notice under the seal of this court, and signed by the clerk thereof, be issued to the claimants, requiring them to produce the invoice or paper aforesaid before this court in the courtrooms thereof in the United States post-office and courthouse building in the city of New York on October 16th, 1884, at eleven o'clock a.m., and thereafter at such other times as the court shall appoint, and that said United States attorney and his assistants and such persons as he shall designate shall be allowed before the court, and under its direction and in the presence of the attorneys for the claimants, if they shall attend, to make examination of said invoice or paper and to take copies thereof; but the claimants or their agents or attorneys shall have, subject to the order of the court, the custody of such invoice or paper, except pending such examination."

The 5th section of the act of June 22, 1874, under which this order was made, is in the following words, to-wit:

"In all suits and proceedings other than criminal arising under any of the revenue laws of the United States, the attorney representing the government, whenever in his belief any business book, invoice, or paper belonging to, or under the control of, the defendant or claimant will tend to prove any allegation made by the United States, may make a written motion particularly describing such book, invoice, or paper and setting forth the allegation which he expects to prove, and thereupon the court in which suit or proceeding is pending may, at its discretion, issue a notice to the defendant or claimant to produce such book, invoice, or paper in court, at a day and hour to be specified in said notice, which, together with a copy of said motion, shall be served formally on the defendant or claimant by the United States marshal by delivering to him a certified copy thereof, or otherwise serving the same as original notices of suit in the same court are served, and if the defendant or claimant shall fail or refuse to produce such book, invoice, or paper in obedience to such notice, the allegations stated in the said motion shall be taken as confessed unless his failure or refusal to produce the same shall be explained to the satisfaction of the court. And if produced, the said attorney shall be permitted, under the direction of the court, to make examination (at which examination the defendant, or claimant, or his agent, may be present) of such entries in said book, invoice, or paper as relate to or tend to prove the allegation aforesaid, and may offer the same in evidence on behalf of the United States. But the owner of said books and papers, his agent or attorney, shall have, subject to the order of the court, the custody of them, except pending their examination in court as aforesaid."

18 Stat. 187.

This section was passed in lieu of the 2d section of the act of March 2, 1867, entitled

"An act to regulate the Disposition of the Proceeds of Fines, Penalties, and forfeitures incurred under the Laws relating to the Customs and for other purposes,"

14 Stat. 547, which section of said last-mentioned statute authorized the district judge, on complaint and affidavit that any fraud on the revenue had been committed by any person interested or engaged in the importation of merchandise, to issue his warrant to the marshal to enter any premises where any invoices, books, or papers were deposited relating to such merchandise, and take possession of such books and papers and produce them before said judge, to be subject to his order, and allowed to be examined by the collector, and to be retained as long as the judge should deem necessary. This law, being in force at the time of the revision, was incorporated into § 3091, 3092, 3093 of the Revised Statutes.

The section last recited was passed in lieu of the the section of the act of March 3, 1863, entitled

"An act to prevent and punish Frauds upon the Revenue, to provide for the more certain and speedy Collection of Claims in Favor of the United States, and for other Purposes."

12 Stat. 737. The 7th section of this act was in substance the same as the 2d section of the act of 1867, except that the warrant was to be directed to the collector instead of the marshal. It was the first legislation of the kind that ever appeared on the statute books of the United States, and, as seen from its date, was adopted at a period of great national excitement, when the powers of the government were subjected to a severe strain to protect the national existence.

The clauses of the Constitution to which it is contended that these laws are repugnant are the Fourth and Fifth Amendments. The Fourth declares,

"The right of the people to be secure in their persons, houses, papers, and effects, against unreasonable searches and seizures, shall not be violated, and no warrants shall issue, but upon probable cause, supported by oath or affirmation, and particularly describing the place to be searched, and the persons or things to be seized."

The Fifth Article, amongst other things, declares that no person "shall be compelled in any criminal case to be a witness against himself."

But, in regard to the Fourth Amendment, it is contended that, whatever might have been alleged against the constitutionality of the acts of 1863 and 1867, that of 1874, under which the order in the present case as made, is free from constitutional objection because it does not authorize the search and seizure of books and papers, but only requires the defendant or claimant to produce them. That is so, but it declares that, if he does not produce them, the allegations which it is affirmed they will prove shall be taken as confessed. This is tantamount to compelling their production, for the prosecuting attorney will always be sure to state the evidence expected to be derived from them as strongly as the case will admit of. It is true that certain aggravating incidents of actual search and seizure, such as forcible entry into a man's house and searching amongst his papers, are wanting, and, to this extent, the proceeding under the act of 1874 is a mitigation of that which was authorized by the former acts; but it accomplishes the substantial object of those acts in forcing from a party evidence against himself. It is our opinion, therefore, that a compulsory production of a man's private papers to establish a criminal charge against him, or to forfeit his property, is within the scope of the Fourth Amendment to the Constitution in all cases in which a search and seizure would be, because it is a material ingredient, and effects the sole object and purpose of search and seizure.

The principal question, however, remains to be considered. Is a search and seizure, or, what is equivalent thereto, a compulsory production of a man's private papers, to be used in evidence against him in a proceeding to forfeit his property for alleged fraud against the revenue laws -- is such a proceeding for such a purpose an "unreasonable search and seizure" within the meaning of the Fourth Amendment of the Constitution? or is it a legitimate proceeding? It is contended by the counsel for the government, that it is a legitimate proceeding, sanctioned by long usage and the authority of judicial decision. No doubt long usage, acquiesced in by the courts, goes a long way to prove that there is some plausible ground or reason for it in the law, or in the historical facts which have imposed a particular construction of the law favorable to such usage. It is a maxim that consuetudo est optimus interpres legum, and another maxim that contemporanea expositio est optima et fortissima in lege. But we do not find any long usage or an contemporary construction of the Constitution which would justify any of the acts of Congress now under consideration As before

stated, the act of 1863 was the first act in this country, and, we might say, either in this country or in England, so far as we have been able to ascertain, which authorized the search and seizure of a man's private papers, or the compulsory production of them, for the purpose of using then in evidence against him in a criminal case or in a proceeding to enforce the forfeiture of his property. Even the act under which the obnoxious writs of assistance were issued [1] did not go as far as this, but only authorized the examination of ships and vessels, and persons found therein, for the purpose of finding goods prohibited to be imported or exported, or on which the duties were not paid, and to enter into and search any suspected vaults, cellars, or warehouses for such goods. The search for and seizure of stolen or forfeited goods, or goods liable to duties and concealed to avoid the payment thereof, are totally different things from a search for and seizure of a man's private books and papers for the purpose of obtaining information therein contained, or of using them as evidence against him. The two things differ toto coelo. In the one case, the government is entitled to the possession of the property; in the other it is not. The seizure of stolen goods is authorized by the common law, and the seizure of goods forfeited for a breach of the revenue laws, or concealed to avoid the duties payable on them, has been authorized by English statutes for at least two centuries past, [2] and the like seizures have been authorized by our own revenue acts from the commencement of the government. The first statute passed by Congress to regulate the collection of duties, the act of July 31, 1789, 1 Stat. 29, 43, contains provisions to this effect. As this act was passed by the same Congress which proposed for adoption the original amendments to the Constitution, it is clear that the members of that body did not regard searches and seizures of this kind as "unreasonable," and they are not embraced within the prohibition of the amendment. So also, the supervision authorized to be exercised by officers of the revenue over the manufacture or custody of excisable articles, and the entries thereof in books required by law to be kept for their inspection, are necessarily excepted out of the category of unreasonable searches and seizures. So also, the laws which provide for the search and seizure of articles and things which it is unlawful for a person to have in his possession for the purpose of issue or disposition, such as counterfeit coin, lottery tickets, implements of gambling, &c., are not within this category. Commonwealth v. Dana, 2 Met. (Mass.) 329. Many other things of this character might be enumerated. The entry upon premises, made by a sheriff or other officer of the law, for the purpose of seizing goods and chattels by virtue of a judicial writ, such as an attachment, a sequestration, or an execution, is not within the prohibition of the Fourth or Fifth Amendment, or any other clause of the Constitution; nor is the examination of a defendant under oath after an ineffectual execution, for the purpose of discovering secreted property or credits, to be applied to the payment of a judgment against him, obnoxious to those amendments.

But, when examined with care, it is manifest that there is a total unlikeness of these official acts and proceedings to that which is now under consideration. In the case of stolen goods, the owner from whom they were stolen is entitled to their possession, and in the case of excisable or dutiable articles, the government has an interest in them for the payment of the duties thereon, and, until such duties are paid, has a right to keep them under observation, or to pursue and drag them from concealment, and, in the case of goods seized on attachment or execution, the creditor is entitled to their seizure in satisfaction of his debt, and the examination of a defendant under oath to obtain a discovery of concealed property or credits is a proceeding merely civil to effect the ends of justice,

and is no more than what the court of chancery would direct on a bill for discovery. Whereas, by the proceeding now under consideration, the court attempts to extort from the party his private books and papers to make him liable for a penalty or to forfeit his property.

In order to ascertain the nature of the proceedings intended by the Fourth Amendment to the Constitution under the terms "unreasonable searches and seizures," it is only necessary to recall the contemporary or then recent history of the controversies on the subject, both in this country and in England. The practice had obtained in the colonies of issuing writs of assistance to the revenue officers, empowering them, in their discretion, to search suspected places for smuggled goods, which James Otis pronounced

"the worst instrument of arbitrary power, the most destructive of English liberty, and the fundamental principles of law, that ever was found in an English law book;"

since they placed "the liberty of every man in the hands of every petty officer." [3] This was in February, 1761, in Boston, and the famous debate in which it occurred was perhaps the most prominent event which inaugurated the resistance of the colonies to the oppressions of the mother country. "Then and there," said John Adams,

"then and there was the first scene of the first act of opposition to the arbitrary claims of Great Britain. Then and there, the child Independence was born."

These things, and the events which took place in England immediately following the argument about writs of assistance in Boston, were fresh in the memories of those who achieved our independence and established our form of government. In the period from 1762, when the North Briton was started by John Wilkes, to April, 1766, when the House of Commons passed resolutions condemnatory of general warrants, whether for the seizure of persons or papers, occurred the bitter controversy between the English government and Wilkes, in which the latter appeared as the champion of popular rights, and was, indeed, the pioneer in the contest which resulted in the abolition of some grievous abuses which had gradually crept into the administration of public affairs. Prominent and principal among these was the practice of issuing general warrants by the Secretary of State for searching private houses for the discovery and seizure of books and papers that might be used to convict their owner of the charge of libel. Certain numbers of the North Briton, particularly No. 45, had been very bold in denunciation of the government, and were esteemed heinously libelous. By authority of the secretary's warrant, Wilkes' house was searched, and his papers were indiscriminately seized. For this outrage, he sued the perpetrators and obtained a verdict of £ 1,000 against Wood, one of the party who made the search, and £ 4,000 against Lord Halifax, the Secretary of State who issued the warrant. The case, however, which will always be celebrated as being the occasion of Lord Camden's memorable discussion of the subject, was that of Entick v. Carrington and Three Other King's Messengers, reported at length in 19 Howell's State Trials 1029. The action was trespass for interfering the plaintiff's dwelling house in November, 1762, and breaking open his desks, boxes, &c., and searching and examining his papers. The jury rendered a special verdict, and the case was twice solemnly argued at the bar. L ord Camden pronounced the judgment of the court in Michaelmas Term, 1765, and the law as expounded by him has been regarded as settled from that time to this, and his great judgment on that occasion is considered as one of the landmarks of English liberty. It was welcomed and applauded by the lovers of liberty in the colonies, as well as in the mother country. It is regarded as one of the permanent monuments of the British Constitution, and is quoted as such by the English authorities on that subject down to the present time. [4]

As every American statesmen, during our revolutionary and formative period as a nation, was undoubtedly familiar with this monument of English freedom, and considered it a the true and ultimate expression of constitutional law, it may be confidently asserted that its propositions were in the minds of those who framed the Fourth Amendment to the Constitution, and were considered as sufficiently explanatory of what was meant by unreasonable searches and seizures. We think, therefore, it is pertinent to the present subject of discussion to quote somewhat largely from this celebrated judgment.

After describing the power claimed by the Secretary of State for issuing general search warrants and the manner in which they were executed, Lord Camden says:

"Such is the power, and, therefore, one would naturally expect that the law to warrant it should be clear in proportion as the power is exorbitant. If it is law, it will be found in our books; if it is not to be found there, it is not law."

"The great end for which men entered into society was to secure their property. That right is preserved sacred and incommunicable in all instances where it has not been taken away or abridged by some public law for the good of the whole. The cases where this right of property is set aside by positive law are various. Distresses, executions, forfeitures, taxes, &c., are all of this description, wherein every man, by common consent, gives up that right for the sake of justice and the general good. By the laws of England, every invasion of private property, be it ever so minute, is a trespass. No man can set his foot upon my ground without my license, but he is liable to an action, though the damage be nothing, which is proved by every declaration in trespass where the defendant is called upon to answer for bruising the grass and even treading upon the soil. If he admits the fact, he is bound to show, by way of justification, that some positive law has justified or excused him. The justification is submitted to the judges, who are to look into the books, and see if such a justification can be maintained by the text of the statute law, or by the principles of the common law. If no such excuse can be found or produced, the silence of the books is an authority, against the defendant, and the plaintiff must have judgment. According to this reasoning, it is now incumbent upon the defendants to show the law by which this seizure is warranted. If that cannot be done, it is a trespass."

"Papers are the owner's goods and chattels; they are his dearest property, and are so far from enduring a seizure that they will hardly bear an inspection, and though the eye cannot by the laws of England be guilty of a trespass, yet where private papers are removed and carried away, the secret nature of those goods will be an aggravation of the trespass, and demand more considerable damages in that respect. Where is the written law that gives any magistrate such a power? I can safely answer there is none; and, therefore, it is too much for us, without such authority, to pronounce a practice legal which would be subversive of all the comforts of society."

"But though it cannot be maintained by any direct law, yet it bears a resemblance, as was urged, to the known case of search and seizure for stolen goods. I answer that the difference is apparent. In the one, I am permitted to seize my own goods, which are placed in the hands of a public officer, till the felon's conviction shall entitle me to restitution. In the other, the party's own property is seized before and without conviction, and he has no power to reclaim his goods, even after his innocence is declared by acquittal."

"The case of searching for stolen goods crept into the law by imperceptible practice. No less a person than my Lord Coke denied its legality, 4 Inst. 176, and, therefore, if the two cases resembled each other more than they do, we have

no right, without an act of Parliament, to adopt a new practice in the criminal law which was never yet allowed from all antiquity. Observe, too, the caution with which the law proceeds in this singular case. There must be a full charge upon oath of a theft committed. The owner must swear that the goods are lodged in such a place. He must attend at the execution of the warrant, to show them to the officer, who must see that they answer the description."

"If it should be said that the same law which has, with so much circumspection, guarded the case of stolen goods from mischief would likewise, in this case, protect the subject by adding proper checks would require proofs beforehand, would call up the servant to stand by and overlook, would require him to take an exact inventory, and deliver a copy, my answer is that all these precautions would have been long since established by law if the power itself had been legal, and that the want of them is an undeniable argument against the legality of the thing."

Then, after showing that these general warrants for search and seizure of papers originated with the Star Chamber, and never had any advocates in Westminster Hall except Chief Justice Scroggs and his associates, Lord Camden proceeds to add:

"Lastly, it is urged, as an argument of utility, that such a search is a means of detecting offenders by discovering evidence. I wish some cases had been shown where the law forceth evidence out of the owner's custody by process. There is no process against papers in civil causes. It has been often tried, but never prevailed. Nay, where the adversary has by force or fraud got possession of your own proper evidence, there is no way to get it back but by action. In the criminal law, such a proceeding was never heard of, and yet there are some crimes, such, for instance, as murder, rape, robbery, and house-breaking, to say nothing of forgery and perjury, that are more atrocious than libeling. But our law has provided no paper search in these cases to help forward the conviction. Whether this proceedeth from the gentleness of the law towards criminals or from a consideration that such a power would be more pernicious to the innocent than useful to the public I will not say. It is very certain that the law obligeth no man to accuse himself, because the necessary means of compelling self-accusation, falling upon the innocent as well as the guilty, would be both cruel and unjust, and it would seem that search for evidence is disallowed upon the same principle. Then too, the innocent would be confounded with the guilty."

After a few further observations, his Lordship concluded thus:

"I have now taken notice of everything that has been urged upon the present point, and, upon the whole, we are all of opinion that the warrant to seize and carry away the party's papers in the case of a seditious libel is illegal and void. [5] "

The principles laid down in this opinion affect the very essence of constitutional liberty and security. They reach farther than the concrete form of the case then before the court, with its adventitious circumstances; they apply to all invasions on the part of the government and its employees of the sanctity of a man's home and the privacies of life. It is not the breaking of his doors and the rummaging of his drawers that constitutes the essence of the offence, but it is the invasion of his indefeasible right of personal security, personal liberty, and private property, where that right has never been forfeited by his conviction of some public offence -- it is the invasion of this sacred right which underlies and constitutes the essence of Lord Camden's judgment. Breaking into a house and opening boxes and drawers are circumstances of aggravation, but any forcible and compulsory extortion of a man's own testimony or of his private papers to be used as evidence to convict him of crime or to forfeit his goods is within the condemnation of that judgment. In this regard, the Fourth and Fifth Amendments run almost into each other.

Can we doubt that, when the Fourth and Fifth Amendments to the Constitution of the United States were penned and adopted, the language of Lord Camden was relied on as expressing the true doctrine on the subject of searches and seizures, and as furnishing the true criteria of the reasonable and "unreasonable" character of such seizures? Could the men who proposed those amendments, in the light of Lord Camden's opinion, have put their hands to a law like those of March 3, 1863, and March 2, 1867, before recited? If they could not, would they have approved the the section of the act of June 22, 1874, which was adopted as a substitute for the previous laws? It seems to us that the question cannot admit of a doubt. They never would have approved of them. The struggles against arbitrary power in which they had been engaged for more than twenty years would have been too deeply engraved in their memories to have allowed them to approve of such insidious disguises of the old grievance which they had so deeply abhorred.

The views of the first Congress on the question of compelling a man to produce evidence against himself may be inferred from a remarkable section of the judiciary act of 1789. The 15th section of that act introduced a great improvement in the law of procedure. The substance of it is found in § 724 of the Revised Statutes, and the section as originally enacted is as follows, to-wit:

"All the said courts of he United States shall have power in the trial of actions at law, on motion and due notice thereof being given, to require the parties to produce books or writings in their possession or power which contain evidence pertinent to the issue,in cases and under circumstances where they might be compelled to produce the same by the ordinary rules of proceeding in chancery, and if a plaintiff shall fail to comply with such order to produce books or writings, it shall be lawful for the courts respectively, on motion, to give the like judgment for the defendant as in cases of nonsuit, and if a defendant shall fail to comply with such order to produce books or writings, it shall be lawful for the courts respectively, on motion as aforesaid, to give judgment against him or her by default. [6]"

The restriction of this proceeding to

"cases and under circumstances where they [the parties] might be compelled to produce the same [books or writings] by the ordinary rules of proceeding in chancery"

shows the wisdom of the Congress of 1789. The court of chancery had, for generations, been weighing and balancing the rules to be observed in granting discovery on bills filed for that purpose in the endeavor to fix upon such as would best secure the ends of justice. To go beyond the point to which that court had gone may well have been thought hazardous. Now it is elementary knowledge that one cardinal rule of the court of chancery is never to decree a discovery which might tend to convict the party of a crime or to forfeit his property. [7] And any compulsory discovery by extorting the party's oath, or compelling the production of his private books and papers, to convict him of crime or to forfeit his property, is contrary to the principles of a free government. It is abhorrent to the instincts of an Englishman; it is abhorrent to the instincts of an American. It may suit the purposes of despotic power, but it cannot abide the pure atmosphere of political liberty and personal freedom.

It is proper to observe that, when the objectionable features of the acts of 1863 and 1867 were brought to the attention of Congress, it passed an act to obviate them. By the act of February 5, 1868, 15 Stat. 37, entitled "An act for the Protection in certain Cases of Persons making Disclosures as Parties, or testifying as Witnesses," the substance of which is incorporated in § 860 of the Revised Statutes, it was enacted

"that no answer or other pleading of any party, and no discovery, or evidence obtained by means of any judicial proceeding from any party or witness in this or any foreign country, shall be given in evidence, or in any manner used against such party or witness, or his property or estate, in any court of the United States, or in any proceeding by or before any officer of the United States, in respect to any crime, or for the enforcement of any penalty or forfeiture by reason of any act or omission of such party or witness."

This act abrogated and repealed the most objectionable part of the act of 1867 (which was then in force), and deprived the government officers of the convenient method afforded by it for getting evidence in suits of forfeiture, and this is probably the reason why the 5th section of the act of 1874 was afterwards passed. No doubt it was supposed that, in this new form, couched as it was in almost the language of the 15th section of the old judiciary act, except leaving out the restriction to cases in which the court of chancery would decree a discovery, it would be free from constitutional objection. But we think it has been made to appear that this result has not been attained, and that the law, though very speciously worded, is still obnoxious to the prohibition of the Fourth Amendment of the Constitution, as well as of the Fifth.

It has been thought by some respectable members of the profession that the two acts, that of 1868 and that of 1874, as being in pari materia, might be construed together so as to restrict the operation of the latter to cases other than those of forfeiture, and that such a construction of the two acts would obviate the necessity of declaring the act of 1874 unconstitutional. But as the act of 1874 was intended as a revisory act on the subject of revenue frauds and prosecutions therefor, and as it expressly repeals the 2d section of the act of 1867, but does not repeal the act of 1868, and expressly excepts criminal suits and proceedings, and does not except suits for penalties and forfeitures, it would hardly be admissible to consider the act of 1868 as having any influence over the construction of the act of 1874. For the purposes of this discussion, we must regard the 5th section of the latter act as independent of the act of 1868.

Reverting then to the peculiar phraseology of this act, and to the information in the present case which is founded on it, we have to deal with an act which expressly excludes criminal proceedings from its operation (though embracing civil suits for penalties and forfeitures), and with an information not technically a criminal proceeding, and neither, therefore, within the literal terms of the Fifth Amendment to the Constitution any more than it is within the literal terms of the Fourth. Does this relieve the proceedings or the law from being obnoxious to the prohibitions of either? We think not; we think they are within the spirit of both.

We have already noticed the intimate relation between the two amendments. They throw great light on each other. For the "unreasonable searches and seizures" condemned in the Fourth Amendment are almost always made for the purpose of compelling a man to give evidence against himself, which, in criminal cases, is condemned in the Fifth Amendment, and compelling a man "in a criminal case to be a witness against himself," which is condemned in the Fifth Amendment, throws light on the question as to what is an "unreasonable search and seizure" within the meaning of the Fourth Amendment. And we have been unable to perceive that the seizure of a man's private books and papers to be used in evidence against him is substantially different from compelling him to be a witness against himself. We think it is within the clear intent and meaning of those terms. We are also clearly of opinion that proceedings instituted for the purpose of declaring the forfeiture of a man's

property by reason of offences committed by him, though they may be civil in form, are in their nature criminal. In this very case, the ground of forfeiture, as declared in the 12th the section of the act of 1874, on which the information is based, consists of certain acts of fraud committed against the public revenue in relation to imported merchandise, which are made criminal by the statute, and it is declared, that the offender shall be fined not exceeding $5,000 nor less than $50, or be imprisoned not exceeding two years, or both, and, in addition to such fine, such merchandise shall be forfeited. These are the penalties affixed to the criminal acts, the forfeiture sought by this suit being one of them. If an indictment had been presented against the claimants, upon conviction, the forfeiture of the goods could have been included in the judgment. If the government prosecutor elects to waive an indictment and to file a civil information against the claimants -- that is, civil in form -- can he, by this device, take from the proceeding its criminal aspect and deprive the claimants of their immunities as citizens, and extort from them a production of their private papers, or, as an alternative, a confession of guilt? This cannot be. The information, though technically a civil proceeding, is, in substance and effect, a criminal one. As showing the close relation between the civil and criminal proceedings on the same statute in such cases, we may refer to the recent case of Coffey v. The United States, ante, 116 U. S. 436, in which we decided that an acquittal on a criminal information was a good plea in bar to a civil information for the forfeiture of goods arising upon the same acts. As, therefore, suits for penalties and forfeitures incurred by the commission of offences against the law are of this quasi-criminal nature, we think that they are within the reason of criminal proceedings for all the purposes of the Fourth Amendment of the Constitution, and of that portion of the Fifth Amendment which declares that no person shall be compelled in any criminal case to be a witness against himself, and we are further of opinion that a compulsory production of the private books and papers of the owner of goods sought to be forfeited in such a suit is compelling him to be a witness against himself within the meaning of the Fifth Amendment to the Constitution, and is the equivalent of a search and seizure -- and an unreasonable search and seizure -- within the meaning of the Fourth Amendment. Though the proceeding in question is divested of many of the aggravating incidents of actual search and seizure, yet, as before said, it contains their substance and essence, and effects their substantial purpose. It may be that it is the obnoxious thing in its mildest and least repulsive form; but illegitimate and unconstitutional practices get their first footing in that way, namely, by silent approaches and slight deviations from legal modes of procedure. This can only be obviated by adhering to the rule that constitutional provisions for the security of person and property should be liberally construed. A close and literal construction deprives them of half their efficacy, and leads to gradual depreciation of the right, as if it consisted more in sound than in substance. It is the duty of courts to be watchful for the constitutional rights of the citizen, and against any stealthy encroachments thereon. Their motto should be obsta principiis. We have no doubt that the legislative body is actuated by the same motives, but the vast accumulation of public business brought before it sometimes prevents it, on a first presentation, from noticing objections which become developed by time and the practical application of the objectionable law.

There have been several decisions in the Circuit and District Courts sustaining the constitutionality of the law under consideration, as well as the prior laws of 1863 and 1867. The principal of these are Stockwell v. United States, 3 Clifford 284; In re Platt and Boyd, 7 Ben. 261; United States v. Hughes, 12 Blatchford 553; United States v. Mason, 6 Bissell 350; United States v. Three Tons of Coal, 6 Bissell 379; United States v. Distillery No. Twenty-eight, 6 Bissell 483. The first and leading case was that of Stockwell v. United States, decided by Mr. Justice Clifford and Judge Shepley, the law under discussion being that of 1867. Justice Clifford delivered the opinion, and relied principally upon the collection statutes, which authorized the seizure of goods liable to duty, as being a contemporaneous exposition of the amendments and as furnishing precedents of analogous laws to that complained of. As we have already considered the bearing of these laws on the subject of discussion, it is unnecessary to say anything more in relation to them. The learned justice seemed to think that the power to institute such searches and seizures as the act of 1867 authorized, was necessary to the efficient collection of the revenue, and that no greater objection can be taken to a warrant to search for books, invoices, and other papers appertaining to an illegal importation than to one authorizing a search for the imported goods, and he concluded that, guarded as the new provision is, it is scarcely possible that the citizen can have any just ground of complaint. It seems to us that these considerations fail to meet the most serious objections to the validity of the law. The other cases followed that of Stockwell v. United States as a precedent, with more or less independent discussion of the subject. The case of Platt and Boyd, decided in the District Court for the Southern District of New York, was also under the act of 1867, and the opinion in that case is quite an elaborate one; but, of course, the previous decision of the Circuit Court in the Stockwell case had a governing influence on the District Court. The other cases referred to were under the 5th section of the act of 1874. The case of United States v. Hughes came up first before Judge Blatchford in the District court in 1875. 8 Ben. 29. It was an action of debt to recover a penalty under the customs act, and the judge held that the 5th section of the act of 1874, in its application to suits for penalties incurred before the passage of the act, was an ex post facto law, and therefore, as to them, was unconstitutional and void; but he granted an order pro forma to produce the books and papers required in order that the objection might come up on the offer to give them in evidence. They were produced in obedience to the order, and offered in evidence by the district attorney, but were not admitted. The district attorney then served upon one of the defendants a subpoena duces tecum requiring him to produce the books and papers, and, this being declined, he moved for an order to compel him to produce them, but the Court refused to make such order. The books and papers referred to had been seized under the act of 1867, but were returned to the defendants under a stipulation to produce them on the trial. The defendants relied not only on the unconstitutionality of the laws, but on the act of 1868, before referred to, which prohibited evidence obtained from a party by a judicial proceeding from being used against him in any prosecution for a crime, penalty, or forfeiture. Judgment being rendered for the defendant, the case was carried to the Circuit Court by writ of error, and, in that court, Mr. Justice Hunt held that the act of 1868 referred only to personal testimony or discovery obtained from a party or witness, and not to books or papers wrested from him; and, as to the constitutionality of the law, he merely referred to the case of Stockwell, and the judgment of the District Court was reversed. In view of what has been already said, we think it unnecessary to make any special observations on this decision. In United States v. Mason, Judge Blodgett took the distinction that, in proceedings in rem for a forfeiture, the parties are not required by a proceeding under the act of 1874 to testify or furnish evidence against themselves, because the suit is not against them, but against the property.

But where the owner of the property has been admitted as a claimant, we cannot see the force of this distinction; nor can we assent to the proposition that the proceeding is not, in effect, a proceeding against the owner of the property, as well as against the goods, for it is his breach of the laws which has to be proved to establish the forfeiture, and it is his property which is sought to be forfeited, and to require such an owner to produce his private books and papers in order to prove his breach of the laws, and thus to establish the forfeiture of his property, is surely compelling him to furnish evidence against himself. In the words of a great judge, "Goods, as goods, cannot offend, forfeit, unlade, pay duties, or the like, but men whose goods they are." [8]

The only remaining case decided in the United States courts to which we shall advert is that of United States v. Distillery No. Twenty-eight. In that case, Judge Gresham adds to the view of Judge Blodgett, in United States v. Mason, the further suggestion, that as in a proceeding in rem the owner is not a party, he might be compelled by a subpoena duces tecum to produce his books and papers like any other witness, and that the warrant or notice for search and seizure, under the act of 1874, does nothing more. But we cannot say that we are any better satisfied with this supposed solution of the difficulty. The assumption that the owner may be cited as a witness in a proceeding to forfeit his property seems to us gratuitous. It begs the question at issue. A witness, as well as a party, is protected by the law from being compelled to give evidence that tends to criminate him or to subject his property to forfeiture. Queen v. Newell, Parker 269; 1 Greenleaf on Evid., §§ 451-453. But, as before said, although the owner of goods, sought to be forfeited by a proceeding in rem is not the nominal party, he is, nevertheless, the substantial party to the suit; he certainly is so after making claim and defence, and, in a case like the present, he is entitled to all the privileges which appertain to a person who is prosecuted for a forfeiture of his property by reason of committing a criminal offence.

We find nothing in the decisions to change our views in relation to the principal question at issue.

We think that the notice to produce the invoice in this case, the order by virtue of which it was issued, and the law which authorized the order were unconstitutional and void, and that the inspection by the district attorney of said invoice, when produced in obedience to said notice, and its admission in evidence by the court, were erroneous and unconstitutional proceedings. We are of opinion, therefore, that

The judgment of the Circuit Court should be reversed, and the cause remanded with directions to award a new trial.

Agnello v. US (Oct 12, 1925)

MR. JUSTICE BUTLER delivered the opinion of the Court.

Thomas Agnello, Frank Agnello, Stephen Alba, Antonio Centorino, and Thomas Pace were indicted in the District Court, Eastern District of New York, under § 37, Criminal Code, 35 Stat. 1088, 1096, c. 321 for a conspiracy to violate the Harrison Act, 38 Stat. 785, c. 1, as amended by §§ 1006, 1007, 1008 of the Revenue Act of 1918, c. 18, 40 Stat. 1057, 1130. The indictment charges that defendants conspired together to sell cocaine without having registered with the collector of internal Revenue and without having paid the prescribed tax. The overt acts charged are that defendants had cocaine in their possession, solicited the sale of it, met in the home of defendant Alba at 138 Union Street, Brooklyn, and made arrangements for the purpose of selling it, brought a large quantity of it to that place, and sold it in violation of the Act. The jury found defendants guilty. Each was sentenced to serve two years in the penitentiary and to pay a fine of $5,000. The circuit court of appeals affirmed the judgment. 290 F. 671.

The evidence introduced by the government was sufficient to warrant a finding of the following facts: Paspuale Napolitano and Nunzio Dispenza, employed by government revenue agents for that purpose, went to the home of Alba, Saturday, January 14, 1922, and there offered by buy narcotics from Alba and Centorino. Alba gave them some samples. They arranged to come again on Monday following. They returned at the time agreed. Six revenue agents and a city policeman followed them and remained on watch outside. Alba left the house and returned with Centorino. They did not then produce any drug. After discussion and the refusal of Napolitano and Dispenza to go to Centorino's house to get the drug, Centorino went to fetch it. He was followed by some of the agents. He first went to his own house, 172 Columbia Street; thence to 167 Columbia Street, one part of which was a grocery store belonging to Pace and Thomas Agnello, and another part of which, connected with the grocery store, was the home of Frank Agnello and Pace. In a short time, Centorino, Pace, and the Agnellos came out of the last-mentioned place, and all went to Alba's house. Looking through the windows, those on watch saw Frank Agnello produce a number of small packages for delivery to Napolitano and saw the letter hand over money to Alba. Upon the apparent consummation of the sale, the agents rushed in and arrested all the defendants. They found some of the packages on the table where the transaction took place, and found others in the pockets of Frank Agnello. All contained cocaine. On searching Alba, they found the money given him by Napolitano.

And, as a part of its case in chief, the government offered testimony tending to show that, while some of the revenue agents were taking the defendants to the police station, the others and the city policeman went to the home of Centorino and searched it, but did not find any narcotics; that they then went to 167 Columbia Street and searched it, and in Frank Agnello's bedroom found a can of cocaine, which was produced and offered in evidence. The evidence was excluded on the ground that the search and seizure were made without a search warrant. In defense, Centorino and others gave testimony to the effect that the packages of cocaine which were brought to and seized in Alba's house at the time of the arrests had been furnished to Centorino by Dispenza to induce an apparent sale of cocaine to Napolitano -- that is, to incite crime or acts having the appearance of crime for the purpose of entrapping and punishing defendants. Centorino testified that, after leaving Napolitano and Dispenza with Alba at the latter's home, he went to his own house and got the packages of cocaine which had been given him by Dispenza, and took them to 167 Columbia Street, and there a gave them to Frank Agnello to be taken to Alba's house. Frank Agnello testified on direct examination that he received the packages from Centorino, but that he did not know their contents, and that he would not have carried them if he had known that they contained cocaine or narcotics. On cross-examination, he said that he had never seen narcotics. Then, notwithstanding objection by defendants, the prosecuting attorney produced the can of cocaine which the government claimed was seized in Agnello's bedroom and asked him whether he had ever seen it. He said he had not, and specifically stated he had never seen it in his house. In rebuttal, over objections of defendants, the government was permitted to put in the evidence of the search and seizure of the can of cocaine in Frank Agnello's room, which theretofore had been offered and excluded.

The case involves the questions whether search of the house of Frank Agnello and seizure of the cocaine there found, without a search warrant, violated the Fourth Amendment, and whether the admission of evidence of such search and seizure violated the Fifth Amendment. The Fourth Amendment is:

"The right of the people to be secure in their persons, houses, papers, and effects, against unreasonable searches and seizures shall not be violated, and no warrants shall issue but upon probable cause, supported by oath or affirmation and particularly describing the place to be searched and the persons or things to be seized."

The provision of the Fifth Amendment invoked is this: "No person . . . shall be compelled in any criminal case to be a witness against himself."

The right without a search warrant contemporaneously to search persons lawfully arrested while committing crime and to search the place where the arrest is made in order to find and seize things connected with the crime as its fruits or as the means by which it was committed, as well as weapons and other things to effect an escape from custody is not to be doubted. See Carroll v. United States, 267 U. S. 132, 267 U. S. 158; Weeks v. United States, 232 U. S. 383, 232 U. S. 392. The legality of the arrests or of the searches and seizures made at the home of Alba is not questioned. Such searches and seizures naturally and usually appertain to and attend such arrests. But the right does not extend to other places. Frank Agnello's house was several blocks distant from Alba's house, where the arrest was made. When it was entered and searched, the conspiracy was ended and the defendants were under arrest and in custody elsewhere. That search cannot be sustained as an incident of the arrests. See Silverthorne Lumber Co. v. United States, 251 U. S. 385, 251 U. S. 391; People v. Conway, 225 Mich. 152; Gamble v. Keyes, 35 S.D. 645, 650.

Under the Harrison Act (§ 8, and § 1 as amended by § 1006), it is unlawful for any person, who has not registered and paid a special tax, to have cocaine in his possession, and all unstamped packages of such drug found in his possession are subject to forfeiture. We assume, as contended by the government, that defendants obtained from Frank Agnello's house the cocaine that was taken to Alba's house and there seized; that the can of cocaine which later was found in Agnello's house was unlawfully in his control and subject to seizure, and that it was a part of the cocaine which was the subject matter of the conspiracy.

The government cites Carroll v. United States, supra, but it does not support the search and seizure complained of. That case involved the legality of a search of an automobile and the seizure of intoxicating liquors being transported therein in violation of the National Prohibition Act. The search and seizure were made by prohibition agents without a warrant. After reference to various acts of Congress relating to the seizure of contraband goods, the Court said (p. 267 U. S. 153):

"We have made a somewhat extended reference to these statutes to show that the guaranty of freedom from unreasonable searches and seizures by the Fourth Amendment has been construed, practically since the beginning of the government, as recognizing a necessary difference between a search of a store, dwelling house, or other structure in respect of which a proper official warrant readily may be obtained, and a search of a ship, motorboat, wagon, or automobile, for contraband goods, where it is not practicable to secure a warrant, because the vehicle can be quickly moved out of the locality or jurisdiction in which the warrant must be sought."

It was held that:

"The facts and circumstances within their knowledge and of which they had reasonably trustworthy information were sufficient in themselves to warrant a man of reasonable caution in the belief that intoxicating liquor was being transported in the automobile which they stopped and searched."

P. 267 U. S. 162. And, on that ground, the Court held the search and seizure without warrant justified.

While the question has never been directly decided by this Court, it has always been assumed that one's house cannot lawfully be searched without a search warrant, except as an incident to a lawful arrest therein. Boyd v. United States, 116 U. S. 616, 116 U. S. 624, et seq., 116 U. S. 630; Weeks v. United States, supra, 232 U. S. 393; Silverthorne Lumber Co. v. United States, supra, 251 U. S. 391; Gouled v. United States, 255 U. S. 298, 255 U. S. 308. The protection of the Fourth Amendment extends to all equally to those justly suspected or accused as well as to the innocent. The search of a private dwelling without a warrant is, in itself, unreasonable and abhorrent to our laws. Congress has never passed an act purporting to authorize the search of a house without a warrant. On the other hand, special limitations have been set about the obtaining of search warrants for that purpose. Thus, the National Prohibition Act, approved October 28, 1919, c. 85, Tit. 2, § 25, 41 Stat. 305, 315, provides that no search warrant shall issue to search any private dwelling occupied as such unless it is being used for the unlawful sale of intoxicating liquor or is in part used for business purposes, such as store, shop, saloon, restaurant, hotel, or boarding house. And later, to the end that government employees without a warrant shall not invade the homes of the people and violate the privacies of life, Congress made it a criminal offense, punishable by heavy penalties, for any officer, agent or employee of the United States engaged in the enforcement of any law to search a private dwelling house without a warrant directing such search. Act of November 23, 1921, c. 134, § 6, 42 Stat. 222, 223. Safeguards similar to the Fourth Amendment are deemed necessary and have been provided in the constitution or laws of every state of the Union. * We think there is no state statute authorizing the search of a house without a warrant, and in a number of state laws recently enacted for the enforcement of prohibition in respect of intoxicating liquors, there are provisions similar to those in § 25 of the National Prohibition Act. Save in certain cases as incident to arrest, there is no sanction in the decisions of the courts, federal or state, for the search of a private dwelling house without a warrant. Absence of any judicial approval is persuasive authority that it is unlawful. See Entick v. Carrington, 19 Howard's state Trials, 1030, 1066. Belief, however well founded, that an article sought is concealed in a dwelling house furnishes no justification for a search of that place without a warrant. And such searches are held unlawful notwithstanding facts unquestionably showing probable cause. See Temperani v. United States, 299 F. 365; United States v. Rembert, 284 F. 996, 1000; Connelly v. United States, 275 F. 509; McClurg v. Brenton, 123 Iowa 368, 372; People v. Margolis, 220 Mich. 431; Childers v. Commonwealth, 198 Ky. 848; State v. Warfield, 184 Wis. 56. The search of Frank Agnello's house and seizure of the can of cocaine violated the Fourth Amendment.

It is well settled that, when properly invoked, the Fifth Amendment protects every person from incrimination by the use of evidence obtained through search or seizure made in violation of his rights under the Fourth Amendment. Boyd v. United States, supra, 116 U. S. 630 et seq.; Weeks v. United States, supra, 232 U. S. 398; Silverthorne Lumber Co. v. United States, supra, 251 U. S. 391-392; Gouled v. United States, supra, 255 U. S. 306; Amos v. United States, 255 U. S. 313, 255 U. S. 316.

The government contends that, even if the search and seizure were unlawful, the evidence was admissible because no application on behalf of defendant was made to the court for the return of the can of cocaine. The reason for such application, where required, is that the court will not pause in a criminal case to determine collateral issues as to how the evidence was obtained. See Adams v. New York, 192 U. S. 585, 192 U. S. 594, aff'g People v. Adams, 176 N.Y. 351. But, in this case, the facts disclosing that the search and seizure violated the Fourth Amendment were not in controversy. They were shown by the examination of the witness called to give the evidence. There was no search warrant, and from the first the position of the government has been that none was necessary. In substance, Frank Agnello testified that he never had possession of the can of cocaine, and never saw it until it was produced in court. There is nothing to show that, in advance of its offer in evidence, he knew that the government claimed it had searched his house and found cocaine there, or that the prosecutor intended to introduce evidence of any search or seizure. It would be unreasonable to hold that he was bound to apply for the return of an article which he maintained he never had. Where, by uncontroverted facts, it appears that a search and seizure were made in violation of the Fourth Amendment, there is no reason why one whose rights have been so violated, and who is sought to be incriminated by evidence so obtained, may not invoke protection of the Fifth Amendment immediately, and without any application for the return of the thing seized. "A rule of practice must not be allowed for any technical reason to prevail over a constitutional right." Gouled v. United States, supra, 255 U. S. 313.

And the contention that the evidence of the search and seizure was admissible in rebuttal is without merit. In his direct examination, Agnello was not asked and did not testify concerning the can of cocaine. In cross-examination, in answer to a question permitted over his objection, he said he had never seen it. He did nothing to waive his constitutional protection or to justify cross-examination in respect of the evidence claimed to have been obtained by the search. As said in Silverthorne Lumber Co. v. United States, supra,

251 U. S. 392:

"The essence of a provision forbidding the acquisition of evidence in a certain way is that not merely evidence so acquired shall not be used before the court, but that it shall not be used at all."

The admission of evidence obtained by the search and seizure was error, and prejudicial to the substantial rights of Frank Agnello. The judgment against him must be set aside, and a new trial awarded.

But the judgment against the other defendants may stand. The introduction of the evidence of the search and seizure did not transgress their constitutional rights. And it was not prejudicial error against them. The possession by Frank Agnello of the can of cocaine which was seized tended to show guilty knowledge and criminal intent on his part; but it was not submitted as attributable to the other defendants. During the summing up of the case to the jury by the prosecuting attorney, the court distinctly indicated that the evidence was admissible only against Frank Agnello. The other defendants did not request any instruction to the jury in reference to the matter, and they do not contend that any erroneous instruction was given. Isaacs v. United States, 159 U. S. 487, 159 U. S. 491.

The packages of cocaine seized at Alba's house were carried to that place by Frank Agnello. He did this at the instance of Centorino, and in his behalf it is claimed he acted innocently and without knowledge of the contents of the package. The evidence of the search and seizure made in his house tended to show that he knew what he was doing and was a willing participant in the conspiracy charged. But, so far as concerns the other defendants, it is immaterial whether he acted innocently and without knowledge of the contents of the package or knowingly to effect the object of the conspiracy. In either case, his act would be equally chargeable to his codefendants. They are not entitled to a new trial. See Rossi v. United States, 278 F. 349, 354; Belfi v. United States, 259 F. 822, 828; Feder et al. v. United States, 257 F. 694; Browne v. United States, 145 F. 1, 13; United States v. Cohn, 128 F. 615, 626.

Judgment against Frank Agnello reversed; judgment against other defendants affirmed.

* See p. 1268, Index Digest of state constitutions (prepared for New York state constitutional Convention Commission, 1915); also, § 8, c. 6, Consolidated Laws, New York, as amended by Laws 1923, c. 80.

Albrecht v. US (Jan 3, 1927)

MR. JUSTICE BRANDEIS delivered the opinion of the Court.

This direct writ of error to the Federal Court for Eastern Illinois was allowed under § 238 of the Judicial Code prior to the amendment of February 13, 1925. Albrecht and his associates were sentenced to either fine or imprisonment upon each of nine counts of an information charging violations of the National Prohibition Act.

There is no contention that the offenses charged could not be prosecuted by information. See Brede v. Powers, 263 U. S. 4, 263 U. S. 10; Rossini v. United States, 6 F.2d 350. The claims mainly urged are that, because of defects in the information and affidavits attached, there was no jurisdiction in the district court, and that rights guaranteed by the Fourth Amendment were violated. Several important questions of practice are presented which have not been passed upon by this Court, and on which there has been diversity of opinion in the lower courts, due in part to language in the opinions in United States v. Morgan, 222 U. S. 274, 222 U. S. 282, and in United States v. Thompson, 251 U. S. 407, 251 U. S. 413-414.

The information recites that it was filed by the United States attorney with leave of the court, and the truth of this allegation has not been questioned. A bench warrant issued, and the marshal executed it by arresting the defendants. When they were brought into court, each gave bond to appear and answer, was released from custody immediately, and was not thereafter in custody by virtue of the warrant or otherwise. At the time of giving the bonds, no objection was made to either the jurisdiction or the service by execution of the warrant, and nothing was done then indicating an intention to enter a special appearance. On a later day, the defendants filed a motion to quash the information, declared in the motion that they "specifically limit their appearance in the cause for the purpose of interposing" it, and protested that the court was without jurisdiction. The main ground urged in support of the objection was that the information had not been verified by the United States attorney; that it recited he "gives the court to understand and be informed, on the affidavit of I. A. Miller and D. P. Coggins," and that these affidavits, which were annexed to the information, had been sworn to before a notary public a state official not authorized to administer oaths in federal criminal proceedings. Compare United States v. Hall, 131 U. S. 50. With leave of court, new oaths to the affidavits were immediately sworn to before the deputy clerk of the court, and additional affidavits, also sworn to before him, were filed. Thereupon, a new motion to quash, setting forth the same grounds, was filed by the defendants, and this motion extended to both the information and the warrant. It also was denied, and a demurrer interposed upon the same ground was overruled. Then, upon a plea of not guilty, the defendants were tried, with the result stated, and a motion in arrest of judgment was denied.

As the affidavits on which the warrant issued had not been properly verified, the arrest was in violation of the clause in the Fourth Amendment, which declares that "no warrants shall issue but upon probable cause, supported by oath or affirmation." See Ex parte Burford, 3 Cranch 448, 7 U. S. 453; United States v. Michalski, 265 F. 839. But it does not follow that, because the arrest was illegal, the information was or became void. The information was filed by leave of court. Despite some practice and statements to the contrary, it may be accepted as settled that leave must be obtained, and that, before granting leave, the court must in some way satisfy itself that there is probable cause for the prosecution. [1] This is done sometimes by a verification of the information and frequently by annexing affidavits thereto. But these are not the only means by which a court may become satisfied that probable cause for the prosecution exists. [2] The United States attorney, like the Attorney General or Solicitor General of England, may file an information under his oath of office, and, if he does so, his official oath may be accepted as sufficient to give verity to the allegations of the information. See Weeks v. United States, 216 F. 292, 302.

It is contended that this information was not presented on the official oath of the United States attorney; that, instead of informing on his official oath, he gave "the court to understand and be informed on the affidavit[s]" referred to, and that, for this reason, the information is to be likened not to those filed in England by the Attorney General or the Solicitor General, but to those exhibited there by Masters of the Crown upon information of a private informer; that the latter class of informations were required by Stat. 4 & 5 W. & M. c. 18, to be supported by affidavit of the person at whose instance they were preferred; that this requirement for informations of that character became a part of our common law; and, that, because the affidavits were not properly verified, the information could not confer jurisdiction.

The practice of prosecuting lesser federal crimes by information, instead of indictment, has been common since 1870. [3] But, in federal proceedings, no trace has been found of the differentiation in informations for such crimes, or of any class of informations instituted by a private informer comparable to those dealt with in England by Stat. 4 & 5 W. & M. c. 18.

The reference to the affidavits in this information is not to be read as indicating that it was presented otherwise than upon the oath of office of the United States attorney. [4] The affidavits were doubtless referred to in the information not as furnishing probable cause for the prosecution, but because it was proposed to use the information and affidavits annexed as the basis for an application for a warrant of arrest. If, before granting the warrant, the defendants had entered a voluntary appearance, the reference and the affidavits could have been treated as surplusage, and would not have vitiated the information. [5] The fact that the information and affidavits were used as a basis for the application for a warrant did not affect the validity of the information as such. [6] Whether the whole proceeding was later vitiated by the false arrest remains to be considered.

The invalidity of the warrant is not comparable to the invalidity of an indictment. A person may not be punished for a crime without a formal and sufficient accusation, even if he voluntarily submits to the jurisdiction of the court. Compare Ex parte Bain, 121 U. S. 1. But a false arrest does not necessarily deprive the court of jurisdiction of the proceeding in which it was made. Where there was an appropriate accusation either by indictment or information, a court may acquire jurisdiction over the person of the defendant by his voluntary appearance. [7] That a defendant may be brought before the court by a summons, without an arrest, is shown by the practice in prosecutions against corporations, which are necessarily commenced by a summons. [8] Here, the court had jurisdiction of the subject matter, and the persons named as defendants were within its territorial jurisdiction. The judgment assailed would clearly have been good if the objection had not been taken until after the verdict. [9] This shows that the irregularity in the warrant was of such a character that it could be waived. Was it waived? And, if not, was it cured?

The bail bonds bound the defendants to "be and appear" in court "from day to day" and "to answer and stand trial upon the information herein and to stand by and abide the orders and judgment of the court in the premises." It is urged there was a waiver by giving the bail bonds without making any objection. We are of the opinion that the failure to take the objection at that time did not waive the invalidity of the warrant or operate as a general appearance. [10] An objection to the illegality of the arrest could have been taken thereafter by a motion to quash the warrants, though technically the defendants were then held under their bonds, the warrants having performed their functions. But the first motion to quash was not directed to the invalidity of the warrant. As that motion to quash was directed solely to the information, it could not raise the question of the validity of the warrant. [11] The motion to quash the warrant was not made until after the government had filed properly verified affidavits by leave of court. Thereby the situation had been changed. The affidavits then on file would have supported a new warrant which, if issued, would plainly have validated the proceedings thenceforward. Compare In re Johnson, 167 U. S. 120. There was no occasion to apply for a new warrant, because the defendants were already in court. [12] The defect in the proceeding by which they had been brought into court had been cured. By failing to move to quash the warrant before the defect had been cured, the defendants lost their right to object. It is thus unnecessary to decide whether it would have been proper to allow the amendment, and deny the motion to quash, if the attack on the warrant had been made before the amendment of the affidavits. [13]

There is a claim of violation of the Fifth Amendment by the imposition of double punishment. This contention rests upon the following facts. Of the nine counts in the information, four charged illegal possession of liquor, four illegal sale, and one maintaining a common nuisance. The contention is that there was double punishment because the liquor which the defendants were convicted for having sold is the same that they were convicted for having possessed. But possessing and selling are distinct offenses. One may obviously possess without selling, and one may sell and cause to be delivered a thing of which he has never had possession, or one may have possession and later sell, as appears to have been done in this case. The fact that the person sells the liquor which he possessed does not render the possession and the sale necessarily a single offense. There is nothing in the Constitution which prevents Congress from punishing separately each step leading to the consummation of a transaction which it has power to prohibit, and punishing also the completed transaction. The precise question does not appear to have been discussed in either this or a lower federal court in connection with the National Prohibition Act, but the general principle is well established.

Compare Burton v. United States, 202 U. S. 344, 202 U. S. 377; Gavieres v. United States, 220 U. S. 338; Morgan v. Devine, 237 U. S. 632.

The remaining objections are unsubstantial, and do not require discussion.

Affirmed.

Oklahoma Press Publishing Co. v. Walling (Feb 11, 1946) [Notes omitted]

MR. JUSTICE RUTLEDGE delivered the opinion of the Court.

These cases bring for decision important questions concerning the Administrator's right to judicial enforcement of subpoenas duces tecum issued by him in the course of investigations conducted pursuant to § 11(a) of the Fair Labor Standards Act, 52 Stat. 1060. His claim is founded directly upon § 9, which incorporates the enforcement provisions of §§ 9 and 10 of the Federal Trade Commission Act, 38 Stat. 717. [1] The subpoenas sought the production of specified records to determine whether petitioners were violating the Fair Labor Standards Act, including records relating to coverage. Petitioners, newspaper publishing corporations, maintain that the Act is not applicable to them, for constitutional and other reasons, and insist that the question of coverage must be adjudicated before the subpoenas may be enforced.

In No. 61, involving the Oklahoma Press Publishing Company, the Circuit Court of Appeals for the Tenth Circuit has rejected this view, holding that the Administrator was entitled to enforcement upon showing of "probable cause," which it found had been made. 147 F.2d 658. Accordingly it affirmed the District Court's order directing that the Administrator be given access to the records and documents specified. [2]

In No. 63, the Circuit Court of Appeals for the Third Circuit likewise rejected the company's position, one judge dissenting on the ground that probable cause had not been shown. 148 F.2d 57. It accordingly reversed the District Court's order of dismissal in the proceeding to show cause, which in effect denied enforcement for want of a showing of coverage. Application of Walling, 49 F.Supp. 659. [3] The Court of Appeals thought that requiring the Administrator

"to make proof of coverage would be to turn the proceeding into a suit to decide a question which must be determined by the Administrator in the course of his investigation"

(148 F.2d 60), and relied upon Endicott Johnson Corp. v. Perkins, 317 U. S. 501, as being

persuasive that this could not be done. Regarding the subpoena as containing no unreasonable demand, it conceived the return and affidavits filed by the company, together with the Administrator's allegations of coverage, [4] as a showing sufficient to require enforcement. Hence, it directed that the District Court's discretion be exercised with that effect.

Because of the importance of the issues for administration of the Act and also on account of the differences in the grounds for the two decisions, as well as between them and decisions from other circuits, [5] certiorari was granted in both cases. 325 U.S. 845.

The issues have taken wide range. They are substantially the same in the two causes, except in one respect to be noted. [6] In addition to an argument from Congress' intent, reliance falls upon various constitutional provisions, including the First, Fourth and Fifth Amendments, as well as the limited reach of the commerce clause, to show that the Administrator's conduct and the relief he seeks are forbidden.

I

Coloring almost all of petitioners' position, as we understand them, is a primary misconception that the First Amendment knocks out any possible application of the Fair Labor Standards Act to the business of publishing and distributing newspapers. The argument has two prongs.

The broadside assertion that petitioners "could not be covered by the Act," for the reason that "application of this Act to its newspaper publishing business would violate its rights as guaranteed by the First Amendment," is without merit. Associated Press v. Labor Board, 301 U. S. 103, and Associated Press v. United States, 326 U. S. 1; Mabee v. White Plains Pub. Co., 327 U. S. 178. [7] If Congress can remove obstructions to commerce by requiring publishers to bargain collectively with employees and refrain from

interfering with their rights of self-organization, matters closely related to eliminating low wages and long hours, Congress likewise may strike directly at those evils when they adversely affect commerce. United States v. Darby, 312 U. S. 100, 312 U. S. 116-117. The Amendment does not forbid this or other regulation which ends in no restraint upon expression or in any other evil outlawed by its terms and purposes. [8]

Petitioners' narrower argument, of allegedly invalid classification, [9] arises from the statutory exemptions and may be shortly dismissed. The intimation that the Act falls by reason of the exclusion of seamen, farm workers and others by § 13(a) is hardly more than a suggestion, and is dismissed accordingly. Cf. Buck v. Bell, 274 U. S. 200, 274 U. S. 208. The contention drawn from the exemption of employees of small newspapers by § 13(a)(8) deserves only slightly more attention. [10] It seems to be two-fold, that the amendment forbids Congress to "regulate the press by classifying it" at all and in any event that it cannot use volume of circulation or size as a factor in the classification. [11]

Reliance upon Grosjean v. American Press Co., 297 U. S. 233, to support these claims is misplaced. There the state statute singled out newspapers for special taxation and was held in effect to graduate the tax in accordance with volume of circulation. Here there was no singling out of the press for treatment different from that accorded other business in general. Rather the Act's purpose was to place publishers of newspapers upon the same plane with other businesses and the exemption for small newspapers had the same object. 83 Cong.Rec. 7445. Nothing in the Grosjean case forbids Congress to exempt some publishers because of size from either a tax or a regulation which would be valid if applied to all.

What has been said also disposes of the

contention drawn from the scope of the commerce power and its applicability to the publishing business considered independently of the Amendment's influence. Associated Press v. Labor Board, supra; Associated Press v. United States, supra.

II

Other questions pertain to whether enforcement of the subpoenas as directed by the Circuit Courts of Appeals will violate any of petitioners' rights secured by the Fourth Amendment and related issues concerning Congress' intent. It is claimed that enforcement would permit the Administrator to conduct general fishing expeditions into petitioners' books, records and papers, in order to secure evidence that they have violated the Act, without a prior charge or complaint and simply to secure information upon which to base one, all allegedly in violation of the Amendment's search and seizure provisions. Supporting this is an argument that Congress did not intend such use to be made of the delegated power, which rests in part upon asserted constitutional implications, but primarily upon the reports of legislative committees, particularly in the House of Representatives, made in passing upon appropriations for years subsequent to the Act's effective date. [12]

The short answer to the Fourth Amendment objections is that the records in these cases present no question of actual search and seizure, but raise only the question whether orders of court for the production of specified records have been validly made; and no sufficient showing appears to justify setting them aside. [13] No officer or other person has sought to enter petitioners' premises against their will, to search them, or to seize or examine their books, records or papers without their assent, otherwise than pursuant to orders of court authorized by law and made after adequate opportunity to present objections, which in fact were made. [14] Nor has any objection been taken to the breadth of the subpoenas or to any other specific defect which would invalidate them. [15]

What petitioners seek is not to prevent an unlawful search and seizure. It is, rather, a total immunity to the Act's provisions, applicable to all others similarly situated, requiring them to submit their pertinent records for the Administrator's inspection under every judicial safeguard, after and only after an order of court made pursuant to and in exact compliance with authority granted by Congress. This broad claim of immunity no doubt is induced by petitioners' First Amendment contentions. But, beyond them, it is rested also upon conceptions of the Fourth Amendment equally lacking in merit.

Petitioners' plea that the Fourth Amendment places them so far above the law that they are beyond the reach of congressional and judicial power as those powers have been exerted here only raises the ghost of controversy long since settled adversely to their claim. [16] They have advanced no claim founded on the Fifth Amendment's somewhat related guaranty against self-incrimination, whether or not for the sufficient reason, among others, that this privilege gives no protection to corporations or their officers against the production of corporate records pursuant to lawful judicial order, which is all these cases involve. [17]

The cited authorities would be sufficient to dispose of the Fourth Amendment argument, and more recent decisions confirm their ruling. [18] Petitioners, however, are insistent, in their contrary views, both upon the constitutional phases and in their asserted bearing upon the intention of Congress. While we think those views reflect a confusion not justified by the actual state of the decisions, the confusion has acquired some currency, as the divided state of opinion among the circuits shows. [19] Since the matter is of some importance, in order to remove any possible basis for like misunderstanding in the future, we give more detailed consideration to the views advanced and to the authorities than would otherwise be necessary.

There are two difficulties with petitioners' theory concerning the intent of Congress. One is that the argument from the so-called legislative history flies in the face of the powers expressly granted to the Administrator and the courts by §§ 9 and 11(a), so flatly that to accept petitioners' view would largely nullify them. [20] Furthermore, the excerpted history from the later appropriation matters does not give the full story, and, when that is considered, the claimed interpretation is not made out, regardless of its retrospective aspect. [21] Moreover, the statute's language leaves no room to doubt that Congress intended to authorize just what the Administrator did and sought to have the courts do. [22]

Section 11(a) expressly authorizes the Administrator to

"enter and inspect such places and such records (and make such transcriptions thereof), question such employees, and investigate such facts, conditions, practices, or matters as he may deem appropriate to determine whether any person has violated any provision of this Act, or which may aid in the enforcement of the provisions of this Act. [23]"

The subpoena power conferred by § 9 (through adoption of § 9 of the Federal Trade Commission Act) is given in aid of this investigation and, in case of disobedience, the District Courts are called upon to enforce the subpoena through their contempt powers, [24] without express condition requiring showing of coverage. [25]

In view of these provisions, with which the Administrator's action was in exact compliance, this case presents an instance of "the most explicit language" [26] which leaves no room for questioning Congress' intent. The very purpose of the subpoena and of the order, as of the authorized investigation, is to discover and procure evidence, not to prove a pending charge or complaint, but upon which to make one if, in the Administrator's judgment, the facts thus discovered should justify doing so.

Accordingly, if §§ 9 and 11(a) are not to be construed as authorizing enforcement of the orders, it must be, as petitioners say, because this construction would make them so dubious constitutionally as to compel resort to an interpretation which saves, rather than to one which destroys or is likely to do so. The Court has adopted this course at least once in this type of case. [27] But, if the same course is followed here, the judgments must be reversed with the effect of cutting squarely into the power of Congress. For to deny the validity of the orders would be in effect to deny not only Congress' power to enact the provisions sustaining them, but also its authority to delegate effective power to investigate violations of its own laws, if not perhaps also its own power to make such investigations.

III

The primary source of misconception concerning the Fourth Amendment's function lies perhaps in the identification of cases involving so-called "figurative" or "constructive" search with cases of actual search and seizure. [28] Only in this analogical sense can any question related to search and seizure be thought to arise in situations which, like the present ones, involve only the validity of authorized judicial orders.

The confusion is due in part to the fact that this is the very kind of situation in which the decisions have moved with variant direction, although without actual conflict when all of the facts in each case are taken into account. Notwithstanding this, emphasis and tone at times are highly contrasting, with consequent overtones of doubt and confusion for validity of the statute or its application. The subject matter perhaps too often has been generative of heat, rather than light, for the border along which the cases lie is one where government intrudes upon different areas of privacy, and the history of such intrusions has brought forth some of the stoutest and most effective instances of resistance to excess of governmental authority. [29]

The matter of requiring the production of books and records to secure evidence is not as one-sided, in this kind of situation, as the most extreme expressions of either emphasis would indicate. With some obvious exceptions, there has always been a real problem of balancing the public interest against private security. The cases for protection of the opposing interests are stated as clearly as anywhere, perhaps, in the summations, quoted in the margin, [30] of two former members of this Court, each of whom was fully alive to the dual necessity of safeguarding adequately the public and the private interest. But emphasis has not always been so aptly placed.

The confusion, obscuring the basic distinction between actual and so-called "constructive" search has been accentuated where the records and papers sought are of corporate character, as in these cases. Historically, private corporations have been subject to broad visitorial power, both in England and in this country. And it long has been established that Congress may exercise wide investigative power over them, analogous to the visitorial power of the incorporating state, [31] when their activities take place within or affect interstate commerce. [32] Correspondingly, it has been settled that corporations are not entitled to all of the constitutional protections which private individuals have in these and related matters. As has been noted, they are not at all within the privilege against self-incrimination, although this Court more than once has said that the privilege runs very closely with the Fourth Amendment's search and seizure provisions. [33] It is also settled

that an officer of the company cannot refuse to produce its records in his possession upon the plea that they either will incriminate him or may incriminate it. [34] And, although the Fourth Amendment has been held applicable to corporations [35] notwithstanding their exclusion from the privilege against self-incrimination, the same leading case of Wilson v. United States, 221 U. S. 361, distinguishing the earlier quite different one of Boyd v. United States, 116 U. S. 616, [36] held the process not invalid under the Fourth Amendment, although it broadly required the production of copies of letters and telegrams

"signed or purport[ed] to be signed by the president of said company during the month[s] of May and June, 1909, in regard to an alleged violation of the statutes of the United States by C. C. Wilson."

221 U.S. at 221 U. S. 368, 221 U. S. 375.

The Wilson case has set the pattern of later decisions and has been followed without qualification of its ruling. [37] Contrary suggestions or implications may be explained as dicta; [38] or by virtue of the presence of an actual illegal search and seizure, the effects of which the Government sought later to overcome by applying the more liberal doctrine devolved in relation to "constructive search"; [39] or by the scope of the subpoena in calling for documents so broadly or indefinitely that it was thought to approach in this respect the character of a general warrant or writ of assistance, odious in both English and American history. [40] But no case has been cited or found in which, upon similar facts, the Wilson doctrine has not been followed. Nor in any has Congress been adjudged to have exceeded its authority, with the single exception of Boyd v. United States, supra, which differed from both the Wilson case and the present ones in providing a drastically incriminating method of enforcement [41] which was applied to the production of partners' business records. Whatever limits there may be to congressional power to provide for the production of corporate or other business records, therefore, they are not to be found, in view of the course of prior decisions, in any such absolute or universal immunity as petitioners seek.

Without attempt to summarize or accurately distinguish all of the cases, the fair distillation, insofar as they apply merely to the production of corporate records and papers in response to a subpoena or order authorized by law and safeguarded by judicial sanction, seems to be that the Fifth Amendment affords no protection by virtue of the self-incrimination provision, whether for the corporation or for its officers; and the Fourth, if applicable, at the most guards against abuse only by way of too much indefiniteness or breadth in the things required to be "particularly described," if also the inquiry is one the demanding agency is authorized by law to make and the materials specified are relevant. The gist of the protection is in the requirement, expressed in terms, that the disclosure sought shall not be unreasonable.

As this has taken from in the decisions, the following specific results have been worked out. It is not necessary, as in the case of a warrant, that a specific charge or complaint of violation of law be pending or that the order be made pursuant to one. It is enough that the investigation be for a lawfully authorized purpose, within the power of Congress to command. This has been ruled most often perhaps in relation to grand jury investigations, [42] but also frequently in respect to general or statistical investigations authorized by Congress. [43] The requirement of "probable cause, supported by oath or affirmation" literally applicable in the case of a warrant is satisfied, in that of an order for production, by the court's determination that the investigation is authorized by Congress, is for a purpose Congress can order, and the documents sought are relevant to the inquiry. [44] Beyond this, the requirement of

reasonableness, including particularity in "describing the place to be searched, and the persons or things to be seized," also literally applicable to warrants, comes down to specification of the documents to be produced adequate, but not excessive, for the purposes of the relevant inquiry. Necessarily, as has been said, this cannot be reduced to formula, for relevancy and adequacy or excess in the breadth of the subpoena are matters variable in relation to the nature, purposes and scope of the inquiry. [45]

When these principles are applied to the facts of the present cases, it is impossible to conceive how a violation of petitioners' rights could have been involved. Both were corporations. The only records or documents sought were corporate ones. No possible element of self-incrimination was therefore presented, or in fact claimed. All the records sought were relevant to the authorized inquiry, [46] the purpose of which was to determine two issues, whether petitioners were subject to the Act and, if so, whether they were violating it. These were subjects of investigation authorized by § 11(a), the latter expressly, the former by necessary implication. [47] It is not to be doubted that Congress could authorize investigation of these matters. In all these respects, [48] the specifications more than meet the requirements long established by many precedents.

More recent confirmation of those rulings may be found in Endicott Johnson Corp. v. Perkins, supra, and Myers v. Bethlehem Corp., 303 U. S. 41. It is true that these cases involved different statutes substantially and procedurally. But, notwithstanding the possible influence of the doctrine of governmental immunity to suit in the Endicott Johnson case, it would be anomalous to hold that, under the Walsh-Healy Act, 49 Stat. 2036, the District Court was not authorized to decide the question of coverage or, on the basis of its adverse decision, to deny enforcement to the

Secretary's subpoena seeking relevant evidence on that question, because Congress had committed its initial determination to him; and at the same time to rule that Congress could not confer the same power upon the Administrator with reference to violations of the Fair Labor Standards Act. [49] The question at issue is not in either case the nature of the legal obligation violation of which the evidence is sought to show. It is rather whether evidence relevant to the violation, whatever the obligation's character, can be drawn forth by the exercise of the subpoena power.

The Myers case did not involve a subpoena duces tecum, but was a suit to enjoin the National Labor Relations Board from holding a hearing upon a complaint against an employer alleged to be engaged in unfair labor practices forbidden by the Wagner Act, 49 Stat. 449. The hearing required an investigation and determination of coverage, involving as in this case the question whether the company was engaged in commerce. It denied this upon allegations thought to sustain the denial, as well as the futility, expensiveness and vexatious character of the hearing to itself. [50] This Court held that the District Court was without jurisdiction to enjoin the hearing. Regarding as appropriate the procedure before the Board and as adequate the provisions for judicial review of its action, including its determination of coverage, the Court sustained the exclusive jurisdiction of the Board, and of the Court of Appeals upon review, to determine that question, with others committed to their judgment, in the statutory proceeding for determining whether violations of the Act exist. The opinion referred to the Board's subpoena power, also to its authority to apply to a District Court for enforcement, and stated that, "to such an application, appropriate defense may be made." But the decision's necessary effect was to rule that it was not "an appropriate defense" that coverage had not been determined prior to the hearing or, it would seem necessarily to follow, prior to the Board's preliminary investigation of violation. If this is true in the case of the Board, it would seem to be equally true in that of the Administrator. [51]

In these results under the later as well as the earlier decisions, the basic compromise has been worked out in a manner to secure the public interest and at the same time to guard the private ones affected against the only abuses from which protection rightfully may be claimed. The latter are not identical with those protected against invasion by actual search and seizure, nor are the threatened abuses the same. They are, rather, the interests of men to be free from officious intermeddling, whether because irrelevant to any lawful purpose or because unauthorized by law, concerning matters which on proper occasion and within lawfully conferred authority of broad limits are subject to public examination in the public interest. Officious examination can be expensive, so much so that it eats up men's substance. It can be time-consuming, clogging the processes of business. It can become persecution when carried beyond reason.

On the other hand, petitioners' view, if accepted, would stop much if not all of investigation in the public interest at the threshold of inquiry and, in the case of the Administrator, is designed avowedly to do so. This would render substantially impossible his effective discharge of the duties of investigation and enforcement which Congress has placed upon him. And if his functions could be thus blocked, so might many others of equal importance.

We think, therefore, that the Courts of Appeals were correct in the view that Congress has authorized the Administrator, rather than the District Courts in the first instance, to determine the question of coverage in the preliminary investigation of possibly existing violations; in doing so to exercise his subpoena power for securing evidence upon that question, by seeking the production of petitioners' relevant books, records and papers; and, in case of refusal to obey his subpoena, issued according to the statute's authorization, to have the aid of the District Court in enforcing it. No constitutional provision forbids Congress to do this. On the contrary, its authority would seem clearly to be comprehended in the "necessary and proper" clause, as incidental to both its general legislative and its investigative powers.

IV

What has been said disposes of petitioners' principal contention upon the sufficiency of the showing. Other assignments, however, present the further questions whether any showing is required beyond the Administrator's allegations of coverage and relevance of the required materials to that question, and, if so, of what character. Stated otherwise, they are whether the court may order enforcement only upon a finding of "probable cause," that is, probability in fact, of coverage, as was held by the Court of Appeals for the Tenth Circuit in No. 61, following the lead of the Eighth Circuit in Walling v. Benson, 137 F.2d 501, or may do so upon the narrower basis accepted by the Third Circuit in No. 63.

The showing in No. 61 was clearly sufficient to constitute "probable cause" in this sense under conceptions of coverage prevailing at the time of the hearing, [52] whether or not that showing was necessary. Accordingly the judgment in that case must be affirmed.

In No. 63, the showing was less extensive, and it is doubtful that it would constitute "probable cause" of coverage as that term was used in the decisions from the Tenth and Eighth Circuits. [53] The Court of Appeals for the Third Circuit did not so label it, but held the showing sufficient.

Congress has made no requirements in terms of any showing of "probable cause", [54] and, in view of what has already been said, any possible constitutional requirement of that sort was satisfied by the Administrator's showing in this case, including not only the allegations concerning coverage, but also that he was proceeding with his investigation in accordance with the mandate of Congress and that the records sought were relevant to that purpose. Actually, in view of today's ruling in Mabee v. White Plains Pub. Co., supra, the showing here, including the facts supplied by the response, was sufficient to establish coverage itself, though that was not required.

The result therefore sustains the Administrator's position that his investigative function, in searching out violations with a view to securing enforcement of the Act, is essentially the same as the grand jury's, or the court's in issuing other pretrial orders for the discovery of evidence, [55] and is governed by the same limitations. These are that he shall not act arbitrarily or in excess of his statutory authority, but this does not mean that his inquiry must be "limited . . . by . . . forecasts of the probable result of the investigation. . . ." Blair v. United States, 250 U. S. 273, 250 U. S. 282; cf. Hale v. Henkel, 201 U. S. 43. Nor is the judicial function either abused or abased, as has been suggested, [56] by leaving to it the determination of the important questions which the Administrator's position concedes the courts may decide. [57]

Petitioner stress that enforcement will subject them to inconvenience, expense and harassment. That argument is answered fully by what was said in Myers v. Bethlehem Corp. [58] There is no harassment when the subpoena is issued and enforced according to law. The Administrator is authorized to enter and inspect, but the Act makes his right to do so subject in all cases to judicial supervision. Persons from whom he seeks relevant information are not required to submit to his demand, if in any respect it is unreasonable or overreaches the authority Congress has given. To it they may make "appropriate defense" surrounded by every safeguard of judicial restraint. In view of these safeguards, the expressed fears of unwarranted intrusions upon personal liberty are effective only to recall Mr. Justice Cardozo's reply to the same exaggerated forebodings in Jones v. Securities & Exchange Commission: "Historians may find hyperbole in the sanguinary simile." [59]

Nor is there room for intimation that the Administrator has proceeded in these cases in any manner contrary to petitioners' fundamental rights or otherwise than strictly according to law. It is to be remembered that petitioners' are not the only rights which may be involved or threatened with possible infringement. Their employees' rights and the public interest under the declared policy of Congress also would be affected if petitioners should enjoy the practically complete immunity they seek.

No sufficient reason was set forth in the returns or the accompanying affidavits for not enforcing the subpoenas, a burden petitioners were required to assume in order to make "appropriate defense."

Accordingly the judgments in both causes, No. 61 and No. 63, are

Affirmed.

Rochin v. California (Jan 2, 1952) [Notes omitted]

MR. JUSTICE FRANKFURTER delivered the opinion of the Court.

Having "some information that [the petitioner here] was selling narcotics," three deputy sheriffs of the County of Los Angeles, on the morning of July 1, 1949, made for the two-story dwelling house in which Rochin lived with his mother, common law wife, brothers and sisters. Finding the outside door open, they entered and then forced open the door to Rochin's room on the second floor. Inside they found petitioner sitting partly dressed on the side of the bed, upon which his wife was lying. On a "night stand" beside the bed, the deputies spied two capsules. When asked "Whose stuff is this?", Rochin seized the capsules and put them in his mouth. A struggle ensued in the course of which the three officers "jumped upon him" and attempted to extract the capsules. The force they applied proved unavailing against Rochin's resistance. He was handcuffed and taken to a hospital. At the direction of one of the officers, a doctor forced an emetic solution through a tube into Rochin's stomach against his will. This "stomach pumping" produced vomiting. In the vomited matter were found two capsules which proved to contain morphine.

Rochin was brought to trial before a California Superior Court, sitting without a jury, on the charge of possessing "a preparation of morphine" in violation of the California Health and Safety Code 1947, § 11500. Rochin was convicted and sentenced to sixty days' imprisonment. The chief evidence against him was the two capsules. They were admitted over petitioner's objection, although the means of obtaining them was frankly set forth in the testimony by one of the deputies, substantially as here narrated.

On appeal, the District Court of Appeal affirmed the conviction, despite the finding that the officer

"were guilty of unlawfully breaking into and entering defendant's room, and were guilty of unlawfully assaulting and battering defendant while in the room,"

and "were guilty of unlawfully assaulting, battering, torturing and falsely imprisoning the defendant at the alleged hospital." 101 Cal.App.2d 140, 143, 225 P.2d 1, 3. One of the three judges, while finding that "the record in this case reveals a shocking series of violations of constitutional rights", concurred only because he felt bound by decisions of his Supreme Court. These, he asserted, "have been looked upon by law enforcement officers as an encouragement, if not an invitation, to the commission of such lawless acts." Ibid. The Supreme Court of California denied without opinion Rochin's petition for a hearing. [1] Two justice dissented from this denial, and, in doing so, expressed themselves thus:

"... a conviction which rests upon evidence of incriminating objects obtained from the body of the accused by physical abuse is as invalid as a conviction which rests upon a verbal confession extracted from him by such abuse.... Had the evidence forced from defendant's lips consisted of an oral confession that he illegally possessed a drug ..., he would have the protection of the rule of law which excludes coerced confessions from evidence. But because the evidence forced from his lips consisted of real objects, the People of this state are permitted to base a conviction upon it. [We] find no valid ground of distinction between a verbal confession extracted by physical abuse and a confession wrested from defendant's body by physical abuse."

101 Cal.App.2d 143, 149-150, 225 P.2d 913, 917-918.

This Court granted certiorari, 341 U.S. 939, because a serious question is raised as to the limitations which the Due Process Clause of the Fourteenth Amendment imposes on the conduct of criminal proceedings by the States.

In our federal system, the administration of criminal justice is predominantly committed to the care of the States. The power to define crimes belongs to Congress only as an appropriate means of carrying into execution its limited grant of legislative powers. U.S.Const. Art. I, § 8, cl. 18. Broadly speaking, crimes in the United States are what the laws of the individual States make them, subject to the limitations of Art. I, § 10, cl. 1, in the original Constitution, prohibiting bills of attainder and ex post facto laws, and of the Thirteenth and Fourteenth Amendments.

These limitations, in the main, concern not restrictions upon the powers of the States to define crime, except in the restricted area where federal authority has preempted the field, but restrictions upon the manner in which the States may enforce their penal codes. Accordingly, in reviewing a State criminal conviction under a claim of right guaranteed by the Due Process Clause of the Fourteenth Amendment, from which is derived the most far-reaching and most frequent federal basis of challenging State criminal justice,

"we must be deeply mindful of the responsibilities of the States for the enforcement of criminal laws, and exercise with due humility our merely negative function in subjecting convictions from state courts to the very narrow scrutiny which the Due Process Clause of the Fourteenth Amendment authorizes."

Malinski v. New York, 324 U. S. 401, 324 U. S. 412, 324 U. S. 418. Due process of law, "itself a historical product," Jackman v. Rosenbaum Co., 260 U. S. 22, 260 U. S. 31, is not to be turned into a destructive dogma against the States in the administration of their systems of criminal justice.

However, this Court too has its responsibility. Regard for the requirements of the Due Process Clause

"inescapably imposes upon this Court an exercise of judgment upon the whole course of the proceedings [resulting in a conviction] in order to ascertain whether they offend those canons of decency and fairness which express the notions of justice of English-speaking peoples even toward those charged with the most heinous offenses."

Malinski v. New York, supra, at 324 U. S. 416-417. These standards of justice are not authoritatively formulated anywhere as though they were specifics. Due process of law is a summarized constitutional guarantee of respect for those personal immunities which, as Mr. Justice Cardozo twice wrote for the Court, are "so rooted in the traditions and conscience of our people as to be ranked as fundamental," Snyder v. Massachusetts, 291 U. S. 97, 291 U. S. 105, or are "implicit in the concept of ordered liberty." Palko v. Connecticut, 302 U. S. 319, 302 U. S. 325. [2]

The Court's function in the observance of this settled conception of the Due Process Clause does not leave us without adequate guides in subjecting State criminal procedures to constitutional judgment. In dealing not with the machinery of government, but with human rights, the absence of formal exactitude, or want of fixity of meaning, is not an unusual, or even regrettable, attribute of constitutional provisions. Words being symbols do not speak without a gloss. On the one hand, the gloss may be the deposit of history, whereby a term gains technical content. Thus the requirements of the Sixth and Seventh Amendments for trial by jury in the federal courts have a rigid meaning. No changes or chances can alter the content of the verbal symbol of "jury" -- a body of twelve men who must reach a unanimous conclusion if the verdict is to go against the defendant. [3] On the other hand, the gloss of some of the verbal symbols of the Constitution does not give them a fixed technical content. It exacts a continuing process of application.

When the gloss has thus not been fixed, but is a function of the process of judgment, the judgment is bound to fall differently at different times and differently at the same time through different judges. Even more specific provisions, such as the guaranty of freedom of speech and the detailed protection against unreasonable searches and seizures, have inevitably evoked as sharp divisions in this Court as the least specific and most comprehensive protection of liberties, the Due Process Clause.

The vague contours of the Due Process Clause do not leave judges at large. [4] We may not draw on our merely personal and private notions and disregard the limits that bind judges in their judicial function. Even though the concept of due process of law is not final and fixed, these limits are derived from considerations that are fused in the whole nature of or judicial process. See Cardozo,

The Nature of the Judicial Process; The Growth of the Law; The Paradoxes of Legal Science. These are considerations deeply rooted in reason and in the compelling traditions of the legal profession. The Due Process Clause places upon this Court the duty of exercising a judgment, within the narrow confines of judicial power in reviewing State convictions, upon interests of society pushing in opposite directions.

Due process of law, thus conceived, is not to be derided as resort to a revival of "natural law." [5] To believe that this judicial exercise of judgment could be avoided by freezing "due process of law" at some fixed stage of time or thought is to suggest that the most important aspect of constitutional adjudication is a function for inanimate machines, and not for judges, for whom the independence safeguarded by Article III of the Constitution was designed and who are presumably guided by established standards of judicial behavior. Even cybernetics has not yet made that haughty claim. To practice the requisite detachment and to achieve sufficient objectivity no doubt demands of judges the habit of self-discipline and self-criticism, incertitude that one's own views are incontestable, and alert tolerance toward views not shared. But these are precisely the presuppositions of our judicial process. They are precisely the qualities society has a right to expect from those entrusted with ultimate judicial power.

Restraints on our jurisdiction are self-imposed only in the sense that there is from our decisions no immediate appeal short of impeachment or constitutional amendment. But that does not make due process of law a matter of judicial caprice. The faculties of the Due Process Clause may be indefinite and vague, but the mode of their ascertainment is not self-willed. In each case, "due process of law" requires an evaluation based on a disinterested inquiry pursued in the spirit of science, on a balanced order of facts exactly and fairly stated, on the detached consideration of conflicting claims, see Hudson County Water Co. v. McCarter, 209 U. S. 349, 209 U. S. 355, on a judgment not ad hoc and episodic, but duly mindful of reconciling the needs both of continuity and of change in a progressive society.

Applying these general considerations to the circumstances of the present case, we are compelled to conclude that the proceedings by which this conviction was obtained do more than offend some fastidious squeamishness or private sentimentalism about combatting crime too energetically. This is conduct that shocks the conscience. Illegally breaking into the privacy of the petitioner, the struggle to open his mouth and remove what was there, the forcible extraction of his stomach's contents -- this course of proceeding by agents of government to obtain evidence is bound to offend even hardened sensibilities. They are methods too close to the rack and the screw to permit of constitutional differentiation.

It has long since ceased to be true that due process of law is heedless of the means by which otherwise relevant and credible evidence is obtained. This was not true even before the series of recent cases enforced the constitutional principle that the States may not base convictions upon confessions, however much verified, obtained by coercion. These decisions are not arbitrary exceptions to the comprehensive right of States to fashion their own rules of evidence for criminal trials. They are not sports in our constitutional law, but applications of a general principle. They are only instances of the general requirement that States, in their prosecutions, respect certain decencies of civilized conduct. Due process of law, as a historic and generative principle, precludes defining, and thereby confining, these standards of conduct more precisely than to say that convictions cannot be brought about by methods that offend "a

sense of justice." See Mr. Chief Justice Hughes, speaking for a unanimous Court in Brown v. Mississippi, 297 U. S. 278, 297 U. S. 285-286. It would be a stultification of the responsibility which the course of constitutional history has cast upon this Court to hold that in order to convict a man the police cannot extract by force what is in his mind but can extract what is in his stomach. [6]

To attempt in this case to distinguish what lawyers call "real evidence" from verbal evidence is to ignore the reasons for excluding coerced confessions. Use of involuntary verbal confessions in State criminal trials is constitutionally obnoxious not only because of their unreliability. They are inadmissible under the Due Process Clause even though statements contained in them may be independently established as true. Coerced confessions offend the community's sense of fair play and decency. So here, to sanction the brutal conduct which, naturally enough, was condemned by the court whose judgment is before us would be to afford brutality the cloak of law. Nothing would be more calculated to discredit law, and thereby to brutalize the temper of a society.

In deciding this, case we do not heedlessly bring into question decisions in many States dealing with essentially different, even if related, problems. We therefore put to one side cases which have arisen in the State courts through use of modern methods and devices for discovering wrongdoers and bringing them to book. It does not fairly represent these decisions to suggest that they legalize force so brutal and so offensive to human dignity in securing evidence from a suspect as is revealed by this record. Indeed, the California Supreme Court has not sanctioned this mode of securing a conviction. It merely exercised its discretion to decline a review of the conviction. All the California judges who have expressed themselves in this case have condemned the conduct in the strongest language.

We are not unmindful that hypothetical

situations can be conjured up standing imperceptibly from the circumstances of this case and, by gradations, producing practical differences despite seemingly logical extensions. But the Constitution is "intended to preserve practical and substantial rights, not to maintain theories." Davis v. Mills, 194 U. S. 451, 194 U. S. 457.

On the facts of this case, the conviction of the petitioner has been obtained by methods that offend the Due Process Clause. The judgment below must be reversed.

Reversed.

On Lee v. US (June 2, 1952)

MR. JUSTICE JACKSON delivered the opinion of the Court.

Petitioner was convicted on a two-count indictment, one charging the substantive offense of selling a pound of opium in violation of 21 U.S.C. §§ 173 and 174, the other conspiring to sell the opium in violation of 18 U.S.C. § 371. The Court of Appeals sustained the conviction by a divided court. [1] We granted certiorari. [2]

The questions raised by petitioner have been considered, but only one is of enough general interest to merit discussion. That concerns admission in evidence of two conversations petitioner had, while at large on bail pending trial, with one Chin Poy. The circumstances are these:

Petitioner, On Lee, had a laundry in Hoboken. A customer's room opened on the street, back of it was a room for ironing tables, and in the rear were his living quarters. Chin Poy, an old acquaintance and former employee, sauntered in and, while customers came and went, engaged the accused in conversation in the course of which petitioner made incriminating statements. He did not know that Chin Poy was what the Government calls "an undercover agent" and what petitioner calls a "stool pigeon" for the Bureau of Narcotics. Neither did he know that Chin Poy was wired for sound, with a small microphone in his inside overcoat pocket and a small antenna running along his arm. Unbeknownst to petitioner, an agent of the Narcotics Bureau named Lawrence Lee had stationed himself outside with a receiving set properly tuned to pick up any sounds the Chin Poy microphone transmitted. Through the large front window, Chin Poy could be seen, and, through the receiving set, his conversation, in Chinese, with petitioner could be heard by agent Lee. A few days later, on the sidewalks of New York, another conversation took place between the two, and damaging admissions were again "audited" by agent Lee.

For reasons left to our imagination, Chin Poy was not called to testify about petitioner's incriminating admissions. Against objection, [3] however, agent Lee was allowed to relate the conversations as heard with aid of his receiving set. Of this testimony, it is enough to say that it was certainly prejudicial if its admission was improper.

Petitioner contends that this evidence should have been excluded because the manner in which it was obtained violates both the search and seizure provisions of the Fourth Amendment, [4] and § 605 of the Federal Communications Act, 47 U.S.C. § 605, [5] and, if not rejected on those grounds, we should pronounce it inadmissible anyway under the judicial power to require fair play in federal law enforcement.

The conduct of Chin Poy and agent Lee did not amount to an unlawful search and seizure such as is proscribed by the Fourth Amendment. In Goldman v. United States, 316 U. S. 129, we held that the action of federal agents in placing a detectaphone on the outer wall of defendant's hotel room, and thereby overhearing conversations held within the room, did not violate the Fourth Amendment. There, the agents had earlier committed a trespass in order to install a listening device within the room itself. Since the device failed to work, the court expressly reserved decision as to the effect on the search and seizure question of a trespass in that situation. Petitioner in the instant case has seized upon that dictum, apparently on the assumption that the presence of a radio set would automatically bring him within the reservation if he can show a trespass.

But petitioner cannot raise the undecided question, for here, no trespass was committed. Chin Poy entered a place of business with the consent, if not by the implied invitation, of the petitioner. Petitioner contends, however, that Chin Poy's subsequent "unlawful conduct" vitiated the consent and rendered his entry a trespass ab initio.

If we were to assume that Chin Poy's conduct was unlawful and consider this argument as an original proposition, it is doubtful that the niceties of tort law initiated almost two and a half centuries ago by the case of the Six Carpenters, 8 Coke 146(a), cited by petitioner, are of much aid in determining rights under the Fourth Amendment. But petitioner's argument comes a quarter of a century too late: this contention was decided adversely to him in McGuire v. United States, 273 U. S. 95, 273 U. S. 98, 273 U. S. 100, where Mr. Justice Stone, speaking for a unanimous Court, said of the doctrine of trespass ab initio:

"This fiction, obviously invoked in support of a policy of penalizing the unauthorized acts of those who had entered under authority of law, has only been applied as a rule of liability in civil actions against them. Its extension is not favored."

He concluded that the Court would not resort to "a fiction whose origin, history, and purpose do not justify its application where the right of the government to make use of evidence is involved." This was followed in Zap v. United States, 328 U. S. 624, 328 U. S. 629.

By the same token, the claim that Chin Poy's entrance was a trespass because consent to his entry was obtained by fraud must be rejected. Whether an entry such as this, without any affirmative misrepresentation, would be a trespass under orthodox tort law is not at all clear. See Prosser on Torts, § 18. But the rational of the McGuire case rejects such fine-spun doctrines for exclusion of evidence. The further contention of petitioner that agent Lee, outside the laundry, was a trespasser because by these aids he overheard what went on inside verges on the frivolous. Only in the case of physical entry, either by force, as in McDonald v. United States, 335 U. S. 451, by unwilling submission to authority, as in Johnson v. United States, 333 U. S. 10, or without any express or implied consent, as in Nueslein v. District of Columbia, 73 App.D.C. 85, 115 F.2d 690, would the problem left undecided in the Goldman case be before the Court.

Petitioner relies on cases relating to the more common and clearly distinguishable problems raised where tangible property is unlawfully seized. Such unlawful seizure may violate the Fourth Amendment, even though the entry itself was by subterfuge or fraud, rather than force. United States v. Jeffers, 342 U. S. 48; Gouled v. United States, 255 U. S. 298 (the authority of the latter case is sharply limited by Olmstead v. United States, 277 U. S. 438, at 277 U. S. 463). But such decisions are inapposite in the field of mechanical or electronic devices designed to overhear or intercept conversation, at least where access to the listening post was not obtained by illegal methods.

Petitioner urges that, if his claim of unlawful search and seizure cannot be sustained on authority, we reconsider the question of Fourth Amendment rights in the field of overheard or intercepted conversations. This apparently is upon the theory that, since there was a radio set involved, he could succeed if he could persuade the Court to overturn the leading case holding wiretapping to be outside the ban of the Fourth Amendment, Olmstead v. United States, 277 U. S. 438, and the cases which have followed it. We need not consider this, however, for success in this attempt, which failed in Goldman v. United States,

316 U. S. 129, would be of no aid to petitioner unless he can show that his situation should be treated as wiretapping. The presence of a radio set is not sufficient to suggest more than the most attenuated analogy to wiretapping. Petitioner was talking confidentially and indiscreetly with one he trusted, and he was overheard. This was due to aid from a transmitter and receiver, to be sure, but with the same effect on his privacy as if agent Lee had been eavesdropping outside an open window. The use of bifocals, field glasses or the telescope to magnify the object of a witness' vision is not a forbidden search or seizure, even if they focus without his knowledge or consent upon what one supposes to be private indiscretions. It would be a dubious service to the genuine liberties protected by the Fourth Amendment to make them bedfellows with spurious liberties improvised by farfetched analogies which would liken eavesdropping on a conversation, with the connivance of one of the parties, to an unreasonable search or seizure. We find no violation of the Fourth Amendment here.

Nor do the facts show a violation of § 605 of the Federal Communications Act. Petitioner had no wires, and no wireless. There was no interference with any communications facility which he possessed or was entitled to use. He was not sending messages to anybody, or using a system of communications within the Act. Goldstein v. United States, 316 U. S. 114.

Finally, petitioner contends that, even though he be overruled in all else, the evidence should be excluded as a means of disciplining law enforcement officers. Cf. McNabb v. United States, 318 U. S. 332. In McNabb, however, we held that, where defendants had been unlawfully detained in violation of the federal statute requiring prompt arraignment before a commissioner, a confession made during the detention would be excluded as evidence in federal courts even though not inadmissible on the ground of any otherwise involuntary character. But here neither agent nor informer violated any federal law, and violation of state law, even had it been shown here, as it was not, would not render the evidence obtained inadmissible in federal courts. Olmstead v. United States, 277 U. S. 438, at 277 U. S. 468.

In order that constitutional or statutory rights may not be undermined, this Court has, on occasion, evolved or adopted from the practice of other courts exclusionary rules of evidence going beyond the requirements of the constitutional or statutory provision. McNabb v. United States, supra; Weeks v. United States, 232 U. S. 383. In so doing, it has, of course, departed from the common law rule under which otherwise admissible evidence was not rendered inadmissible by the fact that it had been illegally obtained. Such departures from the primary evidentiary criteria of relevancy and trustworthiness must be justified by some strong social policy. In discussing the extension of such rules, and the creation of new ones, it is well to remember the remarks of Mr. Justice Stone in McGuire v. United States, 273 U. S. 95, at 273 U. S. 99:

"A criminal prosecution is more than a game in which the government may be checkmated and the game lost merely because its officers have not played according to rule."

Rules of evidence, except where prescribed by statute, are formulated by the courts to some extent, as "a question of sound policy in the administration of the law." Zucker v. Whitridge, 205 N.Y. 50, 65, 98 N.E. 209, 213. Courts which deal with questions of evidence more frequently than we do have found it unwise to multiply occasions when the attention of a trial court in a criminal case must be diverted from the issue of the defendant's guilt to the issue of someone else's misconduct in obtaining evidence. They have considered that

"The underlying principle obviously is that the court, when engaged in trying a criminal cause, will not take notice of the manner in which witnesses have possessed themselves of papers or other articles of personal property which are material and properly offered in evidence."

People v. Adams, 176 N.Y. 351, 358, 68 N.E. 636, 638. However, there is a procedure in federal court by which defendant may protect his right in advance of trial to have returned to him evidence unconstitutionally obtained. Silverthorne Lumber Co. v. United States, 251 U. S. 385. But since we hold here that there was no violation of the Constitution, such a remedy could not be invoked. Exclusion would have to be based on a policy which placed the penalizing of Chin Poy's breach of confidence above ordinary canons of relevancy. For On Lee's statements to Chin Poy were admissions against interest provable against him as an exception to the hearsay rule. The normal manner of proof would be to call Chin Poy and have him relate the conversation. We can only speculate on the reasons why Chin Poy was not called. It seems a not unlikely assumption that the very defects of character and blemishes of record which made On Lee trust him with confidences would make a jury distrust his testimony. Chin Poy was close enough to the underworld to serve as bait, near enough the criminal design so that petitioner would embrace him as a confidante, but too close to it for the Government to vouch for him as a witness. Instead, the Government called agent Lee. We should think a jury probably would find the testimony of agent Lee to have more probative value than the word of Chin Poy.

Society can ill afford to throw away the evidence produced by the falling out, jealousies, and quarrels of those who live by outwitting the law. Certainly no one would foreclose the turning of state's evidence by denizens of the underworld. No good reason of public policy occurs to us why the Government should be deprived of the benefit of On Lee's admissions because he made them to a confidante of shady character.

The trend of the law in recent years has been to turn away from rigid rules of incompetence, in favor of admitting testimony and allowing the trier of fact to judge the weight to be given it. As this Court has pointed out:

"Indeed, the theory of the common law was to admit to the witness stand only those presumably honest, appreciating the sanctity of an oath, unaffected as a party by the result, and free from any of the temptations of interest. The courts were afraid to trust the intelligence of jurors. But the last 50 years have wrought a great change in these respects, and today the tendency is to enlarge the domain of competency, and to submit to the jury for their consideration as to the credibility of the witness those matters which heretofore were ruled sufficient to justify his exclusion. This change has been wrought partially by legislation and partially by judicial construction."

Funk v. United States, 290 U. S. 371, 290 U. S. 376.

The use of informers, accessories, accomplices, false friends, or any of the other betrayals which are "dirty business" may raise serious questions of credibility. To the extent that they do, a defendant is entitled to broad latitude to probe credibility by cross-examination and to have the issues submitted to the jury with careful instructions. But to the extent that the argument for exclusion departs from such orthodox evidentiary canons as relevancy and credibility, it rests solely on the proposition that the Government shall be arbitrarily penalized for the low morals of its informers. However unwilling we as individuals may be to approve conduct such as that of Chin Poy, such disapproval must not be thought to justify a social policy of the magnitude necessary to arbitrarily exclude otherwise relevant evidence. We think the administration of justice is better served if stratagems such as we have here are regarded as raising not questions of law, but issues of credibility. We cannot say that testimony such as this shall, as a matter of law, be refused all hearing.

Judgment affirmed.

Elkins v. US (June 27, 1960) [Appendix omitted]

MR. JUSTICE STEWART delivered the opinion of the Court.

The petitioners were indicted in the United States District Court in Oregon for the offense of intercepting and divulging telephone communications and of conspiracy to do so. 47 U.S.C. §§ 501, 605; 18 U.S.C. § 371. Before trial the petitioners made a motion to suppress as evidence several tape and wire recordings and a recording machine, which had originally been seized by state law enforcement officers in the home of petitioner Clark under circumstances which, two Oregon courts had found, had rendered the search and seizure unlawful. [1] At the hearing on the motion, the district judge assumed, without deciding, that the articles had been obtained as the result of an unreasonable search and seizure, but denied the motion to suppress because there was no evidence that any

"agent of the United States had any knowledge or information or suspicion of any kind that this search was being contemplated or was eventually made by the State officers until they read about it in the newspaper."

At the trial, the articles in question were admitted in evidence against the petitioners, and they were convicted.

The convictions were affirmed by the Court of Appeals for the Ninth Circuit, 266 F.2d 588. That court agreed with the district judge that it was unnecessary to determine whether or not the original state search and seizure had been lawful, because there had been no participation by federal officers.

"Hence the unlawfulness of the State

search and seizure, if indeed they were unlawful, did not entitle defendants to an order of the District Court suppressing the property seized." 266 F.2d at 594.

We granted certiorari, 361 U.S. 810, to consider a question of importance in the administration of federal justice. The question is this: may articles obtained as the result of an unreasonable search and seizure by state officers, without involvement of federal officers, be introduced in evidence against a defendant over his timely objection in a federal criminal trial? In a word, we reexamine here the validity of what has come to be called the "silver platter" doctrine. [2] For the reasons that follow, we conclude that this doctrine can no longer be accepted.

To put the issue in historic perspective, the appropriate starting point must be Weeks v. United States, 232 U.S. 383, decided in 1914. It was there that the Court established the rule which excludes in a federal criminal prosecution evidence obtained by federal agents in violation of the defendant's Fourth Amendment rights. The foundation for that decision was set out in forthright words:

"The effect of the Fourth Amendment is to put the courts of the United States and Federal officials, in the exercise of their power and authority, under limitations and restraints as to the exercise of such power and authority, and to forever secure the people, their persons, houses, papers and effects, against all unreasonable searches and seizures under the guise of law. This protection reaches all alike, whether accused of crime or not, and the duty of giving to it force and effect is obligatory upon all entrusted under our Federal system with the enforcement of the laws. The tendency of those who execute the criminal laws of the country to obtain conviction by means of unlawful seizures and enforced confessions, the latter often obtained after subjecting accused persons to unwarranted practices destructive of rights secured by the Federal Constitution, should find no sanction in the judgments of the courts, which are charged at all times with the support of the Constitution and to which people of all conditions have a right to appeal for the maintenance of such fundamental rights."

"* * * *"

". . . If letters and private documents can thus be seized and held and used in evidence against a citizen accused of an offense, the protection of the Fourth Amendment declaring his right to be secure against such searches and seizures is of no value, and, so far as those thus placed are concerned, might as well be stricken from the Constitution. The efforts of the courts and their officials to bring the guilty to punishment, praiseworthy as they are, are not to be aided by the sacrifice of those great principles established by years of endeavor and suffering which have resulted in their embodiment in the fundamental law of the land."

232 U. S. 232 U.S. 383, 232 U. S. 391-393.

To the exclusionary rule of Weeks v. United States there has been unquestioning adherence for now almost half a century. See Silverthorne Lumber Co. v. United States, 251 U. S. 385; Gouled v. United States, 255 U. S. 298; Amos v. United States, 255 U. S. 313; Agnello v. United States, 269 U. S. 20; Go-Bart Importing Co. v. United States, 282 U. S. 344; Grau v. United States, 287 U. S. 124; McDonald v. United States, 335 U. S. 451; United States v. Jeffers, 342 U. S. 48.

But the Weeks case also announced, unobtrusively but nonetheless definitely, another evidentiary rule. Some of the articles used as evidence against Weeks had been unlawfully seized by local police officers acting on their own account. The Court held that the admission of this evidence was not error for the reason that "the Fourth Amendment is not directed to individual misconduct of such officials. Its limitations reach the Federal government and its agencies." 232 U.S. at 232 U. S. 398. Despite the limited discussion of this second ruling in the Weeks opinion, the right of the prosecutor in a federal criminal trial to avail himself of evidence unlawfully seized by state officers apparently went unquestioned for the next thirty-five years. See, e.g., Byars v. United States, 273 U. S. 28, 273 U. S. 33; Feldman v. United States, 322 U. S. 487, 322 U. S. 492. [3]

That such a rule would engender practical difficulties in an era of expanding federal criminal jurisdiction could not, perhaps, have been foreseen. In any event the difficulties soon appeared. They arose from the entirely commendable practice of state and federal agents to cooperate with each other in the investigation and detection of criminal activity. When in a federal criminal prosecution evidence which had been illegally seized by state officers was sought to be introduced, the question inevitably arose whether there had been such participation by federal agents in the search and seizure as to make applicable the exclusionary rule of Weeks. See Flagg v. United States, 233 F. 481, 483; United States v. Slusser, 270 F. 818, 820; United States v. Falloco, 277 F. 75, 82; Legman v. United States, 295 F. 474, 476-478; Marron v. United States, 8 F.2d 251, 259; United States v. Brown, 8 F.2d 630, 631.

This Court first came to grips with the problem in Byars v. United States, 273 U. S. 28. There it was held that, when the participation of the federal agent in the search was "under color of his federal office" and the search "in substance and effect was a joint operation of the local and federal officers," then the evidence must be excluded, because "the effect is the same as though [the federal agent] had engaged in the undertaking as one exclusively his own." 273 U.S. at 273 U. S. 33. In Gambino v. United States, 275 U. S. 310, the Court went further. There, state officers had seized liquor from the defendants' automobile after an unlawful search in which no federal officers had participated. The liquor was admitted in evidence against the defendants in their subsequent federal trial for violation of the National Prohibition Act. This Court reversed the judgments of conviction, holding that the illegally seized evidence should have been excluded. Pointing out that there was

"no suggestion that the defendants were committing, at the time of the arrest, search, and seizure, any state offense, or that they had done so in the past, or that the [state] troopers believed that they had,' the Court found that '[t]he wrongful arrest, search, and seizure were made solely on behalf of the United States."

275 U.S. at 275 U. S. 314.

Despite these decisions, or perhaps because of them, cases kept arising in which the federal courts were faced with determining whether there had been such participation by federal officers in a lawless state search as to make inadmissible in evidence that which had been seized. And it is fair to say that, in their approach to this recurring question, no less than in their disposition of concrete cases, the federal courts did not find themselves in complete harmony, nor even internally self-consistent. [4] No less difficulty was experienced by the courts in determining whether, even in the absence of actual participation by federal agents, the state officers' illegal search and seizure had nevertheless been made "solely on behalf of the United States." [5]

But difficult and unpredictable as may have been their application to concrete cases, the controlling principles seemed clear up to 1949. Evidence which had been seized by federal officers in violation of the Fourth Amendment could not be used in a federal criminal prosecution. Evidence which had been obtained by state agents in an unreasonable search and seizure was admissible because, as Weeks had pointed out, the Fourth Amendment was not "directed to" the "misconduct of such officials." But if federal agents had

participated in an unreasonable search and seizure by state officers, or if the state officers had acted solely on behalf of the United States, the evidence was not admissible in a federal prosecution.

Then came Wolf v. Colorado, 338 U. S. 25. With the ultimate determination in Wolf -- that the Due Process Clause of the Fourteenth Amendment does not itself require state courts to adopt the exclusionary rule with respect to evidence illegally seized by state agents -- we are not here directly concerned. But nothing could be of greater relevance to the present inquiry than the underlying constitutional doctrine which Wolf established. For there it was unequivocally determined by a unanimous Court that the Federal Constitution, by virtue of the Fourteenth Amendment, prohibits unreasonable searches and seizures by state officers.

"The security of one's privacy against arbitrary intrusion by the police . . . is . . . implicit in 'the concept of ordered liberty,' and, as such, enforceable against the States through the Due Process Clause."

338 U. S. 338 U.S. 25, 338 U. S. 27-28. The Court has subsequently found frequent occasion to reiterate this statement from Wolf. See Stefanelli v. Minard, 342 U. S. 117, 342 U. S. 119; Irvine v. California, 347 U. S. 128, 347 U. S. 132; Frank v. Maryland, 359 U. S. 360, 359 U. S. 362-363.

The foundation upon which the admissibility of state-seized evidence in a federal trial originally rested -- that unreasonable state searches did not violate the Federal Constitution -- thus disappeared in 1949. This removal of the doctrinal underpinning for the admissibility rule has apparently escaped the attention of most of the federal courts, which have continued to approve the admission of evidence illegally seized by state officers without so much as even discussing the impact of Wolf. [6] Only two of the courts of appeals which have adhered to the admissibility rule appear to have recognized that Wolf casts doubt upon its continuing validity. Jones v. United States, 217 F.2d 381; United States v. Benanti, 244 F.2d 389, reversed on other grounds, 355 U. S. 355 U.S. 96. Cf. Kendall v. United States, 272 F.2d 163, 165. The Court of Appeals for the District of Columbia has been alone in squarely holding

"that the Weeks and the Wolf decisions, considered together, make all evidence obtained by unconstitutional search and seizure unacceptable in federal courts."

Hanna v. United States, 104 U.S.App.D.C. 205, 209, 260 F.2d 723, 727.

Yet this Court's awareness that the constitutional doctrine of Wolf operated to undermine the logical foundation of the Weeks admissibility rule has been manifest from the very day that Wolf was decided. In Lustig v. United States, 338 U. S. 74, decided that day, the prevailing opinion carefully left open the question of the continuing validity of the admissibility rule. "Where there is participation on the part of federal officers," the opinion said, "it is not necessary to consider what would be the result if the search had been conducted entirely by State officers." 338 U.S. at 338 U. S. 79. And in Benanti v. United States, 355 U. S. 96, the Court was at pains to point out that

"[i]t has remained an open question in this Court whether evidence obtained solely by state agents in an illegal search may be admissible in federal court . . . ."

355 U.S. at 355 U. S. 102, note 10. There the question has stood for 11 years.

If resolution of the issue were to be dictated solely by principles of logic, it is clear what our decision would have to be. For surely no distinction can logically be drawn between evidence obtained in violation of the Fourth Amendment and that obtained in violation of the Fourteenth. The Constitution is flouted equally in either case. To the victim, it matters not whether his constitutional right has been invaded by a federal agent or by a state officer. [7] It would be a curiously ambivalent rule that would require the courts of the United States to differentiate between unconstitutionally seized evidence upon so arbitrary a basis. Such a distinction indeed would appear to reflect an indefensibly selective evaluation of the provisions of the Constitution. Moreover, it would seem logically impossible to justify a policy that would bar from a federal trial what state officers had obtained in violation of a federal statute, yet would admit that which they had seized in violation of the Constitution itself. Cf. Benanti v. United States, 355 U. S. 96.

Mere logical symmetry and abstract reasoning are perhaps not enough, however, to support a doctrine that would exclude relevant evidence from the trial of a federal criminal case. It is true that there is not involved here an absolute or qualified testimonial privilege such as that accorded a spouse, a patient, or a penitent, which irrevocably bars otherwise admissible evidence because of the status of the witness or his relationship to the defendant. Cf. Hawkins v. United States, 358 U. S. 74. A rule which would exclude evidence if, and only if, government officials in a particular case had chosen to engage in unlawful conduct is of a different order. Yet any apparent limitation upon the process of discovering truth in a federal trial ought to be imposed only upon the basis of considerations which outweigh the general need for untrammeled disclosure of competent and relevant evidence in a court of justice.

What is here invoked is the Court's supervisory power over the administration of criminal justice in the federal courts, under which the Court has "from the very beginning of its history, formulated rules of evidence to be applied in federal criminal prosecutions." McNabb v. United States, 318 U. S. 332, 318 U. S. 341. In devising such evidentiary rules, we are to be governed by "principles of the common law as they may be interpreted . . . in the light of reason and experience." Rule 26, Fed.Rules Crim.Proc. Determination of the issue before us must ultimately depend, therefore, upon evaluation of the exclusionary rule itself in the context here presented.

The exclusionary rule has for decades been the subject of ardent controversy. The arguments of its antagonists and of its proponents have been so many times marshalled as to require no lengthy elaboration here. Most of what has been said in opposition to the rule was distilled in a single Cardozo sentence -- "The criminal is to go free because the constable has blundered." People v. Defore, 242 N.J. 13, 21, 150 N.E. 585, 587. The same point was made at somewhat greater length in the often quoted words of Professor Wigmore:

"Titus, you have been found guilty of conducting a lottery; Flavius, you have confessedly violated the constitution. Titus ought to suffer imprisonment for crime, and Flavius for contempt. But no! We shall let you both go free. We shall not punish Flavius directly, but shall do so by reversing Titus' conviction. This is our way of teaching people like Flavius to behave, and of teaching people like Titus to behave, and incidentally of securing respect for the Constitution. Our way of upholding the Constitution is not to strike at the man who breaks it, but to let off somebody else who broke something else."

8 Wigmore, Evidence (3d ed. 1940), § 2184.

Yet, however felicitous their phrasing, these objections hardly answer the basic postulate of the exclusionary rule itself. The rule is calculated to prevent, not to repair. Its purpose is to deter -- to compel respect for the constitutional guaranty in the only effectively available way -- by removing the incentive to disregard it. See Eleuteri v. Richman, 26 N.J. 506, 513, 141 A.2d 46, 50. Mr. Justice Jackson summed it up well:

"Only occasional and more flagrant abuses come to the attention of the courts, and then only those where the search and seizure yields incriminating evidence and the defendant is at least sufficiently compromised to be indicted. If the officers raid a home, an office, or stop and search an automobile but find nothing incriminating, this invasion of the personal liberty of the innocent too often finds no practical redress. There may be, and I am convinced that there are, many unlawful searches of homes and automobiles of innocent people which turn up nothing incriminating, in which no arrest is made, about which courts do nothing, and about which we never hear."

"Courts can protect the innocent against such invasions only indirectly and through the medium of excluding evidence obtained against those who frequently are guilty."

Brinegar v. United States, 338 U. S. 160, 338 U. S. 181 (dissenting opinion).

Empirical statistics are not available to show that the inhabitants of states which follow the exclusionary rule suffer less from lawless searches and seizures than do those of states which admit evidence unlawfully obtained. Since, as a practical matter, it is never easy to prove a negative, it is hardly likely that conclusive factual data could ever be assembled. For much the same reason, it cannot positively be demonstrated that enforcement of the criminal law is either more or less effective under either rule.

But pragmatic evidence of a sort is not wanting. The federal courts themselves have operated under the exclusionary rule of Weeks for almost half a century, yet it has not been suggested either that the Federal Bureau of Investigation has thereby been rendered ineffective or that the administration of criminal justice in the federal courts has thereby been disrupted. [8] Moreover, the experience of the states is impressive. Not more than half the states continue totally to adhere to the rule that evidence is freely admissible no matter how it was obtained. [9] Most of the others have adopted the exclusionary rule in its entirety; the rest have adopted it in part. [10] The movement towards the rule of exclusion has been halting, but seemingly inexorable. [11] Since the Wolf decision, one state has switched its position in that direction by legislation, [12] and two others by judicial decision. [13] Another state, uncommitted, until 1955, in that year adopted the rule of exclusion. [14] Significantly, most of the exclusionary states which have had to consider the issue have held that evidence obtained by federal officers in a search and seizure unlawful under the Fourth Amendment must be suppressed in a prosecution in the state courts. State v. Arregui, 44 Idaho 43, 254 P. 788; Walters v. Commonwealth, 199 Ky. 182, 250 S.W. 839; Little v. State, 171 Miss. 818, 159 So. 103; State v. Rebasti, 306 Mo. 336, 267 S.W. 858; State v. Hiteshew, 42 Wyo. 147, 292 P. 2; see Ramirez v. State, 123 Tex.Cr.R. 254, 58 S.W.2d 829. Compare Rea v. United States, 350 U. S. 214.

The experience in California has been most illuminating. In 1955, the Supreme Court of that State resolutely turned its back on many years of precedent and adopted the exclusionary rule. People v. Cahan, 44 Cal.2d 434, 282 P.2d 905.

"We have been compelled to reach that conclusion because other remedies have completely failed to secure compliance with the constitutional provisions on the part of police officers, with the attendant result that the courts under the old rule have been constantly required to participate in, and in effect condone, the lawless activities of law enforcement officers. . . . Experience has demonstrated, however, that neither administrative, criminal, nor civil remedies are effective in suppressing lawless searches and seizures. The innocent suffer with the guilty, and we cannot close our eyes to the effect the rule we adopt will have on the rights of those not before the court."

44 Cal.2d 434, at 445, 447, 282 P.2d 905, at 911-912, 913.

The chief law enforcement officer of California was quoted as having made this practical evaluation of the Cahan decision less than two years later:

"The over-all effects of the Cahan decision, particularly in view of the rules now worked out by the Supreme Court, have been excellent. A much greater education is called for on the part of all peace officers of California. As a result, I am confident they will be much better police officers. I think there is more cooperation with the District Attorneys and this will make for better administration of criminal justice. [15]"

Impressive as is this experience of individual states, even more is to be said for adoption of the exclusionary rule in the particular context here presented -- a context which brings into focus considerations of federalism. The very essence of a healthy federalism depends upon the avoidance of needless conflict between state and federal courts. Yet when a federal court sitting in an exclusionary state admits evidence lawlessly seized by state agents, it not only frustrates state policy, but frustrates that policy in a particularly inappropriate and ironic way. For, by admitting the unlawfully seized evidence, the federal court serves to defeat the state's effort to assure obedience to the Federal Constitution. In states which have not adopted the exclusionary rule, on the other hand, it would work no conflict with local policy for a federal court to decline to receive evidence unlawfully seized by state officers. The question with which we deal today affects not at all the freedom of the states to develop and apply their own sanctions in their own way. Cf. Wolf v. Colorado, 338 U. S. 25.

Free and open cooperation between state and federal law enforcement officers is to be commended and encouraged. Yet that kind of cooperation is hardly promoted by a rule that implicitly invites federal officers to withdraw from such association and at least tacitly to encourage state officers in the disregard of constitutionally protected freedom. If, on the other hand, it is understood that the fruit of an unlawful search by state agents will be inadmissible in a federal trial, there can be no inducement to subterfuge and evasion with respect to federal-state cooperation in criminal investigation. Instead, forthright cooperation under constitutional standards will be promoted and fostered.

It must always be remembered that what the Constitution forbids is not all searches and seizures, but unreasonable searches and seizures. Without pausing to analyze individual decisions, it can fairly be said that, in applying the Fourth Amendment, this Court has seldom shown itself unaware of the practical demands of effective criminal investigation and law enforcement. Indeed, there are those who think that some of the Court's decisions have tipped the balance too heavily against the protection of that individual privacy which it was the purpose of the Fourth Amendment to guarantee. See Harris v. United States, 331 U. S. 145, 331 U. S. 155, 331 U. S. 183, 331 U. S. 195 (dissenting opinions); United States v. Rabinowitz, 339 U. S. 56, 339 U. S. 66, 339 U. S. 68 (dissenting opinions). In any event, while individual cases have sometimes evoked "fluctuating differences of view," Abel v. United States, 362 U. S. 217, 362 U. S. 235, it can hardly be said that in the over-all pattern of Fourth Amendment decisions this Court has been either unrealistic or visionary.

These, then, are the considerations of reason and experience which point to the rejection of a doctrine that would freely admit in a federal criminal trial evidence seized by state agents in violation of the defendant's constitutional rights. But there is another consideration -- the imperative of judicial integrity. It was of this that Mr. Justice Holmes and Mr. Justice Brandeis so eloquently spoke in Olmstead v. United States, 277 U. S. 438, 277 U. S. 469, 277 U. S. 471, more than 30 years ago. "For those who agree with me," said Mr. Justice Holmes, "no distinction can be taken between the government as prosecutor and the government as judge." 277 U.S. at 277 U. S. 470. (Dissenting opinion.) "In a government of laws," said Mr. Justice Brandeis,

"existence of the government will be imperilled if it fails to observe the law scrupulously. Our government is the potent, the omnipresent teacher. For good or for ill, it teaches the whole people by its example. Crime is contagious. If the government becomes a lawbreaker, it breeds contempt for law; it invites every man to become a law unto himself; it invites anarchy. To declare that, in the administration of the criminal law, the end justifies the means -- to declare that the government may commit crimes in order to secure the conviction of a private criminal -- would bring terrible retribution. Against that pernicious doctrine this court should resolutely set its face."

277 U.S. at 277 U. S. 485. (Dissenting opinion.)

This basic principle was accepted by the Court in McNabb v. United States, 318 U. S. 332. There it was held that

"a conviction resting on evidence secured through such a flagrant disregard of the procedure which Congress has commanded cannot be allowed to stand without making the courts themselves accomplices in willful disobedience of law."

318 U.S. at 318 U. S. 345. Even less should the federal courts be accomplices in the willful disobedience of a Constitution they are sworn to uphold.

For these reasons, we hold that evidence obtained by state officers during a search which, if conducted by federal officers, would have violated the defendant's immunity from unreasonable searches and seizures under the Fourth Amendment, is inadmissible over the defendant's timely objection in a federal criminal trial. [16] In determining whether there has been an unreasonable search and seizure by state officers, a federal court must make an independent inquiry, whether or not there has been such an inquiry by a state court, and irrespective of how any such inquiry may have turned out. The test is one of federal law, neither enlarged by what one state court may have countenanced, nor diminished by what another may have colorably suppressed.

The judgment of the Court of Appeals is set aside, and the case is remanded to the District Court for further proceedings consistent with this opinion.

Vacated and remanded.

Silverman v. US (March 6, 1961)

MR. JUSTICE STEWART delivered the opinion of the Court.

The petitioners were tried and found guilty in the District Court for the District of Columbia upon three counts of an indictment charging gambling offenses under the District of Columbia Code. At the trial, police officers were permitted to describe incriminating conversations engaged in by the petitioners at their alleged gambling establishment, conversations which the officers had overheard by means of an electronic listening device. The convictions were affirmed by the Court of Appeals, 107 U.S.App.D.C. 144, 275 F.2d 173, and we granted certiorari to consider the contention that the officers' testimony as to what they had heard through the electronic instrument should not have been admitted into evidence. 363 U.S. 801.

The record shows that in the spring of 1958 the District of Columbia police had reason to suspect that the premises at 408 21st Street, N.W., in Washington, were being used as the headquarters of a gambling operation. They gained permission from the owner of the vacant adjoining row house to use it as an observation post. From this vantage point, for a period of at least three consecutive days in April, 1958, the officers employed a so-called "spike mike" to listen to what was going on within the four walls of the house next door.

The instrument in question was a microphone with a spike about a foot long attached to, it together with an amplifier, a power pack, and earphones. The officers inserted the spike under a baseboard in a second-floor room of the vacant house and into a crevice extending several inches into the party wall, until the spike hit something solid "that acted as a very good sounding board." The record clearly indicates that the spike made contact with a heating duct serving the house occupied by the petitioners, thus converting their entire heating system into a conductor of sound. Conversations taking place on both floors of the house were audible to the officers through the earphones, and their testimony regarding these conversations, admitted at the trial over timely objection, played a substantial part in the petitioners' convictions. [1]

Affirming the convictions, the Court of Appeals held that the trial court had not erred in admitting the officers' testimony. The court was of the view that the officers' use of the spike mike had violated neither the Communications Act of 1934, 47 U.S.C. § 605, cf. Nardone v. United States, 302 U. S. 379, nor the petitioners' rights under the Fourth Amendment, cf. Weeks v. United States, 232 U. S. 383.

In reaching these conclusions, the court relied primarily upon our decisions in Goldman v. United States, 316 U. S. 129, and On Lee v. United States, 343 U. S. 747. Judge Washington dissented, believing that, even if the petitioners' Fourth Amendment rights had not been abridged, the officers' conduct had transgressed the standards of due process guaranteed by the Fifth Amendment. Cf. Irvine v. California, 347 U. S. 128.

As to the inapplicability of § 605 of the Communications Act of 1934, we agree with the Court of Appeals. That section provides that

". . . no person not being authorized by the sender shall intercept any communication and divulge or publish the existence, contents, substance, purport, effect, or meaning of such intercepted communication to any person. . . ."

While it is true that much of what the officers heard consisted of the petitioners' share of telephone conversations, we cannot say that the officers intercepted these conversations within the meaning of the statute.

Similar contentions have been rejected here at least twice before. In Irvine v. California, 347 U. S. 128, 347 U. S. 131, the Court said:

"Here the apparatus of the officers was not in any way connected with the telephone facilities, there was no interference with the communications system, there was no interception of any message. All that was heard through the microphone was what an eavesdropper, hidden in the hall, the bedroom, or the closet, might have heard. We do not suppose it is illegal to testify to what another person is heard to say merely because he is saying it into a telephone."

In Goldman v. United States, 316 U. S. 129, 316 U. S. 134, it was said that

"[t]he listening in the next room to the words of [the petitioner] as he talked into the telephone receiver was no more the interception of a wire communication, within the meaning of the Act, than would have been the overhearing of the conversation by one sitting in the same room."

In presenting here the petitioners' Fourth Amendment claim, counsel has painted with a broad brush. We are asked to reconsider our decisions in Goldman v. United States, supra, and On Lee v. United States, supra. We are told that reexamination of the rationale of those cases, and

of Olmstead v. United States, 277 U. S. 438, from which they stemmed, is now essential in the light of recent and projected developments in the science of electronics. We are favoured with a description of "a device known as the parabolic microphone which can pick up a conversation three hundred yards away." We are told of a "still experimental technique whereby a room is flooded with a certain type of sonic wave," which, when perfected, "will make it possible to overhear everything said in a room without ever entering it or even going near it." We are informed of an instrument "which can pick up a conversation through an open office window on the opposite side of a busy street." [2]

The facts of the present case, however, do not require us to consider the large questions which have been argued. We need not here contemplate the Fourth Amendment implications of these and other frightening paraphernalia which the vaunted marvels of an electronic age may visit upon human society. Nor do the circumstances here make necessary a reexamination of the Court's previous decisions in this area. For a fair reading of the record in this case shows that the eavesdropping was accomplished by means of an unauthorized physical penetration into the premises occupied by the petitioners. As Judge Washington pointed out without contradiction in the Court of Appeals:

"Every inference, and what little direct evidence there was, pointed to the fact that the spike made contact with the heating duct, as the police admittedly hoped it would. Once the spike touched the heating duct, the duct became in effect a giant microphone, running through the entire house occupied by appellants."

107 U.S.App.D.C. at 150, 275 F.2d at 179.

Eavesdropping accomplished by means of such a physical intrusion is beyond the pale of even those decisions in which a closely divided Court has held that eavesdropping accomplished by other electronic means did not amount to an invasion of Fourth Amendment rights. In Goldman v. United States, supra, the Court held that placing a detectaphone against an office wall in order to listen to conversations taking place in the office next door did not violate the Amendment. In On Lee v. United States, supra, a federal agent, who was acquainted with the petitioner, entered the petitioner's laundry and engaged him in an incriminating conversation. The agent had a microphone concealed upon his person. Another agent, stationed outside with a radio receiving set, was tuned in on the conversation, and, at the petitioner's subsequent trial, related what he had heard. These circumstances were held not to constitute a violation of the petitioner's Fourth Amendment rights.

But in both Goldman and On Lee, the Court took pains explicitly to point out that the eavesdropping had not been accomplished by means of an unauthorized physical encroachment within a constitutionally protected area. In Goldman, there had, in fact, been a prior physical entry into the petitioner's office for the purpose of installing a different listening apparatus, which had turned out to be ineffective. The Court emphasized that this earlier physical trespass had been of no relevant assistance in the later use of the detectaphone in the adjoining office. 316 U.S. at 316 U. S. 134-135. And in On Lee, as the Court said, ". . . no trespass was committed." The agent went into the petitioner's place of business "with the consent, if not by the implied invitation, of the petitioner." 343 U.S. at 343 U. S. 751-752.

The absence of a physical invasion of the petitioner's premises was also a vital factor in the Court's decision in Olmstead v. United States, 277 U. S. 438. In holding that the wiretapping there did not violate the Fourth Amendment, the Court noted that

"[t]he insertions were made without trespass upon any property of the defendants. They were made in the basement of the large office building. The taps from house lines were made in the streets near the houses."

277 U.S. at 277 U. S. 457. "There was no entry of the houses or offices of the defendants." 277 U.S. at 277 U. S. 464. Relying upon these circumstances, the Court reasoned that "[t]he intervening wires are not part of [the defendant's] house or office any more than are the highways along which they are stretched." 277 U.S. at 277 U. S. 465.

Here, by contrast, the officers overheard the petitioners' conversations only by usurping part of the petitioners' house or office -- a heating system which was an integral part of the premises occupied by the petitioners, a usurpation that was effected without their knowledge and without their consent. In these circumstances, we need not pause to consider whether or not there was a technical trespass under the local property law relating to party walls. [3] Inherent Fourth Amendment rights are not inevitably measurable in terms of ancient niceties of tort or real property law. See Jones v. United States, 362 U. S. 257, 362 U. S. 266; On Lee v. United States, supra, at 343 U. S. 752; Hester v. United States, 265 U. S. 57; United States v. Jeffers, 342 U. S. 48, 342 U. S. 51; McDonald v. United States, 335 U. S. 451, 335 U. S. 454.

The Fourth Amendment, and the personal rights which it secures, have a long history. At the very core stands the right of a man to retreat into his own home and there be free from unreasonable governmental intrusion. Entick v. Carrington, 19 Howell's State Trials 1029, 1066; Boyd v. United States,116 U. S. 616, 116 U. S. 626-630. [4] This Court has never held that a federal officer may, without warrant and without consent, physically entrench into a man's office or home, there secretly observe or listen, and relate at the man's subsequent criminal trial what was seen or heard.

A distinction between the detectaphone

employed in Goldman and the spike mike utilized here seemed to the Court of Appeals too fine a one to draw. The court was "unwilling to believe that the respective rights are to be measured in fractions of inches." But decision here does not turn upon the technicality of a trespass upon a party wall as a matter of local law. It is based upon the reality of an actual intrusion into a constitutionally protected area. What the Court said long ago bears repeating now:

"It may be that it is the obnoxious thing in its mildest and least repulsive form; but illegitimate and unconstitutional practices get their first footing in that way, namely, by silent approaches and slight deviations from legal modes of procedure."

Boyd v. United States,116 U. S. 616, 116 U. S. 635. We find no occasion to reexamine Goldman here, but we decline to go beyond it, by even a fraction of an inch.

Reversed.

Notes

[1] Alleging that the conversations thus overheard had been the basis for a search warrant under which other incriminating evidence was discovered at 408 21st Street, N.W., the petitioners sought unsuccessfully to suppress the evidence obtained upon execution of the warrant. It is the Government's position that there were ample grounds to support the search warrant, even without what was overheard by means of the spike mike. We deal here only with the admissibility at the trial of the officers' testimony as to what they heard by means of the listening device, leaving a determination of the warrant's validity to abide the event of a new trial.

[2] See Hearings before the Subcommittee on Constitutional Rights of the Committee on the Judiciary, United States Senate, 85th Cong., 2d Sess., on Wiretapping, Eavesdropping, and the Bill of Rights; Hearings before Subcommittee No. 5 of the Committee on the Judiciary, House of Representatives, 84th Cong., 1st Sess., on Wiretapping; Dash, Schwartz and Knowlton, The Eavesdroppers (Rutgers University Press, 1959), pp. 346-358.

[3] See Fowler v. Koehler, 43 App.D.C. 349.

[4] William Pitt's eloquent description of this right has been often quoted. The late Judge Jerome Frank made the point in more contemporary language:

"A man can still control a small part of his environment, his house; he can retreat thence from outsiders, secure in the knowledge that they cannot get at him without disobeying the Constitution. That is still a sizable hunk of liberty -- worth protecting from encroachment. A sane, decent, civilized society must provide some such oasis, some shelter from public scrutiny, some insulated enclosure, some enclave, some inviolate place which is a man's castle."

United States v. On Lee, 193 F.2d 306, 315-316 (dissenting opinion).

Ker v. California (June 10, 1963) [Notes omitted]

MR. JUSTICE CLARK delivered the opinion of the Court with reference to the standard by which state searches and seizures must be evaluated (Part I), together with an opinion applying that standard, in which MR. JUSTICE BLACK, MR. JUSTICE STEWART and MR. JUSTICE WHITE join (Parts II-V), and announced the judgment of the Court.

This case raises search and seizure questions under the rule of Mapp v. Ohio, 367 U. S. 643 (1961). Petitioners, husband and wife, were convicted of possession of marijuana in violation of § 11530 of the California Health and Safety Code. The California District Court of Appeal affirmed, 195 Cal.App.2d 246, 15 Cal.Rptr. 767, despite the contention of petitioners that their arrests in their apartment without warrants lacked probable cause, [1] and the evidence seized incident thereto and introduced at their trial was therefore inadmissible. The California Supreme Court denied without opinion a petition for hearing. This being the first case arriving here since our opinion in Mapp which would afford suitable opportunity for further explication of that holding in the light of intervening experience, we granted certiorari. 368 U.S. 974. We affirm the judgment before us.

The state courts' conviction and affirmance are based on these events, which culminated in the petitioners' arrests. Sergeant Cook of the Los Angeles County Sheriff's Office, in negotiating the purchase of marijuana from one Terrhagen, accompanied him to a bowling alley about 7 p.m. on July 26, 1960, where they were to meet Terrhagen's "connection." Terrhagen went inside and returned shortly, pointing to a 1946 DeSoto as his "connection's" automobile and explaining that they were to meet him "up by the oil fields" near Fairfax and Slauson Avenues in Los Angeles. As they neared that location, Terrhagen again pointed out the DeSoto traveling ahead of them, stating that the "connection" kept his supply of narcotics "somewhere up in the hills." They parked near some vacant fields in the vicinity of the intersection of Fairfax and Slauson, and, shortly thereafter, the DeSoto reappeared and pulled up beside them. The deputy then recognized the driver as one Roland Murphy, whose "mug" photograph he had seen and whom he knew from other narcotics officers to be a large-scale seller of marijuana currently out on bail in connection with narcotics charges.

Terrhagen entered the DeSoto and drove off toward the oil fields with Murphy, while the Sergeant waited. They returned shortly, Terrhagen left Murphy's car carrying a package of marijuana and entered his own vehicle, and they drove to Terrhagen's residence. There, Terrhagen cut one pound of marijuana and gave it to Sergeant Cook, who had previously paid him. The Sergeant later reported this occurrence to Los Angles County Officers Berman and Warthen, the latter of whom had observed the occurrences as well.

On the following day, July 27, Murphy was placed under surveillance. Officer Warthen, who had observed the Terrhagen-Murphy episode the previous night, and Officer Markman were assigned this duty . At about 7 p.m. that evening, they followed Murphy's DeSoto as he drove to the same bowling alley in which he had met Terrhagen on the previous evening. Murphy went inside, emerged in about 10 minutes, and drove to a house where he made a brief visit. The officers continued to follow him but, upon losing sight of his vehicle, proceeded to the vicinity of Fairfax and Slauson Avenues, where they parked. There, immediately across the street from the location at which Terrhagen and Sergeant Cook had met Murphy on the previous evening, the officers observed a parked automobile whose lone occupant they later determined to be the petitioner George Douglas Ker.

The officers then saw Murphy drive past them. They followed him but lost sight of him when he extinguished his lights and entered the oil fields. The officers returned to their vantage point and, shortly thereafter, observed Murphy return and park behind Ker. From their location approximately 1,000 feet from the two vehicles, they watched through field glasses. Murphy was seen leaving his DeSoto and walking up to the driver's side of Ker's car, where he "appeared to have conversation with him." It was shortly before 9 p.m., and the distance in the twilight was too great for the officers to see anything pass between Murphy and Ker or whether the former had anything in his hands as he approached.

While Murphy and Ker were talking, the officers had driven past them in order to see their faces closely and in order to take the license number from Ker's vehicle. Soon thereafter, Ker drove away, and the officers followed him, but lost him when he made a U-turn in the middle of the block and drove in the opposite direction. Now, having lost contact with Ker, they checked the registration with the Department of Motor Vehicles and ascertained that the automobile was registered to Douglas Ker at 4801 Slauson. They then communicated this information to Officer Berman, within 15 to 30 minutes after observing the meeting between Ker and Murphy. Though officers Warthen and Markman had no previous knowledge of Ker, Berman had received information at various times, beginning in November of 1959, that Ker was selling marijuana from his apartment and that "he was possibly securing this Marijuana from Ronnie Murphy, who is the alias of Roland Murphy." In early 1960, Officer Berman had received a "mug" photograph of Ker from the Inglewood Police Department. He further testified that, between May and July 27, 1960, he had received information as to Ker from one Robert Black, who had previously given information leading to at least three arrests and whose information was believed by Berman to be reliable. According to Officer Berman, Black had told him on four or five occasions after May, 1960, that Ker and others, including himself, had purchased marijuana from Murphy. [2]

Armed with the knowledge of the meeting between Ker and Murphy and with Berman's information as to Ker's dealings with Murphy, the three officers and a fourth, Officer Love, proceeded immediately to the address which they had obtained through Ker's license number. They found the automobile which they had been following -- and which they had learned was Ker's -- in the parking lot of the multiple-apartment building and also ascertained that there was someone in the Kers' apartment. They then went to the office of the building manager and obtained from him a passkey to the apartment. Officer

Markman was stationed outside the window to intercept any evidence which might be ejected, and the other three officers entered the apartment. Officer Berman unlocked and opened the door, proceeding quietly, he testified, in order to prevent the destruction of evidence, [3] and found petitioner George Ker sitting in the living room. Just as he identified himself, stating that "We are Sheriff's Narcotics Officers, conducting a narcotics investigation," petitioner Diane Ker emerged from the kitchen. Berman testified that he repeated his identification to her and immediately walked to the kitchen. Without entering, he observed through the open doorway a small scale atop the kitchen sink, upon which lay a "brick-like-brick-shaped package containing the green leafy substance" which he recognized as marijuana. He beckoned the petitioners into the kitchen where, following their denial of knowledge of the contents of the two and two-tenths pound package and failure to answer a question as to its ownership, he placed them under arrest for suspicion of violating the State Narcotic Law. Officer Markman testified that he entered the apartment approximately "a minute, minute and a half" after the other officers, at which time Officer Berman was placing the petitioners under arrest. As to this sequence of events, petitioner George Ker testified that his arrest took place immediately upon the officers' entry and before they saw the brick of marijuana in the kitchen.

Subsequent to the arrest and the petitioners' denial of possession of any other narcotics, the officers, proceeding without search warrants, found a half-ounce package of marijuana in the kitchen cupboard and another atop the bedroom dresser. Petitioners were asked if they had any automobile other than the one observed by the officers, and George Ker replied in the negative, while Diane remained silent. On the next day, having learned that an automobile was registered in the name of Diane Ker, Officer

Warthen searched this car without a warrant, finding marijuana and marijuana seeds in the glove compartment and under the rear seat. The marijuana found on the kitchen scale, that found in the kitchen cupboard and in the bedroom, and that found in Diane Ker's automobile [4] were all introduced into evidence against the petitioners.

The California District Court of Appeal in affirming the convictions found that there was probable cause for the arrests; that the entry into the apartment was for the purpose of arrest and was not unlawful; and that the search being incident to the arrests was likewise lawful and its fruits admissible in evidence against petitioners. These conclusions were essential to the affirmance, since the California Supreme Court in 1955 had held that evidence obtained by means of unlawful searches and seizures was inadmissible in criminal trials. People v. Cahan, 44 Cal.2d 434, 282 P.2d 905. The court concluded that, in view of its findings and the implied findings of the trial court, this Court's intervening decision in Mapp v. Ohio, supra, did "not justify a change in our original conclusion." 195 Cal.App.2d, at 257, 15 Cal.Rptr., at 773.

I

In Mapp v. Ohio, at 367 U. S. 646-647, 367 U. S. 657, we followed Boyd v. United States, 116 U. S. 616, 116 U. S. 630 (1886), which held that the Fourth Amendment, [5] implemented by the self-incrimination clause of the Fifth, [6] forbids the Federal Government to convict a man of crime by using testimony or papers obtained from him by unreasonable searches and seizures as defined in the Fourth Amendment. We specifically held in Mapp that this constitutional prohibition is enforceable against the States through the Fourteenth Amendment. [7] This means, as we said in Mapp, that the Fourth Amendment "is enforceable against them (the states) by the same sanction of exclusion as is used against the Federal Government," by the application of the same constitutional standard prohibiting "unreasonable searches and seizures." 367 U.S. at 367 U. S. 655. We now face the specific question as to whether Mapp requires the exclusion of evidence in this case which the California District Court of Appeals has held to be lawfully seized. It is perhaps ironic that the initial test under the Mapp holding comes from California, whose decision voluntarily to adopt the exclusionary rule in 1955 has been commended by us previously. See Mapp v. Ohio, supra, at 367 U. S. 651-652; Elkins v. United States, 364 U. S. 206, 364 U. S. 220 (1960).

Preliminary to our examination of the search and seizures involved here, it might be helpful for us to indicate what was not decided in Mapp. First, it must be recognized that the

"principles governing the admissibility of evidence in federal criminal trials have not been restricted . . . to those derived solely from the Constitution. In the exercise of its supervisory authority over the administration of criminal justice in the federal courts . . . this Court has . . . formulated rules of evidence to be applied in federal criminal prosecutions."

McNabb v. United States, 318 U. S. 332, 318 U. S. 341 (1943); cf. Miller v. United States, 357 U. S. 301 (1958); Nardone v. United States, 302 U. S. 379 (1937). Mapp, however, established no assumption by this Court of supervisory authority over state courts, cf. Cleary v. Bolger, 371 U. S. 392, 371 U. S. 401 (1963), and, consequently, it implied no total obliteration of state laws relating to arrests and searches in favor of federal law. Mapp sounded no death knell for our federalism; rather, it echoed the sentiment of Elkins v. United States, supra, at 364 U. S. 221, that "a healthy federalism depends upon the avoidance of needless conflict between state and federal courts" by itself urging that

"[f]ederal-state cooperation in the solution of crime under constitutional standards will be promoted, if only by recognition of their now mutual obligation to respect the same fundamental criteria in their approaches."

367 U.S. at 367 U. S. 658. (Emphasis added.) Second, Mapp did not attempt the impossible task of laying down a "fixed formula" for the application in specific cases of the constitutional prohibition against unreasonable searches and seizures; it recognized that we would be "met with "recurring questions of the reasonableness of searches," and that, "at any rate, "[r]easonableness is in the first instance for the [trial court] to determine," id., at 367 U. S. 653, thus indicating that the usual weight be given to findings of trial courts.

Mapp, of course, did not lend itself to a detailed explication of standards, since the search involved there was clearly unreasonable, and bore no stamp of legality even from the Ohio Supreme Court. Id., at 367 U. S. 643-645. This is true also of Elkins v. United States, where all of the courts assumed the unreasonableness of the search in question and this Court "invoked" its "supervisory power over the administration of criminal justice in the federal courts," 364 U.S. at 364 U. S. 216, in declaring that the evidence so seized by state officers was inadmissible in a federal prosecution. The prosecution being in a federal court, this Court of course announced that

"[t]he test is one of federal law, neither enlarged by what one state court may have countenanced nor diminished by what another may have colorably suppressed."

Id. at 364 U. S. 224. Significant in the Elkins holding is the statement, apposite here, that

"it can fairly be said that, in applying the Fourth Amendment, this Court has seldom shown itself unaware of the practical demands of effective criminal investigation and law enforcement."

Id. at 364 U. S. 222.

Implicit in the Fourth Amendment's protection from unreasonable searches and seizures is its recognition of individual freedom.

That safeguard has been declared to be "as of the very essence of constitutional liberty," the guaranty of which "is as important and as imperative as are the guaranties of the other fundamental rights of the individual citizen. . . ." Gouled v. United States, 255 U. S. 298, 255 U. S. 304 (1921); cf. 287 U. S. Alabama, 287 U.S. 45, 287 U. S. 65-68 (1932). While the language of the Amendment is "general," it

"forbids every search that is unreasonable; it protects all, those suspected or known as to be offenders as well as the innocent, and unquestionably extends to the premises where the search was made. . . ."

Go-Bart Importing Co. v. United States, 282 U. S. 344, 282 U. S. 357 (1931). MR. JUSTICE Butler there stated for the Court that

"[t]he Amendment is to be liberally construed and all owe the duty of vigilance for its effective enforcement lest there shall be impairment of the rights for the protection of which it was adopted."

Ibid. He also recognized that "[t]here is no formula for the determination of reasonableness. Each case is to be decided on its own facts and circumstances." Ibid.; see United States v. Rabinowitz, 339 U. S. 56, 339 U. S. 63 (1950); Rios v. United States, 364 U. S. 253, 364 U. S. 255 (1960).

This Court's long-established recognition that standards of reasonableness under the Fourth Amendment are not susceptible of Procrustean application is carried forward when that Amendment's proscriptions are enforced against the States through the Fourteenth Amendment. And, although the standard of reasonableness is the same under the Fourth and Fourteenth Amendments, the demands of our federal system compel us to distinguish between evidence held inadmissible because of our supervisory powers over federal courts and that held inadmissible because prohibited by the United States

Constitution. We reiterate that the reasonableness of a search is, in the first instance, a substantive determination to be made by the trial court from the facts and circumstances of the case and in the light of the "fundamental criteria" laid down by the Fourth Amendment and in opinions of this Court applying that Amendment. Findings of reasonableness, of course, are respected only insofar as consistent with federal constitutional guarantees. As we have stated above and in other cases involving federal constitutional rights, findings of state courts are by no means insulated against examination here. See, e.g., Spano v. New York, 360 U. S. 315, 360 U. S. 316 (1959); Thomas v. Arizona, 356 U. S. 390, 356 U. S. 393 (1958); Pierre v. Louisiana, 306 U. S. 354, 306 U. S. 358 (1939). While this Court does not sit as in nisi prius to appraise contradictory factual questions, it will, where necessary to the determination of constitutional rights, make an independent examination of the facts, the findings, and the record so that it can determine for itself whether in the decision as to reasonableness the fundamental -- i.e., constitutional -- criteria established by this Court have been respected. The States are not thereby precluded from developing workable rules governing arrests, searches and seizures to meet "the practical demands of effective criminal investigation and law enforcement" in the States, provided that those rules do not violate the constitutional proscription of unreasonable searches and seizures and the concomitant command that evidence so seized is inadmissible against one who has standing to complain. See Jones v. United States, 362 U. S. 257 (1960). Such a standard implies no derogation of uniformity in applying federal constitutional guarantees, but is only a recognition that conditions and circumstances vary just as do investigative and enforcement techniques.

Applying this federal constitutional standard we proceed to examine the entire record including the findings of California's courts to determine whether the evidence seized from petitioners was constitutionally admissible under the circumstances of this case.

II

The evidence at issue, in order to be admissible, must be the product of a search incident to a lawful arrest, since the officers had no search warrant. The lawfulness of the arrest without warrant, in turn, must be based upon probable cause, which exists

"where 'the facts and circumstances within their [the officers'] knowledge and of which they had reasonably trustworthy information [are] sufficient in themselves to warrant a man of reasonable caution in the belief that' an offense has been or is being committed."

Brinegar v. United States, 338 U. S. 160, 338 U. S. 175-176 (1949), quoting from Carroll v. United States, 267 U. S. 132, 267 U. S. 162 (1925); accord, People v. Fischer, 49 Cal.2d 442, 317 P.2d 967 (1957); Bompensiero v. Superior Court, 44 Cal.2d 178, 281 P.2d 250(1955). The information within the knowledge of the officers at the time they arrived at the Kers' apartment, as California's courts specifically found, clearly furnished grounds for a reasonable belief that petitioner George Ker had committed and was committing the offense of possession of marijuana. Officers Markman and Warthen observed a rendezvous between Murphy and Ker on the evening of the arrest which was a virtual reenactment of the previous night's encounter between Murphy, Terrhagen and Sergeant Cook, which concluded in the sale by Murphy to Terrhagen and the Sergeant of a package of marijuana of which the latter had paid Terrhagen for one pound which he received from Terrhagen after the encounter with Murphy. To be sure, the distance and lack of light prevented the officers from seeing and they did not see any substance pass between the two men, but the virtual identity of the surrounding circumstances warranted a strong suspicion that the one remaining element -- a sale of narcotics -- was a part of this encounter as it was the previous night. But Ker's arrest does not depend on this single episode with Murphy. When Ker's U-turn thwarted the officer's pursuit, they learned his name and address from the Department of Motor Vehicles and reported the occurrence to Officer Berman. Berman, in turn, revealed information from an informer whose reliability had been tested previously, as well as from other sources, not only that Ker had been selling marijuana from his apartment but also that his likely source of supply was Murphy himself. That this information was hearsay does not destroy its role in establishing probable cause. Brinegar v. United States, supra. In Draper v. United States, 358 U. S. 307 (1959), we held that information from a reliable informer, corroborated by the agents' observations as to the accuracy of the informer's description of the accused and of his presence at a particular place, was sufficient to establish probable cause for an arrest without warrant. [8] The corroborative elements in Draper were innocuous in themselves, but here, both the informer's tip and the personal observations connected Ker with specific illegal activities involving the same man, Murphy, a known marijuana dealer. To say that this coincidence of information was sufficient to support a reasonable belief of the officers that Ker was illegally in possession of marijuana is to indulge in understatement.

Probable cause for the arrest of petitioner Diane Ker, while not present at the time the officers entered the apartment to arrest her husband, was nevertheless present at the time of her arrest. Upon their entry and announcement of their identity, the officers were met not only by George Ker, but also by Diane Ker, who was emerging from the kitchen. Officer Berman immediately walked to the doorway from which she emerged and, without entering, observed the brick-shaped package of marijuana in plain view. Even assuming that her presence in a small room with the contraband in a prominent position on the kitchen sink would not alone establish a reasonable ground for the officers' belief that she was in joint possession with her husband, that fact was accompanied by the officers' information that Ker had been using his apartment as a base of operations for his narcotics activities. Therefore, we cannot say that, at the time of her arrest, there were not sufficient grounds for a reasonable belief that Drane Ker, as well as her husband, as committing the offense of possession of marijuana in the presence of the officers.

III

It is contended that the lawfulness of the petitioners arrests, even if they were based upon probable cause, was vitiated by the method of entry. This Court, in cases under the Fourth Amendment, was long recognized that the lawfulness of arrests for federal offenses is to be determined by reference to state law insofar as it is not violative of the Federal Constitution. Miller v. United States, supra; United States v. Di Re, 332 U. S. 581 (1948); Johnson v. United States, 333 U. S. 10, 333 U. S. 15, n. 5 (1948). A fortiori, the lawfulness of these arrests by state officers for state offenses is to be determined by California law. California Penal Code, § 844, [9] permits peace officers to break into a dwelling place for the purpose of arrest after demanding admittance and explaining their purpose. Admittedly the officers did not comply with the terms of this statute since they entered quietly and without announcement, in order to prevent the destruction of contraband. The California District Court of Appeal, however, held that the circumstances here came within a judicial exception which had been engrafted upon the statute by a series of decisions, see, e.g., People v. Ruiz, 146 Cal.App.2d 630, 304 P.2d 1 75 (1956); People v. Maddox, 46 Cal.2d 301, 294 P.2d 6, cert. denied, 352 U.S. 858 (1956), and that the noncompliance was therefore lawful.

Since the petitioner's federal constitutional protection from unreasonable searches and seizures by police officers is here to be determined by whether the search was incident to a lawful arrest, we are warranted in examining that arrest to determine whether, notwithstanding its legality under state law, the method of entering the home may offend federal constitutional standards of reasonableness, and therefore vitiate the legality of an accompanying search. We find no such offensiveness on the facts here. Assuming that the officers' entry by use of a key obtained from the manager is the legal equivalent of a "breaking," see Keiningham v. United States, 109 U.S.App.D.C. 272, 276, 287 F.2d 126, 130 (1960), it has been recognized from the early common law that such breaking is permissible in executing an arrest under certain circumstances. See Wilgus, Arrest Without a Warrant, 22 Mich.L.Rev. 541, 798, 800-806 (1924). Indeed, 18 U.S.C. § 3109, [10] dealing with the execution of search warrants by federal officers, authorizes breaking of doors in words very similar to those of the California statute, both statutes including a requirement of notice of authority and purpose. In Miller v. United States, supra, this Court held unlawful an arrest, and therefore its accompanying search, on the ground that the District of Columbia officers before entering a dwelling did not fully satisfy the requirement of disclosing their identity and purpose. The Court stated that

"the lawfulness of the arrest without warrant is to be determined by reference to state law. . . . By like reasoning the validity of the arrest of petitioner is to be determined by reference to the law of the District of Columbia."

357 U.S. at 357 U. S. 305-306. The parties there conceded and the Court accepted that the criteria for testing the arrest under District of Columbia law were "substantially identical" to the requirements of § 3109. Id. at 357 U. S. 306. Here,

however, the criteria under California law clearly include an exception to the notice requirement where exigent circumstances are present. Moreover, insofar as violation of a federal statute required the exclusion of evidence in Miller, the case is inapposite for state prosecutions, where admissibility is governed by constitutional standards. Finally, the basis of the judicial exception to the California statute, as expressed by Justice Traynor in People v. Maddox, 46 Cal.2d at 306, 294 P.2d, at 9, effectively answers the petitioners' contention:

"It must be borne in mind that the primary purpose of the constitutional guarantees is to prevent unreasonable invasions of the security of the people in their persons, houses, papers, and effects, and when an officer has reasonable cause to enter a dwelling to make an arrest and as an incident to that arrest is authorized to make a reasonable search, his entry and his search are not unreasonable. Suspects have no constitutional right to destroy or dispose of evidence, and no basic constitutional guarantees are violated because an officer succeeds in getting to a place where he is entitled to be more quickly than he would, had he complied with section 844. Moreover, since the demand and explanation requirements of section 844 are a codification of the common law, they may reasonably be interpreted as limited by the common law rules that compliance is not required if the officer's peril would have been increased or the arrest frustrated had he demanded entrance and stated his purpose. (Read v. Case, 4 Conn. 166, 170 [10 Am.Dec. 110]; see Restatement, Torts, § 206, comment d.) Without the benefit of hindsight and ordinarily on the spur of the moment, the officer must decide these questions in the first instance."

No such exigent circumstances as would authorize noncompliance with the California statute were argued in Miller, and the Court expressly refrained from discussing the question, citing the Maddox case without disapproval. 357 U.S. at 357 U. S. 309. [11] Here justification for the officers' failure to give notice is uniquely present. In addition to the officers' belief that Ker was in possession of narcotics, which could be quickly and easily destroyed, Ker's furtive conduct in eluding them shortly before the arrest was ground for the belief that he might well have been expecting the police. [12] We therefore hold that, in the particular circumstances of this case, the officers' method of entry, sanctioned by the law of California, was not unreasonable under the standards of the Fourth Amendment as applied to the States through the Fourteenth Amendment.

IV

Having held the petitioners' arrests lawful, it remains only to consider whether the search which produced the evidence leading to their convictions was lawful as incident to those arrests. The doctrine that a search without warrant may be lawfully conducted if incident to a lawful arrest has long been recognized as consistent with the Fourth Amendment's protection against unreasonable searches and seizures. See Marron v. United States, 275 U. S. 192 (1927); Harris v. United States, 331 U. S. 145 (1947); Abel v. United States, 362 U. S. 217 (1960); Kaplan, Search and Seizure: A No-Man's Land in the Criminal Law, 49 Cal.L.Rev. 474, 490-493 (1961). The cases have imposed no requirement that the arrest be under authority of an arrest warrant, but only that it be lawful. See Marron v. United States, supra, at 275 U. S. 198-199; United States v. Rabinowitz, supra, at 339 U. S. 61; cf. Agnello v. United States, 269 U. S. 20, 269 U. S. 30-31 (1925). The question remains whether the officers' action here exceeded the recognized bounds of an incidental search.

Petitioners contend that the search was unreasonable in that the officers could practicably have obtained a search warrant. The practicability of obtaining a warrant is not the controlling factor when a search is sought to be justified as incident to arrest, United States v. Rabinowitz, supra; but we need not rest the validity of the search here on Rabinowitz, since we agree with the California court that time clearly was of the essence. The officers' observations and their corroboration, which furnished probable cause for George Ker's arrest, occurred at about 9 p.m., approximately one hour before the time of arrest. The officers had reason to act quickly because of Ker's furtive conduct and the likelihood that the marijuana would be distributed or hidden before a warrant could be obtained at that time of night. [13] Thus, the facts bear no resemblance to those in Trupiano v. United States, 334 U. S. 699 (1948), where federal agents for three weeks had been in possession of knowledge sufficient to secure a search warrant.

The search of the petitioners' apartment was well within the limits upheld in Harris v. United States, supra, which also concerned a private apartment dwelling. The evidence here, unlike that in Harris, was the instrumentality of the very crime for which petitioners were arrested, and the record does not indicate that the search here was an extensive in time or in area as that upheld in Harris.

The petitioners' only remaining contention is that the discovery of the brick of marijuana cannot be justified as incidental to arrest since it preceded the arrest. This contention is, of course, contrary to George Ker's testimony, but we reject it in any event. While an arrest may not be used merely as the pretext for a search without warrant, the California court specifically found and the record supports both that the officers entered the apartment for the purpose of arresting George Ker and that they had probable cause to make that arrest prior to the entry. [14] We cannot say that it was unreasonable for Officer Berman, upon seeing Diane Ker emerge from the kitchen, merely to walk to the doorway of that adjacent room. We thus agree with the California court's holding that the discovery of the brick of marijuana did not constitute a search, since the officer merely saw what was placed before him in full view. United States v. Lee, 274 U. S. 559 (1927); United States v. Lefkowitz, 285 U. S. 452, 285 U. S. 465 (1932); People v. West, 144 Cal.App.2d 214, 300 P.2d 729 (1956). Therefore, while California law does not require that an arrest precede an incidental search as long as probable cause exists at the outset, Wilson v. Superior Court, 46 Cal.2d 291, 294 P.2d 36 (1956), the California court did not rely on that rule and we need not reach the question of its status under the Federal Constitution.

V

The petitioners state and the record bears out that the officers searched Diane Ker's automobile on the day subsequent to her arrest. The reasonableness of that search, however, was not raised in the petition for certiorari, nor was it discussed in the brief here. Ordinarily "[w]e do not reach for constitutional questions not raised by the parties," Mazer v. Stein, 347 U. S. 201, 347 U. S. 206, n. 5 (1954), nor extend our review beyond those specific federal questions properly raised in the state court. The record gives no indication that the issue was raised in the trial court or in the District Court of Appeal, the latter court did not adjudicate it and we therefore find no reason to reach it on the record. [15]

For these reasons, the judgment of the California District Court of Appeal is affirmed.

Affirmed.

Hoffa v. US (Dec 12, 1966) [Notes omitted]

MR. JUSTICE STEWART delivered the opinion of the Court.

Over a period of several weeks in the late autumn of 1962, there took place in a federal court in Nashville, Tennessee, a trial by jury in which James Hoffa was charged with violating a provision of the Taft-Hartley Act. That trial, known in the present record as the Test Fleet trial, ended with a hung jury. The petitioners now before us -- James Hoffa, Thomas Parks, Larry Campbell, and Ewing King -- were tried and convicted in 1964 for endeavoring to bribe members of that jury. [1] The convictions were affirmed by the Court of Appeals. [2] A substantial element in the Government's, proof that led to the convictions of these four petitioners was contributed by a witness named Edward Partin, who testified to several incriminating statements which he said petitioners Hoffa and King had made in his presence during the course of the Test Fleet trial. Our grant of certiorari was limited to the single issue of whether the Government's use in this case of evidence supplied by Partin operated to invalidate these convictions. 382 U.S. 1024.

The specific question before us, as framed by counsel for the petitioners, is this:

"Whether evidence obtained by the Government by means of deceptively placing a secret informer in the quarters and councils of a defendant during one criminal trial so violates the defendant's Fourth, Fifth and Sixth Amendment rights that suppression of such evidence is required in a subsequent trial of the same defendant on a different charge."

At the threshold, the Government takes issue with the way this question is worded, refusing to concede that it "placed' the informer anywhere, much less that it did so `deceptively.'" In the view we take of the matter, however, a resolution of this verbal controversy is unnecessary to a decision of the constitutional issues before us. The basic facts are clear enough, and a lengthy discussion of the detailed minutiae to which a large portion of the briefs and oral arguments was addressed would serve only to divert attention from the real issues before us.

The controlling facts can be briefly stated. The Test Fleet trial, in which James Hoffa was the sole individual defendant, was in progress between

October 22 and December 23, 1962, in Nashville, Tennessee. James Hoffa was president of the International Brotherhood of Teamsters. During the course of the trial, he occupied a three-room suite in the Andrew Jackson Hotel in Nashville. One of his constant companions throughout the trial was the petitioner King, president of the Nashville local of the Teamsters Union. Edward Partin, a resident of Baton Rouge, Louisiana, and a local Teamsters Union official there, made repeated visits to Nashville during the period of the trial. On these visits he frequented the Hoffa hotel suite, and was continually in the company of Hoffa and his associates, including King, in and around the hotel suite, the hotel lobby, the courthouse, and elsewhere in Nashville. During this period, Partin made frequent reports to a federal agent named Sheridan concerning conversations he said Hoffa and King had had with him and with each other, disclosing endeavors to bribe members of the Test Fleet jury. Partin's reports and his subsequent testimony at the petitioners' trial unquestionably contributed, directly or indirectly, to the convictions of all four of the petitioners. [3]

The chain of circumstances which led Partin to be in Nashville during the Test Fleet trial extended back at least to September of 1962. At that time, Partin was in jail in Baton Rouge on a state criminal charge. He was also under a federal indictment for embezzling union funds, and other indictments for state offenses were pending against him. Between that time and Partin's initial visit to Nashville on October 22, he was released on bail on the state criminal charge, and proceedings under the federal indictment were postponed. On October 8, Partin telephoned Hoffa in Washington, D.C., to discuss local union matters and Partin's difficulties with the authorities. In the course of this conversation, Partin asked if he could see Hoffa to confer about these problems, and Hoffa acquiesced. Partin again called Hoffa on October 18, and arranged to meet him in Nashville.

During this period, Partin also consulted on several occasions with federal law enforcement agents, who told him that Hoffa might attempt to tamper with the Test Fleet jury and asked him to be on the lookout in Nashville for such attempts, and to report to the federal authorities any evidence of wrongdoing that he discovered. Partin agreed to do so.

After the Test Fleet trial was completed, Partin's wife received four monthly installment payments of $300 from government funds, and the state and federal charges against Partin were either dropped or not actively pursued.

Reviewing these circumstances in detail, the Government insists the fair inference is that Partin went to Nashville on his own initiative to discuss union business and his own problems with Hoffa, that Partin ultimately cooperated closely with federal authorities, only after he discovered evidence of jury tampering in the Test Fleet trial, that the payments to Partin's wife were simply in partial reimbursement of Partin's subsequent out-of-pocket expenses, and that the failure to prosecute Partin on the state and federal charges had no necessary connection with his services as an informer. The findings of the trial court support this version of the facts, [4] and these findings were accepted by the Court of Appeals as "supported by substantial evidence." 349 F.2d at 36. But whether or not the Government "placed" Partin with Hoffa in Nashville during the Test Fleet trial, we proceed upon the premise that Partin was a government informer from the time he first arrived in Nashville on October 22, and that the Government compensated him for his services as such. It is upon that premise that we consider the constitutional issues presented.

Before turning to those issues, we mention an additional preliminary contention of the Government. The petitioner Hoffa was the only individual defendant in the Test Fleet case, and Partin had conversations during the Test Fleet trial only with him and with the petitioner King. So far as appears, Partin never saw either of the other two petitioners during that period. Consequently, the Government argues that, of the four petitioners, only Hoffa has standing to raise a claim that his Sixth Amendment right to counsel in the Test Fleet trial was impaired, and only he and King have standing with respect to the other constitutional claims. Cf. Wong Sun v. United States, 371 U. S. 471, 371 U. S. 487-488, 371 U. S. 491-492; Jones v. United States, 362 U. S. 257, 362 U. S. 259-267. It is clear, on the other hand, that Partin's reports to the agent Sheridan uncovered leads that made possible the development of evidence against petitioners Parks and Campbell. But we need not pursue the nuances of these "standing" questions, because it is evident, in any event, that none of the petitioners can prevail unless the petitioner Hoffa prevails. For that reason, the ensuing discussion is confined to the claims of the petitioner Hoffa (hereinafter petitioner), all of which he clearly has standing to invoke.

I

It is contended that only by violating the petitioner's rights under the Fourth Amendment was Partin able to hear the petitioner's incriminating statements in the hotel suite, and that Partin's testimony was therefore inadmissible under the exclusionary rule of Weeks v. United States, 232 U. S. 383. The argument is that Partin's failure to disclose his role as a government informer vitiated the consent that the petitioner gave to Partin's repeated entries into the suite, and that, by listening to the petitioner's statement,s Partin conducted an illegal "search" for verbal evidence.

The preliminary steps of this argument are on solid ground. A hotel room can clearly be the object of Fourth Amendment protection, as much as a home or an office. United States v. Jeffers, 342 U. S. 48. The Fourth Amendment can certainly be violated by guileful, as well as by forcible, intrusions into a constitutionally protected area. Gouled v. United States, 255 U. S. 298. And the protections of the Fourth Amendment are surely not limited to tangibles, but can extend as well to oral statements. Silverman v. United States, 365 U. S. 505.

Where the argument falls is in its misapprehension of the fundamental nature and scope of Fourth Amendment protection. What the Fourth Amendment protects is the security a man relies upon when he places himself or his property within a constitutionally protected area, be it his home or his office, his hotel room or his automobile. [5] There, he is protected from unwarranted governmental intrusion. And when he puts something in his filing cabinet, in his desk drawer, or in his pocket, he has the right to know it will be secure from an unreasonable search or an unreasonable seizure. So it was that the Fourth Amendment could not tolerate the warrantless search of the hotel room in Jeffers, the purloining of the petitioner's private papers in Gouled, or the surreptitious electronic surveillance in Silverman. Countless other cases which have come to this Court over the years have involved a myriad of differing factual contexts in which the protections of the Fourth Amendment have been appropriately invoked. No doubt the future will bring countless others. By nothing we say here do we either foresee or foreclose factual situations to which the Fourth Amendment may be applicable.

In the present case, however, it is evident that no interest legitimately protected by the Fourth Amendment is involved. It is obvious that the petitioner was not relying on the security of his hotel suite when he made the incriminating statements to Partin or in Partin's presence. Partin did not enter the suite by force or by stealth. He was not a surreptitious eavesdropper. Partin was in the suite by invitation, and every conversation which he heard was either directed to him or knowingly carried on in his presence. The petitioner, in a word, was not relying on the security of the hotel room; he was relying upon his misplaced confidence that Partin would not reveal his wrongdoing. [6] As counsel for the petitioner himself points out, some of the communications with Partin did not take place in the suite at all, but in the "hall of the hotel," in the "Andrew Jackson Hotel lobby," and "at the courthouse."

Neither this Court nor any member of it has ever expressed the view that the Fourth Amendment protects a wrongdoer's misplaced belief that a person to whom he voluntarily confides his wrongdoing will not reveal it. Indeed, the Court unanimously rejected that very contention less than four years ago in Lopez v. United States, 373 U. S. 427. In that case, the petitioner had been convicted of attempted bribery of an internal revenue agent named Davis. The Court was divided with regard to the admissibility in evidence of a surreptitious electronic recording of an incriminating conversation Lopez had had in his private office with Davis. But there was no dissent from the view that testimony about the conversation by Davis himself was clearly admissible.

As the Court put it,

"Davis was not guilty of an unlawful invasion of petitioner's office simply because his apparent willingness to accept a bribe was not real. Compare Wong Sun v. United States, 371 U. S. 471. He was in the office with petitioner's consent, and, while there, he did not violate the privacy of the office by seizing something surreptitiously without petitioner's knowledge. Compare Gouled v. United States, supra. The only evidence obtained consisted of statements made by Lopez to Davis, statements which Lopez knew full well could be used against him by Davis if he wished. . . ."

373 U.S. at 373 U. S. 438. In the words of the dissenting opinion in Lopez,

"The risk of being overheard by an eavesdropper or betrayed by an informer or deceived as to the identity of one with whom one deals is probably inherent in the conditions of human society. It is the kind of risk we necessarily assume whenever we speak."

Id. at 373 U. S. 465. See also Lewis v. United States, ante p. 385 U. S. 206.

Adhering to these views, we hold that no right protected by the Fourth Amendment was violated in the present case.

II

The petitioner argues that his right under the Fifth Amendment not to "be compelled in any criminal case to be a witness against himself" was violated by the admission of Partin's testimony. The claim is without merit.

There have been sharply differing views within the Court as to the ultimate reach of the Fifth Amendment right against compulsory self-incrimination. Some of those differences were aired last Term in Miranda v. Arizona, 384 U. S. 436, 384 U. S. 499, 384 U. S. 504, 384 U. S. 526. But since at least as long ago as 1807, when Chief Justice Marshall first gave attention to the matter in the trial of Aaron Burr, [7] all have agreed that a necessary element of compulsory self-incrimination is some kind of compulsion. Thus, in the Miranda case, dealing with the Fifth Amendment's impact upon police interrogation of persons in custody, the Court predicated its decision upon the conclusion

"that, without proper safeguards, the process of in-custody interrogation of persons suspected or accused of crime contains inherently compelling pressures which work to undermine the individual's will to resist and to compel him to speak where he would not otherwise do so freely. . . ."

384 U.S. at 384 U. S. 467.

In the present case, no claim has been or could be made that the petitioner's incriminating statements were the product of any sort of coercion, legal or factual. The petitioner's conversations with Partin and in Partin's presence were wholly voluntary. For that reason, if for no other, it is clear that no right protected by the Fifth Amendment privilege against compulsory self-incrimination was violated in this case.

III

The petitioner makes two separate claims under the Sixth Amendment, and we give them separate consideration.

A

During the course of the Test Fleet trial, the petitioner's lawyers used his suite as a place to confer with him and with each other, to interview witnesses, and to plan the following day's trial strategy. Therefore, argues the petitioner, Partin's presence in and around the suite violated the petitioner's Sixth Amendment right to counsel, because an essential ingredient thereof is the right of a defendant and his counsel to prepare for trial without intrusion upon their confidential relationship by an agent of the Government, the defendant's trial adversary. Since Partin's presence in the suite thus violated the Sixth Amendment, the argument continues, any evidence acquired by reason of his presence there was constitutionally tainted, and therefore inadmissible against the petitioner in this case. We reject this argument.

In the first place, it is far from clear to what extent Partin was present at conversations or conferences of the petitioner's counsel. Several of the petitioner's Test Fleet lawyers testified at the hearing on the motion to suppress Partin's testimony in the present case. Most of them said that Partin had heard, or had been in a position to hear, at least some of the lawyers' discussions during the Test Fleet trial. On the other hand, Partin himself testified that the lawyers "would move you out" when they wanted to discuss the case, and denied that he made any effort to "get into or be present at any conversations between lawyers or anything of that sort," other than engaging in such banalities as "how things looked," or "how does it look?" He said he might have heard some of the lawyers' conversations, but he didn't know what they were talking about, "because I wasn't interested in what they had to say about the case." He testified that he did not report any of the lawyers' conversations to Sheridan, because the latter "wasn't interested in what the attorneys said." Partin's testimony was largely confirmed by Sheridan. Sheridan did testify, however, to one occasion when Partin told him about a group of prospective character witnesses being interviewed in the suite by one of the petitioner's lawyers, who "was going over" some written "questions and answers" with them. This information was evidently relayed by Sheridan to the chief government attorney at the Test Fleet trial. [8]

The District Court, in the present case, apparently credited Partin's testimony, finding "there has been no interference by the government with any attorney-client relationship of any defendant in this case." The Court of Appeals accepted this finding. 349 F.2d at 36. In view of Sheridan's testimony about Partin's report of the interviews with the prospective character witnesses, however, we proceed here on the hypothesis that Partin did observe and report to Sheridan at least some of the activities of defense counsel in the Test Fleet trial.

The proposition that a surreptitious invasion by a government agent into the legal camp of the defense may violate the protection of the Sixth Amendment has found expression in two cases decided by the Court of Appeals for the District of Columbia Circuit, Caldwell v. United States, 92 U.S.App. D C. 355, 205 F.2d 879, and Coplon v. United States, 89 U.S.App.D.C. 103, 191 F.2d 749. Both of those cases dealt with government intrusion of the grossest kind upon the confidential relationship between the defendant and his counsel. In Coplon, the defendant alleged that government agents deliberately intercepted telephone consultations between the defendant and her lawyer before and during trial. In Caldwell, the agent,

"[i]n his dual capacity as defense assistant and Government agent . . . , gained free access to the planning of the defense. . . . Neither his dealings with the defense nor his reports to the prosecution were limited to the proposed unlawful acts of the defense: they covered many matters connected with the impending trial."

92 U.S.App.D.C. at 356, 205 F.2d at 880.

We may assume that the Coplon and Caldwell cases were rightly decided, and further assume, without deciding, that the Government's activities during the Test Fleet trial were sufficiently similar to what went on in Coplon and Caldwell to invoke the rule of those decisions. Consequently, if the Test Fleet trial had resulted in a conviction, instead of a hung jury, the conviction would presumptively have been set aside as constitutionally defective. Cf. Black v. United States, ante p. 385 U. S. 26.

But a holding that it follows from this presumption that the petitioner's conviction in the present case should be set aside would be both unprecedented and irrational. In Coplon and in Caldwell, the Court of Appeals held that the Government's intrusion upon the defendant's relationship with his lawyer "invalidates the trial at which it occurred." 89 U.S.App.D.C. at 114, 191 F.2d at 759; 92 U.S.App.D.C. at 357, 205 F.2d at 881. In both of those cases, the court directed a new trial, [9] and the second trial in Caldwell resulted in a conviction which this Court declined to review. 95 U.S.App.D.C. 35, 218 F.2d 370, 349 U.S. 930. The argument here, therefore, goes far beyond anything decided in Caldwell or in Coplon. For if the petitioner's argument were accepted, not only could there have been no new conviction on the existing charges in Caldwell, but not even a conviction on other and different charges against the same defendant.

It is possible to imagine a case in which the prosecution might so pervasively insinuate itself into the councils of the defense as to make a new trial on the same charges impermissible under the Sixth Amendment. [10] But even if it were further arguable that a situation could be hypothesized in which the Government's previous activities in undermining a defendant's Sixth Amendment rights at one trial would make evidence obtained thereby inadmissible in a different trial on other charges, the case now before us does not remotely approach such a situation.

This is so because of the clinching basic fact in the present case that none of the petitioner's incriminating statements which Partin heard were made in the presence of counsel, in the hearing of counsel, or in connection in any way with the legitimate defense of the Test Fleet prosecution. The petitioner's statements related to the commission of a quite separate offense -- attempted bribery of jurors -- and the statements were made to Partin out of the presence of any lawyers.

Even assuming, therefore, as we have, that there might have been a Sixth Amendment violation which might have made invalid a conviction, if there had been one, in the Test Fleet case, the evidence supplied by Partin in the present case was in no sense the "fruit" of any such violation. In Wong Sun v. United States, 371 U. S. 471, a case involving exclusion of evidence under the Fourth Amendment, the Court stated that

"the more apt question in such a case is 'whether, granting establishment of the primary illegality, the evidence to which instant objection is made has been come at by exploitation of that illegality, or, instead, by means sufficiently distinguishable to be purged of the primary taint.' Maguire, Evidence of Guilt, 221 (1059)."

371 U.S. at 371 U. S. 488.

Even upon the premise that this same strict standard of excludability should apply under the Sixth Amendment -- a question we need not decide -- it is clear that Partin's evidence in this case was not the consequence of any "exploitation" of a Sixth Amendment violation. The petitioner's incriminating statements to which Partin testified in this case were totally unrelated in both time and subject matter to any assumed intrusion by Partin into the conferences of the petitioner's counsel in the Test Fleet trial. These incriminating statements, all of them made out of the presence or hearing of any of the petitioner's counsel, embodied the very antithesis of any legitimate defense in the Test Fleet trial.

The petitioner's second argument under the Sixth Amendment needs no extended discussion. That argument goes as follows: not later than October 25, 1962, the Government had sufficient ground for taking the petitioner into custody and charging him with endeavors to tamper with the Test Fleet jury. Had the Government done so, it could not have continued to question the petitioner without observance of his Sixth Amendment right to counsel. Massiah v. United States, 377 U. S. 201; Escobedo v. Illinois, 378 U. S. 478. Therefore, the argument concludes, evidence of statements made by the petitioner subsequent to October 25 was inadmissible, because the Government acquired that evidence only by flouting the petitioner's Sixth Amendment right to counsel.

Nothing in Massiah, in Escobedo, or in any other case that has come to our attention even remotely suggests this novel and paradoxical constitutional doctrine, and we decline to adopt it now. There is no constitutional right to be arrested. [11] The police are not required to guess, at their peril, the precise moment at which they have probable cause to arrest a suspect, risking a violation of the Fourth Amendment if they act too soon, and a violation of the Sixth Amendment if they wait too long. Law enforcement officers are under no constitutional duty to call a halt to a criminal investigation the moment they have the

minimum evidence to establish probable cause, a quantum of evidence which may fall far short of the amount necessary to support a criminal conviction.

IV

Finally, the petitioner claims that, even if there was no violation -- "as separately measured by each such Amendment" -- of the Fourth Amendment, the compulsory self-incrimination clause of the Fifth Amendment, or of the Sixth Amendment in this case, the judgment of conviction must nonetheless be reversed. The argument is based upon the Due Process Clause of the Fifth Amendment. The "totality" of the Government's conduct during the Test Fleet trial operated, it is said, to

"'offend those canons of decency and fairness which express the notions of justice of English-speaking peoples even toward those charged with the most heinous offenses' (Rochin v. California, 342 U. S. 165, 342 U. S. 169)."

The argument boils down to a general attack upon the use of a government informer as "a shabby thing in any case," and to the claim that, in the circumstances of this particular case, the risk that Partin's testimony might be perjurious was very high. Insofar as the general attack upon the use of informers is based upon historic "notions" of "English-speaking peoples," it is without historical foundation. In the words of Judge Learned Hand,

"Courts have countenanced the use of informers from time immemorial; in cases of conspiracy, or in other cases when the crime consists of preparing for another crime, it is usually necessary to rely upon them or upon accomplices, because the criminals will almost certainly proceed covertly. . . ."

United States v. Dennis, 183 F.2d 201, at 224.

This is not to say that a secret government informer is to the slightest degree more free from all relevant constitutional restrictions than is any other government agent. See Massiah v. United States, 377 U. S. 201. It is to say that the use of secret informers is not per se unconstitutional.

The petitioner is quite correct in the contention that Partin, perhaps even more than most informers, may have had motives to lie. But it does not follow that his testimony was untrue, nor does it follow that his testimony was constitutionally inadmissible. The established safeguards of the Anglo-American legal system leave the veracity of a witness to be tested by cross-examination, and the credibility of his testimony to be determined by a properly instructed jury. At the trial of this case, Partin was subjected to rigorous cross-examination, and the extent and nature of his dealings with federal and state authorities were insistently explored. [12]

The trial judge instructed the jury, both specifically [13] and generally, [14] with regard to assessing Partin's credibility. The Constitution does not require us to upset the jury's verdict.

Affirmed.

US v. Wade (June 12, 1967) [Notes omitted]

MR. JUSTICE BRENNAN delivered the opinion of the Court.

The question here is whether courtroom identifications of an accused at trial are to be excluded from evidence because the accused was exhibited to the witnesses before trial at a post-indictment lineup conducted for identification purposes without notice to and in the absence of the accused's appointed counsel.

The federally insured bank in Eustace, Texas, was robbed on September 21, 1964. A man with a small strip of tape on each side of his face entered the bank, pointed a pistol at the female cashier and the vice president, the only persons in the bank at the time, and forced them to fill a pillowcase with the bank's money. The man then drove away with an accomplice who had been waiting in a stolen car outside the bank. On March 23, 1965, an indictment was returned against respondent, Wade, and two others for conspiring to rob the bank, and against Wade and the accomplice for the robbery itself. Wade was arrested on April 2, and counsel was appointed to represent him on April 26. Fifteen days later an FBI agent, without notice to Wade's lawyer, arranged to have the two bank employees observe a lineup made up of Wade and five or six other prisoners and conducted in a courtroom of the local county courthouse. Each person in the line wore strips of tape such as allegedly worn by the robber and upon direction each said something like "put the money in the bag," the words allegedly uttered by the robber. Both bank employees identified Wade in the lineup as the bank robber.

At trial, the two employees, when asked on direct examination if the robber was in the courtroom, pointed to Wade. The prior lineup identification was then elicited from both employees on cross-examination. At the close of testimony, Wade's counsel moved for a judgment of acquittal or, alternatively, to strike the bank officials' courtroom identifications on the ground that conduct of the lineup, without notice to and in the absence of his appointed counsel, violated his Fifth Amendment privilege against self-incrimination and his Sixth Amendment right to the assistance of counsel. The motion was denied, and Wade was convicted. The Court of Appeals for the Fifth Circuit reversed the conviction and ordered a new trial at which the in-court identification evidence was to be excluded, holding that, though the lineup did not violate Wade's Fifth Amendment rights, "the lineup, held as it was, in the absence of counsel, already chosen to represent appellant, was a violation of his Sixth Amendment rights . . . ." 358 F. 2d 557, 560. We granted certiorari, 385 U. S. 811, and set the case for oral argument with No. 223, Gilbert v. California, post,

p. 263, and No. 254, Stovall v. Denno, post, p. 293, which present similar questions. We reverse the judgment of the Court of Appeals and remand to that court with direction to enter a new judgment vacating the conviction and remanding the case to the District Court for further proceedings consistent with this opinion.

I.

Neither the lineup itself nor anything shown by this record that Wade was required to do in the lineup violated his privilege against self-incrimination. We have only recently reaffirmed that the privilege "protects an accused only from being compelled to testify against himself, or otherwise provide the State with evidence of a testimonial or communicative nature . . . ." Schmerber v. California, 384 U. S. 757, 761. We there held that compelling a suspect to submit to a withdrawal of a sample of his blood for analysis for alcohol content and the admission in evidence of the analysis report were not compulsion to those ends. That holding was supported by the opinion in Holt v. United States, 218 U. S. 245, in which case a question arose as to whether a blouse belonged to the defendant. A witness testified at trial that the defendant put on the blouse and it had fit him. The defendant argued that the admission of the testimony was error because compelling him to put on the blouse was a violation of his privilege. The Court rejected the claim as "an extravagant extension of the Fifth Amendment," Mr. Justice Holmes saying for the Court:

"[T]he prohibition of compelling a man in a criminal court to be witness against himself is a prohibition of the use of physical or moral compulsion to extort communications from him, not an exclusion of his body as evidence when it may be material." 218 U. S., at 252-253.

The Court in Holt, however, put aside any constitutional questions which might be involved in compelling an accused, as here, to exhibit himself before victims of or witnesses to an alleged crime; the Court stated, "we need not consider how far a court would go in compelling a man to exhibit himself." Id., at 253.[1]

We have no doubt that compelling the accused merely to exhibit his person for observation by a prosecution witness prior to trial involves no compulsion of the accused to give evidence having testimonial significance. It is compulsion of the accused to exhibit his physical characteristics, not compulsion to disclose any knowledge he might have. It is no different from compelling Schmerber to provide a blood sample or Holt to wear the blouse, and, as in those instances, is not within the cover of the privilege. Similarly, compelling Wade to speak within hearing distance of the witnesses, even to utter words purportedly uttered by the robber, was not compulsion to utter statements of a "testimonial" nature; he was required to use his voice as an identifying physical characteristic, not to speak his guilt. We held in Schmerber, supra, at 761, that the distinction to be drawn under the Fifth Amendment privilege against self-incrimination is one between an accused's "communications" in whatever form, vocal or physical, and "compulsion which makes a suspect or accused the source of `real or physical evidence,' " Schmerber, supra, at 764. We recognized that "both federal and state courts have usually held that . . . [the privilege] offers no protection against compulsion to submit to fingerprinting, photography, or measurements, to write or speak for identification, to appear in court, to stand, to assume a stance, to walk, or to make a particular gesture." Id., at 764. None of these activities becomes testimonial within the scope of the privilege because required of the accused in a pretrial lineup.

Moreover, it deserves emphasis that this case presents no question of the admissibility in evidence of anything Wade said or did at the lineup which implicates his privilege. The Government offered no such evidence as part of its case, and what came out about the lineup proceedings on Wade's cross-examination of the bank employees involved no violation of Wade's privilege.

II.

The fact that the lineup involved no violation of Wade's privilege against self-incrimination does not, however, dispose of his contention that the courtroom identifications should have been excluded because the lineup was conducted without notice to and in the absence of his counsel. Our rejection of the right to counsel claim in Schmerber rested on our conclusion in that case that "[n]o issue of counsel's ability to assist petitioner in respect of any rights he did possess is presented." 384 U. S., at 766. In contrast, in this case it is urged that the assistance of counsel at the lineup was indispensable to protect Wade's most basic right as a criminal defendant —his right to a fair trial at which the witnesses against him might be meaningfully cross-examined.

The Framers of the Bill of Rights envisaged a broader role for counsel than under the practice then prevailing in England of merely advising his client in "matters of law," and eschewing any responsibility for "matters of fact."[2] The constitutions in at least 11 of the 13 States expressly or impliedly abolished this distinction. Powell v. Alabama, 287 U. S. 45, 60-65; Note, 73 Yale L. J. 1000, 1030-1033 (1964). "Though the colonial provisions about counsel were in accord on few things, they agreed on the necessity of abolishing the facts-law distinction; the colonists appreciated that if a defendant were forced to stand alone against the state, his case was foredoomed." 73 Yale L. J., supra, at 1033-1034. This background is reflected in the scope given by our decisions to the Sixth Amendment's guarantee to an accused of the assistance of counsel for his defense. When the Bill of Rights was adopted, there were no organized police forces as we know

them today.[3] The accused confronted the prosecutor and the witnesses against him, and the evidence was marshalled, largely at the trial itself. In contrast, today's law enforcement machinery involves critical confrontations of the accused by the prosecution at pretrial proceedings where the results might well settle the accused's fate and reduce the trial itself to a mere formality. In recognition of these realities of modern criminal prosecution, our cases have construed the Sixth Amendment guarantee to apply to "critical" stages of the proceedings. The guarantee reads: "In all criminal prosecutions, the accused shall enjoy the right . . . to have the Assistance of Counsel for his defence." (Emphasis supplied.) The plain wording of this guarantee thus encompasses counsel's assistance whenever necessary to assure a meaningful "defence."

As early as Powell v. Alabama, supra, we recognized that the period from arraignment to trial was "perhaps the most critical period of the proceedings . . .," id., at 57, during which the accused "requires the guiding hand of counsel . . .," id., at 69, if the guarantee is not to prove an empty right. That principle has since been applied to require the assistance of counsel at the type of arraignment —for example, that provided by Alabama—where certain rights might be sacrificed or lost: "What happens there may affect the whole trial. Available defenses may be irretrievably lost, if not then and there asserted . . . ." Hamilton v. Alabama, 368 U. S. 52, 54. See White v. Maryland, 373 U. S. 59. The principle was also applied in Massiah v. United States, 377 U. S. 201, where we held that incriminating statements of the defendant should have been excluded from evidence when it appeared that they were overheard by federal agents who, without notice to the defendant's lawyer, arranged a meeting between the defendant and an accomplice turned informant. We said, quoting a concurring opinion in Spano v. New York, 360 U. S. 315, 326, that "[a]nything less . . . might deny a defendant `effective representation by counsel at the only stage when legal aid and advice would help him.' " 377 U. S., at 204.

In Escobedo v. Illinois, 378 U. S. 478, we drew upon the rationale of Hamilton and Massiah in holding that the right to counsel was guaranteed at the point where the accused, prior to arraignment, was subjected to secret interrogation despite repeated requests to see his lawyer. We again noted the necessity of counsel's presence if the accused was to have a fair opportunity to present a defense at the trial itself:

"The rule sought by the State here, however, would make the trial no more than an appeal from the interrogation; and the `right to use counsel at the formal trial [would be] a very hollow thing [if], for all practical purposes, the conviction is already assured by pretrial examination' . . . . `One can imagine a cynical prosecutor saying: "Let them have the most illustrious counsel, now. They can't escape the noose. There is nothing that counsel can do for them at the trial." ' " 378 U. S., at 487-488.

Finally in Miranda v. Arizona, 384 U. S. 436, the rules established for custodial interrogation included the right to the presence of counsel. The result was rested on our finding that this and the other rules were necessary to safeguard the privilege against self-incrimination from being jeopardized by such interrogation.

Of course, nothing decided or said in the opinions in the cited cases links the right to counsel only to protection of Fifth Amendment rights. Rather those decisions "no more than reflect a constitutional principle established as long ago as Powell v. Alabama . . . ." Massiah v. United States, supra, at 205. It is central to that principle that in addition to counsel's presence at trial,[4] the accused is guaranteed that he need not stand alone against the State at any stage of the prosecution, formal or informal, in court or out,

where counsel's absence might derogate from the accused's right to a fair trial.[5] The security of that right is as much the aim of the right to counsel as it is of the other guarantees of the Sixth Amendment—the right of the accused to a speedy and public trial by an impartial jury, his right to be informed of the nature and cause of the accusation, and his right to be confronted with the witnesses against him and to have compulsory process for obtaining witnesses in his favor. The presence of counsel at such critical confrontations, as at the trial itself, operates to assure that the accused's interests will be protected consistently with out adversary theory of criminal prosecution. Cf. Pointer v. Texas, 380 U. S. 400.

In sum, the principle of Powell v. Alabama and succeeding cases requires that we scrutinize any pretrial confrontation of the accused to determine whether the presence of his counsel is necessary to preserve the defendant's basic right to a fair trial as affected by his right meaningfully to cross-examine the witnesses against him and to have effective assistance of counsel at the trial itself. It calls upon us to analyze whether potential substantial prejudice to defendant's rights inheres in the particular confrontation and the ability of counsel to help avoid that prejudice.

III.

The Government characterizes the lineup as a mere preparatory step in the gathering of the prosecution's evidence, not different—for Sixth Amendment purposes —from various other preparatory steps, such as systematized or scientific analyzing of the accused's fingerprints, blood sample, clothing, hair, and the like. We think there are differences which preclude such stages being characterized as critical stages at which the accused has the right to the presence of his counsel. Knowledge of the techniques of science and technology is sufficiently available, and the variables in techniques few enough, that the accused has the opportunity for a meaningful confrontation of the Government's case at trial through the ordinary processes of cross-examination of the Government's expert witnesses and the presentation of the evidence of his own experts. The denial of a right to have his counsel present at such analyses does not therefore violate the Sixth Amendment; they are not critical stages since there is minimal risk that his counsel's absence at such stages might derogate from his right to a fair trial.

IV.

But the confrontation compelled by the State between the accused and the victim or witnesses to a crime to elicit identification evidence is peculiarly riddled with innumerable dangers and variable factors which might seriously, even crucially, derogate from a fair trial. The vagaries of eyewitness identification are well-known; the annals of criminal law are rife with instances of mistaken identification.[6] Mr. Justice Frankfurter once said: "What is the worth of identification testimony even when uncontradicted? The identification of strangers is proverbially untrustworthy. The hazards of such testimony are established by a formidable number of instances in the records of English and American trials. These instances are recent—not due to the brutalities of ancient criminal procedure." The Case of Sacco and Vanzetti 30 (1927). A major factor contributing to the high incidence of miscarriage of justice from mistaken identification has been the degree of suggestion inherent in the manner in which the prosecution presents the suspect to witnesses for pretrial identification. A commentator has observed that "[t]he influence of improper suggestion upon identifying witnesses probably accounts for more miscarriages of justice than any other single factor— perhaps it is responsible for more such errors than all other factors combined." Wall, Eye-Witness Identification in Criminal Cases 26. Suggestion can be created intentionally or

unintentionally in many subtle ways.[7] And the dangers for the suspect are particularly grave when the witness' opportunity for observation was insubstantial, and thus his susceptibility to suggestion the greatest.

Moreover, "[i]t is a matter of common experience that, once a witness has picked out the accused at the line-up, he is not likely to go back on his word later on, so that in practice the issue of identity may (in the absence of other relevant evidence) for all practical purposes be determined there and then, before the trial."[8]

The pretrial confrontation for purpose of identification may take the form of a lineup, also known as an "identification parade" or "showup," as in the present case, or presentation of the suspect alone to the witness, as in Stovall v. Denno, supra. It is obvious that risks of suggestion attend either form of confrontation and increase the dangers inhering in eyewitness identification.[9] But as is the case with secret interrogations, there is serious difficulty in depicting what transpires at lineups and other forms of identification confrontations. "Privacy results in secrecy and this in turn results in a gap in our knowledge as to what in fact goes on . . . ." Miranda v. Arizona, supra, at 448. For the same reasons, the defense can seldom reconstruct the manner and mode of lineup identification for judge or jury at trial. Those participating in a lineup with the accused may often be police officers;[10] in any event, the participants' names are rarely recorded or divulged at trial.[11] The impediments to an objective observation are increased when the victim is the witness. Lineups are prevalent in rape and robbery prosecutions and present a particular hazard that a victim's understandable outrage may excite vengeful or spiteful motives.[12] In any event, neither witnesses nor lineup participants are apt to be alert for conditions prejudicial to the suspect. And if they were, it would likely be of scant benefit to the suspect since neither witnesses nor lineup participants are likely to be schooled in the detection of suggestive influences.[13] Improper influences may go undetected by a suspect, guilty or not, who experiences the emotional tension which we might expect in one being confronted with potential accusers.[14] Even when he does observe abuse, if he has a criminal record he may be reluctant to take the stand and open up the admission of prior convictions. Moreover, any protestations by the suspect of the fairness of the lineup made at trial are likely to be in vain;[15] the jury's choice is between the accused's unsupported version and that of the police officers present.[16] In short, the accused's inability effectively to reconstruct at trial any unfairness that occurred at the lineup may deprive him of his only opportunity meaningfully to attack the credibility of the witness' courtroom identification.

What facts have been disclosed in specific cases about the conduct of pretrial confrontations for identification illustrate both the potential for substantial prejudice to the accused at that stage and the need for its revelation at trial. A commentator provides some striking examples:

"In a Canadian case . . . the defendant had been picked out of a line-up of six men, of which he was the only Oriental. In other cases, a black-haired suspect was placed among a group of light-haired persons, tall suspects have been made to stand with short non-suspects, and, in a case where the perpetrator of the crime was known to be a youth, a suspect under twenty was placed in a line-up with five other persons, all of whom were forty or over."[17]

Similarly state reports, in the course of describing prior identifications admitted as evidence of guilt, reveal numerous instances of suggestive procedures, for example, that all in the lineup but the suspect were known to the identifying witness,[18] that the other participants in a lineup were grossly dissimilar in appearance to the suspect,[19] that only the suspect was required to wear distinctive clothing which the culprit allegedly wore,[20] that the witness is told by the police that they have caught the culprit after which the defendant is brought before the witness alone or is viewed in jail,[21] that the suspect is pointed out before or during a lineup,[22] and that the participants in the lineup are asked to try on an article of clothing which fits only the suspect.[23]

The potential for improper influence is illustrated by the circumstances, insofar as they appear, surrounding the prior identifications in the three cases we decide today. In the present case, the testimony of the identifying witnesses elicited on cross-examination revealed that those witnesses were taken to the courthouse and seated in the courtroom to await assembly of the lineup. The courtroom faced on a hallway observable to the witnesses through an open door. The cashier testified that she saw Wade "standing in the hall" within sight of an FBI agent. Five or six other prisoners later appeared in the hall. The vice president testified that he saw a person in the hall in the custody of the agent who "resembled the person that we identified as the one that had entered the bank."[24]

The lineup in Gilbert, supra, was conducted in an auditorium in which some 100 witnesses to several alleged state and federal robberies charged to Gilbert made wholesale identifications of Gilbert as the robber in each other's presence, a procedure said to be fraught with dangers of suggestion.[25] And the vice of suggestion created by the identification in Stovall, supra, was the presentation to the witness of the suspect alone handcuffed to police officers. It is hard to imagine a situation more clearly conveying the suggestion to the witness that the one presented is believed guilty by the police. See Frankfurter, The Case of Sacco and Vanzetti 31-32.

The few cases that have surfaced therefore reveal the existence of a process attended with hazards of serious unfairness to the criminal accused and strongly suggest the plight of the more numerous defendants who are unable to ferret out suggestive influences in the secrecy of the confrontation. We do not assume that these risks are the result of police procedures intentionally designed to prejudice an accused. Rather we assume they derive from the dangers inherent in eyewitness identification and the suggestibility inherent in the context of the pretrial identification. Williams & Hammelmann, in one of the most comprehensive studies of such forms of identification, said, "[T]he fact that the police themselves have, in a given case, little or no doubt that the man put up for identification has committed the offense, and that their chief pre-occupation is with the problem of getting sufficient proof, because he has not `come clean,' involves a danger that this persuasion may communicate itself even in a doubtful case to the witness in some way . . . ." Identification Parades, Part I, [1963] Crim. L. Rev. 479, 483.

Insofar as the accused's conviction may rest on a courtroom identification in fact the fruit of a suspect pretrial identification which the accused is helpless to subject to effective scrutiny at trial, the accused is deprived of that right of cross-examination which is an essential safeguard to his right to confront the witnesses against him. Pointer v. Texas, 380 U. S. 400. And even though cross-examination is a precious safeguard to a fair trial, it cannot be viewed as an absolute assurance of accuracy and reliability. Thus in the present context, where so many variables and pitfalls exist, the first line of defense must be the prevention of unfairness and the lessening of the hazards of eyewitness identification at the lineup itself. The trial which might determine the accused's fate may well not be that in the courtroom but that at the pretrial confrontation, with the State aligned against the accused, the witness the sole jury, and the accused unprotected against the overreaching, intentional or unintentional, and with little or no

effective appeal from the judgment there rendered by the witness—"that's the man."

Since it appears that there is grave potential for prejudice, intentional or not, in the pretrial lineup, which may not be capable of reconstruction at trial, and since presence of counsel itself can often avert prejudice and assure a meaningful confrontation at trial,[26] there can be little doubt that for Wade the post-indictment lineup was a critical stage of the prosecution at which he was "as much entitled to such aid [of counsel] . . . as at the trial itself." Powell v. Alabama, 287 U. S. 45, 57. Thus both Wade and his counsel should have been notified of the impending lineup, and counsel's presence should have been a requisite to conduct of the lineup, absent an "intelligent waiver." See Carnley v. Cochran, 369 U. S. 506. No substantial countervailing policy considerations have been advanced against the requirement of the presence of counsel. Concern is expressed that the requirement will forestall prompt identifications and result in obstruction of the confrontations. As for the first, we note that in the two cases in which the right to counsel is today held to apply, counsel had already been appointed and no argument is made in either case that notice to counsel would have prejudicially delayed the confrontations. Moreover, we leave open the question whether the presence of substitute counsel might not suffice where notification and presence of the suspect's own counsel would result in prejudicial delay.[27] And to refuse to recognize the right to counsel for fear that counsel will obstruct the course of justice is contrary to the basic assumptions upon which this Court has operated in Sixth Amendment cases. We rejected similar logic in Miranda v. Arizona concerning presence of counsel during custodial interrogation, 384 U. S., at 480-481:

"[A]n attorney is merely exercising the good professional judgment he has been taught. This is not cause for considering the attorney a menace to law enforcement. He is merely carrying out what he is sworn to do under his oath—to protect to the extent of his ability the rights of his client. In fulfilling this responsibility the attorney plays a vital role in the administration of criminal justice under our Constitution."

In our view counsel can hardly impede legitimate law enforcement; on the contrary, for the reasons expressed, law enforcement may be assisted by preventing the infiltration of taint in the prosecution's identification evidence.[28] That result cannot help the guilty avoid conviction but can only help assure that the right man has been brought to justice.[29]

Legislative or other regulations, such as those of local police departments, which eliminate the risks of abuse and unintentional suggestion at lineup proceedings and the impediments to meaningful confrontation at trial may also remove the basis for regarding the stage as "critical."[30] But neither Congress nor the federal authorities have seen fit to provide a solution. What we hold today "in no way creates a constitutional strait-jacket which will handicap sound efforts at reform, nor is it intended to have this effect." Miranda v. Arizona, supra, at 467.

V.

We come now to the question whether the denial of Wade's motion to strike the courtroom identification by the bank witnesses at trial because of the absence of his counsel at the lineup required, as the Court of Appeals held, the grant of a new trial at which such evidence is to be excluded. We do not think this disposition can be justified without first giving the Government the opportunity to establish by clear and convincing evidence that the in-court identifications were based upon observations of the suspect other than the lineup identification. See Murphy v. Waterfront Commission, 378 U. S. 52, 79, n. 18.[31] Where, as here, the admissibility of evidence of the lineup identification itself is not involved, a per se rule of exclusion of courtroom identification would be unjustified.[32] See Nardone v. United States, 308 U. S. 338, 341. A rule limited solely to the exclusion of testimony concerning identification at the lineup itself, without regard to admissibility of the courtroom identification, would render the right to counsel an empty one. The lineup is most often used, as in the present case, to crystallize the witnesses' identification of the defendant for future reference. We have already noted that the lineup identification will have that effect. The State may then rest upon the witnesses' unequivocal courtroom identification, and not mention the pretrial identification as part of the State's case at trial. Counsel is then in the predicament in which Wade's counsel found himself—realizing that possible unfairness at the lineup may be the sole means of attack upon the unequivocal courtroom identification, and having to probe in the dark in an attempt to discover and reveal unfairness, while bolstering the government witness' courtroom identification by bringing out and dwelling upon his prior identification. Since counsel's presence at the lineup would equip him to attack not only the lineup identification but the courtroom identification as well, limiting the impact of violation of the right to counsel to exclusion of evidence only of identification at the lineup itself disregards a critical element of that right.

We think it follows that the proper test to be applied in these situations is that quoted in Wong Sun v. United States, 371 U. S. 471, 488, " `[W]hether, granting establishment of the primary illegality, the evidence to which instant objection is made has been come at by exploitation of that illegality or instead by means sufficiently distinguishable to be purged of the primary taint.' Maguire, Evidence of Guilt 221 (1959)." See also Hoffa v. United States, 385 U. S. 293, 309. Application of this test in the present context requires consideration of various factors; for example, the prior opportunity to observe the alleged criminal act, the existence of any discrepancy between any pre-lineup description and the defendant's actual description, any identification prior to lineup of another person, the identification by picture of the defendant prior to the lineup, failure to identify the defendant on a prior occasion, and the lapse of time between the alleged act and the lineup identification. It is also relevant to consider those facts which, despite the absence of counsel, are disclosed concerning the conduct of the lineup.[33]

We doubt that the Court of Appeals applied the proper test for exclusion of the in-court identification of the two witnesses. The court stated that "it cannot be said with any certainty that they would have recognized appellant at the time of trial if this intervening lineup had not occurred," and that the testimony of the two witnesses "may well have been colored by the illegal procedure [and] was prejudicial." 358 F. 2d, at 560. Moreover, the court was persuaded, in part, by the "compulsory verbal responses made by Wade at the instance of the Special Agent." Ibid. This implies the erroneous holding that Wade's privilege against self-incrimination was violated so that the denial of counsel required exclusion.

On the record now before us we cannot make the determination whether the in-court identifications had an independent origin. This was not an issue at trial, although there is some evidence relevant to a determination. That inquiry is most properly made in the District Court. We therefore think the appropriate procedure to be followed is to vacate the conviction pending a hearing to determine whether the in-court identifications had an independent source, or whether, in any event, the introduction of the evidence was harmless error, Chapman v. California, 386 U. S. 18, and for the District Court to reinstate the conviction or order a new trial, as may be proper. See United States v. Shotwell Mfg.

Co., 355 U. S. 233, 245-246.

The judgment of the Court of Appeals is vacated and the case is remanded to that court with direction to enter a new judgment vacating the conviction and remanding the case to the District Court for further proceedings consistent with this opinion.

It is so ordered.

Katz v. US (Dec 18, 1967) [Notes omitted]

MR. JUSTICE STEWART delivered the opinion of the Court.

The petitioner was convicted in the District Court for the Southern District of California under an eight-count indictment charging him with transmitting wagering information by telephone from Los Angeles to Miami and Boston, in violation of a federal statute. [n1] At trial, the Government was permitted, over the petitioner's objection, to introduce evidence of the petitioner's end of telephone conversations, overheard by FBI agents who had attached an electronic listening and recording device to the outside of the public telephone booth from which he had placed his calls. In affirming his conviction, the Court of Appeals rejected the contention that the recordings had been obtained in violation of the Fourth Amendment, because "[t]here was no physical entrance into the area occupied by [the petitioner]." [n2] We granted certiorari in order to consider the constitutional questions thus presented. [n3]

The petitioner has phrased those questions as follows:

A. Whether a public telephone booth is a constitutionally protected area so that evidence obtained by attaching an electronic listening recording device to the top of such a booth is obtained in violation of the right to privacy of the user of the booth.

B. Whether physical penetration of a

constitutionally protected area is necessary before a search and seizure can be said to be violative of the Fourth Amendment to the United States Constitution.

We decline to adopt this formulation of the issues. In the first place, the correct solution of Fourth Amendment problems is not necessarily promoted by incantation of the phrase "constitutionally protected area." Secondly, the Fourth Amendment cannot be translated into a general constitutional "right to privacy." That Amendment protects individual privacy against certain kinds of governmental intrusion, but its protections go further, and often have nothing to do with privacy at all. [n4] Other provisions of the Constitution protect personal privacy from other forms of governmental invasion. [n5] But the protection of a person's general right to privacy -- his right to be let alone by other people [n6] -- is, like the protection of his property and of his very life, left largely to the law of the individual States. [n7]

Because of the misleading way the issues have been formulated, the parties have attached great significance to the characterization of the telephone booth from which the petitioner placed his calls. The petitioner has strenuously argued that the booth was a "constitutionally protected area." The Government has maintained with equal vigor that it was not. [n8] But this effort to decide whether or not a given "area," viewed in the abstract, is "constitutionally protected" deflects attention from the problem presented by this case. [n9] For the Fourth Amendment protects people, not places. What a person knowingly exposes to the public, even in his own home or office, is not a subject of Fourth Amendment protection. See Lewis v. United States, 385 U.S. 206, 210; United States v. Lee, 274 U.S. 559, 563. But what he seeks to preserve as private, even in an area accessible to the public, may be constitutionally protected. See Rios v. United States, 364 U.S. 253; Ex parte Jackson, 96 U.S. 727, 733.

The Government stresses the fact that the telephone booth from which the petitioner made his calls was constructed partly of glass, so that he was as visible after he entered it as he would have been if he had remained outside. But what he sought to exclude when he entered the booth was not the intruding eye -- it was the uninvited ear. He did not shed his right to do so simply because he made his calls from a place where he might be seen. No less than an individual in a business office, [n10] in a friend's apartment, [n11] or in a taxicab, [n12] a person in a telephone booth may rely upon the protection of the Fourth Amendment. One who occupies it, shuts the door behind him, and pays the toll that permits him to place a call is surely entitled to assume that the words he utters into the mouthpiece will not be broadcast to the world. To read the Constitution more narrowly is to ignore the vital role that the public telephone has come to play in private communication.

The Government contends, however, that the activities of its agents in this case should not be tested by Fourth Amendment requirements, for the surveillance technique they employed involved no physical penetration of the telephone booth from which the petitioner placed his calls. It is true that the absence of such penetration was at one time thought to foreclose further Fourth Amendment inquiry, Olmstead v. United States, 277 U.S. 438, 457, 464, 466; Goldman v. United States, 316 U.S. 129, 134-136, for that Amendment was thought to limit only searches and seizures of tangible property. [n13] But "[t]he premise that property interests control the right of the Government to search and seize has been discredited." Warden v. Hayden, 387 U.S. 294, 304. Thus, although a closely divided Court supposed in Olmstead that surveillance without any trespass and without the seizure of any material object fell outside the ambit of the

Constitution, we have since departed from the narrow view on which that decision rested. Indeed, we have expressly held that the Fourth Amendment governs not only the seizure of tangible items, but extends as well to the recording of oral statements, overheard without any "technical trespass under . . . local property law." Silverman v. United States, 365 U.S. 505, 511. Once this much is acknowledged, and once it is recognized that the Fourth Amendment protects people -- and not simply "areas" -- against unreasonable searches and seizures, it becomes clear that the reach of that Amendment cannot turn upon the presence or absence of a physical intrusion into any given enclosure.

We conclude that the underpinnings of Olmstead and Goldman have been so eroded by our subsequent decisions that the "trespass" doctrine there enunciated can no longer be regarded as controlling. The Government's activities in electronically listening to and recording the petitioner's words violated the privacy upon which he justifiably relied while using the telephone booth, and thus constituted a "search and seizure" within the meaning of the Fourth Amendment. The fact that the electronic device employed to achieve that end did not happen to penetrate the wall of the booth can have no constitutional significance.

The question remaining for decision, then, is whether the search and seizure conducted in this case complied with constitutional standards. In that regard, the Government's position is that its agents acted in an entirely defensible manner: they did not begin their electronic surveillance until investigation of the petitioner's activities had established a strong probability that he was using the telephone in question to transmit gambling information to persons in other States, in violation of federal law. Moreover, the surveillance was limited, both in scope and in duration, to the specific purpose of establishing the contents of the petitioner's unlawful telephonic communications. The agents confined their surveillance to the brief periods during which he used the telephone booth, [n14] and they took great care to overhear only the conversations of the petitioner himself. [n15]

Accepting this account of the Government's actions as accurate, it is clear that this surveillance was so narrowly circumscribed that a duly authorized magistrate, properly notified of the need for such investigation, specifically informed of the basis on which it was to proceed, and clearly apprised of the precise intrusion it would entail, could constitutionally have authorized, with appropriate safeguards, the very limited search and seizure that the Government asserts, in fact, took place. Only last Term we sustained the validity of such an authorization, holding that, under sufficiently "precise and discriminate circumstances," a federal court may empower government agents to employ a concealed electronic device "for the narrow and particularized purpose of ascertaining the truth of the . . . allegations" of a "detailed factual affidavit alleging the commission of a specific criminal offense." Osborn v. United States, 385 U.S. 323, 329-330. Discussing that holding, the Court in Berger v. New York, 388 U.S. 41, said that "the order authorizing the use of the electronic device" in Osborn "afforded similar protections to those . . . of conventional warrants authorizing the seizure of tangible evidence." Through those protections, "no greater invasion of privacy was permitted than was necessary under the circumstances." Id. at 57. [n16] Here, too, a similar judicial order could have accommodated "the legitimate needs of law enforcement" [n17] by authorizing the carefully limited use of electronic surveillance.

The Government urges that, because its agents relied upon the decisions in Olmstead and Goldman, and because they did no more here than they might properly have done with prior judicial sanction, we should retroactively validate their conduct. That we cannot do. It is apparent that the agents in this case acted with restraint. Yet the inescapable fact is that this restraint was imposed by the agents themselves, not by a judicial officer. They were not required, before commencing the search, to present their estimate of probable cause for detached scrutiny by a neutral magistrate. They were not compelled, during the conduct of the search itself, to observe precise limits established in advance by a specific court order. Nor were they directed, after the search had been completed, to notify the authorizing magistrate in detail of all that had been seized. In the absence of such safeguards, this Court has never sustained a search upon the sole ground that officers reasonably expected to find evidence of a particular crime and voluntarily confined their activities to the least intrusive means consistent with that end. Searches conducted without warrants have been held unlawful "notwithstanding facts unquestionably showing probable cause," Agnello v. United States, 269 U.S. 20, 33, for the Constitution requires "that the deliberate, impartial judgment of a judicial officer . . . be interposed between the citizen and the police. . . ." Wong Sun v. United States, 371 U.S. 471, 481-482. "Over and again, this Court has emphasized that the mandate of the [Fourth] Amendment requires adherence to judicial processes," United States v. Jeffers, 342 U.S. 48, 51, and that searches conducted outside the judicial process, without prior approval by judge or magistrate, are per se unreasonable under the Fourth Amendment [n18] -- subject only to a few specifically established and well delineated exceptions. [n19]

It is difficult to imagine how any of those exceptions could ever apply to the sort of search and seizure involved in this case. Even electronic surveillance substantially contemporaneous with an individual's arrest could hardly be deemed an "incident" of that arrest. [n20] Nor could the use of electronic surveillance without prior authorization

be justified on grounds of "hot pursuit." [n21] And, of course, the very nature of electronic surveillance precludes its use pursuant to the suspect's consent. [n22]

The Government does not question these basic principles. Rather, it urges the creation of a new exception to cover this case. [n23] It argues that surveillance of a telephone booth should be exempted from the usual requirement of advance authorization by a magistrate upon a showing of probable cause. We cannot agree. Omission of such authorization

bypasses the safeguards provided by an objective predetermination of probable cause, and substitutes instead the far less reliable procedure of an after-the-event justification for the . . . search, too likely to be subtly influenced by the familiar shortcomings of hindsight judgment.

Beck v. Ohio, 379 U.S. 89, 96. And bypassing a neutral predetermination of the scope of a search leaves individuals secure from Fourth Amendment violations "only in the discretion of the police." Id. at 97.

These considerations do not vanish when the search in question is transferred from the setting of a home, an office, or a hotel room to that of a telephone booth. Wherever a man may be, he is entitled to know that he will remain free from unreasonable searches and seizures. The government agents here ignored "the procedure of antecedent justification . . . that is central to the Fourth Amendment," [n24] a procedure that we hold to be a constitutional precondition of the kind of electronic surveillance involved in this case. Because the surveillance here failed to meet that condition, and because it led to the petitioner's conviction, the judgment must be reversed.

It is so ordered.

Bumper v. North Carolina (June 3, 1968) [Notes omitted]

MR. JUSTICE STEWART delivered the opinion of the Court.

The petitioner was brought to trial in a North Carolina court upon a charge of rape, an offense punishable in that State by death unless the jury recommends life imprisonment. [1] Among the items of evidence introduced by the prosecution at the trial was a .22-caliber rifle allegedly used in the commission of the crime. The jury found the petitioner guilty, but recommended a sentence of life imprisonment. [2] The trial court-imposed that sentence, and the Supreme Court of North Carolina affirmed the judgment. [3] We granted certiorari [4] to consider two separate constitutional claims pressed unsuccessfully by the petitioner throughout the litigation in the North Carolina courts. First, the petitioner argues that his constitutional right to an impartial jury was violated in this capital case when the prosecution was permitted to challenge for cause all prospective jurors who stated that they were opposed to capital punishment or had conscientious scruples against imposing the death penalty. Secondly, the petitioner contends that the .22-caliber rifle introduced in evidence against him was obtained by the State in a search and seizure violative of the Fourth and Fourteenth Amendments.

I

In Witherspoon v. Illinois, ante, p. 391 U. S. 510, we have held that a death sentence cannot constitutionally be executed if imposed by a jury from which have been excluded for cause those who, without more, are opposed to capital punishment or have conscientious scruples against imposing the death penalty. Our decision in Witherspoon does not govern the present case, because here, the jury recommended a sentence of life imprisonment. The petitioner argues, however, that a jury qualified under such standards must necessarily be biased as well with respect to a defendant's guilt, and that his conviction must

accordingly be reversed because of the denial of his right under the Sixth and Fourteenth Amendments to trial by an impartial jury. Duncan v. Louisiana, ante, p. 391 U. S. 145; Turner v. Louisiana, 379 U. S. 466, 379 U. S. 471-473; Irvin v. Dowd, 366 U. S. 717, 366 U. S. 722-723. We cannot accept that contention in the present case. The petitioner adduced no evidence to support the claim that a jury selected as this one was is necessarily "prosecution prone," [5] and the materials referred to in his brief are no more substantial than those brought to our attention in Witherspoon. [6] Accordingly, we decline to reverse the judgment of conviction upon this basis.

II

The petitioner lived with his grandmother, Mrs. Hattie Leath, a 66-year-old Negro widow, in a house located in a rural area at the end of an isolated mile-long dirt road. Two days after the alleged offense, but prior to the petitioner's arrest, four white law enforcement officers -- the county sheriff, two of his deputies, and a state investigator -- went to this house and found Mrs. Leath there with some young children. She met the officers at the front door. One of them announced, "I have a search warrant to search your house." Mrs. Leath responded, "Go ahead," and opened the door. In the kitchen the officers found the rifle that was later introduced in evidence at the petitioner's trial after a motion to suppress had been denied.

At the hearing on this motion, the prosecutor informed the court that he did not rely upon a warrant to justify the search, but upon the consent of Mrs. Leath. [7] She testified at the hearing, stating, among other things:

"Four of them came. I was busy about my work, and they walked into the house and one of them walked up and said, 'I have a search warrant to search your house,' and I walked out and told them to come on in. . . . He just come on in and said he had a warrant to search the house, and he didn't read it to me or nothing. So, I just told him to come on in and go ahead and search, and I went on about my work. I wasn't concerned what he was about. I was just satisfied. He just told me he had a search warrant, but he didn't read it to me. He did tell me he had a search warrant."

"* * * *"

". . . He said he was the law and had a search warrant to search the house, why I thought he could go ahead. I believed he had a search warrant. I took him at his word. . . . I just seen them out there in the yard. They got through the door when I opened it. At that time, I did not know my grandson had been charged with crime. Nobody told me anything. They didn't tell me anything, just picked it up like that. They didn't tell me nothing about my grandson. [8]"

Upon the basis of Mrs. Leath's testimony, the trial court found that she had given her consent to the search, and denied the motion to suppress. [9] The Supreme Court of North Carolina approved the admission of the evidence on the same basis. [10]

The issue thus presented is whether a search can be justified as lawful on the basis of consent when that "consent" has been given only after the official conducting the search has asserted that he possesses a warrant. [11] We hold that there can be no consent under such circumstances.

When a prosecutor seeks to rely upon consent to justify the lawfulness of a search, he has the burden of proving that the consent was, in fact, freely and voluntarily given. [12] This burden cannot be discharged by showing no more than acquiescence to a claim of lawful authority. [13] A search conducted in reliance upon a warrant cannot later be justified on the basis of consent if it turns out that the warrant was invalid. [14] The result can be no different when it turns out that the State does not even attempt to rely upon the validity of the warrant, or fails to show that there was, in fact, any warrant at all. [15]

When a law enforcement officer claims authority to search a home under a warrant, he announces in effect that the occupant has no right to resist the search. The situation is instinct with coercion -- albeit colorably lawful coercion. Where there is coercion, there cannot be consent.

We hold that Mrs. Leath did not consent to the search, and that it was constitutional error to admit the rifle in evidence against the petitioner. Mapp v. Ohio, 367 U. S. 643. Because the rifle was plainly damaging evidence against the petitioner with respect to all three of the charges against him, its admission at the trial was not harmless error. Chapman v. California, 386 U. S. 18. [16]

The judgment of the Supreme Court of North Carolina is, accordingly, reversed, and the case is remanded for further proceedings not inconsistent with this opinion.

It is so ordered.

Terry v. Ohio (June 10, 1968) [Notes omitted]

MR. CHIEF JUSTICE WARREN delivered the opinion of the Court.

This case presents serious questions concerning the role of the Fourth Amendment in the confrontation on the street between the citizen and the policeman investigating suspicious circumstances.

Petitioner Terry was convicted of carrying a concealed weapon and sentenced to the statutorily prescribed term of one to three years in the penitentiary. [n1] Following the denial of a pretrial motion to suppress, the prosecution introduced in evidence two revolvers and a number of bullets seized from Terry and a codefendant, Richard Chilton, [n2] by Cleveland Police Detective Martin McFadden. At the hearing on the motion to suppress this evidence, Officer McFadden testified that, while he was patrolling in plain clothes in downtown Cleveland at approximately 2:30 in the afternoon of October 31,

1963, his attention was attracted by two men, Chilton and Terry, standing on the corner of Huron Road and Euclid Avenue. He had never seen the two men before, and he was unable to say precisely what first drew his eye to them. However, he testified that he had been a policeman for 39 years and a detective for 35, and that he had been assigned to patrol this vicinity of downtown Cleveland for shoplifters and pickpockets for 30 years. He explained that he had developed routine habits of observation over the years, and that he would "stand and watch people or walk and watch people at many intervals of the day." He added: "Now, in this case, when I looked over, they didn't look right to me at the time."

His interest aroused, Officer McFadden took up a post of observation in the entrance to a store 300 to 400 feet away from the two men. "I get more purpose to watch them when I seen their movements," he testified. He saw one of the men leave the other one and walk southwest on Huron Road, past some stores. The man paused for a moment and looked in a store window, then walked on a short distance, turned around and walked back toward the corner, pausing once again to look in the same store window. He rejoined his companion at the corner, and the two conferred briefly. Then the second man went through the same series of motions, strolling down Huron Road, looking in the same window, walking on a short distance, turning back, peering in the store window again, and returning to confer with the first man at the corner. The two men repeated this ritual alternately between five and six times apiece -- in all, roughly a dozen trips. At one point, while the two were standing together on the corner, a third man approached them and engaged them briefly in conversation. This man then left the two others and walked west on Euclid Avenue. Chilton and Terry resumed their measured pacing, peering, and conferring. After this had gone on for 10 to 12 minutes, the two men walked off together, heading west on Euclid Avenue, following the path taken earlier by the third man.

By this time, Officer McFadden had become thoroughly suspicious. He testified that, after observing their elaborately casual and oft-repeated reconnaissance of the store window on Huron Road, he suspected the two men of "casing a job, a stick-up," and that he considered it his duty as a police officer to investigate further. He added that he feared "they may have a gun." Thus, Officer McFadden followed Chilton and Terry and saw them stop in front of Zucker's store to talk to the same man who had conferred with them earlier on the street corner. Deciding that the situation was ripe for direct action, Officer McFadden approached the three men, identified himself as a police officer and asked for their names. At this point, his knowledge was confined to what he had observed. He was not acquainted with any of the three men by name or by sight, and he had received no information concerning them from any other source. When the men "mumbled something" in response to his inquiries, Officer McFadden grabbed petitioner Terry, spun him around so that they were facing the other two, with Terry between McFadden and the others, and patted down the outside of his clothing. In the left breast pocket of Terry's overcoat, Officer McFadden felt a pistol. He reached inside the overcoat pocket, but was unable to remove the gun. At this point, keeping Terry between himself and the others, the officer ordered all three men to enter Zucker's store. As they went in, he removed Terry's overcoat completely, removed a .38 caliber revolver from the pocket and ordered all three men to face the wall with their hands raised. Officer McFadden proceeded to pat down the outer clothing of Chilton and the third man, Katz. He discovered another revolver in the outer pocket of Chilton's overcoat, but no weapons were found on Katz. The officer testified that he only patted the men down to see whether they had weapons, and that he did not put his hands beneath the outer garments of either Terry or Chilton until he felt their guns. So far as appears from the record, he never placed his hands beneath Katz' outer garments. Officer McFadden seized Chilton's gun, asked the proprietor of the store to call a police wagon, and took all three men to the station, where Chilton and Terry were formally charged with carrying concealed weapons.

On the motion to suppress the guns, the prosecution took the position that they had been seized following a search incident to a lawful arrest. The trial court rejected this theory, stating that it "would be stretching the facts beyond reasonable comprehension" to find that Officer McFadden had had probable cause to arrest the men before he patted them down for weapons. However, the court denied the defendants' motion on the ground that Officer McFadden, on the basis of his experience,

had reasonable cause to believe . . . that the defendants were conducting themselves suspiciously, and some interrogation should be made of their action.

Purely for his own protection, the court held, the officer had the right to pat down the outer clothing of these men, who he had reasonable cause to believe might be armed. The court distinguished between an investigatory "stop" and an arrest, and between a "frisk" of the outer clothing for weapons and a full-blown search for evidence of crime. The frisk, it held, was essential to the proper performance of the officer's investigatory duties, for, without it, "the answer to the police officer may be a bullet, and a loaded pistol discovered during the frisk is admissible."

After the court denied their motion to suppress, Chilton and Terry waived jury trial and pleaded not guilty. The court adjudged them guilty, and the Court of Appeals for the Eighth Judicial District, Cuyahoga County, affirmed. State v. Terry, 5 Ohio App.2d 122, 214 N.E.2d 114 (1966). The Supreme Court of Ohio dismissed their appeal on the ground that no "substantial constitutional question" was involved. We granted certiorari, 387 U.S. 929 (1967), to determine whether the admission of the revolvers in evidence violated petitioner's rights under the Fourth Amendment, made applicable to the States by the Fourteenth. Mapp v. Ohio, 367 U.S. 643 (1961). We affirm the conviction.

I

The Fourth Amendment provides that "the right of the people to be secure in their persons, houses, papers, and effects, against unreasonable searches and seizures, shall not be violated. . . ." This inestimable right of personal security belongs as much to the citizen on the streets of our cities as to the homeowner closeted in his study to dispose of his secret affairs. For as this Court has always recognized,

No right is held more sacred, or is more carefully guarded, by the common law than the right of every individual to the possession and control of his own person, free from all restraint or interference of others, unless by clear and unquestionable authority of law.

Union Pac. R. Co. v. Botsford, 141 U.S. 250, 251 (1891). We have recently held that "the Fourth Amendment protects people, not places," Katz v. United States, 389 U.S. 347, 351 (1967), and wherever an individual may harbor a reasonable "expectation of privacy," id. at 361 (MR. JUSTICE HARLAN, concurring), he is entitled to be free from unreasonable governmental intrusion. Of course, the specific content and incidents of this right must be shaped by the context in which it is asserted. For "what the Constitution forbids is not all searches and seizures, but unreasonable searches and seizures." Elkins v. United States, 364 U.S. 206, 222 (1960). Unquestionably petitioner was entitled to the protection of the Fourth Amendment as he walked down the street in Cleveland. Beck v. Ohio, 379 U.S. 89 (1964); Rios

v. United States, 364 U.S. 253 (1960); Henry v. United States, 361 U.S. 98 (1959); United States v. Di Re, 332 U.S. 581 (1948); Carroll v. United States, 267 U.S. 132 (1925). The question is whether, in all the circumstances of this on-the-street encounter, his right to personal security was violated by an unreasonable search and seizure.

We would be less than candid if we did not acknowledge that this question thrusts to the fore difficult and troublesome issues regarding a sensitive area of police activity -- issues which have never before been squarely presented to this Court. Reflective of the tensions involved are the practical and constitutional arguments pressed with great vigor on both sides of the public debate over the power of the police to "stop and frisk" -- as it is sometimes euphemistically termed -- suspicious persons.

On the one hand, it is frequently argued that, in dealing with the rapidly unfolding and often dangerous situations on city streets, the police are in need of an escalating set of flexible responses, graduated in relation to the amount of information they possess. For this purpose, it is urged that distinctions should be made between a "stop" and an "arrest" (or a "seizure" of a person), and between a "frisk" and a "search." [n3] Thus, it is argued, the police should be allowed to "stop" a person and detain him briefly for questioning upon suspicion that he may be connected with criminal activity. Upon suspicion that the person may be armed, the police should have the power to "frisk" him for weapons. If the "stop" and the "frisk" give rise to probable cause to believe that the suspect has committed a crime, then the police should be empowered to make a formal "arrest," and a full incident "search" of the person. This scheme is justified in part upon the notion that a "stop" and a "frisk" amount to a mere "minor inconvenience and petty indignity," [n4] which can properly be imposed upon the citizen in the interest of effective law enforcement on the basis of a police officer's

suspicion. [n5]

On the other side, the argument is made that the authority of the police must be strictly circumscribed by the law of arrest and search as it has developed to date in the traditional jurisprudence of the Fourth Amendment. [n6] It is contended with some force that there is not -- and cannot be -- a variety of police activity which does not depend solely upon the voluntary cooperation of the citizen, and yet which stops short of an arrest based upon probable cause to make such an arrest. The heart of the Fourth Amendment, the argument runs, is a severe requirement of specific justification for any intrusion upon protected personal security, coupled with a highly developed system of judicial controls to enforce upon the agents of the State the commands of the Constitution. Acquiescence by the courts in the compulsion inherent in the field interrogation practices at issue here, it is urged, would constitute an abdication of judicial control over, and indeed an encouragement of, substantial interference with liberty and personal security by police officers whose judgment is necessarily colored by their primary involvement in "the often competitive enterprise of ferreting out crime." Johnson v. United States, 333 U.S. 10, 14 (1948). This, it is argued, can only serve to exacerbate police-community tensions in the crowded centers of our Nation's cities. [n7]

In this context, we approach the issues in this case mindful of the limitations of the judicial function in controlling the myriad daily situations in which policemen and citizens confront each other on the street. The State has characterized the issue here as

the right of a police officer . . . to make an on-the-street stop, interrogate and pat down for weapons (known in street vernacular as "stop and frisk"). [n8]

But this is only partly accurate. For the issue is not the abstract propriety of the police conduct, but the admissibility against petitioner of the evidence uncovered by the search and seizure. Ever since its inception, the rule excluding evidence seized in violation of the Fourth Amendment has been recognized as a principal mode of discouraging lawless police conduct. See Weeks v. United States, 232 U.S. 383, 391-393 (1914). Thus, its major thrust is a deterrent one, see Linkletter v. Walker, 381 U.S. 618, 629-635 (1965), and experience has taught that it is the only effective deterrent to police misconduct in the criminal context, and that, without it, the constitutional guarantee against unreasonable searches and seizures would be a mere "form of words." Mapp v. Ohio, 367 U.S. 643, 655 (1961). The rule also serves another vital function -- "the imperative of judicial integrity." Elkins v. United States, 364 U.S. 206, 222 (1960). Courts which sit under our Constitution cannot and will not be made party to lawless invasions of the constitutional rights of citizens by permitting unhindered governmental use of the fruits of such invasions. Thus, in our system, evidentiary rulings provide the context in which the judicial process of inclusion and exclusion approves some conduct as comporting with constitutional guarantees and disapproves other actions by state agents. A ruling admitting evidence in a criminal trial, we recognize, has the necessary effect of legitimizing the conduct which produced the evidence, while an application of the exclusionary rule withholds the constitutional imprimatur.

The exclusionary rule has its limitations, however, as a tool of judicial control. It cannot properly be invoked to exclude the products of legitimate police investigative techniques on the ground that much conduct which is closely similar involves unwarranted intrusions upon constitutional protections. Moreover, in some contexts, the rule is ineffective as a deterrent. Street encounters between citizens and police officers are incredibly rich in diversity. They range from wholly friendly exchanges of pleasantries or mutually useful information to hostile confrontations of armed men involving arrests, or injuries, or loss of life. Moreover, hostile confrontations are not all of a piece. Some of them begin in a friendly enough manner, only to take a different turn upon the injection of some unexpected element into the conversation. Encounters are initiated by the police for a wide variety of purposes, some of which are wholly unrelated to a desire to prosecute for crime. [n9] Doubtless some police "field interrogation" conduct violates the Fourth Amendment. But a stern refusal by this Court to condone such activity does not necessarily render it responsive to the exclusionary rule. Regardless of how effective the rule may be where obtaining convictions is an important objective of the police, [n10] it is powerless to deter invasions of constitutionally guaranteed rights where the police either have no interest in prosecuting or are willing to forgo successful prosecution in the interest of serving some other goal.

Proper adjudication of cases in which the exclusionary rule is invoked demands a constant awareness of these limitations. The wholesale harassment by certain elements of the police community, of which minority groups, particularly Negroes, frequently complain, [n11] will not be stopped by the exclusion of any evidence from any criminal trial. Yet a rigid and unthinking application of the exclusionary rule, in futile protest against practices which it can never be used effectively to control, may exact a high toll in human injury and frustration of efforts to prevent crime. No judicial opinion can comprehend the protean variety of the street encounter, and we can only judge the facts of the case before us. Nothing we say today is to be taken as indicating approval of police conduct outside the legitimate investigative sphere. Under our decision, courts still retain their traditional responsibility to guard against police conduct which is overbearing or harassing, or which trenches upon personal security without the objective evidentiary justification which the Constitution requires. When such conduct is identified, it must be condemned by the judiciary, and its fruits must be excluded from evidence in criminal trials. And, of course, our approval of legitimate and restrained investigative conduct undertaken on the basis of ample factual justification should in no way discourage the employment of other remedies than the exclusionary rule to curtail abuses for which that sanction may prove inappropriate.

Having thus roughly sketched the perimeters of the constitutional debate over the limits on police investigative conduct in general and the background against which this case presents itself, we turn our attention to the quite narrow question posed by the facts before us: whether it is always unreasonable for a policeman to seize a person and subject him to a limited search for weapons unless there is probable cause for an arrest. Given the narrowness of this question, we have no occasion to canvass in detail the constitutional limitations upon the scope of a policeman's power when he confronts a citizen without probable cause to arrest him.

II

Our first task is to establish at what point in this encounter the Fourth Amendment becomes relevant. That is, we must decide whether and when Officer McFadden "seized" Terry, and whether and when he conducted a "search." There is some suggestion in the use of such terms as "stop" and "frisk" that such police conduct is outside the purview of the Fourth Amendment because neither action rises to the level of a "search" or "seizure" within the meaning of the Constitution. [n12] We emphatically reject this notion. It is quite plain that the Fourth Amendment governs "seizures" of the person which do not eventuate in a trip to the stationhouse and prosecution for crime -- "arrests" in traditional terminology. It must be recognized that, whenever a police officer accosts an individual and restrains his freedom to walk away, he has "seized" that person. And it is nothing less than sheer torture of the English language to suggest that a careful exploration of the outer surfaces of a person's clothing all over his or her body in an attempt to find weapons is not a "search." Moreover, it is simply fantastic to urge that such a procedure performed in public by a policeman while the citizen stands helpless, perhaps facing a wall with his hands raised, is a "petty indignity." [n13] It is a serious intrusion upon the sanctity of the person, which may inflict great indignity and arouse strong resentment, and it is not to be undertaken lightly. [n14]

The danger in the logic which proceeds upon distinctions between a "stop" and an "arrest," or "seizure" of the person, and between a "frisk" and a "search," is twofold. It seeks to isolate from constitutional scrutiny the initial stages of the contact between the policeman and the citizen. And, by suggesting a rigid all-or-nothing model of justification and regulation under the Amendment, it obscures the utility of limitations upon the scope, as well as the initiation, of police action as a means of constitutional regulation. [n15] This Court has held, in the past that a search which is reasonable at its inception may violate the Fourth Amendment by virtue of its intolerable intensity and scope. Kremen v. United States, 353 U.S. 346 (1957); Go-Bart Importing Co. v. United States, 282 U.S. 344, 356-358 (1931); see United States v. Di Re, 332 U.S. 581, 586-587 (1948). The scope of the search must be "strictly tied to and justified by" the circumstances which rendered its initiation permissible. Warden v. Hayden, 387 U.S. 294, 310 (1967) (MR. JUSTICE FORTAS, concurring); see, e.g., Preston v. United States, 376 U.S. 364, 367-368 (1964); Agnello v. United States, 269 U.S. 20, 30-31 (1925).

The distinctions of classical "stop-and-frisk" theory thus serve to divert attention from the central inquiry under the Fourth Amendment -- the reasonableness in all the circumstances of the particular governmental invasion of a citizen's personal security. "Search" and "seizure" are not talismans. We therefore reject the notions that the Fourth Amendment does not come into play at all as a limitation upon police conduct if the officers stop short of something called a "technical arrest" or a "full-blown search."

In this case, there can be no question, then, that Officer McFadden "seized" petitioner and subjected him to a "search" when he took hold of him and patted down the outer surfaces of his clothing. We must decide whether, at that point, it was reasonable for Officer McFadden to have interfered with petitioner's personal security as he did. [n16] And, in determining whether the seizure and search were "unreasonable," our inquiry is a dual one -- whether the officer's action was justified at its inception, and whether it was reasonably related in scope to the circumstances which justified the interference in the first place.

III

If this case involved police conduct subject to the Warrant Clause of the Fourth Amendment, we would have to ascertain whether "probable cause" existed to justify the search and seizure which took place. However, that is not the case. We do not retreat from our holdings that the police must, whenever practicable, obtain advance judicial approval of searches and seizures through the warrant procedure, see, e.g., Katz v. United States, 389 U.S. 347 (1967); Beck v. Ohio, 379 U.S. 89, 96 (1964); Chapman v. United States, 365 U.S. 610 (1961), or that, in most instances, failure to comply with the warrant requirement can only be excused by exigent circumstances, see, e.g., Warden v. Hayden, 387 U.S. 294 (1967) (hot pursuit); cf. Preston v. United States, 376 U.S. 364, 367-368 (1964). But we deal here with an entire rubric of police conduct -- necessarily swift action predicated upon the on-the-spot observations of the officer on the beat -- which historically has not been, and, as a practical matter, could not be, subjected to the warrant procedure. Instead, the conduct involved in this case must be tested by the Fourth Amendment's general proscription against unreasonable searches and seizures. [n17]

Nonetheless, the notions which underlie both the warrant procedure and the requirement of probable cause remain fully relevant in this context. In order to assess the reasonableness of Officer McFadden's conduct as a general proposition, it is necessary "first to focus upon the governmental interest which allegedly justifies official intrusion upon the constitutionally protected interests of the private citizen," for there is

no ready test for determining reasonableness other than by balancing the need to search [or seize] against the invasion which the search [or seizure] entails.

Camara v. Municipal Court, 387 U.S. 523, 534-535, 536-537 (1967). And, in justifying the particular intrusion, the police officer must be able to point to specific and articulable facts which, taken together with rational inferences from those facts, reasonably warrant that intrusion. [n18] The scheme of the Fourth Amendment becomes meaningful only when it is assured that, at some point, the conduct of those charged with enforcing the laws can be subjected to the more detached, neutral scrutiny of a judge who must evaluate the reasonableness of a particular search or seizure in light of the particular circumstances. [n19] And, in making that assessment, it is imperative that the facts be judged against an objective standard: would the facts available to the officer at the moment of the seizure or the search "warrant a man of reasonable caution in the belief" that the action taken was appropriate? Cf. Carroll v. United States, 267 U.S. 132 (1925); Beck v. Ohio, 379 U.S.

89, 96-97 (1964). [n20] Anything less would invite intrusions upon constitutionally guaranteed rights based on nothing more substantial than inarticulate hunches, a result this Court has consistently refused to sanction. See, e.g., Beck v. Ohio, supra; Rios v. United States, 364 U.S. 253 (1960); Henry v. United States, 361 U.S. 98 (1959). And simple

"good faith on the part of the arresting officer is not enough." . . . If subjective good faith alone were the test, the protections of the Fourth Amendment would evaporate, and the people would be "secure in their persons, houses, papers, and effects," only in the discretion of the police.

Beck v. Ohio, supra, at 97.

Applying these principles to this case, we consider first the nature and extent of the governmental interests involved. One general interest is, of course, that of effective crime prevention and detection; it is this interest which underlies the recognition that a police officer may, in appropriate circumstances and in an appropriate manner, approach a person for purposes of investigating possibly criminal behavior even though there is no probable cause to make an arrest. It was this legitimate investigative function Officer McFadden was discharging when he decided to approach petitioner and his companions. He had observed Terry, Chilton, and Katz go through a series of acts, each of them perhaps innocent in itself, but which, taken together, warranted further investigation. There is nothing unusual in two men standing together on a street corner, perhaps waiting for someone. Nor is there anything suspicious about people in such circumstances strolling up and down the street, singly or in pairs. Store windows, moreover, are made to be looked in. But the story is quite different where, as here, two men hover about a street corner for an extended period of time, at the end of which it becomes apparent that they are not waiting for anyone or anything; where these men

pace alternately along an identical route, pausing to stare in the same store window roughly 24 times; where each completion of this route is followed immediately by a conference between the two men on the corner; where they are joined in one of these conferences by a third man who leaves swiftly, and where the two men finally follow the third and rejoin him a couple of blocks away. It would have been poor police work indeed for an officer of 30 years' experience in the detection of thievery from stores in this same neighborhood to have failed to investigate this behavior further.

The crux of this case, however, is not the propriety of Officer McFadden's taking steps to investigate petitioner's suspicious behavior, but, rather, whether there was justification for McFadden's invasion of Terry's personal security by searching him for weapons in the course of that investigation. We are now concerned with more than the governmental interest in investigating crime; in addition, there is the more immediate interest of the police officer in taking steps to assure himself that the person with whom he is dealing is not armed with a weapon that could unexpectedly and fatally be used against him. Certainly it would be unreasonable to require that police officers take unnecessary risks in the performance of their duties. American criminals have a long tradition of armed violence, and every year in this country many law enforcement officers are killed in the line of duty, and thousands more are wounded. Virtually all of these deaths and a substantial portion of the injuries are inflicted with guns and knives. [n21]

In view of these facts, we cannot blind ourselves to the need for law enforcement officers to protect themselves and other prospective victims of violence in situations where they may lack probable cause for an arrest. When an officer is justified in believing that the individual whose suspicious behavior he is investigating at close range is armed and presently dangerous to the officer or to others, it would appear to be clearly unreasonable to deny the officer the power to take necessary measures to determine whether the person is, in fact, carrying a weapon and to neutralize the threat of physical harm.

We must still consider, however, the nature and quality of the intrusion on individual rights which must be accepted if police officers are to be conceded the right to search for weapons in situations where probable cause to arrest for crime is lacking. Even a limited search of the outer clothing for weapons constitutes a severe, though brief, intrusion upon cherished personal security, and it must surely be an annoying, frightening, and perhaps humiliating experience. Petitioner contends that such an intrusion is permissible only incident to a lawful arrest, either for a crime involving the possession of weapons or for a crime the commission of which led the officer to investigate in the first place. However, this argument must be closely examined.

Petitioner does not argue that a police officer should refrain from making any investigation of suspicious circumstances until such time as he has probable cause to make an arrest; nor does he deny that police officers, in properly discharging their investigative function, may find themselves confronting persons who might well be armed and dangerous. Moreover, he does not say that an officer is always unjustified in searching a suspect to discover weapons. Rather, he says it is unreasonable for the policeman to take that step until such time as the situation evolves to a point where there is probable cause to make an arrest. When that point has been reached, petitioner would concede the officer's right to conduct a search of the suspect for weapons, fruits or instrumentalities of the crime, or "mere" evidence, incident to the arrest.

There are two weaknesses in this line of reasoning, however. First, it fails to take account of traditional limitations upon the scope of searches,

and thus recognizes no distinction in purpose, character, and extent between a search incident to an arrest and a limited search for weapons. The former, although justified in part by the acknowledged necessity to protect the arresting officer from assault with a concealed weapon, Preston v. United States, 376 U.S. 364, 367 (1964), is also justified on other grounds, ibid., and can therefore involve a relatively extensive exploration of the person. A search for weapons in the absence of probable cause to arrest, however, must, like any other search, be strictly circumscribed by the exigencies which justify its initiation. Warden v. Hayden, 387 U.S. 294, 310 (1967) (MR. JUSTICE FORTAS, concurring). Thus, it must be limited to that which is necessary for the discovery of weapons which might be used to harm the officer or others nearby, and may realistically be characterized as something less than a "full" search, even though it remains a serious intrusion.

A second, and related, objection to petitioner's argument is that it assumes that the law of arrest has already worked out the balance between the particular interests involved here -- the neutralization of danger to the policeman in the investigative circumstance and the sanctity of the individual. But this is not so. An arrest is a wholly different kind of intrusion upon individual freedom from a limited search for weapons, and the interests each is designed to serve are likewise quite different. An arrest is the initial stage of a criminal prosecution. It is intended to vindicate society's interest in having its laws obeyed, and it is inevitably accompanied by future interference with the individual's freedom of movement, whether or not trial or conviction ultimately follows. [n22] The protective search for weapons, on the other hand, constitutes a brief, though far from inconsiderable, intrusion upon the sanctity of the person. It does not follow that, because an officer may lawfully arrest a person only when he is apprised of facts sufficient to warrant a belief that the person has committed or is committing a crime, the officer is equally unjustified, absent that kind of evidence, in making any intrusions short of an arrest. Moreover, a perfectly reasonable apprehension of danger may arise long before the officer is possessed of adequate information to justify taking a person into custody for the purpose of prosecuting him for a crime. Petitioner's reliance on cases which have worked out standards of reasonableness with regard to "seizures" constituting arrests and searches incident thereto is thus misplaced. It assumes that the interests sought to be vindicated and the invasions of personal security may be equated in the two cases, and thereby ignores a vital aspect of the analysis of the reasonableness of particular types of conduct under the Fourth Amendment. See Camara v. Municipal Court, supra.

Our evaluation of the proper balance that has to be struck in this type of case leads us to conclude that there must be a narrowly drawn authority to permit a reasonable search for weapons for the protection of the police officer, where he has reason to believe that he is dealing with an armed and dangerous individual, regardless of whether he has probable cause to arrest the individual for a crime. The officer need not be absolutely certain that the individual is armed; the issue is whether a reasonably prudent man, in the circumstances, would be warranted in the belief that his safety or that of others was in danger. Cf. Beck v. Ohio, 379 U.S. 89, 91 (1964); Brinegar v. United States, 338 U.S. 160, 174-176 (1949); Stacey v. Emery, 97 U.S. 642, 645 (1878). [n23] And in determining whether the officer acted reasonably in such circumstances, due weight must be given not to his inchoate and unparticularized suspicion or "hunch," but to the specific reasonable inferences which he is entitled to draw from the facts in light of his experience. Cf. Brinegar v. United States supra.

IV

We must now examine the conduct of Officer McFadden in this case to determine whether his search and seizure of petitioner were reasonable, both at their inception and as conducted. He had observed Terry, together with Chilton and another man, acting in a manner he took to be preface to a "stick-up." We think, on the facts and circumstances Officer McFadden detailed before the trial judge, a reasonably prudent man would have been warranted in believing petitioner was armed, and thus presented a threat to the officer's safety while he was investigating his suspicious behavior. The actions of Terry and Chilton were consistent with McFadden's hypothesis that these men were contemplating a daylight robbery -- which, it is reasonable to assume, would be likely to involve the use of weapons -- and nothing in their conduct from the time he first noticed them until the time he confronted them and identified himself as a police officer gave him sufficient reason to negate that hypothesis. Although the trio had departed the original scene, there was nothing to indicate abandonment of an intent to commit a robbery at some point. Thus, when Officer McFadden approached the three men gathered before the display window at Zucker's store, he had observed enough to make it quite reasonable to fear that they were armed, and nothing in their response to his hailing them, identifying himself as a police officer, and asking their names served to dispel that reasonable belief. We cannot say his decision at that point to seize Terry and pat his clothing for weapons was the product of a volatile or inventive imagination, or was undertaken simply as an act of harassment; the record evidences the tempered act of a policeman who, in the course of an investigation, had to make a quick decision as to how to protect himself and others from possible danger, and took limited steps to do so.

The manner in which the seizure and search were conducted is, of course, as vital a part of the inquiry as whether they were warranted at all. The Fourth Amendment proceeds as much by limitations upon the scope of governmental action as by imposing preconditions upon its initiation. Compare Katz v. United States, 389 U.S. 347, 354-356 (1967). The entire deterrent purpose of the rule excluding evidence seized in violation of the Fourth Amendment rests on the assumption that "limitations upon the fruit to be gathered tend to limit the quest itself." United States v. Poller, 43 F.2d 911, 914 (C.A.2d Cir.1930); see, e.g., Linkletter v. Walker, 381 U.S. 618, 629-635 (1965); Mapp v. Ohio, 367 U.S. 643 (1961); Elkins v. United States, 364 U.S. 206, 216-221 (1960). Thus, evidence may not be introduced if it was discovered by means of a seizure and search which were not reasonably related in scope to the justification for their initiation. Warden v. Hayden, 387 U.S. 294, 310 (1967) (MR. JUSTICE FORTAS, concurring).

We need not develop at length in this case, however, the limitations which the Fourth Amendment places upon a protective seizure and search for weapons. These limitations will have to be developed in the concrete factual circumstances of individual cases. See Sibron v. New York, post, p. 40, decided today. Suffice it to note that such a search, unlike a search without a warrant incident to a lawful arrest, is not justified by any need to prevent the disappearance or destruction of evidence of crime. See Preston v. United States, 376 U.S. 364, 367 (1964). The sole justification of the search in the present situation is the protection of the police officer and others nearby, and it must therefore be confined in scope to an intrusion reasonably designed to discover guns, knives, clubs, or other hidden instruments for the assault of the police officer.

The scope of the search in this case presents no serious problem in light of these standards. Officer McFadden patted down the outer clothing of petitioner and his two companions. He did not place his hands in their pockets or under the outer surface of their garments until he had felt weapons, and then he merely reached for and removed the guns. He never did invade Katz' person beyond the outer surfaces of his clothes, since he discovered nothing in his pat-down which might have been a weapon. Officer McFadden confined his search strictly to what was minimally necessary to learn whether the men were armed and to disarm them once he discovered the weapons. He did not conduct a general exploratory search for whatever evidence of criminal activity he might find.

V

We conclude that the revolver seized from Terry was properly admitted in evidence against him. At the time he seized petitioner and searched him for weapons, Officer McFadden had reasonable grounds to believe that petitioner was armed and dangerous, and it was necessary for the protection of himself and others to take swift measures to discover the true facts and neutralize the threat of harm if it materialized. The policeman carefully restricted his search to what was appropriate to the discovery of the particular items which he sought. Each case of this sort will, of course, have to be decided on its own facts. We merely hold today that, where a police officer observes unusual conduct which leads him reasonably to conclude in light of his experience that criminal activity may be afoot and that the persons with whom he is dealing may be armed and presently dangerous, where, in the course of investigating this behavior, he identifies himself as a policeman and makes reasonable inquiries, and where nothing in the initial stages of the encounter serves to dispel his reasonable fear for his own or others' safety, he is entitled for the protection of himself and others in the area to conduct a carefully limited search of the outer clothing of such persons in an attempt to discover weapons which might be used to assault him. Such a search is a reasonable search under the Fourth Amendment, and any weapons seized may properly be introduced in evidence against the person from whom they were taken.

Affirmed.

Davis v. Mississippi (April 22, 1969) [Notes omitted]

MR. JUSTICE BRENNAN delivered the opinion of the Court.

Petitioner was convicted of rape and sentenced to life imprisonment by a jury in the Circuit Court of Lauderdale County, Mississippi. The only issue before us is whether fingerprints obtained from petitioner should have been excluded from evidence as the product of a detention which was illegal under the Fourth and Fourteenth Amendments.

The rape occurred on the evening of December 2, 1965, at the victim's home in Meridian, Mississippi. The victim could give no better description of her assailant than that he was a Negro youth. Finger and palm prints found on the sill and borders of the window through which the assailant apparently entered the victim's home constituted the only other lead available at the outset of the police investigation. Beginning on December 3, and for a period of about 10 days, the Meridian police, without warrants, took at least 24 Negro youths to police headquarters where they were questioned briefly, fingerprinted, and then released without charge. The police also interrogated 40 or 50 other Negro youths either at police headquarters, at school, or on the street. Petitioner, a 14-year-old youth who had occasionally worked for the victim as a yardboy, was brought in on December 3 and released after being fingerprinted and routinely questioned. Between December 3 and December 7, he was interrogated by the police on several occasions sometimes in his home or in a car, other times at police headquarters. This questioning apparently related primarily to investigation of other potential suspects. Several times during this same period petitioner was exhibited to the victim in her hospital room. A police officer testified that these confrontations were for the purpose of sharpening the victim's description of her assailant by providing "a gauge to go by on size and color." The victim did not identify petitioner as her assailant at any of these confrontations.

On December 12, the police drove petitioner 90 miles to the city of Jackson and confined him overnight in the Jackson jail. The State conceded on oral argument in this Court that there was neither a warrant nor probable cause for this arrest. The next day, petitioner, who had not yet been afforded counsel, took a lie detector test and signed a statement. [1] He was then returned to and confined in the Meridian jail. On December 14, while so confined, petitioner was fingerprinted a second time. That same day, these December 14 prints, together with the fingerprints of 23 other Negro youths apparently still under suspicion, were sent to the Federal Bureau of Investigation in Washington, D.C., for comparison with the latent prints taken from the window of the victim's house. The FBI reported that petitioner's prints matched those taken from the window. Petitioner was subsequently indicted and tried for the rape, and the fingerprint evidence was admitted in evidence at trial over petitioner's timely objections that the fingerprints should be excluded as the product of an unlawful detention. The Mississippi Supreme Court sustained the admission of the fingerprint evidence and affirmed the conviction. 204 So.2d 270 (1967). We granted certiorari. 393 U. S. 821 (1968). We reverse.

At the outset, we find no merit in the suggestion in the Mississippi Supreme Court's opinion that fingerprint evidence, because of its trustworthiness, is not subject to the proscriptions of the Fourth and Fourteenth Amendments. [2]

Our decisions recognize no exception to the rule that illegally seized evidence is inadmissible at trial, however relevant and trustworthy the seized evidence may be as an item of proof. The exclusionary rule was fashioned as a sanction to redress and deter overreaching governmental conduct prohibited by the Fourth Amendment. To make an exception for illegally seized evidence which is trustworthy would fatally undermine these purposes. Thus, in Mapp v. Ohio, 367 U. S. 643, 367 U. S. 655 (1961), we held that "all evidence obtained by searches and seizures in violation of the Constitution is, by that same authority, inadmissible in a state court." (Italics supplied.) Fingerprint evidence is no exception to this comprehensive rule. We agree with and adopt the conclusion of the Court of Appeals for the District of Columbia Circuit in Bynum v. United States, 104 U.S.App.D.C. 368, 370, 262 F.2d 465, 467 (1958):

"True, fingerprints can be distinguished from statements given during detention. They can also be distinguished from articles taken from a prisoner's possession. Both similarities and differences of each type of evidence to and from the others are apparent. But all three have the decisive common characteristic of being something of evidentiary value which the public authorities have caused an arrested person to yield to them during illegal detention. If one such product of illegal detention is proscribed, by the same token all should be proscribed."

We turn then to the question whether the detention of petitioner during which the fingerprints used at trial were taken constituted an unreasonable seizure of his person in violation of the Fourth Amendment. The opinion of the Mississippi Supreme Court proceeded on the mistaken premise that petitioner's prints introduced at trial were taken during his brief detention on December 3. In fact, as both parties before us agree, the fingerprint evidence used at trial was obtained on December 14, while petitioner was still in detention following his December 12 arrest. The legality of his arrest was not determined by the Mississippi Supreme Court. However, on oral argument here, the State conceded that the arrest on December 12 and the ensuing detention through December 14 were based on neither a warrant nor probable cause and were therefore constitutionally invalid. The State argues, nevertheless, that this invalidity should not prevent us from affirming petitioner's conviction. The December 3 prints were validly obtained, it is argued, and "it should make no difference in the practical or legal sense which [fingerprint] card was sent to the F.B.I. for comparison." [3] It may be that it does make a difference in light of the objectives of the exclusionary rule, see Bynum v. United States, supra, at 371-372, 262 F.2d at 468-469, [4] but we need not decide the question since we have concluded that the prints of December 3 were not validly obtained.

The State makes no claim that petitioner voluntarily accompanied the police officers to headquarters on December 3 and willingly submitted to fingerprinting. The State's brief also candidly admits that "[a]ll that the Meridian Police could possibly have known about petitioner at the time . . . would not amount to probable cause for his arrest. . . ." [5] The State argues, however, that the December 3 detention was of a type which does not require probable cause. Two rationales for this position are suggested. First, it is argued that the detention occurred during the investigatory, rather than accusatory, stag,e and thus was not a seizure requiring probable cause. The second and related argument is that, at the least, detention for the sole purpose of obtaining fingerprints does not require probable cause. It is true that, at the time of the December 3 detention, the police had no intention of charging petitioner with the crime, and were far from making him the primary focus of their investigation. But to argue that the Fourth

Amendment does not apply to the investigatory stage is fundamentally to misconceive the purposes of the Fourth Amendment. Investigatory seizures would subject unlimited numbers of innocent persons to the harassment and ignominy incident to involuntary detention. Nothing is more clear than that the Fourth Amendment was meant to prevent wholesale intrusions upon the personal security of our citizenry, whether these intrusions be termed "arrests" or "investigatory detentions." [6] We made this explicit only last Term, in Terry v. Ohio, 392 U. S. 1, 392 U. S. 19 (1968), when we rejected

"the notions that the Fourth Amendment does not come into play at all as a limitation upon police conduct if the officers stop short of something called a 'technical arrest' or a 'full-blown search.'"

Detentions for the sole purpose of obtaining fingerprints are no less subject to the constraints of the Fourth Amendment. It is arguable, however, that, because of the unique nature of the fingerprinting process, such detentions might, under narrowly defined circumstances, be found to comply with the Fourth Amendment even though there is no probable cause in the traditional sense. See Camara v. Municipal Court, 387 U. S. 523 (1967). Detention for fingerprinting may constitute a much less serious intrusion upon personal security than other types of police searches and detentions. Fingerprinting involves none of the probing into an individual's private life and thoughts that marks an interrogation or search. Nor can fingerprint detention be employed repeatedly to harass any individual, since the police need only one set of each person's prints. Furthermore, fingerprinting is an inherently more reliable and effective crime-solving tool than eyewitness identifications or confessions, and is not subject to such abuses as the improper line-up and the "third degree." Finally, because there is no danger of destruction

of fingerprints, the limited detention need not come unexpectedly or at an inconvenient time.

For this same reason, the general requirement that the authorization of a judicial officer be obtained in advance of detention would seem not to admit of any exception in the fingerprinting context.

We have no occasion in this case, however, to determine whether the requirements of the Fourth Amendment could be met by narrowly circumscribed procedures for obtaining, during the course of a criminal investigation, the fingerprints of individuals for whom there is no probable cause to arrest. For it is clear that no attempt was made here to employ procedures which might comply with the requirements of the Fourth Amendment: the detention at police headquarters of petitioner and the other young Negroes was not authorized by a judicial officer; petitioner was unnecessarily required to undergo two fingerprinting sessions, and petitioner was not merely fingerprinted during the December 3 detention, but also subjected to interrogation. The judgment of the Mississippi Supreme Court is therefore

Reversed.

Harris v. New York (Feb 24, 1971)

MR. CHIEF JUSTICE BURGER delivered the opinion of the Court.

We granted the writ in this case to consider petitioner's claim that a statement made by him to police under circumstances rendering it inadmissible to establish the prosecution's case in chief under Miranda v. Arizona, 384 U.S. 436 (1966), may not be used to impeach his credibility.

The State of New York charged petitioner in a two-count indictment with twice selling heroin to an undercover police officer. At a subsequent jury trial, the officer was the State's chief witness, and he testified as to details of the two sales. A second officer verified collateral details of the sales, and a third offered testimony about the chemical analysis of the heroin.

Petitioner took the stand in his own defense. He admitted knowing the undercover police officer, but denied a sale on January 4, 1966. He admitted making a sale of contents of a glassine bag to the officer on January 6, but claimed it was baking powder and part of a scheme to defraud the purchaser.

On cross-examination, petitioner was asked seriatim whether he had made specified statements to the police immediately following his arrest on January 7 -- statements that partially contradicted petitioner's direct testimony at trial. In response to the cross-examination, petitioner testified that he could not remember virtually any of the questions or answers recited by the prosecutor. At the request of petitioner's counsel, the written statement from which the prosecutor had read questions and answers in his impeaching process was placed in the record for possible use on appeal; the statement was not shown to the jury.

The trial judge instructed the jury that the statements attributed to petitioner by the prosecution could be considered only in passing on petitioner's credibility, and not as evidence of guilt. In closing summations, both counsel argued the substance of the impeaching statements. The jury then found petitioner guilty on the second count of the indictment. [n1] The New York Court of Appeals affirmed in a per curiam opinion, 25 N.Y.2d 175, 250 N.E.2d 349 (1969).

At trial, the prosecution made no effort in its case in chief to use the statements allegedly made by petitioner, conceding that they were inadmissible under Miranda v. Arizona, 384 U.S. 436 (1966). The transcript of the interrogation used in the impeachment, but not given to the jury, shows that no warning of a right to appointed counsel was given before questions were put to petitioner when he was taken into custody.

Petitioner makes no claim that the statements made to the police were coerced or involuntary.

Some comments in the Miranda opinion can indeed be read as indicating a bar to use of an uncounseled statement for any purpose, but discussion of that issue was not at all necessary to the Court's holding, and cannot be regarded as controlling. Miranda barred the prosecution from making its case with statements of an accused made while in custody prior to having or effectively waiving counsel. It does not follow from Miranda that evidence inadmissible against an accused in the prosecution's case in chief is barred for all purposes, provided of course that the trustworthiness of the evidence satisfies legal standards.

In Walder v. United States, 347 U.S. 62 (154), the Court permitted physical evidence, inadmissible in the case in chief, to be used for impeachment purposes.

It is one thing to say that the Government cannot make an affirmative use of evidence unlawfully obtained. It is quite another to say that the defendant can turn the illegal method by which evidence in the Government's possession was obtained to his own advantage, and provide himself with a shield against contradiction of his untruths. Such an extension of the Weeks doctrine would be a perversion of the Fourth Amendment.

[T]here is hardly justification for letting the defendant affirmatively resort to perjurious testimony in reliance on the Government's disability to challenge his credibility.

347 U.S. at 65.

It is true that Walder was impeached as to collateral matters included in his direct examination, whereas petitioner here was impeached as to testimony bearing more directly on the crimes charged. We are not persuaded that there is a difference in principle that warrants a result different from that reached by the Court in Walder. Petitioner's testimony in his own behalf concerning the events of January 7 contrasted sharply with what he told the police shortly after his arrest. The impeachment process here undoubtedly provided valuable aid to the jury in assessing petitioner's credibility, and the benefits of this process should not be lost, in our view, because of the speculative possibility that impermissible police conduct will be encouraged thereby. Assuming that the exclusionary rule has a deterrent effect on proscribed police conduct, sufficient deterrence flows when the evidence in question is made unavailable to the prosecution in its case in chief.

Every criminal defendant is privileged to testify in his own defense, or to refuse to do so. But that privilege cannot be construed to include the right to commit perjury. See United States v. Knox, 396 U.S. 77 (1969); cf. Dennis v. United States, 384 U.S. 855 (1966). Having voluntarily taken the stand, petitioner was under an obligation to speak truthfully and accurately, and the prosecution here did no more than utilize the traditional truth-testing devices of the adversary process. [n2] Had inconsistent statements been made by the accused to some third person, it could hardly be contended that the conflict could not be laid before the jury by way of cross-examination and impeachment.

The shield provided by Miranda cannot be perverted into a license to use perjury by way of a defense, free from the risk of confrontation with prior inconsistent utterances. We hold, therefore, that petitioner's credibility was appropriately impeached by use of his earlier conflicting statements.

Affirmed.

Notes

1. No agreement was reached as to the first count. That count was later dropped by the State.

2. If, for example, an accused confessed fully to a homicide and led the police to the body of the victim under circumstances making his confession inadmissible, the petitioner would have us allow that accused to take the stand and blandly deny every fact disclosed to the police or discovered as a "fruit" of his confession, free from confrontation with his prior statements and acts. The voluntariness of the confession would, on this thesis, be totally irrelevant. We reject such an extravagant extension of the Constitution. Compare Killough v. United States, 114 U.S.App.D.C. 305, 315 F.2d 241 (1962).

United States v. White (April 5, 1971) [Judgment and opinion]

MR. JUSTICE WHITE announced the judgment of the Court and an opinion in which THE CHIEF JUSTICE, MR. JUSTICE STEWART, and MR. JUSTICE BLACKMUN join.

In 1966, respondent James A. White was tried and convicted under two consolidated indictments charging various illegal transactions in narcotics violative of 26 U.S.C. § 4705(a) and 21 U.S.C. § 174. He was fined and sentenced as a second offender to 25-year concurrent sentences. The issue before us is whether the Fourth Amendment bars from evidence the testimony of governmental agents who related certain conversations which had occurred between defendant White and a government informant, Harvey Jackson, and which the agents overheard by monitoring the frequency of a radio transmitter carried by Jackson and concealed on his person. [1] On four occasions, the conversations took place in Jackson's home; each of these conversations was overheard by an agent concealed in a kitchen closet with Jackson's consent and by a second agent outside the house using a radio receiver. Four other conversations -- one in respondent's home, one in a restaurant, and two in Jackson's car -- were overheard by the use of radio equipment. The prosecution was unable to locate and produce Jackson at the trial, and the trial court overruled objections to the testimony of the agents who conducted the electronic surveillance. The jury returned a guilty verdict, and defendant appealed.

The Court of Appeals read Katz v. United States, 389 U. S. 347 (1967), as overruling On Lee v. United States, 343 U. S. 747 (1952), and interpreting the Fourth Amendment to forbid the introduction of the agents' testimony in the circumstances of this case. Accordingly, the court reversed, but without adverting to the fact that the transactions at issue here had occurred before Katz was decided in this Court. In our view, the Court of Appeals misinterpreted both the Katz case and the Fourth Amendment and, in any event, erred in applying the Katz case to events that occurred before that decision was rendered by this Court. [2]

I

Until Katz v. United States, neither wiretapping nor electronic eavesdropping violated a defendant's Fourth Amendment rights

"unless there has been an official search and seizure of his person, or such a seizure of his papers or his tangible material effects, or an actual physical invasion of his house 'or curtilage' for the purpose of making a seizure."

Olmstead v. United States, 277 U. S. 438, 277 U. S. 466 (1928); Goldman v. United States, 316 U. S. 129, 316 U. S. 135-136 (1942). But where "eavesdropping was accomplished by means of an unauthorized physical penetration into the premises occupied" by the defendant, although falling short of a "technical trespass under the local property law," the Fourth Amendment was violated, and any evidence of what was seen and heard, as well as tangible objects seized, was considered the inadmissible fruit of an unlawful invasion. Silverman v. United States, 365 U. S. 505, 365 U. S. 509, 511 (1961); see also Wong Sun v. United States, 371 U. S. 471 (1963); Berger v. New York, 388 U. S. 41, 388 U. S. 52 (1967); Alderman v. United States, 394 U. S. 165, 394 U. S.

177-178 (1969).

Katz v. United States, however, finally swept away doctrines that electronic eavesdropping is permissible under the Fourth Amendment unless physical invasion of a constitutionally protected area produced the challenged evidence. In that case, government agents, without petitioner's consent or knowledge, attached a listening device to the outside of a public telephone booth and recorded the defendant's end of his telephone conversations. In declaring the recordings inadmissible in evidence in the absence of a warrant authorizing the surveillance, the Court overruled Olmstead and Goldman and held that the absence of physical intrusion into the telephone booth did not justify using electronic devices in listening to and recording Katz' words, thereby violating the privacy on which he justifiably relied while using the telephone in those circumstances.

The Court of Appeals understood Katz to render inadmissible against White the agents' testimony concerning conversations that Jackson broadcast to them. We cannot agree. Katz involved no revelation to the Government by a party to conversations with the defendant, nor did the Court indicate in any way that a defendant has a justifiable and constitutionally protected expectation that a person with whom he is conversing will not then or later reveal the conversation to the police.

Hoffa v. United States, 385 U. S. 293 (1966), which was left undisturbed by Katz, held that, however strongly a defendant may trust an apparent colleague, his expectations in this respect are not protected by the Fourth Amendment when it turns out that the colleague is a government agent regularly communicating with the authorities. In these circumstances, "no interest legitimately protected by the Fourth Amendment is involved," for that amendment affords no protection to "a wrongdoer's misplaced belief that a person to whom he voluntarily confides his wrongdoing will not reveal it." Hoffa v. United States, at 385 U. S. 302. No warrant to "search and seize" is required in such circumstances, nor is it when the Government sends to defendant's home a secret agent who conceals his identity and makes a purchase of narcotics from the accused, Lewis v. United States, 385 U. S. 206 (1966), or when the same agent, unbeknown to the defendant, carries electronic equipment to record the defendant's words and the evidence so gathered is later offered in evidence. Lopez v. United States, 373 U. S. 427 (1963).

Conceding that Hoffa, Lewis, and Lopez remained unaffected by Katz, [3] the Court of Appeals nevertheless read both Katz and the Fourth Amendment to require a different result if the agent not only records his conversations with the defendant, but instantaneously transmits them electronically to other agents equipped with radio receivers. Where this occurs, the Court of Appeals held, the Fourth Amendment is violated, and the testimony of the listening agents must be excluded from evidence.

To reach this result, it was necessary for the Court of Appeals to hold that On Lee v. United States was no longer good law. In that case, which involved facts very similar to the case before us, the Court first rejected claims of a Fourth Amendment violation because the informer had not trespassed when he entered the defendant's premises and conversed with him. To this extent, the Court's rationale cannot survive Katz. See 389 U.S. at 389 U. S. 352-353. But the Court announced a second and independent ground for its decision; for it went on to say that overruling Olmstead and Goldman would be of no aid to On Lee, since he

"was talking confidentially and indiscreetly with one he trusted, and he was overheard. . . . It would be a dubious service to the genuine liberties protected by the Fourth Amendment to make them bedfellows with spurious liberties improvised by far-fetched analogies which would liken eavesdropping on a conversation, with the connivance of one of the parties, to an unreasonable search or seizure. We find no violation of the Fourth Amendment here."

343 U.S. at 343 U. S. 753-754. We see no indication in Katz that the Court meant to disturb that understanding of the Fourth Amendment or to disturb the result reached in the On Lee case, [4] nor are we now inclined to overturn this view of the Fourth Amendment.

Concededly. a police agent who conceals his police connections may write down for official use his conversations with a defendant and testify concerning them without a warrant authorizing his encounters with the defendant and without otherwise violating the latter's Fourth Amendment rights. Hoffa v. United States, 385 U.S. at 385 U. S. 300-303. For constitutional purposes, no different result is required if the agent, instead of immediately reporting and transcribing his conversations with defendant, either (1) simultaneously records them with electronic equipment which he is carrying on his person, Lopez v. United States, supra; (2) or carries radio equipment which simultaneously transmits the conversations either to recording equipment located elsewhere or to other agents monitoring the transmitting frequency. On Lee v. United States, supra. If the conduct and revelations of an agent operating without electronic equipment do not invade the defendant's constitutionally justifiable expectations of privacy, neither does a simultaneous recording of the same conversations made by the agent or by others from transmissions received from the agent to whom the defendant is talking and whose trustworthiness the defendant necessarily risks.

Our problem is not what the privacy expectations of particular defendants in particular situations may be or the extent to which they may, in fact, have relied on the discretion of their companions. Very probably, individual defendants neither know nor suspect that their colleagues have gone or will go to the police or are carrying recorders or transmitters. Otherwise, conversation would cease, and our problem with these encounters would be nonexistent, or far different from those now before us. Our problem, in terms of the principles announced in Katz, is what expectations of privacy are constitutionally "justifiable" -- what expectations the Fourth Amendment will protect in the absence of a warrant. So far, the law permits the frustration of actual expectations of privacy by permitting authorities to use the testimony of those associates who, for one reason or another, have determined to turn to the police, as well as by authorizing the use of informants in the manner exemplified by Hoffa and Lewis. If the law gives no protection to the wrongdoer whose trusted accomplice is or becomes a police agent, neither should it protect him when that same agent has recorded or transmitted the conversations which are later offered in evidence to prove the State's case. See Lopez v. United States, 373 U. S. 427 (1963).

Inescapably, one contemplating illegal activities must realize and risk that his companions may be reporting to the police. If he sufficiently doubts their trustworthiness, the association will very probably end, or never materialize. But if he has no doubts, or allays them, or risks what doubt he has, the risk is his. In terms of what his course will be, what he will or will not do or say, we are unpersuaded that he would distinguish between probable informers, on the one hand, and probable informers with transmitters, on the other. Given the possibility or probability that one of his colleagues is cooperating with the police, it is only speculation to assert that the defendant's utterances would be substantially different or his sense of security any less if he also thought it possible that the suspected colleague is wired for sound. At least there is no persuasive evidence that the difference in this respect between the electronically equipped and the unequipped agent is substantial enough to require discrete constitutional recognition, particularly under the Fourth Amendment, which is ruled by fluid concepts of "reasonableness."

Nor should we be too ready to erect constitutional barriers to relevant and probative evidence which is also accurate and reliable. An electronic recording will many times produce a more reliable rendition of what a defendant has said than will the unaided memory of a police agent. It may also be that. with the recording in existence. it is less likely that the informant will change his mind, less chance that threat or injury will suppress unfavorable evidence, and less chance that cross-examination will confound the testimony. Considerations like these obviously do not favor the defendant, but we are not prepared to hold that a defendant who has no constitutional right to exclude the informer's unaided testimony nevertheless has a Fourth Amendment privilege against a more accurate version of the events in question.

It is thus untenable to consider the activities and reports of the police agent himself, though acting without a warrant, to be a "reasonable" investigative effort and lawful under the Fourth Amendment, but to view the same agent with a recorder or transmitter as conducting an "unreasonable" and unconstitutional search and seizure. Our opinion is currently shared by Congress and the Executive Branch, Title III, Omnibus Crime Control and Safe Streets Act of 1968, 82 Stat. 212, 18 U.S.C. § 2510 et seq. (1964 ed., Supp. V), and the American Bar Association. Project on Standards for Criminal Justice, Electronic Surveillance § 4.1 (Approved Draft 1971). It is also the result reached by prior cases in this Court. On Lee, supra; Lopez v. United States, supra.

No different result should obtain where, as in On Lee and the instant case, the informer disappears and is unavailable at trial; for the issue of whether specified events on a certain day violate the Fourth Amendment should not be determined by what later happens to the informer. His unavailability at trial and proffering the testimony of other agents may raise evidentiary problems or pose issues of prosecutorial misconduct with respect to the informer's disappearance, but they do not appear critical to deciding whether prior events invaded the defendant's Fourth Amendment rights.

II

The Court of Appeals was in error for another reason. In Desist v. United States, 394 U. S. 244 (1969), we held that our decision in Katz v. United States applied only to those electronic surveillances that occurred subsequent to the date of that decision. Here, the events in question took place in late 1965 and early 1966, long prior to Katz. We adhere to the rationale of Desist, see Williams v. United States, ante, p. 401 U. S. 646. It was error for the Court of Appeals to dispose of this case based on its understanding of the principles announced in the Katz case. The court should have judged this case by the pre-Katz law and under that law, as On Lee clearly holds, the electronic surveillance here involved did not violate White's rights to be free from unreasonable searches and seizures.

The judgment of the Court of Appeals is reversed.

It is so ordered.

Notes

[1] White argues that Jackson, though admittedly "cognizant" of the presence of transmitting devices on his person, did not voluntarily consent thereto. Because the court below did not reach the issue of Jackson's consent, we decline to do so. Similarly, we do not consider White's claim that the Government's actions violated state law.

[2] A panel of three judges on March 18, 1968, reversed the conviction, one judge dissenting. A rehearing en banc was granted, and, on January 7, 1969, the full court followed the panel's decision, three judges dissenting. 405 F.2d 838.

[3] It follows from our opinion that we reject respondent's contentions that Lopez should be overruled.

[4] Other courts of appeals have considered On Lee viable despite Katz. Dancy v. United States, 390 F.2d 370 (CA5 1968); Long v. United States, 387 F.2d 377 (CA5 1967); Koran v. United States, 408 F.2d 1321 (CA5 1969). See also United States v. Kaufer, 406 F.2d 550 (CA2), aff'd per curiam, 394 U. S. 458 (1969); United States v. Jackson, 390 F.2d 317 (CA2 1968); Doty v. United States, 416 F.2d 887 (CA10 1968), id. at 893 (rehearing 1969).

US v. US Dist. Court for Eastern Dist. of Mich. (June 19, 1972) [Notes omitted]

MR. JUSTICE POWELL delivered the opinion of the Court.

The issue before us is an important one for the people of our country and their Government. It involves the delicate question of the President's power, acting through the Attorney General, to authorize electronic surveillance in internal security matters without prior judicial approval. Successive Presidents for more than one-quarter of a century have authorized such surveillance in varying degrees,[1] without guidance from the Congress or a definitive decision of this Court. This case brings the issue here for the first time. Its resolution is a matter of national concern, requiring sensitivity both to the Government's right to protect itself from unlawful subversion and attack and to the citizen's right to be secure in his privacy against unreasonable Government intrusion.

This case arises from a criminal proceeding in the United States District Court for the Eastern District of Michigan, in which the United States charged three defendants with conspiracy to destroy Government property in violation of 18 U. S. C. § 371. One of the defendants, Plamondon, was charged with the dynamite bombing of an office of the Central Intelligence Agency in Ann Arbor, Michigan.

During pretrial proceedings, the defendants moved to compel the United States to disclose certain electronic surveillance information and to conduct a hearing to determine whether this information "tainted" the evidence on which the indictment was based or which the Government intended to offer at trial. In response, the Government filed an affidavit of the Attorney General, acknowledging that its agents had overheard conversations in which Plamondon had participated. The affidavit also stated that the Attorney General approved the wiretaps "to gather intelligence information deemed necessary to protect the nation from attempts of domestic organizations to attack and subvert the existing structure of the Government."[2] The logs of the surveillance were filed in a sealed exhibit for in camera inspection by the District Court.

On the basis of the Attorney General's affidavit and the sealed exhibit, the Government asserted that the surveillance was lawful, though conducted without prior judicial approval, as a reasonable exercise of the President's power (exercised through the Attorney General) to protect the national security. The District Court held that the surveillance violated the Fourth Amendment, and ordered the Government to make full disclosure to Plamondon of his overheard conversations. 321 F. Supp. 1074 (ED Mich. 1971).

The Government then filed in the Court of Appeals for the Sixth Circuit a petition for a writ of mandamus to set aside the District Court order, which was stayed pending final disposition of the case. After concluding that it had jurisdiction,[3] that court held that the surveillance was unlawful and that the District Court had properly required disclosure of the overheard conversations, 444 F. 2d 651 (1971). We granted certiorari, 403 U. S. 930.

I

Title III of the Omnibus Crime Control and Safe Streets Act, 18 U. S. C. §§ 2510-2520, authorizes the use of electronic surveillance for classes of crimes carefully specified in 18 U. S. C. § 2516. Such surveillance is subject to prior court order. Section 2518 sets forth the detailed and particularized application necessary to obtain such an order as well as carefully circumscribed conditions for its use. The Act represents a comprehensive attempt by Congress to promote more effective control of crime while protecting the privacy of individual thought and expression. Much of Title III was drawn to meet the constitutional requirements for electronic surveillance enunciated by this Court in Berger v. New York, 388 U. S. 41 (1967), and Katz v. United States, 389 U. S. 347 (1967).

Together with the elaborate surveillance requirements in Title III, there is the following proviso, 18 U. S. C. § 2511 (3):

"Nothing contained in this chapter or in section 605 of the Communications Act of 1934 (48 Stat. 1143; 47 U. S. C. 605) shall limit the constitutional power of the President to take such measures as he deems necessary to protect the Nation against actual or potential attack or other hostile acts of a foreign power, to obtain foreign intelligence information deemed essential to the security of the United States, or to protect national security information against foreign intelligence activities. Nor shall anything contained in this chapter be deemed to limit the constitutional power of the President to take such measures as he deems necessary to protect the United States against the overthrow of the Government by force or other unlawful means, or against any other clear and present danger to the structure or existence of the Government. The contents of any wire or oral communication intercepted by authority of the President in the exercise of the foregoing powers may be received in evidence in any trial hearing, or other proceeding only where such interception was reasonable, and shall not be otherwise used or disclosed except as is necessary to implement that power." (Emphasis supplied.)

The Government relies on § 2511 (3). It argues that "in excepting national security surveillances from the Act's warrant requirement Congress recognized the President's authority to conduct such surveillances without prior judicial approval." Brief for United States 7, 28. The section thus is viewed as a recognition or affirmance of a constitutional authority in the President to conduct warrantless domestic security surveillance such as that involved in this case.

We think the language of § 2511 (3), as well as the legislative history of the statute, refutes this interpretation. The relevant language is that:

"Nothing contained in this chapter . . . shall limit the constitutional power of the President to take such measures as he deems necessary to protect . . ."

against the dangers specified. At most, this is an implicit recognition that the President does have certain powers in the specified areas. Few would doubt this, as the section refers—among other things—to protection "against actual or potential attack or other hostile acts of a foreign power." But so far as the use of the President's electronic surveillance power is concerned, the language is essentially neutral.

Section 2511 (3) certainly confers no power, as the language is wholly inappropriate for such a purpose. It merely provides that the Act shall not be interpreted to limit or disturb such power as the President may have under the Constitution. In short, Congress simply left presidential powers where it found them. This view is reinforced by the general context of Title III. Section 2511 (1) broadly prohibits the use of electronic surveillance "[e]xcept as otherwise specifically provided in this chapter." Subsection (2) thereof contains four specific exceptions. In each of the specified exceptions, the statutory language is as follows:

"It shall not be unlawful . . . to intercept" the particular type of communication described.[4]

The language of subsection (3), here involved, is to be contrasted with the language of the exceptions set forth in the preceding subsection. Rather than stating that warrantless presidential uses of electronic surveillance "shall not be unlawful" and thus employing the standard language of exception, subsection (3) merely disclaims any intention to "limit the constitutional power of the President."

The express grant of authority to conduct surveillances is found in § 2516, which authorizes the Attorney General to make application to a federal judge when surveillance may provide evidence of certain offenses. These offenses are described with meticulous care and specificity.

Where the Act authorizes surveillance, the procedure to be followed is specified in § 2518. Subsection (1) thereof requires application to a judge of competent jurisdiction for a prior order of approval, and states in detail the information required in such application.[5]

Subsection (3) prescribes the necessary elements of probable cause which the judge must find before issuing an order authorizing an interception. Subsection (4) sets forth the required contents of such an order.

Subsection (5) sets strict time limits on an order. Provision is made in subsection (7) for "an emergency situation" found to exist by the Attorney General (or by the principal prosecuting attorney of a State) "with respect to conspiratorial activities threatening the national security interest." In such a situation, emergency surveillance may be conducted "if an application for an order approving the interception is made . . . within forty-eight hours." If such an order is not obtained, or the application therefore is denied, the interception is deemed to be a violation of the Act.

In view of these and other interrelated provisions delineating permissible interceptions of particular criminal activity upon carefully specified conditions, it would have been incongruous for Congress to have legislated with respect to the important and complex area of national security in a single brief and nebulous paragraph. This would not comport with the sensitivity of the problem involved or with the extraordinary care Congress exercised in drafting other sections of the Act. We therefore think the conclusion inescapable that Congress only intended to make clear that the Act simply did not legislate with respect to national security surveillances.[6]

The legislative history of § 2511 (3) supports this interpretation. Most relevant is the colloquy between Senators Hart, Holland, and McClellan on the Senate floor:

"Mr. HOLLAND. . . . The section [2511 (3)] from which the Senator [Hart] has read does not affirmatively give any power. . . . We are not affirmatively conferring any power upon the President. We are simply saying that nothing herein shall limit such power as the President has under the Constitution.. . . . We certainly do not grant him a thing.

"There is nothing affirmative in this statement.

"Mr. McCLELLAN. Mr. President, we make it understood that we are not trying to take anything away from him.

"Mr. HOLLAND. The Senator is correct.

"Mr. HART. Mr. President, there is no intention here to expand by this language a constitutional power. Clearly we could not do so.

"Mr. McCLELLAN. Even though intended, we could not do so.

"Mr. HART. . . . However, we are agreed that this language should not be regarded as intending to grant any authority, including authority to put a bug on, that the President does not have now.

"In addition, Mr. President, as I think our exchange makes clear, nothing in section 2511 (3) even attempts to define the limits of the President's national security power under present law, which I have always found extremely vague . . . . Section 2511 (3) merely says that if the President has such a power, then its exercise is in no way affected by title III."[7] (Emphasis supplied.)

One could hardly expect a clearer expression of congressional neutrality. The debate above explicitly indicates that nothing in § 2511 (3) was intended to expand or to contract or to define whatever presidential surveillance powers existed in matters affecting the national security. If we could accept the Government's characterization of § 2511 (3) as a congressionally prescribed exception to the general requirement of a warrant, it would be necessary to consider the question of whether the surveillance in this case came within the exception and, if so, whether the statutory exception was itself constitutionally valid. But viewing § 2511 (3) as a congressional disclaimer and expression of neutrality, we hold that the statute is not the measure of the executive authority asserted in this case. Rather, we must look to the constitutional powers of the President.

II

It is important at the outset to emphasize the limited nature of the question before the Court. This case raises no constitutional challenge to electronic surveillance as specifically authorized by Title III of the Omnibus Crime Control and Safe Streets Act of 1968. Nor is there any question or doubt as to the necessity of obtaining a warrant in the surveillance of crimes unrelated to the national security interest. Katz v. United States, 389 U. S. 347 (1967); Berger v. New York, 388 U. S. 41 (1967). Further, the instant case requires no judgment on the scope of the President's surveillance power with respect to the activities of foreign powers, within or without this country. The Attorney General's affidavit in this case states that the surveillances were "deemed necessary to protect the nation from attempts of domestic organizations to attack and subvert the existing structure of Government" (emphasis supplied). There is no evidence of any involvement, directly or indirectly, of a foreign power.[8]

Our present inquiry, though important, is therefore a narrow one. It addresses a question left open by Katz, supra, at 358 n. 23:

"Whether safeguards other than prior authorization by a magistrate would satisfy the Fourth Amendment in a situation involving the national security . . . ."

The determination of this question requires the essential Fourth Amendment inquiry into the "reasonableness" of the search and seizure in question, and the way in which that "reasonableness" derives content and meaning through reference to the warrant clause. Coolidge v. New Hampshire, 403 U. S. 443, 473-484 (1971).

We begin the inquiry by noting that the President of the United States has the fundamental duty, under Art. II, § 1, of the Constitution, to "preserve, protect and defend the Constitution of the United States." Implicit in that duty is the power to protect our Government against those who would subvert or overthrow it by unlawful means. In the discharge of this duty, the President—through the Attorney General— may find it necessary to employ electronic surveillance to obtain intelligence information on the plans of those who plot unlawful acts against the Government.[9] The use of such surveillance in internal security cases has been sanctioned more or less continuously by various Presidents and Attorneys General since July 1946.[10]

Herbert Brownell, Attorney General under President Eisenhower, urged the use of electronic surveillance both in internal and international security matters on the grounds that those acting against the Government

"turn to the telephone to carry on their intrigue. The success of their plans frequently rests upon piecing together shreds of information received from many sources and many nests. The participants in the conspiracy are often dispersed and stationed in various strategic positions in government and industry throughout the country."[11]

Though the Government and respondents debate their seriousness and magnitude, threats and acts of sabotage against the Government exist in sufficient number to justify investigative powers with respect to them.[12] The covertness and complexity of potential unlawful conduct against the Government and the necessary dependency of many conspirators upon the telephone make electronic surveillance an effective investigatory instrument in certain circumstances. The marked acceleration in technological developments and sophistication in their use have resulted in new techniques for the planning, commission, and concealment of criminal activities. It would be contrary to the public interest for Government to deny to itself the prudent and lawful employment of those very techniques which are employed against the Government and its law-abiding citizens.

It has been said that "[t]he most basic function of any government is to provide for the security of the individual and of his property." Miranda v. Arizona, 384 U. S. 436, 539 (1966) (WHITE, J., dissenting). And unless Government safeguards its own capacity to function and to preserve the security of its people, society itself could become so disordered that all rights and liberties would be endangered. As Chief Justice Hughes reminded us in Cox v. New Hampshire, 312 U. S. 569, 574 (1941):

"Civil liberties, as guaranteed by the Constitution, imply the existence of an organized society maintaining public order without which liberty itself would be lost in the excesses of unrestrained abuses."

But a recognition of these elementary truths does not make the employment by Government of electronic surveillance a welcome development—even when employed with restraint and under judicial supervision. There is, understandably, a deep-seated uneasiness and apprehension that this capability will be used to intrude upon cherished privacy of law-abiding citizens.[13] We look to the Bill of Rights to safeguard this privacy. Though physical entry of the home is the chief evil against which the wording of the Fourth Amendment is directed, its broader spirit now shields private speech from unreasonable surveillance. Katz v. United States, supra; Berger v. New York, supra; Silverman v. United States, 365 U. S. 505 (1961). Our decision in Katz refused to lock the Fourth Amendment into instances of actual physical trespass. Rather, the Amendment governs "not only the seizure of tangible items, but extends as well to the recording of oral statements . . . without any `technical trespass under . . . local property law.'" Katz, supra, at 353. That decision implicitly recognized that the broad and unsuspected governmental incursions into conversational privacy which electronic surveillance entails[14] necessitate the application of Fourth Amendment safeguards.

National security cases, moreover, often reflect a convergence of First and Fourth Amendment values not present in cases of "ordinary" crime. Though the investigative duty of the executive may be stronger in such cases, so also is there greater jeopardy to constitutionally protected speech. "Historically the struggle for freedom of speech and press in England was bound up with the issue of the scope of the search and seizure power," Marcus v. Search Warrant, 367 U. S. 717, 724 (1961). History abundantly documents the tendency of Government—however benevolent and benign its motives —to view with suspicion those who most fervently dispute its policies. Fourth Amendment protections become the more necessary when the targets of official surveillance may be those suspected of unorthodoxy in their political beliefs. The danger to political dissent is acute where the Government attempts to act under so vague a concept as the power to protect "domestic security." Given the difficulty of defining the domestic security interest, the danger of abuse in acting to protect that interest becomes apparent. Senator Hart addressed this dilemma in the floor debate on § 2511 (3):

"As I read it—and this is my fear—we are saying that the President, on his motion, could declare— name your favorite poison—draft dodgers, Black Muslims, the Ku Klux Klan, or civil rights activists to be a clear and present danger to the structure or existence of the Government."[15]

The price of lawful public dissent must not be a dread of subjection to an unchecked surveillance power. Nor must the fear of unauthorized official eavesdropping deter vigorous citizen dissent and discussion of Government action in private conversation. For private dissent, no less than open public discourse, is essential to our free society.

III

As the Fourth Amendment is not absolute in its terms, our task is to examine and balance the basic values at stake in this case: the duty of Government to protect the domestic security, and the potential danger posed by unreasonable surveillance to individual privacy and free expression. If the legitimate need of Government to safeguard domestic security requires the use of electronic surveillance, the question is whether the needs of citizens for privacy and free expression may not be better protected by requiring a warrant before such surveillance is undertaken. We must also ask whether a warrant requirement would unduly frustrate the efforts of Government to protect itself from acts of subversion and overthrow directed against it.

Though the Fourth Amendment speaks broadly of "unreasonable searches and seizures," the definition of "reasonableness" turns, at least in part, on the more specific commands of the warrant clause. Some have argued that "[t]he relevant test is not whether it is reasonable to procure a search warrant, but whether the search was reasonable," United States v. Rabinowitz, 339 U. S. 56, 66 (1950).[16] This view, however, overlooks the second clause of the Amendment. The warrant clause of the Fourth Amendment is not dead language. Rather, it has been

"a valued part of our constitutional law for decades, and it has determined the result in scores and scores of cases in courts all over this country. It is not an inconvenience to be somehow `weighed' against the claims of police efficiency. It is, or should be, an important working part of our machinery of government, operating as a matter of course to check the `well-intentioned but mistakenly overzealous executive officers' who are a part of any system of law enforcement." Coolidge v. New Hampshire, 403 U. S., at 481.

See also United States v. Rabinowitz, supra, at 68 (Frankfurter, J., dissenting); Davis v. United States, 328 U. S. 582, 604 (1946) (Frankfurter, J., dissenting).

Over two centuries ago, Lord Mansfield held that common-law principles prohibited warrants that ordered the arrest of unnamed individuals who the officer might conclude were guilty of seditious libel. "It is not fit," said Mansfield, "that the receiving or judging of the information should be left to the discretion of the officer. The magistrate ought to judge; and should give certain directions to the officer." Leach v. Three of the King's Messengers, 19 How. St. Tr. 1001, 1027 (1765).

Lord Mansfield's formulation touches the very heart of the Fourth Amendment directive: that, where practical, a governmental search and seizure should represent both the efforts of the officer to gather evidence of wrongful acts and the judgment of the magistrate that the collected evidence is sufficient to justify invasion of a citizen's private premises or conversation. Inherent in the concept of a warrant is its issuance by a "neutral and detached magistrate." Coolidge v. New Hampshire, supra, at 453; Katz v. United States, supra, at 356. The further requirement of "probable cause" instructs the magistrate that baseless searches shall not proceed.

These Fourth Amendment freedoms cannot properly be guaranteed if domestic security surveillances may be conducted solely within the discretion of the Executive Branch. The Fourth Amendment does not contemplate the executive officers of Government as neutral and disinterested magistrates. Their duty and responsibility are to enforce the laws, to investigate, and to prosecute. Katz v. United States, supra, at 359-360 (DOUGLAS, J., concurring). But those charged with this investigative and prosecutorial duty should not be the sole judges of when to utilize constitutionally sensitive means in pursuing their tasks. The historical judgment, which the Fourth Amendment accepts, is that unreviewed executive discretion may yield too readily to pressures to obtain incriminating evidence and overlook potential invasions of privacy and protected speech.[17]

It may well be that, in the instant case, the Government's surveillance of Plamondon's conversations was a reasonable one which readily would have gained prior judicial approval. But this Court "has never sustained a search upon the sole ground that officers reasonably expected to find evidence of a particular crime and voluntarily confined their activities to the least intrusive means consistent with that end." Katz, supra, at 356-357. The Fourth Amendment contemplates a prior judicial judgment,[18] not the risk that executive discretion may be reasonably exercised. This judicial role accords with our basic constitutional doctrine that individual freedoms will best be preserved through a separation of powers and division of functions among the different branches and levels of Government. Harlan, Thoughts at a Dedication: Keeping the Judicial Function in Balance, 49 A. B. A. J. 943-944 (1963). The independent check upon executive discretion is not satisfied, as the Government argues, by "extremely limited" post-surveillance judicial review.[19] Indeed, post-surveillance review would never reach the surveillances which failed to result in prosecutions. Prior review by a neutral and detached magistrate is the time-tested means of effectuating Fourth Amendment rights. Beck v. Ohio, 379 U. S. 89, 96 (1964).

It is true that there have been some exceptions to the warrant requirement. Chimel v. California, 395 U. S. 752 (1969); Terry v. Ohio, 392 U. S. 1 (1968); McDonald v. United States, 335 U. S. 451 (1948); Carroll v. United States, 267 U. S. 132 (1925). But those exceptions are few in number and carefully delineated, Katz, supra, at 357; in general, they serve the legitimate needs of law enforcement officers to protect their own well-being and preserve evidence from destruction. Even while carving out those exceptions, the Court has reaffirmed the principle that the "police must, whenever practicable, obtain advance judicial approval of searches and seizures through the warrant procedure," Terry v. Ohio, supra, at 20; Chimel v. California, supra, at 762.

The Government argues that the special circumstances applicable to domestic security surveillances necessitate a further exception to the warrant requirement. It is urged that the requirement of prior judicial review would obstruct the President in the discharge of his constitutional duty to protect domestic security. We are told further that these surveillances are directed primarily to the collecting and maintaining of intelligence with respect to subversive forces, and are not an attempt to gather evidence for specific criminal prosecutions. It is said that this type of surveillance should not be subject to traditional warrant requirements which were established to govern investigation of criminal activity, not ongoing intelligence gathering. Brief for United States 15-16, 23-24; Reply Brief for United States 2-3.

The Government further insists that courts "as a practical matter would have neither the knowledge nor the techniques necessary to determine whether there was probable cause to believe that surveillance was necessary to protect national security." These security problems, the Government contends, involve "a large number of complex and subtle factors" beyond the competence of courts to evaluate. Reply Brief for United States 4.

As a final reason for exemption from a warrant requirement, the Government believes that disclosure to a magistrate of all or even a significant portion of the information involved in domestic security surveillances "would create serious potential dangers to the national security and to the lives of informants and agents. . . . Secrecy is the essential ingredient in intelligence gathering; requiring prior judicial authorization would create a greater `danger of leaks . . . , because in addition to the judge, you have the clerk, the stenographer and some other officer like a law assistant or bailiff who may be apprised of the nature' of the surveillance." Brief for United States 24-25.

These contentions in behalf of a complete exemption from the warrant requirement, when urged on behalf of the President and the national security in its domestic implications, merit the most careful consideration. We certainly do not reject them lightly, especially at a time of worldwide ferment and when civil disorders in this country are more prevalent than in the less turbulent periods of our history. There is, no doubt, pragmatic force to the Government's position.

But we do not think a case has been made for the requested departure from Fourth Amendment standards. The circumstances described do not justify complete exemption of domestic security surveillance from prior judicial scrutiny. Official surveillance, whether its purpose be criminal investigation or ongoing intelligence gathering, risks infringement of constitutionally protected privacy of speech. Security surveillances are especially sensitive because of the inherent vagueness of the domestic security concept, the necessarily broad and continuing nature of intelligence gathering, and the temptation to utilize such surveillances to oversee political dissent. We recognize, as we have before, the constitutional basis of the President's domestic security role, but we think it must be exercised in a manner compatible with the Fourth Amendment. In this case we hold that this requires an appropriate prior warrant procedure.

We cannot accept the Government's argument that internal security matters are too subtle and complex for judicial evaluation. Courts regularly deal with the most difficult issues of our society. There is no reason to believe that federal judges will be insensitive to or uncomprehending of the issues involved in domestic security cases. Certainly courts can recognize that domestic security surveillance involves different considerations from the surveillance of "ordinary crime." If the threat is too subtle or complex for our senior law enforcement officers to convey its significance to a court, one may question whether there is probable cause for surveillance.

Nor do we believe prior judicial approval will fracture the secrecy essential to official intelligence gathering. The investigation of criminal activity has long involved imparting sensitive information to judicial officers who have respected the confidentialities involved. Judges may be counted upon to be especially conscious of security requirements in national security cases. Title III of the Omnibus Crime Control and Safe Streets Act already has imposed this responsibility on the judiciary in connection with such crimes as espionage, sabotage, and treason, §§ 2516 (1) (a) and (c), each of which may involve domestic as well as foreign security threats. Moreover, a warrant application involves no public or adversary proceedings: it is an ex parte request before a magistrate or judge. Whatever security dangers clerical and secretarial personnel may pose can be minimized by proper administrative measures, possibly to the point of allowing the Government itself to provide the necessary clerical assistance.

Thus, we conclude that the Government's concerns do not justify departure in this case from the customary Fourth Amendment requirement of judicial approval prior to initiation of a search or surveillance. Although some added burden will be imposed upon the Attorney General, this inconvenience is justified in a free society to protect constitutional values. Nor do we think the Government's domestic surveillance powers will be impaired to any significant degree. A prior warrant establishes presumptive validity of the surveillance and will minimize the burden of justification in post-surveillance judicial review. By no means of least importance will be the reassurance of the public generally that indiscriminate wiretapping and bugging of law-abiding citizens cannot occur.

IV

We emphasize, before concluding this opinion, the scope of our decision. As stated at the outset, this case involves only the domestic aspects of national security. We have not addressed, and express no opinion as to, the issues which may be involved with respect to activities of foreign powers or their agents.[20] Nor does our decision rest on the language of § 2511 (3) or any other section of Title III of the Omnibus Crime Control and Safe Streets Act of 1968. That Act does not attempt to define or delineate the powers of the President to meet domestic threats to the national security.

Moreover, we do not hold that the same type of standards and procedures prescribed by Title III are necessarily applicable to this case. We recognize that domestic security surveillance may involve different policy and practical considerations from the surveillance of "ordinary crime." The gathering of security intelligence is often long range and involves the interrelation of various sources and types of information. The exact targets of such surveillance may be more difficult to identify than in surveillance operations against many types of crime specified in Title III. Often, too, the emphasis of domestic intelligence gathering is on the prevention of unlawful activity or the enhancement of the Government's preparedness for some possible future crisis or emergency. Thus, the focus of domestic surveillance may be less precise than that directed against more conventional types of crime.

Given these potential distinctions between Title III criminal surveillances and those involving the domestic security, Congress may wish to consider protective standards for the latter which differ from those already prescribed for specified crimes in Title III. Different standards may be compatible with the Fourth Amendment if they are reasonable both in relation to the legitimate need of Government for intelligence information and the protected rights of our citizens. For the warrant application may vary according to the governmental interest to be enforced and the nature of citizen rights deserving protection. As the Court said in Camara v. Municipal Court, 387 U. S. 523, 534-535 (1967):

"In cases in which the Fourth Amendment requires that a warrant to search be obtained, `probable cause' is the standard by which a particular decision to search is tested against the constitutional mandate of reasonableness. . . . In determining whether a particular inspection is reasonable—and thus in determining whether there is probable cause to issue a warrant for that inspection—the need for the inspection must be weighed in terms of these reasonable goals of code enforcement."

It may be that Congress, for example, would judge that the application and affidavit showing probable cause need not follow the exact requirements of § 2518 but should allege other circumstances more appropriate to domestic security cases; that the request for prior court authorization could, in sensitive cases, be made to any member of a specially designated court (e. g., the District Court for the District of Columbia or the Court of Appeals for the District of Columbia Circuit); and that the time and reporting requirements need not be so strict as those in § 2518.

The above paragraph does not, of course, attempt to guide the congressional judgment but rather to delineate the present scope of our own opinion. We do not attempt to detail the precise standards for domestic security warrants any more than our decision in Katz sought to set the refined requirements for the specified criminal surveillances which now constitute Title III. We do hold, however, that prior judicial approval is required for the type of domestic security surveillance involved in this case and that such approval may be made in accordance with such reasonable standards as the Congress may prescribe.

V

As the surveillance of Plamondon's

conversations was unlawful, because conducted without prior judicial approval, the courts below correctly held that Alderman v. United States, 394 U. S. 165 (1969), is controlling and that it requires disclosure to the accused of his own impermissibly intercepted conversations. As stated in Alderman, "the trial court can and should, where appropriate, place a defendant and his counsel under enforceable orders against unwarranted disclosure of the materials which they may be entitled to inspect." 394 U. S., at 185.[21]

The judgment of the Court of Appeals is hereby

Affirmed.

Schneckloth v. Bustamonte (May 29, 1973) [Notes omitted]

MR JUSTICE STEWART delivered the opinion of the Court.

It is well settled under the Fourth and Fourteenth Amendments that a search conducted without a warrant issued upon probable cause is "per se unreasonable . . . subject only to a few specifically established and well delineated exceptions." Katz v. United States, 389 U. S. 347, 389 U. S. 357; Coolidge v. New Hampshire, 403 U. S. 443, 403 U. S. 454 455; Chambers v. Maroney, 399 U. S. 42, 399 U. S. 1. It is equally well settled that one of the specifically established exceptions to the requirements of both a warrant and probable cause is a search that is conducted pursuant to consent. Davis v. United States, 328 U. S. 582, 328 U. S. 593-594; Zap v. United States, 328 U. S. 624, 328 U. S. 630. The constitutional question in the present case concerns the definition of "consent" in this Fourth and Fourteenth Amendment context.

I

The respondent was brought to trial in a California court upon a charge of possessing a check with intent to defraud. [1] He moved to suppress the introduction of certain material as evidence against him on the ground that the material had been acquired through an unconstitutional search and seizure. In response to the motion, the trial judge conducted an evidentiary hearing where it was established that the material in question had been acquired by the State under the following circumstances:

While on routine patrol in Sunnyvale, California, at approximately 2:40 in the morning, Police Officer James Rand stopped an automobile when he observed that one headlight and its license plate light were burned out. Six men were in the vehicle. Joe Alcala and the respondent, Robert Bustamonte, were in the front seat with Joe Gonzales, the driver. Three older men were seated in the rear. When, in response to the policeman's question, Gonzales could not produce a driver's license, Officer Rand asked if any of the other five had any evidence of identification. Only Alcala produced a license, and he explained that the car was his brother's. After the six occupants had stepped out of the car at the officer's request, and after two additional policemen had arrived, Officer Rand asked Alcala if he could search the car. Alcala replied, "Sure, go ahead." Prior to the search, no one was threatened with arrest, and, according to Officer Rand's uncontradicted testimony, it "was all very congenial at this time." Gonzales testified that Alcala actually helped in the search of the car by opening the trunk and glove compartment. In Gonzales' words:

"[T]he police officer asked Joe [Alcala], he goes, 'Does the trunk open?' And Joe said, 'Yes.' He went to the car and got the keys and opened up the trunk."

Wadded up under the left rear seat, the police officers found three checks that had previously been stolen from a car wash.

The trial judge denied the motion to suppress, and the checks in question were admitted in evidence at Bustamonte's trial. On the basis of this and other evidence, he was convicted, and the California Court of Appeal for the First Appellate District affirmed the conviction.

270 Cal.App.2d 648, 76 Cal.Rptr. 17. In agreeing that the search and seizure were constitutionally valid, the appellate court applied the standard earlier formulated by the Supreme Court of California in an opinion by then Justice Traynor:

"Whether, in a particular case, an apparent consent was, in fact, voluntarily given, or was in submission to an express or implied assertion of authority, is a question of fact to be determined in the light of all the circumstances."

People v. Michael, 45 Cal.2d 751, 753, 290 P.2d 852, 854. The appellate court found that,

"[i]n the instant case, the prosecution met the necessary burden of showing consent . . . , since there were clearly circumstances from which the trial court could ascertain that consent had been freely given without coercion or submission to authority. Not only officer Rand, but Gonzales, the driver of the automobile, testified that Alcala's assent to the search of his brother's automobile was freely, even casually given. At the time of the request to search the automobile, the atmosphere, according to Rand, was 'congenial,' and there had been no discussion of any crime. As noted, Gonzales said Alcala even attempted to aid in the search."

270 Cal.App.2d at 652, 76 Cal.Rptr. at 20. The California Supreme Court denied review. [2]

Thereafter, the respondent sought a writ of habeas corpus in a federal district court. It was denied. [3] On appeal, the Court of Appeals for the Ninth Circuit, relying on its prior decisions in Cipres v. United States, 343 F.2d 95, and Schoep v. United States, 391 F.2d 390, set aside the District Court's order. 448 F.2d 699. The appellate court reasoned that a consent was a waiver of a person's Fourth and Fourteenth Amendment rights, and that the State was under an obligation to demonstrate, not only that the consent had been uncoerced, but that it had been given with an understanding that it could be freely and effectively withheld. Consent could not be found, the court held, solely from the absence of coercion and a verbal expression of assent. Since the District Court had not determined that Alcala had known that his consent could have been withheld and that he could have refused to have his vehicle searched, the Court of Appeals vacated the order denying the writ and remanded the case for further proceedings. We granted certiorari to determine whether the Fourth and Fourteenth Amendments require the showing thought necessary by the Court of Appeals. 405 U.S. 953.

II

It is important to make it clear at the outset what is not involved in this case. The respondent concedes that a search conducted pursuant to a valid consent is constitutionally permissible. In Katz v. United States, 389 U.S. at 389 U. S. 358, and more recently in Vale v. Louisiana, 399 U. S. 30, 399 U. S. 35, we recognized that a search authorized by consent is wholly valid. See also Davis v. United States, 328 U.S. at 328 U. S. 593-594; Zap v. United States, 328 U.S. at 328 U. S. 630. [4] And similarly, the State concedes that,

"[w]hen a prosecutor seeks to rely upon consent to justify the lawfulness of a search, he has the burden of proving that the consent was, in fact, freely and voluntarily given."

Bumper v. North Carolina, 391 U. S. 543, 391 U. S. 548. See also Johnson v. United States, 333 U. S. 10; Amos v. United States, 255 U. S. 313.

The precise question in this case, then, is what must the prosecution prove to demonstrate that a consent was "voluntarily" given. And, upon that question, there is a square conflict of views between the state and federal courts that have reviewed the search involved in the case before us. The Court of Appeals for the Ninth Circuity concluded that it is an essential part of the State's initial burden to prove that a person knows he has a right to refuse consent. The California courts have followed the rule that voluntariness is a question of fact to be determined from the totality of all the circumstances, and that the state of a defendant's knowledge is only one factor to be taken into account in assessing the voluntariness of a consent. See, e.g., People v. Treymayne, 20 Cal.App.3d 1006, 98 Cal.Rptr. 193; People v. Roberts, 246 Cal.App.2d 715, 55 Cal.Rptr. 62.

A

The most extensive judicial exposition of the meaning of "voluntariness" have been developed in those cases in which the Court has had to determine the "voluntariness" of a defendant's confession for purposes of the Fourteenth Amendment. Almost 40 years ago, in Brown v. Mississippi, 297 U. S. 278, the Court held that a criminal conviction based upon a confession obtained by brutality and violence was constitutionally invalid under the Due Process Clause of the Fourteenth Amendment. In some 30 different cases decided during the era that intervened between Brown and Escobedo v. Illinois, 378 U. S. 478, the Court was faced with the necessity of determining whether in fact the confessions in issue had been "voluntarily" given. [5] It is to that body of case law to which we turn for initial guidance on the meaning of "voluntariness" in the present context. [6]

Those cases yield no talismanic definition of "voluntariness" mechanically applicable to the host of situations where the question has arisen. "The notion of voluntariness,'" Mr. Justice Frankfurter once wrote, "is itself an amphibian." Culombe v. Connecticut, 367 U. S. 568, 367 U. S. 604 605. It cannot be taken literally to mean a "knowing" choice.

"Except where a person is unconscious or drugged or otherwise lacks capacity for conscious choice, all incriminating statements -- even those made under brutal treatment -- are 'voluntary' in the sense of representing a choice of alternatives. On the other hand, if 'voluntariness' incorporates notions of 'but-for' cause, the question should be whether the statement would have been made even absent inquiry or other official action. Under such a test, virtually no statement would be voluntary, because very few people give incriminating statements in the absence of official action of some kind. [7]"

It is thus evident that neither linguistics nor epistemology will provide a ready definition of the meaning of "voluntariness."

Rather, "voluntariness" has reflected an accommodation of the complex of values implicated in police questioning of a suspect. At one end of the spectrum is the acknowledged need for police questioning as a tool for the effective enforcement of criminal laws. See Culombe v. Connecticut, supra, at 367 U. S. 578-580. Without such investigation, those who were innocent might be falsely accused, those who were guilty might wholly escape prosecution, and many crimes would go unsolved. In short, the security of all would be diminished. Haynes v. Washington, 373 U. S. 503, 373 U. S. 515. At the other end of the spectrum is the set of values reflecting society's deeply felt belief that the criminal law cannot be used as an instrument of unfairness, and that the possibility of unfair and even brutal police tactics poses a real and serious threat to civilized notions of justice.

"[I]n cases involving involuntary confessions, this Court enforces the strongly felt attitude of our society that important human values are sacrificed where an agency of the government, in the course of securing a conviction, wrings a confession out of an accused against his will."

Blackburn v. Alabama, 361 U. S. 199, 361 U. S. 206-207. See also Culombe v. Connecticut, supra, at 367 U. S. 581-584; Chambers v. Florida, 309 U. S. 227, 309 U. S. 235-238.

This Court's decisions reflect a frank recognition that the Constitution requires the sacrifice of neither security nor liberty. The Due Process Clause does not mandate that the police forgo all questioning, or that they be given carte blanche to extract what they can from a suspect.

"The ultimate test remains that which has been the only clearly established test in Anglo-American courts for two hundred years: the test of voluntariness. Is the confession the product of an essentially free and unconstrained choice by its maker? If it is, if he has willed to confess, it may be used against him. If it is not, if his will has been overborne and his capacity for self-determination critically impaired, the use of his confession offends due process."

Culombe v. Connecticut, supra, at 367 U. S. 602.

In determining whether a defendant's will was overborne in a particular case, the Court has assessed the totality of all the surrounding circumstances -- both the characteristics of the accused and the details of the interrogation. Some of the factors taken into account have included the youth of the accused, e.g., Haley v. Ohio, 332 U. S. 596; his lack of education, e.g., Payne v. Arkansas, 356 U. S. 560; or his low intelligence, e.g., Fikes v. Alabama, 352 U. S. 191; the lack of any advice to the accused of his constitutional rights, e.g., Davis v. North Carolina, 384 U. S. 737; the length of detention, e.g., Chambers v. Florida, supra; the repeated and prolonged nature of the questioning, e.g., Ashcraft v. Tennessee, 322 U. S. 143; and the use of physical punishment such as the deprivation of food or sleep, e.g., Reck v. Pate, 367 U. S. 433. [8] In all of these cases, the Court determined the factual circumstances surrounding the confession, assessed the psychological impact on the accused, and evaluated the legal significance of how the accused reacted. Culombe v. Connecticut, supra, at 367 U. S. 603.

The significant fact about all of these decisions is that none of them turned on the presence or absence of a single controlling criterion; each reflected a careful scrutiny of all the surrounding circumstances. See Miranda v. Arizona, 384 U. S. 436, 384 U. S. 508 (Harlan, J., dissenting); id. at 384 U. S. 534-535 (WHITE, J., dissenting). In none of them did the Court rule that the Due Process Clause required the prosecution to prove as part of its initial burden that the defendant knew he had a right to refuse to answer the questions that were put. While the state of the accused's mind, and the failure of the police to advise the accused of his rights, were certainly factors to be evaluated in assessing the "voluntariness" of an accused's responses, they were not, in and of themselves, determinative. See, e.g., Davis v. North Carolina, supra; Haynes v. Washington, supra, at 373 U. S. 510-511; Culombe v. Connecticut, supra, at 367 U. S. 610; Turner v. Pennsylvania, 338 U. S. 62, 338 U. S. 64.

B

Similar considerations lead us to agree with the courts of California that the question whether a consent to a search was in fact, "voluntary" or was the product of duress or coercion, express or implied, is a question of fact to be determined from the totality of all the circumstances. While knowledge of the right to refuse consent is one factor to be taken into account, the government need not establish such knowledge as the sine qua non of an effective consent. As with police questioning, two competing concerns must be accommodated in determining the meaning of a "voluntary" consent -- the legitimate need for such searches and the equally important requirement of assuring the absence of coercion.

In situations where the police have some evidence of illicit activity, but lack probable cause to arrest or search, a search authorized by a valid consent may be the only means of obtaining important and reliable evidence. [9] In the present case, for example, while the police had reason to stop the car for traffic violations, the State does not contend that there was probable cause to search the vehicle or that the search was incident to a valid arrest of any of the occupants. [10] Yet the search yielded tangible evidence that served as a basis for a prosecution, and provided some assurance that others, wholly innocent of the crime, were not mistakenly brought to trial. And in those cases where there is probable cause to arrest or search, but where the police lack a warrant, a consent search may still be valuable. If the search is conducted and proves fruitless, that, in itself, may convince the police that an arrest with its possible stigma and embarrassment is unnecessary, or that a far more extensive search pursuant to a warrant is not justified. In short, a search pursuant to consent may result in considerably less inconvenience for the subject of the search, and, properly conducted, is a constitutionally permissible and wholly legitimate aspect of effective police activity.

But the Fourth and Fourteenth Amendments require that a consent not be coerced, by explicit or implicit means, by implied threat or covert force. For no matter how subtly the coercion was applied, the resulting "consent" would be no more than a pretext for the unjustified police intrusion against which the Fourth Amendment is directed. In the words of the classic admonition in Boyd v. United States, 116 U. S. 616, 116 U. S. 635:

"It may be that it is the obnoxious thing in its mildest and least repulsive form; but illegitimate and unconstitutional practices get their first footing in that way, namely, by silent approaches and slight deviations from legal modes of procedure. This can only be obviated by adhering to the rule that constitutional provisions for the security of person and property should be liberally construed. A close and literal construction deprives them of half their efficacy, and leads to gradual depreciation of the right, as if it consisted more in sound than in substance. It is the duty of courts to be watchful for the constitutional rights of the citizen and against any stealthy encroachments thereon."

The problem of reconciling the recognized legitimacy of consent searches with the requirement that they be free from any aspect of official coercion cannot be resolved by any infallible touchstone. To approve such searches without the most careful scrutiny would sanction the possibility of official coercion; to place artificial restrictions upon such searches would jeopardize their basic validity. Just as was true with confessions, the requirement of a "voluntary" consent reflects a fair accommodation of the constitutional requirements involved. In examining all the surrounding circumstances to determine if in fact, the consent to search was coerced, account must be taken of subtly coercive police questions, as well as the possibly vulnerable subjective state of the person who consents. Those searches that are the product of police coercion can thus be filtered out without undermining the continuing validity of consent searches. In sum, there is no reason for us to depart in the area of consent searches, from the traditional definition of "voluntariness."

The approach of the Court of Appeals for the Ninth Circuit finds no support in any of our decisions that have attempted to define the meaning of "voluntariness." Its ruling, that the State must affirmatively prove that the subject of the search knew that he had a right to refuse consent, would, in practice, create serious doubt whether consent searches could continue to be conducted. There might be rare cases where it could be proved from the record that a person in fact, affirmatively knew of his right to refuse -- such as a case where he announced to the police that, if he didn't sign the consent form, "you [police] are going to get a search warrant;" [11] or a case where, by prior experience and training, a person had clearly and convincingly demonstrated such knowledge. [12] But, more commonly, where there was no evidence of any coercion, explicit or implicit, the prosecution would nevertheless be unable to demonstrate that the subject of the search in fact, had known of his right to refuse consent.

The very object of the inquiry -- the nature of a person's subjective understanding -- underlines the difficulty of the prosecution's burden under the rule applied by the Court of Appeals in this case. Any defendant who was the subject of a search authorized solely by his consent could effectively frustrate the introduction into evidence of the fruits of that search by simply failing to testify that he in fact, knew he could refuse to consent. And the near impossibility of meeting this prosecutorial burden suggests why this Court has never accepted any such litmus paper test of voluntariness. It is instructive to recall the fears of then Justice Traynor of the California Supreme Court:

"[I]t is not unreasonable for officers to seek interviews with suspects or witnesses or to call upon them at their homes for such purposes. Such inquiries, although courteously made and not accompanied with any assertion of a right to enter or search or secure answers, would permit the criminal to defeat his prosecution by voluntarily revealing all of the evidence against him and then contending that he acted only in response to an implied assertion of unlawful authority."

People v. Michael, 45 Cal.2d at 754, 290 P.2d at 854.

One alternative that would go far toward proving that the subject of a search did know he had a right to refuse consent would be to advise him of that right before eliciting his consent. That, however, is a suggestion that has been almost universally repudiated by both federal [13] and state courts [14] and, we think, rightly so. For it would be thoroughly impractical to impose on the normal consent search the detailed requirements of an effective warning. Consent searches are part of the standard investigatory techniques of law enforcement agencies. They normally occur on the highway, or in a person's home or office, and under informal and unstructured conditions. The circumstances that prompt the initial request to search may develop quickly or be a logical extension of investigative police questioning. The police may seek to investigate further suspicious circumstances or to follow up leads developed in questioning persons at the scene of a crime. These situations are a far cry from the structured atmosphere of a trial where, assisted by counsel if he chooses, a defendant is informed of his trial rights. Cf. Boykin v. Alabama, 395 U. S. 238, 395 U. S. 243. and, while surely a closer question, these situations are still immeasurably far removed from "custodial interrogation" where, in Miranda v. Arizona, supra, we found that the Constitution required certain now familiar warnings as a prerequisite to police interrogation. Indeed, in language applicable to the typical consent search, we refused to extend the need for warnings:

"Our decision is not intended to hamper the traditional function of police officers in investigating crime. . . . When an individual is in custody on probable cause, the police may, of course, seek out evidence in the field to be used at trial against him. Such investigation may include inquiry of persons not under restraint. General on-the-scene questioning as to facts surrounding a crime or other general questioning of citizens in the factfinding process is not affected by our holding. It is an act of responsible citizenship for individuals to give whatever information they may have to aid in law enforcement."

384 U.S. at 384 U. S. 477-478.

Consequently, we cannot accept the position of the Court of Appeals in this case that proof of knowledge of the right to refuse consent is a necessary prerequisite to demonstrating a "voluntary" consent. Rather, it is only by analyzing all the circumstances of an individual consent that it can be ascertained whether, in fact, it was voluntary or coerced. It is this careful sifting of the unique facts and circumstances of each case that is evidenced in our prior decisions involving consent searches.

For example, in Davis v. United States, 328 U. S. 582, federal agents enforcing wartime gasoline rationing regulations arrested a filling station operator and asked to see his rationing coupons. He eventually unlocked a room where the agents discovered the coupons that formed the basis for his conviction. The District Court found that the petitioner had consented to the search -- that, although he had at first refused to turn the coupons over, he had soon been persuaded to do so, and that force or threat of force had not been employed to persuade him. Concluding that it could not be said that this finding was erroneous, this Court, in an opinion by MR. JUSTICE DOUGLAS that looked to all the circumstances surrounding the consent, affirmed the judgment of conviction:

"The public character of the property, the fact that the demand was made during business hours at the place of business where the coupons were required to be kept, the existence of the right to inspect, the nature of the request, the fact that the initial refusal to turn the coupons over was soon followed by acquiescence in the demand -- these circumstances all support the conclusion of the District Court."

Id. at 328 U. S. 593-594. See also Zap v. United States, 328 U. S. 624.

Conversely, if, under all the circumstances, it has appeared that the consent was not given voluntarily -- that it was coerced by threats or force, or granted only in submission to a claim of lawful authority -- then we have found the consent invalid and the search unreasonable. See, e.g.,

Bumper v. North Carolina, 391 U.S. at 391 U. S. 548-549; Johnson v. United States, 333 U. S. 10; Amos v. United States, 255 U. S. 313. In Bumper, a 66-year-old Negro widow, who lived in a house located in a rural area at the end of an isolated mile-long dirt road, allowed four white law enforcement officials to search her home after they asserted they had a warrant to search the house. We held the alleged consent to be invalid, noting that,

"[w]hen a law enforcement officer claims authority to search a home under a warrant, he announces, in effect, that the occupant has no right to resist the search. The situation is instinct with coercion -- albeit colorably lawful coercion. Where there is coercion, there cannot be consent."

391 U.S. at 391 U. S. 550.

Implicit in all of these cases is the recognition that knowledge of a right to refuse is not a prerequisite of a voluntary consent. If the prosecution were required to demonstrate such knowledge, Davis and Zap could not have found consent without evidence of that knowledge. And similarly, if the failure to prove such knowledge were sufficient to show an ineffective consent, the Amos, Johnson, and Bumper opinions would surely have focused upon the subjective mental state of the person who consented. Yet they did not.

In short, neither this Court's prior cases nor the traditional definition of "voluntariness" requires proof of knowledge of a right to refuse as the sine qua non of an effective consent to a search. [15]

C

It is said, however, that a "consent" is a "waiver" of a person's rights under the Fourth and Fourteenth Amendments. The argument is that, by allowing the police to conduct a search, a person "waives" whatever right he had to prevent the police from searching. It is argued that, under the doctrine of Johnson v. Zerbst, 304 U. S. 458, 304

U. S. 464, to establish such a "waiver," the State must demonstrate "an intentional relinquishment or abandonment of a known right or privilege."

But these standards were enunciated in Johnson in the context of the safeguards of a fair criminal trial. Our cases do not reflect an uncritical demand for a knowing and intelligent waiver in every situation where a person has failed to invoke a constitutional protection. As Mr. Justice Black once observed for the Court: "Waiver' is a vague term used for a great variety of purposes, good and bad, in the law." Green v. United States, 355 U. S. 184, 355 U. S. 191. With respect to procedural due process, for example, the Court has acknowledged that waiver is possible, while explicitly leaving open the question whether a "knowing and intelligent" waiver need be shown. [16] See D. N. Overmyer Co. v. Frick Co., 405 U. S. 174, 405 U. S. 185-186; Fuentes v. Shevin, 407 U. S. 67, 407 U. S. 94-96. [17]

The requirement of a "knowing" and "intelligent" waiver was articulated in a case involving the validity of a defendant's decision to forgo a right constitutionally guaranteed to protect a fair trial and the reliability of the truth-determining process. Johnson v. Zerbst, supra, dealt with the denial of counsel in a federal criminal trial. There, the Court held that, under the Sixth Amendment, a criminal defendant is entitled to the assistance of counsel, and that, if he lacks sufficient funds to retain counsel, it is the Government's obligation to furnish him with a lawyer. As Mr. Justice Black wrote for the Court:

"The Sixth Amendment stands as a constant admonition that, if the constitutional safeguards it provides be lost, justice will not 'still be done.' It embodies a realistic recognition of the obvious truth that the average defendant does not have the professional legal skill to protect himself when brought before a tribunal with power to take his life or liberty, wherein the prosecution is presented by experienced and learned counsel.

That which is simple, orderly and necessary to the lawyer, to the untrained layman may appear intricate, complex and mysterious."

304 U.S. at 304 U. S. 462-463 (footnote omitted). To preserve the fairness of the trial process, the Court established an appropriately heavy burden on the Government before waiver could be found -- "an intentional relinquishment or abandonment of a known right or privilege." Id. at 304 U. S. 464.

Almost without exception, the requirement of a knowing and intelligent waiver has been applied only to those rights which the Constitution guarantees to a criminal defendant in order to preserve a fair trial. [18] Hence, and hardly surprisingly in view of the facts of Johnson itself, the standard of a knowing and intelligent waiver has most often been applied to test the validity of a waiver of counsel, either at trial, [19] or upon a guilty plea. [20] And the Court has also applied the Johnson criteria to assess the effectiveness of a waiver of other trial rights such as the right to confrontation, [21] to a jury trial, [22] and to a speedy trial, [23] and the right to be free from twice being placed in jeopardy. [24] Guilty pleas have been carefully scrutinized to determine whether the accused knew and understood all the rights to which he would be entitled at trial, and that he had intentionally chosen to forgo them. [25] And the Court has evaluated the knowing and intelligent nature of the waiver of trial rights in trial-type situations, such as the waiver of the privilege against compulsory self-incrimination before an administrative agency [26] or a congressional committee, [27] or the waiver of counsel in a juvenile proceeding. [28] The guarantees afforded a criminal defendant at trial also protect him at certain stages before the actual trial, and any alleged waiver must meet the strict standard of an intentional relinquishment of a "known" right. But the "trial" guarantees that have been applied to the "pretrial" stage of the criminal process are similarly designed to protect the fairness of the trial itself.

Hence, in United States v. Wade, 388 U. S. 218, and Gilbert v. California, 388 U. S. 263, the Court held

"that a post-indictment pretrial lineup at which the accused is exhibited to identifying witnesses is a critical stage of the criminal prosecution; that police conduct of such a lineup without notice to and in the absence of his counsel denies the accused his Sixth [and Fourteenth] Amendment right to counsel. . . ."

Id. at 388 U. S. 272. Accordingly, the Court indicated that the standard of a knowing and intelligent waiver must be applied to test the waiver of counsel at such a lineup. See United States v. Wade, supra, at 388 U. S. 237. The Court stressed the necessary interrelationship between the presence of counsel at a postindictment lineup before trial and the protection of the trial process itself:

"Insofar as the accused's conviction may rest on a courtroom identification in fact, the fruit of a suspect pretrial identification which the accused is helpless to subject to effective scrutiny at trial, the accused is deprived of that right of cross-examination which is an essential safeguard to his right to confront the witnesses against him. Pointer v. Texas, 380 U. S. 400. And even though cross-examination is a precious safeguard to a fair trial, it cannot be viewed as an absolute assurance of accuracy and reliability. Thus, in the present context, where so many variables and pitfalls exist, the first line of defense must be the prevention of unfairness and the lessening of the hazards of eyewitness identification at the lineup itself. The trial which might determine the accused's fate may well not be that in the courtroom but that, at the pretrial confrontation, with the State aligned against the accused, the witness the sole jury, and the accused unprotected against the overreaching, intentional or unintentional, and with little or no

effective appeal from the judgment there rendered by the witness -- 'that's the man.'"

Id. at 388 U. S. 235-236.

And in Miranda v. Arizona, 384 U. S. 436, the Court found that custodial interrogation by the police was inherently coercive, and consequently held that detailed warnings were required to protect the privilege against compulsory self-incrimination. The Court made it clear that the basis for decision was the need to protect the fairness of the trial itself:

"That counsel is present when statements are taken from an individual during interrogation obviously enhances the integrity of the factfinding processes in court. The presence of an attorney, and the warnings delivered to the individual, enable the defendant under otherwise compelling circumstances to tell his story without fear, effectively, and in a way that eliminates the evils in the interrogation process. Without the protections flowing from adequate warnings and the rights of counsel,"

"all the careful safeguards erected around the giving of testimony, whether by an accused or any other witness, would become empty formalities in a procedure where the most compelling possible evidence of guilt, a confession, would have already been obtained at the unsupervised pleasure of the police."

Id. at 384 U. S. 466.

The standards of Johnson were, therefore, found to be a necessary prerequisite to a finding of a valid waiver. See 384 U.S. at 384 U. S. 475-479. Cf. Escobedo v. Illinois, 378 U.S. at 378 U. S. 490 n. 14. [29]

There is a vast difference between those rights that protect a fair criminal trial and the rights guaranteed under the Fourth Amendment. Nothing, either in the purposes behind requiring a "knowing" and "intelligent" waiver of trial rights, or in the practical application of such a requirement suggests that it ought to be extended to the constitutional guarantee against unreasonable searches and seizures.

A strict standard of waiver has been applied to those rights guaranteed to a criminal defendant to insure that he will be accorded the greatest possible opportunity to utilize every facet of the constitutional model of a fair criminal trial. Any trial conducted in derogation of that model leaves open the possibility that the trial reached an unfair result precisely because all the protections specified in the Constitution were not provided. A prime example is the right to counsel. For without that right, a wholly innocent accused faces the real and substantial danger that simply because of his lack of legal expertise he may be convicted. As Mr. Justice Harlan once wrote:

"The sound reason why [the right to counsel] is so freely extended for a criminal trial is the severe injustice risked by confronting an untrained defendant with a range of technical points of law, evidence, and tactics familiar to the prosecutor but, not to himself."

Miranda v. Arizona, supra, at 384 U. S. 514 (dissenting opinion). The Constitution requires that every effort be made to see to it that a defendant in a criminal case has not unknowingly relinquished the basic protections that the Framers thought indispensable to a fair trial. [30]

The protections of the Fourth Amendment are of a wholly different order, and have nothing whatever to do with promoting the fair ascertainment of truth at a criminal trial. Rather, as Mr. Justice Frankfurter's opinion for the Court put it in Wolf v. Colorado, 338 U. S. 25, 338 U. S. 27, the Fourth Amendment protects the "security of one's privacy against arbitrary intrusion by the police. . . ." In declining to apply the exclusionary rule of Mapp v. Ohio, 367 U. S. 643, to convictions that had become final before rendition of that decision, the Court emphasized that "there is no likelihood of unreliability or coercion present in a search and seizure case," Linkletter v. Walker, 381 U. S. 618, 381 U. S. 638. In Linkletter, the Court indicated that those cases that had been given retroactive effect went to "the fairness of the trial -- the very integrity of the factfinding process. Here . . . the fairness of the trial is not under attack." Id. at 381 U. S. 639. The Fourth Amendment "is not an adjunct to the ascertainment of truth." The guarantees of the Fourth Amendment stand

"as a protection of quite different constitutional values -- values reflecting the concern of our society for the right of each individual to be let alone. To recognize this is no more than to accord those values undiluted respect."

Tehan v. United States ex rel. Shott, 382 U. S. 406, 382 U. S. 416.

Nor can it even be said that a search, as opposed to an eventual trial, is somehow "unfair" if a person consents to a search. While the Fourth and Fourteenth Amendments limit the circumstances under which the police can conduct a search, there is nothing constitutionally suspect in a person's voluntarily allowing a search. The actual conduct of the search may be precisely the same as if the police had obtained a warrant. And, unlike those constitutional guarantees that protect a defendant at trial, it cannot be said every reasonable presumption ought to be indulged against voluntary relinquishment. We have only recently stated:

"[I]t is no part of the policy underlying the Fourth and Fourteenth Amendments to discourage citizens from aiding to the utmost of their ability in the apprehension of criminals."

Coolidge v. New Hampshire, 403 U.S. at 403 U. S. 488. Rather, the community has a real interest in encouraging consent, for the resulting search may yield necessary evidence for the solution and prosecution of crime, evidence that may insure that a wholly innocent person is not wrongly charged with a criminal offense.

Those cases that have dealt with the

application of the Johnson v. Zerbst rule make clear that it would be next to impossible to apply to a consent search the standard of "an intentional relinquishment or abandonment of a known right or privilege." [31] To be true to Johnson and its progeny, there must be examination into the knowing and understanding nature of the waiver, an examination that was designed for a trial judge in the structured atmosphere of a courtroom. As the Court expressed it in Johnson:

"The constitutional right of an accused to be represented by counsel invokes, of itself, the protection of a trial court, in which the accused -- whose life or liberty is at stake is without counsel. This protecting duty imposes the serious and weighty responsibility upon the trial judge of determining whether there is an intelligent and competent waiver by the accused. While an accused may waive the right to counsel, whether there is a proper waiver should be clearly determined by the trial court, and it would be fitting and appropriate for that determination to appear upon the record."

304 U.S. at 304 U. S. 465. [32]

It would be unrealistic to expect that in the informal, unstructured context of a consent search, a policeman, upon pain of tainting the evidence obtained, could make the detailed type of examination demanded by Johnson. And, if for this reason a diluted form of "waiver" were found acceptable, that would itself be ample recognition of the fact that there is no universal standard that must be applied in every situation where a person forgoes a constitutional right. [33]

Similarly, a "waiver" approach to consent searches would be thoroughly inconsistent with our decisions that have approved "third party consents." In Coolidge v. New Hampshire, 403 U.S. at 403 U. S. 487-490, where a wife surrendered to the police guns and clothing belonging to her husband, we found nothing constitutionally impermissible in the admission of

that evidence at trial, since the wife had not been coerced. Frazier v. Cupp, 394 U. S. 731, 394 U. S. 740, held that evidence seized from the defendant's duffel bag in a search authorized by his cousin's consent was admissible at trial. We found that the defendant had assumed the risk that his cousin, with whom he shared the bag, would allow the police to search it. See also Abel v. United States, 362 U. S. 217. And in Hill v. California, 401 U. S. 797, 401 U. S. 802-805, we held that the police had validly seized evidence from the petitioner's apartment incident to the arrest of a third party, since the police had probable cause to arrest the petitioner and reasonably, though mistakenly, believed the man they had arrested was he. Yet it is inconceivable that the Constitution could countenance the waiver of a defendant's right to counsel by a third party, or that a waiver could be found because a trial judge reasonably, though mistakenly, believed a defendant had waived his right to plead not guilty. [34]

In short, there is nothing in the purposes or application of the waiver requirements of Johnson v. Zerbst that justifies, much less compels, the easy equation of a knowing waiver with a consent search. To make such an equation is to generalize from the broad rhetoric of some of our decisions, and to ignore the substance of the differing constitutional guarantees. We decline to follow what one judicial scholar has termed

"the domino method of constitutional adjudication . . . wherein every explanatory statement in a previous opinion is made the basis for extension to a wholly different situation. [35]"

D

Much of what has already been said disposes of the argument that the Court's decision in the Miranda case requires the conclusion that knowledge of a right to refuse is an indispensable element of a valid consent. The considerations that informed the Court's holding in Miranda are simply inapplicable in the present case.

In Miranda, the Court found that the techniques of police questioning and the nature of custodial surroundings produce an inherently coercive situation. The Court concluded that,

"[u]nless adequate protective devices are employed to dispel the compulsion inherent in custodial surroundings, no statement obtained from the defendant can truly be the product of his free choice."

384 U.S. at 384 U. S. 458. And, at another point, the Court noted that,

"without proper safeguards, the process of in-custody interrogation of persons suspected or accused of crime contains inherently compelling pressures which work to undermine the individual's will to resist and to compel him to speak where he would not otherwise do so freely."

Id. at 384 U. S. 467.

In this case, there is no evidence of any inherently coercive tactics -- either from the nature of the police questioning or the environment in which it took place. Indeed, since consent searches will normally occur on a person's own familiar territory, the specter of incommunicado police interrogation in some remote station house is simply inapposite. [36] There is no reason to believe, under circumstances such as are present here, that the response to a policeman's question is presumptively coerced; and there is, therefore, no reason to reject the traditional test for determining the voluntariness of a person's response. Miranda, of course, did not reach investigative questioning of a person not in custody, which is most directly analogous to the situation of a consent search, and it assuredly did not indicate that such questioning ought to be deemed inherently coercive. See supra at 412 U. S. 232.

It is also argued that the failure to require the Government to establish knowledge as a prerequisite to a valid consent, will relegate the Fourth Amendment to the special province of "the sophisticated, the knowledgeable and the privileged." We cannot agree. The traditional definition of voluntariness we accept today has always taken into account evidence of minimal schooling, low intelligence, and the lack of any effective warnings to a person of his rights; and the voluntariness of any statement taken under those conditions has been carefully scrutinized to determine whether it was in fact, voluntarily given. [37]

E

Our decision today is a narrow one. We hold only that, when the subject of a search is not in custody and the State attempts to justify a search on the basis of his consent, the Fourth and Fourteenth Amendments require that it demonstrate that the consent was in fact, voluntarily given, and not the result of duress or coercion, express or implied. Voluntariness is a question of fact to be determined from all the circumstances, and while the subject's knowledge of a right to refuse is a factor to be taken into account, the prosecution is not required to demonstrate such knowledge as a prerequisite to establishing a voluntary consent. [38] Because the California court followed these principles in affirming the respondent's conviction, and because the Court of Appeals for the Ninth Circuit, in remanding for an evidentiary hearing, required more, its judgment must be reversed.

It so ordered.

Cady v. Dombrowski (June 21, 1973)

Opinion of the Court by MR. JUSTICE REHNQUIST, announced by MR. JUSTICE BLACKMUN.

Respondent Chester J. Dombrowski, was convicted in a Wisconsin state court of first-degree murder of Herbert McKinney and sentenced to life imprisonment. The conviction was upheld on appeal, State v. Dombrowski, 44 Wis.2d 486, 171 N.W.2d 349 (1969), the Wisconsin Supreme Court rejecting respondent's contention that certain evidence admitted at the trial had been unconstitutionally seized. Respondent then filed a petition for a writ of habeas corpus in federal district court, asserting the same constitutional claim. The District Court denied the petition, but the United States Court of Appeals for the Seventh Circuit reversed, holding that one of the searches was unconstitutional under Preston v. United States, 376 U. S. 364 (1964), and the other unconstitutional for unrelated reasons. 471 F.2d 280 (1972). We granted certiorari, 409 U.S. 1059 (1972).

I

On September 9, 1969, respondent was a member of the Chicago, Illinois, police force and either owned or possessed a 1960 Dodge automobile. That day, he drove from Chicago to West Bend, Wisconsin, the county seat of Washington County, located some hundred-odd miles northwest of Chicago. He was identified as having been in two taverns in the small town of Kewaskum, Wisconsin, seven miles north of West Bend, during the late evening of September 9 and the early morning of September 10. At some time before noon on the 10th, respondent's automobile became disabled, and he had it towed to a farm owned by his brother in Fond du Lac County, which adjoins Washington County on the north. He then drove back to Chicago early that, afternoon with his brother in the latter's car.

Just before midnight of the same day, respondent rented a maroon 1967 Ford Thunderbird at O'Hare Field outside of Chicago, and apparently drove back to Wisconsin early the next morning. A tenant on his brother's farm saw a car answering the description of the rented car pull alongside the disabled 1960 Dodge at approximately 4 a.m. At approximately 9:30 a.m. on September 11, respondent purchased two towels, one light brown and the other blue, from a department store in Kewaskum.

From 7 to 10:15 p.m. of the 11th, respondent was in a steak house or tavern in West Bend. He ate dinner and also drank, apparently quite heavily. He left the tavern and drove the 1967 Thunderbird in a direction away from West Bend toward his brother's farm. On the way, respondent had an accident, with the Thunderbird breaking through a guard rail and crashing into a bridge abutment. A passing motorist drove him into Kewaskum, and, after being let off in Kewaskum, respondent telephoned the police. Two police officers picked him up at a tavern and drove to the scene of the accident. On the way, the officers noticed that respondent appeared to be drunk; he offered three conflicting versions of how the accident occurred.

At the scene, the police observed the 1967 Thunderbird and took various measurements relevant to the accident. Respondent was, in the opinion of the officers, drunk. He had informed them that he was a Chicago police officer. The Wisconsin policemen believed that Chicago police officers were required by regulation to carry their service revolvers at all times. After calling a tow truck to remove the disabled Thunderbird, and not finding the revolver on respondent's person, one of the officers looked into the front seat and glove compartment of that car for respondent's service revolver. No revolver was found. The wrecker arrived and the Thunderbird was towed to a privately owned garage in Kewaskum, approximately seven miles from the West Bend police station. It was left outside by the wrecker, and no police guard was posted. At 11:33 p.m. on the 11th, respondent was taken directly to the West Bend police station from the accident scene, and, after being interviewed by an assistant district attorney, to whom respondent again stated he was a Chicago policeman, respondent was formally arrested for drunken driving. Respondent was "in a drunken condition" and "incoherent at times." Because of his injuries sustained in the accident, the same two officers took respondent to a local hospital. He lapsed into an unexplained coma, and a doctor, fearing the possibility of complications, had respondent hospitalized overnight for observation. One of the policemen remained at the hospital as a guard, and the other, Officer Weiss, drove at some time after 2 a.m. on the 12th to the garage to which the 1967 Thunderbird had been towed after the accident.

The purpose of going to the Thunderbird, as developed on the motion to suppress, was to look for respondent's service revolver. Weiss testified that respondent did not have a revolver when he was arrested, and that the West Bend authorities were under the impression that Chicago police officers were required to carry their service revolvers at all times. He stated that the effort to find the revolver was "standard procedure in our department."

Weiss opened the door of the Thunderbird and found, on the floor of the car, a book of Chicago police regulations and, between the two front seats, a flashlight which appeared to have "a few spots of blood on it." He then opened the trunk of the car, which had been locked, and saw various items covered with what was later determined to be type O blood. These included a pair of police uniform trousers, a pair of gray trousers, a nightstick with the name "Dombrowski" stamped on it, a raincoat, a portion of a car floor mat, and a towel. The blood on the car mat was moist. The officer removed these items to the police station.

When, later that day, respondent was confronted with the condition of the items discovered in the trunk, he requested the presence of counsel before making any statement. After conferring with respondent, a lawyer told the police that respondent "authorized me to state he believed there was a body lying near the family picnic area at the north end of his brother's farm."

Fond du Lac County police went to the farm and found, in a dump, the body of a male,

later identified as the decedent McKinney, clad only in a sport shirt. The deceased's head was bloody; a white sock was found near the body. In observing the area, one officer looked through the window of the disabled 1960 Dodge, located not far from where the body was found, and saw a pillowcase, back seat, and briefcase covered with blood. Police officials obtained, on the evening of the 12th, returnable within 48 hours, warrants to search the 1960 Dodge and the 1967 Thunderbird, as well as orders to impound both automobiles. The 1960 Dodge was examined at the farm on the 12th and then towed to the police garage, where it was held as evidence. On the 13th, criminologists came from the Wisconsin Crime Laboratory in Madison and searched the Dodge; they seized the back and front seats, a white sock covered with blood, a part of a bloody rear floor mat, a briefcase, and a front floor mat. A return of the search warrant was filed in the county court on the 14th, but it did not recite that the sock and floor mat had been seized. At a hearing held on the 14th, the sheriff who executed the warrant did not specifically state that these two items had been seized.

At the trial, the State introduced testimony tending to establish that the deceased was first hit over the head and then shot with a .38-caliber gun, dying approximately an hour after the gunshot wound was inflicted; that death occurred at approximately 7 a.m. on the 11th, with a six-hour margin of error either way; that respondent owned two .38-caliber guns; that respondent had type A blood; that the deceased had type O blood and that the bloodstains found in the 1960 Dodge and on the items found in the two cars were type O.

The prosecution introduced the nightstick discovered in the 1967 Thunderbird, and testimony that it had traces of type O blood on it; the portion of the floor mat found in the 1967 car, with testimony that it matched the portion of the floor mat found in the 1960 Dodge; the bloody towel found in the 1967 car, with testimony that it was identical to one of the towels purchased by respondent on the 11th; the police uniform trousers; and the sock found in the 1960 Dodge, with testimony that it was identical in composition and stitching to that found near the body of the deceased.

The State's case was based wholly on circumstantial evidence. The Supreme Court of Wisconsin, in reviewing the conviction on direct appeal, stated that,

"even though the evidence that led to his conviction was circumstantial, we have seldom seen a stronger collection of such evidence assembled and presented by the prosecution."

State v. Dombrowski, 44 Wis.2d at 507, 171 N.W.2d at 360.

II

The Fourth Amendment provides:

"The right of the people to be secure in their persons, houses, papers, and effects, against unreasonable searches and seizures, shall not be violated, and no Warrants shall issue, but upon probable cause, supported by Oath or affirmation, and particularly describing the place to be searched, and the persons or things to be seized."

The ultimate standard set forth in the Fourth Amendment is reasonableness. In construing this command, there has been general agreement that,

"except in certain carefully defined classes of cases, a search of private property without proper consent is 'unreasonable' unless it has been authorized by a valid search warrant."

Camara v. Municipal Court, 387 U. S. 523, 387 U. S. 528-529 (1967). See Coolidge v. New Hampshire, 403 U. S. 443, 403 U. S. 454-455 (1971). One class of cases which constitutes at least a partial exception to this general rule is automobile searches. Although vehicles are "effects" within the meaning of the Fourth Amendment, "for the purposes of the Fourth Amendment, there is a constitutional difference between houses and cars." Chambers v. Maroney, 399 U. S. 42, 399 U. S. 52 (1970). See Carroll v. United States, 267 U. S. 132, 267 U. S. 153-154 (1925). In Cooper v. California, 386 U. S. 58, 386 U. S. 59 (1967), the identical proposition was stated in different language:

"We made it clear in Preston [v. United States] that whether a search and seizure is unreasonable within the meaning of the Fourth Amendment depends upon the facts and circumstances of each case, and pointed out, in particular, that searches of cars that are constantly movable may make the search of a car without a warrant a reasonable one although the result might be the opposite in a search of a home, a store, or other fixed piece of property. 376 U.S. at 376 U. S. 366-367."

While these general principles are easily stated, the decisions of this Court dealing with the constitutionality of warrantless searches, especially when those searches are of vehicles, suggest that this branch of the law is something less than a seamless web.

Since this Court's decision in Mapp v. Ohio, 367 U. S. 643 (1961), which overruled Wolf v. Colorado, 338 U. S. 25 (1949), and held that the provisions of the Fourth Amendment were applicable to the States through the Due Process Clause of the Fourteenth Amendment, the application of Fourth Amendment standards, originally intended to restrict only the Federal Government, to the States presents some difficulty when searches of automobiles are involved. The contact with vehicles by federal law enforcement officers usually, if not always, involves the detection or investigation of crimes unrelated to the operation of a vehicle. Cases such as Carroll v. United States, supra, and Brinegar v. United States, 338 U. S. 160 (1949), illustrate the typical situations in which federal officials come into contact with and search vehicles. In both cases, members of a special federal unit charged with enforcing a particular federal criminal statute stopped and searched a vehicle when they had probable cause to believe that the operator was violating that statute.

As a result of our federal system of government, however, state and local police officers, unlike federal officers, have much more contact with vehicles for reasons related to the operation of vehicles themselves. All States require vehicles to be registered and operators to be licensed. States and localities have enacted extensive and detailed codes regulating the condition and manner in which motor vehicles may be operated on public streets and highways.

Because of the extensive regulation of motor vehicles and traffic, and also because of the frequency with which a vehicle can become disabled or involved in an accident on public highways, the extent of police-citizen contact involving automobiles will be substantially greater than police-citizen contact in a home or office. Some such contacts will occur because the officer may believe the operator has violated a criminal statute, but many more will not be of that nature. Local police officers, unlike federal officers, frequently investigate vehicle accidents in which there is no claim of criminal liability and engage in what, for want of a better term, may be described as community caretaking functions, totally divorced from the detection, investigation, or acquisition of evidence relating to the violation of a criminal statute.

Although the original justification advanced for treating automobiles differently from houses, insofar as warrantless searches of automobiles by federal officers was concerned, was the vagrant and mobile nature of the former, Carroll v. United States, supra; Brinegar v. United States, supra; cf. Coolidge v. New Hampshire, supra; Chambers v. Maroney, supra, warrantless searches of vehicles by state officers have been sustained in cases in which the possibilities of the vehicle's being removed or evidence in it destroyed were remote, if not nonexistent. See Harris v. United States, 390 U. S. 234 (1968) (District of Columbia police), Cooper v. California, supra. The constitutional difference between searches of and seizures from houses and similar structures and from vehicles stems both from the ambulatory character of the latter and from the fact that extensive, and often noncriminal contact with automobiles will bring local officials in "plain view" of evidence, fruits, or instrumentalities of a crime, or contraband. Cf. United States v. Biswell, 406 U. S. 311 (1972).

Here we must decide whether a "search" of the trunk of the 1967 Ford was unreasonable solely because the local officer had not previously obtained a warrant. And, if that be answered in the negative, we must then determine whether the warrantless search was unreasonable within the meaning of the Fourth and Fourteenth Amendments. In answering these questions, two factual considerations deserve emphasis. First, the police had exercised a form of custody or control over the 1967 Thunderbird. Respondent's vehicle was disabled as a result of the accident, and constituted a nuisance along the highway. Respondent, being intoxicated (and later comatose), could not make arrangements to have the vehicle towed and stored. At the direction of the police, and for elemental reasons of safety, the automobile was towed to a private garage. Second, both the state courts and the District Court found as a fact that the search of the trunk to retrieve the revolver was "standard procedure in [that police] department," to protect the public from the possibility that a revolver would fall into untrained or perhaps malicious hands. Although the trunk was locked, the car was left outside, in a lot seven miles from the police station to which respondent had been taken, and no guard was posted over it. For reasons not apparent from the opinion of the

Court of Appeals, that court concluded that, as "no further evidence was needed to sustain" the drunk driving charge, "[t]he search must therefore have been for incriminating evidence of other offenses." 471 F.2d at 283. While that court was obligated to exercise its independent judgment on the underlying constitutional issue presented by the facts of this case, it was not free on this record to disregard these findings of fact. Particularly in nonmetropolitan jurisdictions such as those involved here, enforcement of the traffic laws and supervision of vehicle traffic may be a large part of a police officer's job. We believe that the Court of Appeals should have accepted, as did the state courts and the District Court, the findings with respect to Officer Weiss' specific motivation and the fact that the procedure he followed was "standard."

The Court of Appeals relied, and respondent now relies, primarily on Preston v. United States, 376 U. S. 364 (1964), to conclude that the warrantless search was unconstitutional and the seized items inadmissible. In that case, the police received a telephone all at 3 a.m. from a caller who stated that "three suspicious men acting suspiciously" had been in a car in the business district of Newport, Kentucky, for five hours; four policemen investigated and, after receiving evasive explanations and learning that the suspects were unemployed and apparently indigent, arrested the three for vagrancy. The automobile was cursorily searched, then towed to a police station and ultimately to a garage, where it was searched after the three men had been booked. That search revealed two revolvers in the glove compartment; a subsequent search of the trunk resulted in the seizure of various items later admitted in a prosecution for conspiracy to rob a federally insured bank. In that case, the respondent attempted to justify the warrantless search of the trunk and seizure of the items therein "as incidental to a lawful arrest." Id. at 376 U. S. 367.

The Court rejected the asserted "search incident" justification for the warrantless search in the following terms:

"But these justifications are absent where a search is remote in time or place from the arrest. Once an accused is under arrest and in custody, then a search made at another place, without a warrant is simply not incident to the arrest."

Ibid. It would be possible to interpret Preston broadly, and to argue that it stands for the proposition that, on those facts there could have been no constitutional justification advanced for the search. But we take the opinion as written, and hold that it stands only for the proposition that the search challenged there could not be justified as one incident to an arrest. See Chambers v. Maroney, supra; Cooper v. California, supra. We believe that the instant case is controlled by principles that may be extrapolated from Harris v. United States, supra, and Cooper v. California, supra.

In Harris, petitioner was arrested for robbery. As petitioner's car had been identified leaving the site of the robbery, it was impounded as evidence. A regulation of the District of Columbia Police Department required that an impounded vehicle be searched, that all valuables be removed, and that a tag detailing certain information be placed on the vehicle. In compliance with this regulation, and without a warrant, an officer searched the car and, while opening one of the doors, spotted an automobile registration card, belonging to the victim, lying face up on the metal door stripping. This item was introduced into evidence at petitioner's trial for robbery. In rejecting the contention that the evidence was inadmissible, the Court stated:

"The admissibility of evidence found as a result of a search under the police regulation is not presented by this case. The precise and detailed findings of the District Court, accepted by the Court of Appeals, were to the effect that the discovery of the card was not the result of a search of the car, but of a measure taken to protect the car while it was in police custody. Nothing in the Fourth Amendment requires the police to obtain a warrant in these narrow circumstances."

"Once the door had lawfully been opened, the registration card . . . was plainly visible. It has long been settled that objects falling in the plain view of an officer who has a right to be in the position to have that view are subject to seizure and may be introduced in evidence."

390 U.S. at 390 U. S. 236.

In Cooper, the petitioner was arrested for selling heroin, and his car impounded pending forfeiture proceedings. A week later, a police officer searched the car and found, in the glove compartment, incriminating evidence subsequently admitted at petitioner's trial. This Court upheld the validity of the warrantless search and seizure with the following language:

"This case is not Preston, nor is it controlled by it. Here, the officers seized petitioner's car because they were required to do so by state law. They seized it because of the crime for which they arrested petitioner. They seized it to impound it, and they had to keep it until forfeiture proceedings were concluded. Their subsequent search of the car -- whether the State had 'legal title' to it or not -- was closely related to the reason petitioner was arrested, the reason his car had been impounded, and the reason it was being retained. The forfeiture of petitioner's car did not take place until over four months after it was lawfully seized. It would be unreasonable to hold that the police, having to retain the car in their custody for such a length of time, had no right, even for their own protection, to search it."

386 U.S. at 386 U. S. 61-62.

These decisions, while not on all fours with the instant case, lead us to conclude that the intrusion into the trunk of the 1967 Thunderbird at the garage was not unreasonable within the meaning of the Fourth and Fourteenth Amendments solely because a warrant had not been obtained by Officer Weiss after he left the hospital. The police did not have actual, physical custody of the vehicle, as in Harris and Cooper, but the vehicle had been towed there at the officers' directions. These officers in a rural area were simply reacting to the effect of an accident -- one of the recurring practical situations that results from the operation of motor vehicles and with which local police officers must deal every day. The Thunderbird was not parked adjacent to the dwelling place of the owner, as in Coolidge v. New Hampshire, 403 U. S. 443 (1971), nor simply momentarily unoccupied on a street. Rather, like an obviously abandoned vehicle, it represented a nuisance, and there is no suggestion in the record that the officers' action in exercising control over it by having it towed away was unwarranted either in terms of state law or sound police procedure.

In Harris, the justification for the initial intrusion into the vehicle was to safeguard the owner's property, and in Cooper, it was to guarantee the safety of the custodians. Here, the justification, while different, was as immediate and constitutionally reasonable as those in Harris and Cooper: concern for the safety of the general public who might be endangered if an intruder removed a revolver from the trunk of the vehicle. The record contains uncontradicted testimony to support the findings of the state courts and District Court. Furthermore, although there is no record basis for discrediting such testimony, it was corroborated by the circumstantial fact that, at the time the search was conducted, Officer Weiss was ignorant of the fact that a murder, or any other crime, had been committed. While perhaps, in a metropolitan area, the responsibility to the general public might have been discharged by the posting of a police guard during the night, what might be normal police procedure in such an area may be neither normal nor possible in Kewaskum, Wisconsin. The fact that the protection of the public might, in the abstract, have been accomplished by "less intrusive" means does not, by itself, render the search unreasonable. Cf. Chambers v. Maroney, supra.

The Court's previous recognition of the distinction between motor vehicles and dwelling places leads us to conclude that the type of caretaking "search" conducted here of a vehicle that was neither in the custody nor on the premises of its owner, and that had been placed where it was by virtue of lawful police action, was not unreasonable solely because a warrant had not been obtained. The Framers of the Fourth Amendment have given us only the general standard of "unreasonableness" as a guide in determining whether searches and seizures meet the standard of that Amendment in those cases where a warrant is not required. Very little that has been said in our previous decisions, see Cooper v. California, supra, Harris v. United States, supra, Chambers v. Maroney, supra, and very little that we might say here can usefully refine the language of the Amendment itself in order to evolve some detailed formula for judging cases such as this. Where, as here, the trunk of an automobile, which the officer reasonably believed to contain a gun, was vulnerable to intrusion by vandals, we hold that the search was not "unreasonable" within the meaning of the Fourth and Fourteenth Amendments.

III

The Wisconsin Supreme Court ruled that the sock and the portion of the floor mat were validly seized from the 1960 Dodge. The Fond du Lac county officer who looked through the window of the Dodge after McKinney's body had been found saw the bloody seat and briefcase, but not the sock or floor mat. Consequently, these two items were not listed in the application for the warrant, but the Dodge was the item "particularly described" to be searched in the warrant. The

warrant was validly issued, and the police were authorized to search the car. The reasoning of the Wisconsin Supreme Court was that, although these items were not listed to be seized in the warrant, the warrant was valid and, in executing it, the officers discovered the sock and mat in plain view, and therefore could constitutionally seize them without a warrant.

The Court of Appeals held that the seizure of the two items on September 13 could not be justified under the plain view doctrine. The reasoning of that court hinged on its understanding that the warrant to search the Dodge had been returned and was functus officio by the time Officer Mauer of the Crime Laboratory came upon the sock and the floor mat. The court stated:

"There was no continuing authority under the warrant issued the previous night [the 12th]. First, these items were not described in the warrant, and presumably were not observed that night [the 12th]. Second, when the warrant was returned -- before Mauer came on the scene -- it was functus officio. A 'new ball game,' so to speak, began when Mauer made his 'inspection.'"

471 F.2d at 286.

The record is so indisputably clear that the return of the warrant was filed on the 14th, not sometime prior to Mauer's search on the 13th, that we are somewhat at a loss to understand how the Court of Appeals arrived at its factual conclusion. The warrant to search the Dodge was issued on the 12th, and, although a return of the warrant was prepared by a Fond du Lac County officer at some time on the 13th (whether before or after Mauer's search is impossible to determine), it was not filed in the state court until the 14th, at which time a hearing was held. The seizures of the sock and the floor mat occurred while a valid warrant was outstanding, and thus could not be considered unconstitutional under the theory advanced below. As these items were constitutionally seized, we do not deem it constitutionally significant that they were not listed in the return of the warrant. The ramification of that "defect," if such it was, is purely a question of state law.

We therefore need not reach the question of whether the seizure of the two items from the Dodge would have been valid because the entire car had been validly seized as evidence and impounded pursuant to a valid warrant, cf. Harris v. United States, supra; Cooper v. California, supra, or whether a search of the back seat of this car, located as it was in an open field, required a search warrant at all. See Hester v. United States, 265 U. S. 57, 265 U. S. 59 (1924)

The judgment of the Court of Appeals is Reversed.

* Petitioner argued before this Court that unlocking the trunk of the Ford did not constitute a "search" within the meaning of the Fourth Amendment. The thesis is that only an intrusion into an area in which an individual has a reasonable expectation of privacy, with the specific intent of discovering evidence of a crime, constitutes a search. Compare Haerr v. United States, 240 F.2d 533 (CA5 1957), with District of Columbia v. Little, 85 U.S.App.D.C. 242, 178 F.2d 13 (1949), aff'd on other grounds, 339 U. S. 1 (1950). But see Camara v. Municipal Court, 387 U. S. 523 (1967). Arguing that the officer's conduct constituted an "inspection," rather than a "search," petitioner relies on our decision in Harris v. United States, 390 U. S. 234 (1968), to validate the initial intrusion into the trunk, and then the plain view doctrine to justify the warrantless seizure of the items.

We need not decide this issue. Petitioner conceded in the Court of Appeals that this intrusion was a search. Inasmuch as we believe that Harris and other decisions control this case even if the intrusion is characterized as a search, we need not deal with petitioner's belated contention.

US v. Calandra (Jan 8, 1974) [Notes omitted]

MR. JUSTICE POWELL delivered the opinion of the Court.

This case presents the question whether a witness summoned to appear and testify before a grand jury may refuse to answer questions on the ground that they are based on evidence obtained from an unlawful search and seizure. The issue is of considerable importance to the administration of criminal Justice.

I

On December 11, 1970, federal agents obtained a warrant authorizing a search of respondent John Calandra's place of business, the Royal Machine & Tool Co. in Cleveland, Ohio. The warrant was issued in connection with an extensive investigation of suspected illegal gambling operations. It specified that the object of the search was the discovery and seizure of bookmaking records and wagering paraphernalia. A master affidavit submitted in support of the application for the warrant contained information derived from statements by confidential informants to the Federal Bureau of Investigation (FBI), from physical surveillance conducted by FBI agents, and from court-authorized electronic surveillance. [1]

The Royal Machine & Tool Co. occupies a two-story building. The first floor consists of about 13,000 square feet, and houses industrial machinery and inventory. The second floor contains a general office area of about 1,500 square feet and a small office occupied by Calandra, president of the company, and his secretary. On December 15, 1970, federal agents executed the warrant directed at Calandra's place of business and conducted a thorough, four-hour search of the premises. The record reveals that the agents spent more than three hours searching Calandra's office and files.

Although the agents found no gambling paraphernalia, one discovered, among certain promissory notes, a card indicating that Dr. Walter Loveland had been making periodic payments to Calandra. The agent stated in an affidavit that he was aware that the United States Attorney's office for the Northern District of Ohio was investigating possible violations of 18 U.S.C. §§ 892, 893, and 894, dealing with extortionate credit transactions, and that Dr. Loveland had been the victim of a "loansharking" enterprise then under investigation. The agent concluded that the card bearing Dr. Loveland's name was a loansharking record, and therefore had it seized along with various other items, including books and records of the company, stock certificates, and address books.

On March 1, 1971, a special grand jury was convened in the Northern District of Ohio to investigate possible loansharking activities in violation of federal laws. The grand jury subpoenaed Calandra in order to ask him questions based on the evidence seized during the search of his place of business on December 15, 1970. Calandra appeared before the grand jury on August 17, 1971, but refused to testify, invoking his Fifth Amendment privilege against self-incrimination. The Government then requested the District Court to grant Calandra transactional immunity pursuant to 18 U.S.C. § 2514. Calandra requested and received a postponement of the hearing on the Government's application for the immunity order so that he could prepare a motion to suppress the evidence seized in the search.

Calandra later moved pursuant to Fed.Rule Crim.Proc. 41(e) for suppression and return of the seized evidence on the grounds that the affidavit supporting the warrant was insufficient, and that the search exceeded the scope of the warrant. On August 27, the District Court held a hearing at which Calandra stipulated that he would refuse to answer questions based on the seized materials. On October 1, the District Court entered its judgment ordering the evidence suppressed and returned to Calandra and further ordering that Calandra need not answer any of the grand jury's questions based on the suppressed evidence. 332 F.Supp. 737 (1971). The court held that

"due process . . . allows a witness to litigate the question of whether the evidence which constitutes the basis for the questions asked of him before the grand jury has been obtained in a way which violates the constitutional protection against unlawful search and seizure."

Id. at 742. The court found that the search warrant had been issued without probable cause and that the search had exceeded the scope of the warrant.

The Court of Appeals for the Sixth Circuit affirmed, holding that the District Court had properly entertained the suppression motion and that the exclusionary rule may be invoked by a witness before the grand jury to bar questioning based on evidence obtained in an unlawful search and seizure. [2] 465 F.2d 1218 (1972). The offer to grant Calandra immunity was deemed irrelevant. Id. at 1221.

We granted the Government's petition for certiorari, 410 U.S. 925 (1973). We now reverse.

II

The institution of the grand jury is deeply rooted in Anglo-American history. [3] In England, the grand jury served for centuries both as a body of accusers sworn to discover and present for trial persons suspected of criminal wrongdoing and as a protector of citizens against arbitrary and oppressive governmental action. In this country, the Founders thought the grand jury so essential to basic liberties that they provided in the Fifth Amendment that federal prosecution for serious crimes can only be instituted by "a presentment or indictment of a Grand Jury." Cf. Costello v. United

States, 350 U. S. 359, 350 U. S. 361-362 (1956). The grand jury's historic functions survive to this day. Its responsibilities continue to include both the determination whether there is probable cause to believe a crime has been committed and the protection of citizens against unfounded criminal prosecutions. Branzburg v. Hayes, 408 U. S. 665, 408 U. S. 686-687 (1972).

Traditionally, the grand jury has been accorded wide latitude to inquire into violations of criminal law. No judge presides to monitor its proceedings. It deliberates in secret, and may determine alone the course of its inquiry. The grand jury may compel the production of evidence or the testimony of witnesses as it considers appropriate, and its operation generally is unrestrained by the technical procedural and evidentiary rules governing the conduct of criminal trials.

"It is a grand inquest, a body with powers of investigation and inquisition, the scope of whose inquiries is not to be limited narrowly by questions of propriety or forecasts of the probable result of the investigation, or by doubts whether any particular individual will be found properly subject to an accusation of crime."

Blair v. United States, 250 U. S. 273, 250 U. S. 282 (1919).

The scope of the grand jury's powers reflects its special role in insuring fair and effective law enforcement. A grand jury proceeding is not an adversary hearing in which the guilt or innocence of the accused is adjudicated. Rather, it is an ex parte investigation to determine whether a crime has been committed and whether criminal proceedings should be instituted against any person. The grand jury's investigative power must be broad if its public responsibility is adequately to be discharged. Branzburg v. Hayes, supra, at 408 U. S. 700; Costello v. United States, supra, at 350 U. S. 364.

In Branzburg, the Court had occasion to reaffirm the importance of the grand jury's role:

"[T]he investigation of crime by the grand jury implements a fundamental governmental role of securing the safety of the person and property of the citizen. . . ."

408 U.S. at 408 U. S. 700.

"The role of the grand jury as an important instrument of effective law enforcement necessarily includes an investigatory function with respect to determining whether a crime has been committed and who committed it. . . . 'When the grand jury is performing its investigatory function into a general problem area . . . , society's interest is best served by a thorough and extensive investigation.' Wood v. Georgia, 370 U. S. 375, 370 U. S. 392 (1962). A grand jury investigation 'is not fully carried out until every available clue has been run down and all witnesses examined in every proper way to find if a crime has been committed.' United States v. Stone, 429 F.2d 138, 140 (CA2 1970). Such an investigation may be triggered by tips, rumors, evidence proffered by the prosecutor, or the personal knowledge of the grand jurors. Costello v. United States, 350 U.S. at 350 U. S. 362. It is only after the grand jury has examined the evidence that a determination of whether the proceeding will result in an indictment can be made. . . ."

Id. at 408 U. S. 701-702.

The grand jury's sources of information are widely drawn, and the validity of an indictment is not affected by the character of the evidence considered. Thus, an indictment valid on its face is not subject to challenge on the ground that the grand jury acted on the basis of inadequate or incompetent evidence, Costello v. United States, supra; Holt v. United States, 218 U. S. 245 (1910); or even on the basis of information obtained in violation of a defendant's Fifth Amendment privilege against self-incrimination, Lawn v. United States, 355 U. S. 339 (1958).

The power of a federal court to compel

persons to appear and testify before a grand jury is also firmly established. Kastigar v. United States, 406 U. S. 441 (1972). The duty to testify has long been recognized as a basic obligation that every citizen owes his Government. Blackmer v. United States, 284 U. S. 421, 284 U. S. 438 (1932); United States v. Bryan, 339 U. S. 323, 339 U. S. 331 (1950). In Branzburg v. Hayes, supra, at 408 U. S. 682 and 408 U. S. 688, the Court noted that "[c]itizens generally are not constitutionally immune from grand jury subpoenas . . . ," and that "the longstanding principle that the public . . . has a right to every man's evidence' . . . is particularly applicable to grand jury proceedings." The duty to testify may on occasion be burdensome, and even embarrassing. It may cause injury to a witness' social and economic status. Yet the duty to testify has been regarded as "so necessary to the administration of justice" that the witness' personal interest in privacy must yield to the public's overriding interest in full disclosure. Blair v. United States, 250 U.S. at 250 U. S. 281. Furthermore, a witness may not interfere with the course of the grand jury's inquiry. He "is not entitled to urge objections of incompetency or irrelevancy, such as a party might raise, for this is no concern of his." Id. at 250 U. S. 282. Nor is he entitled "to challenge the authority of the court or of the grand jury" or "to set limits to the investigation that the grand jury may conduct."

Of course, the grand jury's subpoena power is not unlimited. [4] It may consider incompetent evidence, but it may not itself violate a valid privilege, whether established by the Constitution, statutes, or the common law. Branzburg v. Hayes, supra; United States v. Bryan, supra; Blackmer v. United States, supra; 8 J. Wigmore, Evidence §§ 2290-2391 (McNaughton rev. ed.1961). Although, for example, an indictment based on evidence obtained in violation of a defendant's Fifth Amendment privilege is nevertheless valid, Lawn v. United States, supra,

the grand jury may not force a witness to answer questions in violation of that constitutional guarantee. Rather, the grand jury may override a Fifth Amendment claim only if the witness is granted immunity coextensive with the privilege against self-incrimination. Kastigar v. United States, supra. Similarly, a grand jury may not compel a person to produce books and papers that would incriminate him. Boyd v. United States, 116 U. S. 616, 116 U. S. 633-635 (1886). Cf. Couch v. United States, 409 U. S. 322 (1973). The grand jury is also without power to invade a legitimate privacy interest protected by the Fourth Amendment. A grand jury's subpoena duces tecum will be disallowed if it is "far too sweeping in its terms to be regarded as reasonable" under the Fourth Amendment. Hale v. Henkel, 201 U. S. 43, 201 U. S. 76 (1906). Judicial supervision is properly exercised in such cases to prevent the wrong before it occurs.

III

In the instant case, the Court of Appeals held that the exclusionary rule of the Fourth Amendment limits the grand jury's power to compel a witness to answer questions based on evidence obtained from a prior unlawful search and seizure. The exclusionary rule was adopted to effectuate the Fourth Amendment right of all citizens "to be secure in their persons, houses, papers, and effects, against unreasonable searches and seizures. . . ." Under this rule, evidence obtained in violation of the Fourth Amendment cannot be used in a criminal proceeding against the victim of the illegal search and seizure. Weeks v. United States, 232 U. S. 383 (1914); Mapp v. Ohio, 367 U. S. 643 (1961). This prohibition applies as well to the fruits of the illegally seized evidence. Wong Sun v. United States, 371 U. S. 471 (1963); Silverthorne Lumber Co. v. United States, 251 U. S. 385 (1920).

The purpose of the exclusionary rule is not to redress the injury to the privacy of the search victim:

"[T]he ruptured privacy of the victims' homes and effects cannot be restored. Reparation comes too late."

Linkletter v. Walker, 381 U. S. 618, 381 U. S. 637 (1965). Instead, the rule's prime purpose is to deter future unlawful police conduct and thereby effectuate the guarantee of the Fourth Amendment against unreasonable searches and seizures:

"The rule is calculated to prevent, not to repair. Its purpose is to deter -- to compel respect for the constitutional guaranty in the only effectively available way -- by removing the incentive to disregard it."

Elkins v. United States, 364 U. S. 206, 364 U. S. 217 (1960).

Accord, Mapp v. Ohio, supra, at 367 U. S. 656; Tehan v. Schott, 382 U. S. 406, 382 U. S. 416 (1966); Terry v. Ohio, 392 U. S. 1, 392 U. S. 29 (1968). In sum, the rule is a judicially created remedy designed to safeguard Fourth Amendment rights generally through its deterrent effect, rather than a personal constitutional right of the party aggrieved. [5]

Despite its broad deterrent purpose, the exclusionary rule has never been interpreted to proscribe the use of illegally seized evidence in all proceedings or against all persons. As with any remedial device, the application of the rule has been restricted to those areas where its remedial objectives are thought most efficaciously served. The balancing process implicit in this approach is expressed in the contours of the standing requirement. Thus, standing to invoke the exclusionary rule has been confined to situations where the Government seeks to use such evidence to incriminate the victim of the unlawful search. Brown v. United States, 411 U. S. 223 (1973); Alderman v. United States, 394 U. S. 165 (1969); Won Sun v. United States, supra; Jones v. United States, 362 U. S. 257 (1960). This standing rule is premised on a recognition that the need for deterrence, and hence the rationale for excluding the evidence, are strongest where the Government's unlawful conduct would result in imposition of a criminal sanction on the victim of the search. [6]

IV

In deciding whether to extend the exclusionary rule to grand jury proceedings, we must weigh the potential injury to the historic role and functions of the grand jury against the potential benefits of the rule as applied in this context. It is evident that this extension of the exclusionary rule would seriously impede the grand jury. Because the grand jury does not finally adjudicate guilt or innocence, it has traditionally been allowed to pursue its investigative and accusatorial functions unimpeded by the evidentiary and procedural restrictions applicable to a criminal trial. Permitting witnesses to invoke the exclusionary rule before a grand jury would precipitate adjudication of issues hitherto reserved for the trial on the merits, and would delay and disrupt grand jury proceedings. Suppression hearings would halt the orderly progress of an investigation, and might necessitate extended litigation of issues only tangentially related to the grand jury's primary objective. [7] The probable result would be "protracted interruption of grand jury proceedings," Gelbard v. United States, 408 U. S. 41, 408 U. S. 70 (1972) (WHITE, J., concurring), effectively transforming them into preliminary trials on the merits. In some cases, the delay might be fatal to the enforcement of the criminal law. Just last Term, we reaffirmed our disinclination to allow litigious interference with grand jury proceedings:

"Any holding that would saddle a grand jury with mini-trials and preliminary showings would assuredly impede its investigation and frustrate the public's interest in the fair and expeditious administration of the criminal laws."

United States v. Dionisio, 410 U. S. 1, 410 U. S. 17 (1973). Cf. United States v. Ryan, 402 U. S. 530 (1971); Cobbledick v. United States, 309 U. S. 323 (1940). In sum, we believe that allowing a grand jury witness to invoke the exclusionary rule would unduly interfere with the effective and expeditious discharge of the grand jury's duties.

Against this potential damage to the role and functions of the grand jury, we must weigh the benefits to be derived from this proposed extension of the exclusionary rule. Suppression of the use of illegally seized evidence against the search victim in a criminal trial is thought to be an important method of effectuating the Fourth Amendment. But it does not follow that the Fourth Amendment requires adoption of every proposal that might deter police misconduct. In Alderman v. United States, 394 U.S. at 394 U. S. 174-175, for example, this Court declined to extend the exclusionary rule to one who was not the victim of the unlawful search:

"The deterrent values of preventing he incrimination of those whose rights the police have violated have been considered sufficient to justify the suppression of probative evidence even though the case against the defendant is weakened or destroyed. We adhere to that judgment. But we are not convinced that the additional benefits of extending the exclusionary rule to other defendants would justify further encroachment upon the public interest in prosecuting those accused of crime and having them acquitted or convicted on the basis of all the evidence which exposes the truth."

We think this observation equally applicable in the present context.

Any incremental deterrent effect which might be achieved by extending the rule to grand jury proceedings is uncertain, at best. Whatever deterrence of police misconduct may result from the exclusion of illegally seized evidence from criminal trials, it is unrealistic to assume that application of the rule to grand jury proceedings would significantly further that goal. Such an extension would deter only police investigation consciously directed toward the discovery of evidence solely for use in a grand jury investigation. The incentive to disregard the requirement of the Fourth Amendment solely to obtain an indictment from a grand jury is substantially negated by the inadmissibility of the illegally seized evidence in a subsequent criminal prosecution of the search victim. For the most part, a prosecutor would be unlikely to request an indictment where a conviction could not be obtained. We therefore decline to embrace a view that would achieve a speculative and undoubtedly minimal advance in the deterrence of police misconduct at the expense of substantially impeding the role of the grand jury. [8]

V

Respondent also argues that each and every question based on evidence obtained from an illegal search and seizure constitutes a fresh and independent violation of the witness' constitutional rights. [9] Ordinarily, of course, a witness has no right of privacy before the grand jury. Absent some recognized privilege of confidentiality, every man owes his testimony. He may invoke his Fifth Amendment privilege against compulsory self-incrimination, but he may not decline to answer on the grounds that his responses might prove embarrassing or result in an unwelcome disclosure of his personal affairs. Blair v. United States, 250 U. S. 273 (1919). Respondent's claim must be, therefore, not merely that the grand jury's questions invade his privacy but that, because those questions are based on illegally obtained evidence, they somehow constitute distinct violations of his Fourth Amendment rights. We disagree.

The purpose of the Fourth Amendment is to prevent unreasonable governmental intrusions into the privacy of one's person, house, papers, or effects. The wrong condemned is the unjustified governmental invasion of these areas of an individual's life. That wrong, committed in this case, is fully accomplished by the original search without probable cause. Grand jury questions based on evidence obtained thereby involve no independent governmental invasion of one's person, house, papers, or effects, but rather the usual abridgment of personal privacy common to all grand jury questioning. Questions based on illegally obtained evidence are only a derivative use of the product of a past unlawful search and seizure. They work no new Fourth Amendment wrong. Whether such derivative use of illegally obtained evidence by a grand jury should be proscribed presents a question, not of rights, but of remedies.

In the usual context of a criminal trial, the defendant is entitled to the suppression of not only the evidence obtained through an unlawful search and seizure, but also any derivative use of that evidence. The prohibition of the exclusionary rule must reach such derivative use if it is to fulfill its function of deterring police misconduct. In the context of a grand jury proceeding, we believe that the damage to that institution from the unprecedented extension of the exclusionary rule urged by respondent outweighs the benefit of any possible incremental deterrent effect. Our conclusion necessarily controls both the evidence seized during the course of an unlawful search and seizure and any question or evidence derived therefrom (the fruits of the unlawful search). [10] The same considerations of logic and policy apply to both the fruits of an unlawful search and seizure and derivative use of that evidence, and we do not distinguish between them. [11]

The judgment of the Court of Appeals is Reversed.

Cardwell v. Lewis (June 17, 1974) [Notes omitted]

MR. JUSTICE BLACKMUN announced the judgment of the Court and an opinion in which the CHIEF JUSTICE, MR. JUSTICE WHITE, and MR. JUSTICE REHNQUIST join.

This case presents the issue of the legality, under the Fourth and Fourteenth Amendments, of a warrantless seizure of an automobile and the examination of its exterior at a police impoundment area after the car had been removed from a public parking lot.

Evidence obtained upon this examination was introduced at the respondent's state court trial for first-degree murder. He was convicted. The Federal District Court, on a habeas corpus application, ruled that the examination was a search violative of the Fourth and Fourteenth Amendments. 354 F.Supp. 26 (SD Ohio 1972). The United States Court of Appeals for the Sixth Circuit affirmed. 476 F.2d 467 (1973). We granted certiorari, 414 U.S. 1062 (1973), and now conclude that, under the circumstances of this case, there was no violation of the protection afforded by the Amendments.

I

In 1968, respondent Arthur Ben Lewis, Jr., was tried and convicted by a jury in an Ohio state court for the first-degree murder of Paul Radcliffe. On appeal, the Supreme Court of Ohio affirmed the judgment of conviction. State v. Lewis, 22 Ohio St.2d 125, 258 N.E.2d 445 (1970). This Court denied review. Lewis v. Ohio, 400 U.S. 959 (1970).

On respondent's federal habeas application, the District Court, from the record and after an evidentiary hearing, adduced the following facts:

On the afternoon of July 19, 1967, Radcliffe's body was found near his car on the banks of the Olentangy River in Delaware County, Ohio. The car had gone over the embankment and had come to rest in brush. Radcliffe had died from shotgun wounds. Casts were made of tire tracks at the scene, and foreign paint scrapings were removed from the right rear fender of Radcliffe's automobile.

Within five days of Radcliffe's death, the investigation began to focus upon respondent Lewis. It was learned that Lewis knew Radcliffe. Lewis had been negotiating the sale of a business and had executed a contract of sale. The purchaser, Jack Smith, employed Radcliffe,. an accountant, to examine Lewis' books. Police went to Lewis' place of business to question him, and there observed the model and color of his car in the thought that it might have been used to push the Radcliffe vehicle over the embankment. Not until several months later, however, in late September, was Lewis again questioned. On October 9, he was asked to appear the next morning at the Office of the Division of Criminal Activities in Columbus for further interrogation.

On October 10, at 8 am., a warrant for respondent's arrest was obtained. [1] The District Court found that at this time, in addition to probable cause for the arrest, the police also had probable cause to believe that Lewis' car was used in the commission of the crime. An automobile similar to his had been observed leaving the scene; the color of his vehicle was similar to the color of the paint scrapings from the victim's car; in a telephone call to Mrs. Smith, made by a person who said he was Radcliffe but proved not to be, [2] the caller made statements that, if true, would benefit only Lewis; he had had body repair work done on the grille, hood, right front fender, and other parts of his car on the day following the crime; and the victim's desk calendar for the day of his death showed the notation, "Call Ben Lewis." [3]

Respondent Lewis complied with the request to appear. He drove his car to the Activities Office, placed it in a public commercial parking lot a half block away, and arrived shortly after 10 a.m. Although the police were in possession of the arrest warrant for the entire period that Lewis was present, he was not served with that warrant or arrested until late that, afternoon, at approximately 5 p.m. Two hours earlier, Lewis had been permitted to call his lawyer, and two attorneys were present on his behalf in the office at the time of the formal arrest. Upon the arrest, Lewis' car keys and the parking lot claim check were released to the police. A tow truck was dispatched to remove the car from the parking lot to the police impoundment lot.

The impounded car was examined the next day by a technician from the Ohio Bureau of Criminal Investigation. The tread of its right rear tire was found to match the cast of a tire impression made at the scene of the crime. [4] The technician testified that, in his opinion, the foreign paint on the fender of Radcliffe's car was not different from the paint samples taken from respondent's vehicle, that is, there was no difference in color, texture, or order of layering of the paint.

The District Court concluded that the seizure and examination of Lewis' car were violative of the Fourth and Fourteenth Amendments, and that the evidence obtained therefrom should have been excluded at the state court trial. The court, accordingly, issued a writ of habeas corpus requiring the State to "initiate action for a new trial of" respondent within 90 days or, in the alternative, to release him. 354 F.Supp. at 44. The Court of Appeals, in affirming, held that the scraping of paint from the exterior of Lewis' car was, in fact, a search within the meaning of the Fourth Amendment; that there was no consent to that search; that it was not incident to Lewis' arrest; and that the seizure of the car could not be justified on the ground that the vehicle was an instrumentality of the crime in plain view.

II

This case is factually different from prior car search cases decided by this Court. The evidence with which we are concerned is not the product of a "search" that implicates traditional considerations of the owner's privacy interest. It consisted of paint scrapings from the exterior and an observation of the tread of a tire on an operative wheel. The issue, therefore, is whether the examination of an automobile's exterior upon probable cause invades a right to privacy which the interposition of a warrant requirement is meant to protect. This is an issue this Court has not previously addressed.

The common law notion that a warrant to search and seize is dependent upon the assertion of a superior government interest in property, see, e.g., Entick v. Carrington, 19 How.St.Tr. 1029, 1066 (1765), and the proposition that a warrant is valid

"only when a primary right to such search and seizure may be found in the interest which the public or the complainant may have in the property to be seized, or in the right to the possession of it,"

Gouled v. United States, 255 U. S. 298, 255 U. S. 309 (1921), were explicitly rejected as controlling Fourth Amendment considerations in Warden v. Hayden, 387 U. S. 294, 387 U. S. 302-306 (1967). Rather than property rights, the primary object of the Fourth Amendment was determined to be the protection of privacy. Id. at 387 U. S. 305-306. And it had been said earlier:

"The decisions of this Court have time and again underscored the essential purpose of the Fourth Amendment to shield the citizen from unwarranted intrusions into his privacy."

Jones v. United States, 357 U. S. 493, 357 U. S. 498 (1958). See also Schmerber v. California, 384 U. S. 757, 384 U. S. 769-770 (1966); Katz v. United States, 389 U. S. 347, 389 U. S. 350 (1967); United States v. Dionisio, 410 U. S. 1, 410 U. S. 14-15 (1973).

At least since Carroll v. United States, 267 U. S. 132 (1925), the Court has recognized a distinction between the warrantless search and seizure of automobiles or other movable vehicles, on the one hand, and the search of a home or office, on the other. Generally, less stringent warrant requirements have been applied to vehicles. In Chambers v. Maroney, 399 U. S. 42, 399 U. S. 49 (1970), the Court chronicled the development of car searches and seizures. [5] An underlying factor in the Carroll-Chambers line of decisions has been the exigent circumstances that exist in connection with movable vehicles.

"[T]he circumstances that furnish probable cause to search a particular auto for particular articles are most often unforeseeable; moreover, the opportunity to search is fleeting, since a car is readily movable."

Chambers v. Maroney, 399 U.S. at 399 U. S. 50-51. This is strikingly true where the automobile's owner is alerted to police intentions and, as a consequence, the motivation to remove evidence from official grasp is heightened.

There is still another distinguishing factor.

"The search of an automobile is far less intrusive on the rights protected by the Fourth Amendment than the search of one's person or of a building."

Almeida-Sanchez v. United States, 413 U. S. 266, 413 U. S. 279 (1973) (POWELL, J., concurring). One has a lesser expectation of privacy in a motor vehicle because its function is transportation and it seldom serves as one's residence or as the repository of personal effects. A car has little capacity for escaping public scrutiny. It travels public thoroughfares where both its occupants and its contents are in plain view. See People v. Case, 220 Mich. 379, 388-389, 190 N.W. 289, 292 (122). "What a person knowingly exposes to the public, even in his own home or office, is not a subject of Fourth Amendment protection." Katz v. United States, 389 U.S. at 389 U. S. 351; United States v. Dionisio, 410 U.S. at 410 U. S. 14. This is not to say that no part of the interior of an automobile has Fourth Amendment protection; the exercise of a desire to be mobile does not, of course, waive one's right to be free of unreasonable government intrusion. But insofar as Fourth Amendment protection extends to a motor vehicle, it is the right to privacy that is the touchstone of our inquiry.

In the present case, nothing from the interior of the car and no personal effects, which the Fourth Amendment traditionally has been deemed to protect, were searched or seized and introduced in evidence. [6] With the "search" limited to the examination of the tire on the wheel and the taking of paint scrapings from the exterior of the vehicle left in the public parking lot, we fail to comprehend what expectation of privacy was infringed. [7] Stated simply, the invasion of privacy, "if it can be said to exist, is abstract and theoretical." Air Pollution Variance Board v. Western Alfalfa Corp., 416 U. S. 861, 416 U. S. 865 (1974). Under circumstances such as these, where probable cause exists, a warrantless examination of the exterior of a car is not unreasonable under the Fourth and Fourteenth Amendments. [8]

Here, it has been established and is conceded that the police had probable cause to search Lewis' car. An automobile similar in color and model to his car had been seen leaving the scene of the crime. This similarity was corroborated by comparison of the paint scrapings taken from the victim's car with the color and paint of Lewis' automobile. Lewis had had repair work done on his car immediately following the death of the victim. And he had a nexus with Radcliffe on the day of death. All this provided reason to believe that the car was used in the commission of the crime for which Lewis was arrested. Cooper v. California, 386 U. S. 58, 386 U. S. 61 (1967).

III

Concluding, as we have, that the examination of the exterior of the vehicle upon probable cause was reasonable, we have yet to determine whether the prior impoundment of the automobile rendered that examination a violation of the Fourth and Fourteenth Amendments. We do not think that, because the police impounded the car prior to the examination, which they could have made on the spot, there is a constitutional barrier to the use of the evidence obtained thereby. Under the circumstances of this case, the seizure itself was not unreasonable.

Respondent asserts that this case is indistinguishable from Coolidge v. New Hampshire, 403 U. S. 443 (1971). We do not agree. The present case differs from Coolidge both in the scope of the search [9] and in the circumstances of the seizure. Since the Coolidge car was parked on the defendant's driveway, the seizure of that automobile required an entry upon private property. Here, as in Chambers v. Maroney, 399 U. S. 42 (1970), the automobile was seized from a public place where access was not meaningfully restricted. This is, in fact, the ground upon which the Coolidge plurality opinion distinguished Chambers, 403 U.S. at 403 U. S. 463 n. 20. See also Cady v. Dombrowski, 413 U. S. 433, 413 U. S. 446-447 (1973).

In considering whether the lack of a warrant to seize a vehicle invalidates the otherwise legal examination of the car, Chambers is highly pertinent. In Chambers, four men in an automobile were arrested shortly after an armed robbery. The Court concluded that there was probable cause to arrest and probable cause to search the vehicle. The car was taken from the highway to the police station where, some time later, a search producing incriminating evidence, was conducted. We stated:

"For constitutional purposes, we see no difference between, on the one hand, seizing and holding a car before presenting the probable cause issue to a magistrate, and, on the other hand, carrying out an immediate search without a warrant. Given probable cause to search, either course is reasonable under the Fourth

Amendment."

"... The probable cause factor still obtained at the station house, and so did the mobility of the car unless the Fourth Amendment permits a warrantless seizure of the car and the denial of its use to anyone until a warrant is secured. In that event, there is little to choose in terms of practical consequences between an immediate search without a warrant and the car's immobilization until a warrant is obtained."

399 U.S. at 399 U. S. 52.

The fact that the car in Chambers was seized after being stopped on a highway, whereas Lewis' car was seized from a public parking lot, has little, if any, legal significance. [10] The same arguments and considerations of exigency, immobilization on the spot, and posting a guard obtain. In fact, because the interrogation session ended with awareness that Lewis had been arrested and that his car constituted incriminating evidence, the incentive and potential for the car's removal substantially increased. There was testimony at the federal hearing that Lewis asked one of his attorneys to see that his wife and family got the car, and that the attorney relinquished the keys to the police in order to avoid a physical confrontation. 354 F.Supp. at 33. In Chambers, all occupants of the car were in custody and there were no means of relating this fact or the location of the car (if it had not been impounded) to a friend or confederate. Chambers also stated that a search of the car on the spot was impractical because it was dark and the search could not be carefully executed. 399 U.S. at 399 U. S. 52 n. 10. Here too, the seizure facilitated the type of close examination necessary. [11]

Respondent contends that here, unlike Chambers, probable cause to search the car existed for some time prior to arrest and that, therefore, there were no exigent circumstances. Assuming that probable cause previously existed, we know of no case or principle that suggests that the right to

search on probable cause and the reasonableness of seizing a car under exigent circumstances are foreclosed if a warrant was not obtained at the first practicable moment. Exigent circumstances with regard to vehicles are not limited to situations where probable cause is unforeseeable and arises only at the time of arrest. Cf. Chambers, id., at 399 U. S. 50-51. The exigency may arise at any time, and the fact that the police might have obtained a warrant earlier does not negate the possibility of a current situation's necessitating prompt police action. [12] The judgment of the Court of Appeals is reversed.

It is so ordered.

Gerstein v. Pugh (Feb 18, 1975) [Notes omitted]

MR. JUSTICE POWELL delivered the opinion of the Court.

The issue in this case is whether a person arrested and held for trial under a prosecutor's information is constitutionally entitled to a judicial determination of probable cause for pretrial restraint of liberty.

I

In March 1971 respondents Pugh and Henderson were arrested in Dade County, Fla. Each was charged with several offenses under a prosecutor's information.[1] Pugh was denied bail because one of the charges against him carried a potential life sentence, and Henderson remained in custody because he was unable to post a $4,500 bond.

In Florida, indictments are required only for prosecution of capital offenses. Prosecutors may charge all other crimes by information, without a prior preliminary hearing and without obtaining leave of court. Fla. Rule Crim. Proc. 3.140 (a); State v. Hernandez, 217 So. 2d 109 (Fla. 1968); Di Bona v. State, 121 So. 2d 192 (Fla. App. 1960). At the time respondents were arrested, a

Florida rule seemed to authorize adversary preliminary hearings to test probable cause for detention in all cases. Fla. Rule Crim. Proc. 1.122 (before amendment in 1972).

But the Florida courts had held that the filing of an information foreclosed the suspect's right to a preliminary hearing. See State ex rel. Hardy v. Blount, 261 So. 2d 172 (Fla. 1972).[2] They had also held that habeas corpus could not be used, except perhaps in exceptional circumstances, to test the probable cause for detention under an information. See Sullivan v. State ex rel. McCrory, 49 So. 2d 794, 797 (Fla. 1951). The only possible methods for obtaining a judicial determination of probable cause were a special statute allowing a preliminary hearing after 30 days. Fla. Stat. Ann. § 907.045 (1973),[3] and arraignment, which the District Court found was often delayed a month or more after arrest. Pugh v. Rainwater, 332 F. Supp. 1107, 1110 (SD Fla. 1971).[4] As a result, a person charged by information could be detained for a substantial period solely on the decision of a prosecutor.

Respondents Pugh and Henderson filed a class action against Dade Country officials in the Federal District Court,[5] claiming a constitutional right to a judicial hearing on the issue of probable cause and requesting declaratory and injunctive relief.[6] Respondents Turner and Faulk, also in custody under informations, subsequently intervened.[7] Petitioner Gerstein, the State Attorney for Dade County, was one of several defendants.[8]

After an initial delay while the Florida Legislature considered a bill that would have afforded preliminary hearings to persons charged by information, the District Court granted the relief sought. Pugh v. Rainwater, supra. The court certified the case as a class action under Fed. Rule Civ. Proc. 23 (b) (2), and held that the Fourth and Fourteenth Amendments give all arrested persons charged by information a right to a judicial hearing on the question of probable cause. The District Court ordered the Dade County defendants to give the named plaintiffs an immediate preliminary hearing to determine probable cause for further detention.[9] It also ordered them to submit a plan providing preliminary hearings in all cases instituted by information.

The defendants submitted a plan prepared by Sheriff E. Wilson Purdy, and the District Court adopted it with modifications. The final order prescribed a detailed post-arrest procedure. 336 F. Supp. 490 (SD Fla. 1972). Upon arrest the accused would be taken before a magistrate for a "first appearance hearing." The magistrate would explain the charges, advise the accused of his rights, appoint counsel if he was indigent, and proceed with a probable cause determination unless either the prosecutor or the accused was unprepared. If either requested more time, the magistrate would set the date for a "preliminary hearing," to be held within four days if the accused was in custody and within 10 days if he had been released pending trial. The order provided sanctions for failure to hold the hearing at prescribed times. At the "preliminary hearing" the accused would be entitled to counsel, and he would be allowed to confront and cross-examine adverse witnesses, to summon favorable witnesses, and to have a transcript made on request. If the magistrate found no probable cause, the accused would be discharged. He then could not be charged with the same offense by complaint or information, but only by indictment returned within 30 days.

The Court of Appeals for the Fifth Circuit stayed the District Court's order pending appeal, but while the case was awaiting decision, the Dade Country judiciary voluntarily adopted a similar procedure of its own. Upon learning of this development, the Court of Appeals remanded the case for specific findings on the constitutionality of the new Dade County system. Before the District Court issued its findings, however, the Florida

Supreme Court amended the procedural rules governing preliminary hearings statewide, and the parties agreed that the District Court should direct its inquiry to the new rules rather than the Dade County procedures.

Under the amended rules every arrested person must be taken before a judicial officer within 24 hours. Fla. Rule Crim. Proc. 3.130 (b). This "first appearance" is similar to the "first appearance hearing" ordered by the District Court in all respects but the crucial one: the magistrate does not make a determination of probable cause. The rule amendments also changed the procedure for preliminary hearings, restricting them to felony charges and codifying the rule that no hearings are available to persons charged by information or indictment. Rule 3.131; see In re Rule 3.131 (b), Florida Rules of Criminal Procedure, 289 So. 2d 3 (Fla. 1974).

In a supplemental opinion the District Court held that the amended rules had not answered the basic constitutional objection, since a defendant charged by information still could be detained pending trial without a judicial determination of probable cause. 355 F. Supp. 1286 (SD Fla. 1973). Reaffirming its original ruling, the District Court declared that the continuation of this practice was unconstitutional.[10] The Court of Appeals affirmed, 483 F. 2d 778 (1973), modifying the District Court's decree in minor particulars and suggesting that the form of preliminary hearing provided by the amended Florida rules would be acceptable, as long as it was provided to all defendants in custody pending trial. Id., at 788-789.

State Attorney Gerstein petitioned for review, and we granted certiorari because of the importance of the issue.[11] 414 U. S. 1062 (1973). We affirm in part and reverse in part.

II

As framed by the proceedings below, this case presents two issues: whether a person arrested and held for trial on an information is entitled to a judicial determination of probable cause for detention, and if so, whether the adversary hearing ordered by the District Court and approved by the Court of Appeals is required by the Constitution.

A

Both the standards and procedures for arrest and detention have been derived from the Fourth Amendment and its common-law antecedents. See Cupp v. Murphy, 412 U. S. 291, 294-295 (1973); Ex parte Bollman, 4 Cranch 75 (1807); Ex parte Burford, 3 Cranch 448 (1806). The standard for arrest is probable cause, defined in terms of facts and circumstances "sufficient to warrant a prudent man in believing that the [suspect] had committed or was committing an offense." Beck v. Ohio, 379 U. S. 89, 91 (1964). See also Henry v. United States, 361 U. S. 98 (1959); Brinegar v. United States, 338 U. S. 160, 175-176 (1949). This standard, like those for searches and seizures, represents a necessary accommodation between the individual's right to liberty and the State's duty to control crime.

"These long-prevailing standards seek to safeguard citizens from rash and unreasonable interferences with privacy and from unfounded charges of crime. They also seek to give fair leeway for enforcing the law in the community's protection. Because many situations which confront officers in the course of executing their duties are more or less ambiguous, room must be allowed for some mistakes on their part. But the mistakes must be those of reasonable men, acting on facts leading sensibly to their conclusions of probability. The rule of probable cause is a practical, nontechnical conception affording the best compromise that has been found for accommodating these often opposing interests. Requiring more would unduly hamper law enforcement. To allow less would be to leave law-abiding citizens at the mercy of the officers' whim or caprice." Id., at 176.

To implement the Fourth Amendment's protection against unfounded invasions of liberty and privacy, the Court has required that the existence of probable cause be decided by a neutral and detached magistrate whenever possible. The classic statement of this principle appears in Johnson v. United States, 333 U. S. 10, 13-14 (1948):

"The point of the Fourth Amendment, which often is not grasped by zealous officers, is not that it denies law enforcement the support of the usual inferences which reasonable men draw from evidence. Its protection consists in requiring that those inferences be drawn by a neutral and detached magistrate instead of being judged by the officer engaged in the often competitive enterprise of ferreting out crime."

See also Terry v. Ohio, 392 U. S. 1, 20-22 (1968).[12]

Maximum protection of individual rights could be assured by requiring a magistrate's review of the factual justification prior to any arrest, but such a requirement would constitute an intolerable handicap for legitimate law enforcement. Thus, while the Court has expressed a preference for the use of arrest warrants when feasible, Beck v. Ohio, supra, at 96; Wong Sun v. United States, 371 U. S. 471, 479-482 (1963), it has never invalidated an arrest supported by probable cause solely because the officers failed to secure a warrant. See Ker v. California, 374 U. S. 23 (1963); Draper v. United States, 358 U. S. 307 (1959); Trupiano v. United States, 334 U. S. 699, 705 (1948).[13]

Under this practical compromise, a policeman's on-the-scene assessment of probable cause provides legal justification for arresting a person suspected of crime, and for a brief period of detention to take the administrative steps incident to arrest. Once the suspect is in custody, however, the reasons that justify dispensing with the magistrate's neutral judgment evaporate. There no longer is any danger that the suspect will escape or commit further crimes while the police submit their evidence to a magistrate. And, while the State's reasons for taking summary action subside, the suspect's need for a neutral determination of probable cause increases significantly. The consequences of prolonged detention may be more serious than the interference occasioned by arrest. Pretrial confinement may imperil the suspect's job, interrupt his source of income, and impair his family relationships. See R. Goldfarb, Ransom 32-91 (1965); L. Katz, Justice Is the Crime 51-62 (1972). Even pretrial release may be accompanied by burdensome conditions that effect a significant restraint of liberty. See e. g., 18 U. S. C. §§ 3146 (a) (2), (5). When the stakes are this high, the detached judgment of a neutral magistrate is essential if the Fourth Amendment is to furnish meaningful protection from unfounded interference with liberty. Accordingly, we hold that the Fourth Amendment requires a judicial determination of probable cause as a prerequisite to extended restraint of liberty following arrest.

This result has historical support in the common law that has guided interpretation of the Fourth Amendment. See Carroll v. United States, 267 U. S. 132, 149 (1925). At common law it was customary, if not obligatory, for an arrested person to be brought before a justice of the peace shortly after arrest. 2 M. Hale, Pleas of the Crown 77, 81, 95, 121 (1736); 2 W. Hawkins, Pleas of the Crown 116-117 (4th ed. 1762). See also Kurtz v. Moffitt, 115 U. S. 487, 498-499 (1885).[14] The justice of the peace would "examine" the prisoner and the witnesses to determine whether there was reason to believe the prisoner had committed a crime. If there was, the suspect would be committed to jail or bailed pending trial. If not, he would be discharged from custody. 1 M. Hale, supra, at 583-586; 2 W. Hawkins, supra, at 116-119; 1 J. Stephen, History of the Criminal Law of England 233

(1883).[15] The initial determination of probable cause also could be reviewed by higher courts on a writ of habeas corpus. 2 W. Hawkins, supra, at 112-115; 1 J. Stephen, supra, at 243; see Ex parte Bollman, 4 Cranch, at 97-101. This practice furnished the model for criminal procedure in America immediately following the adoption of the Fourth Amendment, see Ex parte Bollman, supra;[16] Ex parte Burford, 3 Cranch 448 (1806); United States v. Hamilton, 3 Dall. 17 (1795), and there are indications that the Framers of the Bill of Rights regarded it as a model for a "reasonable" seizure. See Draper v. United States, 358 U. S., at 317-320 (DOUGLAS, J., dissenting).[17]

B

Under the Florida procedures challenged here, a person arrested without a warrant and charged by information may be jailed or subjected to other restraints pending trial without any opportunity for a probable cause determination.[18] Petitioner defends this practice on the ground that the prosecutor's decision to file an information is itself a determination of probable cause that furnishes sufficient reason to detain a defendant pending trial. Although a conscientious decision that the evidence warrants prosecution affords a measure of protection against unfounded detention, we do not think prosecutorial judgment standing alone meets the requirements of the Fourth Amendment. Indeed, we think the Court's previous decisions compel disapproval of the Florida procedure. In Albrecht v. United States, 273 U. S. 1, 5 (1927), the Court held that an arrest warrant issued solely upon a United States Attorney's information was invalid because the accompanying affidavits were defective. Although the Court's opinion did not explicitly state that the prosecutor's official oath could not furnish probable cause, that conclusion was implicit in the judgment that the arrest was illegal under the Fourth Amendment.[19] More recently, in Coolidge v. New Hampshire, 403 U. S. 443, 449-

453 (1971), the Court held that a prosecutor's responsibility to law enforcement is inconsistent with the constitutional role of a neutral and detached magistrate. We reaffirmed that principle in Shadwick v. City of Tampa, 407 U. S. 345 (1972), and held that probable cause for the issuance of an arrest warrant must be determined by someone independent of police and prosecution. See also United States v. United States District Court, 407 U. S. 297, 317 (1972).[20] The reason for this separation of functions was expressed by Mr. Justice Frankfurter in a similar context:

"A democratic society, in which respect for the dignity of all men is central, naturally guards against the misuse of the law enforcement process. Zeal in tracking down crime is not in itself an assurance of soberness of judgment. Disinterestedness in law enforcement does not alone prevent disregard of cherished liberties. Experience has therefore counselled that safeguards must be provided against the dangers of the overzealous as well as the despotic. The awful instruments of the criminal law cannot be entrusted to a single functionary. The complicated process of criminal justice is therefore divided into different parts, responsibility for which is separately vested in the various participants upon whom the criminal law relies for its vindication." McNabb v. United States, 318 U. S. 332, 343 (1943).

In holding that the prosecutor's assessment of probable cause is not sufficient alone to justify restraint of liberty pending trial, we do not imply that the accused is entitled to judicial oversight or review of the decision to prosecute. Instead, we adhere to the Court's prior holding that a judicial hearing is not prerequisite to prosecution by information. Beck v. Washington, 369 U. S. 541, 545 (1962); Lem Woon v. Oregon, 229 U. S. 586 (1913). Nor do we retreat from the established rule that illegal arrest or detention does not void a subsequent conviction. Frisbie v. Collins, 342 U. S.

519 (1952); Ker v. Illinois, 119 U. S. 436 (1886). Thus, as the Court of Appeals noted below, although a suspect who is presently detained may challenge the probable cause for that confinement, a conviction will not be vacated on the ground that the defendant was detained pending trial without a determination of probable cause. 483 F. 2d, at 786-787. Compare Scarbrough v. Dutton, 393 F. 2d 6 (CA5 1968), with Brown v. Fauntleroy, 143 U. S. App. D. C. 116, 442 F. 2d 838 (1971), and Cooley v. Stone, 134 U. S. App. D. C. 317, 414 F. 2d 1213 (1969).

III

Both the District Court and the Court of Appeals held that the determination of probable cause must be accompanied by the full panoply of adversary safeguards —counsel, confrontation, cross-examination, and compulsory process for witnesses. A full preliminary hearing of this sort is modeled after the procedure used in many states to determine whether the evidence justifies going to trial under an information or presenting the case to a grand jury. See Coleman v. Alabama, 399 U. S. 1 (1970); Y. Kamisar, W. LaFave & J. Israel, Modern Criminal Procedure 957-967, 996-1000 (4th ed. 1974). The standard of proof required of the prosecution is usually referred to as "probable cause," but in some jurisdictions it may approach a prima facie case of guilt. ALI, Model Code of Pre-arraignment Procedure, Commentary on Art. 330, pp. 90-91 (Tent. Draft No. 5, 1972). When the hearing takes this form, adversary procedures are customarily employed. The importance of the issue to both the State and the accused justifies the presentation of witnesses and full exploration of their testimony on cross-examination. This kind of hearing also requires appointment of counsel for indigent defendants. Coleman v. Alabama, supra. And, as the hearing assumes increased importance and the procedures become more complex, the likelihood that it can be held promptly after arrest diminishes. See ALI, Model Code of Pre-arraignment Procedure, supra, at 33-34.

These adversary safeguards are not essential for the probable cause determination required by the Fourth Amendment. The sole issue is whether there is probable cause for detaining the arrested person pending further proceedings. This issue can be determined reliably without an adversary hearing. The standard is the same as that for arrest.[21] That standard—probable cause to believe the suspect has committed a crime—traditionally has been decided by a magistrate in a nonadversary proceeding on hearsay and written testimony, and the Court has approved these informal modes of proof.

"Guilt in a criminal case must be proved beyond a reasonable doubt and by evidence confined to that which long experience in the common-law tradition, to some extent embodied in the Constitution, has crystallized into rules of evidence consistent with that standard. These rules are historically grounded rights of our system, developed to safeguard men from dubious and unjust convictions, with resulting forfeitures of life, liberty and property.

. . . . .

"In dealing with probable cause, however, as the very name implies, we deal with probabilities. These are not technical; they are the factual and practical considerations of everyday life on which reasonable and prudent men, not legal technicians, act. The standard of proof is accordingly correlative to what must be proved." Brinegar v. United States, 338 U. S., at 174-175.

Cf. McCray v. Illinois, 386 U. S. 300 (1967).

The use of an informal procedure is justified not only by the lesser consequences of a probable cause determination but also by the nature of the determination itself. It does not require the fine resolution of conflicting evidence that a reasonable-doubt or even a preponderance standard demands, and credibility determinations are seldom crucial in deciding whether the evidence supports a reasonable belief in guilt. See F. Miller, Prosecution: The Decision to Charge a Suspect with a Crime 64-109 (1969).[22] This is not to say that confrontation and cross-examination might not enhance the reliability of probable cause determinations in some cases. In most cases, however, their value would be too slight to justify holding, as a matter of constitutional principle, that these formalities and safeguards designed for trial must also be employed in making the Fourth Amendment determination of probable cause.[23]

Because of its limited function and its nonadversary character, the probable cause determination is not a "critical stage" in the prosecution that would require appointed counsel. The Court has identified as "critical stages" those pretrial procedures that would impair defense on the merits if the accused is required to proceed without counsel. Coleman v. Alabama, 399 U. S. 1 (1970); United States v. Wade, 388 U. S. 218, 226-227 (1967). In Coleman v. Alabama, where the Court held that a preliminary hearing was a critical stage of an Alabama prosecution, the majority and concurring opinions identified two critical factors that distinguish the Alabama preliminary hearing from the probable cause determination required by the Fourth Amendment. First, under Alabama law the function of the preliminary hearing was to determine whether the evidence justified charging the suspect with an offense. A finding of no probable cause could mean that he would not be tried at all. The Fourth Amendment probable cause determination is addressed only to pretrial custody. To be sure, pretrial custody may affect to some extent the defendant's ability to assist in preparation of his defense, but this does not present the high probability of substantial harm identified as controlling in Wade and Coleman. Second, Alabama allowed the suspect to confront and cross-examine prosecution witnesses at the

preliminary hearing. The Court noted that the suspect's defense on the merits could be compromised if he had no legal assistance for exploring or preserving the witnesses' testimony. This consideration does not apply when the prosecution is not required to produce witnesses for cross-examination.

Although we conclude that the Constitution does not require an adversary determination of probable cause, we recognize that state systems of criminal procedure vary widely. There is no single preferred pretrial procedure and the nature of the probable cause determination usually will be shaped to accord with a State's pretrial procedure viewed as a whole. While we limit our holding to the precise requirement of the Fourth Amendment, we recognize the desirability of flexibility and experimentation by the States. It may be found desirable for example, to make the probable cause determination a the suspect's first appearance before a judicial officer,[24] see McNabb v. United States, 318 U. S., at 342-344, or the determination may be incorporated into the procedure for setting bail or fixing other conditions of pretrial release. In some States, existing procedures may satisfy the requirement of the Fourth Amendment. Others may require only minor adjustment, such as acceleration of existing preliminary hearings. Current proposals for criminal procedure reform suggest other ways of testing probable cause for detention.[25] Whatever procedure a State may adopt, it must provide a fair and reliable determination of probable cause as a condition for any significant pretrial restraint of liberty,[26] and this determination must be made by a judicial officer either before or promptly after arrest.[27]

IV

We agree with the Court of Appeals that the Fourth Amendment requires a timely judicial determination of probable cause as a prerequisite to detention, and we accordingly affirm that much of the judgment. As we do not agree that the Fourth Amendment requires the adversary hearing outlined in the District Court's decree, we reverse in part and remand to the Court of Appeals for further proceedings consistent with this opinion.

It is so ordered.

US v. Brignoni-Ponce (June 30, 1975) [Notes omitted]

MR. JUSTICE POWELL delivered the opinion of the Court.

This case raises questions as to the United States Border Patrol's authority to stop automobiles in areas near the Mexican border. It differs from our decision in Almeida-Sanchez v. United States, 413 U. S. 266 (1973), in that the Border Patrol does not claim authority to search cars, but only to question the occupants about their citizenship and immigration status.

I

As part of its regular traffic-checking operations in southern California, the Border Patrol operates a fixed checkpoint on Interstate Highway 5 south of San Clemente. On the evening of March 11, 1973, the checkpoint was closed because of inclement weather, but two officers were observing northbound traffic from a patrol car parked at the side of the highway. The road was dark, and they were using the patrol car's headlights to illuminate passing cars. They pursued respondent's car and stopped it, saying later that their only reason for doing so was that its three occupants appeared to be of Mexican descent. The officers questioned respondent and his two passengers about their citizenship and learned that the passengers were aliens who had entered the country illegally. All three were then arrested, and respondent was charged with two counts of knowingly transporting illegal immigrants, a violation of § 274(a)(2) of the Immigration and Nationality Act, 66 Stat. 228, 8

U.S.C. § 1324(a)(2). At trial, respondent moved to suppress the testimony of and about the two passengers, claiming that this evidence was the fruit of an illegal seizure. The trial court denied the motion, the aliens testified at trial, and respondent was convicted on both counts.

Respondent's appeal was pending in the Court of Appeals for the Ninth Circuit when we announced our decision in Almeida-Sanchez v. United States, supra, holding that the Fourth Amendment prohibits the use of roving patrols to search vehicles, without a warrant or probable cause, at points removed from the border and its functional equivalents. The Court of Appeals, sitting en banc, held that the stop in this case more closely resembled a roving patrol stop than a stop at a traffic checkpoint, and applied the principles of Almeida-Sanchez. [1]

The court held that the Fourth Amendment, as interpreted in Almeida-Sanchez, forbids stopping a vehicle, even for the limited purpose of questioning its occupants, unless the officers have a "founded suspicion" that the occupants are aliens illegally in the country. The court refused to find that Mexican ancestry alone supported such a "founded suspicion," and held that respondent's motion to suppress should have been granted. [2] 499 F.2d 1109 (1974). We granted certiorari and set the case for oral argument with No. 73-2050, United States v. Ortiz, post, p. 422 U. S. 891, and No. 73-6848, Bowen v. United States, post, p. 422 U. S. 916. 419 U.S. 824 (1974).

The Government does not challenge the Court of Appeals' factual conclusion that the stop of respondent's car was a roving patrol stop, rather than a checkpoint stop. Brief for United States 8. Nor does it challenge the retroactive application of Almeida-Sanchez, supra, Brief for United States 9, or contend that the San Clemente checkpoint is the functional equivalent of the border. The only issue presented for decision is whether a roving patrol may stop a vehicle in an area near the border and question its occupants when the only ground for suspicion is that the occupants appear to be of Mexican ancestry. For the reasons that follow, we affirm the decision of the Court of Appeals.

II

The Government claims two sources of statutory authority for stopping cars without warrants in the border areas. Section 287(a)(1) of the Immigration and Nationality Act, 8 U.S.C. § 1357(a)(1), authorizes any officer or employee of the Immigration and Naturalization Service (INS) without a warrant, "to interrogate any alien or person believed to be an alien as to his right to be or to remain in the United States." There is no geographical limitation on this authority. The Government contends that, at least in the areas adjacent to the Mexican border, a person's apparent Mexican ancestry alone justifies belief that he or she is an alien and satisfies the requirement of this statute. Section 287(a)(3) of the Act, 8 U.S.C. § 1357(a)(3), authorizes agents, without a warrant,

"within a reasonable distance from any external boundary of the United States, to board and search for aliens any vessel within the territorial waters of the United States and any railway car, aircraft, conveyance, or vehicle. . . ."

Under current regulations, this authority may be exercised anywhere within 100 miles of the border. 8 CFR § 287.1(a) (1975). The Border Patrol interprets the statute as granting authority to stop moving vehicles and question the occupants about their citizenship, even when its officers have no reason to believe that the occupants are aliens or that other aliens may be concealed in the vehicle. [3] But "no Act of Congress can authorize a violation of the Constitution," Almeida-Sanchez, supra at 413 U. S. 272, and we must decide whether the Fourth Amendment allows such random vehicle stops in the border areas.

III

The Fourth Amendment applies to all seizures of the person, including seizures that involve only a brief detention short of traditional arrest. Davis v. Mississippi, 394 U. S. 721 (1969); Terry v. Ohio, 392 U. S. 1, 392 U. S. 16-19 (1968). "[W]henever a police officer accosts an individual and restrains his freedom to walk away, he has seized' that person," id. at 392 U. S. 16, and the Fourth Amendment requires that the seizure be "reasonable." As with other categories of police action subject to Fourth Amendment constraints, the reasonableness of such seizures depends on a balance between the public interest and the individual's right to personal security free from arbitrary interference by law officers. Id. at 392 U. S. 20-21; Camara v. Municipal Court, 387 U. S. 523, 387 U. S. 536-537 (1967).

The Government makes a convincing demonstration that the public interest demands effective measures to prevent the illegal entry of aliens at the Mexican border. Estimates of the number of illegal immigrants in the United States vary widely. A conservative estimate in 1972 produced a figure of about one million, but the INS now suggests there may be as many as 10 or 12 million aliens illegally in the country. [4] Whatever the number, these aliens create significant economic and social problems, competing with citizens and legal resident aliens for jobs, and generating extra demand for social services. The aliens themselves are vulnerable to exploitation because they cannot complain of substandard working conditions without risking deportation. See generally Hearings on Illegal Aliens before Subcommittee No. 1 of the House Committee on the Judiciary, 92d Cong., 1st and 2d Sess., ser. 13, pts. 1-5 (1971-1972).

The Government has estimated that 85% of the aliens illegally in the country are from Mexico. United States v. Baca, 368 F.Supp. 398, 402 (SD Cal 1973). [5] The Mexican border is almost 2,000 miles long, and even a vastly reinforced Border Patrol would find it impossible to prevent illegal border crossings. Many aliens cross the Mexican border on foot, miles away from patrolled areas, and then purchase transportation from the border area to inland cities, where they find jobs and elude the immigration authorities. Others gain entry on valid temporary border-crossing permits, but then violate the conditions of their entry. Most of these aliens leave the border area in private vehicles, often assisted by professional "alien smugglers." The Border Patrol's traffic-checking operations are designed to prevent this inland movement. They succeed in apprehending some illegal entrants and smugglers, and they deter the movement of others by threatening apprehension and increasing the cost of illegal transportation.

Against this valid public interest we must weigh the interference with individual liberty that results when an officer stops an automobile and questions its occupants.

The intrusion is modest. The Government tells us that a stop by a roving patrol "usually consumes no more than a minute." Brief for United States 25. There is no search of the vehicle or its occupants, and the visual inspection is limited to those parts of the vehicle that can be seen by anyone standing alongside. [6] According to the Government,

"[a]ll that is required of the vehicle's occupants is a response to a brief question or two and possibly the production of a document evidencing a right to be in the United States."

Ibid.

Because of the limited nature of the intrusion, stops of this sort may be justified on facts that do not amount to the probable cause required for an arrest. In Terry v. Ohio, supra, the Court declined expressly to decide whether facts not amounting to probable cause could justify an "investigative seizure' " short of an arrest, 392 U.S. at 392 U. S. 19 n. 16, but it approved a limited

search -- a pat-down for weapons -- for the protection of an officer investigating suspicious behavior of persons he reasonably believed to be armed and dangerous. The Court approved such a search on facts that did not constitute probable cause to believe the suspects guilty of a crime, requiring only that

"the police officer . . . be able to point to specific and articulable facts which, taken together with rational inferences from those facts, reasonably warrant"

a belief that his safety or that of others is in danger. Id. at 392 U. S. 21; see id. at 392 U. S. 27.

We elaborated on Terry in Adams v. Williams, 407 U. S. 143 (1972), holding that a policeman was justified in approaching the respondent to investigate a tip that he was carrying narcotics and a gun.

"The Fourth Amendment does not require a policeman who lacks the precise level of information necessary for probable cause to arrest to simply shrug his shoulders and allow a crime to occur or a criminal to escape. On the contrary, Terry recognizes that it may be the essence of good police work to adopt an intermediate response. . . . A brief stop of a suspicious individual, in order to determine his identity or to maintain the status quo momentarily while obtaining more information, may be most reasonable in light of the facts known to the officer at the time."

Id. at 407 U. S. 145-146.

These cases together establish that, in appropriate circumstances, the Fourth Amendment allows a properly limited "search" or "seizure" on facts that do not constitute probable cause to arrest or to search for contraband or evidence of crime. In both Terry and Adams v. Williams, the investigating officers had reasonable grounds to believe that the suspects were armed and that they might be dangerous. The limited searches and seizures in those cases were a valid method of protecting the public and preventing crime. In this case as well, because of the importance of the governmental interest at stake, the minimal intrusion of a brief stop, and the absence of practical alternatives for policing the border, we hold that, when an officer's observations lead him reasonably to suspect that a particular vehicle may contain aliens who are illegally in the country, he may stop the car briefly and investigate the circumstances that provoke suspicion. As in Terry, the stop and inquiry must be "reasonably related in scope to the justification for their initiation." 392 U.S. at 392 U. S. 29. The officer may question the driver and passengers about their citizenship and immigration status, and he may ask them to explain suspicious circumstances, but any further detention or search must be based on consent or probable cause.

We are unwilling to let the Border Patrol dispense entirely with the requirement that officers must have a reasonable suspicion to justify roving patrol stops. [7] In the context of border area stops, the reasonableness requirement of the Fourth Amendment demands something more than the broad and unlimited discretion sought by the Government. Roads near the border carry not only aliens seeking to enter the country illegally, but a large volume of legitimate traffic as well. San Diego, with a metropolitan population of 1.4 million, is located on the border. Texas has two fairly large metropolitan areas directly on the border: El Paso, with a population of 360,000, and the Brownsville-McAllen area, with a combined population of 320,000. We are confident that substantially all of the traffic in these cities is lawful, and that relatively few of their residents have any connection with the illegal entry and transportation of aliens. To approve roving patrol stops of all vehicles in the border area, without any suspicion that a particular vehicle is carrying illegal immigrants, would subject the residents of these and other areas to potentially unlimited interference with their use of the highways, solely at the discretion of Border Patrol officers

The only formal limitation on that discretion appears to be the administrative regulation defining the term "reasonable distance" in § 287(a)(3) to mean within 100 air miles from the border. 8 CFR § 287.1(a) (1975). Thus, if we approved the Government's position in this case, Border Patrol officers could stop motorists at random for questioning, day or night, anywhere within 100 air miles of the 2,000-mile border, on a city street, a busy highway, or a desert road, without any reason to suspect that they have violated any law.

We are not convinced that the legitimate needs of law enforcement require this degree of interference with lawful traffic. As we discuss in 422 U. S. infra, the nature of illegal alien traffic and the characteristics of smuggling operations tend to generate articulable grounds for identifying violators. Consequently, a requirement of reasonable suspicion for stops allows the Government adequate means of guarding the public interest and also protects residents of the border areas from indiscriminate official interference. Under the circumstances, and even though the intrusion incident to a stop is modest, we conclude that it is not "reasonable" under the Fourth Amendment to make such stops on a random basis. [8]

The Government also contends that the public interest in enforcing conditions on legal alien entry justifies stopping persons who may be aliens for questioning about their citizenship and immigration status. Although we may assume for purposes of this case that the broad congressional power over immigration, see Klendienst v. Mandel, 408 U. S. 753, 408 U. S. 765-767 (1972), authorizes Congress to admit aliens on condition that they will submit to reasonable questioning about their right to be and remain in the country, this power cannot diminish the Fourth Amendment rights of citizens who may be mistaken for aliens. For the same reasons that the Fourth Amendment forbids stopping vehicles at random to inquire if they are carrying aliens who are illegally in the country, it also forbids stopping or detaining persons for questioning about their citizenship on less than a reasonable suspicion that they may be aliens.

IV

The effect of our decision is to limit exercise of the authority granted by both § 287(a)(1) and § 287(a)(3). Except at the border and its functional equivalents, officers on roving patrol may stop vehicles only if they are aware of specific articulable facts, together with rational inferences from those facts, that reasonably warrant suspicion that the vehicles contain aliens who may be illegally in the country. [9]

Any number of factors may be taken into account in deciding whether there is reasonable suspicion to stop a car in the border area. Officers may consider the characteristics of the area in which they encounter a vehicle. Its proximity to the border, the usual patterns of traffic on the particular road, and previous experience with alien traffic are all relevant. See Carroll v. United States, 267 U. S. 132, 267 U. S. 159-161 (1925); United States v. Jaime-Barrios, 494 F.2d 455 (CA9), cert. denied, 417 U.S. 972 (1974). [10] They also may consider information about recent illegal border crossings in the area. The driver's behavior may be relevant, as erratic driving or obvious attempts to evade officers can support a reasonable suspicion. See United States v. Larios Montes, 500 F.2d 941 (CA9 1974); Duprez v. United States, 435 F.2d 1276 (CA9 1970). Aspects of the vehicle itself may justify suspicion. For instance, officers say that certain station wagons, with large compartments for fold-down seats or spare tires, are frequently used for transporting concealed aliens. See United States v. Bugarin-Casas, 484 F.2d 853 (CA9 1973), cert. denied, 414 U.S. 1136 (1974); United States v. Wright, 476 F.2d 1027 (CA5 1973). The vehicle may appear to be heavily loaded, it may have an extraordinary number of passengers, or the officers may observe persons trying to hide. See United States v. Larios-Montes, supra. The Government also points out that trained officers can recognize the characteristic appearance of persons who live in Mexico, relying on such factors as the mode of dress and haircut. Reply Brief for United States 12-13, in United States v. Ortiz, post, p. 422 U. S. 891. In all situations, the officer is entitled to assess the facts in light of his experience in detecting illegal entry and smuggling. Terry v. Ohio, 392 U.S. at 392 U. S. 27.

In this case, the officers relied on a single factor to justify stopping respondent's car: the apparent Mexican ancestry of the occupants. [11] We cannot conclude that this furnished reasonable grounds to believe that the three occupants were aliens. At best, the officers had only a fleeting glimpse of the persons in the moving car, illuminated by headlights. Even if they saw enough to think that the occupants were of Mexican descent, this factor alone would justify neither a reasonable belief that they were aliens, nor a reasonable belief that the car concealed other aliens who were illegally in the country. Large numbers of native born and naturalized citizens have the physical characteristics identified with Mexican ancestry, and, even in the border area, a relatively small proportion of them are aliens. [12] The likelihood that any given person of Mexican ancestry is an alien is high enough to make Mexican appearance a relevant factor, but, standing alone, it does not justify stopping all Mexican-Americans to ask if they are aliens.

The judgment of the Court of Appeals is Affirmed.

US v. Miller (April 21, 1976) [Notes omitted]

MR. JUSTICE POWELL delivered the opinion of the Court.

Respondent was convicted of possessing

an unregistered still, carrying on the business of a distiller without giving bond and with intent to defraud the Government of whiskey tax, possessing 175 gallons of whiskey upon which no taxes had been paid, and conspiring to defraud the United States of tax revenues. 26 U.S.C. §§ 5179, 5205, 5601 et seq.; 18 U.S.C. § 371. Prior to trial, respondent moved to suppress copies of checks and other bank records obtained by means of allegedly defective subpoenas duces tecum served upon two banks at which he had accounts. The records had been maintained by the banks in compliance with the requirements of the Bank Secrecy Act of 1970, 84 Stat. 1114, 12 U.S.C. § 1829b(d).

The District Court overruled respondent's motion to suppress, and the evidence was admitted. The Court of Appeals for the Fifth Circuit reversed on the ground that a depositor's Fourth Amendment rights are violated when bank records maintained pursuant to the Bank Secrecy Act are obtained by means of a defective subpoena. It held that any evidence so obtained must be suppressed. Since we find that respondent had no protectable Fourth Amendment interest in the subpoenaed documents, we reverse the decision below.

I

On December 18, 1972, in response to an informant's tip, a deputy sheriff from Houston County, Ga. stopped a van-type truck occupied by two of respondent's alleged coconspirators. The truck contained distillery apparatus and raw material. On January 9, 1973, a fire broke out in a Kathleen, Ga., warehouse rented to respondent. During the blaze, firemen and sheriff department officials discovered a 7,500-gallon-capacity distillery, 175 gallons of non-tax-paid whiskey, and related paraphernalia.

Two weeks later, agents from the Treasury Department's Alcohol, Tobacco and Firearms Bureau presented grand jury subpoenas issued in blank by the clerk of the District Court, and completed by the United States Attorney's office, to the presidents of the Citizens & Southern National Bank of Warner Robins and the Bank of Byron, where respondent maintained accounts. The subpoenas required the two presidents to appear on January 24, 1973, and to produce

"all records of accounts, i.e., savings, checking, loan or otherwise, in the name of Mr. Mitch Miller [respondent], 3859 Mathis Street, Macon, Ga. and/or Mitch Miller Associates, 100 Executive Terrace, Warner Robins, Ga. from October 1, 1972, through the present date [January 22, 1973, in the case of the Bank of Byron, and January 23, 1973, in the case of the Citizens & Southern National Bank of Warner Robins]."

The banks did not advise respondent that the subpoenas had been served, but ordered their employees to make the records available and to provide copies of any documents the agents desired. At the Bank of Byron, an agent was shown microfilm records of the relevant account and provided with copies of one deposit slip and one or two checks. At the Citizens & Southern National Bank, microfilm records also were shown to the agent, and he was given copies of the records of respondent's account during the applicable period. These included all checks, deposit slips, two financial statements, and three monthly statements. The bank presidents were then told that it would not be necessary to appear in person before the grand jury.

The grand jury met on February 12, 1973, 19 days after the return date on the subpoenas. Respondent and four others were indicted. The overt acts alleged to have been committed in furtherance of the conspiracy included three financial transactions -- the rental by respondent of the van-type truck, the purchase by respondent of radio equipment, and the purchase by respondent of a quantity of sheet metal and metal pipe. The record does not indicate whether any of the bank records were, in fact, presented to the grand jury. They were used in the investigation and provided "one or two" investigatory leads. Copies of the checks also were introduced at trial to establish the overt acts described above.

In his motion to suppress, denied by the District Court, respondent contended that the bank documents were illegally seized. It was urged that the subpoenas were defective because they were issued by the United States Attorney, rather than a court, no return was made to a court, and the subpoenas were returnable on a date when the grand jury was not in session. The Court of Appeals reversed. 500 F.2d 751 (1974). Citing the prohibition in Boyd v. United States, 116 U. S. 616, 116 U. S. 622 (1886), against "compulsory production of a man's private papers to establish a criminal charge against him," the court held that the Government had improperly circumvented Boyd's protections of respondent's Fourth Amendment right against "unreasonable searches and seizures" by

"first requiring a third party bank to copy all of its depositors' personal checks and then, with an improper invocation of legal process, calling upon the bank to allow inspection and reproduction of those copies."

500 F.2d at 757. The court acknowledged that the recordkeeping requirements of the Bank Secrecy Act had been held to be constitutional on their face in California Bankers Assn. v. Shultz, 416 U. S. 21 (1974), but noted that access to the records was to be controlled by "existing legal process." See id. at 416 U. S. 52. The subpoenas issued here were found not to constitute adequate "legal process." The fact that the bank officers cooperated voluntarily was found to be irrelevant, for "he whose rights are threatened by the improper disclosure here was a bank depositor, not a bank official." 500 F.2d at 758.

The Government contends that the Court of Appeals erred in three respects: (i) in finding that respondent had the Fourth Amendment interest necessary to entitle him to challenge the validity of the subpoenas duces tecum through his motion to suppress; (ii) in holding that the subpoenas were defective; and (iii) in determining that suppression of the evidence obtained was the appropriate remedy if a constitutional violation did the place.

We find that there was no intrusion into any area in which respondent had a protected Fourth Amendment interest, and that the District Court therefore correctly denied respondent's motion to suppress. Because we reverse the decision of the Court of Appeals on that ground alone, we do not reach the Government's latter two contentions.

II

In Hoffa v. United States, 385 U. S. 293, 385 U. S. 301-302 (1966), the Court said that "no interest legitimately protected by the Fourth Amendment" is implicated by governmental investigative activities unless there is an intrusion into a zone of privacy, into "the security a man relies upon when he places himself or his property within a constitutionally protected area." The Court of Appeals, as noted above, assumed that respondent had the necessary Fourth Amendment interest, pointing to the language in Boyd v. United States, supra at 116 U. S. 622, which describes that Amendment's protection against the "compulsory production of a man's private papers." [1] We think that the Court of Appeals erred in finding the subpoenaed documents to fall within a protected zone of privacy.

On their face, the documents subpoenaed here are not respondent's "private papers." Unlike the claimant in Boyd, respondent can assert neither ownership nor possession. Instead, these are the business records of the banks. As we said in California Bankers Assn. v. Shultz, supra at 416 U. S. 48-49,

"[b]anks are . . . not . . . neutrals in

transactions involving negotiable instruments, but parties to the instruments with a substantial stake in their continued availability and acceptance."

The records of respondent's accounts, like "all of the records [which are required to be kept pursuant to the Bank Secrecy Act,] pertain to transactions to which the bank was itself a party." Id. at 416 U. S. 52.

Respondent argues, however, that the Bank Secrecy Act introduces a factor that makes the subpoena in this case the functional equivalent of a search and seizure of the depositor's "private papers." We have held, in California Bankers Assn. v. Shultz, supra at 416 U. S. 54, that the mere maintenance of records pursuant to the requirements of the Act "invade [s] no Fourth Amendment right of any depositor." But respondent contends that the combination of the recordkeeping requirements of the Act and the issuance of a subpoena [2] to obtain those records permits the Government to circumvent the requirements of the Fourth Amendment by allowing it to obtain a depositor's private records without complying with the legal requirements that would be applicable had it proceeded against him directly. [3] Therefore, we must address the question whether the compulsion embodied in the Bank Secrecy Act as exercised in this case creates a Fourth Amendment interest in the depositor where none existed before. This question was expressly reserved in California Bankers Assn., supra at 416 U. S. 53-54, and n. 24.

Respondent urges that he has a Fourth Amendment interest in the records kept by the banks because they are merely copies of personal records that were made available to the banks for a limited purpose and in which he has a reasonable expectation of privacy. He relies on this Court's statement in Katz v. United States, 389 U. S. 347, 389 U. S. 353 (1967), quoting Warden v. Hayden, 387 U. S. 294, 387 U. S. 304 (1967), that "we have . . . departed from the narrow view" that "property

interests control the right of the Government to search and seize,'" and that a "search and seizure" become unreasonable when the Government's activities violate "the privacy upon which [a person] justifiably relie[s]." But in Katz, the Court also stressed that "[w]hat a person knowingly exposes to the public . . . is not a subject of Fourth Amendment protection." 389 U.S. at 389 U. S. 351. We must examine the nature of the particular documents sought to be protected in order to determine whether there is a legitimate "expectation of privacy" concerning their contents. Cf. Couch v. United States, 409 U. S. 322, 409 U. S. 335 (1973).

Even if we direct our attention to the original checks and deposit slips, rather than to the microfilm copies actually viewed and obtained by means of the subpoena, we perceive no legitimate "expectation of privacy" in their contents. The checks are not confidential communications, but negotiable instruments to be used in commercial transactions. All of the documents obtained, including financial statements and deposit slips, contain only information voluntarily conveyed to the banks and exposed to their employees in the ordinary course of business. The lack of any legitimate expectation of privacy concerning the information kept in bank records was assumed by Congress in enacting the Bank Secrecy Act, the expressed purpose of which is to require records to be maintained because they "have a high degree of usefulness in criminal, tax, and regulatory investigations and proceedings." 12 U.S.C. § 1829b(a)(1). Cf. Couch v. United States, supra at 409 U. S. 335.

The depositor takes the risk, in revealing his affairs to another, that the information will be conveyed by that person to the Government. United States v. White, 401 U. S. 745, 401 U. S. 751-752 (1971). This Court has held repeatedly that the Fourth Amendment does not prohibit the obtaining of information revealed to a third party and conveyed by him to Government authorities, even if the information is revealed on the assumption that it will be used only for a limited purpose and the confidence placed in the third party will not be betrayed. Id. at 401 U. S. 752; Hoffa v. United States, 385 U.S. at 385 U. S. 302; Lopez v. United States, 373 U. S. 427 (1963). [4]

This analysis is not changed by the mandate of the Bank Secrecy Act that records of depositors' transactions be maintained by banks. In California Bankers Assn. v. Shultz, 416 U.S. at 416 U. S. 52-53, we rejected the contention that banks, when keeping records of their depositors' transactions pursuant to the Act, are acting solely as agents of the Government. But, even if the banks could be said to have been acting solely as Government agents in transcribing the necessary information and complying without protest [5] with the requirements of the subpoenas, there would be no intrusion upon the depositors' Fourth Amendment rights. See Osborn v. United States, 385 U. S. 323 (1966); Lewis v. United States, 385 U. S. 206 (1966).

III

Since no Fourth Amendment interests of the depositor are implicated here, this case is governed by the general rule that the issuance of a subpoena to a third party to obtain the records of that party does not violate the rights of a defendant, even if a criminal prosecution is contemplated at the time the subpoena is issued. California Bankers Assn. v. Shultz, supra, at 416 U. S. 53; Donaldson v. United States, 400 U. S. 517, 400 U. S. 537 (1971) (Douglas, J., concurring). Under these principles, it was firmly settled, before the passage of the Bank Secrecy Act, that an Internal Revenue Service summons directed to a third-party bank does not violate the Fourth Amendment rights of a depositor under investigation. See First National Bank of Mobile v. United States, 267 U.S. 576 (1925), aff'g 295 F. 142 (SD Ala.1924). See also California Bankers Assn. v.

Shultz, supra, at 416 U. S. 53; Donaldson v. United States, supra at 400 U. S. 522.

Many banks traditionally kept permanent records of their depositors' accounts, although not all banks did so, and the practice was declining in recent years. By requiring that such records be kept by all banks, the Bank Secrecy Act is not a novel means designed to circumvent established Fourth Amendment rights. It is merely an attempt to facilitate the use of a proper and longstanding law enforcement technique by insuring that records are available when they are needed. [6]

We hold that the District Court correctly denied respondent's motion to suppress, since he possessed no Fourth Amendment interest that could be vindicated by a challenge to the subpoenas.

IV

Respondent contends not only that the subpoenas duces tecum directed against the banks infringed his Fourth Amendment rights, but that a subpoena issued to a bank to obtain records maintained pursuant to the Act is subject to more stringent Fourth Amendment requirements than is the ordinary subpoena. In making this assertion, he relies on our statement in California Bankers Assn., supra, at 416 U. S. 52, that access to the records maintained by banks under the Act is to be controlled by "existing legal process." [7]

In Oklahoma Press Pub. Co. v. Walling, 327 U. S. 186, 327 U. S. 208 (1946), the Court said that

"the Fourth [Amendment], if applicable [to subpoenas for the production of business records and papers], at the most guards against abuse only by way of too much indefiniteness or breadth in the things required to be 'particularly described,' if also the inquiry is one the demanding agency is authorized by law to make and the materials specified are relevant."

See also United States v. Dionisio, 410 U. S. 1, 410 U. S. 11-12 (1973). Respondent, citing

United States v. United States District Court, 407 U. S. 297 (1972), in which we discussed the application of the warrant requirements of the Fourth Amendment to domestic security surveillance through electronic eavesdropping, suggests that greater judicial scrutiny, equivalent to that required for a search warrant, is necessary when a subpoena is to be used to obtain bank records of a depositor's account. But in California Bankers Assn., 416 U.S. at 416 U. S. 52, we emphasized only that access to the records was to be in accordance with "existing legal process." There was no indication that a new rule was to be devised, or that the traditional distinction between a search warrant and a subpoena would not be recognized. [8]

In any event, for the reasons stated above, we hold that respondent lacks the requisite Fourth Amendment interest to challenge the validity of the subpoenas. [9]

V

The judgment of the Court of Appeals is reversed. The court deferred decision on whether the trial court had improperly overruled respondent's motion to suppress distillery apparatus and raw material seized from a rented truck. W e remand for disposition of that issue.

So ordered.

Andresen v. Maryland (June 29, 1976) [Notes omitted]

MR. JUSTICE BLACKMUN delivered the opinion of the Court.

This case presents the issue whether the introduction into evidence of a person's business records, seized during a search of his offices, violates the Fifth Amendment's command that "[n]o person . . . shall be compelled in any criminal case to be a witness against himself." We also must determine whether the particular searches and seizures here were "unreasonable," and thus violated the prohibition of the Fourth Amendment.

I

In early 1972, a Bi-County Fraud Unit, acting under the joint auspices of the State's Attorneys' Offices of Montgomery and Prince George's Counties, Md. began an investigation of real estate settlement activities in the Washington, D.C., area. At the time, petitioner Andresen was an attorney who, as a sole practitioner, specialized in real estate settlements in Montgomery County. During the Fraud Unit's investigation, his activities came under scrutiny, particularly in connection with a transaction involving Lot 13T in the Potomac Woods subdivision of Montgomery County. The investigation, which included interviews with the purchaser, the mortgage holder, and other lienholders of Lot 13T, as well as an examination of county land records, disclosed that petitioner, acting as settlement attorney, had defrauded Standard-Young Associates, the purchaser of Lot 13T. Petitioner had represented that the property was free of liens and that, accordingly, no title insurance was necessary, when in fact, he knew that there were two outstanding liens on the property. In addition, investigators learned that the lienholders, by threatening to foreclose their liens, had forced a halt to the purchaser's construction on the property. When Standard-Young had confronted petitioner with this information, he responded by issuing, as an agent of a title insurance company, a title policy guaranteeing clear title to the property. By this action, petitioner also defrauded that insurance company by requiring it to pay the outstanding liens.

The investigators, concluding that there was probable cause to believe that petitioner had committed the state crime of false pretenses, see Md.Ann.Code, Art. 27, § 140 (1976), against Standard-Young, applied for warrants to search petitioner's law office and the separate office of Mount Vernon Development Corporation, of which petitioner was incorporator, sole shareholder, resident agent, and director. The application sought permission to search for specified documents pertaining to the sale and conveyance of Lot 13T. A judge of the Sixth Judicial Circuit of Montgomery County concluded that there was probable cause, and issued the warrants.

The searches of the two offices were conducted simultaneously during daylight hours on October 31, 1972. [1] Petitioner was present during the search of his law office, and was free to move about. Counsel for him was present during the latter half of the search. Between 2% and 3% of the files in the office were seized. A single investigator, in the presence of a police officer, conducted the search of Mount Vernon Development Corporation. This search, taking about four hours, resulted in the seizure of less than 5% of the corporation's files.

Petitioner eventually was charged, partly by information and partly by indictment, with the crime of false pretenses, based on his misrepresentation to Standard-Young concerning Lot 13T, and with fraudulent misappropriation by a fiduciary, based on similar false claims made to three home purchasers. Before trial began, petitioner moved to suppress the seized documents. The trial court held a full suppression hearing. At the hearing, the State returned to petitioner 45 of the 52 items taken from the offices of the corporation. The trial court suppressed six other corporation items on the ground that there was no connection between them and the crimes charged. The net result was that the only item seized from the corporation's offices that was not returned by the State or suppressed was a single file labeled "Potomac Woods General." In addition, the State returned to petitioner seven of the 28 items seized from his law office, and the trial court suppressed four other law office items based on its determination that there was no connection between them and the crime charged.

With respect to all the items not suppressed or returned, the trial court ruled that admitting them into evidence would not violate the Fifth and Fourth Amendments. It reasoned that the searches and seizures did not force petitioner to be a witness against himself, because he had not been required to produce the seized documents, nor would he be compelled to authenticate them. Moreover, the search warrants were based on probable cause, and the documents not returned or suppressed were either directly related to Lot 13T, and therefore within the express language of the warrants, or properly seized and otherwise admissible to show a pattern of criminal conduct relevant to the charge concerning Lot 13T.

At trial, the State proved its case primarily by public land records and by records provided by the complaining purchasers, lienholders, and the title insurance company. It did introduce into evidence, however, a number of the seized items. Three documents from the "Potomac Woods General" file, seized during the search of petitioner's corporation, were admitted. These were notes in the handwriting of an employee who used them to prepare abstracts in the course of his duties as a title searcher and law clerk. The notes concerned deeds of trust affecting the Potomac Woods subdivision and related to the transaction involving Lot 13T. [2] Five items seized from petitioner's law office were also admitted. One contained information relating to the transactions with one of the defrauded home buyers. The second was a file partially devoted to the Lot 13T transaction; among the documents were settlement statements, the deed conveying the property to Standard-Young Associates, and the original and a copy of a notice to the buyer about releases of liens. The third item was a file devoted exclusively to Lot 13T. The fourth item consisted of a copy of a deed of trust, dated March 27, 1972, from the seller of certain lots in the Potomac Woods subdivision to a lienholder. [3] The fifth item contained drafts of documents and memoranda written in petitioner's handwriting.

After a trial by jury, petitioner was found guilty upon five counts of false pretenses and three counts of fraudulent misappropriation by a fiduciary. He was sentenced to eight concurrent two-year prison terms.

On appeal to the Court of Special Appeals of Maryland, four of the five false pretenses counts were reversed because the indictment had failed to allege intent to defraud, a necessary element of the state offense. Only the count pertaining to Standard-Young's purchase of Lot 13T remained. With respect to this count of false pretenses and the three counts of misappropriation by a fiduciary, the Court of Special Appeals rejected petitioner's Fourth and Fifth Amendment Claims. [4] Specifically, it held that the warrants were supported by probable cause, that they did not authorize a general search in violation of the Fourth Amendment, and that the items admitted into evidence against petitioner at trial were within the scope of the warrants or were otherwise properly seized. It agreed with the trial court that the search had not violated petitioner's Fifth Amendment rights because petitioner had not been compelled to do anything. 24 Md.App. 128, 331 A.2d 78 (1975).

We granted certiorari limited to the Fourth and Fifth Amendment issues. 423 U. S. 822 (1975). [5]

II

The Fifth Amendment, made applicable to the States by the Fourteenth Amendment, Malloy v. Hogan, 378 U. S. 1, 378 U. S. 8 (1964), provides that "[n]o person . . . shall be compelled in any criminal case to be a witness against himself." As the Court often has noted, the development of this protection was in part a response to certain historical practices, such as ecclesiastical inquisitions and the proceedings of the Star Chamber, "which placed a premium on compelling subjects of the investigation to admit guilt from their own lips." Michigan v. Tucker, 417 U. S. 433, 417 U. S. 440 (1974). See generally L. Levy, Origins of the Fifth Amendment (1968). The "historic function" of the privilege has been to protect a "natural individual from compulsory incrimination through his own testimony or personal records.'" Bellis v. United States, 417 U. S. 85, 417 U. S. 89-90 (1974), quoting from United States v. White, 322 U. S. 694, 322 U. S. 701 (1944).

There is no question that the records seized from petitioner's offices and introduced against him were incriminating. Moreover, it is undisputed that some of these business records contain statements made by petitioner. Cf. United States v. Mara, 410 U. S. 19, 410 U. S. 21-22 (1973); United States v. Dionisio, 410 U. S. 1 (1973); Gilbert v. California, 388 U. S. 263, 388 U. S. 266-267 (1967); United States v. Wade, 388 U. S. 218 (1967); and Schmerber v. California, 384 U. S. 757 (1966). The question, therefore, is whether the seizure of these business records, and their admission into evidence at his trial, compelled petitioner to testify against himself in violation of the Fifth Amendment. This question may be said to have been reserved in Warden v. Hayden, 387 U. S. 294, 387 U. S. 302-303 (1967), and it was adverted to in United States v. Miller, 425 U. S. 435, 425 U. S. 441 n. 3 (1976).

Petitioner contends that

"the Fifth Amendment prohibition against compulsory self-incrimination applies as well to personal business papers seized from his offices as it does to the same papers being required to be produced under a subpoena."

Brief for Petitioner 9. He bases his argument, naturally, on dicta in a number of cases which imply, or state, that the search for and seizure of a person's private papers violate the privilege against self-incrimination. Thus, in Boyd v. United States, 116 U. S. 616, 116 U. S. 633 (1886), the Court said:

"[W]e have been unable to perceive that the seizure of a man's private books and papers to be used in evidence against him is substantially different from compelling him to be a witness against himself."

And in Hale v. Henkel, 201 U. S. 43, 201 U. S. 76 (1906), it was observed that

"the substance of the offense is the compulsory production of private papers, whether under a search warrant or a subpoena duces tecum, against which the person . . . is entitled to protection."

We do not agree, however, that these broad statements compel suppression of this petitioner's business records as a violation of the Fifth Amendment. In the very recent case of Fisher v. United States, 425 U. S. 391 (1976), the Court held that an attorney's production, pursuant to a lawful summons, of his client's tax records in his hands did not violate the Fifth Amendment privilege of the taxpayer,

"because enforcement against a taxpayer's lawyer would not 'compel' the taxpayer to do anything -- and certainly would not compel him to be a 'witness' against himself."

Id. at 425 U. S. 397. We recognized that the continued validity of the broad statements contained in some of the Court's earlier cases had been discredited by later opinions. Id. at 425 U. S. 407-409. In those earlier cases, the legal predicate for the inadmissibility of the evidence seized was a violation of the Fourth Amendment; the unlawfulness of the search and seizure was thought to supply the compulsion of the accused necessary to invoke the Fifth Amendment. [6] Compulsion of the accused was also absent in Couch v. United States, 409 U. S. 322 (1973), where the Court held that a summons served on a taxpayer's accountant requiring him to produce the taxpayer's personal business records in his possession did not violate the taxpayer's Fifth Amendment rights. [7]

Similarly, in this case, petitioner was not asked to say or to do anything. The records seized contained statements that petitioner had voluntarily committed to writing. The search for and seizure of these records were conducted by law enforcement personnel. Finally, when these records were introduced at trial, they were authenticated by a handwriting expert, not by petitioner. Any compulsion of petitioner to speak, other than the inherent psychological pressure to respond at trial to unfavorable evidence, was not present.

This case thus falls within the principle stated by Mr. Justice Holmes: "A party is privileged from producing the evidence, but not from its production." Johnson v. United States, 228 U. S. 457, 228 U. S. 458 (1913). This principle recognizes that the protection afforded by the Self-Incrimination Clause of the Fifth Amendment "adheres basically to the person, not to information that may incriminate him." Couch v. United States, 409 U.S. at 409 U. S. 328. Thus, although the Fifth Amendment may protect an individual from complying with a subpoena for the production of his personal records in his possession because the very act of production may constitute a compulsory authentication of incriminating information, see Fisher v. United States, supra, a seizure of the same materials by law enforcement officers differs in a crucial respect -- the individual against whom the search is directed is not required to aid in the discovery, production, or authentication of incriminating evidence.

A contrary determination that the seizure of a person's business records and their introduction into evidence at a criminal trial violates the Fifth Amendment, would undermine the principles announced in earlier cases. Nearly a half century ago, in Marron v. United States, 275 U. S. 192 (1927), the Court upheld, against both Fourth and Fifth Amendment claims, the admission into evidence of business records seized during a search of the accused's illegal liquor business. And in Abel v. United States, 362 U. S. 217 (1960), the Court again upheld, against both Fourth and Fifth Amendment claims, the introduction into evidence at an espionage trial of false identity papers and a coded message seized during a search of the accused's hotel room. These cases recognize a general rule:

"There is no special sanctity in papers, as distinguished from other forms of property, to render them immune from search and seizure, if only they fall within the scope of the principles of the cases in which other property may be seized, and if they be adequately described in the affidavit and warrant."

Gouled v. United States, 255 U. S. 298, 255 U. S. 309 (1921).

Moreover, a contrary determination would prohibit the admission of evidence traditionally used in criminal cases and traditionally admissible despite the Fifth Amendment. For example, it would bar the admission of an accused's gambling records in a prosecution for gambling; a note given temporarily to a bank teller during a robbery and subsequently seized in the accused's automobile or home in a prosecution for bank robbery; and incriminating notes prepared, but not sent, by an accused in a kidnaping or blackmail prosecution.

We find a useful analogy to the Fifth Amendment question in those cases that deal with the "seizure" of oral communications. As the Court has explained,

"'[t]he constitutional privilege against self-incrimination . . . is designed to prevent the use of legal process to force from the lips of the accused individual the evidence necessary to convict him or to force him to produce and authenticate any personal documents or effects that might incriminate him.'"

Bellis v. United States, 417 U.S. at 417 U. S. 88, quoting United States v. White, 322 U.S. at 322 U. S. 698. The significant aspect of this principle was apparent and applied in Hoffa v. United States, 385 U. S. 293 (1966), where the Court rejected the contention that an informant's "seizure" of the accused's conversation with him, and his subsequent testimony at trial concerning that conversation, violated the Fifth Amendment. The rationale was that, although the accused's statements may have been elicited by the informant for the purpose of gathering evidence against him, they were made voluntarily. We see no reasoned distinction to be made between the compulsion upon the accused in that case and the compulsion in this one. In each, the communication, whether oral or written, was made voluntarily. The fact that seizure was contemporaneous with the communication in Hoffa but subsequent to the communication here does not affect the question whether the accused was compelled to speak.

Finally, we do not believe that permitting the introduction into evidence of a person's business records seized during an otherwise lawful search would offend or undermine any of the policies undergirding the privilege. Murphy v. Waterfront Comm'n, 378 U. S. 52, 378 U. S. 55 (1964). [8] In this case, petitioner, at the time he recorded his communication, at the time of the search, and at the time the records were admitted at trial, was not subjected to "the cruel trilemma of self-accusation, perjury or contempt." Ibid. Indeed, he was never required to say or to do anything under penalty of sanction. Similarly, permitting the admission of the records in question does not convert our accusatorial system of justice into an inquisitorial system.

"The requirement of specific charges, their proof beyond a reasonable doubt, the protection of the accused from confessions extorted through whatever form of police pressures, the right to a prompt hearing before a magistrate, the right to assistance of counsel, to be supplied by government when circumstances make it necessary, the duty to advise an accused of his constitutional rights -- these are all characteristics of the accusatorial system, and manifestations of its demands."

Watts v. Indiana, 338 U. S. 49, 338 U. S. 54 (1949). None of these attributes is endangered by the introduction of business records "independently secured through skillful investigation." Ibid. Further, the search for and seizure of business records pose no danger greater than that inherent in every search that evidence will be "elicited by inhumane treatment and abuses." 378 U.S. at 378 U. S. 55. In this case, the statements seized were voluntarily committed to paper before the police arrived to search for them, and petitioner was not treated discourteously during the search. Also, the "good cause" to "disturb," ibid., petitioner was independently determined by the judge who issued the warrants; and the State bore the burden of executing them. Finally, there is no chance, in this case, of petitioner's statements being self-deprecatory and untrustworthy because they were extracted from him -- they were already in existence, and had been made voluntarily. We recognize, of course, that the Fifth Amendment protects privacy to some extent. However, "the Court has never suggested that every invasion of privacy violates the privilege." Fisher v. United States, 425 U.S. at 425 U. S. 399. Indeed, we recently held that, unless incriminating testimony is "compelled," any invasion of privacy is outside the scope of the Fifth Amendment's protection, saying that "the Fifth Amendment protects against compelled self-incrimination, not [the disclosure of] private information.'" Id. at 425 U. S. 401. Here, as we have already noted, petitioner was not compelled to testify in any manner. Accordingly, we hold that the search of an individual's office for business records, their seizure, and subsequent introduction into evidence do not offend the Fifth Amendment's proscription that "[n]o person . . . shall be compelled in any criminal case to be a witness against himself."

III

We turn next to petitioner's contention that rights guaranteed him by the Fourth Amendment were violated because the descriptive terms of the search warrants were so broad as to make them impermissible "general" warrants, and because certain items were seized in violation of the principles of Warden v. Hayden, 387 U. S. 294 (1967). [9]

The specificity of the search warrants. Although petitioner concedes that the warrants, for the most part, were models of particularity, Brief for Petitioner 28, he contends that they were rendered fatally "general" by the addition, in each warrant, to the exhaustive list of particularly described documents, of the phrase "together with other fruits, instrumentalities and evidence of crime at this [time] unknown." App. A. 95-A. 96, A. 115. The quoted language, it is argued, must be read in isolation and without reference to the rest of the long sentence at the end of which it appears. When read "properly," petitioner contends, it permits the search for and seizure of any evidence of any crime.

General warrants, of course, are prohibited by the Fourth Amendment.

"[T]he problem [posed by the general warrant] is not that of intrusion per se, but of a general, exploratory rummaging in a person's belongings. . . . [The Fourth Amendment addresses the problem] by requiring a 'particular description' of the things to be seized."

Coolidge v. New Hampshire, 403 U. S. 443, 403 U. S. 467 (1971). This requirement

"'makes general searches . . . impossible and prevents the seizure of one thing under a warrant describing another. As to what is to be taken, nothing is left to the discretion of the officer executing the warrant.'"

Stanford v. Texas, 379 U. S. 476, 379 U. S.

485 (1965), quoting Marron v. United States, 275 U.S. at 275 U. S. 196.

In this case, we agree with the determination of the Court of Special Appeals of Maryland that the challenged phrase must be read as authorizing only the search for and seizure of evidence relating to "the crime of false pretenses with respect to Lot 13T." 24 Md.App. at 167, 331 A.2d at 103. The challenged phrase is not a separate sentence. Instead, it appears in each warrant at the end of a sentence containing a lengthy list of specified and particular items to be seized, all pertaining to Lot 13T. [10] We think it clear from the context that the term "crime" in the warrants refers only to the crime of false pretenses with respect to the sale of Lot 13T. The "other fruits" clause is one of a series that follows the colon after the word "Maryland." All clauses in the series are limited by what precedes that colon, namely, "items pertaining to . . . lot 13, block T." The warrants, accordingly, did not authorize the executing officers to conduct a search for evidence of other crimes but only to search for and seize evidence relevant to the crime of false pretenses and Lot 13T. [11]

The admissibility of certain items of evidence in light of Warden v. Hayden. Petitioner charges that the seizure of documents pertaining to a lot other than Lot 13T violated the principles of Warden v. Hayden, and therefore should have been suppressed. His objection appears to be that these papers were not relevant to the Lot 13T charge, and were admissible only to prove another crime with which he was charged after the search. The fact that these documents were used to help form the evidentiary basis for another charge, it is argued, shows that the documents were seized solely for that purpose.

The State replies that Warden v. Hayden was not violated, and that this is so because the challenged evidence is relevant to the question whether petitioner committed the crime of false pretenses with respect to Lot 13T. In Maryland, the crime is committed when a person makes a false representation of a past or existing fact, with intent to defraud and knowledge of its falsity, and obtains any chattel, money, or valuable security from another, who relies on the false representation o his detriment. Polisher v. State, 11 Md.App. 555, 560, 276 A.2d 102, 104 (1971). Thus, the State is required to prove intent to defraud beyond a reasonable doubt. The State consequently argues that the documents pertaining to another lot in the Potomac Woods subdivision demonstrate that the misrepresentation with respect to Lot 13T was not the result of mistake on the part of petitioner.

In Warden v. Hayden, 387 U.S. at 387 U. S. 307, the Court stated that, when the police seize

"'mere evidence,' probable cause must be examined in terms of cause to believe that the evidence sought will aid in a particular apprehension or conviction. In so doing, consideration of police purposes will be required."

In this case, we conclude that the trained special investigators reasonably could have believed that the evidence specifically dealing with another lot in the Potomac Woods subdivision could be used to show petitioner's intent with respect to the Lot 13T transaction.

The Court has often recognized that proof of similar acts is admissible to show intent or the absence of mistake. In Nye & Nissen v. United States, 336 U. S. 613 (1949), for example, a case involving a scheme of fraudulent conduct, it was said:

"The evidence showed the presentation of eleven other false invoices. . . . The trial court also admitted it at the conclusion of the case 'for the sole purpose of proving guilty intent, motive, or guilty knowledge' of the defendants. Evidence that similar and related offenses were committed in this period tended to show a consistent pattern of conduct highly relevant to the issue of intent."

Id. at 336 U. S. 618.

In the present case, when the special investigators secured the search warrants, they had been informed of a number of similar charges against petitioner arising out of Potomac Woods transactions. And, by reading numerous documents and records supplied by the Lot 13T and other complainants, and by interviewing witnesses, they had become familiar with petitioner's method of operation. Accordingly, the relevance of documents pertaining specifically to a lot other than Lot 13T, and their admissibility to show the Lot 13T offense, would have been apparent. Lot 13T and the other lot had numerous features in common. Both were in the same section of the Potomac Woods subdivision; both had been owned by the same person; and transactions concerning both had been handled extensively by petitioner. Most important was the fact that there were two deeds of trust in which both lots were listed as collateral. Unreleased liens respecting both lots were evidenced by these deeds of trusts. Petitioner's transactions relating to the other lot, subject to the same liens as Lot 13T, therefore, were highly relevant to the question whether his failure to deliver title to Lot 13T free of all encumbrances was mere inadvertence. Although these records subsequently were used to secure additional charges against petitioner, suppression of this evidence in this case was not required. The fact that the records could be used to show intent to defraud with respect to Lot 13T permitted the seizure and satisfied the requirements of Warden v. Hayden.

The judgment of the Court of Special Appeals of Maryland is affirmed.

It is so ordered.

South Dakota v. Opperman (July 6, 1976) [Notes omitted]

MR. CHIEF JUSTICE BURGER delivered the opinion of the Court.

We review the judgment of the Supreme Court of South Dakota, holding that local police violated the Fourth Amendment to the Federal Constitution, as applicable to the States under the Fourteenth Amendment, when they conducted a routine inventory search of an automobile lawfully impounded by police for violations of municipal parking ordinances.

(1)

Local ordinances prohibit parking in certain areas of downtown Vermillion, S.D. between the hours of 2 am. and 6 a.m. During the early morning hours of December 10, 1973, a Vermillion police officer observed respondent's unoccupied vehicle illegally parked in the restricted zone. At approximately 3 a.m., the officer issued an overtime parking ticket and placed it on the car's windshield. The citation warned:

"Vehicles in violation of any parking ordinance may be towed from the area."

At approximately 10 o'clock on the same morning, another officer issued a second ticket for an overtime parking violation. These circumstances were routinely reported to police headquarters, and after the vehicle was inspected, the car was towed to the city impound lot.

From outside the car at the impound lot, a police officer observed a watch on the dashboard and other items of personal property located on the back seat and back floorboard. At the officer's direction, the car door was then unlocked and, using a standard inventory form pursuant to standard police procedures, the officer inventoried the contents of the car, including the contents of the glove compartment, which was unlocked. There he found marihuana contained in a plastic bag. All items, including the contraband, were removed to the police department for safekeeping. [1] During the late afternoon of December 10, respondent appeared at the police department to claim his property. The marihuana was retained by police.

Respondent was subsequently arrested on charges of possession of marihuana. His motion to suppress the evidence yielded by the inventory search was denied; he was convicted after a jury trial and sentenced to a fine of $100 and 14 days' incarceration in the county jail. On appeal, the Supreme Court of South Dakota reversed the conviction. 89 S.D. ___, 228 N.W.2d 152. The court concluded that the evidence had been obtained in violation of the Fourth Amendment prohibition against unreasonable searches and seizures. We granted certiorari, 423 U.S. 923 (1975), and we reverse.

(2)

This Court has traditionally drawn a distinction between automobiles and homes or offices in relation to the Fourth Amendment. Although automobiles are "effects," and thus within the reach of the Fourth Amendment, Cady v. Dombrowski, 413 U. S. 433, 413 U. S. 439 (1973), warrantless examinations of automobiles have been upheld in circumstances in which a search of a home or office would not. Cardwell v. Lewis, 417 U. S. 583, 417 U. S. 589 (1974); Cady v. Dombrowski, supra at 413 U. S. 439-440; Chambers v. Maroney, 399 U. S. 42, 399 U. S. 48 (1970).

The reason for this well settled distinction is twofold. First, the inherent mobility of automobiles creates circumstances of such exigency that, as a practical necessity, rigorous enforcement of the warrant requirement is impossible. Carroll v. United States, 267 U. S. 132, 267 U. S. 153-154 (1925); Coolidge v. New Hampshire, 403 U. S. 443, 403 U. S. 459-460 (1971). But the Court has also upheld warrantless searches where no immediate danger was presented that the car would be removed from the jurisdiction. Chambers v. Maroney, supra at 399 U. S. 51-52; Cooper v. California, 386 U. S. 58 (1967). Besides the element of mobility, less rigorous

warrant requirements govern because the expectation of privacy with respect to one's automobile is significantly less than that relating to one's home or office. [2] In discharging their varied responsibilities for ensuring the public safety, law enforcement officials are necessarily brought into frequent contact with automobiles. Most of this contact is distinctly noncriminal in nature. Cady v. Dombrowski, supra at 413 U. S. 442. Automobiles, unlike homes, are subjected to pervasive and continuing governmental regulation and controls, including periodic inspection and licensing requirements. As an everyday occurrence, police stop and examine vehicles when license plates or inspection stickers have expired, or if other violations, such as exhaust fumes or excessive noise, are noted, or if headlights or other safety equipment are not in proper working order.

The expectation of privacy as to automobiles is further diminished by the obviously public nature of automobile travel. Only two Terms ago, the Court noted:

"One has a lesser expectation of privacy in a motor vehicle because its function is transportation and it seldom serves as one's residence or as the repository of personal effects. . . . It travels public thoroughfares where both its occupants and its contents are in plain view."

Cardwell v. Lewis, supra at 417 U. S. 590.

In the interests of public safety and as part of what the Court has called "community caretaking functions," Cady v. Dombrowski, supra at 413 U. S. 441, automobiles are frequently taken into police custody. Vehicle accidents present one such occasion. To permit the uninterrupted flow of traffic and in some circumstances to preserve evidence, disabled or damaged vehicles will often be removed from the highways or streets at the behest of police engaged solely in caretaking and traffic control activities.

Police will also frequently remove and impound automobiles which violate parking ordinances and which thereby jeopardize both the public safety and the efficient movement of vehicular traffic. [3] The authority of police to seize and remove from the streets vehicles impeding traffic or threatening public safety and convenience is beyond challenge.

When vehicles are impounded, local police departments generally follow a routine practice of securing and inventorying the automobiles' contents. These procedures developed in response to three distinct needs: the protection of the owner's property while it remains in police custody, United States v. Mitchell, 458 F.2d 960, 961 (CA9 1972); the protection of the police against claims or disputes over lost or stolen property, United States v. Kelehar, 470 F.2d 176, 178 (CA5 1972); and the protection of the police from potential danger, Cooper v. California, supra at 386 U. S. 61-62. The practice has been viewed as essential to respond to incidents of theft or vandalism. See Cabbler v. Commonwealth, 212 Va. 520, 522, 184 S.E.2d 781, 782 (1971), cert. denied, 405 U.S. 1073 (1972); Warrix v. State, 50 Wis.2d 368, 376, 184 N.W.2d 189, 194 (1971). In addition, police frequently attempt to determine whether a vehicle has been stolen, and thereafter abandoned.

These caretaking procedures have almost uniformly been upheld by the state courts, which, by virtue of the localized nature of traffic regulation, have had considerable occasion to deal with the issue. [4] Applying the Fourth Amendment standard of "reasonableness," [5] the state courts have overwhelmingly concluded that, even if an inventory is characterized as a "search," [6] the intrusion is constitutionally permissible. See, e.g., City of St. Paul v. Myles, 298 Minn. 298, 300-301, 218 N.W.2d 697, 699 (1974); State v. Tully, 166 Conn.126, 136, 348 A.2d 603, 609 (1974); People v. Trusty, 183 Colo. 291, 296-297, 516 P.2d 423, 425-426 (1973); People v. Sullivan, 29 N.Y.2d 69, 73, 272 N.E.2d 464, 466 (1971); Cabbler v. Commonwealth, supra; Warrix v. State, supra; State v. Wallen, 185 Neb. 44, 173 N.W.2d 372, cert. denied, 399 U.S. 912 (1970); State v. Criscola, 21 Utah 2d 272, 444 P.2d 517 (1968); State v. Montague, 73 Wash.2d 381, 438 P.2d 571 (1968); People v. Clark, 32 Ill.App.3d 898, 336 N.E.2d 892 (1975); State v. Achter, 512 S.W.2d 894 (Mo.Ct.App. 1974); Bennett v. State, 507 P.2d 1252 (Okla.Crim.App. 1973); People v. Willis, 46 Mich.App. 436, 208 N.W.2d 204 (1973); State v. All, 17 N.C. App. 284, 193 S.E.2d 770, cert. denied, 414 U.S. 866 (1973); Godbee v. State, 224 So.2d 441 (Fla.Dist.Ct.App. 1969). Even the seminal state decision relied on by the South Dakota Supreme Court in reaching the contrary result, Mozzetti v. Superior Court, 4 Cal.3d 699, 484 P.2d 84 (1971), expressly approved police caretaking activities resulting in the securing of property within the officer's plain view.

The majority of the Federal Courts of Appeals have likewise sustained inventory procedures as reasonable police intrusions. As Judge Wisdom has observed:

"[W]hen the police take custody of any sort of container [such as] an automobile . . . , it is reasonable to search the container to itemize the property to be held by the police. [This reflects] the underlying principle that the fourth amendment proscribes only unreasonable searches."

United States v. Gravitt, 484 F.2d 375, 378 (CA5 1973), cert. denied, 414 U.S. 1135 (1974) (emphasis in original). See also Cabbler v. Superintendent, 528 F.2d 1142 (CA4 1975), cert. pending, No. 75-1463; Barker v. Johnson, 484 F.2d 941 (CA6 1973); United States v. Mitchell, 458 F.2d 960 (CA9 1972); United States v. Lipscomb, 435 F.2d 795 (CA5 1970), cert. denied, 401 U.S. 980 (1971); United States v. Pennington, 441 F.2d 249 (CA5), cert. denied, 404 U.S. 854 (1971); United States v. Boyd, 436 F.2d 1203 (CA5 1971); Cotton v. United States, 371 F.2d 385 (CA9 1967). Accord, Lowe v. Hopper, 400 F.Supp. 970, 976-977 (SD Ga.1975); United States v. Spitalieri, 391 F.Supp.

167, 169-170 (ND Ohio 1975); United States v. Smith, 340 F.Supp. 1023 (Conn.1972); United States v. Fuller, 277 F.Supp. 97 (DC 1967), conviction aff'd, 139 U.S.App.D.C. 375, 433 F.2d 533 (1970). These cases have recognized that standard inventories often include an examination of the glove compartment, since it is a customary place for documents of ownership and registration, United States v. Pennington, supra at 251, as well as a place for the temporary storage of valuables.

(3)

The decisions of this Court point unmistakably to the conclusion reached by both federal and state courts that inventories pursuant to standard police procedures are reasonable. In the first such case, Mr. Justice Black made plain the nature of the inquiry before us: .

"But the question here is not whether the search was authorized by state law. The question is rather whether the search was reasonable under the Fourth Amendment."

Cooper v. California, 386 U.S. at 386 U. S. 61 (emphasis added).

And, in his last writing on the Fourth Amendment, Mr. Justice Black said:

"[T]he Fourth Amendment does not require that every search be made pursuant to a warrant. It prohibits only 'unreasonable searches and seizures.' The relevant test is not the reasonableness of the opportunity to procure a warrant, but the reasonableness of the seizure under all the circumstances. The test of reasonableness cannot be fixed by per se rules; each case must be decided on its own facts."

Coolidge v. New Hampshire, 403 U.S. at 403 U. S. 509-510 (concurring and dissenting) (emphasis added).

In applying the reasonableness standard adopted by the Framers, this Court has consistently sustained police intrusions into automobiles impounded or otherwise in lawful police custody where the process is aimed at securing or protecting the car and its contents. In Cooper v. California, supra, the Court upheld the inventory of a car impounded under the authority of a state forfeiture statute. Even though the inventory was conducted in a distinctly criminal setting [7] and carried out a week after the car had been impounded, the Court nonetheless found that the car search, including examination of the glove compartment where contraband was found, was reasonable under the circumstances. This conclusion was reached despite the fact that no warrant had issued and probable cause to search for the contraband in the vehicle had not been established. The Court said in language explicitly applicable here:

"It would be unreasonable to hold that the police, having to retain the car in their custody for such a length of time, had no right, even for their own protection, to search it."

386 U.S. at 386 U. S. 61-62. [8]

In the following Term, the Court in Harris v. United States, 390 U. S. 234 (1968), upheld the introduction of evidence, seized by an officer who, after conducting an inventory search of a car and while taking means to safeguard it, observed a car registration card lying on the metal stripping of the car door. Rejecting the argument that a warrant was necessary, the Court held that the intrusion was justifiable, since it was "taken to protect the car while it was in police custody." Id. at 390 U. S. 236. [9] Finally, in Cady v. Dombrowski, supra, the Court upheld a warrantless search of an automobile towed to a private garage even though no probable cause existed to believe that the vehicle contained fruits of a crime. The sole justification for the warrantless incursion was that it was incident to the caretaking function of the local police to protect the community's safety. Indeed, the protective search was instituted solely because local police "were under the impression" that the incapacitated driver, a Chicago police officer, was required to carry his service revolver at all times; the police had reasonable grounds to believe a weapon might be in the car, and thus available to vandals. 413 U.S. at 413 U. S. 436. The Court carefully noted that the protective search was carried out in accordance with standard procedures in the local police department, ibid., a factor tending to ensure that the intrusion would be limited in scope to the extent necessary to carry out the caretaking function. See United States v. Spitalieri, 391 F.Supp. at 169. In reaching this result, the Court in Cady distinguished Preston v. United States, 376 U. S. 364 (1964), on the grounds that the holding, invalidating a car search conducted after a vagrancy arrest, "stands only for the proposition that the search challenged there could not be justified as one incident to an arrest." 413 U.S. at 413 U. S. 444. Preston therefore did not raise the issue of the constitutionality of a protective inventory of a car lawfully within police custody.

The holdings in Cooper, Harris, and Cady point the way to the correct resolution of this ease. None of the three cases, of course, involves the precise situation presented here; but, as in all Fourth Amendment cases, we are obliged to look to all the facts and circumstances of this case in light of the principles set forth in these prior decisions.

"[W]hether a search and seizure is unreasonable within the meaning of the Fourth Amendment depends upon the facts and circumstances of each case. . . ."

Cooper v. California, 386 U.S. at 386 U. S. 59.

The Vermillion police were indisputably engaged in a caretaking search of a lawfully impounded automobile. Cf. United States v.Lawson, 487 F.2d 468, 471 (CA8 1973). The inventory was conducted only after the car had been impounded for multiple parking violations. The owner, having left his car illegally parked for an extended period, and thus subject to impoundment, was not present to make other arrangements for the safekeeping of his belongings. The inventory itself was prompted by the presence in plain view of a number of valuables inside the car. As in Cady, there is no suggestion whatever that this standard procedure, essentially like that followed throughout the country, was a pretext concealing an investigatory police motive. [10]

On this record, we conclude that, in following standard police procedures prevailing throughout the country and approved by the overwhelming majority of courts, the conduct of the police was not "unreasonable" under the Fourth Amendment.

The judgment of the South Dakota Supreme Court is therefore reversed, and the case is remanded for further proceedings not inconsistent with this opinion.

Reversed and remanded.

US v. Janis (July 6, 1976) [Notes omitted]

MR. JUSTICE BLACKMUN delivered the opinion of the Court.

This case presents an issue of the appropriateness of an extension of the judicially created exclusionary rule: is evidence seized by a state criminal law enforcement officer in good faith, but nonetheless unconstitutionally, inadmissible in a civil proceeding by or against the United States?

I

In November, 1968, the Los Angeles police obtained a warrant directing a search for bookmaking paraphernalia at two specified apartment locations in the city and, as well, on the respective persons of Morris Aaron Levine and respondent Max Janis. The warrant was issued by a judge of the Municipal Court of the Los Angeles Judicial District. It was based upon the affidavit of Officer Leonard Weissman. [1] After the search, made pursuant to the warrant, both the respondent and Levine were arrested and the police seized from respondent property consisting of $4,940 in cash and certain wagering records. [2] Soon thereafter, Officer Weissman telephoned an agent of the United States Internal Revenue Service and informed the agent that Janis had been arrested for bookmaking activity. [3] With the assistance of Weissman, who was familiar with bookmakers' codes, the revenue agent analyzed the wagering records that had been seized and determined from them the gross volume of respondent's gambling activity for the five days immediately preceding the seizure. Weissman informed the agent that he had conducted a surveillance of respondent's activities that indicated that respondent had been engaged in bookmaking during the 77-day period from September 14 through November 30, 1968, the day of the arrest.

Respondent had not filed any federal wagering tax return pertaining to bookmaking activities for that 77-day period. Based exclusively upon its examination of the evidence so obtained by the Los Angeles police, the Internal Revenue Service made an assessment jointly against respondent and Levine for wagering taxes, under § 4401 of the Internal Revenue Code of 1954, 26 U.S.C. § 4401, in the amount of $89,026.09, plus interest. The amount of the assessment was computed by first determining respondent's average daily gross proceeds for the five-day period covered by the seized material and analyzed by the agent, and then multiplying the resulting figure by 77, the period of the police surveillance of respondent's activities. [4] The assessment having been made, the Internal Revenue Service exercised its statutory authority, under 26 U.S.C. § 6331, to levy upon the $4,940 in cash in partial satisfaction of the assessment against respondent.

Charges were filed in due course against respondent and Levine in Los Angeles Municipal Court for violation of the local gambling laws. They moved-to quash the search warrant. A suppression hearing was held by the same judge who had issued the warrant. The defendants pressed upon the court the case of Spinelli v. United States, 393 U. S. 410 (1969), which had been decided just three weeks earlier and after the search warrant had been issued. They urged that the Weissman affidavit did not set forth in sufficient detail the underlying circumstances to enable the issuing magistrate to determine independently the reliability of the information supplied by the informants. The judge granted the motion to quash the warrant. He then ordered that all items seized pursuant to it be returned except the cash that had been levied upon by the Internal Revenue Service. App. 78-80.

In June, 1969, respondent filed a claim for refund of the $4,940. The claim was not honored, and, 18 months later, in December, 1970, respondent filed suit for that amount in the United States District Court for the Central District of California. The Government answered and counterclaimed for the substantial unpaid balance of the assessment. [5] In pretrial proceedings, it was agreed that the

"sole basis of the computation of the civil tax assessment . . . was . . . the items obtained pursuant to the search warrant . . . and the information furnished to [the revenue agent] by Officer Weissman with respect to the duration of [respondent's] alleged wagering activities. [6]"

Id. at 18. Respondent then moved to suppress the evidence seized, and all copies thereof in the possession of the Service, and to quash the assessment. Id. at 224.

At the outset of the hearing on the motion, the District Court observed that it was "reluctantly holding that the affidavit supporting the search warrant is insufficient under the Spinelli and Aguilar [v. Texas, 378 U. S. 108 (1964)] doctrines." Id. at 47. It then concluded that "[a]ll of the evidence utilized as the basis" of the assessment "was obtained directly or indirectly as a result of the search pursuant to the defective search warrant," and that, consequently, the assessment

"was based in substantial part, if not completely, on illegally procured evidence . . . in violation of [respondent's] Fourth Amendment rights to be free from unreasonable searches and seizures."

73-1 USTC � 16,083, p. 81,392 (1973). The court concluded that Janis was entitled to a refund of the $4,940, together with interest thereon,

"for the reason that substantially all, if not all, of the evidence utilized by the defendants herein in making their assessment . . . was illegally obtained, and, as such, the assessment was invalid."

Ibid. Further, where, as here, "illegally obtained evidence constitutes the basis of a federal tax assessment," the respondent was "not required to prove the extent of the refund to which he claims he is entitled." Id. at 81,393. Instead, it was sufficient if he prove "that substantially all, if not all, of the evidence upon which the assessment was based was the result of illegally obtained evidence." Accordingly, the court ordered that the civil tax assessment made by the Internal Revenue Service "against all the property and assets of . . . Janis be quashed," and entered judgment for the respondent. Ibid. The Government's counterclaim was dismissed with prejudice. The United States Court of Appeals for the Ninth Circuit, by unpublished memorandum without opinion, affirmed on the basis of the District Court's findings of fact and conclusions of law. Pet. for Cert. 12A.

Because of the obvious importance of the question, we granted certiorari. 421 U.S. 1010 (1975).

II

Some initial observations about the procedural posture of the case in the District Court are indicated. If there is to be no limit to the burden of proof the respondent, as "taxpayer," must carry, then, even though he were to obtain a favorable decision on the inadmissibility of evidence issue, the respondent on this record could not possibly defeat the Government's counterclaim. The Government notes, properly, we think, that the litigation is composed of two separate elements: the refund suit instituted by the respondent, and the collection suit instituted by the United States through its counterclaim. In a refund suit, the taxpayer bears the burden of proving the amount he is entitled to recover. Lewis v. Reynolds, 284 U. S. 281 (1932). It is not enough for him to demonstrate that the assessment of the tax for which refund is sought was erroneous in some respects.

This Court has not spoken with respect to the burden of proof in a tax collection suit. The Government argues here that the presumption of correctness that attaches to the assessment in a refund suit must also apply in a civil collection suit instituted by the United States under the authority granted by §§ 7401 and 7403 of the Code, 26 U.S.C. §§ 7401 and 7403. Thus, it is said, the defendant in a collection suit has the same burden of proving that he paid the correct amount of his tax liability.

The policy behind the presumption of correctness and the burden of proof, see Bull v. United States, 295 U. S. 247, 295 U. S. 259-260 (1935), would appear to be applicable in each situation. It accords, furthermore, with the burden of proof rule which prevails in the usual pre-assessment proceeding in the United States Tax Court. Lucas v. Structural Steel Co., 281 U. S. 264, 281 U. S. 271 (1930); Welch v. Helvering, 290 U. S. 111, 290 U. S. 115 (1933); Rule 142(a) of the Rules of Practice and Procedure of the United States Tax Court (1973). In any event, for purposes of this case, we assume that this is so and that the burden of proof may be said technically to rest with respondent Janis.

Respondent, however, submitted no

evidence tending either to demonstrate that the assessment was incorrect or to show the correct amount of wagering tax liability, if any, on his part. In the usual situation, one might well argue, as the Government does, that the District Court then could not properly grant judgment for the respondent on either aspect of the suit. But the present case may well not be the usual situation. What we have is a "naked" assessment, without any foundation whatsoever if what was seized by the Los Angeles police cannot be used in the formulation of the assessment. [7] The determination of tax due then may be one "without rational foundation and excessive," and not properly subject to the usual rule with respect to the burden of proof in tax cases. Helvering v. Taylor, 293 U. S. 507, 293 U. S. 514-515 (1935). [8] See 9 J. Mertens, Law of Federal Income Taxation § 50.65 (1971).

There appears, indeed, to be some debate among the Federal Courts of Appeals, in different factual contexts, as to the effect upon the burden of proof in a tax case when there is positive evidence that an assessment is incorrect. Some courts indicate that the burden of showing the amount of the deficiency then shifts to the Commissioner. [9] Others hold that the burden of showing the correct amount of the tax remains with the taxpayer. [10] However that may be, the debate does not extend to the situation where the assessment is shown to be naked and without any foundation. The courts then appear to apply the rule of the Taylor case. See United States v. Rexach, 482 F.2d 10, 16-17, n. 3 (CA1), cert. denied, 414 U.S. 1039 (1973); Pizzarello v. United States, 408 F.2d 579 (CA2), cert. denied, 396 U.S. 986 (1969); Suarez v. Commissioner, 58 T.C. 792, 814-815 (1972). But cf. Compton v. United States, 334 F.2d 212, 216 (CA4 1964).

Certainly, proof that an assessment is utterly without foundation is proof that it is arbitrary and erroneous. For purposes of this case, we need not go so far as to accept the Government's argument that the exclusion of the evidence in issue here is insufficient to require judgment for the respondent or even to shift the burden to the Government. We are willing to assume that, if the District Court was correct in ruling that the evidence seized by the Los Angeles police may not be used in formulating the assessment (on which both the levy and the counterclaim were based), then the District Court was also correct in granting judgment for Janis in both aspects of the present suit. This assumption takes us, then, to the primary issue. [11]

III

This Court early pronounced a rule that the Fifth Amendment's command that no person "shall be compelled in any criminal case to be a witness against himself" renders evidence falling within the Amendment's prohibition inadmissible. Boyd v. United States, 116 U. S. 616 (1886). It was not until 1914, however, that the Court held that the Fourth Amendment alone may be the basis for excluding from a federal criminal trial evidence seized by a federal officer in violation solely of that Amendment. Weeks v. United States, 232 U. S. 383. This comparatively late judicial creation of a Fourth Amendment exclusionary rule is not particularly surprising. In contrast to the Fifth Amendment's direct command against the admission of compelled testimony, the issue of admissibility of evidence obtained in violation of the Fourth Amendment is determined after, and apart from, the violation. [12] In Weeks, it was held, however, that the Fourth Amendment did not apply to state officers, and, therefore, that material seized unconstitutionally by a state officer could be admitted in a federal criminal proceeding. This was the "silver platter" doctrine. [13]

In Wolf v. Colorado, 338 U. S. 25 (1949), the Court determined that the Due Process Clause of the Fourteenth Amendment reflected the Fourth Amendment to the extent of providing those protections against intrusions that are "implicit in the concept of ordered liberty.'" Id. at 338 U. S. 27. Nonetheless, the Court, in not applying the Weeks doctrine in a state trial to the product of a state search, held:

"Granting that, in practice, the exclusion of evidence may be an effective way of deterring unreasonable searches, it is not for this Court to condemn as falling below the minimal standards assured by the Due Process Clause a State's reliance upon other methods which, if consistently enforced, would be equally effective."

338 U.S. at 338 U. S. 31.

Not long thereafter, the Court rule that means used by a State to procure evidence could be sufficiently offensive to the concept of ordered liberty as to make admission of the evidence so procured a violation of the Due Process Clause, Rochin v. California, 342 U. S. 165 (1952), but that such a violation would exist only in the most extreme case, Irvine v. California, 347 U. S. 128 (1954).

Thus, as matters then stood, the Fourth Amendment was applicable to the States, but a State could allow an official to engage in a violation thereof with no judicial sanction except in the most extreme case. In addition, federal authorities, if they happened upon a State so inclined, could profit from the State's action by receiving on a silver platter evidence unconstitutionally obtained. The federal authorities, profiting thereby, had no judicially created reason to discourage unconstitutional searches by a State, and the States, having no judicially mandated controls, were free to engage in such searches. [14]

Elkins v. United States, 364 U. S. 206, was decided in 1960. Invoking its "supervisory power over the administration of criminal justice in the federal courts," id. at 364 U. S. 216, the Court held that

"evidence obtained by state officers during a search which, if conducted by federal officers, would have violated the defendant's immunity from unreasonable searches and seizures under the Fourth Amendment, is inadmissible over the defendant's timely objection in a federal criminal trial."

Id. at 364 U. S. 223.

The rule thus announced apparently served two purposes. First, it assured that a State, which could admit the evidence in its own proceedings if it so chose, nevertheless would suffer some deterrence in that its federal counterparts would be unable to use the evidence in federal criminal proceedings. Second, the rule discouraged federal authorities from using a state official to circumvent the restrictions of Weeks.

Only one year later, however, the exclusionary rule was made applicable to state criminal trials. Mapp v. Ohio, 367 U. S. 643 (1961). The Court ruled:

"Since the Fourth Amendment's right of privacy has been declared enforceable against the States through the Due Process Clause of the Fourteenth, it is enforceable against them by the same sanction of exclusion as is used against the Federal Government."

Id. at 367 U. S. 655.

The debate within the Court on the exclusionary rule has always been a warm one. [15] It has been unaided, unhappily, by any convincing empirical evidence on the effects of the rule. The Court, however, has established that the "prime purpose" of the rule, if not the sole one, "is to deter future unlawful police conduct." United States v. Calandra, 414 U. S. 338, 414 U. S. 347 (1974). See United States v. Peltier, 422 U. S. 531, 422 U. S. 536-539 (1975). Thus,

"[i]n sum, the rule is a judicially created remedy designed to safeguard Fourth Amendment rights generally through its deterrent effect, rather than a personal constitutional right of the party aggrieved."

United States v. Calandra, 414 U.S. at 414

U. S. 348.

And

"[a]s with any remedial device, the application of the rule has been restricted to those areas where its remedial objectives are thought most efficaciously served."

Ibid. [16]

In the complex and turbulent history of the rule, the Court never has applied it to exclude evidence from a civil proceeding, federal or state. [17]

IV

In the present case, we are asked to create judicially a deterrent sanction by holding that evidence obtained by a state criminal law enforcement officer in good faith reliance on a warrant that later proved to be defective shall be inadmissible in a federal civil tax proceeding. Clearly, the enforcement of admittedly valid laws would be hampered by so extending the exclusionary rule, and, as is nearly always the case with the rule, concededly relevant and reliable evidence would be rendered unavailable. [18]

In evaluating the need for a deterrent sanction, one must first identify those who are to be deterred. In this case, it is the state officer who is the primary object of the sanction. It is his conduct that is to be controlled. Two factors suggest that a sanction in addition to those that presently exist is unnecessary. First, the local law enforcement official is already "punished" by the exclusion of the evidence in the state criminal trial. [19] That, necessarily, is of substantial concern to him. Second, the evidence is also excludable in the federal criminal trial, Elkins v. United States, supra, so that the entire criminal enforcement process, which is the concern and duty of these officers, is frustrated. [20]

Jurists and scholars uniformly have recognized that the exclusionary rule imposes a substantial cost on the societal interest in law enforcement by its proscription of what concededly is relevant evidence. See, e.g., Bivens v. Six Unknown Fed. Narcotics Agents, 403 U. S. 388, 403 U. S. 411 (1971) (BURGER, C.J., dissenting); Amsterdam, Perspectives on the Fourth Amendment, 58 Minn.L.Rev. 349, 429 (1974). And alternatives that would be less costly to societal interests have been the subject of extensive discussion and exploration. [21]

Equally important, although scholars have attempted to determine whether the exclusionary rule in fact does have any deterrent effect, each empirical study on the subject, in its own way, appears to be flawed. [22] It would not be appropriate to fault those who have attempted empirical studies for their lack of convincing data. The number of variables is substantial, [23] and many cannot be measured or subjected to effective controls. Recordkeeping before Mapp was spotty at best, a fact which thus severely hampers before-and-after studies. Since Mapp, of course, all possibility of broad-scale controlled or even semi-controlled comparison studies has been eliminated. [24] "Response" studies are hampered by the presence of the respondents' interests. [25] And extrapolation studies are rendered highly inconclusive by the changes in legal doctrines and police-citizen relationships that have taken place in the 15 years since Mapp was decided. [26]

We find ourselves, therefore, in no better position than the Court was in 1960 when it said:

"Empirical statistics are not available to show that the inhabitants of states which follow the exclusionary rule suffer less from lawless searches and seizures than do those of states which admit evidence unlawfully obtained. Since, as a practical matter, it is never easy to prove a negative, it is hardly likely that conclusive factual data could ever be assembled. For much the same reason, it cannot positively be demonstrated that enforcement of the criminal law is either more or less effective under either rule."

Elkins v. United States, 364 U.S. at 364 U.

S. 218.

If the exclusionary rule is the "strong medicine" that its proponents claim it to be, then its use in the situations in which it is now applied (resulting, for example, in this case in frustration of the Los Angeles police officers' good faith duties as enforcers of the criminal laws) must be assumed to be a substantial and efficient deterrent. Assuming this efficacy, the additional marginal deterrence provided by forbidding a different sovereign from using the evidence in a civil proceeding surely does not outweigh the cost to society of extending the rule to that situation. [27] If, on the other hand, the exclusionary rule does not result in appreciable deterrence, then, clearly, its use in the instant situation is unwarranted. Under either assumption, therefore, the extension of the rule is unjustified. [28]

In short, we conclude that exclusion from federal civil proceedings of evidence unlawfully seized by a state criminal enforcement officer has not been shown to have a sufficient likelihood of deterring the conduct of the state police so that it outweighs the societal costs imposed by the exclusion. This Court, therefore, is not justified in so extending the exclusionary rule. [29]

Respondent argues, however, that the application of the exclusionary rule to civil proceedings long has been recognized in the federal courts. He cites a number of cases. [30] But respondent does not critically distinguish between those cases in which the officer committing the unconstitutional search or seizure was an agent of the sovereign that sought to use the evidence, on the one hand, and those cases, such as the present one, on the other hand, where the officer has no responsibility or duty to, or agreement with, the sovereign seeking to use the evidence. [31]

The seminal cases that apply the exclusionary rule to a civil proceeding involve "intra-sovereign" violations, [32] a situation we need not consider here. In some cases, the courts have refused to create an exclusionary rule for either inter-sovereign or intra-sovereign violations in proceedings other than strictly criminal prosecutions. See United States ex rel. Sperling v. Fitzpatrick, 426 F.2d 1161 (CA2 1970) (intra-sovereign/parole revocation); United States v. Schipani, 435 F.2d 26 (CA2 1970), cert. denied, 401 U.S. 983 (1971) (inter-sovereign/sentencing). [33] And in Compton v. United States, 334 F.2d 212, 215-216 (1964), a case remarkably like this one, the Fourth Circuit held that the presumption of correctness given a tax assessment was not affected by the fact that the assessment was based upon evidence unconstitutionally seized by state criminal law enforcement officers. Only one case cited by the respondent squarely holds that there must be an exclusionary rule barring use in a civil proceeding by one sovereign of material seized in violation of the Fourth Amendment by an officer of another sovereign. [34] In Suarez v. Commissioner, 58 T.C. 792 (1972) (reviewed by the court, with two judges dissenting), the Tax Court determined that the exclusionary rule should be applied in a situation similar to the one that confronts us here. The court concluded that

"any competing consideration based upon the need for effective enforcement of civil tax liabilities (compare Elkins v. United States . . .) must give way to the higher goal of protection of the individual and the necessity for preserving confidence in, rather than encouraging contempt for, the processes of Government."

Id. at 805. No appeal was taken.

We disagree with the broad implications of this statement of the Tax Court for two reasons. To the extent that the court did not focus on the deterrent purpose of the exclusionary rule, the law has since been clarified. See United States v. Calandra, 414 U. S. 338 (1974); United States v. Peltier, 422 U. S. 531 (1975). Moreover, the court did not distinguish between inter-sovereign and intra-sovereign uses of unconstitutionally seized material. Working, as we must, with the absence of convincing empirical data, common sense dictates that the deterrent effect of the exclusion of relevant evidence is highly attenuated when the "punishment" imposed upon the offending criminal enforcement officer is the removal of that evidence from a civil suit by or against a different sovereign. In Elkins, the Court indicated that the assumed interest of criminal law enforcement officers in the criminal proceedings of another sovereign counterbalanced this attenuation sufficiently to justify an exclusionary rule. Here, however, the attenuation is further augmented by the fact that the proceeding is one to enforce only the civil law of the other sovereign.

This attenuation, coupled with the existing deterrence effected by the denial of use of the evidence by either sovereign in the criminal trials with which the searching officer is concerned, creates a situation in which the imposition of the exclusionary rule sought in this case is unlikely to provide significant, much less substantial, additional deterrence. It falls outside the offending officer's zone of primary interest. The extension of the exclusionary rule, in our view, would be an unjustifiably drastic action by the courts in the pursuit of what is an undesired and undesirable supervisory role over police officers. [35] See Rizzo v. Goode, 423 U. S. 362 (1976).

In the past, this Court has opted for exclusion in the anticipation that law enforcement officers would be deterred from violating Fourth Amendment rights. Then, as now, the Court acted in the absence of convincing empirical evidence and relied, instead, on its own assumptions of human nature and the interrelationship of the various components of the law enforcement system. In the situation before us, we do not find sufficient justification for the drastic measure of an exclusionary rule. There comes a point at which courts, consistent with their duty to administer the law, cannot continue to create barriers to law enforcement in the pursuit of a supervisory role that is properly the duty of the Executive and Legislative Branches. We find ourselves at that point in this case. We therefore hold that the judicially created exclusionary rule should not be extended to forbid the use in the civil proceeding of one sovereign of evidence seized by a criminal law enforcement agent of another sovereign.

The judgment of the Court of Appeals is reversed, and the case is remanded for further proceedings consistent with this opinion

It is so ordered.

Stone v. Powell (July 6, 1976) [Notes omitted]

MR. JUSTICE POWELL delivered the opinion of the Court.

Respondents in these cases were convicted of criminal offenses in state courts, and their convictions were affirmed on appeal. The prosecution in each case relied upon evidence obtained by searches and seizures alleged by respondents to have been unlawful. Each respondent subsequently sought relief in a Federal District Court by filing a petition for a writ of federal habeas corpus under 28 U.S.C. § 2254. The question presented is whether a federal court should consider, in ruling on a petition for habeas corpus relief filed by a state prisoner, a claim that evidence obtained by an unconstitutional search or seizure was introduced at his trial, when he has previously been afforded an opportunity for full and fair litigation of his claim in the state courts. The issue is of considerable importance to the administration of criminal justice.

I

We summarize first the relevant facts and procedural history of these cases.

A

Respondent Lloyd Powell was convicted of murder in June, 1968, after trial in a California state court. At about midnight on February 17, 1968, he and three companions entered the Bonanza Liquor Store in San Bernardino, Cal., where Powell became involved in an altercation with Gerald Parsons, the store manager, over the theft of a bottle of wine. In the scuffling that followed, Powell shot and killed Parsons' wife. Ten hours later, an officer of the Henderson, Nev., Police Department arrested Powell for violation of the Henderson vagrancy ordinance, [1] and in the search incident to the arrest discovered a .38-caliber revolver with six expended cartridges in the cylinder.

Powell was extradited to California and convicted of second-degree murder in the Superior Court of San Bernardino County. Parsons and Powell's accomplices at the liquor store testified against him. A criminologist testified that the revolver found on Powell was the gun that killed Parsons' wife. The trial court rejected Powell's contention that testimony by the Henderson police officer as to the search and the discovery of the revolver should have been excluded because the vagrancy ordinance was unconstitutional. In October, 1969, the conviction was affirmed by a California District Court of Appeal. Although the issue was duly presented, that court found it unnecessary to pass upon the legality of the arrest and search because it concluded that the error, if any, in admitting the testimony of the Henderson officer was harmless beyond a reasonable doubt under Chapman v. California, 386 U. S. 18 (1967). The Supreme Court of California denied Powell's petition for habeas corpus relief.

In August, 1971, Powell filed an amended petition for a writ of federal habeas corpus under 28 U.S.C. § 2254 in the United States District Court for the Northern District of California, contending that the testimony concerning the .38-caliber revolver should have been excluded as the fruit of an illegal search. He argued that his arrest had been unlawful because the Henderson vagrancy ordinance was unconstitutionally vague and that the arresting officer lacked probable cause to believe that he was violating it. The District Court concluded that the arresting officer had probable cause, and held that, even if the vagrancy ordinance was unconstitutional, the deterrent purpose of the exclusionary rule does not require that it be applied to bar admission of the fruits of a search incident to an otherwise valid arrest. In the alternative, that court agreed with the California District Court of Appeal that the admission of the evidence concerning Powell's arrest, if error, was harmless beyond a reasonable doubt.

In December, 1974, the Court of Appeals for the Ninth Circuit reversed. 507 F.2d 93. The court concluded that the vagrancy ordinance was unconstitutionally vague, [2] that Powell's arrest was therefore illegal, and that, although exclusion of the evidence would serve no deterrent purpose with regard to police officers who were enforcing statutes in good faith, exclusion would serve the public interest by deterring legislators from enacting unconstitutional statutes. Id. at 98. After an independent review of the evidence, the court concluded that the admission of the evidence was not harmless error, since it supported the testimony of Parsons and Powell's accomplices. Id. at 99.

B

Respondent David Rice was convicted of murder in April, 1971, after trial in a Nebraska state court. At 2:05 a.m. on August 17, 1970, Omaha police received a telephone call that a woman had been heard screaming at 2867 Ohio Street. As one of the officers sent to that address examined a suitcase lying in the doorway, it exploded, killing him instantly. By August, 22 the investigation of the murder centered on Duane Peak, a 15-year-old member of the National Committee to Combat Fascism (NCCF), and that afternoon, a warrant was issued for Peak's arrest. The investigation also focused on other known members of the NCCF, including Rice, some of whom were believed to be planning to kill Peak before he could incriminate them. In their search for Peak, the police went to Rice's home at 10:30 that night and found lights and a television on, but there was no response to their repeated knocking. While some officers remained to watch the premises, a warrant was obtained to search for explosives and illegal weapons believed to be in Rice's possession. Peak was not in the house, but, upon entering, the police discovered, in plain view, dynamite, blasting caps and other materials useful in the construction of explosive devices. Peak subsequently was arrested, and, on August 27, Rice voluntarily surrendered. The clothes Rice was wearing at that time were subjected to chemical analysis, disclosing dynamite particles.

Rice was tried for first-degree murder in the District Court of Douglas County. At trial, Peak admitted planting the suitcase and making the telephone call, and implicated Rice in the bombing plot. As corroborative evidence the State introduced items seized during the search, as well as the results of the chemical analysis of Rice's clothing. The court denied Rice's motion to suppress this evidence. On appeal, the Supreme Court of Nebraska affirmed the conviction, holding that the search of Rice's home had been pursuant to a valid search warrant. State v. Rice, 188 Neb. 728, 199 N.W.2d 480 (1972).

In September, 1972, Rice filed a petition for a writ of habeas corpus in the United States District Court for Nebraska. Rice's sole contention was that his incarceration was unlawful because the evidence underlying his conviction had been discovered as the result of an illegal search of his home. The District Court concluded that the search warrant was invalid, as the supporting affidavit was defective under Spinelli v. United States, 393 U. S. 410 (1969), and Aguilar v. Texas, 378 U. S. 108 (1964). 388 F.Supp. 185, 19194 (1974). [3] The court also rejected the State's contention that, even

if the warrant was invalid, the search was justified because of the valid arrest warrant for Peak and because of the exigent circumstances of the situation -- danger to Peak and search for bombs and explosives believed in possession of the NCCF. The court reasoned that the arrest warrant did not justify the entry, as the police lacked probable cause to believe Peak was in the house, and further concluded that the circumstances were not sufficiently exigent to justify an immediate warrantless search. Id. at 194-202. [4] The Court of Appeals for the Eighth Circuit affirmed, substantially for the reasons stated by the District Court. 513 F.2d 1280 (1975).

Petitioners Stone and Wolff, the wardens of the respective state prisons where Powell and Rice are incarcerated, petitioned for review of these decisions, raising questions concerning the scope of federal habeas corpus and the role of the exclusionary rule upon collateral review of cases involving Fourth Amendment claims. We granted their petitions for certiorari. 4 22 U.S. 1055 (1975). [5] We now reverse.

II

The authority of federal courts to issue the writ of habeas corpus ad subjiciendum [6] was included in the first grant of federal court jurisdiction, made by the Judiciary Act of 1789, c. 20, § 14, 1 Stat. 81, with the limitation that the writ extend only to prisoners held in custody by the United States. The original statutory authorization did not define the substantive reach of the writ. It merely stated that the courts of the United States "shall have power to issue writs of . . . habeas corpus. . . ." Ibid. The courts defined the scope of the writ in accordance with the common law, and limited it to an inquiry as to the jurisdiction of the sentencing tribunal. See, e.g., 28 U. S. 3 Pet. 193 (1830) (Marshall, C.J.).

In 1867, the writ was extended to state prisoners. Act of Feb. 5, 1867, c. 28, § 1, 14 Stat. 385. Under the 1867 Act, federal courts were authorized to give relief in

"all cases where any person may be restrained of his or her liberty in violation of the constitution, or of any treaty or law of the United States. . . ."

But the limitation of federal habeas corpus jurisdiction to consideration of the jurisdiction of the sentencing court persisted. See, e.g., In re Wood,140 U. S. 278 (1891); In re Rahrer,140 U. S. 545 (1891); Andrews v. Swartz,156 U. S. 272 (1895); Bergemann v. Backer,157 U. S. 655 (1895); Pettibone v. Nichols,203 U. S. 192 (1906). And, although the concept of "jurisdiction" was subjected to considerable strain as the substantive scope of the writ was expanded, [7] this expansion was limited to only a few classes of cases [8] until Frank v. Mangum,237 U. S. 309, in 1915. In Frank, the prisoner had claimed in the state courts that the proceedings which resulted in his conviction for murder had been dominated by a mob. After the State Supreme Court rejected his contentions, Frank unsuccessfully sought habeas corpus relief in the Federal District Court. This Court affirmed the denial of relief because Frank's federal claims had been considered by a competent and unbiased state tribunal. The Court recognized, however, that, if a habeas corpus court found that the State had failed to provide adequate "corrective process" for the full and fair litigation of federal claims, whether or not "jurisdictional," the court could inquire into the merits to determine whether a detention was lawful. Id. at 237 U. S. 333-336.

In the landmark decision in Brown v. Allen,344 U. S. 443, 344 U. S. 482-487 (1953), the scope of the writ was expanded still further. [9] In that case and its companion case, Daniels v. Allen, state prisoners applied for federal habeas corpus relief, claiming that the trial courts had erred in failing to quash their indictments due to alleged discrimination in the selection of grand jurors and in ruling certain confessions admissible. In Brown, the highest court of the State had rejected these claims on direct appeal, State v. Brown, 233 N.C. 202, 63 S.E.2d 99, and this Court had denied certiorari, 341 U.S. 943 (1951). Despite the apparent adequacy of the state corrective process, the Court reviewed the denial of the writ of habeas corpus and held that Brown was entitled to a full reconsideration of these constitutional claims, including, if appropriate, a hearing in the Federal District Court. In Daniels, however, the State Supreme Court, on direct review, had refused to consider the appeal because the papers were filed out of time. This Court held that, since the state court judgment rested on a reasonable application of the State's legitimate procedural rules, a ground that would have barred direct review of his federal claims by this Court, the District Court lacked authority to grant habeas corpus relief. See 344 U.S. at 344 U. S. 458, 486.

This final barrier to broad collateral reexamination of state criminal convictions in federal habeas corpus proceedings was removed in Fay v. Noia,372 U. S. 391 (1963). [10] Noia and two codefendants had been convicted of felony murder. The sole evidence against each defendant was a signed confession. Noia's codefendants, but not Noia himself, appealed their convictions. Although their appeals were unsuccessful, in subsequent state proceedings, they were able to establish that their confessions had been coerced, and their convictions therefore procured in violation of the Constitution. In a subsequent federal habeas corpus proceeding, it was stipulated that Noia's confession also had been coerced, but the District Court followed Daniels in holding that Noia's failure to appeal barred habeas corpus review. See United States v. Fay, 183 F.Supp. 222, 225 (SDNY 1960). The Court of Appeals reversed, ordering that Noia's conviction be set aside and that he be released from custody or that a new trial be granted. This Court affirmed the grant of the writ, narrowly restricting the circumstances in which a federal court may refuse to consider the merits of federal constitutional claims. [11]

During the period in which the substantive scope of the writ was expanded, the Court did not consider whether exceptions to full review might exist with respect to particular categories of constitutional claims. Prior to the Court's decision in Kaufman v. United States,394 U. S. 217 (1969), however, a substantial majority of the Federal Courts of Appeals had concluded that collateral review of search and seizure claims was inappropriate on motions filed by federal prisoners under 28 U.S.C. § 2255, the modern post-conviction procedure available to federal prisoners in lieu of habeas corpus. [12] The primary rationale advanced in support of those decisions was that Fourth Amendment violations are different in kind from denials of Fifth or Sixth Amendment rights, in that claims of illegal search and seizure do not

"impugn the integrity of the factfinding process or challenge evidence as inherently unreliable; rather, the exclusion of illegally seized evidence is simply a prophylactic device intended generally to deter Fourth Amendment violations by law enforcement officers."

394 U.S. at 394 U. S. 224. See Thornton v. United States, 125 U.S.App.D.C. 114, 368 F.2d 822 (1966).

Kaufman rejected this rationale and held that search and seizure claims are cognizable in § 2255 proceedings. The Court noted that "the federal habeas remedy extends to state prisoners alleging that unconstitutionally obtained evidence was admitted against them at trial," 394 U.S. at 394 U. S. 225, citing, e.g., 392 U. S. DeForte, 392 U.S. 364 (1968); Carafas v. LaVallee, 391 U. S. 234 (1968), and concluded, as a matter of statutory construction, that there was no basis for restricting

"access by federal prisoners with illegal search and seizure claims to federal collateral remedies, while placing no similar restriction on access by state prisoners,"

394 U.S. at 394 U. S. 226. Although, in recent years, the view has been expressed that the Court should reexamine the substantive scope of federal habeas jurisdiction and limit collateral review of search and seizure claims

"solely to the question of whether the petitioner was provided a fair opportunity to raise and have adjudicated the question in state courts,"

Schneckloth v. Bustamonte, 412 U. S. 218, 412 U. S. 250 (1973) (POWELL, J., concurring), [13] the Court, without discussion or consideration of the issue, has continued to accept jurisdiction in cases raising such claims. See Lefkowitz v. Newsome, 420 U. S. 283 (1975); Cady v. Dombrowski, 413 U. S. 433 (1973); Cardwell v. Lewis, 417 U. S. 583 (1974) (plurality opinion). [14]

The discussion in Kaufman of the scope of federal habeas corpus rests on the view that the effectuation of the Fourth Amendment, as applied to the States through the Fourteenth Amendment, requires the granting of habeas corpus relief when a prisoner has been convicted in state court on the basis of evidence obtained in an illegal search or seizure, since those Amendments were held in Mapp v. Ohio,367 U. S. 643 (1961), to require exclusion of such evidence at trial and reversal of conviction upon direct review. [15] Until these cases, we have not had occasion fully to consider the validity of this view. See, e.g., Schneckloth v. Bustamonte, supra at 412 U. S. 249 n. 3; Cardwell v. Lewis, supra at 417 U. S. 596, and n. 12. Upon examination, we conclude, in light of the nature and purpose of the Fourth Amendment exclusionary rule, that this view is unjustified. [16] We hold, therefore, that where the State has provided an opportunity for full and fair litigation of a Fourth Amendment claim, the Constitution does not require that a state prisoner be granted federal habeas corpus relief on the ground that evidence obtained in an unconstitutional search or seizure was introduced at his trial. [17]

III

The Fourth Amendment assures the "right

of the people to be secure in their persons, houses, papers, and effects, against unreasonable searches and seizures." The Amendment was primarily a reaction to the evils associated with the use of the general warrant in England and the writs of assistance in the Colonies, Stanford v. Texas,379 U. S. 476, 379 U. S. 481-485 (1965); Frank v. Maryland,359 U. S. 360, 359 U. S. 363-365 (1959), and was intended to protect the "sanctity of a man's home and the privacies of life," Boyd v. United States,116 U. S. 616, 116 U. S. 630 (1886), from searches under unchecked general authority. [18]

The exclusionary rule was a judicially created means of effectuating the rights secured by the Fourth Amendment. Prior to the Court's decisions in Weeks v. United States,232 U. S. 383 (1914), and Gouled v. United States,255 U. S. 298 (1921), there existed no barrier to the introduction in criminal trials of evidence obtained in violation of the Amendment. See Adams v. New York, 192 U. S. 585 (1904). [19] In Weeks, the Court held that the defendant could petition before trial for the return of property secured through an illegal search or seizure conducted by federal authorities. In Gouled, the Court held broadly that such evidence could not be introduced in a federal prosecution. See Warden v. Hayden,387 U. S. 294, 387 U. S. 304-305 (1967). See also Silverthorne Lumber Co. v. United States,251 U. S. 385 (1920) (fruits of illegally seized evidence). Thirty-five years after Weeks, the Court held in Wolf v. Colorado,338 U. S. 25 (1949), that the right to be free from arbitrary intrusion by the police that is protected by the Fourth Amendment is

"implicit in 'the concept of ordered liberty,' and, as such, enforceable against the States through the [Fourteenth Amendment] Due Process Clause."

Id. at 338 U. S. 27-28. The Court concluded, however, that the Weeks exclusionary rule would not be imposed upon the States as "an essential ingredient of [that] right." 338 U.S. at 338 U. S. 29. The full force of Wolf was eroded in subsequent decisions, see Elkins v. United States,364 U. S. 206 (1960); Rea v. United States,350 U. S. 214 (1956), and, a little more than a decade later, the exclusionary rule was held applicable to the States in Mapp v. Ohio,367 U. S. 643 (1961).

Decisions prior to Mapp advanced two principal reasons for application of the rule in federal trials. The Court in Elkins, for example, in the context of its special supervisory role over the lower federal courts, referred to the "imperative of judicial integrity," suggesting that exclusion of illegally seized evidence prevents contamination of the judicial process. 364 U.S. at 364 U. S. 222. [20] But even in that context, a more pragmatic ground was emphasized:

"The rule is calculated to prevent, not to repair. Its purpose is to deter -- to compel respect for the constitutional guaranty in the only effectively available way -- by removing the incentive to disregard it."

Id. at 364 U. S. 217. The Mapp majority justified the application of the rule to the States on several grounds, [21] but relied principally upon the belief that exclusion would deter future unlawful police conduct. 367 U.S. at 367 U. S. 658.

Although our decisions often have alluded to the "imperative of judicial integrity," e.g., United States v. Peltier,422 U. S. 531, 422 U. S. 536-539 (1975), they demonstrate the limited role of this justification in the determination whether to apply the rule in a particular context. [22] Logically extended, this justification would require that courts exclude unconstitutionally seized evidence despite lack of objection by the defendant, or even over his assent. Cf. Henry v. Mississippi,379 U. S. 443 (1965). It also would require abandonment of the standing limitations on who may object to the introduction of unconstitutionally seized evidence, Alderman v. United States,394 U. S. 165 (1969), and retreat from the proposition that judicial proceedings need not abate when the defendant's person is unconstitutionally seized, Gerstein v. Pugh,420 U. S. 103, 420 U. S. 119 (1975); Frisbie v. Collins,342 U. S. 519 (1952). Similarly, the interest in promoting judicial integrity does not prevent the use of illegally seized evidence in grand jury proceedings. United States v. Calandra,414 U. S. 338 (1974). Nor does it require that the trial court exclude such evidence from use for impeachment of a defendant, even though its introduction is certain to result in conviction in some cases. Walder v. United States,347 U. S. 62 (1954). The teaching of these cases is clear. While courts, of course, must ever be concerned with preserving the integrity of the judicial process, this concern has limited force as a justification for the exclusion of highly probative evidence. [23]

The force of this justification becomes minimal where federal habeas corpus relief is sought by a prisoner who previously has been afforded the opportunity for full and fair consideration of his search and seizure claim at trial and on direct review.

The primary justification for the exclusionary rule then is the deterrence of police conduct that violates Fourth Amendment rights. Post-Mapp decisions have established that the rule is not a personal constitutional right. It is not calculated to redress the injury to the privacy of the victim of the search or seizure, for any "[r]eparation comes too late." Linkletter v. Walker,381 U. S. 618, 381 U. S. 637 (196). Instead,

"the rule is a judicially created remedy designed to safeguard Fourth Amendment rights generally through its deterrent effect. . . ."

United States v. Calandra, supra at 414 U. S. 348. Accord, United States v. Peltier, supra at 422 U. S. 538-539; Terry v. Ohio,392 U. S. 1, 392 U. S. 28-29 (1968); Linkletter v. Walker, supra at 381 U. S. 636-637; Tehan v. United States ex rel. Shott,382 U. S. 406, 382 U. S. 416 (1966).

Mapp involved the enforcement of the exclusionary rule at state trials and on direct review. The decision in Kaufman, as noted above, is premised on the view that implementation of the Fourth Amendment also requires the consideration of search and seizure claims upon collateral review of state convictions. But despite the broad deterrent purpose of the exclusionary rule, it has never been interpreted to proscribe the introduction of illegally seized evidence in all proceedings or against all persons. As in the case of any remedial device, "the application of the rule has been restricted to those areas where its remedial objectives are thought most efficaciously served." United States v. Calandra, supra at 414 U. S. 348. [24] Thus, our refusal to extend the exclusionary rule to grand jury proceedings was based on a balancing of the potential injury to the historic role and function of the grand jury by such extension against the potential contribution to the effectuation of the Fourth Amendment through deterrence of police misconduct:

"Any incremental deterrent effect which might be achieved by extending the rule to grand jury proceedings is uncertain, at best. Whatever deterrence of police misconduct may result from the exclusion of illegally seized evidence from criminal trials, it is unrealistic to assume that application of the rule to grand jury proceedings would significantly further that goal. Such an extension would deter only police investigation consciously directed toward the discovery of evidence solely for use in a grand jury investigation. . . . We therefore decline to embrace a view that would achieve a speculative and undoubtedly minimal advance in the deterrence of police misconduct at the expense of substantially impeding the role of the grand jury."

414 U.S. at 414 U. S. 351-352 (footnote omitted).

The same pragmatic analysis of the exclusionary rule's usefulness in a particular context was evident earlier in Walder v. United States, supra, where the Court permitted the Government to use unlawfully seized evidence to impeach the credibility of a defendant who had testified broadly in his own defense. The Court held, in effect, that the interests safeguarded by the exclusionary rule in that context were outweighed by the need to prevent perjury and to assure the integrity of the trial process. The judgment in Walder revealed most clearly that the policies behind the exclusionary rule are not absolute. Rather, they must be evaluated in light of competing policies. In that case, the public interest in determination of truth at trial [25] was deemed to outweigh the incremental contribution that might have been made to the protection of Fourth Amendment values by application of the rule.

The balancing process at work in these cases also finds expression in the standing requirement. Standing to invoke the exclusionary rule has been found to exist only when the Government attempts to use illegally obtained evidence to incriminate the victim of the illegal search. Brown v. United States,411 U. S. 223 (1973); Alderman v. United States,394 U. S. 165 (1969); Wong Sun v. United States,371 U. S. 471, 371 U. S. 491-492 (1963). See Jones v. United States,362 U. S. 257, 362 U. S. 261 (1960). The standing requirement is premised on the view that the "additional benefits of extending the . . . rule" to defendants other than the victim of the search or seizure are outweighed by the

"further encroachment upon the public interest in prosecuting those accused of crime and having them acquitted or convicted on the basis of all the evidence which exposes the truth."

Alderman v. United States, supra at 394 U. S. 174-175. [26]

IV

We turn now to the specific question presented by these cases. Respondents allege violations of Fourth Amendment rights guaranteed them through the Fourteenth Amendment. The question is whether state prisoners -- who have been afforded the opportunity for full and fair consideration of their reliance upon the exclusionary rule with respect to seized evidence by the state courts at trial and on direct review -- may invoke their claim again on federal habeas corpus review. The answer is to be found by weighing the utility of the exclusionary rule against the costs of extending it to collateral review of Fourth Amendment claims.

The costs of applying the exclusionary rule even at trial and on direct review are well known: [27] the focus of the trial, and the attention of the participants therein, are diverted from the ultimate question of guilt or innocence that should be the central concern in a criminal proceeding. [28] Moreover, the physical evidence sought to be excluded is typically reliable and often the most probative information bearing on the guilt or innocence of the defendant. As Mr. Justice Black emphasized in his dissent in Kaufman:

"A claim of illegal search and seizure under the Fourth Amendment is crucially different from many other constitutional rights; ordinarily, the evidence seized can in no way have been rendered untrustworthy by the means of its seizure, and indeed often this evidence alone establishes beyond virtually any shadow of a doubt that the defendant is guilty."

394 U.S. at 394 U. S. 237. Application of the rule thus deflects the truthfinding process, and often frees the guilty. The disparity in particular cases between the error committed by the police officer and the windfall afforded a guilty defendant by application of the rule is contrary to the idea of proportionality that is essential to the concept of justice. [29] Thus, although the rule is thought to deter unlawful police activity in part through the nurturing of respect for Fourth Amendment values, if applied indiscriminately, it may well have the opposite effect of generating disrespect for the

law and administration of justice. [30] These long-recognized costs of the rule persist when a criminal conviction is sought to be overturned on collateral review on the ground that a search and seizure claim was erroneously rejected by two or more tiers of state courts. [31]

Evidence obtained by police officers in violation of the Fourth Amendment is excluded at trial in the hope that the frequency of future violations will decrease. Despite the absence of supportive empirical evidence, [32] we have assumed that the immediate effect of exclusion will be to discourage law enforcement officials from violating the Fourth Amendment by removing the incentive to disregard it. More importantly, over the long-term, this demonstration that our society attaches serious consequences to violation of constitutional rights is thought to encourage those who formulate law enforcement policies, and the officers who implement them, to incorporate Fourth Amendment ideals into their value system. [33]

We adhere to the view that these considerations support the implementation of the exclusionary rule at trial and its enforcement on direct appeal of state court convictions. But the additional contribution, if any, of the consideration of search and seizure claims of state prisoners on collateral review is small in relation to the costs. To be sure, each case in which such claim is considered may add marginally to an awareness of the values protected by the Fourth Amendment. There is no reason to believe, however, that the overall educative effect of the exclusionary rule would be appreciably diminished if search and seizure claims could not be raised in federal habeas corpus review of state convictions. [34] Nor is there reason to assume that any specific disincentive already created by the risk of exclusion of evidence at trial or the reversal of convictions on direct review would be enhanced if there were the further risk that a conviction

obtained in state court and affirmed on direct review might be overturned in collateral proceedings often occurring years after the incarceration of the defendant. The view that the deterrence of Fourth Amendment violations would be furthered rests on the dubious assumption that law enforcement authorities would fear that federal habeas review might reveal flaws in a search or seizure that went undetected at trial and on appeal. [35] Even if one rationally could assume that some additional incremental deterrent effect would be present in isolated cases, the resulting advance of the legitimate goal of furthering Fourth Amendment rights would be outweighed by the acknowledged costs to other values vital to a rational system of criminal justice.

In sum, we conclude that, where the State has provided an opportunity for full and fair litigation of a Fourth Amendment claim, [36] a state prisoner may not be granted federal habeas corpus relief on the ground that evidence obtained in an unconstitutional search or seizure was introduced at his trial. [37] In this context, the contribution of the exclusionary rule, if any, to the effectuation of the Fourth Amendment is minimal, and the substantial societal costs of application of the rule persist with special force. [38]

Accordingly, the judgments of the Courts of Appeals are

Reversed.

US v. Chadwick (June 21, 1977) [Notes omitted]

MR. CHIEF JUSTICE BURGER delivered the opinion of the Court.

We granted certiorari in this case to decide whether a search warrant is required before federal agents may open a locked footlocker which they have lawfully seized at the time of the arrest of its owners, when there is probable cause to believe the footlocker contains contraband.

(1)

On May 8, 1973, Amtrak railroad officials in San Diego observed respondents Gregory Machado and Bridget Leary load a brown footlocker onto a train bound for Boston. Their suspicions were aroused when they noticed that the trunk was unusually heavy for its size, and that it was leaking talcum powder, a substance often used to mask the odor of marihuana or hashish. Because Machado matched a profile used to spot drug traffickers, the railroad officials reported these circumstances to federal agents in San Diego, who, in turn, relayed the information, together with detailed descriptions of Machado and the footlocker, to their counterparts in Boston.

When the train arrived in Boston two days later, federal narcotics agents were on hand. Though the officers had not obtained an arrest or search warrant, they had with them a police dog trained to detect marihuana. The agents identified Machado and Leary and kept them under surveillance as they claimed their suitcases and the footlocker, which had been transported by baggage cart from the train to the departure area. Machado and Leary lifted the footlocker from the baggage cart, placed it on the floor and sat down on it.

The agents then released the dog near the footlocker. Without alerting respondents, the dog signaled the presence of a controlled substance inside. Respondent Chadwick then joined Machado and Leary, and they engaged an attendant to move the footlocker outside to Chadwick's waiting automobile. Machado, Chadwick, and the attendant together lifted the 200-pound footlocker into the trunk of the car while Leary waited in the front seat. At that point, while the trunk of the car was still open and before the car engine had been started, the officers arrested all three. A search disclosed no weapons, but the keys to the footlocker were apparently taken from Machado.

Respondents were taken to the Federal Building in Boston; the agents followed with Chadwick's car and the footlocker. As the Government concedes, from the moment of respondents' arrests at about 9 p.m., the footlocker remained under the exclusive control of law enforcement officers at all times. The footlocker and luggage were placed in the Federal Building, where, as one of the agents later testified, "there was no risk that whatever was contained in the footlocker trunk would be removed by the defendants or their associates." App. 44. The agents had no reason to believe that the footlocker contained explosives or other inherently dangerous items, or that it contained evidence which would lose its value unless the footlocker were opened at once. Facilities were readily available in which the footlocker could have been stored securely; it is not contended that there was any exigency calling for an immediate search.

At the Federal Building an hour and a half after the arrests, the agents opened the footlocker and luggage. They did not obtain respondents' consent; they did not secure a search warrant. The footlocker was locked with a padlock and a regular trunk lock. It is unclear whether it was opened with the keys taken from respondent Machado or by other means. Large amounts of marihuana were found in the footlocker. [1]

Respondents were indicted for possession of marihuana with intent to distribute it in violation of 21 U.S.C. § 841(a)(1), and for conspiracy in violation of 21 U.S.C. § 846. Before trial, they moved to suppress the marihuana obtained from the footlocker. In the District Court, the Government sought to justify its failure to secure a search warrant under the "automobile exception" of Chambers v. Maroney, 399 U. S. 42 (1970), and as a search incident to the arrests. Holding that "[w]arrantless searches are per se unreasonable, subject to a few carefully delineated and limited exceptions," the District Court rejected both justifications. 393 F.Supp. 763, 771

(Mass.1975). The court saw the relationship between the footlocker and Chadwick's automobile as merely coincidental, and held that the double-locked, 200-pound footlocker was not part of "the area from within which [respondents] might gain possession of a weapon or destructible evidence." Chimel v. California, 395 U. S. 752, 395 U. S. 763 (1969).

A divided Court of Appeals for the First Circuit affirmed the suppression of the seized marihuana. The court held that the footlocker had been properly taken into federal custody after respondents' lawful arrest; it also agreed that the agents had probable cause to believe that the footlocker contained a controlled substance when they opened it. But probable cause alone was held not enough to sustain the warrantless search.

On the premise that warrantless searches are per se unreasonable unless they fall within some established exception to the warrant requirement, the Court of Appeals agreed with the District Court that the footlocker search was not justified either under the "automobile exception" or as a search incident to a lawful arrest.

The Court of Appeals then responded to an argument, suggested by the Government for the first time on appeal, that movable personalty lawfully seized in a public place should be subject to search without a warrant if there exists probable cause to believe it contains evidence of a crime. Conceding that such personalty shares some characteristics of mobility which support warrantless automobile searches, the court nevertheless concluded that a rule permitting a search of personalty on probable cause alone had not yet

"received sufficient recognition by the Supreme Court outside the automobile area, or generally, for us to recognize it as a valid exception to the fourth amendment warrant requirement."

532 F.2d 773, 781 (1976). We granted certiorari, 429 U.S. 814 (1976). We affirm.

(2)

In this Court, the Government again contends that the Fourth Amendment Warrant Clause protects only interests traditionally identified with the home. [2] Recalling the colonial writs of assistance, which were often executed in searches of private dwellings, the Government claims that the Warrant Clause was adopted primarily, if not exclusively, in response to unjustified intrusions into private homes on the authority of general warrants. The Government argues there is no evidence that the Framers of the Fourth Amendment intended to disturb the established practice of permitting warrantless searches outside the home, or to modify the initial clause of the Fourth Amendment by making warrantless searches supported by probable cause per se unreasonable.

Drawing on its reading of history, the Government argues that only homes, offices, and private communications implicate interests which lie at the core of the Fourth Amendment. Accordingly, it is only in these contexts that the determination whether a search or seizure is reasonable should turn on whether a warrant has been obtained. In all other situations, the Government contends, less significant privacy values are at stake, and the reasonableness of a government intrusion should depend solely on whether there is probable cause to believe evidence of criminal conduct is present. Where personal effects are lawfully seized outside the home on probable cause, the Government would thus regard searches without a warrant as not "unreasonable."

We do not agree that the Warrant Clause protects only dwellings and other specifically designated locales. As we have noted before, the Fourth Amendment "protects people, not places," Katz v. United States, 389 U. S. 347, 389 U. S. 351 (1967); more particularly, it protects people from unreasonable government intrusions into their legitimate expectations of privacy. In this case, the

Warrant Clause makes a significant contribution to that protection. The question, then, is whether a warrantless search in these circumstances was unreasonable. [3]

(3)

It cannot be doubted that the Fourth Amendment's commands grew in large measure out of the colonists' experience with the writs of assistance and their memories of the general warrants formerly in use in England. These writs, which were issued on executive, rather than judicial, authority, granted sweeping power to customs officials and other agents of the King to search at large for smuggled goods. Though the authority to search granted by the writs was not limited to the home, searches conducted pursuant to them often were carried out in private residences. See generally Stanford v. Texas, 379 U. S. 476, 379 U. S. 481-485 (1965); Marcus v. Search Warrant, 367 U. S. 717, 367 U. S. 724-729 (1961); Frank v. Maryland, 359 U. S. 360 (1959).

Although the searches and seizures which deeply concerned the colonists, and which were foremost in the minds of the Framers, were those involving invasions of the home, it would be a mistake to conclude, as the Government contends, that the Warrant Clause was therefore intended to guard only against intrusions into the home. First, the Warrant Clause does not, in terms, distinguish between searches conducted in private homes and other searches. There is also a strong historical connection between the Warrant Clause and the initial clause of the Fourth Amendment, which draws no distinctions among "persons, houses, papers, and effects" in safeguarding against unreasonable searches and seizures. See United States v. Rabinowitz, 339 U. S. 56, 339 U. S. 68 (1950) (Frankfurter, J., dissenting).

Moreover, if there is little evidence that the Framers intended the Warrant Clause to operate outside the home, there is no evidence at all that they intended to exclude from protection of the Clause all searches occurring outside the home. The absence of a contemporary outcry against warrantless searches in public places was because, aside from searches incident to arrest, such warrantless searches were not a large issue in colonial America. Thus, silence in the historical record tells us little about the Framers' attitude toward application of the Warrant Clause to the search of respondents' footlocker. [4] What we do know is that the Framers were men who focused on the wrongs of that day, but who intended the Fourth Amendment to safeguard fundamental values which would far outlast the specific abuses which gave it birth.

Moreover, in this area, we do not write on a clean slate. Our fundamental inquiry in considering Fourth Amendment issues is whether or not a search or seizure is reasonable under all the circumstances. Cooper v. California, 386 U. S. 58 (1967). The judicial warrant has a significant role to play, in that it provides the detached scrutiny of a neutral magistrate, which is a more reliable safeguard against improper searches than the hurried judgment of a law enforcement officer "engaged in the often competitive enterprise of ferreting out crime." Johnson v. United States, 333 U. S. 10, 333 U. S. 14 (1948). Once a lawful search has begun, it is also far more likely that it will not exceed proper bounds when it is done pursuant to a judicial authorization "particularly describing the place to be searched and the persons or things to be seized." Further, a warrant assures the individual whose property is searched or seized of the lawful authority of the executing officer, his need to search, and the limits of his power to search. Camara v. Municipal Court, 387 U. S. 523, 387 U. S. 532 (1967).

Just as the Fourth Amendment "protects people, not places," the protections a judicial warrant offers against erroneous governmental intrusions are effective whether applied in or out of the home. Accordingly, we have held warrantless searches unreasonable, and therefore unconstitutional, in a variety of settings. [5] A century ago, Mr. Justice Field, speaking for the Court, included within the reach of the Warrant Clause printed matter traveling through the mails within the United States:

"Letters and sealed packages of this kind in the mail are as fully guarded from examination and inspection, except as to their outward form and weight, as if they were retained by the parties forwarding them in their own domiciles. The constitutional guaranty of the right of the people to be secure in their papers against unreasonable searches and seizures extends to their papers, thus closed against inspection, wherever they may be. Whilst in the mail, they can only be opened and examined under like warrant, issued upon similar oath or affirmation, particularly describing the thing to be seized, as is required when papers are subjected to search in one's own household."

Ex parte Jackson, 96 U. S. 727, 96 U. S. 733 (1878). We reaffirmed Jackson in United States v. Van Leeuwen, 397 U. S. 249 (1970), where a search warrant was obtained to open two packages which, on mailing, the sender had declared contained only coins. Judicial warrants have been required for other searches conducted outside the home. E.g., Katz v. United States, 389 U. S. 347 (1967) (electronic interception of conversation in public telephone booth); Coolidge v. New Hampshire, 403 U. S. 443 (1971) (automobile on private premises); Preston v. United States, 376 U. S. 364 (1964) (automobile in custody); United States v. Jeffers, 342 U. S. 48 (1951) (hotel room); G. M. Leasing Corp. v. United States, 429 U. S. 338 (1977) (office); Mancusi v. DeForte, 392 U. S. 364 (1968) (office). These cases illustrate the applicability of the Warrant Clause beyond the narrow limits suggested by the Government. They also reflect the settled constitutional principle, discussed earlier, that a fundamental purpose of the Fourth Amendment is to safeguard individuals from unreasonable government invasions of legitimate privacy interests, [6] and not simply those interests found inside the four walls of the home. Wolf v. Colorado, 338 U. S. 25, 338 U. S. 27 (1949).

In this case, important Fourth Amendment privacy interests were at stake. By placing personal effects inside a double-locked footlocker, respondents manifested an expectation that the contents would remain free from public examination. No less than one who locks the doors of his home against intruders, one who safeguards his personal possessions in this manner is due the protection of the Fourth Amendment Warrant Clause. There being no exigency, it was unreasonable for the Government to conduct this search without the safeguards a judicial warrant provides.

(4)

The Government does not contend that the footlocker's brief contact with Chadwick's car makes this an automobile search, but it is argued that the rationale of our automobile search cases demonstrates the reasonableness of permitting warrantless searches of luggage; the Government views such luggage as analogous to motor vehicles for Fourth Amendment purposes. It is true that, like the footlocker in issue here, automobiles are "effects" under the Fourth Amendment, and searches and seizures of automobiles are therefore subject to the constitutional standard of reasonableness. But this Court has recognized significant differences between motor vehicles and other property which permit warrantless searches of automobiles in circumstances in which warrantless searches would not be reasonable in other contexts. Carroll v. United States, 267 U. S. 132 (1925); Preston v. United States, supra at 376 U. S. 366-367; Chambers v. Maroney, 399 U. S. 42 (1970). See also South Dakota v. Opperman, 428 U. S. 364, 428 U. S. 367 (1976).

Our treatment of automobiles has been

based in part on their inherent mobility, which often makes obtaining a judicial warrant impracticable. Nevertheless, we have also sustained

"warrantless searches of vehicles . . . in cases in which the possibilities of the vehicle's being removed or evidence in it destroyed were remote, if not nonexistent."

Cady v. Dombrowski, 413 U. S. 433, 413 U. S. 441-442 (1973); accord, South Dakota v. Opperman, supra at 428 U. S. 367; see Texas v. White, 423 U. S. 67 (1975); Chambers v. Maroney, supra; Cooper v. California, 386 U. S. 58 (1967).

The answer lies in the diminished expectation of privacy which surrounds the automobile:

"One has a lesser expectation of privacy in a motor vehicle because its function is transportation and it seldom serves as one's residence or as the repository of personal effects. . . . It travels public thoroughfares where both its occupants and its contents are in plain view."

Cardwell v. Lewis, 417 U. S. 583, 417 U. S. 590 (1974) (plurality opinion). Other factors reduce automobile privacy.

"All States require vehicles to be registered and operators to be licensed. States and localities have enacted extensive and detailed codes regulating the condition and manner in which motor vehicles may be operated on public streets and highways."

Cady v. Dombrowski, supra, at 413 U. S. 441. Automobiles periodically undergo official inspection, and they are often taken into police custody in the interests of public safety. South Dakota v. Opperman, supra at 428 U. S. 368.

The factors which diminish the privacy aspects of an automobile do not apply to respondents' footlocker. Luggage contents are not open to public view, except as a condition to a border entry or common carrier travel; nor is luggage subject to regular inspections and official

scrutiny on a continuing basis. Unlike an automobile, whose primary function is transportation, luggage is intended as a repository of personal effects. In sum, a person's expectations of privacy in personal luggage are substantially greater than in an automobile.

Nor does the footlocker's mobility justify dispensing with the added protections of the Warrant Clause. Once the federal agents had seized it at the railroad station and had safely transferred it to the Boston Federal Building under their exclusive control, there was not the slightest danger that the footlocker or its contents could have been removed before a valid search warrant could be obtained. [7] The initial seizure and detention of the footlocker, the validity of which respondents do not contest, were sufficient to guard against any risk that evidence might be lost. With the footlocker safely immobilized, it was unreasonable to undertake the additional and greater intrusion of a search without a warrant. [8]

Finally, the Government urges that the Constitution permits the warrantless search of any property in the possession of a person arrested in public, so long as there is probable cause to believe that the property contains contraband or evidence of crime. Although recognizing that the footlocker was not within respondents' immediate control, the Government insists that the search was reasonable because the footlocker was seized contemporaneously with respondents' arrests, and was searched as soon thereafter as was practicable. The reasons justifying search in a custodial arrest are quite different. When a custodial arrest is made, there is always some danger that the person arrested may seek to use a weapon, or that evidence may be concealed or destroyed. To safeguard himself and others, and to prevent the loss of evidence, it has been held reasonable for the arresting officer to conduct a prompt, warrantless

"search of the arrestee's person and the area 'within his immediate control' -- construing that phrase to mean the area from within which he might gain possession of a weapon or destructible evidence."

Chimel v. California, 395 U.S. at 395 U. S. 763. See also Terry v. Ohio, 392 U. S. 1 (1968). Such searches may be conducted without a warrant, and they may also be made whether or not there is probable cause to believe that the person arrested may have a weapon or is about to destroy evidence. The potential dangers lurking in all custodial arrests make warrantless searches of items within the "immediate control" area reasonable without requiring the arresting officer to calculate the probability that weapons or destructible evidence may be involved. United States v. Robinson, 414 U. S. 218 (1973); Terry v. Ohio, supra. However, warrantless searches of luggage or other property seized at the time of an arrest cannot be justified as incident to that arrest either if the "search is remote in time or place from the arrest," Preston v. United States, 376 U.S. at 376 U. S. 367, or no exigency exists. Once law enforcement officers have reduced luggage or other personal property not immediately associated with the person of the arrestee to their exclusive control, and there is no longer any danger that the arrestee might gain access to the property to seize a weapon or destroy evidence, a search of that property is no longer an incident of the arrest. [9]

Here, the search was conducted more than an hour after federal agents had gained exclusive control of the footlocker and long after respondents were securely in custody; the search therefore cannot be viewed as incidental to the arrest or as justified by any other exigency. Even though on this record the issuance of a warrant by a judicial officer was reasonably predictable, a line must be drawn. In our view, when no exigency is shown to support the need for an immediate search, the Warrant Clause places the line at the point where the property to be searched comes under the exclusive dominion of police authority.

Respondents were therefore entitled to the protection of the Warrant Clause with the evaluation of a neutral magistrate, before their privacy interests in the contents of the footlocker were invaded. [10]

Accordingly, the judgment is Affirmed.

Marshall v. Barlow's, Inc. (May 23, 1978) [Notes omitted]

MR. JUSTICE WHITE delivered the opinion of the Court.

Section 8(a) of the Occupational Safety and Health Act of 1970 (OSHA or Act) [1] empowers agent of the Secretary of Labor (Secretary) to search the work area of any employment facility within the Act's jurisdiction. The purpose of the search is to inspect for safety hazards and violations of OSHA regulations. No search warrant or other process is expressly required under the Act.

On the morning of September 11, 1975, an OSHA inspector entered the customer service area of Barlow's, Inc., an electrical and plumbing installation business located in Pocatello, Idaho. The president and general manager, Ferrol G. "Bill" Barlow, was on hand; and the OSHA inspector, after showing his credentials, [2] informed Mr. Barlow that he wished to conduct a search of the working areas of the business. Mr. Barlow inquired whether any complaint had been received about his company. The inspector answered no, but that Barlow's, Inc., had simply turned up in the agency's selection process. The inspector again asked to enter the nonpublic area of the business; Mr. Barlow's response was to inquire whether the inspector had a search warrant. The inspector had none. Thereupon, Mr. Barlow refused the inspector admission to the employee area of his business. He said he was relying on his rights as guaranteed by the Fourth

Amendment of the United States Constitution.

Three months later, the Secretary petitioned the United States District Court for the District of Idaho to issue an order compelling Mr. Barlow to admit the inspector. [3] The requested order was issued on December 30, 1975, and was presented to Mr. Barlow on January 5, 1976. Mr. Barlow again refused admission, and he sought his own injunctive relief against the warrantless searches assertedly permitted by OSHA. A three-judge court was convened. On December 30, 1976, it ruled in Mr. Barlow's favor. 424 F.Supp. 437. Concluding that Camara v. Municipal Court, 387 U. S. 523, 387 U. S. 528-529 (1967), and See v. Seattle, 387 U. S. 541, 387 U. S. 543 (1967), controlled this case, the court held that the Fourth Amendment required a warrant for the type of search involved here [4] and that the statutory authorization for warrantless inspections was unconstitutional. An injunction against searches or inspections pursuant to § 8(a) was entered. The Secretary appealed, challenging the judgment, and we noted probable jurisdiction. 430 U.S. 964.

I

The Secretary urges that warrantless inspections to enforce OSHA are reasonable within the meaning of the Fourth Amendment. Among other things, he relies on § 8(a) of the Act, 29 U.S.C. § 657(a), which authorizes inspection of business premises without a warrant and which the Secretary urges represents a congressional construction of the Fourth Amendment that the courts should not reject. Regrettably, we are unable to agree.

The Warrant Clause of the Fourth Amendment protects commercial buildings as well as private homes. To hold otherwise would belie the origin of that Amendment, and the American colonial experience. An important forerunner of the first 10 Amendments to the United States Constitution, the Virginia Bill of Rights, specifically opposed "general warrants, whereby an officer or messenger may be commanded to search suspected places without evidence of a fact committed." [5] The general warrant was a recurring point of contention in the Colonies immediately preceding the Revolution. [6] The particular offensiveness it engendered was acutely felt by the merchants and businessmen whose premises and products were inspected for compliance with the several parliamentary revenue measures that most irritated the colonists. [7]

"[T]he Fourth Amendment's commands grew in large measure out of the colonists' experience with the writs of assistance . . . [that] granted sweeping power to customs officials and other agents of the King to search at large for smuggled goods."

United States v. Chadwick, 433 U. S. 1, 433 U. S. 7-8 (1977).

See also G. M. Leasing Corp. v. United States, 429 U. S. 338, 429 U. S. 355 (1977). Against this background, it is untenable that the ban on warrantless searches was not intended to shield places of business as well as of residence.

This Court has already held that warrantless searches are generally unreasonable, and that this rule applies to commercial premises as well as homes. In Camara v. Municipal Court, supra at 387 U. S. 528-529, we held:

"[E]xcept in certain carefully defined classes of cases, a search of private property without proper consent is 'unreasonable' unless it has been authorized by a valid search warrant."

On the same day, we also ruled:

"As we explained in Camara, a search of private houses is presumptively unreasonable if conducted without a warrant. The businessman, like the occupant of a residence, has a constitutional right to go about his business free from unreasonable official entries upon his private commercial property. The businessman, too, has that right placed in jeopardy if the decision to enter and inspect for violation of regulatory laws can be made and enforced by the inspector in the field without official authority evidenced by a warrant."

See v. Seattle, supra at 387 U. S. 543.

These same cases also held that the Fourth Amendment prohibition against unreasonable searches protects against warrantless intrusions during civil, as well as criminal, investigations. Ibid. The reason is found in the

"basic purpose of this Amendment . . . [which] is to safeguard the privacy and security of individuals against arbitrary invasions by governmental officials."

Camara, supra at 387 U. S. 528. If the government intrudes on a person's property, the privacy interest suffers whether the government's motivation is to investigate violations of criminal laws or breaches of other statutory or regulatory standards. It therefore appears that, unless some recognized exception to the warrant requirement applies, See v. Seattle would require a warrant to conduct the inspection sought in this case.

The Secretary urges that an exception from the search warrant requirement has been recognized for "pervasively regulated business[es]," United States v. Biswell, 406 U. S. 311, 406 U. S. 316 (1972), and for "closely regulated" industries "long subject to close supervision and inspection." Colonnade Catering Corp. v. United States, 397 U. S. 72, 397 U. S. 74, 77 (1970). These cases are indeed exceptions, but they represent responses to relatively unique circumstances. Certain industries have such a history of government oversight that no reasonable expectation of privacy, see Katz v. United States, 389 U. S. 347, 389 U. S. 351-352 (1967), could exist for a proprietor over the stock of such an enterprise. Liquor (Colonnade) and firearms (Biswell) are industries of this type; when an entrepreneur embarks upon such a business, he has voluntarily chosen to subject himself to a full arsenal of governmental regulation.

Industries such as these fall within the "certain carefully defined classes of cases," referenced in Camara, 387 U.S. at 387 U. S. 528. The element that distinguishes these enterprises from ordinary businesses is a long tradition of close government supervision, of which any person who chooses to enter such a business must already be aware.

"A central difference between those cases [Colonnade and Biswell] and this one is that businessmen engaged in such federally licensed and regulated enterprises accept the burdens as well as the benefits of their trade, whereas the petitioner here was not engaged in any regulated or licensed business. The businessman in a regulated industry in effect consents to the restrictions placed upon him."

Almeida-Sanchez v. United States, 413 U. S. 266, 413 U. S. 271 (1973).

The clear import of our cases is that the closely regulated industry of the type involved in Colonnade and Biswell is the exception. The Secretary would make it the rule. Invoking the Walsh-Healey Act of 1936, 41 U.S.C. § 35 et seq., the Secretary attempts to support a conclusion that all businesses involved in interstate commerce have long been subjected to close supervision of employee safety and health conditions. But the degree of federal involvement in employee working circumstances has never been of the order of specificity and pervasiveness that OSHA mandates. It is quite unconvincing to argue that the imposition of minimum wages and maximum hours on employers who contracted with the Government under the Walsh-Healey Act prepared the entirety of American interstate commerce for regulation of working conditions to the minutest detail. Nor can any but the most fictional sense of voluntary consent to later searches be found in the single fact that one conducts a business affecting interstate commerce; under current practice and law, few businesses can be conducted without having some effect on interstate commerce.

The Secretary also attempts to derive support for a Colonnde-Biswell type exception by drawing analogies from the field of labor law. In Republic Aviation Corp. v. NLRB, 324 U. S. 793 (1945), this Court upheld the rights of employees to solicit for a union during nonworking time where efficiency was not compromised. By opening up his property to employees, the employer had yielded so much of his private property rights as to allow those employees to exercise § 7 rights under the National Labor Relations Act. But this Court also held that the private property rights of an owner prevailed over the intrusion of nonemployee organizers, even in nonworking area of the plant and during nonworking hours. NLRB v. Babcock & Wilcox Co., 351 U. S. 105 (1956).

The critical fact in this case is that entry over Mr. Barlow's objection is being sought by a Government agent. [8] Employees are not being prohibited from reporting OSHA violations. What they observe in their daily functions is undoubtedly beyond the employer's reasonable expectation of privacy. The Government inspector, however, is not an employee. Without a warrant, he stands in no better position than a member of the public. What is observable by the public is observable, without a warrant, by the Government inspector as well. [9] The owner of a business has not, by the necessary utilization of employees in his operation, thrown open the areas where employees alone are permitted to the warrantless scrutiny of Government agents. That an employee is free to report, and the Government is free to use, any evidence of noncompliance with OSHA that the employee observes furnishes no justification for federal agents to enter a place of business from which the public is restricted and to conduct their own warrantless search. [10]

II

The Secretary nevertheless stoutly argues that the enforcement scheme of the Act requires warrantless searches, and that the restrictions on search discretion contained in the Act and its regulations already protect as much privacy as a warrant would. The Secretary thereby asserts the actual reasonableness of OSHA searches, whatever the general rule against warrantless searches might be. Because "reasonableness is still the ultimate standard," Camara v. Municipal Court, 387 U.S. at 387 U. S. 539, the Secretary suggests that the Court decide whether a warrant is needed by arriving at a sensible balance between the administrative necessities of OSHA inspections and the incremental protection of privacy of business owners a warrant would afford. He suggests that only a decision exempting OSHA inspections from the Warrant Clause would give "full recognition to the competing public and private interests here at stake." Ibid.

The Secretary submits that warrantless inspections are essential to the proper enforcement of OSHA because they afford the opportunity to inspect without prior notice, and hence to preserve the advantages of surprise. While the dangerous conditions outlawed by the Act include structural defects that cannot be quickly hidden or remedied, the Act also regulates a myriad of safety details that may be amenable to speedy alteration or disguise. The risk is that, during the interval between an inspector's initial request to search a plant and his procuring a warrant following the owner's refusal of permission, violations of this latter type could be corrected, and thus escape the inspector's notice. To the suggestion that warrants may be issued ex parte and executed without delay and without prior notice, thereby preserving the element of surprise, the Secretary expresses concern for the administrative strain that would be experienced by the inspection system, and by the courts should ex parte warrants issued in advance become standard practice.

We are unconvinced, however, that requiring warrants to inspect will impose serious burdens on the inspection system or the courts, will prevent inspections necessary to enforce the statute, or will make them less effective. In the first place, the great majority of businessmen can be expected in normal course to consent to inspection without warrant; the Secretary has not brought to this Court's attention any widespread pattern of refusal. [11] In those cases where an owner does insist on a warrant; the Secretary argues that inspection efficiency will be impeded by the advance notice and delay. The Act's penalty provisions for giving advance notice of a search, 29 U.S.C. § 666(f), and the Secretary's own regulations, 29 CFR § 1903.6 (1977), indicate that surprise searches are indeed contemplated. However, the Secretary has also promulgated a regulation providing that, upon refusal to permit an inspector to enter the property or to complete his inspection, the inspector shall attempt to ascertain the reasons for the refusal and report to his superior, who shall "promptly take appropriate action, including compulsory process, if necessary." 29 CFR § 1903.4 (1977). [12] The regulation represents a choice to proceed by process where entry is refused; and, on the basis of evidence available from present practice, the Act's effectiveness has not been crippled by providing those owners who wish to refuse an initial requested entry with a time lapse while the inspector obtains the necessary process. [13] Indeed, the kind of process sought in this case and apparently anticipated by the regulation provides notice to the business operator. [14]

If this safeguard endangers the efficient administration of OSHA, the Secretary should never have adopted it, particularly when the Act does not require it. Nor is it immediately apparent why the advantages of surprise would be lost if, after being refused entry, procedures were available for the Secretary to seek an ex parte warrant and to reappear at the premises without further notice to the establishment being inspected. [15]

Whether the Secretary proceeds to secure a warrant or other process, with or without prior notice, his entitlement to inspect will not depend on his demonstrating probable cause to believe that conditions in violation of OSHA exist on the premises. Probable cause in the criminal law sense is not required. For purposes of an administrative search such as this, probable cause justifying the issuance of a warrant may be based not only on specific evidence of an existing violation, [16] but also on a showing that "reasonable legislative or administrative standards for conducting an . . . inspection are satisfied with respect to a particular [establishment]." Camara v. Municipal Court, 387 U.S. at 387 U. S. 538. A warrant showing that a specific business has been chosen for an OSHA search on the basis of a general administrative plan for the enforcement of the Act derived from neutral sources such as, for example, dispersion of employees in various types of industries across a given area, and the desired frequency of searches in any of the lesser divisions of the area, would protect an employer's Fourth Amendment rights. [17] We doubt that the consumption of enforcement energies in the obtaining of such warrants will exceed manageable proportions.

Finally, the Secretary urges that requiring a warrant for OSHA inspectors will mean that, as a practical matter, warrantless search provisions in other regulatory statutes are also constitutionally infirm. The reasonableness of a warrantless search, however, will depend upon the specific enforcement needs and privacy guarantees of each statute. Some of the statutes cited apply only to a single industry, where regulations might already be so pervasive that a Colonnade-Biswell exception to the warrant requirement could apply. Some statutes already envision resort to federal court enforcement when entry is refused, employing specific language in some cases [18] and general language in others. [19] In short, we base today's opinion on the facts and law concerned with

OSHA, and do not retreat from a holding appropriate to that statute because of its real or imagined effect on other, different administrative schemes.

Nor do we agree that the incremental protections afforded the employer's privacy by a warrant are so marginal that they fail to justify the administrative burdens that may be entailed.

The authority to make warrantless searches devolves almost unbridled discretion upon executive and administrative officers, particularly those in the field, as to when to search and whom to search. A warrant, by contrast, would provide assurances from a neutral officer that the inspection is reasonable under the Constitution, is authorized by statute, and is pursuant to an administrative plan containing specific neutral criteria. [20] Also, a warrant would then and there advise the owner of the scope and objects of the search, beyond which limits the inspector is not expected to proceed. [21] These are important functions for a warrant to perform, functions which underlie the Court's prior decisions that the Warrant Clause applies to inspections for compliance with regulatory statutes. [22] Camara v. Municipal Court, 387 U. S. 523 (1967); See v. Seattle, 387 U. S. 541 (1967). We conclude that the concerns expressed by the Secretary do not suffice to justify warrantless inspections under OSHA or vitiate the general constitutional requirement that for a search to be reasonable a warrant must be obtained.

III

We hold that Barlow's was entitled to a declaratory judgment that the Act is unconstitutional insofar as it purports to authorize inspections without warrant or its equivalent and to an injunction enjoining the Act's enforcement to that extent. [23] The judgment of the District Court is therefore affirmed.

So ordered.

Mincey v. Arizona (June 21, 1978) [Notes omitted]

MR. JUSTICE STEWART delivered the opinion of the Court.

On the afternoon of October 28, 1974, undercover police officer Barry Headricks of the Metropolitan Area Narcotics Squad knocked on the door of an apartment in Tucson, Ariz., occupied by the petitioner, Rufus Mincey. Earlier in the day, Officer Headricks had allegedly arranged to purchase a quantity of heroin from Mincey and had left, ostensibly to obtain money. On his return, he was accompanied by nine other plainclothes policemen and a deputy county attorney. The door was opened by John Hodgman, one of three acquaintances of Mincey who were in the living room of the apartment. Officer Headricks slipped inside and moved quickly into the bedroom. Hodgman attempted to slam the door in order to keep the other officers from entering, but was pushed back against the wall. As the police entered the apartment, a rapid volley of shots was heard from the bedroom. Officer Headricks emerged and collapsed on the floor. When other officers entered the bedroom, they found Mincey lying on the floor, wounded and semiconscious. Officer Headricks died a few hours later in the hospital.

The petitioner was indicted for murder, assault, [n1] and three counts of narcotics offenses. He was tried at a single trial, and convicted on all the charges. At his trial and on appeal, he contended that evidence used against him had been unlawfully seized from his apartment without a warrant, and that statements used to impeach his credibility were inadmissible because they had not been made voluntarily. The Arizona Supreme Court reversed the murder and assault convictions on state law grounds, [n2] but affirmed the narcotics convictions. 115 Ariz. 472, 566 P.2d 273. It held that the warrantless search of a homicide scene is permissible under the Fourth and

Fourteenth Amendments, and that Mincey's statements were voluntary. We granted certiorari to consider these substantial constitutional questions. 434 U.S. 902.

I

The first question presented is whether the search of Mincey's apartment was constitutionally permissible. After the shooting, the narcotics agents, thinking that other persons in the apartment might have been injured, looked about quickly for other victims. They found a young woman wounded in the bedroom closet, and Mincey, apparently unconscious in the bedroom, as well as Mincey's three acquaintances (one of whom had been wounded in the head) in the living room. Emergency assistance was requested, and some medical aid was administered to Officer Headricks. But the agents refrained from further investigation, pursuant to a Tucson Police Department directive that police officers should not investigate incidents in which they are involved. They neither searched further nor seized any evidence; they merely guarded the suspects and the premises.

Within 10 minutes, however, homicide detectives who had heard a radio report of the shooting arrived and took charge of the investigation. They supervised the removal of Officer Headricks and the suspects, trying to make sure that the scene was disturbed as little as possible, and then proceeded to gather evidence. Their search lasted four days, [n3] during which period the entire apartment was searched, photographed, and diagrammed. The officers opened drawers, closets, and cupboards, and inspected their contents; they emptied clothing pockets; they dug bullet fragments out of the walls and floors; they pulled up sections of the carpet and removed them for examination. Every item in the apartment was closely examined and inventoried, and 200 to 300 objects were seized. In short, Mincey's apartment was subjected to an exhaustive and intrusive search. No warrant was ever obtained.

The petitioner's pretrial motion to suppress the fruits of this search was denied after a hearing. Much of the evidence introduced against him at trial (including photographs and diagrams, bullets and shell casings, guns, narcotics, and narcotics paraphernalia) was the product of the four-day search of his apartment. On appeal, the Arizona Supreme Court reaffirmed previous decisions in which it had held that the warrantless search of the scene of a homicide is constitutionally permissible. [n4] It stated its ruling as follows:

We hold a reasonable, warrantless search of the scene of a homicide -- or of a serious personal injury with likelihood of death where there is reason to suspect foul play -- does no violate the Fourth Amendment to the United States Constitution where the law enforcement officers were legally on the premises in the first instance. For the search to be reasonable, the purpose must be limited to determining the circumstances of death and the scope must not exceed that purpose. The search must also begin within a reasonable period following the time when the officials first learn of the murder (or potential murder).

115 Ariz. at 482, 566 P.2d at 283. Since the investigating homicide detectives knew that Officer Headricks was seriously injured, began the search promptly upon their arrival at the apartment, and searched only for evidence either establishing the circumstances of death or "relevant to motive and intent or knowledge (narcotics, e.g.)," id. at 483, 566 P.2d at 284, the court found that the warrantless search of the petitioner's apartment had not violated the Fourth and Fourteenth Amendments.

We cannot agree. The Fourth Amendment proscribes all unreasonable searches and seizures, and it is a cardinal principle that searches conducted outside the judicial process, without prior approval by judge or magistrate, are per se unreasonable under the Fourth Amendment -- subject only to a few specifically established and well delineated exceptions.

Katz v. United States, 389 U.S. 347, 357 (footnotes omitted); see also South Dakota v. Opperman, 428 U.S. 364, 381 (POWELL, J., concurring); Coolidge v. New Hampshire, 403 U.S. 443, 481; Vale v. Louisiana, 399 U.S. 30, 34; Terry v. Ohio, 392 U.S. 1, 20; Trupiano v. United States, 334 U.S. 699, 705. The Arizona Supreme Court did not hold that the search of the petitioner's apartment fell within any of the exceptions to the warrant requirement previously recognized by this Court, but, rather, that the search of a homicide scene should be recognized as an additional exception. Several reasons are advanced by the State to meet its "burden . . . to show the existence of such an exceptional situation" as to justify creating a new exception to the warrant requirement. See Vale v. Louisiana, supra at 34; United States v. Jeffers, 342 U.S. 48, 51. None of these reasons, however, persuades us of the validity of the generic exception delineated by the Arizona Supreme Court.

The first contention is that the search of the petitioner's apartment did not invade any constitutionally protected right of privacy. See Katz v. United States, supra. This argument appears to have two prongs. On the one hand, the State urges that, by shooting Officer Headricks, Mincey forfeited any reasonable expectation of privacy in his apartment. We have recently rejected a similar waiver argument in Michigan v. Tyler, 436 U.S. 499, 505-506; it suffices here to say that this reasoning would impermissibly convict the suspect even before the evidence against him was gathered. [n5] On the other hand, the State contends that the police entry to arrest Mincey was so great an invasion of his privacy that the additional intrusion caused by the search was constitutionally irrelevant. But this claim is hardly tenable in light of the extensive nature of this search. It is one thing to say that one who is legally taken into police custody has a lessened right of privacy in his person. See United States v. Edwards, 415 U.S. 800, 808-809; United States v. Robinson, 414 U.S. 218. It is quite another to argue that he also has a lessened right of privacy in his entire house. Indeed this very argument was rejected when it was advanced to support the warrantless search of a dwelling where a search occurred as "incident" to the arrest of its occupant. Chimel v. California, 395 U.S. 752, 766 n. 12. Thus, this search cannot be justified on the ground that no constitutionally protected right of privacy was invaded.

The State's second argument in support of its categorical exception to the warrant requirement is that a possible homicide presents an emergency situation demanding immediate action. We do not question the right of the police to respond to emergency situations. Numerous state [n6] and federal [n7] cases have recognized that the Fourth Amendment does not bar police officers from making warrantless entries and searches when they reasonably believe that a person within is in need of immediate aid. Similarly, when the police come upon the scene of a homicide, they may make a prompt warrantless search of the area to see if there are other victims or if a killer is still on the premises. Cf. Michigan v. Tyler, supra at 509-510.

The need to protect or preserve life or avoid serious injury is justification for what would be otherwise illegal absent an exigency or emergency.

Wayne v. United States, 115 U.S.App.D.C. 234, 241, 318 F.2d 205, 212 (opinion of Burger, J.). And the police may seize any evidence that is in plain view during the course of their legitimate emergency activities. Michigan v. Tyler, supra at 509-510; Coolidge v. New Hampshire, 403 U.S. at

465-466.

But a warrantless search must be "strictly circumscribed by the exigencies which justify its initiation," Terry v. Ohio, 392 U.S. at 25-26, and it simply cannot be contended that this search was justified by any emergency threatening life or limb. All the persons in Mincey's apartment had been located before the investigating homicide officers arrived there and began their search. And a four-day search that included opening dresser drawers and ripping up carpets can hardly be rationalized in terms of the legitimate concerns that justify an emergency search.

Third, the State points to the vital public interest in the prompt investigation of the extremely serious crime of murder. No one can doubt the importance of this goal. But the public interest in the investigation of other serious crimes is comparable. If the warrantless search of a homicide scene is reasonable, why not the warrantless search of the scene of a rape, a robbery, or a burglary? "No consideration relevant to the Fourth Amendment suggests any point of rational limitation" of such a doctrine. Chimel v. California, supra at 766.

Moreover, the mere fact that law enforcement may be made more efficient can never, by itself, justify disregard of the Fourth Amendment. Cf. Coolidge v. New Hampshire, supra at 481. The investigation of crime would always be simplified if warrants were unnecessary. But the Fourth Amendment reflects the view of those who wrote the Bill of Rights that the privacy of a person's home and property may not be totally sacrificed in the name of maximum simplicity in enforcement of the criminal law. See United States v. Chadwick, 433 U.S. 1, 11. For this reason, warrants are generally required to search a person's home or his person unless "the exigencies of the situation" make the needs of law enforcement so compelling that the warrantless search is objectively reasonable under the Fourth Amendment. McDonald v. United States, 335 U.S. 451, 456; Johnson v. United States, 333 U.S. 10, 14-15. See, e.g., Chimel v. California, supra, (search of arrested suspect and area within his control for weapons or evidence); Warden v. Hayden, 387 U.S. 294, 298-300 ("hot pursuit" of fleeing suspect); Schmerber v. California, 384 U.S. 757, 770-771 (imminent destruction of evidence); see also supra at 392-393.

Except for the fact that the offense under investigation was a homicide, there were no exigent circumstances in this case, as, indeed, the Arizona Supreme Court recognized. 115 Ariz. at 482, 566 P.2d at 283. There was no indication that evidence would be lost, destroyed, or removed during the time required to obtain a search warrant. Indeed, the police guard at the apartment minimized that possibility. And there is no suggestion that a search warrant could not easily and conveniently have been obtained. We decline to hold that the seriousness of the offense under investigation itself creates exigent circumstances of the kind that under the Fourth Amendment justify a warrantless search.

Finally, the State argues that the "murder scene exception" is constitutionally permissible because it is narrowly confined by the guidelines set forth in the decision of the Arizona Supreme Court, see supra at 389-390. [n8] In light of the extensive search that took place in this case, it may be questioned what protection the guidelines afford a person in whose home a homicide or assault occurs. Indeed, these so-called guidelines are hardly so rigidly confining as the State seems to assert. They confer unbridled discretion upon the individual officer to interpret such terms as "reasonable . . . search," "serious personal injury with likelihood of death where there is reason to suspect foul play," and "reasonable period." It is precisely this kind of judgmental assessment of the reasonableness and scope of a proposed search that the Fourth Amendment requires be made by a neutral and objective magistrate, not a police officer. See, e.g., United States v. United States District Court, 407 U.S. 297, 316; Coolidge v. New Hampshire, supra at 449-453; Mancusi v. DeForte, 392 U.S. 364, 371; Wong Sun v. United States, 371 U.S. 471, 481-482.

It may well be that the circumstances described by the Arizona Supreme Court would usually be constitutionally sufficient to warrant a search of substantial scope. But the Fourth Amendment requires that this judgment, in each case, be made in the first instance by a neutral magistrate.

The point of the Fourth Amendment, which often is not grasped by zealous officers, is not that it denies law enforcement the support of the usual inferences which reasonable men draw from evidence. Its protection consists in requiring that those inferences be drawn by a neutral and detached magistrate instead of being judged by the officer engaged in the often competitive enterprise of ferreting out crime.

Johnson v. United States, supra at 13-14.

In sum, we hold that the "murder scene exception" created by the Arizona Supreme Court is inconsistent with the Fourth and Fourteenth Amendments -- that the warrantless search of Mincey's apartment was not constitutionally permissible simply because a homicide had recently occurred there. [n9]

II

Since there will presumably be a new trial in this case, [n10] it is appropriate to consider also the petitioner's contention that statements he made from a hospital bed were involuntary, and therefore could not constitutionally be used against him at his trial.

Mincey was brought to the hospital after the shooting and taken immediately to the emergency room, where he was examined and treated. He had sustained a wound in his hip, resulting in damage to the sciatic nerve and partial paralysis of his right leg. Tubes were inserted into his throat to help him breathe, and through his nose into his stomach to keep him from vomiting; a catheter was inserted into his bladder. He received various drugs, and a device was attached to his arm so that he could be fed intravenously. He was then taken to the intensive care unit.

At about eight o'clock that evening, Detective Hust of the Tucson Police Department came to the intensive care unit to interrogate him. Mincey was unable to talk because of the tube in his mouth, and so he responded to Detective Hust's questions by writing answers on pieces of paper provided by the hospital. [n11] Hust told Mincey he was under arrest for the murder of a police officer, gave him the warnings required by Miranda v. Arizona, 384 U.S. 436, and began to ask questions about the events that had taken place in Mincey's apartment a few hours earlier. Although Mincey asked repeatedly that the interrogation stop until he could get a lawyer, Hust continued to question him until almost midnight.

After a pretrial hearing, see Jackson v. Denno, 378 U.S. 368, the trial court found that Mincey had responded to this interrogation voluntarily. [n12] When Mincey took the witness stand at his trial, his statements in response to Detective Hust's questions were used in an effort to impeach his testimony in several respects. [n13] On appeal, the Arizona Supreme Court indicated its belief that, because Detective Hust had failed to honor Mincey's request for a lawyer, the statements would have been inadmissible as part of the prosecution's case in chief. Miranda v. Arizona, supra. But, relying on Harris v. New York, 401 U.S. 222, and Oregon v. Hass, 420 U.S. 714, it held that, since the trial court's finding of voluntariness was not "clear[ly] and manifest[ly]" erroneous, the statements were properly used for purposes of impeachment. 115 Ariz. at 480, 566 P.2d at 281.

Statements made by a defendant in

circumstances violating the strictures of Miranda v. Arizona, supra, are admissible for impeachment if their "trustworthiness . . . satisfies legal standards." Harris v. New York, supra at 224; Oregon v. Hass, supra at 722. But any criminal trial use against a defendant of his involuntary statement is a denial of due process of law "even though there is ample evidence aside from the confession to support the conviction." Jackson v. Denno, supra at 376; Haynes v. Washington, 373 U.S. 503, 518; Lynumn v. Illinois, 372 U.S. 528, 537; Stroble v. California, 343 U.S. 181, 190; see Chapman v. California, 386 U.S. 18, 23 and n. 8. If, therefore, Mincey's statements to Detective Hust were not "'the product of a rational intellect and a free will,'" Townsend v. Sain, 372 U.S. 293, 307, quoting Blackburn v. Alabama, 361 U.S. 199, 208, his conviction cannot stand. In making this critical determination, we are not bound by the Arizona Supreme Court's holding that the statements were voluntary. Instead, this Court is under a duty to make an independent evaluation of the record. Davis v. North Carolina, 34 U.S. 737, 741-742; Haynes v. Washington, supra at 515-516.

It is hard to imagine a situation less conducive to the exercise of "a rational intellect and a free will" than Mincey's. He had been seriously wounded just a few hours earlier, and had arrived at the hospital "depressed almost to the point of coma," according to his attending physician. Although he had received some treatment, his condition at the time of Hust's interrogation was still sufficiently serious that he was in the intensive care unit. [n14] He complained to Hust that the pain in his leg was "unbearable." He was evidently confused and unable to think clearly about either the events of that afternoon or the circumstances of his interrogation, since some of his written answers were, on their face, not entirely coherent. [n15] Finally, while Mincey was being questioned, he was lying on his back on a hospital bed,

encumbered by tubes, needles, and breathing apparatus. He was, in short, "at the complete mercy" of Detective Hust, unable to escape or resist the thrust of Hust's interrogation. Cf. Beecher v. Alabama, 389 U.S. 35, 38.

In this debilitated and helpless condition, Mincey clearly expressed his wish not to be interrogated. As soon as Hust's questions turned to the details of the afternoon's events, Mincey wrote: "This is all I can say without a lawyer." Hust nonetheless continued to question him, and a nurse who was present suggested it would be best if Mincey answered. Mincey gave unresponsive or uninformative answers to several more questions, and then said again that he did not want to talk without a lawyer. Hust ignored that request and another made immediately thereafter. [n16] Indeed, throughout the interrogation, Mincey vainly asked Hust to desist. Moreover, he complained several times that he was confused or unable to think clearly, or that he could answer more accurately the next day. [n17] But despite Mincey's entreaties to be let alone, Hust ceased the interrogation only during intervals when Mincey lost consciousness or received medical treatment, and, after each such interruption, returned relentlessly to his task. The statements at issue were thus the result of virtually continuous questioning of a seriously and painfully wounded man on the edge of consciousness.

There were not present in this case some of the gross abuses that have led the Court in other cases to find confessions involuntary, such as beatings, see Brown v. Mississippi, 297 U.S. 278, or "truth serums," see Townsend v. Sain, 372 U.S. 293. But "the blood of the accused is not the only hallmark of an unconstitutional inquisition." Blackburn v. Alabama, 361 U.S. at 206. Determination of whether a statement is involuntary "requires more than a mere color-matching of cases." Reck v. Pate, 367 U.S. 433, 442. It requires careful evaluation of all the circumstances of the interrogation. [n18]

It is apparent from the record in this case that Mincey's statements were not "the product of his free and rational choice." Greenwald v. Wisconsin, 390 U.S. 519, 521. To the contrary, the undisputed evidence makes clear that Mincey wanted not to answer Detective Hust. But Mincey was weakened by pain and shock, isolated from family, friends, and legal counsel, and barely conscious, and his will was simply overborne. Due process of law requires that statements obtained as these were cannot be used in any way against a defendant at his trial.

III

For the foregoing reasons, the judgment of the Arizona Supreme Court is reversed, and the case is remanded for further proceedings not inconsistent with this opinion.

It is so ordered.

Franks v. Delaware (June 26, 1978) [Notes and appendices omitted]

MR. JUSTICE BLACKMUN delivered the opinion of the Court.

This case presents an important and longstanding issue of Fourth Amendment law. Does a defendant in a criminal proceeding ever have the right, under the Fourth and Fourteenth Amendments, subsequent to the ex parte issuance of a search warrant, to challenge the truthfulness of factual statements made in an affidavit supporting the warrant?

In the present case the Supreme Court of Delaware held, as a matter of first impression for it, that a defendant under no circumstances may so challenge the veracity of a sworn statement used by police to procure a search warrant. We reverse, and we hold that, where the defendant makes a substantial preliminary showing that a false statement knowingly and intentionally, or with reckless disregard for the truth, was included by

the affiant in the warrant affidavit, and if the allegedly false statement is necessary to the finding of probable cause, the Fourth Amendment requires that a hearing be held at the defendant's request. In the event that, at that hearing, the allegation of perjury or reckless disregard is established by the defendant by a preponderance of the evidence, and, with the affidavit's false material set to one side, the affidavit's remaining content is insufficient to establish probable cause, the search warrant must be voided, and the fruits of the search excluded, to the same extent as if probable cause was lacking on the face of the affidavit.

I

The controversy over the veracity of the search warrant affidavit in this case arose in connection with petitioner Jerome Franks' state conviction for rape, kidnaping, and burglary. On Friday, March 5, 1976, Mrs. Cynthia Bailey told police in Dover, Del., that she had been confronted in her home earlier that morning by a man with a knife, and that he had sexually assaulted her. She described her assailant's age, race, height, build, and facial hair, and gave a detailed description of his clothing as consisting of a white thermal undershirt, black pants with a silver or gold buckle, a brown leather three-quarter-length coat, and a dark knit cap that he wore pulled down around his eyes.

That same day, petitioner Franks coincidentally was taken into custody for an assault involving a 15-year-old girl, Brenda B. ____, six days earlier. After his formal arrest, and while awaiting a bail hearing in Family Court, petitioner allegedly stated to Robert McClements, the youth officer accompanying him, that he was surprised the bail hearing was "about Brenda B. I know her. I thought you said Bailey. I don't know her." Tr. 175, 186. At the time of this statement, the police allegedly had not yet recited to petitioner his rights under Miranda v. Arizona, 384 U. S. 436 (1966).

On the following Monday, March 8, Officer

McClements happened to mention the courthouse incident to a detective, Ronald R. Brooks, who was working on the Bailey case. Tr. 186, 190-191. On March 9, Detective Brooks and Detective Larry D. Gray submitted a sworn affidavit to a Justice of the Peace in Dover, in support of a warrant to search petitioner's apartment. [1] In paragraph 8 of the affidavit's "probable cause page," mention was made of petitioner's statement to McClements. In paragraph 10, it was noted that the description of the assailant given to the police by Mrs. Bailey included the above-mentioned clothing. Finally, the affidavit also described the attempt made by police to confirm that petitioner's typical outfit matched that of the assailant. Paragraph 15 recited:

"On Tuesday, 3/9/76, your affiant contacted Mr. James Williams and Mr. Wesley Lucas of the Delaware Youth Center where Jerome Franks is employed and did have personal conversation with both these people."

Paragraphs 16 and 17 respectively stated:

"Mr. James Williams revealed to your affiant that the normal dress of Jerome Franks does consist of a white knit thermal undershirt and a brown leather jacket,"

and

"Mr. Wesley Lucas revealed to your affiant that in addition to the thermal undershirt and jacket, Jerome Franks often wears a dark green knit hat."

The warrant was issued on the basis of this affidavit. App. 9. Pursuant to the warrant, police searched petitioner's apartment and found a white thermal undershirt, a knit hat, dark pants, and a leather jacket, and, on petitioner's kitchen table, a single-blade knife. All these ultimately were introduced in evidence at trial.

Prior to the trial, however, petitioner's counsel filed a written motion to suppress the clothing and the knife found in the search; this motion alleged that the warrant, on its face, did not show probable cause, and that the search and seizure were in violation of the Fourth and Fourteenth Amendments. Id. at 11-12. At the hearing on the motion to suppress, defense counsel orally amended the challenge to include an attack on the veracity of the warrant affidavit; he also specifically requested the right to call as witnesses Detective Brooks, Wesley Lucas of the Youth Center, and James D. Morrison, formerly of the Youth Center. [2] Id. at 14-17. Counsel asserted that Lucas and Morrison would testify that neither had been personally interviewed by the warrant affiants, and that, although they might have talked to another police officer, any information given by them to that officer was "somewhat different" from what was recited in the affidavit. Id. at 16. Defense counsel charged that the misstatements were included in the affidavit not inadvertently, but in "bad faith." Id. at 25. Counsel also sought permission to call Officer McClements and petitioner as witnesses, to seek to establish that petitioner's courthouse statement to police had been obtained in violation of petitioner's Miranda rights, and that the search warrant was thereby tainted as the fruit of an illegally obtained confession. Id. at 17, 27.

In rebuttal, the State's attorney argued in detail, App. 124, (a) that Del. Code Ann., Tit. 11, §§ 2306, 2307 (1974), contemplated that any challenge to a search warrant was to be limited to questions of sufficiency based on the face of the affidavit; (b) that, purportedly, a majority of the States whose practice was not dictated by statute observed such a rule; [3] and (c) that federal cases on the issue were to be distinguished because of Fed.Rule Crim.Proc. 41(e). [4] He also noted that this Court had reserved the general issue of subfacial challenge to veracity in Rendorf v. United States, 376 U. S. 528, 376 U. S. 531-532 (1964), when it disposed of that case on the ground that, even if a veracity challenge were permitted, the alleged factual inaccuracies in that case's affidavit "were of only peripheral relevancy to the showing of probable cause, and, not being within the personal knowledge of the affiant, did not go to the integrity of the affidavit."

Id. at 376 U. S. 532. The State objected to petitioner's "going behind [the warrant affidavit] in any way," and argued that the court must decide petitioner's motion "on the four corners" of the affidavit. App. 21.

The trial court sustained the State's objection to petitioner's proposed evidence. Id. at 25, 27. The motion to suppress was denied, and the clothing and knife were admitted as evidence at the ensuing trial. Tr.192-196. Petitioner was convicted. In a written motion for judgment of acquittal and/or new trial, Record Doc. No. 23, petitioner repeated his objection to the admission of the evidence, stating that he

"should have been allowed to impeach the Affidavit used in the Search Warrant to show purposeful misrepresentation of information contained therein."

Id. at 2. The motion was denied, and petitioner was sentenced to two consecutive terms of 25 years each and an additional consecutive life sentence.

On appeal, the Supreme Court of Delaware affirmed. 373 A.2d 578 (1977). It agreed with what it deemed to be the "majority rule" that no attack upon the veracity of a warrant affidavit could be made:

"We agree with the majority rule for two reasons. First, it is the function of the issuing magistrate to determine the reliability of information and credibility of affiants in deciding whether the requirement of probable cause has been met. There has been no need demonstrated for interfering with this function. Second, neither the probable cause nor suppression hearings are adjudications of guilt or innocence; the matters asserted by defendant are more properly considered in a trial on the merits."

Id. at 580. Because of this resolution, the Delaware Supreme Court noted that there was no need to consider petitioner's "other contentions, relating to the evidence that would have been introduced for impeachment purposes." Ibid.

Franks' petition for certiorari presented only the issue whether the trial court had erred in refusing to consider his allegation of misrepresentation in the warrant affidavit. [5] Because of the importance of the question, and because of the conflict among both state and federal courts, we granted certiorari. 434 U.S. 889 (1977).

II

It may be well first to note how we are compelled to reach the Fourth Amendment issue proffered in this case. In particular, the State's proposals of an independent and adequate state ground and of harmless error do not dispose of the controversy.

Respondent argues that petitioner's trial counsel, who is not the attorney representing him in this Court, failed to include the challenge to the veracity of the warrant affidavit in the written motion to suppress filed before trial, contrary to the requirement of Del.Super.Ct.Rule Crim.Proc. 41(e) that a motion to suppress "shall state the grounds upon which it is made." The Supreme Court of Delaware, however, disposed of petitioner's Fourth Amendment claim on the merits. A ruling on the merits of a federal question by the highest state court leaves the federal question open to review in this Court. Manhattan Life Ins. Co. v. Cohen, 234 U. S. 123, 234 U. S. 134 (1914); Raley v. Ohio, 360 U. S. 423, 360 U. S. 436-437 (1959); Boykin v. Alabama, 395 U. S. 238, 395 U. S. 241-242 (1969).

Respondent next suggests that any error here was harmless. Assuming, arguendo, respondent says, that petitioner's Fourth Amendment claim was valid, and that the warrant should have been tested for veracity and the evidence excluded, it is still clear beyond a reasonable doubt that the evidence complained of did not contribute to petitioner's conviction. Chambers v. Maroney, 399 U. S. 42, 399 U. S. 52-53 (1970). This contention falls of its own weight. The sole issue at trial was that of consent. Petitioner admitted, App. 37, that he had engaged in sexual relations with Mrs. Bailey on the day in question. She testified, Tr. 50-51, 69-70, that she had not consented to this, and that petitioner, upon first encountering her in the house, had threatened her with a knife to force her to submit. Petitioner claimed that she had given full consent, and that no knife had been present. Id. at 254, 271. To corroborate its contention that consent was lacking, the State introduced in evidence a stainless steel, wooden-handled kitchen knife found by the detectives on the kitchen table in petitioner's apartment four days after the alleged rape. Id. at 195-196; Magistrate's Return on the Search Warrant March 9, 1976, Record Doc. No. 23. Defense counsel objected to its admission, arguing that Mrs. Bailey had not given any detailed description of the knife alleged to be involved in the incident, and had claimed to have seen the knife only in "pitch blackness." Tr.195. The State obtained its admission, however, as a knife that matched the description contained in the search warrant, and Mrs. Bailey testified that the knife allegedly used was, like the knife in evidence, single-edged and not a pocket knife, and that the knife in evidence was the same length and thickness as the knife used in the crime. Id. at 69, 114-115. The State carefully elicited from Detective Brooks the fact that this was the only knife found in petitioner's apartment. Id. at 196. Although respondent argues that the knife was presented to the jury as "merely exemplary of the generic class of weapon testimonially described by the victim," Brief for Respondent 15-16, the State at trial clearly meant to suggest that this was the knife that had been used against Mrs. Bailey. Had the warrant

been quashed, and the knife excluded from the trial as evidence, we cannot say with any assurance that the jury would have reached the same decision on the issue of consent, particularly since there was countervailing evidence on that issue.

We should note, in addition, why this case cannot be treated as was the situation in Rugendorf v. United States. There, the Court held that no Fourth Amendment question was presented when the claimed misstatements in the search warrant affidavit

"were of only peripheral relevancy to the showing of probable cause, and, not being within the personal knowledge of the affiant, did not go to the integrity of the affidavit."

376 U.S. at 532 (emphasis added). Rugendorf emphasized that the "erroneous statements . . . were not those of the affiant," and thus "fail[ed] to show that the affiant was in bad faith or that he made any misrepresentations to the Commissioner in securing the warrant." Id. at 376 U. S. 533. [6] Here, whatever the judgment may be as to the relevancy of the alleged misstatements, the integrity of the affidavit was directly placed in issue by petitioner in his allegation that the affiants did not, as claimed, speak directly to Lucas and Morrison. Whether such conversations took place is surely a matter "within the personal knowledge of the affiant[s]." We also might note that, although respondent's brief puts forth that the alleged misrepresentations in the affidavit were of little importance in establishing probable cause, Brief for Respondent 16, respondent, at oral argument, appeared to disclaim any reliance on Rugendorf. Tr. of Oral Arg. 30.

III

Whether the Fourth and Fourteenth Amendments, and the derivative exclusionary rule made applicable to the States under Mapp v. Ohio, 367 U. S. 643 (1961), ever mandate that a defendant be permitted to attack the veracity of a warrant affidavit after the warrant has been issued and executed, is a question that encounters conflicting values. The bulwark of Fourth Amendment protection, of course, is the Warrant Clause, requiring that, absent certain exceptions, police obtain a warrant from a neutral and disinterested magistrate before embarking upon a search. In deciding today that, in certain circumstances, a challenge to a warrant's veracity must be permitted, we derive our ground from language of the Warrant Clause itself, which surely takes the affiant's good faith as its premise: "[N] o Warrants shall issue, but upon probable cause, supported by Oath or affirmation. . . ." Judge Frankel, in United States v. Halsey, 257 F.Supp. 1002, 1005 (SDNY 1966), aff'd, Docket No. 31369 (CA2, June 12, 1967) (unreported), put the matter simply:

"[W]hen the Fourth Amendment demands a factual showing sufficient to comprise 'probable cause,' the obvious assumption is that there will be a 'truthful showing' (emphasis in original). This does not mean 'truthful' in the sense that every fact recited in the warrant affidavit is necessarily correct, for probable cause may be founded upon hearsay and upon information received from informants, as well as upon information within the affiant's own knowledge that sometimes must be garnered hastily. But surely it is to be 'truthful' in the sense that the information put forth is believed or appropriately accepted by the affiant as true. It is established law, see Nathanson v. United States, 290 U. S. 41, 290 U. S. 47 (1933); Giordenello v. United States, 357 U. S. 480, 357 U. S. 485-486 (1958); Aguilar v. Texas, 378 U. S. 108, 378 U. S. 114-115 (1964), that a warrant affidavit must set forth particular facts and circumstances underlying the existence of probable cause, so as to allow the magistrate to make an independent evaluation of the matter. If an informant's tip is the source of information, the affidavit must recite 'some of the underlying circumstances from which the informant concluded' that relevant evidence might be discovered, and"

"some of the underlying circumstances from which the officer concluded that the informant, whose identity need not be disclosed, . . . was 'credible,' or his information 'reliable.'"

Id. at 378 U. S. 114. Because it is the magistrate who must determine independently whether there is probable cause, Johnson v. United States, 333 U. S. 10, 333 U. S. 13-14 (1948); Jones v. United States, 362 U. S. 257, 362 U. S. 270-271 (1960), it would be an unthinkable imposition upon his authority if a warrant affidavit, revealed after the fact to contain a deliberately or recklessly false statement, were to stand beyond impeachment.

In saying this, however, one must give cognizance to competing values that lead us to impose limitations. They perhaps can best be addressed by noting the arguments of respondent and others against allowing veracity challenges. The arguments are several:

First, respondent argues that the exclusionary rule, created in Weeks v. United States, personal constitutional right, but only a judicially created remedy extended where its benefit as a deterrent promises to outweigh the societal cost of its use; that the Court has declined to apply the exclusionary rule when illegally seized evidence is used to impeach the credibility of a defendant's testimony, Walder v. United States, 347 U. S. 62 (1954), is used in a grand jury proceeding, United States v. Calandra, 414 U. S. 338 (1974), or is used in a civil trial, United States v. Janis, 428 U. S. 433 (1976); and that the Court similarly has restricted application of the Fourth Amendment exclusionary rule in federal habeas corpus review of a state conviction. See Stone v. Powell, 428 U. S. 465 (1976). Respondent argues that applying the exclusionary rule to another situation -- the deterrence of deliberate or reckless untruthfulness in a warrant affidavit -- is not justified for many of the same reasons that led to the above restrictions; interfering with a criminal conviction in order to deter official misconduct is a burden too great to impose on society. Second, respondent argues that a citizen's privacy interests are adequately protected by a requirement that applicants for a warrant submit a sworn affidavit and by the magistrate's independent determination of sufficiency based on the face of the affidavit. Applying the exclusionary rule to attacks upon veracity would weed out a minimal number of perjurious government statements, says respondent, but would overlap unnecessarily with existing penalties against perjury, including criminal prosecutions, departmental discipline for misconduct, contempt of court, and civil actions. Third, it is argued that the magistrate already is equipped to conduct a fairly vigorous inquiry into the accuracy of the factual affidavit supporting a warrant application. He may question the affiant, or summon other persons to give testimony at the warrant proceeding. The incremental gain from a post-search adversary proceeding, it is said, would not be great.

Fourth, it is argued that it would unwisely diminish the solemnity and moment of the magistrate's proceeding to make his inquiry into probable cause reviewable in regard to veracity. The less final, and less deference paid to, the magistrate's determination of veracity, the less initiative will he use in that task. Denigration of the magistrate's function would be imprudent insofar as his scrutiny is the last bulwark preventing any particular invasion of privacy before it happens.

Fifth, it is argued that permitting a post-search evidentiary hearing on issues of veracity would confuse the pressing issue of guilt or innocence with the collateral question as to whether there had been official misconduct in the drafting of the affidavit. The weight of criminal dockets, and the need to prevent diversion of attention from the main issue of guilt or innocence,

militate against such an added burden on the trial courts. And if such hearings were conducted routinely, it is said, they would be misused by defendants as a convenient source of discovery. Defendants might even use the hearings in an attempt to force revelation of the identity of informants.

Sixth and finally, it is argued that a post-search veracity challenge is inappropriate because the accuracy of an affidavit, in large part, is beyond the control of the affiant. An affidavit may properly be based on hearsay, on fleeting observations, and on tips received from unnamed informants whose identity often will be properly protected from revelation under McCray v. Illinois, 386 U. S. 300 (1967).

None of these considerations is trivial. Indeed, because of them, the rule announced today has a limited scope, both in regard to when exclusion of the seized evidence is mandated and when a hearing on allegations of misstatements must be accorded. But neither do the considerations cited by respondent and others have a fully controlling weight; we conclude that they are insufficient to justify an absolute ban on post-search impeachment of veracity. On this side of the balance, also, there are pressing considerations:

First, a at ban on impeachment of veracity could denude the probable cause requirement of all real meaning. The requirement that a warrant not issue "but upon probable cause, supported by Oath or affirmation," would be reduced to a nullity if a police officer was able to use deliberately falsified allegations to demonstrate probable cause, and, having misled the magistrate, then was able to remain confident that the ploy was worthwhile. It is this specter of intentional falsification that, we think, has evoked such widespread opposition to the flat nonimpeachment rule from the commentators, [7] from the American Law Institute in its Model Code of Pre-Arraignment

Procedure, § SS290.3(1) (Prop.Off.Draft 1975), from the federal courts of appeals, and from state courts. On occasion, of course, an instance of deliberate falsity will be exposed and confirmed without a special inquiry either at trial, see United States ex rel. Petillo v. New Jersey, 400 F.Supp. 1152, 1171-1172 (NJ 1975), vacated and remanded by order sub nom. Alanese v. Yeager, 541 F.2d 275 (CA3 1976), or at a hearing on the sufficiency of the affidavit, cf. United States v. Upshaw, 48 F.2d 1218, 1221-1222 (CA5 1971), cert denied, 405 U.S. 934 (1972). A flat nonimpeachment rule would bar reexamination of the warrant even in these cases.

Second, the hearing before the magistrate not always will suffice to discourage lawless or reckless misconduct. The pre-search proceeding is necessarily ex parte, since the subject of the search cannot be tipped off to the application for a warrant, lest he destroy or remove evidence. The usual reliance of our legal system on adversary proceedings itself should be an indication that an ex parte inquiry is likely to be less vigorous. The magistrate has no acquaintance with the information that may contradict the good faith and reasonable basis of the affiant's allegations. The pre-search proceeding will frequently be marked by haste, because of the understandable desire to act before the evidence disappears; this urgency will not always permit the magistrate to make an extended independent examination of the affiant or other witnesses.

Third, the alternative sanctions of a perjury prosecution, administrative discipline, contempt, or a civil suit are not likely to fill the gap. Mapp v. Ohio implicitly rejected the adequacy of these alternatives. Mr. Justice Douglas noted this in his concurrence in Mapp, 367 U.S. at 367 U. S. 670, where he quoted from Wolf v. Colorado, 338 U. S. 25, 338 U. S. 42 (1949):

"'self-scrutiny is a lofty ideal, but its exaltation reaches new heights if we expect a District Attorney to prosecute himself or his associates for well meaning violations of the search and seizure clause during a raid the District Attorney or his associates have ordered.'"

Fourth, allowing an evidentiary hearing, after a suitable preliminary proffer of material falsity, would not diminish the importance and solemnity of the warrant-issuing process. It is the ex parte nature of the initial hearing, rather than the magistrate's capacity, that is the reason for the review. A magistrate's determination is presently subject to review before trial as to sufficiency without any undue interference with the dignity of the magistrate's function. Our reluctance today to extend the rule of exclusion beyond instances of deliberate misstatements, and those of reckless disregard, leaves a broad field where the magistrate is the sole protection of a citizen's Fourth Amendment rights, namely, in instances where police have been merely negligent in checking or recording the facts relevant to a probable cause determination.

Fifth, the claim that a post-search hearing will confuse the issue of the defendant's guilt with the issue of the State's possible misbehavior is footless. The hearing will not be in the presence of the jury. An issue extraneous to guilt already is examined in any probable cause determination or review of probable cause. Nor, if a sensible threshold showing is required and sensible substantive requirements for suppression are maintained, need there be any new large-scale commitment of judicial resources; many claims will wash out at an early stage, and the more substantial ones in any event would require judicial resources for vindication if the suggested alternative sanctions were truly to be effective. The requirement of a substantial preliminary showing should suffice to prevent the misuse of a veracity hearing for purposes of discovery or obstruction. And because we are faced today with only the question of the integrity of the affiant's representations as to his own activities, we need not decide, and we in no way predetermine, the difficult question whether a reviewing court must ever require the revelation of the identity of an informant once a substantial preliminary showing of falsity has been made. McCray v. Illinois, 386 U. S. 300 (1967), the Court's earlier disquisition in this area, concluded only that the Due Process Clause of the Fourteenth Amendment did not require the State to expose an informant's identity routinely, upon a defendant's mere demand, when there was ample evidence in the probable cause hearing to show that the informant was reliable and his information credible.

Sixth and finally, as to the argument that the exclusionary rule should not be extended to a "new" area, we cannot regard any such extension really to be at issue here. Despite the deep skepticism of Members of this Court as to the wisdom of extending the exclusionary rule to collateral areas, such as civil or grand jury proceedings, the Court has not questioned, in the absence of a more efficacious sanction, the continued application of the rule to suppress evidence from the State's case where a Fourth Amendment violation has been substantial and deliberate. See Brewer v. Williams, 430 U. S. 387, 430 U. S. 422 (1977) (BURGER, C.J., dissenting); Stone v. Powell, 428 U.S. at 428 U. S. 538 (WHITE, J., dissenting). We see no principled basis for distinguishing between the question of the sufficiency of an affidavit, which also is subject to a post-search reexamination, and the question of its integrity.

IV

In sum, and to repeat with some embellishment what we stated at the beginning of this opinion: there is, of course, a presumption of validity with respect to the affidavit supporting the search warrant. To mandate an evidentiary hearing, the challenger's attack must be more than conclusory, and must be supported by more than a mere desire to cross-examine. There must be allegations of deliberate falsehood or of reckless disregard for the truth, and those allegations must be accompanied by an offer of proof. They should point out specifically the portion of the warrant affidavit that is claimed to be false; and they should be accompanied by a statement of supporting reasons. Affidavits or sworn or otherwise reliable statements of witnesses should be furnished, or their absence satisfactorily explained. Allegations of negligence or innocent mistake are insufficient. The deliberate falsity or reckless disregard whose impeachment is permitted today is only that of the affiant, not of any nongovernmental informant. Finally, if these requirements are met, and if, when material that is the subject of the alleged falsity or reckless disregard is set to one side, there remains sufficient content in the warrant affidavit to support a finding of probable cause, no hearing is required. [8] On the other hand, if the remaining content is insufficient, the defendant is entitled, under the Fourth and Fourteenth Amendments, to his hearing. Whether he will prevail at that hearing is, of course, another issue.

Because of Delaware's absolute rule, its courts did not have occasion to consider the proffer put forward by petitioner Franks. Since the framing of suitable rules to govern proffers is a matter properly left to the States, we decline ourselves to pass on petitioner's proffer. The judgment of the Supreme Court of Delaware is reversed, and the case is remanded for further proceedings not inconsistent with this opinion.

It is so ordered.

Rakas v. Illinois (Dec 5, 1978) [Notes omitted]

MR. JUSTICE REHNQUIST delivered the opinion of the Court.

Petitioners were convicted of armed robbery in the Circuit Court of Kankakee County,

Ill., and their convictions were affirmed on appeal. At their trial, the prosecution offered into evidence a sawed-off rifle and rifle shells that had been seized by police during a search of an automobile in which petitioners had been passengers. Neither petitioner is the owner of the automobile, and neither has ever asserted that he owned the rifle or shells seized. The Illinois Appellate Court held that petitioners lacked standing to object to the allegedly unlawful search, and seizure and denied their motion to suppress the evidence. We granted certiorari in light of the obvious importance of the issues raised to the administration of criminal justice, 435 U.S. 922 (1978), and now affirm.

I

Because we are not here concerned with the issue of probable cause, a brief description of the events leading to the search of the automobile will suffice. A police officer on a routine patrol received a radio call notifying him of a robbery of a clothing store in Bourbonnais, Ill., and describing the getaway car. Shortly thereafter, the officer spotted an automobile which he thought might be the getaway car. After following the car for some time and after the arrival of assistance, he and several other officers stopped the vehicle. The occupants of the automobile, petitioners and two female companions, were ordered out of the car, and, after the occupants had left the car, two officers searched the interior of the vehicle. They discovered a box of rifle shells in the glove compartment, which had been locked, and a sawed-off rifle under the front passenger seat. App. 111. After discovering the rifle and the shells, the officers took petitioners to the station and placed them under arrest.

Before trial petitioners moved to suppress the rifle and shells seized from the car on the ground that the search violated the Fourth and Fourteenth Amendments. They conceded that they did not own the automobile, and were simply passengers; the owner of the car had been the driver of the vehicle at the time of the search. Nor did they assert that they owned the rifle or the shells seized. [1] The prosecutor challenged petitioners' standing to object to the lawfulness of the search of the car because neither the car, the shells nor the rifle belonged to them. The trial court agreed that petitioners lacked standing, and denied the motion to suppress the evidence. App. 224. In view of this holding, the court did not determine whether there was probable cause for the search and seizure. On appeal after petitioners' conviction, the Appellate Court of Illinois, Third Judicial District, affirmed the trial court's denial of petitioners' motion to suppress because it held that,

"without a proprietary or other similar interest in an automobile, a mere passenger therein lacks standing to challenge the legality of the search of the vehicle. 46 Ill.App.3d 569, 571, 360 N.E.2d 1252, 1253 (1977). The court stated:"

"We believe that defendants failed to establish any prejudice to their own constitutional rights, because they were not persons aggrieved by the unlawful search and seizure. . . . They wrongly seek to establish prejudice only through the use of evidence gathered as a consequence of a search and seizure directed at someone else, and fail to prove an invasion of their own privacy. Alderman v. United States (1969), 394 U. S. 165. . . ."

Id. at 571-572, 360 N.E.2d at 1254. The Illinois Supreme Court denied petitioners leave to appeal.

II

Petitioners first urge us to relax or broaden the rule of standing enunciated in Jones v. United States, 362 U. S. 257 (1960), so that any criminal defendant at whom a search was "directed" would have standing to contest the legality of that search and object to the admission at trial of evidence obtained as a result of the search. Alternatively, petitioners argue that they have standing to object to the search under Jones because they were "legitimately on [the] premises" at the time of the search.

The concept of standing discussed in Jones focuses on whether the person seeking to challenge the legality of a search as a basis for suppressing evidence was himself the "victim" of the search or seizure. Id. at 362 U. S. 261. [2] Adoption of the so-called "target" theory advanced by petitioners would, in effect, permit a defendant to assert that a violation of the Fourth Amendment rights of a third party entitled him to have evidence suppressed at his trial. If we reject petitioners' request for a broadened rule of standing such as this, and reaffirm the holding of Jones and other cases that Fourth Amendment rights are personal rights that may not be asserted vicariously, we will have occasion to reexamine the "standing" terminology emphasized in Jones. For we are not at all sure that the determination of a motion to suppress is materially aided by labeling the inquiry identified in Jones as one of standing, rather than simply recognizing it as one involving the substantive question of whether or not the proponent of the motion to suppress has had his own Fourth Amendment rights infringed by the search and seizure which he seeks to challenge. We shall therefore consider, in turn, petitioners' target theory, the necessity for continued adherence to the notion of standing discussed in Jones as a concept that is theoretically distinct from the merits of a defendant's Fourth Amendment claim, and, finally, the proper disposition of petitioners' ultimate claim in this case.

A

We decline to extend the rule of standing in Fourth Amendment cases in the manner suggested by petitioners. As we stated in Alderman v. United States, 394 U. S. 165, 394 U. S. 174 (1969), "Fourth Amendment rights are personal rights which, like some other constitutional rights, may not be vicariously asserted." See Brown v. United States, 411 U. S. 223, 411 U. S. 230 (1973);

Simmons v. United States, 390 U. S. 377, 390 U. S. 389 (1968); Wong Sun v. United States, 371 U. S. 471, 371 U. S. 492 (1963); cf. Silverman v. United States, 365 U. S. 505, 365 U. S. 511 (1961); Gouled v. United States, 255 U. S. 298, 255 U. S. 304 (1921). A person who is aggrieved by an illegal search and seizure only through the introduction of damaging evidence secured by a search of a third person's premises or property has not had any of his Fourth Amendment rights infringed. Alderman, supra at 394 U. S. 174. And since the exclusionary rule is an attempt to effectuate the guarantees of the Fourth Amendment, United States v. Calandra, 414 U. S. 338, 414 U. S. 347 (1974), it is proper to permit only defendants whose Fourth Amendment rights have been violated to benefit from the rule's protections. [3] See Simmons v. United States, supra at 390 U. S. 389. There is no reason to think that a party whose rights have been infringed will not, if evidence is used against him, have ample motivation to move to suppress it. Alderman, supra at 394 U. S. 174. Even if such a person is not a defendant in the action, he may be able to recover damages for the violation of his Fourth Amendment rights, see Monroe v. Pape, 365 U. S. 167 (1961), or seek redress under state law for invasion of privacy or trespass.

In support of their target theory, petitioners rely on the following quotation from Jones:

"In order to qualify as a 'person aggrieved by an unlawful search and seizure,' one must have been a victim of a search or seizure, one against whom the search was directed, as distinguished from one who claims prejudice only through the use of evidence gathered as a consequence of a search or seizure directed at someone else."

362 U.S. at 362 U. S. 261 (emphasis added). They also rely on Bumper v. North Carolina, 391 U. S. 543, 391 U. S. 548 n. 11 (1968), and United States v. Jeffers, 342 U. S. 48 (1951).

The above-quoted statement from Jones suggests that the italicized language was meant merely as a parenthetical equivalent of the previous phrase "a victim of a search or seizure." To the extent that the language might be read more broadly, it is dictum which was impliedly repudiated in Alderman v. United States, supra, and which we now expressly reject. In Jones, the Court set forth two alternative holdings: it established a rule of "automatic" standing to contest an allegedly illegal search where the same possession needed to establish standing is an essential element of the offense charged, [4] and, second, it stated that "anyone legitimately on premises where a search occurs may challenge its legality by way of a motion to suppress." 362 U.S. at 362 U. S. 264, 362 U. S. 267. See Combs v. United States, 408 U. S. 224, 408 U. S. 227 n. 4 (1972); Mancusi v. DeForte, 392 U. S. 364, 392 U. S. 368 n. 5 (198); Simmons v. United States, supra at 390 U. S. 390. Had the Court intended to adopt the target theory now put forth by petitioners, neither of the above two holdings would have been necessary, since Jones was the "target" of the police search in that case. [5] Nor does United States v. Jeffers, supra, or Bumper v. North Carolina, supra, support the target theory. Standing in Jeffers was based on Jeffers' possessory interest in both the premises searched and the property seized. 342 U.S. at 342 U. S. 49-50, 342 U. S. 54; see Mancusi v. DeForte, supra, at 392 U. S. 367-368; Hoffa v. United States, 385 U. S. 293, 385 U. S. 301 (1966); Lanza v. New York, 370 U. S. 139, 370 U. S. 143, and n. 10 (1962). Similarly, in Bumper, the defendant had a substantial possessory interest in both the house searched and the rifle seized. 391 U.S. at 391 U. S. 548, n. 11.

In Alderman v. United States, Mr. Justice Fortas, in a concurring and dissenting opinion, argued that the Court should "include within the category of those who may object to the introduction of illegal evidence one against whom the search was directed.'" 394 U.S. at 394 U. S. 206-209. The Court did not directly comment on Mr. Justice Fortas' suggestion, but it left no doubt that it rejected this theory by holding that persons who were not parties to unlawfully overheard conversations or who did not own the premises on which such conversations took place did not have standing to contest the legality of the surveillance, regardless of whether or not they were the "targets" of the surveillance. Id. at 394 U. S. 176. Mr. Justice Harlan, concurring and dissenting, did squarely address Mr. Justice Fortas' arguments, and declined to accept them. Id. at 394 U. S. 188-189, n. 1. He identified administrative problems posed by the target theory:

"[T]he [target] rule would entail very substantial administrative difficulties. In the majority of cases, I would imagine that the police plant a bug with the expectation that it may well produce leads to a large number of crimes. A lengthy hearing would, then, appear to be necessary in order to determine whether the police knew of an accused's criminal activity at the time the bug was planted and whether the police decision to plant a bug was motivated by an effort to obtain information against the accused or some other individual. I do not believe that this administrative burden is justified in any substantial degree by the hypothesized marginal increase in Fourth Amendment protection."

Ibid. When we are urged to grant standing to a criminal defendant to assert a violation, not of his own constitutional rights, but of someone else's, we cannot but give weight to practical difficulties such as those foreseen by Mr. Justice Harlan in the quoted language.

Conferring standing to raise vicarious Fourth Amendment claims would necessarily mean a more widespread invocation of the exclusionary rule during criminal trials. The Court's opinion in Alderman counseled against such an extension of the exclusionary rule:

"The deterrent values of preventing the incrimination of those whose rights the police have violated have been considered sufficient to justify the suppression of probative evidence even though the case against the defendant is weakened or destroyed. We adhere to that judgment. But we are not convinced that the additional benefits of extending the exclusionary rule to other defendants would justify further encroachment upon the public interest in prosecuting those accused of crime and having them acquitted or convicted on the basis of all the evidence which exposes the truth."

Id. at 394 U. S. 174-175. Each time the exclusionary rule is applied, it exacts a substantial social cost for the vindication of Fourth Amendment rights. Relevant and reliable evidence is kept from the trier of fact and the search for truth at trial is deflected. See United States v. Ceccolini, 435 U. S. 268, 435 U. S. 275 (1978); Stone v. Powell, 428 U. S. 465, 428 U. S. 489-490 (1976); United States v. Calandra, 414 U.S. at 414 U. S. 348-352. Since our cases generally have held that one whose Fourth Amendment rights are violated may successfully suppress evidence obtained in the course of an illegal search and seizure, misgivings as to the benefit of enlarging the class of persons who may invoke that rule are properly considered when deciding whether to expand standing to assert Fourth Amendment violations. [6]

B

Had we accepted petitioners' request to allow persons other than those whose own Fourth Amendment rights were violated by a challenged search and seizure to suppress evidence obtained in the course of such police activity, it would be appropriate to retain Jones' use of standing in Fourth Amendment analysis. Under petitioners' target theory, a court could determine that a defendant had standing to invoke the exclusionary rule without having to inquire into the substantive question of whether the challenged search or seizure violated the Fourth Amendment rights of that particular defendant. However, having rejected petitioners' target theory and reaffirmed the principle that the

"rights assured by the Fourth Amendment are personal rights, [which] . . . may be enforced by exclusion of evidence only at the instance of one whose own protection was infringed by the search and seizure,"

Simmons v. United States, 390 U.S. at 390 U. S. 389, the question necessarily arises whether it serves any useful analytical purpose to consider this principle a matter of standing, distinct from the merits of a defendant's Fourth Amendment claim. We can think of no decided cases of this Court that would have come out differently had we concluded, as we do now, that the type of standing requirement discussed in Jones and reaffirmed today is more properly subsumed under substantive Fourth Amendment doctrine. Rigorous application of the principle that the rights secured by this Amendment are personal, in place of a notion of "standing," will produce no additional situations in which evidence must be excluded. The inquiry under either approach is the same. [7] But we think the better analysis forthrightly focuses on the extent of a particular defendant's rights under the Fourth Amendment, rather than on any theoretically separate, but invariably intertwined, concept of standing. The Court in Jones also may have been aware that there was a certain artificiality in analyzing this question in terms of standing, because, in at least three separate places in its opinion, the Court placed that term within quotation marks. 362 U.S. at 362 U. S. 261, 362 U. S. 263, 362 U. S. 265.

It should be emphasized that nothing we say here casts the least doubt on cases which recognize that, as a general proposition, the issue of standing involves two inquiries: first, whether the proponent of a particular legal right has alleged "injury in fact," and, second, whether the proponent is asserting his own legal rights and interests, rather than basing his claim for relief upon the rights of third parties. See, e.g., Singleton v. Wulff, 428 U. S. 106, 428 U. S. 112 (1976); Warth v. Seldin, 422 U. S. 490, 439 U. S. 499 (1975); Data Processing Service v. Camp, 397 U. S. 150, 397 U. S. 152-153 (1970). But this Court's long history of insistence that Fourth Amendment rights are personal in nature has already answered many of these traditional standing inquiries, and we think that definition of those rights is more properly placed within the purview of substantive Fourth Amendment law than within that of standing. Cf. id. at 397 U. S. 153, and n. 1; Barrows v. Jackson, 346 U. S. 249, 346 U. S. 256 n. 4 (1953); Hale v. Henkel, 201 U. S. 43, 201 U. S. 69-70 (1906). [8]

Analyzed in these terms, the question is whether the challenged search and seizure violated the Fourth Amendment rights of a criminal defendant who seeks to exclude the evidence obtained during it. That inquiry, in turn, requires a determination of whether the disputed search and seizure has infringed an interest of the defendant which the Fourth Amendment was designed to protect. We are under no illusion that, by dispensing with the rubric of standing used in Jones, we have rendered any simpler the determination of whether the proponent of a motion to suppress is entitled to contest the legality of a search and seizure. But by frankly recognizing that this aspect of the analysis belongs more properly under the heading of substantive Fourth Amendment doctrine than under the heading of standing, we think the decision of this issue will rest on sounder logical footing.

C

Here, petitioners, who were passengers occupying a car which they neither owned nor leased, seek to analogize their position to that of the defendant in Jones v. Unite States.

In Jones, petitioner was present at the time of the search of an apartment which was owned by a friend. The friend had given Jones permission to use the apartment and a key to it, with which Jones had admitted himself on the day of the search. He had a suit and shirt at the apartment, and had slept there "maybe a night," but his home was elsewhere. At the time of the search, Jones was the only occupant of the apartment, because the lessee was away for a period of several days. 362 U.S. at 362 U. S. 259. Under these circumstances, this Court stated that, while one wrongfully on the premises could not move to suppress evidence obtained as a result of searching them, [9] "anyone legitimately on premises where a search occurs may challenge its legality." Id. at 362 U. S. 267. Petitioners argue that their occupancy of the automobile in question was comparable to that of Jones in the apartment, and that they therefore have standing to contest the legality of the search -- or, as we have rephrased the inquiry, that they, like Jones, had their Fourth Amendment rights violated by the search.

We do not question the conclusion in Jones that the defendant in that case suffered a violation of his personal Fourth Amendment rights if the search in question was unlawful.

Nonetheless, we believe that the phrase "legitimately on premises" coined in Jones creates too broad a gauge for measurement of Fourth Amendment right. [10] For example, applied literally, this statement would permit a casual visitor who has never seen, or been permitted to visit, the basement of another's house to object to a search of the basement if the visitor happened to be in the kitchen of the house at the time of the search. Likewise, a casual visitor who walks into a house one minute before a search of the house commences and leaves one minute after the search ends would be able to contest the legality of the search. The first visitor would have absolutely no interest or legitimate expectation of privacy in the basement, the second would have none in the house, and it advances no purpose served by the Fourth Amendment to permit either of them to object to the lawfulness of the search. [11]

We think that Jones, on its facts, merely stands for the unremarkable proposition that a person can have a legally sufficient interest in a place other than his own home so that the Fourth Amendment protects him from unreasonable governmental intrusion into that place. See 362 U.S. at 362 U. S. 263, 362 U. S. 265. In defining the scope of that interest, we adhere to the view expressed in Jones and echoed in later cases that arcane distinctions developed in property and tort law between guests, licensees, invitees, and the like, ought not to control. Id. at 362 U. S. 266; see Mancusi v. DeForte, 392 U. S. 364 (1968); Warden v. Hayden, 387 U. S. 294 (1967); Silverman v. United States, 365 U. S. 505 (1961). But the Jones statement that a person need only be "legitimately on premises" in order to challenge the validity of the search of a dwelling place cannot be taken in its full sweep beyond the facts of that case.

Katz v. United States, 389 U. S. 347 (1967), provides guidance in defining the scope of the interest protected by the Fourth Amendment. In the course of repudiating the doctrine derived from Olmstead v. United States, 277 U. S. 438 (1928), and Goldman v. United States, 316 U. S. 129 (1942), that, if police officers had not been guilty of a common law trespass, they were not prohibited by the Fourth Amendment from eavesdropping, the Court in Katz held that capacity to claim the protection of the Fourth Amendment depends not upon a property right in the invaded place, but upon whether the person who claims the protection of the Amendment has a legitimate expectation of privacy in the invaded place. 389 U.S. at 389 U. S. 353; see United States v. Chadwick, 433 U. S. 1, 433 U. S. 7 (1977); United States v. White, 401 U. S. 745, 401 U. S. 752 (1971).

Viewed in this manner, the holding in Jones can best be explained by the fact that Jones had a legitimate expectation of privacy in the premises he was using, and therefore could claim the protection of the Fourth Amendment with respect to a governmental invasion of those premises even though his "interest" in those premises might not have been a recognized property interest at common law. [12] See Jones v. United States, 362 U.S. at 362 U. S. 261.

Our Brother WHITE, in dissent, expresses the view that, by rejecting the phrase "legitimately on [the] premises" as the appropriate measure of Fourth Amendment rights, we are abandoning a thoroughly workable, "bright line" test in favor of a less certain analysis of whether the facts of a particular case give rise to a legitimate expectation of privacy. Post at 439 U. S. 168. If "legitimately on premises" were the successful litmus test of Fourth Amendment rights that he assumes it is, his approach would have at least the merit of easy application, whatever it lacked in fidelity to the history and purposes of the Fourth Amendment. But a reading of lower court cases that have applied the phrase "legitimately on premises," and of the dissent itself, reveals that this expression is not a shorthand summary for a bright-line rule which somehow encapsulates the "core" of the Fourth Amendment's protections. [13]

The dissent itself shows that the facile consistency it is striving for is illusory. The dissenters concede that "there comes a point when use of an area is shared with so many that one simply cannot reasonably expect seclusion." Post at 439 U. S. 164. But surely the "point" referred to is not one demarcating a line which is black on one side and white on another; it is inevitably a point which separates one shade of gray from another. We are likewise told by the dissent that a person

"legitimately on private premises . . . , though his privacy is not absolute, is entitled to expect that he is sharing it only with those persons [allowed there], and that governmental officials will intrude only with consent or by complying with the Fourth Amendment."

Ibid. (emphasis added). This single sentence describing the contours of the supposedly easily applied rule virtually abounds with unanswered questions: what are "private" premises? Indeed, what are the "premises?" It may be easy to describe the "premises" when one is confronted with a 1-room apartment, but what of the case of a 10-room house, or of a house with an attached garage that is searched? Also, if one's privacy is not absolute, how is it bounded? If he risks governmental intrusion "with consent," who may give that consent?

Again, we are told by the dissent that the Fourth Amendment assures that "some expectations of privacy are justified, and will be protected from official intrusion." Post at 439 U. S. 166 (emphasis added). But we are not told which of many possible expectations of privacy are embraced within this sentence. And our dissenting Brethren concede that "perhaps the Constitution provides some degree less protection for the personal freedom from unreasonable governmental intrusion when one does not have a possessory interest in the invaded private place." Ibid. But how much "less" protection is available when one does not have such a possessory interest?

Our disagreement with the dissent is not that it leaves these questions unanswered, or that the questions are necessarily irrelevant in the context of the analysis contained in this opinion. Our disagreement is rather with the dissent's bland and self-refuting assumption that there will not be fine lines to be drawn in Fourth Amendment cases as in other areas of the law, and that its rubric, rather than a meaningful exegesis of Fourth Amendment doctrine, is more desirable or more easily resolves Fourth Amendment cases. [14] In abandoning "legitimately on premises" for the doctrine that we announce today, we are not forsaking a time-tested and workable rule, which has produced consistent results when applied, solely for the sake of fidelity to the values underlying the Fourth Amendment. Rather, we are rejecting blind adherence to a phrase which, at most, has superficial clarity, and which conceals underneath that thin veneer all of the problems of line drawing which must be faced in any conscientious effort to apply the Fourth Amendment. Where the factual premises for a rule are so generally prevalent that little would be lost and much would be gained by abandoning case-by-case analysis, we have not hesitated to do so. See United States v. Robinson, 414 U. S. 218, 414 U. S. 235 (1973). But the phrase "legitimately on premises" has not been shown to be an easily applicable measure of Fourth Amendment rights so much as it has proved to be simply a label placed by the courts on results which have not been subjected to careful analysis. We would not wish to be understood as saying that legitimate presence on the premises is irrelevant to one's expectation of privacy, but it cannot be deemed controlling.

D

Judged by the foregoing analysis, petitioners' claims must fail. They asserted neither a property nor a possessory interest in the automobile nor an interest in the property seized. And as we have previously indicated, the fact that they were "legitimately on [the] premises" in the sense that they were in the car with the permission of its owner is not determinative of whether they had a legitimate expectation of privacy in the particular areas of the automobile searched. It is unnecessary for us to decide here whether the same expectations of privacy are warranted in a car as would be justified in a dwelling place in analogous circumstances. We have on numerous occasions pointed out that cars are not to be treated identically with houses or apartments for

Fourth Amendment purposes. See United States v. Chadwick, 433 U.S. at 433 U. S. 12; United States v. Martinez-Fuerte, 428 U. S. 543, 428 U. S. 561 (1976); Cardwell v. Lewis, 417 U. S. 583, 417 U. S. 590 (1974) (plurality opinion). [15] But here petitioners' claim is one which would fail even in an analogous situation in a dwelling place, since they made no showing that they had any legitimate expectation of privacy in the glove compartment or area under the seat of the car in which they were merely passengers. Like the trunk of an automobile, these are areas in which a passenger qua passenger simply would not normally have a legitimate expectation of privacy. Supra at 439 U. S. 142.

Jones v. United States, 362 U. S. 257 (1960), and Katz v. United States, 389 U. S. 347 (1967), involved significantly different factual circumstances. Jones not only had permission to use the apartment of his friend, but had a key to the apartment with which he admitted himself on the day of the search and kept possessions in the apartment. Except with respect to his friend, Jones had complete dominion and control over the apartment, and could exclude others from it. Likewise, in Katz, the defendant occupied the telephone booth, shut the door behind him to exclude all others, and paid the toll, which "entitled [him] to assume that the words he utter[ed] into the mouthpiece [would] not be broadcast to the world." Id. at 389 U. S. 352. [16] Katz and Jones could legitimately expect privacy in the areas which were the subject of the search and seizure each sought to contest. No such showing was made by these petitioners with respect to those portions of the automobile which were searched and from which incriminating evidence was seized. [17]

III

The Illinois courts were therefore correct in concluding that it was unnecessary to decide whether the search of the car might have violated the rights secured to someone else by the Fourth and Fourteenth Amendments to the United States Constitution. Since it did not violate any rights of these petitioners, their judgment of conviction is

Affirmed.

Delaware v. Prouse (March 27, 1979)

MR. JUSTICE WHITE delivered the opinion of the Court.

The question is whether it is an unreasonable seizure under the Fourth and Fourteenth Amendments to stop an automobile, being driven on a public highway, for the purpose of checking the driving license of the operator and the registration of the car, where there is neither probable cause to believe nor reasonable suspicion that the car is being driven contrary to the laws governing the operation of motor vehicles or that either the car or any of its occupants is subject to seizure or detention in connection with the violation of any other applicable law.

I

At 7:20 p.m. on November 30, 1976, a New Castle County, Del., patrolman in a police cruiser stopped the automobile occupied by respondent. [n1] The patrolman smelled marihuana smoke as he was walking toward the stopped vehicle, and he seized marihuana in plain view on the car floor. Respondent was subsequently indicted for illegal possession of a controlled substance. At a hearing on respondent's motion to suppress the marihuana seized as a result of the stop, the patrolman testified that, prior to stopping the vehicle, he had observed neither traffic or equipment violations nor any suspicious activity, and that he made the stop only in order to check the driver's license and registration. The patrolman was not acting pursuant to any standards, guidelines, or procedures pertaining to document spot checks, promulgated by either his department or the State Attorney General. Characterizing the stop as "routine," the patrolman explained, "I saw the car in the area and wasn't answering any complaints, so I decided to pull them off." App. A9. The trial court granted the motion to suppress, finding the stop and detention to have been wholly capricious, and therefore violative of the Fourth Amendment.

The Delaware Supreme Court affirmed, noting first that

[t]he issue of the legal validity of systematic, roadblock-type stops of a number of vehicles for license and vehicle registration check is not now before the Court,

382 A.2d 1359, 1362 (1978) (emphasis in original). The court held that

a random stop of a motorist in the absence of specific articulable facts which justify the stop by indicating a reasonable suspicion that a violation of the law has occurred is constitutionally impermissible and violative of the Fourth and Fourteenth Amendments to the United States Constitution.

Id. at 1364. We granted certiorari to resolve the conflict between this decision, which is in accord with decisions in five other jurisdictions, [n2] and the contrary determination in six jurisdictions [n3] that the Fourth Amendment does not prohibit the kind of automobile stop that occurred here. 439 U.S. 816 (1978).

II

Because the Delaware Supreme Court held that the stop at issue not only violated the Federal Constitution but also was impermissible under Art. I, § 6, of the Delaware Constitution, it is urged that the judgment below was based on an independent and adequate state ground, and that we therefore have no jurisdiction in this case. Fox Film Corp. v. Muller, 296 U.S. 207, 210 (1935). At least, it is suggested, the matter is sufficiently uncertain that we should remand for clarification as to the ground upon which the judgment rested. California v. Krivda, 409 U.S. 33, 35 (1972). Based on our reading of the opinion, however, we are satisfied

that, even if the State Constitution would have provided an adequate basis for the judgment, the Delaware Supreme Court did not intend to rest its decision independently on the State Constitution, and that we have jurisdiction of this case.

As we understand the opinion below, Art I, § 6, of the Delaware Constitution will automatically be interpreted at least as broadly as the Fourth Amendment; [n4] that is, every police practice authoritatively determined to be contrary to the Fourth and Fourteenth Amendments will, without further analysis, be held to be contrary to Art. I, § 6. This approach, which is consistent with previous opinions of the Delaware Supreme Court, [n5] was followed in this case. The court analyzed the various decisions interpreting the Federal Constitution, concluded that the Fourth Amendment foreclosed spot checks of automobiles, and summarily held that the State Constitution was therefore also infringed. This is one of those cases where,

at the very least, the [state] court felt compelled by what it understood to be federal constitutional considerations to construe . . . its own law in the manner it did.

Zacchini v. Scripps-Howard Broadcasting Co., 433 U.S. 562, 568 (1977). Had state law not been mentioned at all, there would be no question about our jurisdiction, even though the State Constitution might have provided an independent and adequate state ground. Ibid. The same result should follow here, where the state constitutional holding depended upon the state court's view of the reach of the Fourth and Fourteenth Amendments. If the state court misapprehended federal law, "[i]t should be freed to decide . . . these suits according to its own local law." Missouri ex rel. Southern R. Co. v. Mayfield, 340 U.S. 1, 5 (1950).

III

The Fourth and Fourteenth Amendments are implicated in this case because stopping an automobile and detaining its occupants constitute a "seizure" within the meaning of those Amendments, even though the purpose of the stop is limited and the resulting detention quite brief. United States v. Martinez-Fuerte, 428 U.S. 543, 556-558 (1976); United States v. Brignoni-Ponce, 422 U.S. 873, 878 (1975); cf. Terry v. Ohio, 392 U.S. 1, 16 (1968). The essential purpose of the proscriptions in the Fourth Amendment is to impose a standard of "reasonableness" [n6] upon the exercise of discretion by government officials, including law enforcement agents, in order "'to safeguard the privacy and security of individuals against arbitrary invasions. . . .'" Marshall v. Barlow's, Inc., 436 U.S. 307, 312 (1978), quoting Camara v. Municipal Court, 387 U.S. 523, 528 (1967). [n7] Thus, the permissibility of a particular law enforcement practice is judged by balancing its intrusion on the individual's Fourth Amendment interests against its promotion of legitimate governmental interests. [n8] Implemented in this manner, the reasonableness standard usually requires, at a minimum, that the facts upon which an intrusion is based be capable of measurement against "an objective standard," [n9] whether this be probable cause [n10] or a less stringent test. [n11] In those situations in which the balance of interests precludes insistence upon "some quantum of individualized suspicion," [n12] other safeguards are generally relied upon to assure that the individual's reasonable expectation of privacy is not "subject to the discretion of the official in the field," Camara v. Municipal Court, 387 U.S. at 532. See id. at 534-535; Marshall v. Barlow's, Inc., supra at 320-321; United States v. United States District Court, 407 U.S. 297, 322-323 (1972) (requiring warrants).

In this case, however, the State of Delaware urges that patrol officers be subject to no constraints in deciding which automobiles shall be stopped for a license and registration check because the State's interest in discretionary spot checks as a means of ensuring the safety of its roadways outweighs the resulting intrusion on the privacy and security of the persons detained.

IV

We have only recently considered the legality of investigative stops of automobiles where the officers making the stop have neither probable cause to believe nor reasonable suspicion that either the automobile or its occupants are subject to seizure under the applicable criminal laws. In United State v. Brignoni-Ponce, supra, Border Patrol agents conducting roving patrols in areas near the international border asserted statutory authority to stop at random any vehicle in order to determine whether it contained illegal aliens or was involved in smuggling operations. The practice was held to violate the Fourth Amendment, but the Court did not invalidate all warrantless automobile stops upon less than probable cause. Given

the importance of the governmental interest at stake, the minimal intrusion of a brief stop, and the absence of practical alternatives for policing the border,

422 U.S. at 881, the Court analogized the roving patrol stop to the on-the-street encounter addressed in Terry v. Ohio, supra, and held:

Except at the border and its functional equivalents, officers on roving patrol may stop vehicles only if they are aware of specific articulable facts, together with rational inferences from those facts, that reasonably warrant suspicion that the vehicles contain aliens who may be illegally in the country.

422 U.S. at 884 (footnote omitted). Because

the nature of illegal alien traffic and the characteristics of smuggling operations tend to generate articulable grounds for identifying violators,

id. at 883,

a requirement of reasonable suspicion for stops allows the Government adequate means of guarding the public interest and also protects residents of the border areas from indiscriminate official interference.

Ibid.

The constitutionality of stops by Border Patrol agents was again before the Court in United States v. Martinez-Fuerte, supra, in which we addressed the permissibility of checkpoint operations. This practice involved slowing all oncoming traffic "to a virtual, if not a complete, halt," 428 U.S. at 546, at a highway roadblock, and referring vehicles chosen at the discretion of Border Patrol agents to an area for secondary inspection. See id. at 546, 558. Recognizing that the governmental interest involved was the same as that furthered by roving patrol stops, the Court nonetheless sustained the constitutionality of the Border Patrol's checkpoint operations. The crucial distinction was the lesser intrusion upon the motorist's Fourth Amendment interests:

[The] objective intrusion -- the stop itself, the questioning, and the visual inspection -- also existed in roving patrol stops. But we view checkpoint stops in a different light because the subjective intrusion -- the generating of concern or even freight on the part of lawful traveler -- is appreciably less in the case of a checkpoint stop.

Id. at 558.

Although not dispositive, [n13] these decisions undoubtedly provide guidance in balancing the public interest against the individual's Fourth Amendment interests implicated by the practice of spot checks such as occurred in this case. We cannot agree that stopping or detaining a vehicle on an ordinary city street is less intrusive than a roving patrol stop on a major highway, and that it bears greater resemblance to a permissible stop and secondary detention at a checkpoint near the border. In this regard, we note that Brignoni-Ponce was not limited to roving patrol stops on limited-access roads, but applied to any roving patrol stop by Border Patrol agents on any type of roadway on less than reasonable suspicion. See 422 U.S. at 882-883; United States v. Ortiz, 422 U.S. 891, 894 (1975). We cannot assume that the physical and psychological intrusion visited upon the occupants of a vehicle by a random stop to check documents is of any less moment than that occasioned by a stop by border agents on roving patrol. Both of these stops generally entail law enforcement officers signaling a moving automobile to pull over to the side of the roadway, by means of a possibly unsettling show of authority. Both interfere with freedom of movement, are inconvenient, and consume time. Both may create substantial anxiety. For Fourth Amendment purposes, we also see insufficient resemblance between sporadic and random stops of individual vehicles making their way through city traffic and those stops occasioned by roadblocks where all vehicles are brought to a halt or to a near halt, and all are subjected to a show of the police power of the community.

At traffic checkpoints, the motorist can see that other vehicles are being stopped, he can see visible signs of the officers' authority, and he is much less likely to be frightened or annoyed by the intrusion.

Id. at 894-895, quoted in United States v. Martinez-Fuerte, 428 U.S. at 558.

V

But the State of Delaware urges that, even if discretionary spot checks such as occurred in this case intrude upon motorists as much as or more than do the roving patrols held impermissible in Brignoni-Ponce, these stops are reasonable under the Fourth Amendment because the State's interest in the practice as a means of promoting public safety upon its roads more than outweighs the intrusion entailed. Although the record discloses no statistics concerning the extent of the problem of lack of highway safety, in Delaware or in the Nation as a whole, we are aware of the danger to life [n14] and property posed by vehicular traffic, and of the difficulties that even a cautious and an experienced driver may encounter. We agree that the States have a vital interest in ensuring that only those qualified to do so are permitted to operate motor vehicles, that these vehicles are fit for safe operation, and hence that licensing, registration, and vehicle inspection requirements are being observed. Automobile licenses are issued periodically to evidence that the drivers holding them are sufficiently familiar with the rules of the road and are physically qualified to operate a motor vehicle. [n15] The registration requirement and, more pointedly, the related annual inspection requirement in Delaware, [n16] are designed to keep dangerous automobiles off the road. Unquestionably, these provisions, properly administered, are essential elements in a highway safety program. Furthermore, we note that the State of Delaware requires a minimum amount of insurance coverage as a condition to automobile registration, [n17] implementing its legitimate interest in seeing to it that its citizens have protection when involved in a motor vehicle accident. [n18]

The question remains, however, whether, in the service of these important ends, the discretionary spot check is a sufficiently productive mechanism to justify the intrusion upon Fourth Amendment interests which such stops entail. On the record before us, that question must be answered in the negative. Given the alternative mechanisms available, both those in use and those that might be adopted, we are unconvinced that the incremental contribution to highway safety of the random spot check justifies the practice under the Fourth Amendment.

The foremost method of enforcing traffic and vehicle safety regulations, it must be recalled, is acting upon observed violations. Vehicle stops for traffic violations occur countless times each day; and on these occasions, licenses and registration papers are subject to inspection, and

drivers without them will be ascertained. Furthermore, drivers without licenses are presumably the less safe drivers whose propensities may well exhibit themselves. [n19] Absent some empirical data to the contrary, it must be assumed that finding an unlicensed driver among those who commit traffic violations is a much more likely event than finding an unlicensed driver by choosing randomly from the entire universe of drivers. If this were not so, licensing of drivers would hardly be an effective means of promoting roadway safety. It seems common sense that the percentage of all drivers on the road who are driving without a license is very small, and that the number of licensed drivers who will be stopped in order to find one unlicensed operator will be large indeed. The contribution to highway safety made by discretionary stops selected from among drivers generally will therefore be marginal, at best. Furthermore, and again absent something more than mere assertion to the contrary, we find it difficult to believe that the unlicensed driver would not be deterred by the possibility of being involved in a traffic violation or having some other experience calling for proof of his entitlement to drive, but that he would be deterred by the possibility that he would be one of those chosen for a spot check. In terms of actually discovering unlicensed drivers or deterring them from driving, the spot check does not appear sufficiently productive to qualify as a reasonable law enforcement practice under the Fourth Amendment.

Much the same can be said about the safety aspects of automobiles, as distinguished from drivers. Many violations of minimum vehicle safety requirements are observable, and something can be done about them by the observing officer, directly and immediately. Furthermore, in Delaware, as elsewhere, vehicles must carry and display current license plates, [n20] which themselves evidence that the vehicle is properly registered; [n21] and, under Delaware law, to qualify for annual registration a vehicle must pass the annual safety inspection [n22] and be properly insured. [n23] It does not appear, therefore, that a stop of a Delaware-registered vehicle is necessary in order to ascertain compliance with the State's registration requirements; and, because there is nothing to show that a significant percentage of automobiles from other States do not also require license plates indicating current registration, there is no basis for concluding that stopping even out-of-state cars for document checks substantially promotes the State's interest.

The marginal contribution to roadway safety possibly resulting from a system of spot checks cannot justify subjecting every occupant of every vehicle on the roads to a seizure -- limited in magnitude compared to other intrusions, but nonetheless constitutionally cognizable -- at the unbridled discretion of law enforcement officials. To insist neither upon an appropriate factual basis for suspicion directed at a particular automobile nor upon some other substantial and objective standard or rule to govern the exercise of discretion "would invite intrusions upon constitutionally guaranteed rights based on nothing more substantial than inarticulate hunches. . . ." Terry v. Ohio, 392 U.S. at 22. By hypothesis, stopping apparently safe drivers is necessary only because the danger presented by some drivers is not observable at the time of the stop. When there is not probable cause to believe that a driver is violating any one of the multitude of applicable traffic and equipment regulations [n24] -- or other articulable basis amounting to reasonable suspicion that the driver is unlicensed or his vehicle unregistered -- we cannot conceive of any legitimate basis upon which a patrolman could decide that stopping a particular driver for a spot check would be more productive than stopping any other driver. This kind of standardless and unconstrained discretion is the evil the Court has

discerned when, in previous cases, it has insisted that the discretion of the official in the field be circumscribed, at least to some extent. Almeida-Sanchez v. United States, 413 U.S. 266, 270 (1973); Camara v. Municipal Court, 387 U.S. at 532-533.

VI

The "grave danger" of abuse of discretion, United States v. Martinez-Fuerte, 428 U.S. at 559, does not disappear simply because the automobile is subject to state regulation resulting in numerous instances of police-citizen contact, Cady v. Dombrowski, 413 U.S. 433, 441 (1973). Only last Term, we pointed out that,

if the government intrudes . . . the privacy interest suffers whether the government's motivation is to investigate violations of criminal laws or breaches of other statutory or regulatory standards.

Marshall v. Barlow's, Inc., 436 U.S. at 312-313. There are certain "relatively unique circumstances," id. at 313, in which consent to regulatory restrictions is presumptively concurrent with participation in the regulated enterprise. See United States v. Biswell, 406 U.S. 311 (1972) (federal regulation of firearms); Colonnade Catering Corp. v. United States, 397 U.S. 72 (1970) (federal regulation of liquor). Otherwise, regulatory inspections unaccompanied by any quantum of individualized, articulable suspicion must be undertaken pursuant to previously specified "neutral criteria." Marshall v. Barlow's, Inc., supra at 323.

An individual operating or traveling in an automobile does not lose all reasonable expectation of privacy simply because the automobile and its use are subject to government regulation. [n25] Automobile travel is a basic, pervasive, and often necessary mode of transportation to and from one's home, workplace, and leisure activities. Many people spend more hours each day traveling in cars than walking on the streets. Undoubtedly, many find a greater sense of security and privacy in traveling in an automobile than they do in exposing themselves by pedestrian or other modes of travel. Were the individual subject to unfettered governmental intrusion every time he entered an automobile, the security guaranteed by the Fourth Amendment would be seriously circumscribed. As Terry v. Ohio, supra, recognized, people are not shorn of all Fourth Amendment protection when they step from their homes onto the public sidewalks. Nor are they shorn of those interests when they step from the sidewalks into their automobiles. See Adams v. Williams, 407 U.S. 143, 148 (1972).

VII

Accordingly, we hold that, except in those situations in which there is at least articulable and reasonable suspicion that a motorist is unlicensed or that an automobile is not registered, or that either the vehicle or an occupant is otherwise subject to seizure for violation of law, stopping an automobile and detaining the driver in order to check his driver's license and the registration of the automobile are unreasonable under the Fourth Amendment. This holding does not preclude the State of Delaware or other States from developing methods for spot checks that involve less intrusion or that do not involve the unconstrained exercise of discretion. [n26] Questioning of all oncoming traffic at roadblock-type stops is one possible alternative. We hold only that persons in automobiles on public roadways may not, for that reason alone, have their travel and privacy interfered with at the unbridled discretion of police officers. The judgment below is affirmed.

So ordered.

Notes

1. In its opinion, the Delaware Supreme Court referred to respondent as the operator of the vehicle, see 382 A.2d 1359, 1361 (1978). However, the arresting officer testified: "I don't believe [respondent] was the driver. . . . As I recall, he was in the back seat . . .," App. A12; and the trial court, in its ruling on the motion to suppress, referred to respondent as one of the four "occupants" of the vehicle, id. at A17. The vehicle was registered to respondent. Id. at A10.

2. United States v. Montgomery, 182 U.S.App.D.C. 426, 561 F.2d 875 (1977); People v. Ingle, 36 N.Y.2d 413, 330 N.E.2d 39 (1975); State v. Ochoa, 23 Ariz. App. 510, 534 P.2d 441 (1975), rev'd on other grounds, 112 Ariz. 582, 544 P.2d 1097 (1976); Commonwealth v. Swaner, 453 Pa. 107, 307 A.2d 875 (1973); United States v. Nicholas, 448 F.2d 622 (CA8 1971). See also United States v. Cupps, 503 F.2d 277 (CA6 1974)

3. State v. Holmber, 194 Neb. 337, 231 N.W.2d 672 (1975); State v. Allen, 282 N.C. 503, 194 S.E.2d 9 (1973); Palmore v. United States, 290 A.2d 573 (D.C. App. 1972), aff'd on jurisdictional grounds only, 411 U.S. 389 (1973); Leonard v. State, 496 S.W.2d 576 (Tex.Crim.App. 1973); United States v. Jenkins, 528 F.2d 713 (CA10 1975); Myricks v. United States, 370 F.2d 901 (CA5), cert. dismissed, 386 U.S. 1015 (1967).

4. The court stated:

The Delaware Constitution Article I, § 6 is substantially similar to the Fourth Amendment, and a violation of the latter is necessarily a violation of the former.

382 A.2d at 1362, citing State v. Moore, 55 Del. 356, 187 A.2d 807 (1963).

Moore was decided less than two years after Mapp v. Ohio, 367 U.S. 643 (1961), applied to the States the limitations previously imposed only on the Federal Government. In setting forth the approach reiterated in the opinion below, Moore noted not only the common purposes and wording of the Fourth Amendment and the state constitutional provision, but also the overriding effect of the former. See 55 Del., at 36263, 187 A.2d at 810-811.

5. We have found only one case decided after State v. Moore, supra, in which the court

relied solely on state law in upholding the validity of a search or seizure, and that case involved not only Del.Const. Art. I, § 6, but also state statutory requirements for issuance of a search warrant. Rossitto v. State, 234 A.2d 438 (1967). Moreover, every case holding a search or seizure to be contrary to the state constitutional provision relies on cases interpreting the Fourth Amendment and simultaneously concludes that the search or seizure is contrary to that provision. See, e.g., Young v. State, 339 A.2d 723 (1975); Freeman v. State, 317 A.2d 540 (1974); cf. Bertomeu v. State, 310 A.2d 865 (1973).

6. See Marshall v. Barlow's, Inc., 436 U.S. 307, 315 (1978); United States v. Brignoni-Ponce, 422 U.S. 873, 878 (1975); Cady v. Dombrowski, 413 U.S. 433, 439 (1973); Terry v. Ohio, 392 U.S. 1, 21 (1968); Camara v. Municipal Court, 387 U.S. 523, 539 (1967).

7. See also United States v. Martinez-Fuerte, 428 U.S. 543, 554 (1976); United States v. Ortiz, 422 U.S. 891, 895 (1975); Almeida-Sanchez v. United States, 413 U.S. 266, 270 (1973); Beck v. Ohio, 379 U.S. 89, 97 (1964); McDonald v. United States, 335 U.S. 451, 455-456 (1948).

8. See, e.g., United States v. Ramsey, 431 U.S. 606, 616-619 (1977); United States v. Martinez-Fuerte, supra at 555; cases cited in n. 6, supra.

9. Terry v. Ohio, supra at 21. See also Scott v. United States, 436 U.S. 128, 137 (1978); Beck v. Ohio, supra at 96-97.

10. See, e.g., United States v. Santana, 427 U.S. 38 (1976); United States v. Watson, 423 U.S. 411 (1976); Ker v. California, 374 U.S. 23 (1963) (warrantless arrests requiring probable cause); United States v. Ortiz, supra; Warden v. Hayden, 387 U.S. 294 (1967); Carroll v. United States, 267 U.S. 132 (1925) (warrantless searches requiring probable cause). See also Gerstein v. Pugh, 420 U.S. 103 (1975).

11. See Terry v. Ohio, supra; United States v. Brignoni-Ponce, supra.

In addition, the Warrant Clause of the Fourth Amendment generally requires that prior to a search a neutral and detached magistrate ascertain that the requisite standard is met, see, e.g., Mincey v. Arizona, 437 U.S. 385 (1978).

12. United States v. Martinez-Fuerte, supra at 560.

13. In addressing the constitutionality of Border Patrol practices, we reserved the question of the permissibility of state and local officials stopping motorists for document questioning in a manner similar to checkpoint detention, see 428 U.S. at 560 n. 14, or roving patrol operations, see United States v. Brignoni-Ponce, 422 U.S. at 883 n. 8.

14. In 1977, 47,671 persons died in motor vehicle accidents in this country. U.S. Dept. of Transportation, Highway Safety A-9 (1977).

15. See, e.g., Del.Code Ann., Tit. 21, §§ 2701, 2707 (1974 and Supp. 1977); § 2713 (1974) (Department of Public Safety "shall examine the applicant as to his physical and mental qualifications to operate a motor vehicle in such manner as not to jeopardize the safety of persons or property . . .").

16. § 2143(a) (1974)

17. § 2118 (Supp. 1977); State of Delaware, Department of Public Safety, Division of Motor Vehicles, Driver's Manual 60 (1976).

18. It has been urged that additional state interests are the apprehension of stolen motor vehicles and of drivers under the influence of alcohol or narcotics. The latter interest is subsumed by the interest in roadway safety, as may be the former interest to some extent. The remaining governmental interest in controlling automobile thefts is not distinguishable from the general interest in crime control.

19. United States v. Brignoni-Ponce, supra, at 883

20. Del.Code Ann., Tit.21, § 2126 (1974).

21. §§ 2121(b), (d) (1974)

22. See n. 16, supra, § 2109 (1974).

23. See n. 17, supra, § 2109 (1974).

24. See, e.g., §§ 4101-4199B (1974 and Supp. 1977).

25. Cf. Marshall v. Barlow's, Inc., 436 U.S. 307 (1978) (warrant required for federal inspection under interstate commerce power of health and safety of workplace); See v. Seattle, 387 U.S. 541 (1967) (warrant required for inspection of warehouse for municipal fire code violations); Camara v. Municipal Court, 387 U.S. 523 (1967) (warrant required for inspection of residence for municipal fire code violations).

26. Nor does our holding today cast doubt on the permissibility of roadside truck weigh-stations and inspection checkpoints, at which some vehicles may be subject to further detention for safety and regulatory inspection than are others.

Smith v. Maryland (June 20, 1979)

MR. JUSTICE BLACKMUN delivered the opinion of the Court.

This case presents the question whether the installation and use of a pen register [1] constitutes a "search" within the meaning of the Fourth Amendment, [2] made applicable to the States through the Fourteenth Amendment. Mapp v. Ohio, 367 U. S. 643 (1961).

I

On March 5, 1976, in Baltimore, Md. Patricia McDonough was robbed. She gave the police a description of the robber and of a 1975 Monte Carlo automobile she had observed near the scene of the crime. Tr. 66-68. After the robbery, McDonough began receiving threatening and obscene phone calls from a man identifying himself as the robber. On one occasion, the caller asked that she step out on her front porch; she did so, and saw the 1975 Monte Carlo she had earlier described to police moving slowly past her home.

Id. at 70. On March 16, police spotted a man who met McDonough's description driving a 1975 Monte Carlo in her neighborhood. Id. at 71-72. By tracing the license plate number, police learned that the car was registered in the name of petitioner, Michael Lee Smith. Id. at 72.

The next day, the telephone company, at police request, installed a pen register at its central offices to record the numbers dialed from the telephone at petitioner's home. Id. at 73, 75. The police did not get a warrant or court order before having the pen register installed. The register revealed that, on March 17, a call was placed from petitioner's home to McDonough's phone. Id. at 74. On the basis of this and other evidence, the police obtained a warrant to search petitioner's residence. Id. at 75. The search revealed that a page in petitioner's phone book was turned down to the name and number of Patricia McDonough; the phone book was seized. Ibid. Petitioner was arrested, and a six-man lineup was held on March 19. McDonough identified petitioner as the man who had robbed her. Id. at 70-71.

Petitioner was indicted in the Criminal Court of Baltimore for robbery. By pretrial motion, he sought to suppress "all fruits derived from the pen register" on the ground that the police had failed to secure a warrant prior to its installation. Record 14; Tr. 54 56. The trial court denied the suppression motion, holding that the warrantless installation of the pen register did not violate the Fourth Amendment. Id. at 63.

Petitioner then waived a jury, and the case was submitted to the court on an agreed statement of facts. Id. at 666. The pen register tape (evidencing the fact that a phone call had been made from petitioner's phone to McDonough's phone) and the phone book seized in the search of petitioner's residence were admitted into evidence against him. Id. at 74-76. Petitioner was convicted, id. at 78, and was sentenced to six years. He appealed to the Maryland Court of Special Appeals, but the Court of Appeals of Maryland issued a writ of certiorari to the intermediate court in advance of its decision in order to consider whether the pen register evidence had been properly admitted at petitioner's trial. 283 Md. 156, 160, 389 A.2d 858, 860 (1978).

The Court of Appeals affirmed the judgment of conviction, holding that

"there is no constitutionally protected reasonable expectation of privacy in the numbers dialed into a telephone system, and hence no search within the fourth amendment is implicated by the use of a pen register installed at the central offices of the telephone company."

Id. at 173, 389 A.2d at 867. Because there was no "search," the court concluded, no warrant was needed. Three judges dissented, expressing the view that individuals do have a legitimate expectation of privacy regarding the phone numbers they dial from their homes; that the installation of a pen register thus constitutes a "search"; and that, in the absence of exigent circumstances, the failure of police to secure a warrant mandated that the pen register evidence here be excluded. Id. at 174, 178, 389 A.2d at 868, 870. Certiorari was granted in order to resolve indications of conflict in the decided cases as to the restrictions imposed by the Fourth Amendment on the use of pen registers. [3] 439 U.S. 1001 (1978).

II

A

The Fourth Amendment guarantees "[t]he right of the people to be secure in their persons, houses, papers, and effects, against unreasonable searches and seizures." In determining whether a particular form of government-initiated electronic surveillance is a "search" within the meaning of the Fourth Amendment, [4] our lodestar is Katz v. United States, 389 U. S. 347 (1967). In Katz, Government agents had intercepted the contents of a telephone conversation by attaching an electronic listening device to the outside of a public phone booth. The Court rejected the argument that a "search" can occur only when there has been a "physical intrusion" into a "constitutionally protected area," noting that the Fourth Amendment "protects people, not places." Id. at 389 U. S. 351-353. Because the Government's monitoring of Katz' conversation "violated the privacy upon which he justifiably relied while using the telephone booth," the Court held that it "constituted a search and seizure' within the meaning of the Fourth Amendment." Id. at 389 U. S. 353.

Consistently with Katz, this Court uniformly has held that the application of the Fourth Amendment depends on whether the person invoking its protection can claim a "justifiable," a "reasonable," or a "legitimate expectation of privacy" that has been invaded by government action. E.g., Rakas v. Illinois, 439 U. S. 128, 439 U. S. 143, and n. 12 (1978); id. at 439 U. S. 150, 439 U. S. 151 (concurring opinion); id. at 439 U. S. 164 (dissenting opinion); United States v. Chadwick, 433 U. S. 1, 433 U. S. 7 (1977); United States v. Miller, 425 U. S. 435, 425 U. S. 442 (1976); United States v. Dionisio, 410 U. S. 1, 410 U. S. 14 (1973); Couch v. United States, 409 U. S. 322, 409 U. S. 335-336 (1973); United States v. White, 401 U. S. 745, 401 U. S. 752 (1971) (plurality opinion); Mancusi v. DeForte, 392 U. S. 364, 392 U. S. 368 (1968); Terry v. Ohio, 392 U. S. 1, 392 U. S. 9 (1968). This inquiry, as Mr. Justice Harlan aptly noted in his Katz concurrence, normally embraces two discrete questions. The first is whether the individual, by his conduct, has "exhibited an actual (subjective) expectation of privacy," 389 U.S. at 389 U. S. 361 -- whether, in the words of the Katz majority, the individual has shown that "he seeks to preserve [something] as private." Id. at 389 U. S. 351. The second question is whether the individual's subjective expectation of privacy is "one that society is prepared to recognize as reasonable,'" id. at 389 U. S. 361 --

whether, in the words of the Katz majority, the individual's expectation, viewed objectively, is "justifiable" under the circumstances. Id. at 389 U. S. 353. [5] See Rakas v. Illinois, 439 U.S. at 439 U. S. 143-144, n. 12; id. at 439 U. S. 151 (concurring opinion); United States v. White, 401 U.S. at 401 U. S. 752 (plurality opinion).

B

In applying the Katz analysis to this case, it is important to begin by specifying precisely the nature of the state activity that is challenged. The activity here took the form of installing and using a pen register. Since the pen register was installed on telephone company property at the telephone company's central offices, petitioner obviously cannot claim that his "property" was invaded or that police intruded into a "constitutionally protected area." Petitioner's claim, rather, is that, notwithstanding the absence of a trespass, the State, as did the Government in Katz, infringed a "legitimate expectation of privacy" that petitioner held. Yet a pen register differs significantly from the listening device employed in Katz, for pen registers do not acquire the contents of communications. This Court recently noted:

"Indeed, a law enforcement official could not even determine from the use of a pen register whether a communication existed. These devices do not hear sound. They disclose only the telephone numbers that have been dialed -- a means of establishing communication. Neither the purport of any communication between the caller and the recipient of the call, their identities, nor whether the call was even completed is disclosed by pen registers."

United States v. New York Tel. Co., 434 U. S. 159, 434 U. S. 167 (1977).

Given a pen register's limited capabilities, therefore, petitioner's argument that its installation and use constituted a "search" necessarily rests upon a claim that he had a "legitimate expectation of privacy" regarding the numbers he dialed on his phone.

This claim must be rejected. First, we doubt that people in general entertain any actual expectation of privacy in the numbers they dial. All telephone users realize that they must "convey" phone numbers to the telephone company, since it is through telephone company switching equipment that their calls are completed. All subscribers realize, moreover, that the phone company has facilities for making permanent records of the numbers they dial, for they see a list of their long-distance (toll) calls on their monthly bills. In fact, pen registers and similar devices are routinely used by telephone companies "for the purposes of checking billing operations, detecting fraud, and preventing violations of law." United States v. New York Tel. Co., 434 U.S. at 434 U. S. 174-175. Electronic equipment is used not only to keep billing records of toll calls, but also "to keep a record of all calls dialed from a telephone which is subject to a special rate structure." Hodge v. Mountain States Tel. & Tel. Co., 555 F.2d 254, 266 (CA9 1977) (concurring opinion). Pen registers are regularly employed "to determine whether a home phone is being used to conduct a business, to check for a defective dial, or to check for overbilling." Note, The Legal Constraints upon the Use of the Pen Register as a Law Enforcement Tool, 60 Cornell L.Rev. 1028, 1029 (1975) (footnotes omitted). Although most people may be oblivious to a pen register's esoteric functions, they presumably have some awareness of one common use: to aid in the identification of persons making annoying or obscene calls. See, e.g., Von Lusch v. C & P Telephone Co., 457 F.Supp. 814, 816 (Md.1978); Note, 60 Cornell L.Rev. at 1029-1030, n. 11; Claerhout, The Pen Register, 20 Drake L.Rev. 108, 110-111 (1970). Most phone books tell subscribers, on a page entitled "Consumer Information," that the company "can frequently help in identifying to the authorities the origin of unwelcome and troublesome calls." E.g., Baltimore

Telephone Directory 21 (1978); District of Columbia Telephone Directory 13 (1978). Telephone users, in sum, typically know that they must convey numerical information to the phone company; that the phone company has facilities for recording this information; and that the phone company does in fact record this information for a variety of legitimate business purposes. Although subjective expectations cannot be scientifically gauged, it is too much to believe that telephone subscribers, under these circumstances, harbor any general expectation that the numbers they dial will remain secret.

Petitioner argues, however, that, whatever the expectations of telephone users in general, he demonstrated an expectation of privacy by his own conduct here, since he "us[ed] the telephone in his house to the exclusion of all others." Brief for Petitioner 6 (emphasis added). But the site of the call is immaterial for purposes of analysis in this case. Although petitioner's conduct may have been calculated to keep the contents of his conversation private, his conduct was not and could not have been calculated to preserve the privacy of the number he dialed. Regardless of his location, petitioner had to convey that number to the telephone company in precisely the same way if he wished to complete his call. The fact that he dialed the number on his home phone, rather than on some other phone, could make no conceivable difference, nor could any subscriber rationally think that it would.

Second, even if petitioner did harbor some subjective expectation that the phone numbers he dialed would remain private, this expectation is not "one that society is prepared to recognize as reasonable.'" Katz v. United States, 389 U.S. at 389 U. S. 361. This Court consistently has held that a person has no legitimate expectation of privacy in information he voluntarily turns over to third parties. E.g., United States v. Miller, 425 U.S. at 425 U. S. 442-444; Couch v. United States, 409

U.S. at 409 U. S. 335-336; United States v. White, 401 U.S. at 401 U. S. 752 (plurality opinion); Hoffa v. United States, 385 U. S. 293, 385 U. S. 302 (1966); Lopez v. United States, 373 U. S. 427 (1963). In Miller, for example, the Court held that a bank depositor has no "legitimate `expectation of privacy'" in financial information "voluntarily conveyed to . . . banks and exposed to their employees in the ordinary course of business." 425 U.S. at 425 U. S. 442. The Court explained:

"The depositor takes the risk, in revealing his affairs to another, that the information will be conveyed by that person to the Government. . . . This Court has held repeatedly that the Fourth Amendment does not prohibit the obtaining of information revealed to a third party and conveyed by him to Government authorities, even if the information is revealed on the assumption that it will be used only for a limited purpose and the confidence placed in the third party will not be betrayed."

Id. at 425 U. S. 443. Because the depositor "assumed the risk" of disclosure, the Court held that it would be unreasonable for him to expect his financial records to remain private.

This analysis dictates that petitioner can claim no legitimate expectation of privacy here. When he used his phone, petitioner voluntarily conveyed numerical information to the telephone company and "exposed" that information to its equipment in the ordinary course of business. In so doing, petitioner assumed the risk that the company would reveal to police the numbers he dialed. The switching equipment that processed those numbers is merely the modern counterpart of the operator who, in an earlier day, personally completed calls for the subscriber. Petitioner concedes that, if he had placed his calls through an operator, he could claim no legitimate expectation of privacy. Tr. of Oral Arg. 3 5, 11-12, 32. We are not inclined to hold that a different constitutional result is required because the telephone company has decided to automate.

Petitioner argues, however, that automatic switching equipment differs from a live operator in one pertinent respect. An operator, in theory at least, is capable of remembering every number that is conveyed to him by callers. Electronic equipment, by contrast, can "remember" only those numbers it is programmed to record, and telephone companies, in view of their present billing practices, usually do not record local calls. Since petitioner, in calling McDonough, was making a local call, his expectation of privacy as to her number, on this theory, would be "legitimate."

This argument does not withstand scrutiny. The fortuity of whether or not the phone company in fact elects to make a quasi-permanent record of a particular number dialed does not, in our view, make any constitutional difference. Regardless of the phone company's election, petitioner voluntarily conveyed to it information that it had facilities for recording and that it was free to record. In these circumstances, petitioner assumed the risk that the information would be divulged to police. Under petitioner's theory, Fourth Amendment protection would exist, or not, depending on how the telephone company chose to define local-dialing zones, and depending on how it chose to bill its customers for local calls. Calls placed across town, or dialed directly, would be protected; calls placed across the river, or dialed with operator assistance, might not be. We are not inclined to make a crazy quilt of the Fourth Amendment, especially in circumstances where (as here) the pattern of protection would be dictated by billing practices of a private corporation.

We therefore conclude that petitioner in all probability entertained no actual expectation of privacy in the phone numbers he dialed, and that, even if he did, his expectation was not "legitimate." The installation and use of a pen register, consequently, was not a "search," and no warrant was required. The judgment of the Maryland Court of Appeals is affirmed.

It is so ordered.

Notes

[1] "A pen register is a mechanical device that records the numbers dialed on a telephone by monitoring the electrical impulses caused when the dial on the telephone is released. It does not overhear oral communications and does not indicate whether calls are actually completed."

United States v. New York Tel. Co., 434 U. S. 159, 434 U. S. 161 n. 1 (1977). A pen register is "usually installed at a central telephone facility [and] records on a paper tape all numbers dialed from the line" to which it is attached. United States v. Giordano, 416 U. S. 505, 416 U. S. 549 n. 1 (1974) (opinion concurring in part and dissenting in part). See also United States v. New York Tel. Co., 434 U.S. at 434 U. S. 162.

[2] "The right of the people to be secure in their persons, houses, papers, and effects, against unreasonable searches and seizures, shall not be violated, and no Warrants shall issue, but upon probable cause, supported by Oath or affirmation, and particularly describing the place to be searched, and the persons or things to be seized."

U.S.Const., Amdt. 4.

[3] See Application of United States for Order, 546 F.2d 243, 245 (CA8 1976), cert. denied sub nom. Southwestern Bell Tel. Co. v. United States, 434 U.S. 1008 (1978); Application of United States in Matter of Order, 538 F.2d 956, 959-960 (CA2 1976), rev'd on other grounds sub nom. United States v. New York Tel. Co., 434 U. S. 159 (1977); United States v. Falcone, 505 F.2d 478, 482, and n. 21 (CA3 1974), cert. denied, 420 U.S. 955 (1975); Hodge v. Mountain States Tel. & Tel. Co., 555 F.2d 254, 256 (CA9 1977); id. at 266 (concurring opinion); and United States v. Clegg, 509 F.2d 605, 610 (CA5 1975). In previous decisions, this Court has not found it necessary to consider whether "pen register surveillance [is]

subject to the requirements of the Fourth Amendment." United States v. New York Tel. Co., 434 U.S. at 434 U. S. 165 n. 7. See United States v. Giordano, 416 U.S. at 416 U. S. 554 n. 4 (opinion concurring in part and dissenting in part).

[4] In this case, the pen register was installed, and the numbers dialed were recorded, by the telephone company. Tr. 73-74. The telephone company, however, acted at police request. Id. at 73, 75. In view of this, respondent appears to concede that the company is to be deemed an "agent" of the police for purposes of this case, so as to render the installation and use of the pen register "state action" under the Fourth and Fourteenth Amendments. We may assume that "state action" was present here.

[5] Situations can be imagined, of course, in which Katz' two-pronged inquiry would provide an inadequate index of Fourth Amendment protection. For example, if the Government were suddenly to announce on nationwide television that all homes henceforth would be subject to warrantless entry, individuals thereafter might not in fact entertain any actual expectation of privacy regarding their homes, papers, and effects. Similarly, if a refugee from a totalitarian country, unaware of this Nation's traditions, erroneously assumed that police were continuously monitoring his telephone conversations, a subjective expectation of privacy regarding the contents of his calls might be lacking as well. In such circumstances, where an individual's subjective expectations had been "conditioned" by influences alien to well recognized Fourth Amendment freedoms, those subjective expectations obviously could play no meaningful role in ascertaining what the scope of Fourth Amendment protection was. In determining whether a "legitimate expectation of privacy" existed in such cases, a normative inquiry would be proper.

Ybarra v. Illinois (Nov 28, 1979)

MR. JUSTICE STEWART delivered the opinion of the Court.

An Illinois statute authorizes law enforcement officers to detain and search any person found on premises being searched pursuant to a search warrant, to protect themselves from attack or to prevent the disposal or concealment of anything described in the warrant. [1] The question before us is whether the application of this statute to the facts of the present case violated the Fourth and Fourteenth Amendments.

I

On March 1, 1976, a special agent of the Illinois Bureau of Investigation presented a "Complaint for Search Warrant" to a judge of an Illinois Circuit Court. The complaint recited that the agent had spoken with an informant known to the police to be reliable and:

"3. The informant related . . . that over the weekend of 28 and 29 February he was in the [Aurora Tap Tavern, located in the city of Aurora, Ill.] and observed fifteen to twenty-five tin-foil packets on the person of the bartender 'Greg' and behind the bar. He also has been in the tavern on at least ten other occasions and has observed tin-foil packets on 'Greg' and in a drawer behind the bar. The informant has used heroin in the past and knows that tin-foil packets are a common method of packaging heroin."

"4. The informant advised . . . that over the weekend of 28 and 29 February he had a conversation with 'Greg' and was advised that 'Greg' would have heroin for sale on Monday, March 1, 1976. This conversation took place in the tavern described."

On the strength of this complaint, the judge issued a warrant authorizing the search of "the following person or place: . . . [T]he Aurora Tap Tavern. . . . Also the person of 'Greg,' the bartender, a male white with blondish hair appx. 25 years."

The warrant authorized the police to search for "evidence of the offense of possession of a controlled substance," to-wit,

"[h]eroin, contraband, other controlled substances, money, instrumentalities and narcotics, paraphernalia used in the manufacture, processing and distribution of controlled substances."

In the late afternoon of that day, seven or eight officers proceeded to the tavern. Upon entering it, the officers announced their purpose and advised all those present that they were going to conduct a "cursory search for weapons." One of the officers then proceeded to pat down each of the to 13 customers present in the tavern, while the remaining officers engaged in an extensive search of the premises.

The police officer who frisked the patrons found the appellant, Ventura Ybarra, in front of the bar standing by a pinball machine. In his first pat-down of Ybarra, the officer felt what he described as "a cigarette pack with objects in it." He did not remove this pack from Ybarra's pocket. Instead, he moved on and proceeded to pat down other customers.

After completing this process, the officer returned to Ybarra and frisked him once again. This second search of Ybarra took place approximately 2 to 10 minutes after the first. The officer relocated and retrieved the cigarette pack from Ybarra's pants pocket. Inside the pack, he found six tinfoil packets containing a brown powdery substance which later turned out to be heroin.

Ybarra was subsequently indicted by an Illinois grand jury for the unlawful possession of a controlled substance. He filed a pretrial motion to suppress all the contraband that had been seized from his person at the Aurora Tap Tavern. At the hearing on this motion, the State sought to justify the search by reference to the Illinois statute in question. The trial court denied the motion to suppress, finding that the search had been conducted under the authority of subsection (b) of the statute, to "prevent the disposal or concealment of [the] things particularly described in the warrant." The case proceeded to trial before the court sitting without a jury, and Ybarra was found guilty of the possession of heroin.

On appeal, the Illinois Appellate Court held that the Illinois statute was not unconstitutional "in its application to the facts" of this case. 58 Ill.App.3d 57, 64, 373 N.E.2d 1013, 1017. The court acknowledged that, had the warrant directed that a "large retail or commercial establishment" be searched, the statute could not constitutionally have been read to "authorize a blanket search' of persons or patrons found" therein. Id. at 62, 373 N.E.2d at 1016. The court interpreted the statute as authorizing the search of persons found on premises described in a warrant only if there is

"some showing of a connection with those premises, that the police officer reasonably suspected an attack, or that the person searched would destroy or conceal items described in the warrant."

Id. at 61, 373 N.E.2d at 1016. Accordingly, the State Appellate Court found that the search of Ybarra had been constitutional because it had been "conducted in a one-room bar where it [was] obvious from the complaint . . . that heroin was being sold or dispensed," id. at 62, 373 N.E.2d at 1016, because "the six packets of heroin . . could easily [have been] concealed by the defendant, and thus thwart the purpose of the warrant," id. at 61, 373 N.E.2d at 1016, and because Ybarra was not an "innocent strange[r] having no connection with the premises," ibid. The court, therefore, affirmed Ybarra's conviction, and the Illinois Supreme Court denied his petition for leave to appeal. There followed an appeal to this Court, and we noted probable jurisdiction. 440 U.S. 790.

II

There is no reason to suppose that, when the search warrant was issued on March 1, 1976, the authorities had probable cause to believe that any person found on the premises of the Aurora Tap Tavern, aside from "Greg," would be violating the law. [2] The search warrant complaint did not allege that the bar was frequented by persons illegally purchasing drugs. It did not state that the informant had ever seen a patron of the tavern purchase drugs from "Greg" or from any other person. Nowhere, in fact, did the complaint even mention the patrons of the Aurora Tap Tavern.

Not only was probable cause to search Ybarra absent at the time the warrant was issued, it was still absent when the police executed the warrant. Upon entering the tavern, the police did not recognize Ybarra, and had no reason to believe that he had committed, was committing, or was about to commit any offense under state or federal law. Ybarra made no gestures indicative of criminal conduct, made no movements that might suggest an attempt to conceal contraband, and said nothing of a suspicious nature to the police officers. In short, the agents knew nothing in particular about Ybarra except that he was present, along with several other customers, in a public tavern at a time when the police had reason to believe that the bartender would have heroin for sale.

It is true that the police possessed a warrant based on probable cause to search the tavern in which Ybarra happened to be at the time the warrant was executed. [3] But, a person's mere propinquity to others independently suspected of criminal activity does not, without more, give rise to probable cause to search that person. Sibron v. New York, 392 U. S. 40, 392 U. S. 62-63. Where the standard is probable cause, a search or seizure of a person must be supported by probable cause particularized with respect to that person. This requirement cannot be undercut or avoided by simply pointing to the fact that coincidentally there exists probable cause to search or seize another or to search the premises where the person may happen to be. The Fourth and Fourteenth Amendments protect the "legitimate expectations of privacy" of persons, not places. See Rakas v. Illinois, 439 U. S. 128, 439 U. S. 138-143, 439 U. S. 148-149; Katz v. United States, 389 U. S. 347, 389 U. S. 351-352.

Each patron who walked into the Aurora Tap Tavern on March 1, 1976, was clothed with constitutional protection against an unreasonable search or an unreasonable seizure. That individualized protection was separate and distinct from the Fourth and Fourteenth Amendment protection possessed by the proprietor of the tavern or by "Greg." Although the search warrant, issued upon probable cause, gave the officers authority to search the premises and to search "Greg," it gave them no authority whatever to invade the constitutional protections possessed individually by the tavern's customers. [4]

Notwithstanding the absence of probable cause to search Ybarra, the State argues that the action of the police in searching him and seizing what was found in his pocket was nonetheless constitutionally permissible. We are asked to find that the first pat-down search of Ybarra constituted a reasonable frisk for weapons under the doctrine of Terry v. Ohio, 392 U. S. 1. If this finding is made, it is then possible to conclude, the State argues, that the second search of Ybarra was constitutionally justified. The argument is that the pat-down yielded probable cause to believe that Ybarra was carrying narcotics, and that this probable cause constitutionally supported the second search, no warrant being required in light of the exigencies of the situation coupled with the ease with which Ybarra could have disposed of the illegal substance.

We are unable to take even the first step required by this argument. The initial frisk of Ybarra was simply not supported by a reasonable belief that he was armed and presently dangerous, a belief which this Court has invariably held must form the predicate to a pat-down of a person for weapons. [5] Adams v. Williams, 407 U. S. 143, 407 U. S. 146; Terry v. Ohio, supra at 392 U. S. 21-24, 392 U. S. 27. When the police entered the Aurora Tap Tavern on March 1, 1976, the lighting was sufficient for them to observe the customers. Upon seeing Ybarra, they neither recognized him as a person with a criminal history nor had any particular reason to believe that he might be inclined to assault them. Moreover, as Police Agent Johnson later testified, Ybarra, whose hands were empty, gave no indication of possessing a weapon, made no gestures or other actions indicative of an intent to commit an assault, and acted generally in a manner that was not threatening. At the suppression hearing, the most Agent Johnson could point to was that Ybarra was wearing a 3/4-length lumber jacket, clothing which the State admits could be expected on almost any tavern patron in Illinois in early March. In short, the State is unable to articulate any specific fact that would have justified a police officer at the scene in even suspecting that Ybarra was armed and dangerous.

The Terry case created an exception to the requirement of probable cause, an exception whose "narrow scope" this Court "has been careful to maintain." [6] Under that doctrine, a law enforcement officer, for his own protection and safety, may conduct a pat-down to find weapons that he reasonably believes or suspects are then in the possession of the person he has accosted. See, e.g., Adams v. Williams, supra, (at night, in high-crime district, lone police officer approached person believed by officer to possess gun and narcotics). Nothing in Terry can be understood to allow a generalized "cursory search for weapons" or, indeed, any search whatever for anything but weapons. The "narrow scope" of the Terry exception does not permit a frisk for weapons on less than reasonable belief or suspicion directed at the person to be frisked, even though that person happens to be on premises where an authorized narcotics search is taking place.

What has been said largely disposes of the State's second and alternative argument in this case. Emphasizing the important governmental interest "in effectively controlling traffic in dangerous, hard drugs" and the ease with which the evidence of narcotics possession may be concealed or moved around from person to person, the State contends that the Terry "reasonable belief or suspicion" standard should be made applicable to aid the evidence-gathering function of the search warrant. More precisely, we are asked to construe the Fourth and Fourteenth Amendments to permit evidence searches of persons who, at the commencement of the search, are on "compact" premises subject to a search warrant, at least where the police have a "reasonable belief" that such persons "are connected with" drug trafficking and "may be concealing or carrying away the contraband."

Over 30 years ago, the Court rejected a similar argument in United States v. Di Re, 332 U. S. 581, 332 U. S. 583-587. In that case, a federal investigator had been told by an informant that a transaction in counterfeit gasoline ration coupons was going to occur at a particular place. The investigator went to that location at the appointed time and saw the car of one of the suspected parties to the illegal transaction. The investigator went over to the car and observed a man in the driver's seat, another man (Di Re) in the passenger's seat, and the informant in the back. The informant told the investigator that the person in the driver's seat had given him counterfeit coupons. Thereupon, all three men were arrested and searched. Among the arguments unsuccessfully advanced by the Government to support the constitutionality of the search of Di Re was the contention that the investigator could lawfully have searched the car, since he had reasonable cause to believe that it contained contraband, and correspondingly could have searched any occupant of the car because the contraband sought was of the sort "which could easily be concealed on the person." [7] Not deciding whether or not, under the Fourth Amendment, the car could have been searched, the Court held that it was "not convinced that a person, by mere presence in a suspected car, loses immunities from search of his person to which he would otherwise be entitled." [8]

The Di Re case does not, of course, completely control the case at hand. There the Government investigator was proceeding without a search warrant, and here the police possessed a warrant authorizing the search of the Aurora Tap Tavern. Moreover, in Di Re, the Government conceded that its officers could not search all the persons in a house being searched pursuant to a search warrant. [9] The State makes no such concession in this case. Yet the governing principle in both cases is basically the same, and we follow that principle today. The "long-prevailing" constitutional standard of probable cause embodies

"'the best compromise that has been found for accommodating [the] often opposing interests' in 'safeguard[ing] citizens from rash and unreasonable interferences with privacy' and in 'seek[ing] to give fair leeway for enforcing he law in the community's protection.' [10]"

For these reasons, we conclude that the searches of Ybarra and the seizure of what was in his pocket contravened the Fourth and Fourteenth Amendments. [11] Accordingly, the judgment is reversed, and the case is remanded to the Appellate Court of Illinois, Second District, for further proceedings not inconsistent with this opinion.

It is so ordered.

Notes

[1] The statute in question is Ill.Rev.Stat., ch. 38, § 108-9 (1975), which provides in full:

"In the execution of the warrant the person executing the same may reasonably detain to search any person in the place at the time:"

"(a) To protect himself from attack, or"

"(b) To prevent the disposal or concealment of any instruments, articles or things particularly described in the warrant."

[2] The warrant issued on March 1, 1976, did not itself authorize the search of Ybarra or of any other patron found on the premises of the Aurora Tap Tavern. It directed the police to search "the following person or place : . . . the Aurora Tap Tavern. . . . Also the person of Greg'. . . ." Had the issuing judge intended that the warrant would or could authorize a search of every person found within the tavern, he would hardly have specifically authorized the search of "Greg" alone. "Greg" was an employee of the tavern, and the complaint upon which the search warrant was issued gave every indication that he would be present at the tavern on March 1.

[3] Ybarra concedes that the warrant issued on March 1, 1976, was supported by probable cause insofar as it purported to authorize a search of the premises of the Aurora Tap Tavern and a search of the person of "Greg," the bartender.

[4] The Fourth Amendment directs that

"no Warrants shall issue, but upon probable cause . . . and particularly describing the place to be searched, and the persons or things to be seized."

Thus, "open-ended" or "general" warrants are constitutionally prohibited. See Lo-Ji Sales, Inc. v. New York, 442 U. S. 319; Marshall v. Barlow's, Inc., 436 U. S. 307, 436 U. S. 311; United States v. Chadwick, 433 U. S. 1, 433 U. S. 7-8; Stanford v. Texas, 379 U. S. 476, 379 U. S. 480-482. It follows that a warrant to search a place cannot normally be construed to authorize a search of each individual in that place. The warrant for the Aurora Tap Tavern provided no basis for departing from this general rule. Consequently, we need not consider situations where the warrant itself authorizes the search of unnamed persons in a place and is supported by probable cause to believe that persons who will be in the place at the time of the search will be in possession of illegal drugs.

[5] Since we conclude that the initial pat-down of Ybarra was not justified under the Fourth and Fourteenth Amendments, we need not decide whether or not the presence on Ybarra's person of "a cigarette pack with objects in it" yielded probable cause to believe that Ybarra was carrying any illegal substance.

[6] Dunaway v. New York, 442 U. S. 200, 442 U. S. 210.

[7] 332 U.S. at 332 U. S. 586.

[8] Id. at 332 U. S. 587.

[9] "The Government says it would not contend that, armed with a search warrant for a residence only, it could search all persons found in it. But an occupant of a house could be used to conceal this contraband on his person quite as readily as can an occupant of a car. Necessity, an argument advanced in support of this search, would seem as strong a reason for searching guests of a house for which a search warrant had issued as for search of guests in a car for which none had been issued. By a parity of reasoning with that on which the Government disclaims the right to search occupants of a house, we suppose the Government would not contend that, if it had a valid search warrant for the car only, it could search the occupants as an incident to its execution. How then could we say that the right to search a car without a warrant confers greater latitude to search occupants than a search by warrant would permit?"

Ibid.

[10] Dunaway v. New York, 442 U.S. at 442 U. S. 208, quoting Brinegar v. United States, 338 U. S. 160, 338 U. S. 176.

The circumstances of this case do not remotely approach those in which the Court has said that a search may be made on less than probable cause. In addition to Terry v. Ohio, 392 U. S. 1, see, e.g., Delaware v. Prouse, 440 U. S. 648; Marshall v. Barlow's, Inc., 436 U. S. 307; United States v. Martinez-Fuerte, 428 U. S. 543; South Dakota v. Opperman, 428 U. S. 364; United States v. Brignoni-Ponce, 422 U. S. 873; United States v. Biswell, 406 U. S. 311; Camara v. Municipal Court, 387 U. S. 523.

[11] Our decision last Term in Michigan v. DeFillippo, 443 U. S. 31, does not point in a different direction. There we held that the Fourth and Fourteenth Amendments had not been violated by an arrest based on a police officer's probable cause to believe that the suspect had committed or was committing a substantive criminal offense, even though the statute creating the offense was subsequently declared unconstitutional. Here, the police officers acted on the strength of Ill.Rev.Stat., ch. 38, § 108-9 (1975), but that statute does not define the elements of a substantive criminal offense under state law. The statute purports instead to authorize the police in some circumstances to make searches and seizures without probable cause and without search warrants. This state law, therefore, falls within the category of statutes purporting to authorize searches without probable cause, which the Court has not hesitated to hold invalid as authority for unconstitutional searches. See, e.g., Torres v. Puerto Rico, 442 U. S. 465; Almeida-Sanchez v. United States, 413 U. S. 266; Sibron v. New York, 392 U. S. 40; Berger v. New York, 388 U. S. 41.

Payton v. New York (April 15, 1980) [Notes omitted]

MR. JUSTICE STEVENS delivered the

opinion of the Court.

These appeals challenge the constitutionality of New York statutes that authorize police officers to enter a private residence without a warrant and with force, if necessary, to make a routine felony arrest.

The important constitutional question presented by this challenge has been expressly left open in a number of our prior opinions. In United States v. Watson, 423 U. S. 411, we upheld a warrantless "midday public arrest," expressly noting that the case did not pose "the still unsettled question . . . whether and under what circumstances an officer may enter a suspect's home to make a warrantless arrest.'" Id. at 423 U. S. 418, n. 6. [1] The question has been answered in different ways by other appellate courts. The Supreme Court of Florida rejected the constitutional attack, [2] as did the New York Court of Appeals in this case. The courts of last resort in 10 other States, however, have held that, unless special circumstances are present, warrantless arrests in the home are unconstitutional. [3] Of the seven United States Courts of Appeals that have considered the question, five have expressed the opinion that such arrests are unconstitutional. [4]

Last Term, we noted probable jurisdiction of these appeals in order to address that question. 439 U.S. 1044. After hearing oral argument, we set the case for reargument this Term. 441 U.S. 930. We now reverse the New York Court of Appeals and hold that the Fourth Amendment to the United States Constitution, made applicable to the States by the Fourteenth Amendment, Mapp v. Ohio, 367 U. S. 643; Wolf v. Colorado, 33 U. S. 25, prohibits the police from making a warrantless and nonconsensual entry into a suspect's home in order to make a routine felony arrest.

We first state the facts of both cases in some detail and put to one side certain related questions that are not presented by these records.

We then explain why the New York statutes are not consistent with the Fourth Amendment and why the reasons for upholding warrantless arrests in a public place do not apply to warrantless invasions of the privacy of the home.

I

On January 14, 1970, after two days of intensive investigation, New York detectives had assembled evidence sufficient to establish probable cause to believe that Theodore Payton had murdered the manager of a gas station two days earlier. At about 7:30 a.m. on January 15, six officers went to Payton's apartment in the Bronx, intending to arrest him. They had not obtained a warrant. Although light and music emanated from the apartment, there was no response to their knock on the metal door. They summoned emergency assistance and, about 30 minutes later, used crowbars to break open the door and enter the apartment. No one was there. In plain view, however, was a .30-caliber shell casing that was seized and later admitted into evidence at Payton's murder trial. [5]

In due course, Payton surrendered to the police, was indicted for murder, and moved to suppress the evidence taken from his apartment. The trial judge held that the warrantless and forcible entry was authorized by the New York Code of Criminal Procedure, [6] and that the evidence in plain view was properly seized. He found that exigent circumstances justified the officers' failure to announce their purpose before entering the apartment, as required by the statute. [7] He had no occasion, however, to decide whether those circumstances also would have justified the failure to obtain a warrant, because he concluded that the warrantless entry was adequately supported by the statute without regard to the circumstances. The Appellate Division, First Department, summarily affirmed. [8] On March 14, 1974, Obie Riddick was arrested for the commission of two armed robberies that had occurred in 1971. He had been identified by the victims in June, 1973, and in January, 1974, the police had learned his address. They did not obtain a warrant for his arrest. At about noon on March 14, a detective, accompanied by three other officers, knocked on the door of the Queens house where Riddick was living. When his young son opened the door, they could see Riddick sitting in bed covered by a sheet. They entered the house and placed him under arrest. Before permitting him to dress, they opened a chest of drawers two feet from the bed in search of weapons and found narcotics and related paraphernalia. Riddick was subsequently indicted on narcotics charges. At a suppression hearing, the trial judge held that the warrantless entry into his home was authorized by the revised New York statute, [9] and that the search of the immediate area was reasonable under Chimel v. California, 395 U. S. 752. [10] The Appellate Division, Second Department, affirmed the denial of the suppression motion. [11]

The New York Court of Appeals, in a single opinion, affirmed the convictions of both Payton and Riddick. 45 N.Y.2d 300, 380 N.E.2d 224 (1978). The court recognized that the question whether and under what circumstances an officer may enter a suspect's home to make a warrantless arrest had not been settled either by that court or by this Court. [12] In answering that question, the majority of four judges relied primarily on its perception that there is a

". . . substantial difference between the intrusion which attends an entry for the purpose of searching the premises and that which results from an entry for the purpose of making an arrest, and [a] significant difference in the governmental interest in achieving the objective of the intrusion in the two instances."

Id. at 310, 380 N.E.2d at 228-229. [13]

The majority supported its holding by noting the "apparent historical acceptance" of warrantless entries to make felony arrests, both in the English common law and in the practice of many American States. [14]

Three members of the New York Court of Appeals dissented on this issue because they believed that the Constitution requires the police to obtain a "warrant to enter a home in order to arrest or seize a person, unless there are exigent circumstances." [15] Starting from the premise that, except in carefully circumscribed instances, "the Fourth Amendment forbids police entry into a private home to search for and seize an object without a warrant," [16] the dissenters reasoned that an arrest of the person involves an even greater invasion of privacy, and should therefore be attended with at least as great a measure of constitutional protection. [17] The dissenters noted

"the existence of statutes and the American Law Institute imprimatur codifying the common law rule authorizing warrantless arrests in private homes,"

and acknowledged that "the statutory authority of a police officer to make a warrantless arrest in this State has been in effect for almost 100 years," but concluded that "neither antiquity nor legislative unanimity can be determinative of the grave constitutional question presented," and "can never be a substitute for reasoned analysis." [18]

Before addressing the narrow question presented by these appeals, [19] we put to one side other related problems that are not presented today. Although it is arguable that the warrantless entry to effect Payton's arrest might have been justified by exigent circumstances, none of the New York courts relied on any such justification. The Court of Appeals majority treated both Payton's and Riddick's cases as involving routine arrests in which there was ample time to obtain a warrant, [20] and we will do the same. Accordingly, we have no occasion to consider the sort of emergency or dangerous situation, described in our cases as "exigent circumstances," that would justify a warrantless entry into a home for the purpose of either arrest or search.

Nor do these cases raise any question concerning the authority of the police, without either a search or arrest warrant, to enter a third party's home to arrest a suspect. The police broke into Payton's apartment intending to arrest Payton, and they arrested Riddick in his own dwelling. We also note that in neither case is it argued that the police lacked probable cause to believe that the suspect was at home when they entered. Finally, in both cases we are dealing with entries into homes made without the consent of any occupant. In Payton, the police used crowbars to break down the door, and in Riddick, although his 3-year-old son answered the door, the police entered before Riddick had an opportunity either to object or to consent.

II

It is familiar history that indiscriminate searches and seizures conducted under the authority of "general warrants" were the immediate evils that motivated the framing and adoption of the Fourth Amendment. [21] Indeed, as originally proposed in the House of Representatives, the draft contained only one clause, which directly imposed limitations on the issuance of warrants, but imposed no express restrictions on warrantless searches or seizures. [22] As it was ultimately adopted. however, the Amendment contained two separate clauses, the first protecting the basic right to be free from unreasonable searches and seizures and the second requiring that warrants be particular and supported by probable cause. [23] The Amendment provides:

"The right of the people to be secure in their persons, houses, papers, and effects, against unreasonable searches and seizures, shall not be violated, and no Warrants shall issue, but upon probable cause, supported by Oath or affirmation, and particularly describing the place to be searched, and the persons or things to be seized."

It is thus perfectly clear that the evil the Amendment was designed to prevent was broader than the abuse of a general warrant. Unreasonable searches or seizures conducted without any warrant at all are condemned by the plain language of the first clause of the Amendment. Almost a century ago, the Court stated in resounding terms that the principles reflected in the Amendment "reached farther than the concrete form" of the specific cases that gave it birth, and "apply to all invasions on the part of the government and its employes of the sanctity of a man's home and the privacies of life." Boyd v. United States, 116 U. S. 616, 116 U. S. 630. Without pausing to consider whether that broad language may require some qualification, it is sufficient to note that the warrantless arrest of a person is a species of seizure required by the Amendment to be reasonable. Beck v. Ohio, 379 U. S. 89. Cf. Delaware v. Prouse, 440 U. S. 48. Indeed, as MR. JUSTICE POWELL noted in his concurrence in United States v. Watson, the arrest of a person is "quintessentially a seizure." 423 U.S. at 423 U. S. 428.

The simple language of the Amendment applies equally to seizures of persons and to seizures of property. Our analysis in this case may therefore properly commence with rules that have been well established in Fourth Amendment litigation involving tangible items. As the Court reiterated just a few years ago, the "physical entry of the home is the chief evil against which the wording of the Fourth Amendment is directed." United States v. United States District Court, 407 U. S. 297, 407 U. S. 313. And we have long adhered to the view that the warrant procedure minimizes the danger of needless intrusions of that sort. [24]

It is a "basic principle of Fourth Amendment law" that searches and seizures inside a home without a warrant are presumptively unreasonable. [25] Yet it is also well settled that objects such as weapons or contraband found in a public place may be seized by the police without a warrant. The seizure of property in plain view involve no invasion of privacy and is presumptively reasonable, assuming that there is probable cause to associate the property with criminal activity. The distinction between a warrantless seizure in an open area and such a seizure on private premises was plainly stated in G. M. Leasing Corp. v. United States, 429 U. S. 338, 429 U. S. 354:

"It is one thing to seize without a warrant property resting in an open area or seizable by levy without an intrusion into privacy, and it is quite another thing to effect a warrantless seizure of property, even that owned by a corporation, situated on private premises to which access is not otherwise available for the seizing officer."

As the late Judge Leventhal recognized, this distinction has equal force when the seizure of a person is involved. Writing on the constitutional issue now before us for the United States Court of Appeals for the District of Columbia Circuit sitting en banc, Dorman v. United States, 140 U.S.App.D.C. 313, 435 F.2d 385 (1970), Judge Leventhal first noted the settled rule that warrantless arrests in public places are valid. He immediately recognized, however, that

"[a] greater burden is placed . . . on officials who enter a home or dwelling without consent. Freedom from intrusion into the home or dwelling is the archetype of the privacy protection secured by the Fourth Amendment."

Id. at 317, 435 F.2d at 389. (Footnote omitted.)

His analysis of this question then focused on the long-settled premise that, absent exigent circumstances, a warrantless entry to search for weapons or contraband is unconstitutional even when a felony has been committed and there is probable cause to believe that incriminating evidence will be found within. [26] He reasoned that the constitutional protection afforded to the individual's interest in the privacy of his own home is equally applicable to a warrantless entry for the purpose of arresting a resident of the house; for it is inherent in such an entry that a search for the suspect may be required before he can be apprehended. [27] Judge Leventhal concluded that an entry to arrest and an entry to search for and to seize property implicate the same interest in preserving the privacy and the sanctity of the home, and justify the same level of constitutional protection.

This reasoning has been followed in other Circuits. [28] Thus, the Second Circuit recently summarized its position:

"To be arrested in the home involves not only the invasion attendant to all arrests, but also an invasion of the sanctity of the home. This is simply too substantial an invasion to allow without a warrant, at least in the absence of exigent circumstances, even when it is accomplished under statutory authority and when probable cause is clearly present."

United States v. Reed, 572 F.2d 412, 423 (1978), cert. denied sub nom. Goldsmith v. United States, 439 U.S. 913. We find this reasoning to be persuasive and in accord with this Court's Fourth Amendment decisions.

The majority of the New York Court of Appeals, however, suggested that there is a substantial difference in the relative intrusiveness of an entry to search for property and an entry to search for a person. Seen 13, supra. It is true that the area that may legally be searched is broader when executing a search warrant than when executing an arrest warrant in the home. See Chimel v. California, 395 U. S. 752. This difference may be more theoretical than real, however, because the police may need to check the entire premises for safety reasons, and sometimes they ignore the restrictions on searches incident to arrest. [29]

But the critical point is that any differences

in the intrusiveness of entries to search and entries to arrest are merely ones of degree, rather than kind. The two intrusions share this fundamental characteristic: the breach of the entrance to an individual's home. The Fourth Amendment protects the individual's privacy in a variety of settings. In none is the zone of privacy more clearly defined than when bounded by the unambiguous physical dimensions of an individual's home -- a zone that finds its roots in clear and specific constitutional terms: "The right of the people to be secure in their . . . houses . . . shall not be violated." That language unequivocally establishes the proposition that,

"[a]t the very core [of the Fourth Amendment] stands the right of a man to retreat into his own home and there be free from unreasonable governmental intrusion."

Silverman v. United States, 365 U. S. 505, 365 U. S. 511. In terms that apply equally to seizures of property and to seizures of persons, the Fourth Amendment has drawn a firm line at the entrance to the house. Absent exigent circumstances, that threshold may not reasonably be crossed without a warrant.

III

Without contending that United States v. Watson, 423 U. S. 411, decided the question presented by these appeals, New York argues that the reasons that support the Watson holding require a similar result here. In Watson, the Court relied on (a) the well settled common law rule that. a warrantless arrest in a public place is valid if the arresting officer had probable cause to believe the suspect is a felon; [30] (b) the clear consensus among the States adhering to that well settled common law rule; [31] and (c) the expression of the judgment of Congress that such an arrest is "reasonable." [32] We consider each of these reasons as it applies to a warrantless entry into a home for the purpose of making a routine felony arrest.

A

An examination of the common law understanding of an officer's authority to arrest sheds light on the obviously relevant, if not entirely dispositive, [33] consideration of what the Framers of the Amendment might have thought to be reasonable. Initially, it should be noted that the common law rules of arrest developed in legal contexts that substantially differ from the cases now before us. In these cases, which involve application of the exclusionary rule, the issue is whether certain evidence is admissible at trial. [34] See Weeks v. United States, 232 U. S. 383. At common law, the question whether an arrest was authorized typically arose.in civil damages actions for trespass or false arrest, in which a constable's authority to make the arrest was a defense. See, e.g., Leach v. Money, 19 How. St. Tr. 1001, 97 Eng.Rep. 1075 (K.B. 1765). Additionally, if an officer was killed while attempting to effect an arrest, the question whether the person resisting the arrest was guilty of murder or manslaughter turned on whether the officer was acting within the bounds of his authority. See M. Foster, Crown Law 308, 312 (1762). See also West v. Cabell,153 U. S. 78, 153 U. S. 85.

A study of the common law on the question whether a constable had the authority to make warrantless arrests in the home on mere suspicion of a felony -- as distinguished from an officer's right to arrest for a crime committed in his presence -- reveals a surprising lack of judicial decisions and a deep divergence among scholars.

The most cited evidence of the common law rule consists of an equivocal dictum in a case actually involving the sheriff's authority to enter a home to effect service of civil process. In Semayne's Case, 5 Co.Rep. 91a, 91b, 77 Eng.Rep. 194, 195-196 (K.B. 1603), the Court stated:

"In all cases when the King is party, the Sheriff (if the doors be not open) may break the party's house, either to arrest him, or to do other execution of the K.'s process, if otherwise he cannot enter. But before he breaks it, he ought to signify the cause of his coming, and to make request to open doors; and that appears well by the stat. of Westm. 1. c. 17 (which is but an affirmance of the common law) as hereafter appears, for the law without a default in the owner abhors the destruction or breaking of any house (which is for the habitation and safety of man) by which great damage and inconvenience might ensue to the party, when no default is in him; for perhaps he did not know of the process, of which, if he had notice, it is to be presumed that he would obey it, and that appears by the book in 18 E. 2. Execut. 252, where it is said that the K.'s officer who comes to do execution, &c. may open the doors which are shut, and break them, if he cannot have the keys; which proves, that he ought first to demand them, 7 E. 3. 16."

(Footnotes omitted.) This passage has been read by some as describing an entry without a warrant. The context strongly implies, however, that the court was describing the extent of authority in executing the King's writ. This reading is confirmed by the phrase "either to arrest him, or to do other execution of the K.'s process" and by the further point that notice was necessary because the owner may "not know of the process." In any event, the passage surely cannot be said unambiguously to endorse warrantless entries.

The common law commentators disagreed sharply on the subject. [35] Three distinct views were expressed. Lord Coke, widely recognized by the American colonists "as the greatest authority of his time on the laws of England," [36] clearly viewed a warrantless entry for the purpose of arrest to be illegal. [37]

Burn, Foster, and Hawkins agreed, [38] as did East and Russell, though the latter two qualified their opinions by stating that, if an entry to arrest was made without a warrant, the officer was perhaps immune from liability for the trespass if the suspect was actually guilty. [39] Blackstone, Chitty, and Stephen took the opposite view, that entry to arrest without a warrant was legal, [40] though Stephen relied on Blackstone, who, along with Chitty, in turn relied exclusively on Hale. But Hale's view was not quite so unequivocally expressed. [41]

Further, Hale appears to rely solely on a statement in an early Yearbook, quoted in Burdett v. Abbot, 14 East 1, 155, 104 Eng.Rep. 501, 560 (K.B. 1811): [42]

"that for felony, or suspicion of felony, a man may break open the house to take the felon; for it is for the commonweal to take them."

Considering the diversity of views just describe, however, it is clear that the statement was never deemed authoritative. Indeed, in Burdett, the statement was described as an "extrajudicial opinion." Ibid. [43]

It is obvious that the common law rule on warrantless home arrests was not as clear as the rule on arrests in public places. Indeed, particularly considering the prominence of Lord Coke, the weight of authority as it appeared to the Framers was to the effect that a warrant was required, or, at the minimum, that there were substantial risks in proceeding without one. The common law sources display a sensitivity to privacy interests that could not have been lost on the Framers. The zealous and frequent repetition of the adage that a "man's house is his castle," made it abundantly clear that both in England [44] and in the colonies "the freedom of one's house" was one of the most vital elements of English liberty. [45]

Thus, our study of the relevant common law does not provide the same guidance that was present in Watson. Whereas the rule concerning the validity of an arrest in a public place was supported by cases directly in point and by the unanimous views of the commentators, we have found no direct authority supporting forcible entries into a home to make a routine arrest, and the weight of the scholarly opinion is somewhat to the contrary. Indeed, the absence of any 17th- or 18th-century English cases directly in point, together with the unequivocal endorsement of the tenet that "a man's house is his castle," strongly suggests that the prevailing practice was not to make such arrests except in hot pursuit or when authorized by a warrant. Cf. Agnello v. United States, 269 U. S. 20, 269 U. S. 33. In all events, the issue is not one that can be said to have been definitively settled by the common law at the time the Fourth Amendment was adopted.

B

A majority of the States that have taken a position on the question permit warrantless entry into the home to arrest even in the absence of exigent circumstances. At this time, 24 States permit such warrantless entries; [46] 15 States clearly prohibit them, though 3 States do so on federal constitutional grounds alone; [47] and 11 States have apparently taken no position on the question. [48]

But these current figures reflect a significant decline during the last decade in the number of States permitting warrantless entries for arrest. Recent dicta in this Court raising questions about the practice, seen 1, supra, and Federal Courts of Appeals' decisions on point, seen 4, supra, have led state courts to focus on the issue. Virtually all of the state courts that have had to confront the constitutional issue directly have held warrantless entries into the home to arrest to be invalid in the absence of exigent circumstances. See nn. 23 supra. Three state courts have relied on Fourth Amendment grounds alone, while seven have squarely placed their decisions on both federal and state constitutional grounds. [49] A number of other state courts, though not having had to confront the issue directly, have recognized the serious nature of the constitutional question. [50] Apparently, only the Supreme Court of

Florida and the New York Court of Appeals in this case have expressly upheld warrantless entries to arrest in the face of a constitutional challenge. [51]

A longstanding, widespread practice is not immune from constitutional scrutiny. But neither is it to be lightly brushed aside. This is particularly so when the constitutional standard is as amorphous as the word "reasonable," and when custom and contemporary norms necessarily play such a large role in the constitutional analysis. In this case, although the weight of state law authority is clear, there is by no means the kind of virtual unanimity on this question that was present in United States v. Watson with regard to warrantless arrests in public places. See 423 U.S. at 423 U. S. 422-423. Only 24 of the 50 States currently sanction warrantless entries into the home to arrest, see nn. 46-48supra, and there is an obvious declining trend. Further, the strength of the trend is greater than the numbers alone indicate. Seven state courts have recently held that warrantless home arrests violate their respective State Constitutions. Seen 3, supra. That is significant because, by invoking a state constitutional provision, a state court immunizes its decision from review by this Court. [52] This heightened degree of immutability underscores the depth of the principle underlying the result.

C

No congressional determination that warrantless entries into the home are "reasonable" has been called to our attention. None of the federal statutes cited in the Watson opinion reflects any such legislative judgment. [53] Thus, that support for the Watson holding finds no counterpart in this case.

MR. JUSTICE POWELL,, concurring in United States v. Watson, supra at 423 U. S. 429, stated:

"But logic sometimes must defer to history and experience. The Court's opinion emphasizes the historical sanction accorded warrantless felony arrests [in public places]."

In this case, however, neither history nor this Nation's experience requires us to disregard the overriding respect for the sanctity of the home that has been embedded in our traditions since the origins of the Republic. [54]

IV

The parties have argued at some length about the practical consequences of a warrant requirement as a precondition to a felony arrest in the home. [55] In the absence of any evidence that effective law enforcement has suffered in those States that already have such a requirement, see nn. 347supra, we are inclined to view such arguments with skepticism. More fundamentally, however, such arguments of policy must give way to a constitutional command that we consider to be unequivocal.

Finally, we note the State's suggestion that only a search warrant based on probable cause to believe the suspect is at home at a given time can adequately protect the privacy interests at stake, and since such a warrant requirement is manifestly impractical, there need be no warrant of any kind. We find this ingenious argument unpersuasive. It is true that an arrest warrant requirement may afford less protection than a search warrant requirement, but it will suffice to interpose the magistrate's determination of probable cause between the zealous officer and the citizen. If there is sufficient evidence of a citizen's participation in a felony to persuade a judicial officer that his arrest is justified, it is constitutionally reasonable to require him to open his doors to the officers of the law. Thus, for Fourth Amendment purposes, an arrest warrant founded on probable cause implicitly carries with it the limited authority to enter a dwelling in which the suspect lives when there is reason to believe the suspect is within.

Because no arrest warrant was obtained in either of these cases, the judgments must be reversed and the cases remanded to the New York Court of Appeals for further proceedings not inconsistent with this opinion.

It is so ordered.

US v. Mendenhall (May 27, 1980)

MR. JUSTICE STEWART announced the judgment of the Court and delivered an opinion, in which MR. JUSTICE REHNQUIST joined. *

The respondent was brought to trial in the United States District Court for the Eastern District of Michigan on a charge of possessing heroin with intent to distribute it. She moved to suppress the introduction at trial of the heroin as evidence against her on the ground that it had been acquired from her through an unconstitutional search and seizure by agents of the Drug Enforcement Administration (DEA). The District Court denied the respondent's motion, and she was convicted after a trial upon stipulated facts. The Court of Appeals reversed, finding the search of the respondent's person to have been unlawful. We granted certiorari to consider whether any right of the respondent guaranteed by the Fourth Amendment was violated in the circumstances presented by this case. 444 U.S. 822.

I

At the hearing in the trial court on the respondent's motion to suppress, it was established how the heroin she was charged with possessing had been obtained from her. The respondent arrived at the Detroit Metropolitan Airport on a commercial airline flight from Los Angeles early in the morning on February 10, 1976. As she disembarked from the airplane, she was observed by two agents of the DEA, who were present at the airport for the purpose of detecting unlawful traffic in narcotics. After observing the respondent's conduct, which appeared to the agents to be characteristic of persons unlawfully carrying narcotics, [1] the agents approached her as she was walking through the concourse, identified themselves as federal agents, and asked to see her identification and airline ticket. The respondent produced her driver's license, which was in the name of Sylvia Mendenhall, and, in answer to a question of one of the agents, stated that she resided at the address appearing on the license. The airline ticket was issued in the name of "Annette Ford." When asked why the ticket bore a name different from her own, the respondent stated that she "just felt like using that name." In response to a further question, the respondent indicated that she had been in California only two days. Agent Anderson then specifically identified himself as a federal narcotics agent and, according to his testimony, the respondent "became quite shaken, extremely nervous. She had a hard time speaking."

After returning the airline ticket and driver's license to her, Agent Anderson asked the respondent if she would accompany him to the airport DEA office for further questions. She did so, although the record does not indicate a verbal response to the request. The office, which was located up one flight of stairs about 50 feet from where the respondent had first been approached, consisted of a reception area adjoined by three other rooms. At the office, the agent asked the respondent if she would allow a search of her person and handbag, and told her that she had the right to decline the search if she desired. She responded: "Go ahead." She then handed Agent Anderson her purse, which contained a receipt for an airline ticket that had been issued to "F. Bush" three days earlier for a flight from Pittsburgh through Chicago to Los Angeles. The agent asked whether this was the ticket that she had used for her flight to California, and the respondent stated that it was.

A female police officer then arrived to conduct the search of the respondent's person. She asked the agents if the respondent had consented to be searched. The agents said that she had, and the respondent followed the policewoman into a private room. There the policewoman again asked the respondent if she consented to the search, and the respondent replied that she did. The policewoman explained that the search would require that the respondent remove her clothing. The respondent stated that she had a plane to catch, and was assured by the policewoman that, if she were carrying no narcotics, there would be no problem. The respondent then began to disrobe without further comment. As the respondent removed her clothing, she took from her undergarments two small packages, one of which appeared to contain heroin, and handed both to the policewoman. The agents then arrested the respondent for possessing heroin.

It was on the basis of this evidence that the District Court denied the respondent's motion to suppress. The court concluded that the agents' conduct in initially approaching the respondent and asking to see her ticket and identification was a permissible investigative stop under the standards of Terry v. Ohio, 392 U. S. 1, and United States v. Brignoni-Ponce, 422 U. S. 873, finding that this conduct was based on specific and articulable facts that justified a suspicion of criminal activity. The court also found that the respondent had not been placed under arrest or otherwise detained when she was asked to accompany the agents to the DEA office, but had accompanied the agents "voluntarily in a spirit of apparent cooperation.'" It was the court's view that no arrest occurred until after the heroin had been found. Finally, the trial court found that the respondent "gave her consent to the search [in the DEA office] and . . . such consent was freely and voluntarily given."

The Court of Appeals reversed the respondent's subsequent conviction, stating only that "the court concludes that this case is indistinguishable from United States v McCaleb,"

552 F.2d 717 (CA6 1977). [2] In McCaleb, the Court of Appeals had suppressed heroin seized by DEA agents at the Detroit Airport in circumstances substantially similar to those in the present case. [3] The Court of Appeals there disapproved the Government's reliance on the so-called "drug courier profile," and held that the gents could not reasonably have suspected criminal activity in that case, for the reason that "the activities of the [persons] observed by DEA agents, were consistent with innocent behavior," id. at 720. The Court of Appeals further concluded in McCaleb that, even if the initial approach had been permissible, asking the suspects to accompany the agents to a private room for further questioning constituted an arrest requiring probable cause. Finally, the court in McCaleb held that the consent to the search in that case had not been voluntarily given, principally because it was the fruit of what the court believed to have been an unconstitutional detention.

On rehearing en banc of the present case, the Court of Appeals reaffirmed its original decision, stating simply that the respondent had not validly consented to the search "within the meaning of [McCaleb]." 596 F.2d 706, 707.

II

The Fourth Amendment provides that "the right of the people to be secure in their persons, houses, papers, and effects, against unreasonable searches and seizures, shall not be violated. . . ."

There is no question in this case that the respondent possessed this constitutional right of personal security as she walked through the Detroit Airport, for "the Fourth Amendment protects people, not places," Katz v. United States, 389 U. S. 347, 389 U. S. 351. Here the Government concedes that its agents had neither a warrant nor probable cause to believe that the respondent was carrying narcotics when the agents conducted a search of the respondent's person. It is the Government's position, however, that the search was conducted pursuant to the respondent's consent, [4] and thus was excepted from the requirements of both a warrant and probable cause. See Schneckloth v. Bustamonte, 412 U. S. 218. Evidently, the Court of Appeals concluded that the respondent's apparent consent to the search was in fact not voluntarily given, and was, in any event, the product of earlier official conduct violative of the Fourth Amendment. We must first consider, therefore, whether such conduct occurred, either on the concourse or in the DEA office at the airport.

A

The Fourth Amendment's requirement that searches and seizures be founded upon an objective justification, governs all seizures of the person,

"including seizures that involve only a brief detention short of traditional arrest. Davis v. Mississippi, 394 U. S. 721 (1969); Terry v. Ohio, 392 U. S. 1, 392 U. S. 16-19 (1968)."

United States v. Brignoni-Ponce, supra, at 422 U. S. 878. [5] Accordingly, if the respondent was "seized" when the DEA agents approached her on the concourse and asked questions of her, the agents' conduct in doing so was constitutional only if they reasonably suspected the respondent of wrongdoing. But

"[o]bviously, not all personal intercourse between policemen and citizens involves 'seizures' of persons. Only when the officer, by means of physical force or show of authority, has in some way restrained the liberty of a citizen may we conclude that a 'seizure' has occurred."

Terry v. Ohio, 392 U.S. at 392 U. S. 19, n.16.

The distinction between an intrusion amounting to a "seizure" of the person and an encounter that intrudes upon no constitutionally protected interest is illustrated by the facts of Terry v. Ohio, which the Court recounted as follows:

"Officer McFadden approached the three

men, identified himself as a police officer, and asked for their names. . . . When the men 'mumbled something' in response to his inquiries, Officer McFadden grabbed petitioner Terry, spun him around so that they were facing the other two, with Terry between McFadden and the others, and patted down the outside of his clothing."

Id. at 392 U. S. 6-7. Obviously the officer "seized" Terry and subjected him to a "search" when he took hold of him, spun him around, and patted down the outer surfaces of his clothing, id. at 392 U. S. 19. What was not determined in that case, however, was that a seizure had taken place before the officer physically restrained Terry for purposes of searching his person for weapons. The Court "assume[d] that, up to that point, no intrusion upon constitutionally protected rights had occurred." Id. at 392 U. S. 19, n. 16. The Court's assumption appears entirely correct in view of the fact, noted in the concurring opinion of MR. JUSTICE WHITE, that " [t]here is nothing in the Constitution which prevents a policeman from addressing questions to anyone on the streets," id. at 392 U. S. 34. Police officers enjoy "the liberty (again, possessed by every citizen) to address questions to other persons," id. at 392 U. S. 31, 392 U. S. 32-33 (Harlan, J., concurring), although "ordinarily, the person addressed has an equal right to ignore his interrogator and walk away." Ibid.

Similarly, the Court in Sibron v. New York, 392 U. S. 40, a case decided the same day as Terry v. Ohio, indicated that not every encounter between a police officer and a citizen is an intrusion requiring an objective justification. In that case, a police officer, before conducting what was later found to have been an unlawful search, approached Sibron in a restaurant and told him to come outside, which Sibron did. The Court had no occasion to decide whether there was a "seizure" of Sibron inside the restaurant antecedent to the seizure that accompanied the search. The record was

"barren of any indication whether Sibron accompanied [the officer] outside in submission to a show of force or authority which left him no choice, or whether he went voluntarily in a spirit of apparent cooperation with the officer's investigation."

392 U.S. at 392 U. S. 63 (emphasis added). Plainly, in the latter event, there was no seizure until the police officer in some way demonstrably curtailed Sibron's liberty.

We adhere to the view that a person is "seized" only when, by means of physical force or a show of authority, his freedom of movement is restrained. Only when such restraint is imposed is there any foundation whatever for invoking constitutional safeguards. The purpose of the Fourth Amendment is not to eliminate all contact between the police and the citizenry, but "to prevent arbitrary and oppressive interference by enforcement officials with the privacy and personal security of individuals." United States v. Martinez-Fuerte, 428 U. S. 543, 428 U. S. 554. As long as the person to whom questions are put remains free to disregard the questions and walk away, there has been no intrusion upon that person's liberty or privacy as would under the Constitution require some particularized and objective justification.

Moreover, characterizing every street encounter between a citizen and the police as a "seizure," while not enhancing any interest secured by the Fourth Amendment, would impose wholly unrealistic restrictions upon a wide variety of legitimate law enforcement practices. The Court has on other occasions referred to the acknowledged need for police questioning as a tool in the effective enforcement of the criminal laws.

"Without such investigation, those who were innocent might be falsely accused, those who were guilty might wholly escape prosecution, and many crimes would go unsolved. In short, the security of all would be diminished. Haynes v.

Washington, 373 U. S. 503, 373 U. S. 515."

Schneckloth v. Bustamonte, 412 U.S. at 412 U. S. 225.

We conclude that a person has been "seized" within the meaning of the Fourth Amendment only if, in view of all of the circumstances surrounding the incident, a reasonable person would have believed that he was not free to leave. [6] Examples of circumstances that might indicate a seizure, even where the person did not attempt to leave, would be the threatening presence of several officers, the display of a weapon by an officer, some physical touching of the person of the citizen, or the use of language or tone of voice indicating that compliance with the officer's request might be compelled. See Terry v. Ohio, supra at 392 U. S. 19, n. 16; Dunaway v. New York, 442 U. S. 200, 442 U. S. 207, and n. 6; 3 W. LaFave, Search and Seizure 53-55 (1978). In the absence of some such evidence, otherwise inoffensive contact between a member of the public and the police cannot, as a matter of law, amount to a seizure of that person.

On the facts of this case, no "seizure" of the respondent occurred. The events took place in the public concourse. The agents wore no uniforms, and displayed no weapons. They did not summon the respondent to their presence, but instead approached her and identified themselves as federal agents. They requested, but did not demand, to see the respondent's identification and ticket. Such conduct, without more, did not amount to an intrusion upon any constitutionally protected interest. The respondent was not seized simply by reason of the fact that the agents approached her, asked her if she would show them her ticket and identification, and posed to her a few questions. Nor was it enough to establish a seizure that the person asking the questions was a law enforcement official. See Terry v. Ohio, 392 U.S. at 392 U. S. 31, 392 U. S. 32-33 (Harlan, J., concurring). See also ALI, Model Code of Pre-Arraignment Procedure § 110.1(1) and commentary, at 257-261 (1975). In short, nothing in the record suggests that the respondent had any objective reason to believe that she was not free to end the conversation in the concourse and proceed on her way, and for that reason, we conclude that the agents' initial approach to her was not a seizure.

Our conclusion that no seizure occurred is not affected the fact that the respondent was not expressly told by the agents that she was free to decline to cooperate with their inquiry, for the voluntariness of her responses does not depend upon her having been so informed. See Schneckloth v. Bustamonte, supra. We also reject the argument that the only inference to be drawn from the fact that the respondent acted in a manner so contrary to her self-interest is that she was compelled to answer the agents' questions. It may happen that a person makes statements to law enforcement officials that he later regrets, but the issue in such cases is not whether the statement was self-protective, but rather whether it was made voluntarily.

The Court's decision last Term in Brown v. Texas, 443 U. S. 47, on which the respondent relies, is not apposite. It could not have been plainer under the circumstances there presented that Brown was forcibly detained by the officers. In that case, two police officers approached Brown in an alley, and asked him to identify himself and to explain his reason for being there. Brown "refused to identify himself and angrily asserted that the officers had no right to stop him," id. at 443 U. S. 49. Up to this point, there was no seizure. But after continuing to protest the officers' power to interrogate him, Brown was first frisked, and then arrested for violation of a state statute making it a criminal offense for a person to refuse to give his name and address to an officer "who has lawfully stopped him and requested the information." The Court simply held in that case that, because the officers had no reason to suspect Brown of wrongdoing, there was no basis for detaining him, and therefore no permissible foundation for applying the state statute in the circumstances there presented. Id. at 443 U. S. 52-53.

The Court's decisions involving investigatory stops of automobiles do not point in any different direction. In United States v. Brignoni-Ponce, 422 U. S. 873, the Court held that a roving patrol of law enforcement officers could stop motorists in the general area of an international border for brief inquiry into their residence status only if the officers reasonably suspected that the vehicle might contain aliens who were illegally in the country. Id. at 422 U. S. 881-882. The Government did not contend in that case that the persons whose automobiles were detained were not seized. Indeed, the Government acknowledged that the occupants of a detained vehicle were required to respond to the officers' questions and, on some occasions, to produce documents evidencing their eligibility to be in the United States. Id. at 422 U. S. 880. Moreover stopping or diverting an automobile in transit, with the attendant opportunity for a visual inspection of areas of the passenger compartment not otherwise observable, is materially more intrusive than a question put to a passing pedestrian, and the fact that the former amounts to a seizure tells very little about the constitutional status of the latter. See also Delaware v. Prouse, 440 U. S. 648; United States v. Martinez-Fuerte, 428 U.S. at 428 U. S. 556-559.

B

Although we have concluded that the initial encounter between the DEA agents and the respondent on the concourse at the Detroit Airport did not constitute an unlawful seizure, it is still arguable that the respondent's Fourth Amendment protections were violated when she went from the concourse to the DEA office. Such a violation might in turn infect the subsequent search of the respondent's person.

The District Court specifically found that the respondent accompanied the agents to the office "voluntarily in a spirit of apparent cooperation,'" quoting Sibron v. New York, 392 U.S. at 392 U. S. 63. Notwithstanding this determination by the trial court, the Court of Appeals evidently concluded that the agents' request that the respondent accompany them converted the situation into an arrest requiring probable cause in order to be found lawful. But because the trial court's finding was sustained by the record, the Court of Appeals was mistaken in substituting for that finding its view of the evidence. See Jackson v. United States, 122 U.S.App.D.C. 324, 353 F.2d 862 (1965).

The question whether the respondent's consent to accompany the agents was in fact voluntary or was the product of duress or coercion, express or implied, is to be determined by the totality of all the circumstances, Schneckloth v. Bustamonte, 412 U.S. at 412 U. S. 227, and is a matter which the Government has the burden of proving. Id. at 412 U. S. 222, citing Bumper v. North Carolina, 391 U. S. 543, 391 U. S. 548. The respondent herself did not testify at the hearing. The Government's evidence showed that the respondent was not told that she had to go to the office, but was simply asked if she would accompany the officers. There were neither threats nor any show of force. The respondent had been questioned only briefly, and her ticket and identification were returned to her before she was asked to accompany the officers.

On the other hand, it is argued that the incident would reasonably have appeared coercive to the respondent, who was 22 years old and had not been graduated from high school. It is additionally suggested that the respondent, a female and a Negro, may have felt unusually threatened by the officers, who were white males. While these factors were not irrelevant, see

Schneckloth v. Bustamonte, supra at 412 U. S. 226, neither were they decisive, and the totality of the evidence in this case was plainly adequate to support the District Court's finding that the respondent voluntarily consented to accompany the officers to the DEA office.

C

Because the search of the respondent's person was not preceded by an impermissible seizure of her person, it cannot be contended that her apparent consent to the subsequent search was infected by an unlawful detention. There remains to be considered whether the respondent's consent to the search was for any other reason invalid. The District Court explicitly credited the officers' testimony and found that the "consent was freely and voluntarily given," citing Schneckloth v. Bustamonte, supra. There was more than enough evidence in this case to sustain that view. First, we note that the respondent, who was 22 years old and had an 11th-grade education, was plainly capable of a knowing consent. Second, it is especially significant that the respondent was twice expressly told that she was free to decline to consent to the search, and only thereafter explicitly consented to it. Although the Constitution does not require "proof of knowledge of a right to refuse as the sine qua non of an effective consent to a search," id. at 412 U. S. 234 (footnote omitted), such knowledge was highly relevant to the determination that there had been consent. And, perhaps more important for present purposes, the fact that the officers themselves informed the respondent that she was free to withhold her consent substantially lessened the probability that their conduct could reasonably have appeared to her to be coercive.

Counsel for the respondent has argued that she did, in fact, resist the search, relying principally on the testimony that, when she was told that the search would require the removal of her clothing, she stated to the female police officer that "she had a plane to catch." But the trial court was entitled to view the statement as simply an expression of concern that the search be conducted quickly. The respondent had twice unequivocally indicated her consent to the search, and when assured by the police officer that there would be no problem if nothing were turned up by the search, she began to undress without further comment.

Counsel for the respondent has also argued that, because she was within the DEA office when she consented to the search, her consent may have resulted from the inherently coercive nature of those surroundings. But in view of the District Court's finding that the respondent's presence in the office was voluntary, the fact that she was there is little or no evidence that she was in any way coerced. And in response to the argument that the respondent would not voluntarily have consented to a search that was likely to disclose the narcotics that she carried, we repeat that the question is not whether the respondent acted in her ultimate self-interest, but whether she acted voluntarily. [7]

III

We conclude that the District Court's determination that the respondent consented to the search of her person "freely and voluntarily" was sustained by the evidence and that the Court of Appeals was, therefore, in error in setting it aside. Accordingly, the judgment of the Court of Appeals is reversed, and the case is remanded to that court for further proceedings.

It is so ordered.

* THE CHIEF JUSTICE, MR. JUSTICE BLACKMUN, and MR. JUSTICE POWELL also join all but Part II-A of this opinion.

Notes

[1] The agent testified that the respondent's behavior fit the so-called "drug courier profile" -- an informally compiled abstract of characteristics thought typical of persons carrying illicit drugs. In this case, the agents

thought it relevant that (1) the respondent was arriving on a flight from Los Angeles, a city believed by the agents to be the place of origin for much of the heroin brought to Detroit; (2) the respondent was the last person to leave the plane, "appeared to be very nervous," and "completely scanned the whole area where [the agents] were standing"; (3) after leaving the plane, the respondent proceeded past the baggage area without claiming any luggage; and (4) the respondent changed airlines for her flight out of Detroit.

[2] The opinion of the Court of Appeals and the opinion of the District Court are both unreported.

[3] The McCaleb case, however, involved a circumstance not present here. Although the persons searched in that case were advised of their right to decline to give consent to the search of their luggage, they were also informed that, if they refused, they would be detained while the agents sought a search warrant. 552 F.2d at 719. The Court of Appeals in this case evidently considered the distinction irrelevant.

[4] The Government has made several alternative arguments in this case.

[5] In the District Court and the Court of Appeals, the parties evidently assumed that the respondent was seized when she was approached on the airport concourse and was asked if she would show her identification and airline ticket. In its brief on the merits and oral argument in this Court, however, the Government has argued that no seizure occurred, and the respondent has joined the argument. While the Court ordinarily does not consider matters neither raised before nor decided by the courts below, see Adickes v. Kress & Co., 398 U. S. 144, 398 U. S. 147, n. 2, it has done so in exceptional circumstances. See Youakim v. Miller, 425 U. S. 231, 425 U. S. 234; Duignan v. United States, 274 U. S. 195, 274 U. S. 200. We consider the Government's contention that there was no seizure of the respondent in this case because the contrary assumption, embraced by the trial court and the Court of Appeals, rests on a serious misapprehension of federal constitutional law. And because the determination of the question is essential to the correct disposition of the other issues in the case, we shall treat it as "fairly comprised" by the questions presented in the petition for certiorari. This Court's Rule 23(1)(c). See Procunier v. Navarette, 434 U. S. 555, 434 U. S. 559-560, n. 6; Blonder-Tongue Laboratories, Inc. v. University of Illinois Foundation, 402 U. S. 313, 402 U. S. 320-321, n. 6.

The evidentiary record in the trial court is adequate to permit consideration of the contention. The material facts are not disputed. A major question throughout the controversy has been whether the respondent was at any time detained by the DEA agents. Counsel for the respondent has argued that she was arrested while proceeding through the concourse. The trial court and the Court of Appeals characterized the incident as an "investigatory stop." But the correctness of the legal characterization of the facts appearing in the record is a matter for this Court to determine. See Schneckloth v. Bustamonte, 412 U. S. 218, 412 U. S. 226; Bumper v. North Carolina, 391 U. S. 543, 391 U. S. 548-550.

[6] We agree with the District Court that the subjective intention of the DEA agent in this case to detain the respondent, had she attempted to leave, is irrelevant except insofar as that may have been conveyed to the respondent.

[7] It is arguable that the respondent may have thought she was acting in her self-interest by voluntarily cooperating with the officers in the hope of receiving more lenient treatment.

Walter v. United States (June 20, 1980)

MR. JUSTICE STEVENS announced the judgment of the Court and delivered an opinion, in which MR. JUSTICE STEWART joined.

Having lawfully acquired possession of a dozen cartons of motion pictures, law enforcement officers viewed several reels of 8-millimeter film on a Government projector. Labels on the individual film boxes indicated that they contained obscene pictures. The question is whether the Fourth Amendment required the agents to obtain a warrant before they screened the films.

Only a few of the bizarre facts need be recounted. On September 25, 1975, 12 large, securely sealed packages containing 871 boxes of 8-millimeter film depicting homosexual activities were shipped by private carrier from St. Petersburg, Fla., to Atlanta, Ga. The shipment was addressed to "Leggs, Inc.," [1] but was mistakenly delivered to a substation in the suburbs of Atlanta, where "L'Eggs Products, Inc.," regularly received deliveries. Employees of the latter company opened each of the packages, finding the individual boxes of film. They examined the boxes, on one side of which were suggestive drawings, and on the other were explicit' descriptions of the contents. One employee opened one or two of the boxes, and attempted without success to view portions of the film by holding it up to the light. [2] Shortly thereafter, they called a Federal Bureau of Investigation agent who picked up the packages on October 1, 1975.

Thereafter, without making any effort to obtain a warrant or to communicate with the consignor or the consignee of the shipment, FBI agents viewed the films with a projector. The record does not indicate exactly when they viewed the films, but at least one of them was not screened until more than two months after the FBI had taken possession of the shipment. [3]

On April 6, 1977, petitioners were indicted on obscenity charges relating to the interstate transportation of 5 of the 871 films in the shipment. A motion to suppress and return the films was denied, and petitioners were convicted on multiple counts of violating 18 U.S.C. §§ 371, 1462, and 1465. Over Judge Wisdom's dissent, the Court of Appeals for the Fifth Circuit affirmed, 592 F.2d 788, and rehearing was denied, 597 F.2d 63 (1979). We granted certiorari, 444 U.S. 914, [4] and now reverse.

In his concurrence in Stanley v. Georgia, 394 U. S. 557, 394 U. S. 569, MR. JUSTICE STEWART expressed the opinion that the warrantless projection of motion picture films was an unconstitutional invasion of the privacy of the owner of the films. After noting that the agents in that case were lawfully present in the defendant's home pursuant to a warrant to search for wagering paraphernalia, MR. JUSTICE STEWART wrote:

"This is not a case where agents, in the course of a lawful search, came upon contraband, criminal activity, or criminal evidence in plain view. For the record makes clear that the contents of the films could not be determined by mere inspection. . . . After finding them, the agents spent some 50 minutes exhibiting them by means of the appellant's projector in another upstairs room. Only then did the agents return downstairs and arrest the appellant."

"Even in the much-criticized case of United States v. Rabinowitz, 339 U. S. 56, the Court emphasized that 'exploratory searches . . . cannot be undertaken by officers with or without a warrant.' Id. at 339 U. S. 62. This record presents a bald violation of that basic constitutional rule. To condone what happened here is to invite a government official to use a seemingly precise and legal warrant only as a ticket to get into a man's home, and, once inside, to launch forth upon unconfined searches and indiscriminate seizures as if armed with all the unbridled and illegal power of a general warrant."

"Because the films were seized in violation of the Fourth and Fourteenth Amendments, they were inadmissible in evidence at the appellant's trial."

Id. at 394 U. S. 571-572 (footnote omitted).

Even though the cases before us involve an invasion of the privacy of the home, and notwithstanding that the nature of the contents of these films was indicated by descriptive material on their individual containers, we are nevertheless persuaded that the unauthorized exhibition of the films constituted an unreasonable invasion of their owner's constitutionally protected interest in privacy. It was a search; there was no warrant; the owner had not consented; and there were no exigent circumstances.

It is perfectly obvious that the agents' reason for viewing the films was to determine whether their owner was guilty of a federal offense. To be sure, the labels on the film boxes gave them probable cause to believe that the films were obscene and that their shipment in interstate commerce had offended the federal criminal code. But the labels were not sufficient to support a conviction, and were not mentioned in the indictment. Further investigation -- that is to say, a search of the contents of the films -- was necessary in order to obtain the evidence which was to be used at trial.

The fact that FBI agents were lawfully in possession of the boxes of film did not give them authority to search their contents. Ever since 1878, when Mr. Justice Field's opinion for the Court in Ex parte Jackson, 96 U. S. 727, established that sealed packages in the mail cannot be opened without a warrant, it has been settled that an officer's authority to possess a package is distinct from his authority to examine its contents. [5] See Arkansas v. Sanders, 442 U. S. 753, 442 U. S. 758; United States v. Chadwick, 433 U. S. 1, 433 U. S. 10. When the contents of the package are books or other materials arguably protected by the First Amendment, and when the basis fr the seizure is disapproval of the message contained therein, it is especially important that this requirement be scrupulously observed. [6]

Nor does the fact that the packages and one or more of the boxes had been opened by a private party before they were acquired by the FBI excuse the failure to obtain a search warrant. It has, of course, been settled since Burdeau v. McDowell, 256 U. S. 465, that a wrongful search or seizure conducted by a private party does not violate the Fourth Amendment, and that such private wrongdoing does not deprive the government of the right to use evidence that it has acquired lawfully. See Coolidge v. New Hampshire, 403 U. S. 443, 403 U. S. 487-490. In these cases, there was nothing wrongful about the Government's acquisition of the packages or its examination of their contents to the extent that they had already been examined by third parties. Since that examination had uncovered the labels, and since the labels established probable cause to believe the films were obscene, the Government argues that the limited private search justified an unlimited official search. That argument must fail, whether we view the official search as an expansion of the private search or as an independent search supported by its own probable cause. When an official search is properly authorized -- whether by consent or by the issuance of a valid warrant -- the scope of the search is limited by the terms of its authorization. [7] Consent to search a garage would not implicitly authorize a search of an adjoining house; a warrant to search for a stolen refrigerator would not authorize the opening of desk drawers. Because

"indiscriminate searches and seizures conducted under the authority of 'general warrants' were the immediate evils that motivated the framing and adoption of the Fourth Amendment,"

Payton v. New York, 445 U. S. 573, 445 U. S. 583, that Amendment requires that the scope of every authorized search be particularly described. [8]

If a properly authorized official search is

limited by the particular terms of its authorization, at least the same kind of strict limitation must be applied to any official use of a private party's invasion of another person's privacy. Even though some circumstances -- for example, if the results of the private search are in plain view when materials are turned over to the Government -- may justify the Government's reexamination of the materials, surely the Government may not exceed the scope of the private search unless it has the right to make an independent search. In these cases, the private party had not actually viewed the films. Prior to the Government screening, one could only draw inferences about what was on the films. [9] The projection of the films was a significant expansion of the search that had been conducted previously by a private party, and therefore must be characterized as a separate search. That separate search was not supported by any exigency, or by a warrant, even though one could have easily been obtained. [10]

The Government claims, however, that, because the packages had been opened by a private party, thereby exposing the descriptive labels on the boxes, petitioners no longer had any reasonable expectation of privacy in the films, and that the warrantless screening therefore did not invade any privacy interest protected by the Fourth Amendment. But petitioners expected no one except the intended recipient either to open the 12 packages or to project the films. The 12 cartons were securely wrapped and sealed, with no labels or markings to indicate the character of their contents. [11] There is no reason why the consignor of such a shipment would have any lesser expectation of privacy than the consignor of an ordinary locked suitcase. [12] The fact that the cartons were unexpectedly opened by a third party before the shipment was delivered to its intended consignee does not alter the consignor's legitimate expectation of privacy. The private search merely frustrated that expectation in part. [13] It did not

simply strip the remaining unfrustrated portion of that expectation of all Fourth Amendment protection. [14] Since the additional search conducted by the FBI -- the screening of the films -- was not supported by any justification, it violated that Amendment.

We therefore conclude that the rationale of MR JUSTICE STEWART's concurrence in Stanley v. Georgia, 394 U. S. 557, is applicable to these cases, and that it requires that the judgments of the Court of Appeals be reversed.

It is so ordered.

Notes

[1] There was no "Leggs, Inc." "Leggs" was the nickname of a woman employed by one of petitioners' companies. The packages indicated that the intended recipient would pick them up and pay for them at the carrier's terminal in Atlanta.

[2] Each reel was eight millimeters in width. Petitioner Walter informs us that, excluding three millimeters for sprocketing and one millimeter for the border, the film itself is only four millimeters wide. Brief for Petitioner in No. 797, p. 30, n. 8. Since the scenes depicted within the frame are necessarily even more minute, it is easy to understand why such films cannot be examined successfully with the naked eye.

[3] The FBI had meanwhile received no request from the consignee or the consignor of the films for their return, but the agents had been told by employees of L'Eggs Products, Inc., that inquiries had been made as to their whereabouts.

[4] The petition for certiorari in NO. 79-67 presented 10 separate questions, and the petition in NO. 7148 presented 5 separate questions. Except with respect to the issues discussed in the text, we have determined that certiorari was improvidently granted. We therefore dismiss as to the other questions that have been briefed and argued. For purposes of decision, we accept the

Government's argument that the delivery of the films to the FBI by a third party was not a "seizure" subject to the warrant requirement of the Fourth Amendment.

[5] "In th[e] enforcement [of regulations as to what may be transported in the mails], a distinction is to be made between different kinds of mail matter, -- between what is intended to be kept free from inspection, such as letters, and sealed packages subject to letter postage; and what is open to inspection, such as newspapers, magazines, pamphlets, and other printed matter, purposely left in a condition to be examined. Letters and sealed packages of this kind in the mail are as fully guarded from examination and inspection, except as to their outward form and weight, as if they were retained by the parties forwarding them in their own domiciles. The constitutional guaranty of the right of the people to be secure in their papers against unreasonable searches and seizures extends to their papers, thus closed against inspection, wherever they may be. Whilst in the mail, they can only be opened and examined under like warrant, issued upon similar oath or affirmation, particularly describing the thing to be seized, as is required when papers are subjected to search in one's own household. No law of Congress can place in the hands of officials connected with the postal service any authority to invade the secrecy of letters and such sealed packages in the mail; and all regulations adopted as to mail matter of this kind must be in subordination to the great principle embodied in the fourth amendment of the Constitution."

96 U.S. at 96 U. S. 732-733.

And later in his opinion, Mr. Justice Field again noted that

"regulations excluding matter from the mail cannot be enforced in a way which would require or permit an examination into letters, or sealed packages subject to letter postage, without warrant, issued upon oath or affirmation, in the search for prohibited matter. . . ."

Id. at 96 U. S. 735.

[6] "This is the history which prompted the Court, less than four years ago, to remark that"

"[t]he use by government of the power of search and seizure as an adjunct to a system for the suppression of objectionable publications is not new."

"Marcus v. Search Warrant, 367 U. S. 717, at 376 U. S. 724."

"This history was, of course, part of the intellectual matrix within which our constitutional fabric was shaped. The Bill of Rights was fashioned against the background of knowledge that unrestricted power of search and seizure could also be an instrument for stifling liberty of expression."

"Id. at 367 U. S. 729. As MR. JUSTICE DOUGLAS has put it,"

"The commands of our First Amendment (as well as the prohibitions of the Fourth and the Fifth) reflect the teachings of Entick v. Carrington, [19 How.St.Tr. 1029 (1765)]. These three amendments are indeed closely related, safeguarding not only privacy and protection against self-incrimination but 'conscience and human dignity and freedom of expression as well.'"

"Frank v. Maryland, 359 U. S. 360, 359 U. S. 376 (dissenting opinion)."

"In short, what this history indispensably teaches is that the constitutional requirement that warrants must particularly describe the 'things to be seized' is to be accorded the most scrupulous exactitude when the 'things' are books and the basis for their seizure is the ideas which they contain."

Stanford v. Texas, 379 U. S. 476, 379 U. S. 484-485.

See also Roaden v. Kentucky, 413 U. S. 496, 413 U. S. 501. Although there were 871 reels of film in the shipment, there were only 25 different titles. Since only five of the titles were used as a basis for prosecution, it may be presumed that the other films were not obscene.

[7] "The requirement that warrants shall particularly describe the things to be seized makes general searches under them impossible and prevents the seizure of one thing under a warrant describing another."

Marron v. United States, 275 U. S. 192, 275 U. S. 196.

[8] The Warrant Clause of the Fourth Amendment expressly provides that no warrant may issue except those "particularly describing the place to be searched, and the persons or things to be seized."

[9] Since the viewing was first done by the Government when it screened the films with a projector, we have no occasion to decide whether the Government would have been required to obtain a warrant had the private party been the first to view them.

[10] The fact that the labels on the boxes established probable cause to believe the films were obscene clearly cannot excuse the failure to obtain a warrant; for if probable cause dispensed with the necessity of a warrant, one would never be needed.

Contrary to the dissent, post at 447 U. S. 665-666, n. 3, there were no impracticalities in these cases that would vitiate the warrant requirement. The inability to serve a warrant on the owner of property to be searched does not make execution of the warrant unlawful. See ALI, Model Code of Pre-Arraignment Procedure § 220.3(4) (Prop. Off. Draft 1975). Obviously, such inability does not render a warrant unnecessary under the Fourth Amendment. Nor is it clear in these cases that it would have been impossible to serve petitioners with a search warrant had the FBI made any effort to find them prior to screening the films. See n 3, supra.

[11] For the same reason, one may not deem petitioners to have consented to the screening merely because the labels on the unexposed boxes were explicit.

Nor can petitioners' failure to make a more prompt claim to the Government for return of the films be fairly regarded as an abandonment of their interest in preserving the privacy of the shipment. As subsequent events have demonstrated, such a request could reasonably be expected to precipitate criminal proceedings. We cannot equate an unwillingness to invite a criminal prosecution with a voluntary abandonment of any interest in the contents of the cartons. In any event, the record in these cases does indicate that the defendants made a number of attempts to locate the films before they were examined by the FBI agents.

[12] The consignor's expectation of privacy in the contents of a carton delivered to a private carrier must be measured by the condition of the package at the time it was shipped unless there is reason to assume that it would be opened before it arrived at its destination. Thus, for example if a gun case is delivered to a carrier, there could then be no expectation that the contents would remain private, cf. Arkansas v. Sanders, 442 U. S. 753, 442 U. S. 764-765, n. 13; but if the gun case were enclosed in a locked suitcase, the shipper would surely expect that the privacy of its contents would be respected.

The dissent asserts, post at 447 U. S. 665, that "[a]ny subjective expectation of privacy on the part of petitioners was undone . . . by their own actions and the private search." But it is difficult to understand how petitioners' subjective expectation of privacy could have been altered in any way by subsequent events of which they were obviously unaware.

[13] A partial invasion of privacy cannot automatically justify a total invasion. As Learned Hand noted in a somewhat different context:

"It is true that, when one has been arrested in his home or his office, his privacy has already been invaded; but that interest, though lost, is altogether separate from the interest in protecting his papers from indiscriminate rummage, even though both are customarily grouped together as parts of the 'right of privacy.'"

United States v. Rabinowitz, 176 F.2d 732, 735 (CA2 1949), rev'd, 339 U. S. 339 U.S. 56. Judge Hand's view was ultimately vindicated in Chimel v. California, 395 U. S. 752, 395 U. S. 768, which specifically disapproved this Court's decision in Rabinowitz. See also MR. JUSTICE STEWART's opinion concurring in the result in Stanley v. Georgia, 394 U. S. 557, 394 U. S. 571-572, quoted supra at 447 U. S. 653-654.

[14] It is arguable that a third party's inspection of the contents of "private books, papers, memoranda, etc." could be so complete that there would be no additional search by the FBI when it reexamines the materials. Cf. Burdeau v. McDowell, 256 U. S. 465, 256 U. S. 470. But this is not such a case, because it was clearly necessary for the FBI to screen the films, which the private party had not done, in order to obtain the evidence needed to accomplish its law enforcement objectives.

Michigan v. Summers (June 22, 1981) [Notes omitted]

JUSTICE STEVENS delivered the opinion of the Court.

As Detroit police officers were about to execute a warrant to search a house for narcotics, they encountered respondent descending the front steps. They requested his assistance in gaining entry, and detained him while they searched the premises. After finding narcotics in the basement and ascertaining that respondent owned the house, the police arrested him, searched his person, and found in his coat pocket an envelope containing 8.5 grams of heroin. [1]

Respondent was charged with possession of the heroin found on his person. He moved to suppress the heroin as the product of an illegal search in violation of the Fourth Amendment, [2] and the trial judge granted the motion and quashed the information. That order was affirmed by a divided panel of the Michigan Court of Appeals, 68 Mich.App. 571, 243 N.W.2d 689, and by the Michigan Supreme Court over the dissent of three of its justices. 407 Mich. 432, 286 N.W.2d 226. We granted the State's petition for certiorari, 449 U.S. 898, and now reverse.

I

The dispositive question in this case is whether the initial detention of respondent violated his constitutional right to be secure against an unreasonable seizure of his person. The State attempts to justify the eventual search of respondent's person by arguing that the authority to search premises granted by the warrant implicitly included the authority to search persons on those premises, just as that authority included an authorization to search furniture and containers in which the particular things described might be concealed. But as the Michigan Court of Appeals correctly noted, even if otherwise acceptable, this argument could not justify the initial detention of respondent outside the premises described in the warrant. See 68 Mich.App. at 578-580, 243 N.W. 2d at 62-693. If that detention was permissible, there is no need to reach the question whether a search warrant for premises includes the right to search persons found there, because when the police searched respondent, they had probable cause to arrest him and had done so. [3] Our appraisal of the validity of the search of respondent's person therefore depends upon a determination whether the officers had the authority to require him to reenter the house and to remain there while they conducted their search. [4]

II

In assessing the validity of respondent's initial detention, we note first that it constituted a "seizure" within the meaning of the Fourth Amendment. [5] The State does not contend otherwise, and the record demonstrates that respondent was not free to leave the premises while the officers were searching his home. It is also clear that respondent was not formally arrested until after the search was completed. The dispute therefore involves only the constitutionality of a pre-arrest "seizure," which we assume was unsupported by probable cause.

In Dunaway v. New York, 442 U. S. 200, the Court reaffirmed the general rule that an official seizure of the person must be supported by probable cause, even if no formal arrest is made. In that case, police officers located a murder suspect at a neighbor's house, took him into custody, and transported him to the police station, where interrogation ultimately produced a confession. Because the suspect was not arrested until after he had confessed, and because he presumably would have been set free if probable cause had not been established during his questioning, the State argued that the pre-arrest detention should not be equated with an arrest, and should be upheld as "reasonable" in view of the serious character of the crime and the fact that the police had an articulable basis for suspecting that Dunaway was involved. Id. at 442 U. S. 207. The Court firmly rejected the State's argument, noting that "the detention of petitioner was, in important respects, indistinguishable from a traditional arrest." Id. at 442 U. S. 212. [6] We stated:

"Indeed any 'exception' that could cover a seizure as intrusive as that in this case would threaten to swallow the general rule that Fourth Amendment seizures are 'reasonable' only if based on probable cause."

"The central importance of the probable cause requirement to the protection of a citizen's privacy afforded by the Fourth Amendment's guarantees cannot be compromised in this fashion. "The requirement of probable cause has roots that are deep in our history." Henry v. United States, 361 U. S. 98, 361 U. S. 100 (1959). Hostility to seizures based on mere suspicion was a prime motivation for the adoption of the Fourth Amendment, and decisions immediately after its adoption affirmed that "common rumor or report, suspicion, or even strong reason to suspect' was not adequate to support a warrant for arrest." Id. at 361 U. S. 101 (footnotes omitted). The familiar threshold standard of probable cause for Fourth Amendment seizures reflects the benefit of extensive experience accommodating the factors relevant to the "reasonableness" requirement of the Fourth Amendment, and provides the relative simplicity and clarity necessary to the implementation of a workable rule. See Brinegar v. United States, [338 U.S. at 338 U. S. 175-176]."

Id. at 442 U. S. 213.

Although we refused in Dunaway to find an exception that would swallow the general rule, our opinion recognized that some seizures significantly less intrusive than an arrest have withstood scrutiny under the reasonableness standard embodied in the Fourth Amendment. In these cases, the intrusion on the citizen's privacy "was so much less severe" than that involved in a traditional arrest that "the opposing interests in crime prevention and detection and in the police officer's safety" could support the seizure as reasonable. Id. at 442 U. S. 209.

In the first such case, Terry v. Ohio, 392 U. S. 1, the Court recognized the narrow authority of police officers who suspect criminal activity to make limited intrusions on an individual's personal security based on less than probable cause. The Court approved a "frisk" for weapons as a justifiable response to an officer's reasonable belief that he was dealing with a possibly armed and dangerous suspect. [7] In the second such case, Adams v. Williams, 407 U. S. 143, the Court relied on Terry to hold that an officer could forcibly stop a suspect to investigate an informant's tip that the suspect was armed and carrying narcotics. [8] And in United States v. Brignoni-Ponce, 422 U. S. 873, the Court held that the special enforcement problems confronted by roving Border Patrol agents, though not sufficient to justify random stops of vehicles near the Mexican border to question their occupants about their citizenship, id. at 422 U. S. 882-884, [9] were adequate to support vehicle stops based on the agents' awareness of specific articulable facts indicating that the vehicle contained illegal aliens. The Court reasoned that the difficulty in patrolling the long Mexican border and the interest in controlling the influx of illegal aliens justified the limited intrusion, usually lasting no more than a minute, involved in the stop. Id. at 422 U. S. 878-880. [10] See also United States v. Cortez, 449 U. S. 411.

These cases recognize that some seizures admittedly covered by the Fourth Amendment constitute such limited intrusions on the personal security of those detained, and are justified by such substantial law enforcement interests that they may be made on less than probable cause, so long as police have an articulable basis for suspecting criminal activity. In these cases, as in Dunaway, the Court was applying the ultimate standard of reasonableness embodied in the Fourth Amendment. [11] They are consistent with the general rule that every arrest, and every seizure having the essential attributes of a formal arrest, is unreasonable unless it is supported by probable cause. But they demonstrate that the exception for limited intrusions that may be justified by special law enforcement interests is not confined to the momentary, on-the-street detention accompanied by a frisk for weapons involved in Terry and Adams. [12] Therefore, in order to decide whether this case is controlled by the general rule, it is necessary to examine both the character of the official intrusion and its justification.

III

Of prime importance in assessing the

intrusion is the fact that the police had obtained a warrant to search respondent's house for contraband. A neutral and detached magistrate had found probable cause to believe that the law was being violated in that house, and had authorized a substantial invasion of the privacy of the persons who resided there. The detention of one of the residents while the premises were searched, although admittedly a significant restraint on his liberty, was surely less intrusive than the search itself. [13] Indeed, we may safely assume that most citizens -- unless they intend flight to avoid arrest -- would elect to remain in order to observe the search of their possessions. Furthermore, the type of detention imposed here is not likely to be exploited by the officer or unduly prolonged in order to gain more information, because the information the officers seek normally will be obtained through the search, and not through the detention. [14]

Moreover, because the detention in this case was in respondent's own residence, it could add only minimally to the public stigma associated with the search itself, and would involve neither the inconvenience nor the indignity associated with a compelled visit to the police station. [15] In sharp contrast to the custodial interrogation in Dunaway, the detention of this respondent was "substantially less intrusive" than an arrest. 442 U.S. at 442 U. S. 210. [16]

In assessing the justification for the detention of an occupant of premises being searched for contraband pursuant to a valid warrant, both the law enforcement interest and the nature of the "articulable facts" supporting the detention are relevant. Most obvious is the legitimate law enforcement interest in preventing flight in the event that incriminating evidence is found. Less obvious, but sometimes of greater importance, is the interest in minimizing the risk of harm to the officers. Although no special danger to the police is suggested by the evidence in this record, the execution of a warrant to search for narcotics is the kind of transaction that may give rise to sudden violence or frantic efforts to conceal or destroy evidence. [17] The risk of harm to both the police and the occupants is minimized if the officers routinely exercise unquestioned command of the situation. Cf. 2 W. LaFave Search and Seizure § 4.9, pp. 150-151 (1978). Finally, the orderly completion of the search may be facilitated if the occupants of the premises are present. Their self-interest may induce them to open locked doors or locked containers to avoid the use of force that is not only damaging to property but may also delay the completion of the task at hand.

It is also appropriate to consider the nature of the articulable and individualized suspicion on which the police base the detention of the occupant of a home subject to a search warrant. We have already noted that the detention represents only an incremental intrusion on personal liberty when the search of a home has been authorized by a valid warrant. The existence of a search warrant, however, also provides an objective justification for the detention. A judicial officer has determined that police have probable cause to believe that someone in the home is committing a crime. Thus, a neutral magistrate, rather than an officer in the field, has made the critical determination that the police should be given a special authorization to thrust themselves into the privacy of a home. [18] The connection of an occupant to that home gives the police officer an easily identifiable and certain basis for determining that suspicion of criminal activity justifies a detention of that occupant.

In Payton v. New York, 445 U. S. 573, we held that police officers may not enter a private residence to make a routine felony arrest without first obtaining a warrant. In that case, we rejected the suggestion that only a search warrant could adequately protect the privacy interests at stake, noting that the distinction between a search warrant and an arrest warrant was far less significant than the interposition of the magistrate's determination of probable cause between the zealous officer and the citizen:

"It is true that an arrest warrant requirement may afford less protection than a search warrant requirement, but it will suffice to interpose the magistrate's determination of probable cause between the zealous officer and the citizen. If there is sufficient evidence of a citizen's participation in a felony to persuade a judicial officer that his arrest is justified, it is constitutionally reasonable to require him to open his doors to the officers of the law. Thus, for Fourth Amendment purposes, an arrest warrant founded on probable cause implicitly carries with it the limited authority to enter a dwelling in which the suspect lives when there is reason to believe the suspect is within."

Id. at 445 U. S. 602-603. That holding is relevant today. If the evidence that a citizen's residence is harboring contraband is sufficient to persuade a judicial officer that an invasion of the citizen's privacy is justified, it is constitutionally reasonable to require that citizen to remain while officers of the law execute a valid warrant to search his home. [19] Thus, for Fourth Amendment purposes, we hold that a warrant to search for contraband [20] founded on probable cause implicitly carries with it the limited authority to detain the occupants of the premises while a proper search is conducted. [21]

Because it was lawful to require respondent to reenter and to remain in the house until evidence establishing probable cause to arrest him was found, his arrest and the search incident thereto were constitutionally permissible. The judgment of the Supreme Court of Michigan must therefore be reversed.

It is so ordered.

Robbins v. California (July 1, 1981)

JUSTICE STEWART announced the judgment of the Court and delivered an opinion, in which JUSTICE BRENNAN, JUSTICE WHITE, and JUSTICE MARSHALL joined.

I

On the early morning of January 5, 1975, California Highway Patrol officers stopped the petitioner's car—a 1966 Chevrolet station wagon—because he had been driving erratically. He got out of his vehicle and walked towards the patrol car. When one of the officers asked him for his driver's license and the station wagon's registration, he fumbled with his wallet. When the petitioner opened the car door to get out the registration, the officers smelled marihuana smoke. One of the officers patted down the petitioner, and discovered a vial of liquid. The officer then searched the passenger compartment of the car, and found marihuana as well as equipment for using it.

After putting the petitioner in the patrol car, the officers opened the tailgate of the station wagon, located a handle set flush in the deck, and lifted it up to uncover a recessed luggage compartment. In the compartment were a totebag and two packages wrapped in green opaque plastic.[1] The police unwrapped the packages; each one contained 15 pounds of marihuana.

The petitioner was charged with various drug offenses, his pretrial motion to suppress the evidence found when the packages were unwrapped was denied, and a jury convicted him. In an unpublished opinion, the California Court of Appeal affirmed the judgment in all relevant respects. This Court granted a writ of certiorari, vacated the Court of Appeal's judgment, and remanded the case for further consideration in light of Arkansas v. Sanders, 442 U. S. 753, 443 U. S. 903. On remand, the Court of Appeal again found the warrantless opening of the packages constitutionally permissible, since the trial court "could reasonably [have] conclude[d] that the contents of the packages could have been inferred from their outward appearance, so that appellant could not have held a reasonable expectation of privacy with respect to the contents." 103 Cal. App. 3d 34, 40, 162 Cal. Rptr. 780, 783. Because of continuing uncertainty as to whether closed containers found during a lawful warrantless search of an automobile may themselves be searched without a warrant, this Court granted certiorari. 449 U. S. 1109.

II

The Fourth Amendment to the Constitution, which is made applicable to the States through the Fourteenth Amendment, establishes "[t]he right of the people to be secure in their persons, houses, papers, and effects, against unreasonable searches and seizures." This Court has held that a search is per se unreasonable, and thus violates the Fourth Amendment, if the police making the search have not first secured from a neutral magistrate a warrant that satisfies the terms of the Warrant Clause of the Fourth Amendment. See, e. g., Katz v. United States, 389 U. S. 347, 357; Agnello v. United States, 269 U. S. 20, 33. Although the Court has identified some exceptions to this warrant requirement, the Court has emphasized that these exceptions are "few," "specifically established," and "well-delineated." Katz v. United States, supra, at 357.

Among these exceptions is the so-called "automobile exception." See Colorado v. Bannister, 449 U. S. 1. In Carroll v. United States, 267 U. S. 132, the Court held that a search warrant is unnecessary "where there is probable cause to search an automobile stopped on the highway; the car is movable, the occupants are alerted, and the car's contents may never be found again if a warrant must be obtained." Chambers v. Maroney, 399 U. S. 42, 51. In recent years, we have twice been confronted with the suggestion that this "automobile exception" somehow justifies the warrantless search of a closed container found inside an automobile. Each time, the Court has refused to accept the suggestion.

In United States v. Chadwick, 433 U. S. 1, the Government argued in part that luggage is analogous to motor vehicles for Fourth Amendment purposes, and that the "automobile exception" should thus be extended to encompass closed pieces of luggage. The Court rejected the analogy and insisted that the exception is confined to the special and possibly unique circumstances which were the occasion of its genesis. First, the Court said that "[o]ur treatment of automobiles has been based in part on their inherent mobility, which often makes obtaining a judicial warrant impracticable." Id., at 12. While both cars and luggage may be "mobile," luggage itself may be brought and kept under the control of the police.

Second, the Court acknowledged that "inherent mobility" cannot alone justify the automobile exception, since the Court has sometimes approved warrantless searches in which the automobile's mobility was irrelevant. See Cady v. Dombrowski, 413 U. S. 433, 441-442; South Dakota v. Opperman, 428 U. S. 364, 367. The automobile exception, the Court said, is thus also supported by "the diminished expectation of privacy which surrounds the automobile" and which arises from the facts that a car is used for transportation and not as a residence or a repository of personal effects, that a car's occupants and contents travel in plain view, and that automobiles are necessarily highly regulated by government. United States v. Chadwick, supra, at 12-13. No such diminished expectation of privacy characterizes luggage; on the contrary, luggage typically is a repository of personal effects, the contents of closed pieces of luggage are hidden from view, and luggage is not generally subject to state regulation.

In Arkansas v. Sanders, 442 U. S. 753, the State of Arkansas argued that the "automobile exception" should be extended to allow the warrantless search of everything found in an automobile during a lawful warrantless search of the vehicle itself. The Court rejected this argument for much the same reason it had rejected this Government's argument in Chadwick. Pointing out, first, that "[o]nce police have seized a suitcase, as they did here, the extent of its mobility is in no way affected by the place from which it was taken," the Court said that there generally "is no greater need for warrantless searches of luggage taken from automobiles than of luggage taken from other places." 442 U. S., at 763-764. Second, the Court saw no reason to believe that the privacy expectation in a closed piece of luggage taken from a car is necessarily less than the privacy expectation in closed pieces of luggage found elsewhere.

In the present case, the Court once again encounters the argument—made in the Government's brief as amicus curiae— that the contents of a closed container carried in a vehicle are somehow not fully protected by the Fourth Amendment. But this argument is inconsistent with the Court's decisions in Chadwick and Sanders. Those cases made clear, if it was not clear before, that a closed piece of luggage found in a lawfully searched car is constitutionally protected to the same extent as are closed pieces of luggage found anywhere else.

The respondent, however, proposes that the nature of a container may diminish the constitutional protection to which it otherwise would be entitled—that the Fourth Amendment protects only containers commonly used to transport "personal effects." By personal effects the respondent means property worn on or carried about the person or having some intimate relation to the person. In taking this position, the respondent relies on numerous opinions that have drawn a distinction between pieces of sturdy luggage, like suitcases, and flimsier containers, like cardboard boxes. Compare, e. g., United States v.

Benson, 631 F. 2d 1336 (CA8 1980) (leather totebag); United States v. Miller, 608 F. 2d 1089 (CA5 1979) (plastic portfolio); United States v. Presler, 610 F. 2d 1206 (CA4 1979) (briefcase); United States v. Meier, 602 F. 2d 253 (CA10 1979) (backpack); United States v. Johnson, 588 F. 2d 147 (CA5 1979) (duffelbag); United States v. Stevie, 582 F. 2d 1175 (CA8 1978), with United States v. Mannino, 635 F. 2d 110 (CA2 1980) (plastic bag inside paper bag); United States v. Goshorn, 628 F. 2d 697, 699 (CA1 1980) ("`[t]wo plastic bags, further in three brown paper bags, further in two clear plastic bags'"); United States v. Gooch, 603 F. 2d 122 (CA10 1979) (plastic bag); United States v. Mackey, 626 F. 2d 684 (CA9 1980) (paper bag); United States v. Neumann, 585 F. 2d 355 (CA8 1978) (cardboard box).

The respondent's argument cannot prevail for at least two reasons. First, it has no basis in the language or meaning of the Fourth Amendment. That Amendment protects people and their effects, and it protects those effects whether they are "personal" or "impersonal." The contents of Chadwick's footlocker and Sanders' suitcase were immune from a warrantless search because they had been placed within a closed, opaque container and because Chadwick and Sanders had thereby reasonably "manifested an expectation that the contents would remain free from public examination." United States v. Chadwick, supra, at 11. Once placed within such a container, a diary and a dishpan are equally protected by the Fourth Amendment.

Second, even if one wished to import such a distinction into the Fourth Amendment, it is difficult if not impossible to perceive any objective criteria by which that task might be accomplished. What one person may put into a suitcase, another may put into a paper bag. United States v. Ross, 210 U. S. App. D. C. 342, 655 F. 2d 1159 (1981) (en banc). And as the disparate results in the decided cases indicate, no court, no constable, no citizen, can sensibly be asked to distinguish the relative "privacy interests" in a closed suitcase, briefcase, portfolio, duffelbag, or box.

The respondent protests that footnote 13 of the Sanders opinion says that "[n]ot all containers and packages found by police during the course of a search will deserve the full protection of the Fourth Amendment." 442 U. S., at 764, n. 13. But the exceptions listed in the succeeding sentences of the footnote are the very model of exceptions which prove the rule: "Thus, some containers (for example a kit of burglar tools or a gun case) by their very nature cannot support any reasonable expectation of privacy because their contents can be inferred from their outward appearance. Similarly, in some cases the contents of a package will be open to `plain view,' thereby obviating the need for a warrant." Id., at 764-765, n. 13. The second of these exceptions obviously refers to items in a container that is not closed. The first exception is likewise little more than another variation of the "plain view" exception, since, if the distinctive configuration of a container proclaims its contents, the contents cannot fairly be said to have been removed from a searching officer's view. The same would be true, of course, if the container were transparent, or otherwise clearly revealed its contents. In short, the negative implication of footnote 13 of the Sanders opinion is that, unless the container is such that its contents may be said to be in plain view, those contents are fully protected by the Fourth Amendment.

The California Court of Appeal believed that the packages in the present case fell directly within the second exception described in this footnote, since "[a]ny experienced observer could have inferred from the appearance of the packages that they contained bricks of marijuana." 103 Cal. App. 3d, at 40, 162 Cal. Rptr., at 783. The only evidence the court cited to support this proposition was the testimony of one of the officers who arrested the petitioner. When asked whether there was anything about "these two plastic wrapped green blocks which attracted your attention," the officer replied, somewhat obscurely:

"A. I had previous knowledge of transportation of such blocks. Normally contraband is wrapped this way, merely hearsay. I had never seen them before.

"Q. You had heard contraband was packaged this way?

"A. Yes." Id., at 40, n. 2, 162 Cal. Rptr., at 783, n. 4.

This vague testimony certainly did not establish that marihuana is ordinarily "packaged this way." Expectations of privacy are established by general social norms, and to fall within the second exception of the footnote in question a container must so clearly announce its contents, whether by its distinctive configuration, its transparency, or otherwise, that its contents are obvious to an observer. If indeed a green plastic wrapping reliably indicates that a package could only contain marihuana, that fact was not shown by the evidence of record in this case.[2]

Although the two bricks of marihuana were discovered during a lawful search of the petitioner's car, they were inside a closed, opaque container. We reaffirm today that such a container may not be opened without a warrant, even if it is found during the course of the lawful search of an automobile. Since the respondent does not allege the presence of any circumstances that would constitute a valid exception to this general rule,[3] it is clear that the opening of the closed containers without a search warrant violated the Fourth and Fourteenth Amendments. Accordingly, the judgment of the California Court of Appeal is reversed.

It is so ordered.

Notes

[1] A photograph was made of one of the packages, and it was later described as follows:

"The package visible in the photograph is apparently wrapped or boxed in an opaque material covered by an outer wrapping of transparent, cellophane-type plastic. (The photograph is not in color, and the `green' plastic cannot be seen at all.) Both wrappings are sealed on the outside with at least one strip of opaque tape. As thus wrapped and sealed, the package roughly resembles an oversized, extra-long cigar box with slightly rounded corners and edges. It bears no legend or other written indicia supporting any inference concerning its contents." 103 Cal. App. 3d 34, 44, 162 Cal. Rptr. 780, 785 (Rattigan, J., dissenting).

[2] As Judge Rattigan wrote in his dissenting opinion in the California Court of Appeal: "For all that I see, it could contain books, stationery, canned goods, or any number of other wholly innocuous items which might be heavy in weight. In fact, it bears a remarkable resemblance to an unlabelled carton of emergency highway flares that I bought from a store shelf and have carried in the trunk of my own automobile." 103 Cal. App. 3d, at 44, 162 Cal. Rptr., at 785.

[3] In particular, it is not argued that the opening of the packages was incident to a lawful custodial arrest. Cf. Chimel v. California, 395 U. S. 752. See Arkansas v. Sanders, 442 U. S. 753, 764, n. 11. Further, the respondent does not argue that the petitioner consented to the opening of the packages.

New York v. Belton (July 1, 1981) [Notes omitted]

JUSTICE STEWART delivered the opinion of the Court.

When the occupant of an automobile is subjected to a lawful custodial arrest, does the constitutionally permissible scope of a search incident to his arrest include the passenger compartment of the automobile in which he was riding? That is the question at issue in the present case.

I

On April 9, 1978, Trooper Douglas Nicot, a New York State policeman driving an unmarked car on the New York Thruway, was passed by another automobile traveling at an excessive rate of speed. Nicot gave chase, overtook the speeding vehicle, and ordered its driver to pull it over to the side of the road and stop. There were four men in the car, one of whom was Roger Belton, the respondent in this case. The policeman asked to see the driver's license and automobile registration, and discovered that none of the men owned the vehicle or was related to its owner. Meanwhile, the policeman had smelled burnt marihuana, and had seen on the floor of the car an envelope marked "Supergold" that he associated with marihuana. He therefore directed the men to get out of the car, and placed them under arrest for the unlawful possession of marihuana. He patted down each of the men and "split them up into four separate areas of the Thruway at this time so they would not be in physical touching area of each other." He then picked up the envelope marked "Supergold" and found that it contained marihuana. After giving the arrestees the warnings required by Miranda v. Arizona, 384 U. S. 436, the state policeman searched each one of them. He then searched the passenger compartment of the car. On the back seat, he found a black leather jacket belonging to Belton. He unzipped one of the pockets of the jacket and discovered cocaine. Placing the jacket in his automobile, he drove the four arrestees to a nearby police station.

Belton was subsequently indicted for criminal possession of a controlled substance. In the trial court, he moved that the cocaine the trooper had seized from the jacket pocket be suppressed. The court denied the motion. Belton then pleaded guilty to a lesser included offense, but preserved his claim that the cocaine had been seized in violation of the Fourth and Fourteenth Amendments. See Lefkowitz v. Newsome, 420 U. S. 283. The Appellate Division of the New York Supreme Court upheld the constitutionality of the search and seizure, reasoning that, "[o]nce defendant was validly arrested for possession of marihuana, the officer was justified in searching the immediate area for other contraband." 68 App.Div.2d 198, 201, 416 N.Y.S.2d 922, 925.

The New York Court of Appeals reversed, holding that

"[a] warrantless search of the zippered pockets of an unaccessible jacket may not be upheld as a search incident to a lawful arrest where there is no longer any danger that the arrestee or a confederate might gain access to the article."

50 N.Y.2d 447, 449, 407 N.E.2d 420, 421. Two judges dissented.

They pointed out that the

"search was conducted by a lone peace officer who was in the process of arresting four unknown individuals whom he had stopped in a speeding car owned by none of them and apparently containing an uncertain quantity of a controlled substance. The suspects were standing by the side of the car as the officer gave it a quick check to confirm his suspicions before attempting to transport them to police headquarters. . . ."

Id. at 454, 407 N.E.2d at 424. We granted certiorari to consider the constitutionally permissible scope of a search in circumstances such as these. 449 U.S. 1109.

II

It is a first principle of Fourth Amendment jurisprudence that the police may not conduct a search unless they first convince a neutral magistrate that there is probable cause to do so. This Court has recognized, however, that "the exigencies of the situation" may sometimes make exemption from the warrant requirement "imperative." McDonald v. United States, 335 U. S. 451, 335 U. S. 456. Specifically, the Court held in

Chimel v. California, 395 U. S. 752, that a lawful custodial arrest creates a situation which justifies the contemporaneous search without a warrant of the person arrested and of the immediately surrounding area. Such searches have long been considered valid because of the need "to remove any weapons that [the arrestee] might seek to use in order to resist arrest or effect his escape," and the need to prevent the concealment or destruction of evidence. Id. at 395 U. S. 763.

The Court's opinion in Chimel emphasized the principle that, as the Court had said in Terry v. Ohio, 392 U. S. 1, 392 U. S. 19, "[t]he scope of [a] search must be strictly tied to and justified by' the circumstances which rendered its initiation permissible." Quoted in Chimel v. California, supra, at 395 U. S. 762. Thus, while the Court in Chimel found "ample justification" for a search of "the area from within which [an arrestee] might gain possession of a weapon or destructible evidence," the Court found

"no comparable justification . . . for routinely searching any room other than that in which an arrest occurs -- or, for that matter for searching through all the desk drawers or other closed or concealed areas in that room itself."

395 U.S. at 395 U. S. 763.

Although the principle that limits a search incident to a lawful custodial arrest may be stated clearly enough, courts have discovered the principle difficult to apply in specific cases. Yet, as one commentator has pointed out, the protection of the Fourth and Fourteenth Amendments

"can only be realized if the police are acting under a set of rules which, in most instances, makes it possible to reach a correct determination beforehand as to whether an invasion of privacy is justified in the interest of law enforcement."

LaFave, "Case-By-Case Adjudication" versus "Standardized Procedures": The Robinson Dilemma, 1974 S.Ct.Rev. 127, 142. This is because

"Fourth Amendment doctrine, given force and effect by the exclusionary rule, is primarily intended to regulate the police in their day-to-day activities, and thus ought to be expressed in terms that are readily applicable by the police in the context of the law enforcement activities in which they are necessarily engaged. A highly sophisticated set of rules, qualified by all sorts of ifs, ands, and buts and requiring the drawing of subtle nuances and hairline distinctions, may be the sort of heady stuff upon which the facile minds of lawyers and judges eagerly feed, but they may be 'literally impossible of application by the officer in the field.'"

Id. at 141. In short,

"[a] single familiar standard is essential to guide police officers, who have only limited time and expertise to reflect on and balance the social and individual interests involved in the specific circumstances they confront."

Dunaway v. New York, 442 U. S. 200, 442 U. S. 213-214.

So it was that, in United States v. Robinson, 414 U. S. 218, the Court hewed to a straightforward rule, easily applied, and predictably enforced:

"[I]n the case of a lawful custodial arrest, a full search of the person is not only an exception to the warrant requirement of the Fourth Amendment, but is also a 'reasonable' search under that Amendment."

Id. at 442 U. S. 235. In so holding, the Court rejected the suggestion that

"there must be litigated in each case the issue of whether or not there was present one of the reasons supporting the authority for a search of the person incident to a lawful arrest."

Ibid.

But no straightforward rule has emerged from the litigated cases respecting the question involved here -- the question of the proper scope of a search of the interior of an automobile incident to a lawful custodial arrest of its occupants. The difficulty courts have had is reflected in the conflicting views of the New York judges who dealt with the problem in the present case, and is confirmed by a look at even a small sample drawn from the narrow class of cases in which courts have decided whether, in the course of a search incident to the lawful custodial arrest of the occupants of an automobile, police may search inside the automobile after the arrestees are no longer in it. On the one hand, decisions in cases such as United States v. Sanders, 631 F.2d 1309 (CA8 1980); United States v. Dixon, 558 F.2d 919 (CA9 1977); and United States v. Frick, 490 F.2d 666 (CA5 1973), have upheld such warrantless searches as incident to lawful arrests. On the other hand, in cases such as United States v. Benson, 631 F.2d 1336 (CA8 1980), and United States v. Rigales, 630 F.2d 364 (CA5 1980), such searches, in comparable factual circumstances, have been held constitutionally invalid. [1]

When a person cannot know how a court will apply a settled principle to a recurring factual situation, that person cannot know the scope of his constitutional protection, nor can a policeman know the scope of his authority. While the Chimel case established that a search incident to an arrest may not stray beyond the area within the immediate control of the arrestee, courts have found no workable definition of "the area within the immediate control of the arrestee" when that area arguably includes the interior of an automobile and the arrestee is its recent occupant. Our reading of the cases suggests the generalization that articles inside the relatively narrow compass of the passenger compartment of an automobile are in fact generally, even if not inevitably, within "the area into which an arrestee might reach in order to grab a weapon or evidentiary ite[m]." Chimel, 395 U.S. at 395 U. S. 763. In order to establish the workable rule this category of cases requires, we read Chimel's

definition of the limits of the area that may be searched in light of that generalization. Accordingly, we hold that, when a policeman has made a lawful custodial arrest of the occupant of an automobile, [2] he may, as a contemporaneous incident of that arrest, search the passenger compartment of that automobile. [3]

It follows from this conclusion that the police may also examine the contents of any containers found within the passenger compartment, for if the passenger compartment is within reach of the arrestee, so also will containers in it be within his reach. [4] United States v. Robinson, supra; 358 U. S. S. 461◆ v. United States, 358 U. S. 307. Such a container may, of course, be searched whether it is open or closed, since the justification for the search is not that the arrestee has no privacy interest in the container, but that the lawful custodial arrest justifies the infringement of any privacy interest the arrestee may have. Thus, while the Court in Chimel@ held that the police could not search all the drawers in an arrestee's house simply because the police had arrested him at home, the Court noted that drawers within an arrestee's reach could be searched because of the danger their contents might pose to the police. 395 U.S. at 395 U. S. 763.

It is true, of course, that these containers will sometimes be such that they could hold neither a weapon nor evidence of the criminal conduct for which the suspect was arrested. However, in United States v. Robinson, the Court rejected the argument that such a container -- there a "crumpled up cigarette package" -- located during a search of Robinson incident to his arrest could not be searched:

"The authority to search the person incident to a lawful custodial arrest, while based upon the need to disarm and to discover evidence, does not depend on what a court may later decide was the probability in a particular arrest situation that weapons or evidence would in fact be found upon the person of the suspect. A custodial arrest of a suspect based on probable cause is a reasonable intrusion under the Fourth Amendment; that intrusion being lawful, a search incident to the arrest requires no additional justification."

414 U.S. at 414 U. S. 235.

The New York Court of Appeals relied upon United States v. Chadwick, 433 U. S. 1, and Arkansas v. Sanders, 442 U. S. 753, in concluding that the search and seizure in the present case were constitutionally invalid. [5] But neither of those cases involved an arguably valid search incident to a lawful custodial arrest. As the Court pointed out in the Chadwick case:

"Here the search was conducted more than an hour after federal agents had gained exclusive control of the footlocker and long after respondents were securely in custody; the search therefore cannot be viewed as incidental to the arrest or as justified by any other exigency."

433 U.S. at 433 U. S. 15. And in the Sanders case, the Court explicitly stated that it did not

"consider the constitutionality of searches of luggage incident to the arrest of its possessor. See, e.g., United States v. Robinson, 414 U. S. 218 (1973). The State has not argued that respondent's suitcase was searched incident to his arrest, and it appears that the bag was not within his 'immediate control' at the time of the search."

442 U.S. at 442 U. S. 764, n. 11. (The suitcase in question was in the trunk of the taxicab. See n 4, supra.)

III

It is not questioned that the respondent was the subject of a lawful custodial arrest on a charge of possessing marihuana. The search of the respondent's jacket followed immediately upon that arrest. The jacket was located inside the passenger compartment of the car in which the respondent had been a passenger just before he was arrested. The jacket was thus within the area which we have concluded was "within the arrestee's immediate control" within the meaning of the Chimel case. [6] The search of the jacket, therefore, was a search incident to a lawful custodial arrest, and it did not violate the Fourth and Fourteenth Amendments. Accordingly, the judgment is reversed.

It is so ordered.

US v. Ross (June 1, 1982) [Notes omitted]

JUSTICE STEVENS delivered the opinion of the Court.

In Carroll v. United States, 267 U. S. 132, the Court held that a warrantless search of an automobile stopped by police officers who had probable cause to believe the vehicle contained contraband was not unreasonable within the meaning of the Fourth Amendment. The Court in Carroll did not explicitly address the scope of the search that is permissible. In this case, we consider the extent to which police officers -- who have legitimately stopped an automobile and who have probable cause to believe that contraband is concealed somewhere within it -- may conduct a probing search of compartments and containers within the vehicle whose contents are not in plain view. We hold that they may conduct a search of the vehicle that is as thorough as a magistrate could authorize in a warrant "particularly describing the place to be searched." [1]

I

In the evening of November 27, 1978, an informant who had previously proved to be reliable telephoned Detective Marcum of the District of Columbia Police Department and told him that an individual known as "Bandit" was selling narcotics kept in the trunk of a car parked at 439 Ridge Street. The informant stated that he had just observed "Bandit" complete a sale, and that "Bandit" had told him that additional narcotics were in the trunk. The informant gave Marcum a detailed description of "Bandit" and stated that the car was a "purplish maroon" Chevrolet Malibu with District of Columbia license plates.

Accompanied by Detective Cassidy and Sergeant Gonzales, Marcum immediately drove to the area and found a maroon Malibu parked in front of 439 Ridge Street. A license check disclosed that the car was registered to Albert Ross; a computer check on Ross revealed that he fit the informant's description and used the alias "Bandit." In two passes through the neighborhood the officers did not observe anyone matching the informant's description. To avoid alerting persons on the street, they left the area.

The officers returned five minutes later and observed the maroon Malibu turning off Ridge Street onto Fourth Street. They pulled alongside the Malibu, noticed that the driver matched the informant's description, and stopped the car. Marcum and Cassidy told the driver -- later identified as Albert Ross, the respondent in this action -- to get out of the vehicle. While they searched Ross, Sergeant Gonzales discovered a bullet on the car's front seat. He searched the interior of the car and found a pistol in the glove compartment. Ross then was arrested and handcuffed. Detective Cassidy took Ross' keys and opened the trunk, where he found a closed brown paper bag. He opened the bag and discovered a number of glassine bags containing a white powder. Cassidy replaced the bag, closed the trunk, and drove the car to headquarters.

At the police station, Cassidy thoroughly searched the car. In addition to the "lunch-type" brown paper bag, Cassidy found in the trunk a zippered red leather pouch. He unzipped the pouch and discovered $3,200 in cash. The police laboratory later determined that the powder in the paper bag was heroin. No warrant was obtained.

Ross was charged with possession of heroin with intent to distribute, in violation of 21 U.S.C. § 841(a). Prior to trial, he moved to suppress the heroin found in the paper bag and the currency found in the leather pouch. After an evidentiary hearing, the District Court denied the motion to suppress. The heroin and currency were introduced in evidence at trial, and Ross was convicted.

A three-judge panel of the Court of Appeals reversed the conviction. It held that the police had probable cause to stop and search Ross' car and that, under Carroll v. United States, supra, and Chambers v. Maroney, 399 U. S. 42, the officers lawfully could search the automobile -- including its trunk -- without a warrant. The court considered separately, however, the warrantless search of the two containers found in the trunk. On the basis of Arkansas v. Sanders, 442 U. S. 753, the court concluded that the constitutionality of a warrantless search of a container found in an automobile depends on whether the owner possesses a reasonable expectation of privacy in its contents. Applying that test, the court held that the warrantless search of the paper bag was valid, but the search of the leather pouch was not. The court remanded for a new trial at which the items taken from the paper bag, but not those from the leather pouch, could be admitted. [2]

The entire Court of Appeals then voted to rehear the case en banc. A majority of the court rejected the panel's conclusion that a distinction of constitutional significance existed between the two containers found in respondent's trunk; it held that the police should not have opened either container without first obtaining a warrant. The court reasoned:

"No specific, well delineated exception called to our attention permits the police to dispense with a warrant to open and search 'unworthy' containers. Moreover, we believe that a rule under which the validity of a warrantless search would turn on judgments about the durability of a container would impose an unreasonable and unmanageable burden on police and courts. For these reasons, and because the Fourth Amendment protects all persons, not just those with the resources or fastidiousness to place their effects in containers that decisionmakers would rank in the luggage line, we hold that the Fourth Amendment warrant requirement forbids the warrantless opening of a closed, opaque paper bag to the same extent that it forbids the warrantless opening of a small unlocked suitcase or a zippered leather pouch."

> 210 U.S.App.D.C. 342, 344, 655 F.2d 1159, 1161 (1981) (footnote omitted).

The en banc Court of Appeals considered, and rejected, the argument that it was reasonable for the police to open both the paper bag and the leather pouch because they were entitled to conduct a warrantless search of the entire vehicle in which the two containers were found. The majority concluded that this argument was foreclosed by Sanders.

Three dissenting judges interpreted Sanders differently. [3] Other courts also have read the Sanders opinion in different ways. [4] Moreover, disagreement concerning the proper interpretation of Sanders was at least partially responsible for the fact that Robbins v. California, 453 U. S. 420, was decided last Term without a Court opinion.

There is, however, no dispute among judges about the importance of striving for clarification in this area of the law. For countless vehicles are stopped on highways and public streets every day, and our cases demonstrate that it is not uncommon for police officers to have probable cause to believe that contraband may be found in a stopped vehicle. In every such case, a conflict is presented between the individual's constitutionally protected interest in privacy and the public interest in effective law enforcement. No single rule of law can resolve every conflict, but our conviction that clarification is feasible led us to grant the Government's petition for certiorari in this case and to invite the parties to address the question whether the decision in Robbins should be reconsidered. 454 U.S. 891.

II

We begin with a review of the decision in Carroll itself. In the fall of 1921, federal prohibition agents obtained evidence that George Carroll and John Kiro were "bootleggers" who frequently traveled between Grand Rapids and Detroit in an Oldsmobile Roadster. [5] On December 15, 1921, the agents unexpectedly encountered Carroll and Kiro driving west on that route in that car. The officers gave pursuit, stopped the roadster on the highway, and directed Carroll and Kiro to get out of the car.

No contraband was visible in the front seat of the Oldsmobile, and the rear portion of the roadster was closed. One of the agents raised the rumble, seat but found no liquor. He raised the seat cushion and again found nothing. The officer then struck at the "lazyback" of the seat and noticed that it was "harder than upholstery ordinarily is in those backs." 267 U.S. at 267 U. S. 174. He tore open the seat cushion and discovered 68 bottles of gin and whiskey concealed inside. No warrant had been obtained for the search.

Carroll and Kiro were convicted of transporting intoxicating liquor in violation of the National Prohibition Act. On review of those convictions, this Court ruled that the warrantless search of the roadster was reasonable within the meaning of the Fourth Amendment. In an extensive opinion written by Chief Justice Taft, the Court held:

"On reason and authority, the true rule is that, if the search and seizure without a warrant are made upon probable cause, that is, upon a belief, reasonably arising out of circumstances known to the seizing officer, that an automobile or other vehicle contains that which by law is subject to seizure and destruction, the search and seizure are valid. The Fourth Amendment is to be construed in the light of what was deemed an unreasonable search and seizure when it was adopted, and in a manner which will conserve public interests, as well as the interests and rights of individual citizens."

Id. at 267 U. S. 149.

The Court explained at length the basis for this rule. The Court noted that, historically, warrantless searches of vessels, wagons, and carriages -- as opposed to fixed premises such as a home or other building -- had been considered reasonable by Congress. After reviewing legislation enacted by Congress between 1789 and 1799, [6] the Court stated:

"Thus, contemporaneously with the adoption of the Fourth Amendment, we find in the first Congress, and in the following Second and Fourth Congresses, a difference made as to the necessity for a search warrant between goods subject to forfeiture, when concealed in a dwelling house or similar place, and like goods in course of transportation and concealed in a movable vessel where they readily could be put out of reach of a search warrant."

Id. at 267 U. S. 151. The Court reviewed additional legislation passed by Congress, [7] and again noted that

"the guaranty of freedom from unreasonable searches and seizures by the Fourth Amendment has been construed, practically since the beginning of the Government, as recognizing a necessary difference between a search of a store, dwelling house or other structure in respect of which a proper official warrant readily may be obtained, and a search of a ship, motor boat, wagon or automobile, for contraband goods, where it is not practicable to secure a warrant because the vehicle can be quickly moved out of the locality or jurisdiction in which the warrant must be sought."

Id. at 267 U. S. 153.

Thus, since its earliest days Congress had recognized the impracticability of securing a warrant in cases involving the transportation of contraband goods. [8] It is this impracticability, viewed in historical perspective, that provided the basis for the Carroll decision. Given the nature of an automobile in transit, the Court recognized that an immediate intrusion is necessary if police officers are to secure the illicit substance. In this class of cases, the Court held that a warrantless search of an automobile is not unreasonable. [9]

In defining the nature of this "exception" to the general rule that, "[i]n cases where the securing of a warrant is reasonably practicable, it must be used," id. at 267 U. S. 156, the Court in Carroll emphasized the importance of the requirement that officers have probable cause to believe that the vehicle contains contraband.

"Having thus established that contraband goods concealed and illegally transported in an automobile or other vehicle may be searched for without a warrant, we come now to consider under what circumstances such search may be made. It would be intolerable and unreasonable if a prohibition agent were authorized to stop every automobile on the chance of finding liquor, and thus subject all persons lawfully using the highways to the inconvenience and indignity of such a search. Travelers may be so stopped in crossing an international boundary because of national self-protection reasonably requiring one entering the country to identify himself as entitled to come in, and his belongings as effects which may be lawfully brought in. But those lawfully within the country, entitled to use the public highways, have a right to free passage without interruption or search unless there is known to a competent official authorized to search, probable cause for believing that their vehicles are carrying contraband or illegal merchandise."

Id. at 267 U. S. 153-154. Moreover, the probable cause determination must be based on objective facts that could justify the issuance of a warrant by a magistrate, and not merely on the subjective good faith of the police officers.

"'[A]s we have seen, good faith is not enough to constitute probable cause. That faith must be grounded on facts within knowledge of the [officer] which. in the judgment of the court. would make his faith reasonable.'"

Id. at 267 U. S. 161-162 (quoting Director General of Railroads v. Kastenbaum, 263 U. S. 25, 263 U. S. 28). [10]

In short, the exception to the warrant requirement established in Carroll -- the scope of which we consider in this case -- applies only to searches of vehicles that are supported by probable cause. [11] In this class of cases, a search is not unreasonable if based on facts that would justify the issuance of a warrant, even though a warrant has not actually been obtained. [12]

III

The rationale justifying a warrantless search of an automobile that is believed to be transporting contraband arguably applies with equal force to any movable container that is believed to be carrying an illicit substance. That argument, however, was squarely rejected in United States v. Chadwick, 433 U. S. 1.

Chadwick involved the warrantless search of a 200-pound footlocker secured with two padlocks. Federal railroad officials in San Diego became suspicious when they noticed that a brown footlocker loaded onto a train bound for Boston was unusually heavy and leaking talcum powder, a substance often used to mask the odor of marihuana. Narcotics agents met the train in Boston and a trained police dog signaled the presence of a controlled substance inside the footlocker. The agents did not seize the footlocker, however, at this time; they waited until respondent Chadwick arrived and the footlocker was placed in the trunk of Chadwick's automobile. Before the engine was started, the officers arrested Chadwick and his two companions. The agents then removed the footlocker to a secured place, opened it without a warrant, and discovered a large quantity of marihuana.

In a subsequent criminal proceeding, Chadwick claimed that the warrantless search of the footlocker violated the Fourth Amendment. In the District Court, the Government argued that, as soon as the footlocker was placed in the automobile, a warrantless search was permissible under Carroll. The District Court rejected that argument, [13] and the Government did not pursue it on appeal. [14] Rather, the Government contended in this Court that the warrant requirement of the Fourth Amendment applied only to searches of homes and other "core" areas of privacy. The Court unanimously rejected that contention. [15] Writing for the Court, THE CHIEF JUSTICE stated:

"[I]f there is little evidence that the Framers intended the Warrant Clause to operate outside the home, there is no evidence at all that they intended to exclude from protection of the Clause all searches occurring outside the home. The absence of a contemporary outcry against warrantless searches in public places was because, aside from searches incident to arrest, such warrantless searches were not a large issue in colonial America. Thus, silence in the historical record tells us little about the Framers' attitude toward application of the Warrant Clause to the search of respondents' footlocker. What we do know is that the Framers were men who focused on the wrongs of that day, but who intended the Fourth Amendment to safeguard fundamental values which would far outlast the specific abuses which gave it birth."

433 U.S. at 433 U. S. 8-9 (footnote omitted).

The Court in Chadwick specifically rejected the argument that the warrantless search was "reasonable" because a footlocker has some of the mobile characteristics that support warrantless searches of automobiles. The Court recognized that "a person's expectations of privacy in personal luggage are substantially greater than in an automobile," id. at 433 U. S. 13, and noted that the practical problems associated with the temporary detention of a piece of luggage during the period of time necessary to obtain a warrant are significantly less than those associated with the detention of an automobile. Id. at 433 U. S. 13, n. 7. In ruling that the warrantless search of the footlocker was unjustified, the Court reaffirmed the general principle that closed packages and containers may not be searched without a warrant. Cf. Ex parte Jackson, 96 U. S. 727; United States v. Van Leeuwen, 397 U. S. 249. In sum, the Court in Chadwick declined to extend the rationale of the "automobile exception" to permit a warrantless search of any movable container found in a public place. [16]

The facts in Arkansas v. Sanders, 442 U. S. 753, were similar to those in Chadwick. In Sanders, a Little Rock police officer received information from a reliable informant that Sanders would arrive at the local airport on a specified flight that afternoon carrying a green suitcase containing marihuana. The officer went to the airport. Sanders arrived on schedule, and retrieved a green suitcase from the airline baggage service. Sanders gave the suitcase to a waiting companion, who placed it in the trunk of a taxi. Sanders and his companion drove off in the cab; police officers followed and stopped the taxi several blocks from the airport. The officers opened the trunk, seized the suitcase, and searched it on the scene without a warrant. As predicted, the suitcase contained marihuana.

The Arkansas Supreme Court ruled that the warrantless search of the suitcase was impermissible under the Fourth Amendment, and this Court affirmed. As in Chadwick, the mere fact that the suitcase had been placed in the trunk of the vehicle did not render the automobile exception of Carroll applicable; the police had probable cause to seize the suitcase before it was placed in the trunk of the cab, and did not have probable cause to search the taxi itself. [17] Since the suitcase had been placed in the trunk, no danger existed that its contents could have been secreted elsewhere in the vehicle. [18] As THE CHIEF JUSTICE noted in his opinion concurring in the judgment:

"Because the police officers had probable cause to believe that respondent's green suitcase contained marihuana before it was placed in the trunk of the taxicab, their duty to obtain a search warrant before opening it is clear under United States v. Chadwick, 433 U. S. 1 (1977). . . ."

". . . Here, as in Chadwick, it was the luggage being transported by respondent at the time of the arrest, not the automobile in which it was being carried, that was the suspected locus of the contraband. The relationship between the automobile and the contraband was purely coincidental, as in Chadwick. The fact that the suitcase was resting in the trunk of the automobile at the time of respondent's arrest does not turn this into an 'automobile' exception case. The Court need say no more."

442 U.S. at 442 U. S. 766-767. The Court in Sanders did not, however, rest its decision solely on the authority of Chadwick. In rejecting the State's argument that the warrantless search of the suitcase was justified on the ground that it had been taken from an automobile lawfully stopped on the street, the Court broadly suggested that a warrantless search of a container found in an automobile could never be sustained as part of a warrantless search of the automobile itself. [19] The Court did not suggest that it mattered whether probable cause existed to search the entire vehicle. It is clear, however, that in neither Chadwick nor Sanders did the police have probable cause to search the vehicle or anything within it except the footlocker in the former case and the green

suitcase in the latter.

Robbins v. California, 453 U. S. 420, however, was a case in which suspicion was not directed at a specific container. In that case, the Court for the first time was forced to consider whether police officers who are entitled to conduct a warrantless search of an automobile stopped on a public roadway may open a container found within the vehicle. In the early morning of January 5, 1975, police officers stopped Robbins' station wagon because he was driving erratically. Robbins got out of the car, but later returned to obtain the vehicle's registration papers. When he opened the car door, the officers smelled marihuana smoke. One of the officers searched Robbins and discovered a vial of liquid; in a search of the interior of the car the officer found marihuana. The police officers then opened the tailgate of the station wagon and raised the cover of a recessed luggage compartment. In the compartment, they found two packages wrapped in green opaque plastic. The police unwrapped the packages and discovered a large amount of marihuana in each.

Robbins was charged with various drug offenses, and moved to suppress the contents of the plastic packages. The California Court of Appeal held that "[s]earch of the automobile was proper when the officers learned that appellant was smoking marijuana when they stopped him," [20] and that the warrantless search of the packages was justified because

"the contents of the packages could have been inferred from their outward appearance, so that appellant could not have held a reasonable expectation of privacy with respect to the contents."

People v. Robbins, 103 Cal.App.3d 34, 40, 162 Cal.Rptr. 780, 783 (1980).

This Court reversed. Writing for a plurality, Justice Stewart rejected the argument that the outward appearance of the packages precluded Robbins from having a reasonable expectation of privacy in their contents. He also squarely rejected the argument that there is a constitutional distinction between searches of luggage and searches of "less worthy" containers. Justice Stewart reasoned that all containers are equally protected by the Fourth Amendment unless their contents are in plain view. The plurality concluded that the warrantless search was impermissible because Chadwick and Sanders had established that

"a closed piece of luggage found in a lawfully searched car is constitutionally protected to the same extent as are closed pieces of luggage found anywhere else."

453 U.S. at 453 U. S. 425.

In an opinion concurring in the judgment, JUSTICE POWELL, the author of the Court's opinion in Sanders, stated that

"[t]he plurality's approach strains the rationales of our prior cases, and imposes substantial burdens on law enforcement without vindicating any significant values of privacy."

453 U.S. at 453 U. S. 429. [21] He noted that possibly "the controlling question should be the scope of the automobile exception to the warrant requirement," id. at 453 U. S. 435, and explained that, under that view,

"when the police have probable cause to search an automobile, rather than only to search a particular container that fortuitously is located in it, the exigencies that allow the police to search the entire automobile without a warrant support the warrantless search of every container found therein. See post at 453 U. S. 451, and n. 13 (STEVENS, J., dissenting). This analysis is entirely consistent with the holdings in Chadwick and Sanders, neither of which is an 'automobile case,' because the police there had probable cause to search the double-locked footlocker and the suitcase respectively before either came near an automobile."

Ibid. The parties in Robbins had not

pressed that argument, however, and JUSTICE POWELL concluded that institutional constraints made it inappropriate to reexamine basic doctrine without full adversary presentation. He concurred in the judgment, since it was supported -- although not compelled -- by the Court's opinion in Sanders, and stated that a future case might present a better opportunity for thorough consideration of the basic principles in this troubled area.

That case has arrived. Unlike Chadwick and Sanders, in this case, police officers had probable cause to search respondent's entire vehicle. [22] Unlike Robbins, in this case, the parties have squarely addressed the question whether, in the course of a legitimate warrantless search of an automobile, police are entitled to open containers found within the vehicle. We now address that question. Its answer is determined by the scope of the search that is authorized by the exception to the warrant requirement set forth in Carroll.

IV

In Carroll itself, the whiskey that the prohibition agents seized was not in plain view. It was discovered only after an officer opened the rumble seat and tore open the upholstery of the lazyback. The Court did not find the scope of the search unreasonable. Having stopped Carroll and Kiro on a public road and subjected them to the indignity of a vehicle search -- which the Court found to be a reasonable intrusion on their privacy because it was based on probable cause that their vehicle was transporting contraband -- prohibition agents were entitled to tear open a portion of the roadster itself. The scope of the search was no greater than a magistrate could have authorized by issuing a warrant based on the probable cause that justified the search. Since such a warrant could have authorized the agents to open the rear portion of the roadster and to rip the upholstery in their search for concealed whiskey, the search was constitutionally permissible.

In Chambers v. Maroney, the police found weapons and stolen property "concealed in a compartment under the dashboard." 399 U.S. at 399 U. S. 44. No suggestion was made that the scope of the search was impermissible. It would be illogical to assume that the outcome of Chambers -- or the outcome of Carroll itself -- would have been different if the police had found the secreted contraband enclosed within a secondary container and had opened that container without a warrant. If it was reasonable for prohibition agents to rip open the upholstery in Carroll, it certainly would have been reasonable for them to look into a burlap sack stashed inside; if it was reasonable to open the concealed compartment in Chambers, it would have been equally reasonable to open a paper bag crumpled within it. A contrary rule could produce absurd results inconsistent with the decision in Carroll itself.

In its application of Carroll, this Court, in fact, has sustained warrantless searches of containers found during a lawful search of an automobile. In Husty v. United States, 282 U. S. 694, the Court upheld a warrantless seizure of whiskey found during a search of an automobile, some of which was discovered in "whiskey bags" that could have contained other goods. [23] In Scher v. United States, 305 U. S. 251, federal officers seized and searched packages of unstamped liquor found in the trunk of an automobile searched without a warrant. As described by a police officer who participated in the search:

"I turned the handle and opened the trunk, and found the trunk completely filled with packages wrapped in brown paper and tied with twine; I think somewhere around thirty packages, each one containing six bottles. [24]"

In these cases, it was not contended that police officers needed a warrant to open the whiskey bags or to unwrap the brown paper packages. These decisions nevertheless "have much weight, as they show that this point neither occurred to the bar or the bench." Bank of the United States v. Deveaux, 5 Cranch 61, 88 (Marshall, C.J.). The fact that no such argument was even made illuminates the profession's understanding of the scope of the search permitted under Carroll. Indeed, prior to the decisions in Chadwick and Sanders, courts routinely had held that containers and packages found during a legitimate warrantless search of an automobile also could be searched without a warrant. [25]

As we have stated, the decision in Carroll was based on the Court's appraisal of practical considerations viewed in the perspective of history. It is therefore significant that the practical consequences of the Carroll decision would be largely nullified if the permissible scope of a warrantless search of an automobile did not include containers and packages found inside the vehicle. Contraband goods rarely are strewn across the trunk or floor of a car; since, by their very nature, such goods must be withheld from public view, they rarely can be placed in an automobile unless they are enclosed within some form of container. [26] The Court in Carroll held that "contraband goods concealed and illegally transported in an automobile or other vehicle may be searched for without a warrant." 267 U.S. at 267 U. S. 153 (emphasis added). As we noted in Henry v. United States, 361 U. S. 98, 361 U. S. 104, the decision in Carroll "merely relaxed the requirements for a warrant on grounds of practicability." It neither broadened nor limited the scope of a lawful search based on probable cause.

A lawful search of fixed premises generally extends to the entire area in which the object of the search may be found, and is not limited by the possibility that separate acts of entry or opening may be required to complete the search. [27] Thus, a warrant that authorizes an officer to search a home for illegal weapons also provides authority to open closets, chests, drawers, and containers in which the weapon might be found. A warrant to open a footlocker to search for marihuana would also authorize the opening of packages found inside. A warrant to search a vehicle would support a search of every part of the vehicle that might contain the object of the search. When a legitimate search is under way, and when its purpose and its limits have been precisely defined, nice distinctions between closets, drawers, and containers, in the case of a home, or between glove compartments, upholstered seats, trunks, and wrapped packages, in the case of a vehicle, must give way to the interest in the prompt and efficient completion of the task at hand. [28]

This rule applies equally to all containers, as indeed we believe it must. One point on which the Court was in virtually unanimous agreement in Robbins was that a constitutional distinction between "worthy" and "unworthy" containers would be improper. [29] Even though such a distinction perhaps could evolve in a series of cases in which paper bags, locked trunks, lunch buckets, and orange crates were placed on one side of the line or the other, [30] the central purpose of the Fourth Amendment forecloses such a distinction. For just as the most frail cottage in the kingdom is absolutely entitled to the same guarantees of privacy as the most majestic mansion, [31] so also may a traveler who carries a toothbrush and a few articles of clothing in a paper bag or knotted scarf claim an equal right to conceal his possessions from official inspection as the sophisticated executive with the locked attache case.

As Justice Stewart stated in Robbins, the Fourth Amendment provides protection to the owner of every container that conceals its contents from plain view. 453 U.S. at 453 U. S. 427 (plurality opinion). But the protection afforded by the Amendment varies in different settings. The luggage carried by a traveler entering the country may be searched at random by a customs officer;

the luggage may be searched no matter how great the traveler's desire to conceal the contents may be. A container carried at the time of arrest often may be searched without a warrant and even without any specific suspicion concerning its contents. A container that may conceal the object of a search authorized by a warrant may be opened immediately; the individual's interest in privacy must give way to the magistrate's official determination of probable cause.

In the same manner, an individual's expectation of privacy in a vehicle and its contents may not survive if probable cause is given to believe that the vehicle is transporting contraband. Certainly the privacy interests in a car's trunk or glove compartment may be no less than those in a movable container. An individual undoubtedly has a significant interest that the upholstery of his automobile will not be ripped or a hidden compartment within it opened. These interests must yield to the authority of a search, however, which -- in light of Carroll -- does not itself require the prior approval of a magistrate. The scope of a warrantless search based on probable cause is no narrower -- and no broader -- than the scope of a search authorized by a warrant supported by probable cause. Only the prior approval of the magistrate is waived; the search otherwise is as the magistrate could authorize. [32]

The scope of a warrantless search of an automobile thus is not defined by the nature of the container in which the contraband is secreted. Rather, it is defined by the object of the search and the places in which there is probable cause to believe that it may be found. Just as probable cause to believe that a stolen lawnmower may be found in a garage will not support a warrant to search an upstairs bedroom, probable cause to believe that undocumented aliens are being transported in a van will not justify a warrantless search of a suitcase. Probable cause to believe that a container placed in the trunk of a taxi contains contraband or evidence does not justify a search of the entire cab.

V

Our decision today is inconsistent with the disposition in Robbins v. California and with the portion of the opinion in Arkansas v. Sanders on which the plurality in Robbins relied. Nevertheless, the doctrine of stare decisis does not preclude this action. Although we have rejected some of the reasoning in Sanders, we adhere to our holding in that case; although we reject the precise holding in Robbins, there was no Court opinion supporting a single rationale for its judgment, and the reasoning we adopt today was not presented by the parties in that case. Moreover, it is clear that no legitimate reliance interest can be frustrated by our decision today. [33] Of greatest importance, we are convinced that the rule we apply in this case is faithful to the interpretation of the Fourth Amendment that the Court has followed with substantial consistency throughout our history.

We reaffirm the basic rule of Fourth Amendment jurisprudence stated by Justice Stewart for a unanimous Court in Mincey v. Arizona, 437 U. S. 385, 437 U. S. 390:

"The Fourth Amendment proscribes all unreasonable searches and seizures, and it is a cardinal principle that"

"searches conducted outside the judicial process, without prior approval by judge or magistrate, are per se unreasonable under the Fourth Amendment -- subject only to a few specifically established and well-delineated exceptions."

"Katz v. United States, 389 U. S. 347, 389 U. S. 357 (footnotes omitted)."

The exception recognized in Carroll is unquestionably one that is "specifically established and well delineated." We hold that the scope of the warrantless search authorized by that exception is no broader and no narrower than a magistrate could legitimately authorize by warrant. If probable cause justifies the search of a lawfully stopped vehicle, it justifies the search of every part of the vehicle and its contents that may conceal the object of the search.

The judgment of the Court of Appeals is reversed. The case is remanded for further proceedings consistent with this opinion.

It is so ordered.

US v. Knotts (March 2, 1983)

JUSTICE REHNQUIST delivered the opinion of the Court.

A beeper is a radio transmitter, usually battery operated, which emits periodic signals that can be picked up by a radio receiver. In this case, a beeper was placed in a five-gallon drum containing chloroform purchased by one of respondent's codefendants. By monitoring the progress of a car carrying the chloroform, Minnesota law enforcement agents were able to trace the can of chloroform from its place of purchase in Minneapolis, Minn., to respondent's secluded cabin near Shell Lake, Wis. The issue presented by the case is whether such use of a beeper violated respondent's rights secured by the Fourth Amendment to the United States Constitution.

I

Respondent and two codefendants were charged in the United States District Court for the District of Minnesota with conspiracy to manufacture controlled substances, including but not limited to methamphetamine, in violation of 21 U.S.C. § 846. One of the codefendants, Darryl Petschen, was tried jointly with respondent; the other codefendant, Tristan Armstrong, pleaded guilty and testified for the Government at trial.

Suspicion attached to this trio when the 3M Co., which manufactures chemicals in St. Paul, notified a narcotics investigator for the Minnesota Bureau of Criminal Apprehension that Armstrong, a former 3M employee, had been stealing chemicals which could be used in manufacturing illicit drugs. Visual surveillance of Armstrong revealed that, after leaving the employ of 3M Co., he had been purchasing similar chemicals from the Hawkins Chemical Co. in Minneapolis. The Minnesota narcotics officers observed that, after Armstrong had made a purchase, he would deliver the chemicals to codefendant Petschen.

With the consent of the Hawkins Chemical Co., officers installed a beeper inside a five-gallon container of chloroform, one of the so-called "precursor" chemicals used to manufacture illicit drugs. Hawkins agreed that, when Armstrong next purchased chloroform, the chloroform would be placed in this particular container. When Armstrong made the purchase, officers followed the car in which the chloroform had been placed, maintaining contact by using both visual surveillance and a monitor which received the signals sent from the beeper.

Armstrong proceeded to Petschen's house, where the container was transferred to Petschen's automobile. Officers then followed that vehicle eastward towards the state line, across the St. Croix River, and into Wisconsin. During the latter part of this journey, Petschen began making evasive maneuvers, and the pursuing agents ended their visual surveillance. At about the same time, officers lost the signal from the beeper, but with the assistance of a monitoring device located in a helicopter the approximate location of the signal was picked up again about one hour later. The signal now was stationary, and the location identified was a cabin occupied by respondent near Shell Lake, Wis. The record before us does not reveal that the beeper was used after the location in the area of the cabin had been initially determined. Relying on the location of the chloroform derived through the use of the beeper and additional information obtained during three days of intermittent visual surveillance of respondent's cabin, officers secured a search warrant. During execution of the warrant, officers discovered a fully operable, clandestine drug laboratory in the cabin. In the laboratory area, officers found formulas for amphetamine and methamphetamine, over $10,000 worth of laboratory equipment, and chemicals in quantities sufficient to produce 14 pounds of pure amphetamine. Under a barrel outside the cabin, officers located the five-gallon container of chloroform.

After his motion to suppress evidence based on the warrantless monitoring of the beeper was denied, respondent was convicted for conspiring to manufacture controlled substances in violation of 21 U.S.C. § 846. He was sentenced to five years' imprisonment. A divided panel of the United States Court of Appeals for the Eighth Circuit reversed the conviction, finding that the monitoring of the beeper was prohibited by the Fourth Amendment because its use had violated respondent's reasonable expectation of privacy, and that all information derived after the location of the cabin was a fruit of the illegal beeper monitoring. * 662 F.2d 515 (1981). We granted certiorari, 457 U.S. 1131 (1982), and we now reverse the judgment of the Court of Appeals.

II

In Olmstead v. United States, 277 U. S. 438 (1928), this Court held that the wiretapping of a defendant's private telephone line did not violate the Fourth Amendment because the wiretapping had been effectuated without a physical trespass by the Government. Justice Brandeis, joined by Justice Stone, dissented from that decision, believing that the actions of the Government in that case constituted an "unjustifiable intrusion . . . upon the privacy of the individual," and therefore a violation of the Fourth Amendment. Id. at 277 U. S. 478. Nearly 40 years later, in Katz v. United States, 389 U. S. 347 (1967), the Court overruled Olmstead, saying that the Fourth Amendment's reach "cannot turn upon the presence or absence of a physical intrusion into any given enclosure." 389 U.S. at 389 U. S. 353. The Court said:

"The Government's activities in electronically listening to and recording the petitioner's words violated the privacy upon which he justifiably relied while using the telephone booth, and thus constituted a 'search and seizure' within the meaning of the Fourth Amendment. The fact that the electronic device employed to achieve that end did not happen to penetrate the wall of the booth can have no constitutional significance."

Ibid.

In Smith v. Maryland, 442 U. S. 735 (1979), we elaborated on the principles stated in Katz:

"Consistently with Katz, this Court uniformly has held that the application of the Fourth Amendment depends on whether the person invoking its protection can claim a "justifiable," a "reasonable," or a "legitimate expectation of privacy" that has been invaded by government action. [Citations omitted.] This inquiry, as Mr. Justice Harlan aptly noted in his Katz concurrence, normally embraces two discrete questions. The first is whether the individual, by his conduct, has "exhibited an actual (subjective) expectation of privacy," 389 U.S. at 389 U. S. 361 -- whether, in the words of the Katz majority, the individual has shown that "he seeks to preserve [something] as private." Id. at 389 U. S. 351. The second question is whether the individual's subjective expectation of privacy is "one that society is prepared to recognize as reasonable,'" id. at 389 U. S. 361 -- whether, in the words of the Katz majority, the individual's expectation, viewed objectively, is "justifiable" under the circumstances. Id. at 389 U. S. 353. See Rakas v. Illinois, 439 U.S. at 439 U. S. 143-144, n. 12; id. at 439 U. S. 151 (concurring opinion); United States v. White, 401 U.S. at 401 U. S. 752 (plurality opinion)."

442 U.S. at 442 U. S. 740-741 (footnote

omitted).

The governmental surveillance conducted by means of the beeper in this case amounted principally to the following of an automobile on public streets and highways. We have commented more than once on the diminished expectation of privacy in an automobile:

"One has a lesser expectation of privacy in a motor vehicle because its function is transportation, and it seldom serves as one's residence or as the repository of personal effects. A car has little capacity for escaping public scrutiny. It travels public thoroughfares where both its occupants and its contents are in plain view."

Cardwell v. Lewis, 417 U. S. 583, 417 U. S. 590 (1974) (plurality opinion). See also Rakas v. Illinois, 439 U. S. 128, 439 U. S. 153-154, and n. 2 (1978) (POWELL, J., concurring); South Dakota v. Opperman, 428 U. S. 364, 428 U. S. 368 (1976).

A person traveling in an automobile on public thoroughfares has no reasonable expectation of privacy in his movements from one place to another. When Petschen traveled over the public streets, he voluntarily conveyed to anyone who wanted to look the fact that he was traveling over particular roads in a particular direction, the fact of whatever stops he made, and the fact of his final destination when he exited from public roads onto private property.

Respondent Knotts, as the owner of the cabin and surrounding premises to which Petschen drove, undoubtedly had the traditional expectation of privacy within a dwelling place insofar as the cabin was concerned:

"Crime, even in the privacy of one's own quarters, is, of course, of grave concern to society, and the law allows such crime to be reached on proper showing. The right of officers to thrust themselves into a home is also of grave concern, not only to the individual, but to a society which chooses to dwell in reasonable security and freedom from surveillance. When the right of

privacy must reasonably yield to the right of search is, as a rule, to be decided by a judicial officer, not by a policeman or government enforcement agent."

Johnson v. United States, 333 U. S. 10, 333 U. S. 14 (1948), quoted with approval in Payton v. New York, 445 U. S. 573, 445 U. S. 586 (1980).

But no such expectation of privacy extended to the visual observation of Petschen's automobile arriving on his premises after leaving a public highway, nor to movements of objects such as the drum of chloroform outside the cabin in the "open fields." Hester v. United States, 265 U. S. 57 (1924).

Visual surveillance from public places along Petschen's route or adjoining Knotts' premises would have sufficed to reveal all of these facts to the police. The fact that the officers in this case relied not only on visual surveillance, but also on the use of the beeper to signal the presence of Petschen's automobile to the police receiver, does not alter the situation. Nothing in the Fourth Amendment prohibited the police from augmenting the sensory faculties bestowed upon them at birth with such enhancement as science and technology afforded them in this case. In United States v. Lee, 274 U. S. 559 (1927), the Court said:

"But no search on the high seas is shown. The testimony of the boatswain shows that he used a searchlight. It is not shown that there was any exploration below decks or under hatches. For aught that appears, the cases of liquor were on deck and, like the defendants, were discovered before the motor boat was boarded. Such use of a searchlight is comparable to the use of a marine glass or a field glass. It is not prohibited by the Constitution."

Id. at 563.

We have recently had occasion to deal with another claim which was to some extent a factual counterpart of respondent's assertions here. In Smith v. Maryland, we said:

"This analysis dictates that [Smith] can claim no legitimate expectation of privacy here. When he used his phone, [Smith] voluntarily conveyed numerical information to the telephone company and 'exposed' that information to its equipment in the ordinary course of business. In so doing, [Smith] assumed the risk that the company would reveal to police the numbers he dialed. The switching equipment that processed those numbers is merely the modern counterpart of the operator who, in an earlier day, personally completed calls for the subscriber. [Smith] concedes that, if he had placed his calls through an operator, he could claim no legitimate expectation of privacy. [Citation omitted.] We are not inclined to hold that a different constitutional result is required because the telephone company has decided to automate."

442 U.S. at 442 U. S. 744-745.

Respondent does not actually quarrel with this analysis, though he expresses the generalized view that the result of the holding sought by the Government would be that "twenty-four hour surveillance of any citizen of this country will be possible, without judicial knowledge or supervision." Brief for Respondent 9 (footnote omitted). But the fact is that the "reality hardly suggests abuse," Zurcher v. Stanford Daily, 436 U. S. 547, 436 U. S. 566 (1978); if such dragnet-type law enforcement practices as respondent envisions should eventually occur, there will be time enough then to determine whether different constitutional principles may be applicable. Ibid. Insofar as respondent's complaint appears to be simply that scientific devices such as the beeper enabled the police to be more effective in detecting crime, it simply has no constitutional foundation. We have never equated police efficiency with unconstitutionality, and we decline to do so now.

Respondent specifically attacks the use of the beeper insofar as it was used to determine that the can of chloroform had come to rest on his property at Shell Lake, Wis. He repeatedly challenges the "use of the beeper to determine the location of the chemical drum at Respondent's premises," Brief for Respondent 26; he states that

"[t]he government thus overlooks the fact that this case involves the sanctity of Respondent's residence, which is accorded the greatest protection available under the Fourth Amendment."

Ibid. The Court of Appeals appears to have rested its decision on this ground:

"As noted above, a principal rationale for allowing warrantless tracking of beepers, particularly beepers in or on an auto, is that beepers are merely a more effective means of observing what is already public. But people pass daily from public to private spheres. When police agents track bugged personal property without first obtaining a warrant, they must do so at the risk that this enhanced surveillance, intrusive at best, might push fortuitously and unreasonably into the private sphere protected by the Fourth Amendment."

662 F.2d at 518.

We think that respondent's contentions, and the above-quoted language from the opinion of the Court of Appeals, to some extent lose sight of the limited use which the government made of the signals from this particular beeper. As we have noted, nothing in this record indicates that the beeper signal was received or relied upon after it had indicated that the drum containing the chloroform had ended its automotive journey at rest on respondent's premises in rural Wisconsin. Admittedly, because of the failure of the visual surveillance, the beeper enabled the law enforcement officials in this case to ascertain the ultimate resting place of the chloroform when they would not have been able to do so had they relied solely on their naked eyes. But scientific enhancement of this sort raises no constitutional issues which visual surveillance would not also raise. A police car following Petschen at a distance throughout his journey could have observed him leaving the public highway and arriving at the cabin owned by respondent, with the drum of chloroform still in the car. This fact, along with others, was used by the government in obtaining a search warrant which led to the discovery of the clandestine drug laboratory. But there is no indication that the beeper was used in any way to reveal information as to the movement of the drum within the cabin, or in any way that would not have been visible to the naked eye from outside the cabin. Just as notions of physical trespass based on the law of real property were not dispositive in Katz v. United States, 389 U. S. 347 (1967), neither were they dispositive in Hester v. United States, 265 U. S. 57 (1924).

We thus return to the question posed at the beginning of our inquiry in discussing Katz, supra; did monitoring the beeper signals complained of by respondent invade any legitimate expectation of privacy on his part? For the reasons previously stated, we hold it did not. Since it did not, there was neither a "search" nor a "seizure" within the contemplation of the Fourth Amendment. The judgment of the Court of Appeals is therefore

Reversed.

* Respondent does not challenge the warrantless installation of the beeper in the chloroform container, suggesting in oral argument that he did not believe he had standing to make such a challenge. We note that, while several Courts of Appeals have approved warrantless installations, see United States v. Bernard, 625 F.2d 854 (CA9 1980); United States v. Lewis, 621 F.2d 1382 (CA5 1980), cert. denied, 450 U.S. 935 (1981); United States v. Bruneau, 594 F.2d 1190 (CA8), cert. denied, 444 U.S. 847 (1979); United States v. Miroyan, 577 F.2d 489 (CA9), cert. denied, 439 U.S. 896 (1978); United States v. Cheshire, 569 F.2d 887 (CA5), cert. denied, 437 U.S. 907 (1978); United States v. Curtis, 562 F.2d 1153 (CA9 1977), cert. denied, 439 U.S. 910 (1978); United States v. Ael, 548 F.2d 591 (CA5), cert. denied, 431 U.S. 956 (1977); United States v. Hufford, 539 F.2d 32 (CA9), cert. denied, 429 U.S. 1002 (1976), we have not before, and do not now, pass on the issue.

Florida v. Royer (March 23, 1983)

JUSTICE WHITE announced the judgment of the Court and delivered an opinion, in which JUSTICE MARSHALL, JUSTICE POWELL, and JUSTICE STEVENS joined.

We are required in this case to determine whether the Court of Appeal of Florida, Third District, properly applied the precepts of the Fourth Amendment in holding that respondent Royer was being illegally detained at the time of his purported consent to a search of his luggage.

I

On January 3, 1978, Royer was observed at Miami International Airport by two plainclothes detectives of the Dade County, Fla., Public Safety Department assigned to the county's Organized Crime Bureau, Narcotics Investigation Section. [1] Detectives Johnson and Magdalena believed that Royer's appearance, mannerisms, luggage, and actions fit the so-called "drug courier profile." [2] Royer, apparently unaware of the attention he had attracted, purchased a one-way ticket to New York City and checked his two suitcases, placing on each suitcase an identification tag bearing the name "Holt" and the destination "La Guardia." As Royer made his way to the concourse which led to the airline boarding area, the two detectives approached him, identified themselves as policemen working out of the sheriff's office, and asked if Royer had a "moment" to speak with them; Royer said "Yes."

Upon request, but without oral consent, Royer produced for the detectives his airline ticket and his driver's license. The airline ticket, like the baggage identification tags, bore the name "Holt," while the driver's license carried respondent's correct name, "Royer." When the detectives asked about the discrepancy, Royer explained that a friend had made the reservation in the name of "Holt." Royer became noticeably more nervous during this conversation, whereupon the detectives informed Royer that they were in fact narcotics investigators, and that they had reason to suspect him of transporting narcotics.

The detectives did not return his airline ticket and identification, but asked Royer to accompany them to a room, approximately 40 feet away, adjacent to the concourse. Royer said nothing in response, but went with the officers as he had been asked to do. The room was later described by Detective Johnson as a "large storage closet," located in the stewardesses' lounge and containing a small desk and two chairs. Without Royer's consent or agreement, Detective Johnson, using Royer's baggage check stubs, retrieved the "Holt" luggage from the airline and brought it to the room where respondent and Detective Magdalena were waiting. Royer was asked if he would consent to a search of the suitcases. Without orally responding to this request, Royer produced a key and unlocked one of the suitcases, which one detective then opened without seeking further assent from Royer. Marihuana was found in that suitcase. According to Detective Johnson, Royer stated that he did not know the combination to the lock on the second suitcase. When asked if he objected to the detective opening the second suitcase, Royer said "[n]o, go ahead," and did not object when the detective explained that the suitcase might have to be broken open. The suitcase was pried open by the officers, and more marihuana was found. Royer was then told that he was under arrest. Approximately 15 minutes had elapsed from the time the detectives initially approached respondent until his arrest upon the discovery of the contraband.

Prior to his trial for felony possession of marihuana, [3] Royer made a motion to suppress the evidence obtained in the search of the suitcases. The trial court found that Royer's consent to the search was "freely and voluntarily given," and that, regardless of the consent, the warrantless search was reasonable, because "the officer doesn't have the time to run out and get a search warrant because the plane is going to take off." [4] Following the denial of the motion to suppress, Royer changed his plea from "not guilty" to "nolo contendere," specifically reserving the right to appeal the denial of the motion to suppress. [5] Royer was convicted.

The District Court of Appeal, sitting en banc, reversed Royer's conviction. [6] The court held that Royer had been involuntarily confined within the small room without probable cause; that the involuntary detention had exceeded the limited restraint permitted by Terry v. Ohio, 392 U. S. 1 (1968), at the time his consent to the search was obtained; and that the consent to search was therefore invalid because tainted by the unlawful confinement. [7]

Several factors led the court to conclude that respondent's confinement was tantamount to arrest. Royer had

"found himself in a small enclosed area being confronted by two police officers -- a situation which presents an almost classic definition of imprisonment."

389 So.2d 1007, 1018 (1980). The detectives' statement to Royer that he was suspected of transporting narcotics also bolstered the finding that Royer was "in custody" at the time the consent to search was given. Ibid. In addition, the detectives' possession of Royer's airline ticket and their retrieval and possession of his luggage made it clear, in the District Court of Appeal's view, that Royer was not free to leave. Ibid.

At the suppression hearing, Royer testified

that he was under the impression that he was not free to leave the officers' presence. The Florida District Court of Appeal found that this apprehension "was much more than a well-justified subjective belief," for the State had conceded at oral argument before that court that "the officers would not have permitted Royer to leave the room even if he had erroneously thought he could." Ibid. The nomenclature used to describe Royer's confinement, the court found, was unimportant, because, under Dunaway v. New York, 442 U. S. 200 (1979), "a police confinement which . . . goes beyond the limited restraint of a Terry investigatory stop may be constitutionally justified only by probable cause." 389 So.2d at 1019 (footnote omitted). Detective Johnson, who conducted the search, had specifically stated at the suppression hearing that he did not have probable cause to arrest Royer until the suitcases were opened and their contents revealed.

Ibid. In the absence of probable cause, the court concluded, Royer's consent to search, given only after he had been unlawfully confined, was ineffective to justify the search. Ibid. Because there was no proof at all that a "break in the chain of illegality" had occurred, the court found that Royer's consent was invalid as a matter of law. Id. at 1020. We granted the State's petition for certiorari, 454 U.S. 1079 (1981), and now affirm.

II

Some preliminary observations are in order. First, it is unquestioned that, without a warrant to search Royer's luggage and in the absence of probable cause and exigent circumstances, the validity of the search depended on Royer's purported consent. Neither is it disputed that, where the validity of a search rests on consent, the State has the burden of proving that the necessary consent was obtained and that it was freely and voluntarily given, a burden that is not satisfied by showing a mere submission to a claim of lawful authority. Lo-Ji Sales, Inc. v. New York, 442 U. S. 319, 442 U. S. 329 (1979); Schneckloth v. Bustamonte, 412 U. S. 218, 412 U. S. 233-234 (1973); Bumper v. North Carolina, 391 U. S. 543, 391 U. S. 548-549 (1968); Johnson v. United States, 333 U. S. 10, 333 U. S. 13 (1948); Amos v. United States, 255 U. S. 313, 255 U. S. 317 (1921).

Second, law enforcement officers do not violate the Fourth Amendment by merely approaching an individual on the street or in another public place, by asking him if he is willing to answer some questions, by putting questions to him if the person is willing to listen, or by offering in evidence in a criminal prosecution his voluntary answers to such questions. See Dunaway v. New York, supra, at 442 U. S. 210, n. 12; Terry v. Ohio, 392 U.S. at 392 U. S. 31, 392 U. S. 32-33 (Harlan, J., concurring); id. at 392 U. S. 34 (WHITE, J., concurring). Nor would the fact that the officer identifies himself as a police officer, without more, convert the encounter into a seizure requiring some level of objective justification. United States v. Mendenhall, 446 U. S. 544, 446 U. S. 555 (1980) (opinion of Stewart, J.). The person approached, however, need not answer any question put to him; indeed, he may decline to listen to the questions at all, and may go on his way. Terry v. Ohio, 392 U.S. at 392 U. S. 32-33 (Harlan, J., concurring); id. at 392 U. S. 34 (WHITE, J., concurring). He may not be detained even momentarily without reasonable, objective grounds for doing so; and his refusal to listen or answer does not, without more, furnish those grounds. United States v. Mendenhall, supra, at 446 U. S. 556 (opinion of Stewart, J.). If there is no detention -- no seizure within the meaning of the Fourth Amendment -- then no constitutional rights have been infringed.

Third, it is also clear that not all seizures of the person must be justified by probable cause to arrest for a crime. Prior to Terry v. Ohio, supra, any restraint on the person amounting to a seizure for the purposes of the Fourth Amendment was invalid unless justified by probable cause. Dunaway v. New York, supra, at 442 U. S. 207-209. Terry created a limited exception to this general rule: certain seizures are justifiable under the Fourth Amendment if there is articulable suspicion that a person has committed or is about to commit a crime. In that case, a stop and a frisk for weapons were found unexceptionable. Adams v. Williams, 407 U. S. 143 (1972), applied the same approach in the context of an informant's report that an unnamed individual in a nearby vehicle was carrying narcotics and a gun. Although not expressly authorized in Terry, United States v. Brignoni-Ponce, 422 U. S. 873, 422 U. S. 881-882 (1975), was unequivocal in saying that reasonable suspicion of criminal activity warrants a temporary seizure for the purpose of questioning limited to the purpose of the stop. In Brignoni-Ponce, that purpose was to verify or dispel the suspicion that the immigration laws were being violated, a governmental interest that was sufficient to warrant temporary detention for limited questioning. Royer does not suggest, nor do we, that a similar rationale would not warrant temporary detention for questioning on less than probable cause where the public interest involved is the suppression of illegal transactions in drugs or of any other serious crime.

Michigan v. Summers, 452 U. S. 692 (1981), involved another circumstance in which a temporary detention on less than probable cause satisfied the ultimate test of reasonableness under the Fourth Amendment. There the occupant of a house was detained while a search warrant for the house was being executed. We held that the warrant made the occupant sufficiently suspect to justify his temporary seizure. The "limited intrusio[n] on the personal security" of the person detained was justified "by such substantial law enforcement interests" that the seizure could be made on articulable suspicion not amounting to probable cause. Id. at 452 U. S. 699.

Fourth, Terry and its progeny nevertheless created only limited exceptions to the general rule that seizures of the person require probable cause to arrest. Detentions may be "investigative," yet violative of the Fourth Amendment absent probable cause. In the name of investigating a person who is no more than suspected of criminal activity, the police may not carry out a full search of the person or of his automobile or other effects. Nor may the police seek to verify their suspicions by means that approach the conditions of arrest. Dunaway v. New York, supra, made this clear. There, the suspect was taken to the police station from his home and, without being formally arrested, interrogated for an hour. The resulting incriminating statements were held inadmissible: reasonable suspicion of crime is insufficient to justify custodial interrogation, even though the interrogation is investigative. Id. at 442 U. S. 211-212. Brown v. Illinois, 422 U. S. 590 (1975), and Davis v. Mississippi, 394 U. S. 721 (1969), are to the same effect.

The Fourth Amendment's prohibition against unreasonable searches and seizures has always been interpreted to prevent a search that is not limited to the particularly described "place to be searched, and the persons or things to be seized," U.S.Const., Amdt. 4, even if the search is made pursuant to a warrant and based upon probable cause. The Amendment's protection is not diluted in those situations where it has been determined that legitimate law enforcement interests justify a warrantless search: the search must be limited in scope to that which is justified by the particular purposes served by the exception. For example, a warrantless search is permissible incident to a lawful arrest because of legitimate concerns for the safety of the officer and to prevent the destruction of evidence by the arrestee. E.g., Chimel v. California, 395 U. S. 752, 395 U. S. 763 (1969). Nevertheless, such a search is limited to the person of the arrestee and the area immediately within his control. Id. at 395 U. S. 762. Terry v. Ohio, supra, also embodies this principle: "The scope of the search must be strictly tied to and justified by' the circumstances which rendered its initiation permissible." 392 U.S. at 392 U. S. 19, quoting Warden v. Hayden, 387 U. S. 294, 387 U. S. 310 (1967) (Fortas, J., concurring). The reasonableness requirement of the Fourth Amendment requires no less when the police action is a seizure permitted on less than probable cause because of legitimate law enforcement interests. The scope of the detention must be carefully tailored to its underlying justification.

The predicate permitting seizures on suspicion short of probable cause is that law enforcement interests warrant a limited intrusion on the personal security of the suspect. The scope of the intrusion permitted will vary to some extent with the particular facts and circumstances of each case. This much, however, is clear: an investigative detention must be temporary, and last no longer than is necessary to effectuate the purpose of the stop. Similarly, the investigative methods employed should be the least intrusive means reasonably available to verify or dispel the officer's suspicion in a short period of time. See, e.g., United States v. Brignoni-Ponce, supra, at 422 U. S. 881-882; Adams v. Williams, supra, at 407 U. S. 146. It is the State's burden to demonstrate that the seizure it seeks to justify on the basis of a reasonable suspicion was sufficiently limited in scope and duration to satisfy the conditions of an investigative seizure.

Fifth, Dunaway and Brown hold that statements given during a period of illegal detention are inadmissible, even though voluntarily given, if they are the product of the illegal detention and not the result of an independent act of free will. Dunaway v. New York, 442 U.S. at 442 U. S. 218-219; Brown v. Illinois, supra, at 422 U. S. 601-602. In this respect, those cases reiterated one of the principal holdings of Wong Sun v. United States, 371 U. S. 471 (1963).

Sixth, if the events in this case amounted to no more than a permissible police encounter in a public place or a justifiable Terry-type detention, Royer's consent, if voluntary, would have been effective to legalize the search of his two suitcases. Cf. United States v. Watson, 423 U. S. 411, 423 U. S. 424-425 (1976). The Florida District Court of Appeal in the case before us, however, concluded not only that Royer had been seized when he gave his consent to search his luggage, but also that the bounds of an investigative stop had been exceeded. In its view, the "confinement" in this case went beyond the limited restraint of a Terry investigative stop, and Royer's consent was thus tainted by the illegality, a conclusion that required reversal in the absence of probable cause to arrest. The question before us is whether the record warrants that conclusion. We think that it does.

III

The State proffers three reasons for holding that, when Royer consented to the search of his luggage, he was not being illegally detained. First, it is submitted that the entire encounter was consensual, and hence Royer was not being held against his will at all. We find this submission untenable. Asking for and examining Royer's ticket and his driver's license were, no doubt, permissible in themselves, but when the officers identified themselves as narcotics agents, told Royer that he was suspected of transporting narcotics, and asked him to accompany them to the police room, while retaining his ticket and driver's license and without indicating in any way that he was free to depart, Royer was effectively seized for the purposes of the Fourth Amendment.

These circumstances surely amount to a show of official authority such that "a reasonable person would have believed that he was not free to leave." United States v. Mendenhall, 446 U.S. at 446 U. S. 554 (opinion of Stewart, J.) (footnote omitted).

Second, the State submits that, if Royer was seized, there existed reasonable, articulable suspicion to justify a temporary detention, and that the limits of a Terry-type stop were never exceeded. We agree with the State that, when the officers discovered that Royer was traveling under an assumed name, this fact, and the facts already known to the officers -- paying cash for a one-way ticket, the mode of checking the two bags, and Royer's appearance and conduct in general -- were adequate grounds for suspecting Royer of carrying drugs and for temporarily detaining him and his luggage while they attempted to verify or dispel their suspicions in a manner that did not exceed the limits of an investigative detention. We also agree that, had Royer voluntarily consented to the search of his luggage while he was justifiably being detained on reasonable suspicion, the products of the search would be admissible against him. We have concluded, however, that, at the time Royer produced the key to his suitcase, the detention to which he was then subjected was a more serious intrusion on his personal liberty than is allowable on mere suspicion of criminal activity.

By the time Royer was informed that the officers wished to examine his luggage, he had identified himself when approached by the officers and had attempted to explain the discrepancy between the name shown on his identification and the name under which he had purchased his ticket and identified his luggage. The officers were not satisfied, for they informed him they were narcotics agents and had reason to believe that he was carrying illegal drugs. They requested him to accompany them to the police room. Royer went with them. He found himself in a small room -- a large closet equipped with a desk and two chairs. He was alone with two police officers who again told him that they thought he was carrying narcotics. He also found that the officers, without his consent, had retrieved his checked luggage from the airline. What had begun as a consensual inquiry in a public place had escalated into an investigatory procedure in a police interrogation room, where the police, unsatisfied with previous explanations, sought to confirm their suspicions. The officers had Royer's ticket, they had his identification, and they had seized his luggage. Royer was never informed that he was free to board his plane if he so chose, and he reasonably believed that he was being detained. At least as of that moment, any consensual aspects of the encounter had evaporated, and we cannot fault the Florida District Court of Appeal for concluding that Terry v. Ohio and the cases following it did not justify the restraint to which Royer was then subjected. As a practical matter, Royer was under arrest. Consistent with this conclusion, the State conceded in the Florida courts that Royer would not have been free to leave the interrogation room had he asked to do so. [8] Furthermore, the State's brief in this Court interprets the testimony of the officers at the suppression hearing as indicating that, had Royer refused to consent to a search of his luggage, the officers would have held the luggage and sought a warrant to authorize the search. Brief for Petitioner 6. [9]

We also think that the officers' conduct was more intrusive than necessary to effectuate an investigative detention otherwise authorized by the Terry line of cases. First, by returning his ticket and driver's license, and informing him that he was free to go if he so desired, the officers might have obviated any claim that the encounter was anything but a consensual matter from start to finish. Second, there are undoubtedly reasons of safety and security that would justify moving a suspect from one location to another during an investigatory detention, such as from an airport concourse to a more private area. Cf. Pennsylvania v. Mimms, 434 U. S. 106, 434 U. S. 109-111 (1977) (per curiam). There is no indication in this case that such reasons prompted the officers to transfer the site of the encounter from the concourse to the interrogation room. It appears, rather, that the primary interest of the officers was not in having an extended conversation with Royer, but in the contents of his luggage, a matter which the officers did not pursue orally with Royer until after the encounter was relocated to the police room. The record does not reflect any facts which would support a finding that the legitimate law enforcement purposes which justified the detention in the first instance were furthered by removing Royer to the police room prior to the officers' attempt to gain his consent to a search of his luggage. As we have noted, had Royer consented to a search on the spot, the search could have been conducted with Royer present in the area where the bags were retrieved by Detective Johnson, and any evidence recovered would have been admissible against him. If the search proved negative, Royer would have been free to go much earlier, and with less likelihood of missing his flight, which in itself can be a very serious matter in a variety of circumstances.

Third, the State has not touched on the question whether it would have been feasible to investigate the contents of Royer's bags in a more expeditious way. The courts are not strangers to the use of trained dogs to detect the presence of controlled substances in luggage. [10] There is no indication here that this means was not feasible and available. If it had been used, Royer and his luggage could have been momentarily detained while this investigative procedure was carried out. Indeed, it may be that no detention at all would have been necessary. A negative result would have freed Royer in short order; a positive result would have resulted in his justifiable arrest on probable cause.

We do not suggest that there is a litmus-paper test for distinguishing a consensual encounter from a seizure or for determining when a seizure exceeds the bounds of an investigative stop. Even in the discrete category of airport encounters, there will be endless variations in the facts and circumstances, so much variation that it is unlikely that the courts can reduce to a sentence or a paragraph a rule that will provide unarguable answers to the question whether there has been an unreasonable search or seizure in violation of the Fourth Amendment. Nevertheless, we must render judgment, and we think that the Florida District Court of Appeal cannot be faulted in concluding that the limits of a Terry-stop had been exceeded.

IV

The State's third and final argument is that Royer was not being illegally held when he gave his consent, because there was probable cause to arrest him at that time. Detective Johnson testified at the suppression hearing, and the Florida District Court of Appeal held that there was no probable cause to arrest until Royer's bags were opened, but the fact that the officers did not believe there was probable cause and proceeded on a consensual or Terry-stop rationale would not foreclose the State from justifying Royer's custody by proving probable cause, and hence removing any barrier to relying on Royer's consent to search. Peters v. New York, decided with Sibron v. New York, 392 U. S. 40, 392 U. S. 66-67 (1968). We agree with the Florida District Court of Appeal, however, that probable cause to arrest Royer did not exist at the time he consented to the search of his luggage. The facts are that a nervous young man with two American Tourister bags paid cash for an airline ticket to a "target city." These facts led to inquiry, which in turn revealed that the ticket had been bought under an assumed name. The proffered explanation did not satisfy the officers. We cannot agree with the State, if this is its position, that every nervous young man paying cash for a ticket to New York City under an assumed name and carrying two heavy American Tourister bags may be arrested and held to answer for a serious felony charge.

V

Because we affirm the Florida District Court of Appeal's conclusion that Royer was being illegally detained when he consented to the search of his luggage, we agree that the consent was tainted by the illegality and was ineffective to justify the search. The judgment of the Florida District Court of Appeal is accordingly

Affirmed.

Notes

[1] The facts set forth in this opinion are taken from the en banc decision of the Florida District Court of Appeal, Third District, 389 So.2d 1007, 1015-1018 (1980), and from the transcript of the hearing on the motion to suppress contained in the joint appendix. App. 11A-116A.

[2] The "drug courier profile" is an abstract of characteristics found to be typical of persons transporting illegal drugs. In Royer's case, the detectives attention was attracted by the following facts which were considered to be within the profile: (a) Royer was carrying American Tourister luggage, which appeared to be heavy, (b) he was young, apparently between 25-35, (c) he was casually dressed, (d) he appeared pale and nervous, looking around at other people, (e) he paid for his ticket in cash with a large number of bills, and (f) rather than completing the airline identification tag to be attached to checked baggage, which had space for a name, address, and telephone number, he wrote only a name and the destination. 389 So.2d at 1016; App. 27A-40A.

[3] Fla.Stat. § 893.13(1)(a)(2) (1975).

[4] App. 114A-116A.

[5] Under Florida law, a plea of nolo contendere is equivalent to a plea of guilty.

[6] On appeal, a panel of the District Court of Appeal of Florida found that, viewing the totality of the circumstances, the finding of consent by the trial court was supported by clear and convincing evidence. 389 So.2d 1007 (1979). The panel decision was vacated, and rehearing en banc granted. Id. at 1015 (1980). It is the decision of the en banc court that is reviewed here.

[7] The Florida court was also of the opinion that "a mere similarity with the contents of the drug courier profile is insufficient even to constitute the articulable suspicion required to justify" the stop authorized by Terry v. Ohio. It went on to hold that, even if it followed a contrary rule, or even if articulable suspicion occurred at some point prior to Royer's consent to search, the facts did not amount to probable cause that would justify the restraint imposed on Royer. 389 So.2d at 1019. As will become clear, we disagree on the reasonable suspicion issue, but do concur that probable cause to arrest was lacking.

[8] In its brief and at oral argument before this Court, the State contests whether this concession was ever made. We have no basis to question the statement of the Florida court.

[9] Our decision here is consistent with the Court's judgment in United States v. Mendenhall, 446 U. S. 544 (1980). In Mendenhall, the respondent was walking along an airport concourse when she was approached by two federal Drug Enforcement Agency (DEA) officers. As in the present case, the officers asked for Mendenhall's airline ticket and some identification; the names on the ticket and identification did not match. When one of the agents specifically identified himself as attached to the DEA, Mendenhall became visibly shaken and nervous. Id. at 446 U. S. 548.

After returning the ticket and identification, one officer asked Mendenhall if she would accompany him to the DEA airport office, 50 feet away, for further questions. Once in the office, Mendenhall was asked to consent to a search of her person and her handbag; she was advised of her right to decline. Ibid. In a private room, following further assurance from Mendenhall that she consented to the search, a policewoman began the search of Mendenhall's person by requesting that Mendenhall disrobe. As she began to undress, Mendenhall removed two concealed packages that appeared to contain heroin and handed them to the policewoman. Id. at 446 U. S. 549. The Court of Appeals determined that the initial "stop" of Mendenhall was unlawful because not based upon a reasonable suspicion of criminal activity. In the alternative, the court found that, even if the initial stop was permissible, the officer's request that Mendenhall accompany him to the DEA office constituted an arrest without probable cause.

This Court reversed. Two Justices were of the view that the entire encounter was consensual, and that no seizure had taken place. Three other Justices assumed that there had been a seizure, but would have held that there was reasonable suspicion to warrant it; hence, a voluntary consent to search was a valid basis for the search. Thus, the five Justices voting to reverse appeared to agree that Mendenhall was not being illegally detained when she consented to be searched. The four dissenting Justices also assumed that there had been a detention, but were of the view that reasonable grounds for suspecting Mendenhall did not exist, and concluded that Mendenhall was thus being illegally detained at the time of her consent.

The case before us differs in important respects. Here, Royer's ticket and identification remained in the possession of the officers throughout the encounter; the officers also seized and had possession of his luggage. As a practical matter, Royer could not leave the airport without them. In Mendenhall, no luggage was involved, the ticket and identification were immediately returned, and the officers were careful to advise that the suspect could decline to be searched. Here, the officers had seized Royer's luggage and made no effort to advise him that he need not consent to the search.

[10] Courts of Appeals are in disagreement as to whether using a dog to detect drugs in luggage is a search, but no Court of Appeals has held that more than an articulable suspicion is necessary to justify this kind of a warrantless search, if indeed it is a search. See, e.g., United States v. Sullivan, 625 F.2d 9, 13 (CA4 1980) (no search), cert. denied, 450 U.S. 923 (1981); United States v. Burns, 624 F.2d 95, 101 (CA10 1980) (same); United States v. Beale, 674 F.2d 1327, 1335 (CA9 1982) (sniff is an intrusion requiring reasonable suspicion), cert. pending, No. 82-674. Furthermore, the law of the Circuit from which this case comes was and is that "use of [drug-detecting canines] constitute[s] neither a search nor a seizure under the Fourth Amendment." United States v. Goldstein, 635 F.2d 356, 361 (CA5), cert. denied, 452 U.S. 962 (1981). See United States v. Viera, 644 F.2d 509, 510 (CA5), cert. denied, 454 U.S. 867 (1981). Decisions of the United States Court of Appeals for the Fifth Circuit rendered prior to September 30, 1981, are binding precedent on the United States Court of Appeals for the Eleventh Circuit. Bonner v. City of Prichard, 661 F.2d 1206, 1207 (CA11 1981).

In any event, we hold here that the officers had reasonable suspicion to believe that Royer's luggage contained drugs, and we assume that the use of dogs in the investigation would not have entailed any prolonged detention of either Royer or his luggage which may involve other Fourth Amendment concerns. In United State v. Beale, supra, for example, after briefly questioning two suspects who had checked baggage for a flight from the Fort Lauderdale, Fla., airport, the officers proceeded to the baggage area, where a trained dog alerted to one of the checked bags. Meanwhile, the suspects had boarded their plane for California, where their bags were again sniffed by a trained dog, and they were arrested. The Court of Appeals for the Ninth Circuit vacated a judgment convicting the suspects on the ground that articulable suspicion was necessary to justify the use of a trained dog to sniff luggage, and that the existence or not of that requirement should have been determined in the District Court. 674 F.2d at 1335. In the case before us, the officers, with founded suspicion, could have detained Royer for the brief period during which Florida authorities at busy airports seem able to carry out the dog-sniffing procedure.

Texas v. Brown (April 19, 1983)

JUSTICE REHNQUIST announced the judgment of the Court and delivered an opinion, in which THE CHIEF JUSTICE, JUSTICE WHITE, and JUSTICE O'CONNOR joined.

Respondent Clifford James Brown was convicted in the District Court of Tarrant County, Tex., for possession of heroin in violation of state law. The Texas Court of Criminal Appeals reversed his conviction, holding that certain evidence should have been suppressed because it was obtained in violation of the Fourth Amendment to the United States Constitution. [1] 617 S.W.2d 196. That court rejected the State's contention that the so-called "plain view" doctrine justified the police seizure. Because of apparent uncertainty concerning the scope and applicability of this doctrine, we granted certiorari, 457 U.S. 1116, and now reverse the judgment of the Court of Criminal Appeals.

On a summer evening in June, 1979, Tom Maples, an officer of the Fort Worth police force, assisted in setting up a routine driver's license checkpoint on East Allen Street in that city. Shortly before midnight, Maples stopped an automobile driven by respondent Brown, who was alone. Standing alongside the driver's window of Brown's car, Maples asked him for his driver's license. At roughly the same time, Maples shined his flashlight into the car and saw Brown withdraw his right hand from his right pants pocket. Caught between the two middle fingers of the hand was an opaque, green party balloon, knotted about one-half inch from the tip. Brown let the balloon fall to the seat beside his leg, and then reached across the passenger seat and opened the glove compartment.

Because of his previous experience in arrests for drug offenses, Maples testified that he was aware that narcotics frequently were packaged in balloons like the one in Brown's hand. When he saw the balloon, Maples shifted his position in order to obtain a better view of the interior of the glove compartment. He noticed that it contained several small plastic vials, quantities of loose white powder, and an open bag of party balloons. After rummaging briefly through the glove compartment, Brown told Maples that he had no driver's license in his possession. Maples then instructed him to get out of the car and stand at its rear. Brown complied, and, before following him to the rear of the car, Maples reached into the car and picked up the green balloon; there seemed to be a sort of powdery substance within the tied-off portion of the balloon.

Maples then displayed the balloon to a fellow officer who indicated that he "understood the situation." The two officers then advised Brown that he was under arrest. [2] They also conducted an on-the-scene inventory of Brown's car, discovering several plastic bags containing a green leafy substance and a large bottle of milk sugar. These items, like the balloon, were seized by the officers. At the suppression hearing conducted by the District Court, a police department chemist testified that he had examined the substance in the balloon seized by Maples, and determined that it was heroin. He also testified that narcotics frequently were packaged in ordinary party balloons.

The Court of Criminal Appeals, discussing the Fourth Amendment issue, observed that "plain view alone is never enough to justify the warrantless seizure of evidence.'" 617 S.W.2d at 200, quoting Coolidge v. New Hampshire, 403 U. S. 443, 403 U. S. 468 (1971) (opinion of Stewart, J., joined by Douglas, BRENNAN, and MARSHALL, JJ.) It further concluded that "Officer Maples had to know that `incriminatory evidence was before him when he seized the balloon.'" 617 S.W.2d at 200 (emphasis supplied), quoting DeLao v. State, 550 S.W.2d 289, 291 (Tex.Crim.App.1977). On the State's petition for rehearing, three judges dissented, stating their view that

"[t]he issue turns on whether an officer, relying on years of practical experience and knowledge commonly accepted, has probable cause to seize the balloon in plain view."

617 S.W.2d at 201.

Because the "plain view" doctrine generally is invoked in conjunction with other Fourth Amendment principles, such as those relating to warrants, probable cause, and search incident to arrest, we rehearse briefly these better understood principles of Fourth Amendment law. That Amendment secures the persons, houses, papers, and effects of the people against unreasonable searches and seizures, and requires the existence of probable cause before a warrant shall issue. Our cases hold that procedure by way of a warrant is preferred, although in a wide range of diverse situations we have recognized flexible, common-sense exceptions to this requirement. See, e.g., Warden v. Hayden, 387 U. S. 294 (1967) (hot pursuit); United States v. Jeffers, 342 U. S. 48, 342 U. S. 51-52 (1951) (exigent circumstances); United States v. Ross, 456 U. S. 798 (1982) (automobile search); Chimel v. California, 395 U. S. 752 (1969), United States v. Robinson, 414 U. S. 218 (1973), and New York v. Belton, 453 U. S. 454 (1981) (search of person and surrounding area incident to arrest); Almeida-Sanchez v. United States, 413 U. S. 266 (1973) (search at border or "functional equivalent"); Zap v. United States, 328 U. S. 624, 328 U. S. 630 (1946) (consent). We have also held to be permissible intrusions less severe than full-scale searches or seizures without the necessity of a warrant. See, e.g., Terry v. Ohio, 392 U. S. 1 (1968) (stop and frisk); United States v. Brignoni-Ponce, 422 U. S. 873 (1975) (seizure for questioning); Delaware v. Prouse, 440 U. S. 648 (1979) (roadblock). One frequently mentioned "exception to the warrant requirement," Coolidge v. New Hampshire, supra, at 403 U. S. 456, is the so-called "plain view" doctrine, relied upon by the State in this case.

While conceding that the green balloon seized by Officer Maples was clearly visible to him, the Court of Criminal Appeals held that the State might not avail itself of the "plain view" doctrine. That court said:

"For the plain view doctrine to apply, not only must the officer be legitimately in a position to view the object, but it must be immediately apparent to the police that they have evidence before them. This 'immediately apparent' aspect is central to the plain view exception, and is here relied upon by appellant. [Citation omitted.] In this case then, Officer Maples had to know that 'incriminatory evidence was before him when he seized the balloon.'"

617 S.W.2d at 200. The Court of Criminal Appeals based its conclusion primarily on the plurality portion of the opinion of this Court in Coolidge v. New Hampshire, supra. In the Coolidge plurality's view, the "plain view" doctrine permits the warrantless seizure by police of private possessions where three requirements are satisfied. [3] First, the police officer must lawfully make an "initial intrusion" or otherwise properly be in a position from which he can view a particular area. Id. at 403 U. S. 465-468. Second, the officer must discover incriminating evidence "inadvertently," which is to say, he may not "know in advance the location of [certain] evidence and intend to seize it," relying on the plain view doctrine only as a pretext. Id. at 403 U. S. 470. Finally, it must be "immediately apparent" to the police that the items they observe may be evidence of a crime, contraband, or otherwise subject to

seizure. Id. at 403 U. S. 466. While the lower courts generally have applied the Coolidge plurality's discussion of "plain view," it has never been expressly adopted by a majority of this Court. On the contrary, the plurality's formulation was sharply criticized at the time, see Coolidge v. New Hampshire, 403 U.S. at 403 U. S. 506 (Black, J., dissenting); id. at 403 U. S. 516-521 (WHITE, J., dissenting). While not a binding precedent, as the considered opinion of four Members of this Court, it should obviously be the point of reference for further discussion of the issue.

The Coolidge plurality observed:

"it is important to keep in mind that, in the vast majority of cases, any evidence seized by the police will be in plain view, at least at the moment of seizure,"

simply as "the normal concomitant of any search, legal or illegal." Id. at 403 U. S. 465. The question whether property in plain view of the police may be seized therefore must turn on the legality of the intrusion that enables them to perceive and physically seize the property in question. The Coolidge plurality, while following this approach to "plain view," characterized it as an independent exception to the warrant requirement. At least from an analytical perspective, this description may be somewhat inaccurate. We recognized in Payton v. New York, 445 U. S. 573, 445 U. S. 587 (1980), the well-settled rule that

"objects such as weapons or contraband found in a public place may be seized by the police without a warrant. The seizure of property in plain view involves no invasion of privacy, and is presumptively reasonable, assuming that there is probable cause to associate the property with criminal activity."

A different situation is presented, however, when the property in open view is "situated on private premises to which access is not otherwise available for the seizing officer.'" Ibid., quoting G.

M. Leasing Corp. v. United States, 429 U. S. 338, 429 U. S. 354 (1977). As these cases indicate, "plain view" provides grounds for seizure of an item when an officer's access to an object has some prior justification under the Fourth Amendment. [4] "Plain view" is perhaps better understood, therefore, not as an independent "exception" to the Warrant Clause, but simply as an extension of whatever the prior justification for an officer's "access to an object" may be.

The principle is grounded on the recognition that, when a police officer has observed an object in "plain view," the owner's remaining interests in the object are merely those of possession and ownership, see Coolidge v. New Hampshire, supra, at 403 U. S. 515 (WHITE, J., dissenting). Likewise, it reflects the fact that requiring police to obtain a warrant once they have obtained a first-hand perception of contraband, stolen property, or incriminating evidence generally would be a "needless inconvenience," 403 U.S. at 403 U. S. 468, that might involve danger to the police and public. Ibid. We have said previously that

"the permissibility of a particular law enforcement practice is judged by balancing its intrusion on . . . Fourth Amendment interests against its promotion of legitimate governmental interests."

Delaware v. Prouse, 440 U.S. at 440 U. S. 654. In light of the private and governmental interests just outlined, our decisions have come to reflect the rule that, if, while lawfully engaged in an activity in a particular place, police officers perceive a suspicious object, they may seize it immediately. See Marron v. United States, 275 U. S. 192 (1927); Go-Bart Importing Co. v. United States, 282 U. S. 344, 282 U. S. 358 (1931); United States v. Lefkowitz, 285 U. S. 452, 285 U. S. 465 (1932); Harris v. United States, 390 U. S. 234, 390 U. S. 236 (1968); Frazier v. Cupp, 394 U. S. 731 (1969). This rule merely reflects an application of the Fourth Amendment's central requirement of reasonableness to the law governing seizures of property.

Applying these principles, we conclude that Officer Maples properly seized the green balloon from Brown's automobile. The Court of Criminal Appeals stated that it did not "question . . . the validity of the officer's initial stop of appellant's vehicle as a part of a license check," 617 S.W.2d at 200, and we agree. Delaware v. Prouse, supra, at 440 U. S. 654-655. It is likewise beyond dispute that Maples' action in shining his flashlight to illuminate the interior of Brown's car trenched upon no right secured to the latter by the Fourth Amendment. The Court said in United States v. Lee, 274 U. S. 559, 274 U. S. 563 (1927): "[The] use of a searchlight is comparable to the use of a marine glass or a field glass. It is not prohibited by the Constitution." Numerous other courts have agreed that the use of artificial means to illuminate a darkened area simply does not constitute a search, and thus triggers no Fourth Amendment protection. [5]

Likewise, the fact that Maples "changed [his] position" and "bent down at an angle so [he] could see what was inside" Brown's car, App. 16, is irrelevant to Fourth Amendment analysis. The general public could peer into the interior of Brown's automobile from any number of angles; there is no reason Maples should be precluded from observing as an officer what would be entirely visible to him as a private citizen. There is no legitimate expectation of privacy, Katz v. United States, 389 U. S. 347, 389 U. S. 361 (1967) (Harlan, J., concurring); Smith v. Maryland, 442 U. S. 735, 442 U. S. 739-745 (1979), shielding that portion of the interior of an automobile which may be viewed from outside the vehicle by either inquisitive passersby or diligent police officers. In short, the conduct that enabled Maples to observe the interior of Brown's car and of his open glove compartment was not a search within the meaning of the Fourth Amendment.

Thus, there can be no dispute here as to the presence of the first of the three requirements held necessary by the Coolidge plurality to invoke the "plain view" doctrine. [6] But the Court of Criminal Appeals, as we have noted, felt the State's case ran aground on the requirement that the incriminating nature of the items be "immediately apparent" to the police officer. To the Court of Criminal Appeals, this apparently meant that the officer must be possessed of near certainty as to the seizable nature of the items. Decisions by this Court since Coolidge indicate that the use of the phrase "immediately apparent" was very likely an unhappy choice of words, since it can be taken to imply that an unduly high degree of certainty as to the incriminatory character of evidence is necessary for an application of the "plain view" doctrine.

In Colorado v. Bannister, 449 U. S. 1, 449 U. S. 3-4 (1980), we applied what was, in substance, the plain view doctrine to an officer's seizure of evidence from an automobile. Id. at 449 U. S. 4, n. 4. The officer noticed that the occupants of the automobile matched a description of persons suspected of a theft and that auto parts in the open glove compartment of the car similarly resembled ones reported stolen. The Court held that these facts supplied the officer with "probable cause," id. at 449 U. S. 4, and therefore, that he could seize the incriminating items from the car without a warrant. Plainly, the Court did not view the "immediately apparent" language of Coolidge as establishing any requirement that a police officer "know" that certain items are contraband or evidence of a crime. Indeed, Colorado v. Bannister, supra, was merely an application of the rule, set forth in Payton v. New York, 445 U. S. 573 (1980), that

"[t]he seizure of property in plain view involves no invasion of privacy, and is presumptively reasonable, assuming that there is probable cause to associate the property with criminal activity."

Id. at 445 U. S. 587 (emphasis added). We think this statement of the rule from Payton, supra, requiring probable cause for seizure in the ordinary case, [7] is consistent with the Fourth Amendment, and we reaffirm it here.

As the Court frequently has remarked, probable cause is a flexible, common-sense standard. It merely required that the facts available to the officer would "warrant a man of reasonable caution in the belief," Carroll v. United States, 267 U. S. 132, 267 U. S. 162 (1925), that certain items may be contraband or stolen property or useful as evidence of a crime; it does not demand any showing that such a belief be correct, or more likely true than false. A "practical, nontechnical" probability that incriminating evidence is involved is all that is required. Brinegar v. United States, 338 U. S. 160, 338 U. S. 176 (1949). Moreover, our observation in United States v. Cortez, 449 U. S. 411, 449 U. S. 418 (1981), regarding "particularized suspicion," is equally applicable to the probable cause requirement:

"This process does not deal with hard certainties, but with probabilities. Long before the law of probabilities was articulated as such, practical people formulated certain common-sense conclusions about human behavior; jurors as factfinders are permitted to do the same -- and so are law enforcement officers. Finally, the evidence thus collected must be seen and weighed not in terms of library analysis by scholars, but as understood by those versed in the field of law enforcement."

With these considerations in mind, it is plain that Officer Maples possessed probable cause to believe that the balloon in Brown's hand contained an illicit substance. Maples testified that he was aware, both from his participation in previous narcotics arrests and from discussions with other officers, that balloons tied in the manner of the one possessed by Brown were frequently used to carry narcotics. This testimony was corroborated by that of a police department chemist who noted that it was "common" for balloons to be used in packaging narcotics. In addition, Maples was able to observe the contents of the glove compartment of Brown's car, which revealed further suggestions that Brown was engaged in activities that might involve possession of illicit substances. The fact that Maples could not see through the opaque fabric of the balloon is all but irrelevant: the distinctive character of the balloon itself spoke volumes as to its contents -- particularly to the trained eye of the officer.

In addition to its statement that for seizure of objects in plain view to be justified, the basis upon which they might be seized had to be "immediately apparent," and the requirement that the initial intrusion be lawful, both of which requirements we hold were satisfied here, the Coolidge plurality also stated that the police must discover incriminating evidence "inadvertently," which is to say they may not "know in advance the location of [certain] evidence and intend to seize it," relying on the plain-view doctrine only as a pretext. 430 U.S. at 430 U. S. 470. Whatever may be the final disposition of the "inadvertence" element of "plain view," [8] it clearly was no bar to the seizure here. The circumstances of this meeting between Maples and Brown give no suggestion that the roadblock was a pretext whereby evidence of narcotics violation might be uncovered in "plain view" in the course of a check for driver's licenses. Here, although the officers no doubt had an expectation that some of the cars they halted on East Allen Street -- which was part of a "medium" area of narcotics traffic, App. 33 -- would contain narcotics or parapernalia, there is no indication in the record that they had anything beyond this generalized expectation. Likewise, there is no indication that Maples had any reason to believe that any particular object would be in Brown's glove compartment or elsewhere in his automobile. The "inadvertence" requirement of "plain view," properly understood, was no bar to the seizure here.

Maples lawfully viewed the green balloon in the interior of Brown's car, and had probable cause to believe that it was subject to seizure under the Fourth Amendment. The judgment of the Texas Court of Criminal Appeals is accordingly reversed, and the case is remanded for further proceedings.

It is so ordered.

Notes

[1] Brown argues that the decision below rested on an independent and adequate state ground, and therefore that this Court lacks jurisdiction. Fox Film Corp. v. Muller, 296 U. S. 207, 296 U. S. 210 (1935). The position is untenable. The opinion of the Texas Court of Criminal Appeals rests squarely on the interpretation of the Fourth Amendment to the United States Constitution in Coolidge v. New Hampshire, 403 U. S. 443 (1971), and on Texas cases interpreting that decision, e.g., Howard v. State, 599 S.W.2d 597 (Tex.Crim.App.1979); DeLao v. State, 550 S.W.2d 289 (Tex.Crim.App.1977); Duncan v. State, 549 S.W.2d 730 (Tex.Crim.App.1977); and Nicholas v. State, 502 S.W.2d 169 (Tex.Crim.App.1973). The only mention of the Texas Constitution occurs in a summary of Brown's contentions at the outset of the lower court's opinion.

Brown relies principally on Howard v. State, supra, and Duncan v. State, supra. Neither decision supports the proposition that the Texas Court of Criminal Appeals based its decision upon state law. In Howard, the State argued that the plain view doctrine justified the seizure of a closed translucent medicine jar from an automobile. The Court of Criminal Appeals rejected the claim, relying on Coolidge v. New Hampshire, supra, and

stating that the State's arguments "cannot be squared with the Supreme Court's interpretation of the plain view doctrine." 599 S.W.2d at 602. The court also relied on Thomas v. State, 572 S.W.2d 507 (Tex.Crim.App.1976), which it characterized as "[f]ollowing the teachings of Coolidge v. New Hampshire." 599 S.W.2d at 602. An additional opinion of the court on the State's motion for rehearing merely elaborated upon the application of the plain view doctrine set forth in the court's original opinion. Similarly, in Duncan, the Court of Criminal Appeals rejected the State's reliance on the plain view theory, citing to Coolidge for a statement of the applicable law, as well as to Nicholas v. State, supra. Like the court's other decisions in the area, Nicholas relied only on Coolidge.

[2] It is not clear on the record before us when Brown was arrested. The Court of Criminal Appeals stated at one point in its opinion that it did not question "the propriety of the arrest, since appellant failed to produce a driver's license." 617 S.W.2d 196, 200. This statement might be read to suggest that Brown was arrested upon his failure to produce a license, instead of at some point following seizure of the balloon from the car. The transcript of the suppression hearing, however, indicates rather clearly that Brown was not formally arrested until after seizure of the balloon. App. 28-31. In the face of such indications, we decline to interpret the above-quoted clause from the Court of Criminal Appeals' opinion as evidencing a belief that an arrest occurred prior to seizure of the balloon. Rather, we think it likely that the court was simply reasoning that Brown's arrest, whenever it may have taken place, was justified because of his failure to produce a driver's license.

We do not address the argument that seizure of the balloon would have been justified under New York v. Belton, 453 U. S. 454 (1981), which permits warrantless searches of the passenger compartment of an automobile incident to an arrest, because of the absence of clear factual findings regarding the time at which, and the reason for which, Brown was arrested, and because the lower court was not able to consider that decision.

[3] The plurality also remarked that "plain view alone is never enough to justify the warrantless seizure of evidence." 403 U.S. at 403 U. S. 468. The court below appeared to understand this phrase to impose an independent limitation upon the scope of the plain view doctrine articulated in Coolidge. The context in which the plurality used the phrase, however, indicates that it was merely a rephrasing of its conclusion, discussed below, that in order for the plain view doctrine to apply, a police officer must be engaged in a lawful intrusion or must otherwise legitimately occupy the position affording him a "plain view."

[4] Thus, police may perceive an object while executing a search warrant, or they may come across an item while acting pursuant to some exception to the Warrant Clause, e.g., Warden v. Hayden, 387 U. S. 294 (1967); Terry v. Ohio, 392 U. S. 1 (1968). Alternatively, police may need no justification under the Fourth Amendment for their access to an item, such as when property is left in a public place, see Payton v. New York, 445 U. S. 573, 445 U. S. 587 (1980).

It is important to distinguish "plain view," as used in Coolidge to justify seizure of an object, from an officer's mere observation of an item left in plain view. Whereas the latter generally involves no Fourth Amendment search, see infra at 460 U. S. 740; Katz v. United States, 389 U. S. 347 (1967), the former generally does implicate the Amendment's limitations upon seizures of personal property. The information obtained as a result of observation of an object in plain sight may be the basis for probable cause or reasonable suspicion of illegal activity. In turn, these levels of suspicion may, in some cases, see, e.g., Terry v.

Ohio, supra; United States v. Ross, 456 U. S. 798 (1982), justify police conduct affording them access to a particular item.

[5] E.g., United States v. Chesher, 678 F.2d 1353, 1356-1357, n. 2 (CA9 1982); United States v. Ocampo, 650 F.2d 421, 427 (CA2 1981); United States v. Pugh, 566 F.2d 626, 627, n. 2 (CA8 1977), cert. denied, 435 U.S. 1010 (1978); United States v. Coplen, 541 F.2d 211 (CA9 1976), cert. denied, 429 U.S. 1073 (1977); United States v. Lara, 517 F.2d 209 (CA5 1975); United States v. Johnson, 506 F.2d 674 (CA8 1974), cert. denied, 421 U.S. 917 (1975); United States v. Booker, 461 F.2d 990, 992 (CA6 1972); United States v. Hanahan, 442 F.2d 649 (CA7 1971); People v. Waits, 196 Colo. 35, 580 P.2d 391 (1978); Redd v. State, 240 Ga. 753, 243 S.E.2d 16 (1978); State v. Chattley, 390 A.2d 472 (Me.1978); State v. Vohnoutka, 292 N.W.2d 756 (Minn.1980); Dick v. State, 596 P.2d 1265 (Okla.Crim.App.1979); State v. Miller, 45 Ore.App. 407, 608 P.2d 595 (1980); Albo v. State, 379 So.2d 648 (Fla.1980).

[6] While seizure of the balloon required a warrantless, physical intrusion into Brown's automobile, this was proper, assuming that the remaining requirements of the plain view doctrine were satisfied. United States v. Ross, 456 U. S. 798 (1982).

[7] We need not address whether, in some circumstances, a degree of suspicion lower than probable cause would be sufficient basis for a seizure in certain cases.

[8] See State v. King, 191 N.W.2d 650, 655 (Iowa 1971); United States v. Santana, 485 F.2d 365, 369-370 (CA2 1973), cert. denied, 415 U.S. 931 (1974); United States v. Bradshaw, 490 F.2d 1097, 1101, n. 3 (CA4), cert. denied, 419 U.S. 895 (1974); North v. Superior Ct., 8 Cal.3d 301, 306-307, 502 P.2d 1305, 1308 (1972).

Illinois v. Gates (June 8, 1983)

JUSTICE REHNQUIST delivered the opinion of the Court.

Respondents Lance and Susan Gates were indicted for violation of state drug laws after police officers, executing a search warrant, discovered marihuana and other contraband in their automobile and home. Prior to trial, the Gateses moved to suppress evidence seized during this search. The Illinois Supreme Court affirmed the decisions of lower state courts granting the motion. 85 Ill.2d 376, 423 N.E.2d 887 (1981). It held that the affidavit submitted in support of the State's application for a warrant to search the Gateses' property was inadequate under this Court's decisions in Aguilar v. Texas, 378 U. S. 108 (1964), and Spinelli v. United States, 393 U. S. 410 (1969).

We granted certiorari to consider the application of the Fourth Amendment to a magistrate's issuance of a search warrant on the basis of a partially corroborated anonymous informant's tip. 454 U.S. 1140 (1982). After receiving briefs and hearing oral argument on this question, however, we requested the parties to address an additional question:

"[W]hether the rule requiring the exclusion at a criminal trial of evidence obtained in violation of the Fourth Amendment, Mapp v. Ohio, 367 U. S. 643 (1961); Weeks v. United States, 232 U. S. 383 (1914), should to any extent be modified, so as, for example, not to require the exclusion of evidence obtained in the reasonable belief that the search and seizure at issue was consistent with the Fourth Amendment."

459 U.S. 1028 (1982).

We decide today, with apologies to all, that the issue we framed for the parties was not presented to the Illinois courts and, accordingly, do not address it. Rather, we consider the question originally presented in the petition for certiorari, and conclude that the Illinois Supreme Court read the requirements of our Fourth Amendment decisions too restrictively. Initially, however, we set forth our reasons for not addressing the question regarding modification of the exclusionary rule framed in our order of November 29, 1982. Ibid.

I

Our certiorari jurisdiction over decisions from state courts derives from 28 U.S.C. § 1257, which provides that

"[f]inal judgments or decrees rendered by the highest court of a State in which a decision could be had, may be reviewed by the Supreme Court as follows: . . . (3) By writ of certiorari, . . . where any title, right, privilege or immunity is specially set up or claimed under the Constitution, treaties or statutes of . . . the United States."

The provision derives, albeit with important alterations, see, e.g., Act of Dec. 23, 1914, ch. 2, 38 Stat. 790; Act of June 25, 1948, § 1257, 62 Stat. 929, from the Judiciary Act of 1789, § 25, 1 Stat. 85.

Although we have spoken frequently on the meaning of § 1257 and its predecessors, our decisions are in some respects not entirely clear. We held early on that § 25 of the Judiciary Act of 1789 furnished us with no jurisdiction unless a federal question had been both raised and decided in the state court below. As Justice Story wrote in Crowell v. Randell, 10 Pet. 368, 35 U. S. 392 (1836): "If both of these requirements do not appear on the record, the appellate jurisdiction fails." See also Owings v. Norwood's Lessee, 5 Cranch 344 (1809). [1]

More recently, in McGoldrick v. Compagnie Generale Transatlantique, 309 U. S. 430, 309 U. S. 434-435 (1940), the Court observed:

"But it is also the settled practice of this Court, in the exercise of its appellate jurisdiction, that it is only in exceptional cases, and then only in cases coming from the federal courts, that it considers questions urged by a petitioner or appellant not pressed or passed upon in the courts below. . . . In cases coming here from state courts in which a state statute is assailed as unconstitutional, there are reasons of peculiar force which should lead us to refrain from deciding questions not presented or decided in the highest court of the state whose judicial action we are called upon to review. Apart from the reluctance with which every court should proceed to set aside legislation as unconstitutional on grounds not properly presented, due regard for the appropriate relationship of this Court to state courts requires us to decline to consider and decide questions affecting the validity of state statutes not urged or considered there. It is for these reasons that this Court, where the constitutionality of a statute has been upheld in the state court, consistently refuses to consider any grounds of attack not raised or decided in that court."

Finally, the Court seemed to reaffirm the jurisdictional character of the rule against our deciding claims "not pressed nor passed upon" in state court in State Farm Mutual Automobile Ins. Co. v. Duel, 324 U. S. 154, 324 U. S. 160 (1945), where we explained that, "[s]ince the [State] Supreme Court did not pass on the question, we may not do so." See also Hill v. California, 401 U. S. 797, 401 U. S. 805-806 (1971).

Notwithstanding these decisions, however, several of our more recent cases have treated the so-called "not pressed or passed upon below" rule as merely a prudential restriction. In Terminiello v. Chicago, 337 U. S. 1 (1949), the Court reversed a state criminal conviction on a ground not urged in state court, nor even in this Court. Likewise, in Vachon v. New Hampshire, 414 U. S. 478 (1974), the Court summarily reversed a state criminal conviction on the ground, not raised in state court, or here, that it had been obtained in violation of the Due Process Clause of the Fourteenth Amendment. The Court indicated in a footnote, id. at 414 U. S. 479, n. 3, that it possessed discretion to ignore the failure to raise in state court the

question on which it decided the case.

In addition to this lack of clarity as to the character of the "not pressed or passed upon below" rule, we have recognized that it often may be unclear whether the particular federal question presented in this Court was raised or passed upon below. In Dewey v. Des Moines, 173 U. S. 193, 173 U. S. 197-198 (1899), the fullest treatment of the subject, the Court said that,

"[i]f the question were only an enlargement of the one mentioned in the assignment of errors, or if it were so connected with it in substance as to form but another ground or reason for alleging the invalidity of the [lower court's] judgment, we should have no hesitation in holding the assignment sufficient to permit the question to be now raised and argued. Parties are not confined here to the same arguments which were advanced in the courts below upon a Federal question there discussed. [2]"

We have not attempted, and likely would not have been able, to draw a clear-cut line between cases involving only an "enlargement" of questions presented below and those involving entirely new questions.

The application of these principles in the instant case is not entirely straightforward. It is clear in this case that respondents expressly raised, at every level of the Illinois judicial system, the claim that the Fourth Amendment had been violated by the actions of the Illinois police and that the evidence seized by the officers should be excluded from their trial. It also is clear that the State challenged, at every level of the Illinois court system, respondents' claim that the substantive requirements of the Fourth Amendment had been violated. The State never, however, raised or addressed the question whether the federal exclusionary rule should be modified in any respect, and none of the opinions of the Illinois courts give any indication that the question was considered.

The case, of course, is before us on the State's petition for a writ of certiorari. Since the Act of Dec. 23, 1914, ch. 2, 38 Stat. 790, jurisdiction has been vested in this Court to review state court decisions even when a claimed federal right has been upheld. Our prior decisions interpreting the "not pressed or passed on below" rule have not, however, involved a State's failure to raise a defense to a federal right or remedy asserted below. As explained below, however, we can see no reason to treat the State's failure to have challenged an asserted federal claim differently from the failure of the proponent of a federal claim to have raised that claim.

We have identified several purposes underlying the "not pressed or passed upon" rule: for the most part, these are as applicable to the State's failure to have opposed the assertion of a particular federal right as to a party's failure to have asserted the claim. First, "[q]uestions not raised below are those on which the record is very likely to be inadequate, since it certainly was not compiled with those questions in mind." Cardinale v. Louisiana, 394 U. S. 437, 394 U. S. 439 (1969). Exactly the same difficulty exists when the State urges modification of an existing constitutional right or accompanying remedy. Here, for example, the record contains little, if anything, regarding the subjective good faith of the police officers that searched the Gateses' property -- which might well be an important consideration in determining whether to fashion a good faith exception to the exclusionary rule. Our consideration of whether to modify the exclusionary rule plainly would benefit from a record containing such facts.

Likewise, "due regard for the appropriate relationship of this Court to state courts," McGoldrick v. Compagnie Generale Transatlantique, 309 U.S. at 309 U. S. 434-435, demands that those courts be given an opportunity to consider the constitutionality of the actions of state officials, and, equally important, proposed changes in existing remedies for unconstitutional actions. Finally, by requiring that the State first argue to the state courts that the federal exclusionary rule should be modified, we permit a state court, even if it agrees with the State as a matter of federal law, to rest its decision on an adequate and independent state ground. See Cardinale, supra, at 394 U. S. 439. Illinois, for example, adopted an exclusionary rule as early as 1923, see People v. Brocamp, 307 Ill. 448, 138 N.E. 728 (1923), and might adhere to its view even if it thought we would conclude that the federal rule should be modified. In short, the reasons supporting our refusal to hear federal claims not raised in state court apply with equal force to the State's failure to challenge the availability of a well-settled federal remedy. Whether the "not pressed or passed upon below" rule is jurisdictional, as our earlier decisions indicate, see supra at 462 U. S. 217-219, or prudential, as several of our later decisions assume, or whether its character might be different in cases like this from its character elsewhere, we need not decide. Whatever the character of the rule may be, consideration of the question presented in our order of November 29, 1982, would be contrary to the sound justifications for the "not pressed or passed upon below" rule, and we thus decide not to pass on the issue.

The fact that the Illinois courts affirmatively applied the federal exclusionary rule -- suppressing evidence against respondents -- does not affect our conclusion. In Morrison v. Watson, 154 U. S. 111 (1894), the Court was asked to consider whether a state statute impaired the plaintiff in error's contract with the defendant in error. It declined to hear the case because the question presented here had not been pressed or passed on below. The Court acknowledged that the lower court's opinion had restated the conclusion, set forth in an earlier decision of that court, that the state statute did not impermissibly impair contractual obligations. Nonetheless, it held that there was no showing that "there was any real contest at any stage of this case upon the point," id. at 154 U. S. 115, and that without such a contest, the routine restatement and application of settled law by an appellate court did not satisfy the "not pressed or passed upon below" rule. Similarly, in the present case, although the Illinois courts applied the federal exclusionary rule, there was never "any real contest" upon the point. The application of the exclusionary rule was merely a routine act, once a violation of the Fourth Amendment had been found, and not the considered judgment of the Illinois courts on the question whether application of a modified rule would be warranted on the facts of this case. In such circumstances, absent the adversarial dispute necessary to apprise the state court of the arguments for not applying the exclusionary rule, we will not consider the question whether the exclusionary rule should be modified.

Likewise, we do not believe that the State's repeated opposition to respondents' substantive Fourth Amendment claims suffices to have raised the question whether the exclusionary rule should be modified. The exclusionary rule is "a judicially created remedy designed to safeguard Fourth Amendment rights generally," and not "a personal constitutional right of the party aggrieved." United States v. Calandra, 414 U. S. 338, 414 U. S. 348 (1974). The question whether the exclusionary rule's remedy is appropriate in a particular context has long been regarded as an issue separate from the question whether the Fourth Amendment rights of the party seeking to invoke the rule were violated by police conduct. See, e.g., United States v. Havens, 446 U. S. 620 (1980); United States v. Ceccolini, 435 U. S. 268 (1978); United States v. Calandra, supra; Stone v. Powell, 428 U. S. 465 (1976). Because of this distinction, we cannot say that modification or abolition of the exclusionary rule is "so connected with [the substantive Fourth Amendment right at issue] as to form but another

ground or reason for alleging the invalidity" of the judgment. Dewey v. Des Moines, 173 U.S. at 173 U. S. 197-198. Rather, the rule's modification was, for purposes of the "not pressed or passed upon below" rule, a separate claim that had to be specifically presented to the state courts.

Finally, weighty prudential considerations militate against our considering the question presented in our order of November 29, 1982. The extent of the continued vitality of the rules that have developed from our decisions in Weeks v. United States, 232 U. S. 383 (1914), and Mapp v. Ohio, 367 U. S. 643 (1961), is an issue of unusual significance. Sufficient evidence of this lies just in the comments on the issue that Members of this Court recently have made, e.g., Bivens v. Six Unknown Fed. Narcotics Agents, 403 U. S. 388, 403 U. S. 415 (1971) (BURGER, C.J., dissenting); Coolidge v. New Hampshire, 403 U. S. 443, 403 U. S. 490 (1971) (Harlan, J., concurring); id. at 403 U. S. 502 (Black, J., dissenting); Stone v. Powell, supra, at 428 U. S. 537-539 (WHITE, J., dissenting); Brewer v. Williams, 430 U. S. 387, 430 U. S. 413-414 (1977) (POWELL, J., concurring); Robbins v. California, 453 U. S. 420, 453 U. S. 437, 453 U. S. 443-444 (1981) (REHNQUIST, J., dissenting). Where difficult issues of great public importance are involved, there are strong reasons to adhere scrupulously to the customary limitations on our discretion. By doing so, we "promote respect . . . for the Court's adjudicatory process [and] the stability of [our] decisions." Mapp v. Ohio, 367 U.S. at 367 U. S. 677 (Harlan, J., dissenting). Moreover, fidelity to the rule guarantees that a factual record will be available to us, thereby discouraging the framing of broad rules, seemingly sensible on one set of facts, which may prove ill-considered in other circumstances. In Justice Harlan's words, adherence to the rule lessens the threat of "untoward practical ramifications," id. at 367 U. S. 676 (dissenting opinion), not foreseen at the time of decision. The public importance of our decisions in Weeks and Mapp and the emotions engendered by the debate surrounding these decisions counsel that we meticulously observe our customary procedural rules. By following this course, we promote respect for the procedures by which our decisions are rendered, as well as confidence in the stability of prior decisions. A wise exercise of the powers confided in this Court dictates that we reserve for another day the question whether the exclusionary rule should be modified.

II

We now turn to the question presented in the State's original petition for certiorari, which requires us to decide whether respondents' rights under the Fourth and Fourteenth Amendments were violated by the search of their car and house. A chronological statement of events usefully introduces the issues at stake. Bloomingdale, Ill., is a suburb of Chicago located in Du Page County. On May 3, 1978, the Bloomingdale Police Department received by mail an anonymous handwritten letter which read as follows:

"This letter is to inform you that you have a couple in your town who strictly make their living on selling drugs. They are Sue and Lance Gates, they live on Greenway, off Bloomingdale Rd. in the condominiums. Most of their buys are done in Florida. Sue his wife drives their car to Florida, where she leaves it to be loaded up with drugs, then Lance flys down and drives it back. Sue flys back after she drops the car off in Florida. May 3 she is driving down there again and Lance will be flying down in a few days to drive it back. At the time Lance drives the car back he has the trunk loaded with over $100,000.00 in drugs. Presently they have over $100,000.00 worth of drugs in their basement."

"They brag about the fact they never have to work, and make their entire living on pushers."

"I guarantee if you watch them carefully you will make a big catch. They are friends with some big drugs dealers, who visit their house often."

"Lance & Susan Gates"

"Greenway"

"in Condominiums"

The letter was referred by the Chief of Police of the Bloomingdale Police Department to Detective Mader, who decided to pursue the tip. Mader learned, from the office of the Illinois Secretary of State, that an Illinois driver's license had been issued to one Lance Gates, residing at a stated address in Bloomingdale. He contacted a confidential informant, whose examination of certain financial records revealed a more recent address for the Gateses, and he also learned from a police officer assigned to O'Hare Airport that "L. Gates" had made a reservation on Eastern Airlines Flight 245 to West Palm Beach, Fla., scheduled to depart from Chicago on May 5 at 4:15 p. m.

Mader then made arrangements with an agent of the Drug Enforcement Administration for surveillance of the May 5 Eastern Airlines flight. The agent later reported to Mader that Gates had boarded the flight, and that federal agents in Florida had observed him arrive in West Palm Beach and take a taxi to the nearby Holiday Inn. They also reported that Gates went to a room registered to one Susan Gates and that, at 7 o'clock the next morning, Gates and an unidentified woman left the motel in a Mercury bearing Illinois license plates and drove north-bound on an interstate highway frequently used by travelers to the Chicago area. In addition, the DEA agent informed Mader that the license plate number on the Mercury was registered to a Hornet station wagon owned by Gates. The agent also advised Mader that the driving time between West Palm Beach and Bloomingdale was approximately 22 to 24 hours.

Mader signed an affidavit setting forth the foregoing facts, and submitted it to a judge of the Circuit Court of Du Page County, together with a copy of the anonymous letter. The judge of that court thereupon issued a search warrant for the Gateses' residence and for their automobile. The judge, in deciding to issue the warrant, could have determined that the modus operandi of the Gateses had been substantially corroborated. As the anonymous letter predicted, Lance Gates had flown from Chicago to West Palm Beach late in the afternoon of May 5th, had checked into a hotel room registered in the name of his wife, and, at 7 o'clock the following morning, had headed north, accompanied by an unidentified woman, out of West Palm Beach on an interstate highway used by travelers from South Florida to Chicago in an automobile bearing a license plate issued to him.

At 5:15 a.m. on March 7, only 36 hours after he had flown out of Chicago, Lance Gates, and his wife, returned to their home in Bloomingdale, driving the car in which they had left West Palm Beach some 22 hours earlier. The Bloomingdale police were awaiting them, searched the trunk of the Mercury, and uncovered approximately 350 pounds of marihuana. A search of the Gateses' home revealed marihuana, weapons, and other contraband. The Illinois Circuit Court ordered suppression of all these items, on the ground that the affidavit submitted to the Circuit Judge failed to support the necessary determination of probable cause to believe that the Gateses' automobile and home contained the contraband in question. This decision was affirmed in turn by the Illinois Appellate Court, 82 Ill.App.3d 749, 403 N.E.2d 77 (1980), and by a divided vote of the Supreme Court of Illinois. 85 Ill.2d 376, 423 N.E.2d 887 (1981).

The Illinois Supreme Court concluded -- and we are inclined to agree -- that, standing alone, the anonymous letter sent to the Bloomingdale Police Department would not provide the basis for a magistrate's determination that there was probable cause to believe contraband would be found in the Gateses' car and home. The letter

provides virtually nothing from which one might conclude that its author is either honest or his information reliable; likewise, the letter gives absolutely no indication of the basis for the writer's predictions regarding the Gateses' criminal activities. Something more was required, then, before a magistrate could conclude that there was probable cause to believe that contraband would be found in the Gateses' home and car. See Aguilar v. Texas, 378 U.S. at 378 U. S. 109, n. 1; Nathanson v. United States, 290 U. S. 41 (1933).

The Illinois Supreme Court also properly recognized that Detective Mader's affidavit might be capable of supplementing the anonymous letter with information sufficient to permit a determination of probable cause. See Whiteley v. Warden, 401 U. S. 560, 401 U. S. 567 (1971). In holding that the affidavit in fact did not contain sufficient additional information to sustain a determination of probable cause, the Illinois court applied a "two-pronged test," derived from our decision in Spinelli v. United States, 393 U. S. 410 (1969). [3] The Illinois Supreme Court, like some others, apparently understood Spinelli as requiring that the anonymous letter satisfy each of two independent requirements before it could be relied on. 85 Ill.2d at 383, 423 N.E.2d at 890. According to this view, the letter, as supplemented by Mader's affidavit, first had to adequately reveal the "basis of knowledge" of the letterwriter -- the particular means by which he came by the information given in his report. Second, it had to provide facts sufficiently establishing either the "veracity" of the affiant's informant, or, alternatively, the "reliability" of the informant's report in this particular case.

The Illinois court, alluding to an elaborate set of legal rules that have developed among various lower courts to enforce the "two-pronged test," [4] found that the test had not been satisfied. First, the "veracity" prong was not satisfied because "[t]here was simply no basis [for] conclud[ing] that the anonymous person [who wrote the letter to the Bloomingdale Police Department] was credible."

Id. at 385, 423 N.E.2d at 891. The court indicated that corroboration by police of details contained in the letter might never satisfy the "veracity" prong, and in any event, could not do so if, as in the present case, only "innocent" details are corroborated. Id. at 390, 423 N.E.2d at 893. In addition, the letter gave no indication of the basis of its writer's knowledge of the Gateses' activities. The Illinois court understood Spinelli as permitting the detail contained in a tip to be used to infer that the informant had a reliable basis for his statements, but it thought that the anonymous letter failed to provide sufficient detail to permit such an inference. Thus, it concluded that no showing of probable cause had been made.

We agree with the Illinois Supreme Court that an informant's "veracity," "reliability," and "basis of knowledge" are all highly relevant in determining the value of his report. We do not agree, however, that these elements should be understood as entirely separate and independent requirements to be rigidly exacted in every case, [5] which the opinion of the Supreme Court of Illinois would imply. Rather, as detailed below, they should be understood simply as closely intertwined issues that may usefully illuminate the common sense, practical question whether there is "probable cause" to believe that contraband or evidence is located in a particular place.

III

This totality-of-the-circumstances approach is far more consistent with our prior treatment of probable cause [6] than is any rigid demand that specific "tests" be satisfied by every informant's tip. Perhaps the central teaching of our decisions bearing on the probable cause standard is that it is a "practical, nontechnical conception." Brinegar v. United States, 338 U. S. 160, 338 U. S. 176 (1949).

"In dealing with probable cause, . . . as the very name implies, we deal with probabilities. These are not technical; they are the factual and practical considerations of everyday life on which reasonable and prudent men, not legal technicians, act."

Id. at 338 U. S. 175. Our observation in United States v. Cortez, 449 U. S. 411, 449 U. S. 418 (1981), regarding "particularized suspicion," is also applicable to the probable cause standard:

"The process does not deal with hard certainties, but with probabilities. Long before the law of probabilities was articulated as such, practical people formulated certain common sense conclusions about human behavior; jurors as factfinders are permitted to do the same – and so are law enforcement officers. Finally, the evidence thus collected must be seen and weighed not in terms of library analysis by scholars, but as understood by those versed in the field of law enforcement."

As these comments illustrate, probable cause is a fluid concept -- turning on the assessment of probabilities in particular factual contexts -- not readily, or even usefully, reduced to a neat set of legal rules. Informants' tips doubtless come in many shapes and sizes from many different types of persons. As we said in Adams v. Williams, 407 U. S. 143, 407 U. S. 147 (1972):

"Informants' tips, like all other clues and evidence coming to a policeman on the scene, may vary greatly in their value and reliability."

Rigid legal rules are ill-suited to an area of such diversity. "One simple rule will not cover every situation." Ibid. [7]

Moreover, the "two-pronged test" directs analysis into two largely independent channels -- the informant's "veracity" or "reliability" and his "basis of knowledge." See nn. 4 and | 4 and S. 213fn5|>5, supra. There are persuasive arguments against according these two elements such independent status. Instead, they are better understood as relevant considerations in the totality-of-the-circumstances analysis that traditionally has guided probable cause determinations: a deficiency in one may be compensated for, in determining the overall reliability of a tip, by a strong showing as to the other, or by some other indicia of reliability. See, e.g., Adams v. Williams, supra, at 407 U. S. 146-147; United States v. Harris, 403 U. S. 573 (1971).

If, for example, a particular informant is known for the unusual reliability of his predictions of certain types of criminal activities in a locality, his failure, in a particular case, to thoroughly set forth the basis of his knowledge surely should not serve as an absolute bar to a finding of probable cause based on his tip. See United States v. Sellers, 483 F.2d 37 (CA5 1973). [8] Likewise, if an unquestionably honest citizen comes forward with a report of criminal activity -- which, if fabricated, would subject him to criminal liability -- we have found rigorous scrutiny of the basis of his knowledge unnecessary. Adams v. Williams, supra. Conversely, even if we entertain some doubt as to an informant's motives, his explicit and detailed description of alleged wrongdoing, along with a statement that the event was observed first-hand, entitles his tip to greater weight than might otherwise be the case. Unlike a totality-of-the-circumstances analysis, which permits a balanced assessment of the relative weights of all the various indicia of reliability (and unreliability) attending an informant's tip, the "two-pronged test" has encouraged an excessively technical dissection of informants' tips, [9] with undue attention's being focused on isolated issues that cannot sensibly be divorced from the other facts presented to the magistrate.

As early as Locke v. United States, 7 Cranch 339, 11 U. S. 348 (1813), Chief Justice Marshall observed, in a closely related context:

"[T]he term 'probable cause,' according to its usual acceptation, means less than evidence which would justify condemnation. . . . It imports a seizure made under circumstances which warrant suspicion."

More recently, we said that "the quanta . . . of proof" appropriate in ordinary judicial proceedings are inapplicable to the decision to issue a warrant. Brinegar, 338 U.S. at 338 U. S. 173. Finely tuned standards such as proof beyond a reasonable doubt or by a preponderance of the evidence, useful in formal trials, have no place in the magistrate's decision. While an effort to fix some general, numerically precise degree of certainty corresponding to "probable cause" may not be helpful, it is clear that "only the probability, and not a prima facie showing, of criminal activity, is the standard of probable cause." Spinelli, 393 U.S. at 393 U. S. 419. See Model Code of Pre-Arraignment Procedure § 210.1(7) (Prop.Off.Draft 1972); 1 W. LaFave, Search and Seizure § 3.2(e) (1978).

We also have recognized that affidavits

"are normally drafted by nonlawyers in the midst and haste of a criminal investigation. Technical requirements of elaborate specificity once exacted under common law pleadings have no proper place in this area."

United States v. Ventresca, 380 U. S. 102, 380 U. S. 108 (1965). Likewise, search and arrest warrants long have been issued by persons who are neither lawyers nor judges, and who certainly do not remain abreast of each judicial refinement of the nature of "probable cause." See Shadwick v. City of Tampa, 407 U. S. 345, 407 U. S. 348-350 (1972). The rigorous inquiry into the Spinelli prongs and the complex superstructure of evidentiary and analytical rules that some have seen implicit in our Spinelli decision, cannot be reconciled with the fact that many warrants are -- quite properly, 407 U.S. at 407 U. S. 348-350 -- issued on the basis of nontechnical, common sense judgments of laymen applying a standard less demanding than those used in more formal legal proceedings. Likewise, given the informal, often hurried context in which it must be applied, the "built-in subtleties," Stanley v. State, 19 Md.App. 507, 528, 313 A.2d 847, 860 (1974), of the "two-pronged test" are particularly unlikely to assist magistrates in determining probable cause.

Similarly, we have repeatedly said that after-the-fact scrutiny by courts of the sufficiency of an affidavit should not take the form of de novo review. A magistrate's "determination of probable cause should be paid great deference by reviewing courts." Spinelli, supra, at 393 U. S. 419. "A grudging or negative attitude by reviewing courts toward warrants," Ventresca, 380 U.S. at 380 U. S. 108, is inconsistent with the Fourth Amendment's strong preference for searches conducted pursuant to a warrant; "courts should not invalidate warrant[s] by interpreting affidavit[s] in a hypertechnical, rather than a common sense, manner." Id. at 380 U. S. 109.

If the affidavits submitted by police officers are subjected to the type of scrutiny some courts have deemed appropriate, police might well resort to warrantless searches, with the hope of relying on consent or some other exception to the Warrant Clause that might develop at the time of the search. In addition, the possession of a warrant by officers conducting an arrest or search greatly reduces the perception of unlawful or intrusive police conduct, by assuring

"the individual whose property is searched or seized of the lawful authority of the executing officer, his need to search, and the limits of his power to search."

United States v. Chadwick, 433 U. S. 1, 433 U. S. 9 (1977). Reflecting this preference for the warrant process, the traditional standard for review of an issuing magistrate's probable cause determination has been that, so long as the magistrate had a "substantial basis for . . . conclud[ing]" that a search would uncover evidence of wrongdoing, the Fourth Amendment requires no more. Jones v. United States, 362 U. S. 257, 362 U. S. 271 (1960). See United States v. Harris, 403 U.S. at 403 U. S. 577-583. [10] We think reaffirmation of this standard better serves the purpose of encouraging recourse to the warrant procedure and is more consistent with our traditional deference to the probable cause determinations of magistrates than is the "two-pronged test."

Finally, the direction taken by decisions following Spinelli poorly serves "[t]he most basic function of any government:" "to provide for the security of the individual and of his property." Miranda v. Arizona, 384 U. S. 436, 384 U. S. 539 (1966) (WHITE, J., dissenting). The strictures that inevitably accompany the "two-pronged test" cannot avoid seriously impeding the task of law enforcement, see, e.g., n 9, supra. If, as the Illinois Supreme Court apparently thought, that test must be rigorously applied in every case, anonymous tips would be of greatly diminished value in police work. Ordinary citizens, like ordinary witnesses, see Advisory Committee's Notes on Fed.Rule Evid. 701, 28 U.S.C.App. p. 570, generally do not provide extensive recitations of the basis of their everyday observations. Likewise, as the Illinois Supreme Court observed in this case, the veracity of persons supplying anonymous tips is, by hypothesis, largely unknown, and unknowable. As a result, anonymous tips seldom could survive a rigorous application of either of the Spinelli prongs. Yet such tips, particularly when supplemented by independent police investigation, frequently contribute to the solution of otherwise "perfect crimes." While a conscientious assessment of the basis for crediting such tips is required by the Fourth Amendment, a standard that leaves virtually no place for anonymous citizen informants is not. For all these reasons, we conclude that it is wiser to abandon the "two-pronged test" established by our decisions in

Aguilar and Spinelli. [11] In its place, we reaffirm the totality-of-the-circumstances analysis that traditionally has informed probable cause determinations. See Jones v. United States, supra; United States v. Ventresca, 380 U. S. 102 (1965); Brinegar v. United States, 338 U. S. 160 (1949). The task of the issuing magistrate is simply to make a practical, common sense decision whether, given all the circumstances set forth in the affidavit before him, including the "veracity" and "basis of knowledge" of persons supplying hearsay information, there is a fair probability that contraband or evidence of a crime will be found in a particular place. And the duty of a reviewing court is simply to ensure that the magistrate had a "substantial basis for . . . conclud[ing]" that probable cause existed. Jones v. United States, 362 U. S. at 362 U. S. 271. We are convinced that this flexible, easily applied standard will better achieve the accommodation of public and private interests that the Fourth Amendment requires than does the approach that has developed from Aguilar and Spinelli.

Our earlier cases illustrate the limits beyond which a magistrate may not venture in issuing a warrant. A sworn statement of an affiant that "he has cause to suspect and does believe" that liquor illegally brought into the United States is located on certain premises will not do. Nathanson v. United States, 290 U. S. 41 (1933). An affidavit must provide the magistrate with a substantial basis for determining the existence of probable cause, and the wholly conclusory statement at issue in Nathanson failed to meet this requirement. An officer's statement that "[a]ffiants have received reliable information from a credible person and do believe" that heroin is stored in a home, is likewise inadequate. Aguilar v. Texas, 378 U. S. 108 (1964). As in Nathanson, this is a mere conclusory statement that gives the magistrate virtually no basis at all for making a judgment regarding probable cause. Sufficient information

must be presented to the magistrate to allow that official to determine probable cause; his action cannot be a mere ratification of the bare conclusions of others. In order to ensure that such an abdication of the magistrate's duty does not occur, courts must continue to conscientiously review the sufficiency of affidavits on which warrants are issued. But when we move beyond the "bare bones" affidavits present in cases such as Nathanson and Aguilar, this area simply does not lend itself to a prescribed set of rules, like that which had developed from Spinelli. Instead, the flexible, common sense standard articulated in Jones, Ventresca, and Brinegar better serves the purposes of the Fourth Amendment's probable cause requirement.

JUSTICE BRENNAN's dissent suggests in several places that the approach we take today somehow downgrades the role of the neutral magistrate, because Aguilar and Spinelli "preserve the role of magistrates as independent arbiters of probable cause. . . ." Post at 462 U. S. 287. Quite the contrary, we believe, is the case. The essential protection of the warrant requirement of the Fourth Amendment, as stated in Johnson v. United States, 333 U. S. 10 (1948), is in

"requiring that [the usual inferences which reasonable men draw from evidence] be drawn by a neutral and detached magistrate, instead of being judged by the officer engaged in the often competitive enterprise of ferreting out crime."

Id. at 333 U. S. 13-14. Nothing in our opinion in any way lessens the authority of the magistrate to draw such reasonable inferences as he will from the material supplied to him by applicants for a warrant; indeed, he is freer than under the regime of Aguilar and Spinelli to draw such inferences, or to refuse to draw them if he is so minded.

The real gist of JUSTICE BRENNAN's criticism seems to be a second argument, somewhat at odds with the first, that magistrates should be restricted in their authority to make probable cause determinations by the standards laid down in Aguilar and Spinelli, and that such findings

"should not be authorized unless there is some assurance that the information on which they are based has been obtained in a reliable way by an honest or credible person."

Post at 462 U. S. 283. However, under our opinion, magistrates remain perfectly free to exact such assurances as they deem necessary, as well as those required by this opinion, in making probable cause determinations. JUSTICE BRENNAN would apparently prefer that magistrates be restricted in their findings of probable cause by the development of an elaborate body of case law dealing with the "veracity" prong of the Spinelli test, which in turn is broken down into two "spurs" -- the informant's "credibility" and the "reliability" of his information, together with the "basis of knowledge" prong of the Spinelli test. See n 4, supra. That such a labyrinthine body of judicial refinement bears any relationship to familiar definitions of probable cause is hard to imagine. As previously noted, probable cause deals

"with probabilities. These are not technical; they are the factual and practical considerations of everyday life on which reasonable and prudent men, not legal technicians, act,"

Brinegar v. United States, 338 U.S. at 338 U. S. 175.

JUSTICE BRENNAN's dissent also suggests that

"[w]ords such as 'practical,' 'nontechnical,' and 'common sense,' as used in the Court's opinion, are but code words for an overly permissive attitude towards police practices in derogation of the rights secured by the Fourth Amendment."

Post at 462 U. S. 290. An easy, but not a complete, answer to this rather florid statement would be that nothing we know about Justice Rutledge suggests that he would have used the words he chose in Brinegar in such a manner. More fundamentally, no one doubts that,

"under our Constitution, only measures consistent with the Fourth Amendment may be employed by government to cure [the horrors of drug trafficking],"

post at 462 U. S. 290; but this agreement does not advance the inquiry as to which measures are, and which measures are not, consistent with the Fourth Amendment. "Fidelity" to the commands of the Constitution suggests balanced judgment, rather than exhortation. The highest "fidelity" is not achieved by the judge who instinctively goes furthest in upholding even the most bizarre claim of individual constitutional rights, any more than it is achieved by a judge who instinctively goes furthest in accepting the most restrictive claims of governmental authorities. The task of this Court, as of other courts, is to "hold the balance true," and we think we have done that in this case.

IV

Our decisions applying the totality-of-the-circumstances analysis outlined above have consistently recognized the value of corroboration of details of an informant's tip by independent police work. In Jones v. United States, 362 U.S. at 362 U. S. 269, we held that an affidavit relying on hearsay "is not to be deemed insufficient on that score so long as a substantial basis for crediting the hearsay is presented." We went on to say that, even in making a warrantless arrest, an officer

"may rely upon information received through an informant, rather than upon his direct observations, so long as the informant's statement is reasonably corroborated by other matters within the officer's knowledge."

Ibid. Likewise, we recognized the probative value of corroborative efforts of police officials in Aguilar -- the source of the "two-pronged test" -- by observing that, if the police had made some effort to corroborate the informant's report at issue, "an entirely different case" would have been presented. Aguilar, 378 U.S. at 378 U. S. 109, n. 1.

Our decision in Draper v. United States, 358 U. S. 307 (1959), however, is the classic case on the value of corroborative efforts of police officials. There, an informant named Hereford reported that Draper would arrive in Denver on a train from Chicago on one of two days, and that he would be carrying a quantity of heroin. The informant also supplied a fairly detailed physical description of Draper, and predicted that he would be wearing a light colored raincoat, brown slacks, and black shoes, and would be walking "real fast." Id. at 358 U. S. 309. Hereford gave no indication of the basis for his information. [12]

On one of the stated dates, police officers observed a man matching this description exit a train arriving from Chicago; his attire and luggage matched Hereford's report, and he was walking rapidly. We explained in Draper that, by this point in his investigation, the arresting officer

"had personally verified every facet of the information given him by Hereford except whether petitioner had accomplished his mission, and had the three ounces of heroin on his person or in his bag. And surely, with every other bit of Hereford's information being thus personally verified, [the officer] had 'reasonable grounds' to believe that the remaining unverified bit of Hereford's information -- that Draper would have the heroin with him -- was likewise true,"

id. at 358 U. S. 313.

The showing of probable cause in the present case was fully as compelling as that in Draper. Even standing alone, the facts obtained through the independent investigation of Mader and the DEA at least suggested that the Gateses were involved in drug trafficking. In addition to being a popular vacation site, Florida is well known as a source of narcotics and other illegal drugs. See United States v. Mendenhall, 446 U. S. 544, 446 U. S. 562 (1980) (POWELL, J., concurring in part and concurring in judgment); DEA, Narcotics Intelligence Estimate, The Supply of Drugs to the U.S. Illicit Market From Foreign and Domestic Sources in 1980, pp. 8-9. Lance Gates' flight to West Palm Beach, his brief, overnight stay in a motel, and apparent immediate return north to Chicago in the family car, conveniently awaiting him in West Palm Beach, is as suggestive of a prearranged drug run, as it is of an ordinary vacation trip.

In addition, the judge could rely on the anonymous letter, which had been corroborated in major part by Mader's efforts -- just as had occurred in Draper. [13] The Supreme Court of Illinois reasoned that Draper involved an informant who had given reliable information on previous occasions, while the honesty and reliability of the anonymous informant in this case were unknown to the Bloomingdale police. While this distinction might be an apt one at the time the Police Department received the anonymous letter, it became far less significant after Mader's independent investigative work occurred. The corroboration of the letter's predictions that the Gateses' car would be in Florida, that Lance Gates would fly to Florida in the next day or so, and that he would drive the car north toward Bloomingdale all indicated, albeit not with certainty, that the informant's other assertions also were true. "[B]ecause an informant is right about some things, he is more probably right about other facts," Spinelli, 393 U.S. at 393 U. S. 427 (WHITE, J., concurring) -- including the claim regarding the Gateses' illegal activity. This may well not be the type of "reliability" or "veracity" necessary to satisfy some views of the "veracity prong" of Spinelli, but we think it suffices for the practical, common sense judgment called for in making a probable cause determination. It is enough, for purposes of assessing probable cause, that "[c]orroboration through other sources of information reduced the chances of a reckless or prevaricating tale," thus providing "a substantial basis for crediting the hearsay." Jones v. United States, 362 U.S. at 362 U. S. 269, 362 U. S. 271.

Finally, the anonymous letter contained a range of details relating not just to easily obtained facts and conditions existing at the time of the tip, but to future actions of third parties ordinarily not easily predicted. The letterwriter's accurate information as to the travel plans of each of the Gateses was of a character likely obtained only from the Gateses themselves, or from someone familiar with their not entirely ordinary travel plans. If the informant had access to accurate information of this type a magistrate could properly conclude that it was not unlikely that he also had access to reliable information of the Gateses' alleged illegal activities. [14] Of course, the Gateses' travel plans might have been learned from a talkative neighbor or travel agent; under the "two-pronged test" developed from Spinelli, the character of the details in the anonymous letter might well not permit a sufficiently clear inference regarding the letterwriter's "basis of knowledge." But, as discussed previously, supra, at 462 U. S. 235, probable cause does not demand the certainty we associate with formal trials. It is enough that there was a fair probability that the writer of the anonymous letter had obtained his entire story either from the Gateses or someone they trusted. And corroboration of major portions of the letter's predictions provides just this probability. It is apparent, therefore, that the judge issuing the warrant had a "substantial basis for . . . conclud[ing]" that probable cause to search the Gateses' home and car existed. The judgment of the Supreme Court of Illinois therefore must be

Reversed.

Notes

[1] The apparent rule of Crowell v. Randell that a federal claim have been both raised and addressed in state court was generally not understood in the literal fashion in which it was phrased. See R. Robertson & F. Kirkham, Jurisdiction of the Supreme Court of the United States § 60 (1951). Instead, the Court developed the rule that a claim would not be considered here unless it had been either raised or squarely considered and resolved in state court. See, e.g., McGoldrick v. Compagnie Generale Transatlantique, 309 U. S. 430, 309 U. S. 434-435 (1940); State Farm Mutual Ins. Co. v. Duel, 324 U. S. 154, 324 U. S. 160 (1945).

[2] In Dewey, certain assessments had been levied against the owner of property abutting a street paved by the city; a state trial court ordered that the property be forfeited when the assessments were not paid, and in addition, held the plaintiff in error personally liable for the amount by which the assessments exceeded the value of the lots. In state court, the plaintiff in error argued that the imposition of personal liability against him violated the Due Process Clause of the Fourteenth Amendment, because he had not received personal notice of the assessment proceedings. In this Court, he also attempted to argue that the assessment itself constituted a taking under the Fourteenth Amendment. The Court held that, beyond arising from a single factual occurrence, the two claims "are not in anywise necessarily connected," 173 U.S. at 173 U. S. 198. Because of this, we concluded that the plaintiff in error's taking claim could not be considered.

[3] In Spinelli, police officers observed Mr. Spinelli going to and from a particular apartment, which the telephone company said contained two telephones with stated numbers. The officers also were "informed by a confidential reliable informant that William Spinelli [was engaging in illegal gambling activities]" at the apartment, and

that he used two phones, with numbers corresponding to those possessed by the police. 393 U.S. at 393 U. S. 414. The officers submitted an affidavit with this information to a magistrate and obtained a warrant to search Spinelli's apartment. We held that the magistrate could have made his determination of probable cause only by "abdicating his constitutional function," id. at 393 U. S. 416. The Government's affidavit contained absolutely no information regarding the informant's reliability. Thus, it did not satisfy Aguilar's requirement that such affidavits contain "some of the underlying circumstances" indicating that "the informant . . . was credible'" or that "his information [was] `reliable.'" Aguilar v. Texas, 378 U. S. 108, 378 U. S. 114 (1964). In addition, the tip failed to satisfy Aguilar's requirement that it detail "some of the underlying circumstances from which the informant concluded that . . . narcotics were where he claimed they were." Ibid. We also held that, if the tip concerning Spinelli had contained "sufficient detail" to permit the magistrate to conclude

"that he [was] relying on something more substantial than a casual rumor circulating in the underworld or an accusation based merely on an individual's general reputation,"

393 U.S. at 393 U. S. 416, then he properly could have relied on it; we thought, however, that the tip lacked the requisite detail to permit this "self-verifying detail" analysis.

[4] See, e.g., Stanley v. State, 19 Md.App. 507, 313 A.2d 847 (1974). In summary, these rules posit that the "veracity" prong of the Spinelli test has two "spurs" -- the informant's "credibility" and the "reliability" of his information. Various interpretations are advanced for the meaning of the "reliability" spur of the "veracity" prong. Both the "basis of knowledge" prong and the "veracity" prong are treated as entirely separate requirements, which must be independently satisfied in every case in order to sustain a determination of probable cause. See n 5, infra. Some ancillary doctrines are relied on to satisfy certain of the foregoing requirements. For example, the "self-verifying detail" of a tip may satisfy the "basis of knowledge" requirement, although not the "credibility" spur of the "veracity" prong. See 85 Ill.2d at 388, 423 N.E.2d at 892. Conversely, corroboration would seem not capable of supporting the "basis of knowledge" prong, but only the "veracity" prong. Id. at 390, 423 N.E.2d at 893.

The decision in Stanley, while expressly approving and conscientiously attempting to apply the "two-pronged test," observes that "[t]he built-in subtleties [of the test] are such, however, that a slipshod application calls down upon us the fury of Murphy's Law." 19 Md.App. at 528, 313 A.2d at 860 (footnote omitted). The decision also suggested that it is necessary to "evolve analogous guidelines [to hearsay rules employed in trial settings] for the reception of hearsay in a probable cause setting." Id. at 522, n. 12, 313 A.2d at 857, n. 12.

[5] The entirely independent character that the Spinelli prongs have assumed is indicated both by the opinion of the Illinois Supreme Court in this case, and by decisions of other courts. One frequently cited decision Stanley v. State, supra, at 530, 313 A.2d at 861 (footnote omitted), remarks that

"the dual requirements represented by the 'two-pronged test' are 'analytically severable,' and an 'overkill' on one prong will not carry over to make up for a deficit on the other prong."

See also n 9, infra.

[6] Our original phrasing of the so-called "two-pronged test" in Aguilar v. Texas, supra, suggests that the two prongs were intended simply as guides to a magistrate's determination of probable cause, not as inflexible, independent requirements applicable in every case. In Aguilar, we required only that

"the magistrate must be informed of some of the underlying circumstances from which the informant concluded that . . . narcotics were where he claimed they were, and some of the underlying circumstances from which the officer concluded that the informant . . . was 'credible' or his information 'reliable.'"

Id. at 378 U. S. 114 (emphasis added). As our language indicates, we intended neither a rigid compartmentalization of the inquiries into an informant's "veracity," "reliability," and "basis of knowledge," nor that these inquiries be elaborate exegeses of an informant's tip. Rather, we required only that some facts bearing on two particular issues be provided to the magistrate. Our decision in Jaben v. United States, 381 U. S. 214 (1965), demonstrated this latter point. We held there that a criminal complaint showed probable cause to believe the defendant had attempted to evade the payment of income taxes. We commented:

"Obviously, any reliance upon factual allegations necessarily entails some degree of reliability upon the credibility of the source. . . . Nor does it indicate that each factual allegation which the affiant puts forth must be independently documented, or that each and every fact which contributed to his conclusions be spelled out in the complaint. . . . It simply requires that enough information be presented to the Commissioner to enable him to make the judgment that the charges are not capricious and are sufficiently supported to justify bringing into play the further steps of the criminal process."

Id. at 378 U. S. 224-225 (emphasis added).

[7] The diversity of informants' tips, as well as the usefulness of the totality-of-the-circumstances approach to probable cause, is reflected in our prior decisions on the subject. In Jones v. United States, 362 U. S. 257, 362 U. S. 271 (1960), we held that probable cause to search petitioners' apartment was established by an affidavit based principally on an informant's tip.

The unnamed informant claimed to have purchased narcotics from petitioners at their apartment; the affiant stated that he had been given correct information from the informant on a prior occasion. This, and the fact that petitioners had admitted to police officers on another occasion that they were narcotics users, sufficed to support the magistrate's determination of probable cause.

Likewise, in Rugendorf v. United States, 376 U. S. 528 (1964), the Court upheld a magistrate's determination that there was probable cause to believe that certain stolen property would be found in petitioner's apartment. The affidavit submitted to the magistrate stated that certain furs had been stolen, and that a confidential informant, who previously had furnished confidential information, said that he saw the furs in petitioner's home. Moreover, another confidential informant, also claimed to be reliable, stated that one Schweihs had stolen the furs. Police reports indicated that petitioner had been seen in Schweihs' company, and a third informant stated that petitioner was a fence for Schweihs.

Finally, in Ker v. California, 374 U. S. 23 (1963), we held that information within the knowledge of officers who searched the Kers' apartment provided them with probable cause to believe drugs would be found there. The officers were aware that one Murphy had previously sold marihuana to a police officer; the transaction had occurred in an isolated area, to which Murphy had led the police. The night after this transaction, police observed Mr. Ker and Murphy meet in the same location. Murphy approached Ker's car, and, although police could see nothing change hands, Murphy's modus operandi was identical to what it had been the night before. Moreover, when police followed Ker from the scene of the meeting with Murphy, he managed to lose them after performing an abrupt U-turn. Finally, the police had a statement from an informant who had provided reliable information previously, that Ker was engaged in selling marihuana, and that his source was Murphy. We concluded that

"[t]o say that this coincidence of information was sufficient to support a reasonable belief of the officers that Ker was illegally in possession of marijuana is to indulge in understatement."

Id. at 374 U. S. 36.

[8] Compare Stanley v. State, 19 Md.App. at 530, 313 A.2d at 861, reasoning that,

"[e]ven assuming 'credibility' amounting to sainthood, the judge still may not accept the bare conclusion . . . of a sworn and known and trusted police affiant."

[9] Some lower court decisions, brought to our attention by the State, reflect a rigid application of such rules. In Bridger v. State, 503 S.W.2d 801 (Tex.Crim.App.1974), the affiant had received a confession of armed robbery from one of two suspects in the robbery; in addition, the suspect had given the officer $800 in cash stolen during the robbery. The suspect also told the officer that the gun used in the robbery was hidden in the other suspect's apartment. A warrant issued on the basis of this was invalidated on the ground that the affidavit did not satisfactorily describe how the accomplice had obtained his information regarding the gun.

Likewise, in People v. Palanza, 55 Ill.App.3d 1028, 371 N.E.2d 687 (1978), the affidavit submitted in support of an application for a search warrant stated that an informant of proven and uncontested reliability had seen, in specifically described premises,

"a quantity of a white crystalline substance which was represented to the informant by a white male occupant of the premises to be cocaine. Informant has observed cocaine on numerous occasions in the past and is thoroughly familiar with its appearance. The informant states that the white crystalline powder he observed in the above described premises appeared to him to be cocaine."

Id. at 1029, 371 N.E.2d at 688. The warrant issued on the basis of the affidavit was invalidated because

"[t]here is no indication as to how the informant or for that matter any other person could tell whether a white substance was cocaine and not some other substance such as sugar or salt."

Id. at 1030, 371 N.E.2d at 689.

Finally, in People v. Brethauer, 174 Colo. 29, 482 P.2d 369 (1971), an informant, stated to have supplied reliable information in the past, claimed that L.S.D. and marihuana were located on certain premises. The informant supplied police with drugs, which were tested by police and confirmed to be illegal substances. The affidavit setting forth these, and other, facts was found defective under both prongs of Spinelli.

[10] We also have said that,

"[a]lthough in a particular case it may not be easy to determine when an affidavit demonstrates the existence of probable cause, the resolution of doubtful or marginal cases in this area should be largely determined by the preference to be accorded to warrants,"

United States v. Ventresca, 380 U. S. 102, 380 U. S. 109 (1965). This reflects both a desire to encourage use of the warrant process by police officers and a recognition that, once a warrant has been obtained, intrusion upon interests protected by the Fourth Amendment is less severe than otherwise may be the case. Even if we were to accept the premise that the accurate assessment of probable cause would be furthered by the "two-pronged test," which we do not, these Fourth Amendment policies would require a less rigorous standard than that which appears to have been read into Aguilar and Spinelli.

[11] The Court's decision in Spinelli has been the subject of considerable criticism, both by Members of this Court and others. JUSTICE

BLACKMUN, concurring in United States v. Harris, 403 U. S. 573, 403 U. S. 585-586 (1971), noted his long-held view "that Spinelli . . . was wrongly decided" by this Court. Justice Black similarly would have overruled that decision. Id. at 403 U. S. 585. Likewise, a noted commentator has observed that "[t]he Aguilar-Spinelli formulation has provoked apparently ceaseless litigation." 8A J. Moore, Moore's Federal Practice � 41.04, p. 41-43 (1982).

Whether the allegations submitted to the magistrate in Spinelli would, under the view we now take, have supported a finding of probable cause, we think it would not be profitable to decide. There are so many variables in the probable cause equation that one determination will seldom be a useful "precedent" for another. Suffice it to say that, while we in no way abandon Spinelli's concern for the trustworthiness of informers and for the principle that it is the magistrate who must ultimately make a finding of probable cause, we reject the rigid categorization suggested by some of its language.

[12] The tip in Draper might well not have survived the rigid application of the "two-pronged test" that developed following Spinelli. The only reference to Hereford's reliability was that he had

"been engaged as a 'special employee' of the Bureau of Narcotics at Denver for about six months, and from time to time gave information to [the police for] small sums of money, and that [the officer] had always found the information given by Hereford to be accurate and reliable."

358 U.S. at 358 U. S. 309. Likewise, the tip gave no indication of how Hereford came by his information. At most, the detailed and accurate predictions in the tip indicated that, however Hereford obtained his information, it was reliable.

[13] The Illinois Supreme Court thought that the verification of details contained in the anonymous letter in this case amounted only to "[t]he corroboration of innocent activity," 85 Ill.2d

376, 390, 423 N.E.2d 887, 893 (1981), and that this was insufficient to support a finding of probable cause. We are inclined to agree, however, with the observation of Justice Moran in his dissenting opinion that "[i]n this case, just as in Draper, seemingly innocent activity became suspicious in light of the initial tip." Id. at 396, 423 N.E.2d at 896. And it bears noting that all of the corroborating detail established in Draper was of entirely innocent activity -- a fact later pointed out by the Court in both Jones v. United States, 362 U.S. at 362 U. S. 269-270, and Ker v. California, 374 U.S. at 374 U. S. 36.

This is perfectly reasonable. As discussed previously, probable cause requires only a probability or substantial chance of criminal activity, not an actual showing of such activity. By hypothesis, therefore, innocent behavior frequently will provide the basis for a showing of probable cause; to require otherwise would be to sub silentio impose a drastically more rigorous definition of probable cause than the security of our citizens' demands. We think the Illinois court attempted a too rigid classification of the types of conduct that may be relied upon in seeking to demonstrate probable cause. See Brown v. Texas, 443 U. S. 47, 443 U. S. 52, n. 2 (1979). In making a determination of probable cause, the relevant inquiry is not whether particular conduct is "innocent" or "guilty," but the degree of suspicion that attaches to particular types of noncriminal acts.

[14] JUSTICE STEVENS' dissent seizes on one inaccuracy in the anonymous informant's letter -- its statement that Sue Gates would fly from Florida to Illinois, when in fact she drove -- and argues that the probative value of the entire tip was undermined by this allegedly "material mistake." We have never required that informants used by the police be infallible, and can see no reason to impose such a requirement in this case. Probable cause, particularly when police have

obtained a warrant, simply does not require the perfection the dissent finds necessary.

Likewise, there is no force to the dissent's argument that the Gateses' action in leaving their home unguarded undercut the informant's claim that drugs were hidden there. Indeed, the line-by-line scrutiny that the dissent applies to the anonymous letter is akin to that which we find inappropriate in reviewing magistrates' decisions. The dissent apparently attributes to the judge who issued the warrant in this case the rather implausible notion that persons dealing in drugs always stay at home, apparently out of fear that to leave might risk intrusion by criminals. If accurate, one could not help sympathizing with the self-imposed isolation of people so situated. In reality, however, it is scarcely likely that the judge ever thought that the anonymous tip "kept one spouse" at home, much less that he relied on the theory advanced by the dissent. The letter simply says that Sue would fly from Florida to Illinois, without indicating whether the Gateses made the bitter choice of leaving the drugs in their house, or those in their car, unguarded. The judge's determination that there might be drugs or evidence of criminal activity in the Gateses' home was well supported by the less speculative theory, noted in text, that, if the informant could predict with considerable accuracy the somewhat unusual travel plans of the Gateses, he probably also had a reliable basis for his statements that the Gateses kept a large quantity of drugs in their home and frequently were visited by other drug traffickers there.

Michigan v. Long (July 6, 1983) [Notes omitted]

JUSTICE O'CONNOR delivered the opinion of the Court.

In Terry v. Ohio, 392 U. S. 1 (1968), we upheld the validity of a protective search for weapons in the absence of probable cause to arrest because it is unreasonable to deny a police officer the right "to neutralize the threat of physical harm," id. at 392 U. S. 24, when he possesses an articulable suspicion that an individual is armed and dangerous. We did not, however, expressly address whether such a protective search for weapons could extend to an area beyond the person in the absence of probable cause to arrest. In the present case, respondent David Long was convicted for possession of marihuana found by police in the passenger compartment and trunk of the automobile that he was driving. The police searched the passenger compartment because they had reason to believe that the vehicle contained weapons potentially dangerous to the officers. We hold that the protective search of the passenger compartment was reasonable under the principles articulated in Terry and other decisions of this Court. We also examine Long's argument that the decision below rests upon an adequate and independent state ground, and we decide in favor of our jurisdiction.

I

Deputies Howell and Lewis were on patrol in a rural area one evening when, shortly after midnight, they observed a car traveling erratically and at excessive speed. [1] The officers observed the car turning down a side road, where it swerved off into a shallow ditch. The officers stopped to investigate. Long, the only occupant of the automobile, met the deputies at the rear of the car, which was protruding from the ditch onto the road. The door on the driver's side of the vehicle was left open.

Deputy Howell requested Long to produce his operator's license, but he did not respond. After the request was repeated, Long produced his license. Long again failed to respond when Howell requested him to produce the vehicle registration. After another repeated request, Long, who Howell thought "appeared to be under the influence of something," 413 Mich. 461, 469, 320 N.W.2d 866,

868 (1982), turned from the officers and began walking toward the open door of the vehicle. The officers followed Long, and both observed a large hunting knife on the floorboard of the driver's side of the car. The officers then stopped Long's progress and subjected him to a Terry protective patdown, which revealed no weapons.

Long and Deputy Lewis then stood by the rear of the vehicle while Deputy Howell shined his flashlight into the interior of the vehicle, but did not actually enter it. The purpose of Howell's action was "to search for other weapons." 413 Mich., at 469, 320 N.W.2d at 868. The officer noticed that something was protruding from under the armrest on the front seat. He knelt in the vehicle and lifted the armrest. He saw an open pouch on the front seat, and upon flashing his light on the pouch, determined that it contained what appeared to be marihuana. After Deputy Howell showed the pouch and its contents to Deputy Lewis, Long was arrested for possession of marihuana. A further search of the interior of the vehicle, including the glovebox, revealed neither more contraband nor the vehicle registration. The officers decided to impound the vehicle. Deputy Howell opened the trunk, which did not have a lock, and discovered inside it approximately 75 pounds of marihuana.

The Barry County Circuit Court denied Long's motion to suppress the marihuana taken from both the interior of the car and its trunk. He was subsequently convicted of possession of marihuana. The Michigan Court of Appeals affirmed Long's conviction, holding that the search of the passenger compartment was valid as a protective search under Terry, supra, and that the search of the trunk was valid as an inventory search under South Dakota v. Opperman, 428 U. S. 364 (1976). See 94 Mich.App. 338, 288 N.W.2d 629 (1979). The Michigan Supreme Court reversed. The court held that "the sole justification of the Terry search, protection of the police officers and

others nearby, cannot justify the search in this case." 413 Mich. at 472, 320 N.W.2d at 869. The marihuana found in Long's trunk was considered by the court below to be the "fruit" of the illegal search of the interior, and was also suppressed. [2]

We granted certiorari in this case to consider the important question of the authority of a police officer to protect himself by conducting a Terry-type search of the passenger compartment of a motor vehicle during the lawful investigatory stop of the occupant of the vehicle. 459 U.S. 904 (1982).

II

Before reaching the merits, we must consider Long's argument that we are without jurisdiction to decide this case because the decision below rests on an adequate and independent state ground. The court below referred twice to the State Constitution in its opinion, but otherwise relied exclusively on federal law. [3] Long argues that the Michigan courts have provided greater protection from searches and seizures under the State Constitution than is afforded under the Fourth Amendment, and the references to the State Constitution therefore establish an adequate and independent ground for the decision below.

It is, of course,

"incumbent upon this Court . . . to ascertain for itself . . . whether the asserted nonfederal ground independently and adequately supports the judgment."

Abie State Bank v. Bryan, 282 U. S. 765, 282 U. S. 773 (1931). Although we have announced a number of principles in order to help us determine whether various forms of references to state law constitute adequate and independent state grounds, [4] we openly admit that we have thus far not developed a satisfying and consistent approach for resolving this vexing issue. In some instances, we have taken the strict view that, if the ground of decision was at all unclear, we would dismiss the case. See, e.g., Lynch v. New York ex rel. Pierson, 293 U. S. 52 (1934). In other instances, we have vacated, see, e.g., Minnesota v. National Tea Co., 309 U. S. 551 (1940), or continued a case, see, e.g., Herb v. Pitcairn, 324 U. S. 117 (1945), in order to obtain clarification about the nature of a state court decision. See also California v. Krivda, 409 U. S. 33 (1972). In more recent cases, we have ourselves examined state law to determine whether state courts have used federal law to guide their application of state law or to provide the actual basis for the decision that was reached. See Texas v. Brown, 460 U. S. 730, 460 U. S. 732-733, n. 1 (1983) (plurality opinion). Cf. South Dakota v. Neville, 459 U. S. 553, 459 U. S. 569 (1983) (STEVENS, J., dissenting). In Oregon v. Kennedy, 456 U. S. 667, 456 U. S. 670-671 (1982), we rejected an invitation to remand to the state court for clarification even when the decision rested in part on a case from the state court, because we determined that the state case itself rested upon federal grounds. We added that,

"[e]ven if the case admitted of more doubt as to whether federal and state grounds for decision were intermixed, the fact that the state court relied to the extent it did on federal grounds requires us to reach the merits."

Id. at 456 U. S. 671.

This ad hoc method of dealing with cases that involve possible adequate and independent state grounds is antithetical to the doctrinal consistency that is required when sensitive issues of federal-state relations are involved. Moreover, none of the various methods of disposition that we have employed thus far recommends itself as the preferred method that we should apply to the exclusion of others, and we therefore determine that it is appropriate to reexamine our treatment of this jurisdictional issue in order to achieve the consistency that is necessary.

The process of examining state law is unsatisfactory because it requires us to interpret state laws with which we are generally unfamiliar, and which often, as in this case, have not been discussed at length by the parties. Vacation and continuance for clarification have also been unsatisfactory, both because of the delay and decrease in efficiency of judicial administration, see Dixon v. Duffy, 344 U. S. 143 (1952), [5] and, more important, because these methods of disposition place significant burdens on state courts to demonstrate the presence or absence of our jurisdiction. See Philadelphia Newspapers, Inc. v. Jerome, 434 U. S. 241, 434 U. S. 244 (1978) (REHNQUIST, J., dissenting); Department of Motor Vehicles v. Rios, 410 U. S. 425, 410 U. S. 427 (973) (Douglas, J., dissenting). Finally, outright dismissal of cases is clearly not a panacea, because it cannot be doubted that there is an important need for uniformity in federal law, and that this need goes unsatisfied when we fail to review an opinion that rests primarily upon federal grounds and where the independence of an alleged state ground is not apparent from the four corners of the opinion. We have long recognized that dismissal is inappropriate "where there is strong indication . . . that the federal constitution as judicially construed controlled the decision below." National Tea Co., supra, at 309 U. S. 556.

Respect for the independence of state courts, as well as avoidance of rendering advisory opinions, have been the cornerstones of this Court's refusal to decide cases where there is an adequate and independent state ground. It is precisely because of this respect for state courts, and this desire to avoid advisory opinions, that we do not wish to continue to decide issues of state law that go beyond the opinion that we review, or to require state courts to reconsider cases to clarify the grounds of their decisions. Accordingly, when, as in this case, a state court decision fairly appears to rest primarily on federal law, or to be interwoven with the federal law, and when the adequacy and independence of any possible state law ground is not clear from the face of the opinion, we will accept as the most reasonable explanation that the state court decided the case the way it did because it believed that federal law required it to do so. If a state court chooses merely to rely on federal precedents as it would on the precedents of all other jurisdictions, then it need only make clear by a plain statement in its judgment or opinion that the federal cases are being used only for the purpose of guidance, and do not themselves compel the result that the court has reached. In this way, both justice and judicial administration will be greatly improved. If the state court decision indicates clearly and expressly that it is alternatively based on bona fide separate, adequate, and independent grounds, we, of course, will not undertake to review the decision.

This approach obviates in most instances the need to examine state law in order to decide the nature of the state court decision, and will at the same time avoid the danger of our rendering advisory opinions. [6] It also avoids the unsatisfactory and intrusive practice of requiring state courts to clarify their decisions to the satisfaction of this Court. We believe that such an approach will provide state judges with a clearer opportunity to develop state jurisprudence unimpeded by federal interference, and yet will preserve the integrity of federal law.

"It is fundamental that state courts be left free and unfettered by us in interpreting their state constitutions. But it is equally important that ambiguous or obscure adjudications by state courts do not stand as barriers to a determination by this Court of the validity under the federal constitution of state action."

National Tea Co., supra, at 309 U. S. 557.

The principle that we will not review judgments of state courts that rest on adequate and independent state grounds is based, in part, on "the limitations of our own jurisdiction." Herb v. Pitcairn, 324 U. S. 117, 324 U. S. 125 (1945). [7]

The jurisdictional concern is that we not

"render an advisory opinion, and if the same judgment would be rendered by the state court after we corrected its views of federal laws, our review could amount to nothing more than an advisory opinion."

Id. at 324 U. S. 126. Our requirement of a "plain statement" that a decision rests upon adequate and independent state grounds does not in any way authorize the rendering of advisory opinions. Rather, in determining, as we must, whether we have jurisdiction to review a case that is alleged to rest on adequate and independent state grounds, see Abie State Bank v. Bryan, 282 U.S. at 282 U. S. 773, we merely assume that there are no such grounds when it is not clear from the opinion itself that the state court relied upon an adequate and independent state ground and when it fairly appears that the state court rested its decision primarily on federal law. [8]

Our review of the decision below under this framework leaves us unconvinced that it rests upon an independent state ground. Apart from its two citations to the State Constitution, the court below relied exclusively on its understanding of Terry and other federal cases. Not a single state case was cited to support the state court's holding that the search of the passenger compartment was unconstitutional. [9] Indeed, the court declared that the search in this case was unconstitutional because "[t]he Court of Appeals erroneously applied the principles of Terry v. Ohio . . . to the search of the interior of the vehicle in this case." 413 Mich. at 471, 320 N.W.2d at 869. The references to the State Constitution in no way indicate that the decision below rested on grounds in any way independent from the state court's interpretation of federal law. Even if we accept that the Michigan Constitution has been interpreted to provide independent protection for certain rights also secured under the Fourth Amendment, it fairly appears in this case that the Michigan

Supreme Court rested its decision primarily on federal law.

Rather than dismissing the case, or requiring that the state court reconsider its decision on our behalf solely because of a mere possibility that an adequate and independent ground supports the judgment, we find that we have jurisdiction in the absence of a plain statement that the decision below rested on an adequate and independent state ground. It appears to us that the state court "felt compelled by what it understood to be federal constitutional considerations to construe . . . its own law in the manner it did." Zacchini v. Scripps-Howard Broadcasting Co., 433 U. S. 562, 433 U. S. 568 (1977). [10]

III

The court below held, and respondent Long contends, that Deputy Howell's entry into the vehicle cannot be justified under the principles set forth in Terry, because "Terry authorized only a limited pat-down search of a person suspected of criminal activity," rather than a search of an area. 413 Mich. at 472, 320 N.W.2d at 869 (footnote omitted). Brief for Respondent 10. Although Terry did involve the protective frisk of a person, we believe that the police action in this case is justified by the principles that we have already established in Terry and other cases.

In Terry, the Court examined the validity of a "stop and frisk" in the absence of probable cause and a warrant. The police officer in Terry detained several suspects to ascertain their identities after the officer had observed the suspects for a brief period of time and formed the conclusion that they were about to engage in criminal activity. Because the officer feared that the suspects were armed, he patted down the outside of the suspects' clothing and discovered two revolvers.

Examining the reasonableness of the officer's conduct in Terry, [11] we held that there is

"'no ready test for determining reasonableness other than by balancing the need to search [or seize] against the invasion which the search [or seizure] entails.'"

392 U.S. at 392 U. S. 21 (quoting Camara v. Municipal Court, 387 U. S. 523, 387 U. S. 536-537 (1967)). Although the conduct of the officer in Terry involved a "severe, though brief, intrusion upon cherished personal security," 392 U.S. at 392 U. S. 24-25, we found that the conduct was reasonable when we weighed the interest of the individual against the legitimate interest in "crime prevention and detection," id. at 392 U. S. 22, and the

"need for law enforcement officers to protect themselves and other prospective victims of violence in situations where they may lack probable cause for an arrest."

Id. at 392 U. S. 24. When the officer has a reasonable belief

"that the individual whose suspicious behavior he is investigating at close range is armed and presently dangerous to the officer or to others, it would appear to be clearly unreasonable to deny the officer the power to take necessary measures to determine whether the person is in fact carrying a weapon and to neutralize the threat of physical harm."

Ibid.

Although Terry itself involved the stop and subsequent patdown search of a person, we were careful to note that

"[w]e need not develop at length in this case, however, the limitations which the Fourth Amendment places upon a protective search and seizure for weapons. These limitations will have to be developed in the concrete factual circumstances of individual cases."

Id. at 392 U. S. 29. Contrary to Long's view, Terry need not be read as restricting the preventative search to the person of the detained suspect. [12]

In two cases in which we applied Terry to specific factual situations, we recognized that investigative detentions involving suspects in vehicles are especially fraught with danger to police officers. In Pennsylvania v. Mimms, 434 U. S. 106 (1977), we held that police may order persons out of an automobile during a stop for a traffic violation, and may frisk those persons for weapons if there is a reasonable belief that they are armed and dangerous. Our decision rested in part on the "inordinate risk confronting an officer as he approaches a person seated in an automobile." Id. at 434 U. S. 110. In Adams v. Williams, 407 U. S. 143 (1972), we held that the police, acting on an informant's tip, may reach into the passenger compartment of an automobile to remove a gun from a driver's waistband even where the gun was not apparent to police from outside the car and the police knew of its existence only because of the tip. Again, our decision rested in part on our view of the danger presented to police officers in "traffic stop" and automobile situations. [13]

Finally, we have also expressly recognized that suspects may injure police officers and others by virtue of their access to weapons, even though they may not themselves be armed. In the Term following Terry, we decided Chimel v. California, 395 U. S. 752 (1969), which involved the limitations imposed on police authority to conduct a search incident to a valid arrest. Relying explicitly on Terry, we held that, when an arrest is made, it is reasonable for the arresting officer to search

"the arrestee's person and the area 'within his immediate control' -- construing that phrase to mean the area from within which he might gain possession of a weapon or destructible evidence."

395 U.S. at 395 U. S. 763. We reasoned that

"[a] gun on a table or in a drawer in front of one who is arrested can be as dangerous to the arresting officer as one concealed in the clothing of the person arrested."

Ibid. In New York v. Belton, 453 U. S. 454 (1981), we determined that the lower courts

"have found no workable definition of 'the area within the immediate control of the arrestee' when that area arguably includes the interior of an automobile and the arrestee is its recent occupant."

Id. at 453 U. S. 460. In order to provide a "workable rule," ibid., we held that

"articles inside the relatively narrow compass of the passenger compartment of an automobile are in fact generally, even if not inevitably, within 'the area into which an arrestee might reach in order to grab a weapon.' . . ."

Ibid. (quoting Chimel, supra, at 395 U. S. 763). We also held that the police may examine the contents of any open or closed container found within the passenger compartment, "for if the passenger compartment is within the reach of the arrestee, so will containers in it be within his reach." 453 U.S. at 453 U. S. 460 (footnote omitted). See also Michigan v. Summers, 452 U. S. 692, 452 U. S. 702 (1981).

Our past cases indicate, then, that protection of police and others can justify protective searches when police have a reasonable belief that the suspect poses a danger, that roadside encounters between police and suspects are especially hazardous, and that danger may arise from the possible presence of weapons in the area surrounding a suspect. These principles compel our conclusion that the search of the passenger compartment of an automobile, limited to those areas in which a weapon may be placed or hidden, is permissible if the police officer possesses a reasonable belief based on "specific and articulable facts which, taken together with the rational inferences from those facts, reasonably warrant" the officer in believing that the suspect is dangerous and the suspect may gain immediate control of weapons. [14] See Terry, 392 U.S. at 392 U. S. 21.

"[T]he issue is whether a reasonably prudent man in the circumstances would be warranted in the belief that his safety or that of others was in danger."

Id. at 392 U. S. 27. If a suspect is "dangerous," he is no less dangerous simply because he is not arrested. If, while conducting a legitimate Terry search of the interior of the automobile, the officer should, as here, discover contraband other than weapons, he clearly cannot be required to ignore the contraband, and the Fourth Amendment does not require its suppression in such circumstances. Coolidge v. New Hampshire, 403 U. S. 443, 403 U. S. 465 (1971); Michigan v. Tyler, 436 U. S. 499, 436 U. S. 509 (1978); Texas v. Brown, 460 U.S. at 460 U. S. 739 (plurality opinion by REHNQUIST, J.); id. at 460 U. S. 746 (POWELL, J., concurring in judgment).

The circumstances of this case clearly justified Deputies Howell and Lewis in their reasonable belief that Long posed a danger if he were permitted to reenter his vehicle. The hour was late, and the area rural. Long was driving his automobile at excessive speed, and his car swerved into a ditch. The officers had to repeat their questions to Long, who appeared to be "under the influence" of some intoxicant. Long was not frisked until the officers observed that there was a large knife in the interior of the car into which Long was about to reenter. The subsequent search of the car was restricted to those areas to which Long would generally have immediate control, and that could contain a weapon. The trial court determined that the leather pouch containing marihuana could have contained a weapon. App. 64a. [15] It is clear that the intrusion was "strictly circumscribed by the exigencies which justifi[ed] its initiation." Terry, supra, at 392 U. S. 26.

In evaluating the validity of an officer's investigative or protective conduct under Terry, the

"[t]ouchstone of our analysis . . . is always 'the reasonableness in all the circumstances of the particular governmental invasion of a citizen's personal security.'"

Pennsylvania v. Mimms, 434 U.S. at 434 U. S. 108-109 (quoting Terry, supra, at 392 U. S. 19). In this case, the officers did not act unreasonably in taking preventive measures to ensure that there were no other weapons within Long's immediate grasp before permitting him to reenter his automobile. Therefore, the balancing required by Terry clearly weighs in favor of allowing the police to conduct an area search of the passenger compartment to uncover weapons, as long as they possess an articulable and objectively reasonable belief that the suspect is potentially dangerous.

The Michigan Supreme Court appeared to believe that it was not reasonable for the officers to fear that Long could injure them, because he was effectively under their control during the investigative stop and could not get access to any weapons that might have been located in the automobile. See 413 Mich. at 472, 320 N.W.2d at 869. This reasoning is mistaken in several respects. During any investigative detention, the suspect is "in the control" of the officers in the sense that he "may be briefly detained against his will. . . ." Terry, supra, at 392 U. S. 34 (WHITE, J., concurring). Just as a Terry suspect on the street may, despite being under the brief control of a police officer, reach into his clothing and retrieve a weapon, so might a Terry suspect in Long's position break away from police control and retrieve a weapon from his automobile. See United State v. Rainone, 586 F.2d 1132 1134 (CA7 1978), cert. denied, 440 U.S. 980 (1979). In addition, if the suspect is not placed under arrest, he will be permitted to reenter his automobile, and he will then have access to any weapons inside. United States v. Powless, 546 F.2d 792, 795-796 (CA8), cert. denied, 430 U.S. 910 (1977). Or, as here, the suspect may be permitted to reenter the vehicle before the Terry investigation is over, and again, may have access to weapons. In any event, we stress that a Terry investigation, such as the one that occurred here, involves a police investigation "at close range," Terry, 392 U.S. at 392 U. S. 24, when the officer remains particularly vulnerable in part because a full custodial arrest has not been effected, and the officer must make a "quick decision as to how to protect himself and others from possible danger. . . ." Id. at 392 U. S. 28. In such circumstances, we have not required that officers adopt alternative means to ensure their safety in order to avoid the intrusion involved in a Terry encounter. [16]

IV

The trial court and the Court of Appeals upheld the search of the trunk as a valid inventory search under this Court's decision in South Dakota v. Opperman, 428 U. S. 364 (1976). The Michigan Supreme Court did not address this holding, and instead suppressed the marihuana taken from the trunk as a fruit of the illegal search of the interior of the automobile. Our holding that the initial search was justified under Terry makes it necessary to determine whether the trunk search was permissible under the Fourth Amendment. However, we decline to address this question, because it was not passed upon by the Michigan Supreme Court, whose decision we review in this case. See Cardinale v. Louisiana, 394 U. S. 437, 394 U. S. 438 (1969). We remand this issue to the court below, to enable it to determine whether the trunk search was permissible under Opperman, supra, or other decisions of this Court. See, e.g., United States v. Ross, 456 U. S. 798 (1982). [17]

The judgment of the Michigan Supreme Court is reversed, and the case is remanded for further proceedings not inconsistent with this opinion.

It is so ordered.

Oliver v. US (April 17, 1984)

JUSTICE POWELL delivered the opinion of the Court.

The "open fields" doctrine, first enunciated by this Court in Hester v. United States, 265 U. S. 57 (1924), permits police officers to enter and search a field without a warrant. We granted certiorari in these cases to clarify confusion that has arisen as to the continued vitality of the doctrine.

I

No. 8215. Acting on reports that marihuana was being raised on the farm of petitioner Oliver, two narcotics agents of the Kentucky State Police went to the farm to investigate. [1] Arriving at the farm, they drove past petitioner's house to a locked gate with a "No Trespassing" sign. A footpath led around one side of the gate. The agents walked around the gate and along the road for several hundred yards, passing a barn and a parked camper. At that point, someone standing in front of the camper shouted: "No hunting is allowed, come back up here." The officers shouted back that they were Kentucky State Police officers, but found no one when they returned to the camper. The officers resumed their investigation of the farm and found a field of marihuana over a mile from petitioner's home.

Petitioner was arrested and indicted for "manufactur[ing]" a "controlled substance." 21 U.S.C. § 841(a)(1). After a pretrial hearing, the District Court suppressed evidence of the discovery of the marihuana field. Applying Katz v. United States, 389 U. S. 347, 389 U. S. 357 (1967), the court found that petitioner had a reasonable expectation that the field would remain private because petitioner "had done all that could be expected of him to assert his privacy in the area of farm that was searched." He had posted "No Trespassing" signs at regular intervals and had locked the gate at the entrance to the center of the farm. App. to Pet. for Cert. in No. 82-15, pp. 23-24. Further, the court noted that the field itself is highly secluded: it is bounded on all sides by woods, fences, and embankments, and cannot be seen from any point of public access. The court concluded that this was not an "open" field that invited casual intrusion.

The Court of Appeals for the Sixth Circuit, sitting en banc, reversed the District Court. 686 F.2d 356 (1982). [2] The court concluded that Katz, upon which the District Court relied, had not impaired the vitality of the open fields doctrine of Hester. Rather, the open fields doctrine was entirely compatible with Katz' emphasis on privacy. The court reasoned that the "human relations that create the need for privacy do not ordinarily take place" in open fields, and that the property owner's common law right to exclude trespassers is insufficiently linked to privacy to warrant the Fourth Amendment's protection. 686 F.2d at 360. [3] We granted certiorari. 459 U.S. 1168 (1983).

No. 82-1273. After receiving an anonymous tip that marihuana was being grown in the woods behind respondent Thornton's residence, two police officers entered the woods by a path between this residence and a neighboring house. They followed a footpath through the woods until they reached two marihuana patches fenced with chicken wire. Later, the officers determined that the patches were on the property of respondent, obtained a warrant to search the property, and seized the marihuana. On the basis of this evidence, respondent was arrested and indicted.

The trial court granted respondent's motion to suppress the fruits of the second search. The warrant for this search was premised on information that the police had obtained during their previous warrantless search, that the court found to be unreasonable. [4] "No Trespassing" signs and the secluded location of the marihuana

patches evinced a reasonable expectation of privacy. Therefore, the court held, the open fields doctrine did not apply.

The Maine Supreme Judicial Court affirmed. 453 A.2d 489 (1982). It agreed with the trial court that the correct question was whether the search "is a violation of privacy on which the individual justifiably relied," id. at 493, and that the search violated respondent's privacy. The court also agreed that the open fields doctrine did not justify the search. That doctrine applies, according to the court, only when officers are lawfully present on property and observe "open and patent" activity. Id. at 495. In this case, the officers had trespassed upon defendant's property, and the respondent had made every effort to conceal his activity. We granted certiorari. 460 U.S. 1068 (1983). [5]

II

The rule announced in Hester v. United States was founded upon the explicit language of the Fourth Amendment. That Amendment indicates with some precision the places and things encompassed by its protections. As Justice Holmes explained for the Court in his characteristically laconic style:

"[T]he special protection accorded by the Fourth Amendment to the people in their 'persons, houses, papers, and effects' is not extended to the open fields. The distinction between the latter and the house is as old as the common law."

Hester v. United States, 265 U.S. at 265 U. S. 59. [6]

Nor are the open fields "effects" within the meaning of the Fourth Amendment. In this respect, it is suggestive that James Madison's proposed draft of what became the Fourth Amendment preserves

"[t]he rights of the people to be secured in their persons, their houses, their papers, and their other property, from all unreasonable searches and seizures. . . ."

See N. Lasson, The History and Development of the Fourth Amendment to the United States Constitution 100, n. 77 (1937). Although Congress' revisions of Madison's proposal broadened the scope of the Amendment in some respects, id. at 100-103, the term "effects" is less inclusive than "property," and cannot be said to encompass open fields. [7] We conclude, as did the Court in deciding Hester v. United States, that the government's intrusion upon the open fields is not one of those "unreasonable searches" proscribed by the text of the Fourth Amendment.

III

This interpretation of the Fourth Amendment's language is consistent with the understanding of the right to privacy expressed in our Fourth Amendment jurisprudence. Since Katz v. United States, 389 U. S. 347 (1967), the touchstone of Amendment analysis has been the question whether a person has a "constitutionally protected reasonable expectation of privacy." Id. at 389 U. S. 360 (Harlan, J., concurring). The Amendment does not protect the merely subjective expectation of privacy, but only those "expectation[s] that society is prepared to recognize as reasonable.'" Id. at 389 U. S. 361. See also Smith v. Maryland, 442 U. S. 735, 442 U. S. 740-741 (1979).

A

No single factor determines whether an individual legitimately may claim under the Fourth Amendment that a place should be free of government intrusion not authorized by warrant. See Rakas v. Illinois, 439 U. S. 128, 439 U. S. 152-153 (1978) (POWELL, J., concurring). In assessing the degree to which a search infringes upon individual privacy, the Court has given weight to such factors as the intention of the Framers of the Fourth Amendment, e.g., United States v. Chadwick, 433 U. S. 1, 433 U. S. 7-8 (1977), the uses to which the individual has put a location, e.g., Jones v. United States, 362 U. S. 257, 362 U.

S. 265 (1960), and our societal understanding that certain areas deserve the most scrupulous protection from government invasion, e.g., Payton v. New York, 445 U. S. 573 (1980). These factors are equally relevant to determining whether the government's intrusion upon open fields without a warrant or probable cause violates reasonable expectations of privacy, and is therefore a search proscribed by the Amendment.

In this light, the rule of Hester v. United States, supra, that we reaffirm today, may be understood as providing that an individual may not legitimately demand privacy for activities conducted out of doors in fields, except in the area immediately surrounding the home. See also Air Pollution Variance Bd. v. Western Alfalfa Corp., 416 U. S. 861, 416 U. S. 865 (1974). This rule is true to the conception of the right to privacy embodied in the Fourth Amendment. The Amendment reflects the recognition of the Framers that certain enclaves should be free from arbitrary government interference. For example, the Court, since the enactment of the Fourth Amendment, has stressed "the overriding respect for the sanctity of the home that has been embedded in our traditions since the origins of the Republic." Payton v. New York, supra, at 445 U. S. 601. [8] See also Silverman v. United States, 365 U. S. 505, 365 U. S. 511 (1961); United States v. United States District Court, 407 U. S. 297, 407 U. S. 313 (1972).

In contrast, open fields do not provide the setting for those intimate activities that the Amendment is intended to shelter from government interference or surveillance. There is no societal interest in protecting the privacy of those activities, such as the cultivation of crops, that occur in open fields. Moreover, as a practical matter, these lands usually are accessible to the public and the police in ways that a home, an office, or commercial structure would not be. It is not generally true that fences or "No Trespassing" signs effectively bar the public from viewing open fields in rural areas. And both petitioner Oliver and respondent Thornton concede that the public and police lawfully may survey lands from the air. [9] For these reasons, the asserted expectation of privacy in open fields is not an expectation that "society recognizes as reasonable." [10]

The historical underpinnings of the open fields doctrine also demonstrate that the doctrine is consistent with respect for "reasonable expectations of privacy." As Justice Holmes, writing for the Court, observed in Hester, 265 U.S. at 265 U. S. 59, the common law distinguished "open fields" from the "curtilage," the land immediately surrounding and associated with the home. See 4 W. Blackstone, Commentaries *225. The distinction implies that only the curtilage, not the neighboring open fields, warrants the Fourth Amendment protections that attach to the home. At common law, the curtilage is the area to which extends the intimate activity associated with the "sanctity of a man's home and the privacies of life," Boyd v. United States, 116 U. S. 616, 116 U. S. 630 (1886), and therefore has been considered part of the home itself for Fourth Amendment purposes. Thus, courts have extended Fourth Amendment protection to the curtilage; and they have defined the curtilage, as did the common law, by reference to the factors that determine whether an individual reasonably may expect that an area immediately adjacent to the home will remain private. See, e.g., United States v. Van Dyke, 643 F.2d 992, 993-994 (CA4 1981); United States v. Williams, 581 F.2d 451, 453 (CA5 1978); Care v. United States, 231 F.2d 22, 25 (CA10), cert. denied, 351 U.S. 932 (1956). Conversely, the common law implies, as we reaffirm today, that no expectation of privacy legitimately attaches to open fields. [11]

We conclude, from the text of the Fourth Amendment and from the historical and contemporary understanding of its purposes, that an individual has no legitimate expectation that open fields will remain free from warrantless intrusion by government officers.

B

Petitioner Oliver and respondent Thornton contend, to the contrary, that the circumstances of a search sometimes may indicate that reasonable expectations of privacy were violated, and that courts therefore should analyze these circumstances on a case-by-case basis. The language of the Fourth Amendment itself answers their contention.

Nor would a case-by-case approach provide a workable accommodation between the needs of law enforcement and the interests protected by the Fourth Amendment. Under this approach, police officers would have to guess before every search whether landowners had erected fences sufficiently high, posted a sufficient number of warning signs, or located contraband in an area sufficiently secluded to establish a right of privacy. The lawfulness of a search would turn on

"'[a] highly sophisticated set of rules, qualified by all sorts of ifs, ands, and buts, and requiring the drawing of subtle nuances and hairline distinctions. . . .'"

New York v. Belton, 453 U. S. 454, 453 U. S. 458 (1981) (quoting LaFave, "Case-By-Case Adjudication" versus "Standardized Procedures": The Robinson Dilemma, 1974 S.Ct.Rev. 127, 142). This Court repeatedly has acknowledged the difficulties created for courts, police, and citizens by an ad hoc, case-by-case definition of Fourth Amendment standards to be applied in differing factual circumstances. See Belton, supra, at 453 U. S. 458-460; Robbins v. California, 453 U. S. 420, 453 U. S. 430 (1981) (POWELL, J., concurring in judgment); Dunaway v. New York, 442 U. S. 200, 442 U. S. 213-214 (1979); United States v. Robinson, 414 U. S. 218, 414 U. S. 235 (1973). The ad hoc approach not only makes it difficult for the policeman to discern the scope of his authority, Belton, supra, at 453 U. S. 460; it also creates a danger that constitutional rights will be arbitrarily and inequitably enforced. Cf. Smith v. Goguen, 415 U. S. 566, 415 U. S. 572-573 (1974). [12]

IV

In any event, while the factors that petitioner Oliver and respondent Thornton urge the courts to consider may be relevant to Fourth Amendment analysis in some contexts, these factors cannot be decisive on the question whether the search of an open field is subject to the Amendment. Initially, we reject the suggestion that steps taken to protect privacy establish that expectations of privacy in an open field are legitimate. It is true, of course, that petitioner Oliver and respondent Thornton, in order to conceal their criminal activities, planted the marihuana upon secluded land and erected fences and "No Trespassing" signs around the property. And it may be that, because of such precautions, few members of the public stumbled upon the marihuana crops seized by the police. Neither of these suppositions demonstrates, however, that the expectation of privacy was legitimate in the sense required by the Fourth Amendment. The test of legitimacy is not whether the individual chooses to conceal assertedly "private" activity. [13] Rather, the correct inquiry is whether the government's intrusion infringes upon the personal and societal values protected by the Fourth Amendment. As we have explained, we find no basis for concluding that a police inspection of open fields accomplishes such an infringement.

Nor is the government's intrusion upon an open field a "search" in the constitutional sense because that intrusion is a trespass at common law. The existence of a property right is but one element in determining whether expectations of privacy are legitimate. "The premise that property interests control the right of the Government to search and seize has been discredited.'" Katz, 389 U.S. at 389 U. S. 353 (quoting Warden v. Hayden, 387 U. S. 294, 387 U. S. 304 (1967)).

"[E]ven a property interest in premises may not be sufficient to establish a legitimate expectation of privacy with respect to particular items located on the premises or activity conducted thereon."

Rakas v. Illinois, 439 U.S. at 439 U. S. 144, n. 12.

The common law may guide consideration of what areas are protected by the Fourth Amendment by defining areas whose invasion by others is wrongful. Id. at 430 U. S. 153 (POWELL, J., concurring). [14] The law of trespass, however, forbids intrusions upon land that the Fourth Amendment would not proscribe. For trespass law extends to instances where the exercise of the right to exclude vindicates no legitimate privacy interest. [15] Thus, in the case of open fields, the general rights of property protected by the common law of trespass have little or no relevance to the applicability of the Fourth Amendment.

V

We conclude that the open fields doctrine, as enunciated in Hester, is consistent with the plain language of the Fourth Amendment and its historical purposes. Moreover, Justice Holmes' interpretation of the Amendment in Hester accords with the "reasonable expectation of privacy" analysis developed in subsequent decisions of this Court. We therefore affirm Oliver v. United States; Maine v. Thornton is reversed and remanded for further proceedings not inconsistent with this opinion.

It is so ordered.

Notes

[1] It is conceded that the police did not have a warrant authorizing the search, that there was no probable cause for the search, and that no exception to the warrant requirement is applicable.

[2] A panel of the Sixth Circuit had affirmed the suppression order. 657 F.2d 85 (1981).

[3] The four dissenting judges contended

that the open fields doctrine did not apply where, as in this case, "reasonable effort[s] [have] been made to exclude the public." 686 F.2d at 372. To that extent, the dissent considered that Katz v. United States implicitly had overruled previous holdings of this Court. The dissent then concluded that petitioner had established a "reasonable expectation of privacy" under the Katz standard. Judge Lively also wrote separately to argue that the open fields doctrine applied only to lands that could be viewed by the public.

[4] The court also discredited other information, supplied by a confidential informant, upon which the police had based their warrant application.

[5] Respondent contends that the decision below rests upon adequate and independent state law grounds. We do not read that decision, however, as excluding the evidence because the search violated the State Constitution. The Maine Supreme Judicial Court referred only to the Fourth Amendment of the Federal Constitution, and purported to apply the Katz test; the prior state cases that the court cited also construed the Federal Constitution. In any case, the Maine Supreme Judicial Court did not articulate an independent state ground with the clarity required by Michigan v. Long, 463 U. S. 1032 (1983).

Contrary to respondent's assertion, we do not review here the state courts' finding as a matter of "fact" that the area searched was not an "open field." Rather, the question before us is the appropriate legal standard for determining whether search of that area without a warrant was lawful under the Federal Constitution.

The conflict between the two cases that we review here is illustrative of the confusion the open fields doctrine has generated among the state and federal courts. Compare, e.g., State v. Byers, 359 So.2d 84 (La.1978) (refusing to apply open fields doctrine); State v. Brady, 406 So.2d 1093 (Fla.1981) (same), with United States v. Lace, 669 F.2d 46, 50-51 (CA2 1982); United States v. Freie, 545 F.2d 1217 (CA9 1976); United States v. Brown, 473 F.2d 952, 954 (CA5 1973); Atwell v. United States, 414 F.2d 136, 138 (CA5 1969).

[6] The dissent offers no basis for its suggestion that Hester rests upon some narrow, unarticulated principle, rather than upon the reasoning enunciated by the Court's opinion in that case. Nor have subsequent cases discredited Hester's reasoning. This Court frequently has relied on the explicit language of the Fourth Amendment as delineating the scope of its affirmative protections. See, e.g., Robbins v. California, 453 U. S. 420, 453 U. S. 426 (1981) (opinion of Stewart, J.); Payton v. New York, 445 U. S. 573, 445 U. S. 589-590 (1980); Alderman v. United States, 394 U. S. 165, 394 U. S. 178-180 (1969). As these cases, decided after Katz, indicate, Katz' "reasonable expectation of privacy" standard did not sever Fourth Amendment doctrine from the Amendment's language. Katz itself construed the Amendment's protection of the person against unreasonable searches to encompass electronic eavesdropping of telephone conversations sought to be kept private; and Katz' fundamental recognition that "the Fourth Amendment protects people -- and not simply areas' -- against unreasonable searches and seizures," see 389 U.S. at 389 U. S. 353, is faithful to the Amendment's language. As Katz demonstrates, the Court fairly may respect the constraints of the Constitution's language without wedding itself to an unreasoning literalism. In contrast, the dissent's approach would ignore the language of the Constitution itself, as well as overturn this Court's governing precedent.

[7] The Framers would have understood the term "effects" to be limited to personal, rather than real, property. See generally Doe v. Dring, 2 M. & S. 448, 454, 105 Eng.Rep. 447, 449 (K. B. 1814) (discussing prior cases); 2 W. Blackstone, Commentaries *16, *384-*385.

[8] The Fourth Amendment's protection of offices and commercial buildings, in which there may be legitimate expectations of privacy, is also based upon societal expectations that have deep roots in the history of the Amendment. See Marshall v. Barlow's, Inc., 436 U. S. 307, 436 U. S. 311 (1978); G. M. Leasing Corp. v. United States, 429 U. S. 338, 429 U. S. 355 (1977).

[9] Tr. of Oral Arg. 14-15, 58. See, e.g., United States v. Allen, 675 F.2d 1373, 1380-1381 (CA9 1980); United States v. DeBacker, 493 F.Supp. 1078, 1081 (WD Mich.1980). In practical terms, petitioner Oliver's and respondent Thornton's analysis merely would require law enforcement officers, in most situations, to use aerial surveillance to gather the information necessary to obtain a warrant or to justify warrantless entry onto the property. It is not easy to see how such a requirement would advance legitimate privacy interests.

[10] The dissent conceives of open fields as bustling with private activity as diverse as lovers' trysts and worship services. Post at 466 U. S. 191-193. But in most instances, police will disturb no one when they enter upon open fields. These fields, by their very character as open and unoccupied, are unlikely to provide the setting for activities whose privacy is sought to be protected by the Fourth Amendment. One need think only of the vast expanse of some western ranches or of the undeveloped woods of the Northwest to see the unreality of the dissent's conception. Further, the Fourth Amendment provides ample protection to activities in the open fields that might implicate an individual's privacy. An individual who enters a place defined to be "public" for Fourth Amendment analysis does not lose all claims to privacy or personal security. Cf. Arkansas v. Sanders, 442 U. S. 753, 442 U. S. 766-767 (1979) (BURGER, C.J., concurring in judgment). For example, the Fourth Amendment's protections against unreasonable arrest or unreasonable

seizure of effects upon the person remain fully applicable. See, e.g., United States v. Watson, 423 U. S. 411 (1976).

[11] Neither petitioner Oliver nor respondent Thornton has contended that the property searched was within the curtilage. Nor is it necessary in these cases to consider the scope of the curtilage exception to the open fields doctrine or the degree of Fourth Amendment protection afforded the curtilage, as opposed to the home itself. It is clear, however, that the term "open fields" may include any unoccupied or undeveloped area outside of the curtilage. An open field need be neither "open" nor a "field" as those terms are used in common speech. For example, contrary to respondent Thornton's suggestion, Tr. of Oral Arg. 21-22, a thickly wooded area nonetheless may be an open field as that term is used in construing the Fourth Amendment. See, e.g., United States v. Pruitt, 464 F.2d 494 (CA9 1972); Bedell v. State, 257 Ark. 895, 521 S.W.2d 200 (1975).

[12] The clarity of the open fields doctrine that we reaffirm today is not sacrificed, as the dissent suggests, by our recognition that the curtilage remains within the protections of the Fourth Amendment. Most of the many millions of acres that are "open fields" are not close to any structure, and so not arguably within the curtilage. And, for most homes, the boundaries of the curtilage will be clearly marked; and the conception defining the curtilage -- as the area around the home to which the activity of home life extends -- is a familiar one easily understood from our daily experience. The occasional difficulties that courts might have in applying this, like other, legal concepts do not argue for the unprecedented expansion of the Fourth Amendment advocated by the dissent.

[13] Certainly the Framers did not intend that the Fourth Amendment should shelter criminal activity wherever persons with criminal

intent choose to erect barriers and post "No Trespassing" signs.

[14] As noted above, the common law conception of the "curtilage" has served this function.

[15] The law of trespass recognizes the interest in possession and control of one's property, and for that reason permits exclusion of unwanted intruders. But it does not follow that the right to exclude conferred by trespass law embodies a privacy interest also protected by the Fourth Amendment. To the contrary, the common law of trespass furthers a range of interests that have nothing to do with privacy, and that would not be served by applying the strictures of trespass law to public officers. Criminal laws against trespass are prophylactic: they protect against intruders who poach, steal livestock and crops, or vandalize property. And the civil action of trespass serves the important function of authorizing an owner to defeat claims of prescription by asserting his own title. See, e.g., O. Holmes, The Common Law 98-100, 244-246 (1881). In any event, unlicensed use of property by others is presumptively unjustified, as anyone who wishes to use the property is free to bargain for the right to do so with the property owner, cf. R. Posner, Economic Analysis of Law 10-13, 21 (1973). For these reasons, the law of trespass confers protections from intrusion by others far broader than those required by Fourth Amendment interests.

Welsh v. Wisconsin (May 15, 1984)

JUSTICE BRENNAN delivered the opinion of the Court.

Payton v. New York, 445 U. S. 573 (1980), held that, absent probable cause and exigent circumstances, warrantless arrests in the home are prohibited by the Fourth Amendment.

But the Court in that case explicitly refused

"to consider the sort of emergency or dangerous situation, described in our cases as 'exigent circumstances,' that would justify a warrantless entry into a home for the purpose of either arrest or search."

Id. at 445 U. S. 583. Certiorari was granted in this case to decide at least one aspect of the unresolved question: whether, and if so under what circumstances, the Fourth Amendment prohibits the police from making a warrantless night entry of a person's home in order to arrest him for a nonjailable traffic offense.

I

A

Shortly before 9 o'clock on the rainy night of April 24, 1978, a lone witness, Randy Jablonic, observed a car being driven erratically. After changing speeds and veering from side to side, the car eventually swerved off the road and came to a stop in an open field. No damage to any person or property occurred. Concerned about the driver and fearing that the car would get back on the highway, Jablonic drove his truck up behind the car so as to block it from returning to the road. Another passerby also stopped at the scene, and Jablonic asked her to call the police. Before the police arrived, however, the driver of the car emerged from his vehicle, approached Jablonic's truck, and asked Jablonic for a ride home. Jablonic instead suggested that they wait for assistance in removing or repairing the car. Ignoring Jablonic's suggestion, the driver walked away from the scene.

A few minutes later, the police arrived and questioned Jablonic. He told one officer what he had seen, specifically noting that the driver was either very inebriated or very sick. The officer checked the motor vehicle registration of the abandoned car and learned that it was registered to the petitioner, Edward G. Welsh. In addition, the officer noted that the petitioner's residence was a short distance from the scene, and therefore easily within walking distance.

Without securing any type of warrant, the police proceeded to the petitioner's home, arriving about 9 p.m. When the petitioner's stepdaughter answered the door, the police gained entry into the house. [1] Proceeding upstairs to the petitioner's bedroom, they found him lying naked in bed. At this point, the petitioner was placed under arrest for driving or operating a motor vehicle while under the influence of an intoxicant, in violation of Wis.Stat. § 346.63(1) (1977). [2] The petitioner was taken to the police station, where he refused to submit to a breath-analysis test.

B

As a result of these events, the petitioner was subjected to two separate but related proceedings: one concerning his refusal to submit to a breath test and the other involving the alleged code violation for driving while intoxicated. Under the Wisconsin Vehicle Code in effect in April 1978, one arrested for driving while intoxicated under § 346.63(1) could be requested by a law enforcement officer to provide breath, blood, or urine samples for the purpose of determining the presence or quantity of alcohol. Wis.Stat. § 343.305(1) (1975). If such a request was made, the arrestee was required to submit to the appropriate testing or risk a revocation of operating privileges. Cf. South Dakota v. Neville, 459 U. S. 553 (1983) (admission into evidence of a defendant's refusal to submit to a blood alcohol test does not offend constitutional right against self-incrimination). The arrestee could challenge the officer's request, however, by refusing to undergo testing and then asking for a hearing to determine whether the refusal was justified. If, after the hearing, it was determined that the refusal was not justified, the arrestee's operating privileges would be revoked for 60 days. [3]

The statute also set forth specific criteria to be applied by a court when determining whether an arrestee's refusal to take a breath test was justified. Included among these criteria was a requirement that, before revoking the arrestee's operating privileges, the court determine that "the refusal . . . to submit to a test was unreasonable." § 343.305(2)(b)(5) (1975). It is not disputed by the parties that an arrestee's refusal to take a breath test would be reasonable, and therefore operating privileges could not be revoked, if the underlying arrest was not lawful. Indeed, state law has consistently provided that a valid arrest is a necessary prerequisite to the imposition of a breath test. See Scales v. State, 64 Wis.2d 485, 494, 219 N.W.2d 286, 292 (1974). [4] Although the statute in effect in April, 1978, referred to reasonableness, the current version of § 343.305 explicitly recognizes that one of the issues that an arrestee may raise at a refusal hearing is "whether [he] was lawfully placed under arrest for violation of s.346.63(1)." §§ 343.305(3)(b)(5)(a), (8)(b) (1981-1982). See also 67 Op.Wis.Atty.Gen. No. 93-78 (1978) ("statutory scheme . . . contemplates that a lawful arrest be made prior to a request for submission to a test"). [5]

Separate statutory provisions control the penalty that might be imposed for the substantive offense of driving while intoxicated. At the time in question, the Vehicle Code provided that a first offense for driving while intoxicated was a noncriminal violation subject to a civil forfeiture proceeding for a maximum fine of $200; a second or subsequent offense in the previous five years was a potential misdemeanor that could be punished by imprisonment for up to one year and a maximum fine of $500. Wis.Stat. § 346.65(2) (1975). Since that time, the State has made only minor amendments to these penalty provisions. Indeed, the statute continues to categorize a first offense as a civil violation that allows for only a monetary forfeiture of no more than $300. § 346.65(2)(a) (Supp.1983-1984). See State v. Albright, 98 Wis.2d 663, 672-673, 298 N.W.2d 196, 202 (App.1980).

C

As noted, in this case, the petitioner refused to submit to a breath test; he subsequently filed a timely request for a refusal hearing. Before that hearing was held, however, the State filed a criminal complaint against the petitioner for driving while intoxicated. [6] The petitioner responded by filing a motion to dismiss the complaint, relying on his contention that the underlying arrest was invalid. After receiving evidence at a hearing on this motion in July, 1980, the trial court concluded that the criminal complaint would not be dismissed because the existence of both probable cause and exigent circumstances justified the warrantless arrest. The decision at the refusal hearing, which was not held until September, 1980, was therefore preordained. In fact, the primary issue at the refusal hearing -- whether the petitioner acted reasonably in refusing to submit to a breath test because he was unlawfully placed under arrest, see supra at 466 U. S. 744-746 -- had already been determined two months earlier by the same trial court.

As expected, after the refusal hearing, the trial court concluded that the arrest of the petitioner was lawful and that the petitioner's refusal to take the breath test was therefore unreasonable. [7] Accordingly, the court issued an order suspending the petitioner's operating license for 60 days. On appeal, the suspension order was vacated by the Wisconsin Court of Appeals. See State v. Welsh, No. 80-1686 (May 26, 1981), App. 114-125. Contrary to the trial court, the appellate court concluded that the warrantless arrest of the petitioner in his home violated the Fourth Amendment because the State, although demonstrating probable cause to arrest, had not established the existence of exigent circumstances. The petitioner's refusal to submit to a breath test was therefore reasonable. [8] The Supreme Court of Wisconsin, in turn, reversed the Court of Appeals, relying on the existence of three factors that it believed constituted exigent circumstances: the need for "hot pursuit" of a suspect, the need to prevent physical harm to the offender and the public, and the need to prevent destruction of evidence. See 108 Wis.2d 319, 336-338, 321 N.W.2d 245, 254-255 (1982). Because of the important Fourth Amendment implications of the decision below, we granted certiorari. 459 U.S. 1200 (1983). [9]

II

It is axiomatic that the "physical entry of the home is the chief evil against which the wording of the Fourth Amendment is directed." United States v. United States District Court, 407 U. S. 297, 407 U. S. 313 (1972). And a principal protection against unnecessary intrusions into private dwellings is the warrant requirement imposed by the Fourth Amendment on agents of the government who seek to enter the home for purposes of search or arrest. See Johnson v. United States, 333 U. S. 10, 333 U. S. 13-14 (1948). [10] It is not surprising, therefore, that the Court has recognized, as

"a 'basic principle of Fourth Amendment law[,]' that searches and seizures inside a home without a warrant are presumptively unreasonable."

Payton v. New York, 445 U.S. at 445 U. S. 586. See Coolidge v. New Hampshire, 403 U. S. 443, 403 U. S. 474-475 (1971) ("a search or seizure carried out on a suspect's premises without a warrant is per se unreasonable, unless the police can show . . . the presence of exigent circumstances'"). See also Michigan v. Clifford, 464 U. S. 287, 464 U. S. 296-297 (1984) (plurality opinion); Steagald v. United States, 451 U. S. 204, 451 U. S. 211-212 (1981); McDonald v. United States, 335 U. S. 451, 335 U. S. 456 (1948); Johnson v. United States, supra, at 333 U. S. 13-15; Boyd v. United States, 116 U. S. 616, 116 U. S. 630 (1886).

Consistently with these long-recognized

principles, the Court decided in Payton v. New York, supra, that warrantless felony arrests in the home are prohibited by the Fourth Amendment, absent probable cause and exigent circumstances. Id. at 445 U. S. 583-590. At the same time, the Court declined to consider the scope of any exception for exigent circumstances that might justify warrantless home arrests, id. at 445 U. S. 583, thereby leaving to the lower courts the initial application of the exigent circumstances exception. [11] Prior decisions of this Court, however, have emphasized that exceptions to the warrant requirement are "few in number and carefully delineated," United States v. United States District Court, supra, at 407 U. S. 318, and that the police bear a heavy burden when attempting to demonstrate an urgent need that might justify warrantless searches or arrests. Indeed, the Court has recognized only a few such emergency conditions, see, e.g., United States v. Santana, 427 U. S. 38, 427 U. S. 42-43 (1976) (hot pursuit of a fleeing felon); Warden v. Hayden, 387 U. S. 294, 387 U. S. 298-299 (1967) (same); Schmerber v. California, 384 U. S. 757, 384 U. S. 770-771 (1966) (destruction of evidence); Michigan v. Tyler, 436 U. S. 499, 436 U. S. 509 (1978) (ongoing fire), and has actually applied only the "hot pursuit" doctrine to arrests in the home, see Santana, supra.

Our hesitation in finding exigent circumstances, especially when warrantless arrests in the home are at issue, is particularly appropriate when the underlying offense for which there is probable cause to arrest is relatively minor. Before agents of the government may invade the sanctity of the home, the burden is on the government to demonstrate exigent circumstances that overcome the presumption of unreasonableness that attaches to all warrantless home entries. See Payton v. New York, supra, at 445 U. S. 586. When the government's interest is only to arrest for a minor offense, [12] that presumption of unreasonableness is difficult to rebut, and the government usually should be allowed to make such arrests only with a warrant issued upon probable cause by a neutral and detached magistrate.

This is not a novel idea. Writing in concurrence in McDonald v. United States, 335 U. S. 451 (1948), Justice Jackson explained why a finding of exigent circumstances to justify a warrantless home entry should be severely restricted when only a minor offense has been committed:

"Even if one were to conclude that urgent circumstances might justify a forced entry without a warrant, no such emergency was present in this case. This method of law enforcement displays a shocking lack of all sense of proportion. Whether there is reasonable necessity for a search without waiting to obtain a warrant certainly depends somewhat upon the gravity of the offense thought to be in progress as well as the hazards of the method of attempting to reach it. . . . It is to me a shocking proposition that private homes, even quarters in a tenement, may be indiscriminately invaded at the discretion of any suspicious police officer engaged in following up offenses that involve no violence or threats of it. While I should be human enough to apply the letter of the law with some indulgence to officers acting to deal with threats or crimes of violence which endanger life or security, it is notable that few of the searches found by this Court to be unlawful dealt with that category of crime. . . . While the enterprise of parting fools from their money by the 'numbers' lottery is one that ought to be suppressed, I do not think its suppression is more important to society than the security of the people against unreasonable searches and seizures. When an officer undertakes to act as his own magistrate, he ought to be in a position to justify it by pointing to some real immediate and serious consequences if he postponed action to get a warrant."

Id. at 335 U. S. 459-460 (footnote

omitted).

Consistently with this approach, the lower courts have looked to the nature of the underlying offense as an important factor to be considered in the exigent circumstances calculus. In a leading federal case defining exigent circumstances, for example, the en banc United States Court of Appeals for the District of Columbia Circuit recognized that the gravity of the underlying offense was a principal factor to be weighed. Dorman v. United States, 140 U.S.App.D.C. 313, 320, 435 F.2d 385, 392 (1970). [13] Without approving all of the factors included in the standard adopted by that court, it is sufficient to note that many other lower courts have also considered the gravity of the offense an important part of their constitutional analysis.

For example, courts have permitted warrantless home arrests for major felonies if identifiable exigencies, independent of the gravity of the offense, existed at the time of the arrest. Compare United States v. Campbell, 581 F.2d 22 (CA2 1978) (allowing warrantless home arrest for armed robbery when exigent circumstances existed), with Commonwealth v. Williams, 483 Pa. 293, 396 A.2d 1177 (1978) (disallowing warrantless home arrest for murder due to absence of exigent circumstances). But of those courts addressing the issue, most have refused to permit warrantless home arrests for nonfelonious crimes. See, e.g., State v. Gertin, 190 Conn.440, 453, 461 A.2d 963, 970 (1983) ("The [exigent circumstances] exception is narrowly drawn to cover cases of real, and not contrived, emergencies. The exception is limited to the investigation of serious crimes; misdemeanors are excluded"); People v. Strelow, 96 Mich.App. 182, 190-193, 292 N.W.2d 517, 521-522 (1980). See also People v. Sanders, 59 Ill.App.3d 6, 374 N.E.2d 1315 (1978) (burglary without weapons not grave offense of violence for this purpose); State v. Bennett, 295 N.W.2d 5 (S.D.1980) (distribution of controlled substances not a grave offense for these purposes). But cf. State v. Penas, 200 Neb. 387, 263 N.W.2d 835 (1978) (allowing warrantless home arrest upon hot pursuit from commission of misdemeanor in the officer's presence; decided before Payton); State v. Niedermeyer, 48 Ore.App. 665, 617 P.2d 911 (1980) (allowing warrantless home arrest upon hot pursuit from commission of misdemeanor in the officer's presence). The approach taken in these cases should not be surprising. Indeed, without necessarily approving any of these particular holdings or considering every possible factual situation, we note that it is difficult to conceive of a warrantless home arrest that would not be unreasonable under the Fourth Amendment when the underlying offense is extremely minor.

We therefore conclude that the common-sense approach utilized by most lower courts is required by the Fourth Amendment prohibition on "unreasonable searches and seizures," and hold that an important factor to be considered when determining whether any exigency exists is the gravity of the underlying offense for which the arrest is being made. Moreover, although no exigency is created simply because there is probable cause to believe that a serious crime has been committed, see Payton, application of the exigent circumstances exception in the context of a home entry should rarely be sanctioned when there is probable cause to believe that only a minor offense, such as the kind at issue in this case, has been committed.

Application of this principle to the facts of the present case is relatively straightforward. The petitioner was arrested in the privacy of his own bedroom for a noncriminal, traffic offense. The State attempts to justify the arrest by relying on the hot-pursuit doctrine, on the threat to public safety, and on the need to preserve evidence of the petitioner's blood alcohol level. On the facts of this case, however, the claim of hot pursuit is unconvincing, because there was no immediate or continuous pursuit of the petitioner from the scene of a crime. Moreover, because the petitioner had already arrived home, and had abandoned his car at the scene of the accident, there was little remaining threat to the public safety. Hence, the only potential emergency claimed by the State was the need to ascertain the petitioner's blood alcohol level.

Even assuming, however, that the underlying facts would support a finding of this exigent circumstance, mere similarity to other cases involving the imminent destruction of evidence is not sufficient. The State of Wisconsin has chosen to classify the first offense for driving while intoxicated as a noncriminal, civil forfeiture offense for which no imprisonment is possible. See Wis.Stat. § 346.65(2) (1975); § 346.65(2)(a) (Supp.1983-1984); supra at 466 U. S. 746. This is the best indication of the State's interest in precipitating an arrest, and is one that can be easily identified both by the courts and by officers faced with a decision to arrest. See n 6, supra. Given this expression of the State's interest, a warrantless home arrest cannot be upheld simply because evidence of the petitioner's blood alcohol level might have dissipated while the police obtained a warrant. [14] To allow a warrantless home entry on these facts would be to approve unreasonable police behavior that the principles of the Fourth Amendment will not sanction.

III

The Supreme Court of Wisconsin let stand a warrantless, night-time entry into the petitioner's home to arrest him for a civil traffic offense. Such an arrest, however, is clearly prohibited by the special protection afforded the individual in his home by the Fourth Amendment. The petitioner's arrest was therefore invalid, the judgment of the Supreme Court of Wisconsin is vacated, and the case is remanded for further proceedings not inconsistent with this opinion. [15]

It is so ordered.

THE CHIEF JUSTICE would dismiss the writ as having been improvidently granted and defer resolution of the question presented to a more appropriate case.

Notes

[1] The state trial court never decided whether there was consent to the entry, because it deemed decision of that issue unnecessary in light of its finding that exigent circumstances justified the warrantless arrest. After reversing the lower court's finding of exigent circumstances, the Wisconsin Court of Appeals remanded for full consideration of the consent issue. See State v. Welsh, No. 80-1686 (May 26, 1981), App. 114-125. That remand never occurred, however, because the Supreme Court of Wisconsin reversed the Court of Appeals and reinstated the trial court's judgment. See 108 Wis.2d 319, 321 N.W.2d 245 (1982). For purposes of this decision, therefore, we assume that there was no valid consent to enter the petitioner's home.

[2] Since the petitioner's arrest, § 346.63 has been amended to provide that it is a code violation to drive or operate a motor vehicle while under the influence of an intoxicant or while evidencing certain blood or breath alcohol levels. See Wis.Stat. §§ 346.63(1)(a), (b) (1981-1982). This amendment, however, has no bearing on the issues raised by the present case.

[3] Since the petitioner's arrest, this statute also has been amended, with the current version found at Wis.Stat. § 343.305 (1981-1982). Although the procedures to be followed by the law enforcement officer and the arrestee have remained essentially unchanged, §§ 343.305(3), (8), the potential length of any revocation of operating privileges has been increased, depending on the arrestee's prior driving record, §§ 343.305(9)(a), (b). An arrestee who improperly refuses to submit to a required test may also be required to comply with an assessment order and a

driver safety plan, §§ 343.305(9)(c)(e). These amendments, however, also have no direct bearing on the issues raised by the present case.

[4] "The implied consent law does not limit the right to take a blood sample as an incident to a lawful arrest. It should be emphasized, however, that the arrest, and therefore probable cause for making it, must precede the taking of the blood sample. We conclude that the sample was constitutionally taken incident to the lawful arrest."

64 Wis.2d at 494, 219 N.W.2d at 292 (emphasis added).

Nor is there any doubt that the Supreme Court of Wisconsin applies federal constitutional standards when determining whether an arrest, even for a nonjailable traffic offense, is lawful. The court, for example, explained the basis for its holding in this case as follows:

"The trial court revoked the defendant's motor vehicle operator's license for sixty days pursuant to his unreasonable refusal to submit to a breathalyzer test, as required by [state statute]."

"The defendant challenges the officer's warrantless arrest in his residence as violating the Fourth Amendment of the United States Constitution and Article I, section 11 of the Wisconsin Constitution. The [trial court] upheld this warrantless arrest, concluding that probable cause to believe that the defendant had been operating a motor vehicle while under the influence of an intoxicant, coupled with the existence of exigent circumstances, justified the officers' entry into the defendant's residence.... [T]he court of appeals reversed the trial court, holding that, although the officers' warrantless arrest was unreasonable, thereby violating the Fourth and Fourteenth Amendments, the absence of a finding regarding the consensual entry necessitated remanding the case on that issue. We affirm the findings of the [trial court], holding that the coexistence of probable cause and exigent

circumstances in this case justifies the warrantless arrest...."

"* * * *"

"To prevail in this case, the state must prove the coexistence of probable cause and exigent circumstances, justifying the officer's conduct at the defendant's residence. We hold that there was ample evidence supporting the trial court's ruling that the officer's entry was justified on the basis of both probable cause and exigent circumstances. Entry to effect a warrantless arrest in a residence is subject to the limitations imposed by both the United States and the Wisconsin Constitutions. U.S.Const. amend. IV; Wis. Const. art. 1, sec. 11."

108 Wis.2d at 320-321, 326-327, 321 N.W.2d at 246-247, 249-250 (emphasis added) (citations and footnotes omitted).

[5] Because state law provides that evidence of the petitioner's refusal to submit to a breath test is inadmissible if the underlying arrest was unlawful, this case does not implicate the exclusionary rule under the Federal Constitution.

[6] The petitioner was charged with a criminal misdemeanor because this was his second such citation in the previous five years. See § 346.65(2) (1975). Although the petitioner was subject to a criminal charge, the police conducting the warrantless entry of his home did not know that the petitioner had ever been charged with, or much less convicted of, a prior violation for driving while intoxicated. It must be assumed, therefore, that, at the time of the arrest, the police were acting as if they were investigating and eventually arresting for a nonjailable traffic offense that constituted only a civil violation under the applicable state law. See Beck v. Ohio, 379 U. S. 89, 379 U. S. 91, 96 (1964).

[7] When ruling from the bench after the refusal hearing, the trial judge specifically indicated:

"[T]he Court is bound by its earlier ruling

that that was a valid arrest. And, I think [counsel for the petitioner] certainly will have the right to challenge that on appeal if he appeals this matter, as well as the previous ruling should there be a conviction on the underlying charge."

App. 111. See also id. at 112-113.

[8] The court remanded the case for further findings as to whether the police had entered the petitioner's home with consent. See n 1, supra.

[9] Although the state courts differed in their respective conclusions concerning exigent circumstances, they each found that the facts known to the police at the time of the warrantless home entry were sufficient to establish probable cause to arrest. The petitioner has not challenged that finding before this Court.

The parallel criminal proceedings against the petitioner, see supra at 466 U. S. 746-747, and n. 6, resulted in a misdemeanor conviction for driving while intoxicated. During the jury trial, held in early 1982, the State introduced evidence of the petitioner's refusal to submit to a breath test. His appeal from that conviction, now before the Wisconsin Court of Appeals, has been stayed pending our decision in this case. See Brief for Petitioner 17, n. 5.

[10] In Johnson, Justice Jackson eloquently explained the warrant requirement in the context of a home search:

"The point of the Fourth Amendment, which often is not grasped by zealous officers, is not that it denies law enforcement the support of the usual inferences which reasonable men draw from evidence. Its protection consists in requiring that those inferences be drawn by a neutral and detached magistrate, instead of being judged by the officer engaged in the often competitive enterprise of ferreting out crime. . . . The right of officers to thrust themselves into a home is . . . a grave concern, not only to the individual but to a society which chooses to dwell in reasonable

security and freedom from surveillance. When the right of privacy must reasonably yield to the right of search is, as a rule, to be decided by a judicial officer, not by a policeman or government enforcement agent."

333 U.S. at 333 U. S. 13-14 (footnote omitted).

[11] Our decision in Payton, allowing warrantless home arrests upon a showing of probable cause and exigent circumstances, was also expressly limited to felony arrests. See, e.g., 445 U.S. at 445 U. S. 574, 445 U. S. 602. Because we conclude that, in the circumstances presented by this case, there were no exigent circumstances sufficient to justify a warrantless home entry, we have no occasion to consider whether the Fourth Amendment may impose an absolute ban on warrantless home arrests for certain minor offenses.

[12] Even the dissenters in Payton, although believing that warrantless home arrests are not prohibited by the Fourth Amendment, recognized the importance of the felony limitation on such arrests. See id. at 445 U. S. 616-617 (WHITE, J., joined by BURGER, C.J., and REHNQUIST, J., dissenting) ("The felony requirement guards against abusive or arbitrary enforcement and ensures that invasions of the home occur only in case of the most serious crimes").

[13] See generally Donnino & Girese, Exigent Circumstances for a Warrantless Home Arrest, 45 Albany L.Rev. 90 (1980); Harbaugh & Faust, "Knock on Any Door" -- Home Arrests After Paton and Steagald, 86 Dick.L.Rev. 191, 220-233 (1982); Note, Exigent Circumstances for Warrantless Home Arrests, 23 Ariz.L.Rev. 1171 (1981).

[14] Nor do we mean to suggest that the prevention of drunken driving is not properly of major concern to the States. The State of Wisconsin, however, along with several other

States, see, e.g., Minn.Stat. § 169.121 subd. 4 (1982); Neb.Rev.Stat. § 39-669.07(1) (Supp.1983); S.D.Codified Laws § 32-23-2 (Supp.1983), has chosen to limit severely the penalties that may be imposed after a first conviction for driving while intoxicated. Given that the classification of state crimes differs widely among the States, the penalty that may attach to any particular offense seems to provide the clearest and most consistent indication of the State's interest in arresting individuals suspected of committing that offense.

[15] On remand, the state courts may consider whether the petitioner's arrest was justified because the police had validly obtained consent to enter his home. See n 1, supra.

Segura v. United States (July 5, 1984) [Judgment and opinion]

CHIEF JUSTICE BURGER delivered the opinion of the Court.

We granted certiorari to decide whether, because of an earlier illegal entry, the Fourth Amendment requires suppression of evidence seized later from a private residence pursuant to a valid search warrant which was issued on information obtained by the police before the entry into the residence.

I

Resolution of this issue requires us to consider two separate questions: first, whether the entry and internal securing of the premises constituted an impermissible seizure of all the contents of the apartment, seen and unseen; second, whether the evidence first discovered during the search of the apartment pursuant to a valid warrant issued the day after the entry should have been suppressed as "fruit" of the illegal entry. Our disposition of both questions is carefully limited.

The Court of Appeals affirmed the District Court's holding that there were no exigent circumstances to justify the warrantless entry into petitioners' apartment. That issue is not before us, and we have no reason to question the courts' holding that that search was illegal. The ensuing interference with petitioners' possessory interests in their apartment, however, is another matter. On this first question, we conclude that, assuming that there was a seizure of all the contents of the petitioners' apartment when agents secured the premises from within, that seizure did not violate the Fourth Amendment. Specifically, we hold that, where officers, having probable cause, enter premises and, with probable cause, arrest the occupants who have legitimate possessory interests in its contents and take them into custody and, for no more than the period here involved, secure the premises from within to preserve the status quo while others, in good faith, are in the process of obtaining a warrant, they do not violate the Fourth Amendment's proscription against unreasonable seizures. [1]

The illegality of the initial entry, as we will show, has no bearing on the second question. The resolution of this second question requires that we determine whether the initial entry tainted the discovery of the evidence now challenged. On this issue, we hold that the evidence discovered during the subsequent search of the apartment the following day pursuant to the valid search warrant issued wholly on information known to the officers before the entry into the apartment need not have been suppressed as "fruit" of the illegal entry, because the warrant and the information on which it was based were unrelated to the entry, and therefore constituted an independent source for the evidence under Silverthorne Lumber Co. v. United States, 251 U. S. 385 (1920).

II

In January, 1981, the New York Drug Enforcement Task Force received information indicating that petitioners Andres Segura and Luz Marina Colon probably were trafficking in cocaine from their New York apartment. Acting on this information, Task Force agents maintained continuing surveillance over petitioners until their arrest on February 12, 1981. On February 9, agents observed a meeting between Segura and Enrique Rivudalla-Vidal, during which, as it later developed, the two discussed the possible sale of cocaine by Segura to Rivudalla-Vidal. Three days later, February 12, Segura telephoned Rivudalla-Vidal and agreed to provide him with cocaine. The two agreed that the delivery would be made at 5 p.m. that day at a designated fast-food restaurant in Queens, N.Y. Rivudalla-Vidal and one Esther Parra arrived at the restaurant at 5 p.m., as agreed. While Segura and Rivudalla-Vidal visited inside the restaurant, agents observed Colon deliver a bulky package to Parra, who had remained in Rivudalla-Vidal's car in the restaurant parking lot. A short time after the delivery of the package, Rivudalla-Vidal and Parra left the restaurant and proceeded to their apartment. Task Force agents followed. The agents stopped the couple as they were about to enter Rivudalla-Vidal's apartment. Parra was found to possess cocaine; both Rivudalla-Vidal and Parra were immediately arrested.

After Rivudalla-Vidal and Parra were advised of their constitutional rights, Rivudalla-Vidal agreed to cooperate with the agents. He admitted that he had purchased the cocaine from Segura and he confirmed that Colon had made the delivery at the fast-food restaurant earlier that day, as the agents had observed. Rivudalla-Vidal informed the agents that Segura was to call him at approximately 10 o'clock that evening to learn if Rivudalla-Vidal had sold the cocaine, in which case Segura was to deliver additional cocaine.

Between 6:30 and 7 p.m. the same day, Task Force agents sought and received authorization from an Assistant United States Attorney to arrest Segura and Colon. The agents were advised by the Assistant United States Attorney that, because of the lateness of the hour, a search warrant for petitioners' apartment probably could not be obtained until the following day, but that the agents should proceed to secure the premises to prevent the destruction of evidence.

At about 7:30 p.m., the agents arrived at petitioners' apartment and established external surveillance. At 11:15 p.m., Segura, alone, entered the lobby of the apartment building, where he was immediately arrested by agents. He first claimed he did not reside in the building. The agents took him to his third floor apartment, and when they knocked on the apartment door, a woman later identified as Colon appeared; the agents then entered with Segura, without requesting or receiving permission. There were three persons in the living room of the apartment in addition to Colon. Those present were informed by the agents that Segura was under arrest and that a search warrant for the apartment was being obtained.

Following this brief exchange in the living room, the agents conducted a limited security check of the apartment to ensure that no one else was there who might pose a threat to their safety or destroy evidence. In the process, the agents observed, in a bedroom in plain view, a triple-beam scale, jars of lactose, and numerous small cellophane bags, all accouterments of drug trafficking. None of these items was disturbed by the agents. After this limited security check, Colon was arrested. In the search incident to her arrest, agents found in her purse a loaded revolver and more than $2,000 in cash. Colon, Segura, and the other occupants of the apartment were taken to Drug Enforcement Administration headquarters.

Two Task Force agents remained in petitioners' apartment awaiting the warrant. Because of what is characterized as "administrative delay," the warrant application was not presented to the Magistrate until 5 p.m. the next day. The warrant was issued, and the search was performed at approximately 6 p.m., some 19 hours after the agents' initial entry into the apartment. In the search pursuant to the warrant, agents discovered almost three pounds of cocaine, 18 rounds of .38-caliber ammunition fitting the revolver agents had found in Colon's possession at the time of her arrest, more than $50,000 cash, and records of narcotics transactions. Agents seized these items, together with those observed during the security check the previous night.

Before trial in the United States District Court in the Eastern District of New York, petitioners moved to suppress all of the evidence seized from the apartment -- the items discovered in plain view during the initial security check and those not in plain view first discovered during the subsequent warrant search. [2] After a full evidentiary hearing, the District Court granted petitioners' motion. The court ruled that there were no exigent circumstances justifying the initial entry into the apartment. Accordingly, it held that the entry, the arrest of Colon and search incident to her arrest, and the effective seizure of the drug paraphernalia in plain view were illegal. The District Court ordered this evidence suppressed as "fruits" of illegal searches.

The District Court held that the warrant later issued was supported by information sufficient to establish probable cause; however, it read United States v. Griffin, 502 F.2d 959 (CA6), cert. denied, 419 U.S. 1050 (1974), as requiring suppression of the evidence seized under the valid warrant. [3] The District Court reasoned that this evidence would not necessarily have been discovered, because, absent the illegal entry and "occupation" of the apartment, Colon might have arranged to have the drugs removed or destroyed, in which event they would not have been in the apartment when the warrant search was made. Under this analysis, the District Court held that even the drugs seized under the valid warrant were "fruit of the poisonous tree."

On an appeal limited to the admissibility of the incriminating evidence, the Court of Appeals affirmed in part and reversed in part. 663 F.2d 411 (1981). It affirmed the District Court holding that the initial warrantless entry was not justified by exigent circumstances and that the evidence discovered in plain view during the initial entry must be suppressed. [4] The Court of Appeals rejected the argument advanced by the United States that the evidence in plain view should not be excluded because it was not actually "seized" until after the search warrant was secured.

Relying upon its holding in United States v. Agapito, 620 F.2d 324 (CA2), cert. denied, 449 U.S. 834 (1980), [5] the Court of Appeals reversed the District Court's holding requiring suppression of the evidence seized under the valid warrant executed on the day following the initial entry. The Court of Appeals described as "prudentially unsound" the District Court's decision to suppress that evidence simply because it could have been destroyed had the agents not entered.

Petitioners were convicted of conspiring to distribute cocaine, in violation of 21 U.S.C. § 846, and of distributing and possessing with intent to distribute cocaine, in violation of 21 U.S.C. § 841(a)(1). On the subsequent review of these convictions, the Second Circuit affirmed, 697 F.2d 300 (1982), rejecting claims by petitioners that the search warrant was procured through material misrepresentations and that the evidence at trial was insufficient as a matter of law to support their convictions. We granted certiorari, 459 U.S. 1200 (1983), and we affirm.

III

At the outset, it is important to focus on the narrow and precise question now before us. As we have noted, the Court of Appeals agreed with the District Court that the initial warrantless entry and the limited security search were not justified by exigent circumstances, and were therefore illegal. No review of that aspect of the case was sought by the Government, and no issue concerning items observed during the initial entry is before the Court. The only issue here is whether drugs and the other items not observed during the initial entry and first discovered by the agents the day after the entry, under an admittedly valid search warrant, should have been suppressed.

The suppression or exclusionary rule is a judicially prescribed remedial measure, and, as

"with any remedial device, the application of the rule has been restricted to those areas where its remedial objectives are thought most efficaciously served."

United States v. Calandra, 414 U. S. 338, 414 U. S. 348 (1974). Under this Court's holdings, the exclusionary rule reaches not only primary evidence obtained as a direct result of an illegal search or seizure, Weeks v. United States, 232 U. S. 383 (1914), but also evidence later discovered and found to be derivative of an illegality or "fruit of the poisonous tree." Nardone v. United States, 308 U. S. 338, 308 U. S. 341 (1939). It "extends as well to the indirect as the direct products" of unconstitutional conduct. Wong Sun v. United States, 371 U. S. 471, 371 U. S. 484 (1963).

Evidence obtained as a direct result of an unconstitutional search or seizure is plainly subject to exclusion. The question to be resolved when it is claimed that evidence subsequently obtained is "tainted" or is "fruit" of a prior illegality is whether the challenged evidence was "come at by exploitation of [the initial] illegality, or instead by means sufficiently distinguishable to be purged of the primary taint.'" Id. at 371 U. S. 488 (citation omitted; emphasis added).

It has been well established for more than 60 years that evidence is not to be excluded if the connection between the illegal police conduct and the discovery and seizure of the evidence is "so attenuated as to dissipate the taint," Nardone v. United States, supra, at 306 U. S. 341. It is not to be excluded, for example, if police had an "independent source" for discovery of the evidence:

"The essence of a provision forbidding the acquisition of evidence in a certain way is that not merely evidence so acquired shall not be used before the Court, but that it shall not be used at all. Of course this does not mean that the facts thus obtained become sacred and inaccessible. If knowledge of them is gained from an independent source, they may be proved like any others."

Silverthorne Lumber Co. v. United States, 251 U.S. at 251 U. S. 392 (emphasis added). In short, it is clear from our prior holdings that "the exclusionary rule has no application [where] the Government learned of the evidence from an independent source.'" Wong Sun, supra, at 371 U. S. 487 (quoting Silverthorne Lumber Co., supra, at 251 U. S. 392); see also United States v. Crews, 445 U. S. 463 (1980); United States v. Wade, 388 U. S. 218, 388 U. S. 242 (1967); Costello v. United States, 365 U. S. 265, 365 U. S. 278-280 (1961).

IV

Petitioners argue that all of the contents of the apartment, seen and not seen, including the evidence now in question, were "seized" when the agents entered and remained on the premises while the lawful occupants were away from the apartment in police custody. The essence of this argument is that, because the contents were then under the control of the agents and no one would have been permitted to remove the incriminating evidence from the premises or destroy it, a "seizure" took place. Plainly, this argument is advanced to avoid the Silverthorne "independent source" exception. If all the contents of the apartment were "seized" at the time of the illegal entry and securing, presumably the evidence now challenged would be suppressible as primary evidence obtained as a direct result of that entry.

We need not decide whether, when the agents entered the apartment and secured the premises, they effected a seizure of the cocaine, the cash, the ammunition, and the narcotics records within the meaning of the Fourth Amendment. By its terms, the Fourth Amendment forbids only "unreasonable" searches and seizures. Assuming, arguendo, that the agents seized the entire apartment and its contents, as petitioners suggest, the seizure was not unreasonable under the totality of the circumstances.

Different interests are implicated by a seizure than by a search. United States v. Jacobsen, 466 U. S. 109, 466 U. S. 113, and n. 5, 466 U. S. 122-126 (1984); Texas v. Brown, 460 U. S. 730 (1983); id. at 460 U. S. 747-748 (STEVENS, J., concurring in judgment); United States v. Chadwick, 433 U. S. 1, 433 U. S. 13-14, n. 8 (1977); Chambers v. Maroney, 399 U. S. 42, 399 U. S. 51-52 (1970). A seizure affects only the person's possessory interests; a search affects a person's privacy interests. United States v. Jacobsen, supra, at 466 U. S. 113, and n. 5; United States v. Chadwick, supra, at 433 U. S. 13-14, n. 8; see generally Texas v. Brown, supra, at 460 U. S. 747-751 (STEVENS, J., concurring in judgment). Recognizing the generally less intrusive nature of a seizure, Chadwick, supra, at 433 U. S. 13-14, n. 8; Chambers v. Maroney, supra, at 399 U. S. 51, the Court has frequently approved warrantless seizures of property, on the basis of probable cause, for the time necessary to secure a warrant, where a warrantless search was either held to be or likely would have been held impermissible. Chambers v. Maroney, supra; United States v. Chadwick, supra; Arkansas v. Sanders, 442 U. S. 753 (1979). [6]

We focused on the issue notably in Chambers, holding that it was reasonable to seize and impound an automobile, on the basis of probable cause, for "whatever period is necessary to obtain a warrant for the search." 399 U.S. at 399 U. S. 51 (footnote omitted). We acknowledged in Chambers that following the car until a warrant could be obtained was an alternative to impoundment, albeit an impractical one. But we

allowed the seizure nonetheless, because otherwise the occupants of the car could have removed the "instruments or fruits of crime" before the search. Id. at 399 U. S. 51, n. 9. The Court allowed the warrantless seizure to protect the evidence from destruction, even though there was no immediate fear that the evidence was in the process of being destroyed or otherwise lost. The Chambers Court declared:

"For constitutional purposes, we see no difference between, on the one hand, seizing and holding the car before presenting the probable cause issue to a magistrate and, on the other hand, carrying out an immediate search without a warrant. Given probable cause to search, either course is reasonable under the Fourth Amendment."

Id. at 52 (emphasis added)

In Chadwick, we held that the warrantless search of the footlocker after it had been seized and was in a secure area of the Federal Building violated the Fourth Amendment's proscription against unreasonable searches, but neither the respondents nor the Court questioned the validity of the initial warrantless seizure of the footlocker on the basis of probable cause. The seizure of Chadwick's footlocker clearly interfered with his use and possession of the footlocker -- his possessory interest -- but we held that this did not "diminish [his] legitimate expectation that the footlocker's contents would remain private." 433 U.S. at 433 U. S. 13-14, n. 8 (emphasis added). And again, in Arkansas v. Sanders, supra, we held that, absent exigent circumstances, a warrant was required to search luggage seized from an automobile which was already in the possession and control of police at the time of the search. However, we expressly noted that the police acted not only "properly," but "commendably" in seizing the suitcase without a warrant on the basis of probable cause to believe that it contained drugs. 442 U.S. at 442 U. S. 761. The taxi into which the suitcase had been placed was about to drive away. However, just as there was no immediate threat of loss or destruction of evidence in Chambers -- since officers could have followed the car until a warrant issued -- so too, in Sanders, officers could have followed the taxicab. Indeed, there arguably was even less fear of immediate loss of the evidence in Sanders, because the suitcase at issue had been placed in the vehicle's trunk, thus rendering immediate access unlikely before police could act.

Underlying these decisions is a belief that society's interest in the discovery and protection of incriminating evidence from removal or destruction can supersede, at least for a limited period, a person's possessory interest in property, provided that there is probable cause to believe that that property is associated with criminal activity. See United States v. Place, 462 U. S. 696 (1983).

The Court has not had occasion to consider whether, when officers have probable cause to believe that evidence of criminal activity is on the premises, the temporary securing of a dwelling to prevent the removal or destruction of evidence violates the Fourth Amendment. However, in two cases, we have suggested that securing of premises under these circumstances does not violate the Fourth Amendment, at least when undertaken to preserve the status quo while a search warrant is being sought. In Mincey v. Arizona, 437 U. S. 385 (1978), we noted with approval that, to preserve evidence, a police guard had been stationed at the entrance to an apartment in which a homicide had been committed, even though

"[t]here was no indication that evidence would be lost, destroyed, or removed during the time required to obtain a search warrant."

Id. at 437 U. S. 394. Similarly, in Rawlings v. Kentucky, 448 U. S. 98 (1980), although officers secured, from within, the home of a person for whom they had an arrest warrant, and detained all occupants while other officers were obtaining a search warrant, the Court did not question the admissibility of evidence discovered pursuant to the warrant later issued. [7]

We see no reason, as Mincey and Rawlings would suggest, why the same principle applied in Chambers, Chadwick, and Sanders should not apply where a dwelling is involved. The sanctity of the home is not to be disputed. But the home is sacred in Fourth Amendment terms not primarily because of the occupants' possessory interests in the premises, but because of their privacy interests in the activities that take place within. "[T]he Fourth Amendment protects people, not places." Katz v. United States, 389 U. S. 347, 389 U. S. 351 (1967); see also Payton v. New York, 445 U. S. 573, 445 U. S. 615 (1980) (WHITE, J., dissenting).

As we have noted, however, a seizure affects only possessory interests, not privacy interests. Therefore, the heightened protection we accord privacy interests is simply not implicated where a seizure of premises, not a search, is at issue. We hold, therefore, that securing a dwelling, on the basis of probable cause, to prevent the destruction or removal of evidence while a search warrant is being sought is not itself an unreasonable seizure of either the dwelling or its contents. We reaffirm at the same time, however, that, absent exigent circumstances, a warrantless search -- such as that invalidated in Vale v. Louisiana, 399 U. S. 30, 399 U. S. 33-34 (1970) -- is illegal.

Here, the agents had abundant probable cause in advance of their entry to believe that there was a criminal drug operation being carried on in petitioners' apartment; indeed, petitioners do not dispute the probable cause determination. The agents had maintained surveillance over petitioners for weeks, and had observed petitioners leave the apartment to make sales of cocaine. Wholly apart from observations made during that extended surveillance, Rivudalla-Vidal had told agents after his arrest on February 13 that petitioners had supplied him with cocaine earlier that day, that he had not purchased all of the cocaine offered by Segura, and that Segura probably had more cocaine in the apartment. On the basis of this information, a Magistrate duly issued a search warrant, the validity of which was upheld by both the District Court and the Court of Appeals, and which is not before us now.

In this case, the agents entered and secured the apartment from within. Arguably, the wiser course would have been to depart immediately and secure the premises from the outside by a "stakeout" once the security check revealed that no one other than those taken into custody were in the apartment. But the method actually employed does not require a different result under the Fourth Amendment, insofar as the seizure is concerned. As the Court of Appeals held, absent exigent circumstances, the entry may have constituted an illegal search, or interference with petitioners' privacy interests, requiring suppression of all evidence observed during the entry. Securing of the premises from within, however, was no more an interference with the petitioners' possessory interests in the contents of the apartment than a perimeter "stakeout." In other words, the initial entry -- legal or not -- does not affect the reasonableness of the seizure. Under either method -- entry and securing from within or a perimeter stakeout -- agents control the apartment pending arrival of the warrant; both an internal securing and a perimeter stakeout interfere to the same extent with the possessory interests of the owners.

Petitioners argue that we heighten the possibility of illegal entries by a holding that the illegal entry and securing of the premises from the inside do not themselves render the seizure any more unreasonable than had the agents staked out the apartment from the outside. We disagree. In the first place, an entry in the absence of exigent circumstances is illegal. We are unwilling to believe that officers will routinely and purposely violate the law as a matter of course. Second, as a practical matter, officers who have probable cause and who are in the process of obtaining a warrant have no reason to enter the premises before the warrant issues, absent exigent circumstances, which, of course, would justify the entry. United States v. Santana, 427 U. S. 38 (1976); Johnson v. United States, 333 U. S. 10 (1948). Third, officers who enter illegally will recognize that whatever evidence they discover as a direct result of the entry may be suppressed, as it was by the Court of Appeals in this case. Finally, if officers enter without exigent circumstances to justify the entry, they expose themselves to potential civil liability under 42 U.S.C. § 1983. Bivens v. Six Unknown Federal Narcotics Agents, 403 U. S. 388 (1971).

Of course, a seizure reasonable at its inception because based upon probable cause may become unreasonable as a result of its duration or for other reasons. Cf. United States v. Place, 462 U. S. 696 (1983). Here, because of the delay in securing the warrant, the occupation of the apartment continued throughout the night and into the next day. Such delay in securing a warrant in a large metropolitan center unfortunately is not uncommon; this is not, in itself, evidence of bad faith. And there is no suggestion that the officers, in bad faith, purposely delayed obtaining the warrant. The asserted explanation is that the officers focused first on the task of processing those whom they had arrested before turning to the task of securing the warrant. It is not unreasonable for officers to believe that the former should take priority, given, as was the case here, that the proprietors of the apartment were in the custody of the officers throughout the period in question.

There is no evidence that the agents in any way exploited their presence in the apartment; they simply awaited issuance of the warrant.

Moreover, more than half of the 19-hour delay was between 10 p.m. and 10 a. m. the following day, when it is reasonable to assume that judicial officers are not as readily available for consideration of warrant requests. Finally, and most important, we observed in United States v. Place, supra, at 462 U. S. 705, that

"[t]he intrusion on possessory interests occasioned by a seizure . . . can vary both in its nature and extent. The seizure may be made after the owner has relinquished control of the property to a third party or . . . from the immediate custody and control of the owner."

Here, of course, Segura and Colon, whose possessory interests were interfered with by the occupation, were under arrest and in the custody of the police throughout the entire period the agents occupied the apartment. The actual interference with their possessory interests in the apartment and its contents was, thus, virtually nonexistent. Cf. United States v. Van Leeuwen, 397 U. S. 249 (1970). We are not prepared to say under these limited circumstances that the seizure was unreasonable under the Fourth Amendment. [8]

V

Petitioners also argue that, even if the evidence was not subject to suppression as primary evidence "seized" by virtue of the initial illegal entry and occupation of the premises, it should have been excluded as "fruit" derived from that illegal entry. Whether the initial entry was illegal or not is irrelevant to the admissibility of the challenged evidence, because there was an independent source for the warrant under which that evidence was seized. Exclusion of evidence as derivative or "fruit of the poisonous tree" is not warranted here because of that independent source.

None of the information on which the warrant was secured was derived from or related in any way to the initial entry into petitioners' apartment; the information came from sources wholly unconnected with the entry, and was known to the agents well before the initial entry. No information obtained during the initial entry or occupation of the apartment was needed or used by the agents to secure the warrant. It is therefore beyond dispute that the information possessed by the agents before they entered the apartment constituted an independent source for the discovery and seizure of the evidence now challenged. This evidence was discovered the day following the entry, during the search conducted under a valid warrant; it was the product of that search, wholly unrelated to the prior entry. The valid warrant search was a "means sufficiently distinguishable" to purge the evidence of any "taint" arising from the entry. Wong Sun, 371 U.S. at 371 U. S. 488. [9] Had police never entered the apartment, but instead conducted a perimeter stakeout to prevent anyone from entering the apartment and destroying evidence, the contraband now challenged would have been discovered and seized precisely as it was here. The legality of the initial entry is, thus, wholly irrelevant under Wong Sun, supra, and Silverthorne Lumber Co. v. United States, 251 U. S. 385 (1920). [10]

Our conclusion that the challenged evidence was admissible is fully supported by our prior cases going back more than a half century. The Court has never held that evidence is "fruit of the poisonous tree" simply because "it would not have come to light but for the illegal actions of the police." See Wong Sun, supra, at 371 U. S. 487-488; Rawlings v. Kentucky, 448 U. S. 98 (1980); Brown v. Illinois, 422 U. S. 590, 422 U. S. 599 (1975). That would squarely conflict with Silverthorne and our other cases allowing admission of evidence, notwithstanding a prior illegality, when the link between the illegality and that evidence was sufficiently attenuated to dissipate the taint. By the same token, our cases make clear that evidence will not be excluded as "fruit" unless the illegality is at least the "but for" cause of the discovery of the evidence. Suppression is not justified unless "the challenged evidence is in some sense the product of illegal governmental activity." United States v. Crews, 445 U.S. at 445 U. S. 471. The illegal entry into petitioners' apartment did not contribute in any way to discovery of the evidence seized under the warrant; it is clear, therefore, that not even the threshold "but for" requirement was met in this case.

The dissent contends that the initial entry and securing of the premises are the "but for" causes of the discovery of the evidence in that, had the agents not entered the apartment, but instead secured the premises from the outside, Colon or her friends, if alerted, could have removed or destroyed the evidence before the warrant issued. While the dissent embraces this "reasoning," petitioners do not press this argument.

The Court of Appeals rejected this argument as "prudentially unsound," and because it rested on "wholly speculative assumptions." Among other things, the Court of Appeals suggested that, had the agents waited to enter the apartment until the warrant issued, they might not have decided to take Segura to the apartment, and thereby alert Colon. Or, once alerted by Segura's failure to appear, Colon might have attempted to remove the evidence, rather than destroy it, in which event the agents could have intercepted her and the evidence.

We agree fully with the Court of Appeals that the District Court's suggestion that Colon and her cohorts would have removed or destroyed the evidence was pure speculation. Even more important, however, we decline to extend the exclusionary rule, which already exacts an enormous price from society and our system of justice, to further "protect" criminal activity, as the dissent would have us do.

It may be that, if the agents had not entered the apartment, petitioners might have

arranged for the removal or destruction of the evidence, and that, in this sense, the agents' actions could be considered the "but for" cause for discovery of the evidence. But at this juncture we are reminded of Justice Frankfurter's warning that

"[s]ophisticated argument may prove a causal connection between information obtained through [illegal conduct] and the Government's proof,"

and his admonition that the courts should consider whether, "[a]s a matter of good sense, . . . such connection may have become so attenuated as to dissipate the taint." Nardone, 308 U.S. at 308 U. S. 341. The essence of the dissent is that there is some "constitutional right" to destroy evidence. This concept defies both logic and common sense.

VI

We agree with the Court of Appeals that the cocaine, cash records, and ammunition were properly admitted into evidence. Accordingly, the judgment is affirmed.

It is so ordered.

* JUSTICE WHITE, JUSTICE POWELL, and JUSTICE REHNQUIST join all but Part IV of this opinion.

Notes

[1] See Griswold, Criminal Procedure, -- 1969 Is It a Means or an End?, 29 Md.L.Rev. 307, 317 (1969); see generally 2 W. LaFave, Search and Seizure § 6.5 (1978).

[2] Rivudalla-Vidal and Parra were indicted with petitioners and were charged with one count of possession with intent to distribute one-half kilogram of cocaine on one occasion and one kilogram on another occasion. Both pleaded guilty to the charges. They moved in the District Court to suppress the one-half kilogram of cocaine found on Parra's person at the time of their arrests on the ground that the Task Force agents had stopped them in violation of Terry v. Ohio, 392 U. S. 1 (1968). The court denied the motion.

Rivudalla-Vidal and Parra absconded prior to sentencing by the District Court.

[3] In Griffin, absent exigent circumstances, police officers forcibly entered an apartment and discovered in plain view narcotics and related paraphernalia. The entry took place while other officers sought a search warrant. The Court of Appeals for the Sixth Circuit affirmed the District Court's grant of the defendant's suppression motion.

[4] Both the District Court and the Court of Appeals held that the initial entry into the apartment was not justified by exigent circumstances, and thus that the items discovered in plain view during the limited security check had to be suppressed to effect the purposes of the Fourth Amendment. The United States, although it does not concede the correctness of this holding, does not contest it in this Court. Because the Government has decided not to press its argument that exigent circumstances existed, we need not and do not address this aspect of the Court of Appeals decision. We are concerned only with whether the Court of Appeals properly determined that the Fourth Amendment did not require suppression of the evidence seized during execution of the valid warrant.

[5] In Agapito, DEA agents, following a 2-day surveillance of the defendant's hotel room, arrested the suspected occupants of the room in the lobby of the hotel. After the arrests, the agents entered the hotel room and remained within, with the exception of periodic departures, for almost 24 hours until a search warrant issued. During their stay in the room, the agents seized but did not open a suitcase found in the room. In the search pursuant to the warrant, the agents found cocaine in the suitcase. Although the Second Circuit held that the initial entry was illegal, it held that the cocaine need not be suppressed because it was discovered in the search under the valid warrant.

[6] In two instances, the Court has allowed temporary seizures and limited detentions of property based upon less than probable cause. In United States v. Van Leeuwen, 397 U. S. 249 (1970), the Court refused to invalidate the seizure and detention -- on the basis of only reasonable suspicion -- of two packages delivered to a United States Post Office for mailing. One of the packages was detained on mere suspicion for only 1 1/2 hours; by the end of that period, enough information had been obtained to establish probable cause that the packages contained stolen coins. But the other package was detained for 29 hours before a search warrant was finally served. Both seizures were held reasonable. In fact, the Court suggested that both seizures and detentions for these "limited times" were "prudent" under the circumstances.

Only last Term, in United States v. Place, 462 U. S. 696 (1983), we considered the validity of a brief seizure and detention of a traveler's luggage on the basis of a reasonable suspicion that the luggage contained contraband; the purpose of the seizure and brief detention was to investigate further the causes for the suspicion. Although we held that the 90-minute detention of the luggage in the airport was, under the circumstances, unreasonable, we held that the rationale of Terry v. Ohio, 392 U. S. 1 (1968), applies to permit an officer, on the basis of reasonable suspicion that a traveler is carrying luggage containing contraband, to seize and detain the luggage briefly to "investigate the circumstances that aroused his suspicion." 462 U.S. at 462 U. S. 706.

[7] A distinguished constitutional scholar raised the question whether a seizure of premises might not be appropriate to preserve the status quo and protect valuable evidence while police officers in good faith seek a warrant.

"Here there is a very real practical problem. Does the police officer have any power to maintain the status quo while he, or a colleague of his, is taking the time necessary to draw up a sufficient affidavit to support an application for a search warrant, and then finding a magistrate, submitting the application to him, obtaining the search warrant if it is issued, and then bringing it to the place where the arrest was made. It seems inevitable that a minimum of several hours will be required for this process, at the very best. Unless there is some kind of a power to prevent removal of material from the premises, or destruction of material during this time, the search warrant will almost inevitably be fruitless."

Griswold, 29 Md.L.Rev. at 317 (emphasis added).

Justice Black posed essentially the same question in his dissent in Vale v. Louisiana, 399 U. S. 30, 399 U. S. 36 (1970). After pointing out that Vale's arrest just outside his residence was

"plainly visible to anyone within the house, and the police had every reason to believe that someone in the house was likely to destroy the contraband if the search were postponed,"

he noted:

"This case raises most graphically the question how does a policeman protect evidence necessary to the State if he must leave the premises to get a warrant, allowing the evidence he seeks to be destroyed. The Court's answer to that question makes unnecessarily difficult the conviction of those who prey upon society."

Id. at 399 U. S. 41.

[8] Our decision in United States v. Place, 462 U. S. 696 (1983), is not inconsistent with this conclusion. There, we found unreasonable a 90-minute detention of a traveler's luggage. But the detention was based only on a suspicion that the luggage contained contraband, not on probable cause. After probable cause was established, authorities held the unopened luggage for almost three days before a warrant was obtained. It was not suggested that this delay presented an independent basis for suppression of the evidence eventually discovered.

[9] Our holding in this respect is consistent with the vast majority of Federal Courts of Appeals which have held that evidence obtained pursuant to a valid warrant search need not be excluded because of a prior illegal entry. See, e.g., United States v. Perez, 700 F.2d 1232 (CA8 1983); United States v. Kinney, 638 F.2d 941 (CA6), cert. denied, 452 U.S. 918 (1981); United States v. Fitzharris, 633 F.2d 416 (CA5 1980), cert. denied, 451 U.S. 988 (1981); United States v. Agapito, 620 F.2d 324 (CA2 1980); United States v. Bosby, 675 F.2d 1174 (CA11 1982) (dictum). The only Federal Court of Appeals to hold otherwise is the Ninth Circuit. See United States v. Lomas, 706 F.2d 886 (1983); United States v. Allard, 634 F.2d 1182 (1980).

[10] It is important to note that the dissent stresses the legal status of the agents' initial entry and occupation of the apartment; however, this case involves only evidence seized in the search made subsequently under a valid warrant. Implicit in the dissent is that the agents' presence in the apartment denied petitioners some legal "right" to arrange to have the incriminating evidence concealed or destroyed.

US v. Leon (July 5, 1984) [Notes omitted]

JUSTICE WHITE delivered the opinion of the Court.

This case presents the question whether the Fourth Amendment exclusionary rule should be modified so as not to bar the use in the prosecution's case in chief of evidence obtained by officers acting in reasonable reliance on a search warrant issued by a detached and neutral magistrate but ultimately found to be unsupported by probable cause. To resolve this question, we must consider once again the tension between the sometimes competing goals of, on the one hand, deterring official misconduct and removing inducements to unreasonable invasions of privacy and, on the other, establishing procedures under which criminal defendants are "acquitted or convicted on the basis of all the evidence which exposes the truth." Alderman v. United States, 394 U. S. 165, 394 U. S. 175 (1969).

I

In August, 1981, a confidential informant of unproven reliability informed an officer of the Burbank Police Department that two persons known to him as "Armando" and "Patsy" were selling large quantities of cocaine and methaqualone from their residence at 620 Price Drive in Burbank, Cal. The informant also indicated that he had witnessed a sale of methaqualone by "Patsy" at the residence approximately five months earlier, and had observed at that time a shoebox containing a large amount of cash that belonged to "Patsy." He further declared that "Armando" and "Patsy" generally kept only small quantities of drugs at their residence and stored the remainder at another location in Burbank.

On the basis of this information, the Burbank police initiated an extensive investigation focusing first on the Price Drive residence and later on two other residences as well. Cars parked at the Price Drive residence were determined to belong to respondents Armando Sanchez, who had previously been arrested for possession of marihuana, and Patsy Stewart, who had no criminal record. During the course of the investigation, officers observed an automobile belonging to respondent Ricardo Del Castillo, who had previously been arrested for possession of 50 pounds of marihuana, arrive at the Price Drive residence. The driver of that car entered the house, exited shortly thereafter carrying a small paper sack, and drove away. A check of Del Castillo's probation records led the officers to respondent Alberto Leon, whose telephone number Del Castillo had listed as his employer's. Leon had been arrested in 1980 on drug charges, and a

companion had informed the police at that time that Leon was heavily involved in the importation of drugs into this country. Before the current investigation began, the Burbank officers had learned that an informant had told a Glendale police officer that Leon stored a large quantity of methaqualone at his residence in Glendale. During the course of this investigation, the Burbank officers learned that Leon was living at 716 South Sunset Canyon in Burbank.

Subsequently, the officers observed several persons, at least one of whom had prior drug involvement, arriving at the Price Drive residence and leaving with small packages; observed a variety of other material activity at the two residences as well as at a condominium at 7902 Via Magdalena; and witnessed a variety of relevant activity involving respondents' automobiles. The officers also observed respondents Sanchez and Stewart board separate flights for Miami. The pair later returned to Los Angeles together, consented to a search of their luggage that revealed only a small amount of marihuana, and left the airport. Based on these and other observations summarized in the affidavit, App. 34, Officer Cyril Rombach of the Burbank Police Department, an experienced and well-trained narcotics investigator, prepared an application for a warrant to search 620 Price Drive, 716 South Sunset Canyon, 7902 Via Magdalena, and automobiles registered to each of the respondents for an extensive list of items believed to be related to respondents' drug trafficking activities. Officer Rombach's extensive application was reviewed by several Deputy District Attorneys.

A facially valid search warrant was issued in September, 1981, by a State Superior Court Judge. The ensuing searches produced large quantities of drugs at the Via Magdalena and Sunset Canyon addresses and a small quantity at the Price Drive residence. Other evidence was discovered at each of the residences and in

Stewart's and Del Castillo's automobiles. Respondents were indicted by a grand jury in the District Court for the Central District of California and charged with conspiracy to possess and distribute cocaine and a variety of substantive counts.

The respondents then filed motions to suppress the evidence seized pursuant to the warrant. [1] The District Court held an evidentiary hearing and, while recognizing that the case was a close one, see id. at 131, granted the motions to suppress in part. It concluded that the affidavit was insufficient to establish probable cause, [2] but did not suppress all of the evidence as to all of the respondents because none of the respondents had standing to challenge all of the searches. [3] In response to a request from the Government, the court made clear that Officer Rombach had acted in good faith, but it rejected the Government's suggestion that the Fourth Amendment exclusionary rule should not apply where evidence is seized in reasonable, good faith reliance on a search warrant. [4] The District Court denied the Government's motion for reconsideration, id. at 147, and a divided panel of the Court of Appeals for the Ninth Circuit affirmed, judgt. order reported at 701 F.2d 187 (1983). The Court of Appeals first concluded that Officer Rombach's affidavit could not establish probable cause to search the Price Drive residence. To the extent that the affidavit set forth facts demonstrating the basis of the informant's knowledge of criminal activity, the information included was fatally stale. The affidavit, moreover, failed to establish the informant's credibility. Accordingly, the Court of Appeals concluded that the information provided by the informant was inadequate under both prongs of the two-part test established in Aguilar v. Texas, 378 U. S. 108 (1964), and Spinelli v. United States, 393 U. S. 410 (1969). [5] The officers' independent investigation neither cured the staleness nor corroborated the details of the informant's declarations. The Court of Appeals then considered whether the affidavit formed a proper basis for the search of the Sunset Canyon residence. In its view, the affidavit included no facts indicating the basis for the informants' statements concerning respondent Leon's criminal activities, and was devoid of information establishing the informants' reliability. Because these deficiencies had not been cured by the police investigation, the District Court properly suppressed the fruits of the search. The Court of Appeals refused the Government's invitation to recognize a good faith exception to the Fourth Amendment exclusionary rule. App. to Pet. for Cert. 4a.

The Government's petition for certiorari expressly declined to seek review of the lower courts' determinations that the search warrant was unsupported by probable cause, and presented only the question

"[w]hether the Fourth Amendment exclusionary rule should be modified so as not to bar the admission of evidence seized in reasonable, good faith reliance on a search warrant that is subsequently held to be defective."

We granted certiorari to consider the propriety of such a modification. 463 U.S. 1206 (1983). Although it undoubtedly is within our power to consider the question whether probable cause existed under the "totality of the circumstances" test announced last Term in Illinois v. Gates, 462 U. S. 213 (1983), that question has not been briefed or argued; and it is also within our authority, which we choose to exercise, to take the case as it comes to us, accepting the Court of Appeals' conclusion that probable cause was lacking under the prevailing legal standards. See this Court's Rule 21. 1(a).

We have concluded that, in the Fourth Amendment context, the exclusionary rule can be modified somewhat without jeopardizing its ability to perform its intended functions. Accordingly, we reverse the judgment of the Court of Appeals.

II

Language in opinions of this Court and of individual Justices has sometimes implied that the exclusionary rule is a necessary corollary of the Fourth Amendment, Mapp v. Ohio, 367 U. S. 643, 367 U. S. 651, 655-657 (1961); Olmstead v. United States, 277 U. S. 438, 277 U. S. 462-463 (1928), or that the rule is required by the conjunction of the Fourth and Fifth Amendments. Mapp v. Ohio, supra, at 367 U. S. 661-662 (Black, J., concurring); Agnello v. United States, 269 U. S. 20, 269 U. S. 33-34 (1925). These implications need not detain us long. The Fifth Amendment theory has not withstood critical analysis or the test of time, see Andresen v. Maryland, 427 U. S. 463 (1976), and the Fourth Amendment "has never been interpreted to proscribe the introduction of illegally seized evidence in all proceedings or against all persons." Stone v. Powell, 428 U. S. 465, 428 U. S. 486 (1976).

A

The Fourth Amendment contains no provision expressly precluding the use of evidence obtained in violation of its commands, and an examination of its origin and purposes makes clear that the use of fruits of a past unlawful search or seizure "work[s] no new Fourth Amendment wrong." United States v. Calandra, 414 U. S. 338, 414 U. S. 354 (1974). The wrong condemned by the Amendment is "fully accomplished" by the unlawful search or seizure itself, ibid., and the exclusionary rule is neither intended nor able to "cure the invasion of the defendant's rights which he has already suffered." Stone v. Powell, supra, at 428 U. S. 540 (WHITE, J., dissenting). The rule thus operates as "a judicially created remedy designed to safeguard Fourth Amendment rights generally through its deterrent effect, rather than a personal constitutional right of the party aggrieved." United States v. Calandra, supra, at 414 U. S. 348.

Whether the exclusionary sanction is appropriately imposed in a particular case, our decisions make clear, is

"an issue separate from the question whether the Fourth Amendment rights of the party seeking to invoke the rule were violated by police conduct."

Illinois v. Gates, supra, at 462 U. S. 223. Only the former question is currently before us, and it must be resolved by weighing the costs and benefits of preventing the use in the prosecution's case in chief of inherently trustworthy tangible evidence obtained in reliance on a search warrant issued by a detached and neutral magistrate that ultimately is found to be defective.

The substantial social costs exacted by the exclusionary rule for the vindication of Fourth Amendment rights have long been a source of concern.

"Our cases have consistently recognized that unbending application of the exclusionary sanction to enforce ideals of governmental rectitude would impede unacceptably the truthfinding functions of judge and jury."

United States v. Payner, 447 U. S. 727, 447 U. S. 734 (1980). An objectionable collateral consequence of this interference with the criminal justice system's truthfinding function is that some guilty defendants may go free or receive reduced sentences as a result of favorable plea bargains. [6] Particularly when law enforcement officers have acted in objective good faith or their transgressions have been minor, the magnitude of the benefit conferred on such guilty defendants offends basic concepts of the criminal justice system. Stone v. Powell, 428 U.S. at 428 U. S. 490. Indiscriminate application of the exclusionary rule, therefore, may well "generat[e] disrespect for the law and administration of justice." Id. at 428 U. S. 491. Accordingly,

"[a]s with any remedial device, the application of the rule has been restricted to those areas where its remedial objectives are thought most efficaciously served."

United States v. Calandra, supra, at 414 U. S. 348; see Stone v. Powell, supra, at 428 U. S. 486-487; United States v. Janis, 428 U. S. 433, 428 U. S. 447 (1976).

B

Close attention to those remedial objectives has characterized our recent decisions concerning the scope of the Fourth Amendment exclusionary rule. The Court has, to be sure, not seriously questioned,

"in the absence of a more efficacious sanction, the continued application of the rule to suppress evidence from the [prosecution's] case where a Fourth Amendment violation has been substantial and deliberate. . . ."

Franks v. Delaware, 438 U. S. 154, 438 U. S. 171 (1978); Stone v. Powell, supra, at 428 U. S. 492. Nevertheless, the balancing approach that has evolved in various contexts -- including criminal trials --

"forcefully suggest[s] that the exclusionary rule be more generally modified to permit the introduction of evidence obtained in the reasonable good faith belief that a search or seizure was in accord with the Fourth Amendment."

Illinois v. Gates, 462 U.S. at 462 U. S. 255 (WHITE, J., concurring in judgment).

In Stone v. Powell, supra, the Court emphasized the costs of the exclusionary rule, expressed its view that limiting the circumstances under which Fourth Amendment claims could be raised in federal habeas corpus proceedings would not reduce the rule's deterrent effect, id. at 428 U. S. 489-495, and held that a state prisoner who has been afforded a full and fair opportunity to litigate a Fourth Amendment claim may not obtain federal habeas relief on the ground that unlawfully obtained evidence had been introduced at his trial. Cf. Rose v. Mitchell, 443 U. S. 545, 443 U. S. 560-563 (1979). Proposed extensions of the exclusionary rule to proceedings other than the criminal trial itself have been evaluated and rejected under the same analytic approach. In United States v. Calandra, for example, we declined to allow grand jury witnesses to refuse to answer questions based on evidence obtained from an unlawful search or seizure, since "[a]ny incremental deterrent effect which might be achieved by extending the rule to grand jury proceedings is uncertain, at best." 414 U.S. at 414 U. S. 348. Similarly, in United States v. Janis, supra, we permitted the use in federal civil proceedings of evidence illegally seized by state officials, since the likelihood of deterring police misconduct through such an extension of the exclusionary rule was insufficient to outweigh its substantial social costs. In so doing, we declared that,

"[i]f . . . the exclusionary rule does not result in appreciable deterrence, then, clearly, its use in the instant situation is unwarranted."

Id. at 428 U. S. 454.

As cases considering the use of unlawfully obtained evidence in criminal trials themselves make clear, it does not follow from the emphasis on the exclusionary rule's deterrent value that "anything which deters illegal searches is thereby commanded by the Fourth Amendment." Alderman v. United States, 394 U.S. at 394 U. S. 174. In determining whether persons aggrieved solely by the introduction of damaging evidence unlawfully obtained from their coconspirators or codefendants could seek suppression, for example, we found that the additional benefits of such an extension of the exclusionary rule would not outweigh its costs. Id. at 394 U. S. 174-175. Standing to invoke the rule has thus been limited to cases in which the prosecution seeks to use the fruits of an illegal search or seizure against the victim of police misconduct. Rakas v. Illinois, 439 U. S. 128 (1978); Brown v. United States, 411 U. S. 223 (1973); Wong Sun v. United States, 371 U. S.

471, 371 U. S. 491-492 (1963). Cf. United States v. Payner, 447 U. S. 727 (1980).

Even defendants with standing to challenge the introduction in their criminal trials of unlawfully obtained evidence cannot prevent every conceivable use of such evidence. Evidence obtained in violation of the Fourth Amendment and inadmissible in the prosecution's case in chief may be used to impeach a defendant's direct testimony. Walder v. United States, 347 U. S. 62 (1954). See also Oregon v. Hass, 420 U. S. 714 (1975); Harris v. New York, 401 U. S. 222 (1971). A similar assessment of the "incremental furthering" of the ends of the exclusionary rule led us to conclude in United States v. Havens, 446 U. S. 620, 446 U. S. 627 (1980), that evidence inadmissible in the prosecution's case in chief or otherwise as substantive evidence of guilt may be used to impeach statements made by a defendant in response to "proper cross-examination reasonably suggested by the defendant's direct examination." Id. at 446 U. S. 627-628.

When considering the use of evidence obtained in violation of the Fourth Amendment in the prosecution's case in chief, moreover, we have declined to adopt a per se or "but for" rule that would render inadmissible any evidence that came to light through a chain of causation that began with an illegal arrest. Brown v. Illinois, 422 U. S. 590 (1975); Wong Sun v. United States, supra, at 371 U. S. 487-488. We also have held that a witness' testimony may be admitted even when his identity was discovered in an unconstitutional search. United States v. Ceccolini, 435 U. S. 268 (1978). The perception underlying these decisions -- that the connection between police misconduct and evidence of crime may be sufficiently attenuated to permit the use of that evidence at trial -- is a product of considerations relating to the exclusionary rule and the constitutional principles it is designed to protect. Dunaway v. New York, 442 U. S. 200, 442 U. S. 217-218 (1979); United States v. Ceccolini, supra, at 435 U. S. 279. [7] In short, the "dissipation of the taint" concept that the Court has applied in deciding whether exclusion is appropriate in a particular case

"attempts to mark the point at which the detrimental consequences of illegal police action become so attenuated that the deterrent effect of the exclusionary rule no longer justifies its cost."

Brown v. Illinois, supra, at 411 U. S. 609 (POWELL, J., concurring in part). Not surprisingly in view of this purpose, an assessment of the flagrancy of the police misconduct constitutes an important step in the calculus. Dunaway v. New York, supra, at 442 U. S. 218; Brown v. Illinois, supra, at 411 U. S. 603-604.

The same attention to the purposes underlying the exclusionary rule also has characterized decisions not involving the scope of the rule itself. We have not required suppression of the fruits of a search incident to an arrest made in good faith reliance on a substantive criminal statute that subsequently is declared unconstitutional. Michigan v. DeFillippo, 443 U. S. 31 (1979). [8] Similarly, although the Court has been unwilling to conclude that new Fourth Amendment principles are always to have only prospective effect, United States v. Johnson, 457 U. S. 537, 457 U. S. 560 (1982), [9] no Fourth Amendment decision marking a "clear break with the past" has been applied retroactively. See United States v. Peltier, 422 U. S. 531 (1975); Desist v. United States, 394 U. S. 244 (1969); Linkletter v. Walker, 381 U. S. 618 (1965). [10] The propriety of retroactive application of a newly announced Fourth Amendment principle, moreover, has been assessed largely in terms of the contribution retroactivity might make to the deterrence of police misconduct. United States v. Johnson, supra, at 457 U. S. 560-561; United States v. Peltier, supra, at 422 U. S. 536-539, 422 U. S. 542.

As yet, we have not recognized any form of

good faith exception to the Fourth Amendment exclusionary rule. [11] But the balancing approach that has evolved during the years of experience with the rule provides strong support for the modification currently urged upon us. As we discuss below, our evaluation of the costs and benefits of suppressing reliable physical evidence seized by officers reasonably relying on a warrant issued by a detached and neutral magistrate leads to the conclusion that such evidence should be admissible in the prosecution's case in chief.

III

A

Because a search warrant

"provides the detached scrutiny of a neutral magistrate, which is a more reliable safeguard against improper searches than the hurried judgment of a law enforcement officer 'engaged in the often competitive enterprise of ferreting out crime,'"

United States v. Chadwick, 433 U. S. 1, 433 U. S. 9 (1977) (quoting Johnson v. United States, 333 U. S. 10, 333 U. S. 14 (1948)), we have expressed a strong preference for warrants, and declared that, "in a doubtful or marginal case, a search under a warrant may be sustainable where without one it would fall." United States v. Ventresca, 380 U. S. 102, 380 U. S. 106 (1965). See Aguilar v. Texas, 378 U.S. at 378 U. S. 111. Reasonable minds frequently may differ on the question whether a particular affidavit establishes probable cause, and we have thus concluded that the preference for warrants is most appropriately effectuated by according "great deference" to a magistrate's determination. Spinelli v. United States, 393 U.S. at 393 U. S. 419. See Illinois v. Gates, 462 U.S. at 462 U. S. 236; United States v. Ventresca, supra, at 380 U. S. 108-109.

Deference to the magistrate, however, is not boundless. It is clear, first, that the deference accorded to a magistrate's finding of probable cause does not preclude inquiry into the knowing or reckless falsity of the affidavit on which that determination was based. Franks v. Delaware, 438 U. S. 154 (1978). [12] Second, the courts must also insist that the magistrate purport to "perform his neutral and detached' function and not serve merely as a rubber stamp for the police." Aguilar v. Texas, supra, at 378 U. S. 111. See Illinois v. Gates, supra, at 462 U. S. 239. A magistrate failing to "manifest that neutrality and detachment demanded of a judicial officer when presented with a warrant application" and who acts instead as "an adjunct law enforcement officer" cannot provide valid authorization for an otherwise unconstitutional search. Lo-Ji Sales, Inc. v. New York, 442 U. S. 319, 442 U. S. 326-327 (1979).

Third, reviewing courts will not defer to a warrant based on an affidavit that does not "provide the magistrate with a substantial basis for determining the existence of probable cause." Illinois v. Gates, 462 U.S. at 462 U. S. 239.

"Sufficient information must be presented to the magistrate to allow that official to determine probable cause; his action cannot be a mere ratification of the bare conclusions of others."

Ibid. See Aguilar v. Texas, supra, at 378 U. S. 114-115; Giordenello v. United States, 357 U. S. 480 (1958); Nathanson v. United States, 290 U. S. 41 (1933). [13] Even if the warrant application was supported by more than a "bare bones" affidavit, a reviewing court may properly conclude that, notwithstanding the deference that magistrates deserve, the warrant was invalid because the magistrate's probable cause determination reflected an improper analysis of the totality of the circumstances, Illinois v. Gates, supra, at 462 U. S. 238-239, or because the form of the warrant was improper in some respect.

Only in the first of these three situations, however, has the Court set forth a rationale for suppressing evidence obtained pursuant to a search warrant; in the other areas, it has simply excluded such evidence without considering whether Fourth Amendment interests will be advanced. To the extent that proponents of exclusion rely on its behavioral effects on judges and magistrates in these areas, their reliance is misplaced. First, the exclusionary rule is designed to deter police misconduct, rather than to punish the errors of judges and magistrates. Second, there exists no evidence suggesting that judges and magistrates are inclined to ignore or subvert the Fourth Amendment, or that lawlessness among these actors requires application of the extreme sanction of exclusion. [14]

Third, and most important, we discern no basis, and are offered none, for believing that exclusion of evidence seized pursuant to a warrant will have a significant deterrent effect on the issuing judge or magistrate. [15] Many of the factors that indicate that the exclusionary rule cannot provide an effective "special" or "general" deterrent for individual offending law enforcement officers [16] apply as well to judges or magistrates. And, to the extent that the rule is thought to operate as a "systemic" deterrent on a wider audience, [17] it clearly can have no such effect on individuals empowered to issue search warrants. Judges and magistrates are not adjuncts to the law enforcement team; as neutral judicial officers, they have no stake in the outcome of particular criminal prosecutions. The threat of exclusion thus cannot be expected significantly to deter them. Imposition of the exclusionary sanction is not necessary meaningfully to inform judicial officers of their errors, and we cannot conclude that admitting evidence obtained pursuant to a warrant while at the same time declaring that the warrant was somehow defective will in any way reduce judicial officers' professional incentives to comply with the Fourth Amendment, encourage them to repeat their mistakes, or lead to the granting of all colorable warrant requests. [18]

B

If exclusion of evidence obtained pursuant to a subsequently invalidated warrant is to have any deterrent effect, therefore, it must alter the behavior of individual law enforcement officers or the policies of their departments. One could argue that applying the exclusionary rule in cases where the police failed to demonstrate probable cause in the warrant application deters future inadequate presentations or "magistrate shopping," and thus promotes the ends of the Fourth Amendment. Suppressing evidence obtained pursuant to a technically defective warrant supported by probable cause also might encourage officers to scrutinize more closely the form of the warrant, and to point out suspected judicial errors. We find such arguments speculative, and conclude that suppression of evidence obtained pursuant to a warrant should be ordered only on a case-by-case basis, and only in those unusual cases in which exclusion will further the purposes of the exclusionary rule. [19]

We have frequently questioned whether the exclusionary rule can have any deterrent effect when the offending officers acted in the objectively reasonable belief that their conduct did not violate the Fourth Amendment.

"No empirical researcher, proponent or opponent of the rule has yet been able to establish with any assurance whether the rule has a deterrent effect. . . ."

United States v. Janis, 428 U.S. at 428 U. S. 452, n. 22. But even assuming that the rule effectively deters some police misconduct and provides incentives for the law enforcement profession as a whole to conduct itself in accord with the Fourth Amendment, it cannot be expected, and should not be applied, to deter objectively reasonable law enforcement activity.

As we observed in Michigan v. Tucker, 417 U. S. 433, 417 U. S. 447 (1974), and reiterated in United States v. Peltier, 422 U.S. at 422 U. S. 539:

"The deterrent purpose of the exclusionary rule necessarily assumes that the police have engaged in willful, or at the very least negligent, conduct which has deprived the defendant of some right. By refusing to admit evidence gained as a result of such conduct, the courts hope to instill in those particular investigating officers, or in their future counterparts, a greater degree of care toward the rights of an accused. Where the official action was pursued in complete good faith, however, the deterrence rationale loses much of its force."

The Peltier Court continued, id. at 422 U. S. 542:

"If the purpose of the exclusionary rule is to deter unlawful police conduct, then evidence obtained from a search should be suppressed only if it can be said that the law enforcement officer had knowledge, or may properly be charged with knowledge, that the search was unconstitutional under the Fourth Amendment."

See also Illinois v. Gates, 462 U.S. at 462 U. S. 260-261 (WHITE, J., concurring in judgment); United States v. Janis, supra, at 428 U. S. 459; Brown v. Illinois, 422 U.S. at 422 U. S. 610-611 (POWELL, J., concurring in part). [20] In short, where the officer's conduct is objectively reasonable,

"excluding the evidence will not further the ends of the exclusionary rule in any appreciable way; for it is painfully apparent that . . . the officer is acting as a reasonable officer would and should act in similar circumstances. Excluding the evidence can in no way affect his future conduct unless it is to make him less willing to do his duty."

Stone v. Powell, 428 U.S. at 428 U. S. 539-540 (WHITE, J., dissenting).

This is particularly true, we believe, when an officer, acting with objective good faith, has obtained a search warrant from a judge or magistrate and acted within its scope. [21] In most such cases, there is no police illegality, and thus nothing to deter. It is the magistrate's responsibility to determine whether the officer's allegations establish probable cause and, if so, to issue a warrant comporting in form with the requirements of the Fourth Amendment. In the ordinary case, an officer cannot be expected to question the magistrate's probable cause determination or his judgment that the form of the warrant is technically sufficient. "[O]nce the warrant issues, there is literally nothing more the policeman can do in seeking to comply with the law." Id. at 428 U. S. 498 (BURGER, C.J., concurring). Penalizing the officer for the magistrate's error, rather than his own, cannot logically contribute to the deterrence of Fourth Amendment violations. [22]

C

We conclude that the marginal or nonexistent benefits produced by suppressing evidence obtained in objectively reasonable reliance on a subsequently invalidated search warrant cannot justify the substantial costs of exclusion. We do not suggest, however, that exclusion is always inappropriate in cases where an officer has obtained a warrant and abided by its terms. "[S]earches pursuant to a warrant will rarely require any deep inquiry into reasonableness," Illinois v. Gates, 462 U.S. at 462 U. S. 267 (WHITE, J., concurring in judgment), for "a warrant issued by a magistrate normally suffices to establish" that a law enforcement officer has "acted in good faith in conducting the search." United States v. Ross, 456 U. S. 798, 456 U. S. 823, n. 32 (1982). Nevertheless, the officer's reliance on the magistrate's probable cause determination and on the technical sufficiency of the warrant he issues must be objectively reasonable, cf. Harlow v. Fitzgerald, 457 U. S. 800, 457 U. S. 815-819 (1982), [23] and it is clear that, in some circumstances the officer [24] will have no reasonable grounds for believing that the warrant was properly issued.

Suppression therefore remains an appropriate remedy if the magistrate or judge in issuing a warrant was misled by information in an affidavit that the affiant knew was false or would have known was false except for his reckless disregard of the truth. Franks v. Delaware, 438 U. S. 154 (1978). The exception we recognize today will also not apply in cases where the issuing magistrate wholly abandoned his judicial role in the manner condemned in Lo-Ji Sales, Inc. v. New York, 442 U. S. 319 (1979); in such circumstances, no reasonably well-trained officer should rely on the warrant. Nor would an officer manifest objective good faith in relying on a warrant based on an affidavit "so lacking in indicia of probable cause as to render official belief in its existence entirely unreasonable." Brown v. Illinois, 422 U.S. at 422 U. S. 610-611 (POWELL, J., concurring in part); see Illinois v. Gates, supra, at 462 U. S. 263-264 (WHITE, J., concurring in judgment). Finally, depending on the circumstances of the particular case, a warrant may be so facially deficient -- i.e., in failing to particularize the place to be searched or the things to be seized -- that the executing officers cannot reasonably presume it to be valid. Cf. Massachusetts v. Sheppard, post at 468 U. S. 988-991.

In so limiting the suppression remedy, we leave untouched the probable cause standard and the various requirements for a valid warrant. Other objections to the modification of the Fourth Amendment exclusionary rule we consider to be insubstantial. The good faith exception for searches conducted pursuant to warrants is not intended to signal our unwillingness strictly to enforce the requirements of the Fourth Amendment, and we do not believe that it will have this effect. As we have already suggested, the good faith exception, turning as it does on objective reasonableness, should not be difficult to apply in practice. When officers have acted pursuant to a warrant, the prosecution should ordinarily be able to establish objective good faith without a substantial expenditure of judicial time.

Nor are we persuaded that application of a good faith exception to searches conducted pursuant to warrants will preclude review of the constitutionality of the search or seizure, deny needed guidance from the courts, or freeze Fourth Amendment law in its present state. [25] There is no need for courts to adopt the inflexible practice of always deciding whether the officers' conduct manifested objective good faith before turning to the question whether the Fourth Amendment has been violated. Defendants seeking suppression of the fruits of allegedly unconstitutional searches or seizures undoubtedly raise live controversies which Art. III empowers federal courts to adjudicate. As cases addressing questions of good faith immunity under 42 U.S.C. § 1983, compare O'Connor v. Donaldson, 422 U. S. 563 (1975), with Procunier v. Navarette, 434 U. S. 555, 434 U. S. 566, n. 14 (1978), and cases involving the harmless error doctrine, compare Milton v. Wainwright, 407 U. S. 371, 407 U. S. 372 (1972), with Coleman v. Alabama, 399 U. S. 1 (1970), make clear, courts have considerable discretion in conforming their decisionmaking processes to the exigencies of particular cases.

If the resolution of a particular Fourth Amendment question is necessary to guide future action by law enforcement officers and magistrates, nothing will prevent reviewing courts from deciding that question before turning to the good faith issue. [26] Indeed, it frequently will be difficult to determine whether the officers acted reasonably without resolving the Fourth Amendment issue. Even if the Fourth Amendment question is not one of broad import, reviewing courts could decide in particular cases that magistrates under their supervision need to be informed of their errors, and so evaluate the officers' good faith only after finding a violation. In other circumstances, those courts could reject suppression motions posing no important Fourth Amendment questions by turning immediately to a consideration of the officers' good faith. We have no reason to believe that our Fourth Amendment jurisprudence would suffer by allowing reviewing courts to exercise an informed discretion in making this choice.

IV

When the principles we have enunciated today are applied to the facts of this case, it is apparent that the judgment of the Court of Appeals cannot stand. The Court of Appeals applied the prevailing legal standards to Officer Rombach's warrant application, and concluded that the application could not support the magistrate's probable cause determination. In so doing, the court clearly informed the magistrate that he had erred in issuing the challenged warrant. This aspect of the court's judgment is not under attack in this proceeding.

Having determined that the warrant should not have issued, the Court of Appeals understandably declined to adopt a modification of the Fourth Amendment exclusionary rule that this Court had not previously sanctioned. Although the modification finds strong support in our previous cases, the Court of Appeals' commendable self-restraint is not to be criticized. We have now reexamined the purposes of the exclusionary rule and the propriety of its application in cases where officers have relied on a subsequently invalidated search warrant. Our conclusion is that the rule's purposes will only rarely be served by applying it in such circumstances.

In the absence of an allegation that the magistrate abandoned his detached and neutral role, suppression is appropriate only if the officers were dishonest or reckless in preparing their affidavit or could not have harbored an objectively reasonable belief in the existence of probable cause. Only respondent Leon has contended that no reasonably well trained police officer could have believed that there existed probable cause to search his house; significantly, the other

respondents advance no comparable argument. Officer Rombach's application for a warrant clearly was supported by much more than a "bare bones" affidavit. The affidavit related the results of an extensive investigation and, as the opinions of the divided panel of the Court of Appeals make clear, provided evidence sufficient to create disagreement among thoughtful and competent judges as to the existence of probable cause. Under these circumstances, the officers' reliance on the magistrate's determination of probable cause was objectively reasonable, and application of the extreme sanction of exclusion is inappropriate.

Accordingly, the judgment of the Court of Appeals is

Reversed.

Nix v. Williams (June 11, 1984)

CHIEF JUSTICE BURGER delivered the opinion of the Court.

We granted certiorari to consider whether, at respondent Williams' second murder trial in state court, evidence pertaining to the discovery and condition of the victim's body was properly admitted on the ground that it would ultimately or inevitably have been discovered even if no violation of any constitutional or statutory provision had taken place.

I

A

On December 24, 1968, 10-year-old Pamela Powers disappeared from a YMCA building in Des Moines, Iowa, where she had accompanied her parents to watch an athletic contest. Shortly after she disappeared, Williams was seen leaving the YMCA carrying a large bundle wrapped in a blanket; a 14-year-old boy who had helped Williams open his car door reported that he had seen "two legs in it and they were skinny and white."

Williams' car was found the next day 160

miles east of Des Moines in Davenport, Iowa. Later, several items of clothing belonging to the child, some of Williams' clothing, and an army blanket like the one used to wrap the bundle that Williams carried out of the YMCA were found at a rest stop on Interstate 80 near Grinnell, between Des Moines and Davenport. A warrant was issued for Williams' arrest.

Police surmised that Williams had left Pamela Powers or her body somewhere between Des Moines and the Grinnell rest stop where some of the young girl's clothing had been found. On December 26, the Iowa Bureau of Criminal Investigation initiated a large-scale search. Two hundred volunteers divided into teams began the search 21 miles east of Grinnell, covering an area several miles to the north and south of Interstate 80. They moved westward from Poweshiek County, in which Grinnell was located, into Jasper County. Searchers were instructed to check all roads, abandoned farm buildings, ditches, culverts, and any other place in which the body of a small child could be hidden.

Meanwhile, Williams surrendered to local police in Davenport, where he was promptly arraigned. Williams contacted a Des Moines attorney, who arranged for an attorney in Davenport to meet Williams at the Davenport police station. Des Moines police informed counsel they would pick Williams up in Davenport and return him to Des Moines without questioning him. Two Des Moines detectives then drove to Davenport, took Williams into custody, and proceeded to drive him back to Des Moines.

During the return trip, one of the policemen, Detective Leaming, began a conversation with Williams, saying:

"I want to give you something to think about while we're traveling down the road. . . . They are predicting several inches of snow for tonight, and I feel that you yourself are the only person that knows where this little girl's body is . . .

and if you get a snow on top of it, you yourself may be unable to find it. And since we will be going right past the area [where the body is] on the way into Des Moines, I feel that we could stop and locate the body, that the parents of this little girl should be entitled to a Christian burial for the little girl who was snatched away from them on Christmas [E]ve and murdered. . . . "

"[A]fter a snow storm, [we may not be] able to find it at all."

Leaming told Williams he knew the body was in the area of Mitchellville -- a town they would be passing on the way to Des Moines. He concluded the conversation by saying: "I do not want you to answer me. . . . Just think about it. . . ."

Later, as the police car approached Grinnell, Williams asked Leaming whether the police had found the young girl's shoes. After Leaming replied that he was unsure, Williams directed the police to a point near a service station where he said he had left the shoes; they were not found. As they continued the drive to Des Moines, Williams asked whether the blanket had been found, and then directed the officers to a rest area in Grinnell where he said he had disposed of the blanket; they did not find the blanket. At this point, Leaming and his party were joined by the officers in charge of the search. As they approached Mitchellville, Williams, without any further conversation, agreed to direct the officers to the child's body.

The officers directing the search had called off the search at 3 p. m., when they left the Grinnell Police Department to join Leaming at the rest area. At that time, one search team near the Jasper County-Polk County line was only two and one-half miles from where Williams soon guided Leaming and his party to the body. The child's body was found next to a culvert in a ditch beside a gravel road in Polk County, about two miles south of Interstate 80, and essentially within the area to be searched.

B

First Trial

In February, 1969, Williams was indicted for first-degree murder. Before trial in the Iowa court, his counsel moved to suppress evidence of the body and all related evidence, including the condition of the body as shown by the autopsy. The ground for the motion was that such evidence was the "fruit" or product of Williams' statements made during the automobile ride from Davenport to Des Moines and prompted by Leaming's statements. The motion to suppress was denied.

The jury found Williams guilty of first-degree murder; the judgment of conviction was affirmed by the Iowa Supreme Court. State v. Williams, 182 N.W.2d 396 (1970). Williams then sought release on habeas corpus in the United States District Court for the Southern District of Iowa. That court concluded that the evidence in question had been wrongly admitted at Williams' trial, Williams v. Brewer, 375 F.Supp. 170 (1974); a divided panel of the Court of Appeals for the Eighth Circuit agreed. 509 F.2d 227 (1974).

We granted certiorari, 423 U.S. 1031 (1975), and a divided Court affirmed, holding that Detective Leaming had obtained incriminating statements from Williams by what was viewed as interrogation in violation of his right to counsel. Brewer v. Williams, 430 U. S. 387 (1977). This Court's opinion noted, however, that although Williams' incriminating statements could not be introduced into evidence at a second trial, evidence of the body's location and condition

"might well be admissible on the theory that the body would have been discovered in any event, even had incriminating statements not been elicited from Williams."

Id. at 430 U. S. 407, n. 12.

C

Second Trial

At Williams' second trial in 1977 in the Iowa court, the prosecution did not offer Williams' statements into evidence, nor did it seek to show that Williams had directed the police to the child's body. However, evidence of the condition of her body as it was found, articles and photographs of her clothing, and the results of post mortem medical and chemical tests on the body were admitted. The trial court concluded that the State had proved by a preponderance of the evidence that, if the search had not been suspended and Williams had not led the police to the victim, her body would have been discovered "within a short time" in essentially the same condition as it was actually found. The trial court also ruled that, if the police had not located the body,

"the search would clearly have been taken up again where it left off, given the extreme circumstances of this case, and the body would [have] been found in short order."

App. 86 (emphasis added).

In finding that the body would have been discovered in essentially the same condition as it was actually found, the court noted that freezing temperatures had prevailed and tissue deterioration would have been suspended. Id. at 87. The challenged evidence was admitted, and the jury again found Williams guilty of first-degree murder; he was sentenced to life in prison.

On appeal, the Supreme Court of Iowa again affirmed. 285 N.W.2d 248 (1979). That court held that there was, in fact, a "hypothetical independent source" exception to the exclusionary rule:

"After the defendant has shown unlawful conduct on the part of the police, the State has the burden to show by a preponderance of the evidence that (1) the police did not act in bad faith for the purpose of hastening discovery of the evidence in question, and (2) that the evidence in question would have been discovered by lawful means."

Id. at 260. As to the first element, the Iowa Supreme Court, having reviewed the relevant cases, stated:

"The issue of the propriety of the police conduct in this case, as noted earlier in this opinion, has caused the closest possible division of views in every appellate court which has considered the question. In light of the legitimate disagreement among individuals well versed in the law of criminal procedure who were given the opportunity for calm deliberation, it cannot be said that the actions of the police were taken in bad faith."

Id. at 260-261.

The Iowa court then reviewed the evidence de novo [1] and concluded that the State had shown by a preponderance of the evidence that, even if Williams had not guided police to the child's body, it would inevitably have been found by lawful activity of the search party before its condition had materially changed.

In 1980, Williams renewed his attack on the state court conviction by seeking a writ of habeas corpus in the United States District Court for the Southern District of Iowa. The District Court conducted its own independent review of the evidence and concluded, as had the state courts, that the body would inevitably have been found by the searchers in essentially the same condition it was in when Williams led police to its discovery. The District Court denied Williams' petition. 528 F.Supp. 664 (1981).

The Court of Appeals for the Eighth Circuit reversed, 700 F.2d 1164 (1983); an equally divided court denied rehearing en banc. Id. at 1175. That court assumed, without deciding, that there is an inevitable discovery exception to the exclusionary rule, and that the Iowa Supreme Court correctly stated that exception to require proof that the police did not act in bad faith and that the evidence would have been discovered absent any constitutional violation. In reversing the District Court's denial of habeas relief, the Court of Appeals stated:

"We hold that the State has not met the first requirement. It is therefore unnecessary to decide whether the state courts' finding that the body would have been discovered anyway is fairly supported by the record. It is also unnecessary to decide whether the State must prove the two elements of the exception by clear and convincing evidence, as defendant argues, or by a preponderance of the evidence, as the state courts held."

"The state trial court, in denying the motion to suppress, made no finding one way or the other on the question of bad faith. Its opinion does not even mention the issue, and seems to proceed on the assumption -- contrary to the rule of law later laid down by the Supreme Court of Iowa -- that the State needed to show only that the body would have been discovered in any event. The Iowa Supreme Court did expressly address the issue . . . , and a finding by an appellate court of a state is entitled to the same presumption of correctness that attaches to trial court findings under 28 U.S.C. § 2254(d). . . . We conclude, however, that the state Supreme Court's finding that the police did not act in bad faith is not entitled to the shield of § 2254(d). . . ."

Id. at 1169-1170 (footnotes omitted).

We granted the State's petition for certiorari, 461 U.S. 956 (1983), and we reverse.

II

A

The Iowa Supreme Court correctly stated that the "vast majority" of all courts, both state and federal, recognize an inevitable discovery exception to the exclusionary rule. [2] We are now urged to adopt and apply the so-called ultimate or inevitable discovery exception to the exclusionary rule.

Williams contends that evidence of the body's location and condition is "fruit of the poisonous tree," i.e., the "fruit" or product of Detective Leaming's plea to help the child's parents give her "a Christian burial," which this Court had already held equated to interrogation. He contends that admitting the challenged evidence violated the Sixth Amendment whether it would have been inevitably discovered or not. Williams also contends that, if the inevitable discovery doctrine is constitutionally permissible, it must include a threshold showing of police good faith.

B

The doctrine requiring courts to suppress evidence as the tainted "fruit" of unlawful governmental conduct had its genesis in Silverthorne Lumber Co. v. United States, 251 U. S. 385 (1920); there, the Court held that the exclusionary rule applies not only to the illegally obtained evidence itself, but also to other incriminating evidence derived from the primary evidence. The holding of Silverthorne was carefully limited, however, for the Court emphasized that such information does not automatically become "sacred and inaccessible." Id. at 251 U. S. 392.

"If knowledge of [such facts] is gained from an independent source, they may be proved like any others. . . ."

Ibid. (emphasis added).

Wong Sun v. United States, 371 U. S. 471 (1963), extended the exclusionary rule to evidence that was the indirect product or "fruit" of unlawful police conduct, but there again the Court emphasized that evidence that has been illegally obtained need not always be suppressed, stating:

"We need not hold that all evidence is 'fruit of the poisonous tree' simply because it would not have come to light but for the illegal actions of the police. Rather, the more apt question in such a case is"

"whether, granting establishment of the primary illegality, the evidence to which instant objection is made has been come at by exploitation of that illegality, or instead by means sufficiently distinguishable to be purged of the primary taint."

Id. at 371 U. S. 487-488 (emphasis added)

(quoting J. Maguire, Evidence of Guilt 221 (1959)). The Court thus pointedly negated the kind of good faith requirement advanced by the Court of Appeals in reversing the District Court.

Although Silverthorne and Wong Sun involved violations of the Fourth Amendment, the "fruit of the poisonous tree" doctrine has not been limited to cases in which there has been a Fourth Amendment violation. The Court has applied the doctrine where the violations were of the Sixth Amendment, see United States v. Wade, 388 U. S. 218 (1967), as well as of the Fifth Amendment. [3]

The core rationale consistently advanced by this Court for extending the exclusionary rule to evidence that is the fruit of unlawful police conduct has been that this admittedly drastic and socially costly course is needed to deter police from violations of constitutional and statutory protections. This Court has accepted the argument that the way to ensure such protections is to exclude evidence seized as a result of such violations notwithstanding the high social cost of letting persons obviously guilty go unpunished for their crimes. On this rationale, the prosecution is not to be put in a better position than it would have been in if no illegality had transpired.

By contrast, the derivative evidence analysis ensures that the prosecution is not put in a worse position simply because of some earlier police error or misconduct. The independent source doctrine allows admission of evidence that has been discovered by means wholly independent of any constitutional violation. That doctrine, although closely related to the inevitable discovery doctrine, does not apply here; Williams' statements to Leaming indeed led police to the child's body, but that is not the whole story. The independent source doctrine teaches us that the interest of society in deterring unlawful police conduct and the public interest in having juries receive all probative evidence of a crime are properly balanced by putting the police in the same, not a worse, position that they would have been in if no police error or misconduct had occurred. [4] See Murphy v. Waterfront Comm'n of New York Harbor, 378 U. S. 52, 378 U. S. 79 (1964); Kastigar v. United States, 406 U. S. 441, 406 U. S. 457, 406 U. S. 458-459 (1972). When the challenged evidence has an independent source, exclusion of such evidence would put the police in a worse position than they would have been in absent any error or violation. There is a functional similarity between these two doctrines in that exclusion of evidence that would inevitably have been discovered would also put the government in a worse position, because the police would have obtained that evidence if no misconduct had taken place. Thus, while the independent source exception would not justify admission of evidence in this case, its rationale is wholly consistent with, and justifies, our adoption of the ultimate or inevitable discovery exception to the exclusionary rule.

It is clear that the cases implementing the exclusionary rule "begin with the premise that the challenged evidence is, in some sense, the product of illegal governmental activity." United States v. Crews, 445 U. S. 463, 445 U. S. 471 (1980) (emphasis added). Of course, this does not end the inquiry. If the prosecution can establish by a preponderance of the evidence that the information ultimately or inevitably would have been discovered by lawful means -- here, the volunteers' search -- then the deterrence rationale has so little basis that the evidence should be received. [5] Anything less would reject logic, experience, and common sense.

The requirement that the prosecution must prove the absence of bad faith, imposed here by the Court of Appeals, would place courts in the position of withholding from juries relevant and undoubted truth that would have been available to police absent any unlawful police activity. Of course, that view would put the police in a worse position than they would have been in if no unlawful conduct had transpired. And, of equal importance, it wholly fails to take into account the enormous societal cost of excluding truth in the search for truth in the administration of justice. Nothing in this Court's prior holdings supports any such formalistic, pointless, and punitive approach.

The Court of Appeals concluded, without analysis, that, if an absence-of-bad-faith requirement were not imposed,

"the temptation to risk deliberate violations of the Sixth Amendment would be too great, and the deterrent effect of the Exclusionary Rule reduced too far."

700 F.2d at 1169, n. 5. We reject that view. A police officer who is faced with the opportunity to obtain evidence illegally will rarely, if ever, be in a position to calculate whether the evidence sought would inevitably be discovered. Cf. United States v. Ceccolini, 435 U. S. 268, 435 U. S. 283 (1978):

"[T]he concept of effective deterrence assumes that the police officer consciously realizes the probable consequences of a presumably impermissible course of conduct."

(Opinion concurring in judgment.) On the other hand, when an officer is aware that the evidence will inevitably be discovered, he will try to avoid engaging in any questionable practice. In that situation, there will be little to gain from taking any dubious "shortcuts" to obtain the evidence. Significant disincentives to obtaining evidence illegally -- including the possibility of departmental discipline and civil liability -- also lessen the likelihood that the ultimate or inevitable discovery exception will promote police misconduct. See Bivens v. Six Unknown Federal Narcotics Agents, 403 U. S. 388, 403 U. S. 397 (1971). In these circumstances, the societal costs of the exclusionary rule far outweigh any possible benefits to deterrence that a good faith requirement might produce.

Williams contends that, because he did not

waive his right to the assistance of counsel, the Court may not balance competing values in deciding whether the challenged evidence was properly admitted. He argues that, unlike the exclusionary rule in the Fourth Amendment context, the essential purpose of which is to deter police misconduct, the Sixth Amendment exclusionary rule is designed to protect the right to a fair trial and the integrity of the factfinding process. Williams contends that, when those interests are at stake, the societal costs of excluding evidence obtained from responses presumed involuntary are irrelevant in determining whether such evidence should be excluded. We disagree.

Exclusion of physical evidence that would inevitably have been discovered adds nothing to either the integrity or fairness of a criminal trial. The Sixth Amendment right to counsel protects against unfairness by preserving the adversary process in which the reliability of proffered evidence may be tested in cross-examination. See United States v. Ash, 413 U. S. 300, 413 U. S. 314 (1973); Schneckloth v. Bustamonte, 412 U. S. 218, 412 U. S. 241 (1973). Here, however, Detective Leaming's conduct did nothing to impugn the reliability of the evidence in question -- the body of the child and its condition as it was found, articles of clothing found on the body, and the autopsy. No one would seriously contend that the presence of counsel in the police car when Leaming appealed to Williams' decent human instincts would have had any bearing on the reliability of the body as evidence. Suppression, in these circumstances, would do nothing whatever to promote the integrity of the trial process, but would inflict a wholly unacceptable burden on the administration of criminal justice.

Nor would suppression ensure fairness on the theory that it tends to safeguard the adversary system of justice. To assure the fairness of trial proceedings, this Court has held that assistance of counsel must be available at pretrial confrontations, where

"the subsequent trial [cannot] cure a[n otherwise] one-sided confrontation between prosecuting authorities and the uncounseled defendant."

United States v. Ash, supra, at 413 U. S. 315. Fairness can be assured by placing the State and the accused in the same positions they would have been in had the impermissible conduct not taken place. However, if the government can prove that the evidence would have been obtained inevitably and, therefore, would have been admitted regardless of any overreaching by the police, there is no rational basis to keep that evidence from the jury in order to ensure the fairness of the trial proceedings. In that situation, the State has gained no advantage at trial and the defendant has suffered no prejudice. Indeed, suppression of the evidence would operate to undermine the adversary system by putting the State in a worse position than it would have occupied without any police misconduct. Williams' argument that inevitable discovery constitutes impermissible balancing of values is without merit.

More than a half century ago, Judge, later Justice, Cardozo made his seminal observation that, under the exclusionary rule, "[t]he criminal is to go free because the constable has blundered." People v. Defore, 242 N.Y. 13, 21, 150 N.E. 585, 587 (1926). Prophetically, he went on to consider "how far-reaching in its effect upon society" the exclusionary rule would be when

"[t]he pettiest peace officer would have it in his power, through overzeal or indiscretion, to confer immunity upon an offender for crimes the most flagitious."

Id. at 23, 150 N.E. at 588. Some day, Cardozo speculated, some court might press the exclusionary rule to the outer limits of its logic -- or beyond -- and suppress evidence relating to the "body of a murdered" victim because of the means by which it was found. Id. at 23-24, 150 N.E. at 588. Cardozo's prophecy was fulfilled in Killough v. United States, 114 U.S.App.D.C. 305, 309, 315 F.2d 241, 245 (1962) (en banc). But when, as here, the evidence in question would inevitably have been discovered without reference to the police error or misconduct, there is no nexus sufficient to provide a taint, and the evidence is admissible.

C

The Court of Appeals did not find it necessary to consider whether the record fairly supported the finding that the volunteer search party would ultimately or inevitably have discovered the victim's body. However, three courts independently reviewing the evidence have found that the body of the child inevitably would have been found by the searchers. Williams challenges these findings, asserting that the record contains only the "post hoc rationalization" that the search efforts would have proceeded two and one-half miles into Polk County where Williams had led police to the body.

When that challenge was made at the suppression hearing preceding Williams' second trial, the prosecution offered the testimony of Agent Ruxlow of the Iowa Bureau of Criminal Investigation. Ruxlow had organized and directed some 200 volunteers who were searching for the child's body. Tr. of Hearings on Motion to Suppress in State v. Williams, No. CR 55805, p. 34 (May 31, 1977). The searchers were instructed "to check all the roads, the ditches, any culverts. . . . If they came upon any abandoned farm buildings, they were instructed to go onto the property and search those abandoned farm buildings or any other places where a small child could be secreted." Id. at 35. Ruxlow testified that he marked off highway maps of Poweshiek and Jasper Counties in grid fashion, divided the volunteers into teams of four to six persons, and assigned each team to search specific grid areas. Id. at 34. Ruxlow also testified that, if the search had not been suspended because of Williams' promised cooperation, it would have continued into Polk County, using the same grid system. Id. at 36, 39-40. Although he had previously marked off into grids only the highway maps of Poweshiek and Jasper Counties, Ruxlow had obtained a map of Polk County, which he said he would have marked off in the same manner had it been necessary for the search to continue. Id. at 39.

The search had commenced at approximately 10 a. m. and moved westward through Poweshiek County into Jasper County. At approximately 3 p. m., after Williams had volunteered to cooperate with the police, Detective Leaming, who was in the police car with Williams, sent word to Ruxlow and the other Special Agent directing the search to meet him at the Grinnell truck stop, and the search was suspended at that time. Id. at 51-52. Ruxlow also stated that he was "under the impression that there was a possibility" that Williams would lead them to the child's body at that time. Id. at 61. The search was not resumed once it was learned that Williams had led the police to the body, id. at 57, which was found two and one-half miles from where the search had stopped in what would have been the easternmost grid to be searched in Polk County, id. at 39. There was testimony that it would have taken an additional three to five hours to discover the body if the search had continued, id. at 41; the body was found near a culvert, one of the kinds of places the teams had been specifically directed to search.

On this record, it is clear that the search parties were approaching the actual location of the body, and we are satisfied, along with three courts earlier, that the volunteer search teams would have resumed the search had Williams not earlier led the police to the body, and the body inevitably would have been found. The evidence asserted by Williams as newly discovered, i.e., certain photographs of the body and deposition testimony of Agent Ruxlow made in connection with the federal habeas proceeding, does not demonstrate that the material facts were inadequately developed in the suppression hearing in state court, or that Williams was denied a full, fair, and adequate opportunity to present all relevant facts at the suppression hearing. [6]

The judgment of the Court of Appeals is reversed, and the case is remanded for further proceedings consistent with this opinion. [7]

It is so ordered.

Notes

[1] Iowa law provides for de novo appellate review of factual as well as legal determinations in cases raising constitutional challenges. See, e.g., Amelto v. Baughman, 290 N.W.2d 11, 15 (Iowa 1980); State v. Ege, 274 N.W.2d 350, 352 (Iowa 1979).

[2] Every Federal Court of Appeals having jurisdiction over criminal matters, including the Eighth Circuit in a case decided after the instant case, has endorsed the inevitable discovery doctrine. See Wayne v. United States, 115 U.S.App.D.C. 234, 238, 318 F.2d 205, 209, cert. denied, 375 U.S. 860 (1963); United States v. Bienvenue, 632 F.2d 910, 914 (CA1 1980); United States v. Fisher, 700 F.2d 780, 784 (CA2 1983); Government of Virgin Islands v. Gereau, 502 F.2d 914, 927-928 (CA3 1974), cert. denied, 420 U.S. 909 (1975); United States v. Seohnlein, 423 F.2d 1051, 1053 (CA4), cert. denied, 399 U.S. 913 (1970); United States v. Brookins, 614 F.2d 1037, 1042, 1044 (CA5 1980); Papp v. Jago, 656 F.2d 221, 222 (CA6 1981); United States ex rel. Owens v. Twomey, 508 F.2d 858, 865-866 (CA7 1974); United States v. Apker, 705 F.2d 293, 306-307 (CA8 1983); United States v. Schmidt, 573 F.2d 1057, 1065-1066, n. 9 (CA9), cert. denied, 439 U.S. 881 (1978); United States v. Romero, 692 F.2d 699, 704 (CA10 1982); United States v. Roper, 681 F.2d 1354, 1358 (CA11 1982).

[3] In Murphy v. Waterfront Comm'n of New York Harbor, 378 U. S. 52, 378 U. S. 79 (1964), the Court held that

"a state witness may not be compelled to give testimony which may be incriminating under federal law unless the compelled testimony and its fruits cannot be used in any manner by federal officials in connection with a criminal prosecution against him."

The Court added, however, that,

"[o]nce a defendant demonstrates that he has testified, under a state grant of immunity, to matters related to the federal prosecution, the federal authorities have the burden of showing that their evidence is not tainted by establishing that they had an independent, legitimate source for the disputed evidence."

Id. at 378 U. S. 79, n. 18; see id. at 378 U. S. 103 (WHITE, J., concurring). Application of the independent source doctrine in the Fifth Amendment context was reaffirmed in Kastigar v. United States, 406 U. S. 441, 406 U. S. 460-461 (1972).

[4] The ultimate or inevitable discovery exception to the exclusionary rule is closely related in purpose to the harmless error rule of Chapman v. California, 386 U. S. 18, 386 U. S. 22 (1967). The harmless constitutional error rule

"serve[s] a very useful purpose insofar as [it] block[s] setting aside convictions for small errors or defects that have little, if any, likelihood of having changed the result of the trial."

The purpose of the inevitable discovery rule is to block setting aside convictions that would have been obtained without police misconduct.

[5] As to the quantum of proof, we have already established some relevant guidelines. In United States v. Matlock, 415 U. S. 164, 415 U. S. 178, n. 14 (1974) (emphasis added), we stated that

"the controlling burden of proof at suppression hearings should impose no greater burden than proof by a preponderance of the evidence."

In Lego v. Twomey, 404 U. S. 477, 404 U. S. 488 (1972), we observed

"from our experience [that] no substantial evidence has accumulated that federal rights have suffered from determining admissibility by a preponderance of the evidence,"

and held that the prosecution must prove by a preponderance of the evidence that a confession sought to be used at trial was voluntary. We are unwilling to impose added burdens on the already difficult task of proving guilt in criminal cases by enlarging the barrier to placing evidence of unquestioned truth before juries.

Williams argues that the preponderance of the evidence standard used by the Iowa courts is inconsistent with United States v. Wade, 388 U. S. 218 (1967). In requiring clear and convincing evidence of an independent source for an in-court identification, the Court gave weight to the effect an uncounseled pretrial identification has in "crystaliz[ing] the witnesses' identification of the defendant for future reference." Id. at 388 U. S. 240. The Court noted as well that possible unfairness at the lineup "may be the sole means of attack upon the unequivocal courtroom identification," ibid., and recognized the difficulty of determining whether an in-court identification was based on independent recollection unaided by the lineup identification, id. at 388 U. S. 240-241. By contrast, inevitable discovery involves no speculative elements, but focuses on demonstrated historical facts capable of ready verification or impeachment and does not require a departure from the usual burden of proof at suppression hearings.

[6] Williams had presented to the District Court newly discovered evidence consisting of

"previously overlooked photographs of the body at the site of its discovery and recent deposition testimony of the investigative officer in charge of the search [Ruxlow]."

528 F.Supp. at 671, n. 6. He contends that Ruxlow's testimony was no more than "post hoc rationalization," and challenges Ruxlow's credibility. However, the state trial court and Federal District Court that heard Ruxlow's testimony credited it. The District Court found that the newly discovered evidence "neither adds much to nor subtracts much from the suppression hearing evidence." Ibid.

[7] In view of our holding that the challenged evidence was admissible under the inevitable discovery exception to the exclusionary rule, we find it unnecessary to decide whether Stone v. Powell, 428 U. S. 465 (1976), should be extended to bar federal habeas corpus review of Williams' Sixth Amendment claim, and we express no view on that issue.

Winston v. Lee (March 20, 1985)

JUSTICE BRENNAN delivered the opinion of the Court.

Schmerber v. California, 384 U. S. 757 (1966), held, inter alia, that a State may, over the suspect's protest, have a physician extract blood from a person suspected of drunken driving without violation of the suspect's right secured by the Fourth Amendment not to be subjected to unreasonable searches and seizures. However, Schmerber cautioned:

"That we today hold that the Constitution does not forbid the States['] minor intrusions into an individual's body under stringently limited conditions in no way indicates that it permits more substantial intrusions, or intrusions under other conditions."

Id. at 384 U. S. 772. In this case, the Commonwealth of Virginia seeks to compel the respondent Rudolph Lee, who is suspected of attempting to commit armed robbery, to undergo a surgical procedure under a general anesthetic for removal of a bullet lodged in his chest. Petitioners allege that the bullet will provide evidence of respondent's guilt or innocence. We conclude that the procedure sought here is an example of the "more substantial intrusion" cautioned against in Schmerber, and hold that to permit the procedure would violate respondent's right to be secure in his person guaranteed by the Fourth Amendment.

I

A

At approximately 1 a. m. on July 18, 1982, Ralph E. Watkinson was closing his shop for the night. As he was locking the door, he observed someone armed with a gun coming toward him from across the street. Watkinson was also armed, and when he drew his gun, the other person told him to freeze. Watkinson then fired at the other person, who returned his fire. Watkinson was hit in the legs, while the other individual, who appeared to be wounded in his left side, ran from the scene. The police arrived on the scene shortly thereafter, and Watkinson was taken by ambulance to the emergency room of the Medical College of Virginia (MCV) Hospital.

Approximately 20 minutes later, police officers responding to another call found respondent eight blocks from where the earlier shooting occurred. Respondent was suffering from a gunshot wound to his left chest area, and told the police that he had been shot when two individuals attempted to rob him. An ambulance took respondent to the MCV Hospital. Watkinson was still in the MCV emergency room and, when respondent entered that room, said "[t]hat's the man that shot me." App. 14. After an investigation, the police decided that respondent's story of having been himself the victim of a robbery was untrue, and charged respondent with attempted robbery, malicious wounding, and two counts of using a firearm in the commission of a felony.

B

The Commonwealth shortly thereafter moved in state court for an order directing respondent to undergo surgery to remove an object thought to be a bullet lodged under his left collarbone. The court conducted several evidentiary hearings on the motion. At the first hearing, the Commonwealth's expert testified that the surgical procedure would take 45 minutes and would involve a three to four percent chance of temporary nerve damage, a one percent chance of permanent nerve damage, and a one-tenth of one percent chance of death. At the second hearing, the expert testified that, on reexamination of respondent, he discovered that the bullet was not "back inside close to the nerves and arteries," id. at 52, as he originally had thought. Instead, he now believed the bullet to be located "just beneath the skin." Id. at 57. He testified that the surgery would require an incision of only one and one-half centimeters (slightly more than one-half inch), could be performed under local anesthesia, and would result in "no danger on the basis that there's no general anesthesia employed." Id. at 51.

The state trial judge granted the motion to compel surgery. Respondent petitioned the Virginia Supreme Court for a writ of prohibition and/or a writ of habeas corpus, both of which were denied. Respondent then brought an action in the United States District Court for the Eastern District of Virginia to enjoin the pending operation on Fourth Amendment grounds. The court refused to issue a preliminary injunction, holding that respondent's cause had little likelihood of success on the merits. 551 F.Supp. 247, 247-253 (1982). [1]

On October 18, 1982, just before the surgery was scheduled, the surgeon ordered that X-rays be taken of respondent's chest. The X-rays revealed that the bullet was in fact lodged two and one-half to three centimeters (approximately one inch) deep in muscular tissue in respondent's chest, substantially deeper than had been thought when the state court granted the motion to compel surgery. The surgeon now believed that a general anesthetic would be desirable for medical reasons.

Respondent moved the state trial court for

a rehearing based on the new evidence. After holding an evidentiary hearing, the state trial court denied the rehearing, and the Virginia Supreme Court affirmed. Respondent then returned to federal court, where he moved to alter or amend the judgment previously entered against him. After an evidentiary hearing, the District Court enjoined the threatened surgery. 551 F.Supp. at 253-261 (supplemental opinion). [2]

A divided panel of the Court of Appeals for the Fourth Circuit affirmed. 717 F.2d 888 (1983). [3] We granted certiorari, 466 U.S. 942 (1984), to consider whether a State may, consistently with the Fourth Amendment, compel a suspect to undergo surgery of this kind in a search for evidence of a crime.

II

The Fourth Amendment protects "expectations of privacy," see Katz v. United States, 389 U. S. 347 (1967) --the individual's legitimate expectations that, in certain places and at certain times, he has "the right to be let alone -- the most comprehensive of rights and the right most valued by civilized men." Olmstead v. United States, 277 U. S. 438, 277 U. S. 478 (1928) (Brandeis, J., dissenting). Putting to one side the procedural protections of the warrant requirement, the Fourth Amendment generally protects the "security" of "persons, houses, papers, and effects" against official intrusions up to the point where the community's need for evidence surmounts a specified standard, ordinarily "probable cause." Beyond this point, it is ordinarily justifiable for the community to demand that the individual give up some part of his interest in privacy and security to advance the community's vital interests in law enforcement; such a search is generally "reasonable" in the Amendment's terms.

A compelled surgical intrusion into an individual's body for evidence, however, implicates expectations of privacy and security of such magnitude that the intrusion may be "unreasonable" even if likely to produce evidence of a crime. In Schmerber v. California, 384 U. S. 757 (1966), we addressed a claim that the State had breached the Fourth Amendment's protection of the "right of the people to be secure in their persons . . . against unreasonable searches and seizures" (emphasis added) when it compelled an individual suspected of drunken driving to undergo a blood test. Schmerber had been arrested at a hospital while receiving treatment for injuries suffered when the automobile he was driving struck a tree. Id. at 384 U. S. 758. Despite Schmerber's objection, a police officer at the hospital had directed a physician to take a blood sample from him. Schmerber subsequently objected to the introduction at trial of evidence obtained as a result of the blood test.

The authorities in Schmerber clearly had probable cause to believe that he had been driving while intoxicated, id. at 384 U. S. 768, and to believe that a blood test would provide evidence that was exceptionally probative in confirming this belief. Id. at 384 U. S. 770. Because the case fell within the exigent circumstances exception to the warrant requirement, no warrant was necessary. Ibid. The search was not more intrusive than reasonably necessary to accomplish its goals. Nonetheless, Schmerber argued that the Fourth Amendment prohibited the authorities from intruding into his body to extract the blood that was needed as evidence.

Schmerber noted that

"[t]he overriding function of the Fourth Amendment is to protect personal privacy and dignity against unwarranted intrusion by the State."

Id. at 384 U. S. 767. Citing Wolf v. Colorado, 338 U. S. 25, 338 U. S. 27 (1949), and Mapp v. Ohio, 367 U. S. 643 (1961), we observed that these values were "basic to a free society." We also noted that,

"[b]ecause we are dealing with intrusions

into the human body, rather than with state interferences with property relationships or private papers -- 'houses, papers, and effects' -- we write on a clean slate."

384 U.S. at 384 U. S. 767-768. The intrusion perhaps implicated Schmerber's most personal and deep-rooted expectations of privacy, and the Court recognized that Fourth Amendment analysis thus required a discerning inquiry into the facts and circumstances to determine whether the intrusion was justifiable. The Fourth Amendment neither forbids nor permits all such intrusions; rather, the Amendment's

"proper function is to constrain, not against all intrusions as such, but against intrusions which are not justified in the circumstances, or which are made in an improper manner."

Id. at 384 U. S. 768.

The reasonableness of surgical intrusions beneath the skin depends on a case-by-case approach, in which the individual's interests in privacy and security are weighed against society's interests in conducting the procedure. In a given case, the question whether the community's need for evidence outweighs the substantial privacy interests at stake is a delicate one admitting of few categorical answers. We believe that Schmerber, however, provides the appropriate framework of analysis for such cases.

Schmerber recognized that the ordinary requirements of the Fourth Amendment would be the threshold requirements for conducting this kind of surgical search and seizure. We noted the importance of probable cause. Id. at 384 U. S. 768-769.

And we pointed out:

"Search warrants are ordinarily required for searches of dwellings, and, absent an emergency, no less could be required where intrusions into the human body are concerned. . . . The importance of informed, detached and deliberate determinations of the issue whether or not to invade another's body in search of evidence of guilt is indisputable and great."

Id. at 384 U. S. 770.

Beyond these standards, Schmerber's inquiry considered a number of other factors in determining the "reasonableness" of the blood test. A crucial factor in analyzing the magnitude of the intrusion in Schmerber is the extent to which the procedure may threaten the safety or health of the individual. "[F]or most people, [a blood test] involves virtually no risk, trauma, or pain." Id. at 384 U. S. 771. Moreover, all reasonable medical precautions were taken, and no unusual or untested procedures were employed in Schmerber; the procedure was performed "by a physician in a hospital environment according to accepted medical practices." Ibid. Notwithstanding the existence of probable cause, a search for evidence of a crime may be unjustifiable if it endangers the life or health of the suspect. [4]

Another factor is the extent of intrusion upon the individual's dignitary interests in personal privacy and bodily integrity. Intruding into an individual's living room, See Payton v. New York, 445 U. S. 573 (1980), eavesdropping upon an individual's telephone conversations, see Katz v. United States, 389 U.S. at 389 U. S. 361, or forcing an individual to accompany police officers to the police station, see Dunaway v. New York, 442 U. S. 200 (1979), typically do not injure the physical person of the individual. Such intrusions do, however, damage the individual's sense of personal privacy and security, and are thus subject to the Fourth Amendment's dictates. In noting that a blood test was "a commonplace in these days of periodic physical examinations," 384 U.S. at 384 U. S. 771, Schmerber recognized society's judgment that blood tests do not constitute an unduly extensive imposition on an individual's personal privacy and bodily integrity. [5]

Weighed against these individual interests

is the community's interest in fairly and accurately determining guilt or innocence. This interest is of course of great importance. We noted in Schmerber that a blood test is "a highly effective means of determining the degree to which a person is under the influence of alcohol." Id. at 384 U. S. 771. Moreover, there was "a clear indication that in fact [desired] evidence [would] be found" if the blood test were undertaken. Id. at 384 U. S. 770.

Especially given the difficulty of proving drunkenness by other means, these considerations showed that results of the blood test were of vital importance if the State were to enforce its drunken driving laws. In Schmerber, we concluded that this state interest was sufficient to justify the intrusion, and the compelled blood test was thus "reasonable" for Fourth Amendment purposes.

III

Applying the Schmerber balancing test in this case, we believe that the Court of Appeals reached the correct result. The Commonwealth plainly had probable cause to conduct the search. In addition, all parties apparently agree that respondent has had a full measure of procedural protections, and has been able fully to litigate the difficult medical and legal questions necessarily involved in analyzing the reasonableness of a surgical incision of this magnitude. [6] Our inquiry therefore must focus on the extent of the intrusion on respondent's privacy interests and on the State's need for the evidence.

The threats to the health or safety of respondent posed by the surgery are the subject of sharp dispute between the parties. Before the new revelations of October 18, the District Court found that the procedure could be carried out "with virtually no risk to [respondent]." 551 F.Supp. at 252. On rehearing, however, with new evidence before it, the District Court held that "the risks previously involved have increased in magnitude even as new risks are being added." Id. at 260.

The Court of Appeals examined the medical evidence in the record and found that respondent would suffer some risks associated with the surgical procedure. [7] One surgeon had testified that the difficulty of discovering the exact location of the bullet "could require extensive probing and retracting of the muscle tissue," carrying with it

"the concomitant risks of injury to the muscle, as well as injury to the nerves, blood vessels and other tissue in the chest and pleural cavity."

717 F.2d at 900. The court further noted that "the greater intrusion and the larger incisions increase the risks of infection." Ibid. Moreover, there was conflict in the testimony concerning the nature and the scope of the operation. One surgeon stated that it would take 15-20 minutes, while another predicted the procedure could take up to two and one-half hours. Ibid. The court properly took the resulting uncertainty about the medical risks into account. [8]

Both lower courts in this case believed that the proposed surgery, which for purely medical reasons required the use of a general anesthetic, [9] would be an "extensive" intrusion on respondent's personal privacy and bodily integrity. Ibid.

When conducted with the consent of the patient, surgery requiring general anesthesia is not necessarily demeaning or intrusive. In such a case, the surgeon is carrying out the patient's own will concerning the patient's body, and the patient's right to privacy is therefore preserved. In this case, however, the Court of Appeals noted that the Commonwealth proposes to take control of respondent's body, to "drug this citizen -- not yet convicted of a criminal offense -- with narcotics and barbiturates into a state of unconsciousness," id. at 901, and then to search beneath his skin for evidence of a crime. This kind of surgery involves a virtually total divestment of respondent's ordinary control over surgical probing beneath his skin.

The other part of the balance concerns the Commonwealth's need to intrude into respondent's body to retrieve the bullet. The Commonwealth claims to need the bullet to demonstrate that it was fired from Watkinson's gun, which in turn would show that respondent was the robber who confronted Watkinson. However, although we recognize the difficulty of making determinations in advance as to the strength of the case against respondent, petitioners' assertions of a compelling need for the bullet are hardly persuasive. The very circumstances relied on in this case to demonstrate probable cause to believe that evidence will be found tend to vitiate the Commonwealth's need to compel respondent to undergo surgery. The Commonwealth has available substantial additional evidence that respondent was the individual who accosted Watkinson on the night of the robbery. No party in this case suggests that Watkinson's entirely spontaneous identification of respondent at the hospital would be inadmissible. In addition, petitioners can no doubt prove that Watkinson was found a few blocks from Watkinson's store shortly after the incident took place. And petitioners can certainly show that the location of the bullet (under respondent's left collarbone) seems to correlate with Watkinson's report that the robber "jerked" to the left. App. 13. The fact that the Commonwealth has available such substantial evidence of the origin of the bullet restricts the need for the Commonwealth to compel respondent to undergo the contemplated surgery. [10]

In weighing the various factors in this case, we therefore reach the same conclusion as the courts below. The operation sought will intrude substantially on respondent's protected interests. The medical risks of the operation, although apparently not extremely severe, are a subject of considerable dispute; the very uncertainty militates against finding the operation to be "reasonable." In addition, the intrusion on respondent's privacy interests entailed by the operation can only be characterized as severe. On the other hand, although the bullet may turn out to be useful to the Commonwealth in prosecuting respondent, the Commonwealth has failed to demonstrate a compelling need for it. We believe that, in these circumstances, the Commonwealth has failed to demonstrate that it would be "reasonable" under the terms of the Fourth Amendment to search for evidence of this crime by means of the contemplated surgery.

IV

The Fourth Amendment is a vital safeguard of the right of the citizen to be free from unreasonable governmental intrusions into any area in which he has a reasonable expectation of privacy. Where the Court has found a lesser expectation of privacy, see, e.g., Rakas v. Illinois, 439 U. S. 128 (1978); South Dakota v. Opperman, 428 U. S. 364 (1976), or where the search involves a minimal intrusion on privacy interests, see, e.g., United States v. Hensley, 469 U. S. 221 (1985); Dunaway v. New York, 442 U.S. at 442 U. S. 210-211; United States v. Brignoni-Ponce, 422 U. S. 873, 422 U. S. 880 (1975); Adams v. Williams, 407 U. S. 143 (1972); Terry v. Ohio, 392 U. S. 1 (1968), the Court has held that the Fourth Amendment's protections are correspondingly less stringent. Conversely, however, the Fourth Amendment's command that searches be "reasonable" requires that, when the State seeks to intrude upon an area in which our society recognizes a significantly heightened privacy interest, a more substantial justification is required to make the search "reasonable." Applying these principles, we hold that the proposed search in this case would be "unreasonable" under the Fourth Amendment.

Affirmed.

JUSTICE BLACKMUN and JUSTICE REHNQUIST concur in the judgment.

Notes

[1] Respondent's action in the District Court was styled as a petition for habeas corpus and an action under 42 U.S.C. § 1983 for a preliminary injunction. Because the District Court denied the relief sought, it found it unnecessary to consider whether res judicata, see Allen v. McCurry, 449 U. S. 90 (1980), would bar consideration of the § 1983 claim. 551 F.Supp. at 252, n. 4.

[2] Respondent had moved to reopen the petition for habeas corpus, as well as to alter or amend the judgment. Petitioners moved to dismiss the petition for habeas on the ground that respondent was not at that time "in custody" for purposes of 28 U.S.C. § 2241. The District Court rejected this contention, holding that habeas was available because respondent was objecting to a future custody that would take place when the operation was to be performed. 551 F.Supp. at 257-259. The Court of Appeals held that respondent's claim was cognizable only under § 1983. 717 F.2d 888, 893 (1983). Respondent has not cross-petitioned for review of this holding, and it is therefore not before us.

[3] The Fourth Circuit held that Allen v. McCurry, supra, did not bar respondent's attempt to relitigate in federal court the same Fourth Amendment issues previously litigated in state court. The court agreed with the District Court's conclusion, see 551 F.Supp. at 258-259, that respondent had not had a full and fair opportunity to litigate in the state trial court. 717 F.2d at 895-899. Respondent filed his motion for rehearing in state court on October 18, the day he was informed of the changed circumstances regarding the removal of the bullet. On October 19, the state court ordered an evidentiary hearing to be held on October 21. The Court of Appeals was

"satisfied from the record that counsel was not able, despite obviously diligent effort, to obtain an independent review of the medical record by outside physicians, nor was he able to consult with the independent expert in anesthesiology in order to prepare a presentation on the risks of general anesthesia."

Id. at 897. Yet, despite the crucial nature of the medical evidence, the state court refused to grant respondent's repeated request for a continuance. Because

"[t]he arbitrary truncation of preparation time deprived [respondent] of a fair opportunity to determine the crucial factors relevant to his claim and to obtain independent expert witnesses to testify about those factors,"

id. at 898-899, the Court of Appeals refused to grant preclusive effect to the state court's findings. Petitioners do not challenge this ruling.

[4] Numerous courts have recognized the crucial importance of this factor. See, e.g., Bowden v. State, 256 Ark. 820, 823, 510 S.W.2d 879, 882 (1974) (refusing to order surgery because of medical risk); People v. Smith, 80 Misc.2d 210, 362 N.Y.S.2d 909 (1974) (same); State v. Allen, 277 S.C. 595, 291 S.E.2d 459 (1982) (same); see also 717 F.2d 888, 900 (CA4 1983) (case below); id. at 905-908 (Widener, J., dissenting); United States v. Crowder, 177 U.S. App.D.C. 165, 169, 543 F.2d 312, 316 (1976) (en banc), cert. denied, 429 U.S. 1062 (1977); State v. Overstreet, 551 S.W.2d 621, 628 (Mo.1977) (en banc). See generally Note, 68 Marq.L.Rev. 130, 135 (1984) (discussing cases involving bodily intrusions); Note, 60 Notre Dame L.Rev. 149, 152-156 (1984) (same); Note, 55 Texas L.Rev. 147 (1976) (same); Mandell & Richardson, Surgical Search: Removing a Scar on the Fourth Amendment, 75 J.Crim.L. & C., No. 3, p. 525 (1984).

[5] See also Schmerber, 384 U.S. at 384 U. S. 771, n. 13 ("The blood test procedure has become routine in our everyday life. It is a ritual for those going into the military service as well as those applying for marriage licenses. Many colleges require such tests before permitting entrance, and

literally millions of us have voluntarily gone through the same, though a longer, routine in becoming blood donors'") (quoting Breithaupt v. Abram, 352 U. S. 432, 352 U. S. 436 (1957)). The degree of intrusion in Schmerber was minimized as well by the fact that a blood test "involves virtually no risk, trauma, or pain," 384 U.S. at 384 U. S. 771, and by the fact that the blood test was conducted "in a hospital environment according to accepted medical practices." Ibid. As such, the procedure in Schmerber contrasted sharply with the practice in Rochin v. California, 342 U. S. 165 (1952), in which police officers broke into a suspect's room, attempted to extract narcotics capsules he had put into his mouth, took him to a hospital, and directed that an emetic be administered to induce vomiting. Id. at 342 U. S. 166. Rochin, recognizing the individual's interest in "human dignity," id. at 342 U. S. 174, held the search and seizure unconstitutional under the Due Process Clause.

[6] Because the State has afforded respondent the benefit of a full adversary presentation and appellate review, we do not reach the question whether the State may compel a suspect to undergo a surgical search of this magnitude for evidence absent such special procedural protections. Cf. United States v. Crowder, supra, at 169, 543 F.2d at 316; State v. Lawson, 187 N.J.Super. 25, 28-29, 453 A.2d 556, 558 (App.Div.1982).

[7] The Court of Appeals concluded, however, that "the specific physical risks from putting [respondent] under general anesthesia may therefore be considered minimal." 717 F.2d at 900. Testimony had shown that

"the general risks of harm or death from general anesthesia are quite low, and that [respondent] was in the statistical group of persons with the lowest risk of injury from general anesthesia."

Ibid.

[8] One expert testified that this would be "minor" surgery. See App. 99. The question whether the surgery is to be characterized in medical terms as "major" or "minor" is not controlling. We agree with the Court of Appeals and the District Court in this case that

"there is no reason to suppose that the definition of a medical term of art should coincide with the parameters of a constitutional standard."

551 F.Supp. at 260 (quoted at 717 F.2d at 901); accord, State v. Overstreet, 551 S.W.2d at 628. This does not mean that the application of medical concepts in such cases is to be ignored. However, no specific medical categorization can control the multifaceted legal inquiry that the court must undertake.

[9] Somewhat different issues would be raised if the use of a general anesthetic became necessary because of the patient's refusal to cooperate. Cf. State v. Lawson, supra.

[10] There are also some questions concerning the probative value of the bullet, even if it could be retrieved. The evidentiary value of the bullet depends on a comparison between markings, if any, on the bullet in respondent's shoulder and markings, if any, found on a test bullet that the police could fire from Watkinson's gun. However, the record supports some doubt whether this kind of comparison is possible. This is because the bullet's markings may have been corroded in the time that the bullet has been in respondent's shoulder, thus making it useless for comparison purposes. See 717 F.2d at 901, n. 15. In addition, respondent argues that any given gun may be incapable of firing bullets that have a consistent set of markings. See Joling, An Overview of Firearms Identification Evidence for Attorneys I: Salient Features of Firearms Evidence, 26 J.Forensic Sci. 153, 154 (1981). The record is devoid of any evidence that the police have attempted to test-fire Watkinson's gun, and there thus remains the additional possibility that a

comparison of bullets is impossible because Watkinson's gun does not consistently fire bullets with the same markings. However, because the courts below made no findings on this point, we hesitate to give it significant weight in our analysis.

Arizona v. Hicks (March 3, 1987)

JUSTICE SCALIA delivered the opinion of the Court.

In Coolidge v. New Hampshire, 403 U. S. 443 (1971), we said that, in certain circumstances, a warrantless seizure by police of an item that comes within plain view during their lawful search of a private area may be reasonable under the Fourth Amendment. See id. at 403 U. S. 465-471 (plurality opinion); id. at 465 U. S. 505-506 (Black, J., concurring and dissenting); id. at 465 U. S. 521-522 (WHITE, J., concurring and dissenting). We granted certiorari, 475 U.S. 1107 (1986), in the present case to decide whether this "plain view" doctrine may be invoked when the police have less than probable cause to believe that the item in question is evidence of a crime or is contraband.

I

On April 18, 1984, a bullet was fired through the floor of respondent's apartment, striking and injuring a man in the apartment below. Police officers arrived and entered respondent's apartment to search for the shooter, for other victims, and for weapons. They found and seized three weapons, including a sawed-off rifle, and in the course of their search also discovered a stocking-cap mask.

One of the policemen, Officer Nelson, noticed two sets of expensive stereo components, which seemed out of place in the squalid and otherwise ill-appointed four-room apartment. Suspecting that they were stolen, he read and recorded their serial numbers -- moving some of the components, including a Bang and Olufsen turntable, in order to do so -- which he then reported by phone to his headquarters. On being advised that the turntable had been taken in an armed robbery, he seized it immediately. It was later determined that some of the other serial numbers matched those on other stereo equipment taken in the same armed robbery, and a warrant was obtained and executed to seize that equipment as well. Respondent was subsequently indicted for the robbery.

The state trial court granted respondent's motion to suppress the evidence that had been seized. The Court of Appeals of Arizona affirmed. It was conceded that the initial entry and search, although warrantless, were justified by the exigent circumstance of the shooting. The Court of Appeals viewed the obtaining of the serial numbers, however, as an additional search, unrelated to that exigency. Relying upon a statement in Mincey v. Arizona, 437 U. S. 385 (1978), that a "warrantless search must be strictly circumscribed by the exigencies which justify its initiation,'" id. at 437 U. S. 393 (citation omitted), the Court of Appeals held that the police conduct violated the Fourth Amendment, requiring the evidence derived from that conduct to be excluded. 146 Ariz. 533, 534-535, 707 P.2d 331, 332-333 (1985). Both courts -- the trial court explicitly and the Court of Appeals by necessary implication -- rejected the State's contention that Officer Nelson's actions were justified under the "plain view" doctrine of Coolidge v. New Hampshire, supra. The Arizona Supreme Court denied review, and the State filed this petition.

II

As an initial matter, the State argues that Officer Nelson's actions constituted neither a "search" nor a "seizure" within the meaning of the Fourth Amendment. We agree that the mere recording of the serial numbers did not constitute a seizure. To be sure, that was the first step in a process by which respondent was eventually deprived of the stereo equipment. In and of itself, however, it did not "meaningfully interfere" with respondent's possessory interest in either the serial numbers or the equipment, and therefore did not amount to a seizure. See Maryland v. Macon, 472 U. S. 463, 472 U. S. 469 (1985).

Officer Nelson's moving of the equipment, however, did constitute a "search" separate and apart from the search for the shooter, victims, and weapons that was the lawful objective of his entry into the apartment. Merely inspecting those parts of the turntable that came into view during the latter search would not have constituted an independent search, because it would have produced no additional invasion of respondent's privacy interest. See Illinois v. Andreas, 463 U. S. 765, 463 U. S. 771 (1983). But taking action, unrelated to the objectives of the authorized intrusion, which exposed to view concealed portions of the apartment or its contents, did produce a new invasion of respondent's privacy unjustified by the exigent circumstance that validated the entry. This is why, contrary to JUSTICE POWELL's suggestion, post at 480 U. S. 333, the "distinction between looking' at a suspicious object in plain view and `moving' it even a few inches" is much more than trivial for purposes of the Fourth Amendment. It matters not that the search uncovered nothing of any great personal value to respondent -- serial numbers rather than (what might conceivably have been hidden behind or under the equipment) letters or photographs. A search is a search, even if it happens to disclose nothing but the bottom of a turntable.

III

The remaining question is whether the search was "reasonable" under the Fourth Amendment.

On this aspect of the case, we reject, at the outset, the apparent position of the Arizona Court of Appeals that, because the officers' action directed to the stereo equipment was unrelated to the justification for their entry into respondent's apartment, it was ipso facto unreasonable. That lack of relationship always exists with regard to action validated under the "plain view" doctrine; where action is taken for the purpose justifying the entry, invocation of the doctrine is superfluous. Mincey v. Arizona, supra, in saying that a warrantless search must be "strictly circumscribed by the exigencies which justify its initiation," 437 U.S. at 437 U. S. 393 (citation omitted), was addressing only the scope of the primary search itself, and was not overruling by implication the many cases acknowledging that the "plain view" doctrine can legitimate action beyond that scope.

We turn, then, to application of the doctrine to the facts of this case. "It is well established that, under certain circumstances, the police may seize evidence in plain view without a warrant," Coolidge v. New Hampshire, 403 U.S. at 403 U. S. 465 (plurality opinion) (emphasis added). Those circumstances include situations

"[w]here the initial intrusion that brings the police within plain view of such [evidence] is supported . . . by one of the recognized exceptions to the warrant requirement,"

ibid., such as the exigent circumstances intrusion here. It would be absurd to say that an object could lawfully be seized and taken from the premises, but could not be moved for closer examination. It is clear, therefore, that the search here was valid if the "plain view" doctrine would have sustained a seizure of the equipment.

There is no doubt it would have done so if Officer Nelson had probable cause to believe that the equipment was stolen. The State has conceded, however, that he had only a "reasonable suspicion," by which it means something less than probable cause. See Brief for Petitioner 18-19. * We have not ruled on the question whether probable cause is required in order to invoke the "plain view" doctrine. Dicta in Payton v. New York, 445 U. S. 573, 445 U. S. 587 (1980), suggested that the standard of probable cause must be met, but our later opinions in Texas v. Brown, 460 U. S. 730 (1983), explicitly regarded the issue as unresolved, see id. at 460 U. S. 742, n. 7 (plurality opinion); id. at 460 U. S. 746 (STEVENS, J., concurring in judgment).

We now hold that probable cause is required. To say otherwise would be to cut the "plain view" doctrine loose from its theoretical and practical moorings. The theory of that doctrine consists of extending to nonpublic places such as the home, where searches and seizures without a warrant are presumptively unreasonable, the police's longstanding authority to make warrantless seizures in public places of such objects as weapons and contraband. See Payton v. New York, supra, at 445 U. S. 586-587. And the practical justification for that extension is the desirability of sparing police, whose viewing of the object in the course of a lawful search is as legitimate as it would have been in a public place, the inconvenience and the risk -- to themselves or to preservation of the evidence -- of going to obtain a warrant. See Coolidge v. New Hampshire, supra, at 403 U. S. 468 (plurality opinion). Dispensing with the need for a warrant is worlds apart from permitting a lesser standard of cause for the seizure than a warrant would require, i.e., the standard of probable cause. No reason is apparent why an object should routinely be seizable on lesser grounds, during an unrelated search and seizure, than would have been needed to obtain a warrant for that same object if it had been known to be on the premises.

We do not say, of course, that a seizure can never be justified on less than probable cause. We have held that it can -- where, for example, the seizure is minimally intrusive and operational necessities render it the only practicable means of detecting certain types of crime. See, e.g., United States v. Cortez, 449 U. S. 411 (1981) (investigative detention of vehicle suspected to be transporting

illegal aliens); United States v. Brignoni-Ponce, 422 U. S. 873 (1975) (same); United States v. Place, 462 U. S. 696, 462 U. S. 709, and n. 9 (1983) (dictum) (seizure of suspected drug dealer's luggage at airport to permit exposure to specially trained dog). No special operational necessities are relied on here, however -- but rather the mere fact that the items in question came lawfully within the officer's plain view. That alone cannot supplant the requirement of probable cause.

The same considerations preclude us from holding that, even though probable cause would have been necessary for a seizure, the search of objects in plain view that occurred here could be sustained on lesser grounds. A dwelling place search, no less than a dwelling place seizure, requires probable cause, and there is no reason in theory or practicality why application of the "plain view" doctrine would supplant that requirement. Although the interest protected by the Fourth Amendment injunction against unreasonable searches is quite different from that protected by its injunction against unreasonable seizures, see Texas v. Brown, supra, at 460 U. S. 747-748 (STEVENS, J., concurring in judgment), neither the one nor the other is of inferior worth or necessarily requires only lesser protection. We have not elsewhere drawn a categorical distinction between the two insofar as concerns the degree of justification needed to establish the reasonableness of police action, and we see no reason for a distinction in the particular circumstances before us here. Indeed, to treat searches more liberally would especially erode the plurality's warning in Coolidge that

"the 'plain view' doctrine may not be used to extend a general exploratory search from one object to another until something incriminating at last emerges."

403 U.S. at 403 U. S. 466. In short, whether legal authority to move the equipment could be found only as an inevitable concomitant

of the authority to seize it, or also as a consequence of some independent power to search certain objects in plain view, probable cause to believe the equipment was stolen was required.

JUSTICE O'CONNOR's dissent suggests that we uphold the action here on the ground that it was a "cursory inspection," rather than a "full-blown search," and could therefore be justified by reasonable suspicion instead of probable cause. As already noted, a truly cursory inspection -- one that involves merely looking at what is already exposed to view, without disturbing it -- is not a "search" for Fourth Amendment purposes, and therefore does not even require reasonable suspicion. We are unwilling to send police and judges into a new thicket of Fourth Amendment law, to seek a creature of uncertain description that is neither a "plain view" inspection nor yet a "full-blown search." Nothing in the prior opinions of this Court supports such a distinction, not even the dictum from Justice Stewart's concurrence in Stanley v. Georgia, 394 U. S. 557, 394 U. S. 571 (1969), whose reference to a "mere inspection" describes, in our view, close observation of what lies in plain sight.

JUSTICE POWELL's dissent reasonably asks what it is we would have had Officer Nelson do in these circumstances. Post at 480 U. S. 332. The answer depends, of course, upon whether he had probable cause to conduct a search, a question that was not preserved in this case. If he had, then he should have done precisely what he did. If not, then he should have followed up his suspicions, if possible, by means other than a search -- just as he would have had to do if, while walking along the street, he had noticed the same suspicious stereo equipment sitting inside a house a few feet away from him, beneath an open window. It may well be that, in such circumstances, no effective means short of a search exist. But there is nothing new in the realization that the Constitution sometimes insulates the criminality of a few in order to protect the privacy of us all. Our disagreement with the dissenters pertains to where the proper balance should be struck; we choose to adhere to the textual and traditional standard of probable cause.

The State contends that, even if Officer Nelson's search violated the Fourth Amendment, the court below should have admitted the evidence thus obtained under the "good faith" exception to the exclusionary rule. That was not the question on which certiorari was granted, and we decline to consider it.

For the reasons stated, the judgment of the Court of Appeals of Arizona is

Affirmed.

* Contrary to the suggestion in JUSTICE O'CONNOR's dissent, post at 480 U. S. 339, this concession precludes our considering whether the probable cause standard was satisfied in this case.

California v. Greenwood (May 16, 1988)

JUSTICE WHITE delivered the opinion of the Court.

The issue here is whether the Fourth Amendment prohibits the warrantless search and seizure of garbage left for collection outside the curtilage of a home. We conclude, in accordance with the vast majority of lower courts that have addressed the issue, that it does not.

I

In early 1984, Investigator Jenny Stracner of the Laguna Beach Police Department received information indicating that respondent Greenwood might be engaged in narcotics trafficking. Stracner learned that a criminal suspect had informed a federal drug enforcement agent in February, 1984, that a truck filled with illegal drugs was en route to the Laguna Beach address at which Greenwood resided. In addition, a neighbor complained of heavy vehicular traffic late at night in front of Greenwood's single-family home. The neighbor reported that the vehicles remained at

Greenwood's house for only a few minutes.

Stracner sought to investigate this information by conducting a surveillance of Greenwood's home. She observed several vehicles make brief stops at the house during the late-night and early-morning hours, and she followed a truck from the house to a residence that had previously been under investigation as a narcotics trafficking location.

On April 6, 1984, Stracner asked the neighborhood's regular trash collector to pick up the plastic garbage bags that Greenwood had left on the curb in front of his house and to turn the bags over to her without mixing their contents with garbage from other houses. The trash collector cleaned his truck bin of other refuse, collected the garbage bags from the street in front of Greenwood's house, and turned the bags over to Stracner. The officer searched through the rubbish and found items indicative of narcotics use. She recited the information that she had gleaned from the trash search in an affidavit in support of a warrant to search Greenwood's home.

Police officers encountered both respondents at the house later that day when they arrived to execute the warrant. The police discovered quantities of cocaine and hashish during their search of the house. Respondents were arrested on felony narcotics charges. They subsequently posted bail.

The police continued to receive reports of many late-night visitors to the Greenwood house. On May 4, Investigator Robert Rahaeuser obtained Greenwood's garbage from the regular trash collector in the same manner as had Stracner. The garbage again contained evidence of narcotics use.

Rahaeuser secured another search warrant for Greenwood's home based on the information from the second trash search. The police found more narcotics and evidence of narcotics trafficking when they executed the warrant. Greenwood was again arrested.

The Superior Court dismissed the charges against respondents on the authority of People v. Krivda, 5 Cal.3d 357, 486 P.2d 1262 (1971), which held that warrantless trash searches violate the Fourth Amendment and the California Constitution. The court found that the police would not have had probable cause to search the Greenwood home without the evidence obtained from the trash searches.

The Court of Appeal affirmed. 182 Cal.App.3d 729, 227 Cal.Rptr. 539 (1986). The court noted at the outset that the fruits of warrantless trash searches could no longer be suppressed if Krivda were based only on the California Constitution, because, since 1982, the State has barred the suppression of evidence seized in violation of California law but not federal law. See Cal.Const., Art. I, § 28(d); In re Lance W., 37 Cal.3d 873, 694 P.2d 744 (1985). But Krivda, a decision binding on the Court of Appeal, also held that the fruits of warrantless trash searches were to be excluded under federal law. Hence, the Superior Court was correct in dismissing the charges against respondents. 182 Cal.App.3d at 735, 227 Cal.Rptr, at 542. [1]

The California Supreme Court denied the State's petition for review of the Court of Appeal's decision. We granted certiorari, 483 U.S. 1019, and now reverse.

II

The warrantless search and seizure of the garbage bags left at the curb outside the Greenwood house would violate the Fourth Amendment only if respondents manifested a subjective expectation of privacy in their garbage that society accepts as objectively reasonable. O'Connor v. Ortega, 480 U. S. 709, 480 U. S. 715 (1987); California v. Ciraolo, 476 U. S. 207, 476 U. S. 211 (1986); Oliver v. United States, 466 U. S. 170, 466 U. S. 177 (1984); Katz v. United States, 389 U. S. 347, 389 U. S. 361 (1967) (Harlan, J., concurring). Respondents do not disagree with this standard.

They assert, however, that they had, and exhibited, an expectation of privacy with respect to the trash that was searched by the police: the trash, which was placed on the street for collection at a fixed time, was contained in opaque plastic bags, which the garbage collector was expected to pick up, mingle with the trash of others, and deposit at the garbage dump. The trash was only temporarily on the street, and there was little likelihood that it would be inspected by anyone.

It may well be that respondents did not expect that the contents of their garbage bags would become known to the police or other members of the public. An expectation of privacy does not give rise to Fourth Amendment protection, however, unless society is prepared to accept that expectation as objectively reasonable.

Here, we conclude that respondents exposed their garbage to the public sufficiently to defeat their claim to Fourth Amendment protection. It is common knowledge that plastic garbage bags left on or at the side of a public street are readily accessible to animals, [2] children, scavengers, [3] snoops, [4] and other members of the public. See Krivda, 5 Cal.3d at 367, 486 P.2d at 1269. Moreover, respondents placed their refuse at the curb for the express purpose of conveying it to a third party, the trash collector, who might himself have sorted through respondents' trash or permitted others, such as the police, to do so. Accordingly, having deposited their garbage

"in an area particularly suited for public inspection and, in a manner of speaking, public consumption, for the express purpose of having strangers take it,"

United States v. Reicherter, 647 F.2d 397, 399 (CA3 1981), respondents could have had no reasonable expectation of privacy in the inculpatory items that they discarded.

Furthermore, as we have held, the police cannot reasonably be expected to avert their eyes from evidence of criminal activity that could have been observed by any member of the public. Hence, "[w]hat a person knowingly exposes to the public, even in his own home or office, is not a subject of Fourth Amendment protection." Katz v. United States, supra, at 389 U. S. 351. We held in Smith v. Maryland, 442 U. S. 735 (1979), for example, that the police did not violate the Fourth Amendment by causing a pen register to be installed at the telephone company's offices to record the telephone numbers dialed by a criminal suspect. An individual has no legitimate expectation of privacy in the numbers dialed on his telephone, we reasoned, because he voluntarily conveys those numbers to the telephone company when he uses the telephone. Again, we observed that "a person has no legitimate expectation of privacy in information he voluntarily turns over to third parties." Id. at 442 U. S. 743-744.

Similarly, we held in California v. Ciraolo, supra, that the police were not required by the Fourth Amendment to obtain a warrant before conducting surveillance of the respondent's fenced backyard from a private plane flying at an altitude of 1,000 feet. We concluded that the respondent's expectation that his yard was protected from such surveillance was unreasonable, because "[a]ny member of the public flying in this airspace who glanced down could have seen everything that these officers observed." Id. at 476 U. S. 213-214.

Our conclusion that society would not accept as reasonable respondents' claim to an expectation of privacy in trash left for collection in an area accessible to the public is reinforced by the unanimous rejection of similar claims by the Federal Courts of Appeals. See United States v. Dela Espriella, 781 F.2d 1432, 1437 (CA9 1986); United States v. O'Bryant, 775 F.2d 1528, 1533-1534 (CA11 1985); United States v. Michaels, 726 F.2d 1307, 1312-1313 (CA8), cert. denied, 469 U.S. 820 (1984); United States v. Kramer, 711 F.2d 789, 791-794 (CA7), cert. denied, 464 U.S. 962 (1983);

United States v. Terry, 702 F.2d 299, 308-309 (CA2), cert. denied sub nom. Williams v. United States, 461 U.S. 931 (1983); United States v. Reicherter, supra, at 399; United States v. Vahalik, 606 F.2d 99, 100-101 (CA5 1979) (per curiam), cert. denied, 444 U.S. 1081 (1980); United States v. Crowell, 586 F.2d 1020, 1025 (CA4 1978), cert. denied, 440 U.S. 959 (1979); Magda v. Benson, 536 F.2d 111, 112-113 (CA6 1976) (per curiam); United States v. Mustone, 469 F.2d 970, 972-974 (CA1 1972). In United States v. Thornton, 241 U.S.App.D.C. 46, 56, and n. 11, 746 F.2d 39, 49, and n. 11 (1984), the court observed that

"the overwhelming weight of authority rejects the proposition that a reasonable expectation of privacy exists with respect to trash discarded outside the home and the curtilege [sic] thereof."

In addition, of those state appellate courts that have considered the issue, the vast majority have held that the police may conduct warrantless searches and seizures of garbage discarded in public areas. See Commonwealth v. Chappee, 397 Mass. 508, 512-513, 492 N.E.2d 719, 721-722 (1986); Cooks v. State, 699 P.2d 653, 656 (Okla. Crim.), cert. denied, 474 U.S. 935 (1985); State v. Stevens, 123 Wis.2d 303, 314-317, 367 N.W.2d 788, 794-797, cert. denied, 474 U.S. 852 (1985); State v. Ronngren, 361 N.W.2d 224, 228-230 (N.D.1985); State v. Brown, 20 Ohio App.3d 36, 37-38, 484 N.E.2d 215, 217-218 (1984); State v. Oquist, 327 N.W.2d 587 (Minn.1982); People v. Whotte, 113 Mich.App. 12, 317 N.W.2d 266 (1982); Commonwealth v. Minton, 288 Pa.Super. 381, 391, 432 A.2d 212, 217 (1981); State v. Schultz, 388 So.2d 1326 (Fla.App.1980); People v. Huddleston, 38 Ill.App.3d 277, 347 N.E.2d 76 (1976); Willis v. State, 518 S.W.2d 247, 249 (Tex.Crim.App.1975); Smith v. State, 510 P.2d 793 (Alaska), cert. denied, 414 U.S. 1086 (1973); State v. Fassler, 108 Ariz. 586, 592-593, 503 P.2d 807, 813-814 (1972); Croker v. State, 477 P.2d 122, 125-126 (Wyo.1970);

State v. Purvis, 249 Ore. 404, 411, 438 P.2d 1002, 1005 (1968). But see State v. Tanaka, 67 Haw. 658, 701 P.2d 1274 (1985); People v. Krivda, 5 Cal.3d 729, 486 P.2d 1262 (1971). [5]

III

We reject respondent Greenwood's alternative argument for affirmance: that his expectation of privacy in his garbage should be deemed reasonable as a matter of federal constitutional law because the warrantless search and seizure of his garbage was impermissible as a matter of California law. He urges that the state law right of Californians to privacy in their garbage, announced by the California Supreme Court in Krivda, supra, survived the subsequent state constitutional amendment eliminating the suppression remedy as a means of enforcing that right. See In re Lance W., 37 Cal.3d at 886-887, 694 P.2d at 752-753. Hence, he argues that the Fourth Amendment should itself vindicate that right.

Individual States may surely construe their own constitutions as imposing more stringent constraints on police conduct than does the Federal Constitution. We have never intimated, however, that whether or not a search is reasonable within the meaning of the Fourth Amendment depends on the law of the particular State in which the search occurs. We have emphasized instead that the Fourth Amendment analysis must turn on such factors as "our societal understanding that certain areas deserve the most scrupulous protection from government invasion." Oliver v. United States, 466 U.S. at 466 U. S. 178 (emphasis added). See also Rakas v. Illinois, 439 U. S. 128, 439 U. S. 143-144, n. 12 (1978). We have already concluded that society as a whole possesses no such understanding with regard to garbage left for collection at the side of a public street. Respondent's argument is no less than a suggestion that concepts of privacy under the laws of each State are to determine the reach of the

Fourth Amendment. We do not accept this submission.

IV

Greenwood finally urges as an additional ground for affirmance that the California constitutional amendment eliminating the exclusionary rule for evidence seized in violation of state but not federal law violates the Due Process Clause of the Fourteenth Amendment. In his view, having recognized a state law right to be free from warrantless searches of garbage, California may not under the Due Process Clause deprive its citizens of what he describes as "the only effective deterrent" to violations of this right. Greenwood concedes that no direct support for his position can be found in the decisions of this Court. He relies instead on cases holding that individuals are entitled to certain procedural protections before they can be deprived of a liberty or property interest created by state law. See Hewitt v. Helms, 459 U. S. 460 (1983); Vitek v. Jones, 445 U. S. 480 (1980).

We see no merit in Greenwood's position. California could amend its Constitution to negate the holding in Krivda that state law forbids warrantless searches of trash. We are convinced that the State may likewise eliminate the exclusionary rule as a remedy for violations of that right. At the federal level, we have not required that evidence obtained in violation of the Fourth Amendment be suppressed in all circumstances. See, e.g., United States v. Leon, 468 U. S. 897 (1984); United States v. Janis, 428 U. S. 433 (1976); United States v. Calandra, 414 U. S. 338 (1974). Rather, our decisions concerning the scope of the Fourth Amendment exclusionary rule have balanced the benefits of deterring police misconduct against the costs of excluding reliable evidence of criminal activity. See Leon, 468 U.S. at 468 U. S. 908-913. We have declined to apply the exclusionary rule indiscriminately "when law enforcement officers have acted in objective good faith or their transgressions have been minor," because

"the magnitude of the benefit conferred on . . . guilty defendants [in such circumstances] offends basic concepts of the criminal justice system."

Id. at 468 U. S. 908 (citing Stone v. Powell, 428 U. S. 465, 428 U. S. 490 (1976)).

The States are not foreclosed by the Due Process Clause from using a similar balancing approach to delineate the scope of their own exclusionary rules. Hence, the people of California could permissibly conclude that the benefits of excluding relevant evidence of criminal activity do not outweigh the costs when the police conduct at issue does not violate federal law.

V

The judgment of the California Court of Appeal is therefore reversed, and this case is remanded for further proceedings not inconsistent with this opinion.

It is so ordered.

Notes

[1] The Court of Appeal also held that respondent Van Houten had standing to seek the suppression of evidence discovered during the April 4 search of Greenwood's home. 182 Cal.App.3d at 735, 227 Cal.Rptr. at 542-543.

[2] For example, State v. Ronngren, 361 N.W.2d 224 (N. D.1985), involved the search of a garbage bag that a dog, acting "at the behest of no one," id. at 228, had dragged from the defendants' yard into the yard of a neighbor. The neighbor deposited the bag in his own trash can, which he later permitted the police to search. The North Dakota Supreme Court held that the search of the garbage bag did not violate the defendants' Fourth Amendment rights.

[3] It is not only the homeless of the Nation's cities who make use of others' refuse. For example, a nationally syndicated consumer

columnist has suggested that apartment dwellers obtain cents-off coupons by "mak[ing] friends with the fellow who handles the trash" in their buildings, and has recounted the tale of

"the 'Rich lady' from Westmont who, once a week, puts on rubber gloves and hip boots and wades into the town garbage dump looking for labels and other proofs of purchase"

needed to obtain manufacturers' refunds. M. Sloane, "The Supermarket Shopper's" 1980 Guide to Coupons and Refunds 74, 161 (1980).

[4] Even the refuse of prominent Americans has not been invulnerable. In 1975, for example, a reporter for a weekly tabloid seized five bags of garbage from the sidewalk outside the home of Secretary of State Henry Kissinger. Washington Post, July 9, 1975, p. A1, col. 8. A newspaper editorial criticizing this journalistic "trash-picking" observed that "[e]vidently . . . everybody does it.'" Washington Post, July 10, 1975, p. A18, col. 1. We of course do not, as the dissent implies, "bas[e] [our] conclusion" that individuals have no reasonable expectation of privacy in their garbage on this "sole incident." Post at 486 U. S. 51.

[5] Given that the dissenters are among the tiny minority of judges whose views are contrary to ours, we are distinctly unimpressed with the dissent's prediction that "society will be shocked to learn" of today's decision. Post at 486 U. S. 46.

Michigan v. Chesternut (June 13, 1988)

JUSTICE BLACKMUN delivered the opinion of the Court.

In this case, we review a determination by the Michigan Court of Appeals that any "investigatory pursuit" of a person undertaken by the police necessarily constitutes a seizure under the Fourth Amendment of the Constitution. We conclude that the police conduct in this case did not amount to a seizure, for it would not have communicated to a reasonable person that he was not at liberty to ignore the police presence and go about his business.

I

Early on the afternoon of December 19, 1984, four officers riding in a marked police cruiser were engaged in routine patrol duties in Metropolitan Detroit. As the cruiser came to an intersection, one of the officers observed a car pull over to the curb. A man got out of the car and approached respondent Michael Mose Chesternut, who was standing alone on the corner. When respondent saw the patrol car nearing the corner where he stood, he turned and began to run. As Officer Peltier, one of those in the car, later testified, the patrol car followed respondent around the corner "to see where he was going." App. 25. The cruiser quickly caught up with respondent and drove alongside him for a short distance. As they drove beside him, the officers observed respondent discard a number of packets he pulled from his right-hand pocket. Officer Peltier got out of the cruiser to examine the packets. He discovered that they contained pills. While Peltier was engaged in this inspection, respondent, who had run only a few paces farther, stopped. Surmising on the basis of his experience as a paramedic that the pills contained codeine, Officer Peltier arrested respondent for the possession of narcotics and took him to the station house. During an ensuing search, the police discovered in respondent's hatband another packet of pills, a packet containing heroin, and a hypodermic needle. Respondent was charged with knowingly and intentionally possessing heroin, tablets containing codeine, and tablets containing diazepam, all in violation of Mich.Comp.Laws § 333.7403(2) (1980).

At a preliminary hearing, at which Officer Peltier was the only witness, respondent moved to dismiss the charges on the ground that he had been unlawfully seized during the police pursuit preceding his disposal of the packets. The presiding Magistrate granted the motion and dismissed the complaint. [1] Relying on People v. Terrell, 77 Mich.App. 676, 259 N.W.2d 187 (1977), [2] the Magistrate ruled from the bench that a police "chase" like the one involved in this case implicated Fourth Amendment protections and could not be justified by the mere fact that the suspect ran at the sight of the police. App. 31-35. Applying a clearly erroneous standard to the Magistrate's ruling, the trial court upheld the dismissal order. Id. at 2-10.

The Michigan Court of Appeals "reluctantly" affirmed, 157 Mich.App. 181, 184, 403 N.W.2d 74, 76 (1986), noting that

"although we find the result unfortunate, we cannot say that the lower court's ruling was clearly erroneous under the present law or the facts presented."

Id. at 183, 403 N.W. 2d at 75. Like the courts below it, the Court of Appeals rested its ruling on state precedents interpreting the Fourth Amendment. [3] The court determined, first, that any "investigatory pursuit" amounts to a seizure under Terry v. Ohio, 392 U. S. 1 (1968). "As soon as the officers began their pursuit," the court explained, "defendant's freedom was restricted." 157 Mich.App. at 183, 403 N.W.2d at 75. The court went on to conclude that respondent's flight from the police was insufficient, by itself, to give rise to the particularized suspicion necessary to justify this kind of seizure. Because "the police saw [respondent] do absolutely nothing illegal, nor did they observe other suspicious activity," the court determined that the investigatory pursuit had violated the Fourth Amendment's prohibition against unreasonable seizures. Id. at 184, 403 N.W.2d at 76.

After the Michigan Supreme Court denied petitioner leave to appeal, [4] App. to Pet. for Cert. 9a, petitioner sought review here. We granted a writ of certiorari, 484 U.S. 895 (1987), to consider whether the officers' pursuit of respondent constituted a seizure implicating Fourth Amendment protections, and, if so, whether the act of fleeing, by itself, was sufficient to constitute reasonable suspicion justifying that seizure. Because we conclude that the officers' conduct did not constitute a seizure, we need not reach the second question.

II

A

Petitioner argues that the Fourth Amendment is never implicated until an individual stops in response to the police's show of authority. Thus, petitioner would have us rule that a lack of objective and particularized suspicion would not poison police conduct, no matter how coercive, as long as the police did not succeed in actually apprehending the individual. Respondent contends, in sharp contrast, that any and all police "chases" are Fourth Amendment seizures. Respondent would have us rule that the police may never pursue an individual absent a particularized and objective basis for suspecting that he is engaged in criminal activity.

Both petitioner and respondent, it seems to us, in their attempts to fashion a bright-line rule applicable to all investigatory pursuits, have failed to heed this Court's clear direction that any assessment as to whether police conduct amounts to a seizure implicating the Fourth Amendment must take into account "all of the circumstances surrounding the incident'" in each individual case. INS v. Delgado, 466 U. S. 210, 466 U. S. 215 (1984), quoting United States v. Mendenhall, 446 U. S. 544, 446 U. S. 554 (1980) (opinion of Stewart, J.). Rather than adopting either rule proposed by the parties and determining that an investigatory pursuit is or is not necessarily a seizure under the Fourth Amendment, we adhere to our traditional contextual approach and determine only that, in this particular case, the police conduct in question did not amount to a seizure.

B

In Terry v. Ohio, 392 U. S. 1 (1968), the Court noted:

"Obviously, not all personal intercourse between policemen and citizens involves 'seizures' of persons. Only when the officer, by means of physical force or show of authority, has in some way restrained the liberty of a citizen may we conclude that a 'seizure' has occurred."

Id. at 392 U. S. 19, n. 16. A decade later, in United States v. Mendenhall, Justice Stewart, writing for himself and then-JUSTICE REHNQUIST, first transposed this analysis into a test to be applied in determining whether "a person has been seized' within the meaning of the Fourth Amendment." 446 U.S. at 446 U. S. 554. [5] The test provides that the police can be said to have seized an individual "only if, in view of all of the circumstances surrounding the incident, a reasonable person would have believed that he was not free to leave." Ibid. The Court has since embraced this test. See INS v. Delgado, 466 U.S. at 466 U. S. 215. See also Florida v. Royer, 460 U. S. 491, 460 U. S. 502 (1983) (plurality opinion); id. at 460 U. S. 514 (BLACKMUN, J., dissenting).

The test is necessarily imprecise, because it is designed to assess the coercive effect of police conduct, taken as a whole, rather than to focus on particular details of that conduct in isolation. Moreover, what constitutes a restraint on liberty prompting a person to conclude that he is not free to "leave" will vary, not only with the particular police conduct at issue, but also with the setting in which the conduct occurs. Compare United States v. Mendenhall, supra, (considering whether police request to see identification and ticket of individual who stopped upon police's approach constituted seizure), with INS v. Delgado, supra, (considering whether INS "factory survey" conducted while employees continued to move about constituted seizure of entire workforce).

While the test is flexible enough to be applied to the whole range of police conduct in an equally broad range of settings, it calls for consistent application from one police encounter to the next, regardless of the particular individual's response to the actions of the police. The test's objective standard -- looking to the reasonable man's interpretation of the conduct in question -- allows the police to determine in advance whether the conduct contemplated will implicate the Fourth Amendment. 3 W. LaFave, Search and Seizure § 9.2(h), pp. 407-408 (2d ed.1987 and Supp.1988). This "reasonable person" standard also ensures that the scope of Fourth Amendment protection does not vary with the state of mind of the particular individual being approached.

C

Applying the Court's test to the facts of this case, we conclude that respondent was not seized by the police before he discarded the packets containing the controlled substance. Although Officer Peltier referred to the police conduct as a "chase," and the Magistrate who originally dismissed the complaint was impressed by this description, [6] the characterization is not enough, standing alone, to implicate Fourth Amendment protections. Contrary to respondent's assertion that a chase necessarily communicates that detention is intended and imminent, Brief for Respondent 9, the police conduct involved here would not have communicated to the reasonable person an attempt to capture or otherwise intrude upon respondent's freedom of movement. [7] The record does not reflect that the police activated a siren or flashers; or that they commanded respondent to halt, or displayed any weapons; or that they operated the car in an aggressive manner to block respondent's course or otherwise control the direction or speed of his movement. Tr. of Oral Arg. 2, 11, 20. [8] While the very presence of a police car driving parallel to a running pedestrian could be somewhat intimidating, this kind of police presence does not, standing alone, constitute a seizure. [9] Cf. United States v. Knotts, 460 U. S. 276 (1983) (holding that continuous surveillance on public thoroughfares by visual observation and electronic "beeper" does not constitute seizure); Florida v. Royer, 460 U.S. at 460 U. S. 497 (plurality opinion) (noting that mere approach by law enforcement officers, identified as such, does not constitute seizure). Without more, the police conduct here -- a brief acceleration to catch up with respondent, followed by a short drive alongside him -- was not "so intimidating" that respondent could reasonably have believed that he was not free to disregard the police presence and go about his business. INS v. Delgado, 466 U.S. at 466 U. S. 216. The police therefore were not required to have "a particularized and objective basis for suspecting [respondent] of criminal activity," in order to pursue him. United States v. Cortez, 449 U. S. 411, 449 U. S. 417-418 (1981).

III

Because respondent was not unlawfully seized during the initial police pursuit, we conclude that charges against him were improperly dismissed. Accordingly, we reverse the judgment of the Michigan Court of Appeals and remand the case to that court for further proceedings not inconsistent with this opinion.

It is so ordered.

Notes

[1] The Magistrate did not independently consider whether the codeine pills, if lawfully seized, established probable cause justifying respondent's arrest. The Fourth Amendment issue before us is therefore limited to the police conduct preceding and including respondent's disposal of the packets.

[2] In Terrell, a police officer got out of his unmarked car and "gave chase" on foot after allegedly observing the defendant stick his hand in his pocket and run at the sight of the officer. 77 Mich.App. at 678, 259 N.W.2d at 188. According to the officer, the defendant ran into an apartment building where the officer observed him drop a clear envelope containing a brown powdery substance. Having determined that the package might contain heroin, the officer arrested the defendant. At a pretrial hearing, the trial court granted the defendant's motion to suppress the envelope and its contents. The Michigan Court of Appeals affirmed, finding that the police "investigatory pursuit" constituted a seizure that was unjustified by any particularized suspicion that the defendant was engaged in criminal activity. Id. at 679-680, 259 N.W.2d at 188-189.

[3] The Michigan Court of Appeals rested its holding on People v. Terrell, supra, and People v. Shabaz, 424 Mich. 42, 378 N.W.2d 451 (1985), cert. dism'd (in view of that respondent's death), 478 U.S. 1017 (1986), both of which were to the effect that the defendant in question had been seized in violation of the Fourth Amendment of the United States Constitution. In Shabaz, the Michigan Supreme Court quoted "Michigan's analogous [constitutional] provision," without elaboration, in a footnote following a recitation of the Fourth Amendment. 424 Mich. at 52, n. 4, 378 N.W.2d at 455, n. 4. The Supreme Court said nothing to suggest that the Michigan Constitution's seizure provision provided an independent source of relief, and the court's entire analysis rested expressly on the Fourth Amendment and federal cases. Similarly, in Terrell, the Michigan Court of Appeals stated that the suppression of evidence and dismissal of charges against the defendant "was soundly based on existing law, state and Federal," but made clear that the scope of the right in question was defined "by the Fourth Amendment's general proscription against unreasonable searches and seizures." 77 Mich.App. at 679, 259 N.W.2d at 188, citing Terry v. Ohio, 392 U. S. 1, 392 U. S. 20 (1968). In light of the

bases for the courts' decisions in Shabaz and Terrell, we readily conclude that the decision below likewise rests on the Michigan courts' interpretation of the Federal Constitution, and not on any adequate and independent state ground. See Michigan v. Long, 463 U. S. 1032 (1983). The defense in effect concedes this. See Tr. of Oral Arg. 38-39.

[4] Two justices of the Michigan Supreme Court would have granted leave to appeal. See App. to Pet. for Cert. 10a.

[5] Three other Justices, otherwise in the majority, chose not to reach the question whether the federal officers had seized respondent. 446 U.S. at 560 (opinion concurring in part and concurring in the judgment).

[6] At the preliminary hearing, the Magistrate interrupted the State's attorney, who was asserting that the police were simply performing routine patrolling duties, with the following:

"That would be fine until the Officer said we were chasing him in the car, otherwise I would agree with you. My ears picked up when the Officer said that, you know. He said we went around. I asked him why were you chasing him in the car, why were you chasing him, and he said because he was running, and we wanted to see where he was going."

App. 29-30.

[7] As Officer Peltier explained, the goal of the "chase" was not to capture respondent, but "to see where he was going." Id. at 25. Of course, the subjective intent of the officers is relevant to an assessment of the Fourth Amendment implications of police conduct only to the extent that that intent has been conveyed to the person confronted. United States v. Mendenhall, 446 U.S. at 446 U. S. 554, n. 6 (opinion of Stewart, J.). See also 3 W. LaFave, Search and Seizure § 9.2(h), p. 407 (2d ed.1987 and Supp.1988) (uncommunicated intent of police irrelevant to determination of whether seizure occurred).

[8] The facts of this case are not identical to the facts involved in both Terrell and Shabaz, upon which the Michigan courts relied in finding a seizure in this case. In both Terrell and Shabaz, a police officer got out of the car to chase the pedestrian suspect on foot, after which the defendant abandoned the inculpatory evidence. People v. Terrell, 77 Mich.App. at 678, 259 N.W.2d at 188; People v. Shabaz, 424 Mich., at 47-48, 378 N.W.2d at 453. In Shabaz, the State appears to have stipulated that the chase, whose clear object was to apprehend the defendant, constituted a seizure. Id. at 52, 378 N.W.2d at 455. While no similar stipulation was entered in Terrell, the goal of that chase appears to have been equally clear. We, of course, intimate no view as to the federal constitutional correctness of either of those Michigan state court cases.

[9] The United States, which has submitted a brief as amicus curiae, suggests that, in some circumstances, police pursuit "will amount to a stop from the outset or from an early point in the chase, if the police command the person to halt and indicate that he is not free to go." Brief for United States as Amicus Curiae 13. Of course, such circumstances are not before us in this case. We therefore leave to another day the determination of the circumstances in which police pursuit could amount to a seizure under the Fourth Amendment.

Murray v. United States (June 27, 1988)

JUSTICE SCALIA delivered the opinion of the Court.

In Segura v. United States, 468 U. S. 796 (1984), we held that police officers' illegal entry upon private premises did not require suppression of evidence subsequently discovered at those premises when executing a search warrant obtained on the basis of information wholly unconnected with the initial entry. In these consolidated cases, we are faced with the question whether, again assuming evidence obtained pursuant to an independently obtained search warrant, the portion of such evidence that had been observed in plain view at the time of a prior illegal entry must be suppressed.

I

Both cases arise out of the conviction of petitioner Michael F. Murray, petitioner James D. Carter, and others for conspiracy to possess and distribute illegal drugs. Insofar as relevant for our purposes, the facts are as follows: based on information received from informants, federal law enforcement agents had been surveiling petitioner Murray and several of his coconspirators. At about 1:45 p.m. on April 6, 1983, they observed Murray drive a truck and Carter drive a green camper, into a warehouse in South Boston. When the petitioners drove the vehicles out about 20 minutes later, the surveiling agents saw within the warehouse two individuals and a tractor-trailer rig bearing a long, dark container. Murray and Carter later turned over the truck and camper to other drivers, who were in turn followed and ultimately arrested, and the vehicles lawfully seized. Both vehicles were found to contain marijuana.

After receiving this information, several of the agents converged on the South Boston warehouse and forced entry. They found the warehouse unoccupied, but observed in plain view numerous burlap-wrapped bales that were later found to contain marijuana. They left without disturbing the bales, kept the warehouse under surveillance, and did not reenter it until they had a search warrant. In applying for the warrant, the agents did not mention the prior entry, and did not rely on any observations made during that entry. When the warrant was issued -- at 10:40 p.m., approximately eight hours after the initial entry -- the agents immediately reentered the warehouse and seized 270 bales of marijuana and notebooks listing customers for whom the bales were

destined.

Before trial, petitioners moved to suppress the evidence found in the warehouse. The District Court denied the motion, rejecting petitioners' arguments that the warrant was invalid because the agents did not inform the Magistrate about their prior warrantless entry, and that the warrant was tainted by that entry. United States v. Carter, No. 83102-S (Mass., Dec. 23, 1983), App. to Pet. for Cert. 44a-45a. The First Circuit affirmed, assuming for purposes of its decision that the first entry into the warehouse was unlawful. United States v. Moscatiello, 771 F.2d 589 (1985). Murray and Carter then separately filed petitions for certiorari, which we granted, [1] 480 U.S. 916 (1987), and have consolidated here.

II

The exclusionary rule prohibits introduction into evidence of tangible materials seized during an unlawful search, Weeks v. United States, 232 U. S. 383 (1914), and of testimony concerning knowledge acquired during an unlawful search, Silverman v. United States, 365 U. S. 505 (1961). Beyond that, the exclusionary rule also prohibits the introduction of derivative evidence, both tangible and testimonial, that is the product of the primary evidence, or that is otherwise acquired as an indirect result of the unlawful search, up to the point at which the connection with the unlawful search becomes "so attentuated as to dissipate the taint," Nardone v. United States, 308 U. S. 338, 308 U. S. 341 (1939). See Wong Sun v. United States, 371 U. S. 471, 371 U. S. 484-485 (1963).

Almost simultaneously with our development of the exclusionary rule, in the first quarter of this century, we also announced what has come to be known as the "independent source" doctrine. See Silverthorne Lumber Co. v. United States, 251 U. S. 385, 251 U. S. 392 (1920). That doctrine, which has been applied to evidence acquired not only through Fourth Amendment violations, but also through Fifth and Sixth Amendment violations, has recently been described as follows:

"[T]he interest of society in deterring unlawful police conduct and the public interest in having juries receive all probative evidence of a crime are properly balanced by putting the police in the same, not a worse, position that they would have been in if no police error or misconduct had occurred. . . . When the challenged evidence has an independent source, exclusion of such evidence would put the police in a worse position than they would have been in absent any error or violation."

Nix v. Williams, 467 U. S. 431, 467 U. S. 443 (1984). The dispute here is over the scope of this doctrine. Petitioners contend that it applies only to evidence obtained for the first time during an independent lawful search. The Government argues that it applies also to evidence initially discovered during, or as a consequence of, an unlawful search, but later obtained independently from activities untainted by the initial illegality. We think the Government's view has better support in both precedent and policy.

Our cases have used the concept of "independent source" in a more general and a more specific sense. The more general sense identifies all evidence acquired in a fashion untainted by the illegal evidence-gathering activity. Thus, where an unlawful entry has given investigators knowledge of facts x and y, but fact z has been learned by other means, fact z can be said to be admissible because derived from an "independent source." This is how we used the term in Segura v. United States, 468 U. S. 796 (1984). In that case, agents unlawfully entered the defendant's apartment and remained there until a search warrant was obtained. The admissibility of what they discovered while waiting in the apartment was not before us, id. at 468 U. S. 802-803, n. 4, but we held that the evidence found for the first time during the execution of the valid and untainted search warrant was admissible because it was discovered pursuant to an "independent source," id. at 468 U. S. 813-814. See also United States v. Wade, 388 U. S. 218, 388 U. S. 240-242 (1967); Costello v. United States, 365 U. S. 265, 365 U. S. 280 (1961); Nardone v. United States, supra, at 308 U. S. 341.

The original use of the term, however, and its more important use for purposes of this case, was more specific. It was originally applied in the exclusionary rule context, by Justice Holmes, with reference to that particular category of evidence acquired by an untainted search which is identical to the evidence unlawfully acquired -- that is, in the example just given, to knowledge of facts x and y derived from an independent source:

"The essence of a provision forbidding the acquisition of evidence in a certain way is that not merely evidence so acquired shall not be used before the Court, but that it shall not be used at all. Of course this does not mean that the facts thus obtained become sacred and inaccessible. If knowledge of them is gained from an independent source, they may be proved like any others."

Silverthorne Lumber, supra, at 251 U. S. 392.

As the First Circuit has observed,

"[i]n the classic independent source situation, information which is received through an illegal source is considered to be cleanly obtained when it arrives through an independent source."

United States v. Silvestri, 787 F.2d 736, 739 (1986). We recently assumed this application of the independent source doctrine (in the Sixth Amendment context) in Nix v. Williams, supra. There, incriminating statements obtained in violation of the defendant's right to counsel had led the police to the victim's body. The body had not in fact been found through an independent source as well, and so the independent source doctrine was not itself applicable. We held, however, that evidence concerning the body was nonetheless admissible because a search had been under way which would have discovered the body, had it not been called off because of the discovery produced by the unlawfully obtained statements. 467 U.S. at 476 U. S. 448-450. This "inevitable discovery" doctrine obviously assumes the validity of the independent source doctrine as applied to evidence initially acquired unlawfully. It would make no sense to admit the evidence because the independent search, had it not been aborted, would have found the body, but to exclude the evidence if the search had continued and had in fact found the body. The inevitable discovery doctrine, with its distinct requirements, is in reality an extrapolation from the independent source doctrine: since the tainted evidence would be admissible if in fact discovered through an independent source, it should be admissible if it inevitably would have been discovered.

Petitioners' asserted policy basis for excluding evidence which is initially discovered during an illegal search, but is subsequently acquired through an independent and lawful source, is that a contrary rule will remove all deterrence to, and indeed positively encourage, unlawful police searches. As petitioners see the incentives, law enforcement officers will routinely enter without a warrant to make sure that what they expect to be on the premises is in fact there. If it is not, they will have spared themselves the time and trouble of getting a warrant; if it is, they can get the warrant and use the evidence despite the unlawful entry. Brief for Petitioners 42. We see the incentives differently. An officer with probable cause sufficient to obtain a search warrant would be foolish to enter the premises first in an unlawful manner. By doing so, he would risk suppression of all evidence on the premises, both seen and unseen, since his action would add to the normal burden of convincing a magistrate that there is probable cause the much more onerous burden of convincing a trial court that no information gained from the illegal entry affected either the law enforcement officers' decision to seek a warrant or the magistrate's decision to grant it. See 487 U. S. infra. Nor would the officer without sufficient probable cause to obtain a search warrant have any added incentive to conduct an unlawful entry, since whatever he finds cannot be used to establish probable cause before a magistrate. [2]

It is possible to read petitioners' briefs as asserting the more narrow position that the "independent source" doctrine does apply to independent acquisition of evidence previously derived indirectly from the unlawful search, but does not apply to what they call "primary evidence," that is, evidence acquired during the course of the search itself. In addition to finding no support in our precedent, see Silverthorne Lumber, 251 U.S. at 251 U. S. 392 (referring specifically to evidence seized during an unlawful search), this strange distinction would produce results bearing no relation to the policies of the exclusionary rule. It would mean, for example, that the government's knowledge of the existence and condition of a dead body, knowledge lawfully acquired through independent sources, would have to be excluded if government agents had previously observed the body during an unlawful search of the defendant's apartment; but not if they had observed a notation that the body was buried in a certain location, producing consequential discovery of the corpse.

III

To apply what we have said to the present cases: knowledge that the marijuana was in the warehouse was assuredly acquired at the time of the unlawful entry. But it was also acquired at the time of entry pursuant to the warrant, and if that later acquisition was not the result of the earlier entry, there is no reason why the independent source doctrine should not apply. Invoking the exclusionary rule would put the police (and society) not in the same position they would have occupied if no violation occurred, but in a worse one. See Nix v. Williams, 467 U.S. at 467 U. S. 443.

We think this is also true with respect to the tangible evidence, the bales of marijuana. It would make no more sense to exclude that than it would to exclude tangible evidence found upon the corpse in Nix, if the search in that case had not been abandoned and had in fact come upon the body. The First Circuit has discerned a difference between tangible and intangible evidence that has been tainted, in that objects "once seized cannot be cleanly reseized without returning the objects to private control." United States v. Silvestri, 787 F.2d at 739. It seems to us, however, that reseizure of tangible evidence already seized is no more impossible than rediscovery of intangible evidence already discovered. The independent source doctrine does not rest upon such metaphysical analysis, but upon the policy that, while the government should not profit from its illegal activity, neither should it be placed in a worse position than it would otherwise have occupied. So long as a later, lawful seizure is genuinely independent of an earlier, tainted one (which may well be difficult to establish where the seized goods are kept in the police's possession), there is no reason why the independent source doctrine should not apply.

The ultimate question, therefore, is whether the search pursuant to warrant was, in fact, a genuinely independent source of the information and tangible evidence at issue here. This would not have been the case if the agents' decision to seek the warrant was prompted by what they had seen during the initial entry, [3] or if information obtained during that entry was presented to the Magistrate and affected his decision to issue the warrant. On this point, the Court of Appeals said the following:

"[W]e can be absolutely certain that the warrantless entry in no way contributed in the slightest either to the issuance of a warrant or to the discovery of the evidence during the lawful search that occurred pursuant to the warrant."

"* * * *"

"This is as clear a case as can be imagined where the discovery of the contraband in plain view was totally irrelevant to the later securing of a warrant and the successful search that ensued. As there was no causal link whatever between the illegal entry and the discovery of the challenged evidence, we find no error in the court's refusal to suppress."

United States v. Moscatiello, 771 F.2d at 603, 604. Although these statements can be read to provide emphatic support for the Government's position, it is the function of the District Court, rather than the Court of Appeals, to determine the facts, and we do not think the Court of Appeals' conclusions are supported by adequate findings. The District Court found that the agents did not reveal their warrantless entry to the Magistrate, App. to Pet. for Cert. 43a, and that they did not include in their application for a warrant any recitation of their observations in the warehouse, id. at 44a-45a. It did not, however, explicitly find that the agents would have sought a warrant if they had not earlier entered the warehouse. The Government concedes this in its brief. Brief for United States 17, n. 5. To be sure, the District Court did determine that the purpose of the warrantless entry was, in part, "to guard against the destruction of possibly critical evidence," App. to Pet. for Cert. 42a, and one could perhaps infer from this that the agents who made the entry already planned to obtain that "critical evidence" through a warrant-authorized search. That inference is not, however, clear enough to justify the conclusion that the District Court's findings amounted to a determination of independent source.

Accordingly, we vacate the judgment and remand these cases to the Court of Appeals with instructions that it remand to the District Court for determination whether the warrant-authorized search of the warehouse was an independent source of the challenged evidence in the sense we have described.

It is so ordered.

Notes

[1] The original petitions raised both the present Fourth Amendment claim and a Speedy Trial Act claim. We granted the petitions, vacated the judgment below, and remanded for reconsideration of the Speedy Trial Act issue in light of Henderson v. United States, 476 U. S. 321 (1986). Carter v. United States and Murray v. United States, 476 U.S. 1138 (1986). On remand, the Court of Appeals again rejected the Speedy Trial Act claim, and did not reexamine its prior ruling on the Fourth Amendment question. 803 F.2d 20 (1986). Petitioners again sought writs of certiorari, which we granted limited to the Fourth Amendment question.

[2] JUSTICE MARSHALL argues, in effect, that where the police cannot point to some historically verifiable fact demonstrating that the subsequent search pursuant to a warrant was wholly unaffected by the prior illegal search -- e.g., that they had already sought the warrant before entering the premises -- we should adopt a per se rule of inadmissibilty. See post at 487 U. S. 549. We do not believe that such a prophylatic exception to the independent source rule is necessary. To say that a district court must be satisfied that a warrant would have been sought without the illegal entry is not to give dispositive effect to police officers' assurances on the point. Where the facts render those assurances implausible, the independent source doctrine will not apply.

We might note that there is no basis for pointing to the present cases as an example of a "search first, warrant later" mentality. The District Court found that the agents entered the warehouse

"in an effort to apprehend any participants who might have remained inside and to guard against the destruction of possibly critical evidence."

United States v. Carter, No. 83-102-S (Mass., Dec. 23, 1983), App. to Pet. for Cert. 42a. While they may have misjudged the existence of sufficient exigent circumstances to justify the warrantless entry (the Court of Appeals did not reach that issue, and neither do we), there is nothing to suggest that they went in merely to see if there was anything worth getting a warrant for.

[3] JUSTICE MARSHALL argues that

"the relevant question [is] whether, even if the initial entry uncovered no evidence, the officers would return immediately with a warrant to conduct a second search."

Post at 487 U. S. 548, n. 2; see post at 487 U. S. 549-550, n. 4. We do not see how this is "relevant" at all. To determine whether the warrant was independent of the illegal entry, one must ask whether it would have been sought even if what actually happened had not occurred -- not whether it would have been sought if something else had happened. That is to say, what counts is whether the actual illegal search had any effect in producing the warrant, not whether some hypothetical illegal search would have aborted the warrant. Only that much is needed to assure that what comes before the court is not the product of illegality; to go further than that would be to expand our existing exclusionary rule.

Florida v. Riley (Jan 23, 1989) [Notes omitted]

JUSTICE WHITE announced the judgment of the Court and delivered an opinion, in which THE CHIEF JUSTICE, JUSTICE SCALIA, and JUSTICE KENNEDY join.

On certification to it by a lower state court,

the Florida Supreme Court addressed the following question:

"Whether surveillance of the interior of a partially covered greenhouse in a residential backyard from the vantage point of a helicopter located 400 feet above the greenhouse constitutes a 'search' for which a warrant is required under the Fourth Amendment and Article I, § 12 of the Florida Constitution."

511 So.2d 282 (1987). The court answered the question in the affirmative, and we granted the State's petition for certiorari challenging that conclusion. 484 U.S. 1058 (1988). [1]

Respondent Riley lived in a mobile home located on five acres of rural property. A greenhouse was located 10 to 20 feet behind the mobile home. Two sides of the greenhouse were enclosed. The other two sides were not enclosed, but the contents of the greenhouse were obscured from view from surrounding property by trees, shrubs, and the mobile home. The greenhouse was covered by corrugated roofing panels, some translucent and some opaque. At the time relevant to this case, two of the panels, amounting to approximately 10% of the roof area, were missing. A wire fence surrounded the mobile home and the greenhouse, and the property was posted with a "DO NOT ENTER" sign.

This case originated with an anonymous tip to the Pasco County Sheriff's office that marijuana was being grown on respondent's property. When an investigating officer discovered that he could not see the contents of the greenhouse from the road, he circled twice over respondent's property in a helicopter at the height of 400 feet. With his naked eye, he was able to see through the openings in the roof and one or more of the open sides of the greenhouse and to identify what he thought was marijuana growing in the structure. A warrant was obtained based on these observations, and the ensuing search revealed marijuana growing in the greenhouse. Respondent was charged with possession of marijuana under Florida law. The trial court granted his motion to suppress; the Florida Court of Appeals reversed, but certified the case to the Florida Supreme Court, which quashed the decision of the Court of Appeals and reinstated the trial court's suppression order.

We agree with the State's submission that our decision in California v. Ciraolo, 476 U. S. 207 (1986), controls this case. There, acting on a tip, the police inspected the backyard of a particular house while flying in a fixed-wing aircraft at 1,000 feet. With the naked eye the officers saw what they concluded was marijuana growing in the yard. A search warrant was obtained on the strength of this airborne inspection, and marijuana plants were found. The trial court refused to suppress this evidence, but a state appellate court held that the inspection violated the Fourth and Fourteenth Amendments to the United States Constitution, and that the warrant was therefore invalid. We in turn reversed, holding that the inspection was not a search subject to the Fourth Amendment. We recognized that the yard was within the curtilage of the house, that a fence shielded the yard from observation from the street, and that the occupant had a subjective expectation of privacy. We held, however, that such an expectation was not reasonable, and not one "that society is prepared to honor." Id. at 476 U. S. 214. Our reasoning was that the home and its curtilage are not necessarily protected from inspection that involves no physical invasion. "What a person knowingly exposes to the public, even in his own home or office, is not a subject of Fourth Amendment protection.'" Id. at 213, quoting Katz v. United States, 389 U. S. 347, 389 U. S. 351 (1967). As a general proposition, the police may see what may be seen "from a public vantagepoint where [they have] a right to be," 476 U.S. at 476 U. S. 213. Thus the police, like the public, would have been free to inspect the backyard garden from the street if their view had been unobstructed. They were likewise free to inspect the yard from the vantage point of an aircraft flying in the navigable airspace as this plane was.

"In an age where private and commercial flight in the public airways is routine, it is unreasonable for respondent to expect that his marijuana plants were constitutionally protected from being observed with the naked eye from an altitude of 1,000 feet. The Fourth Amendment simply does not require the police traveling in the public airways at this altitude to obtain a warrant in order to observe what is visible to the naked eye."

Id. at 476 U. S. 215.

We arrive at the same conclusion in the present case. In this case, as in Ciraolo, the property surveyed was within the curtilage of respondent's home. Riley no doubt intended and expected that his greenhouse would not be open to public inspection, and the precautions he took protected against ground-level observation. Because the sides and roof of his greenhouse were left partially open, however, what was growing in the greenhouse was subject to viewing from the air. Under the holding in Ciraolo, Riley could not reasonably have expected the contents of his greenhouse to be immune from examination by an officer seated in a fixed-wing aircraft flying in navigable airspace at an altitude of 1,000 feet or, as the Florida Supreme Court seemed to recognize, at an altitude of 500 feet, the lower limit of the navigable airspace for such an aircraft. 511 So.2d at 288. Here, the inspection was made from a helicopter, but, as is the case with fixed-wing planes, "private and commercial flight [by helicopter] in the public airways is routine" in this country, Ciraolo, supra, at 476 U. S. 215, and there is no indication that such flights are unheard of in Pasco County, Florida. [2] Riley could not reasonably have expected that his greenhouse was protected from public or official observation from a helicopter had it been flying within the navigable airspace for fixed-wing aircraft.

Nor on the facts before us, does it make a difference for Fourth Amendment purposes that the helicopter was flying at 400 feet when the officer saw what was growing in the greenhouse through the partially open roof and sides of the structure. We would have a different case if flying at that altitude had been contrary to law or regulation. But helicopters are not bound by the lower limits of the navigable airspace allowed to other aircraft. [3] Any member of the public could legally have been flying over Riley's property in a helicopter at the altitude of 400 feet, and could have observed Riley's greenhouse. The police officer did no more. This is not to say that an inspection of the curtilage of a house from an aircraft will always pass muster under the Fourth Amendment simply because the plane is within the navigable airspace specified by law. But it is of obvious importance that the helicopter in this case was not violating the law, and there is nothing in the record or before us to suggest that helicopters flying at 400 feet are sufficiently rare in this country to lend substance to respondent's claim that he reasonably anticipated that his greenhouse would not be subject to observation from that altitude. Neither is there any intimation here that the helicopter interfered with respondent's normal use of the greenhouse or of other parts of the curtilage. As far as this record reveals, no intimate details connected with the use of the home or curtilage were observed, and there was no undue noise, and no wind, dust, or threat of injury. In these circumstances, there was no violation of the Fourth Amendment.

The judgment of the Florida Supreme Court is accordingly reversed.

So ordered.

James v. Illinois (Jan 10, 1990) [Notes omitted]

JUSTICE BRENNAN delivered the opinion of the Court.

The impeachment exception to the exclusionary rule permits the prosecution in a criminal proceeding to introduce illegally obtained evidence to impeach the defendant's own testimony. The Illinois Supreme Court extended this exception to permit the prosecution to impeach the testimony of all defense witnesses with illegally obtained evidence. 123 Ill. 2d 523, 528 N. E. 2d 723 (1988). Finding this extension inconsistent with the balance of values underlying our previous applications of the exclusionary rule, we reverse.

I

On the night of August 30, 1982, eight young boys returning home from a party were confronted by a trio of other boys who demanded money. When the eight boys refused to comply, one member of the trio produced a gun and fired into the larger group, killing one boy and seriously injuring another. When the police arrived, the remaining members of the larger group provided eyewitness accounts of the event and descriptions of the perpetrators.

The next evening, two detectives of the Chicago Police Department took 15-year-old Darryl James into custody as a suspect in the shooting. James was found at his mother's beauty parlor sitting under a hair dryer; when he emerged, his hair was black and curly. After placing James in their car, the detectives questioned him about his prior hair color. He responded that the previous day his hair had been reddish brown, long, and combed straight back. The detectives questioned James again later at the police station, and he further stated that he had gone to the beauty parlor in order to have his hair "dyed black and curled in order to change his appearance." App. 11.

The State subsequently indicted James for murder and attempted murder. Prior to trial, James moved to suppress the statements regarding his hair, contending that they were the fruit of a Fourth Amendment violation because the detectives lacked probable cause for his warrantless arrest. After an evidentiary hearing, the trial court sustained this motion and ruled that the statements would be inadmissible at trial.

At trial, five members of the larger group of boys testified for the State, and each made an in-court identification of the defendant. Each testified that the person responsible for the shooting had "reddish" hair, worn shoulder length in a slicked-back "butter" style. Each also recalled having seen James several weeks earlier at a parade, at which time James had the aforementioned hair color and style. At trial, however, his hair was black and worn in a "natural" style. Despite the discrepancy between the witnesses' description and his present appearance, the witnesses stood firm in their conviction that James had been present and had fired the shots.

James did not testify in his own defense. He called as a witness Jewel Henderson, a fried of his family. Henderson testified that on the day of the shooting she had taken James to register for high school and that, at that time, his hair was black. The State then sought, over James' objection, to introduce his illegally obtained statements as a means of impeaching the credibility of Henderson's testimony. After determining that the suppressed statements had been made voluntarily, the trial court overruled James' objection. One of the interrogating detectives then reported James' prior admissions that he had reddish hair the night of the shooting and he dyed and curled his hair the next day in order to change his appearance. James ultimately was convicted of both murder and attempted murder and sentenced to 30 years' imprisonment.

On appeal, the Illinois Appellate Court reversed James' convictions and ordered a new trial. 153 Ill. App. 3d 131, 505 N. E. 2d 1118 (1987). The appellate court held that the exclusionary rule barred admission of James' illegally obtained statements for the purpose of impeaching a defense witness' testimony and that the resulting constitutional error was not harmless. However, the Illinois Supreme Court reversed.

The court reasoned that, in order to deter the defendant from engaging in perjury "by proxy," the impeachment exception to the exclusionary rule ought to be expanded to allow the State to introduce illegally obtained evidence to impeach the testimony of defense witnesses other than the defendant himself. The court therefore ordered James' convictions reinstated. We granted certiorari. 489 U. S. 1010 (1989).

II

"There is no gainsaying that arriving at the truth is a fundamental goal of our legal system." United States v. Havens, 446 U. S. 620, 626 (1980). But various constitutional rules limit the means by which government may conduct this search for truth in order to promote other values embraced by the Framers and cherished throughout our Nation's history. "Ever since its inception, the rule excluding evidence seized in violation of the Fourth Amendment has been recognized as a principal mode of discouraging lawless police conduct. . . . [W]ithout it the constitutional guarantee against unreasonable searches and seizures would be a mere `form of words.' " Terry v. Ohio, 392 U. S. 1, 12 (1968), quoting Mapp v. Ohio, 367 U. S. 643, 655 (1961). The occasional suppression of illegally obtained yet probative evidence has long been considered a necessary cost of preserving overriding constitutional values: "[T]here is nothing new in the realization that the Constitution sometimes insulates the criminality of a few in order to protect the privacy of us all." Arizona v. Hicks, 480 U. S. 321, 329 (1987).

This Court has carved out exceptions to the exclusionary rule, however, where the introduction of reliable and probative evidence would significantly further the truth-seeking function of a criminal trial and the likelihood that admissibility of such evidence would encourage police misconduct is but a "speculative possibility." Harris v. New York, 401 U. S. 222, 225 (1971).[1] One exception to the rule permits prosecutors to introduce illegally obtained evidence for the limited purpose of impeaching the credibility of the defendant's own testimony. This Court first recognized this exception in Walder v. United States, 347 U. S. 62 (1954), permitting the prosecutor to introduce into evidence heroin obtained through an illegal search to undermine the credibility of the defendant's claim that he had never possessed narcotics. The Court explained that a defendant

"must be free to deny all the elements of the case against him without thereby giving leave to the Government to introduce by way of rebuttal evidence illegally secured by it, and therefore not available for its case in chief. Beyond that, however, there is hardly justification for letting the defendant affirmatively resort to perjurious testimony in reliance on the Government's disability to challenge his credibility." Id., at 65.

In Harris v. New York, supra, and Oregon v. Hass, 420 U. S. 714 (1975), the Court applied the exception to permit prosecutors to impeach defendants using incriminating yet voluntary and reliable statements elicited in violation of Miranda requirements.[2] Finally, in United States v. Havens, supra, the Court expanded the exception to permit prosecutors to introduce illegally obtained evidence in order to impeach a defendant's "answers to questions put to him on cross-examination that are plainly within the scope of the defendant's direct examination." Id., at 627.

This Court insisted throughout this line of cases that "evidence that has been illegally obtained . . . is inadmissible on the government's direct case, or otherwise, as substantive evidence of guilt." Id., at 628.[3] However, because the

Court believed that permitting the use of such evidence to impeach defendants' testimony would further the goal of truthseeking by preventing defendants from perverting the exclusionary rule " `into a license to use perjury by way of a defense,' " id., at 626 (citation omitted), and because the Court further believed that permitting such use would create only a "speculative possibility that impermissible police conduct will be encouraged thereby," Harris, supra, at 225, the Court concluded that the balance of values underlying the exclusionary rule justified an exception covering impeachment of defendants' testimony.

III

In this case, the Illinois Supreme Court held that our balancing approach in Walder and its progeny justifies expanding the scope of the impeachment exception to permit prosecutors to use illegally obtained evidence to impeach the credibility of defense witnesses. We disagree. Expanding the class of impeachable witnesses from the defendant alone to all defense witnesses would create different incentives affecting the behavior of both defendants and law enforcement officers. As a result, this expansion would not promote the truth-seeking function to the same extent as did creation of the original exception, and yet it would significantly undermine the deterrent effect of the general exclusionary rule. Hence, we believe that this proposed expansion would frustrate rather than further the purposes underlying the exclusionary rule.

The previously recognized exception penalizes defendants for committing perjury by allowing the prosecution to expose their perjury through impeachment using illegally obtained evidence. Thus defendants are discouraged in the first instance from "affirmatively resort[ing] to perjurious testimony." Walder, supra, at 65. But the exception leaves defendants free to testify truthfully on their own behalf; they can offer probative and exculpatory evidence to the jury without opening the door to impeachment by carefully avoiding any statements that directly contradict the suppressed evidence. The exception thus generally discourages perjured testimony without discouraging truthful testimony.

In contrast, expanding the impeachment exception to encompass the testimony of all defense witnesses would not have the same beneficial effects. First, the mere threat of a subsequent criminal prosecution for perjury is far more likely to deter a witness from intentionally lying on a defendant's behalf than to deter a defendant, already facing conviction for the underlying offense, from lying on his own behalf. Hence the Illinois Supreme Court's underlying premise that a defendant frustrated by our previous impeachment exception can easily find a witness to engage in "perjury by proxy" is suspect.[4]

More significantly, expanding the impeachment exception to encompass the testimony of all defense witnesses likely would chill some defendants from presenting their best defense — and sometimes any defense at all — through the testimony of others. Whenever police obtained evidence illegally, defendants would have to assess prior to trial the likelihood that the evidence would be admitted to impeach the otherwise favorable testimony of any witness they call. Defendants might reasonably fear that one or more of their witnesses, in a position to offer truthful and favorable testimony, would also make some statement in sufficient tension with the tainted evidence to allow the prosecutor to introduce that evidence for impeachment. First, defendants sometimes need to call "reluctant" or "hostile" witnesses to provide reliable and probative exculpatory testimony, and such witnesses likely will not share the defendants' concern for avoiding statements that invite impeachment through contradictory evidence. Moreover, defendants often cannot trust even "friendly" witnesses to testify without subjecting themselves to impeachment, simply due to insufficient care or attentiveness. This concern is magnified in those occasional situations when defendants must call witnesses to testify despite having had only a limited opportunity to consult with or prepare them in advance. For these reasons, we have recognized in a variety of contexts that a party "cannot be absolutely certain that his witnesses will testify as expected." Brooks v. Tennessee, 406 U. S. 605, 609 (1972).[5] As a result, an expanded impeachment exception likely would chill some defendants from calling witnesses who would otherwise offer probative evidence.[6]

This realization alters the balance of values underlying the current impeachment exception governing defendants' testimony. Our prior cases make clear that defendants ought not be able to "pervert" the exclusion of illegally obtained evidence into a shield for perjury, but it seems no more appropriate for the State to brandish such evidence as a sword with which to dissuade defendants from presenting a meaningful defense through other witnesses. Given the potential chill created by expanding the impeachment exception, the conceded gains to the truth-seeking process from discouraging or disclosing perjured testimony would be offset to some extent by the concomitant loss of probative witness testimony. Thus, the truth-seeking rationale supporting the impeachment of defendants in Walder and its progeny does not apply to other witnesses with equal force.

Moreover, the proposed expansion of the current impeachment exception would significantly weaken the exclusionary rule's deterrent effect on police misconduct. This Court has characterized as a mere "speculative possibility," Harris v. New York, 401 U. S., at 225, the likelihood that permitting prosecutors to impeach defendants with illegally obtained evidence would encourage police misconduct. Law enforcement officers will think it unlikely that the defendant will first decide to testify at trial and will also open the door inadvertently to admission of any illegally obtained evidence. Hence, the officers' incentive to acquire evidence through illegal means is quite weak.

In contrast, expanding the impeachment exception to all defense witnesses would significantly enhance the expected value to the prosecution of illegally obtained evidence. First, this expansion would vastly increase the number of occasions on which such evidence could be used. Defense witnesses easily outnumber testifying defendants, both because many defendants do not testify themselves and because many if not most defendants call multiple witnesses on their behalf. Moreover, due to the chilling effect identified above, see supra, at 315-316, illegally obtained evidence holds even greater value to the prosecution for each individual witness than for each defendant. The prosecutor's access to impeachment evidence would not just deter perjury; it would also deter defendants from calling witnesses in the first place, thereby keeping from the jury much probative exculpatory evidence. For both of these reasons, police officers and their superiors would recognize that obtaining evidence through illegal means stacks the deck heavily in the prosecution's favor. It is thus far more than a "speculative possibility" that police misconduct will be encouraged by permitting such use of illegally obtained evidence.

The United States argues that this result is constitutionally acceptable because excluding illegally obtained evidence solely from the prosecution's case in chief would still provide a quantum of deterrence sufficient to protect the privacy interests underlying the exclusionary rule.[7] We disagree. Of course, a police officer might in certain situations believe that obtaining particular evidence through illegal means, resulting in its suppression from the case in chief, would prevent the prosecution from establishing a prima facie case to take to a jury. In such situations, the officer likely would be deterred from obtaining the evidence illegally for fear of jeopardizing the entire case. But much if not most of the time, police officers confront opportunities to obtain evidence illegally after they have already legally obtained (or know that they have other means of legally obtaining) sufficient evidence to sustain a prima facie case. In these situations, a rule requiring exclusion of illegally obtained evidence from only the government's case in chief would leave officers with little to lose and much to gain by overstepping constitutional limits on evidence gathering.[8] Narrowing the exclusionary rule in this manner, therefore, would significantly undermine the rule's ability "to compel respect for the constitutional guaranty in the only effectively available way — by removing the incentive to disregard it." Elkins v. United States, 364 U. S. 206, 217 (1960). So long as we are committed to protecting the people from the disregard of their constitutional rights during the course of criminal investigations, inadmissibility of illegally obtained evidence must remain the rule, not the exception.

IV

The cost to the truth-seeking process of evidentiary exclusion invariably is perceived more tangibly in discrete prosecutions than is the protection of privacy values through deterrence of future police misconduct. When defining the precise scope of the exclusionary rule, however, we must focus on systemic effects of proposed exceptions to ensure that individual liberty from arbitrary or oppressive police conduct does not succumb to the inexorable pressure to introduce all incriminating evidence, no matter how obtained, in each and every criminal case. Our previous recognition of an impeachment exception limited to the testimony of defendants reflects a careful weighing of the competing values. Because

expanding the exception to encompass the testimony of all defense witnesses would not further the truth-seeking value with equal force but would appreciably undermine the deterrent effect of the exclusionary rule, we adhere to the line drawn in our previous cases.

Accordingly, we hold that the Illinois Supreme Court erred in affirming James' convictions despite the prosecutor's use of illegally obtained statements to impeach a defense witness' testimony. The court's judgment is reversed, and the case is remanded for further proceedings not inconsistent with this opinion.

It is so ordered.

Minnesota v. Olson (April 18, 1990)

Justice WHITE delivered the opinion of the Court.

The police in this case made a warrantless, nonconsensual entry into a house where respondent Robert Olson was an overnight guest and arrested him. The issue is whether the arrest violated Olson's Fourth Amendment rights. We hold that it did.

* Shortly before 6 a.m. on Saturday, July 18, 1987, a lone gunman robbed an Amoco gasoline station in Minneapolis, Minnesota, and fatally shot the station manager. A police officer heard the police dispatcher report and suspected Joseph Ecker. The officer and his partner drove immediately to Ecker's home, arriving at about the same time that an Oldsmobile arrived. The driver of the Oldsmobile took evasive action, and the car spun out of control and came to a stop. Two men fled the car on foot. Ecker, who was later identified as the gunman, was captured shortly thereafter inside his home. The second man escaped.

Inside the abandoned Oldsmobile, police found a sack of money and the murder weapon. They also found a title certificate with the name Rob Olson crossed out as a secured party, a letter addressed to a Roger R. Olson of 3151 Johnson Street, and a videotape rental receipt made out to Rob Olson and dated two days earlier. The police verified that a Robert Olson lived at 3151 Johnson Street.

The next morning, Sunday, July 19, a woman identifying herself as Dianna Murphy called the police and said that a man by the name of Rob drove the car in which the gas station killer left the scene and that Rob was planning to leave town by bus. About noon, the same woman called again, gave her address and phone number, and said that a man named Rob had told a Maria and two other women, Louanne and Julie, that he was the driver in the Amoco robbery. The caller stated that Louanne was Julie's mother and that the two women lived at 2406 Fillmore Northeast. The detective-in-charge who took the second phone call sent police officers to 2406 Fillmore to check out Louanne and Julie. When police arrived they determined that the dwelling was a duplex and that Louanne Bergstrom and her daughter Julie lived in the upper unit but were not home. Police spoke to Louanne's mother, Helen Niederhoffer, who lived in the lower unit. She confirmed that a Rob Olson had been staying upstairs but was not then in the unit. She promised to call the police when Olson returned. At 2 p.m., a pickup order, or "probable cause arrest bulletin," was issued for Olson's arrest. The police were instructed to stay away from the duplex.

At approximately 2:45 p.m., Niederhoffer called police and said Olson had returned. The detective-in-charge instructed police officers to go to the house and surround it. He then telephoned Julie from headquarters and told her Rob should come out of the house. The detective heard a male voice say, "tell them I left." Julie stated that Rob had left, whereupon at 3 p.m. the detective ordered the police to enter the house. Without seeking permission and with weapons drawn, the police entered the upper unit and found respondent

hiding in a closet. Less than an hour after his arrest, respondent made an inculpatory statement at police headquarters.

The Hennepin County trial court held a hearing and denied respondent's motion to suppress his statement. App. 3-13. The statement was admitted into evidence at Olson's trial, and he was convicted on one count of first-degree murder, three counts of armed robbery, and three counts of second-degree assault. On appeal, the Minnesota Supreme Court reversed. 436 N.W.2d 92 (1989). The court ruled that respondent had a sufficient interest in the Bergstrom home to challenge the legality of his warrantless arrest there, that the arrest was illegal because there were no exigent circumstances to justify a warrantless entry, 1 and that respondent's statement was tainted by that illegality and should have been suppressed. 2 Because the admission of the statement was not harmless beyond reasonable doubt, the court reversed Olson's conviction and remanded for a new trial. 3

We granted the State's petition for certiorari, 493 U.S. 806, 110 S.Ct. 46, 107 L.Ed.2d 15 (1989), and now affirm.

II

It was held in Payton v. New York, 445 U.S. 573, 100 S.Ct. 1371, 63 L.Ed.2d 639 (1980), that a suspect should not be arrested in his house without an arrest warrant, even though there is probable cause to arrest him. The purpose of the decision was not to protect the person of the suspect but to protect his home from entry in the absence of a magistrate's finding of probable cause. In this case, the court below held that Olson's warrantless arrest was illegal because he had a sufficient connection with the premises to be treated like a householder. The State challenges that conclusion.

Since the decision in Katz v. United States, 389 U.S. 347, 88 S.Ct. 507, 19 L.Ed.2d 576 (1967), it has been the law that "capacity to claim the protection of the Fourth Amendment depends . . . upon whether the person who claims the protection of the Amendment has a legitimate expectation of privacy in the invaded place." Rakas v. Illinois, 439 U.S. 128, 143, 99 S.Ct. 421, 430, 58 L.Ed.2d 387 (1978). A subjective expectation of privacy is legitimate if it is " 'one that society is prepared to recognize as "reasonable," ' " id., at 143-144, n. 12, 99 S.Ct., at 430, n. 12, quoting Katz, supra, at 361, 88 S.Ct., at 516 (Harlan, J., concurring).

The State argues that Olson's relationship to the premises does not satisfy the 12 factors which in its view determine whether a dwelling is a "home." 4 Aside from the fact that it is based on the mistaken premise that a place must be one's "home" in order for one to have a legitimate expectation of privacy there, 5 the State's proposed test is needlessly complex. We need go no further than to conclude, as we do, that Olson's status as an overnight guest is alone enough to show that he had an expectation of privacy in the home that society is prepared to recognize as reasonable.

As recognized by the Minnesota Supreme Court, the facts of this case are similar to those in Jones v. United States, 362 U.S. 257, 80 S.Ct. 725, 4 L.Ed.2d 697 (1960). In Jones, the defendant was arrested in a friend's apartment during the execution of a search warrant and sought to challenge the warrant as not supported by probable cause. ·

"Jones testified that the apartment belonged to a friend, Evans, who had given him the use of it, and a key, with which Jones had admitted himself on the day of the arrest. On cross-examination Jones testified that he had a suit and shirt at the apartment, that his home was elsewhere, that he paid nothing for the use of the apartment, that Evans had let him use it 'as a friend,' that he had slept there 'maybe a night,' and that at the time of the search Evans had been away in Philadelphia for about five days." Id., at 259, 80 S.Ct., at 730. 6

The Court ruled that Jones could challenge the search of the apartment because he was "legitimately on the premises," id., at 267, 80 S.Ct., at 734. Although the "legitimately on the premises" standard was rejected in Rakas as too broad, 439 U.S., at 142-148, 99 S.Ct., at 429-433, the Rakas Court explicitly reaffirmed the factual holding in Jones:

"We do not question the conclusion in Jones that the defendant in that case suffered a violation of his personal Fourth Amendment rights if the search in question was unlawful. . . .

"We think that Jones on its facts merely stands for the unremarkable proposition that a person can have a legally sufficient interest in a place other than his own home so that the Fourth Amendment protects him from unreasonable governmental intrusion into that place." 439 U.S., at 141-142, 99 S.Ct., at 429-430.

Rakas thus recognized that, as an overnight guest, Jones was much more than just legitimately on the premises.

The distinctions relied on by the State between this case and Jones are not legally determinative. The State emphasizes that in this case Olson was never left alone in the duplex or given a key, whereas in Jones the owner of the apartment was away and Jones had a key with which he could come and go and admit and exclude others. These differences are crucial, it is argued, because in not disturbing the holding in Jones, the Court pointed out that while his host was away, Jones had complete dominion and control over the apartment and could exclude others from it. Rakas, 439 U.S., at 149, 99 S.Ct., at 433. We do not understand Rakas, however, to hold that an overnight guest can never have a legitimate expectation of privacy except when his host is away and he has a key, or that only when those facts are present may an overnight guest assert the "unremarkable proposition," id., at 142,

99 S.Ct., at 430, that a person may have a sufficient interest in a place other than his home to enable him to be free in that place from unreasonable searches and seizures.

To hold that an overnight guest has a legitimate expectation of privacy in his host's home merely recognizes the everyday expectations of privacy that we all share. Staying overnight in another's home is a longstanding social custom that serves functions recognized as valuable by society. We stay in others' homes when we travel to a strange city for business or pleasure, when we visit our parents, children, or more distant relatives out of town, when we are in between jobs or homes, or when we house-sit for a friend. We will all be hosts and we will all be guests many times in our lives. From either perspective, we think that society recognizes that a houseguest has a legitimate expectation of privacy in his host's home.

From the overnight guest's perspective, he seeks shelter in another's home precisely because it provides him with privacy, a place where he and his possessions will not be disturbed by anyone but his host and those his host allows inside. We are at our most vulnerable when we are asleep because we cannot monitor our own safety or the security of our belongings. It is for this reason that, although we may spend all day in public places, when we cannot sleep in our own home we seek out another private place to sleep, whether it be a hotel room, or the home of a friend. Society expects at least as much privacy in these places as in a telephone booth—"a temporarily private place whose momentary occupants' expectations of freedom from intrusion are recognized as reasonable," Katz, 389 U.S., at 361, 88 S.Ct., at 517 (Harlan, J., concurring).

That the guest has a host who has ultimate control of the house is not inconsistent with the guest having a legitimate expectation of privacy. The houseguest is there with the permission of his host, who is willing to share his house and his privacy with his guest. It is unlikely that the guest will be confined to a restricted area of the house; and when the host is away or asleep, the guest will have a measure of control over the premises. The host may admit or exclude from the house as he prefers, but it is unlikely that he will admit someone who wants to see or meet with the guest over the objection of the guest. On the other hand, few houseguests will invite others to visit them while they are guests without consulting their hosts; but the latter, who have the authority to exclude despite the wishes of the guest, will often be accommodating. The point is that hosts will more likely than not respect the privacy interests of their guests, who are entitled to a legitimate expectation of privacy despite the fact that they have no legal interest in the premises and do not have the legal authority to determine who may or may not enter the household. If the untrammeled power to admit and exclude were essential to Fourth Amendment protection, an adult daughter temporarily living in the home of her parents would have no legitimate expectation of privacy because her right to admit or exclude would be subject to her parents' veto.

Because respondent's expectation of privacy in the Bergstrom home was rooted in "understandings that are recognized and permitted by society," Rakas, supra, at 144, n. 12, 99 S.Ct., at 431, n. 12, it was legitimate, and respondent can claim the protection of the Fourth Amendment.

III

In Payton v. New York, the Court had no occasion to "consider the sort of emergency or dangerous situation, described in our cases as 'exigent circumstances,' that would justify a warrantless entry into a home for the purpose of either arrest or search," 445 U.S., at 583, 100 S.Ct., at 1378. This case requires us to determine whether the Minnesota Supreme Court was correct in holding that there were no exigent circumstances that justified the warrantless entry into the house to make the arrest.

The Minnesota Supreme Court applied essentially the correct standard in determining whether exigent circumstances existed. The court observed that "a warrantless intrusion may be justified by hot pursuit of a fleeing felon, or imminent destruction of evidence, Welsh v. Wisconsin, 466 U.S. 740 104 S.Ct. 2091, 80 L.Ed.2d 732 (1984), or the need to prevent a suspect's escape, or the risk of danger to the police or to other persons inside or outside the dwelling." 436 N.W.2d, at 97. The court also apparently thought that in the absence of hot pursuit there must be at least probable cause to believe that one or more of the other factors justifying the entry were present and that in assessing the risk of danger, the gravity of the crime and likelihood that the suspect is armed should be considered. Applying this standard, the state court determined that exigent circumstances did not exist.

We are not inclined to disagree with this fact-specific application of the proper legal standard. The court pointed out that although a grave crime was involved, respondent "was known not to be the murderer but thought to be the driver of the getaway car," ibid., and that the police had already recovered the murder weapon, ibid. "The police knew that Louanne and Julie were with the suspect in the upstairs duplex with no suggestion of danger to them. Three or four Minneapolis police squads surrounded the house. The time was 3 p.m., Sunday. . . . It was evident the suspect was going nowhere. If he came out of the house he would have been promptly apprehended." Ibid. We do not disturb the state court's judgment that these facts do not add up to exigent circumstances.

IV

We therefore affirm the judgment of the Minnesota Supreme Court.

It is so ordered.

Florida v. Jimeno (May 23, 1991)

Chief Justice Rehnquist delivered the opinion of the Court.

In this case we decide whether a criminal suspect's Fourth Amendment right to be free from unreasonable searches is violated when, after he gives a police officer permission to search his automobile, the officer opens a closed container found within the car that might reasonably hold the object of the search. We find that it is not. The Fourth Amendment is satisfied when, under the circumstances, it is objectively reasonable for the officer to believe that the scope of the suspect's consent permitted him to open a particular container within the automobile.

This case began when a Dade County police officer, Frank Trujillo, overheard respondent, Enio Jimeno, arranging what appeared to be a drug transaction over a public telephone. Believing that respondent might be involved in illegal drug trafficking, Officer Trujillo followed his car. The officer observed respondent make a right turn at a red light without stopping. He then pulled respondent over to the side of the road in order to issue him a traffic citation. Officer Trujillo told respondent that he had been stopped for committing a traffic infraction. The officer went on to say that he had rea- son to believe that respondent was carrying narcotics in his car, and asked permission to search the car. He explained that respondent did not have to consent to a search of the car. Respondent stated that he had nothing to hide, and gave Trujillo permission to search the automobile. After two passengers stepped out of respondent's car, Officer Trujillo went to the passenger side, opened the door, and saw a folded, brown paper bag on the floorboard. The officer picked up the bag, opened it, and found a kilogram of cocaine inside.

Respondent was charged with possession with intent to distribute cocaine in violation of

Florida law. Before trial, he moved to suppress the cocaine found in the bag on the ground that his consent to search the car did not extend to the closed paper bag inside of the car. The trial court granted the motion. It found that although respondent "could have assumed that the officer would have searched the bag" at the time he gave his consent, his mere consent to search the car did not carry with it specific consent to open the bag and examine its contents. No. 88-23967 (Cir. Ct. Dade Cty., Fla., Mar. 21, 1989); App. to Pet. for Cert. A-6.

The Florida District Court of Appeal affirmed the trial court's decision to suppress the evidence of the cocaine. 550 So. 2d 1176 (Fla. 3d DCA 1989). In doing so, the court established a per se rule that "consent to a general search for narcotics does not extend to `sealed containers within the general area agreed to by the defendant.' " Ibid. (citation omitted). The Florida Supreme Court affirmed, relying upon its decision in State v. Wells, 539 So. 2d 464 (1989) aff'd on other grounds, 495 U. S. --- (1990). 564 So. 2d 1083 (1990). We granted certiorari to determine whether consent to search a vehicle may extend to closed containers found inside the vehicle. 498 U. S. --- (1990), and we now reverse the judgment of the Supreme Court of Florida.

The touchstone of the Fourth Amendment is reasonable- ness. Katz v. United States, 389 U.S. 347, 360 (1967). The Fourth Amendment does not proscribe all state-initiated searches and seizures; it merely proscribes those which are unreasonable. Illinois v. Rodriguez, 497 U. S. --- (1990). Thus, we have long approved consensual searches because it is no doubt reasonable for the police to conduct a search once they have been permitted to do so. Schneckloth v. Bustamonte, 412 U.S. 218, 219 (1973). The standard for measuring the scope of a suspect's consent under the Fourth Amendment is that of "objective" reasonableness -- what would the typical reasonable person have understood by

the exchange between the officer and the suspect? Illinois v. Rodriguez, supra, at --- - --- (slip op., at 5-11); Florida v. Royer, 460 U.S. 491, 501-502 (1983) (opinion of White, J.); id., at 514 (Blackmun, J., dissenting). The question before us, then, is whether it is reasonable for an officer to consider a suspect's general consent to a search of his car to include consent to examine a paper bag lying on the floor of the car. We think that it is.

The scope of a search is generally defined by its expressed object. United States v. Ross, 456 U.S. 798 (1982). In this case, the terms of the search's authorization were simple. Respondent granted Officer Trujillo permission to search his car, and did not place any explicit limitation on the scope of the search. Trujillo had informed respondent that he believed respondent was carrying narcotics, and that he would be looking for narcotics in the car. We think that it was objectively reasonable for the police to conclude that the general consent to search respondent's car included consent to search containers within that car which might bear drugs. A reasonable person may be expected to know that narcotics are generally carried in some form of a container. "Contraband goods rarely are strewn across the trunk or floor of a car." Id., at 820. The authorization to search in this case, therefore, extended beyond the surfaces of the car's interior to the paper bag lying on the car's floor.

The facts of this case are therefore different from those in State v. Wells, supra, on which the Supreme Court of Florida relied in affirming the suppression order in this case. There the Supreme Court of Florida held that consent to search the trunk of a car did not include authorization to pry open a locked briefcase found inside the trunk. It is very likely unreasonable to think that a suspect, by consenting to the search of his trunk, has agreed to the breaking open of a locked briefcase within the trunk, but it is otherwise with respect to a closed paper bag.

Respondent argues, and the Florida trial court agreed with him, that if the police wish to search closed containers within a car they must separately request permission to search each container. But we see no basis for adding this sort of super- structure to the Fourth Amendment's basic test of objective reasonableness. Cf. Illinois v. Gates, 462 U.S. 213 (1983). A suspect may of course delimit as he chooses the scope of the search to which he consents. But if his consent would reasonably be understood to extend to a particular container, the Fourth Amendment provides no grounds for requiring a more explicit authorization. "[T]he community has a real interest in encouraging consent, for the resulting search may yield necessary evidence for the solution and prosecution of crime, evidence that may ensure that a wholly innocent person is not wrongly charged with a criminal offense." Schneckloth v. Bustamonte, supra, at 243.

The judgment of the Supreme Court of Florida is accordingly reversed, and the case remanded for further proceedings not inconsistent with this opinion.

California v. Acevedo (May 30, 1991)

JUSTICE BLACKMUN delivered the opinion of the Court.

This case requires us once again to consider the so-called "automobile exception" to the warrant requirement of the Fourth Amendment and its application to the search of a closed container in the trunk of a car.

I

On October 28, 1987, Officer Coleman of the Santa Ana, Cal., Police Department received a telephone call from a federal drug enforcement agent in Hawaii. The agent informed Coleman that he had seized a package containing marijuana which was to have been delivered to the Federal Express Office in Santa Ana and which was addressed to J.R. Daza at 805 West Stevens Avenue in that city. The agent arranged to send the package to Coleman instead. Coleman then was to take the package to the Federal Express office and arrest the person who arrived to claim it.

Coleman received the package on October 29, verified its contents, and took it to the Senior Operations Manager at the Federal Express office. At about 10:30 a.m. on October 30, a man, who identified himself as Jamie Daza, arrived to claim the package. He accepted it and drove to his apartment on West Stevens. He carried the package into the apartment.

At 11:45 a.m., officers observed Daza leave the apartment and drop the box and paper that had contained the marijuana into a trash bin. Coleman at that point left the scene to get a search warrant. About 12:05 p.m., the officers saw Richard St. George leave the apartment carrying a blue knapsack which appeared to be half full. The officers stopped him as he was driving off, searched the knapsack, and found 1 1/2 pounds of marijuana.

At 12:30 p.m., respondent Charles Steven Acevedo arrived. He entered Daza's apartment, stayed for about 10 minutes, and reappeared carrying a brown paper bag that looked full. The officers noticed that the bag was the size of one of the wrapped marijuana packages sent from Hawaii. Acevedo walked to a silver Honda in the parking lot. He placed the bag in the trunk of the car and started to drive away. Fearing the loss of evidence, officers in a marked police car stopped him. They opened the trunk and the bag, and found marijuana. [1]

Respondent was charged in state court with possession of marijuana for sale, in violation of Cal.Health & Safety Code Ann. § 11359 (West Supp.1987). App. 2. He moved to suppress the marijuana found in the car. The motion was denied. He then pleaded guilty, but appealed the denial of the suppression motion.

The California Court of Appeal, Fourth District, concluded that the marijuana found in the paper bag in the car's trunk should have been suppressed. People v. Acevedo, 216 Cal.App.3d 586, 265 Cal.Rptr. 23 (1990). The court concluded that the officers had probable cause to believe that the paper bag contained drugs, but lacked probable cause to suspect that Acevedo's car, itself, otherwise contained contraband. Because the officers' probable cause was directed specifically at the bag, the court held that the case was controlled by United States v. Chadwick, 433 U. S. 1 (1977), rather than by United States v. Ross, 456 U. S. 798 (1982). Although the court agreed that the officers could seize the paper bag, it held that, under Chadwick, they could not open the bag without first obtaining a warrant for that purpose. The court then recognized "the anomalous nature" of the dichotomy between the rule in Chadwick and the rule in Ross. 216 Cal.App.3d at 592, 265 Cal.Rptr. at 27. That dichotomy dictates that, if there is probable cause to search a car, then the entire car -- including any closed container found therein -- may be searched without a warrant, but if there is probable cause only as to a container in the car, the container may be held, but not searched, until a warrant is obtained.

The Supreme Court of California denied the State's petition for review. App. to Pet. for Cert. 33. On May 14, 1990, JUSTICE O'CONNOR stayed enforcement of the Court of Appeal's judgment pending the disposition of the State's petition for certiorari, and, if that petition were granted, the issuance of the mandate of this Court.

We granted certiorari, 498 U.S. 807 (1990), to reexamine the law applicable to a closed container in an automobile, a subject that has troubled courts and law enforcement officers since it was first considered in Chadwick.

II

The Fourth Amendment protects the "right of the people to be secure in their persons, houses, papers, and effects, against unreasonable searches and seizures." Contemporaneously with the adoption of the Fourth Amendment, the First Congress, and, later, the Second and Fourth Congresses, distinguished between the need for a warrant to search for contraband concealed in "a dwelling house or similar place" and the need for a warrant to search for contraband concealed in a movable vessel. See Carroll v. United States, 267 U. S. 132, 267 U. S. 151 (1925). See also Boyd v. United States, 116 U. S. 616, 116 U. S. 623-624 (1886). In Carroll, this Court established an exception to the warrant requirement for moving vehicles, for it recognized

"a necessary difference between a search of a store, dwelling house or other structure in respect of which a proper official warrant readily may be obtained, and a search of a ship, motor boat, wagon or automobile, for contraband goods, where it is not practicable to secure a warrant because the vehicle can be quickly moved out of the locality or jurisdiction in which the warrant must be sought."

267 U.S. at 267 U. S. 153. It therefore held that a warrantless search of an automobile based upon probable cause to believe that the vehicle contained evidence of crime in the light of an exigency arising out of the likely disappearance of the vehicle did not contravene the Warrant Clause of the Fourth Amendment. See id. at 267 U. S. 158-159.

The Court refined the exigency requirement in Chambers v. Maroney, 399 U. S. 42 (1970), when it held that the existence of exigent circumstances was to be determined at the time the automobile is seized. The car search at issue in Chambers took place at the police station, where the vehicle was immobilized, some time after the driver had been arrested. Given probable cause and exigent circumstances at the time the vehicle was first stopped, the Court held that the later warrantless search at the station passed constitutional muster. The validity of the later search derived from the ruling in Carroll that an immediate search without a warrant at the moment of seizure would have been permissible. See Chambers, 399 U.S. at 399 U. S. 51. The Court reasoned in Chambers that the police could search later whenever they could have searched earlier, had they so chosen. Id. at 399 U. S. 51-52. Following Chambers, if the police have probable cause to justify a warrantless seizure of an automobile on a public roadway, they may conduct either an immediate or a delayed search of the vehicle.

In United States v. Ross, 456 U. S. 798, decided in 1982, we held that a warrantless search of an automobile under the Carroll doctrine could include a search of a container or package found inside the car when such a search was supported by probable cause. The warrantless search of Ross' car occurred after an informant told the police that he had seen Ross complete a drug transaction using drugs stored in the trunk of his car. The police stopped the car, searched it, and discovered in the trunk a brown paper bag containing drugs. We decided that the search of Ross' car was not unreasonable under the Fourth Amendment:

"The scope of a warrantless search based on probable cause is no narrower -- and no broader -- than the scope of a search authorized by a warrant supported by probable cause."

Id. at 456 U. S. 823. Thus,

"[i]f probable cause justifies the search of a lawfully stopped vehicle, it justifies the search of every part of the vehicle and its contents that may conceal the object of the search."

Id. at 456 U. S. 825. In Ross, therefore, we clarified the scope of the Carroll doctrine as properly including a "probing search" of compartments and containers within the automobile so long as the search is supported by probable cause. Id. at 456 U. S. 800.

In addition to this clarification, Ross

distinguished the Carroll doctrine from the separate rule that governed the search of closed containers. See 456 U.S. at 456 U. S. 817. The Court had announced this separate rule, unique to luggage and other closed packages, bags, and containers, in United States v. Chadwick, 433 U. S. 1 (1977). In Chadwick, federal narcotics agents had probable cause to believe that a 200-pound double-locked footlocker contained marijuana. The agents tracked the locker as the defendants removed it from a train and carried it through the station to a waiting car. As soon as the defendants lifted the locker into the trunk of the car, the agents arrested them, seized the locker, and searched it. In this Court, the United States did not contend that the locker's brief contact with the automobile's trunk sufficed to make the Carroll doctrine applicable. Rather, the United States urged that the search of movable luggage could be considered analogous to the search of an automobile. 433 U.S. at 433 U. S. 11-12.

The Court rejected this argument because, it reasoned, a person expects more privacy in his luggage and personal effects than he does in his automobile. Id. at 433 U. S. 13. Moreover, it concluded that, as "may often not be the case when automobiles are seized," secure storage facilities are usually available when the police seize luggage. Id. at 433 U. S. 13, n. 7.

In Arkansas v. Sanders, 442 U. S. 753 (1979), the Court extended Chadwick's rule to apply to a suitcase actually being transported in the trunk of a car. In Sanders, the police had probable cause to believe a suitcase contained marijuana. They watched as the defendant placed the suitcase in the trunk of a taxi and was driven away. The police pursued the taxi for several blocks, stopped it, found the suitcase in the trunk, and searched it. Although the Court had applied the Carroll doctrine to searches of integral parts of the automobile itself, (indeed, in Carroll, contraband whiskey was in the upholstery of the seats, see 267 U.S. at 267 U. S. 136), it did not extend the doctrine to the warrantless search of personal luggage "merely because it was located in an automobile lawfully stopped by the police." 442 U.S. at 442 U. S. 765. Again, the Sanders majority stressed the heightened privacy expectation in personal luggage, and concluded that the presence of luggage in an automobile did not diminish the owner's expectation of privacy in his personal items. Id. at 442 U. S. 764-765. Cf. California v. Carney, 471 U. S. 386 (1985).

In Ross, the Court endeavored to distinguish between Carroll, which governed the Ross automobile search, and Chadwick, which governed the Sanders automobile search. It held that the Carroll doctrine covered searches of automobiles when the police had probable cause to search an entire vehicle, but that the Chadwick doctrine governed searches of luggage when the officers had probable cause to search only a container within the vehicle. Thus, in a Ross situation, the police could conduct a reasonable search under the Fourth Amendment without obtaining a warrant, whereas in a Sanders situation, the police had to obtain a warrant before they searched.

JUSTICE STEVENS is correct, of course, that Ross involved the scope of an automobile search. See post at 500 U. S. 592. Ross held that closed containers encountered by the police during a warrantless search of a car pursuant to the automobile exception could also be searched. Thus, this Court in Ross took the critical step of saying that closed containers in cars could be searched without a warrant because of their presence within the automobile. Despite the protection that Sanders purported to extend to closed containers, the privacy interest in those closed containers yielded to the broad scope of an automobile search.

III

The facts in this case closely resemble the facts in Ross. In Ross, the police had probable cause to believe that drugs were stored in the trunk of a particular car. See 456 U.S. at 456 U. S. 800. Here, the California Court of Appeal concluded that the police had probable cause to believe that respondent was carrying marijuana in a bag in his car's trunk. [2] 216 Cal.App.3d at 590, 265 Cal.Rptr. at 25. Furthermore, for what it is worth, in Ross, as here, the drugs in the trunk were contained in a brown paper bag.

This Court in Ross rejected Chadwick's distinction between containers and cars. It concluded that the expectation of privacy in one's vehicle is equal to one's expectation of privacy in the container, and noted that "the privacy interests in a car's trunk or glove compartment may be no less than those in a movable container." 456 U.S. at 456 U. S. 823. It also recognized that it was arguable that the same exigent circumstances that permit a warrantless search of an automobile would justify the warrantless search of a movable container. Id. at 456 U. S. 809. In deference to the rule of Chadwick and Sanders, however, the Court put that question to one side. Id. at 456 U. S. 809-810. It concluded that the time and expense of the warrant process would be misdirected if the police could search every cubic inch of an automobile until they discovered a paper sack, at which point the Fourth Amendment required them to take the sack to a magistrate for permission to look inside. We now must decide the question deferred in Ross: whether the Fourth Amendment requires the police to obtain a warrant to open the sack in a movable vehicle simply because they lack probable cause to search the entire car. We conclude that it does not.

IV

Dissenters in Ross asked why the suitcase in Sanders was

"more private, less difficult for police to seize and store, or in any other relevant respect more properly subject to the warrant requirement, than a container that police discover in a probable cause search of an entire automobile?"

Id. 456 U.S. at 456 U. S. 839-840. We now agree that a container found after a general search of the automobile and a container found in a car after a limited search for the container are equally easy for the police to store and for the suspect to hide or destroy. In fact, we see no principled distinction in terms of either the privacy expectation or the exigent circumstances between the paper bag found by the police in Ross and the paper bag found by the police here. Furthermore, by attempting to distinguish between a container for which the police are specifically searching and a container which they come across in a car, we have provided only minimal protection for privacy, and have impeded effective law enforcement.

The line between probable cause to search a vehicle and probable cause to search a package in that vehicle is not always clear, and separate rules that govern the two objects to be searched may enable the police to broaden their power to make warrantless searches and disserve privacy interests. We noted this in Ross in the context of a search of an entire vehicle. Recognizing that, under Carroll, the "entire vehicle itself . . . could be searched without a warrant," we concluded that

"prohibiting police from opening immediately a container in which the object of the search is most likely to be found, and instead forcing them first to comb the entire vehicle, would actually exacerbate the intrusion on privacy interests."

456 U.S. at 456 U. S. 821, n. 28. At the moment when officers stop an automobile, it may be less than clear whether they suspect with a high degree of certainty that the vehicle contains drugs in a bag or simply contains drugs. If the police know that they may open a bag only if they are actually searching the entire car, they may search more extensively than they otherwise would in order to establish the general probable cause

required by Ross.

Such a situation is not far-fetched. In United States v. Johns, 469 U. S. 478 (1985), customs agents saw two trucks drive to a private airstrip and approach two small planes. The agents drew near the trucks, smelled marijuana, and then saw in the backs of the trucks packages wrapped in a manner that marijuana smugglers customarily employed. The agents took the trucks to headquarters and searched the packages without a warrant. Id. at 469 U. S. 481. Relying on Chadwick, the defendants argued that the search was unlawful. Id. at 469 U. S. 482. The defendants contended that Ross was inapplicable because the agents lacked probable cause to search anything but the packages themselves, and supported this contention by noting that a search of the entire vehicle never occurred. Id. at 469 U. S. 483. We rejected that argument, and found Chadwick and Sanders inapposite because the agents had probable cause to search the entire body of each truck, although they had chosen not to do so. Id. at 469 U. S. 482-483. We cannot see the benefit of a rule that requires law enforcement officers to conduct a more intrusive search in order to justify a less intrusive

To the extent that the Chadwick-Sanders rule protects privacy, its protection is minimal. Law enforcement officers may seize a container and hold it until they obtain a search warrant. Chadwick, 433 U.S. at 433 U. S. 13.

"Since the police, by hypothesis, have probable cause to seize the property, we can assume that a warrant will be routinely forthcoming in the overwhelming majority of cases."

Sanders, 442 U.S. at 442 U. S. 770 (dissenting opinion). And the police often will be able to search containers without a warrant, despite the Chadwick-Sanders rule, as a search incident to a lawful arrest. In New York v. Belton, 453 U. S. 454 (1981), the Court said:

"[W]e hold that, when a policeman has made a lawful custodial arrest of the occupant of an automobile, he may, as a contemporaneous incident of that arrest, search the passenger compartment of that automobile."

"It follows from this conclusion that the police may also examine the contents of any containers found within the passenger compartment."

Id. at 453 U. S. 460 (footnote omitted). Under Belton, the same probable cause to believe that a container holds drugs will allow the police to arrest the person transporting the container and search it.

Finally, the search of a paper bag intrudes far less on individual privacy than does the incursion sanctioned long ago in Carroll. In that case, prohibition agents slashed the upholstery of the automobile. This Court nonetheless found their search to be reasonable under the Fourth Amendment. If destroying the interior of an automobile is not unreasonable, we cannot conclude that looking inside a closed container is. In light of the minimal protection to privacy afforded by the Chadwick-Sanders rule, and our serious doubt whether that rule substantially serves privacy interests, we now hold that the Fourth Amendment does not compel separate treatment for an automobile search that extends only to a container within the vehicle.

V

The Chadwick-Sanders rule not only has failed to protect privacy, but it has also confused courts and police officers and impeded effective law enforcement. The conflict between the Carroll doctrine cases and the Chadwick-Sanders line has been criticized in academic commentary. See, e.g., Gardner, Searches and Seizures of Automobiles and Their Contents: Fourth Amendment Considerations in a Post-Ross World, 62 Neb.L.Rev. 1 (1983); Latzer, Searching Cars and Their Contents, 18 Crim.L.Bull. 381 (1982);

Kamisar, The "Automobile Search" Cases: The Court Does Little to Clarify the "Labyrinth" of Judicial Uncertainty, in 3 The Supreme Court: Trends and Developments 1980-1981, p. 69 (1982). One leading authority on the Fourth Amendment, after comparing Chadwick and Sanders with Carroll and its progeny, observed:

"These two lines of authority cannot be completely reconciled, and thus how one comes out in the container-in-the-car situation depends upon which line of authority is used as a point of departure."

3 W. LaFave, Search & Seizure 53 (2d ed.1987).

The discrepancy between the two rules has led to confusion for law enforcement officers. For example, when an officer, who has developed probable cause to believe that a vehicle contains drugs, begins to search the vehicle and immediately discovers a closed container, which rule applies? The defendant will argue that the fact that the officer first chose to search the container indicates that his probable cause extended only to the container and that Chadwick and Sanders therefore require a warrant. On the other hand, the fact that the officer first chose to search in the most obvious location should not restrict the propriety of the search. The Chadwick rule, as applied in Sanders, has devolved into an anomaly such that the more likely the police are to discover drugs in a container, the less authority they have to search it. We have noted the virtue of providing ""clear and unequivocal" guidelines to the law enforcement profession.'" Minnick v. Mississippi, 498 U. S. 146, 498 U. S. 151 (1990) quoting Arizona v. Roberson, 486 U. S. 675, 486 U. S. 682 (1988). The Chadwick-Sanders rule is the antithesis of a "`clear and unequivocal' guideline."

JUSTICE STEVENS argues that the decisions of this Court evince a lack of confusion about the automobile exception. See post at 500 U. S. 594. The first case cited by the dissent, United

States v. Place, 462 U. S. 696 (1983), however, did not involve an automobile at all. We considered in Place the temporary detention of luggage in an airport. Not only was no automobile involved, but the defendant, Place, was waiting at the airport to board his plane, rather than preparing to leave the airport in a car. Any similarity to Sanders, in which the defendant was leaving the airport in a car, is remote, at best. Place had nothing to do with the automobile exception, and is inapposite.

Nor does JUSTICE STEVENS's citation to Oklahoma v. Castleberry, 471 U.S. 146 (1985), support its contention. Castleberry presented the same question about the application of the automobile exception to the search of a closed container that we face here. In Castleberry, we affirmed by an equally divided court. That result illustrates this Court's continued struggle with the scope of the automobile exception, rather than the absence of confusion in applying it.

JUSTICE STEVENS also argues that law enforcement has not been impeded because the Court has decided 29 Fourth Amendment cases since Ross in favor of the government. See post at 500 U. S. 600. In each of these cases, the government appeared as the petitioner. The dissent fails to explain how the loss of 29 cases below, not to mention the many others which this Court did not hear, did not interfere with law enforcement. The fact that the state courts and the federal courts of appeals have been reversed in their Fourth Amendment holdings 29 times since 1982 further demonstrates the extent to which our Fourth Amendment jurisprudence has confused the courts.

Most important, with the exception of Johns, supra, and Texas v. Brown, 460 U. S. 730 (1983), the Fourth Amendment cases cited by the dissent do not concern automobiles or the automobile exception . From Carroll through Ross, this Court has explained that automobile searches differ from other searches. The dissent fails to

acknowledge this basic principle, and so misconstrues and misapplies our Fourth Amendment case law.

The Chadwick dissenters predicted that the container rule would have "the perverse result of allowing fortuitous circumstances to control the outcome" of various searches. 433 U.S. at 433 U. S. 22. The rule also was so confusing that, within two years after Chadwick, this Court found it necessary to expound on the meaning of that decision and explain its application to luggage in general. Sanders, 442 U.S. at 442 U. S. 761-764. Again, dissenters bemoaned the "inherent opaqueness" of the difference between the Carroll and Chadwick principles, and noted "the confusion to be created for all concerned." Id. at 442 U. S. 771. See also Robbins v. California, 453 U. S. 420, 453 U. S. 425-426 (1981) (listing cases decided by Federal Courts of Appeals since Chadwick had been announced). Three years after Sanders, we returned in Ross to "this troubled area," 456 U.S. at 456 U. S. 817, in order to assert that Sanders had not cut back on Carroll.

Although we have recognized firmly that the doctrine of stare decisis serves profoundly important purposes in our legal system, this Court has overruled a prior case on the comparatively rare occasion when it has bred confusion or been a derelict or led to anomalous results. See, e.g., Complete Auto Transit, Inc. v. Brady, 430 U. S. 274, 430 U. S. 288-289 (1977). Sanders was explicitly undermined in Ross, 456 U.S. at 456 U. S. 824, and the existence of the dual regimes for automobile searches that uncover containers has proved as confusing as the Chadwick and Sanders dissenters predicted. We conclude that it is better to adopt one clear-cut rule to govern automobile searches and eliminate the warrant requirement for closed containers set forth in Sanders.

VI

The interpretation of the Carroll doctrine set forth in Ross now applies to all searches of containers found in an automobile. In other words, the police may search without a warrant if their search is supported by probable cause. The Court in Ross put it this way:

"The scope of a warrantless search of an automobile . . . is not defined by the nature of the container in which the contraband is secreted. Rather, it is defined by the object of the search and the places in which there is probable cause to believe that it may be found."

456 U.S. at 456 U. S. 824. It went on to note:

"Probable cause to believe that a container placed in the trunk of a taxi contains contraband or evidence does not justify a search of the entire cab."

Ibid. We reaffirm that principle. In the case before us, the police had probable cause to believe that the paper bag in the automobile's trunk contained marijuana. That probable cause now allows a warrantless search of the paper bag. The facts in the record reveal that the police did not have probable cause to believe that contraband was hidden in any other part of the automobile and a search of the entire vehicle would have been without probable cause and unreasonable under the Fourth Amendment.

Our holding today neither extends the Carroll doctrine nor broadens the scope of the permissible automobile search delineated in Carroll, Chambers, and Ross. It remains a

"cardinal principle that 'searches conducted outside the judicial process, without prior approval by judge or magistrate, are per se unreasonable under the Fourth Amendment -- subject only to a few specifically established and well-delineated exceptions.'"

Mincey v. Arizona, 437 U.S. 385, 437 U. S. 390 (1978), quoting Katz v. United States, 389 U. S. 347, 389 U. S. 357 (1967) (footnote omitted). We held in Ross: "The exception recognized in Carroll is unquestionably one that is specifically

established and well delineated.'" 456 U.S. at 456 U. S. 825.

Until today, this Court has drawn a curious line between the search of an automobile that coincidentally turns up a container and the search of a container that coincidentally turns up in an automobile. The protections of the Fourth Amendment must not turn on such coincidences. We therefore interpret Carroll as providing one rule to govern all automobile searches. The police may search an automobile and the containers within it where they have probable cause to believe contraband or evidence is contained.

The judgment of the California Court of Appeal is reversed, and the case is remanded to that court for further proceedings not inconsistent with this opinion.

It is so ordered.

Notes

[1] When Officer Coleman returned with a warrant, the apartment was searched and bags of marijuana were found there. We are here concerned, of course, only with what was discovered in the automobile.

[2] Although respondent now challenges this holding, we decline to second-guess the California courts, which have found probable cause. Respondent did not raise the probable cause question in his Brief in Opposition, nor did he cross-petition for resolution of the issue. He also did not raise the point in a cross-petition to the Supreme Court of California. We therefore do not consider the issue here. See Lytle v. Household Mfg., Inc., 494 U. S. 545, 494 U. S. 551, n. 3 (1990); Heckler v. Campbell, 461 U. S. 458, 461 U. S. 468-469, n. 12 (1983).

Soldal v. Cook County (Dec 8, 1992)

JUSTICE WHITE delivered the opinion of the Court.

I

Edward Soldal and his family resided in their trailer home, which was located on a rented lot in the Willoway Terrace mobile home park in Elk Grove, Illinois. In May 1987, Terrace Properties, the owner of the park, and Margaret Hale, its manager, filed an eviction proceeding against the Soldals in an Illinois state court. Under the Illinois Forcible Entry and Detainer Act, Ill.Rev.Stat., ch. 110, 9-101 et seq. (1991), a tenant cannot be dispossessed absent a judgment of eviction. The suit was dismissed on June 2, 1987. A few months later, in August 1987, the owner brought a second proceeding of eviction, claiming nonpayment of rent. The case was set for trial on September 22, 1987.

Rather than await judgment in their favor, Terrace Properties and Hale, contrary to Illinois law, chose to evict the Soldals forcibly two weeks prior to the scheduled hearing. On September 4, Hale notified the Cook County's Sheriff's Department that she was going to remove the trailer home from the park, and requested the presence of sheriff deputies to forestall any possible resistance. Later that day, two Terrace Properties employees arrived at the Soldals' home accompanied by Cook County Deputy Sheriff O'Neil. The employees proceeded to wrench the sewer and water connections off the side of the trailer home, disconnect the phone, tear off the trailer's canopy and skirting, and hook the home to a tractor. Meanwhile, O'Neil explained to Edward Soldal that "`he was there to see that [Soldal] didn't interfere with [Willoway's] work.'" Brief for Petitioner 6.

By this time, two more deputy sheriffs had arrived at the scene, and Soldal told them that he wished to file a complaint for criminal trespass. They referred him to deputy Lieutenant Jones, who was in Hale's office. Jones asked Soldal to wait outside while he remained closeted with Hale and other Terrace Properties employees for over 20 minutes. After talking to a district attorney and making Soldal wait another half hour, Jones told Soldal that he would not accept a complaint because "`it was between the landlord and the tenant . . . [and] they were going to go ahead and continue to move out the trailer.'" Id., at 8. 1 Throughout this period, the deputy sheriffs knew that Terrace Properties did not have an eviction order and that its actions were unlawful. Eventually, and in the presence of an additional two deputy sheriffs, the Willoway workers pulled the trailer free of its moorings and towed it onto the street. Later, it was hauled to a neighboring property.

On September 9, the state judge assigned to the pending eviction proceedings ruled that the eviction had been unauthorized, and ordered Terrace Properties to return the Soldals' home to the lot. The home, however, was badly damaged. 2 The Soldals brought this action under 42 U.S.C. 1983, alleging a violation of their rights under the Fourth and Fourteenth Amendments. They claimed that Terrace Properties and Hale had conspired with Cook County deputy sheriffs to unreasonably seize and remove the Soldals' trailer home. The District Judge granted defendants' motion for summary judgment on the grounds that the Soldals had failed to adduce any evidence to support their conspiracy theory and, therefore, the existence of state action necessary under 1983. 3

The Court of Appeals for the Seventh Circuit, construing the facts in petitioners' favor, accepted their contention that there was state action. However, it went on to hold that the removal of the Soldals' trailer did not constitute a seizure for purposes of the Fourth Amendment or a deprivation of due process for purposes of the Fourteenth.

On rehearing, a majority of the Seventh Circuit, sitting en banc, reaffirmed the panel decision. 4 Acknowledging that what had occurred was a "seizure" in the literal sense of the word, the court reasoned that, because it was not made in the course of public law enforcement, and because it did not invade the Soldals' privacy, it was not a seizure as contemplated by the Fourth Amendment. 942 F.2d 1073, 1076 (1991). Interpreting prior cases of this Court, the Seventh Circuit concluded that, absent interference with privacy or liberty, a "pure deprivation of property" is not cognizable under the Fourth Amendment. Id., at 1078-1079. Rather, petitioners' property interests were protected only by the Due Process Clauses of the Fifth and Fourteenth Amendments. 5

We granted certiorari to consider whether the seizure and removal of the Soldals' trailer home implicated their Fourth Amendment rights, 503 U.S. 918 (1992), and now reverse. 6

II

The Fourth Amendment, made applicable to the States by the Fourteenth, Ker v. California, 374 U.S. 23, 30 (1963), provides in pertinent part that the "right of the people to be secure in their persons, houses, papers, and effects, against unreasonable searches and seizures, shall not be violated. . . ."

A "seizure" of property, we have explained, occurs when "there is some meaningful interference with an individual's possessory interests in that property." United States v. Jacobsen, 466 U.S. 109, 113 (1984). In addition, we have emphasized that "at the very core" of the Fourth Amendment "stands the right of a man to retreat into his own home." Silverman v. United States, 365 U.S. 505, 511 (1961). See also Oliver v. United States, 466 U.S. 170, 178 -179 (1984); Wyman v. James, 400 U.S. 309, 316 (1971); Payton v. New York, 445 U.S. 573, 601 (1980).

As a result of the state action in this case, the Soldals' domicile was not only seized, it literally was carried away, giving new meaning to the term "mobile home." We fail to see how being unceremoniously dispossessed of one's home in the manner alleged to have occurred here can be viewed as anything but a seizure invoking the protection of the Fourth Amendment. Whether the Amendment was in fact violated is, of course, a different question that requires determining if the seizure was reasonable. That inquiry entails the weighing of various factors, and is not before us.

The Court if Appeals recognized that there had been a seizure, but concluded that it was a seizure only in a "technical" sense, not within the meaning of the Fourth Amendment. This conclusion followed from a narrow reading of the Amendment, which the court construed to safeguard only privacy and liberty interests, while leaving unprotected possessory interests where neither privacy nor liberty was at stake. Otherwise, the court said,

"a constitutional provision enacted two centuries ago [would] make every repossession and eviction with police assistance actionable under - of all things - the Fourth Amendment[, which] would both trivialize the amendment and gratuitously shift a large body of routine commercial litigation from the state courts to the federal courts. That trivializing, this shift, can be prevented by recognizing the difference between possessory and privacy interests." 942 F.2d, at 1077.

Because the officers had not entered Soldal's house, rummaged through his possessions, or, in the Court of Appeals' view, interfered with his liberty in the course of the eviction, the Fourth Amendment offered no protection against the "grave deprivation" of property that had occurred. Ibid.

We do not agree with this interpretation of the Fourth Amendment. The Amendment protects the people from unreasonable searches and seizures of "their persons, houses, papers, and effects." This language surely cuts against the novel holding below, and our cases unmistakably hold that the Amendment protects property as well as privacy. 7 This much was made clear in Jacobsen, supra, where we explained that the first Clause of the Fourth Amendment

"protects two types of expectations, one involving "searches," the other "seizures." A "search" occurs when an expectation of privacy that society is prepared to consider reasonable is infringed. A "seizure" of property occurs where there is some meaningful interference with an individual's possessory interests in that property." 466 U.S., at 113 (footnote omitted).

See also id., at 120; Horton v. California, 496 U.S. 128, 133 (1990); Arizona v. Hicks, 480 U.S. 321, 328 (1987); Maryland v. Macon, 472 U.S. 463, 469 (1985); Texas v. Brown, 460 U.S. 730, 747 -748 (1983) (STEVENS, J., concurring in judgment); United States v. Salvucci, 448 U.S. 83, 91, n. 6 (1980). Thus, having concluded that chemical testing of powder found in a package did not compromise its owner's privacy, the Court in Jacobsen did not put an end to its inquiry, as would be required under the view adopted by the Court of Appeals and advocated by respondents. Instead, adhering to the teachings of United States v. Place, 462 U.S. 696 (1983), it went on to determine whether the invasion of the owners' "possessory interests" occasioned by the destruction of the powder was reasonable under the Fourth Amendment. Jacobsen, supra, at 124-125. In Place, although we found that subjecting luggage to a "dog sniff" did not constitute a search for Fourth Amendment purposes because it did not compromise any privacy interest, taking custody of Place's suitcase was deemed an unlawful seizure, for it unreasonably infringed "the suspect's possessory interest in his luggage." 462 U.S., at 708 . 8 Although lacking a privacy component, the property rights in both instances nonetheless were not disregarded, but rather were afforded Fourth Amendment protection.

Respondents rely principally on precedents such as Katz v. United States, 389 U.S. 347 (1967), Warden, Maryland Penitentiary v. Hayden, 387 U.S. 294 (1967), and Cardwell v. Lewis, 417 U.S. 583 (1974), to demonstrate that the Fourth Amendment is only marginally concerned with property rights. But the message of those cases is that property rights are not the sole measure of Fourth Amendment violations. The Warden opinion thus observed, citing Jones v. United States, 362 U.S. 257 (1960), and Silverman v. United States, 365 U.S. 505 (1961), that the "principal" object of the Amendment is the protection of privacy, rather than property, and that "this shift in emphasis from property to privacy has come about through a subtle interplay of substantive and procedural reform." 387 U.S., at 304 . There was no suggestion that this shift in emphasis had snuffed out the previously recognized protection for property under the Fourth Amendment. Katz, in declaring violative of the Fourth Amendment the unwarranted overhearing of a telephone booth conversation, effectively ended any lingering notions that the protection of privacy depended on trespass into a protected area. In the course of its decision, the Katz Court stated that the Fourth Amendment can neither be translated into a provision dealing with constitutionally protected areas nor into a general constitutional right to privacy. The Amendment, the Court said, protects individual privacy against certain kinds of governmental intrusion, "but its protections go further, and often have nothing to do with privacy at all." 389 U.S., at 350 .

As for Cardwell, a plurality of this Court held in that case that the Fourth Amendment did not bar the use in evidence of paint scrapings taken from and tire treads observed on the defendant's automobile, which had been seized in a parking lot and towed to a police lockup. Gathering this evidence was not deemed to be a search, for nothing from the interior of the car and "no personal effects, which the Fourth Amendment traditionally has been deemed to protect" were searched or seized. 417 U.S., at 591 (opinion of BLACKMUN, J.). No meaningful privacy rights were invaded. But this left the argument, pressed by the dissent, that the evidence gathered was the product of a warrantless, and hence illegal, seizure of the car from the parking lot where the defendant had left it. However, the plurality was of the view that, because, under the circumstances of the case, there was probable cause to seize the car as an instrumentality of the crime, Fourth Amendment precedent permitted the seizure without a warrant. Id., at 593. Thus, both the plurality and dissenting Justices considered the defendant's auto deserving of Fourth Amendment protection even though privacy interests were not at stake. They differed only in the degree of protection that the Amendment demanded.

The Court of Appeals appeared to find more specific support for confining the protection of the Fourth Amendment to privacy interests in our decision in Hudson v. Palmer, 468 U.S. 517 (1984). There, a state prison inmate sued, claiming that prison guards had entered his cell without consent and had seized and destroyed some of his personal effects. We ruled that an inmate, because of his status, enjoyed neither a right to privacy in his cell nor protection against unreasonable seizures of his personal effects. Id., at 526-528, and n. 8; id., at 538 (O'CONNOR, J., concurring). Whatever else the case held, it is of limited usefulness outside the prison context with respect to the coverage of the Fourth Amendment.

We thus are unconvinced that any of the Court's prior cases supports the view that the Fourth Amendment protects against unreasonable seizures of property only where privacy or liberty is also implicated. What is more, our "plain view" decisions make untenable such a construction of the Amendment. Suppose, for example, that police officers lawfully enter a house, by either complying with the warrant requirement or satisfying one of its recognized exceptions - e.g., through a valid

consent or a showing of exigent circumstances. If they come across some item in plain view and seize it, no invasion of personal privacy has occurred. Horton, 496 U.S., at 133 -134; Brown, supra, at 739 (opinion of REHNQUIST, J.). If the boundaries of the Fourth Amendment were defined exclusively by rights of privacy, "plain view" seizures would not implicate that constitutional provision at all. Yet, far from being automatically upheld, "plain view" seizures have been scrupulously subjected to Fourth Amendment inquiry. Thus, in the absence of consent or a warrant permitting the seizure of the items in question, such seizures can be justified only if they meet the probable-cause standard, Arizona v. Hicks, 480 U.S. 321, 326 -327 (1987), 9 and if they are unaccompanied by unlawful trespass, Horton, 496 U.S., at 136 -137. 10 That is because, the absence of a privacy interest notwithstanding, "[a] seizure of the article . . . would obviously invade the owner's possessory interest." Id., at 134; see also Brown, 460 U.S., at 739 (opinion of REHNQUIST, J.). The plain-view doctrine "merely reflects an application of the Fourth Amendment's central requirement of reasonableness to the law governing seizures of property." Ibid.; Coolidge v. New Hampshire, 403 U.S. 443, 468 (1971); id., at 516 (WHITE, J., concurring and dissenting).

The Court of Appeals understandably found it necessary to reconcile its holding with our recognition in the plain-view cases that the Fourth Amendment protects property as such. In so doing, the court did not distinguish this case on the ground that the seizure of the Soldals' home took place in a noncriminal context. Indeed, it acknowledged what is evident from our precedents - that the Amendment's protection applies in the civil context as well. See O'Connor v. Ortega, 480 U.S. 709 (1987); New Jersey v. T.L.O., 469 U.S. 325, 334 -335 (1985); Michigan v. Tyler, 436 U.S. 499, 504 -506 (1978); Marshall v. Barlow's, Inc., 436 U.S. 307, 312 -313 (1978); Camara v.

Municipal Court of San Francisco, 387 U.S. 523, 528 (1967). 11

Nor did the Court of Appeals suggest that the Fourth Amendment applied exclusively to law enforcement activities. It observed, for example, that the Amendment's protection would be triggered "by a search or other entry into the home incident to an eviction or repossession," 942 F.2d, at 1077. 12 Instead, the court sought to explain why the Fourth Amendment protects against seizures of property in the plain-view context, but not in this case, as follows:

"[S]eizures made in the course of investigations by police or other law enforcement officers are almost always, as in the plain view cases, the culmination of searches. The police search in order to seize, and it is the search and ensuing seizure that the Fourth Amendment, by its reference to "searches and seizures," seeks to regulate. Seizure means one thing when it is the outcome of a search; it may mean something else when it stands apart from a search or any other investigative activity. The Fourth Amendment may still nominally apply, but, precisely because there is no invasion of privacy, the usual rules do not apply." Id., at 1079 (emphasis in original).

We have difficulty with this passage. The court seemingly construes the Amendment to protect only against seizures that are the outcome of a search. But our cases are to the contrary, and hold that seizures of property are subject to Fourth Amendment scrutiny even though no search within the meaning of the Amendment has taken place. See, e.g., Jacobsen, 466 U.S., at 120 -125; Place, 462 U.S., at 706 -707; Cardwell, 417 U.S., at 588 - 589. 13 More generally, an officer who happens to come across an individual's property in a public area could seize it only if Fourth Amendment standards are satisfied - for example, if the items are evidence of a crime or contraband. Cf. Payton v. New York, 445 U.S., at 587 . We are also puzzled by the last sentence of the excerpt, where the court announces that the "usual rules" of the Fourth Amendment are inapplicable if the seizure is not the result of a search or any other investigative activity "precisely because there is no invasion of privacy." For the plain-view cases clearly state that, notwithstanding the absence of any interference with privacy, seizures of effects that are not authorized by a warrant are reasonable only because there is probable cause to associate the property with criminal activity. The seizure of the weapons in Horton, for example, occurred in the midst of a search, yet we emphasized that it did not "involve any invasion of privacy." 496 U.S., at 133 . In short, our statement that such seizures must satisfy the Fourth Amendment and will be deemed reasonable only if the item's incriminating character is "immediately apparent," id., at 136- 137, is at odds with the Court of Appeals' approach.

The Court of Appeals' effort is both interesting and creative, but, at bottom, it simply reasserts the earlier thesis that the Fourth Amendment protects privacy, but not property. We remain unconvinced, and see no justification for departing from our prior cases. In our view, the reason why an officer might enter a house or effectuate a seizure is wholly irrelevant to the threshold question whether the Amendment applies. What matters is the intrusion on the people's security from governmental interference. Therefore, the right against unreasonable seizures would be no less transgressed if the seizure of the house was undertaken to collect evidence, verify compliance with a housing regulation, effect an eviction by the police, or on a whim, for no reason at all. As we have observed on more than one occasion, it would be "anomalous to say that the individual and his private property are fully protected by the Fourth Amendment only when the individual is suspected of criminal behavior." Camara 387 U.S., at 530; see also O'Connor, 480 U.S., at 715; T.L.O., 469 U.S., at 335 .

The Court of Appeals also stated that, even

if, contrary to its previous rulings, "there is some element or tincture of a Fourth Amendment seizure, it cannot carry the day for the Soldals." 942 F.2d, at 1080. Relying on our decision in Graham v. Connor, 490 U.S. 386 (1989), the court reasoned that it should look at the "dominant character of the conduct challenged in a section 1983 case [to] determine the constitutional standard under which it is evaluated." 942 F.2d, at 1080. Believing that the Soldals' claim was more akin to a challenge against the deprivation of property without due process of law than against an unreasonable seizure, the court concluded that they should not be allowed to bring their suit under the guise of the Fourth Amendment.

But we see no basis for doling out constitutional protections in such fashion. Certain wrongs affect more than a single right, and, accordingly, can implicate more than one of the Constitution's commands. Where such multiple violations are alleged, we are not in the habit of identifying, as a preliminary matter, the claim's "dominant" character. Rather, we examine each constitutional provision in turn. See, e.g., Hudson v. Palmer, 468 U.S. 517 (1984) (Fourth Amendment and Fourteenth Amendment Due Process Clause); Ingraham v. Wright, 430 U.S. 651 (1977) (Eighth Amendment and Fourteenth Amendment Due Process Clause). Graham is not to the contrary. Its holding was that claims of excessive use of force should be analyzed under the Fourth Amendment's reasonableness standard, rather than the Fourteenth Amendment's substantive due process test. We were guided by the fact that, in that case, both provisions targeted the same sort of governmental conduct and, as a result, we chose the more "explicit textual source of constitutional protection" over the "more generalized notion of `substantive due process.'" 490 U.S., at 394 -395. Surely, Graham does not bar resort in this case to the Fourth Amendment's specific protection for "houses, papers, and

effects," rather than the general protection of property in the Due Process Clause.

III

Respondents are fearful, as was the Court of Appeals, that applying the Fourth Amendment in this context inevitably will carry it into territory unknown and unforeseen: routine repossessions, negligent actions of public employees that interfere with individuals' right to enjoy their homes, and the like, thereby federalizing areas of law traditionally the concern of the States. For several reasons, we think the risk is exaggerated. To begin, our decision will have no impact on activities such as repossessions or attachments if they involve entry into the home, intrusion on individuals' privacy, or interference with their liberty, because they would implicate the Fourth Amendment even on the Court of Appeals' own terms. This was true of the Tenth Circuit's decision in Specht, with which, as we previously noted, the Court of Appeals expressed agreement.

More significantly, "reasonableness is still the ultimate standard" under the Fourth Amendment, Camara, supra, at 539, which means that numerous seizures of this type will survive constitutional scrutiny. As is true in other circumstances, the reasonableness determination will reflect a "careful balancing of governmental and private interests." T.L.O., supra, at 341. Assuming, for example, that the officers were acting pursuant to a court order, as in Specht v. Jensen, 832 F.2d 1516 (CA10 1987), or Fuentes v. Shevin, 407 U.S. 67, (1972), and, as often would be the case, a showing of unreasonableness on these facts would be a laborious task indeed. Cf. Simms v. Slacum, 3 Cranch 300, 301 (1806). Hence, while there is no guarantee against the filing of frivolous suits, had the ejection in this case properly awaited the state court's judgment, it is quite unlikely that the federal court would have been bothered with a 1983 action alleging a Fourth Amendment violation.

Moreover, we doubt that the police will often choose to further an enterprise knowing that it is contrary to the law, or proceed to seize property in the absence of objectively reasonable grounds for doing so. In short, our reaffirmance of Fourth Amendment principles today should not foment a wave of new litigation in the federal courts.

IV

The complaint here alleges that respondents, acting under color of state law, dispossessed the Soldals of their trailer home by physically tearing it from its foundation and towing it to another lot. Taking these allegations as true, this was no "garden variety" landlord-tenant or commercial dispute. The facts alleged suffice to constitute a "seizure" within the meaning of the Fourth Amendment, for they plainly implicate the interests protected by that provision. The judgment of the Court of Appeals is, accordingly, reversed, and the case is remanded for further proceedings consistent with this opinion.

So ordered.

Notes

[1] Jones' statement was prompted by a district attorney's advice that no criminal charges could be brought because, under Illinois law, a criminal action cannot be used to determine the right of possession. See Ill.Rev.Stat. ch. 110, 9-101 et seq. (1991); People v. Evans, 163 Ill.App. 3d 561, 114 Ill.Dec. 662, 516 N.E.2d 817 (1st Dist. 1987).

[2] The Soldals ultimately were evicted per court order in December 1987.

[3] Title 42 U.S.C. 1983 provides that:

"Every person who, under color of any statute, ordinance, regulation, custom or usage, of any State . . . subjects, or causes to be subjected, any citizen of the United States . . . to the deprivation of any rights, privileges, or immunities secured by the Constitution and laws, shall be liable to the party injured in an action at law, suit

in equity, or other proper proceeding for redress."

[4] The court reiterated the panel's conclusion that a conspiracy must be assumed on the state of the record and, therefore, that the case must be treated in its current posture "as if the deputy sheriffs themselves seized the trailer, disconnected it from the utilities, and towed it away." 942 F.2d 1073, 1075 (CA7 1991) (en banc).

[5] The court noted that, in light of the existence of adequate judicial remedies under state law, a claim for deprivation of property without due process of law was unlikely to succeed. Id., at 1075-1076. See Parratt v. Taylor, 451 U.S. 527 (1981). In any event, the Soldals did not claim a violation of their procedural rights. As noted, the Seventh Circuit also held that respondents had not violated the Soldals' substantive due process rights under the Fourteenth Amendment. Petitioners assert that this was error, but, in view of our disposition of the case, we need not address the question at this time.

[6] Under 42 U.S.C. 1983, the Soldals were required to establish that the respondents, acting under color of state law, deprived them of a constitutional right, in this instance, their Fourth and Fourteenth Amendment freedom from unreasonable seizures by the State. See Monroe v. Pape, 365 U.S. 167, 184 (1961). Respondents request that we affirm on the ground that the Court of Appeals erred in holding that there was sufficient state action to support a 1983 action. The alleged injury to the Soldals, it is urged, was inflicted by private parties for whom the county is not responsible. Although respondents did not cross-petition, they are entitled to ask us to affirm on that ground if such action would not enlarge the judgment of the Court of Appeals in their favor. The Court of Appeals found that, because the police prevented Soldal from using reasonable force to protect his home from private action that the officers knew was illegal, there was sufficient evidence of conspiracy between the private parties

and the officers to foreclose summary judgment for respondents. We are not inclined to review that holding. See Adickes v. S.H. Kress & Co., 398 U.S. 144, 152 -161 (1970).

[7] In holding that the Fourth Amendment's reach extends to property as such, we are mindful that the Amendment does not protect possessory interests in all kinds of property. See, e.g., Oliver v. United States, 466 U.S. 170, 176 -177 (1984). This case, however, concerns a house, which the Amendment's language explicitly includes, as it does a person's effects.

[8] Place also found that to detain luggage for 90 minutes was an unreasonable deprivation of the individual's "liberty interest in proceeding with his itinerary," which also is protected by the Fourth Amendment. 462 U.S., at 708 -710.

[9] When "operational necessities" exist, seizures can be justified on less than probable cause. 480 U.S., at 327 . That in no way affects our analysis, for even then it is clear that the Fourth Amendment applies. Ibid; see also United States v. Place, 462 U.S. 696, at 703 (1983).

[10] Of course, if the police officers' presence in the home itself entailed a violation of the Fourth Amendment, no amount of probable cause to believe that an item in plain view constitutes incriminating evidence will justify its seizure. Horton, 496 U.S., at 136 -137.

[11] It is true that Murray's Lessee v. Hoboken Land & Improvement Co., 18 How. 272 (1856), cast some doubt on the applicability of the Amendment to noncriminal encounters such as this. Id., 18 How. at 285. But cases since that time have shed a different light, making clear that Fourth Amendment guarantees are triggered by governmental searches and seizures "without regard to the use to which [houses, papers, and effects] are applied." Warden, Maryland Penitentiary v. Hayden, 387 U.S. 294, 301 (1967). Murray's Lessee's broad statement that the Fourth

Amendment "has no reference to civil proceedings for the recovery of debt" arguably only meant that the warrant requirement did not apply, as was suggested in G.M. Leasing Corp. v. United States, 429 U.S. 338, 352 (1977). Whatever its proper reading, we reaffirm today our basic understanding that the protection against unreasonable searches and seizures fully applies in the civil context.

[12] This was the view expressed by the Court of Appeals for the Tenth Circuit in Specht v. Jensen, 832 F.2d 1516 (1987), remanded on unrelated grounds, 853 F.2d 805 (1988) (en banc), with which the Seventh Circuit expressly agreed. 942 F.2d, at 1076.

[13] The officers in these cases were engaged in law enforcement, and were looking for something that was found and seized. In this broad sense, the seizures were the result of "searches," but not in the Fourth Amendment sense. That the Court of Appeals might have been suggesting that the plain-view cases are explainable because they almost always occur in the course of law enforcement activities receives some support from the penultimate sentence of the quoted passage, where the court states that the word "seizure" might lose its usual meaning "when it stands apart from a search or any other investigative activity." Id., at 1079 (emphasis added). And, in the following paragraph, it observes that, "[o]utside of the law enforcement area, the Fourth Amendment retains its force as a protection against searches, because they invade privacy. That is why we decline to confine the amendment to the law enforcement setting." Id., at 1079-1080. Even if the court meant that seizures of property in the course of law enforcement activities, whether civil or criminal, implicate interests safeguarded by the Fourth Amendment, but that pure property interests are unprotected in the non-law-enforcement setting, we are not in accord, as indicated in the body of this opinion.

Arizona v. Evans (March 1, 1995)

Chief Justice Rehnquist delivered the opinion of the Court.

This case presents the question whether evidence seized in violation of the Fourth Amendment by an officer who acted in reliance on a police record indicating the existence of an outstanding arrest warrant--a record that is later determined to be erroneous--must be suppressed by virtue of the exclusionary rule regardless of the source of the error. The Supreme Court of Arizona held that the exclusionary rule required suppression of evidence even if the erroneous information resulted from an error committed by an employee of the office of the Clerk of Court. We disagree.

In January 1991, Phoenix police officer Bryan Sargent observed respondent Evans driving the wrong way on a one way street in front of the police station. The officer stopped respondent and asked to see his driver's license. After respondent told him that his license had been suspended, the officer entered respondent's name into a computer data terminal located in his patrol car. The computer inquiry confirmed that respondent's license had been suspended and also indicated that there was an outstanding misdemeanor warrant for his arrest. Based upon the outstanding warrant, Officer Sargent placed respondent under arrest. While being handcuffed, respondent dropped a hand rolled cigarette that the officers determined smelled of marijuana. Officers proceeded to search his car and discovered a bag of marijuana under the passenger's seat.

The State charged respondent with possession of marijuana. When the police notified the Justice Court that they had arrested him, the Justice Court discovered that the arrest warrant previously had been quashed and so advised the police. Respondent argued that because his arrest was based on a warrant that had been quashed 17 days prior to his arrest, the marijuana seized incident to the arrest should be suppressed as the fruit of an unlawful arrest. Respondent also argued that "[t]he `good faith' exception to the exclusionary rule [was] inapplicable . . . because it was police error, not judicial error, which caused the invalid arrest." App. 5.

At the suppression hearing, the Chief Clerk of the Justice Court testified that a Justice of the Peace had issued the arrest warrant on December 13, 1990, because respondent had failed to appear to answer for several traffic violations. On December 19, 1990, respondent appeared before a pro tem Justice of the Peace who entered a notation in respondent's file to "quash warrant." Id., at 13.

The Chief Clerk also testified regarding the standard court procedure for quashing a warrant. Under that procedure a justice court clerk calls and informs the warrant section of the Sheriff's Office when a warrant has been quashed. The Sheriff's Office then removes the warrant from its computer records. After calling the Sheriff's Office, the clerk makes a note in the individual's file indicating the clerk who made the phone call and the person at the Sheriff's Office to whom the clerk spoke. The Chief Clerk testified that there was no indication in respondent's file that a clerk had called and notified the Sheriff's Office that his arrest warrant had been quashed. A records clerk from the Sheriff's Office also testified that the Sheriff's Office had no record of a telephone call informing it that respondent's arrest warrant had been quashed. Id., at 42-43.

At the close of testimony, respondent argued that the evidence obtained as a result of the arrest should be suppressed because "the purposes of the exclusionary rule would be served here by making the clerks for the court, or the clerk for the Sheriff's office, whoever is responsible for this mistake, to be more careful about making sure that warrants are removed from the records." Id., at 47. The trial court granted the motion to suppress because it concluded that the State had been at fault for failing to quash the warrant. Presumably because it could find no "distinction between State action, whether it happens to be the police department or not," id., at 52, the trial court made no factual finding as to whether the Justice Court or Sheriff's Office was responsible for the continued presence of the quashed warrant in the police records.

A divided panel of the Arizona Court of Appeals reversed because it "believe[d] that the exclusionary rule [was] not intended to deter justice court employees or Sheriff's Office employees who are not directly associated with the arresting officers or the arresting officers' police department." 172 Ariz. 314, 317, 836 P. 2d 1024, 1027 (1992). Therefore, it concluded, "the purpose of the exclusionary rule would not be served by excluding the evidence obtained in this case." Ibid.

The Arizona Supreme Court reversed. 177 Ariz. 201, 866 P. 2d 869 (1994). The court rejected the "distinction drawn by the court of appeals . . . between clerical errors committed by law enforcement personnel and similar mistakes by court employees." Id., at 203, 866 P. 2d, at 871. The court predicted that application of the exclusionary rule would "hopefully serve to improve the efficiency of those who keep records in our criminal justice system." Id., at 204, 866 P. 2d, at 872. Finally, the Court concluded that "[e]ven assuming that deterrence is the principal reason for application of the exclusionary rule, we disagree with the court of appeals that such a purpose would not be served where carelessness by a court clerk results in an unlawful arrest." Ibid.

We granted certiorari to determine whether the exclusionary rule requires suppression of evidence seized incident to an arrest resulting from an inaccurate computer record, regardless of whether police personnel or court personnel were responsible for the record's continued presence in the police computer. 511 U. S. ___ (1994). [n.1] We now reverse.

We first must consider whether we have jurisdiction to review the Arizona Supreme Court's decision. Respondent argues that we lack jurisdiction under 28 U.S.C. § 1257 because the Arizona Supreme Court never passed upon the Fourth Amendment issue and instead based its decision on the Arizona good faith statute, Ariz. Rev. Stat. Ann. §13-3925 (1993), an adequate and independent state ground. In the alternative, respondent asks that we remand to the Arizona Supreme Court for clarification.

In Michigan v. Long, 463 U.S. 1032 (1983), we adopted a standard for determining whether a state court decision rested upon an adequate and independent state ground. When "a state court decision fairly appears to rest primarily on federal law, or to be interwoven with the federal law, and when the adequacy and independence of any possible state law ground is not clear from the face of the opinion, we will accept as the most reasonable explanation that the state court decided the case the way it did because it believed that federal law required it to do so." Id., at 1040-1041. We adopted this practice, in part, to obviate the "unsatisfactory and intrusive practice of requiring state courts to clarify their decisions to the satisfaction of this Court." Id., at 1041. We also concluded that this approach would "provide state judges with a clearer opportunity to develop state jurisprudence unimpeded by federal interference, and yet will preserve the integrity of federal law." Ibid.

Justice Ginsburg would overrule Michigan v. Long, supra, because she believes that the rule of that case "impedes the States' ability to serve as laboratories for testing solutions to novel legal problems." Post, at 2. [n.2] The opinion in Long describes the 60 year history of the Court's differing approaches to the determination whether the judgment of the highest court of a State rested on federal or nonfederal grounds. 463 U. S., at 1038-1040. When we were in doubt, on some occasions we dismissed the writ of certiorari; on other occasions we vacated the judgment of the state court and remanded so that it might clarify the basis for its decision. See ibid. The latter approach did not always achieve the desired result and burdened the state courts with additional work. Ibid.

We believe that Michigan v. Long properly serves its purpose and should not be disturbed. Under it, state courts are absolutely free to interpret state constitutional provisions to accord greater protection to individual rights than do similar provisions of the United States Constitution. They also are free to serve as experimental laboratories, in the sense that Justice Brandeis used that term in his dissenting opinion in New State Ice Co. v. Liebmann, 285 U.S. 262, 311 (1932) (urging that the Court not impose federal constitutional restraints on the efforts of a State to "serve as a laboratory"). Under our decision today, the State of Arizona remains free to seek whatever solutions it chooses to problems of law enforcement posed by the advent of computerization. [n.3] Indeed, it is freer to do so because it is disabused of its erroneous view of what the United States Constitution requires.

State courts, in appropriate cases, are not merely free to--they are bound to--interpret the United States Constitution. In doing so, they are not free from the final authority of this Court. This principle was enunciated in Cohens v. Virginia, 6 Wheat. 264 (1821), and presumably Justice Ginsburg does not quarrel with it. [n.4] In Minnesota v. National Tea Co., 309 U.S. 551 (1940), we recognized that our authority as final arbiter of the United States Constitution could be eroded by a lack of clarity in state court decisions.

"It is fundamental that state courts be left free and unfettered by us in interpreting their state constitutions. But it is equally important that ambiguous or obscure adjudications by state courts do not stand as barriers to a determination by this Court of the validity under the federal constitution of state action. Intelligent exercise of our appellate powers compels us to ask for the elimination of the obscurities and ambiguities from the opinions in such cases. . . . For no other course assures that important federal issues, such as have been argued here, will reach this Court for adjudication; that state courts will not be the final arbiters of important issues under the federal constitution; and that we will not encroach on the constitutional jurisdiction of the states." Id., at 557.

We therefore adhere to the standard adopted in Michigan v. Long, supra.

Applying that standard here, we conclude that we have jurisdiction. In reversing the Court of Appeals, the Arizona Supreme Court stated that "[w]hile it may be inappropriate to invoke the exclusionary rule where a magistrate has issued a facially valid warrant (a discretionary judicial function) based on an erroneous evaluation of the facts, the law, or both, Leon, 468 U.S. 897 . . . (1984), it is useful and proper to do so where negligent record keeping (a purely clerical function) results in an unlawful arrest." 177 Ariz., at 204, 866 P. 2d, at 872. Thus, the Arizona Supreme Court's decision to suppress the evidence was based squarely upon its interpretation of federal law. See ibid. Nor did it offer a plain statement that its references to federal law were "being used only for the purpose of guidance, and d[id] not themselves compel the result that [it] reached." Long, supra, at 1041.

The Fourth Amendment states that "[t]he right of the people to be secure in their persons, houses, papers, and effects, against unreasonable searches and seizures, shall not be violated, and no Warrants shall issue, but upon probable cause, supported by Oath or affirmation, and particularly describing the place to be searched, and the persons or things to be seized." U. S. Const. We have recognized, however, that the Fourth Amendment contains no provision expressly precluding the use of evidence obtained in violation of its commands. See United States v. Leon, 468 U.S. 897, 906 (1984). "The wrong condemned by the [Fourth] Amendment is `fully accomplished' by the unlawful search or seizure itself," ibid. (quoting United States v. Calandra, 414 U.S. 338, 354 (1974)), and the use of the fruits of a past unlawful search or seizure " `work[s] no new Fourth Amendment wrong,' " Leon, supra, at 906 (quoting Calandra, supra, at 354).

"The question whether the exclusionary rule's remedy is appropriate in a particular context has long been regarded as an issue separate from the question whether the Fourth Amendment rights of the party seeking to invoke the rule were violated by police conduct." Illinois v. Gates, 462 U.S. 213, 223 (1983); see also United States v. Havens, 446 U.S. 620, 627-628 (1980); Stone v. Powell, 428 U.S. 465, 486-487 (1976); Calandra, supra, at 348. The exclusionary rule operates as a judicially created remedy designed to safeguard against future violations of Fourth Amendment rights through the rule's general deterrent effect. Leon, supra, at 906; Calandra, supra, at 348. As with any remedial device, the rule's application has been restricted to those instances where its remedial objectives are thought most efficaciously served. Leon, supra, at 908; Calandra, supra, at 348. Where "the exclusionary rule does not result in appreciable deterrence, then, clearly, its use. . . is unwarranted." United States v. Janis, 428 U.S. 433, 454 (1976).

In Leon, we applied these principles to the context of a police search in which the officers had acted in objectively reasonable reliance on a search warrant, issued by a neutral and detached Magistrate, that later was determined to be invalid. 468 U. S., at 905. On the basis of three factors, we determined that there was no sound reason to apply the exclusionary rule as a means of deterring misconduct on the part of judicial officers who are responsible for issuing warrants. See Illinois v. Krull, 480 U.S. 340, 348 (1987) (analyzing Leon, supra). First, we noted that the exclusionary rule was historically designed " `to deter police misconduct rather than to punish the errors of judges and magistrates.' " Krull, supra, at 348 (quoting Leon, supra, at 916). Second, there was " `no evidence suggesting that judges and magistrates are inclined to ignore or subvert the Fourth Amendment or that lawlessness among these actors requires the application of the extreme sanction of exclusion.' " Krull, supra, at 348 (quoting Leon, supra, at 916). Third, and of greatest importance, there was no basis for believing that exclusion of evidence seized pursuant to a warrant would have a significant deterrent effect on the issuing judge or magistrate. Krull, supra, at 348.

The Leon Court then examined whether application of the exclusionary rule could be expected to alter the behavior of the law enforcement officers. We concluded:

"[W]here the officer's conduct is objectively reasonable, `excluding the evidence will not further the ends of the exclusionary rule in any appreciable way; for it is painfully apparent that . . . the officer is acting as a reasonable officer would and should act in similar circumstances. Excluding the evidence can in no way affect his future conduct unless it is to make him less willing to do his duty.' " Leon, supra, at 919-920 (quoting Stone v. Powell, supra, at 539-540 (White, J., dissenting)).

See also Massachusetts v. Sheppard, 468 U.S. 981, 990-991 (1984) ("[S]uppressing evidence because the judge failed to make all the necessary clerical corrections despite his assurances that such changes would be made will not serve the deterrent function that the exclusionary rule was designed to achieve"). Thus, we held that the "marginal or nonexistent benefits produced by suppressing evidence obtained in objectively reasonable reliance on a subsequently invalidated search warrant cannot justify the substantial costs of exclusion." Leon, supra, at 922.

Respondent relies on United States v. Hensley, 469 U.S. 221 (1985), and argues that the evidence seized incident to his arrest should be suppressed because he was the victim of a Fourth Amendment violation. Brief for Respondent 10-12, 21-22. In Hensley, the Court determined that evidence uncovered as a result of a Terry stop was admissible because the officers who made the stop acted in objectively reasonable reliance on a flyer that had been issued by officers of another police department who possessed a reasonable suspicion to justify a Terry stop. 469 U. S., at 231. Because the Hensley Court determined that there had been no Fourth Amendment violation, id., at 236, the Court never considered whether the seized evidence should have been excluded. Hensley does not contradict our earlier pronouncements that "[t]he question whether the exclusionary rule's remedy is appropriate in a particular context has long been regarded as an issue separate from the question whether the Fourth Amendment rights of the party seeking to invoke the rule were violated by police conduct." Gates, supra, at 223; see also Stone v. Powell, supra, at 486-487; Calandra, 414 U. S., at 348. Respondent also argues that Whiteley v. Warden, Wyoming State Penitentiary, 401 U.S. 560 (1971), compels exclusion of the evidence. In Whiteley, the Court determined that the Fourth Amendment had been violated when police officers arrested Whiteley and recovered inculpatory evidence based upon a radio report that two suspects had been involved in two robberies. Id., at 568-569. Although the "police were entitled to act on the strength of the radio bulletin," the Court determined that there had been a Fourth Amendment violation because the initial complaint, upon which the arrest warrant and subsequent radio bulletin were based, was insufficient to support an independent judicial assessment of probable cause. Id., at 568. The Court concluded that "an otherwise illegal arrest cannot be insulated from challenge by the decision of the instigating officer to rely on fellow officers to make the arrest." Ibid. Because the "arrest violated [Whiteley's] constitutional rights under the Fourth and Fourteenth Amendments; the evidence secured as an incident thereto should have been excluded from his trial. Mapp v. Ohio, 367 U.S. 643 (1961)." Whiteley, supra, at 568-569.

Although Whiteley clearly retains relevance in determining whether police officers have violated the Fourth Amendment, see Hensley, supra, at 230-231, its precedential value regarding application of the exclusionary rule is dubious. In Whiteley, the Court treated identification of a Fourth Amendment violation as synonymous with application of the exclusionary rule to evidence secured incident to that violation. 401 U. S., at 568-569. Subsequent case law has rejected this reflexive application of the exclusionary rule. Cf. Krull, supra; Sheppard, supra; United States v. Leon, 468 U.S. 897 (1984); Calandra, supra. These later cases have emphasized that the issue of exclusion is separate from whether the Fourth Amendment has been violated, see e.g., Leon, supra, at 906, and exclusion is appropriate only if the remedial objectives of the rule are thought most efficaciously served, see Calandra, supra, at 348.

Our approach is consistent with the dissenting Justices' position in Illinois v. Krull, our only major case since Leon and Sheppard involving the good faith exception to the exclusionary rule. In that case, the Court found that the good faith exception applies when an officer conducts a search in objectively reasonable reliance on the constitutionality of a statute that subsequently is declared unconstitutional. Krull, 480 U. S., at 346. Even the dissenting Justices in Krull agreed that

Leon provided the proper framework for analyzing whether the exclusionary rule applied; they simply thought that "application of Leon's stated rationales le[d] to a contrary result." 480 U. S., at 362 (O'Connor, J., dissenting). In sum, respondent does not persuade us to abandon the Leon framework.

Applying the reasoning of Leon to the facts of this case, we conclude that the decision of the Arizona Supreme Court must be reversed. The Arizona Supreme Court determined that it could not "support the distinction drawn . . . between clerical errors committed by law enforcement personnel and similar mistakes by court employees," 177 Ariz., at 203, 866 P. 2d, at 871, and that "even assuming . . . that responsibility for the error rested with the justice court, it does not follow that the exclusionary rule should be inapplicable to these facts," ibid.

This holding is contrary to the reasoning of Leon, supra; Massachusetts v. Sheppard, 480 U.S. 981 (1984); and, Krull, supra. If court employees were responsible for the erroneous computer record, the exclusion of evidence at trial would not sufficiently deter future errors so as to warrant such a severe sanction. First, as we noted in Leon, the exclusionary rule was historically designed as a means of deterring police misconduct, not mistakes by court employees. See Leon, supra, at 916; see also Krull, supra, at 350. Second, respondent offers no evidence that court employees are inclined to ignore or subvert the Fourth Amendment or that lawlessness among these actors requires application of the extreme sanction of exclusion. See Leon, supra, at 916, and n. 14; see also Krull, supra, at 350-351. To the contrary, the Chief Clerk of the Justice Court testified at the suppression hearing that this type of error occurred once every three or four years. App. 37.

Finally, and most important, there is no basis for believing that application of the exclusionary rule in these circumstances will have a significant effect on court employees responsible for informing the police that a warrant has been quashed. Because court clerks are not adjuncts to the law enforcement team engaged in the often competitive enterprise of ferreting out crime, see Johnson v. United States, 333 U.S. 10, 14 (1948), they have no stake in the outcome of particular criminal prosecutions. Cf. Leon, supra, at 917; Krull, supra, at 352. The threat of exclusion of evidence could not be expected to deter such individuals from failing to inform police officials that a warrant had been quashed. Cf. Leon, supra, at 917; Krull, supra, at 352.

If it were indeed a court clerk who was responsible for the erroneous entry on the police computer, application of the exclusionary rule also could not be expected to alter the behavior of the arresting officer. As the trial court in this case stated: "I think the police officer [was] bound to arrest. I think he would [have been] derelict in his duty if he failed to arrest." App. 51. Cf. Leon, supra, at 920 (" `Excluding the evidence can in no way affect [the officer's] future conduct unless it is to make him less willing to do his duty.' " quoting Stone v. Powell, 428 U. S., at 540 (White, J., dissenting)). The Chief Clerk of the Justice Court testified that this type of error occurred "on[c]e every three or four years." App. 37. In fact, once the court clerks discovered the error, they immediately corrected it, id., at 30, and then proceeded to search their files to make sure that no similar mistakes had occurred, id., at 37. There is no indication that the arresting officer was not acting objectively reasonably when he relied upon the police computer record. Application of the Leon framework supports a categorical exception to the exclusionary rule for clerical errors of court employees. See Leon, 468 U. S., at 916-922; Sheppard, supra, at 990-991. [n.5]

The judgment of the Supreme Court of Arizona is therefore reversed, and the case is remanded to that court for proceedings not inconsistent with this opinion.

It is so ordered.

Notes

1 Petitioner has conceded that respondent's arrest violated the Fourth Amendment. Brief for Petitioner 10. We decline to review that determination. Cf. United States v. Leon, 468 U.S. 897, 905 (1984); Illinois v. Krull, 480 U.S. 340, 357, n. 13 (1987).

2 Justice Ginsburg certainly is correct when she notes that " `[s]ince Long, we repeatedly have followed [its] "plain statement" requirement.' " Post, at 11 (quoting Harris v. Reed, 489 U.S. 255, 261, n. 7 (1989) (opinion of Blackmun, J.)); see also Illinois v. Rodriguez, 497 U.S. 177, 182 (1990) (opinion of Scalia, J.); Pennsylvania v. Muniz, 496 U.S. 582, 588, n. 4 (1990) (opinion of Brennan, J.); Maryland v. Garrison, 480 U.S. 79, 83-84 (1987) (opinion of Stevens, J.); Caldwell v. Mississippi, 472 U.S. 320, 327-328 (1985) (opinion of Marshall, J.); California v. Carney, 471 U.S. 386, 389, n. 1 (1985) (opinion of Burger, C. J.); Ohio v. Johnson, 467 U.S. 493, 497-498, n. 7 (1984) (opinion of Rehnquist, J.); Oliver v. United States, 466 U.S. 170, 175-176, n. 5 (1984) (opinion of Powell, J.); cf. Coleman v. Thompson, 501 U.S. 722, 740 (1991) (opinion of O'Connor, J.) (declining to expand the Long and Harris presumption to instances "where the relevant state court decision does not fairly appear to rest primarily on federal law or to be interwoven with such law").

3 Justice Ginsburg acknowledges as much when she states that since Long, "state courts, on remand, have reinstated their prior judgments after clarifying their reliance on state grounds." Post, at 10 (citing statistics).

4 Surely if we have jurisdiction to vacate and remand a state court judgment for clarification, post, at 12, n. 7, we also must have jurisdiction to determine whether a state court judgment is based upon an adequate and independent state ground. See Abie State Bank v. Bryan, 282 U.S. 765, 773 (1931).

5 The Solicitor General, as amicus curiae, argues that an analysis similar to that we apply here to court personnel also would apply in order to determine whether the evidence should be suppressed if police personnel were responsible for the error. As the State has not made any such argument here, we agree that "[t]he record in this case . . . does not adequately present that issue for the Court's consideration." Brief for United States as Amicus Curiae 13. Accordingly, we decline to address that question.

Maryland v. Wilson (Feb 19, 1997)

Chief Justice Rehnquist delivered the opinion of the Court.

In this case we consider whether the rule of Pennsylvania v. Mimms, 434 U.S. 106 (1977), that a police officer may as a matter of course order the driver of a lawfully stopped car to exit his vehicle, extends to passengers as well. We hold that it does.

At about 7:30 p.m. on a June evening, Maryland state trooper David Hughes observed a passenger car driving southbound on I-95 in Baltimore County at a speed of 64 miles per hour. The posted speed limit was 55 miles per hour, and the car had no regular license tag; there was a torn piece of paper reading "Enterprise Rent A Car" dangling from its rear. Hughes activated his lights and sirens, signaling the car to pull over, but it continued driving for another mile and a half until it finally did so.

During the pursuit, Hughes noticed that there were three occupants in the car and that the two passengers turned to look at him several times, repeatedly ducking below sight level and then reappearing. As Hughes approached the car on foot, the driver alighted and met him halfway. The driver was trembling and appeared extremely nervous, but nonetheless produced a valid Connecticut driver's license. Hughes instructed him to return to the car and retrieve the rental documents, and he complied. During this encounter, Hughes noticed that the front seat passenger, respondent Jerry Lee Wilson, was sweating and also appeared extremely nervous. While the driver was sitting in the driver's seat looking for the rental papers, Hughes ordered Wilson out of the car.

When Wilson exited the car, a quantity of crack cocaine fell to the ground. Wilson was then arrested and charged with possession of cocaine with intent to distribute. Before trial, Wilson moved to suppress the evidence, arguing that Hughes' ordering him out of the car constituted an unreasonable seizure under the Fourth Amendment. The Circuit Court for Baltimore County agreed, and granted respondent's motion to suppress. On appeal, the Court of Special Appeals of Maryland affirmed, 106 Md. App. 24, 664 A. 2d 1 (1995), ruling that Pennsylvania v. Mimms does not apply to passengers. The Court of Appeals of Maryland denied certiorari. 340 Md. 502, 667 A. 2d 342 (1995). We granted certiorari, 518 U. S. ____ (1996), and now reverse.

In Mimms, we considered a traffic stop much like the one before us today. There, Mimms had been stopped for driving with an expired license plate, and the officer asked him to step out of his car. When Mimms did so, the officer noticed a bulge in his jacket that proved to be a .38-caliber revolver, whereupon Mimms was arrested for carrying a concealed deadly weapon. Mimms, like Wilson, urged the suppression of the evidence on the ground that the officer's ordering him out of the car was an unreasonable seizure, and the Pennsylvania Supreme Court, like the Court of Special Appeals of Maryland, agreed.

We reversed, explaining that "[t]he touchstone of our analysis under the Fourth Amendment is always `the reasonableness in all the circumstances of the particular governmental invasion of a citizen's personal security,' "434 U. S., at 108-109 (quoting Terry v. Ohio, 392 U.S. 1, 19 (1968)), and that reasonableness "depends `on a balance between the public interest and the individual's right to personal security free from arbitrary interference by law officers,' " id., at 109 (quoting United States v. Brignoni-Ponce, 422 U.S. 873, 878 (1975)). On the public interest side of the balance, we noted that the State "freely concede[d]" that there had been nothing unusual or suspicious to justify ordering Mimms out of the car, but that it was the officer's "practice to order all drivers [stopped in traffic stops] out of their vehicles as a matter of course" as a "precautionary measure" to protect the officer's safety. Id., at 109-110. We thought it "too plain for argument" that this justification--officer safety--was "both legitimate and weighty." Id., at 110. In addition, we observed that the danger to the officer of standing by the driver's door and in the path of oncoming traffic might also be "appreciable." Id., at 111.

On the other side of the balance, we considered the intrusion into the driver's liberty occasioned by the officer's ordering him out of the car. Noting that the driver's car was already validly stopped for a traffic infraction, we deemed the additional intrusion of asking him to step outside his car "de minimis." Ibid. Accordingly, we concluded that "once a motor vehicle has been lawfully detained for a traffic violation, the police officers may order the driver to get out of the vehicle without violating the Fourth Amendment's proscription of unreasonable seizures." Id., at 111, n. 6.

Respondent urges, and the lower courts agreed, that this per se rule does not apply to Wilson because he was a passenger, not the driver. Maryland, in turn, argues that we have already implicitly decided this question by our statement in Michigan v. Long, 463 U.S. 1032 (1983), that "[i]n [Mimms], we held that police may order persons out of an automobile during a stop for a traffic violation," id., at 1047-1048 (emphasis added), and by Justice Powell's statement in Rakas v. Illinois, 439 U.S. 128 (1978), that "this Court determined in [Mimms] that passengers in automobiles have no Fourth Amendment right not to be ordered from their vehicle, once a proper stop is made," id., at 155, n. 4 (Powell, J., joined by Burger, C. J., concurring) (emphasis added). We agree with respondent that the former statement was dictum, and the latter was contained in a concurrence, so that neither constitutes binding precedent.

We must therefore now decide whether the rule of Mimms applies to passengers as well as to drivers. [n.1] On the public interest side of the balance, the same weighty interest in officer safety is present regardless of whether the occupant of the stopped car is a driver or passenger. Regrettably, traffic stops may be dangerous encounters. In 1994 alone, there were 5,762 officer assaults and 11 officers killed during traffic pursuits and stops. Federal Bureau of Investigation, Uniform Crime Reports: Law Enforcement Officers Killed and Assaulted 71, 33 (1994). In the case of passengers, the danger of the officer's standing in the path of oncoming traffic would not be present except in the case of a passenger in the left rear seat, but the fact that there is more than one occupant of the vehicle increases the possible sources of harm to the officer. [n.2]

On the personal liberty side of the balance, the case for the passengers is in one sense stronger than that for the driver. There is probable cause to believe that the driver has committed a minor vehicular offense, but there is no such reason to stop or detain the passengers. But as a practical matter, the passengers are already stopped by virtue of the stop of the vehicle. The only change in their circumstances which will result from ordering them out of the car is that they will be outside of, rather than inside of, the stopped car. Outside the car, the passengers will be denied access to any possible weapon that might be concealed in the interior of the passenger compartment. It would seem that the possibility of a violent encounter stems not from the ordinary reaction of a motorist stopped for a speeding violation, but from the fact that evidence of a more serious crime might be uncovered during the stop. And the motivation of a passenger to employ violence to prevent apprehension of such a crime is every bit as great as that of the driver.

We think that our opinion in Michigan v. Summers, 452 U.S. 692 (1981), offers guidance by analogy here. There the police had obtained a search warrant for contraband thought to be located in a residence, but when they arrived to execute the warrant they found Summers coming down the front steps. The question in the case depended "upon a determination whether the officers had the authority to require him to re enter the house and to remain there while they conducted their search." Id., at 695. In holding as it did, the Court said:

"Although no special danger to the police is suggested by the evidence in this record, the execution of a warrant to search for narcotics is the kind of transaction that may give rise to sudden violence or frantic efforts to conceal or destroy evidence. The risk of harm to both the police and the occupants is minimized if the officers routinely exercise unquestioned command of the situation." Id., at 702-703 (footnote omitted).

In summary, danger to an officer from a traffic stop is likely to be greater when there are passengers in addition to the driver in the stopped car. While there is not the same basis for ordering the passengers out of the car as there is for ordering the driver out, the additional intrusion on the passenger is minimal. We therefore hold that an officer making a traffic stop may order passengers to get out of the car pending completion of the stop. [n.3]

The judgment of the Court of Special Appeals of Maryland is reversed, and the case is remanded for proceedings not inconsistent with this opinion.

It is so ordered.

Notes

1 Respondent argues that, because we have generally eschewed bright line rules in the Fourth Amendment context, see, e.g., Ohio v. Robinette, 519 U. S. ____ (1996), we should not here conclude that passengers may constitutionally be ordered out of lawfully stopped vehicles. But, that we typically avoid per se rules concerning searches and seizures does not mean that we have always done so; Mimms itself drew a bright line, and we believe the principles that underlay that decision apply to passengers as well.

2 Justice Stevens' dissenting opinion points out, post, at 2-3, that these statistics are not further broken down as to assaults by passengers and assaults by drivers. It is, indeed, regrettable that the empirical data on a subject such as this are sparse, but we need not ignore the data which do exist simply because further refinement would be even more helpful. Justice Stevens agrees that there is "a strong public interest in minimizing" the number of assaults on law officers, post, at 2, and we believe that our holding today is more likely to accomplish that result than would be the case if his views were to prevail.

3 Maryland urges us to go further and hold that an officer may forcibly detain a passenger for the entire duration of the stop. But respondent was subjected to no detention based on the stopping of the car once he had left it; his arrest was based on probable cause to believe that he was guilty of possession of cocaine with intent to distribute. The question which Maryland wishes answered, therefore, is not presented by this case, and we express no opinion upon it.

Chandler v. Miller (April 15, 1997) [Notes omitted]

Justice Ginsburg delivered the opinion of the Court.

The Fourth Amendment requires government to respect "[t]he right of the people to be secure in their persons . . . against unreasonable searches and seizures." This restraint on government conduct generally bars officials from undertaking a search or seizure absent individualized suspicion. Searches conducted without grounds for suspicion of particular individuals have been upheld, however, in "certain limited circumstances." See Treasury Employees v. Von Raab, 489 U.S. 656, 668 (1989). These circumstances include brief stops for questioning or observation at a fixed Border Patrol checkpoint, United States v. Martinez Fuerte, 428 U.S. 543, 545-550, 566-567 (1976), or at a sobriety checkpoint, Michigan Dept. of State Police v. Sitz, 496 U.S. 444, 447, 455 (1990), and administrative inspections in "closely regulated" businesses, New York v. Burger, 482 U.S. 691, 703-704 (1987).

Georgia requires candidates for designated state offices to certify that they have taken a drug test and that the test result was negative. Ga. Code Ann. §21-2-140 (1993) (hereinafter §21-2-140). We confront in this case the question whether that requirement ranks among the limited circumstances in which suspicionless searches are warranted. Relying on this Court's precedents sustaining drug testing programs for student athletes, customs employees, and railway employees, see Vernonia School Dist. 47J v. Acton, 515 U. S. ____, ____ (1995) (slip op., at 3, 19-20) (random drug testing of students who participate in interscholastic sports); Von Raab, 489 U. S., at 659 (drug tests for United States Customs Service employees who seek transfer or promotion to certain positions); Skinner v. Railway Labor Executives' Assn., 489 U.S. 602, 608-613 (1989) (drug and alcohol tests for railway employees involved in train accidents and for those who violate particular safety rules), the United States Court of Appeals for the Eleventh Circuit judged Georgia's law constitutional. We reverse that judgment. Georgia's requirement that candidates for state office pass a drug test, we hold, does not fit within the closely guarded category of constitutionally permissible suspicionless searches.

The prescription at issue, approved by the Georgia Legislature in 1990, orders that "[e]ach candidate seeking to qualify for nomination or election to a state office shall as a condition of such qualification be required to certify that such candidate has tested negative for illegal drugs." §21-2-140(b). Georgia was the first, and apparently remains the only, State to condition candidacy for state office on a drug test.

Under the Georgia statute, to qualify for a place on the ballot, a candidate must present a certificate from a state approved laboratory, in a form approved by the Secretary of State, reporting that the candidate submitted to a urinalysis drug test within 30 days prior to qualifying for nomination or election and that the results were negative. §21-2-140(c). The statute lists as "[i]llegal drug[s]": marijuana, cocaine, opiates, amphetamines, and phencyclidines. §21-2-140(a)(3). The designated state offices are: "the Governor, Lieutenant Governor, Secretary of State, Attorney General, State School Superintendent, Commissioner of Insurance, Commissioner of Agriculture, Commissioner of Labor, Justices of the Supreme Court, Judges of the Court of Appeals, judges of the superior courts, district attorneys, members of the General Assembly, and members of the Public Service Commission." §21-2-140(a)(4).

Candidate drug tests are to be administered in a manner consistent with the United States Department of Health and Human Services Guidelines, 53 Fed. Reg. 11979-11989 (1988), or other professionally valid procedures approved by Georgia's Commissioner of Human Resources. See §21-2-140(a)(2). A candidate may provide the test specimen at a laboratory approved by the State, or at the office of the candidate's personal physician, see App. 4-5 (Joint Statement of Undisputed Facts). Once a urine sample is obtained, an approved laboratory determines whether any of the five specified illegal drugs are present, id., at 5; §21-2-140(c), and prepares a certificate reporting the test results to the candidate.

Petitioners were Libertarian Party nominees in 1994 for state offices subject to the requirements of §21-2-140. The Party nominated Walker L. Chandler for the office of Lieutenant Governor, Sharon T. Harris for the office of Commissioner of Agriculture, and James D. Walker for the office of member of the General Assembly. In May 1994, about one month before the deadline for submission of the certificates required by §21-2-140, petitioners Chandler, Harris, and Walker filed this action in the United States District Court for the Northern District of Georgia. They asserted, inter alia, that the drug tests required by §21-2-140 violated their rights under the First, Fourth, and Fourteenth Amendments to the United States Constitution. Naming as defendants Governor Zell D. Miller and two other state officials involved in the administration of §21-2-140, petitioners requested declaratory and injunctive relief barring enforcement of the statute.

In June 1994, the District Court denied petitioners' motion for a preliminary injunction. Stressing the importance of the state offices sought and the relative unintrusiveness of the testing procedure, the court found it unlikely that petitioners would prevail on the merits of their claims. App. to Pet. for Cert. 5B. Petitioners apparently submitted to the drug tests, obtained the certificates required by §21-2-140, and appeared on the ballot. See Tr. of Oral Arg. 5. After the 1994 election, the parties jointly moved for the entry of final judgment on stipulated facts. In January 1995, the District Court entered final judgment for respondents.

A divided Eleventh Circuit panel affirmed. 73 F. 3d 1543 (1996). It is settled law, the court accepted, that the drug tests required by the statute rank as searches. But, as was true of the drug testing programs at issue in Skinner and Von Raab, the court reasoned, §21-2-140 serves "special needs," interests other than the ordinary needs of law enforcement. The court therefore endeavored to " `balance the individual's privacy expectations against the Government's interests to determine whether it [was] impractical to require a warrant or some level of individualized suspicion in the particular context.' " 73 F. 3d, at 1545 (quoting Von Raab, 489 U. S., at 665-666).

Examining the state interests involved, the court acknowledged the absence of any record of drug abuse by elected officials in Georgia. Nonetheless, the court observed, "[t]he people of Georgia place in the trust of their elected officials . . . their liberty, their safety, their economic well being, [and] ultimate responsibility for law enforcement." 73 F. 3d, at 1546. Consequently, "those vested with the highest executive authority to make public policy in general and frequently to supervise Georgia's drug interdiction efforts in particular must be persons appreciative of the perils of drug use." Ibid. The court further noted that "[t]he nature of high public office in itself demands the highest levels of honesty, clear sightedness, and clear thinking." Ibid. Reciting responsibilities of the offices petitioners sought, the Court of Appeals perceived those "positions [as] particularly susceptible to the `risks of bribery and blackmail against which the Government is

entitled to guard.' " Ibid. (quoting Von Raab, 489 U. S., at 674).

Turning to petitioners' privacy interests, the Eleventh Circuit emphasized that the tests could be conducted in the office of the candidate's private physician, making the "intrusion here . . . even less than that approved in Von Raab." 73 F. 3d, at 1547. The court also noted the statute's reference to federally approved drug testing guidelines. Ibid. The drug test itself would reveal only the presence or absence of indicia of the use of particular drugs, and not any other information about the health of the candidate. Furthermore, the candidate would control release of the test results: Should the candidate test positive, he or she could forfeit the opportunity to run for office, and in that event, nothing would be divulged to law enforcement officials. Ibid. Another consideration, the court said, is the reality that "candidates for high office must expect the voters to demand some disclosures about their physical, emotional, and mental fitness for the position." Ibid. Concluding that the State's interests outweighed the privacy intrusion caused by the required certification, the court held the statute, as applied to petitioners, not inconsistent with the Fourth and Fourteenth Amendments. Ibid. [n.1]

Judge Barkett dissented. In her view, a balance of the State's and candidates' interests was not appropriate, for the State had failed to establish a special governmental need for the regime. "There is nothing so special or immediate about the generalized governmental interests involved here," she observed, "as to warrant suspension of the Fourth Amendment's requirement of individualized suspicion for searches and seizures." Id., at 1551.

We granted the petition for certiorari, 518 U. S. ____ (1996), and now reverse. [n.2]

We begin our discussion of this case with an uncontested point: Georgia's drug testing requirement, imposed by law and enforced by state officials, effects a search within the meaning of the Fourth and Fourteenth Amendments. See Skinner, 489 U. S., at 617; Tr. of Oral Arg. 36; Brief for United States as Amicus Curiae 10 (collection and testing of urine to meet Georgia's certification statute "constitutes a search subject to the demands of the Fourth Amendment" (internal quotation marks omitted)). As explained in Skinner, government ordered "collection and testing of urine intrudes upon expectations of privacy that society has long recognized as reasonable." 489 U. S., at 617. Because "these intrusions [are] searches under the Fourth Amendment," ibid., we focus on the question: Are the searches reasonable?

To be reasonable under the Fourth Amendment, a search ordinarily must be based on individualized suspicion of wrongdoing. See Vernonia, 515 U. S., at ____--____ (slip op., at 5-6). But particularized exceptions to the main rule are sometimes warranted based on "special needs, beyond the normal need for law enforcement." Skinner, 489 U. S., at 619 (internal quotation marks omitted). When such "special needs"-- concerns other than crime detection--are alleged in justification of a Fourth Amendment intrusion, courts must undertake a context specific inquiry, examining closely the competing private and public interests advanced by the parties. See Von Raab, 489 U. S., at 665-666; see also id., at 668. As Skinner stated: "In limited circumstances, where the privacy interests implicated by the search are minimal, and where an important governmental interest furthered by the intrusion would be placed in jeopardy by a requirement of individualized suspicion, a search may be reasonable despite the absence of such suspicion." 489 U. S., at 624.

In evaluating Georgia's ballot access, drug testing statute--a measure plainly not tied to individualized suspicion--the Eleventh Circuit sought to " `balance the individual's privacy expectations against the [State's] interests,' " 73 F.

3d, at 1545 (quoting Von Raab, 489 U. S., at 665), in line with our precedents most immediately in point: Skinner, Von Raab, and Vernonia. We review those decisions before inspecting Georgia's law.

Skinner concerned Federal Railroad Administration (FRA) regulations that required blood and urine tests of rail employees involved in train accidents; the regulations also authorized railroads to administer breath and urine tests to employees who violated certain safety rules. 489 U. S., at 608-612. The FRA adopted the drug testing program in response to evidence of drug and alcohol abuse by some railroad employees, the obvious safety hazards posed by such abuse, and the documented link between drug and alcohol impaired employees and the incidence of train accidents. Id., at 607-608. Recognizing that the urinalysis tests, most conspicuously, raised evident privacy concerns, the Court noted two offsetting considerations: First, the regulations reduced the intrusiveness of the collection process, id., at 626; and, more important, railway employees, "by reason of their participation in an industry that is regulated pervasively to ensure safety," had diminished expectations of privacy, id., at 627.

"[S]urpassing safety interests," the Court concluded, warranted the FRA testing program. Id., at 634. The drug tests could deter illegal drug use by railroad employees, workers positioned to "cause great human loss before any signs of impairment become noticeable to supervisors." Id., at 628. The program also helped railroads to obtain invaluable information about the causes of major train accidents. See id., at 630. Testing without a showing of individualized suspicion was essential, the Court explained, if these vital interests were to be served. See id., at 628. Employees could not forecast the timing of an accident or a safety violation, events that would trigger testing. The employee's inability to avoid detection simply by staying drug free at a prescribed test time significantly enhanced the deterrent effect of the program. See ibid. Furthermore, imposing an individualized suspicion requirement for a drug test in the chaotic aftermath of a train accident would seriously impede an employer's ability to discern the cause of the accident; indeed, waiting until suspect individuals could be identified "likely would result in the loss or deterioration of the evidence furnished by the tests." Id., at 631.

In Von Raab, the Court sustained a United States Customs Service program that made drug tests a condition of promotion or transfer to positions directly involving drug interdiction or requiring the employee to carry a firearm. 489 U. S., at 660-661, 667-677. [n.3] While the Service's regime was not prompted by a demonstrated drug abuse problem, id., at 660, it was developed for an agency with an "almost unique mission," id., at 674, as the "first line of defense" against the smuggling of illicit drugs into the United States, id. at 668. Work directly involving drug interdiction and posts that require the employee to carry a firearm pose grave safety threats to employees who hold those positions, and also expose them to large amounts of illegal narcotics and to persons engaged in crime; illicit drug users in such high risk positions might be unsympathetic to the Service's mission, tempted by bribes, or even threatened with blackmail. See id., at 668-671. The Court held that the government had a "compelling" interest in assuring that employees placed in these positions would not include drug users. See id., at 670-671. Individualized suspicion would not work in this setting, the Court determined, because it was "not feasible to subject [these] employees and their work product to the kind of day to day scrutiny that is the norm in more traditional office environments." Id., at 674.

Finally, in Vernonia, the Court sustained a random drug testing program for high school students engaged in interscholastic athletic competitions. The program's context was critical, for local governments bear large "responsibilities, under a public school system, as guardian and tutor of children entrusted to its care." 515 U. S., at ____ (slip op., at 19). An "immediate crisis," id., at ____ (slip op., at 17), caused by "a sharp increase in drug use" in the school district, id., at ____ (slip op., at 1), sparked installation of the program. District Court findings established that student athletes were not only "among the drug users," they were "leaders of the drug culture." Id., at ____ (slip op., at 2). Our decision noted that " `students within the school environment have a lesser expectation of privacy than members of the population generally.' " Id., at ____ (slip op., at 10) (quoting New Jersey v. T. L. O., 469 U.S. 325, 348 (1985) (Powell, J., concurring)). We emphasized the importance of deterring drug use by schoolchildren and the risk of injury a drug using student athlete cast on himself and those engaged with him on the playing field. See Vernonia, 515 U. S., at ____ (slip op., at 16).

Respondents urge that the precedents just examined are not the sole guides for assessing the constitutional validity of the Georgia statute. The "special needs" analysis, they contend, must be viewed through a different lens because §21-2-140 implicates Georgia's sovereign power, reserved to it under the Tenth Amendment, to establish qualifications for those who seek state office. Respondents rely on Gregory v. Ashcroft, 501 U.S. 452 (1991), which upheld against federal statutory and Equal Protection Clause challenges Missouri's mandatory retirement age of 70 for state judges. The Court found this age classification reasonable and not barred by the federal legislation. See id., at 473. States, Gregory reaffirmed, enjoy wide latitude to establish conditions of candidacy for state office, but in setting such conditions, they may not disregard basic constitutional protections. See id., at 463; McDaniel v. Paty, 435 U.S. 618 (1978) (invalidating state provision prohibiting members of clergy from serving as delegates to state constitutional convention); Communist Party of Ind. v. Whitcomb, 414 U.S. 441 (1974) (voiding loyalty oath as a condition of ballot access); Bond v. Floyd, 385 U.S. 116 (1966) (Georgia Legislature could not exclude elected representative on ground that his antiwar statements cast doubt on his ability to take an oath). We are aware of no precedent suggesting that a State's power to establish qualifications for state offices--any more than its sovereign power to prosecute crime--diminishes the constraints on state action imposed by the Fourth Amendment. We therefore reject respondents' invitation to apply in this case a framework extraordinarily deferential to state measures setting conditions of candidacy for state office. Our guides remain Skinner, Von Raab, and Vernonia.

Turning to those guides, we note, first, that the testing method the Georgia statute describes is relatively noninvasive; therefore, if the "special need" showing had been made, the State could not be faulted for excessive intrusion. Georgia's statute invokes the drug testing guidelines applicable to the federal programs upheld in Skinner and Von Raab. See Brief for United States as Amicus Curiae 20-21; Von Raab, 489 U. S., at 661-662, n. 1. The State permits a candidate to provide the urine specimen in the office of his or her private physician; and the results of the test are given first to the candidate, who controls further dissemination of the report. Because the State has effectively limited the invasiveness of the testing procedure, we concentrate on the core issue: Is the certification requirement warranted by a special need?

Our precedents establish that the proffered special need for drug testing must be substantial--important enough to override the individual's acknowledged privacy interest, sufficiently vital to suppress the Fourth Amendment's normal requirement of individualized suspicion. See supra, at 7-11. Georgia has failed to show, in justification of §21-2-140, a special need of that kind.

Respondents' defense of the statute rests primarily on the incompatibility of unlawful drug use with holding high state office. The statute is justified, respondents contend, because the use of illegal drugs draws into question an official's judgment and integrity; jeopardizes the discharge of public functions, including antidrug law enforcement efforts; and undermines public confidence and trust in elected officials. Brief for Respondents 11-18. The statute, according to respondents, serves to deter unlawful drug users from becoming candidates and thus stops them from attaining high state office. Id., at 17-18. Notably lacking in respondents' presentation is any indication of a concrete danger demanding departure from the Fourth Amendment's main rule.

Nothing in the record hints that the hazards respondents broadly describe are real and not simply hypothetical for Georgia's polity. The statute was not enacted, as counsel for respondents readily acknowledged at oral argument, in response to any fear or suspicion of drug use by state officials:

"QUESTION: Is there any indication anywhere in this record that Georgia has a particular problem here with State officeholders being drug abusers?

"[COUNSEL FOR RESPONDENTS]: No, there is no such evidence. . . . and to be frank, there is no such problem as we sit here today." Tr. of Oral Arg. 32.

See also id., at 31 (counsel for respondents affirms absence of evidence that state officeholders in Georgia have drug problems). A demonstrated problem of drug abuse, while not in all cases necessary to the validity of a testing regime, see Von Raab, 489 U. S., at 673-675, would shore up an assertion of special need for a suspicionless general search program. Proof of unlawful drug use may help to clarify--and to substantiate--the precise hazards posed by such use. Thus, the evidence of drug and alcohol use by railway employees engaged in safety sensitive tasks in Skinner, see 489 U. S., at 606-608, and the immediate crisis prompted by a sharp rise in students' use of unlawful drugs in Vernonia, see 515 U. S., at ____--____ (slip op., at 16-17), bolstered the government's and school officials' arguments that drug testing programs were warranted and appropriate.

In contrast to the effective testing regimes upheld in Skinner, Von Raab, and Vernonia, Georgia's certification requirement is not well designed to identify candidates who violate antidrug laws. Nor is the scheme a credible means to deter illicit drug users from seeking election to state office. The test date--to be scheduled by the candidate anytime within 30 days prior to qualifying for a place on the ballot--is no secret. As counsel for respondents acknowledged at oral argument, users of illegal drugs, save for those prohibitively addicted, could abstain for a pretest period sufficient to avoid detection. See Tr. of Oral Arg. 44-46. [n.4] Even if we indulged respondents' argument that one purpose of §21-2-140 might be to detect those unable so to abstain, see Tr. of Oral Arg. 46, respondents have not shown or argued that such persons are likely to be candidates for public office in Georgia. Moreover, respondents have offered no reason why ordinary law enforcement methods would not suffice to apprehend such addicted individuals, should they appear in the limelight of a public stage. Section 21-2-140, in short, is not needed and cannot work to ferret out lawbreakers, and respondents barely attempt to support the statute on that ground.

Respondents and the United States as amicus curiae rely most heavily on our decision in Von Raab, which sustained a drug testing program for Customs Service officers prior to promotion or transfer to certain high risk positions, despite the absence of any documented drug abuse problem among Service employees. 489 U. S., at 660; see Brief for Respondents 12-14; Brief for United States as Amicus Curiae 18; see also 73 F. 3d, at 1546. The posts in question in Von Raab directly involved drug interdiction or otherwise required the Service member to carry a firearm. See 489 U. S., at 670 ("Government has a compelling interest in ensuring that front line interdiction personnel are physically fit, and have unimpeachable integrity and judgment."); id., at 670-671 ("[T]he public should not bear the risk that employees who may suffer from impaired perception and judgment will be promoted to positions where they may need to employ deadly force.").

Hardly a decision opening broad vistas for suspicionless searches, Von Raab must be read in its unique context. As the Customs Service reported in announcing the testing program, "[Customs employees], more than any other Federal workers, are routinely exposed to the vast network of organized crime that is inextricably tied to illegal drug use." National Treasury Employees Union v. Von Raab, 816 F. 2d 170, 173 (CA51987) (internal quotation marks omitted), aff'd in part, vacated in part, 489 U.S. 656 (1989). We stressed that "[d]rug interdiction ha[d] become the agency's primary enforcement mission," id., at 660, and that the employees in question would have "access to vast sources of valuable contraband," id., at 669. Furthermore, Customs officers "ha[d] been the targets of bribery by drug smugglers on numerous occasions," and several had succumbed to the temptation. Ibid.

Respondents overlook a telling difference between Von Raab and Georgia's candidate drug testing program. In Von Raab it was "not feasible to subject employees [required to carry firearms or concerned with interdiction of controlled substances] and their work product to the kind of day to day scrutiny that is the norm in more traditional office environments." Id., at 674.

Candidates for public office, in contrast, are subject to relentless scrutiny--by their peers, the public, and the press. Their day-to-day conduct attracts attention notably beyond the norm in ordinary work environments.

What is left, after close review of Georgia's scheme, is the image the State seeks to project. By requiring candidates for public office to submit to drug testing, Georgia displays its commitment to the struggle against drug abuse. The suspicionless tests, according to respondents, signify that candidates, if elected, will be fit to serve their constituents free from the influence of illegal drugs. But Georgia asserts no evidence of a drug problem among the State's elected officials, those officials typically do not perform high risk, safety sensitive tasks, and the required certification immediately aids no interdiction effort. The need revealed, in short, is symbolic, not "special," as that term draws meaning from our case law.

In Von Raab, the Customs Service had defended its officer drug test program in part as a way to demonstrate the agency's commitment to enforcement of the law. See Brief for United States in Treasury Employees v. Von Raab, O. T. 1988, No. 86-1879, pp. 35-36. The Von Raab Court, however, did not rely on that justification. Indeed, if a need of the "set a good example" genre were sufficient to overwhelm a Fourth Amendment objection, then the care this Court took to explain why the needs in Skinner, Von Raab, and Vernonia ranked as "special" wasted many words in entirely unnecessary, perhaps even misleading, elaborations.

In a pathmarking dissenting opinion, Justice Brandeis recognized the importance of teaching by example: "Our Government is the potent, the omnipresent teacher. For good or for ill, it teaches the whole people by its example." Olmstead v. United States, 277 U.S. 438, 485 (1928). Justice Brandeis explained in Olmstead why the Government set a bad example when it introduced in a criminal proceeding evidence obtained through an unlawful Government wiretap:

"[I]t is . . . immaterial that the intrusion was in aid of law enforcement. Experience should teach us to be most on our guard to protect liberty when the Government's purposes are beneficent. Men born to freedom are naturally alert to repel invasion of their liberty by evil minded rulers. The greatest dangers to liberty lurk in insidious encroachment by men of zeal, well meaning but without understanding." Id., at 479.

However well meant, the candidate drug test Georgia has devised diminishes personal privacy for a symbol's sake. The Fourth Amendment shields society against that state action.

We note, finally, matters this opinion does not treat. Georgia's singular drug test for candidates is not part of a medical examination designed to provide certification of a candidate's general health, and we express no opinion on such examinations. Nor do we touch on financial disclosure requirements, which implicate different concerns and procedures. See, e.g., Barry v. City of New York, 712 F. 2d 1554 (CA2 1983) (upholding city's financial disclosure law for elected and appointed officials, candidates for city office, and certain city employees); Plante v. Gonzalez, 575 F. 2d 1119 (CA5 1978) (upholding Florida's financial disclosure requirements for certain public officers, candidates, and employees). And we do not speak to drug testing in the private sector, a domain unguarded by Fourth Amendment constraints. See United States v. Jacobsen, 466 U.S. 109, 113 (1984).

We reiterate, too, that where the risk to public safety is substantial and real, blanket suspicionless searches calibrated to the risk may rank as "reasonable"--for example, searches now routine at airports and at entrances to courts and other official buildings. See Von Raab, 489 U. S., at

674-676, and n. 3. But where, as in this case, public safety is not genuinely in jeopardy, the Fourth Amendment precludes the suspicionless search, no matter how conveniently arranged.

* * *

For the reasons stated, the judgment of the Court of Appeals for the Eleventh Circuit is Reversed.

Minnesota v. Carter (Dec 1, 1998)

Chief Justice Rehnquist delivered the opinion of the Court.

Respondents and the lessee of an apartment were sitting in one of its rooms, bagging cocaine. While so engaged they were observed by a police officer, who looked through a drawn window blind. The Supreme Court of Minnesota held that the officer's viewing was a search which violated respondents' Fourth Amendment rights. We hold that no such violation occurred.

James Thielen, a police officer in the Twin Cities' suburb of Eagan, Minnesota, went to an apartment building to investigate a tip from a confidential informant. The informant said that he had walked by the window of a ground-floor apartment and had seen people putting a white powder into bags. The officer looked in the same window through a gap in the closed blind and observed the bagging operation for several minutes. He then notified headquarters, which began preparing affidavits for a search warrant while he returned to the apartment building. When two men left the building in a previously identified Cadillac, the police stopped the car. Inside were respondents Carter and Johns. As the police opened the door of the car to let Johns out, they observed a black zippered pouch and a handgun, later determined to be loaded, on the vehicle's floor. Carter and Johns were arrested, and a later police search of the vehicle the next day discovered pagers, a scale, and 47 grams of cocaine in plastic sandwich bags.

After seizing the car, the police returned to Apartment 103 and arrested the occupant, Kimberly Thompson, who is not a party to this appeal. A search of the apartment pursuant to a warrant revealed cocaine residue on the kitchen table and plastic baggies similar to those found in the Cadillac. Thielen identified Carter, Johns, and Thompson as the three people he had observed placing the powder into baggies. The police later learned that while Thompson was the lessee of the apartment, Carter and Johns lived in Chicago and had come to the apartment for the sole purpose of packaging the cocaine. Carter and Johns had never been to the apartment before and were only in the apartment for approximately 2½ hours. In return for the use of the apartment, Carter and Johns had given Thompson one-eighth of an ounce of the cocaine.

Carter and Johns were charged with conspiracy to commit controlled substance crime in the first degree and aiding and abetting in a controlled substance crime in the first degree, in violation of Minn. Stat. § 152.021, subd. 1(1), subd. 3(a) (1996); §609.05. They moved to suppress all evidence obtained from the apartment and the Cadillac, as well as to suppress several post-arrest incriminating statements they had made. They argued that Thielen's initial observation of their drug packaging activities was an unreasonable search in violation of the Fourth Amendment and that all evidence obtained as a result of this unreasonable search was inadmissible as fruit of the poisonous tree. The Minnesota trial court held that since, unlike the defendant in Minnesota v. Olson, 495 U.S. 91 (1990), Carter and Johns were not overnight social guests but temporary out-of-state visitors, they were not entitled to claim the protection of the Fourth Amendment against the government intrusion into the apartment. The trial court also concluded that Thielen's observation was not a search within the meaning of the Fourth

Amendment. After a trial, Carter and Johns were each convicted of both offenses. The Minnesota Court of Appeals held that the respondent Carter did not have "standing" to object to Thielen's actions because his claim that he was predominantly a social guest was "inconsistent with the only evidence concerning his stay in the apartment, which indicates that he used it for a business purpose–to package drugs." State v. Carter, 545 N. W. 2d 695, 698 (1996). In a separate appeal, the Court of Appeals also affirmed Johns' conviction, without addressing what it termed the "standing" issue. State v. Johns, No. C9-95-1765 (Minn. Ct. App., June 11, 1996), App. D-1, D-3 (unpublished).

A divided Minnesota Supreme Court reversed, holding that respondents had "standing" to claim the protection of the Fourth Amendment because they had " 'a legitimate expectation of privacy in the invaded place.' " 569 N. W. 2d 169, 174 (1997) (quoting Rakas v. Illinois, 439 U.S. 128, 143 (1978)). The court noted that even though "society does not recognize as valuable the task of bagging cocaine, we conclude that society does recognize as valuable the right of property owners or leaseholders to invite persons into the privacy of their homes to conduct a common task, be it legal or illegal activity. We, therefore, hold that [respondents] had standing to bring [their] motion to suppress the evidence gathered as a result of Thielen's observations." 569 N. W. 2d, at 176; see also 569 N. W.2d 180, 181. Based upon its conclusion that the respondents had "standing" to raise their Fourth Amendment claims, the court went on to hold that Thielen's observation constituted a search of the apartment under the Fourth Amendment, and that the search was unreasonable. Id., at 176—179. We granted certiorari, 523 U.S. ____ (1998), and now reverse.

The Minnesota courts analyzed whether respondents had a legitimate expectation of privacy under the rubric of "standing" doctrine, an analysis which this Court expressly rejected 20 years ago in Rakas. 439 U.S., at 139-140. In that case, we held that automobile passengers could not assert the protection of the Fourth Amendment against the seizure of incriminating evidence from a vehicle where they owned neither the vehicle nor the evidence. Ibid. Central to our analysis was the idea that in determining whether a defendant is able to show the violation of his (and not someone else's) Fourth Amendment rights, the "definition of those rights is more properly placed within the purview of substantive Fourth Amendment law than within that of standing." 439 U.S., at 140. Thus, we held that in order to claim the protection of the Fourth Amendment, a defendant must demonstrate that he personally has an expectation of privacy in the place searched, and that his expectation is reasonable; i.e., one which has "a source outside of the Fourth Amendment, either by reference to concepts of real or personal property law or to understandings that are recognized and permitted by society." Id., at 143—144, and n. 12. See also Smith v. Maryland, 442 U.S. 735, 740-741 (1979).

The Fourth Amendment guarantees: "The right of the people to be secure in their persons, houses, papers, and effects, against unreasonable searches and seizures, shall not be violated, and no Warrants shall issue, but upon probable cause, supported by Oath or affirmation, and particularly describing the place to be searched, and the persons or things to be seized." The Amendment protects persons against unreasonable searches of "their persons [and] houses" and thus indicates that the Fourth Amendment is a personal right that must be invoked by an individual. See Katz v. United States, 389 U.S. 347, 351 (1967) ("[T]he Fourth Amendment protects people, not places"). But the extent to which the Fourth Amendment protects people may depend upon where those people are. We have held that "capacity to claim the protection of the Fourth Amendment depends ... upon whether the person who claims the protection of the Amendment has a legitimate expectation of privacy in the invaded place." Rakas, supra, at 143. See also Rawlings v. Kentucky, 448 U.S. 98, 106 (1980).

The text of the Amendment suggests that its protections extend only to people in "their" houses. But we have held that in some circumstances a person may have a legitimate expectation of privacy in the house of someone else. In Minnesota v. Olson, 495 U.S. 91 (1990), for example, we decided that an overnight guest in a house had the sort of expectation of privacy that the Fourth Amendment protects. We said:

"To hold that an overnight guest has a legitimate expectation of privacy in his host's home merely recognizes the every day expectations of privacy that we all share. Staying overnight in another's home is a long-standing social custom that serves functions recognized as valuable by society. We stay in others' homes when we travel to a strange city for business or pleasure, we visit our parents, children, or more distant relatives out of town, when we are in between jobs, or homes, or when we house-sit for a friend... .

"From the overnight guest's perspective, he seeks shelter in another's home precisely because it provides him with privacy, a place where he and his possessions will not be disturbed by anyone but his host and those his host allows inside. We are at our most vulnerable when we are asleep because we cannot monitor our own safety or the security of our belongings. It is for this reason that, although we may spend all day in public places, when we cannot sleep in our own home we seek out another private place to sleep, whether it be a hotel room, or the home of a friend." Id., at 98—99.

In Jones v. United States, 362 U.S. 257, 259 (1960), the defendant seeking to exclude evidence resulting from a search of an apartment had been given the use of the apartment by a friend. He had clothing in the apartment, had slept there " 'maybe a night,' " and at the time was the sole occupant of the apartment. But while the holding of Jones—that a search of the apartment violated the defendant's Fourth Amendment rights—is still valid, its statement that "anyone legitimately on the premises where a search occurs may challenge its legality," id., at 267, was expressly repudiated in Rakas v. Illinois, 439 U.S. 128 (1978). Thus an overnight guest in a home may claim the protection of the Fourth Amendment, but one who is merely present with the consent of the householder may not.

Respondents here were obviously not overnight guests, but were essentially present for a business transaction and were only in the home a matter of hours. There is no suggestion that they had a previous relationship with Thompson, or that there was any other purpose to their visit. Nor was there anything similar to the overnight guest relationship in Olson to suggest a degree of acceptance into the household.1 While the apartment was a dwelling place for Thompson, it was for these respondents simply a place to do business.

Property used for commercial purposes is treated differently for Fourth Amendment purposes than residential property. "An expectation of privacy in commercial premises, however, is different from, and indeed less than, a similar expectation in an individual's home." New York v. Burger, 482 U.S. 691, 700 (1987). And while it was a "home" in which respondents were present, it was not their home. Similarly, the Court has held that in some circumstances a worker can claim Fourth Amendment protection over his own workplace. See, e.g., O'Connor v. Ortega, 480 U.S. 709 (1987). But there is no indication that respondents in this case had nearly as significant a connection to Thompson's apartment as the worker in O'Connor had to his own private office.

See id., at 716-17.

If we regard the overnight guest in Minnesota v. Olson as typifying those who may claim the protection of the Fourth Amendment in the home of another, and one merely "legitimately on the premises" as typifying those who may not do so, the present case is obviously somewhere in between. But the purely commercial nature of the transaction engaged in here, the relatively short period of time on the premises, and the lack of any previous connection between respondents and the householder, all lead us to conclude that respondents' situation is closer to that of one simply permitted on the premises. We therefore hold that any search which may have occurred did not violate their Fourth Amendment rights.

Because we conclude that respondents had no legitimate expectation of privacy in the apartment, we need not decide whether the police officer's observation constituted a "search." The judgment of the Supreme Court of Minnesota is accordingly reversed, and the cause is remanded for proceedings not inconsistent with this opinion.

Notes

1. Justice Ginsburg's dissent would render the operative language in Minnesota v. Olson, post p. 5, almost entirely superfluous. There, we explained the justification for extending Fourth Amendment protection to the overnight visitor: "Staying overnight in another's home is a long-standing social custom that serves functions recognized as valuable by society. ... We are at our most vulnerable when we are asleep because we cannot monitor our own safety or the security of our belongings." 495 U.S., at 98-99. If any short-term business visit by a stranger entitles the visitor to share the Fourth Amendment protection of the lease holder's home, the Court's explanation of its holding in Olson was quite unnecessary.

Illinois v. Wardlow (Jan 12, 2000)

Chief Justice Rehnquist delivered the opinion of the Court.

Respondent Wardlow fled upon seeing police officers patrolling an area known for heavy narcotics trafficking. Two of the officers caught up with him, stopped him and conducted a protective pat-down search for weapons. Discovering a .38-caliber handgun, the officers arrested Wardlow. We hold that the officers' stop did not violate the Fourth Amendment to the United States Constitution.

On September 9, 1995, Officers Nolan and Harvey were working as uniformed officers in the special operations section of the Chicago Police Department. The officers were driving the last car of a four car caravan converging on an area known for heavy narcotics trafficking in order to investigate drug transactions. The officers were traveling together because they expected to find a crowd of people in the area, including lookouts and customers.

As the caravan passed 4035 West Van Buren, Officer Nolan observed respondent Wardlow standing next to the building holding an opaque bag. Respondent looked in the direction of the officers and fled. Nolan and Harvey turned their car southbound, watched him as he ran through the gangway and an alley, and eventually cornered him on the street. Nolan then exited his car and stopped respondent. He immediately conducted a protective pat-down search for weapons because in his experience it was common for there to be weapons in the near vicinity of narcotics transactions. During the frisk, Officer Nolan squeezed the bag respondent was carrying and felt a heavy, hard object similar to the shape of a gun. The officer then opened the bag and discovered a .38-caliber handgun with five live rounds of ammunition. The officers arrested Wardlow.

The Illinois trial court denied

respondent's motion to suppress, finding the gun was recovered during a lawful stop and frisk. App. 14. Following a stipulated bench trial, Wardlow was convicted of unlawful use of a weapon by a felon. The Illinois Appellate Court reversed Wardlow's conviction, concluding that the gun should have been suppressed because Officer Nolan did not have reasonable suspicion sufficient to justify an investigative stop pursuant to Terry v. Ohio, 392 U.S. 1 (1968). 287 Ill. App. 3d 367, 678 N. E. 2d 65 (1997).

The Illinois Supreme Court agreed. 183 Ill. 2d 306, 701 N. E. 2d 484 (1998). While rejecting the Appellate Court's conclusion that Wardlow was not in a high crime area, the Illinois Supreme Court determined that sudden flight in such an area does not create a reasonable suspicion justifying a Terry stop. Id., at 310, 701 N. E. 2d, at 486. Relying on Florida v. Royer, 460 U.S. 491 (1983), the court explained that although police have the right to approach individuals and ask questions, the individual has no obligation to respond. The person may decline to answer and simply go on his or her way, and the refusal to respond, alone, does not provide a legitimate basis for an investigative stop. 183 Ill. 2d, at 311—312, 701 N. E. 2d, at 486—487. The court then determined that flight may simply be an exercise of this right to "go on one's way," and, thus, could not constitute reasonable suspicion justifying a Terry stop. Id., at 312, 701 N. E. 2d, at 487.

The Illinois Supreme Court also rejected the argument that flight combined with the fact that it occurred in a high crime area supported a finding of reasonable suspicion because the "high crime area" factor was not sufficient standing alone to justify a Terry stop. Finding no independently suspicious circumstances to support an investigatory detention, the court held that the stop and subsequent arrest violated the Fourth Amendment. We granted certiorari, 526 U.S. ____ (1999), and now reverse.1

This case, involving a brief encounter between a citizen and a police officer on a public street, is governed by the analysis we first applied in Terry. In Terry, we held that an officer may, consistent with the Fourth Amendment, conduct a brief, investigatory stop when the officer has a reasonable, articulable suspicion that criminal activity is afoot. Terry, supra, at 30. While "reasonable suspicion" is a less demanding standard than probable cause and requires a showing considerably less than preponderance of the evidence, the Fourth Amendment requires at least a minimal level of objective justification for making the stop. United States v. Sokolow, 490 U.S. 1, 7 (1989). The officer must be able to articulate more than an "inchoate and unparticularized suspicion or 'hunch' " of criminal activity. Terry, supra, at 27.2

Nolan and Harvey were among eight officers in a four car caravan that was converging on an area known for heavy narcotics trafficking, and the officers anticipated encountering a large number of people in the area, including drug customers and individuals serving as lookouts. App. 8. It was in this context that Officer Nolan decided to investigate Wardlow after observing him flee. An individual's presence in an area of expected criminal activity, standing alone, is not enough to support a reasonable, particularized suspicion that the person is committing a crime. Brown v. Texas, 443 U.S. 47 (1979). But officers are not required to ignore the relevant characteristics of a location in determining whether the circumstances are sufficiently suspicious to warrant further investigation. Accordingly, we have previously noted the fact that the stop occurred in a "high crime area" among the relevant contextual considerations in a Terry analysis. Adams v. Williams, 407 U.S. 143, 144 and 147—148 (1972).

In this case, moreover, it was not merely respondent's presence in an area of heavy narcotics trafficking that aroused the officers' suspicion but his unprovoked flight upon noticing the police. Our cases have also recognized that nervous, evasive behavior is a pertinent factor in determining reasonable suspicion. United States v. Brignoni-Ponce, 422 U.S. 873, 885 (1975); Florida v. Rodriguez, 469 U.S. 1, 6 (1984) (per curiam); United States v. Sokolow, supra, at 8—9. Headlong flight—wherever it occurs—is the consummate act of evasion: it is not necessarily indicative of wrongdoing, but it is certainly suggestive of such. In reviewing the propriety of an officer's conduct, courts do not have available empirical studies dealing with inferences drawn from suspicious behavior, and we cannot reasonably demand scientific certainty from judges or law enforcement officers where none exists. Thus, the determination of reasonable suspicion must be based on commonsense judgments and inferences about human behavior. See United States v. Cortez, 449 U.S. 411, 418 (1981). We conclude Officer Nolan was justified in suspecting that Wardlow was involved in criminal activity, and, therefore, in investigating further.

Such a holding is entirely consistent with our decision in Florida v. Royer, 460 U.S. 491 (1983), where we held that when an officer, without reasonable suspicion or probable cause, approaches an individual, the individual has a right to ignore the police and go about his business. Id., at 498. And any "refusal to cooperate, without more, does not furnish the minimal level of objective justification needed for a detention or seizure." Florida v. Bostick, 501 U.S. 429, 437 (1991). But unprovoked flight is simply not a mere refusal to cooperate. Flight, by its very nature, is not "going about one's business"; in fact, it is just the opposite. Allowing officers confronted with such flight to stop the fugitive and investigate further is quite consistent with the individual's right to go about his business or to stay put and remain silent in the face of police questioning.

Respondent and amici also argue that there are innocent reasons for flight from police and that, therefore, flight is not necessarily indicative of ongoing criminal activity. This fact is undoubtedly true, but does not establish a violation of the Fourth Amendment. Even in Terry, the conduct justifying the stop was ambiguous and susceptible of an innocent explanation. The officer observed two individuals pacing back and forth in front of a store, peering into the window and periodically conferring. Terry, 392 U.S., at 5—6. All of this conduct was by itself lawful, but it also suggested that the individuals were casing the store for a planned robbery. Terry recognized that the officers could detain the individuals to resolve the ambiguity. Id., at 30.

In allowing such detentions, Terry accepts the risk that officers may stop innocent people. Indeed, the Fourth Amendment accepts that risk in connection with more drastic police action; persons arrested and detained on probable cause to believe they have committed a crime may turn out to be innocent. The Terry stop is a far more minimal intrusion, simply allowing the officer to briefly investigate further. If the officer does not learn facts rising to the level of probable cause, the individual must be allowed to go on his way. But in this case the officers found respondent in possession of a handgun, and arrested him for violation of an Illinois firearms statute. No question of the propriety of the arrest itself is before us.

The judgment of the Supreme Court of Illinois is reversed, and the cause is remanded for further proceedings not inconsistent with this opinion.

It is so ordered.

Notes

1. The state courts have differed on whether unprovoked flight is sufficient grounds to constitute reasonable suspicion. See, e.g., State v.

Anderson, 155 Wis. 2d 77, 454 N. W. 2d 763 (Wis. 1990) (flight alone is sufficient); Platt v. State, 589 N. E. 2d 222 (Ind. 1992) (same); Harris v. State, 205 Ga. App. 813, 423 S. E. 2d 723 (1992) (flight in high crime area sufficient); State v. Hicks, 241 Neb. 357, 488 N. W. 2d 359 (1992) (flight is not enough); State v. Tucker, 136 N. J. 158, 642 A. 2d 401 (1994) (same); People v. Shabaz, 424 Mich. 42, 378 N. W. 2d 451 (1985) (same); People v. Wilson, 784 P.2d 325 (Colo. 1989) (same).

2. We granted certiorari solely on the question of whether the initial stop was supported by reasonable suspicion. Therefore, we express no opinion as to the lawfulness of the frisk independently of the stop.

Bond v. United States (April 17, 2000)

Chief Justice Rehnquist delivered the opinion of the Court.

This case presents the question whether a law enforcement officer's physical manipulation of a bus passenger's carry-on luggage violated the Fourth Amendment's proscription against unreasonable searches. We hold that it did.

Petitioner Steven Dewayne Bond was a passenger on a Greyhound bus that left California bound for Little Rock, Arkansas. The bus stopped, as it was required to do, at the permanent Border Patrol checkpoint in Sierra Blanca, Texas. Border Patrol Agent Cesar Cantu boarded the bus to check the immigration status of its passengers. After reaching the back of the bus, having satisfied himself that the passengers were lawfully in the United States, Agent Cantu began walking toward the front. Along the way, he squeezed the soft luggage which passengers had placed in the overhead storage space above the seats.

Petitioner was seated four or five rows from the back of the bus. As Agent Cantu inspected the luggage in the compartment above petitioner's seat, he squeezed a green canvas bag and noticed that it contained a "brick-like" object. Petitioner admitted that the bag was his and agreed to allow Agent Cantu to open it.[1] Upon opening the bag, Agent Cantu discovered a "brick" of methamphetamine. The brick had been wrapped in duct tape until it was oval-shaped and then rolled in a pair of pants.

Petitioner was indicted for conspiracy to possess, and possession with intent to distribute, methamphetamine in violation of 84 Stat. 1260, 21 U. S. C. §841(a)(1). He moved to suppress the drugs, arguing that Agent Cantu conducted an illegal search of his bag. Petitioner's motion was denied, and the District Court found him guilty on both counts and sentenced him to 57 months in prison. On appeal, he conceded that other passengers had access to his bag, but contended that Agent Cantu manipulated the bag in a way that other passengers would not. The Court of Appeals rejected this argument, stating that the fact that Agent Cantu's manipulation of petitioner's bag was calculated to detect contraband is irrelevant for Fourth Amendment purposes. 167 F.3d 225, 227 (CA5 1999) (citing California v. Ciraolo, 476 U.S. 207 (1986)). Thus, the Court of Appeals affirmed the denial of the motion to suppress, holding that Agent Cantu's manipulation of the bag was not a search within the meaning of the Fourth Amendment. 167 F.3d, at 227. We granted certiorari, 528 U.S. ____ (1999), and now reverse.

The Fourth Amendment provides that "[t]he right of the people to be secure in their persons, houses, papers, and effects, against unreasonable searches and seizures, shall not be violated ... ." A traveler's personal luggage is clearly an "effect" protected by the Amendment. See United States v. Place, 462 U.S. 696, 707 (1983). Indeed, it is undisputed here that petitioner possessed a privacy interest in his bag.

But the Government asserts that by

exposing his bag to the public, petitioner lost a reasonable expectation that his bag would not be physically manipulated. The Government relies on our decisions in California v. Ciraolo, supra, and Florida v. Riley, 488 U.S. 445 (1989), for the proposition that matters open to public observation are not protected by the Fourth Amendment. In Ciraolo, we held that police observation of a backyard from a plane flying at an altitude of 1,000 feet did not violate a reasonable expectation of privacy. Similarly, in Riley, we relied on Ciraolo to hold that police observation of a greenhouse in a home's curtilage from a helicopter passing at an altitude of 400 feet did not violate the Fourth Amendment. We reasoned that the property was "not necessarily protected from inspection that involves no physical invasion," and determined that because any member of the public could have lawfully observed the defendants' property by flying overhead, the defendants' expectation of privacy was "not reasonable and not one 'that society is prepared to honor.'" See Riley, supra, at 449 (explaining and relying on Ciraolo's reasoning).

But Ciraolo and Riley are different from this case because they involved only visual, as opposed to tactile, observation. Physically invasive inspection is simply more intrusive than purely visual inspection. For example, in Terry v. Ohio, 392 U.S. 1, 17—18 (1968), we stated that a "careful [tactile] exploration of the outer surfaces of a person's clothing all over his or her body" is a "serious intrusion upon the sanctity of the person, which may inflict great indignity and arouse strong resentment, and is not to be undertaken lightly." Although Agent Cantu did not "frisk" petitioner's person, he did conduct a probing tactile examination of petitioner's carry-on luggage. Obviously, petitioner's bag was not part of his person. But travelers are particularly concerned about their carry-on luggage; they generally use it to transport personal items that, for whatever reason, they prefer to keep close at hand.

Here, petitioner concedes that, by placing his bag in the overhead compartment, he could expect that it would be exposed to certain kinds of touching and handling. But petitioner argues that Agent Cantu's physical manipulation of his luggage "far exceeded the casual contact [petitioner] could have expected from other passengers." Brief for Petitioner 18—19. The Government counters that it did not.

Our Fourth Amendment analysis embraces two questions. First, we ask whether the individual, by his conduct, has exhibited an actual expectation of privacy; that is, whether he has shown that "he [sought] to preserve [something] as private." Smith v. Maryland, 442 U.S. 735, 740 (1979) (internal quotation marks omitted). Here, petitioner sought to preserve privacy by using an opaque bag and placing that bag directly above his seat. Second, we inquire whether the individual's expectation of privacy is "one that society is prepared to recognize as reasonable." Ibid. (internal quotation marks omitted).[2] When a bus passenger places a bag in an overhead bin, he expects that other passengers or bus employees may move it for one reason or another. Thus, a bus passenger clearly expects that his bag may be handled. He does not expect that other passengers or bus employees will, as a matter of course, feel the bag in an exploratory manner. But this is exactly what the agent did here. We therefore hold that the agent's physical manipulation of petitioner's bag violated the Fourth Amendment.

The judgment of the Court of Appeals is Reversed.

Notes

1. The Government has not argued here that petitioner's consent to Agent Cantu's opening the bag is a basis for admitting the evidence.

2. The parties properly agree that the subjective intent of the law enforcement officer is

irrelevant in determining whether that officer's actions violate the Fourth Amendment. Brief for Petitioner 14; Brief for United States 33–34; see Whren v. United States, 517 U.S. 806, 813 (1996) (stating that "we have been unwilling to entertain Fourth Amendment challenges based on the actual motivations of individual officers"); California v. Ciraolo, 476 U.S. 207, 212 (1986) (rejecting respondent's challenge to "the authority of government to observe his activity from any vantage point or place if the viewing is motivated by a law enforcement purpose, and not the result of a casual, accidental observation"). This principle applies to the agent's acts in this case as well; the issue is not his state of mind, but the objective effect of his actions.

City of Indianapolis v. Edmond (Nov 28, 2000)

JUSTICE O'CONNOR delivered the opinion of the Court.

In Michigan Dept. of State Police v. Sitz, 496 U. S. 444 (1990), and United States v. Martinez-Fuerte, 428 U. S. 543 (1976), we held that brief, suspicionless seizures at highway checkpoints for the purposes of combating drunk driving and intercepting illegal immigrants were constitutional. We now consider the constitutionality of a highway checkpoint program whose primary purpose is the discovery and interdiction of illegal narcotics.

I

In August 1998, the city of Indianapolis began to operate vehicle checkpoints on Indianapolis roads in an effort to interdict unlawful drugs. The city conducted six such roadblocks between August and November that year, stopping

*Briefs of amici curiae urging reversal were filed for the State of Kansas et al. by Carla J. Stovall, Attorney General of Kansas, Stephen R.

McAllister, State Solicitor, Jared S. Maag, Assistant Attorney General, and John M. Bailey, Chief State's Attorney of Connecticut, and by the Attorneys General for their respective States as follows: Bill Pryor of Alabama, Janet Napolitano of Arizona, Mark Pryor of Arkansas, Bill Lockyer of California, Robert A. Butterworth of Florida, James E. Ryan of Illinois, Karen M. Freeman-Wilson of Indiana, Thomas J. Miller of Iowa, Michael C. Moore of Mississippi, Don Stenberg of Nebraska, W A. Drew Edmondson of Oklahoma, Jan Graham of Utah, and Mark L. Earley of Virginia; for the National League of Cities et al. by Richard Ruda and James I. Crowley; and for the Washington Legal Foundation et al. by Daniel J. Popeo.

Briefs of amici curiae urging affirmance were filed for the National Association of Criminal Defense Lawyers et al. by Wesley MacNeil Oliver and Barbara Bergman; and for the Rutherford Institute by John W Whitehead and Steven H. Aden.

Wayne W Schmidt, James P. Manak, Richard Weintraub, and Bernard J. Farber filed a brief for Americans for Effective Law Enforcement, Inc., et al. as amici curiae.

1,161 vehicles and arresting 104 motorists. Fifty-five arrests were for drug-related crimes, while 49 were for offenses unrelated to drugs. Edmond v. Goldsmith, 183 F.3d 659, 661 (CA7 1999). The overall "hit rate" of the program was thus approximately nine percent.

The parties stipulated to the facts concerning the operation of the checkpoints by the Indianapolis Police Department (IPD) for purposes of the preliminary injunction proceedings instituted below. At each checkpoint location, the police stop a predetermined number of vehicles. Approximately 30 officers are stationed at the checkpoint. Pursuant to written directives issued by the chief of police, at least one officer approaches the vehicle, advises the driver that he or she is being stopped briefly at a drug checkpoint, and asks the driver to produce a license and registration. The officer also looks for signs of impairment and conducts an open-view examination of the vehicle from the outside. A narcoticsdetection dog walks around the outside of each stopped vehicle.

The directives instruct the officers that they may conduct a search only by consent or based on the appropriate quantum of particularized suspicion. The officers must conduct each stop in the same manner until particularized suspicion develops, and the officers have no discretion to stop any vehicle out of sequence. The city agreed in the stipulation to operate the checkpoints in such a way as to ensure that the total duration of each stop, absent reasonable suspicion or probable cause, would be five minutes or less.

The affidavit of Indianapolis Police Sergeant Marshall DePew, although it is technically outside the parties' stipulation, provides further insight concerning the operation of the checkpoints. According to Sergeant DePew, checkpoint locations are selected weeks in advance based on such considerations as area crime statistics and traffic flow. The checkpoints are generally operated during daylight hours and are identified with lighted signs reading, "'NARCOTICS CHECKPOINT __ MILE AHEAD, NARCOTICS K-9 IN USE, BE PREPARED TO STOP.'" App. to Pet. for Cert. 57a. Once a group of cars has been stopped, other traffic proceeds without interruption until all the stopped cars have been processed or diverted for further processing. Sergeant DePew also stated that the average stop for a vehicle not subject to further processing lasts two to three minutes or less.

Respondents James Edmond and J oell Palmer were each stopped at a narcotics checkpoint in late September 1998. Respondents then filed a lawsuit on behalf of themselves and the class of all motorists who had been stopped or were subject to being stopped in the future at the Indianapolis drug checkpoints. Respondents claimed that the roadblocks violated the Fourth Amendment of the United States Constitution and the search and seizure provision of the Indiana Constitution. Respondents requested declaratory and injunctive relief for the class, as well as damages and attorney's fees for themselves.

Respondents then moved for a preliminary injunction.

Although respondents alleged that the officers who stopped them did not follow the written directives, they agreed to the stipulation concerning the operation of the checkpoints for purposes of the preliminary injunction proceedings. The parties also stipulated to certification of the plaintiff class. The United States District Court for the Southern District of Indiana agreed to class certification and denied the motion for a preliminary injunction, holding that the checkpoint program did not violate the Fourth Amendment. Edmond v. Goldsmith, 38 F. Supp. 2d 1016 (1998). A divided panel of the United States Court of Appeals for the Seventh Circuit reversed, holding that the checkpoints contravened the Fourth Amendment. 183 F.3d 659 (1999). The panel denied rehearing. We granted certiorari, 528 U. S. 1153 (2000), and now affirm.

II

The Fourth Amendment requires that searches and seizures be reasonable. A search or seizure is ordinarily unreasonable in the absence of individualized suspicion of wrongdoing. Chandler v. Miller, 520 U. S. 305, 308 (1997). While such suspicion is not an "irreducible" component of reasonableness, Martinez-Fuerte, 428 U. S., at 561, we have recognized only limited circumstances in which the usual rule does not apply. For example, we have upheld certain regimes of suspicionless searches where the program was designed to serve "special needs, beyond the normal need for law enforcement." See, e. g., Vernonia School Dist. J,7J v. Acton, 515 U. S. 646 (1995) (random drug testing of studentathletes); Treasury Employees v. Von Raab, 489 U. S. 656 (1989) (drug tests for United States Customs Service employees seeking transfer or promotion to certain positions); Skinner v. Railway Labor Executives' Assn., 489 U. S. 602 (1989) (drug and alcohol tests for railway employees involved in train accidents or found to be in violation of particular safety regulations). We have also allowed searches for certain administrative purposes without particularized suspicion of misconduct, provided that those searches are appropriately limited. See, e. g., New York v. Burger, 482 U. S. 691, 702-704 (1987) (warrantless administrative inspection of premises of "closely regulated" business); Michigan v. Tyler, 436 U. S. 499, 507-509, 511-512 (1978) (administrative inspection of fire-damaged premises to determine cause of blaze); Camara v. Municipal Court of City and County of San Francisco, 387 U. S. 523, 534-539 (1967) (administrative inspection to ensure compliance with city housing code).

We have also upheld brief, suspicionless seizures of motorists at a fixed Border Patrol checkpoint designed to intercept illegal aliens, Martinez-Fuerte, supra, and at a sobriety checkpoint aimed at removing drunk drivers from the road, Michigan Dept. of State Police v. Sitz, 496 U. S. 444 (1990). In addition, in Delaware v. Prouse, 440 U. S. 648, 663 (1979), we suggested that a similar type of roadblock with the purpose of verifying drivers' licenses and vehicle registrations would be permissible. In none of these cases, however, did we indicate approval of a checkpoint program whose primary purpose was to detect evidence of ordinary criminal wrongdoing.

In Martinez-Fuerte, we entertained Fourth Amendment challenges to stops at two permanent immigration checkpoints located on major United States highways less than 100 miles from the Mexican border. We noted at the outset the particular context in which the constitutional question arose, describing in some detail the "formidable law enforcement problems" posed by the northbound tide of illegal entrants into the United States. 428 U. S., at 551-554. These problems had also been the focus of several earlier cases addressing the constitutionality of other Border Patrol traffic-checking operations. See United States v. Ortiz, 422 U. S. 891 (1975); United States v. Brignoni-Ponce, 422 U. S. 873 (1975); Almeida-Sanchez v. United States, 413 U. S. 266 (1973). In Martinez-Fuerte, we found that the balance tipped in favor of the Government's interests in policing the Nation's borders. 428 U. S., at 561-564. In so finding, we emphasized the difficulty of effectively containing illegal immigration at the border itself. Id., at 556. We also stressed the impracticality of the particularized study of a given car to discern whether it was transporting illegal aliens, as well as the relatively modest degree of intrusion entailed by the stops. Id., at 556-564.

Our subsequent cases have confirmed that considerations specifically related to the need to police the border were a significant factor in our Martinez-Fuerte decision. For example, in United States v. Montoya de Hernandez, 473 U. S. 531,538 (1985), we counted Martinez-Fuerte as one of a number of Fourth Amendment cases that "reflect longstanding concern for the protection of the integrity of the border." Although the stops in Martinez-Fuerte did not occur at the border itself, the checkpoints were located near the border and served a border control function made necessary by the difficulty of guarding the border's entire length. See Martinez-Fuerte, supra, at 556.

In Sitz, we evaluated the constitutionality of a Michigan highway sobriety checkpoint program. The Sitz checkpoint involved brief, suspicionless stops of motorists so that police officers could detect signs of intoxication and remove impaired drivers from the road. 496 U. S., at 447-448. Motorists who exhibited signs of intoxication were diverted for a license and registration check and, if warranted, further sobriety tests. Id., at 447. This checkpoint program was clearly aimed at reducing the immediate hazard posed by the presence of drunk drivers on the highways, and there was an obvious connection between the imperative of highway safety and the law enforcement practice at issue. The gravity of the drunk driving problem and the magnitude of the State's interest in getting drunk drivers off the road weighed heavily in our determination that the program was constitutional. See id., at 451.

In Prouse, we invalidated a discretionary, suspicionless stop for a spot check of a motorist's driver's license and vehicle registration. The officer's conduct in that case was unconstitutional primarily on account of his exercise of "standardless and unconstrained discretion." 440 U. S., at 661. We nonetheless acknowledged the States' "vital interest in ensuring that only those qualified to do so are permitted to operate motor vehicles, that these vehicles are fit for safe operation, and hence that licensing, registration, and vehicle inspection requirements are being observed." Id., at 658. Accordingly, we suggested that "[q]uestioning of all oncoming traffic at roadblock-type stops" would be a lawful means of serving this interest in highway safety. Id., at 663.

We further indicated in Prouse that we considered the purposes of such a hypothetical roadblock to be distinct from a general purpose of investigating crime. The State proffered the additional interests of "the apprehension of stolen motor vehicles and of drivers under the influence of alcohol or narcotics" in its effort to justify the discretionary spot check. Id., at 659, n. 18. We attributed the entirety of the latter interest to the State's interest in roadway safety. Ibid. We also noted that the interest in apprehending stolen vehicles may be partly subsumed by the interest in roadway safety. Ibid. We observed, however, that "[t]he remaining governmental interest in controlling automobile thefts is not distinguishable from the general interest in crime control." Ibid. Not only does the common thread of highway safety thus run through Sitz and Prouse, but Prouse itself reveals a difference in the Fourth Amendment significance of highway safety interests and the general interest in crime control.

III

It is well established that a vehicle stop at a highway checkpoint effectuates a seizure within the meaning of the Fourth Amendment. See, e. g., Sitz, supra, at 450. The fact that officers walk a narcotics-detection dog around the exterior of each car at the Indianapolis checkpoints does not transform the seizure into a search. See United States v. Place, 462 U. S. 696, 707 (1983). Just as in Place, an exterior sniff of an automobile does not require entry into the car and is not designed to disclose any information other than the presence or absence of narcotics. See ibid. Like the dog sniff in Place, a sniff by a dog that simply walks around a car is "much less intrusive than a typical search." Ibid. Cf. United States v. Turpin, 920 F.2d 1377, 1385 (CA8 1990). Rather, what principally distinguishes these checkpoints from those we have previously approved is their primary purpose.

As petitioners concede, the Indianapolis checkpoint program unquestionably has the primary purpose of interdicting illegal narcotics. In their stipulation of facts, the parties repeatedly refer to the checkpoints as "drug checkpoints" and describe them as "being operated by the City of Indianapolis in an effort to interdict unlawful drugs in Indianapolis." App. to Pet. for Cert. 51a-52a. In addition, the first document attached to the parties' stipulation is entitled "DRUG CHECKPOINT CONTACT OFFICER DIRECTIVES BY ORDER OF THE CHIEF OF POLICE." Id., at 53a. These directives instruct officers to "[a]dvise the citizen that they are being stopped briefly at a drug checkpoint." Ibid. The second document attached to the stipulation is entitled "1998 Drug Road Blocks" and contains a statistical breakdown of information relating to the checkpoints conducted. Id., at 55a. Further, according to Sergeant DePew, the checkpoints are identified with lighted signs reading, "'NARCOTICS CHECKPOINT ___ MILE AHEAD, NARCOTICS K-9 IN USE, BE PREPARED TO STOP.'" Id., at 57a. Finally, both the District Court and the Court of Appeals recognized that the primary purpose of the roadblocks is the interdiction of narcotics. 38 F. Supp. 2d, at 1026 (noting that both parties "stress the primary purpose of the roadblocks as the interdiction of narcotics" and that "[t]he IPD has made it clear that the purpose for its checkpoints is to interdict narcotics traffic"); 183 F. 3d, at 665 (observing that "the City concedes that its proximate goal is to catch drug offenders").

We have never approved a checkpoint program whose primary purpose was to detect evidence of ordinary criminal wrongdoing. Rather, our checkpoint cases have recognized only limited exceptions to the general rule that a seizure must be accompanied by some measure of individualized suspicion. We suggested in Prouse that we would not credit the "general interest in crime control" as justification for a regime of suspicionless stops. 440 U. S., at 659, n. 18. Consistent with this suggestion, each of the checkpoint programs that we have approved was designed primarily to serve purposes closely related to the problems of policing the border or the necessity of ensuring roadway safety. Because the primary purpose of the Indianapolis narcotics checkpoint program is to uncover evidence of ordinary criminal wrongdoing, the program contravenes the Fourth Amendment.

Petitioners propose several ways in which the narcotics detection purpose of the instant checkpoint program may instead resemble the primary purposes of the checkpoints in Sitz and Martinez-Fuerte. Petitioners state that the checkpoints in those cases had the same ultimate purpose of arresting those suspected of committing crimes. Brief for Petitioners 22. Securing the border and apprehending drunk drivers are, of course, law enforcement activities, and law enforcement officers employ arrests and criminal prosecutions in pursuit of these goals. See Sitz, 496 U. S., at 447, 450; Martinez-Fuerte, 428 U. S., at 545-550. If we were to rest the case at this high level of generality, there would be little check on the ability of the authorities to construct roadblocks for almost any conceivable law enforcement purpose. Without drawing the line at roadblocks designed primarily to serve the general interest in crime control, the Fourth Amendment would do little to prevent such intrusions from becoming a routine part of American life.

Petitioners also emphasize the severe and intractable nature of the drug problem as justification for the checkpoint program. Brief for Petitioners 14-17, 31. There is no doubt that traffic in illegal narcotics creates social harms of the first magnitude. Cf. Von Raab, 489 U. S., at 668. The law enforcement problems that the drug trade creates likewise remain daunting and complex, particularly in light of the myriad forms of spin-off crime that it spawns. Cf. M ontoya de Hernandez, 473 U. S., at 538. The same can be said of various other illegal activities, if only to a lesser degree. But the gravity of the threat alone cannot be dispositive of questions concerning what means law enforcement officers may employ to pursue a given purpose. Rather, in determining whether individualized suspicion is required, we must consider the nature of the interests threatened and their connection to the particular law enforcement practices at issue. We are particularly reluctant to recognize exceptions to the general rule of individualized suspicion where governmental authorities primarily pursue their general crime control ends.

Nor can the narcotics-interdiction purpose of the checkpoints be rationalized in terms of a highway safety concern similar to that present in Sitz. The detection and punishment of almost any criminal offense serves broadly the safety of the community, and our streets would no doubt be safer but for the scourge of illegal drugs. Only with respect to a smaller class of offenses, however, is society confronted with the type of immediate, vehicle-bound threat to life and limb that the sobriety checkpoint in Sitz was designed to eliminate.

Petitioners also liken the anticontraband agenda of the Indianapolis checkpoints to the antismuggling purpose of the checkpoints in Martinez-Fuerte. Brief for Petitioners 1516. Petitioners cite this Court's conclusion in Martinez-Fuerte that the flow of traffic was too heavy to permit "particularized study of a given car that would enable it to be identified as a possible carrier of illegal aliens," 428 U. S., at 557, and claim that this logic has even more force here. The problem with this argument is that the same logic prevails any time a vehicle is employed to conceal contraband or other evidence of a crime. This type of connection to the roadway is very different from the close connection to roadway safety that was present in Sitz and Prouse. Further, the Indianapolis checkpoints are far removed from the border context that was crucial in Martinez-Fuerte. While the difficulty of examining each passing car was an important factor in validating the law enforcement technique employed in Martinez-Fuerte, this factor alone cannot justify a regime of suspicionless searches or seizures. Rather, we must look more closely at the nature of the public interests that such a regime is designed principally to serve.

The primary purpose of the Indianapolis narcotics checkpoints is in the end to advance "the general interest in crime control," Prouse, 440 U. S., at 659, n. 18. We decline to suspend the usual requirement of individualized suspicion where the police seek to employ a checkpoint primarily for the ordinary enterprise of investigating crimes. We cannot sanction stops justified only by the generalized and everpresent possibility that interrogation and inspection may reveal that any given motorist has committed some crime.

Of course, there are circumstances that may justify a law enforcement checkpoint where the primary purpose would otherwise, but for some emergency, relate to ordinary crime control. For example, as the Court of Appeals noted, the Fourth Amendment would almost certainly permit an appropriately tailored roadblock set up to thwart an imminent terrorist attack or to catch a dangerous criminal who is likely to flee by way of a particular route. See 183 F. 3d, at 662663. The exigencies created by these scenarios are far removed from the circumstances under which authorities might simply stop cars as a matter of course to see if there just happens to be a felon leaving the jurisdiction. While we do not limit the purposes that may justify a checkpoint program to any rigid set of categories, we decline to approve a program whose primary purpose is ultimately indistinguishable from the general interest in crime control.l

Petitioners argue that our prior cases preclude an inquiry into the purposes of the checkpoint program. For example, they cite Whren v. United States, 517 U. S. 806 (1996), and Bond v. United States, 529 U. S. 334 (2000), to support the proposition that "where the government articulates and pursues a legitimate interest for a suspicionless stop, courts should not look behind that interest to determine whether the government's 'primary purpose' is valid." Brief for Petitioners 34; see also id., at 9. These cases, however, do not control the instant situation.

In Whren, we held that an individual officer's subjective intentions are irrelevant to the

Fourth Amendment validity of a traffic stop that is justified objectively by probable cause to believe that a traffic violation has occurred. 517 U. S., at 810-813. We observed that our prior cases "foreclose any argument that the constitutional reasonableness of traffic stops depends on the actual motivations of the individual officers involved." Id., at 813. In so holding, we expressly distinguished cases where we had addressed the validity of searches conducted in the absence of probable cause. See id., at 811-812 (distinguishing Florida v. Wells, 495 U. S. 1, 4 (1990) (stating that "an inventory search must not be a ruse for a general rummaging in order to discover incriminating evidence"), Colorado v. Bertine, 479 U. S. 367, 372 (1987) (suggesting that the absence of bad faith and the lack of a purely investigative purpose were relevant to the validity of an inventory search), and Burger, 482 U. S., at 716-717, n. 27 (observing that a valid administrative inspection conducted with neither a warrant nor probable cause did not appear to be a pretext for gathering evidence of violations of the penal laws)).

Whren therefore reinforces the principle that, while "[sJubjective intentions play no role in ordinary, probablecause Fourth Amendment analysis," 517 U. S., at 813, programmatic purposes may be relevant to the validity of Fourth Amendment intrusions undertaken pursuant to a general scheme without individualized Suspicion. Accordingly, Whren does not preclude an inquiry into programmatic purpose in such contexts. Cf. Chandler v. Miller, 520 U. S. 305 (1997); Treasury Employees v. Von Raab, 489 U. S. 656 (1989); Burger, supra; Michigan v. Tyler, 436 U. S. 499 (1978); Camara v. Municipal Court of City and County of San Francisco, 387 U. S. 523 (1967). It likewise does not preclude an inquiry into programmatic purpose here.

Last Term in Bond, we addressed the question whether a law enforcement officer violated a reasonable expectation of privacy in conducting a tactile examination of carry-on luggage in the overhead compartment of a bus. In doing so, we simply noted that the principle of Whren rendered the subjective intent of an officer irrelevant to this analysis. 529 U. S., at 338, n. 2. While, as petitioners correctly observe, the analytical rubric of Bond was not "ordinary, probable-cause Fourth Amendment analysis," Whren, supra, at 813, nothing in Bond suggests that we would extend the principle of Whren to all situations where individualized suspicion was lacking. Rather, subjective intent was irrelevant in Bond because the inquiry that our precedents required focused on the objective effects of the actions of an individual officer. By contrast, our cases dealing with intrusions that occur pursuant to a general scheme absent individualized suspicion have often required an inquiry into purpose at the programmatic level.

Petitioners argue that the Indianapolis checkpoint program is justified by its lawful secondary purposes of keeping impaired motorists off the road and verifying licenses and registrations. Brief for Petitioners 31-34. If this were the case, however, law enforcement authorities would be able to establish checkpoints for virtually any purpose so long as they also included a license or sobriety check. For this reason, we examine the available evidence to determine the primary purpose of the checkpoint program. While we recognize the challenges inherent in a purpose inquiry, courts routinely engage in this enterprise in many areas of constitutional jurisprudence as a means of sifting abusive governmental conduct from that which is lawful. Cf. 183 F. 3d, at 665. As a result, a program driven by an impermissible purpose may be proscribed while a program impelled by licit purposes is permitted, even though the challenged conduct may be outwardly similar. While reasonableness under the Fourth Amendment is predominantly an objective inquiry, our special needs and administrative search cases demonstrate that purpose is often relevant when suspicionless intrusions pursuant to a general scheme are at issue.2

It goes without saying that our holding today does nothing to alter the constitutional status of the sobriety and border checkpoints that we approved in Sitz and Martinez-Fuerte, or of the type of traffic checkpoint that we suggested would be lawful in Prouse. The constitutionality of such checkpoint programs still depends on a balancing of the competing interests at stake and the effectiveness of the program. See Sitz, 496 U. S., at 450-455; Martinez-Fuerte, 428 U. S., at 556-564. When law enforcement authorities pursue primarily general crime control purposes at checkpoints such as here, however, stops can only be justified by some quantum of individualized suspicion.

Our holding also does not affect the validity of border searches or searches at places like airports and government buildings, where the need for such measures to ensure public safety can be particularly acute. Nor does our opinion speak to other intrusions aimed primarily at purposes beyond the general interest in crime control. Our holding also does not impair the ability of police officers to act appropriately upon information that they properly learn during a checkpoint stop justified by a lawful primary purpose, even where such action may result in the arrest of a motorist for an offense unrelated to that purpose. Finally, we caution that the purpose inquiry in this context is to be conducted only at the programmatic level and is not an invitation to probe the minds of individual officers acting at the scene. Cf. Whren, supra.

Because the primary purpose of the Indianapolis checkpoint program is ultimately indistinguishable from the general interest in crime control, the checkpoints violate the Fourth Amendment. The judgment of the Court of Appeals is, accordingly, affirmed.

It is so ordered.

Notes

1 THE CHIEF JUSTICE'S dissent erroneously characterizes our opinion as resting on the application of a "non-law-enforcement primary purpose test." Post, at 53. Our opinion nowhere describes the purposes of the Sitz and Martinez-Fuerte checkpoints as being "not primarily related to criminal law enforcement." Post, at 50. Rather, our judgment turns on the fact that the primary purpose of the Indianapolis checkpoints is to advance the general interest in crime control.

THE CHIEF JUSTICE'S dissent also erroneously characterizes our opinion as holding that the "use of a drug-sniffing dog ... annuls what is otherwise plainly constitutional under our Fourth Amendment jurisprudence." Post, at 48. Again, the constitutional defect of the program is that its primary purpose is to advance the general interest in crime control.

2 Because petitioners concede that the primary purpose of the Indianapolis checkpoints is narcotics detection, we need not decide whether the State may establish a checkpoint program with the primary purpose of checking licenses or driver sobriety and a secondary purpose of interdicting narcotics. Specifically, we express no view on the question whether police may expand the scope of a license or sobriety checkpoint seizure in order to detect the presence of drugs in a stopped car. Cf. New Jersey v. T. L. O, 469 U. S. 325, 341 (1985) (search must be "'reasonably related in scope to the circumstances which justified the interference in the first place'" (quoting Terry v. Ohio, 392 U. S. 1, 20 (1968))); Michigan v. Clifford, 464 U. S. 287, 294-295 (1984) (plurality opinion).

Ferguson v. Charleston (March 21, 2001)

Justice Stevens delivered the opinion of the Court.

In this case, we must decide whether a state hospital's performance of a diagnostic test to obtain evidence of a patient's criminal conduct for law enforcement purposes is an unreasonable search if the patient has not consented to the procedure. More narrowly, the question is whether the interest in using the threat of criminal sanctions to deter pregnant women from using cocaine can justify a departure from the general rule that an official nonconsensual search is unconstitutional if not authorized by a valid warrant.

I

In the fall of 1988, staff members at the public hospital operated in the city of Charleston by the Medical University of South Carolina (MUSC) became concerned about an apparent increase in the use of cocaine by patients who were receiving prenatal treatment.1 In response to this perceived increase, as of April 1989, MUSC began to order drug screens to be performed on urine samples from maternity patients who were suspected of using cocaine. If a patient tested positive, she was then referred by MUSC staff to the county substance abuse commission for counseling and treatment. However, despite the referrals, the incidence of cocaine use among the patients at MUSC did not appear to change.

Some four months later, Nurse Shirley Brown, the case manager for the MUSC obstetrics department, heard a news broadcast reporting that the police in Greenville, South Carolina, were arresting pregnant users of cocaine on the theory that such use harmed the fetus and was therefore child abuse.2 Nurse Brown discussed the story with MUSC's general counsel, Joseph C. Good, Jr., who then contacted Charleston Solicitor Charles Condon in order to offer MUSC's cooperation in prosecuting mothers whose children tested positive for drugs at birth.3

After receiving Good's letter, Solicitor Condon took the first steps in developing the policy at issue in this case. He organized the initial meetings, decided who would participate, and issued the invitations, in which he described his plan to prosecute women who tested positive for cocaine while pregnant. The task force that Condon formed included representatives of MUSC, the police, the County Substance Abuse Commission and the Department of Social Services. Their deliberations led to MUSC's adoption of a 12-page document entitled "POLICY M—7," dealing with the subject of "Management of Drug Abuse During Pregnancy." App. to Pet. for Cert. A—53.

The first three pages of Policy M—7 set forth the procedure to be followed by the hospital staff to "identify/assist pregnant patients suspected of drug abuse." Id., at A—53 to A—56. The first section, entitled the "Identification of Drug Abusers," provided that a patient should be tested for cocaine through a urine drug screen if she met one or more of nine criteria.4 It also stated that a chain of custody should be followed when obtaining and testing urine samples, presumably to make sure that the results could be used in subsequent criminal proceedings. The policy also provided for education and referral to a substance abuse clinic for patients who tested positive. Most important, it added the threat of law enforcement intervention that "provided the necessary ' leverage' to make the [p]olicy effective." Brief for Respondents 8. That threat was, as respondents candidly acknowledge, essential to the program's success in getting women into treatment and keeping them there.

The threat of law enforcement involvement was set forth in two protocols, the first dealing with the identification of drug use during pregnancy, and the second with identification of drug use after labor. Under the latter protocol, the police were to be notified without delay and the patient promptly arrested. Under the former, after the initial positive drug test, the police were to be notified (and the patient arrested) only if the patient tested positive for cocaine a second time or if she missed an appointment with a substance abuse counselor.5 In 1990, however, the policy was modified at the behest of the solicitor's office to give the patient who tested positive during labor, like the patient who tested positive during a prenatal care visit, an opportunity to avoid arrest by consenting to substance abuse treatment.

The last six pages of the policy contained forms for the patients to sign, as well as procedures for the police to follow when a patient was arrested. The policy also prescribed in detail the precise offenses with which a woman could be charged, depending on the stage of her pregnancy. If the pregnancy was 27 weeks or less, the patient was to be charged with simple possession. If it was 28 weeks or more, she was to be charged with possession and distribution to a person under the age of 18–in this case, the fetus. If she delivered "while testing positive for illegal drugs," she was also to be charged with unlawful neglect of a child. App. to Pet. for Cert. A—62. Under the policy, the police were instructed to interrogate the arrestee in order "to ascertain the identity of the subject who provided illegal drugs to the suspect." Id., at A—63. Other than the provisions describing the substance abuse treatment to be offered to women who tested positive, the policy made no mention of any change in the prenatal care of such patients, nor did it prescribe any special treatment for the newborns.

II

Petitioners are 10 women who received obstetrical care at MUSC and who were arrested after testing positive for cocaine. Four of them were arrested during the initial implementation of the policy; they were not offered the opportunity to receive drug treatment as an alternative to arrest. The others were arrested after the policy was modified in 1990; they either failed to comply with the terms of the drug treatment program or tested positive for a second time. Respondents include the city of Charleston, law enforcement officials who helped develop and enforce the policy, and representatives of MUSC.

Petitioners' complaint challenged the validity of the policy under various theories, including the claim that warrantless and nonconsensual drug tests conducted for criminal investigatory purposes were unconstitutional searches. Respondents advanced two principal defenses to the constitutional claim: (1) that, as a matter of fact, petitioners had consented to the searches; and (2) that, as a matter of law, the searches were reasonable, even absent consent, because they were justified by special non-law-enforcement purposes. The District Court rejected the second defense because the searches in question "were not done by the medical university for independent purposes. [Instead,] the police came in and there was an agreement reached that the positive screens would be shared with the police." App. 1248—1249. Accordingly, the District Court submitted the factual defense to the jury with instructions that required a verdict in favor of petitioners unless the jury found consent.6 The jury found for respondents.

Petitioners appealed, arguing that the evidence was not sufficient to support the jury's consent finding. The Court of Appeals for the Fourth Circuit affirmed, but without reaching the question of consent. 186 F.3d 469 (1999). Disagreeing with the District Court, the majority of the appellate panel held that the searches were reasonable as a matter of law under our line of cases recognizing that "special needs" may, in certain exceptional circumstances, justify a search policy designed to serve non-law-enforcement ends.7 On the understanding "that MUSC personnel conducted the urine drug screens for medical purposes wholly independent of an intent to aid law enforcement efforts,"[8] id., at 477, the majority applied the balancing test used in Treasury Employees v. Von Raab, 489 U.S. 656 (1989), and Vernonia School Dist. 47J v. Acton, 515 U.S. 646 (1995), and concluded that the interest in curtailing the pregnancy complications and medical costs associated with maternal cocaine use outweighed what the majority termed a minimal intrusion on the privacy of the patients. In dissent, Judge Blake concluded that the "special needs" doctrine should not apply and that the evidence of consent was insufficient to sustain the jury's verdict. 186 F.3d, at 487–488.

We granted certiorari, 528 U.S. 1187 (2000), to review the appellate court's holding on the "special needs" issue. Because we do not reach the question of the sufficiency of the evidence with respect to consent, we necessarily assume for purposes of our decision–as did the Court of Appeals–that the searches were conducted without the informed consent of the patients. We conclude that the judgment should be reversed and the case remanded for a decision on the consent issue.

III

Because MUSC is a state hospital, the members of its staff are government actors, subject to the strictures of the Fourth Amendment. New Jersey v. T. L. O., 469 U.S. 325, 335–337 (1985). Moreover, the urine tests conducted by those staff members were indisputably searches within the meaning of the Fourth Amendment. Skinner v. Railway Labor Executives' Assn., 489 U.S. 602, 617 (1989).[9] Neither the District Court nor the Court of Appeals concluded that any of the nine criteria used to identify the women to be searched provided either probable cause to believe that they were using cocaine, or even the basis for a reasonable suspicion of such use. Rather, the District Court and the Court of Appeals viewed the case as one involving MUSC's right to conduct searches without warrants or probable cause.[10] Furthermore, given the posture in which the case

comes to us, we must assume for purposes of our decision that the tests were performed without the informed consent of the patients.[11]

Because the hospital seeks to justify its authority to conduct drug tests and to turn the results over to law enforcement agents without the knowledge or consent of the patients, this case differs from the four previous cases in which we have considered whether comparable drug tests "fit within the closely guarded category of constitutionally permissible suspicionless searches." Chandler v. Miller, 520 U.S. 305, 309 (1997). In three of those cases, we sustained drug tests for railway employees involved in train accidents, Skinner v. Railway Labor Executives' Assn., 489 U.S. 602 (1989), for United States Customs Service employees seeking promotion to certain sensitive positions, Treasury Employees v. Von Raab, 489 U.S. 656 (1989), and for high school students participating in interscholastic sports, Vernonia School Dist. 47J v. Acton, 515 U.S. 646 (1995). In the fourth case, we struck down such testing for candidates for designated state offices as unreasonable. Chandler v. Miller, 520 U.S. 305 (1997).

In each of those cases, we employed a balancing test that weighed the intrusion on the individual's interest in privacy against the "special needs" that supported the program. As an initial matter, we note that the invasion of privacy in this case is far more substantial than in those cases. In the previous four cases, there was no misunderstanding about the purpose of the test or the potential use of the test results, and there were protections against the dissemination of the results to third parties.[12] The use of an adverse test result to disqualify one from eligibility for a particular benefit, such as a promotion or an opportunity to participate in an extracurricular activity, involves a less serious intrusion on privacy than the unauthorized dissemination of such results to third parties. The reasonable expectation of privacy enjoyed by the typical patient undergoing diagnostic tests in a hospital is that the results of those tests will not be shared with nonmedical personnel without her consent. See Brief for American Medical Association et al. as Amici Curiae 11; Brief for American Public Health Association et al. as Amici Curiae 6, 17—19.13 In none of our prior cases was there any intrusion upon that kind of expectation.14

The critical difference between those four drug-testing cases and this one, however, lies in the nature of the "special need" asserted as justification for the warrantless searches. In each of those earlier cases, the "special need" that was advanced as a justification for the absence of a warrant or individualized suspicion was one divorced from the State's general interest in law enforcement.15 This point was emphasized both in the majority opinions sustaining the programs in the first three cases,16 as well as in the dissent in the Chandler case.17 In this case, however, the central and indispensable feature of the policy from its inception was the use of law enforcement to coerce the patients into substance abuse treatment. This fact distinguishes this case from circumstances in which physicians or psychologists, in the course of ordinary medical procedures aimed at helping the patient herself, come across information that under rules of law or ethics is subject to reporting requirements, which no one has challenged here. See, e.g., Council on Ethical and Judicial Affairs, American Medical Association, PolicyFinder, Current Opinions E—5.05 (2000) (requiring reporting where "a patient threatens to inflict serious bodily harm to another person or to him or herself and there is a reasonable probability that the patient may carry out the threat"); Ark. Code Ann. §12—12—602 (1999) (requiring reporting of intentionally inflicted knife or gunshot wounds); Ariz. Rev. Stat. Ann. §13—3620 (Supp. 2000) (requiring "any . . . person having responsibility for the care or treatment of children" to report suspected abuse or neglect to a peace officer or child protection agency).18

Respondents argue in essence that their ultimate purpose–namely, protecting the health of both mother and child–is a benificent one. In Chandler, however, we did not simply accept the State's invocation of a "special need." Instead, we carried out a "close review" of the scheme at issue before concluding that the need in question was not "special," as that term has been defined in our cases. 520 U.S., at 322. In this case, a review of the M—7 policy plainly reveals that the purpose actually served by the MUSC searches "is ultimately indistinguishable from the general interest in crime control." Indianapolis v. Edmond, 531 U.S. ___, ___ (2000) (slip op., at 15).

In looking to the programmatic purpose, we consider all the available evidence in order to determine the relevant primary purpose. See, e.g., id., at ___—___ (slip op., at 12—14). In this case, as Judge Blake put it in her dissent below, "it . . . is clear from the record that an initial and continuing focus of the policy was on the arrest and prosecution of drug-abusing mothers . . . ." 186 F.3d, at 484. Tellingly, the document codifying the policy incorporates the police's operational guidelines. It devotes its attention to the chain of custody, the range of possible criminal charges, and the logistics of police notification and arrests. Nowhere, however, does the document discuss different courses of medical treatment for either mother or infant, aside from treatment for the mother's addiction.

Moreover, throughout the development and application of the policy, the Charleston prosecutors and police were extensively involved in the day-to-day administration of the policy. Police and prosecutors decided who would receive the reports of positive drug screens and what information would be included with those reports. App. 78—80, 145—146, 1058—1060. Law enforcement officials also helped determine the procedures to be followed when performing the screens.19 Id., at 1052—1053. See also id., at 26—27, 945. In the course of the policy's administration, they had access to Nurse Brown's medical files on the women who tested positive, routinely attended the substance abuse team's meetings, and regularly received copies of team documents discussing the women's progress. Id., at 122—124, 609—610. Police took pains to coordinate the timing and circumstances of the arrests with MUSC staff, and, in particular, Nurse Brown. Id., at 1057—1058.

While the ultimate goal of the program may well have been to get the women in question into substance abuse treatment and off of drugs, the immediate objective of the searches was to generate evidence for law enforcement purposes20 in order to reach that goal.21 The threat of law enforcement may ultimately have been intended as a means to an end, but the direct and primary purpose of MUSC's policy was to ensure the use of those means. In our opinion, this distinction is critical. Because law enforcement involvement always serves some broader social purpose or objective, under respondents' view, virtually any nonconsensual suspicionless search could be immunized under the special needs doctrine by defining the search solely in terms of its ultimate, rather than immediate, purpose.22 Such an approach is inconsistent with the Fourth Amendment. Given the primary purpose of the Charleston program, which was to use the threat of arrest and prosecution in order to force women into treatment, and given the extensive involvement of law enforcement officials at every stage of the policy, this case simply does not fit within the closely guarded category of "special needs."23

The fact that positive test results were turned over to the police does not merely provide a basis for distinguishing our prior cases applying the "special needs" balancing approach to the determination of drug use. It also provides an affirmative reason for enforcing the strictures of the Fourth Amendment. While state hospital employees, like other citizens, may have a duty to provide the police with evidence of criminal conduct that they inadvertently acquire in the course of routine treatment, when they undertake to obtain such evidence from their patients for the specific purpose of incriminating those patients, they have a special obligation to make sure that the patients are fully informed about their constitutional rights, as standards of knowing waiver require.24 Cf. Miranda v. Arizona, 384 U.S. 436 (1966).

As respondents have repeatedly insisted, their motive was benign rather than punitive. Such a motive, however, cannot justify a departure from Fourth Amendment protections, given the pervasive involvement of law enforcement with the development and application of the MUSC policy. The stark and unique fact that characterizes this case is that Policy M—7 was designed to obtain evidence of criminal conduct by the tested patients that would be turned over to the police and that could be admissible in subsequent criminal prosecutions. While respondents are correct that drug abuse both was and is a serious problem, "the gravity of the threat alone cannot be dispositive of questions concerning what means law enforcement officers may employ to pursue a given purpose." Indianapolis v. Edmond, 531 U.S., at ___—____ (slip op., at 9—10). The Fourth Amendment's general prohibition against nonconsensual, warrantless, and suspicionless searches necessarily applies to such a policy. See, e.g., Chandler, 520 U.S., at 308; Skinner 498 U.S., at 619.

Accordingly, the judgment of the Court of Appeals is reversed, and the case is remanded for further proceedings consistent with this opinion.

It is so ordered.

Notes

1. As several witnesses testified at trial, the problem of "crack babies" was widely perceived in the late 1980's as a national epidemic, prompting considerable concern both in the medical community and among the general populace.

2. Under South Carolina law, a viable fetus has historically been regarded as a person; in 1995, the South Carolina Supreme Court held that the ingestion of cocaine during the third trimester of pregnancy constitutes criminal child neglect. Whitner v. South Carolina, 328 S. C. 1, 492 S. E. 2d 777 (1995), cert. denied, 523 U.S. 1145 (1998).

3. In his letter dated August 23, 1989, Good wrote: " Please advise us if your office is anticipating future criminal action and what if anything our Medical Center needs to do to assist you in this matter." App. to Pet. for Cert. A—67.

4. Those criteria were as follows: "1. No prenatal care "2. Late prenatal care after 24 weeks gestation "3. Incomplete prenatal care "4. Abruptio placentae "5. Intrauterine fetal death "6. Preterm labor ' of no obvious cause' "7. IUGR [intrauterine growth retardation] ' of no obvious cause' "8. Previously known drug or alcohol abuse "9. Unexplained congenital anomalies." Id., at A—53 to A—54.

5. Despite the conditional description of the first category, when the policy was in its initial stages, a positive test was immediately reported to the police, who then promptly arrested the patient.

6. The instructions read: "THERE WERE NO SEARCH WARRANTS ISSUED BY A MAGISTRATE OR ANY OTHER PROPER JUDICIAL OFFICER TO PERMIT THESE URINE SCREENS TO BE TAKEN. THERE NOT BEING A WARRANT ISSUED, THEY ARE UNREASONABLE AND IN VIOLATION OF THE CONSTITUTION OF THE UNITED STATES, UNLESS THE DEFENDANTS HAVE SHOWN BY THE GREATER WEIGHT OR PREPONDERANCE OF THE EVIDENCE THAT THE PLAINTIFFS CONSENTED TO THOSE SEARCHES." App. 1314—1315. Under the judge's instructions, in order to find that the plaintiffs had consented to the searches, it was necessary for the jury to find that they had consented to the taking of the samples, to the testing for evidence of cocaine, and to the possible disclosure of the test results to the police. Respondents have not argued, as Justice Scalia does, that it is permissible for members of the staff of a public hospital to use diagnostic tests "deceivingly" to obtain incriminating evidence from their patients. See post, at 3 (dissenting opinion).

7. The term "special needs" first appeared in Justice Blackmun's opinion concurring in the judgment in New Jersey v. T. L. O., 469 U.S. 325, 351 (1985). In his concurrence, Justice Blackmun agreed with the Court that there are limited exceptions to the probable-cause requirement, in which reasonableness is determined by "a careful balancing of governmental and private interests," but concluded that such a test should only be applied "in those exceptional circumstances in which special needs, beyond the normal need for law enforcement, make the warrant and probable-cause requirement impracticable . . . ." Ibid. This Court subsequently adopted the "special needs" terminology in O'Connor v. Ortega, 480 U.S. 709, 720 (1987) (plurality opinion), and Griffin v. Wisconsin, 483 U.S. 868, 873 (1987), concluding that, in limited circumstances, a search unsupported by either warrant or probable cause can be constitutional when "special needs" other than the normal need for law enforcement provide sufficient justification. See also Vernonia School District 47J v. Acton, 515 U.S. 646, 652—653 (1995).

8. The majority stated that the District Court had made such a finding. 186 F.3d 469, 477 (CA4 1999). The text of the relevant finding, made in the context of petitioners' now abandoned Title

VI claim, reads as follows: "The policy was applied in all maternity departments at MUSC. Its goal was not to arrest patients but to facilitate their treatment and protect both the mother and unborn child." App. to Pet. for Cert. A—38. That finding, however, must be read in light of this comment by the District Court with respect to the Fourth Amendment claim: ". . . THESE SEARCHES WERE NOT DONE BY THE MEDICAL UNIVERSITY FOR INDEPENDENT PURPOSES. IF THEY HAD BEEN, THEN THEY WOULD NOT IMPLICATE THE FOURTH AMENDMENT. OBVIOUSLY AS I POINT OUT THERE ON PAGE 4, NORMALLY URINE SCREENS AND BLOOD TESTS AND THAT TYPE OF THING CAN BE TAKEN BY HEALTH CARE PROVIDERS WITHOUT HAVING TO WORRY ABOUT THE FOURTH AMENDMENT. THE ONLY REASON THE FOURTH AMENDMENT IS IMPLICATED HERE IS THAT THE POLICE CAME IN AND THERE WAS AN AGREEMENT REACHED THAT THE POSITIVE SCREENS WOULD BE SHARED WITH THE POLICE. AND THEN THE SCREEN IS NOT DONE INDEPENDENT OF POLICE, IT'S DONE IN CONJUNCTION WITH THE POLICE AND THAT IMPLICATES THE FOURTH AMENDMENT." App. 1247—1249.

9.   In arguing that the urine tests at issue were not searches, the dissent attempts to disaggregate the taking and testing of the urine sample from the reporting of the results to the police. See post, at 2. However, in our special needs cases, we have routinely treated urine screens taken by state agents as searches within the meaning of the Fourth Amendment even though the results were not reported to the police, see, e.g., Chandler v. Miller, 520 U.S. 305 (1997); Vernonia School Dist. 47J v. Acton, 515 U.S. 646 (1995); Skinner v. Railway Labor Executives' Assn., 489 U.S. 602, 617 (1989); Treasury Employees v. Von Raab, 489 U.S. 656 (1989), and respondents here do not contend that the tests were not

searches. Rather, they argue that the searches were justified by consent and/or by special needs.

10.   In a footnote to their brief, respondents do argue that the searches were not entirely suspicionless. Brief for Respondents 23, n. 13. They do not, however, point to any evidence in the record indicating that any of the nine search criteria was more apt to be caused by cocaine use than by some other factor, such as malnutrition, illness, or indigency. More significantly, their legal argument and the reasoning of the majority panel opinion rest on the premise that the policy would be valid even if the tests were conducted randomly.

11.   The dissent would have us do otherwise and resolve the issue of consent in favor of respondents. Because the Court of Appeals did not discuss this issue, we think it more prudent to allow that court to resolve the legal and factual issues in the first instance, and we express no view on those issues. See, e.g., Glover v. United States, 531 U.S. ___ (2001); National Collegiate Athletic Assn. v. Smith, 525 U.S. 459, 470 (1999).

12.   Chandler, 520 U.S., at 312, 318; Acton, 515 U.S., at 658; Skinner, 489 U.S., at 621, n. 5, 622, n. 6; Von Raab, 489 U.S., at 663, 666—667, 672, n. 2.

13.   There are some circumstances in which state hospital employees, like other citizens, may have a duty to provide law enforcement officials with evidence of criminal conduct acquired in the course of routine treatment, see, e.g., S. C. Code Ann. §20—7—510 (2000) (physicians and nurses required to report to child welfare agency or law enforcement authority "when in the person's professional capacity the person" receives information that a child has been abused or neglected). While the existence of such laws might lead a patient to expect that members of the hospital staff might turn over evidence acquired in the course of treatment to which the patient had consented, they surely would not lead a patient to anticipate that hospital staff would

intentionally set out to obtain incriminating evidence from their patients for law enforcement purposes.

14. In fact, we have previously recognized that an intrusion on that expectation may have adverse consequences because it may deter patients from receiving needed medical care. Whalen v. Roe, 429 U.S. 589, 599—600 (1977). Cf. Poland, Dombrowski, Ager, & Sokol, Punishing pregnant drug users: enhancing the flight from care, 31 Drug and Alcohol Dependence 199—203 (1993).

15. As the Chief Justice recently noted: "The ' special needs' doctrine, which has been used to uphold certain suspicionless searches performed for reasons unrelated to law enforcement, is an exception to the general rule that a search must be based on individualized suspicion of wrongdoing." Indianapolis v. Edmond, 531 U.S. __, ____ (2000) (slip op., at 7) (dissenting opinion); see also nn. 16—17, infra. In T. L. O., we made a point of distinguishing searches "carried out by school authorities acting alone and on their own authority" from those conducted "in conjunction with or at the behest of law enforcement agencies." 469 U.S., at 341, n. 7. The dissent, however, relying on Griffin v. Wisconsin, 483 U.S. 868 (1987), argues that the special needs doctrine "is ordinarily employed, precisely to enable searches by law enforcement officials who, of course, ordinarily have a law enforcement objective." Post, at 7. Viewed in the context of our special needs case law and even viewed in isolation, Griffin does not support the proposition for which the dissent invokes it. In other special needs cases, we have tolerated suspension of the Fourth Amendment's warrant or probable cause requirement in part because there was no law enforcement purpose behind the searches in those cases, and there was little, if any, entanglement with law enforcement. See Skinner, 489 U.S., at 620—621; Von Raab, 489 U.S., at 665—666; Acton, 515 U.S., at 658.

Moreover, after our decision in Griffin, we reserved the question whether "routine use in criminal prosecutions of evidence obtained pursuant to the administrative scheme would give rise to an inference of pretext, or otherwise impugn the administrative nature of the . . . program." Skinner, 489 U.S., at 621, n. 5. In Griffin itself, this Court noted that "[a]lthough a probation officer is not an impartial magistrate, neither is he the police officer who normally conducts searches against the ordinary citizen." 483 U.S., at 876. Finally, we agree with petitioners that Griffin is properly read as limited by the fact that probationers have a lesser expectation of privacy than the public at large. Id., at 874—875.

16. In Skinner v. Railway Labor Executives' Assn., 489 U.S. 602 (1989), this Court noted that "[t]he FRA has prescribed toxicological tests, not to assist in the prosecution of employees, but rather 'to prevent accidents and casualties in railroad operations that result from impairment of employees by alcohol or drugs.' " Id., at 620—621 (quoting 49 CFR § 219.1(a) (1987)). Similarly, in Treasury Employees v. Von Raab, 489 U.S. 656 (1989), we concluded that it was "clear that the Customs Service's drug-testing program is not designed to serve the ordinary needs of law enforcement. Test results may not be used in a criminal prosecution of the employee without the employee's consent." Id., at 665—666. In the same vein, in Acton, 515 U.S., at 658, we relied in part on the fact that "the results of the tests are disclosed only to a limited class of school personnel who have a need to know; and they are not turned over to law enforcement authorities or used for any internal disciplinary function" in finding the searches reasonable.

17. "Today's opinion speaks of a 'closely guarded' class of permissible suspicionless searches which must be justified by a 'special need.' But this term, as used in Skinner and Von Raab and on which the Court now relies, was used

456

in a quite different sense than it is used by the Court today. In Skinner and Von Raab it was used to describe a basis for a search apart from the regular needs of law enforcement, Skinner, [489 U.S.], at 620; Von Raab, [489 U.S.], at 669. The 'special needs' inquiry as delineated there has not required especially great 'importan[ce],' [520 U.S.], at 318, unless one considers 'the supervision of probationers,' or the 'operation of a government office,' Skinner, supra, at 620, to be especially 'important.' Under our precedents, if there was a proper governmental purpose other than law enforcement, there was a 'special need,' and the Fourth Amendment then required the familiar balancing between that interest and the individual's privacy interest." Chandler v. Miller, 520 U.S., at 325 (Rehnquist, C. J., dissenting).

18. Our emphasis on this distinction should make it clear that, contrary to the hyperbole in the dissent, we do not view these reporting requirements as "clearly bad." See post, at 5, n. 3. Those requirements are simply not in issue here.

19. Accordingly, the police organized a meeting with the staff of the police and hospital laboratory staffs, as well as Nurse Brown, in which the police went over the concept of a chain of custody system with the MUSC staff. App. 1052–1053.

20. We italicize those words lest our reasoning be misunderstood. See post, at 1–2 (Kennedy, J., concurring in judgment). In none of our previous special needs cases have we upheld the collection of evidence for criminal law enforcement purposes. Our essential point is the same as Justice Kennedy's–the extensive entanglement of law enforcement cannot be justified by reference to legitimate needs. According to the dissent, the fact that MUSC performed tests prior to the development of Policy M–7 should immunize any subsequent testing policy despite the presence of a law enforcement purpose and extensive law enforcement

involvement. See post, at 8–10. To say that any therapeutic purpose did not disappear is simply to miss the point. What matters is that under the new policy developed by the solicitor's office and MUSC, law enforcement involvement was the means by which that therapeutic purpose was to be met. Policy M–7 was, at its core, predicated on the use of law enforcement. The extensive involvement of law enforcement and the threat of prosecution were, as respondents admitted, essential to the program's success.

21. Accordingly, this case differs from New York v. Burger, 482 U.S. 691 (1987), in which the Court upheld a scheme in which police officers were used to carry out administrative inspections of vehicle dismantling businesses. That case involved an industry in which the expectation of privacy in commercial premises was "particularly attenuated" given the extent to which the industry in question was closely regulated. Id., at 700. More important for our purposes, the Court relied on the "plain administrative purposes" of the scheme to reject the contention that the statute was in fact "designed to gather evidence to enable convictions under the penal laws . . . ." Id., at 715. The discovery of evidence of other violations would have been merely incidental to the purposes of the administrative search. In contrast, in this case, the policy was specifically designed to gather evidence of violations of penal laws. This case also differs from the handful of seizure cases in which we have applied a balancing test to determine Fourth Amendment reasonableness. See, e.g., Michigan Dept. of State Police v. Sitz, 496 U.S. 444, 455 (1990); United States v. Martinez-Fuerte, 428 U.S. 543 (1976). First, those cases involved roadblock seizures, rather than "the intrusive search of the body or the home." See Indianapolis v. Edmond, 531 U.S., at ___–___ (slip op., at 7–8) (Rehnquist, C. J., dissenting); Martinez-Fuerte, 428 U.S., at 561 ("[W]e deal neither with searches nor with the sanctity of private dwellings, ordinarily afforded

the most stringent Fourth Amendment protection"). Second, the Court explicitly distinguished the cases dealing with checkpoints from those dealing with "special needs." Sitz, 496 U.S., at 450.

22. Thus, under respondents' approach, any search to generate evidence for use by the police in enforcing general criminal laws would be justified by reference to the broad social benefits that those laws might bring about (or, put another way, the social harms that they might prevent).

23. It is especially difficult to argue that the program here was designed simply to save lives. Amici claim a near consensus in the medical community that programs of the sort at issue, by discouraging women who use drugs from seeking prenatal care, harm, rather than advance, the cause of prenatal health. See Brief for American Medical Association as Amicus Curiae 6—22; Brief for American Public Health Association et al. as Amici Curiae 17—21; Brief for NARAL Foundation et al. as Amici Curiae 18—19.

24. In fact, some MUSC staff made this distinction themselves. See Pl. Exh. No. 14, Hulsey, 11—17—89, Coke Committee, 1—2 ("The use of medically indicated tests for substance abuse, obtained in conventional manners, must be distinguished from mandatory screening and collection of evidence using such methods as chain of custody, etc. . . . The question is raised as to whether pediatricians should function as law enforcement officials. While the reporting of criminal activity to appropriate authorities may be required and/or ethically just, the active pursuit of evidence to be used against individuals presenting for medical care may not be proper"). The dissent, however, mischaracterizes our opinion as holding that "material which a person voluntarily entrusts to someone else cannot be given by that person to the police and used for whatever evidence it may contain." Post, at 4. But, as we have noted elsewhere, given the posture of the case, we must assume for purposes of decision that the patients did not consent to the searches, and we leave the question of consent for the Court of Appeals to determine. See n. 11, supra. The dissent further argues that our holding "leaves law enforcement officials entirely in the dark as to when they can use incriminating evidence obtained from 'trusted' sources." See post, at 5. With all due respect, we disagree. We do not address a case in which doctors independently complied with reporting requirements. Rather, as we point out above, in this case, medical personnel used the criteria set out in n. 4, supra, to collect evidence for law enforcement purposes, and law enforcement officers were extensively involved in the initiation, design, and implementation of the program. In such circumstances, the Fourth Amendment's general prohibition against nonconsensual, warrantless, and suspicionless searches applies in the absence of consent. We decline to accept the dissent's invitation to make a foray into dicta and address other situations not before us.

Gail Atwater v. City of Lago Vista (April 24, 2001) [Appendix omitted]

Justice Souter delivered the opinion of the Court.

The question is whether the Fourth Amendment forbids a warrantless arrest for a minor criminal offense, such as a misdemeanor seatbelt violation punishable only by a fine. We hold that it does not.

I

A

In Texas, if a car is equipped with safety belts, a front-seat passenger must wear one, Tex. Tran. Code Ann. §545.413(a) (1999), and the driver must secure any small child riding in front, §545.413(b). Violation of either provision is "a misdemeanor punishable by a fine not less than $25 or more than $50." §545.413(d). Texas law expressly authorizes "[a]ny peace officer [to] arrest without warrant a person found committing a violation" of these seatbelt laws, §543.001, although it permits police to issue citations in lieu of arrest, §§543.003–543.005.

In March 1997, Petitioner Gail Atwater was driving her pickup truck in Lago Vista, Texas, with her 3-year-old son and 5-year-old daughter in the front seat. None of them was wearing a seatbelt. Respondent Bart Turek, a Lago Vista police officer at the time, observed the seatbelt violations and pulled Atwater over. According to Atwater's complaint (the allegations of which we assume to be true for present purposes), Turek approached the truck and "yell[ed]" something to the effect of "[w]e've met before" and "[y]ou're going to jail." App. 20.1 He then called for backup and asked to see Atwater's driver's license and insurance documentation, which state law required her to carry. Tex. Tran. Code Ann. §§521.025, 601.053 (1999). When Atwater told Turek that she did not have the papers because her purse had been stolen the day before, Turek said that he had "heard that story two-hundred times." App. 21.

Atwater asked to take her "frightened, upset, and crying" children to a friend's house nearby, but Turek told her, "[y]ou're not going anywhere." Ibid. As it turned out, Atwater's friend learned what was going on and soon arrived to take charge of the children. Turek then handcuffed Atwater, placed her in his squad car, and drove her to the local police station, where booking officers had her remove her shoes, jewelry, and eyeglasses, and empty her pockets. Officers took Atwater's "mug shot" and placed her, alone, in a jail cell for about one hour, after which she was taken before a magistrate and released on $310 bond.

Atwater was charged with driving without her seatbelt fastened, failing to secure her children in seatbelts, driving without a license, and failing to provide proof of insurance. She ultimately pleaded no contest to the misdemeanor seatbelt offenses and paid a $50 fine; the other charges were dismissed.

B

Atwater and her husband, petitioner Michael Haas, filed suit in a Texas state court under 42 U.S.C. § 1983 against Turek and respondents City of Lago Vista and Chief of Police Frank Miller. So far as concerns us, petitioners (whom we will simply call Atwater) alleged that respondents (for simplicity, the City) had violated Atwater's Fourth Amendment "right to be free from unreasonable seizure," App. 23, and sought compensatory and punitive damages.

The City removed the suit to the United States District Court for the Western District of Texas. Given Atwater's admission that she had "violated the law" and the absence of any allegation "that she was harmed or detained in any way inconsistent with the law," the District Court ruled the Fourth Amendment claim "meritless" and granted the City's summary judgment motion. No. A–97 CA 679 SS (WD Tex., Feb. 13, 1999), App. to Pet. for Cert. 50a–63a. A panel of the United States Court of Appeals for the Fifth Circuit reversed. 165 F.3d 380 (1999). It concluded that "an arrest for a first-time seat belt offense" was an unreasonable seizure within the meaning of the Fourth Amendment, id., at 387, and held that Turek was not entitled to qualified immunity, id., at 389.

Sitting en banc, the Court of Appeals vacated the panel's decision and affirmed the District Court's summary judgment for the City. 195 F.3d 242 (CA5 1999). Relying on Whren v. United States, 517 U.S. 806 (1996), the en banc court observed that, although the Fourth Amendment generally requires a balancing of individual and governmental interests, where "an arrest is based on probable cause then 'with rare exceptions ... the result of that balancing is not in doubt.' " 195 F.3d, at 244 (quoting Whren, supra, at 817). Because "[n]either party dispute[d] that

Officer Turek had probable cause to arrest Atwater," and because "there [was] no evidence in the record that Officer Turek conducted the arrest in an 'extraordinary manner, unusually harmful' to Atwater's privacy interests," the en banc court held that the arrest was not unreasonable for Fourth Amendment purposes. 195 F.3d, at 245—246 (quoting Whren, supra, at 818).

Three judges issued dissenting opinions. On the understanding that citation is the "usual procedure" in a traffic stop situation, Judge Reynaldo Garza thought Atwater's arrest unreasonable, since there was no particular reason for taking her into custody. 195 F.3d, at 246—247. Judge Weiner likewise believed that "even with probable cause, [an] officer must have a plausible, articulable reason" for making a custodial arrest. Id., at 251. Judge Dennis understood the Fourth Amendment to have incorporated an earlier, common-law prohibition on warrantless arrests for misdemeanors that do not amount to or involve a "breach of the peace." Ibid.

We granted certiorari to consider whether the Fourth Amendment, either by incorporating common-law restrictions on misdemeanor arrests or otherwise, limits police officers' authority to arrest without warrant for minor criminal offenses. 530 U.S. 1260 (2000). We now affirm.

II

The Fourth Amendment safeguards "[t]he right of the people to be secure in their persons, houses, papers, and effects, against unreasonable searches and seizures." In reading the Amendment, we are guided by "the traditional protections against unreasonable searches and seizures afforded by the common law at the time of the framing," Wilson v. Arkansas, 514 U.S. 927, 931 (1995), since "[a]n examination of the common-law understanding of an officer's authority to arrest sheds light on the obviously relevant, if not entirely dispositive, consideration of what the Framers of the Amendment might have thought to be reasonable," Payton v. New York, 445 U.S. 573, 591 (1980) (footnote omitted). Thus, the first step here is to assess Atwater's claim that peace officers' authority to make warrantless arrests for misdemeanors was restricted at common law (whether "common law" is understood strictly as law judicially derived or, instead, as the whole body of law extant at the time of the framing). Atwater's specific contention is that "founding-era common-law rules" forbade peace officers to make warrantless misdemeanor arrests except in cases of "breach of the peace," a category she claims was then understood narrowly as covering only those nonfelony offenses "involving or tending toward violence." Brief for Petitioners 13. Although her historical argument is by no means insubstantial, it ultimately fails.

A

We begin with the state of pre-founding English common law and find that, even after making some allowance for variations in the common-law usage of the term "breach of the peace,"[2] the "founding-era common-law rules" were not nearly as clear as Atwater claims; on the contrary, the common-law commentators (as well as the sparsely reported cases) reached divergent conclusions with respect to officers' warrantless misdemeanor arrest power. Moreover, in the years leading up to American independence, Parliament repeatedly extended express warrantless arrest authority to cover misdemeanor-level offenses not amounting to or involving any violent breach of the peace.

1

Atwater's historical argument begins with our quotation from Halsbury in Carroll v. United States, 267 U.S. 132 (1925), that

" '[i]n cases of misdemeanor, a peace officer like a private person has at common law no power of arresting without a warrant except when a breach of the peace has been committed in his presence or there is reasonable ground for supposing that a breach of peace is about to be committed or renewed in his presence.' " Id., at 157 (quoting 9 Halsbury, Laws of England §612, p. 299 (1909)).

But the isolated quotation tends to mislead. In Carroll itself we spoke of the common-law rule as only "sometimes expressed" that way, 267 U.S., at 157, and, indeed, in the very same paragraph, we conspicuously omitted any reference to a breach-of-the-peace limitation in stating that the "usual rule" at common law was that "a police officer [could] arrest without warrant ... one guilty of a misdemeanor if committed in his presence." Id., at 156—157. Thus, what Carroll illustrates, and what others have recognized, is that statements about the common law of warrantless misdemeanor arrest simply are not uniform. Rather, "[a]t common law there is a difference of opinion among the authorities as to whether this right to arrest [without a warrant] extends to all misdemeanors." American Law Institute, Code of Criminal Procedure, Commentary to §21, p. 231 (1930).

On one side of the divide there are certainly eminent authorities supporting Atwater's position. In addition to Lord Halsbury, quoted in Carroll, James Fitzjames Stephen and Glanville Williams both seemed to indicate that the common law confined warrantless misdemeanor arrests to actual breaches of the peace. See 1 J. Stephen, A History of the Criminal Law of England 193 (1883) ("The common law did not authorise the arrest of persons guilty or suspected of misdemeanours, except in cases of an actual breach of the peace either by an affray or by violence to an individual"); G. Williams, Arrest for Breach of the Peace, 1954 Crim. L. Rev. 578, 578 ("Apart from arrest for felony ..., the only power of arrest at common law is in respect of breach of the peace"). See also Queen v. Tooley, 2 Ld. Raym. 1296, 1301, 92 Eng. Rep. 349, 352 (Q. B. 1710) ("[A] constable cannot arrest, but when he sees an actual breach of the peace; and if the affray be over, he cannot arrest").

Sir William Blackstone and Sir Edward East might also be counted on Atwater's side, although they spoke only to the sufficiency of breach of the peace as a condition to warrantless misdemeanor arrest, not to its necessity. Blackstone recognized that at common law "[t]he constable ... hath great original and inherent authority with regard to arrests," but with respect to nonfelony offenses said only that "[h]e may, without warrant, arrest any one for breach of the peace, and carry him before a justice of the peace." 4 Blackstone 289. Not long after the framing of the Fourth Amendment, East characterized peace officers' common-law arrest power in much the same way: "A constable or other known conservator of the peace may lawfully interpose upon his own view to prevent a breach of the peace, or to quiet an affray ... ." 1 E. East, Pleas of the Crown §71, p. 303 (1803).

The great commentators were not unanimous, however, and there is also considerable evidence of a broader conception of common-law misdemeanor arrest authority unlimited by any breach-of-the-peace condition. Sir Matthew Hale, Chief Justice of King's Bench from 1671 to 1676,3 wrote in his History of the Pleas of the Crown that, by his "original and inherent power," a constable could arrest without a warrant "for breach of the peace and some misdemeanors, less than felony." 2 M. Hale, The History of the Pleas of the Crown 88 (1736). Hale's view, posthumously published in 1736, reflected an understanding dating back at least 60 years before the appearance of his Pleas yet sufficiently authoritative to sustain a momentum extending well beyond the framing era in this country. See The Compleat Parish-Officer 11 (1744) ("[T]he Constable ... may for Breach of the Peace, and some Misdemeanors less than Felony, imprison a

Man"); R. Burn, The Justice of the Peace 271 (1837) ("A constable ... may at common law, for treason, felony, breach of the peace, and some misdemeanors less than felony, committed in his view, apprehend the supposed offender without any warrant") (italics in original); 1 J. Chitty, A Practical Treatise on the Criminal Law 20 (5th ed. 1847) ("[A constable] may for treason, felony, breach of the peace, and some misdemeanors less than felony, committed in his view, apprehend the supposed offender virtiute officii, without any warrant"); 1 W. Russell, Crimes and Misdemeanors 725 (7th ed. 1909) (officer "may arrest any person who in his presence commits a misdemeanor or breach of the peace").4

As will be seen later, the view of warrantless arrest authority as extending to at least "some misdemeanors" beyond breaches of the peace was undoubtedly informed by statutory provisions authorizing such arrests, but it reflected common law in the strict, judge-made sense as well, for such was the holding of at least one case reported before Hale had even become a judge but which, like Hale's own commentary, continued to be cited well after the ratification of the Fourth Amendment. In Holyday v. Oxenbridge, Cro. Car. 234, 79 Eng. Rep. 805 (K.B. 1631), the Court of King's Bench held that even a private person (and thus a fortiori a peace officer5) needed no warrant to arrest a "common cheater" whom he discovered "cozen[ing] with false dice." The court expressly rejected the contention that warrantless arrests were improper "unless in felony," and said instead that "there was good cause [for] staying" the gambler and, more broadly, that "it is pro bono publico to stay such offenders." Id., at 805—806. In the edition nearest to the date of the Constitution's framing, Sergeant William Hawkins's widely-read Treatise of the Pleas of the Crown generalized from Holyday that "from the reason of this case it seems to follow, That the [warrantless] arrest of any other offenders ... for

offenses in like manner scandalous and prejudicial to the public, may be justified." 2 Hawkins, ch. 12, §20, p. 122. A number of other common-law commentaries shared Hawkins's broad reading of Holyday. See The Law of Arrests 205 (2d ed. 1753) (In light of Holyday, "an Arrest of an Offender ... for any Crime prejudicial to the Publick, seems to be justifiable"); 1 T. Cunningham, A New and Complete Law Dictionary (1771) (definition of "arrest") (same); 1 G. Jacob, The Law Dictionary 129 (1st Am. ed., 1811) (same). See generally C. Greaves, Law of Arrest Without a Warrant, in The Criminal Law Consolidation Acts, p. lxiii (1870) ("[Holyday] is rested upon the broad ground that 'it is pro bono publico to stay such offenders,' which is equally applicable to every case of misdemeanor ... ").6

We thus find disagreement, not unanimity, among both the common-law jurists and the text-writers who sought to pull the cases together and summarize accepted practice. Having reviewed the relevant English decisions, as well as English and colonial American legal treatises, legal dictionaries, and procedure manuals, we simply are not convinced that Atwater's is the correct, or even necessarily the better, reading of the common-law history.

2

A second, and equally serious, problem for Atwater's historical argument is posed by the "divers Statutes," M. Dalton, Country Justice ch. 170, §4, p. 582 (1727), enacted by Parliament well before this Republic's founding that authorized warrantless misdemeanor arrests without reference to violence or turmoil. Quite apart from Hale and Blackstone, the legal background of any conception of reasonableness the Fourth Amendment's Framers might have entertained would have included English statutes, some centuries old, authorizing peace officers (and even private persons) to make warrantless arrests for all sorts of relatively minor offenses unaccompanied by violence. The so-called "nightwalker" statutes are perhaps the most notable examples. From the enactment of the Statute of Winchester in 1285, through its various readoptions and until its repeal in 1827,7 night watchmen were authorized and charged "as ... in Times past" to "watch the Town continually all Night, from the Sun-setting unto the Sun-rising" and were directed that "if any Stranger do pass by them, he shall be arrested until Morning ... ." 13 Edw. I, ch. 4, §§5—6, 1 Statutes at Large 232—233; see also 5 Edw. III, ch. 14, 1 Statutes at Large 448 (1331) (confirming and extending the powers of watchmen). Hawkins emphasized that the Statute of Winchester "was made" not in derogation but rather "in affirmance of the common law," for "every private person may by the common law arrest any suspicious night-walker, and detain him till he give good account of himself ... ." 2 Hawkins, ch. 13, §6, p. 130. And according to Blackstone, these watchmen had virtually limitless warrantless nighttime arrest power: "Watchmen, either those appointed by the statute of Winchester ... or such as are merely assistants to the constable, may virtute officii arrest all offenders, and particularly nightwalkers, and commit them to custody till the morning." 4 Blackstone 289; see also 2 Hale, History of the Pleas of the Crown, at 97 (describing broad arrest powers of watchmen even over and above those conferred by the Statute of Winchester).8 The Statute of Winchester, moreover, empowered peace officers not only to deal with nightwalkers and other nighttime "offenders," but periodically to "make Inquiry of all Persons being lodged in the Suburbs, or in foreign Places of the Towns." On that score, the Statute provided that "if they do find any that have lodged or received any Strangers or suspicious Person, against the Peace, the Bailiffs shall do Right therein," 13 Edw. I, ch. 4, §§3—4, 1 Statutes at Large 232—233, which Hawkins understood "surely" to mean that officers could "lawfully arrest and detain any such stranger[s]," 2

Hawkins, ch. 13, §12, at 134.

Nor were the nightwalker statutes the only legislative sources of warrantless arrest authority absent real or threatened violence, as the parties and their amici here seem to have assumed. On the contrary, following the Edwardian legislation and throughout the period leading up to the framing, Parliament repeatedly extended warrantless arrest power to cover misdemeanor-level offenses not involving any breach of the peace. One 16th-century statute, for instance, authorized peace officers to arrest persons playing "unlawful game[s]" like bowling, tennis, dice, and cards, and for good measure extended the authority beyond players to include persons "haunting" the "houses, places and alleys where such games shall be suspected to be holden, exercised, used or occupied." 33 Hen. VIII, ch. 9, §§11—16, 5 Statutes at Large 84—85 (1541). A 17th-century act empowered "any person ... whatsoever to seize and detain any ... hawker, pedlar, petty chapman, or other trading person" found selling without a license. 8 & 9 Wm. III, ch. 25, §§3, 8, 10 Statutes at Large 81—83 (1697). And 18th-century statutes authorized the warrantless arrest of "rogues, vagabonds, beggars, and other idle and disorderly persons" (defined broadly to include jugglers, palm-readers, and unlicensed play-actors), 17 Geo. II, ch. 5, §§1—2, 5, 18 Statutes at Large 144, 145—147 (1744); "horrid" persons who "profanely swear or curse," 19 Geo. II, ch. 21, §3, 18 Statutes at Large 445 (1746); individuals obstructing "publick streets, lanes or open passages" with "pipes, butts, barrels, casks or other vessels" or an "empty cart, car, dray or other carriage," 30 Geo. II, ch. 22, §§5, 13, 22 Statutes at Large 107—108, 111 (1757); and, most significantly of all given the circumstances of the case before us, negligent carriage drivers, 27 Geo. II, ch. 16, §7, 21 Statutes at Large 188 (1754). See generally S. Blackerby, The Justice of Peace: His Companion, or a Summary of all the Acts of Parliament (1723) (cataloguing statutes); S. Welch, An Essay on the Office of Constable 19—22 (1758) (describing same).

The significance of these early English statutes lies not in proving that any common-law rule barring warrantless misdemeanor arrests that might have existed would have been subject to statutory override; the sovereign Parliament could of course have wiped away any judge-made rule. The point is that the statutes riddle Atwater's supposed common-law rule with enough exceptions to unsettle any contention that the law of the mother country would have left the Fourth Amendment's Framers of a view that it would necessarily have been unreasonable to arrest without warrant for a misdemeanor unaccompanied by real or threatened violence.

B

An examination of specifically American evidence is to the same effect. Neither the history of the framing era nor subsequent legal development indicates that the Fourth Amendment was originally understood, or has traditionally been read, to embrace Atwater's position.

1

To begin with, Atwater has cited no particular evidence that those who framed and ratified the Fourth Amendment sought to limit peace officers' warrantless misdemeanor arrest authority to instances of actual breach of the peace, and our own review of the recent and respected compilations of framing-era documentary history has likewise failed to reveal any such design. See The Complete Bill of Rights 223—263 (N. Cogan ed. 1997) (collecting original sources); 5 The Founders' Constitution 219—244 (P. Kurland & R. Lerner eds. 1987) (same). Nor have we found in any of the modern historical accounts of the Fourth Amendment's adoption any substantial indication that the Framers intended such a restriction. See, e.g., L. Levy, Origins of the Bill of

Rights 150—179 (1999); T. Taylor, Two Studies in Constitutional Interpretation 19—93 (1969); J. Landynski, Search and Seizure and the Supreme Court 19—48 (1966); N. Lasson, History and Development of the Fourth Amendment to the United States Constitution 79—105 (1937); Davies, Recovering the Original Fourth Amendment, 98 Mich. L. Rev. 547 (1999); Amar, Fourth Amendment First Principles, 107 Harv. L. Rev. 757 (1994); Bradley, Constitutional Theory of the Fourth Amendment, 38 DePaul L. Rev. 817 (1989). Indeed, to the extent these modern histories address the issue, their conclusions are to the contrary. See Landynski, supra, at 45 (Fourth Amendment arrest rules are "based on common-law practice," which "dispensed with" a warrant requirement for misdemeanors "committed in the presence of the arresting officer"); Davies, supra, at 551 ("[T]he Framers did not address warrantless intrusions at all in the Fourth Amendment or in the earlier state provisions; thus, they never anticipated that 'unreasonable' might be read as a standard for warrantless intrusions").

The evidence of actual practice also counsels against Atwater's position. During the period leading up to and surrounding the framing of the Bill of Rights, colonial and state legislatures, like Parliament before them, supra, at 11—14, regularly authorized local peace officers to make warrantless misdemeanor arrests without conditioning statutory authority on breach of the peace. See, e.g., First Laws of the State of Connecticut 214—215 (Cushing ed. 1982) (1784 compilation; exact date of Act unknown) (authorizing warrantless arrests of "all Persons unnecessarily travelling on the Sabbath or Lord's Day"); id., at 23 ("such as are guilty of Drunkenness, profane Swearing, Sabbath-breaking, also vagrant Persons [and] unseasonable Night-walkers"); Digest of the Laws of the State of Georgia 1755—1800, p. 411 (H. Marbury & W. Crawford eds. 1802) (1762 Act) (breakers of the

Sabbath laws); id., at 252 (1764 Act) (persons "gaming … in any licensed public house, or other house selling liquors"); Colonial Laws of Massachusetts 139 (1889) (1646 Act) ("such as are overtaken with drink, swearing, Sabbath breaking, Lying, vagrant persons, [and] night-walkers"); Laws of the State of New Hampshire 549 (1800) (1799 Act) (persons "travelling unnecessarily" on Sunday); Digest of the Laws of New Jersey 1709—1838, pp. 585—586 (L. Elmer ed. 1838) (1799 Act) ("vagrants or vagabonds, common drunkards, common night-walkers, and common prostitutes," as well as fortune-tellers and other practitioners of "crafty science"); Laws of the State of New York, 1777—1784, pp. 358—359 (1886) (1781 Act) ("hawker[s]" and "pedlar[s]"); Earliest Printed Laws of New York, 1665—1693, p. 133 (J. Cushing, ed., 1978) (Duke of York's Laws, 1665—1675) ("such as are overtaken with Drink, Swearing, Sabbath breaking, Vagrant persons or night walkers"); 3 Laws of the Commonwealth of Pennsylvania 177—183 (1810) (1794 Act) (persons "profanely curs[ing]," drinking excessively, "cock-fighting," or "play[ing] at cards, dice, billiards, bowls, shuffle-boards, or any game of hazard or address, for money").9

What we have here, then, is just the opposite of what we had in Wilson v. Arkansas. There, we emphasized that during the founding era a number of States had "enacted statutes specifically embracing" the common-law knock-and-announce rule, 514 U.S., at 933; here, by contrast, those very same States passed laws extending warrantless arrest authority to a host of nonviolent misdemeanors, and in so doing acted very much inconsistently with Atwater's claims about the Fourth Amendment's object. Of course, the Fourth Amendment did not originally apply to the States, see Barron v. Mayor of Baltimore, 7 Pet. 243 (1833), but that does not make state practice irrelevant in unearthing the Amendment's original meaning. A number of state constitutional search-and-seizure provisions served as models for the Fourth Amendment, see, e.g., N. H. Const. of 1784, pt. I, Art. XIX; Pa. Const. of 1776 (Declaration of Rights), Art. X, and the fact that many of the original States with such constitutional limitations continued to grant their own peace officers broad warrantless misdemeanor arrest authority undermines Atwater's contention that the founding generation meant to bar federal law enforcement officers from exercising the same authority. Given the early state practice, it is likewise troublesome for Atwater's view that just one year after the ratification of the Fourth Amendment, Congress vested federal marshals with "the same powers in executing the laws of the United States, as sheriffs and their deputies in the several states have by law, in executing the laws of their respective states." Act of May 2, 1792, ch. 28, §9, 1 Stat. 265. Thus, as we have said before in only slightly different circumstances, the Second Congress apparently "saw no inconsistency between the Fourth Amendment and legislation giving United States marshals the same power as local peace officers" to make warrantless arrests. United States v. Watson, 423 U.S. 411, 420 (1976).10

The record thus supports Justice Powell's observation that "[t]here is no historical evidence that the Framers or proponents of the Fourth Amendment, outspokenly opposed to the infamous general warrants and writs of assistance, were at all concerned about warrantless arrests by local constables and other peace officers." Id., at 429 (concurring opinion). We simply cannot conclude that the Fourth Amendment, as originally understood, forbade peace officers to arrest without a warrant for misdemeanors not amounting to or involving breach of the peace.

2

Nor does Atwater's argument from tradition pick up any steam from the historical record as it has unfolded since the framing, there being no indication that her claimed rule has ever become "woven ... into the fabric" of American law. Wilson, supra, at 933; see also Payton v. New York, 445 U.S., at 590 (emphasizing "a clear consensus among the States adhering to [a] well-settled common-law rule"). The story, on the contrary, is of two centuries of uninterrupted (and largely unchallenged) state and federal practice permitting warrantless arrests for misdemeanors not amounting to or involving breach of the peace.

First, there is no support for Atwater's position in this Court's cases (apart from the isolated sentence in Carroll, already explained). Although the Court has not had much to say about warrantless misdemeanor arrest authority, what little we have said tends to cut against Atwater's argument. In discussing this authority, we have focused on the circumstance that an offense was committed in an officer's presence, to the omission of any reference to a breach-of-the-peace limitation.11 See, e.g., United States v. Watson, supra, at 418 ("The cases construing the Fourth Amendment thus reflect the ancient common-law rule that a peace officer was permitted to arrest without a warrant for a misdemeanor or felony committed in his presence ..."); Carroll, 267 U.S., at 156—157 ("The usual rule is that a police officer may arrest without a warrant one ... guilty of a misdemeanor if committed in his presence"); Bad Elk v. United States, 177 U.S. 529, 534, 536, n. 1 (1900) (noting common-law pedigree of state statute permitting warrantless arrest "[f]or a public offense committed or attempted in [officer's] presence"); Kurtz v. Moffitt, 115 U.S. 487, 499 (1885) (common-law presence requirement); cf. also Welsh v. Wisconsin, 466 U.S. 740, 756 (1984) (White, J., dissenting) (" '[A]uthority to arrest without a warrant in misdemeanor cases may be enlarged by statute' ").

Second, and again in contrast with Wilson, it is not the case here that "[e]arly American courts ... embraced" an accepted common-law rule with anything approaching unanimity. Wilson v. Arkansas, 514 U.S., at 933. To be sure, Atwater has cited several 19th-century decisions that, at least at first glance, might seem to support her contention that "warrantless misdemeanor arrest was unlawful when not [for] a breach of the peace." Brief for Petitioners 17 (citing Pow v. Beckner, 3 Ind. 475, 478 (1852), Commonwealth v. Carey, 66 Mass. 246, 250 (1853), and Robison v. Miner, 68 Mich. 549, 556—559, 37 N. W. 21, 25 (1888)). But none is ultimately availing. Pow is fundamentally a "presence" case; it stands only for the proposition, not at issue here, see n. 11, supra, that a nonfelony arrest should be made while the offense is "in [the officer's] view and ... still continuing" and not subsequently "upon vague information communicated to him." 3 Ind., at 478. The language Atwater attributes to Carey ("[E]ven if he were a constable, he had no power to arrest for any misdemeanor without a warrant, except to stay a breach of the peace, or to prevent the commission of such an offense") is taken from the reporter's summary of one of the party's arguments, not from the opinion of the court. While the court in Carey (through Chief Justice Shaw) said that "the old established rule of the common law" was that "a constable or other peace officer could not arrest one without a warrant ... if such crime were not an offence amounting in law to felony," it said just as clearly that the common-law rule could be "altered by the legislature" (notwithstanding Massachusetts's own Fourth Amendment equivalent in its state constitution). 66 Mass., at 252. Miner, the third and final case upon which Atwater relies, was expressly overruled just six years after it was decided. In Burroughs v. Eastman, 101 Mich. 419 (1894), the Supreme Court of Michigan held that the language from Miner upon which the plaintiff there (and presumably Atwater here) relied "should not be followed," and then went on to offer the following: "[T]he question has arisen in many of our sister states, and the power to authorize arrest on view for offenses not amounting to breaches of the peace has been affirmed. Our attention has been called to no case, nor have we in our research found one, in which the contrary doctrine has been asserted." 101 Mich., at 425 (collecting cases from, e.g., Illinois, Indiana, Massachusetts, Minnesota, Missouri, New Hampshire, New York, Ohio, and Texas).

The reports may well contain early American cases more favorable to Atwater's position than the ones she has herself invoked. But more to the point, we think, are the numerous early- and mid-19th-century decisions expressly sustaining (often against constitutional challenge) state and local laws authorizing peace officers to make warrantless arrests for misdemeanors not involving any breach of the peace. See, e.g., Mayo v. Wilson, 1 N. H. 53 (1817) (upholding statute authorizing warrantless arrests of those unnecessarily traveling on Sunday against challenge based on state due process and search-and-seizure provisions); Holcomb v. Cornish, 8 Conn. 375 (1831) (upholding statute permitting warrantless arrests for "drunkenness, profane swearing, cursing or sabbath-breaking" against argument that "[t]he power of a justice of the peace to arrest and detain a citizen without complaint or warrant against him, is surely not given by the common law"); Jones v. Root, 72 Mass. 435 (1856) (rebuffing constitutional challenge to statute authorizing officers "without a warrant [to] arrest any person or persons whom they may find in the act of illegally selling, transporting, or distributing intoxicating liquors"); Main v. McCarty, 15 Ill. 441 (1854) (concluding that a law expressly authorizing arrests for city-ordinance violations was "not repugnant to the constitution or the general provisions of law"); White v. Kent, 11 Ohio St. 550 (1860) (upholding municipal ordinance permitting warrantless arrest of any person found violating any city ordinance or state law); Davis v. American

Soc. for Prevention of Cruelty to Animals, 75 N. Y. 362 (1878) (upholding statute permitting warrantless arrest for misdemeanor violation of cruelty-to-animals prohibition). See generally Wilgus, Arrest Without a Warrant, 22 Mich. L. Rev. 541, 550, and n. 54 (1924) (collecting cases and observing that "[t]he states may, by statute, enlarge the common law right to arrest without a warrant, and have quite generally done so or authorized municipalities to do so, as for example, an officer may be authorized by statute or ordinance to arrest without a warrant for various misdemeanors and violations of ordinances, other than breaches of the peace, if committed in his presence"); id., at 706, nn. 570, 571 (collecting cases); 1 J. Bishop, New Criminal Procedure §§181, 183, pp. 101, n. 2, 103, n. 5 (4th ed. 1895) (same); W. Clark, Handbook of Criminal Procedure §12, p. 50, n. 8 (2d ed. 1918) (same).

Finally, both the legislative tradition of granting warrantless misdemeanor arrest authority and the judicial tradition of sustaining such statutes against constitutional attack are buttressed by legal commentary that, for more than a century now, has almost uniformly recognized the constitutionality of extending warrantless arrest power to misdemeanors without limitation to breaches of the peace. See, e.g., E. Fisher, Laws of Arrest §59, p. 130 (1967) ("[I]t is generally recognized today that the common law authority to arrest without a warrant in misdemeanor cases may be enlarged by statute, and this has been done in many of the states"); Wilgus, supra, at 705—706 ("Statutes and municipal charters have quite generally authorized an officer to arrest for any misdemeanor whether a breach of the peace or not, without a warrant, if committed in the officer's presence. Such statutes are valid"); Clark, supra, §12, at 50 ("In most, if not all, the states there are statutes and city ordinances, which are clearly valid, authorizing officers to arrest for certain misdemeanors without a warrant, when committed in their presence"); J. Beale, Criminal Pleading and Practice §21, p. 20, and n. 7 (1899) ("By statute the power of peace officers to arrest without a warrant is often extended to all misdemeanors committed in their presence." "Such a statute is constitutional"); 1 Bishop, supra, §183, at 103 ("[T]he power of arrest extends, possibly, to any indictable wrong in [an officer's] presence.... And statutes and ordinances widely permit these arrests for violations of municipal by-laws"); J. Bassett, Criminal Pleading and Practice §89, p. 104 (2d ed. 1885) ("[A]s to the lesser misdemeanors, except breaches of the peace, the power extends only so far as some statute gives it"). But cf. H. Vorhees, Law of Arrest §131, pp. 78—79 (1904) (acknowledging that "by authority of statute, city charter, or ordinance, [an officer] may arrest without a warrant, one who ... commits a misdemeanor other than a breach of the peace," but suggesting that courts look with "disfavor" on such legislative enactments "as interfering with the constitutional liberties of the subject").

Small wonder, then, that today statutes in all 50 States and the District of Columbia permit warrantless misdemeanor arrests by at least some (if not all) peace officers without requiring any breach of the peace,12 as do a host of congressional enactments.13 The American Law Institute has long endorsed the validity of such legislation, see American Law Institute, Code of Criminal Procedure §21(a), p. 28 (1930); American Law Institute, Model Code of Pre-Arraignment Procedure §120.1(1)(c), p. 13 (1975), and the consensus, as stated in the current literature, is that statutes "remov[ing] the breach of the peace limitation and thereby permit[ting] arrest without warrant for any misdemeanor committed in the arresting officer's presence" have " 'never been successfully challenged and stan[d] as the law of the land.' " 3 W. LaFave, Search and Seizure §5.1(b), pp. 13—14, and n. 76 (1996) (quoting Higbee v. San Diego, 911 F.2d 377, 379 (CA9

1990)) (emphasis in original; footnote omitted). This, therefore, simply is not a case in which the claimant can point to "a clear answer [that] existed in 1791 and has been generally adhered to by the traditions of our society ever since." County of Riverside v. McLaughlin, 500 U.S. 44, 60 (1991) (Scalia, J., dissenting).

III

While it is true here that history, if not unequivocal, has expressed a decided, majority view that the police need not obtain an arrest warrant merely because a misdemeanor stopped short of violence or a threat of it, Atwater does not wager all on history.14 Instead, she asks us to mint a new rule of constitutional law on the understanding that when historical practice fails to speak conclusively to a claim grounded on the Fourth Amendment, courts are left to strike a current balance between individual and societal interests by subjecting particular contemporary circumstances to traditional standards of reasonableness. See Wyoming v. Houghton, 526 U.S. 295, 299—300 (1999); Vernonia School Dist. 47J v. Acton, 515 U.S. 646, 652—653 (1995). Atwater accordingly argues for a modern arrest rule, one not necessarily requiring violent breach of the peace, but nonetheless forbidding custodial arrest, even upon probable cause, when conviction could not ultimately carry any jail time and when the government shows no compelling need for immediate detention.15

If we were to derive a rule exclusively to address the uncontested facts of this case, Atwater might well prevail. She was a known and established resident of Lago Vista with no place to hide and no incentive to flee, and common sense says she would almost certainly have buckled up as a condition of driving off with a citation. In her case, the physical incidents of arrest were merely gratuitous humiliations imposed by a police officer who was (at best) exercising extremely poor judgment. Atwater's claim to live free of pointless indignity and confinement clearly outweighs anything the City can raise against it specific to her case.

But we have traditionally recognized that a responsible Fourth Amendment balance is not well served by standards requiring sensitive, case-by-case determinations of government need, lest every discretionary judgment in the field be converted into an occasion for constitutional review. See, e.g., United States v. Robinson, 414 U.S. 218, 234–235 (1973). Often enough, the Fourth Amendment has to be applied on the spur (and in the heat) of the moment, and the object in implementing its command of reasonableness is to draw standards sufficiently clear and simple to be applied with a fair prospect of surviving judicial second-guessing months and years after an arrest or search is made. Courts attempting to strike a reasonable Fourth Amendment balance thus credit the government's side with an essential interest in readily administrable rules. See New York v. Belton, 453 U.S. 454, 458 (1981) (Fourth Amendment rules " 'ought to be expressed in terms that are readily applicable by the police in the context of the law enforcement activities in which they are necessarily engaged' " and not " 'qualified by all sorts of ifs, ands, and buts' ").16

At first glance, Atwater's argument may seem to respect the values of clarity and simplicity, so far as she claims that the Fourth Amendment generally forbids warrantless arrests for minor crimes not accompanied by violence or some demonstrable threat of it (whether "minor crime" be defined as a fine-only traffic offense, a fine-only offense more generally, or a misdemeanor17). But the claim is not ultimately so simple, nor could it be, for complications arise the moment we begin to think about the possible applications of the several criteria Atwater proposes for drawing a line between minor crimes with limited arrest authority and others not so restricted.

One line, she suggests, might be between "jailable" and "fine-only" offenses, between those for which conviction could result in commitment and those for which it could not. The trouble with this distinction, of course, is that an officer on the street might not be able to tell. It is not merely that we cannot expect every police officer to know the details of frequently complex penalty schemes, see Berkemer v. McCarty, 468 U.S. 420, 431, n. 13 (1984) ("[O]fficers in the field frequently 'have neither the time nor the competence to determine' the severity of the offense for which they are considering arresting a person"), but that penalties for ostensibly identical conduct can vary on account of facts difficult (if not impossible) to know at the scene of an arrest. Is this the first offense or is the suspect a repeat offender?18 Is the weight of the marijuana a gram above or a gram below the fine-only line?19 Where conduct could implicate more than one criminal prohibition, which one will the district attorney ultimately decide to charge?20 And so on.

But Atwater's refinements would not end there. She represents that if the line were drawn at nonjailable traffic offenses, her proposed limitation should be qualified by a proviso authorizing warrantless arrests where "necessary for enforcement of the traffic laws or when [an] offense would otherwise continue and pose a danger to others on the road." Brief for Petitioners 46. (Were the line drawn at misdemeanors generally, a comparable qualification would presumably apply.) The proviso only compounds the difficulties. Would, for instance, either exception apply to speeding? At oral argument, Atwater's counsel said that "it would not be reasonable to arrest a driver for speeding unless the speeding rose to the level of reckless driving." Tr. of Oral Arg. 16. But is it not fair to expect that the chronic speeder will speed again despite a citation in his pocket, and should that not qualify as showing that the "offense would ... continue" under Atwater's rule? And why, as a constitutional matter, should we assume that only reckless driving will "pose a danger to others on the road" while speeding will not?

There is no need for more examples to show that Atwater's general rule and limiting proviso promise very little in the way of administrability. It is no answer that the police routinely make judgments on grounds like risk of immediate repetition; they surely do and should. But there is a world of difference between making that judgment in choosing between the discretionary leniency of a summons in place of a clearly lawful arrest, and making the same judgment when the question is the lawfulness of the warrantless arrest itself. It is the difference between no basis for legal action challenging the discretionary judgment, on the one hand, and the prospect of evidentiary exclusion or (as here) personal §1983 liability for the misapplication of a constitutional standard, on the other. Atwater's rule therefore would not only place police in an almost impossible spot but would guarantee increased litigation over many of the arrests that would occur.21 For all these reasons, Atwater's various distinctions between permissible and impermissible arrests for minor crimes strike us as "very unsatisfactory line[s]" to require police officers to draw on a moment's notice. Carroll v. United States, 267 U.S., at 157.

One may ask, of course, why these difficulties may not be answered by a simple tie breaker for the police to follow in the field: if in doubt, do not arrest. The first answer is that in practice the tie breaker would boil down to something akin to a least-restrictive-alternative limitation, which is itself one of those "ifs, ands, and buts" rules, New York v. Belton, 453 U.S., at 458, generally thought inappropriate in working out Fourth Amendment protection. See, e.g., Skinner v. Railway Labor Executives' Assn., 489 U.S. 602, 629 n. 9 (1989) (collecting cases); United States v. Martinez-Fuerte, 428 U.S. 543, 557—558,

n. 12 (1976) ("The logic of such elaborate less-restrictive-alternative arguments could raise insuperable barriers to the exercise of virtually all search-and-seizure powers"). Beyond that, whatever help the tie breaker might give would come at the price of a systematic disincentive to arrest in situations where even Atwater concedes that arresting would serve an important societal interest. An officer not quite sure that the drugs weighed enough to warrant jail time or not quite certain about a suspect's risk of flight would not arrest, even though it could perfectly well turn out that, in fact, the offense called for incarceration and the defendant was long gone on the day of trial. Multiplied many times over, the costs to society of such underenforcement could easily outweigh the costs to defendants of being needlessly arrested and booked, as Atwater herself acknowledges.22

Just how easily the costs could outweigh the benefits may be shown by asking, as one Member of this Court did at oral argument, "how bad the problem is out there." Tr. of Oral Arg. 20. The very fact that the law has never jelled the way Atwater would have it leads one to wonder whether warrantless misdemeanor arrests need constitutional attention, and there is cause to think the answer is no. So far as such arrests might be thought to pose a threat to the probable-cause requirement, anyone arrested for a crime without formal process, whether for felony or misdemeanor, is entitled to a magistrate's review of probable cause within 48 hours, County of Riverside v. McLaughlin, 500 U.S., at 55—58, and there is no reason to think the procedure in this case atypical in giving the suspect a prompt opportunity to request release, see Tex. Tran. Code Ann. §543.002 (1999) (persons arrested for traffic offenses to be taken "immediately" before a magistrate). Many jurisdictions, moreover, have chosen to impose more restrictive safeguards through statutes limiting warrantless arrests for minor offenses. See, e.g., Ala. Code §32—1—4 (1999); Cal. Veh. Code Ann. §40504 (West 2000); Ky. Rev. Stat. Ann. §§431.015(1), (2) (Michie 1999); La. Rev. Stat. Ann. §32:391 (West 1989); Md. Transp. Code Ann. §26—202(a)(2) (1999); S. D. Codified Laws §32—33—2 (1998); Tenn. Code Ann. §40—7—118(b)(1) (1997); Va. Code Ann. §46.2—936 (Supp. 2000). It is of course easier to devise a minor-offense limitation by statute than to derive one through the Constitution, simply because the statute can let the arrest power turn on any sort of practical consideration without having to subsume it under a broader principle. It is, in fact, only natural that States should resort to this sort of legislative regulation, for, as Atwater's own amici emphasize, it is in the interest of the police to limit petty-offense arrests, which carry costs that are simply too great to incur without good reason. See Brief for Institute on Criminal Justice at the University of Minnesota Law School and Eleven Leading Experts on Law Enforcement and Corrections Administration and Policy as Amici Curiae 11 (the use of custodial arrests for minor offenses "[a]ctually [c]ontradicts [l]aw [e]nforcement [i]nterests"). Finally, and significantly, under current doctrine the preference for categorical treatment of Fourth Amendment claims gives way to individualized review when a defendant makes a colorable argument that an arrest, with or without a warrant, was "conducted in an extraordinary manner, unusually harmful to [his] privacy or even physical interests." Whren v. United States, 517 U.S., at 818; see also Graham v. Connor, 490 U.S. 386, 395—396 (1989) (excessive force actionable under §1983).

The upshot of all these influences, combined with the good sense (and, failing that, the political accountability) of most local lawmakers and law-enforcement officials, is a dearth of horribles demanding redress. Indeed, when Atwater's counsel was asked at oral argument for any indications of comparably foolish, warrantless misdemeanor arrests, he could offer only one.23 We are sure that there are others,24 but just as surely the country is not confronting anything like an epidemic of unnecessary minor-offense arrests.25 That fact caps the reasons for rejecting Atwater's request for the development of a new and distinct body of constitutional law.

Accordingly, we confirm today what our prior cases have intimated: the standard of probable cause "applie[s] to all arrests, without the need to 'balance' the interests and circumstances involved in particular situations." Dunaway v. New York, 442 U.S. 200, 208 (1979). If an officer has probable cause to believe that an individual has committed even a very minor criminal offense in his presence, he may, without violating the Fourth Amendment, arrest the offender.

IV

Atwater's arrest satisfied constitutional requirements. There is no dispute that Officer Turek had probable cause to believe that Atwater had committed a crime in his presence. She admits that neither she nor her children were wearing seat belts, as required by Tex. Tran. Code Ann. §545.413 (1999). Turek was accordingly authorized (not required, but authorized) to make a custodial ar-

rest without balancing costs and benefits or determin-

ing whether or not Atwater's arrest was in some sense necessary.

Nor was the arrest made in an "extraordinary manner, unusually harmful to [her] privacy or ... physical interests." Whren v. United States, 517 U.S., at 818. As our citations in Whren make clear, the question whether a search or seizure is "extraordinary" turns, above all else, on the manner in which the search or seizure is executed. See id., at 818 (citing Tennessee v. Garner, 471 U.S. 1 (1985) ("seizure by means of deadly force"), Wilson v. Arkansas, 514 U.S. 927

(1995) ("unannounced entry into a home"), Welsh v. Wisconsin, 466 U.S. 740 (1984) ("entry into a home without a warrant"), and Winston v. Lee, 470 U.S. 753 (1985) ("physical penetration of the body")). Atwater's arrest was surely "humiliating," as she says in her brief, but it was no more "harmful to ... privacy or ... physical interests" than the normal custodial arrest. She was handcuffed, placed in a squad car, and taken to the local police station, where officers asked her to remove her shoes, jewelry, and glasses, and to empty her pockets. They then took her photograph and placed her in a cell, alone, for about an hour, after which she was taken before a magistrate, and released on $310 bond. The arrest and booking were inconvenient and embarrassing to Atwater, but not so extraordinary as to violate the Fourth Amendment.

The Court of Appeals's en banc judgment is affirmed.

It is so ordered.

Notes

1. Turek had previously stopped Atwater for what he had thought was a seatbelt violation, but had realized that Atwater's son, although seated on the vehicle's armrest, was in fact belted in. Atwater acknowledged that her son's seating position was unsafe, and Turek issued a verbal warning. See Record 379.

2. The term apparently meant very different things in different common-law contexts. For instance, under a statute enacted during the reign of Charles II forbidding service of any warrant or other court process on Sunday "except in cases of treason, felony or breach of the peace," 29 Car. II, ch. 7, §6, 8 Statutes at Large 414 (1676), "it was held that every indictable offense was constructively a breach of the peace," Wilgus, Arrest Without a Warrant, 22 Mich. L. Rev. 541, 574 (1924); see also Ex parte Whitchurch, 1 Atk. 56, 58, 26 Eng. Rep. 37, 39 (Ch. 1749). The term carried a similarly broad meaning when employed to define the jurisdiction of justices of the peace, see 2 W. Hawkins, Pleas of the Crown, ch. 8, §38, p. 60 (6th ed. 1787) (hereinafter Hawkins), or to delimit the scope of parliamentary privilege, see Williamson v. United States, 207 U.S. 425, 435–446 (1908) (discussing common-law origins of Arrest Clause, U.S. Const., Art. I, §6, cl. 1). Even when used to describe common-law arrest authority, the term's precise import is not altogether clear. See J. Turner, Kenny's Outlines of Criminal Law §695, p. 537 (17th ed. 1958) ("Strangely enough what constitutes a 'breach of the peace' has not been authoritatively laid down"); G. Williams, Arrest for Breach of the Peace, 1954 Crim. L. Rev. 578, 578–579 ("The expression 'breach of the peace' seems clearer than it is and there is a surprising lack of authoritative definition of what one would suppose to be a fundamental concept in criminal law"); Wilgus, supra, at 573 ("What constitutes a breach of peace is not entirely certain"). More often than not, when used in reference to common-law arrest power, the term seemed to connote an element of violence. See, e.g., M. Dalton, Country Justice, ch. 3, p. 9 (1727) ("The Breach of th[e] Peace seemeth to be any injurious Force or Violence moved against the Person of another, his Goods, Lands, or other Possessions, whether by threatening words, or by furious Gesture, or Force of the Body, or any other Force used in terrorem"). On occasion, however, common-law commentators included in their descriptions of breaches of the peace offenses that do not necessarily involve violence or a threat thereof. See M. Hale, A Methodical Summary of the Principal Matters Relating to the Pleas of the Crown *134 (7th ed. 1773) ("Barretries"); 4 W. Blackstone, Commentaries on the Laws of England 149 (1769) (hereinafter Blackstone) ("[s]preading false news"). For purposes of this case, it is unnecessary to reach a definitive resolution of the

uncertainty. As stated in the text, we will assume that as used in the context of common-law arrest, the phrase "breach of the peace" was understood narrowly, as entailing at least a threat of violence.

3. E. Foss, The Judges of England 113 (1864).

4. Cf. E. Trotter, Seventeenth Century Life in the Country Parish: With Special Reference to Local Government 88 (1919) (describing broad authority of local constables and concluding that "[i]n short, the constable must apprehend, take charge of and present for trial all persons who broke the laws, written or unwritten, against the King's peace or against the statutes of the realm ...").

5. See 2 Hawkins, ch. 13, §1, at 129 ("[W]herever any [warrantless] arrest may be justified by a private person, in every such case à fortiori it may be justified by any [peace] officer").

6. King v. Wilkes, 2 Wils. K. B. 151, 95 Eng. Rep. 737 (1763), and Money v. Leach, 3 Burr. 1742, 97 Eng. Rep. 1075 (K. B. 1765), two of the decisions arising out of the controversy that generated Wilkes v. Wood, Lofft 1, 98 Eng. Rep. 489 (C. P. 1763), the "paradigm search and seizure case for Americans" of the founding generation, Amar, Fourth Amendment First Principles, 107 Harv. L. Rev. 757, 772 (1994), also contain dicta suggesting a somewhat broader conception of common-law arrest power than the one Atwater advances. See, e.g., King v. Wilkes, 2 Wils. K.B., at 158, 95 Eng. Rep., at 741 ("[I]f a crime be done in his sight," a justice of the peace "may commit the criminal upon the spot"); Money v. Leach, 3 Burr., at 1766, 97 Eng. Rep., at 1088 ("The common law, in many cases, gives authority to arrest without a warrant; more especially, where taken in the very act ...").

7. 7 & 8 Geo. IV, ch. 27, 67 Statutes at Large 153.

8. Atwater seeks to distinguish the nightwalker statutes by arguing that they "just reflected the reasonable notion that, in an age before lighting, finding a person walking about in the dead of night equaled probable suspicion that the person was a felon." Reply Brief for Petitioners 7, n. 6. Hale indicates, however, that nightwalkers and felons were not considered to be one and the same. 2 Hale, History of the Pleas of the Crown, at 97 ("And such a watchman may apprehend night-walkers and commit them to custody till the morning, and also felons and persons suspected of felony").

9. Given these early colonial and state laws, the fact that a number of States that ratified the Fourth Amendment generally incorporated common-law principles into their own constitutions or statutes, see Wilson v. Arkansas, 514 U.S. 927, 934 (1995), cannot aid Atwater here. Founding-era receptions of common law, whether by state constitution or state statute, generally provided that common-law rules were subject to statutory alteration. See, e.g., Del. Const., Art. 25 (1776), 2 W. Swindler, Sources and Documents of United States Constitutions 203 (1973) (hereinafter Swindler) ("The common law of England ... shall remain in force, unless [it] shall be altered by a future law of the legislature"); N. J. Const., Art. XXII (1776), 6 Swindler 452 ("[T]he common law of England ... shall still remain in force, until [it] shall be altered by a future law of the Legislature"); N. Y. Const., Art. XXXV (1777), 7 Swindler 177—178 ("[S]uch parts of the common law of England, and of the statute law of England and Great Britain ... as together did form the law of [New York on April 19, 1775,] shall be and continue the law of this State, subject to such alterations and provisions as the legislature of this State shall, from time to time, make concerning the same"); N. C. Laws 1778, ch. V, in 1 First Laws of the State of North Carolina 353 (J. Cushing ed. 1984) ("[A]ll such ... Parts of the Common Law, as were heretofore in Force and Use within this Territory ... which have not been ... abrogated [or] repealed ...

are hereby declared to be in full Force within this State"); Ordinances of May 1776, ch. 5, §6, 9 Statutes at Large of Virginia 127 (W. Hening ed. 1821) ("[T]he common law of England ... shall be the rule of decision, and shall be considered in full force, until the same shall be altered by the legislative power of this colony").

10. Courts and commentators alike have read the 1792 Act as conferring broad warrantless arrest authority on federal officers, and, indeed, the Act's passage "so soon after the adoption of the Fourth Amendment itself underscores the probability that the constitutional provision was intended to restrict entirely different practices." Watson, 423 U.S., at 429 (Powell, J., concurring); see also Amar, Fourth Amendment First Principles, 107 Harv. L. Rev., at 764, and n. 14.

11. We need not, and thus do not, speculate whether the Fourth Amendment entails an "in the presence" requirement for purposes of misdemeanor arrests. Cf. Welsh v. Wisconsin, 466 U.S. 740, 756 (1984) (White, J., dissenting) ("[T]he requirement that a misdemeanor must have occurred in the officer's presence to justify a warrantless arrest is not grounded in the Fourth Amendment").

12. See Appendix, infra.

13. See, e.g., 18 U.S.C. § 3052 (Federal Bureau of Investigation agents authorized to "make arrests without warrant for any offense against the United States committed in their presence"); §3053 (same, for United States marshals and deputies); §3056(c)(1)(C) (same, for Secret Service agents); §3061(a)(2) (same, for postal inspectors); §3063(a)(3) (same, for Environmental Protection Agency officers); 19 U.S.C. § 1589a(3) (same, for customs officers); 21 U.S.C. § 878(a)(3) (same, for Drug Enforcement Administration agents); 25 U.S.C. § 2803(3)(A) (same, for Bureau of Indian Affairs officers).

14. And, indeed, the dissent chooses not to deal with history at all. See post (O'Connor, J.,

dissenting). As is no doubt clear from the text, the historical record is not nearly as murky as the dissent suggests. See, e.g., supra, at 11—14 (parliamentary statutes clearly authorizing warrantless arrests for misdemeanor-level offenses), 15—16 (colonial and founding-era state statutes clearly authorizing same). History, moreover, is not just "one of the tools" relevant to a Fourth Amendment inquiry, post, at 2. Justice O'Connor herself has observed that courts must be "reluctant ... to conclude that the Fourth Amendment proscribes a practice that was accepted at the time of adoption of the Bill of Rights and has continued to receive the support of many state legislatures," Tennessee v. Garner, 471 U.S. 1, 26 (1985) (dissenting opinion), as the practice of making warrantless misdemeanor arrests surely was and has, see supra, at 15—24. Because here the dissent "claim[s] that [a] practice[] accepted when the Fourth Amendment was adopted [is] now constitutionally impermissible," the dissent bears the "heavy burden" of justifying a departure from the historical understanding. Ibid.

15. Although it is unclear from Atwater's briefs whether the rule she proposes would bar custodial arrests for fine-only offenses even when made pursuant to a warrant, at oral argument Atwater's counsel "concede[d] that if a warrant were obtained, this arrest ... would ... be reasonable." Tr. of Oral Arg. 5.

16. Terry v. Ohio, 392 U.S. 1 (1968), upon which the dissent relies, see post, at 7—8, is not to the contrary. Terry certainly supports a more finely tuned approach to the Fourth Amendment when police act without the traditional justification that either a warrant (in the case of a search) or probable cause (in the case of arrest) provides; but at least in the absence of "extraordinary" circumstances, Whren v. United States, 517 U.S. 806, 818 (1996), there is no comparable cause for finicking when police act with such justification.

17. Compare, e.g., Brief for Petitioners 46 ("fine-only") with, e.g., Tr. of Oral Arg. 11 (misdemeanors). Because the difficulties attendant to any major crime-minor crime distinction are largely the same, we treat them together.

18. See, e.g., Welsh, 466 U.S., at 756 (first DUI offense subject to maximum fine of $200; subsequent offense punishable by one year's imprisonment); Carroll v. United States, 267 U.S. 132, 154 (1925) (first offense of smuggling liquor subject to maximum fine of $500; subsequent offense punishable by 90 days' imprisonment); 21 U.S.C. § 844a(a), (c) (first offense for possession of "personal use amount" of controlled substance subject to maximum $10,000 fine; subsequent offense punishable by imprisonment); Tex. Penal Code Ann. §§42.01, 49.02, 12.23, 12.43 (1994 and Supp. 2001) (first public drunkenness or disorderly conduct offense subject to maximum $500 fine; third offense punishable by 180 days' imprisonment).

19. See, e.g., 21 U.S.C. § 844 844a (possession of "personal use amount" of a controlled substance subject to maximum $10,000 fine; possession of larger amount punishable by one year's imprisonment); Tex. Health & Safety Code Ann. §481.121(b) (Supp. 2001) (possession of four ounces or less of marijuana a misdemeanor; possession of more than four ounces a felony). See generally National Survey of State Laws 151—188 (3d R. Leiter ed. 1999) (surveying state laws concerning drug possession).

20. For instance, the act of allowing a small child to stand unrestrained in the front seat of a moving vehicle at least arguably constitutes child endangerment, which under Texas law is a state jail felony. Tex. Penal Code Ann. §§22.041(c), (f) (Supp. 2001). Cf. also 21 Am. Jur. 2d Criminal Law §28 (1998) ("[S]ome statutory schemes permit courts in their discretion to term certain offenses as felonies or as misdemeanors").

21. See United States v. Watson, 423 U.S. 411, 423—424 (1976) ("[T]he judgment of the Nation and Congress has ... long been to authorize warrantless public arrests on probable cause rather than to encumber criminal prosecutions with endless litigation with respect to the existence of exigent circumstances, whether it was practicable to get a warrant, whether the suspect was about to flee, and the like").

22. The doctrine of qualified immunity is not the panacea the dissent believes it to be. See post, at 8—9. As the dissent itself rightly acknowledges, even where personal liability does not ultimately materialize, the mere "specter of liability" may inhibit public officials in the discharge of their duties, post, at 9, for even those officers with airtight qualified immunity defenses are forced to incur "the expenses of litigation" and to endure the "diversion of [their] official energy from pressing public issues," Harlow v. Fitzgerald, 457 U.S. 800, 814 (1982). Further, and somewhat perversely, the disincentive to arrest produced by Atwater's opaque standard would be most pronounced in the very situations in which police officers can least afford to hesitate: when acting "on the spur (and in the heat) of the moment," supra, at 26. We could not seriously expect that when events were unfolding fast, an officer would be able to tell with much confidence whether a suspect's conduct qualified, or even "reasonably" qualified, under one of the exceptions to Atwater's general no-arrests rule.

23. He referred to a newspaper account of a girl taken into custody for eating french fries in a Washington, D. C., subway station. Tr. of Oral Arg. 20—21; see also Washington Post, Nov. 16, 2000, p. A1 (describing incident). Not surprisingly, given the practical and political considerations discussed in text, the Washington Metro Transit Police recently revised their "zero-tolerance" policy to provide for citation in lieu of custodial arrest of subway snackers. Washington Post, Feb. 27, 2001, at B1.

24. One of Atwater's amici described a handful in its brief. Brief for American Civil Liberties Union et al. as Amici Curiae 7—8 (reporting arrests for littering, riding a bicycle without a bell or gong, operating a business without a license, and "walking as to create a hazard").

25. The dissent insists that a minor traffic infraction "may serve as an excuse" for harassment, and that fine-only misdemeanor prohibitions "may be enforced" in an arbitrary manner. Post, at 13—14. Thus, the dissent warns, the rule that we recognize today "has potentially serious consequences for the everyday lives of Americans" and "carries with it grave potential for abuse." Post, at 12—13. But the dissent's own language (e.g., "may," "potentially") betrays the speculative nature of its claims. Noticeably absent from the parade of horribles is any indication that the "potential for abuse" has ever ripened into a reality. In fact, as we have pointed out in text, there simply is no evidence of widespread abuse of minor-offense arrest authority.

Kyllo v. United States (June 11, 2001)

Justice Scalia delivered the opinion of the Court.

This case presents the question whether the use of a thermal-imaging device aimed at a private home from a public street to detect relative amounts of heat within the home constitutes a "search" within the meaning of the Fourth Amendment.

I

In 1991 Agent William Elliott of the United States Department of the Interior came to suspect that marijuana was being grown in the home belonging to petitioner Danny Kyllo, part of a triplex on Rhododendron Drive in Florence, Oregon. Indoor marijuana growth typically requires high-intensity lamps. In order to determine whether an amount of heat was emanating from petitioner's home consistent with the use of such lamps, at 3:20 a.m. on January 16, 1992, Agent Elliott and Dan Haas used an Agema Thermovision 210 thermal imager to scan the triplex. Thermal imagers detect infrared radiation, which virtually all objects emit but which is not visible to the naked eye. The imager converts radiation into images based on relative warmth–black is cool, white is hot, shades of gray connote relative differences; in that respect, it operates somewhat like a video camera showing heat images. The scan of Kyllo's home took only a few minutes and was performed from the passenger seat of Agent Elliott's vehicle across the street from the front of the house and also from the street in back of the house. The scan showed that the roof over the garage and a side wall of petitioner's home were relatively hot compared to the rest of the home and substantially warmer than neighboring homes in the triplex. Agent Elliott concluded that petitioner was using halide lights to grow marijuana in his house, which indeed he was. Based on tips from informants, utility bills, and the thermal imaging, a Federal Magistrate Judge issued a warrant authorizing a search of petitioner's home, and the agents found an indoor growing operation involving more than 100 plants. Petitioner was indicted on one count of manufacturing marijuana, in violation of 21 U.S.C. § 841(a)(1). He unsuccessfully moved to suppress the evidence seized from his home and then entered a conditional guilty plea.

The Court of Appeals for the Ninth Circuit remanded the case for an evidentiary hearing regarding the intrusiveness of thermal imaging. On remand the District Court found that the Agema 210 "is a non-intrusive device which emits no rays or beams and shows a crude visual image of the heat being radiated from the outside of the house"; it "did not show any people or activity within the walls of the structure"; "[t]he device used cannot penetrate walls or windows to reveal conversations or human activities"; and "[n]o intimate details of the home were observed." Supp. App. to Pet. for Cert. 39—40. Based on these findings, the District Court upheld the validity of the warrant that relied in part upon the thermal imaging, and reaffirmed its denial of the motion to suppress. A divided Court of Appeals initially reversed, 140 F.3d 1249 (1998), but that opinion was withdrawn and the panel (after a change in composition) affirmed, 190 F.3d 1041 (1999), with Judge Noonan dissenting. The court held that petitioner had shown no subjective expectation of privacy because he had made no attempt to conceal the heat escaping from his home, id., at 1046, and even if he had, there was no objectively reasonable expectation of privacy because the imager "did not expose any intimate details of Kyllo's life," only "amorphous 'hot spots' on the roof and exterior wall," id., at 1047. We granted certiorari. 530 U.S. 1305 (2000).

II

The Fourth Amendment provides that "[t]he right of the people to be secure in their persons, houses, papers, and effects, against unreasonable searches and seizures, shall not be violated." "At the very core" of the Fourth Amendment "stands the right of a man to retreat into his own home and there be free from unreasonable governmental intrusion." Silverman v. United States, 365 U.S. 505, 511 (1961). With few exceptions, the question whether a warrantless search of a home is reasonable and hence constitutional must be answered no. See Illinois v. Rodriguez, 497 U.S. 177, 181 (1990); Payton v. New York, 445 U.S. 573, 586 (1980).

On the other hand, the antecedent question of whether or not a Fourth Amendment "search" has occurred is not so simple under our precedent. The permissibility of ordinary visual surveillance of a home used to be clear because, well into the 20th century, our Fourth Amendment jurisprudence was tied to common-law trespass. See, e.g., Goldman v. United States, 316 U.S. 129, 134—136 (1942); Olmstead v. United States, 277 U.S. 438, 464—466 (1928). Cf. Silverman v. United States, supra, at 510—512 (technical trespass not necessary for Fourth Amendment violation; it suffices if there is "actual intrusion into a constitutionally protected area"). Visual surveillance was unquestionably lawful because " 'the eye cannot by the laws of England be guilty of a trespass.' " Boyd v. United States, 116 U.S. 616, 628 (1886) (quoting Entick v. Carrington, 19 How. St. Tr. 1029, 95 Eng. Rep. 807 (K. B. 1765)). We have since decoupled violation of a person's Fourth Amendment rights from trespassory violation of his property, see Rakas v. Illinois, 439 U.S. 128, 143 (1978), but the lawfulness of warrantless visual surveillance of a home has still been preserved. As we observed in California v. Ciraolo, 476 U.S. 207, 213 (1986), "[t]he Fourth Amendment protection of the home has never been extended to require law enforcement officers to shield their eyes when passing by a home on public thoroughfares."

One might think that the new validating rationale would be that examining the portion of a house that is in plain public view, while it is a "search"1 despite the absence of trespass, is not an "unreasonable" one under the Fourth Amendment. See Minnesota v. Carter, 525 U.S. 83, 104 (1998) (Breyer, J., concurring in judgment). But in fact we have held that visual observation is no "search" at all—perhaps in order to preserve somewhat more intact our doctrine that warrantless searches are presumptively unconstitutional. See Dow Chemical Co. v. United States, 476 U.S. 227, 234—235, 239 (1986). In assessing when a search is not a search, we have applied somewhat in reverse the principle first enunciated in Katz v. United States, 389 U.S. 347 (1967). Katz involved eavesdropping by means of an electronic listening device placed on the outside of a telephone booth—a location not within the catalog ("persons, houses, papers, and effects") that the Fourth Amendment protects against unreasonable searches. We held that the Fourth Amendment nonetheless protected Katz from the warrantless eavesdropping because he "justifiably relied" upon the privacy of the telephone booth. Id., at 353. As Justice Harlan's oft-quoted concurrence described it, a Fourth Amendment search occurs when the government violates a subjective expectation of privacy that society recognizes as reasonable. See id., at 361. We have subsequently applied this principle to hold that a Fourth Amendment search does not occur–even when the explicitly protected location of a house is concerned–unless "the individual manifested a subjective expectation of privacy in the object of the challenged search," and "society [is] willing to recognize that expectation as reasonable." Ciraolo, supra, at 211. We have applied this test in holding that it is not a search for the police to use a pen register at the phone company to determine what numbers were dialed in a private home, Smith v. Maryland, 442 U.S. 735, 743–744 (1979), and we have applied the test on two different occasions in holding that aerial surveillance of private homes and surrounding areas does not constitute a search, Ciraolo, supra; Florida v. Riley, 488 U.S. 445 (1989).

The present case involves officers on a public street engaged in more than naked-eye surveillance of a home. We have previously reserved judgment as to how much technological enhancement of ordinary perception from such a vantage point, if any, is too much. While we upheld enhanced aerial photography of an industrial complex in Dow Chemical, we noted that we found "it important that this is not an area immediately adjacent to a private home, where privacy expectations are most heightened," 476 U.S., at 237, n. 4 (emphasis in original).

III

It would be foolish to contend that the degree of privacy secured to citizens by the Fourth Amendment has been entirely unaffected by the advance of technology. For example, as the cases discussed above make clear, the technology enabling human flight has exposed to public view (and hence, we have said, to official observation) uncovered portions of the house and its curtilage that once were private. See Ciraolo, supra, at 215. The question we confront today is what limits there are upon this power of technology to shrink the realm of guaranteed privacy.

The Katz test–whether the individual has an expectation of privacy that society is prepared to recognize as reasonable–has often been criticized as circular, and hence subjective and unpredictable. See 1 W. LaFave, Search and Seizure §2.1(d), pp. 393–394 (3d ed. 1996); Posner, The Uncertain Protection of Privacy by the Supreme Court, 1979 S. Ct. Rev. 173, 188; Carter, supra, at 97 (Scalia, J., concurring). But see Rakas, supra, at 143–144, n. 12. While it may be difficult to refine Katz when the search of areas such as telephone booths, automobiles, or even the curtilage and uncovered portions of residences are at issue, in the case of the search of the interior of homes–the prototypical and hence most commonly litigated area of protected privacy– there is a ready criterion, with roots deep in the common law, of the minimal expectation of privacy that exists, and that is acknowledged to be reasonable. To withdraw protection of this minimum expectation would be to permit police technology to erode the privacy guaranteed by the Fourth Amendment. We think that obtaining by sense-enhancing technology any information regarding the interior of the home that could not otherwise have been obtained without physical "intrusion into a constitutionally protected area," Silverman, 365 U.S., at 512, constitutes a search–at least where (as here) the technology in question is not in general public use. This assures preservation of that degree of privacy against government that existed when the Fourth Amendment was adopted. On the basis of this criterion, the information obtained by the thermal imager in this case was the product of a search.2

The Government maintains, however, that the thermal imaging must be upheld because it detected "only heat radiating from the external surface of the house," Brief for United States 26. The dissent makes this its leading point, see post, at 1, contending that there is a fundamental difference between what it calls "off-the-wall" observations and "through-the-wall surveillance." But just as a thermal imager captures only heat emanating from a house, so also a powerful directional microphone picks up only sound emanating from a house—and a satellite capable of scanning from many miles away would pick up only visible light emanating from a house. We rejected such a mechanical interpretation of the Fourth Amendment in Katz, where the eavesdropping device picked up only sound waves that reached the exterior of the phone booth. Reversing that approach would leave the homeowner at the mercy of advancing technology—including imaging technology that could discern all human activity in the home. While the technology used in the present case was relatively crude, the rule we adopt must take account of more sophisticated systems that are already in use or in development.3 The dissent's reliance on the distinction between "off-the-wall" and "through-the-wall" observation is entirely incompatible with the dissent's belief, which we discuss below, that thermal-imaging observations of the intimate details of a home are impermissible. The most sophisticated thermal imaging devices continue to measure heat "off-the-wall" rather than "through-the-wall"; the dissent's disapproval of those more sophisticated thermal-imaging devices, see post, at 10, is an acknowledgement that there is no substance to this distinction. As for the dissent's extraordinary assertion that anything learned through "an inference" cannot be a search, see post, at 4—5, that would validate even the "through-the-wall" technologies that the dissent purports to disapprove. Surely the dissent does not believe that the through-the-wall radar or ultrasound technology produces an 8-by-10 Kodak glossy that needs no analysis (i.e., the making of inferences). And, of course, the novel proposition that inference insulates a search is blatantly contrary to United States v. Karo, 468 U.S. 705 (1984), where the police "inferred" from the activation of a beeper that a certain can of ether was in the home. The police activity was held to be a search, and the search was held unlawful.4

The Government also contends that the thermal imaging was constitutional because it did not "detect private activities occurring in private areas," Brief for United States 22. It points out that in Dow Chemical we observed that the enhanced aerial photography did not reveal any "intimate details." 476 U.S., at 238. Dow Chemical, however, involved enhanced aerial photography of an industrial complex, which does not share the Fourth Amendment sanctity of the home. The Fourth Amendment's protection of the home has never been tied to measurement of the quality or quantity of information obtained. In Silverman, for example, we made clear that any physical invasion of the structure of the home, "by even a fraction of an inch," was too much, 365 U.S., at 512, and there is certainly no exception to the warrant requirement for the officer who barely cracks open the front door and sees nothing but the nonintimate rug on the vestibule floor. In the home, our cases show, all details are intimate details, because the entire area is held safe from prying government eyes. Thus, in Karo, supra, the only thing detected was a can of ether in the home; and in Arizona v. Hicks, 480 U.S. 321 (1987), the only thing detected by a physical search that went beyond what officers lawfully present could observe in "plain view" was the registration number of a phonograph turntable. These were intimate details because they were details of the home, just as was the detail of how warm–or even how relatively warm–Kyllo was heating his residence.5

Limiting the prohibition of thermal imaging to "intimate details" would not only be wrong in principle; it would be impractical in application, failing to provide "a workable accommodation between the needs of law enforcement and the interests protected by the Fourth Amendment," Oliver v. United States, 466 U.S. 170, 181 (1984). To begin with, there is no necessary connection between the sophistication of the surveillance equipment and the "intimacy" of the details that it observes–which means that one cannot say (and the police cannot be assured) that use of the relatively crude equipment at issue here will always be lawful. The Agema Thermovision 210 might disclose, for example, at what hour each night the lady of the house takes her daily sauna and bath–a detail that many would consider "intimate"; and a much more sophisticated system might detect nothing more intimate than the fact that someone left a closet light on. We could not, in other words, develop a rule approving only that through-the-wall surveillance which identifies objects no smaller than 36 by 36 inches, but would have to develop a jurisprudence specifying which home activities are "intimate" and which are not. And even when (if ever) that jurisprudence were fully developed, no police officer would be able to know in advance whether his through-the-wall surveillance picks up "intimate" details–and thus would be unable to know in advance whether it is constitutional.

The dissent's proposed standard– whether the technology offers the "functional equivalent of actual presence in the area being searched," post, at 7–would seem quite similar to our own at first blush. The dissent concludes that Katz was such a case, but then inexplicably asserts

that if the same listening device only revealed the volume of the conversation, the surveillance would be permissible, post, at 10. Yet if, without technology, the police could not discern volume without being actually present in the phone booth, Justice Stevens should conclude a search has occurred. Cf. Karo, supra, at 735 (Stevens, J., concurring in part and dissenting in part) ("I find little comfort in the Court's notion that no invasion of privacy occurs until a listener obtains some significant information by use of the device... . A bathtub is a less private area when the plumber is present even if his back is turned"). The same should hold for the interior heat of the home if only a person present in the home could discern the heat. Thus the driving force of the dissent, despite its recitation of the above standard, appears to be a distinction among different types of information–whether the "homeowner would even care if anybody noticed," post, at 10. The dissent offers no practical guidance for the application of this standard, and for reasons already discussed, we believe there can be none. The people in their houses, as well as the police, deserve more precision.6

We have said that the Fourth Amendment draws "a firm line at the entrance to the house," Payton, 445 U.S., at 590. That line, we think, must be not only firm but also bright–which requires clear specification of those methods of surveillance that require a warrant. While it is certainly possible to conclude from the videotape of the thermal imaging that occurred in this case that no "significant" compromise of the homeowner's privacy has occurred, we must take the long view, from the original meaning of the Fourth Amendment forward.

"The Fourth Amendment is to be construed in the light of what was deemed an unreasonable search and seizure when it was adopted, and in a manner which will conserve public interests as well as the interests and rights of individual citizens." Carroll v. United States, 267 U.S. 132, 149 (1925).

Where, as here, the Government uses a device that is not in general public use, to explore details of the home that would previously have been unknowable without physical intrusion, the surveillance is a "search" and is presumptively unreasonable without a warrant.

Since we hold the Thermovision imaging to have been an unlawful search, it will remain for the District Court to determine whether, without the evidence it provided, the search warrant issued in this case was supported by probable cause—and if not, whether there is any other basis for supporting admission of the evidence that the search pursuant to the warrant produced.

* * *

The judgment of the Court of Appeals is reversed; the case is remanded for further proceedings consistent with this opinion.

It is so ordered.

Notes

1. When the Fourth Amendment was adopted, as now, to "search" meant "[t]o look over or through for the purpose of finding something; to explore; to examine by inspection; as, to search the house for a book; to search the wood for a thief." N. Webster, An American Dictionary of the English Language 66 (1828) (reprint 6th ed. 1989).

2. The dissent's repeated assertion that the thermal imaging did not obtain information regarding the interior of the home, post, at 3, 4 (opinion of Stevens, J.), is simply inaccurate. A thermal imager reveals the relative heat of various rooms in the home. The dissent may not find that information particularly private or important, see post, at 4, 5, 10, but there is no basis for saying it is not information regarding the interior of the home. The dissent's comparison of the thermal imaging to various circumstances in which outside observers might be able to perceive, without

technology, the heat of the home—for example, by observing snowmelt on the roof, post, at 3—is quite irrelevant. The fact that equivalent information could sometimes be obtained by other means does not make lawful the use of means that violate the Fourth Amendment. The police might, for example, learn how many people are in a particular house by setting up year-round surveillance; but that does not make breaking and entering to find out the same information lawful. In any event, on the night of January 16, 1992, no outside observer could have discerned the relative heat of Kyllo's home without thermal imaging.

3. The ability to "see" through walls and other opaque barriers is a clear, and scientifically feasible, goal of law enforcement research and development. The National Law Enforcement and Corrections Technology Center, a program within the United States Department of Justice, features on its Internet Website projects that include a "Radar-Based Through-the-Wall Surveillance System," "Handheld Ultrasound Through the Wall Surveillance," and a "Radar Flashlight" that "will enable law officers to detect individuals through interior building walls." www.nlectc.org/techproj/ (visited May 3, 2001). Some devices may emit low levels of radiation that travel "through-the-wall," but others, such as more sophisticated thermal imaging devices, are entirely passive, or "off-the-wall" as the dissent puts it.

4. The dissent asserts, post, at 5, n. 3, that we have misunderstood its point, which is not that inference insulates a search, but that inference alone is not a search. If we misunderstood the point, it was only in a good-faith effort to render the point germane to the case at hand. The issue in this case is not the police's allegedly unlawful inferencing, but their allegedly unlawful thermal-imaging measurement of the emanations from a house. We say such measurement is a search; the dissent says it is not, because an inference is not a search. We took that to mean that, since the

technologically enhanced emanations had to be the basis of inferences before anything inside the house could be known, the use of the emanations could not be a search. But the dissent certainly knows better than we what it intends. And if it means only that an inference is not a search, we certainly agree. That has no bearing, however, upon whether hi-tech measurement of emanations from a house is a search.

5. The Government cites our statement in California v. Ciraolo, 476 U.S. 207 (1986), noting apparent agreement with the State of California that aerial surveillance of a house's curtilage could become " 'invasive' " if " 'modern technology' " revealed " 'those intimate associations, objects or activities otherwise imperceptible to police or fellow citizens.' " Id., at 215, n. 3 (quoting brief of the State of California). We think the Court's focus in this second-hand dictum was not upon intimacy but upon otherwise-imperceptibility, which is precisely the principle we vindicate today.

6. The dissent argues that we have injected potential uncertainty into the constitutional analysis by noting that whether or not the technology is in general public use may be a factor. See post, at 7—8. That quarrel, however, is not with us but with this Court's precedent. See Ciraolo, supra, at 215 ("In an age where private and commercial flight in the public airways is routine, it is unreasonable for respondent to expect that his marijuana plants were constitutionally protected from being observed with the naked eye from an altitude of 1,000 feet"). Given that we can quite confidently say that thermal imaging is not "routine," we decline in this case to reexamine that factor.

Bd of Ed. of Indept. School Dist. No. 92 of Pottawatomie County v Earls (June 27, 2002)

Justice Thomas delivered the opinion of the Court.

The Student Activities Drug Testing Policy implemented by the Board of Education of Independent School District No. 92 of Pottawatomie County (School District) requires all students who participate in competitive extracurricular activities to submit to drug testing. Because this Policy reasonably serves the School District's important interest in detecting and preventing drug use among its students, we hold that it is constitutional.

I

The city of Tecumseh, Oklahoma, is a rural community located approximately 40 miles southeast of Oklahoma City. The School District administers all Tecumseh public schools. In the fall of 1998, the School District adopted the Student Activities Drug Testing Policy (Policy), which requires all middle and high school students to consent to drug testing in order to participate in any extracurricular activity. In practice, the Policy has been applied only to competitive extracurricular activities sanctioned by the Oklahoma Secondary Schools Activities Association, such as the Academic Team, Future Farmers of America, Future Homemakers of America, band, choir, pom pon, cheerleading, and athletics. Under the Policy, students are required to take a drug test before participating in an extracurricular activity, must submit to random drug testing while participating in that activity, and must agree to be tested at any time upon reasonable suspicion. The urinalysis tests are designed to detect only the use of illegal drugs, including amphetamines, marijuana, cocaine, opiates, and barbituates, not medical conditions or the presence of authorized prescription medications.

At the time of their suit, both respondents attended Tecumseh High School. Respondent Lindsay Earls was a member of the show choir, the marching band, the Academic

Team, and the National Honor Society. Respondent Daniel James sought to participate in the Academic Team.1 Together with their parents, Earls and James brought a 42 U.S.C. § 1983 action against the School District, challenging the Policy both on its face and as applied to their participation in extracurricular activities.2 They alleged that the Policy violates the Fourth Amendment as incorporated by the Fourteenth Amendment and requested injunctive and declarative relief. They also argued that the School District failed to identify a special need for testing students who participate in extracurricular activities, and that the "Drug Testing Policy neither addresses a proven problem nor promises to bring any benefit to students or the school." App. 9.

Applying the principles articulated in Vernonia School Dist. 47J v. Acton, 515 U.S. 646 (1995), in which we upheld the suspicionless drug testing of school athletes, the United States District Court for the Western District of Oklahoma rejected respondents' claim that the Policy was unconstitutional and granted summary judgment to the School District. The court noted that "special needs" exist in the public school context and that, although the School District did "not show a drug problem of epidemic proportions," there was a history of drug abuse starting in 1970 that presented "legitimate cause for concern." 115 F. Supp. 2d 1281, 1287 (2000). The District Court also held that the Policy was effective because "[i]t can scarcely be disputed that the drug problem among the student body is effectively addressed by making sure that the large number of students participating in competitive, extracurricular activities do not use drugs." Id., at 1295.

The United States Court of Appeals for the Tenth Circuit reversed, holding that the Policy violated the Fourth Amendment. The Court of Appeals agreed with the District Court that the Policy must be evaluated in the "unique environment of the school setting," but reached a different conclusion as to the Policy's constitutionality. 242 F.3d 1264, 1270 (2001). Before imposing a suspicionless drug testing program, the Court of Appeals concluded that a school "must demonstrate that there is some identifiable drug abuse problem among a sufficient number of those subject to the testing, such that testing that group of students will actually redress its drug problem." Id., at 1278. The Court of Appeals then held that because the School District failed to demonstrate such a problem existed among Tecumseh students participating in competitive extracurricular activities, the Policy was unconstitutional. We granted certiorari, 534 U.S. 1015 (2001), and now reverse.

II

The Fourth Amendment to the United States Constitution protects "[t]he right of the people to be secure in their persons, houses, papers, and effects, against unreasonable searches and seizures." Searches by public school officials, such as the collection of urine samples, implicate Fourth Amendment interests. See Vernonia, supra, at 652; cf. New Jersey v. T. L. O., 469 U.S. 325, 334 (1985). We must therefore review the School District's Policy for "reasonableness," which is the touchstone of the constitutionality of a governmental search.

In the criminal context, reasonableness usually requires a showing of probable cause. See, e.g., Skinner v. Railway Labor Executives' Assn., 489 U.S. 602, 619 (1989). The probable-cause standard, however, "is peculiarly related to criminal investigations" and may be unsuited to determining the reasonableness of administrative searches where the "Government seeks to prevent the development of hazardous conditions." Treasury Employees v. Von Raab, 489 U.S. 656, 667—668 (1989) (internal quotation marks and citations omitted) (collecting cases). The Court has also held that a warrant and finding of probable cause are unnecessary in the public school context because such requirements " 'would unduly interfere with the maintenance of the swift and informal disciplinary procedures [that are] needed.' " Vernonia, supra, at 653 (quoting T. L. O., supra, at 340—341).

Given that the School District's Policy is not in any way related to the conduct of criminal investigations, see Part II—B, infra, respondents do not contend that the School District requires probable cause before testing students for drug use. Respondents instead argue that drug testing must be based at least on some level of individualized suspicion. See Brief for Respondents 12—14. It is true that we generally determine the reasonableness of a search by balancing the nature of the intrusion on the individual's privacy against the promotion of legitimate governmental interests. See Delaware v. Prouse, 440 U.S. 648, 654 (1979). But we have long held that "the Fourth Amendment imposes no irreducible requirement of [individualized] suspicion." United States v. Martinez-Fuerte, 428 U.S. 543, 561 (1976). "[I]n certain limited circumstances, the Government's need to discover such latent or hidden conditions, or to prevent their development, is sufficiently compelling to justify the intrusion on privacy entailed by conducting such searches without any measure of individualized suspicion." Von Raab, supra, at 668; see also Skinner, supra, at 624. Therefore, in the context of safety and administrative regulations, a search unsupported by probable cause may be reasonable "when 'special needs, beyond the normal need for law enforcement, make the warrant and probable-cause requirement impracticable.' " Griffin v. Wisconsin, 483 U.S. 868, 873 (1987) (quoting T. L. O., supra, at 351 (Blackmun, J., concurring in judgment)); see also Vernonia, supra, at 653; Skinner, supra, at 619.

Significantly, this Court has previously held that "special needs" inhere in the public school context. See Vernonia, supra, at 653; T. L.

O., supra, at 339—340. While schoolchildren do not shed their constitutional rights when they enter the schoolhouse, see Tinker v. Des Moines Independent Community School Dist., 393 U.S. 503, 506 (1969), "Fourth Amendment rights ... are different in public schools than elsewhere; the 'reasonableness' inquiry cannot disregard the schools' custodial and tutelary responsibility for children." Vernonia, supra, at 656. In particular, a finding of individualized suspicion may not be necessary when a school conducts drug testing.

In Vernonia, this Court held that the suspicionless drug testing of athletes was constitutional. The Court, however, did not simply authorize all school drug testing, but rather conducted a fact-specific balancing of the intrusion on the children's Fourth Amendment rights against the promotion of legitimate governmental interests. See 515 U.S., at 652—653. Applying the principles of Vernonia to the somewhat different facts of this case, we conclude that Tecumseh's Policy is also constitutional.

A

We first consider the nature of the privacy interest allegedly compromised by the drug testing. See id., at 654. As in Vernonia, the context of the public school environment serves as the backdrop for the analysis of the privacy interest at stake and the reasonableness of the drug testing policy in general. See ibid. ("Central ... is the fact that the subjects of the Policy are (1) children, who (2) have been committed to the temporary custody of the State as schoolmaster"); see also id., at 665 ("The most significant element in this case is the first we discussed: that the Policy was undertaken in furtherance of the government's responsibilities, under a public school system, as guardian and tutor of children entrusted to its care"); ibid. ("[W]hen the government acts as guardian and tutor the relevant question is whether the search is one that a reasonable guardian and tutor might undertake").

A student's privacy interest is limited in a public school environment where the State is responsible for maintaining discipline, health, and safety. Schoolchildren are routinely required to submit to physical examinations and vaccinations against disease. See id., at 656. Securing order in the school environment sometimes requires that students be subjected to greater controls than those appropriate for adults. See T. L. O., supra, at 350 (Powell, J., concurring) ("Without first establishing discipline and maintaining order, teachers cannot begin to educate their students. And apart from education, the school has the obligation to protect pupils from mistreatment by other children, and also to protect teachers themselves from violence by the few students whose conduct in recent years has prompted national concern").

Respondents argue that because children participating in nonathletic extracurricular activities are not subject to regular physicals and communal undress, they have a stronger expectation of privacy than the athletes tested in Vernonia. See Brief for Respondents 18—20. This distinction, however, was not essential to our decision in Vernonia, which depended primarily upon the school's custodial responsibility and authority.3

In any event, students who participate in competitive extracurricular activities voluntarily subject themselves to many of the same intrusions on their privacy as do athletes.4 Some of these clubs and activities require occasional off-campus travel and communal undress. All of them have their own rules and requirements for participating students that do not apply to the student body as a whole. 115 F. Supp. 2d, at 1289—1290. For example, each of the competitive extracurricular activities governed by the Policy must abide by the rules of the Oklahoma Secondary Schools Activities Association, and a faculty sponsor monitors the students for compliance with the various rules dictated by the clubs and activities. See id., at 1290. This regulation of extracurricular activities further diminishes the expectation of privacy among schoolchildren. Cf. Vernonia, supra, at 657 ("Somewhat like adults who choose to participate in a closely regulated industry, students who voluntarily participate in school athletics have reason to expect intrusions upon normal rights and privileges, including privacy" (internal quotation marks omitted)). We therefore conclude that the students affected by this Policy have a limited expectation of privacy.

B

Next, we consider the character of the intrusion imposed by the Policy. See Vernonia, supra, at 658. Urination is "an excretory function traditionally shielded by great privacy." Skinner, 489 U.S., at 626. But the "degree of intrusion" on one's privacy caused by collecting a urine sample "depends upon the manner in which production of the urine sample is monitored." Vernonia, supra, at 658.

Under the Policy, a faculty monitor waits outside the closed restroom stall for the student to produce a sample and must "listen for the normal sounds of urination in order to guard against tampered specimens and to insure an accurate chain of custody." App. 199. The monitor then pours the sample into two bottles that are sealed and placed into a mailing pouch along with a consent form signed by the student. This procedure is virtually identical to that reviewed in Vernonia, except that it additionally protects privacy by allowing male students to produce their samples behind a closed stall. Given that we considered the method of collection in Vernonia a "negligible" intrusion, 515 U.S., at 658, the method here is even less problematic.

In addition, the Policy clearly requires that the test results be kept in confidential files separate from a student's other educational records and released to school personnel only on a "need to know" basis. Respondents nonetheless contend that the intrusion on students' privacy is significant because the Policy fails to protect effectively against the disclosure of confidential information and, specifically, that the school "has been careless in protecting that information: for example, the Choir teacher looked at students' prescription drug lists and left them where other students could see them." Brief for Respondents 24. But the choir teacher is someone with a "need to know," because during off-campus trips she needs to know what medications are taken by her students. Even before the Policy was enacted the choir teacher had access to this information. See App. 132. In any event, there is no allegation that any other student did see such information. This one example of alleged carelessness hardly increases the character of the intrusion.

Moreover, the test results are not turned over to any law enforcement authority. Nor do the test results here lead to the imposition of discipline or have any academic consequences. Cf. Vernonia, supra, at 658, and n. 2. Rather, the only consequence of a failed drug test is to limit the student's privilege of participating in extracurricular activities. Indeed, a student may test positive for drugs twice and still be allowed to participate in extracurricular activities. After the first positive test, the school contacts the student's parent or guardian for a meeting. The student may continue to participate in the activity if within five days of the meeting the student shows proof of receiving drug counseling and submits to a second drug test in two weeks. For the second positive test, the student is suspended from participation in all extracurricular activities for 14 days, must complete four hours of substance abuse counseling, and must submit to monthly drug tests. Only after a third positive test will the student be suspended from participating in any extracurricular activity for the remainder of the school year, or 88 school days, whichever is longer.

See App. 201-202.

Given the minimally intrusive nature of the sample collection and the limited uses to which the test results are put, we conclude that the invasion of students' privacy is not significant.

C

Finally, this Court must consider the nature and immediacy of the government's concerns and the efficacy of the Policy in meeting them. See Vernonia, 515 U.S., at 660. This Court has already articulated in detail the importance of the governmental concern in preventing drug use by schoolchildren. See id., at 661—662. The drug abuse problem among our Nation's youth has hardly abated since Vernonia was decided in 1995. In fact, evidence suggests that it has only grown worse.5 As in Vernonia, "the necessity for the State to act is magnified by the fact that this evil is being visited not just upon individuals at large, but upon children for whom it has undertaken a special responsibility of care and direction." Id., at 662. The health and safety risks identified in Vernonia apply with equal force to Tecumseh's children. Indeed, the nationwide drug epidemic makes the war against drugs a pressing concern in every school.

Additionally, the School District in this case has presented specific evidence of drug use at Tecumseh schools. Teachers testified that they had seen students who appeared to be under the influence of drugs and that they had heard students speaking openly about using drugs. See, e.g., App. 72 (deposition of Dean Rogers); id., at 115 (deposition of Sheila Evans). A drug dog found marijuana cigarettes near the school parking lot. Police officers once found drugs or drug paraphernalia in a car driven by a Future Farmers of America member. And the school board president reported that people in the community were calling the board to discuss the "drug situation." See 115 F. Supp. 2d, at 1285—1286. We decline to second- guess the finding of the District

Court that "[v]iewing the evidence as a whole, it cannot be reasonably disputed that the [School District] was faced with a 'drug problem' when it adopted the Policy." Id., at 1287.

Respondents consider the proffered evidence insufficient and argue that there is no "real and immediate interest" to justify a policy of drug testing nonathletes. Brief for Respondents 32. We have recognized, however, that "[a] demonstrated problem of drug abuse ... [is] not in all cases necessary to the validity of a testing regime," but that some showing does "shore up an assertion of special need for a suspicionless general search program." Chandler v. Miller, 520 U.S. 305, 319 (1997). The School District has provided sufficient evidence to shore up the need for its drug testing program.

Furthermore, this Court has not required a particularized or pervasive drug problem before allowing the government to conduct suspicionless drug testing. For instance, in Von Raab the Court upheld the drug testing of customs officials on a purely preventive basis, without any documented history of drug use by such officials. See 489 U.S., at 673. In response to the lack of evidence relating to drug use, the Court noted generally that "drug abuse is one of the most serious problems confronting our society today," and that programs to prevent and detect drug use among customs officials could not be deemed unreasonable. Id., at 674; cf. Skinner, 489 U.S., at 607, and n. 1 (noting nationwide studies that identified on-the-job alcohol and drug use by railroad employees). Likewise, the need to prevent and deter the substantial harm of childhood drug use provides the necessary immediacy for a school testing policy. Indeed, it would make little sense to require a school district to wait for a substantial portion of its students to begin using drugs before it was allowed to institute a drug testing program designed to deter drug use.

Given the nationwide epidemic of drug use, and the evidence of increased drug use in Tecumseh schools, it was entirely reasonable for the School District to enact this particular drug testing policy. We reject the Court of Appeals' novel test that "any district seeking to impose a random suspicionless drug testing policy as a condition to participation in a school activity must demonstrate that there is some identifiable drug abuse problem among a sufficient number of those subject to the testing, such that testing that group of students will actually redress its drug problem." 242 F.3d, at 1278. Among other problems, it would be difficult to administer such a test. As we cannot articulate a threshold level of drug use that would suffice to justify a drug testing program for schoolchildren, we refuse to fashion what would in effect be a constitutional quantum of drug use necessary to show a "drug problem."

Respondents also argue that the testing of nonathletes does not implicate any safety concerns, and that safety is a "crucial factor" in applying the special needs framework. Brief for Respondents 25—27. They contend that there must be "surpassing safety interests," Skinner, supra, at 634, or "extraordinary safety and national security hazards," Von Raab, supra, at 674, in order to override the usual protections of the Fourth Amendment. See Brief for Respondents 25—26. Respondents are correct that safety factors into the special needs analysis, but the safety interest furthered by drug testing is undoubtedly substantial for all children, athletes and nonathletes alike. We know all too well that drug use carries a variety of health risks for children, including death from overdose.

We also reject respondents' argument that drug testing must presumptively be based upon an individualized reasonable suspicion of wrongdoing because such a testing regime would be less intrusive. See id., at 12—16. In this context, the Fourth Amendment does not require a finding of individualized suspicion, see supra, at 5, and we decline to impose such a requirement on schools attempting to prevent and detect drug use by students. Moreover, we question whether testing based on individualized suspicion in fact would be less intrusive. Such a regime would place an additional burden on public school teachers who are already tasked with the difficult job of maintaining order and discipline. A program of individualized suspicion might unfairly target members of unpopular groups. The fear of lawsuits resulting from such targeted searches may chill enforcement of the program, rendering it ineffective in combating drug use. See Vernonia, 515 U.S., at 663—664 (offering similar reasons for why "testing based on 'suspicion' of drug use would not be better, but worse"). In any case, this Court has repeatedly stated that reasonableness under the Fourth Amendment does not require employing the least intrusive means, because "[t]he logic of such elaborate less-restrictive-alternative arguments could raise insuperable barriers to the exercise of virtually all search-and-seizure powers." Martinez-Fuerte, 428 U.S., at 556—557, n. 12; see also Skinner, supra, at 624 ("[A] showing of individualized suspicion is not a constitutional floor, below which a search must be presumed unreasonable").

Finally, we find that testing students who participate in extracurricular activities is a reasonably effective means of addressing the School District's legitimate concerns in preventing, deterring, and detecting drug use. While in Vernonia there might have been a closer fit between the testing of athletes and the trial court's finding that the drug problem was "fueled by the 'role model' effect of athletes' drug use," such a finding was not essential to the holding. 515 U.S., at 663; cf. id., at 684—685 (O'Connor, J., dissenting) (questioning the extent of the drug problem, especially as applied to athletes). Vernonia did not require the school to test the group of students most likely to use drugs, but

rather considered the constitutionality of the program in the context of the public school's custodial responsibilities. Evaluating the Policy in this context, we conclude that the drug testing of Tecumseh students who participate in extracurricular activities effectively serves the School District's interest in protecting the safety and health of its students.

III

Within the limits of the Fourth Amendment, local school boards must assess the desirability of drug testing schoolchildren. In upholding the constitutionality of the Policy, we express no opinion as to its wisdom. Rather, we hold only that Tecumseh's Policy is a reasonable means of furthering the School District's important interest in preventing and deterring drug use among its schoolchildren. Accordingly, we reverse the judgment of the Court of Appeals.

It is so ordered.

Notes

1. The District Court noted that the School District's allegations concerning Daniel James called his standing to sue into question because his failing grades made him ineligible to participate in any interscholastic competition. See 115 F. Supp. 2d 1281, 1282, n. 1 (WD Okla. 2000). The court noted, however, that the dispute need not be resolved because Lindsay Earls had standing, and therefore the court was required to address the constitutionality of the drug testing policy. See ibid. Because we are likewise satisfied that Earls has standing, we need not address whether James also has standing.

2. The respondents did not challenge the Policy either as it applies to athletes or as it provides for drug testing upon reasonable, individualized suspicion. See App. 28.

3. Justice Ginsburg argues that Vernonia School Dist. 47J v. Acton, 515 U.S. 646 (1995), depended on the fact that the drug testing program

applied only to student athletes. But even the passage cited by the dissent manifests the supplemental nature of this factor, as the Court in Vernonia stated that "[l]egitimate privacy expectations are even less with regard to student athletes." See post, at 5 (citing Vernonia, 515 U.S., at 657) (emphasis added). In upholding the drug testing program in Vernonia, we considered the school context "[c]entral" and "[t]he most significant element." 515 U.S., at 654, 665. This hefty weight on the side of the school's balance applies with similar force in this case even though we undertake a separate balancing with regard to this particular program.

4. Justice Ginsburg's observations with regard to extracurricular activities apply with equal force to athletics. See post, at 4 ("Participation in such [extracurricular] activities is a key component of school life, essential in reality for students applying to college, and, for all participants, a significant contributor to the breadth and quality of the educational experience").

5. For instance, the number of 12th graders using any illicit drug increased from 48.4 percent in 1995 to 53.9 percent in 2001. The number of 12th graders reporting they had used marijuana jumped from 41.7 percent to 49.0 percent during that same period. See Department of Health and Human Services, Monitoring the Future: National Results on Adolescent Drug Use, Overview of Key Findings (2001) (Table 1).

Maryland v. Pringle (Dec 15, 2003)

Chief Justice Rehnquist delivered the opinion of the Court.

In the early morning hours a passenger car occupied by three men was stopped for speeding by a police officer. The officer, upon searching the car, seized $763 of rolled-up cash from the glove compartment and five glassine baggies of cocaine from between the back-seat armrest and the back seat. After all three men denied ownership of the cocaine and money, the officer arrested each of them. We hold that the officer had probable cause to arrest Pringle—one of the three men.

At 3:16 a.m. on August 7, 1999, a Baltimore County Police officer stopped a Nissan Maxima for speeding. There were three occupants in the car: Donte Partlow, the driver and owner, respondent Pringle, the front-seat passenger, and Otis Smith, the back-seat passenger. The officer asked Partlow for his license and registration. When Partlow opened the glove compartment to retrieve the vehicle registration, the officer observed a large amount of rolled-up money in the glove compartment. The officer returned to his patrol car with Partlow's license and registration to check the computer system for outstanding violations. The computer check did not reveal any violations. The officer returned to the stopped car, had Partlow get out, and issued him an oral warning.

After a second patrol car arrived, the officer asked Partlow if he had any weapons or narcotics in the vehicle. Partlow indicated that he did not. Partlow then consented to a search of the vehicle. The search yielded $763 from the glove compartment and five plastic glassine baggies containing cocaine from behind the back-seat armrest. When the officer began the search the armrest was in the upright position flat against the rear seat. The officer pulled down the armrest and found the drugs, which had been placed between the armrest and the back seat of the car.

The officer questioned all three men about the ownership of the drugs and money, and told them that if no one admitted to ownership of the drugs he was going to arrest them all. The men offered no information regarding the ownership of the drugs or money. All three were placed under arrest and transported to the police station.

Later that morning, Pringle waived his

rights under Miranda v. Arizona, 384 U.S. 436 (1966), and gave an oral and written confession in which he acknowledged that the cocaine belonged to him, that he and his friends were going to a party, and that he intended to sell the cocaine or "[u]se it for sex." App. 26. Pringle maintained that the other occupants of the car did not know about the drugs, and they were released.

The trial court denied Pringle's motion to suppress his confession as the fruit of an illegal arrest, holding that the officer had probable cause to arrest Pringle. A jury convicted Pringle of possession with intent to distribute cocaine and possession of cocaine. He was sentenced to 10 years' incarceration without the possibility of parole. The Court of Special Appeals of Maryland affirmed. 141 Md. App. 292, 785 A. 2d 790 (2001).

The Court of Appeals of Maryland, by divided vote, reversed, holding that, absent specific facts tending to show Pringle's knowledge and dominion or control over the drugs, "the mere finding of cocaine in the back armrest when [Pringle] was a front seat passenger in a car being driven by its owner is insufficient to establish probable cause for an arrest for possession." 370 Md. 525, 545, 805 A. 2d 1016, 1027 (2002). We granted certiorari, 538 U.S. 921 (2003), and now reverse.

Under the Fourth Amendment, made applicable to the States by the Fourteenth Amendment, Mapp v. Ohio, 367 U.S. 643 (1961), the people are "to be secure in their persons, houses, papers, and effects, against unreasonable searches and seizures, ... and no Warrants shall issue, but upon probable cause ... ." U.S. Const., Amdt. 4. Maryland law authorizes police officers to execute warrantless arrests, inter alia, for felonies committed in an officer's presence or where an officer has probable cause to believe that a felony has been committed or is being committed in the officer's presence. Md. Ann. Code, Art. 27, §594B (1996) (repealed 2001). A warrantless arrest of an individual in a public place for a felony, or a misdemeanor committed in the officer's presence, is consistent with the Fourth Amendment if the arrest is supported by probable cause. United States v. Watson, 423 U.S. 411, 424 (1976); see Atwater v. Lago Vista, 532 U.S. 318, 354 (2001) (stating that "[i]f an officer has probable cause to believe that an individual has committed even a very minor criminal offense in his presence, he may, without violating the Fourth Amendment, arrest the offender").

It is uncontested in the present case that the officer, upon recovering the five plastic glassine baggies containing suspected cocaine, had probable cause to believe a felony had been committed. Md. Ann. Code, Art. 27, §287 (1996) (repealed 2002) (prohibiting possession of controlled dangerous substances). The sole question is whether the officer had probable cause to believe that Pringle committed that crime.1

The long-prevailing standard of probable cause protects "citizens from rash and unreasonable interferences with privacy and from unfounded charges of crime," while giving "fair leeway for enforcing the law in the community's protection." Brinegar v. United States, 338 U.S. 160, 176 (1949). On many occasions, we have reiterated that the probable-cause standard is a " 'practical, nontechnical conception' " that deals with " 'the factual and practical considerations of everyday life on which reasonable and prudent men, not legal technicians, act.' " Illinois v. Gates, 462 U.S. 213, 231 (1983) (quoting Brinegar, supra, at 175–176); see, e.g., Ornelas v. United States, 517 U.S. 690, 695 (1996); United States v. Sokolow, 490 U.S. 1, 7–8 (1989). "[P]robable cause is a fluid concept–turning on the assessment of probabilities in particular factual contexts–not readily, or even usefully, reduced to a neat set of legal rules." Gates, 462 U.S., at 232.

The probable-cause standard is incapable of precise definition or quantification into percentages because it deals with probabilities and depends on the totality of the circumstances. See ibid.; Brinegar, 338 U.S., at 175. We have stated, however, that "[t]he substance of all the definitions of probable cause is a reasonable ground for belief of guilt," ibid. (internal quotation marks and citations omitted), and that the belief of guilt must be particularized with respect to the person to be searched or seized, Ybarra v. Illinois, 444 U.S. 85, 91 (1979). In Illinois v. Gates, we noted:

"As early as Locke v. United States, 7 Cranch 339, 348 (1813), Chief Justice Marshall observed, in a closely related context: '[T]he term "probable cause," according to its usual acceptation, means less than evidence which would justify condemnation ... . It imports a seizure made under circumstances which warrant suspicion.' More recently, we said that 'the quanta ... of proof' appropriate in ordinary judicial proceedings are inapplicable to the decision to issue a warrant. Brinegar, 338 U.S., at 173. Finely tuned standards such as proof beyond a reasonable doubt or by a preponderance of the evidence, useful in formal trials, have no place in the [probable-cause] decision." 462 U.S., at 235.

To determine whether an officer had probable cause to arrest an individual, we examine the events leading up to the arrest, and then decide "whether these historical facts, viewed from the standpoint of an objectively reasonable police officer, amount to" probable cause, Ornelas, supra, at 696.

In this case, Pringle was one of three men riding in a Nissan Maxima at 3:16 a.m. There was $763 of rolled-up cash in the glove compartment directly in front of Pringle.2 Five plastic glassine baggies of cocaine were behind the back-seat armrest and accessible to all three men. Upon questioning, the three men failed to offer any information with respect to the ownership of the cocaine or the money.

We think it an entirely reasonable inference from these facts that any or all three of the occupants had knowledge of, and exercised dominion and control over, the cocaine. Thus a reasonable officer could conclude that there was probable cause to believe Pringle committed the crime of possession of cocaine, either solely or jointly.

Pringle's attempt to characterize this case as a guilt-by-association case is unavailing. His reliance on Ybarra v. Illinois, supra, and United States v. Di Re, 332 U.S. 581 (1948), is misplaced. In Ybarra, police officers obtained a warrant to search a tavern and its bartender for evidence of possession of a controlled substance. Upon entering the tavern, the officers conducted patdown searches of the customers present in the tavern, including Ybarra. Inside a cigarette pack retrieved from Ybarra's pocket, an officer found six tinfoil packets containing heroin. We stated:

"[A] person's mere propinquity to others independently suspected of criminal activity does not, without more, give rise to probable cause to search that person. Sibron v. New York, 392 U.S. 40, 62–63 (1968). Where the standard is probable cause, a search or seizure of a person must be supported by probable cause particularized with respect to that person. This requirement cannot be undercut or avoided by simply pointing to the fact that coincidentally there exists probable cause to search or seize another or to search the premises where the person may happen to be." 444 U.S., at 91.

We held that the search warrant did not permit body searches of all of the tavern's patrons and that the police could not pat down the patrons for weapons, absent individualized suspicion. Id., at 92.

This case is quite different from Ybarra. Pringle and his two companions were in a relatively small automobile, not a public tavern. In Wyoming v. Houghton, 526 U.S. 295 (1999), we noted that "a car passenger—unlike the unwitting tavern patron in Ybarra—will often be engaged in a common enterprise with the driver, and have the same interest in concealing the fruits or the evidence of their wrongdoing." Id., at 304—305. Here we think it was reasonable for the officer to infer a common enterprise among the three men. The quantity of drugs and cash in the car indicated the likelihood of drug dealing, an enterprise to which a dealer would be unlikely to admit an innocent person with the potential to furnish evidence against him.

In Di Re, a federal investigator had been told by an informant, Reed, that he was to receive counterfeit gasoline ration coupons from a certain Buttitta at a particular place. The investigator went to the appointed place and saw Reed, the sole occupant of the rear seat of the car, holding gasoline ration coupons. There were two other occupants in the car: Buttitta in the driver's seat and Di Re in the front passenger's seat. Reed informed the investigator that Buttitta had given him counterfeit coupons. Thereupon, all three men were arrested and searched. After noting that the officers had no information implicating Di Re and no information pointing to Di Re's possession of coupons, unless presence in the car warranted that inference, we concluded that the officer lacked probable cause to believe that Di Re was involved in the crime. 332 U.S., at 592—594. We said "[a]ny inference that everyone on the scene of a crime is a party to it must disappear if the Government informer singles out the guilty person." Id., at 594. No such singling out occurred in this case; none of the three men provided information with respect to the ownership of the cocaine or money.

We hold that the officer had probable cause to believe that Pringle had committed the crime of possession of a controlled substance. Pringle's arrest therefore did not contravene the Fourth and Fourteenth Amendments. Accordingly, the judgment of the Court of Appeals of Maryland is reversed, and the case is remanded for further proceedings not inconsistent with this opinion.

It is so ordered.

Notes

1. Maryland law defines "possession" as "the exercise of actual or constructive dominion or control over a thing by one or more persons." Md. Ann. Code, Art. 27, §277(s) (1996) (repealed 2002).

2. The Court of Appeals of Maryland dismissed the $763 seized from the glove compartment as a factor in the probable-cause determination, stating that "[m]oney, without more, is innocuous." 370 Md. 524, 546, 805 A. 2d 1016, 1028 (2002). The court's consideration of the money in isolation, rather than as a factor in the totality of the circumstances, is mistaken in light of our precedents. See, e.g., Illinois v. Gates, 462 U.S. 213, 230—231 (1983) (opining that the totality of the circumstances approach is consistent with our prior treatment of probable cause); Brinegar v. United States, 338 U.S. 160, 175—176 (1949) ("Probable cause exists where 'the facts and circumstances within their [the officers'] knowledge and of which they had reasonably trustworthy information [are] sufficient in themselves to warrant a man of reasonable caution in the belief that' an offense has been or is being committed"). We think it is abundantly clear from the facts that this case involves more than money alone.

Groh v. Ramirez (Feb 24, 2004)

Justice Stevens delivered the opinion of the Court.

Petitioner conducted a search of respondents' home pursuant to a warrant that failed to describe the "persons or things to be seized." U.S. Const., Amdt. 4. The questions presented are (1) whether the search violated the

Fourth Amendment, and (2) if so, whether petitioner nevertheless is entitled to qualified immunity, given that a Magistrate Judge (Magistrate), relying on an affidavit that particularly described the items in question, found probable cause to conduct the search.

I

Respondents, Joseph Ramirez and members of his family, live on a large ranch in Butte-Silver Bow County, Montana. Petitioner, Jeff Groh, has been a Special Agent for the Bureau of Alcohol, Tobacco and Firearms (ATF) since 1989. In February 1997, a concerned citizen informed petitioner that on a number of visits to respondents' ranch the visitor had seen a large stock of weaponry, including an automatic rifle, grenades, a grenade launcher, and a rocket launcher.1 Based on that information, petitioner prepared and signed an application for a warrant to search the ranch. The application stated that the search was for "any automatic firearms or parts to automatic weapons, destructive devices to include but not limited to grenades, grenade launchers, rocket launchers, and any and all receipts pertaining to the purchase or manufacture of automatic weapons or explosive devices or launchers." App. to Pet. for Cert. 28a. Petitioner supported the application with a detailed affidavit, which he also prepared and executed, that set forth the basis for his belief that the listed items were concealed on the ranch. Petitioner then presented these documents to a Magistrate, along with a warrant form that petitioner also had completed. The Magistrate signed the warrant form.

Although the application particularly described the place to be searched and the contraband petitioner expected to find, the warrant itself was less specific; it failed to identify any of the items that petitioner intended to seize. In the portion of the form that called for a description of the "person or property" to be seized, petitioner typed a description of respondents' two-story blue house rather than the alleged stockpile of firearms.2 The warrant did not incorporate by reference the itemized list contained in the application. It did, however, recite that the Magistrate was satisfied the affidavit established probable cause to believe that contraband was concealed on the premises, and that sufficient grounds existed for the warrant's issuance.3

The day after the Magistrate issued the warrant, petitioner led a team of law enforcement officers, including both federal agents and members of the local sheriff's department, in the search of respondents' premises. Although respondent Joseph Ramirez was not home, his wife and children were. Petitioner states that he orally described the objects of the search to Mrs. Ramirez in person and to Mr. Ramirez by telephone. According to Mrs. Ramirez, however, petitioner explained only that he was searching for " 'an explosive device in a box.' " Ramirez v. Butte-Silver Bow County, 298 F.3d 1022, 1026 (CA9 2002). At any rate, the officers' search uncovered no illegal weapons or explosives. When the officers left, petitioner gave Mrs. Ramirez a copy of the search warrant, but not a copy of the application, which had been sealed. The following day, in response to a request from respondents' attorney, petitioner faxed the attorney a copy of the page of the application that listed the items to be seized. No charges were filed against the Ramirezes.

Respondents sued petitioner and the other officers under Bivens v. Six Unknown Fed. Narcotics Agents, 403 U.S. 388 (1971), and Rev. Stat. §1979, 42 U.S.C. § 1983 raising eight claims, including violation of the Fourth Amendment. App. 17—27. The District Court entered summary judgment for all defendants. The court found no Fourth Amendment violation, because it considered the case comparable to one in which the warrant contained an inaccurate address, and in such a case, the court reasoned, the warrant is sufficiently detailed if the executing officers can locate the correct house. App. to Pet. for Cert. 20a—

22a. The court added that even if a constitutional violation occurred, the defendants were entitled to qualified immunity because the failure of the warrant to describe the objects of the search amounted to a mere "typographical error." Id., at 22a—24a.

The Court of Appeals affirmed the judgment with respect to all defendants and all claims, with the exception of respondents' Fourth Amendment claim against petitioner. 298 F.3d, at 1029—1030. On that claim, the court held that the warrant was invalid because it did not "describe with particularity the place to be searched and the items to be seized," and that oral statements by petitioner during or after the search could not cure the omission. Id., at 1025—1026. The court observed that the warrant's facial defect "increased the likelihood and degree of confrontation between the Ramirezes and the police" and deprived respondents of the means "to challenge officers who might have exceeded the limits imposed by the magistrate." Id., at 1027. The court also expressed concern that "permitting officers to expand the scope of the warrant by oral statements would broaden the area of dispute between the parties in subsequent litigation." Ibid. The court nevertheless concluded that all of the officers except petitioner were protected by qualified immunity. With respect to petitioner, the court read our opinion in United States v. Leon, 468 U.S. 897 (1984), as precluding qualified immunity for the leader of a search who fails to "read the warrant and satisfy [himself] that [he] understand[s] its scope and limitations, and that it is not defective in some obvious way." 298 F.3d, at 1027. The court added that "[t]he leaders of the search team must also make sure that a copy of the warrant is available to give to the person whose property is being searched at the commencement

of the search, and that such copy has no missing pages or other obvious defects." Ibid. (footnote omitted). We granted certiorari. 537 U.S. 1231 (2003).

II

The warrant was plainly invalid. The Fourth Amendment states unambiguously that "no Warrants shall issue, but upon probable cause, supported by Oath or affirmation, and particularly describing the place to be searched, and the persons or things to be seized." (Emphasis added.) The warrant in this case complied with the first three of these requirements: It was based on probable cause and supported by a sworn affidavit, and it described particularly the place of the search. On the fourth requirement, however, the warrant failed altogether. Indeed, petitioner concedes that "the warrant … was deficient in particularity because it provided no description of the type of evidence sought." Brief for Petitioner 10.

The fact that the application adequately described the "things to be seized" does not save the warrant from its facial invalidity. The Fourth Amendment by its terms requires particularity in the warrant, not in the supporting documents. See Massachusetts v. Sheppard, 468 U.S. 981, 988, n. 5 (1984) ("[A] warrant that fails to conform to the particularity requirement of the Fourth Amendment is unconstitutional"); see also United States v. Stefonek, 179 F.3d 1030, 1033 (CA7 1999) ("The Fourth Amendment requires that the warrant particularly describe the things to be seized, not the papers presented to the judicial officer … asked to issue the warrant"). And for good reason: "The presence of a search warrant serves a high function," McDonald v. United States, 335 U.S. 451, 455 (1948), and that high function is not necessarily vindicated when some other document, somewhere, says something about the objects of the search, but the contents of that document are neither known to the person whose home is being searched nor available for her inspection. We do not say that the Fourth Amendment forbids a warrant from cross-referencing other documents. Indeed, most Courts of Appeals have held that a court may construe a warrant with reference to a supporting application or affidavit if the warrant uses appropriate words of incorporation, and if the supporting document accompanies the warrant. See, e.g., United States v. McGrew, 122 F.3d 847, 849—850 (CA9 1997); United States v. Williamson, 1 F.3d 1134, 1136, n. 1 (CA10 1993); United States v. Blakeney, 942 F.2d 1001, 1025—1026 (CA6 1991); United States v. Maxwell, 920 F.2d 1028, 1031 (CADC 1990); United States v. Curry, 911 F.2d 72, 76—77 (CA8 1990); United States v. Roche, 614 F.2d 6, 8 (CA1 1980). But in this case the warrant did not incorporate other documents by reference, nor did either the affidavit or the application (which had been placed under seal) accompany the warrant. Hence, we need not further explore the matter of incorporation.

Petitioner argues that even though the warrant was invalid, the search nevertheless was "reasonable" within the meaning of the Fourth Amendment. He notes that a Magistrate authorized the search on the basis of adequate evidence of probable cause, that petitioner orally described to respondents the items to be seized, and that the search did not exceed the limits intended by the Magistrate and described by petitioner. Thus, petitioner maintains, his search of respondents' ranch was functionally equivalent to a search authorized by a valid warrant.

We disagree. This warrant did not simply omit a few items from a list of many to be seized, or misdescribe a few of several items. Nor did it make what fairly could be characterized as a mere technical mistake or typographical error. Rather, in the space set aside for a description of the items to be seized, the warrant stated that the items consisted of a "single dwelling residence ... items to be seized, the warrant stated that the items consisted of a "single dwelling residence ...

blue in color." In other words, the warrant did not describe the items to be seized at all. In this respect the warrant was so obviously deficient that we must regard the search as "warrantless" within the meaning of our case law. See Leon, 468 U.S., at 923; cf. Maryland v. Garrison, 480 U.S. 79, 85 (1987); Steele v. United States, 267 U.S. 498, 503—504 (1925). "We are not dealing with formalities." McDonald, 335 U.S., at 455. Because " 'the right of a man to retreat into his own home and there be free from unreasonable governmental intrusion' " stands " '[a]t the very core' of the Fourth Amendment," Kyllo v. United States, 533 U.S. 27, 31 (2001) (quoting Silverman v. United States, 365 U.S. 505, 511 (1961)), our cases have firmly established the " 'basic principle of Fourth Amendment law' that searches and seizures inside a home without a warrant are presumptively unreasonable," Payton v. New York, 445 U.S. 573, 586 (1980) (footnote omitted). Thus, "absent exigent circumstances, a warrantless entry to search for weapons or contraband is unconstitutional even when a felony has been committed and there is probable cause to believe that incriminating evidence will be found within." Id., at 587—588 (footnote omitted). See Kyllo, 533 U.S., at 29; Illinois v. Rodriguez, 497 U.S. 177, 181 (1990); Chimel v. California, 395 U.S. 752, 761—763 (1969); McDonald, 335 U.S., at 454; Johnson v. United States, 333 U.S. 10 (1948).

We have clearly stated that the presumptive rule against warrantless searches applies with equal force to searches whose only defect is a lack of particularity in the warrant. In Sheppard, for instance, the petitioner argued that even though the warrant was invalid for lack of particularity, "the search was constitutional because it was reasonable within the meaning of the Fourth Amendment." 468 U.S., at 988, n. 5. In squarely rejecting that position, we explained:

"The uniformly applied rule is that a search conducted pursuant to a warrant that fails to conform to the particularity requirement of the Fourth Amendment is unconstitutional. Stanford v. Texas, 379 U.S. 476 (1965); United States v. Cardwell, 680 F.2d 75, 77—78 (CA9 1982); United States v. Crozier, 674 F.2d 1293, 1299 (CA9 1982); United States v. Klein, 565 F.2d 183, 185 (CA1 1977); United States v. Gardner, 537 F.2d 861, 862 (CA6 1976); United States v. Marti, 421 F.2d 1263, 1268—1269 (CA2 1970). That rule is in keeping with the well-established principle that 'except in certain carefully defined classes of cases, a search of private property without proper consent is "unreasonable" unless it has been authorized by a valid search warrant.' Camara v. Municipal Court, 387 U.S. 523, 528—529 (1967). See Steagald v. United States, 451 U.S. 204, 211—212 (1981); Jones v. United States, 357 U.S. 493, 499 (1958)." Ibid.

Petitioner asks us to hold that a search conducted pursuant to a warrant lacking particularity should be exempt from the presumption of unreasonableness if the goals served by the particularity requirement are otherwise satisfied. He maintains that the search in this case satisfied those goals–which he says are "to prevent general searches, to prevent the seizure of one thing under a warrant describing another, and to prevent warrants from being issued on vague or dubious information," Brief for Petitioner 16–because the scope of the search did not exceed the limits set forth in the application. But unless the particular items described in the affidavit are also set forth in the warrant itself (or at least incorporated by reference, and the affidavit present at the search), there can be no written assurance that the Magistrate actually found probable cause to search for, and to seize, every item mentioned in the affidavit. See McDonald, 335 U.S., at 455 ("Absent some grave emergency, the Fourth Amendment has interposed a magistrate between the citizen and the police. This was done ... so that an objective mind might weigh the need to invade [the citizen's] privacy in order

to enforce the law"). In this case, for example, it is at least theoretically possible that the Magistrate was satisfied that the search for weapons and explosives was justified by the showing in the affidavit, but not convinced that any evidentiary basis existed for rummaging through respondents' files and papers for receipts pertaining to the purchase or manufacture of such items. Cf. Stanford v. Texas, 379 U.S. 476, 485—486 (1965). Or, conceivably, the Magistrate might have believed that some of the weapons mentioned in the affidavit could have been lawfully possessed and therefore should not be seized. See 26 U.S.C. § 5861 (requiring registration, but not banning possession of, certain firearms). The mere fact that the Magistrate issued a warrant does not necessarily establish that he agreed that the scope of the search should be as broad as the affiant's request. Even though petitioner acted with restraint in conducting the search, "the inescapable fact is that this restraint was imposed by the agents themselves, not by a judicial officer." Katz v. United States, 389 U.S. 347, 356 (1967).[4]

We have long held, moreover, that the purpose of the particularity requirement is not limited to the prevention of general searches. See Garrison, 480 U.S., at 84. A particular warrant also "assures the individual whose property is searched or seized of the lawful authority of the executing officer, his need to search, and the limits of his power to search." United States v. Chadwick, 433 U.S. 1, 9 (1977) (citing Camara v. Municipal Court of City and County of San Francisco, 387 U.S. 523, 532 (1967)), abrogated on other grounds, California v. Acevedo, 500 U.S. 565 (1991). See also Illinois v. Gates, 462 U.S. 213, 236 (1983) ("[P]ossession of a warrant by officers conducting an arrest or search greatly reduces the perception of unlawful or intrusive police conduct").[5]

Petitioner argues that even if the goals of the particularity requirement are broader than he acknowledges, those goals nevertheless were served because he orally described to respondents the items for which he was searching. Thus, he submits, respondents had all of the notice that a proper warrant would have accorded. But this case presents no occasion even to reach this argument, since respondents, as noted above, dispute petitioner's account. According to Mrs. Ramirez, petitioner stated only that he was looking for an " 'explosive device in a box.' " 298 F.3d, at 1026. Because this dispute is before us on petitioner's motion for summary judgment, App. to Pet. for Cert. 13a, "[t]he evidence of the nonmovant is to be believed, and all justifiable inferences are to be drawn in [her] favor," Anderson v. Liberty Lobby, Inc., 477 U.S. 242, 255 (1986) (citation omitted). The posture of the case therefore obliges us to credit Mrs. Ramirez's account, and we find that petitioner's description of " 'an explosive device in a box' " was little better than no guidance at all. See Stefonek, 179 F.3d, at 1032–1033 (holding that a search warrant for " 'evidence of crime' " was "[s]o open-ended" in its description that it could "only be described as a general warrant").

It is incumbent on the officer executing a search warrant to ensure the search is lawfully authorized and lawfully conducted.6 Because petitioner did not have in his possession a warrant particularly describing the things he intended to seize, proceeding with the search was clearly "unreasonable" under the Fourth Amendment. The Court of Appeals correctly held that the search was unconstitutional.

III

Having concluded that a constitutional violation occurred, we turn to the question whether petitioner is entitled to qualified immunity despite that violation. See Wilson v. Layne, 526 U.S. 603, 609 (1999). The answer depends on whether the right that was transgressed was " 'clearly established' "–that is, "whether it would be clear to a reasonable officer that his conduct was unlawful in the situation he

confronted." Saucier v. Katz, 533 U.S. 194, 202 (2001).

Given that the particularity requirement is set forth in the text of the Constitution, no reasonable officer could believe that a warrant that plainly did not comply with that requirement was valid. See Harlow v. Fitzgerald, 457 U.S. 800, 818–819 (1982) ("If the law was clearly established, the immunity defense ordinarily should fail, since a reasonably competent public official should know the law governing his conduct"). Moreover, because petitioner himself prepared the invalid warrant, he may not argue that he reasonably relied on the Magistrate's assurance that the warrant contained an adequate description of the things to be seized and was therefore valid. Cf. Sheppard, 468 U.S., at 989–990. In fact, the guidelines of petitioner's own department placed him on notice that he might be liable for executing a manifestly invalid warrant. An ATF directive in force at the time of this search warned: "Special agents are liable if they exceed their authority while executing a search warrant and must be sure that a search warrant is sufficient on its face even when issued by a magistrate." Searches and Examinations, ATF Order O 3220.1(7)(d) (Feb. 13, 1997). See also id., at 3220.1(23)(b) ("If any error or deficiency is discovered and there is a reasonable probability that it will invalidate the warrant, such warrant shall not be executed. The search shall be postponed until a satisfactory warrant has been obtained").7 And even a cursory reading of the warrant in this case–perhaps just a simple glance– would have revealed a glaring deficiency that any reasonable police officer would have known was constitutionally fatal.

No reasonable officer could claim to be unaware of the basic rule, well established by our cases, that, absent consent or exigency, a warrantless search of the home is presumptively unconstitutional. See Payton, 445 U.S., at 586–

588. Indeed, as we noted nearly 20 years ago in Sheppard: "The uniformly applied rule is that a search conducted pursuant to a warrant that fails to conform to the particularity requirement of the Fourth Amendment is unconstitutional." 468 U.S., at 988, n. 5.8   Because not a word in any of our cases would suggest to a reasonable officer that this case fits within any exception to that fundamental tenet, petitioner is asking us, in effect, to craft a new exception. Absent any support for such an exception in our cases, he cannot reasonably have relied on an expectation that we would do so.

Petitioner contends that the search in this case was the product, at worst, of a lack of due care, and that our case law requires more than negligent behavior before depriving an official of qualified immunity. See Malley v. Briggs, 475 U.S. 335, 341 (1986). But as we observed in the companion case to Sheppard, "a warrant may be so facially deficient–i.e., in failing to particularize the place to be searched or the things to be seized–that the executing officers cannot reasonably presume it to be valid." Leon, 468 U.S., at 923. This is such a case.9

Accordingly, the judgment of the Court of Appeals is affirmed.

It is so ordered.

Notes

1. Possession of these items, if unregistered, would violate 18 U.S.C. § 922(o)(1) and 26 U.S.C. § 5861.

2. The warrant stated: "[T]here is now concealed [on the specified premises] a certain person or property, namely [a] single dwelling residence two story in height which is blue in color and has two additions attached to the east. The front entrance to the residence faces in a southerly direction." App. to Pet. for Cert. 26a.

3. The affidavit was sealed. Its sufficiency is not disputed.

4. For this reason petitioner's argument that any constitutional error was committed by the Magistrate, not petitioner, is misplaced. In Massachusetts v. Sheppard, 468 U.S. 981 (1984), we suggested that "the judge, not the police officers," may have committed "[a]n error of constitutional dimension," id., at 990, because the judge had assured the officers requesting the warrant that he would take the steps necessary to conform the warrant to constitutional requirements, id., at 986. Thus, "it was not unreasonable for the police in [that] case to rely on the judge's assurances that the warrant authorized the search they had requested." Id., at 990, n. 6. In this case, by contrast, petitioner did not alert the Magistrate to the defect in the warrant that petitioner had drafted, and we therefore cannot know whether the Magistrate was aware of the scope of the search he was authorizing. Nor would it have been reasonable for petitioner to rely on a warrant that was so patently defective, even if the Magistrate was aware of the deficiency. See United States v. Leon, 468 U.S. 897, 915, 922, n. 23 (1984).

5. It is true, as petitioner points out, that neither the Fourth Amendment nor Rule 41 of the Federal Rules of Criminal Procedure requires the executing officer to serve the warrant on the owner before commencing the search. Rule 41(f)(3) provides that "[t]he officer executing the warrant must: (A) give a copy of the warrant and a receipt for the property taken to the person from whom, or from whose premises, the property was taken; or (B) leave a copy of the warrant and receipt at the place where the officer took the property." Quite obviously, in some circumstances–a surreptitious search by means of a wiretap, for example, or the search of empty or abandoned premises–it will be impracticable or imprudent for the officers to show the warrant in advance. See Katz v. United States, 389 U.S. 347, 355, n. 16 (1967); Ker v. California, 374 U.S. 23, 37–41 (1963). Whether it would be

unreasonable to refuse a request to furnish the warrant at the outset of the search when, as in this case, an occupant of the premises is present and poses no threat to the officers' safe and effective performance of their mission, is a question that this case does not present.

6. The Court of Appeals' decision is consistent with this principle. Petitioner mischaracterizes the court's decision when he contends that it imposed a novel proofreading requirement on officers executing warrants. The court held that officers leading a search team must "mak[e] sure that they have a proper warrant that in fact authorizes the search and seizure they are about to conduct." 298 F.3d 1022, 1027 (CA9 2002). That is not a duty to proofread; it is, rather, a duty to ensure that the warrant conforms to constitutional requirements.

7. We do not suggest that an official is deprived of qualified immunity whenever he violates an internal guideline. We refer to the ATF Order only to underscore that petitioner should have known that he should not execute a patently defective warrant.

8. Although both Sheppard and Leon involved the application of the "good faith" exception to the Fourth Amendment's general exclusionary rule, we have explained that "the same standard of objective reasonableness that we applied in the context of a suppression hearing in Leon defines the qualified immunity accorded an officer." Malley v. Briggs, 475 U.S. 335, 344 (1986) (citation omitted).

9. Justice Kennedy argues in dissent that we have not allowed " 'ample room for mistaken judgments,' " post, at 6 (quoting Malley, 475 U.S., at 343), because "difficult and important tasks demand the officer's full attention in the heat of an ongoing and often dangerous criminal investigation," post, at 3. In this case, however, petitioner does not contend that any sort of exigency existed when he drafted the affidavit, the warrant application, and the warrant, or when he conducted the search. This is not the situation, therefore, in which we have recognized that "officers in the dangerous and difficult process of making arrests and executing search warrants" require "some latitude." Maryland v. Garrison, 480 U.S. 79, 87 (1987). Nor are we according "the correctness of paper forms" a higher status than "substantive rights." Post, at 6. As we have explained, the Fourth Amendment's particularity requirement assures the subject of the search that a magistrate has duly authorized the officer to conduct a search of limited scope. This substantive right is not protected when the officer fails to take the time to glance at the authorizing document and detect a glaring defect that Justice Kennedy agrees is of constitutional magnitude, post, at 1.

Brosseau v. Haugen (Dec 13, 2004) [Notes omitted]

Per Curiam.

Officer Rochelle Brosseau, a member of the Puyallup, Washington, Police Department, shot Kenneth Haugen in the back as he attempted to flee from law enforcement authorities in his vehicle. Haugen subsequently filed this action in the United States District Court for the Western District of Washington pursuant to Rev. Stat. §1979, 42 U.S.C. § 1983. He alleged that the shot fired by Brosseau constituted excessive force and violated his federal constitutional rights.[1] The District Court granted summary judgment to Brosseau after finding she was entitled to qualified immunity. The Court of Appeals for the Ninth Circuit reversed. 339 F.3d 857 (2003). Following the two-step process set out in Saucier v. Katz, 533 U.S. 194 (2001), the Court of Appeals found, first, that Brosseau had violated Haugen's Fourth Amendment right to be free from excessive force and, second, that the right violated was clearly established and thus Brosseau was not entitled to qualified immunity. Brosseau then petitioned for writ of certiorari, requesting that we review both of the Court of Appeals' determinations. We grant the petition on the second, qualified immunity question and reverse.

The material facts, construed in a light most favorable to Haugen, are as follows.[2]

On the day before the fracas, Glen Tamburello went to the police station and reported to Brosseau that Haugen, a former crime partner of his, had stolen tools from his shop. Brosseau later learned that there was a felony no-bail warrant out for Haugen's arrest on drug and other offenses. The next morning, Haugen was spray-painting his Jeep Cherokee in his mother's driveway. Tamburello learned of Haugen's whereabouts, and he and cohort Matt Atwood drove a pickup truck to Haugen's mother's house to pay Haugen a visit. A fight ensued, which was witnessed by a neighbor who called 911.

Brosseau heard a report that the men were fighting in Haugen's mother's yard and responded. When she arrived, Tamburello and Atwood were attempting to get Haugen into Tamburello's pickup. Brosseau's arrival created a distraction, which provided Haugen the opportunity to get away. Haugen ran through his mother's yard and hid in the neighborhood. Brosseau requested assistance, and, shortly thereafter, two officers arrived with a K—9 to help track Haugen down. During the search, which lasted about 30 to 45 minutes, officers instructed Tamburello and Atwood to remain in Tamburello's pickup. They instructed Deanna Nocera, Haugen's girlfriend who was also present with her 3-year-old daughter, to remain in her small car with her daughter. Tamburello's pickup was parked in the street in front of the driveway; Nocera's small car was parked in the driveway in front of and facing the Jeep; and the Jeep was in the driveway facing Nocera's car and angled somewhat to the left. The Jeep was parked about 4 feet away from Nocera's car and 20 to 30 feet away from Tamburello's pickup.

An officer radioed from down the street that a neighbor had seen a man in her backyard. Brosseau ran in that direction, and Haugen appeared. He ran past the front of his mother's house and then turned and ran into the driveway. With Brosseau still in pursuit, he jumped into the driver's side of the Jeep and closed and locked the door. Brosseau believed that he was running to the Jeep to retrieve a weapon.

Brosseau arrived at the Jeep, pointed her gun at Haugen, and ordered him to get out of the vehicle. Haugen ignored her command and continued to look for the keys so he could get the Jeep started. Brosseau repeated her commands and hit the driver's side window several times with her handgun, which failed to deter Haugen. On the third or fourth try, the window shattered. Brosseau unsuccessfully attempted to grab the keys and struck Haugen on the head with the barrel and butt of her gun. Haugen, still undeterred, succeeded in starting the Jeep. As the Jeep started or shortly after it began to move, Brosseau jumped back and to the left. She fired one shot through the rear driver's side window at a forward angle, hitting Haugen in the back. She later explained that she shot Haugen because she was " 'fearful for the other officers on foot who [she] believed were in the immediate area, [and] for the occupied vehicles in [Haugen's] path and for any other citizens who might be in the area.' " 339 F.3d, at 865.

Despite being hit, Haugen, in his words, " 'st[ood] on the gas' "; navigated the " 'small, tight space' " to avoid the other vehicles; swerved across the neighbor's lawn; and continued down the street. Id., at 882. After about a half block, Haugen realized that he had been shot and brought the Jeep to a halt. He suffered a collapsed lung and was airlifted to a hospital. He survived the shooting and subsequently pleaded guilty to the felony of "eluding." Wash. Rev. Code §46.61.024

(1994). By so pleading, he admitted that he drove his Jeep in a manner indicating "a wanton or wilful disregard for the lives . . . of others." Ibid. He subsequently brought this §1983 action against Brosseau.

***

When confronted with a claim of qualified immunity, a court must ask first the following question: "Taken in the light most favorable to the party asserting the injury, do the facts alleged show the officer's conduct violated a constitutional right?" Saucier v. Katz, 533 U.S., at 201. As the Court of Appeals recognized, the constitutional question in this case is governed by the principles enunciated in Tennessee v. Garner, 471 U.S. 1 (1985), and Graham v. Connor, 490 U.S. 386 (1989). These cases establish that claims of excessive force are to be judged under the Fourth Amendment's " 'objective reasonableness' " standard. Id., at 388. Specifically with regard to deadly force, we explained in Garner that it is unreasonable for an officer to "seize an unarmed, nondangerous suspect by shooting him dead." 471 U.S., at 11. But "[w]here the officer has probable cause to believe that the suspect poses a threat of serious physical harm, either to the officer or to others, it is not constitutionally unreasonable to prevent escape by using deadly force." Ibid.

We express no view as to the correctness of the Court of Appeals' decision on the constitutional question itself. We believe that, however that question is decided, the Court of Appeals was wrong on the issue of qualified immunity.3

Qualified immunity shields an officer from suit when she makes a decision that, even if constitutionally deficient, reasonably misapprehends the law governing the circumstances she confronted. Saucier v. Katz, 533 U.S., at 206 (qualified immunity operates "to protect officers from the sometimes 'hazy border between excessive and acceptable force' "). Because the focus is on whether the officer had fair notice that her conduct was unlawful, reasonableness is judged against the backdrop of the law at the time of the conduct. If the law at that time did not clearly establish that the officer's conduct would violate the Constitution, the officer should not be subject to liability or, indeed, even the burdens of litigation.

It is important to emphasize that this inquiry "must be undertaken in light of the specific context of the case, not as a broad general proposition." Id., at 201. As we previously said in this very context:

"[T]here is no doubt that Graham v. Connor, supra, clearly establishes the general proposition that use of force is contrary to the Fourth Amendment if it is excessive under objective standards of reasonableness. Yet that is not enough. Rather, we emphasized in Anderson [v. Creighton,] 'that the right the official is alleged to have violated must have been "clearly established" in a more particularized, and hence more relevant, sense: The contours of the right must be sufficiently clear that a reasonable official would understand that what he is doing violates that right.' 483 U.S. [635,] 640 [(1987)]. The relevant, dispositive inquiry in determining whether a right is clearly established is whether it would be clear to a reasonable officer that his conduct was unlawful in the situation he confronted." Id., at 201–202.

The Court of Appeals acknowledged this statement of law, but then proceeded to find fair warning in the general tests set out in Graham and Garner. 339 F.3d, at 873–874. In so doing, it was mistaken. Graham and Garner, following the lead of the Fourth Amendment's text, are cast at a high level of generality. See Graham v. Connor, supra, at 396 (" '[T]he test of reasonableness under the Fourth Amendment is not capable of precise definition or mechanical application' "). Of course, in an obvious case, these standards can "clearly establish" the answer, even without a body of relevant case law. See Hope v. Pelzer, 536 U.S. 730, 738 (2002) (noting in a case where the Eighth Amendment violation was "obvious" that there need not be a materially similar case for the right to be clearly established). See also Pace v. Capobianco, 283 F.3d 1275, 1283 (CA11 2002) (explaining in a Fourth Amendment case involving an officer shooting a fleeing suspect in a vehicle that, "when we look at decisions such as Garner and Graham, we see some tests to guide us in determining the law in many different kinds of circumstances; but we do not see the kind of clear law (clear answers) that would apply" to the situation at hand). The present case is far from the obvious one where Graham and Garner alone offer a basis for decision.

We therefore turn to ask whether, at the time of Brosseau's actions, it was " ' "clearly established" ' " in this more " 'particularized' " sense that she was violating Haugen's Fourth Amendment right. Saucier v. Katz, 533 U.S., at 202. The parties point us to only a handful of cases relevant to the "situation [Brosseau] confronted": whether to shoot a disturbed felon, set on avoiding capture through vehicular flight, when persons in the immediate area are at risk from that flight.4 Ibid. Specifically, Brosseau points us to Cole v. Bone, 993 F.2d 1328 (CA8 1993), and Smith v. Freland, 954 F.2d 343 (CA6 1992).

In these cases, the courts found no Fourth Amendment violation when an officer shot a fleeing suspect who presented a risk to others. Cole v. Bone, supra, at 1333 (holding the officer "had probable cause to believe that the truck posed an imminent threat of serious physical harm to innocent motorists as well as to the officers themselves"); Smith v. Freland, 954 F.2d, at 347 (noting "a car can be a deadly weapon" and holding the officer's decision to stop the car from possibly injuring others was reasonable). Smith is closer to this case. There, the officer and suspect engaged in

a car chase, which appeared to be at an end when the officer cornered the suspect at the back of a dead-end residential street. The suspect, however, freed his car and began speeding down the street. At this point, the officer fired a shot, which killed the suspect. The court held the officer's decision was reasonable and thus did not violate the Fourth Amendment. It noted that the suspect, like Haugen here, "had proven he would do almost anything to avoid capture" and that he posed a major threat to, among others, the officers at the end of the street. Ibid.

Haugen points us to Estate of Starks v. Enyart, 5 F.3d 230 (CA7 1993), where the court found summary judgment inappropriate on a Fourth Amendment claim involving a fleeing suspect. There, the court concluded that the threat created by the fleeing suspect's failure to brake when an officer suddenly stepped in front of his just-started car was not a sufficiently grave threat to justify the use of deadly force. Id., at 234.

These three cases taken together undoubtedly show that this area is one in which the result depends very much on the facts of each case. None of them squarely governs the case here; they do suggest that Brosseau's actions fell in the " 'hazy border between excessive and acceptable force.' " Saucier v. Katz, supra, at 206. The cases by no means "clearly establish" that Brosseau's conduct violated the Fourth Amendment.

The judgment of the United States Court of Appeals for the Ninth Circuit is therefore reversed, and the case is remanded for further proceedings consistent with this opinion.

It is so ordered.

Devenpeck v. Alford (Dec 13, 2004) [Notes omitted]

Justice Scalia delivered the opinion of the Court.

This case presents the question whether

an arrest is lawful under the Fourth Amendment when the criminal offense for which there is probable cause to arrest is not "closely related" to the offense stated by the arresting officer at the time of arrest.

I

A

On the night of November 22, 1997, a disabled automobile and its passengers were stranded on the shoulder of State Route 16, a divided highway, in Pierce County, Washington. Alford v. Haner, 333 F.3d 972, 974 (CA9 2003); App. 94, 98. Respondent Jerome Alford pulled his car off the road behind the disabled vehicle, activating his "wig-wag" headlights (which flash the left and right lights alternately). As he pulled off the road, Officer Joi Haner of the Washington State Patrol, one of the two petitioners here, passed the disabled car from the opposite direction. 333 F.3d, at 974. He turned around to check on the motorists at the first opportunity, and when he arrived, respondent, who had begun helping the motorists change a flat tire, hurried back to his car and drove away. Ibid. The stranded motorists asked Haner if respondent was a "cop"; they said that respondent's statements, and his flashing, wig-wag headlights, had given them that impression. Ibid.; App. 96. They also informed Haner that as respondent hurried off he left his flashlight behind. Id., at 97.

On the basis of this information, Haner radioed his supervisor, Sergeant Gerald Devenpeck, the other petitioner here, that he was concerned respondent was an "impersonator" or "wannabe cop." Id., at 97—98. He pursued respondent's vehicle and pulled it over. 333 F.3d, at 975. Through the passenger-side window, Haner observed that respondent was listening to the Kitsap County Sheriff's Office police frequency on a special radio, and that handcuffs and a hand-held police scanner were in the car. Ibid. These facts bolstered Haner's suspicion that respondent was impersonating a police officer. App. 106, 107. Haner thought, moreover, that respondent seemed untruthful and evasive: He told Haner that he had worked previously for the "State Patrol," but under further questioning, claimed instead to have worked in law enforcement in Texas and at a shipyard. Ibid. He claimed that his flashing headlights were part of a recently installed car-alarm system, and acted as though he was unable to trigger the system; but during these feigned efforts Haner noticed that respondent avoided pushing a button near his knee, which Haner suspected (correctly) to be the switch for the lights. 333 F.3d, at 975; App. 108.

Sergeant Devenpeck arrived on the scene a short time later. After Haner informed Devenpeck of the basis for his belief that respondent had been impersonating a police officer, id., at 110, Devenpeck approached respondent's vehicle and inquired about the wig-wag headlights, 333 F.3d, at 975. As before, respondent said that the headlights were part of his alarm system and that he did not know how to activate them. App. 52, 138—139. Like Haner, Devenpeck was skeptical of respondent's answers. In the course of his questioning, Devenpeck noticed a tape recorder on the passenger seat of respondent's car, with the play and record buttons depressed. 333 F.3d, at 975. He ordered Haner to remove respondent from the car, played the recorded tape, and found that respondent had been recording his conversations with the officers. Devenpeck informed respondent that he was under arrest for a violation of the Washington Privacy Act, Wash. Rev. Code §9.73.030 (1994). 333 F.3d, at 975; App. 144—145. Respondent protested that a state court-of-appeals decision, a copy of which he claimed was in his glove compartment, permitted him to record roadside conversations with police officers. 333 F.3d, at 975; App. 42, 67—68. Devenpeck returned to his car, reviewed the language of the Privacy Act, and attempted unsuccessfully to reach a prosecutor to confirm that the arrest was lawful. Id., at 151—154. Believing that the text of the Privacy Act confirmed that respondent's recording was unlawful,1 he directed Officer Haner to take respondent to jail. Id., at 154.

A short time later, Devenpeck reached by phone Mark Lindquist, a deputy county prosecutor, to whom he recounted the events leading to respondent's arrest. 333 F.3d, at 975. The two discussed a series of possible criminal offenses, including violation of the Privacy Act, impersonating a police officer, and making a false representation to an officer. App. 177—178. Lindquist advised that there was "clearly probable cause," id., at 179, and suggested that respondent also be charged with "obstructing a public servant" "based on the runaround [he] gave [Devenpeck]," id., at 157. Devenpeck rejected this suggestion, explaining that the State Patrol does not, as a matter of policy, "stack charges" against an arrestee. Id., at 157—158.

At booking, Haner charged respondent with violating the State Privacy Act, id., at 32—33, and issued a ticket to respondent for his flashing headlights under Wash. Rev. Code §46.37.280(3) (1994), App. 24—25. Under state law, respondent could be detained on the latter offense only for the period of time "reasonably necessary" to issue a citation. §46.64.015 (1994). The state trial court subsequently dismissed both charges. App. 10, 29.

B

Respondent filed suit against petitioners in Federal District Court. He asserted a federal cause of action under Rev. Stat. §1979, 42 U.S.C. § 1983 and a state cause of action for unlawful arrest and imprisonment, both claims resting upon the allegation that petitioners arrested him without probable cause in violation of the Fourth and Fourteenth Amendments. 333 F.3d, at 975. The District Court denied petitioners' motion for summary judgment on grounds of qualified

immunity, and the case proceeded to trial. Alford v. Washington State Police, Case No. C99—5586RJB (WD Wash., Nov. 30, 2000), App. to Pet. for Cert. 40a. The jury was instructed that, for respondent to prevail on either his federal- or state-law claim, he must demonstrate that petitioners arrested him without probable cause, App. 199—201; and that probable cause exists "if the facts and circumstances within the arresting officer's knowledge are sufficient to warrant a prudent person to conclude that the suspect has committed, is committing, or was about to commit a crime," id., at 201. The jury was also instructed that, at the time of respondent's arrest, a State Court-of-Appeals decision, State v. Flora, 68 Wash. App. 802, 845 P.2d 1355 (1992), had clearly established that respondent's taping of petitioners was not a crime, App. 202. And the jury was directed that it must find for petitioners if a reasonable officer in the same circumstances would have believed respondent's detention was lawful. Id., at 200. Respondent did not object to any of these instructions. The jury returned a unanimous verdict in favor of petitioners. 333 F.3d, at 975. The District Court denied respondent's motion for judgment as a matter of law or, in the alternative, a new trial, and respondent appealed. Ibid.; App. to Pet. for Cert. 25a.

A divided panel of the Court of Appeals for the Ninth Circuit reversed, finding "no evidence to support the jury's verdict," 333 F.3d, at 975. The majority concluded that petitioners could not have had probable cause to arrest because they cited only the Privacy Act charge and "[t]ape recording officers conducting a traffic stop is not a crime in Washington." Id., at 976. The majority rejected petitioners' claim that probable cause existed to arrest respondent for the offenses of impersonating a law-enforcement officer, Wash. Rev. Code §9A.60.040(3) (1994), and obstructing a law-enforcement officer, §9A.76.020, because it said, those offenses were not "closely related" to the offense invoked by Devenpeck as he took respondent into custody, 333 F.3d, at 976—977. The majority also held that there was no evidence to support petitioners' claim of qualified immunity, since, given the Washington Court of Appeals' decision in Flora, "no objectively reasonable officer could have concluded that arresting [respondent] for taping the traffic stop was permissible," 333 F.3d, at 979. Judge Gould dissented on the ground that it was objectively reasonable for petitioners to believe that respondent had violated the Privacy Act. See id., at 980. We granted certiorari. 541 U.S. 987 (2004).

II

The Fourth Amendment protects "[t]he right of the people to be secure in their persons, houses, papers, and effects, against unreasonable searches and seizures." In conformity with the rule at common law, a warrantless arrest by a law officer is reasonable under the Fourth Amendment where there is probable cause to believe that a criminal offense has been or is being committed. See United States v. Watson, 423 U.S. 411, 417—424 (1976); Brinegar v. United States, 338 U.S. 160, 175—176 (1949). Whether probable cause exists depends upon the reasonable conclusion to be drawn from the facts known to the arresting officer at the time of the arrest. Maryland v. Pringle, 540 U.S. 366, 371 (2003). In this case, the Court of Appeals held that the probable-cause inquiry is further confined to the known facts bearing upon the offense actually invoked at the time of arrest, and that (in addition) the offense supported by these known facts must be "closely related" to the offense that the officer invoked. 333 F.3d, at 976. We find no basis in precedent or reason for this limitation.

Our cases make clear that an arresting officer's state of mind (except for the facts that he knows) is irrelevant to the existence of probable cause. See Whren v. United States, 517 U.S. 806, 812—813 (1996) (reviewing cases); Arkansas v. Sullivan, 532 U.S. 769 (2001) (per curiam). That is to say, his subjective reason for making the arrest need not be the criminal offense as to which the known facts provide probable cause. As we have repeatedly explained, " 'the fact that the officer does not have the state of mind which is hypothecated by the reasons which provide the legal justification for the officer's action does not invalidate the action taken as long as the circumstances, viewed objectively, justify that action.' " Whren, supra, at 813 (quoting Scott v. United States, 436 U.S. 128, 138 (1978)). "[T]he Fourth Amendment's concern with 'reasonableness' allows certain actions to be taken in certain circumstances, whatever the subjective intent." Whren, supra, at 814. "[E]venhanded law enforcement is best achieved by the application of objective standards of conduct, rather than standards that depend upon the subjective state of mind of the officer." Horton v. California, 496 U.S. 128, 138 (1990).

The rule that the offense establishing probable cause must be "closely related" to, and based on the same conduct as, the offense identified by the arresting officer at the time of arrest is inconsistent with this precedent.2 Such a rule makes the lawfulness of an arrest turn upon the motivation of the arresting officer—eliminating, as validating probable cause, facts that played no part in the officer's expressed subjective reason for making the arrest, and offenses that are not "closely related" to that subjective reason. See, e.g., Sheehy v. Plymouth, 191 F.3d 15, 20 (CA1 1999); Trejo v. Perez, 693 F.2d 482, 485—486 (CA5 1982). This means that the constitutionality of an arrest under a given set of known facts will "vary from place to place and from time to time," Whren, supra, at 815, depending on whether the arresting officer states the reason for the detention and, if so, whether he correctly identifies a general class of offense for which probable cause exists. An arrest made by a knowledgeable, veteran officer would be valid, whereas an arrest made by a rookie in precisely the same circumstances would not. We see no reason to ascribe to the Fourth Amendment such arbitrarily variable protection.

Those who support the "closely related offense" rule say that, although it is aimed at rooting out the subjective vice of arrests made for the wrong reason, it does so by objective means— that is, by reference to the arresting officer's statement of his reason. The same argument was made in Whren, supra, in defense of the proposed rule that a traffic stop can be declared invalid for malicious motivation when it is justified only by an offense which standard police practice does not make the basis for a stop. That rule, it was said, "attempt[s] to root out subjective vices through objective means," id., at 814. We rejected the argument there, and we reject it again here. Subjective intent of the arresting officer, however it is determined (and of course subjective intent is always determined by objective means), is simply no basis for invalidating an arrest. Those are lawfully arrested whom the facts known to the arresting officers give probable cause to arrest.

Finally, the "closely related offense" rule is condemned by its perverse consequences. While it is assuredly good police practice to inform a person of the reason for his arrest at the time he is taken into custody, we have never held that to be constitutionally required.3 Hence, the predictable consequence of a rule limiting the probable-cause inquiry to offenses closely related to (and supported by the same facts as) those identified by the arresting officer is not, as respondent contends, that officers will cease making sham arrests on the hope that such arrests will later be validated, but rather that officers will cease providing reasons for arrest. And even if this option were to be foreclosed by adoption of a statutory or constitutional requirement, officers would simply give every reason for which probable cause could conceivably exist.

The facts of this case exemplify the arbitrary consequences of a "closely related offense" rule. Officer Haner's initial stop of respondent was motivated entirely by the suspicion that he was impersonating a police officer. App. 106. Before pulling respondent over, Haner indicated by radio that this was his concern; during the stop, Haner asked respondent whether he was actively employed in law enforcement and why his car had wig-wag headlights; and when Sergeant Devenpeck arrived, Haner told him why he thought respondent was a "wannabe cop," id., at 98. In addition, in the course of interrogating respondent, both officers became convinced that he was not answering their questions truthfully and, with respect to the wig-wag headlights, that he was affirmatively trying to mislead them. Only after these suspicions had developed did Devenpeck discover the taping, place respondent under arrest, and offer the Privacy Act as the reason. Because of the "closely related offense" rule, Devenpeck's actions render irrelevant both Haner's developed suspicions that respondent was impersonating a police officer and the officers' shared belief that respondent obstructed their investigation. If Haner, rather than Devenpeck, had made the arrest, on the stated basis of his suspicions; if Devenpeck had not abided the county's policy against "stacking" charges; or if either officer had made the arrest without stating the grounds; the outcome under the "closely related offense" rule might well have been different. We have consistently rejected a conception of the Fourth Amendment that would produce such haphazard results, see Whren, 517 U.S., at 815.

* * *

Respondent contended below that petitioners lacked probable cause to arrest him for obstructing a law-enforcement officer or for impersonating a law-enforcement officer. Because the Court of Appeals held that those offenses were legally irrelevant, it did not decide the question. We decline to engage in this inquiry for the first time here. Accordingly, we reverse the judgment of the Ninth Circuit and remand the case for further proceedings consistent with this opinion.

It is so ordered.

Illinois v. Cabelles (Jan 24, 2005)

Justice Stevens delivered the opinion of the Court.

Illinois State Trooper Daniel Gillette stopped respondent for speeding on an interstate highway. When Gillette radioed the police dispatcher to report the stop, a second trooper, Craig Graham, a member of the Illinois State Police Drug Interdiction Team, overheard the transmission and immediately headed for the scene with his narcotics-detection dog. When they arrived, respondent's car was on the shoulder of the road and respondent was in Gillette's vehicle. While Gillette was in the process of writing a warning ticket, Graham walked his dog around respondent's car. The dog alerted at the trunk. Based on that alert, the officers searched the trunk, found marijuana, and arrested respondent. The entire incident lasted less than 10 minutes.

Respondent was convicted of a narcotics offense and sentenced to 12 years' imprisonment and a $256,136 fine. The trial judge denied his motion to suppress the seized evidence and to quash his arrest. He held that the officers had not unnecessarily prolonged the stop and that the dog alert was sufficiently reliable to provide probable cause to conduct the search. Although the Appellate Court affirmed, the Illinois Supreme Court reversed, concluding that because the canine sniff was performed without any " 'specific and articulable facts' " to suggest drug activity, the use of the dog "unjustifiably enlarg[ed] the scope of a routine traffic stop into a drug investigation." 207 Ill. 2d 504, 510, 802 N. E. 2d 202, 205 (2003).

The question on which we granted certiorari, 541 U.S. 972 (2004), is narrow: "Whether the Fourth Amendment requires reasonable, articulable suspicion to justify using a drug-detection dog to sniff a vehicle during a legitimate traffic stop." Pet. for Cert. i. Thus, we proceed on the assumption that the officer conducting the dog sniff had no information about respondent except that he had been stopped for speeding; accordingly, we have omitted any reference to facts about respondent that might have triggered a modicum of suspicion.

Here, the initial seizure of respondent when he was stopped on the highway was based on probable cause, and was concededly lawful. It is nevertheless clear that a seizure that is lawful at its inception can violate the Fourth Amendment if its manner of execution unreasonably infringes interests protected by the Constitution. United States v. Jacobsen, 466 U.S. 109, 124 (1984). A seizure that is justified solely by the interest in issuing a warning ticket to the driver can become unlawful if it is prolonged beyond the time reasonably required to complete that mission. In an earlier case involving a dog sniff that occurred during an unreasonably prolonged traffic stop, the Illinois Supreme Court held that use of the dog and the subsequent discovery of contraband were the product of an unconstitutional seizure. People v. Cox, 202 Ill. 2d 462, 782 N. E. 2d 275 (2002). We may assume that a similar result would be warranted in this case if the dog sniff had been conducted while respondent was being unlawfully detained.

In the state-court proceedings, however, the judges carefully reviewed the details of Officer Gillette's conversations with respondent and the precise timing of his radio transmissions to the dispatcher to determine whether he had improperly extended the duration of the stop to enable the dog sniff to occur. We have not recounted those details because we accept the state court's conclusion that the duration of the stop in this case was entirely justified by the traffic offense and the ordinary inquiries incident to such a stop.

Despite this conclusion, the Illinois Supreme Court held that the initially lawful traffic stop became an unlawful seizure solely as a result of the canine sniff that occurred outside respondent's stopped car. That is, the court characterized the dog sniff as the cause rather than the consequence of a constitutional violation. In its view, the use of the dog converted the citizen-police encounter from a lawful traffic stop into a drug investigation, and because the shift in purpose was not supported by any reasonable suspicion that respondent possessed narcotics, it was unlawful. In our view, conducting a dog sniff would not change the character of a traffic stop that is lawful at its inception and otherwise executed in a reasonable manner, unless the dog sniff itself infringed respondent's constitutionally protected interest in privacy. Our cases hold that it did not.

Official conduct that does not "compromise any legitimate interest in privacy" is not a search subject to the Fourth Amendment. Jacobsen, 466 U.S., at 123. We have held that any interest in possessing contraband cannot be deemed "legitimate," and thus, governmental conduct that only reveals the possession of contraband "compromises no legitimate privacy interest." Ibid. This is because the expectation "that certain facts will not come to the attention of the authorities" is not the same as an interest in "privacy that society is prepared to consider reasonable." Id., at 122 (punctuation omitted). In United States v. Place, 462 U.S. 696 (1983), we treated a canine sniff by a well-trained narcotics-detection dog as "sui generis" because it "discloses only the presence or absence of narcotics, a contraband item." Id., at 707; see also Indianapolis v. Edmond, 531 U.S. 32, 40 (2000). Respondent

likewise concedes that "drug sniffs are designed, and if properly conducted are generally likely, to reveal only the presence of contraband." Brief for Respondent 17. Although respondent argues that the error rates, particularly the existence of false positives, call into question the premise that drug-detection dogs alert only to contraband, the record contains no evidence or findings that support his argument. Moreover, respondent does not suggest that an erroneous alert, in and of itself, reveals any legitimate private information, and, in this case, the trial judge found that the dog sniff was sufficiently reliable to establish probable cause to conduct a full-blown search of the trunk.

Accordingly, the use of a well-trained narcotics-detection dog—one that "does not expose noncontraband items that otherwise would remain hidden from public view," Place, 462 U.S., at 707—during a lawful traffic stop, generally does not implicate legitimate privacy interests. In this case, the dog sniff was performed on the exterior of respondent's car while he was lawfully seized for a traffic violation. Any intrusion on respondent's privacy expectations does not rise to the level of a constitutionally cognizable infringement.

This conclusion is entirely consistent with our recent decision that the use of a thermal-imaging device to detect the growth of marijuana in a home constituted an unlawful search. Kyllo v. United States, 533 U.S. 27 (2001). Critical to that decision was the fact that the device was capable of detecting lawful activity—in that case, intimate details in a home, such as "at what hour each night the lady of the house takes her daily sauna and bath." Id., at 38. The legitimate expectation that information about perfectly lawful activity will remain private is categorically distinguishable from respondent's hopes or expectations concerning the nondetection of contraband in the trunk of his car. A dog sniff conducted during a concededly lawful traffic stop that reveals no information other than the location of a substance that no individual has any right to possess does not violate the Fourth Amendment.

The judgment of the Illinois Supreme Court is vacated, and the case is remanded for further proceedings not inconsistent with this opinion.

It is so ordered.

Georgia v. Randolph (March 22, 2006) [Notes omitted]

Justice Souter delivered the opinion of the Court.

The Fourth Amendment recognizes a valid warrantless entry and search of premises when police obtain the voluntary consent of an occupant who shares, or is reasonably believed to share, authority over the area in common with a co-occupant who later objects to the use of evidence so obtained. Illinois v. Rodriguez, 497 U. S. 177 (1990); United States v. Matlock, 415 U. S. 164 (1974). The question here is whether such an evidentiary seizure is likewise lawful with the permission of one occupant when the other, who later seeks to suppress the evidence, is present at the scene and expressly refuses to consent. We hold that, in the circumstances here at issue, a physically present co-occupant's stated refusal to permit entry prevails, rendering the warrantless search unreasonable and invalid as to him.

I

Respondent Scott Randolph and his wife, Janet, separated in late May 2001, when she left the marital residence in Americus, Georgia, and went to stay with her parents in Canada, taking their son and some belongings. In July, she returned to the Americus house with the child, though the record does not reveal whether her object was reconciliation or retrieval of remaining possessions.

On the morning of July 6, she complained to the police that after a domestic dispute her husband took their son away, and when officers reached the house she told them that her husband was a cocaine user whose habit had caused financial troubles. She mentioned the marital problems and said that she and their son had only recently returned after a stay of several weeks with her parents. Shortly after the police arrived, Scott Randolph returned and explained that he had removed the child to a neighbor's house out of concern that his wife might take the boy out of the country again; he denied cocaine use, and countered that it was in fact his wife who abused drugs and alcohol.

One of the officers, Sergeant Murray, went with Janet Randolph to reclaim the child, and when they returned she not only renewed her complaints about her husband's drug use, but also volunteered that there were " 'items of drug evidence' " in the house. Brief for Petitioner 3. Sergeant Murray asked Scott Randolph for permission to search the house, which he unequivocally refused.

The sergeant turned to Janet Randolph for consent to search, which she readily gave. She led the officer upstairs to a bedroom that she identified as Scott's, where the sergeant noticed a section of a drinking straw with a powdery residue he suspected was cocaine. He then left the house to get an evidence bag from his car and to call the district attorney's office, which instructed him to stop the search and apply for a warrant. When Sergeant Murray returned to the house, Janet Randolph withdrew her consent. The police took the straw to the police station, along with the Randolphs. After getting a search warrant, they returned to the house and seized further evidence of drug use, on the basis of which Scott Randolph was indicted for possession of cocaine.

He moved to suppress the evidence, as products of a warrantless search of his house unauthorized by his wife's consent over his express refusal. The trial court denied the motion, ruling that Janet Randolph had common authority to consent to the search.

The Court of Appeals of Georgia reversed, 264 Ga. App. 396, 590 S. E. 2d 834 (2003), and was itself sustained by the State Supreme Court, principally on the ground that "the consent to conduct a warrantless search of a residence given by one occupant is not valid in the face of the refusal of another occupant who is physically present at the scene to permit a warrantless search." 278 Ga. 614, 604 S. E. 2d 835, 836 (2004). The Supreme Court of Georgia acknowledged this Court's holding in Matlock, 415 U. S. 164, that "the consent of one who possesses common authority over premises or effects is valid as against the absent, nonconsenting person with whom that authority is shared," id., at 170, and found Matlock distinguishable just because Scott Randolph was not "absent" from the colloquy on which the police relied for consent to make the search. The State Supreme Court stressed that the officers in Matlock had not been "faced with the physical presence of joint occupants, with one consenting to the search and the other objecting." 278 Ga., at 615, 604 S. E. 2d, at 837. It held that an individual who chooses to live with another assumes a risk no greater than " 'an inability to control access to the premises during [his] absence,' " ibid. (quoting 3 W. LaFave, Search and Seizure §8.3(d), p. 731 (3d ed. 1996) (hereinafter LaFave)), and does not contemplate that his objection to a request to search commonly shared premises, if made, will be overlooked.

We granted certiorari to resolve a split of authority on whether one occupant may give law enforcement effective consent to search shared premises, as against a co-tenant who is present and states a refusal to permit the search.[1] 544 U. S. 973 (2005). We now affirm.

II

To the Fourth Amendment rule ordinarily prohibiting the warrantless entry of a person's house as unreasonable per se, Payton v. New York, 445 U. S. 573, 586 (1980); Coolidge v. New Hampshire, 403 U. S. 443, 454–455 (1971), one "jealously and carefully drawn" exception, Jones v. United States, 357 U. S. 493, 499 (1958), recognizes the validity of searches with the voluntary consent of an individual possessing authority, Rodriguez, 497 U. S., at 181. That person might be the householder against whom evidence is sought, Schneckloth v. Bustamonte, 412 U. S. 218, 222 (1973), or a fellow occupant who shares common authority over property, when the suspect is absent, Matlock, supra, at 170, and the exception for consent extends even to entries and searches with the permission of a co-occupant whom the police reasonably, but erroneously, believe to possess shared authority as an occupant, Rodriguez, supra, at 186. None of our co-occupant consent-to-search cases, however, has presented the further fact of a second occupant physically present and refusing permission to search, and later moving to suppress evidence so obtained.[2] The significance of such a refusal turns on the underpinnings of the co-occupant consent rule, as recognized since Matlock.

A

The defendant in that case was arrested in the yard of a house where he lived with a Mrs. Graff and several of her relatives, and was detained in a squad car parked nearby. When the police went to the door, Mrs. Graff admitted them and consented to a search of the house. 415 U. S., at 166. In resolving the defendant's objection to use of the evidence taken in the warrantless search, we said that "the consent of one who possesses common authority over premises or effects is valid as against the absent, nonconsenting person with whom that authority is shared." Id., at 170. Consistent with our prior understanding that Fourth Amendment rights are not limited by the law of property, cf. Katz v. United States, 389 U. S. 347, 352–353 (1967), we explained that the third party's "common authority" is not synonymous with a technical property interest:

"The authority which justified the third-party consent does not rest upon the law of property, with its attendant historical and legal refinement, but rests rather on mutual use of the property by persons generally having joint access or control for most purposes, so that it is reasonable to recognize that any of the co-inhabitants has the right to permit the inspection in his own right and that the others have assumed the risk that one of their number might permit the common area to be searched." 415 U. S., at 171, n. 7 (citations omitted).

See also Frazier v. Cupp, 394 U. S. 731, 740 (1969) ("[I]n allowing [his cousin to share use of a duffel bag] and in leaving it in his house, [the suspect] must be taken to have assumed the risk that [the cousin] would allow someone else to look inside"). The common authority that counts under the Fourth Amendment may thus be broader than the rights accorded by property law, see Rodriguez, supra, at 181–182 (consent is sufficient when given by a person who reasonably appears to have common authority but who, in fact, has no property interest in the premises searched), although its limits, too, reflect specialized tenancy arrangements apparent to the police, see Chapman v. United States, 365 U. S. 610 (1961) (landlord could not consent to search of tenant's home).

The constant element in assessing Fourth Amendment reasonableness in the consent cases, then, is the great significance given to widely shared social expectations, which are naturally enough influenced by the law of property, but not controlled by its rules. Cf. Rakas v. Illinois, 439 U. S. 128, n. 12 (1978) (an expectation of privacy is reasonable if it has "a source outside of the Fourth Amendment, either by reference to concepts of real or personal property law or to understandings that are recognized and permitted by society"). Matlock accordingly not only holds that a solitary co-inhabitant may sometimes consent to a search of shared premises, but stands for the proposition that the reasonableness of such a search is in significant part a function of commonly held understanding about the authority that co-inhabitants may exercise in ways that affect each other's interests.

B

Matlock's example of common understanding is readily apparent. When someone comes to the door of a domestic dwelling with a baby at her hip, as Mrs. Graff did, she shows that she belongs there, and that fact standing alone is enough to tell a law enforcement officer or any other visitor that if she occupies the place along with others, she probably lives there subject to the assumption tenants usually make about their common authority when they share quarters. They understand that any one of them may admit visitors, with the consequence that a guest obnoxious to one may nevertheless be admitted in his absence by another. As Matlock put it, shared tenancy is understood to include an "assumption of risk," on which police officers are entitled to rely, and although some group living together might make an exceptional arrangement that no one could admit a guest without the agreement of all, the chance of such an eccentric scheme is too remote to expect visitors to investigate a particular household's rules before accepting an invitation to come in. So, Matlock relied on what was usual and placed no burden on the police to eliminate the possibility of atypical arrangements, in the absence of reason to doubt that the regular scheme was in place.

It is also easy to imagine different facts on which, if known, no common authority could sensibly be suspected. A person on the scene who identifies himself, say, as a landlord or a hotel manager calls up no customary understanding of authority to admit guests without the consent of the current occupant. See Chapman v. United

States, supra (landlord); Stoner v. California, 376 U. S. 483 (1964) (hotel manager). A tenant in the ordinary course does not take rented premises subject to any formal or informal agreement that the landlord may let visitors into the dwelling, Chapman, supra, at 617, and a hotel guest customarily has no reason to expect the manager to allow anyone but his own employees into his room, see Stoner, supra, at 489; see also United States v. Jeffers, 342 U. S. 48, 51 (1951) (hotel staff had access to room for purposes of cleaning and maintenance, but no authority to admit police). In these circumstances, neither state-law property rights, nor common contractual arrangements, nor any other source points to a common understanding of authority to admit third parties generally without the consent of a person occupying the premises. And when it comes to searching through bureau drawers, there will be instances in which even a person clearly belonging on premises as an occupant may lack any perceived authority to consent; "a child of eight might well be considered to have the power to consent to the police crossing the threshold into that part of the house where any caller, such as a pollster or salesman, might well be admitted," 4 LaFave §8.4(c), at 207 (4th ed. 2004), but no one would reasonably expect such a child to be in a position to authorize anyone to rummage through his parents' bedroom.

C

Although we have not dealt directly with the reasonableness of police entry in reliance on consent by one occupant subject to immediate challenge by another, we took a step toward the issue in an earlier case dealing with the Fourth Amendment rights of a social guest arrested at premises the police entered without a warrant or the benefit of any exception to the warrant requirement. Minnesota v. Olson, 495 U. S. 91 (1990), held that overnight houseguests have a legitimate expectation of privacy in their temporary quarters because "it is unlikely that [the host] will admit someone who wants to see or meet with the guest over the objection of the guest," id., at 99. If that customary expectation of courtesy or deference is a foundation of Fourth Amendment rights of a houseguest, it presumably should follow that an inhabitant of shared premises may claim at least as much, and it turns out that the co-inhabitant naturally has an even stronger claim.

To begin with, it is fair to say that a caller standing at the door of shared premises would have no confidence that one occupant's invitation was a sufficiently good reason to enter when a fellow tenant stood there saying, "stay out." Without some very good reason, no sensible person would go inside under those conditions. Fear for the safety of the occupant issuing the invitation, or of someone else inside, would be thought to justify entry, but the justification then would be the personal risk, the threats to life or limb, not the disputed invitation.3

The visitor's reticence without some such good reason would show not timidity but a realization that when people living together disagree over the use of their common quarters, a resolution must come through voluntary accommodation, not by appeals to authority. Unless the people living together fall within some recognized hierarchy, like a household of parent and child or barracks housing military personnel of different grades, there is no societal understanding of superior and inferior, a fact reflected in a standard formulation of domestic property law, that "[e]ach cotenant . . . has the right to use and enjoy the entire property as if he or she were the sole owner, limited only by the same right in the other cotenants." 7 R. Powell, Powell on Real Property §50.03[1], p. 50–14 (M. Wolf gen. ed. 2005). The want of any recognized superior authority among disagreeing tenants is also reflected in the law's response when the disagreements cannot be resolved. The law does not ask who has the better side of the conflict; it simply provides a right to any co-tenant, even the most unreasonable, to obtain a decree partitioning the property (when the relationship is one of co-ownership) and terminating the relationship. See, e.g., 2 H. Tiffany, Real Property §§468, 473, 474, pp. 297, 307–309 (3d ed. 1939 and 2006 Cum. Supp.). And while a decree of partition is not the answer to disagreement among rental tenants, this situation resembles co-ownership in lacking the benefit of any understanding that one or the other rental co-tenant has a superior claim to control the use of the quarters they occupy together. In sum, there is no common understanding that one co-tenant generally has a right or authority to prevail over the express wishes of another, whether the issue is the color of the curtains or invitations to outsiders.

D

Since the co-tenant wishing to open the door to a third party has no recognized authority in law or social practice to prevail over a present and objecting co-tenant, his disputed invitation, without more, gives a police officer no better claim to reasonableness in entering than the officer would have in the absence of any consent at all. Accordingly, in the balancing of competing individual and governmental interests entailed by the bar to unreasonable searches, Camara v. Municipal Court of City and County of San Francisco, 387 U. S. 523, 536–537 (1967), the cooperative occupant's invitation adds nothing to the government's side to counter the force of an objecting individual's claim to security against the government's intrusion into his dwelling place. Since we hold to the "centuries-old principle of respect for the privacy of the home," Wilson v. Layne, 526 U. S. 603, 610 (1999), "it is beyond dispute that the home is entitled to special protection as the center of the private lives of our people," Minnesota v. Carter, 525 U. S. 83, 99 (1998) (Kennedy, J., concurring). We have, after all, lived our whole national history with an understanding of "the ancient adage that a man's home is his castle [to the point that t]he poorest man may in his cottage bid defiance to all the forces of the Crown," Miller v. United States, 357 U. S. 301, 307 (1958) (internal quotation marks omitted).4

Disputed permission is thus no match for this central value of the Fourth Amendment, and the State's other countervailing claims do not add up to outweigh it.5 Yes, we recognize the consenting tenant's interest as a citizen in bringing criminal activity to light, see Coolidge, 403 U. S., at 488 ("[I]t is no part of the policy underlying the Fourth ... Amendmen[t] to discourage citizens from aiding to the utmost of their ability in the apprehension of criminals"). And we understand a co-tenant's legitimate self-interest in siding with the police to deflect suspicion raised by sharing quarters with a criminal, see 4 LaFave §8.3(d), at 162, n. 72 ("The risk of being convicted of possession of drugs one knows are present and has tried to get the other occupant to remove is by no means insignificant"); cf. Schneckloth, 412 U. S., at 243 (evidence obtained pursuant to a consent search "may insure that a wholly innocent person is not wrongly charged with a criminal offense").

But society can often have the benefit of these interests without relying on a theory of consent that ignores an inhabitant's refusal to allow a warrantless search. The co-tenant acting on his own initiative may be able to deliver evidence to the police, Coolidge, supra, at 487–489 (suspect's wife retrieved his guns from the couple's house and turned them over to the police),and can tell the police what he knows, for use before a magistrate in getting a warrant.6 The reliance on a co-tenant's information instead of disputed consent accords with the law's general partiality toward "police action taken under a warrant [as against] searches and seizures without one," United States v. Ventresca, 380 U. S. 102, 107

(1965); "the informed and deliberate determinations of magistrates empowered to issue warrants as to what searches and seizures are permissible under the Constitution are to be preferred over the hurried action of officers," United States v. Lefkowitz, 285 U. S. 452, 464 (1932).

Nor should this established policy of Fourth Amendment law be undermined by the principal dissent's claim that it shields spousal abusers and other violent co-tenants who will refuse to allow the police to enter a dwelling when their victims ask the police for help, post, at 12 (opinion of Roberts, C. J.) (hereinafter the dissent). It is not that the dissent exaggerates violence in the home; we recognize that domestic abuse is a serious problem in the United States. See U. S. Dept. of Justice, National Institute of Justice, P. Tjaden & N. Thoennes, Full Report of the Prevalence, Incidence, and Consequence of Violence Against Women 25–26 (2000) (noting that over 20 million women and 6 million men will, in the course of their lifetimes, be the victims of intimate-partner abuse); U. S. Dept. of Health and Human Services, Centers for Disease Control and Prevention, National Center for Injury Prevention and Control, Costs of Intimate Partner Violence Against Women in the United States 19 (2003) (finding that nearly 5.3 million intimate partner victimizations, which result in close to 2 million injuries and 1300 deaths, occur among women in the United States each year); U. S. Dept. of Justice, Bureau of Justice Statistics, Crime Data Brief, C. Rennison, Intimate Partner Violence, 1993–2001 (Feb. 2003) (noting that in 2001 intimate partner violence made up 20% of violent crime against women); see also Becker, The Politics of Women's Wrongs and the Bill of "Rights": A Bicentennial Perspective, 59 U. Chi. L. Rev. 454, 507–508 (1992) (noting that women may feel physical insecurity in their homes as a result of abuse from domestic partners).

But this case has no bearing on the capacity of the police to protect domestic victims. The dissent's argument rests on the failure to distinguish two different issues: when the police may enter without committing a trespass, and when the police may enter to search for evidence. No question has been raised, or reasonably could be, about the authority of the police to enter a dwelling to protect a resident from domestic violence; so long as they have good reason to believe such a threat exists, it would be silly to suggest that the police would commit a tort by entering, say, to give a complaining tenant the opportunity to collect belongings and get out safely, or to determine whether violence (or threat of violence) has just occurred or is about to (or soon will) occur, however much a spouse or other co-tenant objected. (And since the police would then be lawfully in the premises, there is no question that they could seize any evidence in plain view or take further action supported by any consequent probable cause, see Texas v. Brown, 460 U. S. 730, 737–739 (1983) (plurality opinion).) Thus, the question whether the police might lawfully enter over objection in order to provide any protection that might be reasonable is easily answered yes. See 4 LaFave §8.3(d), at 161 ("[E]ven when . . . two persons quite clearly have equal rights in the place, as where two individuals are sharing an apartment on an equal basis, there may nonetheless sometimes exist a basis for giving greater recognition to the interests of one over the other. . . . [W]here the defendant has victimized the third-party . . . the emergency nature of the situation is such that the third-party consent should validate a warrantless search despite defendant's objections" (internal quotation marks omitted; third omission in original)). The undoubted right of the police to enter in order to protect a victim, however, has nothing to do with the question in this case, whether a search with the consent of one co-tenant is good against another, standing at the door and expressly refusing consent.7

None of the cases cited by the dissent support its improbable view that recognizing limits on merely evidentiary searches would compromise the capacity to protect a fearful occupant. In the circumstances of those cases, there is no danger that the fearful occupant will be kept behind the closed door of the house simply because the abusive tenant refuses to consent to a search. See United States v. Donlin, 982 F. 2d 31, 32 (CA1 1992) (victimized individual was already outside of her apartment when police arrived and, for all intents and purposes, within the protective custody of law enforcement officers); United States v. Hendrix, 595 F. 2d 883, 885–886 (CADC 1979) (per curiam) (even if the consent of the threatened co-occupant did not justify a warrantless search, the police entry was nevertheless allowable on exigent-circumstances grounds); People v. Sanders, 904 P. 2d 1311, 1313–1315 (Colo. 1995) (victimized individual gave her consent-to-search away from her home and was not present at the time of the police visit; alternatively, exigent circumstances existed to satisfy the warrantless exception); Brandon v. State, 778 P. 2d 221, 223–224 (Alaska App. 1989) (victimized individual consented away from her home and was not present at the time of the police visit); United States v. Davis, 290 F. 3d 1239, 1241 (CA10 2002) (immediate harm extinguished after husband "order[ed]" wife out of the home).

The dissent's red herring aside, we know, of course, that alternatives to disputed consent will not always open the door to search for evidence that the police suspect is inside. The consenting tenant may simply not disclose enough information, or information factual enough, to add up to a showing of probable cause, and there may be no exigency to justify fast action. But nothing in social custom or its reflection in private law argues for placing a higher value on delving into private premises to search for evidence in the face of disputed consent, than on requiring clear justification before the government searches private living quarters over a resident's objection. We therefore hold that a warrantless search of a shared dwelling for evidence over the express refusal of consent by a physically present resident cannot be justified as reasonable as to him on the basis of consent given to the police by another resident.8

E

There are two loose ends, the first being the explanation given in Matlock for the constitutional sufficiency of a co-tenant's consent to enter and search: it "rests ... on mutual use of the property by persons generally having joint access or control for most purposes, so that it is reasonable to recognize that any of the co-inhabitants has the right to permit the inspection in his own right ... ." 415 U. S., at 171, n. 7. If Matlock's co-tenant is giving permission "in his own right," how can his "own right" be eliminated by another tenant's objection? The answer appears in the very footnote from which the quoted statement is taken: the "right" to admit the police to which Matlock refers is not an enduring and enforceable ownership right as understood by the private law of property, but is instead the authority recognized by customary social usage as having a substantial bearing on Fourth Amendment reasonableness in specific circumstances. Thus, to ask whether the consenting tenant has the right to admit the police when a physically present fellow tenant objects is not to question whether some property right may be divested by the mere objection of another. It is, rather, the question whether customary social understanding accords the consenting tenant authority powerful enough to prevail over the co-tenant's objection. The Matlock Court did not purport to answer this question, a point made clear by another statement (which the dissent does not quote): the Court described the co-tenant's consent as good against "the absent, nonconsenting" resident." Id., at 170.

The second loose end is the significance of Matlock and Rodriguez after today's decision. Although the Matlock defendant was not present with the opportunity to object, he was in a squad car not far away; the Rodriguez defendant was actually asleep in the apartment, and the police might have roused him with a knock on the door before they entered with only the consent of an apparent co-tenant. If those cases are not to be undercut by today's holding, we have to admit that we are drawing a fine line; if a potential defendant with self-interest in objecting is in fact at the door and objects, the co-tenant's permission does not suffice for a reasonable search, whereas the potential objector, nearby but not invited to take part in the threshold colloquy, loses out.

This is the line we draw, and we think the formalism is justified. So long as there is no evidence that the police have removed the potentially objecting tenant from the entrance for the sake of avoiding a possible objection, there is practical value in the simple clarity of complementary rules, one recognizing the co-tenant's permission when there is no fellow occupant on hand, the other according dispositive weight to the fellow occupant's contrary indication when he expresses it. For the very reason that Rodriguez held it would be unjustifiably impractical to require the police to take affirmative steps to confirm the actual authority of a consenting individual whose authority was apparent, we think it would needlessly limit the capacity of the police to respond to ostensibly legitimate opportunities in the field if we were to hold that reasonableness required the police to take affirmative steps to find a potentially objecting co-tenant before acting on the permission they had already received. There is no ready reason to believe that efforts to invite a refusal would make a difference in many cases, whereas every co-tenant consent case would turn into a test about the adequacy of the police's efforts to consult with a potential objector. Better to accept the formalism of distinguishing Matlock from this case than to impose a requirement, time-consuming in the field and in the courtroom, with no apparent systemic justification. The pragmatic decision to accept the simplicity of this line is, moreover, supported by the substantial number of instances in which suspects who are asked for permission to search actually consent,[9] albeit imprudently, a fact that undercuts any argument that the police should try to locate a suspected inhabitant because his denial of consent would be a foregone conclusion.

III

This case invites a straightforward application of the rule that a physically present inhabitant's express refusal of consent to a police search is dispositive as to him, regardless of the consent of a fellow occupant. Scott Randolph's refusal is clear, and nothing in the record justifies the search on grounds independent of Janet Randolph's consent. The State does not argue that she gave any indication to the police of a need for protection inside the house that might have justified entry into the portion of the premises where the police found the powdery straw (which, if lawfully seized, could have been used when attempting to establish probable cause for the warrant issued later). Nor does the State claim that the entry and search should be upheld under the rubric of exigent circumstances, owing to some apprehension by the police officers that Scott Randolph would destroy evidence of drug use before any warrant could be obtained.

The judgment of the Supreme Court of Georgia is therefore affirmed.

It is so ordered.

Brigham City v. Stuart (May 22, 2006)

Chief Justice Roberts delivered the opinion of the Court.

In this case we consider whether police may enter a home without a warrant when they have an objectively reasonable basis for believing that an occupant is seriously injured or imminently threatened with such injury. We conclude that they may.

I

This case arises out of a melee that occurred in a Brigham City, Utah, home in the early morning hours of July 23, 2000. At about 3 a.m., four police officers responded to a call regarding a loud party at a residence. Upon arriving at the house, they heard shouting from inside, and proceeded down the driveway to investigate. There, they observed two juveniles drinking beer in the backyard. They entered the backyard, and saw—through a screen door and windows—an altercation taking place in the kitchen of the home. According to the testimony of one of the officers, four adults were attempting, with some difficulty, to restrain a juvenile. The juvenile eventually "broke free, swung a fist and struck one of the adults in the face." 2005 UT 13, ¶2, 122 P. 3d 506, 508. The officer testified that he observed the victim of the blow spitting blood into a nearby sink. App. 40. The other adults continued to try to restrain the juvenile, pressing him up against a refrigerator with such force that the refrigerator began moving across the floor. At this point, an officer opened the screen door and announced the officers' presence. Amid the tumult, nobody noticed. The officer entered the kitchen and again cried out, and as the occupants slowly became aware that the police were on the scene, the altercation ceased.

The officers subsequently arrested respondents and charged them with contributing to the delinquency of a minor, disorderly conduct, and intoxication. In the trial court, respondents filed a motion to suppress all evidence obtained after the officers entered the home, arguing that the warrantless entry violated the Fourth Amendment. The court granted the motion, and the Utah Court of Appeals affirmed.

Before the Supreme Court of Utah, Brigham City argued that although the officers lacked a warrant, their entry was nevertheless reasonable on either of two grounds. The court rejected both contentions and, over two dissenters, affirmed. First, the court held that the injury caused by the juvenile's punch was insufficient to trigger the so-called "emergency aid doctrine" because it did not give rise to an " objectively reasonable belief that an unconscious, semi-conscious, or missing person feared injured or dead [was] in the home." 122 P. 3d, at 513 (internal quotation marks omitted). Furthermore, the court suggested that the doctrine was inapplicable because the officers had not sought to assist the injured adult, but instead had acted "exclusively in their law enforcement capacity." Ibid.

The court also held that the entry did not fall within the exigent circumstances exception to the warrant requirement. This exception applies, the court explained, where police have probable cause and where "a reasonable person [would] believe that the entry was necessary to prevent physical harm to the officers or other persons." Id., at 514 (internal quotation marks omitted). Under this standard, the court stated, the potential harm need not be as serious as that required to invoke the emergency aid exception. Although it found the case "a close and difficult call," the court nevertheless concluded that the officers' entry was not justified by exigent circumstances. Id., at 515.

We granted certiorari, 546 U. S. ____ (2006), in light of differences among state courts and the Courts of Appeals concerning the appropriate Fourth Amendment standard governing warrantless entry by law enforcement in an emergency situation. Compare In re Sealed Case 96–3167, 153 F. 3d 759, 766 (CADC 1998)

("[T]he standard for exigent circumstances is an objective one") and People v. Hebert, 46 P. 3d 473, 480 (Colo. 2002) (en banc) (considering the circumstances as they "would have been objectively examined by a prudent and trained police officer"), with United States v. Cervantes, 219 F. 3d 882, 890 (CA9 2000) ("[U]nder the emergency doctrine, '[a] search must not be primarily motivated by intent to arrest and seize evidence' " (quoting People v. Mitchell, 39 N. Y. 2d 173, 177, 347 N. E. 2d 607, 609 (1976)) and State v. Mountford, 171 Vt. 487, 492, 769 A. 2d 639, 645 (2000) (Mitchell test "requir[es] courts to find that the primary subjective motivation behind such searches was to provide emergency aid").

II

It is a " ' basic principle of Fourth Amendment law that searches and seizures inside a home without a warrant are presumptively unreasonable.' " Groh v. Ramirez, 540 U. S. 551, 559 (2004) (quoting Payton v. New York, 445 U. S. 573, 586 (1980) (some internal quotation marks omitted)). Nevertheless, because the ultimate touchstone of the Fourth Amendment is "reasonableness," the warrant requirement is subject to certain exceptions. Flippo v. West Virginia, 528 U. S. 11, 13 (1999) (per curiam); Katz v. United States, 389 U. S. 347, 357 (1967). We have held, for example, that law enforcement officers may make a warrantless entry onto private property to fight a fire and investigate its cause, Michigan v. Tyler, 436 U. S. 499, 509 (1978), to prevent the imminent destruction of evidence, Ker v. California, 374 U. S. 23, 40 (1963), or to engage in "hot pursuit" of a fleeing suspect, United States v. Santana, 427 U. S. 38, 42–43 (1976). "[W]arrants are generally required to search a person's home or his person unless 'the exigencies of the situation' make the needs of law enforcement so compelling that the warrantless search is objectively reasonable under the Fourth Amendment." Mincey v. Arizona, 437 U. S. 385, 393–394 (1978).

One exigency obviating the requirement of a warrant is the need to assist persons who are seriously injured or threatened with such injury. " 'The need to protect or preserve life or avoid serious injury is justification for what would be otherwise illegal absent an exigency or emergency.' " Id., at 392 (quoting Wayne v. United States, 318 F. 2d 205, 212 (CADC 1963) (Burger, J.)); see also Tyler, supra, at 509. Accordingly, law enforcement officers may enter a home without a warrant to render emergency assistance to an injured occupant or to protect an occupant from imminent injury. Mincey, supra, at 392; see also Georgia v. Randolph, 547 U. S. ___, ___ (2006) (slip op., at 13–14) ("[I]t would be silly to suggest that the police would commit a tort by entering ... to determine whether violence (or threat of violence) has just occurred or is about to (or soon will) occur").

Respondents do not take issue with these principles, but instead advance two reasons why the officers' entry here was unreasonable. First, they argue that the officers were more interested in making arrests than quelling violence. They urge us to consider, in assessing the reasonableness of the entry, whether the officers were "indeed motivated primarily by a desire to save lives and property." Brief for Respondents 3; see also Brief for National Association of Criminal Defense Lawyers as Amicus Curiae 6 (entry to render emergency assistance justifies a search "only when the searching officer is acting outside his traditional law-enforcement capacity"). The Utah Supreme Court also considered the officers' subjective motivations relevant. See 122 P. 3d, at 513 (search under the "emergency aid doctrine" may not be "primarily motivated by intent to arrest and seize evidence" (internal quotation marks omitted)).

Our cases have repeatedly rejected this approach. An action is "reasonable" under the

Fourth Amendment, regardless of the individual officer's state of mind, "as long as the circumstances, viewed objectively, justify [the] action." Scott v. United States, 436 U. S. 128, 138 (1978) (emphasis added). The officer's subjective motivation is irrelevant. See Bond v. United States, 529 U. S. 334, n. 2 (2000) ("The parties properly agree that the subjective intent of the law enforcement officer is irrelevant in determining whether that officer's actions violate the Fourth Amendment ...; the issue is not his state of mind, but the objective effect of his actions"); Whren v. United States, 517 U. S. 806, 813 (1996) ("[W]e have been unwilling to entertain Fourth Amendment challenges based on the actual motivations of individual officers"); Graham v. Connor, 490 U. S. 386, 397 (1989) ("[O]ur prior cases make clear" that "the subjective motivations of the individual officers ... ha[ve] no bearing on whether a particular seizure is 'unreasonable' under the Fourth Amendment").It therefore does not matter here—even if their subjective motives could be so neatly unraveled—whether the officers entered the kitchen to arrest respondents and gather evidence against them or to assist the injured and prevent further violence.

As respondents note, we have held in the context of programmatic searches conducted without individualized suspicion—such as checkpoints to combat drunk driving or drug trafficking—that "an inquiry into programmatic purpose" is sometimes appropriate. Indianapolis v. Edmond, 531 U. S. 32, 46 (2000) (emphasis added); see also Florida v. Wells, 495 U. S. 1, 4 (1990) (an inventory search must be regulated by "standardized criteria" or "established routine" so as not to "be a ruse for a general rummaging in order to discover incriminating evidence"). But this inquiry is directed at ensuring that the purpose behind the program is not "ultimately indistinguishable from the general interest in crime control." Edmond, 531 U. S., at 44. It has nothing to do with discerning what is in the mind of the individual officer conducting the search. Id., at 48.

Respondents further contend that their conduct was not serious enough to justify the officers' intrusion into the home. They rely on Welsh v. Wisconsin, 466 U. S. 740, 753 (1984), in which we held that "an important factor to be considered when determining whether any exigency exists is the gravity of the underlying offense for which the arrest is being made." This contention, too, is misplaced. Welsh involved a warrantless entry by officers to arrest a suspect for driving while intoxicated. There, the "only potential emergency" confronting the officers was the need to preserve evidence (i.e., the suspect's blood-alcohol level)—an exigency that we held insufficient under the circumstances to justify entry into the suspect's home. Ibid. Here, the officers were confronted with ongoing violence occurring within the home. Welsh did not address such a situation.

We think the officers' entry here was plainly reasonable under the circumstances. The officers were responding, at 3 o'clock in the morning, to complaints about a loud party. As they approached the house, they could hear from within "an altercation occurring, some kind of a fight." App. 29. "It was loud and it was tumultuous." Id., at 33. The officers heard "thumping and crashing" and people yelling "stop, stop" and "get off me." Id., at 28, 29. As the trial court found, "it was obvious that ... knocking on the front door" would have been futile. Id., at 92. The noise seemed to be coming from the back of the house; after looking in the front window and seeing nothing, the officers proceeded around back to investigate further. They found two juveniles drinking beer in the backyard. From there, they could see that a fracas was taking place inside the kitchen. A juvenile, fists clenched, was being held back by several adults. As the officers watch, he breaks free and strikes one of the adults in the face, sending the adult to the sink spitting blood.

In these circumstances, the officers had an objectively reasonable basis for believing both that the injured adult might need help and that the violence in the kitchen was just beginning. Nothing in the Fourth Amendment required them to wait until another blow rendered someone "unconscious" or "semi-conscious" or worse before entering. The role of a peace officer includes preventing violence and restoring order, not simply rendering first aid to casualties; an officer is not like a boxing (or hockey) referee, poised to stop a bout only if it becomes too one-sided.

The manner of the officers' entry was also reasonable. After witnessing the punch, one of the officers opened the screen door and "yelled in police." Id., at 40. When nobody heard him, he stepped into the kitchen and announced himself again. Only then did the tumult subside. The officer's announcement of his presence was at least equivalent to a knock on the screen door. Indeed, it was probably the only option that had even a chance of rising above the din. Under these circumstances, there was no violation of the Fourth Amendment's knock-and-announce rule. Furthermore, once the announcement was made, the officers were free to enter; it would serve no purpose to require them to stand dumbly at the door awaiting a response while those within brawled on, oblivious to their presence.

Accordingly, we reverse the judgment of the Supreme Court of Utah, and remand the case for further proceedings not inconsistent with this opinion.

It is so ordered.

Hudson v. Michigan (June 15, 2006) [Notes omitted]

Justice Scalia delivered the opinion of the Court, except as to Part IV.

We decide whether violation of the "knock-and-announce" rule requires the suppression of all evidence found in the search.

I

Police obtained a warrant authorizing a search for drugs and firearms at the home of petitioner Booker Hudson. They discovered both. Large quantities of drugs were found, including cocaine rocks in Hudson's pocket. A loaded gun was lodged between the cushion and armrest of the chair in which he was sitting. Hudson was charged under Michigan law with unlawful drug and firearm possession.

This case is before us only because of the method of entry into the house. When the police arrived to execute the warrant, they announced their presence, but waited only a short time— perhaps "three to five seconds," App. 15—before turning the knob of the unlocked front door and entering Hudson's home. Hudson moved to suppress all the inculpatory evidence, arguing that the premature entry violated his Fourth Amendment rights.

The Michigan trial court granted his motion. On interlocutory review, the Michigan Court of Appeals reversed, relying on Michigan Supreme Court cases holding that suppression is inappropriate when entry is made pursuant to warrant but without proper " 'knock and announce.' " App. to Pet. for Cert. 4 (citing People v. Vasquez, 461 Mich. 235, 602 N. W. 2d 376 (1999) (per curiam); People v. Stevens, 460 Mich. 626, 597 N. W. 2d 53 (1999)). The Michigan Supreme Court denied leave to appeal. 465 Mich. 932, 639 N. E. 2d 255 (2001). Hudson was convicted of drug possession. He renewed his Fourth Amendment claim on appeal, but the Court of Appeals rejected it and affirmed the conviction. App. to Pet. for Cert. 1–2. The Michigan Supreme Court again declined review. 472 Mich. 862, 692 N. W. 2d 385 (2005). We granted certiorari. 545 U. S. ___ (2005).

II

The common-law principle that law enforcement officers must announce their presence and provide residents an opportunity to open the door is an ancient one. See Wilson v. Arkansas, 514 U. S. 927, 931–932 (1995) . Since 1917, when Congress passed the Espionage Act, this traditional protection has been part of federal statutory law, see 40 Stat. 229, and is currently codified at 18 U. S. C. §3109. We applied that statute in Miller v. United States, 357 U. S. 301 (1958) , and again in Sabbath v. United States, 391 U. S. 585 (1968) . Finally, in Wilson, we were asked whether the rule was also a command of the Fourth Amendment . Tracing its origins in our English legal heritage, 514 U. S., at 931–936, we concluded that it was.

We recognized that the new constitutional rule we had announced is not easily applied. Wilson and cases following it have noted the many situations in which it is not necessary to knock and announce. It is not necessary when "circumstances presen[t] a threat of physical violence," or if there is "reason to believe that evidence would likely be destroyed if advance notice were given," id., at 936, or if knocking and announcing would be "futile," Richards v. Wisconsin, 520 U. S. 385, 394 (1997) . We require only that police "have a reasonable suspicion ... under the particular circumstances" that one of these grounds for failing to knock and announce exists, and we have acknowledged that "[t]his showing is not high." Ibid.

When the knock-and-announce rule does apply, it is not easy to determine precisely what officers must do. How many seconds' wait are too few? Our "reasonable wait time" standard, see United States v. Banks, 540 U. S. 31, 41 (2003) , is necessarily vague. Banks (a drug case, like this one) held that the proper measure was not how long it would take the resident to reach the door, but how long it would take to dispose of the suspected drugs—but that such a time (15 to 20 seconds in that case) would necessarily be extended when, for instance, the suspected contraband was not easily concealed. Id., at 40–41. If our ex post evaluation is subject to such calculations, it is unsurprising that, ex ante, police officers about to encounter someone who may try to harm them will be uncertain how long to wait.

Happily, these issues do not confront us here. From the trial level onward, Michigan has conceded that the entry was a knock-and-announce violation. The issue here is remedy. Wilson specifically declined to decide whether the exclusionary rule is appropriate for violation of the knock-and-announce requirement. 514 U. S., at 937, n. 4. That question is squarely before us now.

III

A

In Weeks v. United States, 232 U. S. 383 (1914) , we adopted the federal exclusionary rule for evidence that was unlawfully seized from a home without a warrant in violation of the Fourth Amendment . We began applying the same rule to the States, through the Fourteenth Amendment , in Mapp v. Ohio, 367 U. S. 643 (1961) .

Suppression of evidence, however, has always been our last resort, not our first impulse. The exclusionary rule generates "substantial social costs," United States v. Leon, 468 U. S. 897, 907 (1984) , which sometimes include setting the guilty free and the dangerous at large. We have therefore been "cautio[us] against expanding" it, Colorado v. Connelly, 479 U. S. 157, 166 (1986) , and "have repeatedly emphasized that the rule's 'costly toll' upon truth-seeking and law enforcement objectives presents a high obstacle for those urging [its] application," Pennsylvania Bd. of Probation and Parole v. Scott, 524 U. S. 357, 364–365 (1998) (citation omitted). We have rejected "[i]ndiscriminate application" of the rule, Leon, supra, at 908, and have held it to be applicable only "where its remedial objectives are thought most efficaciously served," United States v. Calandra, 414 U. S. 338, 348 (1974) —that is, "where its deterrence benefits outweigh its 'substantial social costs,' " Scott, supra, at 363 (quoting Leon, supra, at 907).

We did not always speak so guardedly. Expansive dicta in Mapp, for example, suggested wide scope for the exclusionary rule. See, e.g., 367 U. S., at 655 ("[A]ll evidence obtained by searches and seizures in violation of the Constitution is, by that same authority, inadmissible in a state court"). Whiteley v. Warden, Wyo. State Penitentiary, 401 U. S. 560, 568–569 (1971), was to the same effect. But we have long since rejected that approach. As explained in Arizona v. Evans, 514 U. S. 1, 13 (1995): "In Whiteley, the Court treated identification of a Fourth Amendment violation as synonymous with application of the exclusionary rule to evidence secured incident to that violation. Subsequent case law has rejected this reflexive application of the exclusionary rule." (Citation omitted.) We had said as much in Leon, a decade earlier, when we explained that "[w]hether the exclusionary sanction is appropriately imposed in a particular case, . . . is 'an issue separate from the question whether the Fourth Amendment rights of the party seeking to invoke the rule were violated by police conduct.' " 468 U. S., at 906 (quoting Illinois v. Gates, 462 U. S. 213, 223 (1983)).

In other words, exclusion may not be premised on the mere fact that a constitutional violation was a "but-for" cause of obtaining evidence. Our cases show that but-for causality is only a necessary, not a sufficient, condition for suppression. In this case, of course, the constitutional violation of an illegal manner of entry was not a but-for cause of obtaining the evidence. Whether that preliminary misstep had occurred or not, the police would have executed the warrant they had obtained, and would have discovered the gun and drugs inside the house. But even if the illegal entry here could be characterized as a but-for cause of discovering what was inside, we have "never held that evidence is 'fruit of the poisonous tree' simply because 'it would not have come to light but for the illegal actions of the police.' " Segura v. United States, 468 U. S. 796, 815 (1984) . See also id., at 829 (Stevens, J., dissenting) ("We have not ... mechanically applied the [exclusionary] rule to every item of evidence that has a causal connection with police misconduct"). Rather, but-for cause, or "causation in the logical sense alone," United States v. Ceccolini, 435 U. S. 268, 274 (1978) , can be too attenuated to justify exclusion, id., at 274–275. Even in the early days of the exclusionary rule, we declined to

"hold that all evidence is 'fruit of the poisonous tree' simply because it would not have come to light but for the illegal actions of the police. Rather, the more apt question in such a case is 'whether, granting establishment of the primary illegality, the evidence to which instant objection is made has been come at by exploitation of that illegality or instead by means sufficiently distinguishable to be purged of the primary taint.' " Wong Sun v. United States, 371 U. S. 471, 487–488 (1963) (quoting J. Maguire, Evidence of Guilt 221 (1959) (emphasis added)).

Attenuation can occur, of course, when the causal connection is remote. See, e.g., Nardone v. United States, 308 U. S. 338, 341 (1939) . Attenuation also occurs when, even given a direct causal connection, the interest protected by the constitutional guarantee that has been violated would not be served by suppression of the evidence obtained. "The penalties visited upon the Government, and in turn upon the public, because its officers have violated the law must bear some relation to the purposes which the law is to serve." Ceccolini, supra, at 279. Thus, in New York v. Harris, 495 U. S. 14 (1990) , where an illegal warrantless arrest was made in Harris' house, we held that

"suppressing [Harris'] statement taken outside the house would not serve the purpose of the rule that made Harris' in-house arrest illegal. The warrant requirement for an arrest in the home is imposed to protect the home, and anything incriminating the police gathered from arresting Harris in his home, rather than elsewhere, has been excluded, as it should have been; the purpose of the rule has thereby been vindicated." Id., at 20.

For this reason, cases excluding the fruits of unlawful warrantless searches, see, e.g., Boyd v. United States, 116 U. S. 616 (1886) ; Weeks, 232 U. S. 383 ; Silverthorne Lumber Co. v. United States, 251 U. S. 385 (1920) ; Mapp, supra, say nothing about the appropriateness of exclusion to vindicate the interests protected by the knock-and-announce requirement. Until a valid warrant has issued, citizens are entitled to shield "their persons, houses, papers, and effects," U. S. Const., Amdt. 4, from the government's scrutiny. Exclusion of the evidence obtained by a warrantless search vindicates that entitlement. The interests protected by the knock-and-announce requirement are quite different—and do not include the shielding of potential evidence from the government's eyes.

One of those interests is the protection of human life and limb, because an unannounced entry may provoke violence in supposed self-defense by the surprised resident. See, e.g., McDonald v. United States, 335 U. S. 451, 460–461 (1948) (Jackson, J., concurring). See also Sabbath, 391 U. S., at 589; Miller, 357 U. S., at 313, n. 12. Another interest is the protection of property. Breaking a house (as the old cases typically put it) absent an announcement would penalize someone who " 'did not know of the process, of which, if he had notice, it is to be presumed that he would obey it ... .' " Wilson, 514 U. S., at 931–932 (quoting Semayne's Case, 5 Co. Rep. 91a, 91b, 77 Eng. Rep. 194, 195–196 (K. B. 1603)). The knock-and-announce rule gives individuals "the opportunity

to comply with the law and to avoid the destruction of property occasioned by a forcible entry." Richards, 520 U. S., at 393, n. 5. See also Banks, 540 U. S., at 41. And thirdly, the knock-and-announce rule protects those elements of privacy and dignity that can be destroyed by a sudden entrance. It gives residents the "opportunity to prepare themselves for" the entry of the police. Richards, 520 U. S., at 393, n. 5. "The brief interlude between announcement and entry with a warrant may be the opportunity that an individual has to pull on clothes or get out of bed." Ibid. In other words, it assures the opportunity to collect oneself before answering the door.

What the knock-and-announce rule has never protected, however, is one's interest in preventing the government from seeing or taking evidence described in a warrant. Since the interests that were violated in this case have nothing to do with the seizure of the evidence, the exclusionary rule is inapplicable.

B

Quite apart from the requirement of unattenuated causation, the exclusionary rule has never been applied except "where its deterrence benefits outweigh its 'substantial social costs,' " Scott, 524 U. S., at 363 (quoting Leon, 468 U. S., at 907). The costs here are considerable. In addition to the grave adverse consequence that exclusion of relevant incriminating evidence always entails (viz., the risk of releasing dangerous criminals into society), imposing that massive remedy for a knock-and-announce violation would generate a constant flood of alleged failures to observe the rule, and claims that any asserted Richards justification for a no-knock entry, see 520 U. S., at 394, had inadequate support. Cf. United States v. Singleton, 441 F. 3d 290, 293–294 (CA4 2006). The cost of entering this lottery would be small, but the jackpot enormous: suppression of all evidence, amounting in many cases to a get-out-of-jail-free card. Courts would experience as never before the reality that "[t]he exclusionary rule frequently requires extensive litigation to determine whether particular evidence must be excluded." Scott, supra, at 366. Unlike the warrant or Miranda requirements, compliance with which is readily determined (either there was or was not a warrant; either the Miranda warning was given, or it was not), what constituted a "reasonable wait time" in a particular case, Banks, supra, at 41 (or, for that matter, how many seconds the police in fact waited), or whether there was "reasonable suspicion" of the sort that would invoke the Richards exceptions, is difficult for the trial court to determine and even more difficult for an appellate court to review.

Another consequence of the incongruent remedy Hudson proposes would be police officers' refraining from timely entry after knocking and announcing. As we have observed, see supra, at 3, the amount of time they must wait is necessarily uncertain. If the consequences of running afoul of the rule were so massive, officers would be inclined to wait longer than the law requires—producing preventable violence against officers in some cases, and the destruction of evidence in many others. See Gates, 462 U. S., at 258. We deemed these consequences severe enough to produce our unanimous agreement that a mere "reasonable suspicion" that knocking and announcing "under the particular circumstances, would be dangerous or futile, or that it would inhibit the effective investigation of the crime," will cause the requirement to yield. Richards, supra, at 394.

Next to these "substantial social costs" we must consider the deterrence benefits, existence of which is a necessary condition for exclusion. (It is not, of course, a sufficient condition: "[I]t does not follow that the Fourth Amendment requires adoption of every proposal that might deter police misconduct." Calandra, 414 U. S., at 350; see also Leon, supra, at 910.) To begin with, the value of deterrence depends upon the strength of the incentive to commit the forbidden act. Viewed from this perspective, deterrence of knock-and-announce violations is not worth a lot. Violation of the warrant requirement sometimes produces incriminating evidence that could not otherwise be obtained. But ignoring knock-and-announce can realistically be expected to achieve absolutely nothing except the prevention of destruction of evidence and the avoidance of life-threatening resistance by occupants of the premises—dangers which, if there is even "reasonable suspicion" of their existence, suspend the knock-and-announce requirement anyway. Massive deterrence is hardly required.

It seems to us not even true, as Hudson contends, that without suppression there will be no deterrence of knock-and-announce violations at all. Of course even if this assertion were accurate, it would not necessarily justify suppression. Assuming (as the assertion must) that civil suit is not an effective deterrent, one can think of many forms of police misconduct that are similarly "undeterred." When, for example, a confessed suspect in the killing of a police officer, arrested (along with incriminating evidence) in a lawful warranted search, is subjected to physical abuse at the station house, would it seriously be suggested that the evidence must be excluded, since that is the only "effective deterrent"? And what, other than civil suit, is the "effective deterrent" of police violation of an already-confessed suspect's Sixth Amendment rights by denying him prompt access to counsel? Many would regard these violated rights as more significant than the right not to be intruded upon in one's nightclothes—and yet nothing but "ineffective" civil suit is available as a deterrent. And the police incentive for those violations is arguably greater than the incentive for disregarding the knock-and-announce rule.

We cannot assume that exclusion in this context is necessary deterrence simply because we found that it was necessary deterrence in different contexts and long ago. That would be forcing the public today to pay for the sins and inadequacies of a legal regime that existed almost half a century ago. Dollree Mapp could not turn to 42 U. S. C. §1983 for meaningful relief; Monroe v. Pape, 365 U. S. 167 (1961), which began the slow but steady expansion of that remedy, was decided the same Term as Mapp. It would be another 17 years before the §1983 remedy was extended to reach the deep pocket of municipalities, Monell v. New York City Dept. of Social Servs., 436 U. S. 658 (1978). Citizens whose Fourth Amendment rights were violated by federal officers could not bring suit until 10 years after Mapp, with this Court's decision in Bivens v. Six Unknown Fed. Narcotics Agents, 403 U. S. 388 (1971).

Hudson complains that "it would be very hard to find a lawyer to take a case such as this," Tr. of Oral Arg. 7, but 42 U. S. C. §1988(b) answers this objection. Since some civil-rights violations would yield damages too small to justify the expense of litigation, Congress has authorized attorney's fees for civil-rights plaintiffs. This remedy was unavailable in the heydays of our exclusionary-rule jurisprudence, because it is tied to the availability of a cause of action. For years after Mapp, "very few lawyers would even consider representation of persons who had civil rights claims against the police," but now "much has changed. Citizens and lawyers are much more willing to seek relief in the courts for police misconduct." M. Avery, D. Rudovsky, & K. Blum, Police Misconduct: Law and Litigation, p. v (3d ed. 2005); see generally N. Aron, Liberty and Justice for All: Public Interest Law in the 1980s and Beyond (1989) (describing the growth of public-interest law). The number of public-interest law firms and lawyers who specialize in civil-rights grievances has greatly expanded.

Hudson points out that few published decisions to date announce huge awards for knock-and-announce violations. But this is an unhelpful statistic. Even if we thought that only large damages would deter police misconduct (and that police somehow are deterred by "damages" but indifferent to the prospect of large §1988 attorney's fees), we do not know how many claims have been settled, or indeed how many violations have occurred that produced anything more than nominal injury. It is clear, at least, that the lower courts are allowing colorable knock-and-announce suits to go forward, unimpeded by assertions of qualified immunity. See, e.g., Green v. Butler, 420 F. 3d 689, 700–701 (CA7 2005) (denying qualified immunity in a knock-and-announce civil suit); Holland ex rel. Overdorff v. Harrington, 268 F. 3d 1179, 1193–1196 (CA10 2001) (same); Mena v. Simi Valley, 226 F. 3d 1031, 1041–1042 (CA9 2000) (same); Gould v. Davis, 165 F. 3d 265, 270–271 (CA4 1998) (same). As far as we know, civil liability is an effective deterrent here, as we have assumed it is in other contexts. See, e.g., Correctional Services Corp. v. Malesko, 534 U. S. 61, 70 (2001) ("[T]he threat of litigation and liability will adequately deter federal officers for Bivens purposes no matter that they may enjoy qualified immunity" (as violators of knock-and-announce do not)); see also Nix v. Williams, 467 U. S. 431, 446 (1984).

Another development over the past half-century that deters civil-rights violations is the increasing professionalism of police forces, including a new emphasis on internal police discipline. Even as long ago as 1980 we felt it proper to "assume" that unlawful police behavior would "be dealt with appropriately" by the authorities, United States v. Payner, 447 U. S. 727, n. 5 (1980), but we now have increasing evidence that police forces across the United States take the constitutional rights of citizens seriously. There have been "wide-ranging reforms in the education, training, and supervision of police officers." S. Walker, Taming the System: The Control of Discretion in Criminal Justice 1950–1990, p. 51

(1993). Numerous sources are now available to teach officers and their supervisors what is required of them under this Court's cases, how to respect constitutional guarantees in various situations, and how to craft an effective regime for internal discipline. See, e.g., D. Waksman & D. Goodman, The Search and Seizure Handbook (2d ed. 2006); A. Stone & S. DeLuca, Police Administration: An Introduction (2d ed. 1994); E. Thibault, L. Lynch, & R. McBridge, Proactive Police Management (4th ed. 1998). Failure to teach and enforce constitutional requirements exposes municipalities to financial liability. See Canton v. Harris, 489 U. S. 378, 388 (1989) . Moreover, modern police forces are staffed with professionals; it is not credible to assert that internal discipline, which can limit successful careers, will not have a deterrent effect. There is also evidence that the increasing use of various forms of citizen review can enhance police accountability.

In sum, the social costs of applying the exclusionary rule to knock-and-announce violations are considerable; the incentive to such violations is minimal to begin with, and the extant deterrences against them are substantial— incomparably greater than the factors deterringwarrantless entries when Mapp was decided. Resort to the massive remedy of suppressing evidence of guilt is unjustified.

IV

A trio of cases—Segura v. United States, 468 U. S. 796 (1984) ; New York v. Harris, 495 U. S. 14 (1990) ; and United States v. Ramirez, 523 U. S. 65 (1998) —confirms our conclusion that suppression is unwarranted in this case.

Like today's case, Segura involved a concededly illegal entry. Police conducting a drug crime investigation waited for Segura outside an apartment building; when he arrived, he denied living there. The police arrested him and brought him to the apartment where they suspected illegal activity. An officer knocked. When someone inside opened the door, the police entered, taking Segura with them. They had neither a warrant nor consent to enter, and they did not announce themselves as police—an entry as illegal as can be. Officers then stayed in the apartment for 19 hours awaiting a search warrant. 468 U. S., at 800–801; id., at 818–819 (Stevens, J., dissenting). Once alerted that the search warrant had been obtained, the police—still inside, having secured the premises so that no evidence could be removed—conducted a search. Id., at 801. We refused to exclude the resulting evidence. We recognized that only the evidence gained from the particular violation could be excluded, see id., at 799, 804–805, and therefore distinguished the effects of the illegal entry from the effects of the legal search: "None of the information on which the warrant was secured was derived from or related in any way to the initial entry into petitioners' apartment . . . ." Id., at 814. It was therefore "beyond dispute that the information possessed by the agents before they entered the apartment constituted an independent source for the discovery and seizure of the evidence now challenged." Ibid.

If the search in Segura could be "wholly unrelated to the prior entry," ibid., when the only entry was warrantless, it would be bizarre to treat more harshly the actions in this case, where the only entry was with a warrant. If the probable cause backing a warrant that was issued later in time could be an "independent source" for a search that proceeded after the officers illegally entered and waited, a search warrant obtained before going in must have at least this much effect.1

In the second case, Harris, the police violated the defendant's Fourth Amendment rights by arresting him at home without a warrant, contrary to Payton v. New York, 445 U. S. 573 (1980) . Once taken to the station house, he gave an incriminating statement. See 495 U. S., at 15– 16. We refused to exclude it. Like the illegal entry which led to discovery of the evidence in today's case, the illegal arrest in Harris began a process that culminated in acquisition of the evidence sought to be excluded. While Harris's statement was "the product of an arrest and being in custody," it "was not the fruit of the fact that the arrest was made in the house rather than someplace else." Id., at 20. Likewise here: While acquisition of the gun and drugs was the product of a search pursuant to warrant, it was not the fruit of the fact that the entry was not preceded by knock and announce.2

United States v. Ramirez, supra, involved a claim that police entry violated the Fourth Amendment because it was effected by breaking a window. We ultimately concluded that the property destruction was, under all the circumstances, reasonable, but in the course of our discussion we unanimously said the following: "[D]estruction of property in the course of a search may violate the Fourth Amendment , even though the entry itself is lawful and the fruits of the search are not subject to suppression." Id., at 71. Had the breaking of the window been unreasonable, the Court said, it would have been necessary to determine whether there had been a "sufficient causal relationship between the breaking of the window and the discovery of the guns to warrant suppression of the evidence." Id., at 72, n. 3. What clearer expression could there be of the proposition that an impermissible manner of entry does not necessarily trigger the exclusionary rule?

*   *   *

For the foregoing reasons we affirm the judgment of the Michigan Court of Appeals.

It is so ordered.

Samson v. California (June 19, 2006) [Notes omitted]

Justice Thomas delivered the opinion of the Court.

California law provides that every prisoner eligible for release on state parole "shall agree in writing to be subject to search or seizure by a parole officer or other peace officer at any time of the day or night, with or without a search warrant and with or without cause." Cal. Penal Code Ann. §3067(a) (West 2000). We granted certiorari to decide whether a suspicionless search, conducted under the authority of this statute, violates the Constitution. We hold that it does not.

I

In September 2002, petitioner Donald Curtis Samson was on state parole in California, following a conviction for being a felon in possession of a firearm. On September 6, 2002, Officer Alex Rohleder of the San Bruno Police Department observed petitioner walking down a street with a woman and a child. Based on a prior contact with petitioner, Officer Rohleder was aware that petitioner was on parole and believed that he was facing an at large warrant. Accordingly, Officer Rohleder stopped petitioner and asked him whether he had an outstanding parole warrant. Petitioner responded that there was no outstanding warrant and that he "was in good standing with his parole agent." Brief for Petitioner 4. Officer Rohleder confirmed, by radio dispatch, that petitioner was on parole and that he did not have an outstanding warrant. Nevertheless, pursuant to Cal. Penal Code Ann. §3067(a) (West 2000) and based solely on petitioner's status as a parolee, Officer Rohleder searched petitioner. During the search, Officer Rohleder found a cigarette box in petitioner's left breast pocket. Inside the box he found a plastic baggie containing methamphetamine.

The State charged petitioner with possession of methamphetamine pursuant to Cal. Health & Safety Code Ann. §11377(a) (West 1991). The trial court denied petitioner's motion to suppress the methamphetamine evidence, finding that Cal. Penal Code Ann. §3067(a) (West 2000) authorized the search and that the search was not "arbitrary or capricious." App. 62–63 (Proceedings on Motion to Supress). A jury convicted petitioner of the possession charge and the trial court sentenced him to seven years' imprisonment.

The California Court of Appeal affirmed. Relying on People v. Reyes, 19 Cal. 4th 743, 968 P. 2d 445 (1998), the court held that suspicionless searches of parolees are lawful under California law; that " '[s]uch a search is reasonable within the meaning of the Fourth Amendment as long as it is not arbitrary, capricious or harassing' "; and that the search in this case was not arbitrary, capricious, or harassing. No. A102394 (Ct. App. Cal., 1st App. Dist., Oct. 14, 2004), App. 12–14.

We granted certiorari, 545 U. S. ____ (2005), to answer a variation of the question this Court left open in United States v. Knights, 534 U. S. 112 , n. 6 (2001)—whether a condition of release can so diminish or eliminate a released prisoner's reasonable expectation of privacy that a suspicionless search by a law enforcement officer would not offend the Fourth Amendment .1 Answering that question in the affirmative today, we affirm the judgment of the California Court of Appeal.

II

"[U]nder our general Fourth Amendment approach" we "examin[e] the totality of the circumstances" to determine whether a search is reasonable within the meaning of the Fourth Amendment . Id., at 118 (internal quotation marks omitted). Whether a search is reasonable "is determined by assessing, on the one hand, the degree to which it intrudes upon an individual's privacy and, on the other, the degree to which it is needed for the promotion of legitimate governmental interests." Id., at 118–119 (internal quotation marks omitted).

We recently applied this approach in United States v. Knights. In that case, California law required Knights, as a probationer, to " '[s]ubmit his ... person, property, place of residence, vehicle, personal effects, to search anytime, with or without a search warrant, warrant of arrest or reasonable cause by any probation officer or law enforcement officer.' " Id., at 114 (brackets in original). Several days after Knights had been placed on probation, police suspected that he had been involved in several incidents of arson and vandalism. Based upon that suspicion and pursuant to the search condition of his probation, a police officer conducted a warrantless search of Knights' apartment and found arson and drug paraphernalia. Id., at 115–116.

We concluded that the search of Knights' apartment was reasonable. In evaluating the degree of intrusion into Knights' privacy, we found Knights' probationary status "salient," id., at 118, observing that "[p]robation is 'one point . . . on a continuum of possible punishments ranging from solitary confinement in a maximum-security facility to a few hours of mandatory community service.' " Id., at 119 (quoting Griffin v. Wisconsin, 483 U. S. 868, 874 (1987)). Cf. Hudson v. Palmer, 468 U. S. 517, 530 (1984) (holding that prisoners have no reasonable expectation of privacy). We further observed that, by virtue of their status alone, probationers " 'do not enjoy "the absolute liberty to which every citizen is entitled," ' " Knights, supra, at 119 (quoting Griffin, supra, at 874, in turn quoting Morrissey v. Brewer, 408 U. S. 471, 480 (1972)), justifying the "impos[ition] [of] reasonable conditions that deprive the offender of some freedoms enjoyed by law-abiding citizens." Knights, supra, at 119. We also considered the facts that Knights' probation order clearly set out the probation search condition, and that Knights was clearly informed of the condition. See Knights,534 U. S., at 119. We concluded that under these circumstances, Knights' expectation of privacy was significantly diminished. See id., at 119–120.

We also concluded that probation searches, such as the search of Knights' apartment, are necessary to the promotion of legitimate governmental interests. Noting the State's dual interest in integrating probationers back into the community and combating recidivism, see id., at 120–121, we credited the " 'assumption' " that, by virtue of his status, a probationer " 'is more likely than the ordinary citizen to violate the law.' " Id., at 120 (quoting Griffin, supra, at 880). We further found that "probationers have even more of an incentive to conceal their criminal activities and quickly dispose of incriminating evidence than the ordinary criminal because probationers are aware that they may be subject to supervision and face revocation of probation, and possible incarceration, in proceedings in which the trial rights of a jury and proof beyond a reasonable doubt, among other things, do not apply." Knights, 534 U. S., at 120. We explained that the State did not have to ignore the reality of recidivism or suppress its interests in "protecting potential victims of criminal enterprise" for fear of running afoul of the Fourth Amendment . Id., at 121.

Balancing these interests, we held that "[w]hen an officer has reasonable suspicion that a probationer subject to a search condition is engaged in criminal activity, there is enough likelihood that criminal conduct is occurring that an intrusion on the probationer's significantly diminished privacy interests is reasonable." Ibid. Because the search at issue in Knights was predicated on both the probation search condition and reasonable suspicion, we did not reach the question whether the search would have been reasonable under the Fourth Amendment had it been solely predicated upon the condition of probation. Id., at 120, n. 6. Our attention is directed to that question today, albeit in the context of a parolee search.

III

As we noted in Knights, parolees are on the "continuum" of state-imposed punishments. Id., at 119 (internal quotation marks omitted). On this continuum, parolees have fewer expectations of privacy than probationers, because parole is more akin to imprisonment than probation is to imprisonment. As this Court has pointed out, "parole is an established variation on imprisonment of convicted criminals.... . The essence of parole is release from prison, before the completion of sentence, on the condition that the prisoner abides by certain rules during the balance of the sentence." Morrissey, supra, at 477. "In most cases, the State is willing to extend parole only because it is able to condition it upon compliance with certain requirements." Pennsylvania Bd. of Probation and Parole v. Scott, 524 U. S. 357, 365 (1998) . See also United States v. Reyes, 283 F. 3d 446, 461 (CA2 2002) ("[F]ederal supervised release, ... in contrast to probation, is meted out in addition to, not in lieu of, incarceration" (citation and internal quotation marks omitted)); United States v. Cardona, 903 F. 2d 60, 63 (CA1 1990) ("[O]n the Court's continuum of possible punishments, parole is the stronger medicine; ergo, parolees enjoy even less of the average citizen's absolute liberty than do probationers" (internal quotation marks and citation omitted)).[2]

California's system of parole is consistent with these observations: A California inmate may serve his parole period either in physical custody, or elect to complete his sentence out of physical custody and subject to certain conditions. Cal. Penal Code Ann. §3060.5 (West 2000). Under the latter option, an inmate-turned-parolee remains in the legal custody of the California Department of Corrections through the remainder of his term, §3056, and must comply with all of the terms and conditions of parole, including mandatory drug tests, restrictions on association with felons or gang members, and mandatory meetings with parole officers, Cal. Code Regs., tit. 15, §2512 (2005); Cal. Penal Code Ann. §3067 (West 2000). See also Morrissey, supra, at 478 (discussing other permissible terms and conditions of parole). General conditions of parole also require a parolee to report to his assigned parole officer immediately upon release, inform the parole officer within 72 hours of any change in employment status, request permission to travel a distance of more than 50 miles from the parolee's home, and refrain from criminal conduct and possession of firearms, specified weapons, or knives unrelated to employment. Cal. Code Regs., tit. 15, §2512. Parolees may also be subject to special conditions, including psychiatric treatment programs, mandatory abstinence from alcohol, residence approval, and "[a]ny other condition deemed necessary by the Board [of Parole Hearings] or the Department [of Corrections and Rehabilitation] due to unusual circumstances." §2513. The extent and reach of these conditions clearly demonstrate that parolees like petitioner have severely diminished expectations of privacy by virtue of their status alone.

Additionally, as we found "salient" in Knights with respect to the probation search condition, the parole search condition under California law—requiring inmates who opt for parole to submit to suspicionless searches by a parole officer or other peace officer "at any time," Cal. Penal Code Ann. §3067(a) (West 2000)—was "clearly expressed" to petitioner. Knights, 534 U. S., at 119. He signed an order submitting to the condition and thus was "unambiguously" aware of it. Ibid. In Knights, we found that acceptance of a clear and unambiguous search condition "significantly diminished Knights' reasonable expectation of privacy." Id., at 120. Examining the totality of the circumstances pertaining to petitioner's status as a parolee, "an established variation on imprisonment," Morrissey, 408 U. S., at 477, including the plain terms of the parole search condition, we conclude that petitioner did not have an expectation of privacy that society would recognize as legitimate.3

The State's interests, by contrast, are substantial. This Court has repeatedly acknowledged that a State has an "overwhelming interest" in supervising parolees because "parolees... are more likely to commit future criminal offenses." Pennsylvania Bd. of Probation and Parole, 524 U. S., at 365 (explaining that the interest in combating recidivism "is the very premise behind the system of close parole supervision"). Similarly, this Court has repeatedly acknowledged that a State's interests in reducing recidivism and thereby promoting reintegration and positive citizenship among probationers and parolees warrant privacy intrusions that would not otherwise be tolerated under the Fourth Amendment . See Griffin, 483 U. S., at 879; Knights, supra, at 121.

The empirical evidence presented in this case clearly demonstrates the significance of these interests to the State of California. As of November 30, 2005, California had over 130,000 released parolees. California's parolee population has a 68-to-70 percent recidivism rate. See California Attorney General, Crime in California 37 (Apr. 2001) (explaining that 68 percent of adult parolees are returned to prison, 55 percent for a parole violation, 13 percent for the commission of a new felony offense); J. Petersilia, Challenges of Prisoner Reentry and Parole in California, 12 California Policy Research Center Brief, p. 2 (June 2000), available at http://www.ucop.edu/cprc/parole.pdf (as visited June 15, 2006, and available in Clerk of Court's case file) ("70% of the state's paroled felons reoffend within 18 months—the highest recidivism rate in the nation"). This Court has acknowledged the grave safety concerns that attend recidivism. See Ewing v. California, 538 U. S. 11, 26 (2003) (plurality opinion) ("Recidivism is a serious public safety concern in California and throughout the Nation").

As we made clear in Knights, the Fourth Amendment does not render the States powerless to address these concerns effectively. See 534 U. S., at 121. Contrary to petitioner's contention, California's ability to conduct suspicionless searches of parolees serves its interest in reducing recidivism, in a manner that aids, rather than hinders, the reintegration of parolees into productive society.

In California, an eligible inmate serving a determinate sentence may elect parole when the actual days he has served plus statutory time credits equal the term imposed by the trial court, Cal. Penal Code Ann. §§2931, 2933, 3000(b)(1) (West 2000), irrespective of whether the inmate is capable of integrating himself back into productive society. As the recidivism rate demonstrates, most parolees are ill prepared to handle the pressures of reintegration. Thus, most parolees require intense supervision. The California Legislature has concluded that, given the number of inmates the State paroles and its high recidivism rate, a requirement that searches be based on individualized suspicion would undermine the State's ability to effectively supervise parolees and protect the public from criminal acts by reoffenders. This conclusion makes eminent sense. Imposing a reasonable suspicion requirement, as urged by petitioner, would give parolees greater opportunity to anticipate searches and conceal criminality. See Knights, supra, at 120; Griffin, 483 U. S., at 879. This Court concluded that the incentive-to-conceal concern justified an "intensive" system for supervising probationers in Griffin, id., at 875. That concern applies with even greater force to a system of supervising parolees. See United States v. Reyes, 283 F. 3d, at 461 (observing that the Griffin rationale "appl[ies] a fortiori" to "federal supervised release, which, in contrast to probation, is 'meted out in addition to, not in lieu of, incareration' "); United States v. Crawford, 372 F. 3d 1048, 1077 (CA9 2004) (en banc) (Kleinfeld, J., concurring) (explaining that parolees, in contrast to probationers, "have been

sentenced to prison for felonies and released before the end of their prison terms" and are "deemed to have acted more harmfully than anyone except those felons not released on parole"); Hudson, 468 U. S., at 526 (persons sentenced to terms of imprisonment have been "deemed to have acted more harmfully than anyone except those felons not released on parole"); id., at 529 (observing that it would be "naive" to institute a system of " 'planned random searches' " as that would allow prisoners to "anticipate" searches, thus defeating the purpose of random searches).

Petitioner observes that the majority of States and the Federal Government have been able to further similar interests in reducing recidivism and promoting re-integration, despite having systems that permit parolee searches based upon some level of suspicion. Thus, petitioner contends, California's system is constitutionally defective by comparison. Petitioner's reliance on the practices of jurisdictions other than California, however, is misplaced. That some States and the Federal Government require a level of individualized suspicion is of little relevance to our determination whether California's supervisory system is drawn to meet its needs and is reasonable, taking into account a parolee's substantially diminished expectation of privacy.[4]

Nor is there merit to the argument that California's parole search law permits "a blanket grant of discretion untethered by any procedural safeguards," post, at 1 (Stevens, J., dissenting). The concern that California's suspicionless search system gives officers unbridled discretion to conduct searches, thereby inflicting dignitary harms that arouse strong resentment in parolees and undermine their ability to reintegrate into productive society, is belied by California's prohibition on "arbitrary, capricious or harassing" searches. See Reyes, 19 Cal. 4th, at 752, 753–754, 968 P. 2d, at 450, 451; People v. Bravo, 43 Cal. 3d

600, 610, 738 P. 2d 336, 342 (1987) (probation); see also Cal. Penal Code Ann. §3067(d) (West 2000) ("It is not the intent of the Legislature to authorize law enforcement officers to conduct searches for the sole purpose of harassment").5 The dissent's claim that parolees under California law are subject to capricious searches conducted at the unchecked "whim" of law enforcement officers, post, at 3, 4, ignores this prohibition. Likewise, petitioner's concern that California's suspicionless search law frustrates reintegration efforts by permitting intrusions into the privacy interests of third parties is also unavailing because that concern would arise under a suspicion-based regime as well.

IV

Thus, we conclude that the Fourth Amendment does not prohibit a police officer from conducting a suspicionless search of a parolee. Accordingly, we affirm the judgment of the California Court of Appeal.

It is so ordered.

Scott v. Harris (April 30, 2007) [Notes omitted]

Justice Scalia delivered the opinion of the Court.

We consider whether a law enforcement official can, consistent with the Fourth Amendment, attempt to stop a fleeing motorist from continuing his public-endangering flight by ramming the motorist's car from behind. Put another way: Can an officer take actions that place a fleeing motorist at risk of serious injury or death in order to stop the motorist's flight from endangering the lives of innocent bystanders?

I

In March 2001, a Georgia county deputy clocked respondent's vehicle traveling at 73 miles per hour on a road with a 55-mile-per-hour speed limit. The deputy activated his blue flashing lights indicating that respondent should pull over. Instead, respondent sped away, initiating a chase down what is in most portions a two-lane road, at speeds exceeding 85 miles per hour. The deputy radioed his dispatch to report that he was pursuing a fleeing vehicle, and broadcast its license plate number. Petitioner, Deputy Timothy Scott, heard the radio communication and joined the pursuit along with other officers. In the midst of the chase, respondent pulled into the parking lot of a shopping center and was nearly boxed in by the various police vehicles. Respondent evaded the trap by making a sharp turn, colliding with Scott's police car, exiting the parking lot, and speeding off once again down a two-lane highway.

Following respondent's shopping center maneuvering, which resulted in slight damage to Scott's police car, Scott took over as the lead pursuit vehicle. Six minutes and nearly 10 miles after the chase had begun, Scott decided to attempt to terminate the episode by employing a "Precision Intervention Technique ('PIT') maneuver, which causes the fleeing vehicle to spin to a stop." Brief for Petitioner 4. Having radioed his supervisor for permission, Scott was told to " '[g]o ahead and take him out.' " Harris v. Coweta County, 433 F. 3d 807, 811 (CA11 2005). Instead, Scott applied his push bumper to the rear of respondent's vehicle.1 As a result, respondent lost control of his vehicle, which left the roadway, ran down an embankment, overturned, and crashed. Respondent was badly injured and was rendered a quadriplegic.

Respondent filed suit against Deputy Scott and others under Rev. Stat. §1979, 42 U. S. C. §1983, alleging, inter alia, a violation of his federal constitutional rights, viz. use of excessive force resulting in an unreasonable seizure under the Fourth Amendment . In response, Scott filed a motion for summary judgment based on an assertion of qualified immunity. The District Court denied the motion, finding that "there are material issues of fact on which the issue of qualified immunity turns which present sufficient disagreement to require submission to a jury." Harris v. Coweta County, No. 3:01–CV–148–WBH (ND Ga., Sept. 23, 2003), App. to Pet. for Cert. 41a–42a. On interlocutory appeal,2 the United States Court of Appeals for the Eleventh Circuit affirmed the District Court's decision to allow respondent's Fourth Amendment claim against Scott to proceed to trial.3 Taking respondent's view of the facts as given, the Court of Appeals concluded that Scott's actions could constitute "deadly force" under Tennessee v. Garner, 471 U. S. 1 (1985) , and that the use of such force in this context "would violate [respondent's] constitutional right to be free from excessive force during a seizure. Accordingly, a reasonable jury could find that Scott violated [respondent's] Fourth Amendment rights." 433 F. 3d, at 816. The Court of Appeals further concluded that "the law as it existed [at the time of the incident], was sufficiently clear to give reasonable law enforcement officers 'fair notice' that ramming a vehicle under these circumstances was unlawful." Id., at 817. The Court of Appeals thus concluded that Scott was not entitled to qualified immunity. We granted certiorari, 549 U. S. __ (2006), and now reverse.

II

In resolving questions of qualified immunity, courts are required to resolve a "threshold question: Taken in the light most favorable to the party asserting the injury, do the facts alleged show the officer's conduct violated a constitutional right? This must be the initial inquiry." Saucier v. Katz, 533 U. S. 194, 201 (2001) . If, and only if, the court finds a violation of a constitutional right, "the next, sequential step is to ask whether the right was clearly established ... in light of the specific context of the case." Ibid. Although this ordering contradicts "[o]ur policy of avoiding unnecessary adjudication of constitutional issues," United States v. Treasury

Employees, 513 U. S. 454, 478 (1995) (citing Ashwander v. TVA, 297 U. S. 288, 346–347 (1936) (Brandeis, J., concurring)), we have said that such a departure from practice is "necessary to set forth principles which will become the basis for a [future] holding that a right is clearly established." Saucier, supra, at 201.4 We therefore turn to the threshold inquiry: whether Deputy Scott's actions violated the Fourth Amendment.

III

A

The first step in assessing the constitutionality of Scott's actions is to determine the relevant facts. As this case was decided on summary judgment, there have not yet been factual findings by a judge or jury, and respondent's version of events (unsurprisingly) differs substantially from Scott's version. When things are in such a posture, courts are required to view the facts and draw reasonable inferences "in the light most favorable to the party opposing the [summary judgment] motion." United States v. Diebold, Inc., 369 U. S. 654, 655 (1962) (per curiam); Saucier, supra, at 201. In qualified immunity cases, this usually means adopting (as the Court of Appeals did here) the plaintiff's version of the facts.

There is, however, an added wrinkle in this case: existence in the record of a videotape capturing the events in question. There are no allegations or indications that this videotape was doctored or altered in any way, nor any contention that what it depicts differs from what actually happened. The videotape quite clearly contradicts the version of the story told by respondent and adopted by the Court of Appeals.5 For example, the Court of Appeals adopted respondent's assertions that, during the chase, "there was little, if any, actual threat to pedestrians or other motorists, as the roads were mostly empty and [respondent] remained in control of his vehicle." 433 F. 3d, at 815. Indeed, reading the lower court's opinion, one gets the impression that respondent, rather than fleeing from police, was attempting to pass his driving test:

"[T]aking the facts from the non-movant's viewpoint, [respondent] remained in control of his vehicle, slowed for turns and intersections, and typically used his indicators for turns. He did not run any motorists off the road. Nor was he a threat to pedestrians in the shopping center parking lot, which was free from pedestrian and vehicular traffic as the center was closed. Significantly, by the time the parties were back on the highway and Scott rammed [respondent], the motorway had been cleared of motorists and pedestrians allegedly because of police blockades of the nearby intersections." Id., at 815–816 (citations omitted).

The videotape tells quite a different story. There we see respondent's vehicle racing down narrow, two-lane roads in the dead of night at speeds that are shockingly fast. We see it swerve around more than a dozen other cars, cross the double-yellow line, and force cars traveling in both directions to their respective shoulders to avoid being hit.6 We see it run multiple red lights and travel for considerable periods of time in the occasional center left-turn-only lane, chased by numerous police cars forced to engage in the same hazardous maneuvers just to keep up. Far from being the cautious and controlled driver the lower court depicts, what we see on the video more closely resembles a Hollywood-style car chase of the most frightening sort, placing police officers and innocent bystanders alike at great risk of serious injury.7

At the summary judgment stage, facts must be viewed in the light most favorable to the nonmoving party only if there is a "genuine" dispute as to those facts. Fed. Rule Civ. Proc. 56(c). As we have emphasized, "[w]hen the moving party has carried its burden under Rule 56(c), its opponent must do more than simply show that there is some metaphysical doubt as to the material facts... . Where the record taken as a whole could not lead a rational trier of fact to find for the nonmoving party, there is no 'genuine issue for trial.' " Matsushita Elec. Industrial Co. v. Zenith Radio Corp., 475 U. S. 574, 586–587 (1986) (footnote omitted). "[T]he mere existence of some alleged factual dispute between the parties will not defeat an otherwise properly supported motion for summary judgment; the requirement is that there be no genuine issue of material fact." Anderson v. Liberty Lobby, Inc., 477 U. S. 242, 247–248 (1986). When opposing parties tell two different stories, one of which is blatantly contradicted by the record, so that no reasonable jury could believe it, a court should not adopt that version of the facts for purposes of ruling on a motion for summary judgment.

That was the case here with regard to the factual issue whether respondent was driving in such fashion as to endanger human life. Respondent's version of events is so utterly discredited by the record that no reasonable jury could have believed him. The Court of Appeals should not have relied on such visible fiction; it should have viewed the facts in the light depicted by the videotape.

B

Judging the matter on that basis, we think it is quite clear that Deputy Scott did not violate the Fourth Amendment. Scott does not contest that his decision to terminate the car chase by ramming his bumper into respondent's vehicle constituted a "seizure." "[A] Fourth Amendment seizure [occurs] ... when there is a governmental termination of freedom of movement through means intentionally applied." Brower v. County of Inyo, 489 U. S. 593, 596–597 (1989) (emphasis deleted). See also id., at 597 ("If ... the police cruiser had pulled alongside the fleeing car and sideswiped it, producing the crash, then the termination of the suspect's freedom of movement would have been a seizure"). It is also conceded, by both sides, that a claim of "excessive force in the course of making [a] ...'seizure' of [the] person ... [is] properly analyzed under the Fourth Amendment 's 'objective reasonableness' standard." Graham v. Connor, 490 U. S. 386, 388 (1989) . The question we need to answer is whether Scott's actions were objectively reasonable.8

1

Respondent urges us to analyze this case as we analyzed Garner, 471 U. S. 1. See Brief for Respondent 16–29. We must first decide, he says, whether the actions Scott took constituted "deadly force." (He defines "deadly force" as "any use of force which creates a substantial likelihood of causing death or serious bodily injury," id., at 19.) If so, respondent claims that Garner prescribes certain preconditions that must be met before Scott's actions can survive Fourth Amendment scrutiny: (1) The suspect must have posed an immediate threat of serious physical harm to the officer or others; (2) deadly force must have been necessary to prevent escape;9 and (3) where feasible, the officer must have given the suspect some warning. See Brief for Respondent 17–18 (citing Garner, supra, at 9–12). Since these Garner preconditions for using deadly force were not met in this case, Scott's actions were per se unreasonable.

Respondent's argument falters at its first step; Garner did not establish a magical on/off switch that triggers rigid preconditions whenever an officer's actions constitute "deadly force." Garner was simply an application of the Fourth Amendment 's "reasonableness" test, Graham, supra, at 388, to the use of a particular type of force in a particular situation. Garner held that it was unreasonable to kill a "young, slight, and unarmed" burglary suspect, 471 U. S., at 21, by shooting him "in the back of the head" while he was running away on foot, id., at 4, and when the officer "could not reasonably have believed that [the suspect] ... posed any threat," and "never

attempted to justify his actions on any basis other than the need to prevent an escape," id., at 21. Whatever Garner said about the factors that might have justified shooting the suspect in that case, such "preconditions" have scant applicability to this case, which has vastly different facts. "Garner had nothing to do with one car striking another or even with car chases in general ... . A police car's bumping a fleeing car is, in fact, not much like a policeman's shooting a gun so as to hit a person." Adams v. St. Lucie County Sheriff's Dept., 962 F. 2d 1563, 1577 (CA11 1992) (Edmondson, J., dissenting), adopted by 998 F. 2d 923 (CA11 1993) (en banc) (per curiam). Nor is the threat posed by the flight on foot of an unarmed suspect even remotely comparable to the extreme danger to human life posed by respondent in this case. Although respondent's attempt to craft an easy-to-apply legal test in the Fourth Amendment context is admirable, in the end we must still slosh our way through the factbound morass of "reasonableness." Whether or not Scott's actions constituted application of "deadly force," all that matters is whether Scott's actions were reasonable.

2

In determining the reasonableness of the manner in which a seizure is effected, "[w]e must balance the nature and quality of the intrusion on the individual's Fourth Amendment interests against the importance of the governmental interests alleged to justify the intrusion." United States v. Place, 462 U. S. 696, 703 (1983) . Scott defends his actions by pointing to the paramount governmental interest in ensuring public safety, and respondent nowhere suggests this was not the purpose motivating Scott's behavior. Thus, in judging whether Scott's actions were reasonable, we must consider the risk of bodily harm that Scott's actions posed to respondent in light of the threat to the public that Scott was trying to eliminate. Although there is no obvious way to quantify the risks on either side, it is clear from the videotape that respondent posed an actual and imminent threat to the lives of any pedestrians who might have been present, to other civilian motorists, and to the officers involved in the chase. See Part III–A, supra. It is equally clear that Scott's actions posed a high likelihood of serious injury or death to respondent—though not the near certainty of death posed by, say, shooting a fleeing felon in the back of the head, see Garner, supra, at 4, or pulling alongside a fleeing motorist's car and shooting the motorist, cf. Vaughan v. Cox, 343 F. 3d 1323, 1326–1327 (CA11 2003). So how does a court go about weighing the perhaps lesser probability of injuring or killing numerous bystanders against the perhaps larger probability of injuring or killing a single person? We think it appropriate in this process to take into account not only the number of lives at risk, but also their relative culpability. It was respondent, after all, who intentionally placed himself and the public in danger by unlawfully engaging in the reckless, high-speed flight that ultimately produced the choice between two evils that Scott confronted. Multiple police cars, with blue lights flashing and sirens blaring, had been chasing respondent for nearly 10 miles, but he ignored their warning to stop. By contrast, those who might have been harmed had Scott not taken the action he did were entirely innocent. We have little difficulty in concluding it was reasonable for Scott to take the action that he did.10

But wait, says respondent: Couldn't the innocent public equally have been protected, and the tragic accident entirely avoided, if the police had simply ceased their pursuit? We think the police need not have taken that chance and hoped for the best. Whereas Scott's action—ramming respondent off the road—was certain to eliminate the risk that respondent posed to the public, ceasing pursuit was not. First of all, there would have been no way to convey convincingly to respondent that the chase was off, and that he was free to go. Had respondent looked in his rear-view mirror and seen the police cars deactivate their flashing lights and turn around, he would have had no idea whether they were truly letting him get away, or simply devising a new strategy for capture. Perhaps the police knew a shortcut he didn't know, and would reappear down the road to intercept him; or perhaps they were setting up a roadblock in his path. Cf. Brower, 489 U. S., at 594. Given such uncertainty, respondent might have been just as likely to respond by continuing to drive recklessly as by slowing down and wiping his brow.11

Second, we are loath to lay down a rule requiring the police to allow fleeing suspects to get away whenever they drive so recklessly that they put other people's lives in danger. It is obvious the perverse incentives such a rule would create: Every fleeing motorist would know that escape is within his grasp, if only he accelerates to 90 miles per hour, crosses the double-yellow line a few times, and runs a few red lights. The Constitution assuredly does not impose this invitation to impunity-earned-by-recklessness. Instead, we lay down a more sensible rule: A police officer's attempt to terminate a dangerous high-speed car chase that threatens the lives of innocent bystanders does not violate the Fourth Amendment , even when it places the fleeing motorist at risk of serious injury or death.

*   *   *

The car chase that respondent initiated in this case posed a substantial and immediate risk of serious physical injury to others; no reasonable jury could conclude otherwise. Scott's attempt to terminate the chase by forcing respondent off the road was reasonable, and Scott is entitled to summary judgment. The Court of Appeals' decision to the contrary is reversed.

It is so ordered.

Brendlin v. California (June 18, 2007)

[Notes omitted]

Justice Souter delivered the opinion of the Court.

When a police officer makes a traffic stop, the driver of the car is seized within the meaning of the Fourth Amendment. The question in this case is whether the same is true of a passenger. We hold that a passenger is seized as well and so may challenge the constitutionality of the stop.

I

Early in the morning of November 27, 2001, Deputy Sheriff Robert Brokenbrough and his partner saw a parked Buick with expired registration tags. In his ensuing conversation with the police dispatcher, Brokenbrough learned that an application for renewal of registration was being processed. The officers saw the car again on the road, and this time Brokenbrough noticed its display of a temporary operating permit with the number "11," indicating it was legal to drive the car through November. App. 115. The officers decided to pull the Buick over to verify that the permit matched the vehicle, even though, as Brokenbrough admitted later, there was nothing unusual about the permit or the way it was affixed. Brokenbrough asked the driver, Karen Simeroth, for her license and saw a passenger in the front seat, petitioner Bruce Brendlin, whom he recognized as "one of the Brendlin brothers." Id., at 65. He recalled that either Scott or Bruce Brendlin had dropped out of parole supervision and asked Brendlin to identify himself.1 Brokenbrough returned to his cruiser, called for backup, and verified that Brendlin was a parole violator with an outstanding no-bail warrant for his arrest. While he was in the patrol car, Brokenbrough saw Brendlin briefly open and then close the passenger door of the Buick. Once reinforcements arrived, Brokenbrough went to the passenger side of the Buick, ordered him out of the car at gunpoint, and declared him under arrest. When the police searched Brendlin incident to arrest, they found an orange syringe cap on his person. A patdown search of Simeroth revealed syringes and a plastic bag of a green leafy substance, and she was also formally arrested. Officers then searched the car and found tubing, a scale, and other things used to produce methamphetamine.

Brendlin was charged with possession and manufacture of methamphetamine, and he moved to suppress the evidence obtained in the searches of his person and the car as fruits of an unconstitutional seizure, arguing that the officers lacked probable cause or reasonable suspicion to make the traffic stop. He did not assert that his Fourth Amendment rights were violated by the search of Simeroth's vehicle, cf. Rakas v. Illinois, 439 U. S. 128 (1978), but claimed only that the traffic stop was an unlawful seizure of his person. The trial court denied the suppression motion after finding that the stop was lawful and Brendlin was not seized until Brokenbrough ordered him out of the car and formally arrested him. Brendlin pleaded guilty, subject to appeal on the suppression issue, and was sentenced to four years in prison.

The California Court of Appeal reversed the denial of the suppression motion, holding that Brendlin was seized by the traffic stop, which they held unlawful. 8 Cal. Rptr. 3d 882 (2004) (officially depublished). By a narrow majority, the Supreme Court of California reversed. The State Supreme Court noted California's concession that the officers had no reasonable basis to suspect unlawful operation of the car, 38 Cal. 4th 1107, 1114, 136 P. 3d 845, 848 (2006),2 but still held suppression unwarranted because a passenger "is not seized as a constitutional matter in the absence of additional circumstances that would indicate to a reasonable person that he or she was the subject of the peace officer's investigation or show of authority," id., at 1111, 136 P. 3d, at 846. The court reasoned that Brendlin was not seized by the traffic stop because Simeroth was its exclusive target, id., at 1118, 136 P. 3d, at 851, that a passenger cannot submit to an officer's show of authority while the driver controls the car, id., at 1118–1119, 135 P. 3d, at 851–852, and that once a car has been pulled off the road, a passenger "would feel free to depart or otherwise to conduct his or her affairs as though the police were not present," id., at 1119, 136 P. 3d, at 852. In dissent, Justice Corrigan said that a traffic stop entails the seizure of a passenger even when the driver is the sole target of police investigation because a passenger is detained for the purpose of ensuring an officer's safety and would not feel free to leave the car without the officer's permission. Id., at 1125, 136 P. 3d, at 856.

We granted certiorari to decide whether a traffic stop subjects a passenger, as well as the driver, to Fourth Amendment seizure, 549 U. S. ___ (2007). We now vacate.

II

A

A person is seized by the police and thus entitled to challenge the government's action under the Fourth Amendment when the officer, " 'by means of physical force or show of authority,' " terminates or restrains his freedom of movement, Florida v. Bostick, 501 U. S. 429, 434 (1991) (quoting Terry v. Ohio, 392 U. S. 1, 19, n. 16 (1968)), "through means intentionally applied," Brower v. County of Inyo, 489 U. S. 593, 597 (1989) (emphasis in original). Thus, an "unintended person ... [may be] the object of the detention," so long as the detention is "willful" and not merely the consequence of "an unknowing act." Id., at 596; cf. County of Sacramento v. Lewis, 523 U. S. 833, 844 (1998) (no seizure where a police officer accidentally struck and killed a motorcycle passenger during a high-speed pursuit). A police officer may make a seizure by a show of authority and without the use of physical force, but there is

no seizure without actual submission; otherwise, there is at most an attempted seizure, so far as the Fourth Amendment is concerned. See California v. Hodari D., 499 U. S. 621 , n. 2 (1991); Lewis, supra, at 844, 845, n. 7.

When the actions of the police do not show an unambiguous intent to restrain or when an individual's submission to a show of governmental authority takes the form of passive acquiescence, there needs to be some test for telling when a seizure occurs in response to authority, and when it does not. The test was devised by Justice Stewart in United States v. Mendenhall, 446 U. S. 544 (1980) , who wrote that a seizure occurs if "in view of all of the circumstances surrounding the incident, a reasonable person would have believed that he was not free to leave," id., at 554 (principal opinion). Later on, the Court adopted Justice Stewart's touchstone, see, e.g., Hodari D., supra, at 627; Michigan v. Chesternut, 486 U. S. 567, 573 (1988) ; INS v. Delgado, 466 U. S. 210, 215 (1984) , but added that when a person "has no desire to leave" for reasons unrelated to the police presence, the "coercive effect of the encounter" can be measured better by asking whether "a reasonable person would feel free to decline the officers' requests or otherwise terminate the encounter," Bostick, supra, at 435–436; see also United States v. Drayton, 536 U. S. 194, 202 (2002) .

The law is settled that in Fourth Amendment terms a traffic stop entails a seizure of the driver "even though the purpose of the stop is limited and the resulting detention quite brief." Delaware v. Prouse, 440 U. S. 648, 653 (1979) ; see also Whren v. United States, 517 U. S. 806, 809–810 (1996) . And although we have not, until today, squarely answered the question whether a passenger is also seized, we have said over and over in dicta that during a traffic stop an officer seizes everyone in the vehicle, not just the driver. See, e.g., Prouse, supra, at 653 ("[S]topping an automobile and detaining its occupants constitute a 'seizure' within the meaning of [the Fourth and Fourteenth] Amendments"); Colorado v. Bannister, 449 U. S. 1, 4, n. 3 (1980) (per curiam) ("There can be no question that the stopping of a vehicle and the detention of its occupants constitute a 'seizure' within the meaning of the Fourth Amendment "); Berkemer v. McCarty, 468 U. S. 420, 436–437 (1984) ("[W]e have long acknowledged that stopping an automobile and detaining its occupants constitute a seizure" (internal quotation marks omitted)); United States v. Hensley, 469 U. S. 221, 226 (1985) ("[S]topping a car and detaining its occupants constitute a seizure"); Whren, supra, at 809–810 ("Temporary detention of individuals during the stop of an automobile by the police, even if only for a brief period and for a limited purpose, constitutes a 'seizure' of 'persons' within the meaning of [the Fourth Amendment]").

We have come closest to the question here in two cases dealing with unlawful seizure of a passenger, and neither time did we indicate any distinction between driver and passenger that would affect the Fourth Amendment analysis. Delaware v. Prouse considered grounds for stopping a car on the road and held that Prouse's suppression motion was properly granted. We spoke of the arresting officer's testimony that Prouse was in the back seat when the car was pulled over, see 440 U. S., at 650, n. 1, described Prouse as an occupant, not as the driver, and referred to the car's "occupants" as being seized, id., at 653. Justification for stopping a car was the issue again in Whren v. United States, where we passed upon a Fourth Amendment challenge by two petitioners who moved to suppress drug evidence found during the course of a traffic stop. See 517 U. S., at 809. Both driver and passenger claimed to have been seized illegally when the police stopped the car; we agreed and held suppression unwarranted only because the stop rested on probable cause. Id., at 809–810, 819.

B

The State concedes that the police had no adequate justification to pull the car over, see n. 2, supra, but argues that the passenger was not seized and thus cannot claim that the evidence was tainted by an unconstitutional stop. We resolve this question by asking whether a reasonable person in Brendlin's position when the car stopped would have believed himself free to "terminate the encounter" between the police and himself. Bostick, supra, at 436. We think that in these circumstances any reasonable passenger would have understood the police officers to be exercising control to the point that no one in the car was free to depart without police permission.

A traffic stop necessarily curtails the travel a passenger has chosen just as much as it halts the driver, diverting both from the stream of traffic to the side of the road, and the police activity that normally amounts to intrusion on "privacy and personal security" does not normally (and did not here) distinguish between passenger and driver. United States v. Martinez-Fuerte, 428 U. S. 543, 554 (1976) . An officer who orders one particular car to pull over acts with an implicit claim of right based on fault of some sort, and a sensible person would not expect a police officer to allow people to come and go freely from the physical focal point of an investigation into faulty behavior or wrongdoing. If the likely wrongdoing is not the driving, the passenger will reasonably feel subject to suspicion owing to close association; but even when the wrongdoing is only bad driving, the passenger will expect to be subject to some scrutiny, and his attempt to leave the scene would be so obviously likely to prompt an objection from the officer that no passenger would feel free to leave in the first place. Cf. Drayton, supra, at 197–199, 203–204 (finding no seizure when police officers boarded a stationary bus and asked passengers for permission to search for drugs).[3]

It is also reasonable for passengers to expect that a police officer at the scene of a crime, arrest, or investigation will not let people move around in ways that could jeopardize his safety. In Maryland v. Wilson, 519 U. S. 408 (1997), we held that during a lawful traffic stop an officer may order a passenger out of the car as a precautionary measure, without reasonable suspicion that the passenger poses a safety risk. Id., at 414–415; cf. Pennsylvania v. Mimms, 434 U. S. 106 (1977) (per curiam) (driver may be ordered out of the car as a matter of course). In fashioning this rule, we invoked our earlier statement that " '[t]he risk of harm to both the police and the occupants is minimized if the officers routinely exercise unquestioned command of the situation.' " Wilson, supra, at 414 (quoting Michigan v. Summers, 452 U. S. 692, 702–703 (1981)). What we have said in these opinions probably reflects a societal expectation of " 'unquestioned [police] command' " at odds with any notion that a passenger would feel free to leave, or to terminate the personal encounter any other way, without advance permission. Wilson, supra, at 414.4

Our conclusion comports with the views of all nine Federal Courts of Appeals, and nearly every state court, to have ruled on the question. See United States v. Kimball, 25 F. 3d 1, 5 (CA1 1994); United States v. Mosley, 454 F. 3d 249, 253 (CA3 2006); United States v. Rusher, 966 F. 2d 868, 874, n. 4 (CA4 1992); United States v. Grant, 349 F. 3d 192, 196 (CA5 2003); United States v. Perez, 440 F. 3d 363, 369 (CA6 2006); United States v. Powell, 929 F. 2d 1190, 1195 (CA7 1991); United States v. Ameling, 328 F. 3d 443, 446–447, n. 3 (CA8 2003); United States v. Twilley, 222 F. 3d 1092, 1095 (CA9 2000); United States v. Eylicio-Montoya, 70 F. 3d 1158, 1163–1164 (CA10 1995); State v. Bowers, 334 Ark. 447, 451–452, 976 S. W. 2d 379, 381–382 (1998); State v. Haworth, 106 Idaho 405, 405–406, 679 P. 2d 1123, 1123–1124 (1984); People v. Bunch, 207 Ill. 2d 7, 13, 796

N. E. 2d 1024, 1029 (2003); State v. Eis, 348 N. W. 2d 224, 226 (Iowa 1984); State v. Hodges, 252 Kan. 989, 1002–1005, 851 P. 2d 352, 361–362 (1993); State v. Carter, 69 Ohio St. 3d 57, 63, 630 N. E. 2d 355, 360 (1994) (per curiam); State v. Harris, 206 Wis. 2d 243, 253–258, 557 N. W. 2d 245, 249–251 (1996). And the treatise writers share this prevailing judicial view that a passenger may bring a Fourth Amendment challenge to the legality of a traffic stop. See, e.g., 6 W. LaFave, Search and Seizure §11.3(e), pp. 194, 195, and n. 277 (4th ed. 2004 and Supp. 2007) ("If either the stopping of the car, the length of the passenger's detention thereafter, or the passenger's removal from it are unreasonable in a Fourth Amendment sense, then surely the passenger has standing to object to those constitutional violations and to have suppressed any evidence found in the car which is their fruit" (footnote omitted)); 1 W. Ringel, Searches & Seizures, Arrests and Confessions §11:20, p. 11–98 (2d ed. 2007) ("[A] law enforcement officer's stop of an automobile results in a seizure of both the driver and the passenger").5

C

The contrary conclusion drawn by the Supreme Court of California, that seizure came only with formal arrest, reflects three premises as to which we respectfully disagree. First, the State Supreme Court reasoned that Brendlin was not seized by the stop because Deputy Sheriff Brokenbrough only intended to investigate Simeroth and did not direct a show of authority toward Brendlin. The court saw Brokenbrough's "flashing lights [as] directed at the driver," and pointed to the lack of record evidence that Brokenbrough "was even aware [Brendlin] was in the car prior to the vehicle stop." 38 Cal. 4th, at 1118, 136 P. 3d, at 851. But that view of the facts ignores the objective Mendenhall test of what a reasonable passenger would understand. To the extent that there is anything ambiguous in the show of force (was it fairly seen as directed only at the driver or at the car and its occupants?), the test resolves the ambiguity, and here it leads to the intuitive conclusion that all the occupants were subject to like control by the successful display of authority. The State Supreme Court's approach, on the contrary, shifts the issue from the intent of the police as objectively manifested to the motive of the police for taking the intentional action to stop the car, and we have repeatedly rejected attempts to introduce this kind of subjectivity into Fourth Amendment analysis. See, e.g., Whren, 517 U. S., at 813 ("Subjective intentions play no role in ordinary, probable-cause Fourth Amendment analysis"); Chesternut, 486 U. S., at 575, n. 7 ("[T]he subjective intent of the officers is relevant to an assessment of the Fourth Amendment implications of police conduct only to the extent that that intent has been conveyed to the person confronted"); Mendenhall, 446 U. S., at 554, n. 6 (principal opinion) (disregarding a Government agent's subjective intent to detain Mendenhall); cf. Rakas, 439 U. S., at 132–135 (rejecting the "target theory" of Fourth Amendment standing, which would have allowed "any criminal defendant at whom a search was directed" to challenge the legality of the search (internal quotation marks omitted)).

California defends the State Supreme Court's ruling on this point by citing our cases holding that seizure requires a purposeful, deliberate act of detention. See Brief for Respondent 9–14. But Chesternut, supra, answers that argument. The intent that counts under the Fourth Amendment is the "intent [that] has been conveyed to the person confronted," id., at 575, n. 7, and the criterion of willful restriction on freedom of movement is no invitation to look to subjective intent when determining who is seized. Our most recent cases are in accord on this point. In Lewis, 523 U. S. 833 , we considered whether a seizure occurred when an officer accidentally ran

over a passenger who had fallen off a motorcycle during a high-speed chase, and in holding that no seizure took place, we stressed that the officer stopped Lewis's movement by accidentally crashing into him, not "through means intentionally applied." Id., at 844 (emphasis deleted). We did not even consider, let alone emphasize, the possibility that the officer had meant to detain the driver only and not the passenger. Nor is Brower, 489 U. S. 593 , to the contrary, where it was dispositive that "Brower was meant to be stopped by the physical obstacle of the roadblock—and that he was so stopped." Id., at 599. California reads this language to suggest that for a specific occupant of the car to be seized he must be the motivating target of an officer's show of authority, see Brief for Respondent 12, as if the thrust of our observation were that Brower, and not someone else, was "meant to be stopped." But our point was not that Brower alone was the target but that officers detained him "through means intentionally applied"; if the car had had another occupant, it would have made sense to hold that he too had been seized when the car collided with the roadblock. Neither case, then, is at odds with our holding that the issue is whether a reasonable passenger would have perceived that the show of authority was at least partly directed at him, and that he was thus not free to ignore the police presence and go about his business.

Second, the Supreme Court of California assumed that Brendlin, "as the passenger, had no ability to submit to the deputy's show of authority" because only the driver was in control of the moving vehicle. 38 Cal. 4th, at 1118, 1119, 136 P. 3d, at 852. But what may amount to submission depends on what a person was doing before the show of authority: a fleeing man is not seized until he is physically overpowered, but one sitting in a chair may submit to authority by not getting up to run away. Here, Brendlin had no effective way to signal submission while the car was still moving on the roadway, but once it came to a stop he could, and apparently did, submit by staying inside.

Third, the State Supreme Court shied away from the rule we apply today for fear that it "would encompass even those motorists following the vehicle subject to the traffic stop who, by virtue of the original detention, are forced to slow down and perhaps even come to a halt in order to accommodate that vehicle's submission to police authority." Id., at 1120, 136 P. 3d, at 853. But an occupant of a car who knows that he is stuck in traffic because another car has been pulled over (like the motorist who can't even make out why the road is suddenly clogged) would not perceive a show of authority as directed at him or his car. Such incidental restrictions on freedom of movement would not tend to affect an individual's "sense of security and privacy in traveling in an automobile." Prouse, 440 U. S., at 662. Nor would the consequential blockage call for a precautionary rule to avoid the kind of "arbitrary and oppressive interference by [law] enforcement officials with the privacy and personal security of individuals" that the Fourth Amendment was intended to limit. Martinez-Fuerte, 428 U. S., at 554.6

Indeed, the consequence to worry about would not flow from our conclusion, but from the rule that almost all courts have rejected. Holding that the passenger in a private car is not (without more) seized in a traffic stop would invite police officers to stop cars with passengers regardless of probable cause or reasonable suspicion of anything illegal.7 The fact that evidence uncovered as a result of an arbitrary traffic stop would still be admissible against any passengers would be a powerful incentive to run the kind of "roving patrols" that would still violate the driver's Fourth Amendment right. See, e.g., Almeida-Sanchez v. United States, 413 U. S. 266, 273 (1973) (stop and search by Border Patrol agents without a warrant or probable cause violated the Fourth Amendment); Prouse, supra, at 663 (police spot check of driver's license and registration without reasonable suspicion violated the Fourth Amendment).

*   *   *

Brendlin was seized from the moment Simeroth's car came to a halt on the side of the road, and it was error to deny his suppression motion on the ground that seizure occurred only at the formal arrest. It will be for the state courts to consider in the first instance whether suppression turns on any other issue. The judgment of the Supreme Court of California is vacated, and the case is remanded for further proceedings not inconsistent with this opinion.

It is so ordered.

Herring v. US (Jan 14, 2009) [Notes omitted]

Chief Justice Roberts delivered the opinion of the Court.

The Fourth Amendment forbids "unreasonable searches and seizures," and this usually requires the police to have probable cause or a warrant before making an arrest. What if an officer reasonably believes there is an outstanding arrest warrant, but that belief turns out to be wrong because of a negligent bookkeeping error by another police employee? The parties here agree that the ensuing arrest is still a violation of the Fourth Amendment, but dispute whether contraband found during a search incident to that arrest must be excluded in a later prosecution.

Our cases establish that such suppression is not an automatic consequence of a Fourth Amendment violation. Instead, the question turns on the culpability of the police and the potential of exclusion to deter wrongful police conduct. Here the error was the result of isolated negligence attenuated from the arrest. We hold that in these circumstances the jury should not be barred from considering all the evidence.

I

On July 7, 2004, Investigator Mark Anderson learned that Bennie Dean Herring had driven to the Coffee County Sheriff's Department to retrieve something from his impounded truck. Herring was no stranger to law enforcement, and Anderson asked the county's warrant clerk, Sandy Pope, to check for any outstanding warrants for Herring's arrest. When she found none, Anderson asked Pope to check with Sharon Morgan, her counterpart in neighboring Dale County. After checking Dale County's computer database, Morgan replied that there was an active arrest warrant for Herring's failure to appear on a felony charge. Pope relayed the information to Anderson and asked Morgan to fax over a copy of the warrant as confirmation. Anderson and a deputy followed Herring as he left the impound lot, pulled him over, and arrested him. A search incident to the arrest revealed methamphetamine in Herring's pocket, and a pistol (which as a felon he could not possess) in his vehicle. App. 17–23.

There had, however, been a mistake about the warrant. The Dale County sheriff's computer records are supposed to correspond to actual arrest warrants, which the office also maintains. But when Morgan went to the files to retrieve the actual warrant to fax to Pope, Morgan was unable to find it. She called a court clerk and learned that the warrant had been recalled five months earlier. Normally when a warrant is recalled the court clerk's office or a judge's chambers calls Morgan, who enters the information in the sheriff's computer database and disposes of the physical copy. For whatever reason, the information about the recall of the warrant for Herring did not appear in the database. Morgan immediately called Pope to alert her to the mixup, and Pope contacted Anderson over a secure radio. This all unfolded in 10 to 15 minutes, but Herring had already been arrested and found with the gun and drugs, just a few hundred yards from the sheriff's office. Id., at 26, 35–42, 54–55.

Herring was indicted in the District Court for the Middle District of Alabama for illegally possessing the gun and drugs, violations of 18 U. S. C. §922(g)(1) and 21 U. S. C. §844(a). He moved to suppress the evidence on the ground that his initial arrest had been illegal because the warrant had been rescinded. The Magistrate Judge recommended denying the motion because the arresting officers had acted in a good-faith belief that the warrant was still outstanding. Thus, even if there were a Fourth Amendment violation, there was "no reason to believe that application of the exclusionary rule here would deter the occurrence of any future mistakes." App. 70. The District Court adopted the Magistrate Judge's recommendation, 451 F. Supp. 2d 1290 (2005), and the Court of Appeals for the Eleventh Circuit affirmed, 492 F. 3d 1212 (2007).

The Eleventh Circuit found that the arresting officers in Coffee County "were entirely innocent of any wrongdoing or carelessness." id., at 1218. The court assumed that whoever failed to update the Dale County sheriff's records was also a law enforcement official, but noted that "the conduct in question [wa]s a negligent failure to act, not a deliberate or tactical choice to act." Ibid. Because the error was merely negligent and attenuated from the arrest, the Eleventh Circuit concluded that the benefit of suppressing the evidence "would be marginal or nonexistent," ibid. (internal quotation marks omitted), and the evidence was therefore admissible under the good-faith rule of United States v. Leon, 468 U. S. 897 (1984).

Other courts have required exclusion of evidence obtained through similar police errors, e.g., Hoay v. State, 348 Ark. 80, 86–87, 71 S. W. 3d 573, 577 (2002), so we granted Herring's petition for certiorari to resolve the conflict, 552 U. S. ____ (2008). We now affirm the Eleventh Circuit's judgment.

II

When a probable-cause determination was based on reasonable but mistaken assumptions, the person subjected to a search or seizure has not necessarily been the victim of a constitutional violation. The very phrase "probable cause" confirms that the Fourth Amendment does not demand all possible precision. And whether the error can be traced to a mistake by a state actor or some other source may bear on the analysis. For purposes of deciding this case, however, we accept the parties' assumption that there was a Fourth Amendment violation. The issue is whether the exclusionary rule should be applied.

A

The Fourth Amendment protects "[t]he right of the people to be secure in their persons, houses, papers, and effects, against unreasonable searches and seizures," but "contains no provision expressly precluding the use of evidence obtained in violation of its commands," Arizona v. Evans, 514 U. S. 1, 10 (1995) . Nonetheless, our decisions establish an exclusionary rule that, when applicable, forbids the use of improperly obtained evidence at trial. See, e.g., Weeks v. United States, 232 U. S. 383, 398 (1914) . We have stated that this judicially created rule is "designed to safeguard Fourth Amendment rights generally through its deterrent effect." United States v. Calandra, 414 U. S. 338, 348 (1974) .

In analyzing the applicability of the rule, Leon admonished that we must consider the actions of all the police officers involved. 468 U. S., at 923, n. 24 ("It is necessary to consider the objective reasonableness, not only of the officers who eventually executed a warrant, but also of the officers who originally obtained it or who provided information material to the probable-cause determination"). The Coffee County officers did nothing improper. Indeed, the error was noticed so quickly because Coffee County requested a faxed confirmation of the warrant.

The Eleventh Circuit concluded, however, that somebody in Dale County should have updated the computer database to reflect the recall of the arrest warrant. The court also concluded that this error was negligent, but did not find it to be reckless or deliberate. 492 F. 3d, at 1218.1 That fact is crucial to our holding that this error is not enough by itself to require "the extreme sanction of exclusion." Leon, supra, at 916.

B

1. The fact that a Fourth Amendment violation occurred—i.e., that a search or arrest was unreasonable—does not necessarily mean that the exclusionary rule applies. Illinois v. Gates, 462 U. S. 213, 223 (1983) . Indeed, exclusion "has always been our last resort, not our first impulse," Hudson v. Michigan, 547 U. S. 586, 591 (2006) , and our precedents establish important principles that constrain application of the exclusionary rule.

First, the exclusionary rule is not an individual right and applies only where it " 'result[s] in appreciable deterrence.' " Leon, supra, at 909 (quoting United States v. Janis, 428 U. S. 433, 454 (1976)). We have repeatedly rejected the argument that exclusion is a necessary consequence of a Fourth Amendment violation. Leon, supra, at 905–906; Evans, supra, at 13–14; Pennsylvania Bd. of Probation and Parole v. Scott, 524 U. S. 357, 363 (1998) . Instead we have focused on the efficacy of the rule in deterring Fourth Amendment violations in the future. See Calandra, supra, at 347–355; Stone v. Powell, 428 U. S. 465, 486 (1976) .2

In addition, the benefits of deterrence must outweigh the costs. Leon, supra, at 910. "We have never suggested that the exclusionary rule must apply in every circumstance in which it might provide marginal deterrence." Scott, supra, at 368. "[T]o the extent that application of the exclusionary rule could provide some incremental deterrent, that possible benefit must be weighed against [its] substantial social costs." Illinois v.

Krull, 480 U. S. 340, 352–353 (1987) (internal quotation marks omitted). The principal cost of applying the rule is, of course, letting guilty and possibly dangerous defendants go free—something that "offends basic concepts of the criminal justice system." Leon, supra, at 908. "[T]he rule's costly toll upon truth-seeking and law enforcement objectives presents a high obstacle for those urging [its] application." Scott, supra, at 364–365 (internal quotation marks omitted); see also United States v. Havens, 446 U. S. 620, 626–627 (1980) ; United States v. Payner, 447 U. S. 727, 734 (1980) .

These principles are reflected in the holding of Leon: When police act under a warrant that is invalid for lack of probable cause, the exclusionary rule does not apply if the police acted "in objectively reasonable reliance" on the subsequently invalidated search warrant. 468 U. S.,at 922. We (perhaps confusingly) called this objectively reasonable reliance "good faith." Ibid., n. 23. In a companion case, Massachusetts v. Sheppard, 468 U. S. 981 (1984) , we held that the exclusionary rule did not apply when a warrant was invalid because a judge forgot to make "clerical corrections" to it. Id., at 991.

Shortly thereafter we extended these holdings to warrantless administrative searches performed in good-faith reliance on a statute later declared unconstitutional. Krull, supra, at 349–350. Finally, in Evans, 514 U. S. 1 , we applied this good-faith rule to police who reasonably relied on mistaken information in a court's database that an arrest warrant was outstanding. We held that a mistake made by a judicial employee could not give rise to exclusion for three reasons: The exclusionary rule was crafted to curb police rather than judicial misconduct; court employees were unlikely to try to subvert the Fourth Amendment ; and "most important, there [was] no basis for believing that application of the exclusionary rule in [those] circumstances" would have any

significant effect in deterring the errors. Id., at 15. Evans left unresolved "whether the evidence should be suppressed if police personnel were responsible for the error,"3 an issue not argued by the State in that case, id., at 16, n. 5, but one that we now confront.

2. The extent to which the exclusionary rule is justified by these deterrence principles varies with the culpability of the law enforcement conduct. As we said in Leon, "an assessment of the flagrancy of the police misconduct constitutes an important step in the calculus" of applying the exclusionary rule. 468 U. S., at 911. Similarly, in Krull we elaborated that "evidence should be suppressed 'only if it can be said that the law enforcement officer had knowledge, or may properly be charged with knowledge, that the search was unconstitutional under the Fourth Amendment .' " 480 U. S., at 348–349 (quoting United States v. Peltier, 422 U. S. 531, 542 (1975)).

Anticipating the good-faith exception to the exclusionary rule, Judge Friendly wrote that "[t]he beneficent aim of the exclusionary rule to deter police misconduct can be sufficiently accomplished by a practice . . . outlawing evidence obtained by flagrant or deliberate violation of rights." The Bill of Rights as a Code of Criminal Procedure, 53 Calif. L. Rev. 929, 953 (1965) (footnotes omitted); see also Brown v. Illinois, 422 U. S. 590, 610–611 (1975) (Powell, J., concurring in part) ("[T]he deterrent value of the exclusionary rule is most likely to be effective" when "official conduct was flagrantly abusive of Fourth Amendment rights").

Indeed, the abuses that gave rise to the exclusionary rule featured intentional conduct that was patently unconstitutional. In Weeks, 232 U. S. 383 , a foundational exclusionary rule case, the officers had broken into the defendant's home (using a key shown to them by a neighbor), confiscated incriminating papers, then returned again with a U. S. Marshal to confiscate even more.

Id., at 386. Not only did they have no search warrant, which the Court held was required, but they could not have gotten one had they tried. They were so lacking in sworn and particularized information that "not even an order of court would have justified such procedure." Id., at 393–394. Silverthorne Lumber Co. v. United States, 251 U. S. 385 (1920), on which petitioner repeatedly relies, was similar; federal officials "without a shadow of authority" went to the defendants' office and "made a clean sweep" of every paper they could find. Id., at 390. Even the Government seemed to acknowledge that the "seizure was an outrage." Id., at 391.

Equally flagrant conduct was at issue in Mapp v. Ohio, 367 U. S. 643 (1961), which overruled Wolf v. Colorado, 338 U. S. 25 (1949), and extended the exclusionary rule to the States. Officers forced open a door to Ms. Mapp's house, kept her lawyer from entering, brandished what the court concluded was a false warrant, then forced her into handcuffs and canvassed the house for obscenity. 367 U. S., at 644–645. See Friendly, supra, at 953, and n. 127 ("[T]he situation in Mapp" featured a "flagrant or deliberate violation of rights"). An error that arises from nonrecurring and attenuated negligence is thus far removed from the core concerns that led us to adopt the rule in the first place. And in fact since Leon, we have never applied the rule to exclude evidence obtained in violation of the Fourth Amendment, where the police conduct was no more intentional or culpable than this.

3. To trigger the exclusionary rule, police conduct must be sufficiently deliberate that exclusion can meaningfully deter it, and sufficiently culpable that such deterrence is worth the price paid by the justice system. As laid out in our cases, the exclusionary rule serves to deter deliberate, reckless, or grossly negligent conduct, or in some circumstances recurring or systemic negligence. The error in this case does not rise to that level.[4]

Our decision in Franks v. Delaware, 438 U. S. 154 (1978), provides an analogy. Cf. Leon, supra, at 914. In Franks, we held that police negligence in obtaining a warrant did not even rise to the level of a Fourth Amendment violation, let alone meet the more stringent test for triggering the exclusionary rule. We held that the Constitution allowed defendants, in some circumstances, "to challenge the truthfulness of factual statements made in an affidavit supporting the warrant," even after the warrant had issued. 438 U. S., at 155–156. If those false statements were necessary to the Magistrate Judge's probable-cause determination, the warrant would be "voided." Ibid. But we did not find all false statements relevant: "There must be allegations of deliberate falsehood or of reckless disregard for the truth," and "[a]llegations of negligence or innocent mistake are insufficient." Id., at 171.

Both this case and Franks concern false information provided by police. Under Franks, negligent police miscommunications in the course of acquiring a warrant do not provide a basis to rescind a warrant and render a search or arrest invalid. Here, the miscommunications occurred in a different context—after the warrant had been issued and recalled—but that fact should not require excluding the evidence obtained.

The pertinent analysis of deterrence and culpability is objective, not an "inquiry into the subjective awareness of arresting officers," Reply Brief for Petitioner 4–5. See also post, at 10, n. 7 (Ginsburg, J., dissenting). We have already held that "our good-faith inquiry is confined to the objectively ascertainable question whether a reasonably well trained officer would have known that the search was illegal" in light of "all of the circumstances." Leon, 468 U. S., at 922, n. 23. These circumstances frequently include a particular officer's knowledge and experience, but that does not make the test any more subjective than the one for probable cause, which looks to an officer's knowledge and experience, Ornelas v. United States, 517 U. S. 690, 699–700 (1996), but not his subjective intent, Whren v. United States, 517 U. S. 806, 812–813 (1996).

4. We do not suggest that all recordkeeping errors by the police are immune from the exclusionary rule. In this case, however, the conduct at issue was not so objectively culpable as to require exclusion. In Leon we held that "the marginal or nonexistent benefits produced by suppressing evidence obtained in objectively reasonable reliance on a subsequently invalidated search warrant cannot justify the substantial costs of exclusion." 468 U. S., at 922. The same is true when evidence is obtained in objectively reasonable reliance on a subsequently recalled warrant.

If the police have been shown to be reckless in maintaining a warrant system, or to have knowingly made false entries to lay the groundwork for future false arrests, exclusion would certainly be justified under our cases should such misconduct cause a Fourth Amendment violation. We said as much in Leon, explaining that an officer could not "obtain a warrant on the basis of a 'bare bones' affidavit and then rely on colleagues who are ignorant of the circumstances under which the warrant was obtained to conduct the search." Id., at 923, n. 24 (citing Whiteley v. Warden, Wyo. State Penitentiary, 401 U. S. 560, 568 (1971)). Petitioner's fears that our decision will cause police departments to deliberately keep their officers ignorant, Brief for Petitioner 37–39, are thus unfounded.

The dissent also adverts to the possible unreliability of a number of databases not relevant to this case. Post, at 8–9. In a case where systemic errors were demonstrated, it might be reckless for officers to rely on an unreliable warrant system. See Evans, 514 U. S., at 17 (O'Connor, J., concurring) ("Surely it would not be reasonable for the police to rely . . . on a recordkeeping system . . . that routinely leads to false arrests" (second emphasis added)); Hudson, 547 U. S., at 604 (Kennedy, J., concurring) ("If a widespread pattern of violations were shown ... there would be reason for grave concern" (emphasis added)). But there is no evidence that errors in Dale County's system are routine or widespread. Officer Anderson testified that he had never had reason to question information about a Dale County warrant, App. 27, and both Sandy Pope and Sharon Morgan testified that they could remember no similar miscommunication ever happening on their watch, id., at 33, 61–62. That is even less error than in the database at issue in Evans, where we also found reliance on the database to be objectively reasonable. 514 U. S., at 15 (similar error "every three or four years"). Because no such showings were made here, see 451 F. Supp. 2d, at 1292, 5 the Eleventh Circuit was correct to affirm the denial of the motion to suppress.

* * *

Petitioner's claim that police negligence automatically triggers suppression cannot be squared with the principles underlying the exclusionary rule, as they have been explained in our cases. In light of our repeated holdings that the deterrent effect of suppression must be substantial and outweigh any harm to the justice system, e.g., Leon, 468 U. S., at 909–910, we conclude that when police mistakes are the result of negligence such as that described here, rather than systemic error or reckless disregard of constitutional requirements, any marginal deterrence does not "pay its way." Id., at 907–908, n. 6 (internal quotation marks omitted). In such a case, the criminal should not "go free because the constable has blundered." People v. Defore, 242 N. Y. 13, 21, 150 N. E. 585, 587 (1926) (opinion of the Court by Cardozo, J.).

The judgment of the Court of Appeals for the Eleventh Circuit is affirmed.

It is so ordered.

Pearson v. Callahan (Jan 21, 2009)

Justice Alito delivered the opinion of the Court.

This is an action brought by respondent under Rev. Stat. §1979, 42 U. S. C. §1983, against state law enforcement officers who conducted a warrantless search of his house incident to his arrest for the sale of methamphetamine to an undercover informant whom he had voluntarily admitted to the premises. The Court of Appeals held that petitioners were not entitled to summary judgment on qualified immunity grounds. Following the procedure we mandated in Saucier v. Katz, 533 U. S. 194 (2001), the Court of Appeals held, first, that respondent adduced facts sufficient to make out a violation of the Fourth Amendment and, second, that the unconstitutionality of the officers' conduct was clearly established. In granting review, we required the parties to address the additional question whether the mandatory procedure set out in Saucier should be retained.

We now hold that the Saucier procedure should not be regarded as an inflexible requirement and that petitioners are entitled to qualified immunity on the ground that it was not clearly established at the time of the search that their conduct was unconstitutional. We therefore reverse.

I
A

The Central Utah Narcotics Task Force is charged with investigating illegal drug use and sales. In 2002, Brian Bartholomew, who became an informant for the task force after having been charged with the unlawful possession of methamphetamine, informed Officer Jeffrey Whatcott that respondent Afton Callahan had arranged to sell Bartholomew methamphetamine later that day.

That evening, Bartholomew arrived at respondent's residence at about 8 p.m. Once there, Bartholomew went inside and confirmed that respondent had methamphetamine available for sale. Bartholomew then told respondent that he needed to obtain money to make his purchase and left.

Bartholomew met with members of the task force at about 9 p.m. and told them that he would be able to buy a gram of methamphetamine for $100. After concluding that Bartholomew was capable of completing the planned purchase, the officers searched him, determined that he had no controlled substances on his person, gave him a marked $100 bill and a concealed electronic transmitter to monitor his conversations, and agreed on a signal that he would give after completing the purchase.

The officers drove Bartholomew to respondent's trailer home, and respondent's daughter let him inside. Respondent then retrieved a large bag containing methamphetamine from his freezer and sold Bartholomew a gram of methamphetamine, which he put into a small plastic bag. Bartholomew gave the arrest signal to the officers who were monitoring the conversation, and they entered the trailer through a porch door. In the enclosed porch, the officers encountered Bartholomew, respondent, and two other persons, and they saw respondent drop a plastic bag, which they later determined contained methamphetamine. The officers then conducted a protective sweep of the premises. In addition to the large bag of meth-amphetamine, the officers recovered the marked bill from respondent and a small bag containing meth-amphetamine from Bartholomew, and they found drug syringes in the residence. As a result, respondent was charged with the unlawful possession and distribution of methamphetamine.

B

The trial court held that the warrantless

arrest and search were supported by exigent circumstances. On respondent's appeal from his conviction, the Utah attorney general conceded the absence of exigent circumstances, but urged that the inevitable discovery doctrine justified introduction of the fruits of the warrantless search. The Utah Court of Appeals disagreed and vacated respondent's conviction. See State v. Callahan, 2004 LIT App. 164, 93 P. 3d 103. Respondent then brought this damages action under 42 U. S. C. §1983 in the United States District Court for the District of Utah, alleging that the officers had violated the Fourth Amendment by entering his home without a warrant. See Callahan v. Millard Cty., No. 2:04–CV–00952, 2006WL 1409130 (2006).

In granting the officers' motion for summary judgment, the District Court noted that other courts had adopted the "consent-once-removed" doctrine, which permits a warrantless entry by police officers into a home when consent to enter has already been granted to an undercover officer or informant who has observed contraband in plain view. Believing that this doctrine was in tension with our intervening decision in Georgia v. Randolph, 547 U. S. 103 (2006), the District Court concluded that "the simplest approach is to assume that the Supreme Court will ultimately reject the [consent-once-removed] doctrine and find that searches such as the one in this case are not reasonable under the Fourth Amendment ." 2006 WL 1409130, at *8. The Court then held that the officers were entitled to qualified immunity because they could reasonably have believed that the consent-once-removed doctrine authorized their conduct.

On appeal, a divided panel of the Tenth Circuit held that petitioners' conduct violated respondent's Fourth Amendment rights. Callahan v. Millard Cty., 494 F. 3d 891, 895–899 (2007). The panel majority stated that "[t]he 'consent-once-removed' doctrine applies when an undercover officer enters a house at the express invitation of someone with authority to consent, establishes probable cause to arrest or search, and then immediately summons other officers for assistance." Id., at 896. The majority took no issue with application of the doctrine when the initial consent was granted to an undercover law enforcement officer, but the majority disagreed with decisions that "broade[n] this doctrine to grant informants the same capabilities as undercover officers." Ibid.

The Tenth Circuit panel further held that the Fourth Amendment right that it recognized was clearly established at the time of respondent's arrest. Id., at 898–899. "In this case," the majority stated, "the relevant right is the right to be free in one's home from unreasonable searches and arrests." Id., at 898. The Court determined that, under the clearly established precedents of this Court and the Tenth Circuit, "warrantless entries into a home are per se unreasonable unless they satisfy the established exceptions." Id., at 898–899. In the panel's words, "the Supreme Court and the Tenth Circuit have clearly established that to allow police entry into a home, the only two exceptions to the warrant requirement are consent and exigent circumstances." Id., at 899. Against that backdrop, the panel concluded, petitioners could not reasonably have believed that their conduct was lawful because petitioners "knew (1) they had no warrant; (2) [respondent] had not consented to their entry; and (3) [respondent's] consent to the entry of an informant could not reasonably be interpreted to extend to them." Ibid.

In dissent, Judge Kelly argued that "no constitutional violation occurred in this case" because, by inviting Bartholomew into his house and participating in a narcotics transaction there, respondent had compromised the privacy of the residence and had assumed the risk that Bartholomew would reveal their dealings to the police. Id., at 903. Judge Kelly further concluded that, even if petitioners' conduct had been unlawful, they were nevertheless entitled to qualified immunity because the constitutional right at issue—"the right to be free from the warrantless entry of police officers into one's home to effectuate an arrest after one has granted voluntary, consensual entry to a confidential informant and undertaken criminal activity giving rise to probable cause"—was not "clearly established" at the time of the events in question. Id., at 903–904.

As noted, the Court of Appeals followed the Saucier procedure. The Saucier procedure has been criticized by Members of this Court and by lower court judges, who have been required to apply the procedure in a great variety of cases and thus have much firsthand experience bearing on its advantages and disadvantages. Accordingly, in granting certiorari, we directed the parties to address the question whether Saucier should be overruled. 552 U. S. ___ (2008).

II

A

The doctrine of qualified immunity protects government officials "from liability for civil damages insofar as their conduct does not violate clearly established statutory or constitutional rights of which a reasonable person would have known." Harlow v. Fitzgerald, 457 U. S. 800, 818 (1982) . Qualified immunity balances two important interests—the need to hold public officials accountable when they exercise power irresponsibly and the need to shield officials from harassment, distraction, and liability when they perform their duties reasonably. The protection of qualified immunity applies regardless of whether the government official's error is "a mistake of law, a mistake of fact, or a mistake based on mixed questions of law and fact." Groh v. Ramirez, 540 U. S. 551, 567 (2004) (Kennedy, J., dissenting) (citing Butz v. Economou, 438 U. S. 478, 507 (1978) (noting that qualified immunity covers "mere

mistakes in judgment, whether the mistake is one of fact or one of law")).

Because qualified immunity is "an immunity from suit rather than a mere defense to liability ... it is effectively lost if a case is erroneously permitted to go to trial." Mitchell v. Forsyth, 472 U. S. 511, 526 (1985) (emphasis deleted). Indeed, we have made clear that the "driving force" behind creation of the qualified immunity doctrine was a desire to ensure that " 'insubstantial claims' against government officials [will] be resolved prior to discovery." Anderson v. Creighton, 483 U. S. 635 , n. 2 (1987). Accordingly, "we repeatedly have stressed the importance of resolving immunity questions at the earliest possible stage in litigation." Hunter v. Bryant, 502 U. S. 224, 227 (1991) (per curiam).

In Saucier, 533 U. S. 194 , this Court mandated a two-step sequence for resolving government officials' qualified immunity claims. First, a court must decide whether the facts that a plaintiff has alleged (see Fed. Rules Civ. Proc. 12(b)(6), (c)) or shown (see Rules 50, 56) make out a violation of a constitutional right. 533 U. S., at 201. Second, if the plaintiff has satisfied this first step, the court must decide whether the right at issue was "clearly established" at the time of defendant's alleged misconduct. Ibid. Qualified immunity is applicable unless the official's conduct violated a clearly established constitutional right. Anderson, supra, at 640.

Our decisions prior to Saucier had held that "the better approach to resolving cases in which the defense of qualified immunity is raised is to determine first whether the plaintiff has alleged a deprivation of a constitutional right at all." County of Sacramento v. Lewis, 523 U. S. 833 , n. 5 (1998). Saucier made that suggestion a mandate. For the first time, we held that whether "the facts alleged show the officer's conduct violated a constitutional right ... must be the initial inquiry" in every qualified immunity case. 533 U.

S., at 20 (emphasis added). Only after completing this first step, we said, may a court turn to "the next, sequential step," namely, "whether the right was clearly established." Ibid.

This two-step procedure, the Saucier Court reasoned, is necessary to support the Constitution's "elaboration from case to case" and to prevent constitutional stagnation. Ibid. "The law might be deprived of this explanation were a court simply to skip ahead to the question whether the law clearly established that the officer's conduct was unlawful in the circumstances of the case." Ibid.

B

In considering whether the Saucier procedure should be modified or abandoned, we must begin with the doctrine of stare decisis. Stare decisis "promotes the evenhanded, predictable, and consistent development of legal principles, fosters reliance on judicial decisions, and contributes to the actual and perceived integrity of the judicial process." Payne v. Tennessee, 501 U. S. 808, 827 (1991) . Although "[w]e approach the reconsideration of [our] decisions ... with the utmost caution," "[s]tare decisis is not an inexorable command." State Oil Co. v. Khan, 522 U. S. 3, 20 (1997) (internal quotation marks omitted). Revisiting precedent is particularly appropriate where, as here, a departure would not upset expectations, the precedent consists of a judge-made rule that was recently adopted to improve the operation of the courts, and experience has pointed up the precedent's shortcomings.

"Considerations in favor of stare decisis are at their acme in cases involving property and contract rights, where reliance interests are involved; the opposite is true in cases ... involving procedural and evidentiary rules" that do not produce such reliance. Payne, supra, at 828 (citations omitted). Like rules governing procedures and the admission of evidence in the trial courts, Saucier's two-step protocol does not affect the way in which parties order their affairs. Withdrawing from Saucier's categorical rule would not upset settled expectations on anyone's part. See United States v. Gaudin, 515 U. S. 506, 521 (1995) .

Nor does this matter implicate "the general presumption that legislative changes should be left to Congress." Khan, supra, at 20. We recognize that "considerations of stare decisis weigh heavily in the area of statutory construction, where Congress is free to change this Court's interpretation of its legislation." Illinois Brick Co. v. Illinois, 431 U. S. 720, 736 (1977) . But the Saucier rule is judge made and implicates an important matter involving internal Judicial Branch operations. Any change should come from this Court, not Congress.

Respondent argues that the Saucier procedure should not be reconsidered unless we conclude that its justification was "badly reasoned" or that the rule has proved to be "unworkable," see Payne, supra, at 827, but those standards, which are appropriate when a constitutional or statutory precedent is challenged, are out of place in the present context. Because of the basis and the nature of the Saucier two-step protocol, it is sufficient that we now have a considerable body of new experience to consider regarding the consequences of requiring adherence to this inflexible procedure. This experience supports our present determination that a mandatory, two-step rule for resolving all qualified immunity claims should not be retained.

Lower court judges, who have had the task of applying the Saucier rule on a regular basis for the past eight years, have not been reticent in their criticism of Saucier's "rigid order of battle." See, e.g., Purtell v. Mason, 527 F. 3d 615, 622 (CA7 2008) ("This 'rigid order of battle' has been criticized on practical, procedural, and substantive grounds"); Leval, Judging Under the Constitution:

Dicta About Dicta, 81 N. Y. U. L. Rev. 1249, 1275, 1277 (2006) (referring to Saucier's mandatory two-step framework as "a new and mischievous rule" that amounts to "a puzzling misadventure in constitutional dictum"). And application of the rule has not always been enthusiastic. See Higazy v. Templeton, 505 F. 3d 161, 179, n. 19 (CA2 2007) ("We do not reach the issue of whether [plaintiff's] Sixth Amendment rights were violated, because principles of judicial restraint caution us to avoid reaching constitutional questions when they are unnecessary to the disposition of a case"); Cherrington v. Skeeter, 344 F. 3d 631, 640 (CA6 2003) ("[I]t ultimately is unnecessary for us to decide whether the individual Defendants did or did not heed the Fourth Amendment command ... because they are entitled to qualified immunity in any event"); Pearson v. Ramos, 237 F. 3d 881, 884 (CA7 2001) ("Whether [the Saucier] rule is absolute may be doubted").

Members of this Court have also voiced criticism of the Saucier rule. See Morse v. Frederick, 551 U. S. ____, ____ (2007) (slip op., at 8) (Breyer, J., concurring in judgment in part and dissenting in part) ("I would end the failed Saucier experiment now"); Bunting v. Mellen, 541 U. S. 1019 (2004) (Stevens, J., joined by Ginsburg and Breyer, JJ., respecting denial of certiorari) (criticizing the "unwise judge-made rule under which courts must decide whether the plaintiff has alleged a constitutional violation before addressing the question whether the defendant state actor is entitled to qualified immunity"); Id., at 1025 (Scalia, J., joined by Rehnquist, C. J., dissenting from denial of certiorari) ("We should either make clear that constitutional determinations are not insulated from our review ... or else drop any pretense at requiring the ordering in every case" (emphasis in original)); Brosseau v. Haugen, 543 U. S. 194, 201–202 (2004) (Breyer, J., joined by Scalia and Ginsburg, JJ., concurring) (urging Court to reconsider Saucier's "rigid 'order of battle,' " which "requires courts unnecessarily to decide difficult constitutional questions when there is available an easier basis for the decision (e.g., qualified immunity) that will satisfactorily resolve the case before the court"); Saucier, 533 U. S., at 210 (Ginsburg, J., concurring in judgment) ("The two-part test today's decision imposes holds large potential to confuse").

Where a decision has "been questioned by Members of the Court in later decisions and [has] defied consistent application by the lower courts," these factors weigh in favor of reconsideration. Payne, 501 U. S., at 829–830; see also Crawford v. Washington, 541 U. S. 36, 60 (2004) . Collectively, the factors we have noted make our present reevaluation of the Saucier two-step protocol appropriate.

III

On reconsidering the procedure required in Saucier, we conclude that, while the sequence set forth there is often appropriate, it should no longer be regarded as mandatory. The judges of the district courts and the courts of appeals should be permitted to exercise their sound discretion in deciding which of the two prongs of the qualified immunity analysis should be addressed first in light of the circumstances in the particular case at hand.

A

Although we now hold that the Saucier protocol should not be regarded as mandatory in all cases, we continue to recognize that it is often beneficial. For one thing, there are cases in which there would be little if any conservation of judicial resources to be had by beginning and ending with a discussion of the "clearly established" prong. "[I]t often may be difficult to decide whether a right is clearly established without deciding precisely what the constitutional right happens to be." Lyons v. Xenia, 417 F. 3d 565, 581 (CA6 2005) (Sutton, J., concurring). In some cases, a discussion of why the relevant facts do not violate clearly established law may make it apparent that in fact the relevant facts do not make out a constitutional violation at all. In addition, the Saucier Court was certainly correct in noting that the two-step procedure promotes the development of constitutional precedent and is especially valuable with respect to questions that do not frequently arise in cases in which a qualified immunity defense is unavailable.

B

At the same time, however, the rigid Saucier procedure comes with a price. The procedure sometimes results in a substantial expenditure of scarce judicial resources on difficult questions that have no effect on the outcome of the case. There are cases in which it is plain that a constitutional right is not clearly established but far from obvious whether in fact there is such a right. District courts and courts of appeals with heavy caseloads are often understandably unenthusiastic about what may seem to be an essentially academic exercise.

Unnecessary litigation of constitutional issues also wastes the parties' resources. Qualified immunity is "an immunity from suit rather than a mere defense to liability." Mitchell, 472 U. S., at 526 (emphasis deleted). Saucier's two-step protocol "disserve[s] the purpose of qualified immunity" when it "forces the parties to endure additional burdens of suit—such as the costs of litigating constitutional questions and delays attributable to resolving them—when the suit otherwise could be disposed of more readily." Brief for Nat. Assn. of Criminal Defense Lawyers as Amicus Curiae 30.

Although the first prong of the Saucier procedure is intended to further the development of constitutional precedent, opinions following that procedure often fail to make a meaningful contribution to such development. For one thing, there are cases in which the constitutional question is so fact-bound that the decision provides little guidance for future cases. See Scott v. Harris, 550

U. S. 372, 388 (2007) (Breyer, J., concurring) (counseling against the Saucier two-step protocol where the question is "so fact dependent that the result will be confusion rather than clarity"); Buchanan v. Maine, 469 F. 3d 158, 168 (CA1 2006) ("We do not think the law elaboration purpose will be well served here, where the Fourth Amendment inquiry involves a reasonableness question which is highly idiosyncratic and heavily dependent on the facts").

A decision on the underlying constitutional question in a §1983 damages action or a Bivens v. Six Unknown Fed. Narcotics Agents, 403 U. S. 388 (1971) ,1 action may have scant value when it appears that the question will soon be decided by a higher court. When presented with a constitutional question on which this Court had just granted certiorari, the Ninth Circuit elected to "bypass Saucier's first step and decide only whether [the alleged right] was clearly established." Motley v. Parks, 432 F. 3d 1072, 1078, and n. 5 (2005) (en banc). Similar considerations may come into play when a court of appeals panel confronts a constitutional question that is pending before the court en banc or when a district court encounters a constitutional question that is before the court of appeals.

A constitutional decision resting on an uncertain interpretation of state law is also of doubtful precedential importance. As a result, several courts have identified an "exception" to the Saucier rule for cases in which resolution of the constitutional question requires clarification of an ambiguous state statute. Egolf v. Witmer, 526 F. 3d 104, 109–111 (CA3 2008); accord, Tremblay v. McClellan, 350 F. 3d 195, 200 (CA1 2003); Ehrlich v. Glastonbury, 348 F. 3d 48, 57–60 (CA2 2003). Justifying the decision to grant qualified immunity to the defendant without first resolving, under Saucier's first prong, whether the defendant's conduct violated the Constitution, these courts have observed that Saucier's "underlying principle" of encouraging federal courts to decide unclear legal questions in order to clarify the law for the future "is not meaningfully advanced ... when the definition of constitutional rights depends on a federal court's uncertain assumptions about state law." Egolf, supra, at 110; accord, Tremblay, supra, at 200; Ehrlich, supra, at 58.

When qualified immunity is asserted at the pleading stage, the precise factual basis for the plaintiff's claim or claims may be hard to identify. See Lyons, supra, at 582 (Sutton, J., concurring); Kwai Fun Wong v. United States, 373 F. 3d 952, 957 (CA9 2004); Mollica v. Volker, 229 F. 3d 366, 374 (CA2 2000). Accordingly, several courts have recognized that the two-step inquiry "is an uncomfortable exercise where ... the answer [to] whether there was a violation may depend on a kaleidoscope of facts not yet fully developed" and have suggested that "[i]t may be that Saucier was not strictly intended to cover" this situation. Dirrane v. Brookline Police Dept., 315 F. 3d 65, 69–70 (CA1 2002); see also Robinette v. Jones, 476 F. 3d 585, 592, n. 8 (CA8 2007) (declining to follow Saucier because "the parties have provided very few facts to define and limit any holding" on the constitutional question).

There are circumstances in which the first step of the Saucier procedure may create a risk of bad decisionmaking. The lower courts sometimes encounter cases in which the briefing of constitutional questions is woefully inadequate. See Lyons, 417 F. 3d, at 582 (Sutton, J., concurring) (noting the "risk that constitutional questions may be prematurely and incorrectly decided in cases where they are not well presented"); Mollica, supra, at 374.

Although the Saucier rule prescribes the sequence in which the issues must be discussed by a court in its opinion, the rule does not—and obviously cannot—specify the sequence in which judges reach their conclusions in their own internal thought processes. Thus, there will be cases in which a court will rather quickly and easily decide that there was no violation of clearly established law before turning to the more difficult question whether the relevant facts make out a constitutional question at all. In such situations, there is a risk that a court may not devote as much care as it would in other circumstances to the decision of the constitutional issue. See Horne v. Coughlin, 191 F. 3d, 244, 247 (CA2 1999) ("Judges risk being insufficiently thoughtful and cautious in uttering pronouncements that play no role in their adjudication"); Leval 1278–1279.

Rigid adherence to the Saucier rule may make it hard for affected parties to obtain appellate review of constitutional decisions that may have a serious prospective effect on their operations. Where a court holds that a defendant committed a constitutional violation but that the violation was not clearly established, the defendant may face a difficult situation. As the winning party, the defendant's right to appeal the adverse holding on the constitutional question may be contested. See Bunting, 541 U. S., at 1025 (Scalia, J., dissenting from denial of certiorari) ("The perception of unreviewability undermines adherence to the sequencing rule we . . . created" in Saucier);2 see also Kalka v. Hawk, 215 F. 3d 90, 96, n. 9 (CADC 2000) (noting that "[n]ormally, a party may not appeal from a favorable judgment" and that the Supreme Court "has apparently never granted the certiorari petition of a party who prevailed in the appellate court"). In cases like Bunting, the "prevailing" defendant faces an unenviable choice: "compl[y] with the lower court's advisory dictum without opportunity to seek appellate [or certiorari] review," or "def[y] the views of the lower court, adher[e] to practices that have been declared illegal, and thus invit[e] new suits" and potential "punitive damages." Horne, supra, at 247–248.

Adherence to Saucier's two-step protocol departs from the general rule of constitutional avoidance and runs counter to the "older, wiser judicial counsel 'not to pass on questions of constitutionality ... unless such adjudication is unavoidable.' " Scott, 550 U. S., at 388 (Breyer, J., concurring) (quoting Spector Motor Service, Inc. v. McLaughlin, 323 U. S. 101, 105 (1944)); see Ashwander v. TVA, 297 U. S. 288, 347 (1936) (Brandeis, J., concurring) ("The Court will not pass upon a constitutional question although properly presented by the record, if there is also present some other ground upon which the case may be disposed of ").

In other analogous contexts, we have appropriately declined to mandate the order of decision that the lower courts must follow. For example, in Strickland v. Washington, 466 U. S. 668 (1984) , we recognized a two-part test for determining whether a criminal defendant was denied the effective assistance of counsel: The defendant must demonstrate (1) that his counsel's performance fell below what could be expected of a reasonably competent practitioner; and (2) that he was prejudiced by that substandard performance. Id., at 687. After setting forth and applying the analytical framework that courts must use in evaluating claims of ineffective assistance of counsel, we left it to the sound discretion of lower courts to determine the order of decision. Id., at 697 ("Although we have discussed the performance component of an ineffectiveness claim prior to the prejudice component, there is no reason for a court deciding an ineffective assistance claim to approach the inquiry in the same order or even to address both components of the inquiry if the defendant makes an insufficient showing on one").

In United States v. Leon, 468 U. S. 897 (1984) , we created an exception to the exclusionary rule when officers reasonably rely on a facially valid search warrant. Id., at 913. In that context, we recognized that a defendant challenging a search will lose if either: (1) the warrant issued was supported by probable cause;

or (2) it was not, but the officers executing it reasonably believed that it was. Again, after setting forth and applying the analytical framework that courts must use in evaluating the good-faith exception to the Fourth Amendment warrant requirement, we left it to the sound discretion of the lower courts to determine the order of decision. Id., at 924, 925 ("There is no need for courts to adopt the inflexible practice of always deciding whether the officers' conduct manifested objective good faith before turning to the question whether the Fourth Amendment has been violated").

This flexibility properly reflects our respect for the lower federal courts that bear the brunt of adjudicating these cases. Because the two-step Saucier procedure is often, but not always, advantageous, the judges of the district courts and the courts of appeals are in the best position to determine the order of decisionmaking will best facilitate the fair and efficient disposition of each case.

C

Any misgivings concerning our decision to withdraw from the mandate set forth in Saucier are unwarranted. Our decision does not prevent the lower courts from following the Saucier procedure; it simply recognizes that those courts should have the discretion to decide whether that procedure is worthwhile in particular cases. Moreover, the development of constitutional law is by no means entirely dependent on cases in which the defendant may seek qualified immunity. Most of the constitutional issues that are presented in §1983 damages actions and Bivens cases also arise in cases in which that defense is not available, such as criminal cases and §1983 cases against a municipality, as well as §1983 cases against individuals where injunctive relief is sought instead of or in addition to damages. See Lewis, 523 U. S., at 841, n. 5 (noting that qualified immunity is unavailable "in a suit to enjoin future conduct, in an action against a municipality, or in litigating a suppression motion").

We also do not think that relaxation of Saucier's mandate is likely to result in a proliferation of damages claims against local governments. Compare Brief for Nat. Assn. of Counties et al., as Amici Curiae 29, 30 ("[T]o the extent that a rule permitting courts to bypass the merits makes it more difficult for civil rights plaintiffs to pursue novel claims, they will have greater reason to press custom, policy, or practice [damages] claims against local governments"). It is hard to see how the Saucier procedure could have a significant effect on a civil rights plaintiff's decision whether to seek damages only from a municipal employee or also from the municipality. Whether the Saucier procedure is mandatory or discretionary, the plaintiff will presumably take into account the possibility that the individual defendant will be held to have qualified immunity, and presumably the plaintiff will seek damages from the municipality as well as the individual employee if the benefits of doing so (any increase in the likelihood of recovery or collection of damages) outweigh the litigation costs.

Nor do we think that allowing the lower courts to exercise their discretion with respect to the Saucier procedure will spawn "a new cottage industry of litigation ... over the standards for deciding whether to reach the merits in a given case." Brief for Nat. Assn. of Counties et al. as Amici Curiae 29, 30. It does not appear that such a "cottage industry" developed prior to Saucier, and we see no reason why our decision today should produce such a result.

IV

Turning to the conduct of the officers here, we hold that petitioners are entitled to qualified immunity because the entry did not violate clearly established law. An officer conducting a search is entitled to qualified immunity where clearly established law does not show that the search violated the Fourth Amendment . See Anderson, 483 U. S., at 641. This inquiry turns on the "objective legal reasonableness of the action, assessed in light of the legal rules that were clearly established at the time it was taken." Wilson v. Layne, 526 U. S. 603, 614 (1999) (internal quotation marks omitted); see Hope v. Pelzer, 536 U. S. 730, 739 (2002) ("[Q]ualified immunity operates to ensure that before they are subjected to suit, officers are on notice their conduct is unlawful" (internal quotation marks omitted)).

When the entry at issue here occurred in 2002, the "consent-once-removed" doctrine had gained acceptance in the lower courts. This doctrine had been considered by three Federal Courts of Appeals and two State Supreme Courts starting in the early 1980's. See, e.g., United States v. Diaz, 814 F. 2d 454, 459 (CA7), cert. denied, 484 U. S. 857 (1987) ; United States v. Bramble, 103 F. 3d 1475 (CA9 1996); United States v. Pollard, 215 F. 3d 643, 648–649 (CA6), cert. denied, 531 U. S. 999 (2000) ; State v. Henry, 133 N. J. 104, 627 A. 2d 125 (1993); State v. Johnston, 184 Wis. 2d 794, 518 N. W. 2d 759 (1994). It had been accepted by every one of those courts. Moreover, the Seventh Circuit had approved the doctrine's application to cases involving consensual entries by private citizens acting as confidential informants. See United States v. Paul, 808 F. 2d, 645, 648 (1986). The Sixth Circuit reached the same conclusion after the events that gave rise to respondent's suit, see United States v. Yoon, 398 F. 3d 802, 806–808, cert. denied, 546 U. S. 977 (2005) , and prior to the Tenth Circuit's decision in the present case, no court of appeals had issued a contrary decision.

The officers here were entitled to rely on these cases, even though their own Federal Circuit had not yet ruled on "consent-once-removed" entries. The principles of qualified immunity shield an officer from personal liability when an officer reasonably believes that his or her conduct complies with the law. Police officers are entitled to rely on existing lower court cases without facing personal liability for their actions. In Wilson, we explained that a Circuit split on the relevant issue had developed after the events that gave rise to suit and concluded that "[i]f judges thus disagree on a constitutional question, it is unfair to subject police to money damages for picking the losing side of the controversy." 526 U. S., at 618. Likewise, here, where the divergence of views on the consent-once-removed doctrine was created by the decision of the Court of Appeals in this case, it is improper to subject petitioners to money damages for their conduct.

Because the unlawfulness of the officers' conduct in this case was not clearly established, petitioners are entitled to qualified immunity. We therefore reverse the judgment of the Court of Appeals.

It is so ordered.

Notes

1 See Harlow v. Fitzgerald, 457 U. S. 800 , and n. 30 (1982) (noting that the Court's decisions equate the qualified immunity of state officials sued under 42 U. S. C. §1983 with the immunity of federal officers sued directly under the Constitution).

2 In Bunting, the Court of Appeals followed the Saucier two-step protocol and first held that the Virginia Military Institute's use of the word "God" in a "supper roll call" ceremony violated the Establishment Clause, but then granted the defendants qualified immunity because the law was not clearly established at the relevant time. Mellen v. Bunting, 327 F. 3d 355, 365–376 (CA4 2003), cert. denied, 541 U. S. 1019 (2004). Although they had a judgment in their favor below, the defendants asked this Court to review the adverse constitutional ruling. Dissenting from the denial of certiorari, Justice Scalia, joined by Chief Justice Rehnquist, criticized "a perceived procedural tangle of the Court's own

making." 541 U. S., at 1022. The "tangle" arose from the Court's " 'settled refusal' to entertain an appeal by a party on an issue as to which he prevailed" below, a practice that insulates from review adverse merits decisions that are "locked inside" favorable qualified immunity rulings. Id., at 1023, 1024.

Safford Unified School District #1 v. Redding (June 25, 2009) [Notes omitted]

Justice Souter delivered the opinion of the Court.

The issue here is whether a 13-year-old student's Fourth Amendment right was violated when she was subjected to a search of her bra and underpants by school officials acting on reasonable suspicion that she had brought forbidden prescription and over-the-counter drugs to school. Because there were no reasons to suspect the drugs presented a danger or were concealed in her underwear, we hold that the search did violate the Constitution, but because there is reason to question the clarity with which the right was established, the official who ordered the unconstitutional search is entitled to qualified immunity from liability.

I

The events immediately prior to the search in question began in 13-year-old Savana Redding's math class at Safford Middle School one October day in 2003. The assistant principal of the school, Kerry Wilson, came into the room and asked Savana to go to his office. There, he showed her a day planner, unzipped and open flat on his desk, in which there were several knives, lighters, a permanent marker, and a cigarette. Wilson asked Savana whether the planner was hers; she said it was, but that a few days before she had lent it to her friend, Marissa Glines. Savana stated that none of the items in the planner belonged to her.

Wilson then showed Savana four white

prescription-strength ibuprofen 400-mg pills, and one over-the-counter blue naproxen 200-mg pill, all used for pain and inflammation but banned under school rules without advance permission. He asked Savana if she knew anything about the pills. Savana answered that she did not. Wilson then told Savana that he had received a report that she was giving these pills to fellow students; Savana denied it and agreed to let Wilson search her belongings. Helen Romero, an administrative assistant, came into the office, and together with Wilson they searched Savana's backpack, finding nothing.

At that point, Wilson instructed Romero to take Savana to the school nurse's office to search her clothes for pills. Romero and the nurse, Peggy Schwallier, asked Savana to remove her jacket, socks, and shoes, leaving her in stretch pants and a T-shirt (both without pockets), which she was then asked to remove. Finally, Savana was told to pull her bra out and to the side and shake it, and to pull out the elastic on her underpants, thus exposing her breasts and pelvic area to some degree. No pills were found.

Savana's mother filed suit against Safford Unified School District #1, Wilson, Romero, and Schwallier for conducting a strip search in violation of Savana's Fourth Amendment rights. The individuals (hereinafter petitioners) moved for summary judgment, raising a defense of qualified immunity. The District Court for the District of Arizona granted the motion on the ground that there was no Fourth Amendment violation, and a panel of the Ninth Circuit affirmed. 504 F. 3d 828 (2007).

A closely divided Circuit sitting en banc, however, reversed. Following the two-step protocol for evaluating claims of qualified immunity, see Saucier v. Katz, 533 U. S. 194, 200 (2001), the Ninth Circuit held that the strip search was unjustified under the Fourth Amendment test for searches of children by school officials set out in New Jersey v. T. L. O., 469 U. S. 325 (1985). 531 F. 3d 1071, 1081–1087 (2008). The Circuit then applied the test for qualified immunity, and found that Savana's right was clearly established at the time of the search: " '[t]hese notions of personal privacy are "clearly established" in that they inhere in all of us, particularly middle school teenagers, and are inherent in the privacy component of the Fourth Amendment 's proscription against unreasonable searches.' " Id., at 1088–1089 (quoting Brannum v. Overton Cty. School Bd., 516 F. 3d 489, 499 (CA6 2008)). The upshot was reversal of summary judgment as to Wilson, while affirming the judgments in favor of Schwallier, the school nurse, and Romero, the administrative assistant, since they had not acted as independent decisionmakers. 531 F. 3d, at 1089.

We granted certiorari, 555 U. S. ____ (2009), and now affirm in part, reverse in part, and remand.

II

The Fourth Amendment "right of the people to be secure in their persons ... against unreasonable searches and seizures" generally requires a law enforcement officer to have probable cause for conducting a search. "Probable cause exists where 'the facts and circumstances within [an officer's] knowledge and of which [he] had reasonably trustworthy information [are] sufficient in themselves to warrant a man of reasonable caution in the belief that' an offense has been or is being committed," Brinegar v. United States, 338 U. S. 160, 175–176 (1949) (quoting Carroll v. United States, 267 U. S. 132, 162 (1925)), and that evidence bearing on that offense will be found in the place to be searched.

In T. L. O., we recognized that the school setting "requires some modification of the level of suspicion of illicit activity needed to justify a search," 469 U. S., at 340, and held that for searches by school officials "a careful balancing of governmental and private interests suggests that the public interest is best served by a Fourth Amendment standard of reasonableness that stops short of probable cause," id., at 341. We have thus applied a standard of reasonable suspicion to determine the legality of a school administrator's search of a student, id., at 342, 345, and have held that a school search "will be permissible in its scope when the measures adopted are reasonably related to the objectives of the search and not excessively intrusive in light of the age and sex of the student and the nature of the infraction," id., at 342.

A number of our cases on probable cause have an implicit bearing on the reliable knowledge element of reasonable suspicion, as we have attempted to flesh out the knowledge component by looking to the degree to which known facts imply prohibited conduct, see, e.g., Adams v. Williams, 407 U. S. 143, 148 (1972); id., at 160, n. 9 (Marshall, J., dissenting), the specificity of the information received, see, e.g., Spinelli v. United States, 393 U. S. 410, 416–417 (1969), and the reliability of its source, see, e.g., Aguilar v. Texas, 378 U. S. 108, 114 (1964). At the end of the day, however, we have realized that these factors cannot rigidly control, Illinois v. Gates, 462 U. S. 213, 230 (1983), and we have come back to saying that the standards are "fluid concepts that take their substantive content from the particular contexts" in which they are being assessed. Ornelas v. United States, 517 U. S. 690, 696 (1996).

Perhaps the best that can be said generally about the required knowledge component of probable cause for a law enforcement officer's evidence search is that it raise a "fair probability," Gates, 462 U. S., at 238, or a "substantial chance," id., at 244, n. 13, of discovering evidence of criminal activity. The lesser standard for school searches could as readily be described as a moderate chance of finding evidence of wrongdoing.

III

A

In this case, the school's policies strictly prohibit the nonmedical use, possession, or sale of any drug on school grounds, including " '[a]ny prescription or over-the-counter drug, except those for which permission to use in school has been granted pursuant to Board policy.' " App. to Pet. for Cert. 128a.1 A week before Savana was searched, another student, Jordan Romero (no relation of the school's administrative assistant), told the principal and Assistant Principal Wilson that "certain students were bringing drugs and weapons on campus," and that he had been sick after taking some pills that "he got from a classmate." App. 8a. On the morning of October 8, the same boy handed Wilson a white pill that he said Marissa Glines had given him. He told Wilson that students were planning to take the pills at lunch.

Wilson learned from Peggy Schwallier, the school nurse, that the pill was Ibuprofen 400 mg, available only by prescription. Wilson then called Marissa out of class. Outside the classroom, Marissa's teacher handed Wilson the day planner, found within Marissa's reach, containing various contraband items. Wilson escorted Marissa back to his office.

In the presence of Helen Romero, Wilson requested Marissa to turn out her pockets and open her wallet. Marissa produced a blue pill, several white ones, and a razor blade. Wilson asked where the blue pill came from, and Marissa answered, " 'I guess it slipped in when she gave me the IBU 400s.' " Id., at 13a. When Wilson asked whom she meant, Marissa replied, " 'Savana Redding.' " Ibid. Wilson then enquired about the day planner and its contents; Marissa denied knowing anything about them. Wilson did not ask Marissa any followup questions to determine whether there was any likelihood that Savana presently had pills: neither asking when Marissa received the pills from Savana nor where Savana might be hiding them.

Schwallier did not immediately recognize the blue pill, but information provided through a poison control hotline2 indicated that the pill was a 200-mg dose of an antiinflammatory drug, generically called naproxen, available over the counter. At Wilson's direction, Marissa was then subjected to a search of her bra and underpants by Romero and Schwallier, as Savana was later on. The search revealed no additional pills.

It was at this juncture that Wilson called Savana into his office and showed her the day planner. Their conversation established that Savana and Marissa were on friendly terms: while she denied knowledge of the contraband, Savana admitted that the day planner was hers and that she had lent it to Marissa. Wilson had other reports of their friendship from staff members, who had identified Savana and Marissa as part of an unusually rowdy group at the school's opening dance in August, during which alcohol and cigarettes were found in the girls' bathroom. Wilson had reason to connect the girls with this contraband, for Wilson knew that Jordan Romero had told the principal that before the dance, he had been at a party at Savana's house where alcohol was served. Marissa's statement that the pills came from Savana was thus sufficiently plausible to warrant suspicion that Savana was involved in pill distribution.

This suspicion of Wilson's was enough to justify a search of Savana's backpack and outer clothing.3 If a student is reasonably suspected of giving out contraband pills, she is reasonably suspected of carrying them on her person and in the carryall that has become an item of student uniform in most places today. If Wilson's reasonable suspicion of pill distribution were not understood to support searches of outer clothes and backpack, it would not justify any search

worth making. And the look into Savana's bag, in her presence and in the relative privacy of Wilson's office, was not excessively intrusive, any more than Romero's subsequent search of her outer clothing.

B

Here it is that the parties part company, with Savana's claim that extending the search at Wilson's behest to the point of making her pull out her underwear was constitutionally unreasonable. The exact label for this final step in the intrusion is not important, though strip search is a fair way to speak of it. Romero and Schwallier directed Savana to remove her clothes down to her underwear, and then "pull out" her bra and the elastic band on her underpants. Id., at 23a. Although Romero and Schwallier stated that they did not see anything when Savana followed their instructions, App. to Pet. for Cert. 135a, we would not define strip search and its Fourth Amendment consequences in a way that would guarantee litigation about who was looking and how much was seen. The very fact of Savana's pulling her underwear away from her body in the presence of the two officials who were able to see her necessarily exposed her breasts and pelvic area to some degree, and both subjective and reasonable societal expectations of personal privacy support the treatment of such a search as categorically distinct, requiring distinct elements of justification on the part of school authorities for going beyond a search of outer clothing and belongings.

Savana's subjective expectation of privacy against such a search is inherent in her account of it as embarrassing, frightening, and humiliating. The reasonableness of her expectation (required by the Fourth Amendment standard) is indicated by the consistent experiences of other young people similarly searched, whose adolescent vulnerability intensifies the patent intrusiveness of the exposure. See Brief for National Association of Social Workers et al. as Amici Curiae 6–14; Hyman & Perone, The Other Side of School Violence:

Educator Policies and Practices that may Contribute to Student Misbehavior, 36 J. School Psychology 7, 13 (1998) (strip search can "result in serious emotional damage"). The common reaction of these adolescents simply registers the obviously different meaning of a search exposing the body from the experience of nakedness or near undress in other school circumstances. Changing for gym is getting ready for play; exposing for a search is responding to an accusation reserved for suspected wrongdoers and fairly understood as so degrading that a number of communities have decided that strip searches in schools are never reasonable and have banned them no matter what the facts maybe, see, e.g., New York City Dept. of Education, Reg. No. A–432, p. 2 (2005), online at http://docs.nycenet.edu/docushare/dsweb/Get/D ocument-21/A-432.pdf ("Under no circumstances shall a strip-search of a student be conducted").

The indignity of the search does not, of course, outlaw it, but it does implicate the rule of reasonableness as stated in T. L. O., that "the search as actually conducted [be] reasonably related in scope to the circumstances which justified the interference in the first place." 469 U. S., at 341 (internal quotation marks omitted). The scope will be permissible, that is, when it is "not excessively intrusive in light of the age and sex of the student and the nature of the infraction." Id., at 342.

Here, the content of the suspicion failed to match the degree of intrusion. Wilson knew beforehand that the pills were prescription-strength ibuprofen and over-the-counter naproxen, common pain relievers equivalent to two Advil, or one Aleve.[4] He must have been aware of the nature and limited threat of the specific drugs he was searching for, and while just about anything can be taken in quantities that will do real harm, Wilson had no reason to suspect that large amounts of the drugs were being passed around, or that individual students were receiving great numbers of pills.

Nor could Wilson have suspected that Savana was hiding common painkillers in her underwear. Petitioners suggest, as a truth universally acknowledged, that "students ... hid[e] contraband in or under their clothing," Reply Brief for Petitioners 8, and cite a smattering of cases of students with contraband in their underwear, id., at 8–9. But when the categorically extreme intrusiveness of a search down to the body of an adolescent requires some justification in suspected facts, general background possibilities fall short; a reasonable search that extensive calls for suspicion that it will pay off. But nondangerous school contraband does not raise the specter of stashes in intimate places, and there is no evidence in the record of any general practice among Safford Middle School students of hiding that sort of thing in underwear; neither Jordan nor Marissa suggested to Wilson that Savana was doing that, and the preceding search of Marissa that Wilson ordered yielded nothing. Wilson never even determined when Marissa had received the pills from Savana; if it had been a few days before, that would weigh heavily against any reasonable conclusion that Savana presently had the pills on her person, much less in her underwear.

In sum, what was missing from the suspected facts that pointed to Savana was any indication of danger to the students from the power of the drugs or their quantity, and any reason to suppose that Savana was carrying pills in her underwear. We think that the combination of these deficiencies was fatal to finding the search reasonable.

In so holding, we mean to cast no ill reflection on the assistant principal, for the record raises no doubt that his motive throughout was to eliminate drugs from his school and protect students from what Jordan Romero had gone through. Parents are known to overreact to protect their children from danger, and a school official with responsibility for safety may tend to do the same. The difference is that the Fourth Amendment places limits on the official, even with the high degree of deference that courts must pay to the educator's professional judgment.

We do mean, though, to make it clear that the T. L. O. concern to limit a school search to reasonable scope requires the support of reasonable suspicion of danger or of resort to underwear for hiding evidence of wrongdoing before a search can reasonably make the quantum leap from outer clothes and backpacks to exposure of intimate parts. The meaning of such a search, and the degradation its subject may reasonably feel, place a search that intrusive in a category of its own demanding its own specific suspicions.

IV

A school official searching a student is "entitled to qualified immunity where clearly established law does not show that the search violated the Fourth Amendment ." Pearson v. Callahan, 555 U. S. ___, ___ (2009) (slip op., at 18). To be established clearly, however, there is no need that "the very action in question [have] previously been held unlawful." Wilson v. Layne, 526 U. S. 603, 615 (1999). The unconstitutionality of outrageous conduct obviously will be unconstitutional, this being the reason, as Judge Posner has said, that "[t]he easiest cases don't even arise." K. H. v. Morgan, 914 F. 2d 846, 851 (CA7 1990). But even as to action less than an outrage, "officials can still be on notice that their conduct violates established law ... in novel factual circumstances." Hope v. Pelzer, 536 U. S. 730, 741 (2002).

T. L. O. directed school officials to limit the intrusiveness of a search, "in light of the age and sex of the student and the nature of the infraction," 469 U. S., at 342, and as we have just said at some length, the intrusiveness of the strip search here cannot be seen as justifiably related to the circumstances. But we realize that the lower courts have reached divergent conclusions regarding how the T. L. O. standard applies to such searches.

A number of judges have read T. L. O. as the en banc minority of the Ninth Circuit did here. The Sixth Circuit upheld a strip search of a high school student for a drug, without any suspicion that drugs were hidden next to her body. Williams v. Ellington, 936 F. 2d 881, 882–883, 887 (1991). And other courts considering qualified immunity for strip searches have read T. L. O. as "a series of abstractions, on the one hand, and a declaration of seeming deference to the judgments of school officials, on the other," Jenkins v. Talladega City Bd. of Ed., 115 F. 3d 821, 828 (CA11 1997) (en banc), which made it impossible "to establish clearly the contours of a Fourth Amendment right ... [in] the wide variety of possible school settings different from those involved in T. L. O." itself. Ibid. See also Thomas v. Roberts, 323 F. 3d 950 (CA11 2003) (granting qualified immunity to a teacher and police officer who conducted a group strip search of a fifth grade class when looking for a missing $26).

We think these differences of opinion from our own are substantial enough to require immunity for the school officials in this case. We would not suggest that entitlement to qualified immunity is the guaranteed product of disuniform views of the law in the other federal, or state, courts, and the fact that a single judge, or even a group of judges, disagrees about the contours of a right does not automatically render the law unclear if we have been clear. That said, however, the cases viewing school strip searches differently from the way we see them are numerous enough, with well-reasoned majority and dissenting opinions, to counsel doubt that we were sufficiently clear in the prior statement of law. We conclude that qualified immunity is warranted.

V

The strip search of Savana Redding was

unreasonable and a violation of the Fourth Amendment, but petitioners Wilson, Romero, and Schwallier are nevertheless protected from liability through qualified immunity. Our conclusions here do not resolve, however, the question of the liability of petitioner Safford Unified School District #1 under Monell v. New York City Dept. of Social Servs., 436 U. S. 658, 694 (1978), a claim the Ninth Circuit did not address. The judgment of the Ninth Circuit is therefore affirmed in part and reversed in part, and this case is remanded for consideration of the Monell claim.

It is so ordered.

Ontario v. Quon (June 17, 2010)

Justice Kennedy delivered the opinion of the Court.

This case involves the assertion by a government employer of the right, in circumstances to be described, to read text messages sent and received on a pager the employer owned and issued to an employee. The employee contends that the privacy of the messages is protected by the ban on "unreasonable searches and seizures" found in the Fourth Amendment to the United States Constitution, made applicable to the States by the Due Process Clause of the Fourteenth Amendment. Mapp v. Ohio, 367 U. S. 643 (1961). Though the case touches issues of far- reaching significance, the Court concludes it can be resolved by settled principles determining when a search is reasonable.

I

A

The City of Ontario (City) is a political subdivision of the State of California. The case arose out of incidents in 2001 and 2002 when respondent Jeff Quon was employed by the Ontario Police Department (OPD). He was a police sergeant and member of OPD's Special Weapons and Tactics (SWAT) Team. The City, OPD, and OPD's Chief, Lloyd Scharf, are petitioners here. As will be discussed, two respondents share the last name Quon. In this opinion "Quon" refers to Jeff Quon, for the relevant events mostly revolve around him.

In October 2001, the City acquired 20 alphanumeric pagers capable of sending and receiving text messages. Arch Wireless Operating Company provided wireless service for the pagers. Under the City's service contract with Arch Wireless, each pager was allotted a limited number of characters sent or received each month. Usage in excess of that amount would result in an additional fee. The City issued pagers to Quon and other SWAT Team members in order to help the SWAT Team mobilize and respond to emergency situations.

Before acquiring the pagers, the City announced a "Computer Usage, Internet and E-Mail Policy" (Computer Policy) that applied to all employees. Among other provisions, it specified that the City "reserves the right to monitor and log all network activity including e-mail and Internet use, with or without notice. Users should have no expectation of privacy or confidentiality when using these resources." App. to Pet. for Cert. 152a. In March 2000, Quon signed a statement acknowledging that he had read and understood the Computer Policy.

The Computer Policy did not apply, on its face, to text messaging. Text messages share similarities with e-mails, but the two differ in an important way. In this case, for instance, an e-mail sent on a City computer was transmitted through the City's own data servers, but a text message sent on one of the City's pagers was transmitted using wireless radio frequencies from an individual pager to a receiving station owned by Arch Wireless. It was routed through Arch Wireless' computer network, where it remained until the recipient's pager or cellular telephone was ready to receive the message, at which point Arch Wireless transmitted the message from the transmitting station nearest to the recipient. After delivery, Arch Wireless retained a copy on its computer servers. The message did not pass through computers owned by the City.

Although the Computer Policy did not cover text messages by its explicit terms, the City made clear to employees, including Quon, that the City would treat text messages the same way as it treated e-mails. At an April 18, 2002, staff meeting at which Quon was present, Lieutenant Steven Duke, the OPD officer responsible for the City's contract with Arch Wireless, told officers that messages sent on the pagers "are considered e-mail messages. This means that [text] messages would fall under the City's policy as public information and [would be] eligible for auditing." App. 30. Duke's comments were put in writing in a memorandum sent on April 29, 2002, by Chief Scharf to Quon and other City personnel.

Within the first or second billing cycle after the pagers were distributed, Quon exceeded his monthly text message character allotment. Duke told Quon about the overage, and reminded him that messages sent on the pagers were "considered e-mail and could be audited." Id., at 40. Duke said, however, that "it was not his intent to audit [an] employee's text messages to see if the overage [was] due to work related transmissions." Ibid. Duke suggested that Quon could reimburse the City for the overage fee rather than have Duke audit the messages. Quon wrote a check to the City for the overage. Duke offered the same arrangement to other employees who incurred overage fees.

Over the next few months, Quon exceeded his character limit three or four times. Each time he reimbursed the City. Quon and another officer again incurred overage fees for their pager usage in August 2002. At a meeting in October, Duke told Scharf that he had become "'tired of being a bill collector.'" Id., at 91. Scharf decided to determine whether the existing character limit was too low—that is, whether officers such as Quon were having to pay fees for sending work-related messages—or if the overages were for personal messages. Scharf told Duke to request transcripts of text messages sent in August and September by Quon and the other employee who had exceeded the character allowance.

At Duke's request, an administrative assistant employed by OPD contacted Arch Wireless. After verifying that the City was the subscriber on the accounts, Arch Wireless provided the desired transcripts. Duke reviewed the transcripts and discovered that many of the messages sent and received on Quon's pager were not work related, and some were sexually explicit. Duke reported his findings to Scharf, who, along with Quon's immediate supervisor, reviewed the transcripts himself. After his review, Scharf referred the matter to OPD's internal affairs division for an investigation into whether Quon was violating OPD rules by pursuing personal matters while on duty.

The officer in charge of the internal affairs review was Sergeant Patrick McMahon. Before conducting a review, McMahon used Quon's work schedule to redact the transcripts in order to eliminate any messages Quon sent while off duty. He then reviewed the content of the messages Quon sent during work hours. McMahon's report noted that Quon sent or received 456 messages during work hours in the month of August 2002, of which no more than 57 were work related; he sent as many as 80 messages during a single day at work; and on an average workday, Quon sent or received 28 messages, of which only 3 were related to police business. The report concluded that Quon had violated OPD rules. Quon was allegedly disciplined.

B

Raising claims under Rev. Stat. §1979,

42 U. S. C. §1983; 18 U. S. C. §2701 et seq. , popularly known as the Stored Communications Act (SCA); and California law, Quon filed suit against petitioners in the United States District Court for the Central District of California. Arch Wireless and an individual not relevant here were also named as defendants. Quon was joined in his suit by another plaintiff who is not a party before this Court and by the other respondents, each of whom exchanged text messages with Quon during August and September 2002: Jerilyn Quon, Jeff Quon's then-wife, from whom he was separated; April Florio, an OPD employee with whom Jeff Quon was romantically involved; and Steve Trujillo, another member of the OPD SWAT Team. Among the allegations in the complaint was that petitioners violated respondents' Fourth Amendment rights and the SCA by obtaining and reviewing the transcript of Jeff Quon's pager messages and that Arch Wireless had violated the SCA by turning over the transcript to the City.

The parties filed cross-motions for summary judgment. The District Court granted Arch Wireless' motion for summary judgment on the SCA claim but denied petitioners' motion for summary judgment on the Fourth Amendment claims. Quon v. Arch Wireless Operating Co., 445 F. Supp. 2d 1116 (CD Cal. 2006). Relying on the plurality opinion in O'Connor v. Ortega , 480 U. S. 709, 711 (1987) , the District Court determined that Quon had a reasonable expectation of privacy in the content of his text messages. Whether the audit of the text messages was nonetheless reasonable, the District Court concluded, turned on Chief Scharf's intent: "[I]f the purpose for the audit was to determine if Quon was using his pager to 'play games' and 'waste time,' then the audit was not constitutionally reasonable"; but if the audit's purpose "was to determine the efficacy of the existing character limits to ensure that officers were not paying hidden work-related costs, ... no constitutional violation occurred." 445 F. Supp. 2d,

at 1146.

The District Court held a jury trial to determine the purpose of the audit. The jury concluded that Scharf ordered the audit to determine the efficacy of the character limits. The District Court accordingly held that petitioners did not violate the Fourth Amendment . It entered judgment in their favor.

The United States Court of Appeals for the Ninth Circuit reversed in part. 529 F. 3d 892 (2008). The panel agreed with the District Court that Jeff Quon had a reasonable expectation of privacy in his text messages but disagreed with the District Court about whether the search was reasonable. Even though the search was conducted for "a legitimate work-related rationale," the Court of Appeals concluded, it "was not reasonable in scope." Id., at 908. The panel disagreed with the District Court's observation that "there were no less-intrusive means" that Chief Scharf could have used "to verify the efficacy of the 25,000 character limit ... without intruding on [respondents'] Fourth Amendment rights." Id., at 908–909. The opinion pointed to a "host of simple ways" that the chief could have used instead of the audit, such as warning Quon at the beginning of the month that his future messages would be audited, or asking Quon himself to redact the transcript of his messages. Id., at 909. The Court of Appeals further concluded that Arch Wireless had violated the SCA by turning over the transcript to the City.

The Ninth Circuit denied a petition for rehearing en banc. Quon v. Arch Wireless Operating Co., 554 F. 3d 769 (2009). Judge Ikuta, joined by six other Circuit Judges, dissented. Id., at 774–779. Judge Wardlaw concurred in the denial of rehearing, defending the panel's opinion against the dissent. Id., at 769–774.

This Court granted the petition for certiorari filed by the City, OPD, and Chief Scharf challenging the Court of Appeals' holding that they violated the Fourth Amendment . 558 U. S. ____

(2009). The petition for certiorari filed by Arch Wireless challenging the Ninth Circuit's ruling that Arch Wireless violated the SCA was denied. USA Mobility Wireless, Inc. v. Quon, 558 U. S. ____ (2009).

II

The Fourth Amendment states: "The right of the people to be secure in their persons, houses, papers, and effects, against unreasonable searches and seizures, shall not be violated ... ." It is well settled that the Fourth Amendment 's protection extends beyond the sphere of criminal investigations. Camara v. Municipal Court of City and County of San Francisco , 387 U. S. 523, 530 (1967) . "The Amendment guarantees the privacy, dignity, and security of persons against certain arbitrary and invasive acts by officers of the Government," without regard to whether the government actor is investigating crime or performing another function. Skinner v. Railway Labor Executives' Assn. , 489 U. S. 602, 613–614 (1989) . The Fourth Amendment applies as well when the Government acts in its capacity as an employer. Treasury Employees v. Von Raab , 489 U. S. 656, 665 (1989) .

The Court discussed this principle in O'Connor. There a physician employed by a state hospital alleged that hospital officials investigating workplace misconduct had violated his Fourth Amendment rights by searching his office and seizing personal items from his desk and filing cabinet. All Members of the Court agreed with the general principle that "[i]ndividuals do not lose Fourth Amendment rights merely because they work for the government instead of a private employer." 480 U. S., at 717 (plurality opinion); see also id., at 731 (Scalia , J., concurring in judgment); id., at 737 (Blackmun, J., dissenting). A majority of the Court further agreed that " 'special needs, beyond the normal need for law enforcement,' " make the warrant and probable-cause requirement impracticable for government employers. Id., at 725 (plurality opinion) (quoting New Jersey v. T. L. O. , 469 U. S. 325, 351 (1985) (Blackmun, J., concurring in judgment); 480 U. S. , at 732 (opinion of Scalia , J.) (quoting same).

The O'Connor Court did disagree on the proper analytical framework for Fourth Amendment claims against government employers. A four-Justice plurality concluded that the correct analysis has two steps. First, because "some government offices may be so open to fellow employees or the public that no expectation of privacy is reasonable," id., at 718, a court must consider "[t]he operational realities of the workplace" in order to determine whether an employee's Fourth Amendment rights are implicated, id., at 717. On this view, "the question whether an employee has a reasonable expectation of privacy must be addressed on a case-by-case basis." Id., at 718. Next, where an employee has a legitimate privacy expectation, an employer's intrusion on that expectation "for noninvestigatory, work-related purposes, as well as for investigations of work-related misconduct, should be judged by the standard of reasonableness under all the circumstances." Id., at 725–726.

Justice Scalia, concurring in the judgment, outlined a different approach. His opinion would have dispensed with an inquiry into "operational realities" and would conclude "that the offices of government employees ... are covered by Fourth Amendment protections as a general matter." Id., at 731. But he would also have held "that government searches to retrieve work-related materials or to investigate violations of workplace rules—searches of the sort that are regarded as reasonable and normal in the private-employer context—do not violate the Fourth Amendment ." Id., at 732.

Later, in the Von Raab decision, the Court explained that "operational realities" could diminish an employee's privacy expectations, and that this diminution could be taken into consideration when assessing the reasonableness of a workplace search. 489 U. S., at 671. In the two decades since O'Connor , however, the threshold test for determining the scope of an employee's Fourth Amendment rights has not been clarified further. Here, though they disagree on whether Quon had a reasonable expectation of privacy, both petitioners and respondents start from the premise that the O'Connor plurality controls. See Brief for Petitioners 22–28; Brief for Respondents 25–32. It is not necessary to resolve whether that premise is correct. The case can be decided by determining that the search was reasonable even assuming Quon had a reasonable expectation of privacy. The two O'Connor approaches—the plurality's and Justice Scalia 's—therefore lead to the same result here.

III

A

Before turning to the reasonableness of the search, it is instructive to note the parties' disagreement over whether Quon had a reasonable expectation of privacy. The record does establish that OPD, at the outset, made it clear that pager messages were not considered private. The City's Computer Policy stated that "[u]sers should have no expectation of privacy or confidentiality when using" City computers. App. to Pet. for Cert. 152a. Chief Scharf's memo and Duke's statements made clear that this official policy extended to text messaging. The disagreement, at least as respondents see the case, is over whether Duke's later statements overrode the official policy. Respondents contend that because Duke told Quon that an audit would be unnecessary if Quon paid for the overage, Quon reasonably could expect that the contents of his messages would remain private.

At this point, were we to assume that inquiry into "operational realities" were called for, compare O'Connor , 480 U. S., at 717 (plurality opinion), with id., at 730–731 (opinion of Scalia ,

J.); see also id., at 737–738 (Blackmun, J., dissenting), it would be necessary to ask whether Duke's statements could be taken as announcing a change in OPD policy, and if so, whether he had, in fact or appearance, the authority to make such a change and to guarantee the privacy of text messaging. It would also be necessary to consider whether a review of messages sent on police pagers, particularly those sent while officers are on duty, might be justified for other reasons, including performance evaluations, litigation concerning the lawfulness of police actions, and perhaps compliance with state open records laws. See Brief for Petitioners 35–40 (citing Cal. Public Records Act, Cal. Govt. Code Ann. §6250 et seq. (West 2008)). These matters would all bear on the legitimacy of an employee's privacy expectation.

The Court must proceed with care when considering the whole concept of privacy expectations in communications made on electronic equipment owned by a government employer. The judiciary risks error by elaborating too fully on the Fourth Amendment implications of emerging technology before its role in society has become clear. See, e.g., Olmstead v. United States , 277 U. S. 438 (1928) , overruled by Katz v. United States , 389 U. S. 347, 353 (1967) . In Katz , the Court relied on its own knowledge and experience to conclude that there is a reasonable expectation of privacy in a telephone booth. See id., at 360–361 (Harlan, J., concurring). It is not so clear that courts at present are on so sure a ground. Prudence counsels caution before the facts in the instant case are used to establish far-reaching premises that define the existence, and extent, of privacy expectations enjoyed by employees when using employer-provided communication devices.

Rapid changes in the dynamics of communication and information transmission are evident not just in the technology itself but in what society accepts as proper behavior. As one amici brief notes, many employers expect or at least tolerate personal use of such equipment by employees because it often increases worker efficiency. See Brief for Electronic Frontier Foundation et al. 16–20. Another amicus points out that the law is beginning to respond to these developments, as some States have recently passed statutes requiring employers to notify employees when monitoring their electronic communications. See Brief for New York Intellectual Property Law Association 22 (citing Del. Code Ann., Tit. 19, §705 (2005); Conn. Gen. Stat. Ann. §31–48d (West 2003)). At present, it is uncertain how workplace norms, and the law's treatment of them, will evolve.

Even if the Court were certain that the O'Connor plurality's approach were the right one, the Court would have difficulty predicting how employees' privacy expectations will be shaped by those changes or the degree to which society will be prepared to recognize those expectations as reasonable. See 480 U. S., at 715. Cell phone and text message communications are so pervasive that some persons may consider them to be essential means or necessary instruments for self-expression, even self-identification. That might strengthen the case for an expectation of privacy. On the other hand, the ubiquity of those devices has made them generally affordable, so one could counter that employees who need cell phones or similar devices for personal matters can purchase and pay for their own. And employer policies concerning communications will of course shape the reasonable expectations of their employees, especially to the extent that such policies are clearly communicated.

A broad holding concerning employees' privacy expectations vis-À-vis employer-provided technological equipment might have implications for future cases that cannot be predicted. It is preferable to dispose of this case on narrower grounds. For present purposes we assume several propositions arguendo: First, Quon had a reasonable expectation of privacy in the text messages sent on the pager provided to him by the City; second, petitioners' review of the transcript constituted a search within the meaning of the Fourth Amendment ; and third, the principles applicable to a government employer's search of an employee's physical office apply with at least the same force when the employer intrudes on the employee's privacy in the electronic sphere.

B

Even if Quon had a reasonable expectation of privacy in his text messages, petitioners did not necessarily violate the Fourth Amendment by obtaining and reviewing the transcripts. Although as a general matter, warrantless searches "are per se unreasonable under the Fourth Amendment ," there are "a few specifically established and well-delineated exceptions" to that general rule. Katz, supra, at 357. The Court has held that the " 'special needs' " of the workplace justify one such exception. O'Connor , 480 U. S., at 725 (plurality opinion); id., at 732 (Scalia, J., concurring in judgment); Von Raab, 489 U. S., at 666–667.

Under the approach of the O'Connor plurality, when conducted for a "noninvestigatory, work-related purpos[e]" or for the "investigatio[n] of work-related misconduct," a government employer's warrantless search is reasonable if it is " 'justified at its inception' " and if " 'the measures adopted are reasonably related to the objectives of the search and not excessively intrusive in light of' " the circumstances giving rise to the search. 480 U. S., at 725–726. The search here satisfied the standard of the O'Connor plurality and was reasonable under that approach.

The search was justified at its inception because there were "reasonable grounds for suspecting that the search [was] necessary for a noninvestigatory work-related purpose." Id., at 726. As a jury found, Chief Scharf ordered the search in order to determine whether the character limit on the City's contract with Arch Wireless was sufficient to meet the City's needs. This was, as the Ninth Circuit noted, a "legitimate work-related rationale." 529 F. 3d, at 908. The City and OPD had a legitimate interest in ensuring that employees were not being forced to pay out of their own pockets for work-related expenses, or on the other hand that the City was not paying for extensive personal communications.

As for the scope of the search, reviewing the transcripts was reasonable because it was an efficient and expedient way to determine whether Quon's overages were the result of work-related messaging or personal use. The review was also not " 'excessively intrusive.' " O'Connor, supra, at 726 (plurality opinion). Although Quon had gone over his monthly allotment a number of times, OPD requested transcripts for only the months of August and September 2002. While it may have been reasonable as well for OPD to review transcripts of all the months in which Quon exceeded his allowance, it was certainly reasonable for OPD to review messages for just two months in order to obtain a large enough sample to decide whether the character limits were efficacious. And it is worth noting that during his internal affairs investigation, McMahon redacted all messages Quon sent while off duty, a measure which reduced the intrusiveness of any further review of the transcripts.

Furthermore, and again on the assumption that Quon had a reasonable expectation of privacy in the contents of his messages, the extent of an expectation is relevant to assessing whether the search was too intrusive. See Von Raab, supra, at 671; cf. Vernonia School Dist. 47J v. Acton, 515 U. S. 646, 654–657 (1995). Even if he could assume some level of privacy would inhere in his messages, it would not have been reasonable for Quon to conclude that his messages were in all circumstances immune from scrutiny. Quon was told that his messages were

subject to auditing. As a law enforcement officer, he would or should have known that his actions were likely to come under legal scrutiny, and that this might entail an analysis of his on-the-job communications. Under the circumstances, a reasonable employee would be aware that sound management principles might require the audit of messages to determine whether the pager was being appropriately used. Given that the City issued the pagers to Quon and other SWAT Team members in order to help them more quickly respond to crises—and given that Quon had received no assurances of privacy—Quon could have anticipated that it might be necessary for the City to audit pager messages to assess the SWAT Team's performance in particular emergency situations.

From OPD's perspective, the fact that Quon likely had only a limited privacy expectation, with boundaries that we need not here explore, lessened the risk that the review would intrude on highly private details of Quon's life. OPD's audit of messages on Quon's employer-provided pager was not nearly as intrusive as a search of his personal e-mail account or pager, or a wiretap on his home phone line, would have been. That the search did reveal intimate details of Quon's life does not make it unreasonable, for under the circumstances a reasonable employer would not expect that such a review would intrude on such matters. The search was permissible in its scope.

The Court of Appeals erred in finding the search unreasonable. It pointed to a "host of simple ways to verify the efficacy of the 25,000 character limit ... without intruding on [respondents'] Fourth Amendment rights." 529 F. 3d, at 909. The panel suggested that Scharf "could have warned Quon that for the month of September he was forbidden from using his pager for personal communications, and that the contents of all his messages would be reviewed to ensure the pager was used only for work-related purposes during that time frame. Alternatively, if [OPD] wanted to review past usage, it could have asked Quon to count the characters himself, or asked him to redact personal messages and grant permission to [OPD] to review the redacted transcript." Ibid.

This approach was inconsistent with controlling precedents. This Court has "repeatedly refused to declare that only the 'least intrusive' search practicable can be reasonable under the Fourth Amendment ." Vernonia , supra, at 663; see also, e.g. , Board of Ed. of Independent School Dist. No. 92 of Pottawatomie Cty. v. Earls, 536 U. S. 822, 837 (2002); Illinois v. Lafayette , 462 U. S. 640, 647 (1983). That rationale "could raise insuperable barriers to the exercise of virtually all search-and-seizure powers," United States v. Martinez-Fuerte , 428 U. S. 543 , n. 12 (1976), because "judges engaged in post hoc evaluations of government conduct can almost always imagine some alternative means by which the objectives of the government might have been accomplished," Skinner , 489 U. S., at 629, n. 9 (internal quotation marks and brackets omitted). The analytic errors of the Court of Appeals in this case illustrate the necessity of this principle. Even assuming there were ways that OPD could have performed the search that would have been less intrusive, it does not follow that the search as conducted was unreasonable.

Respondents argue that the search was per se unreasonable in light of the Court of Appeals' conclusion that Arch Wireless violated the SCA by giving the City the transcripts of Quon's text messages. The merits of the SCA claim are not before us. But even if the Court of Appeals was correct to conclude that the SCA forbade Arch Wireless from turning over the transcripts, it does not follow that petitioners' actions were unreasonable. Respondents point to no authority for the proposition that the existence of statutory protection renders a search per se unreasonable

under the Fourth Amendment . And the precedents counsel otherwise. See Virginia v. Moore , 553 U. S. 164, 168 (2008) (search incident to an arrest that was illegal under state law was reasonable); California v. Greenwood , 486 U. S. 35, 43 (1988) (rejecting argument that if state law forbade police search of individual's garbage the search would violate the Fourth Amendment). Furthermore, respondents do not maintain that any OPD employee either violated the law him- or herself or knew or should have known that Arch Wireless, by turning over the transcript, would have violated the law. The otherwise reasonable search by OPD is not rendered unreasonable by the assumption that Arch Wireless violated the SCA by turning over the transcripts.

Because the search was motivated by a legitimate work-related purpose, and because it was not excessive in scope, the search was reasonable under the approach of the O'Connor plurality. 480 U. S., at 726. For these same reasons—that the employer had a legitimate reason for the search, and that the search was not excessively intrusive in light of that justification— the Court also concludes that the search would be "regarded as reasonable and normal in the private- employer context" and would satisfy the approach of Justice Scalia 's concurrence. Id., at 732. The search was reasonable, and the Court of Appeals erred by holding to the contrary. Petitioners did not violate Quon's Fourth Amendment rights.

C

Finally, the Court must consider whether the search violated the Fourth Amendment rights of Jerilyn Quon, Florio, and Trujillo, the respondents who sent text messages to Jeff Quon. Petitioners and respondents disagree whether a sender of a text message can have a reasonable expectation of privacy in a message he knowingly sends to someone's employer-provided pager. It is not necessary to resolve this question in order to dispose of the case, however. Respondents argue that because "the search was unreasonable as to Sergeant Quon, it was also unreasonable as to his correspondents." Brief for Respondents 60 (some capitalization omitted; boldface deleted). They make no corollary argument that the search, if reasonable as to Quon, could nonetheless be unreasonable as to Quon's correspondents. See id., at 65–66. In light of this litigating position and the Court's conclusion that the search was reasonable as to Jeff Quon, it necessarily follows that these other respondents cannot prevail.

*   *   *

Because the search was reasonable, petitioners did not violate respondents' Fourth Amendment rights, and the court below erred by concluding otherwise. The judgment of the Court of Appeals for the Ninth Circuit is reversed, and the case is remanded for further proceedings consistent with this opinion.

It is so ordered.

NASA v. Nelson (Jan 19, 2011) [Notes omitted]

Justice Alito delivered the opinion of the Court.

In two cases decided more than 30 years ago, this Court referred broadly to a constitutional privacy "interest in avoiding disclosure of personal matters." Whalen v. Roe, 429 U. S. 589, 599–600 (1977); Nixon v. Administrator of General Services, 433 U. S. 425, 457 (1977). Respondents in this case, federal contract employees at a Government laboratory, claim that two parts of a standard employment background investigation violate their rights under Whalen and Nixon. Respondents challenge a section of a form questionnaire that asks employees about treatment or counseling for recent illegal-drug use. They also object to certain open-ended questions on a form sent to employees' designated references.

We assume, without deciding, that the Constitution protects a privacy right of the sort mentioned in Whalen and Nixon. We hold, however, that the challenged portions of the Government's background check do not violate this right in the present case. The Government's interests as employer and proprietor in managing its internal operations, combined with the protections against public dissemination provided by the Privacy Act of 1974, 5 U. S. C. §552a, satisfy any "interest in avoiding disclosure" that may "arguably ha[ve] its roots in the Constitution." Whalen , supra , at 599, 605.

I

A

The National Aeronautics and Space Administration (NASA) is an independent federal agency charged with planning and conducting the Government's "space activities." Pub. L. 111–314, §3, 124 Stat. 3333, 51 U. S. C. §20112(a)(1). NASA's workforce numbers in the tens of thousands of employees. While many of these workers are federal civil servants, a substantial majority are employed directly by Government contractors. Contract employees play an important role in NASA's mission, and their duties are functionally equivalent to those performed by civil servants.

One NASA facility, the Jet Propulsion Laboratory (JPL) in Pasadena, California, is staffed exclusively by contract employees. NASA owns JPL, but the California Institute of Technology (Cal Tech) operates the facility under a Government contract. JPL is the lead NASA center for deep-space robotics and communications. Most of this country's unmanned space missions—from the Explorer 1 satellite in 1958 to the Mars Rovers of today—have been developed and run by JPL. JPL scientists contribute to NASA earth-observation and technology-development projects. Many JPL employees also engage in pure scientific research on topics like "the star formation history of the universe" and "the fundamental properties of quantum fluids." App. 64–65, 68.

Twenty-eight JPL employees are respondents here. Many of them have worked at the lab for decades, and none has ever been the subject of a Government background investigation. At the time when respondents were hired, background checks were standard only for federal civil servants. See Exec. Order No. 10450, 3 CFR 936 (1949–1953 Comp.). In some instances, individual contracts required background checks for the employees of federal contractors, but no blanket policy was in place.

The Government has recently taken steps to eliminate this two-track approach to background investigations. In 2004, a recommendation by the 9/11 Commission prompted the President to order new, uniform identification standards for "[f]ederal employees," including "contractor employees." Homeland Security Presidential Directive/HSPD–12—Policy for a Common Identification Standard for Federal Employees and Contractors, Public Papers of the President, George W. Bush, Vol. 2, Aug. 27, p. 1765 (2007) (hereinafter HSPD–12), App. 127. The Department of Commerce implemented this directive by mandating that contract employees with long-term access to federal facilities complete a standard background check, typically the National Agency Check with Inquiries (NACI). National Inst. of Standards and Technology, Personal Identity Verification of Federal Employees & Contractors, pp. iii–vi, 1–8, 6 (FIPS PUB 201–1, Mar. 2006) (hereinafter FIPS PUB 201–1), App. 131–150, 144–145. 1

An October 2007 deadline was set for completion of these investigations. Memorandum from Joshua B. Bolten, Director, OMB, to the Heads of all Departments and Agencies (Aug. 5, 2005), App. 112. In January 2007, NASA modified its contract with Cal Tech to reflect the new background-check requirement. JPL management informed employees that anyone failing to complete the NACI process by October 2007 would be denied access to JPL and would face termination by Cal Tech.

B

The NACI process has long been the standard background investigation for prospective civil servants. The process begins when the applicant or employee fills out a form questionnaire. Employees who work in "non-sensitive" positions (as all respondents here do) complete Standard Form 85 (SF–85). Office of Personnel Management (OPM), Standard Form 85, Questionnaire for Non-Sensitive Positions, App. 88–95. 2

Most of the questions on SF–85 seek basic biographical information: name, address, prior residences, education, employment history, and personal and professional references. The form also asks about citizenship, selective-service registration, and military service. The last question asks whether the employee has "used, possessed, supplied, or manufactured illegal drugs" in the last year. Id., at 94. If the answer is yes, the employee must provide details, including information about "any treatment or counseling received." Ibid. A "truthful response," the form notes, cannot be used as evidence against the employee in a criminal proceeding. Ibid. The employee must certify that all responses on the form are true and must sign a release authorizing the Government to obtain personal information from schools, employers, and others during its investigation.

Once a completed SF–85 is on file, the "agency check" and "inquiries" begin. 75 Fed. Reg. 5359 (2010). The Government runs the information provided by the employee through FBI and other federal-agency databases. It also sends out form questionnaires to the former employers, schools, landlords, and references listed on SF–85. The particular form at issue in this case—the Investigative Request for Personal Information, Form 42—goes to the employee's former landlords and references. Ibid . 3

Form 42 is a two-page document that takes about five minutes to complete. See ibid . It explains to the reference that "[y]our name has been provided by" a particular employee or applicant to help the Government determine that person's "suitability for employment or a security clearance." App. 96–97. After several preliminary questions about the extent of the reference's associations with the employee, the form asks if the reference has "any reason to question" the employee's "honesty or trustworthiness." Id., at 97. It also asks if the reference knows of any "adverse information" concerning the employee's "violations of the law," "financial integrity," "abuse of alcohol and/or drugs," "mental or emotional stability," "general behavior or conduct," or "other matters." Ibid . If "yes" is checked for any of these categories, the form calls for an explanation in the space below. That space is also available for providing "additional information" ("derogatory" or "favorable") that may bear on "suitability for government employment or a security clearance." Ibid.

All responses to SF–85 and Form 42 are subject to the protections of the Privacy Act. The Act authorizes the Government to keep records pertaining to an individual only when they are "relevant and necessary" to an end "required to be accomplished" by law. 5 U. S. C. §552a(e)(1). Individuals are permitted to access their records and request amendments to them. §§552a(d)(1),(2). Subject to certain exceptions, the Government may not disclose records pertaining to an individual without that individual's written consent. §552a(b).

C

About two months before the October 2007 deadline for completing the NACI, respondents brought this suit, claiming, as relevant here, that the background-check process violates a constitutional right to informational privacy. App.

82 (Complaint for Injunctive and Declaratory Relief). 4 The District Court denied respondents' motion for a preliminary injunction, but the Ninth Circuit granted an injunction pending appeal, 506 F. 3d 713 (2007), and later reversed the District Court's order. The court held that portions of both SF–85 and Form 42 are likely unconstitutional and should be preliminarily enjoined. 512 F. 3d 1134, vacated and superseded, 530 F. 3d 865 (2008).

Turning first to SF–85, the Court of Appeals noted respondents' concession "that most of the questions" on the form are "unproblematic" and do not "implicate the constitutional right to informational privacy." 530 F. 3d, at 878. But the court determined that the "group of questions concerning illegal drugs" required closer scrutiny. Ibid . Applying Circuit precedent, the court upheld SF–85's inquiries into recent involvement with drugs as "necessary to further the government's legitimate interest" in combating illegal-drug use. Id. , at 879. The court went on to hold, however, that the portion of the form requiring disclosure of drug "treatment or counseling" furthered no legitimate interest and was thus likely to be held unconstitutional. Ibid .

Form 42, in the Court of Appeals' estimation, was even "more problematic." Ibid. The form's "open-ended and highly private" questions, the court concluded, were not "narrowly tailored" to meet the Government's interests in verifying contractors' identities and "ensuring the security of the JPL." Id. , at 881, 880. As a result, the court held, these "open-ended" questions, like the drug-treatment question on SF–85, likely violate respondents' informational-privacy rights. 5

Over the dissents of five judges, the Ninth Circuit denied rehearing en banc. 568 F. 3d 1028 (2009). We granted certiorari. 559 U. S. ____ (2010).

II

As noted, respondents contend that

portions of SF–85 and Form 42 violate their "right to informational privacy." Brief for Respondents 15. This Court considered a similar claim in Whalen , 429 U. S. 589 , which concerned New York's practice of collecting "the names and addresses of all persons" prescribed dangerous drugs with both "legitimate and illegitimate uses." Id ., at 591. In discussing that claim, the Court said that "[t]he cases sometimes characterized as protecting 'privacy' " actually involved "at least two different kinds of interests": one, an "interest in avoiding disclosure of personal matters"; 6 the other, an interest in "making certain kinds of important decisions" free from government interference. 7 The patients who brought suit in Whalen argued that New York's statute "threaten[ed] to impair" both their "nondisclosure" interests and their interests in making healthcare decisions independently. Id. , at 600. The Court, however, upheld the statute as a "reasonable exercise of New York's broad police powers." Id. , at 598.

Whalen acknowledged that the disclosure of "private information" to the State was an "unpleasant invasion of privacy," id. , at 602, but the Court pointed out that the New York statute contained "security provisions" that protected against "public disclosure" of patients' information, id. , at 600–601. This sort of "statutory or regulatory duty to avoid unwarranted disclosures" of "accumulated private data" was sufficient, in the Court's view, to protect a privacy interest that "arguably ha[d] its roots in the Constitution." Id. , at 605–606. The Court thus concluded that the statute did not violate "any right or liberty protected by the Fourteenth Amendment ." Id ., at 606.

Four months later, the Court referred again to a constitutional "interest in avoiding disclosure." Nixon, 433 U. S., at 457 (internal quotation marks omitted). Former President Nixon brought a challenge to the Presidential Recordings and Materials Preservation Act, 88 Stat. 1695, note following 44 U. S. C. §2111, a statute that required him to turn over his presidential papers and tape recordings for archival review and screening. 433 U. S., at 455–465. In a section of the opinion entitled "Privacy," the Court addressed a combination of claims that the review required by this Act violated the former President's "Fourth and Fifth Amendmen[t]" rights. Id. , at 455, and n. 18, 458–459. The Court rejected those challenges after concluding that the Act at issue, like the statute in Whalen , contained protections against "undue dissemination of private materials." 433 U. S., at 458. Indeed, the Court observed that the former President's claim was "weaker" than the one "found wanting . . . in Whalen ," as the Government was required to return immediately all "purely private papers and recordings" identified by the archivists. Id., at 458–459. Citing Fourth Amendment precedent, the Court also stated that the public interest in preserving presidential papers outweighed any "legitimate expectation of privacy" that the former President may have enjoyed. Id., at 458 (citing Katz v. United States, 389 U. S. 347 (1967); Camara v. Municipal Court of City and County of San Francisco, 387 U. S. 523 (1967); and Terry v. Ohio, 392 U. S. 1 (1968)). 8

The Court announced the decision in Nixon in the waning days of October Term 1976. Since then, the Court has said little else on the subject of an "individual interest in avoiding disclosure of personal matters." Whalen, supra, at 599; Nixon, supra, at 457. A few opinions have mentioned the concept in passing and in other contexts. See Department of Justice v. Reporters Comm. for Freedom of Press , 489 U. S. 749, 762–763 (1989); New York v. Ferber, 458 U. S. 747 , n. 10 (1982). But no other decision has squarely addressed a constitutional right to informational privacy. 9

III

As was our approach in Whalen, we will assume for present purposes that the Government's challenged inquiries implicate a privacy interest of constitutional significance. 429 U. S., at 599, 605. 10 We hold, however, that, whatever the scope of this interest, it does not prevent the Government from asking reasonable questions of the sort included on SF–85 and Form 42 in an employment background investigation that is subject to the Privacy Act's safeguards against public disclosure.

A

1

As an initial matter, judicial review of the Government's challenged inquiries must take into account the context in which they arise. When the Government asks respondents and their references to fill out SF–85 and Form 42, it does not exercise its sovereign power "to regulate or license." Cafeteria & Restaurant Workers v. McElroy , 367 U. S. 886, 896 (1961) . Rather, the Government conducts the challenged background checks in its capacity "as proprietor" and manager of its "internal operation." Ibid . Time and again our cases have recognized that the Government has a much freer hand in dealing "with citizen employees than it does when it brings its sovereign power to bear on citizens at large." Engquist v. Oregon Dept. of Agriculture , 553 U. S. 591, 598 (2008) ; Waters v. Churchill , 511 U. S. 661, 674 (1994) (plurality opinion). This distinction is grounded on the "common-sense realization" that if every "employment decision became a constitutional matter," the Government could not function. See Connick v. Myers , 461 U. S. 138, 143 (1983) ; see also Bishop v. Wood , 426 U. S. 341, 350 (1976) ("The Due Process Clause . . . is not a guarantee against incorrect or ill-advised personnel decisions").

An assessment of the constitutionality of the challenged portions of SF–85 and Form 42 must account for this distinction. The questions challenged by respondents are part of a standard employment background check of the sort used by millions of private employers. See Brief for Consumer Data Indus. Assn. et al. as Amici Curiae 2 (hereinafter CDIA Brief) ("[M]ore than 88% of U. S. companies ... perform background checks on their employees"). The Government itself has been conducting employment investigations since the earliest days of the Republic. L. White, The Federalists: A Study in Administrative History 262–263 (1948); see OPM, Biography of An Ideal: History of the Federal Civil Service 8 (2002) (noting that President Washington "set a high standard" for federal office and finalized appointments only after "investigating [candidates'] capabilities and reputations"). Since 1871, the President has enjoyed statutory authority to "ascertain the fitness of applicants" for the civil service "as to age, health, character, knowledge and ability for the employment sought," Act of Mar. 3, 1871, Rev. Stat. §1753, as amended, 5 U. S. C. §3301(2), and that Act appears to have been regarded as a codification of established practice. 11 Standard background investigations similar to those at issue here became mandatory for all candidates for the federal civil service in 1953. Exec. Order No. 10450, 3 CFR 936. And the particular investigations challenged in this case arose from a decision to extend that requirement to federal contract employees requiring long-term access to federal facilities. See HSPD–12, at 1765, App. 127; FIPS PUB 201–1, at iii–vi, 1–8, App. 131–150.

As this long history suggests, the Government has an interest in conducting basic employment background checks. Reasonable investigations of applicants and employees aid the Government in ensuring the security of its facilities and in employing a competent, reliable workforce. See Engquist , supra , at 598–599. Courts must keep those interests in mind when asked to go line-by-line through the Government's employment forms and to scrutinize the choice and wording of the questions they contain.

Respondents argue that, because they are contract employees and not civil servants, the Government's broad authority in managing its affairs should apply with diminished force. But the Government's interest as "proprietor" in managing its operations, Cafeteria & Restaurant Workers, supra , at 896, does not turn on such formalities. See Board of Comm'rs, Wabaunsee Cty. v. Umbehr , 518 U. S. 668, 678, 679 (1996) (formal distinctions such as whether a "service provider" has a "contract of employment or a contract for services" with the government is a "very poor proxy" for constitutional interests at stake). The fact that respondents' direct employment relationship is with Cal Tech—which operates JPL under a Government contract—says very little about the interests at stake in this case. The record shows that, as a "practical matter," there are no "[r]elevant distinctions" between the duties performed by NASA's civil-service workforce and its contractor workforce. App. 221. The two classes of employees perform "functionally equivalent duties," and the extent of employees' "access to NASA ... facilities" turns not on formal status but on the nature of "the jobs they perform." Ibid .

At JPL, in particular, the work that contract employees perform is critical to NASA's mission. Respondents in this case include "the lead trouble-shooter for ... th[e] $568 [million]" Kepler space observatory, 7 Record 396; the leader of the program that "tests ... all new technology that NASA will use in space," App. 60; and one of the lead "trajectory designers for ... the Galileo Project and the Apollo Moon landings," id., at 62. This is important work, and all of it is funded with a multibillion dollar investment from the American taxpayer. See NASA, Jet Propulsion Laboratory Annual Report 09, p. 35 (2010), online at http://www.jpl.nasa.gov/annualreport/2009-report.pdf. The Government has a strong interest in conducting basic background checks into the contract employees minding the store at JPL. 12

2

With these interests in view, we conclude that the challenged portions of both SF–85 and Form 42 consist of reasonable, employment-related inquiries that further the Government's interests in managing its internal operations. See Engquist , 553 U. S., at 598–599; Whalen, 429 U. S., at 597–598. As to SF–85, the only part of the form challenged here is its request for information about "any treatment or counseling received" for illegal-drug use within the previous year. The "treatment or counseling" question, however, must be considered in context. It is a followup to SF–85's inquiry into whether the employee has "used, possessed, supplied, or manufactured illegal drugs" during the past year. The Government has good reason to ask employees about their recent illegal-drug use. Like any employer, the Government is entitled to have its projects staffed by reliable, law-abiding persons who will " 'efficiently and effectively' " discharge their duties. See Engquist , supra , at 598–599. Questions about illegal-drug use are a useful way of figuring out which persons have these characteristics. See, e.g. , Breen & Matusitz, An Updated Examination of the Effects of Illegal Drug Use in the Workplace, 19 J. Human Behavior in the Social Environment, 434 (2009) (illicit drug use negatively correlated with workplace productivity).

In context, the follow-up question on "treatment or counseling" for recent illegal-drug use is also a reasonable, employment-related inquiry. The Government, recognizing that illegal-drug use is both a criminal and a medical issue, seeks to separate out those illegal-drug users who are taking steps to address and overcome their problems. The Government thus uses responses to the "treatment or counseling" question as a mitigating factor in determining whether to grant contract employees long-term access to federal facilities. 13

This is a reasonable, and indeed a humane, approach, and respondents do not dispute the legitimacy of the Government's decision to use drug treatment as a mitigating factor in its contractor credentialing decisions. Respondents' argument is that, if drug treatment is only used to mitigate, then the Government should change the mandatory phrasing of SF–85— "Include [in your answer] any treatment or counseling received"—so as to make a response optional. App. 94. As it stands, the mandatory "treatment or counseling" question is unconstitutional, in respondents' view, because it is "more intrusive than necessary to satisfy the government's objective." Brief for Respondents 26; 530 F. 3d, at 879 (holding that "treatment or counseling" question should be enjoined because the form "appears to compel disclosure").

We reject the argument that the Government, when it requests job-related personal information in an employment background check, has a constitutional burden to demonstrate that its questions are "necessary" or the least restrictive means of furthering its interests. So exacting a standard runs directly contrary to Whalen. The patients in Whalen , much like respondents here, argued that New York's statute was unconstitutional because the State could not "demonstrate the necessity" of its program. 429 U. S., at 596. The Court quickly rejected that argument, concluding that New York's collection of patients' prescription information could "not be held unconstitutional simply because" a court viewed it as "unnecessary, in whole or in part." Id., at 596–597.

That analysis applies with even greater force where the Government acts, not as a regulator, but as the manager of its internal affairs. See Engquist, supra , at 598–599. SF–85's "treatment or counseling" question reasonably seeks to identify a subset of acknowledged drug users who are attempting to overcome their problems. The Government's considered position is that phrasing the question in more permissive terms would result in a lower response rate, and the question's effectiveness in identifying illegal-drug users who are suitable for employment would be "materially reduced." Reply Brief for Petitioners 19. That is a reasonable position, falling within the " 'wide latitude' " granted the Government in its dealings with employees. See Engquist, supra , at 600.

3

The Court of Appeals also held that the broad, "open-ended questions" on Form 42 likely violate respondents' informational-privacy rights. Form 42 asks applicants' designated references and landlords for "information" bearing on "suitability for government employment or a security clearance." App. 97. In a series of questions, the Government asks if the reference has any "adverse information" about the applicant's "honesty or trustworthiness," "violations of the law," "financial integrity," "abuse of alcohol and/or drugs," "mental or emotional stability," "general behavior or conduct," or "other matters." Ibid.

These open-ended inquiries, like the drug-treatment question on SF–85, are reasonably aimed at identifying capable employees who will faithfully conduct the Government's business. See Engquist, supra , at 598–599. Asking an applicant's designated references broad, open-ended questions about job suitability is an appropriate tool for separating strong candidates from weak ones. It would be a truly daunting task to catalog all the reasons why a person might not be suitable for a particular job, and references do not have all day to answer a laundry list of specific questions. See CDIA Brief 6–7 (references "typically have limited time to answer questions from potential employers," and "open-ended questions" yield more relevant information than narrow inquiries). Form 42, by contrast, takes just five minutes to complete. 75 Fed. Reg. 5359.

The reasonableness of such open-ended questions is illustrated by their pervasiveness in the public and private sectors. Form 42 alone is sent out by the Government over 1.8 million times annually. Ibid. In addition, the use of open-ended questions in employment background checks appears to be equally commonplace in the private sector. See, e.g. , S. Bock et al., Mandated Benefits 2008 Compliance Guide, Exh. 20.1, A Sample Policy on Reference Checks on Job Applicants ("Following are the guidelines for conducting a telephone reference check: … Ask open-ended questions, then wait for the respondent to answer"); M. Zweig, Human Resources Management 87 (1991) ("Also ask, 'Is there anything else I need to know about [candidate's name]?' This kind of open-ended question may turn up all kinds of information you wouldn't have gotten any other way"). The use of similar open-ended questions by the Government is reasonable and furthers its interests in managing its operations.

B

1

Not only are SF–85 and Form 42 reasonable in light of the Government interests at stake, they are also subject to substantial protections against disclosure to the public. Both Whalen and Nixon recognized that government "accumulation" of "personal information" for "public purposes" may pose a threat to privacy. Whalen , 429 U. S., at 605; see Nixon 433 U. S., at 457–458, 462. But both decisions also stated that a "statutory or regulatory duty to avoid unwarranted disclosures" generally allays these privacy concerns. Whalen , supra , at 605; Nixon , supra, at 458–459. The Court in Whalen , relying on New York's "security provisions" prohibiting public disclosure, turned aside a challenge to the collection of patients' prescription information.

429 U. S., at 594, and n. 12, 600–601, 605. In Nixon, the Court rejected what it regarded as an even "weaker" claim by the former President because the Presidential Recordings and Materials Preservation Act "[n]ot only . . . mandate[d] regulations" against "undue dissemination," but also required immediate return of any "purely private" materials flagged by the Government's archivists. 433 U. S., at 458–459.

Respondents in this case, like the patients in Whalen and former President Nixon, attack only the Government's collection of information on SF–85 and Form 42. And here, no less than in Whalen and Nixon , the information collected is shielded by statute from "unwarranted disclosur[e]." See Whalen , supra, at 605. The Privacy Act, which covers all information collected during the background-check process, allows the Government to maintain records "about an individual" only to the extent the records are "relevant and necessary to accomplish" a purpose authorized by law. 5 U. S. C. §552a(e)(1). The Act requires written consent before the Government may disclose records pertaining to any individual. §552a(b). And the Act imposes criminal liability for willful violations of its nondisclosure obligations. §552a(i)(1). These requirements, as we have noted, give "forceful recognition" to a Government employee's interest in maintaining the "confidentiality of sensitive information . . . in his personnel files." Detroit Edison Co. v. NLRB , 440 U. S. 301 , n. 16 (1979). Like the protections against disclosure in Whalen and Nixon, they "evidence a proper concern" for individual privacy. Whalen, supra, at 605; Nixon, supra, at 458–459.

2

Notwithstanding these safeguards, respondents argue that statutory exceptions to the Privacy Act's disclosure bar, see §§552a(b)(1)–(12), leave its protections too porous to supply a meaningful check against "unwarranted disclosures," Whalen , supra , at 605. Respondents point in particular to what they describe as a "broad" exception for "routine use[s]," defined as uses that are "compatible with the purpose for which the record was collected." §§552a(b)(3), (a)(7).

Respondents' reliance on these exceptions rests on an incorrect reading of both our precedents and the terms of the Privacy Act. As to our cases, the Court in Whalen and Nixon referred approvingly to statutory or regulatory protections against " unwarranted disclosures" and " undue dissemination" of personal information collected by the Government. Whalen , supra , at 605; Nixon , supra , at 458. Neither case suggested that an ironclad disclosure bar is needed to satisfy privacy interests that may be "root[ed] in the Constitution." Whalen , supra , at 605. In Whalen , the New York statute prohibiting "[p]ublic disclosure of the identity of patients" was itself subject to several exceptions. 429 U. S., at 594–595, and n. 12. In Nixon , the protections against "undue dissemination" mentioned in the opinion were not even before the Court, but were to be included in forthcoming regulations "mandate[d]" by the challenged Act. 433 U. S., at 458; see id. , at 437–439 (explaining that the Court was limiting its review to the Act's "facial validity" and was not considering the Administrator's forthcoming regulations). Thus, the mere fact that the Privacy Act's nondisclosure requirement is subject to exceptions does not show that the statute provides insufficient protection against public disclosure.

Nor does the substance of the "routine use" exception relied on by respondents create any undue risk of public dissemination. None of the authorized "routine use[s]" of respondents' background-check information allows for release to the public. 71 Fed. Reg. 45859–45860, 45862 (2006); 60 Fed. Reg. 63084 (1995), as amended, 75 Fed. Reg. 28307 (2010). Rather, the established "routine use[s]" consist of limited, reasonable steps designed to complete the background-check process in an efficient and orderly manner. See Whalen , supra , at 602 (approving disclosures to authorized New York Department of Health employees that were not "meaningfully distinguishable" from routine disclosures "associated with many facets of health care"). One routine use, for example, involves a limited disclosure to persons filling out Form 42 so that designated references can "identify the individual" at issue and can understand the "nature and purpose of the investigation." App. 89. Authorized JPL employees also review each completed SF–85 to verify that all requested information has been provided. Id., at 211. These designated JPL employees may not "disclose any information contained in the form to anyone else," ibid ., and Cal Tech is not given access to adverse information uncovered during the Government's background check, id., at 207–208. The "remote possibility" of public disclosure created by these narrow "routine use[s]" does not undermine the Privacy Act's substantial protections. See Whalen , 429 U. S., at 601–602 ("remote possibility" that statutory security provisions will "provide inadequate protection against unwarranted disclosures" not a sufficient basis for striking down statute).

Citing past violations of the Privacy Act, 14 respondents note that it is possible that their personal information could be disclosed as a result of a similar breach. But data breaches are a possibility any time the Government stores information. As the Court recognized in Whalen , the mere possibility that security measures will fail provides no "proper ground" for a broad-based attack on government information-collection practices. Ibid. Respondents also cite a portion of SF–85 that warns of possible disclosure "[t]o the news media or the general public." App. 89. By its terms, this exception allows public disclosure only where release is "in the public interest" and would not result in "an unwarranted invasion of personal privacy." Ibid . Respondents have not cited any example of such a disclosure, nor have they identified any plausible scenario in which their information might be unduly disclosed under this exception. 15

In light of the protection provided by the Privacy Act's nondisclosure requirement, and because the challenged portions of the forms consist of reasonable inquiries in an employment background check, we conclude that the Government's inquiries do not violate a constitutional right to informational privacy. Whalen , supra , at 605.

*   *   *

For these reasons, the judgment of the Court of Appeals is reversed, and the case is remanded for further proceedings consistent with this opinion.

It is so ordered.

Kentucky v. King (May 16, 2011) [Notes omitted]

Justice Alito delivered the opinion of the Court.

It is well established that "exigent circumstances," including the need to prevent the destruction of evidence, permit police officers to conduct an otherwise permissible search without first obtaining a warrant. In this case, we consider whether this rule applies when police, by knocking on the door of a residence and announcing their presence, cause the occupants to attempt to destroy evidence. The Kentucky Supreme Court held that the exigent circumstances rule does not apply in the case at hand because the police should have foreseen that their conduct would prompt the occupants to attempt to destroy evidence. We reject this interpretation of the exigent circumstances rule. The conduct of the police prior to their entry into the apartment was entirely lawful. They did not violate the Fourth Amendment or threaten to do so. In such a situation, the exigent circumstances rule applies.

I

A

This case concerns the search of an apartment in Lexington, Kentucky. Police officers set up a controlled buy of crack cocaine outside an apartment complex. Undercover Officer Gibbons watched the deal take place from an unmarked car in a nearby parking lot. After the deal occurred, Gibbons radioed uniformed officers to move in on the suspect. He told the officers that the suspect was moving quickly toward the breezeway of an apartment building, and he urged them to "hurry up and get there" before the suspect entered an apartment. App. 20.

In response to the radio alert, the uniformed officers drove into the nearby parking lot, left their vehicles, and ran to the breezeway. Just as they entered the breezeway, they heard a door shut and detected a very strong odor of burnt marijuana. At the end of the breezeway, the officers saw two apartments, one on the left and one on the right, and they did not know which apartment the suspect had entered. Gibbons had radioed that the suspect was running into the apartment on the right, but the officers did not hear this statement because they had already left their vehicles. Because they smelled marijuana smoke emanating from the apartment on the left, they approached the door of that apartment.

Officer Steven Cobb, one of the uniformed officers who approached the door, testified that the officers banged on the left apartment door "as loud as [they] could" and announced, " 'This is the police' " or " 'Police, police, police.' " Id., at 22–23. Cobb said that "[a]s soon as [the officers] started banging on the door," they "could hear people inside moving," and "[i]t sounded as [though] things were being moved inside the apartment." Id., at 24. These noises, Cobb testified, led the officers to believe that drug-related evidence was about to be destroyed.

At that point, the officers announced that they "were going to make entry inside the apartment." Ibid. Cobb then kicked in the door, the officers entered the apartment, and they found three people in the front room: respondent Hollis King, respondent's girlfriend, and a guest who was smoking marijuana. 1 The officers performed a protective sweep of the apartment during which they saw marijuana and powder cocaine in plain view. In a subsequent search, they also discovered crack cocaine, cash, and drug paraphernalia.

Police eventually entered the apartment on the right. Inside, they found the suspected drug dealer who was the initial target of their investigation.

B

In the Fayette County Circuit Court, a grand jury charged respondent with trafficking in marijuana, first-degree trafficking in a controlled substance, and second-degree persistent felony offender status. Respondent filed a motion to suppress the evidence from the warrantless search, but the Circuit Court denied the motion. The Circuit Court concluded that the officers had probable cause to investigate the marijuana odor and that the officers "properly conducted [the investigation] by initially knocking on the door of the apartment unit and awaiting the response or consensual entry." App. to Pet. for Cert. 9a. Exigent circumstances justified the warrantless entry, the court held, because "there was no response at all to the knocking," and because "Officer Cobb heard movement in the apartment which he reasonably concluded were persons in the act of destroying evidence, particularly narcotics because of the smell." Ibid. Respondent then entered a conditional guilty plea, reserving his right to appeal the denial of his suppression motion. The court sentenced respondent to 11 years' imprisonment.

The Kentucky Court of Appeals affirmed. It held that exigent circumstances justified the warrantless entry because the police reasonably believed that evidence would be destroyed. The police did not impermissibly create the exigency, the court explained, because they did not deliberately evade the warrant requirement.

The Supreme Court of Kentucky reversed. 302 S. W. 3d 649 (2010). As a preliminary matter, the court observed that there was "certainly some question as to whether the sound of persons moving [inside the apartment] was sufficient to establish that evidence was being destroyed." Id., at 655. But the court did not answer that question. Instead, it "assume[d] for the purpose of argument that exigent circumstances existed." Ibid.

To determine whether police impermissibly created the exigency, the Supreme Court of Kentucky announced a two-part test. First, the court held, police cannot "deliberately creat[e] the exigent circumstances with the bad faith intent to avoid the warrant requirement." Id. , at 656 (internal quotation marks omitted). Second, even absent bad faith, the court concluded, police may not rely on exigent circumstances if "it was reasonably foreseeable that the investigative tactics employed by the police would create the exigent circumstances." Ibid. (internal quotation marks omitted). Although the court found no evidence of bad faith, it held that exigent circumstances could not justify the search because it was reasonably foreseeable that the occupants would destroy evidence when the police knocked on the door and announced their presence. Ibid.

We granted certiorari. 561 U. S. ____ (2010). 2

II

A

The Fourth Amendment provides:

"The right of the people to be secure in their persons, houses, papers, and effects, against unreasonable searches and seizures, shall not be violated, and no Warrants shall issue, but upon probable cause, supported by Oath or affirmation, and particularly describing the place to be searched, and the persons or things to be seized."

The text of the Amendment thus expressly imposes two requirements. First, all searches and seizures must be reasonable. Second, a warrant may not be issued unless probable cause is properly established and the scope of the authorized search is set out with particularity. See Payton v. New York , 445 U. S. 573, 584 (1980) .

Although the text of the Fourth Amendment does not specify when a search warrant must be obtained, this Court has inferred that a warrant must generally be secured. "It is a 'basic principle of Fourth Amendment law,' " we have often said, " 'that searches and seizures inside a home without a warrant are presumptively unreasonable.' " Brigham City v. Stuart , 547 U. S. 398, 403 (2006) (quoting Groh v. Ramirez , 540 U. S. 551, 559 (2004)). But we have also recognized that this presumption may be overcome in some circumstances because "[t]he ultimate touchstone of the Fourth Amendment is 'reasonableness.' " Brigham City , supra, at 403; see also Michigan v. Fisher , 558 U. S. ____, ____ (2009) (per curiam) (slip op., at 2). Accordingly, the warrant requirement is subject to certain reasonable exceptions. Brigham City , supra , at 403.

One well-recognized exception applies when " 'the exigencies of the situation' make the needs of law en-forcement so compelling that [a] warrantless search is objectively reasonable under the Fourth Amendment ." Mincey v. Arizona , 437 U. S. 385, 394 (1978) ; see also Payton , supra, at 590 ("[T]he Fourth Amendment has drawn a firm line at the entrance to the house. Absent exigent circumstances, that threshold may not reasonably be crossed without a warrant").

This Court has identified several exigencies that may justify a warrantless search of a home. See Brigham City , 547 U. S., at 403. Under the "emergency aid" exception, for example,

"officers may enter a home without a warrant to render emergency assistance to an injured occupant or to protect an occupant from imminent injury." Ibid.; see also, e.g., Fisher , supra, at ____ (slip op., at 5) (upholding warrantless home entry based on emergency aid exception). Police officers may enter premises without a warrant when they are in hot pursuit of a fleeing suspect. See United States v. Santana , 427 U. S. 38, 42–43 (1976) . And—what is relevant here—the need "to prevent the imminent destruction of evidence" has long been recognized as a sufficient justification for a warrantless search. Brigham City , supra, at 403; see also Georgia v. Randolph , 547 U. S. 103 , n. 6 (2006); Minnesota v. Olson , 495 U. S. 91, 100 (1990) . 3

B

Over the years, lower courts have developed an exception to the exigent circumstances rule, the so-called "police-created exigency" doctrine. Under this doctrine, police may not rely on the need to prevent destruction of evidence when that exigency was "created" or "manufactured" by the conduct of the police. See, e.g., United States v. Chambers , 395 F. 3d 563, 566 (CA6 2005) ("[F]or a warrantless search to stand, law enforcement officers must be responding to an unanticipated exigency rather than simply creating the exigency for themselves"); United States v. Gould , 364 F. 3d 578, 590 (CA5 2004) (en banc) ("[A]lthough exigent circumstances may justify a warrantless probable cause entry into the home, they will not do so if the exigent circumstances were manufactured by the agents" (internal quotation marks omitted)).

In applying this exception for the "creation" or "manufacturing" of an exigency by the police, courts require something more than mere proof that fear of detection by the police caused the destruction of evidence. An additional showing is obviously needed because, as the Eighth Circuit has recognized, "in some sense the police always create the exigent circumstances." United States v. Duchi , 906 F. 2d 1278, 1284 (CA8 1990). That is to say, in the vast majority of cases in which evidence is destroyed by persons who are engaged in illegal conduct, the reason for the destruction is fear that the evidence will fall into the hands of law enforcement. Destruction of evidence issues probably occur most frequently in drug cases because drugs may be easily destroyed by flushing them down a toilet or rinsing them down a drain. Persons in possession of valuable drugs are unlikely to destroy them unless they fear discovery by the police. Consequently, a rule that precludes the police from making a warrantless entry to prevent the destruction of evidence whenever their conduct causes the exigency would unreasonably shrink the reach of this well-established exception to the warrant requirement.

Presumably for the purpose of avoiding such a result, the lower courts have held that the police-created exigency doctrine requires more than simple causation, but the lower courts have not agreed on the test to be applied. Indeed, the petition in this case maintains that "[t]here are currently five different tests being used by the United States Courts of Appeals," Pet. for Cert. 11, and that some state courts have crafted additional tests, id. , at 19–20.

III

A

Despite the welter of tests devised by the lower courts, the answer to the question presented in this case follows directly and clearly from the principle that permits warrantless searches in the first place. As previously noted, warrantless searches are allowed when the circumstances make it reasonable, within the meaning of the Fourth Amendment , to dispense with the warrant requirement. Therefore, the answer to the question before us is that the exigent circumstances rule justifies a warrantless search when the conduct of the police preceding the

exigency is reasonable in the same sense. Where, as here, the police did not create the exigency by engaging or threatening to engage in conduct that violates the Fourth Amendment , warrantless entry to prevent the destruction of evidence is reasonable and thus allowed. 4

We have taken a similar approach in other cases involving warrantless searches. For example, we have held that law enforcement officers may seize evidence in plain view, provided that they have not violated the Fourth Amendment in arriving at the spot from which the observation of the evidence is made. See Horton v. California , 496 U. S. 128, 136–140 (1990) . As we put it in Horton , "[i]t is … an essential predicate to any valid warrantless seizure of incriminating evidence that the officer did not violate the Fourth Amendment in arriving at the place from which the evidence could be plainly viewed." Id., at 136. So long as this prerequisite is satisfied, however, it does not matter that the officer who makes the observation may have gone to the spot from which the evidence was seen with the hope of being able to view and seize the evidence. See id., at 138 ("The fact that an officer is interested in an item of evidence and fully expects to find it in the course of a search should not invalidate its seizure"). Instead, the Fourth Amendment requires only that the steps preceding the seizure be lawful. See id., at 136–137.

Similarly, officers may seek consent-based encounters if they are lawfully present in the place where the consensual encounter occurs. See INS v. Delgado , 466 U. S. 210, 217, n. 5 (1984) (noting that officers who entered into consent-based encounters with employees in a factory building were "lawfully present [in the factory] pursuant to consent or a warrant"). If consent is freely given, it makes no difference that an officer may have approached the person with the hope or expectation of obtaining consent. See id., at 216 ("While most citizens will respond to a police request, the fact that people do so, and do so without being told they are free not to respond, hardly eliminates the consensual nature of the response").

B

Some lower courts have adopted a rule that is similar to the one that we recognize today. See United States v. MacDonald , 916 F. 2d 766, 772 (CA2 1990) (en banc) (law enforcement officers "do not impermissibly create exigent circumstances" when they "act in an entirely lawful manner"); State v. Robinson , 2010 WI 80, ¶32, 327 Wis. 2d 302, 326–328, 786 N. W. 2d 463, 475–476 (2010). But others, including the Kentucky Supreme Court, have imposed additional requirements that are unsound and that we now reject.

Bad faith . Some courts, including the Kentucky Supreme Court, ask whether law enforcement officers " 'deliberately created the exigent circumstances with the bad faith intent to avoid the warrant requirement.' " 302 S. W. 3d, at 656 (quoting Gould , 364 F. 3d, at 590); see also, e.g., Chambers , 395 F. 3d, at 566; United States v. Socey , 846 F. 2d 1439, 1448 (CADC 1988); United States v. Rengifo , 858 F. 2d 800, 804 (CA1 1988).

This approach is fundamentally inconsistent with our Fourth Amendment jurisprudence. "Our cases have repeatedly rejected" a subjective approach, asking only whether "the circumstances, viewed objectively , justify the action." 'Brigham City , 547 U. S., at 404 (alteration and internal quotation marks omitted); see also Fisher , 558 U. S., at ____ (slip op., at 3–5). Indeed, we have never held, outside limited contexts such as an "inventory search or administrative inspection ... , that an officer's motive invalidates objectively justifiable behavior under the Fourth Amendment ." Whren v. United States , 517 U. S. 806, 812 (1996) ; see also Brigham City, supra, at 405.

The reasons for looking to objective factors, rather than subjective intent, are clear. Legal tests based on reasonableness are generally objective, and this Court has long taken the view that "evenhanded law enforcement is best achieved by the application of objective standards of conduct, rather than standards that depend upon the subjective state of mind of the officer." Horton , supra, at 138.

Reasonable foreseeability . Some courts, again including the Kentucky Supreme Court, hold that police may not rely on an exigency if " 'it was reasonably foreseeable that the investigative tactics employed by the police would create the exigent circumstances.' " 302 S. W. 3d, at 656 (quoting Mann v . State , 357 Ark. 159, 172, 161 S. W. 3d 826, 834 (2004)); see also, e.g., United States v. Mowatt , 513 F. 3d 395, 402 (CA4 2008). Courts applying this test have invalidated warrantless home searches on the ground that it was reasonably foreseeable that police officers, by knocking on the door and announcing their presence, would lead a drug suspect to destroy evidence. See, e.g., id. , at 402–403; 302 S. W. 3d, at 656.

Contrary to this reasoning, however, we have rejected the notion that police may seize evidence without a warrant only when they come across the evidence by happenstance. In Horton , as noted, we held that the police may seize evidence in plain view even though the officers may be "interested in an item of evidence and fully expec[t] to find it in the course of a search." 496 U. S., at 138.

Adoption of a reasonable foreseeability test would also introduce an unacceptable degree of unpredictability. For example, whenever law enforcement officers knock on the door of premises occupied by a person who may be involved in the drug trade, there is some possibility that the occupants may possess drugs and may seek to destroy them. Under a reasonable foreseeability test, it would be necessary to quantify the degree of predictability that must be reached before the police-created exigency doctrine comes into play.

A simple example illustrates the difficulties that such an approach would produce. Suppose that the officers in the present case did not smell marijuana smoke and thus knew only that there was a 50% chance that the fleeing suspect had entered the apartment on the left rather than the apartment on the right. Under those circumstances, would it have been reasonably foreseeable that the occupants of the apartment on the left would seek to destroy evidence upon learning that the police were at the door? Or suppose that the officers knew only that the suspect had disappeared into one of the apartments on a floor with 3, 5, 10, or even 20 units? If the police chose a door at random and knocked for the purpose of asking the occupants if they knew a person who fit the description of the suspect, would it have been reasonably foreseeable that the occupants would seek to destroy evidence?

We have noted that "[t]he calculus of reasonableness must embody allowance for the fact that police officers are often forced to make split-second judgments—in circumstances that are tense, uncertain, and rapidly evolving." Graham v. Connor , 490 U. S. 386, 396–397 (1989) . The reasonable foreseeability test would create unacceptable and unwarranted difficulties for law enforcement officers who must make quick decisions in the field, as well as for judges who would be required to determine after the fact whether the destruction of evidence in response to a knock on the door was reasonably foreseeable based on what the officers knew at the time.

Probable cause and time to secure a warrant . Some courts, in applying the police-created exigency doctrine, fault law enforcement officers if, after acquiring evidence that is sufficient to establish probable cause to search particular premises, the officers do not seek a warrant but instead knock on the door and seek either to speak with an occupant or to obtain consent to search. See, e.g., Chambers , supra, at 569 (citing "[t]he failure to seek a warrant in the face of plentiful probable cause" as a factor indicating that the police deliberately created the exigency).

This approach unjustifiably interferes with legitimate law enforcement strategies. There are many entirely proper reasons why police may not want to seek a search warrant as soon as the bare minimum of evidence needed to establish probable cause is acquired. Without attempting to provide a comprehensive list of these reasons, we note a few.

First, the police may wish to speak with the occupants of a dwelling before deciding whether it is worthwhile to seek authorization for a search. They may think that a short and simple conversation may obviate the need to apply for and execute a warrant. See Schneckloth v. Bustamonte , 412 U. S. 218, 228 (1973) . Second, the police may want to ask an occupant of the premises for consent to search because doing so is simpler, faster, and less burdensome than applying for a warrant. A consensual search also "may result in considerably less inconvenience" and embarrassment to the occupants than a search conducted pursuant to a warrant. Ibid. Third, law enforcement officers may wish to obtain more evidence before submitting what might otherwise be considered a marginal warrant application. Fourth, prosecutors may wish to wait until they acquire evidence that can justify a search that is broader in scope than the search that a judicial officer is likely to authorize based on the evidence then available. And finally, in many cases, law enforcement may not want to execute a search that will disclose the existence of an investigation because doing so may interfere with the acquisition of additional evidence against those already under suspicion or evidence about additional but as yet unknown participants in a criminal scheme.

We have said that "[l]aw enforcement officers are under no constitutional duty to call a halt to criminal investigation the moment they have the minimum evidence to establish probable cause." Hoffa v. United States , 385 U. S. 293, 310 (1966) . Faulting the police for failing to apply for a search warrant at the earliest possible time after obtaining probable cause imposes a duty that is nowhere to be found in the Constitution.

<tab>Standard or good investigative tactics . Finally, some lower court cases suggest that law enforcement officers may be found to have created or manufactured an exigency if the court concludes that the course of their investigation was "contrary to standard or good law enforcement practices (or to the policies or practices of their jurisdictions)." Gould , 364 F. 3d, at 591. This approach fails to provide clear guidance for law enforcement officers and authorizes courts to make judgments on matters that are the province of those who are responsible for federal and state law enforcement agencies.

C

Respondent argues for a rule that differs from those discussed above, but his rule is also flawed. Respondent contends that law enforcement officers impermissibly create an exigency when they "engage in conduct that would cause a reasonable person to believe that entry is imminent and inevitable." Brief for Respondent 24. In respondent's view, relevant factors include the officers' tone of voice in announcing their presence and the forcefulness of their knocks. But the ability of law enforcement officers to respond to an exigency cannot turn on such subtleties.

Police officers may have a very good reason to announce their presence loudly and to knock on the door with some force. A forceful knock may be necessary to alert the occupants that someone is at the door. Cf. United States v. Banks ,

540 U. S. 31, 33 (2003) (Police "rapped hard enough on the door to be heard by officers at the back door" and announced their presence, but defendant "was in the shower and testified that he heard nothing"). Furthermore, unless police officers identify themselves loudly enough, occupants may not know who is at their doorstep. Officers are permitted—indeed, encouraged—to identify themselves to citizens, and "in many circumstances this is cause for assurance, not discomfort." United States v. Drayton , 536 U. S. 194, 204 (2002) . Citizens who are startled by an unexpected knock on the door or by the sight of unknown persons in plain clothes on their doorstep may be relieved to learn that these persons are police officers. Others may appreciate the opportunity to make an informed decision about whether to answer the door to the police.

If respondent's test were adopted, it would be extremely difficult for police officers to know how loudly they may announce their presence or how forcefully they may knock on a door without running afoul of the police-created exigency rule. And in most cases, it would be nearly impossible for a court to determine whether that threshold had been passed. The Fourth Amendment does not require the nebulous and impractical test that respondent proposes. 5

D

For these reasons, we conclude that the exigent circumstances rule applies when the police do not gain entry to premises by means of an actual or threatened violation of the Fourth Amendment . This holding provides ample protection for the privacy rights that the Amendment protects.

When law enforcement officers who are not armed with a warrant knock on a door, they do no more than any private citizen might do. And whether the person who knocks on the door and requests the opportunity to speak is a police officer or a private citizen, the occupant has no obligation to open the door or to speak. Cf. Florida v. Royer , 460 U. S. 491, 497–498 (1983) . ("[H]e may decline to listen to the questions at all and may go on his way"). When the police knock on a door but the occupants choose not to respond or to speak, "the investigation will have reached a conspicuously low point," and the occupants "will have the kind of warning that even the most elaborate security system cannot provide." Chambers , 395 F. 3d, at 577 (Sutton, J., dissenting). And even if an occupant chooses to open the door and speak with the officers, the occupant need not allow the officers to enter the premises and may refuse to answer any questions at any time.

Occupants who choose not to stand on their constitutional rights but instead elect to attempt to destroy evidence have only themselves to blame for the warrantless exigent-circumstances search that may ensue.

IV

We now apply our interpretation of the police-created exigency doctrine to the facts of this case.

A

We need not decide whether exigent circumstances existed in this case. Any warrantless entry based on exigent circumstances must, of course, be supported by a genuine exigency. See Brigham City , 547 U. S., at 406 . The trial court and the Kentucky Court of Appeals found that there was a real exigency in this case, but the Kentucky Supreme Court expressed doubt on this issue, observing that there was "certainly some question as to whether the sound of persons moving [inside the apartment] was sufficient to establish that evidence was being destroyed." 302 S. W. 3d, at 655. The Kentucky Supreme Court "assum[ed] for the purpose of argument that exigent circumstances existed," ibid., and it held that the police had impermissibly manufactured the exigency.

We, too, assume for purposes of argument that an exigency existed. We decide only the question on which the Kentucky Supreme Court ruled and on which we granted certiorari: Under what circumstances do police impermissibly create an exigency? Any question about whether an exigency actually existed is better addressed by the Kentucky Supreme Court on remand. See Kirk v. Louisiana , 536 U. S. 635, 638 (2002) (per curiam) (reversing state-court judgment that exigent circumstances were not required for warrantless home entry and remanding for state court to determine whether exigent circumstances were present).

B

In this case, we see no evidence that the officers either violated the Fourth Amendment or threatened to do so prior to the point when they entered the apartment. Officer Cobb testified without contradiction that the officers "banged on the door as loud as [they] could" and announced either " 'Police, police, police' " or " 'This is the police.' " App. 22–23. This conduct was entirely consistent with the Fourth Amendment , and we are aware of no other evidence that might show that the officers either violated the Fourth Amendment or threatened to do so (for example, by announcing that they would break down the door if the occupants did not open the door voluntarily).

Respondent argues that the officers "demanded" entry to the apartment, but he has not pointed to any evidence in the record that supports this assertion. He relies on a passing statement made by the trial court in its opinion denying respondent's motion to suppress. See App. to Pet. for Cert. 3a–4a. In recounting the events that preceded the search, the judge wrote that the officers "banged on the door of the apartment on the back left of the breezeway identifying themselves as police officers and demanding that the door be opened by the persons inside." Ibid .

(emphasis added and deleted). However, at a later point in this opinion, the judge stated that the officers "initially knock[ed] on the door of the apartment unit and await[ed] the response or consensual entry." Id. , at 9a. This later statement is consistent with the testimony at the suppression hearing and with the findings of the state appellate courts. See 302 S. W. 3d, at 651 (The officers "knocked loudly on the back left apartment door and announced 'police' "); App. to Pet. for Cert. 14a (The officers "knock[ed] on the door and announc[ed] themselves as police"); App. 22–24. There is no evidence of a "demand" of any sort, much less a demand that amounts to a threat to violate the Fourth Amendment . If there is contradictory evidence that has not been brought to our attention, the state court may elect to address that matter on remand.

Finally, respondent claims that the officers "explained to [the occupants that the officers] were going to make entry inside the apartment," id., at 24, but the record is clear that the officers did not make this statement until after the exigency arose. As Officer Cobb testified, the officers "knew that there was possibly something that was going to be destroyed inside the apartment," and " [a]t that point , ... [they] explained ... [that they] were going to make entry." Ibid. (emphasis added). Given that this announcement was made after the exigency arose, it could not have created the exigency.

* * *

Like the court below, we assume for purposes of argument that an exigency existed. Because the officers in this case did not violate or threaten to violate the Fourth Amendment prior to the exigency, we hold that the exigency justified the warrantless search of the apartment.

The judgment of the Kentucky Supreme Court is reversed, and the case is remanded for further proceedings not inconsistent with this opinion.

It is so ordered.

US v. Jones (Jan 23, 2012) [Notes omitted]

Justice Scalia delivered the opinion of the Court.

We decide whether the attachment of a Global-Positioning-System (GPS) tracking device to an individual's vehicle, and subsequent use of that device to monitor the vehicle's movements on public streets, constitutes a search or seizure within the meaning of the Fourth Amendment.

I

In 2004 respondent Antoine Jones, owner and operator of a nightclub in the District of Columbia, came under suspicion of trafficking in narcotics and was made the target of an investigation by a joint FBI and Metropolitan Police Department task force. Officers employed various investigative techniques, including visual surveillance of the nightclub, installation of a camera focused on the front door of the club, and a pen register and wiretap covering Jones's cellular phone.

Based in part on information gathered from these sources, in 2005 the Government applied to the United States District Court for the District of Columbia for a warrant authorizing the use of an electronic tracking device on the Jeep Grand Cherokee registered to Jones's wife. A warrant issued, authorizing installation of the de-vice in the District of Columbia and within 10 days.

On the 11th day, and not in the District of Columbia but in Maryland, 1 agents installed a GPS tracking device on the undercarriage of the Jeep while it was parked in a public parking lot. Over the next 28 days, the Government used the device to track the vehicle's movements, and once had to replace the device's battery when the vehicle was parked in a different public lot in Maryland. By means of signals from multiple satellites, the device established the vehicle's location within 50 to 100 feet, and communicated that location by cellular phone to a Government computer. It relayed more than 2,000 pages of data over the 4-week period.

The Government ultimately obtained a multiple-count indictment charging Jones and several alleged co-conspirators with, as relevant here, conspiracy to distribute and possess with intent to distribute five kilograms or more of cocaine and 50 grams or more of cocaine base, in violation of 21 U. S. C. §§841 and 846. Before trial, Jones filed a motion to suppress evidence obtained through the GPS device. The District Court granted the motion only in part, suppressing the data obtained while the vehicle was parked in the garage adjoining Jones's residence. 451 F. Supp. 2d 71, 88 (2006). It held the remaining data admissible, because " '[a] person traveling in an automobile on public thoroughfares has no reasonable expectation of privacy in his movements from one place to another.' " Ibid. (quoting United States v. Knotts, 460 U. S. 276, 281 (1983)). Jones's trial in October 2006 produced a hung jury on the conspiracy count.

In March 2007, a grand jury returned another indictment, charging Jones and others with the same conspiracy. The Government introduced at trial the same GPS-derived locational data admitted in the first trial, which connected Jones to the alleged conspirators' stash house that contained $850,000 in cash, 97 kilograms of cocaine, and 1 kilogram of cocaine base. The jury returned a guilty verdict, and the District Court sentenced Jones to life imprisonment.

The United States Court of Appeals for the District of Columbia Circuit reversed the conviction because of admission of the evidence obtained by warrantless use of the GPS device which, it said, violated the Fourth Amend-ment. United States v. Maynard, 615 F. 3d 544 (2010). The D. C. Circuit denied the Government's petition for rehearing en banc, with four judges dissenting. 625 F. 3d 766 (2010). We granted certiorari, 564 U. S. ____ (2011).

II

A

The Fourth Amendment provides in relevant part that "[t]he right of the people to be secure in their persons, houses, papers, and effects, against unreasonable searches and seizures, shall not be violated." It is beyond dispute that a vehicle is an "effect" as that term is used in the Amendment. United States v. Chadwick, 433 U. S. 1, 12 (1977). We hold that the Government's installation of a GPS device on a target's vehicle, 2 and its use of that device to monitor the vehicle's movements, constitutes a "search."

It is important to be clear about what occurred in this case: The Government physically occupied private property for the purpose of obtaining information. We have no doubt that such a physical intrusion would have been considered a "search" within the meaning of the Fourth Amendment when it was adopted. Entick v. Carrington, 95 Eng. Rep. 807 (C. P. 1765), is a "case we have described as a 'monument of English freedom' 'undoubtedly familiar' to 'every American statesman' at the time the Constitution was adopted, and considered to be 'the true and ultimate expression of constitutional law' " with regard to search and seizure. Brower v. County of Inyo, 489 U. S. 593, 596 (1989) (quoting Boyd v. United States, 116 U. S. 616, 626 (1886)). In that case, Lord Camden expressed in plain terms the significance of property rights in search-and-seizure analysis:

"[O]ur law holds the property of every man so sacred, that no man can set his foot upon his neighbour's close without his leave; if he does he is a trespasser, though he does no damage at all; if he will tread upon his neighbour's ground, he must justify it by law." Entick, supra, at 817.

The text of the Fourth Amendment reflects

its close connection to property, since otherwise it would have referred simply to "the right of the people to be secure against unreasonable searches and seizures"; the phrase "in their persons, houses, papers, and effects" would have been superfluous.

Consistent with this understanding, our Fourth Amendment jurisprudence was tied to common-law trespass, at least until the latter half of the 20th century. Kyllo v. United States, 533 U. S. 27, 31 (2001); Kerr, The Fourth Amendment and New Technologies: Constitutional Myths and the Case for Caution, 102 Mich. L. Rev. 801, 816 (2004). Thus, in Olmstead v. United States, 277 U. S. 438 (1928), we held that wiretaps attached to telephone wires on the public streets did not constitute a Fourth Amendment search because "[t]here was no entry of the houses or offices of the defendants," id., at 464.

Our later cases, of course, have deviated from that exclusively property-based approach. In Katz v. United States, 389 U. S. 347, 351 (1967), we said that "the Fourth Amendment protects people, not places," and found a violation in attachment of an eavesdropping device to a public telephone booth. Our later cases have applied the analysis of Justice Harlan's concurrence in that case, which said that a violation occurs when government officers violate a person's "reasonable expectation of privacy," id., at 360. See, e.g., Bond v. United States, 529 U. S. 334 (2000); California v. Ciraolo, 476 U. S. 207 (1986); Smith v. Maryland, 442 U. S. 735 (1979).

The Government contends that the Harlan standard shows that no search occurred here, since Jones had no "reasonable expectation of privacy" in the area of the Jeep accessed by Government agents (its underbody) and in the locations of the Jeep on the public roads, which were visible to all. But we need not address the Government's contentions, because Jones's Fourth Amendment rights do not rise or fall with the Katz formulation. At bottom, we must "assur[e] preservation of that degree of privacy against government that existed when the Fourth Amendment was adopted." Kyllo, supra, at 34. As explained, for most of our history the Fourth Amendment was understood to embody a particular concern for government trespass upon the areas ("persons, houses, papers, and effects") it enumerates. 3 Katz did not repudiate that understanding. Less than two years later the Court upheld defendants' contention that the Government could not introduce against them conversations between other people obtained by warrantless placement of electronic surveillance devices in their homes. The opinion rejected the dissent's contention that there was no Fourth Amendment violation "unless the conversational privacy of the homeowner himself is invaded." 4 Alderman v. United States, 394 U. S. 165, 176 (1969). "[W]e [do not] believe that Katz, by holding that the Fourth Amendment protects persons and their private conversations, was intended to withdraw any of the protection which the Amendment extends to the home . . . ." Id., at 180.

More recently, in Soldal v. Cook County, 506 U. S. 56 (1992), the Court unanimously rejected the argument that although a "seizure" had occurred "in a 'technical' sense" when a trailer home was forcibly removed, id., at 62, no Fourth Amendment violation occurred because law enforcement had not "invade[d] the [individuals'] privacy," id., at 60. Katz, the Court explained, established that "property rights are not the sole measure of Fourth Amendment violations," but did not "snuf[f] out the previously recognized protection for property." 506 U. S., at 64. As Justice Brennan explained in his concurrence in Knotts, Katz did not erode the principle "that, when the Government does engage in physical intrusion of a constitutionally protected area in order to obtain information, that intrusion may constitute a violation of the Fourth Amendment." 460 U. S., at 286 (opinion concurring in judgment). We have embodied that preservation of past rights in our very definition of "reasonable expectation of privacy" which we have said to be an expectation "that has a source outside of the Fourth Amendment, either by reference to concepts of real or personal property law or to understandings that are recognized and permitted by society." Minnesota v. Carter, 525 U. S. 83, 88 (1998) (internal quotation marks omitted). Katz did not narrow the Fourth Amendment's scope. 5

The Government contends that several of our post-Katz cases foreclose the conclusion that what occurred here constituted a search. It relies principally on two cases in which we rejected Fourth Amendment challenges to "beepers," electronic tracking devices that represent another form of electronic monitoring. The first case, Knotts, upheld against Fourth Amendment challenge the use of a "beeper" that had been placed in a container of chloroform, allowing law enforcement to monitor the location of the container. 460 U. S., at 278. We said that there had been no infringement of Knotts' reasonable expectation of privacy since the information obtained—the location of the automobile carrying the container on public roads, and the location of the off-loaded container in open fields near Knotts' cabin—had been voluntarily conveyed to the public. 6 Id., at 281–282. But as we have discussed, the Katz reasonable-expectation-of-privacy test has been added to, not substituted for, the common-law trespassory test. The holding in Knotts addressed only the former, since the latter was not at issue. The beeper had been placed in the container before it came into Knotts' possession, with the consent of the then-owner. 460 U. S., at 278. Knotts did not challenge that installation, and we specifically declined to consider its effect on the Fourth Amendment analysis. Id., at 279, n. Knotts would be relevant, perhaps, if the Government were making the argument that what would otherwise be an unconstitutional search is not such where it produces only public information. The Government does not make that argument, and we know of no case that would support it.

The second "beeper" case, United States v. Karo, 468 U. S. 705 (1984), does not suggest a different conclusion. There we addressed the question left open by Knotts, whether the installation of a beeper in a container amounted to a search or seizure. 468 U. S., at 713. As in Knotts, at the time the beeper was installed the container belonged to a third party, and it did not come into possession of the defendant until later. 468 U. S., at 708. Thus, the specific question we considered was whether the installation "with the consent of the original owner constitute[d] a search or seizure . . . when the container is delivered to a buyer having no knowledge of the presence of the beeper." Id., at 707 (emphasis added). We held not. The Government, we said, came into physical contact with the container only before it belonged to the defendant Karo; and the transfer of the container with the unmonitored beeper inside did not convey any information and thus did not invade Karo's privacy. See id., at 712. That conclusion is perfectly consistent with the one we reach here. Karo accepted the container as it came to him, beeper and all, and was therefore not entitled to object to the beeper's presence, even though it was used to monitor the container's location. Cf. On Lee v. United States, 343 U. S. 747–752 (1952) (no search or seizure where an informant, who was wearing a concealed microphone, was invited into the defendant's business). Jones, who possessed the Jeep at the time the Government trespassorily inserted the information-gathering device, is on much different footing.

The Government also points to our exposition in New York v. Class, 475 U. S. 106 (1986), that "[t]he exterior of a car . . . is thrust into the public eye, and thus to examine it does not constitute a 'search.'" Id., at 114. That statement is of marginal relevance here since, as the

Government acknowledges, "the officers in this case did more than conduct a visual inspection of respondent's vehicle," Brief for United States 41 (emphasis added). By attaching the device to the Jeep, officers encroached on a protected area. In Class itself we suggested that this would make a difference, for we concluded that an officer's momentary reaching into the interior of a vehicle did constitute a search. 7 475 U. S., at 114–115.

Finally, the Government's position gains little support from our conclusion in Oliver v. United States, 466 U. S. 170 (1984), that officers' information-gathering intrusion on an "open field" did not constitute a Fourth Amendment search even though it was a trespass at common law, id., at 183. Quite simply, an open field, unlike the curtilage of a home, see United States v. Dunn, 480 U. S. 294, 300 (1987), is not one of those protected areas enumerated in the Fourth Amendment. Oliver, supra, at 176–177. See also Hester v. United States, 265 U. S. 57, 59 (1924). The Government's physical intrusion on such an area—unlike its intrusion on the "effect" at issue here—is of no Fourth Amendment significance. 8

B

The concurrence begins by accusing us of applying "18th-century tort law." Post, at 1. That is a distortion. What we apply is an 18th-century guarantee against un-reasonable searches, which we believe must provide at a minimum the degree of protection it afforded when it was adopted. The concurrence does not share that belief. It would apply exclusively Katz's reasonable-expectation-of-privacy test, even when that eliminates rights that previously existed.

The concurrence faults our approach for "present[ing] particularly vexing problems" in cases that do not involve physical contact, such as those that involve the transmission of electronic signals. Post, at 9. We entirely fail to understand that point. For unlike the concurrence, which would make Katz the exclusive test, we do not make trespass the exclusive test. Situations involving merely the transmission of electronic signals without trespass would remain subject to Katz analysis.

In fact, it is the concurrence's insistence on the exclusivity of the Katz test that needlessly leads us into "particularly vexing problems" in the present case. This Court has to date not deviated from the understanding that mere visual observation does not constitute a search. See Kyllo, 533 U. S., at 31–32. We accordingly held in Knotts that "[a] person traveling in an automobile on public thoroughfares has no reasonable expectation of privacy in his movements from one place to another." 460 U. S., at 281. Thus, even assuming that the concurrence is correct to say that "[t]raditional surveillance" of Jones for a 4-week period "would have required a large team of agents, multiple vehicles, and perhaps aerial assistance," post, at 12, our cases suggest that such visual observation is constitutionally permissible. It may be that achieving the same result through electronic means, without an accompanying trespass, is an unconstitutional invasion of privacy, but the present case does not require us to answer that question.

And answering it affirmatively leads us needlessly into additional thorny problems. The concurrence posits that "relatively short-term monitoring of a person's movements on public streets" is okay, but that "the use of longer term GPS monitoring in investigations of most offenses" is no good. Post, at 13 (emphasis added). That introduces yet another novelty into our jurisprudence. There is no precedent for the proposition that whether a search has occurred depends on the nature of the crime being investigated. And even accepting that novelty, it remains unexplained why a 4-week investigation is "surely" too long and why a drug-trafficking conspiracy involving substantial amounts of cash and narcotics is not an "extra-ordinary offens[e]" which may permit longer observation. See post, at 13–14. What of a 2-day monitoring of asuspected purveyor of stolen electronics? Or of a 6-month monitoring of a suspected terrorist? We may have to grapple with these "vexing problems" in some future case where a classic trespassory search is not involved and resort must be had to Katz analysis; but there is no reason for rushing forward to resolve them here.

III

The Government argues in the alternative that even if the attachment and use of the device was a search, it was reasonable—and thus lawful—under the Fourth Amendment because "officers had reasonable suspicion, and in-deed probable cause, to believe that [Jones] was a leader in a large-scale cocaine distribution conspiracy." Brief for United States 50–51. We have no occasion to consider this argument. The Government did not raise it below, and the D. C. Circuit therefore did not address it. See 625 F. 3d, at 767 (Ginsburg, Tatel, and Griffith, JJ., concurring in denial of rehearing en banc). We consider the argument forfeited. See Sprietsma v. Mercury Marine, 537 U. S. 51, n. 4 (2002).

*   *   *

The judgment of the Court of Appeals for the D. C. Circuit is affirmed.

It is so ordered.

Ryburn v. Huff (Jan 23, 2012)

Per Curiam.

Petitioners Darin Ryburn and Edmundo Zepeda, along with two other officers from the Burbank Police Department, responded to a call from Bellarmine-Jefferson High School in Burbank, California. When the officers arrived at the school, the principal informed them that a student, Vincent Huff, was rumored to have written a letter threatening to "shoot up" the school. App. to Pet. for Cert. 2. The principal reported that many parents, after hearing the rumor, had decided to keep their children at home. Ibid. The principal expressed concern for the safety of her students and requested that the officers investigate the threat. Id., at 42, 54–55.

In the course of conducting interviews with the principal and two of Vincent's classmates, the officers learned that Vincent had been absent from school for two days andthat he was frequently subjected to bullying. Id., at 2. Theofficers additionally learned that one of Vincent's classmates believed that Vincent was capable of carrying out the alleged threat. Id., at 44. The officers found Vincent's absences from school and his history of being subjected to bullying as cause for concern. The officers had received training on targeted school violence and were aware that these characteristics are common among perpetrators of school shootings. Id., at 56–58, 63.

The officers decided to continue the investigation by interviewing Vincent. When the officers arrived at Vincent's house, Officer Zepeda knocked on the door and announced several times that the officers were with the Burbank Police Department. No one answered the door or otherwise responded to Officer Zepeda's knocks. Sergeant Ryburn then called the home telephone. The officers could hear the phone ringing inside the house, but no one answered. Id., at 2.

Sergeant Ryburn next tried calling the cell phone of Vincent's mother, Mrs. Huff. When Mrs. Huff answered the phone, Sergeant Ryburn identified himself and inquired about her location. Mrs. Huff informed Sergeant Ryburn that she was inside the house. Sergeant Ryburn then inquired about Vincent's location, and Mrs. Huff informed him that Vincent was inside with her. Sergeant Ryburn told Mrs. Huff that he and the other officers were outside and requested to speak with her, but Mrs. Huff hung up the phone. Id., at 2–3.

One or two minutes later, Mrs. Huff and Vincent walked out of the house and stood on the front steps. Officer Zepeda advised Vincent that he and the other officers were there to discuss the threats. Vincent, apparently aware of the rumor that was circulating at his school, responded, "I can't believe you're here for that." Id., at 3. Sergeant Ryburn asked Mrs. Huff if they could continue the discussion inside the house, but she refused. Ibid. In Sergeant Ryburn's experience as a juvenile bureau sergeant, it was "extremely unusual" for a parent to decline an officer's request to interview a juvenile inside. Id., at 3, 73–74. Sergeant Ryburn also found it odd that Mrs. Huff never asked the officers the reason for their visit. Id., at 73–74.

After Mrs. Huff declined Sergeant Ryburn's request to continue the discussion inside, Sergeant Ryburn asked her if there were any guns in the house. Mrs. Huff responded by "immediately turn[ing] around and r[unning] into the house." Id., at 3. Sergeant Ryburn, who was "scared because [he] didn't know what was in that house" and had "seen too many officers killed," entered the house behind her. Id., at 75. Vincent entered the house behind Sergeant Ryburn, and Officer Zepeda entered after Vincent. Officer Zepeda was concerned about "officer safety" and did not want Sergeant Ryburn to enter the house alone. Id., at 3. The two remaining officers, who had been standing out of earshot while Sergeant Ryburn and Officer Zepeda talked to Vincent and Mrs. Huff, entered the house last, on the assumption that Mrs. Huff had given Sergeant Ryburn and Officer Zepeda permission to enter. Id., at 3–4.

Upon entering the house, the officers remained in the living room with Mrs. Huff and Vincent. Eventually, Vincent's father entered the room and challenged the officers' authority to be there. The officers remained in-side the house for a total of 5 to 10 minutes. During that time, the officers talked to Mr. Huff and Vincent. They did not conduct any search of Mr. Huff, Mrs. Huff, or Vincent, or any of their property. The officers

ultimately concluded that the rumor about Vincent was false, and they reported their conclusion to the school. Id., at 4.

The Huffs brought this action against the officers under Rev. Stat. §1979, 42 U. S. C. §1983. The complaint alleges that the officers violated the Huffs' Fourth Amendment rights by entering their home without a warrant. Following a 2-day bench trial, the District Court entered judgment in favor of the officers. The District Court resolved conflicting testimony regarding Mrs. Huff's response to Sergeant Ryburn's inquiry about guns by finding that Mrs. Huff "immediately turned around and ran into the house." App. to Pet. for Cert. 3. The District Court concluded that the officers were entitled to qualified immunity because Mrs. Huff's odd behavior, combined with the information the officers gathered at the school, could have led reason-able officers to believe "that there could be weapons inside the house, and that family members or the officers themselves were in danger." Id., at 6. The District Court noted that "[w]ithin a very short period of time, the officers were confronted with facts and circumstances giving rise to grave concern about the nature of the danger they were confronting." Id., at 6–7. With respect to this kind of "rapidly evolving incident," the District Court explained, courts should be especially reluctant "to fault the police for not obtaining a warrant." Id., at 7.

A divided panel of the Ninth Circuit affirmed the District Court as to the two officers who entered the house on the assumption that Mrs. Huff had consented, but reversed as to petitioners. The majority upheld the District Court's findings of fact, but disagreed with the District Court's conclusion that petitioners were entitled to qualified immunity. The majority acknowledged that police officers are allowed to enter a home without a warrant if they reasonably believe that immediate entry is necessary to protect themselves or others from serious harm, even if the officers lack probable cause to believe that a crime has been or is about to be committed. Id., at 24. But the majority determined that, in this case, "any belief thatthe officers or other family members were in serious, im-minent harm would have been objectively unreasonable" given that "[Mrs. Huff] merely asserted her right to end her conversation with the officers and returned to her home." Id., at 25.

Judge Rawlinson dissented. She explained that "the discrete incident that precipitated the entry in this case was Mrs. Huff's response to the question regarding whether there were guns in the house." Id., at 31. She faulted the majority for "recit[ing] a sanitized account of this event" that differed markedly from the District Court's findings of fact, which the majority had conceded must be credited. Judge Rawlinson looked to "cases that specifi-cally address the scenario where officer safety concerns prompted the entry" and concluded that, under the rationale articulated in those cases, "a police officer could have reasonably believed that he was justified in making a warrantless entry to ensure that no one inside the house had a gun after Mrs. Huff ran into the house without answering the question of whether anyone had a weapon." Id., at 31, 33, 37.

Judge Rawlinson's analysis of the qualified immunity issue was correct. No decision of this Court has found a Fourth Amendment violation on facts even roughly comparable to those present in this case. On the contrary, some of our opinions may be read as pointing in the opposition direction.

In Brigham City v. Stuart, 547 U. S. 398, 400 (2006), we held that officers may enter a residence without a warrant when they have "an objectively reasonable basis for believing that an occupant is . . . imminently threatened with [serious injury]." We explained that " '[t]he need to protect or preserve life or avoid serious injury is justificationfor what would be otherwise illegal absent an exigency or emergency.' " Id., at 403 (quoting Mincey v. Arizona, 437 U. S. 385, 392 (1978)). In addition, in Georgia v. Randolph, 547 U. S. 103, 118 (2006) , the Court stated that "it would be silly to suggest that the police would commit a tort by entering [a residence] . . . to determine whether violence . . . is about to (or soon will) occur."

A reasonable police officer could read these decisions to mean that the Fourth Amendment permits an officer to en-ter a residence if the officer has a reasonable basis for concluding that there is an imminent threat of violence. In this case, the District Court concluded that petitioners had such an objectively reasonable basis for reaching such a conclusion. The District Court wrote:

"[T]he officers testified that a number of factors led them to be concerned for their own safety and for the safety of other persons in the residence: the unusual behavior of the parents in not answering the door or the telephone; the fact that Mrs. Huff did not inquire about the reason for their visit or express concern that they were investigating her son; the fact that she hung up the telephone on the officer; the fact thatshe refused to tell them whether there were guns in the house; and finally, the fact that she ran back into the house while being questioned. That behavior, combined with the information obtained at the school—that Vincent was a student who was a victim of bullying, who had been absent from school for two days, and who had threatened to 'shoot up' the school—led the officers to believe that there could be weapons inside the house, and that family members or the officers themselves were in danger." App. to Pet. for Cert. 6.

This belief, the District Court held, was "objectively reasonable," particularly since the situation was "rapidly evolving" and the officers had to make quick decisions. Id., at 6–7.

The panel majority—far removed from the

scene and with the opportunity to dissect the elements of the situation—confidently concluded that the officers really had no reason to fear for their safety or that of anyone else. As the panel majority saw things, it was irrelevant that the Huffs did not respond when the officers knocked on the door and announced their presence and when they called the home phone because the Huffs had no legal obligation to respond to a knock on the door or to answer the phone. The majority attributed no significance to the fact that, when the officers finally reached Mrs. Huff on her cell phone, she abruptly hung up in the middle of their conversation. And, according to the majority, the officers should not have been concerned by Mrs. Huff's reaction when they asked her if there were any guns in the house because Mrs. Huff "merely asserted her right to end her conversation with the officers and returned to her home." Id., at 25.

Confronted with the facts found by the District Court, reasonable officers in the position of petitioners could have come to the conclusion that there was an imminent threat to their safety and to the safety of others. The Ninth Circuit's contrary conclusion was flawed for numerous reasons.

First, although the panel majority purported to accept the findings of the District Court, it changed those findings in several key respects. As Judge Rawlinson correctly observed, "the discrete incident that precipitated the entry in this case was Mrs. Huff's response to the question regarding whether there were guns in the house." Id., at 31. The District Court's finding that Mrs. Huff "immediately turned around and ran into the house" implicitly rejected Mrs. Huff's contrary testimony that she walked into the house after telling the officers that she was going to get her husband. Id., at 3. The panel majority upheld the District Court's findings of fact and acknowledged that it could not reverse the District Court simply because it "may have weighed the testimony of the witnesses and other evidence in another manner." Id., at 15. But the panel majority's determination that petitioners were not entitled to qualified immunity rested on an account of the facts that differed markedly from the District Court's finding. According to the panel majority, Mrs. Huff "merely asserted her right to end her conversation with the officers and returned to her home" after telling the officers "that she would go get her husband." Id., at 12, 25.

Second, the panel majority appears to have taken the view that conduct cannot be regarded as a matter of concern so long as it is lawful. Accordingly, the panel ma-jority concluded that Mrs. Huff's response to the question whether there were any guns in the house (immediately turning around and running inside) was not a reason for alarm because she was under no legal obligation to continue her conversation with the police. It should go without saying, however, that there are many circumstances in which lawful conduct may portend imminent violence.

Third, the panel majority's method of analyzing the string of events that unfolded at the Huff residence was entirely unrealistic. The majority looked at each separate event in isolation and concluded that each, in itself, did not give cause for concern. But it is a matter of common sense that a combination of events each of which is mundane when viewed in isolation may paint an alarming picture.

Fourth, the panel majority did not heed the District Court's wise admonition that judges should be cautious about second-guessing a police officer's assessment, made on the scene, of the danger presented by a particular situation. With the benefit of hindsight and calm deliberation, the panel majority concluded that it was unreasonable for petitioners to fear that violence was imminent. But we have instructed that reasonableness "must be judged from the perspective of a reasonable officer on the scene, rather than with the 20/20 vision of hindsight" and that "[t]he calculus of reasonableness must embody allowance for the fact that police officers are often forced to make split-second judgments—in circumstances that are tense, uncertain, and rapidly evolving." Graham v. Connor, 490 U. S. 386–397 (1989). Judged from the proper perspective of a reasonable officer forced to make a split-second decision in response to a rapidly unfolding chain of events that culminated with Mrs. Huff turning and running into the house after refusing to answer a question about guns, petitioners' belief that entry was necessary to avoid injury to themselves or others was imminently reasonable.

In sum, reasonable police officers in petitioners' position could have come to the conclusion that the Fourth Amendment permitted them to enter the Huff residence if there was an objectively reasonable basis for fearing that violence was imminent. And a reasonable officer could have come to such a conclusion based on the facts as found by the District Court.

The petition for certiorari is granted, the judgment of the Ninth Circuit is reversed, and the case is remanded for the entry of judgment in favor of petitioners.

It is so ordered.

Messerschmidt v. Millender (Feb 22, 2012) [Notes omitted]

Chief Justice Roberts delivered the opinion of the Court.

Petitioner police officers conducted a search of respondents' home pursuant to a warrant issued by a neutral magistrate. The warrant authorized a search for all guns and gang-related material, in connection with the investigation of a known gang member for shooting at his ex-girlfriend with a pistol-gripped sawed-off shotgun, because she had "call[ed] the cops" on him. App. 56. Respondents brought an action seeking to hold the officers personally liable under 42 U. S. C. §1983, alleging that the search violated their Fourth Amendment rights because there was not sufficient probable cause to believe the items sought were evidence of a crime. In particular, respondents argued that there was no basis to search for all guns simply because the suspect owned and had used a sawed-off shotgun, and no reason to search for gang material because the shooting at the ex-girlfriend for "call[ing] the cops" was solely a domestic dispute. The Court of Appeals for the Ninth Circuit held that the warrant was invalid, and that the officers were not entitled to immunity from personal liability because this invalidity was so obvious that any reasonable officer would have recognized it, despite the magistrate's approval. We disagree and reverse.

I

A

Shelly Kelly decided to break off her romantic relationship with Jerry Ray Bowen and move out of her apartment, to which Bowen had a key. Kelly feared an attack from Bowen, who had previously assaulted her and had been convicted of multiple violent felonies. She therefore asked officers from the Los Angeles County Sheriff's Department to accompany her while she gathered her things. Deputies from the Sheriff's Department came to assist Kelly but were called away to respond to an emergency before the move was complete.

As soon as the officers left, an enraged Bowen appeared at the bottom of the stairs to the apartment, yelling "I told you never to call the cops on me bitch!" App. 39, 56. Bowen then ran up the stairs to Kelly, grabbed her by her shirt, and tried to throw her over the railing of the second-story landing. When Kelly successfully resisted, Bowen bit her on the shoulder and attempted to drag her inside the apartment by her hair. Kelly again managed to escape Bowen's grasp, and ran to her car. By that time, Bowen had retrieved a black sawed-off shotgun with a pistol grip. He ran in front of Kelly's car, pointed the shotgun at her, and told Kelly that if she tried to leave he would kill her. Kelly leaned over, fully depressed the gas pedal, and sped away. Bowen fired at the car a total of five times, blowing out the car's left front tire in the process, but Kelly managed to escape.

Kelly quickly located police officers and reported the assault. She told the police what had happened—that Bowen had attacked her after becoming "angry because she had called the Sheriff's Department"—and she mentioned that Bowen was "an active member of the 'Mona Park Crips,' " a local street gang. Id., at 39. Kelly also provided the officers with photographs of Bowen.

Detective Curt Messerschmidt was assigned to investigate the incident. Messerschmidt met with Kelly to obtain details of the assault and information about Bowen. Kelly described the attack and informed Messerschmidt that she thought Bowen was staying at his foster mother's homeat 2234 East 120th Street. Kelly also informed Messerschmidt of Bowen's previous assaults on her and of his gang ties.

Messerschmidt then conducted a background check on Bowen by consulting police records, California Department of Motor Vehicles records, and the "cal-gang" database. Based on this research, Messerschmidt confirmed Bowen's connection to the 2234 East 120th Street address. He also confirmed that Bowen was an "active" member of the Mona Park Crips and a "secondary" member of the Dodge City Crips. Id., at 64. Finally, Messerschmidt learned that Bowen had been arrested and convicted for numerous violent and firearm-related offenses. Indeed, at the time of the investigation, Bowen's "rapsheet" spanned over 17 printed pages, and indicated that he had been arrested at least 31 times. Nine of these arrests were for firearms offenses and six were for violent crimes, including three arrests for assault with a deadly weapon (firearm). Id., at 72–81.

Messerschmidt prepared two warrants: one to authorize Bowen's arrest and one to authorize the search of 2234 East 120th Street. An attachment to the search warrant described the property that would be the object of the search:

"All handguns, rifles, or shotguns of any caliber, or any firearms capable of firing ammunition, or firearms or devices modified or designed to allow it [sic] to fire ammunition. All caliber of ammunition, miscellaneous gun parts, gun cleaning kits, holsters which could hold or have held any caliber handgun being sought. Any receipts or paperwork, showing the purchase, ownership, or possession of the handguns being sought. Any firearm for which there is no proof of ownership. Any firearm capable of firing or chambered to fire any caliber ammunition.

"Articles of evidence showing street gang membership or affiliation with any Street Gang to include but not limited to any reference to 'Mona Park Crips', including writings or graffiti depicting gang membership, activity or identity. Articles of personal property tending to establish the identity of person [sic] in control of the premise or premises. Any photographs or photograph albums depicting persons, vehicles, weapons or locations, which may appear relevant to gang membership, or which may depict the item being sought and or believed to be evidence in the case being investigated on this warrant, or which may depict evidence of criminal activity. Additionally to include any gang indicia that would establish the persons being sought in this warrant, affiliation or membership with the 'Mona Park Crips' street gang." Id., at 52.

Two affidavits accompanied Messerschmidt's warrant ap-plications. The first affidavit described Messerschmidt's extensive law enforcement experience, including that he had served as a peace officer for 14 years, that he was then assigned to a "specialized unit" "investigating gang related crimes and arresting gang members for various violations of the law," that he had been involved in "hundreds of gang related incidents, contacts, and or arrests" during his time on the force, and that he had "received specialized training in the field of gang related crimes" and training in "gang related shootings." Id., at 53–54.

The second affidavit—expressly incorporated into the search warrant—explained why Messerschmidt believed there was sufficient probable cause to support the warrant. That affidavit described the facts of the incident involving Kelly and Bowen in great detail, including the weapon used in the assault. The affidavit recounted that Kelly had identified Bowen as the assailant and that she thought Bowen might be found at 2234 East 120th Street. It also reported that Messerschmidt had "conducted an extensive background search on the suspect by utilizing departmental records, state computer records, and other police agency records," and that from that information he had concluded that Bowen resided at 2234 East 120th Street. Id., at 58.

The affidavit requested that the search warrant be endorsed for night service because "information provided by the victim and the cal-gang data base" indicated that Bowen had "gang ties to the Mona Park Crip gang" and that "night service would provide an added element of safety to the community as well as for the deputy personnel serving the warrant." Id., at 59. The affidavit concluded by noting that Messerschmidt "believe[d] that the items sought" would be in Bowen's possession and that "recovery of the weapon could be invaluable in the successful prosecution of the suspect involved in this case, and the curtailment of further crimes being committed." Ibid.

Messerschmidt submitted the warrants to his super-visors—Sergeant Lawrence and Lieutenant Ornales—for review. Deputy District Attorney Janet Wilson also reviewed the materials and initialed the search warrant, indicating that she agreed with Messerschmidt's assessment of probable cause. Id., at 27, 47. Finally, Messerschmidt submitted the warrants to a magistrate. The magistrate approved the warrants and authorized night service.

The search warrant was served two days later by a team of officers that included Messerschmidt and Lawrence. Sheriff's deputies forced open the front door of 2234 East 120th Street and encountered Augusta Millender—a woman in her seventies—and Millender's daughter and grandson. As instructed by the police, the Millenders went outside while the residence was secured but remained in the living room while the search was conducted. Bowen was not found in the residence. The search did, however, result in the seizure of Augusta Millender's shotgun, a California Social Services letter addressed to Bowen, and a box of .45-caliber ammunition.

Bowen was arrested two weeks later after Messerschmidt found him hiding under a bed in a motel room.

B

The Millenders filed suit in Federal District Court against the County of Los Angeles, the sheriff's department, the sheriff, and a number of individual officers, including Messerschmidt and Lawrence. The complaint alleged, as relevant here, that the search warrant was invalid under the Fourth Amendment. It sought damages from Messerschmidt and Lawrence, among others.

The parties filed cross motions for summary judgment on the validity of the search warrant. The District Court found the warrant defective in two respects. The District Court concluded that the warrant's authorization to search for firearms was unconstitutionally overbroad because the "crime specified here was a physical assault with a very specific weapon"—a black sawed-off shotgun with a pistol grip—negating any need to "search for all firearms." Millender v. County of Los Angeles, Civ. No. 05–

2298 (CD Cal., Mar. 15, 2007), App. to Pet. for Cert. 106, 157, 2007 WL 7589200, *21. The court also foundthe warrant overbroad with respect to the search for gang-related materials, because there "was no evidence that the crime at issue was gang-related." App. to Pet. for Cert. 157. As a result, the District Court granted summary judgment to the Millenders on their constitutional challenges to the firearm and gang material aspects of the search warrant. Id., at 160. The District Court also rejected the officers' claim that they were entitled to qualified immunity from damages. Id., at 171.

Messerschmidt and Lawrence appealed, and a divided panel of the Court of Appeals for the Ninth Circuit reversed the District Court's denial of qualified immunity. 564 F. 3d 1143 (2009). The court held that the officers were entitled to qualified immunity because "they reasonably relied on the approval of the warrant by a deputy district attorney and a judge." Id., at 1145.

The Court of Appeals granted rehearing en banc and affirmed the District Court's denial of qualified immunity. 620 F. 3d 1016 (CA9 2010). The en banc court concluded that the warrant's authorization was unconstitutionally overbroad because the affidavit and the warrant failed to "establish[ ] probable cause that the broad categories of firearms, firearm-related material, and gang-related material described in the warrant were contraband or evidence of a crime." Id., at 1033. In the en banc court's view, "the deputies had probable cause to search for a single, identified weapon . . . . They had no probable cause to search for the broad class of firearms and firearm-related materials described in the warrant." Id., at 1027. In addition, "[b]ecause the deputies failed to establish any link between gang-related materials and a crime, the warrant authorizing the search and seizure of all gang-related evidence [was] likewise invalid." Id., at 1031. Concluding that "a reasonable officer in the deputies' position would have been

well aware of this deficiency," the en banc court held that the officers were not entitled to qualified immunity. Id., at 1033–1035.

There were two separate dissenting opinions. Judge Callahan determined that "the officers had probable cause to search for and seize any firearms in the home in which Bowen, a gang member and felon, was thought to reside." Id., at 1036. She also concluded that "the officers reasonably relied on their superiors, the district attorney, and the magistrate to correct" any overbreadth in the warrant, and that the officers were entitled to qualified immunity because their actions were not objectively unreasonable. Id., at 1044, 1049. Judge Silverman also dissented, concluding that the "deputies' belief in the validity of . . . the warrant was entirely reasonable" and that the "record [wa]s totally devoid of any evidence that the deputies acted other than in good faith." Id., at 1050. Judge Tallman joined both dissents.

We granted certiorari. 564 U. S. ____ (2011).

II

The Millenders allege that they were subjected to an unreasonable search in violation of the Fourth Amendment because the warrant authorizing the search of their home was not supported by probable cause. They seek damages from Messerschmidt and Lawrence for their roles in obtaining and executing this warrant. The validity of the warrant is not before us. The question instead is whether Messerschmidt and Lawrence are entitled to im-munity from damages, even assuming that the warrant should not have been issued.

"The doctrine of qualified immunity protects government officials 'from liability for civil damages insofar as their conduct does not violate clearly established statutory or constitutional rights of which a reasonable person would have known.' " Pearson v. Callahan, 555 U.

S. 223, 231 (2009) (quoting Harlow v. Fitzgerald, 457 U. S. 800, 818 (1982)). Qualified immunity "gives government officials breathing room to make reasonable but mistaken judgments," and "protects 'all but the plainly incompetent or those who knowingly violate the law.' " Ashcroft v. al-Kidd, 563 U. S. ___, ___ (2011) (slip op., at 12) (quoting Malley v. Briggs, 475 U. S. 335, 341 (1986)). "[W]hether an official protected by qualified immunity may be held personally liable for an allegedly unlawful official action generally turns on the 'objective legal reasonableness' of the action, assessed in light of the legal rules that were 'clearly established' at the time it was taken." Anderson v. Creighton, 483 U. S. 635, 639 (1987) (citation omitted).

Where the alleged Fourth Amendment violation involves a search or seizure pursuant to a warrant, the fact that a neutral magistrate has issued a warrant is the clearest indication that the officers acted in an objectively reasonable manner or, as we have sometimes put it, in "objective good faith." United States v. Leon, 468 U. S. 897–923 (1984). 1 Nonetheless, under our precedents, the fact that a neutral magistrate has issued a warrant authorizing the allegedly unconstitutional search or seizure does not end the inquiry into objective reasonableness. Rather, we have recognized an exception allowing suit when "it is obvious that no reasonably competent officer would have concluded that a warrant should issue." Malley, 475 U. S., at 341. The "shield of immunity" otherwise conferred by the warrant, id., at 345, will be lost, for example, where the warrant was "based on an affidavit so lacking in indicia of probable cause as to render official belief in its existence entirely unreasonable." Leon, 468 U. S., at 923 (internal quotation marks omitted). 2

Our precedents make clear, however, that the threshold for establishing this exception is a high one, and it should be. As we explained in Leon, "[i]n the ordinary case, an officer cannot be expected to question the magistrate's probable-cause determination" because "[i]t is the magistrate's responsibility to determine whether the officer's allegations establish probable cause and, if so, to issue a warrant comporting in form with the requirements of the Fourth Amendment." Id., at 921; see also Malley, supra, at 346, n. 9 ("It is a sound presumption that the magistrate is more qualified than the police officer to make a probable cause determination, and it goes without saying that where a magistrate acts mistakenly in issuing a warrant but within the range of professional competence of a magistrate, the officer who requested the warrant cannot be held liable" (internal quotation marks and citation omitted)).

III

The Millenders contend, and the Court of Appeals held, that their case falls into this narrow exception. According to the Millenders, the officers "failed to provide any facts or circumstances from which a magistrate could properly conclude that there was probable cause to seize the broad classes of items being sought," and "[n]o reasonable officer would have presumed that such a warrant was valid." Brief for Respondents 27. We disagree.

A

With respect to the warrant's authorization to search for and seize all firearms, the Millenders argue that "a reasonably well-trained officer would have readily perceived that there was no probable cause to search the house for all firearms and firearm-related items." Id., at 32. Noting that "the affidavit indicated exactly what item was evidence of a crime—the 'black sawed off shotgun with a pistol grip,' " they argue that "[n]o facts established that Bowen possessed any other firearms, let alone that such firearms (if they existed) were 'contraband or evidence of a crime.' " Ibid. (quoting App. 56).

Even if the scope of the warrant were overbroad in authorizing a search for all guns when there was information only about a specific one, that specific one was a sawed-off shotgun with a pistol grip, owned by a known gang member, who had just fired the weapon five times in public in an attempt to murder another person, on the asserted ground that she had "call[ed] the cops" on him. Id., at 56. Under these circumstances—set forth in the warrant—it would not have been unreasonable for an officer to conclude that there was a "fair probability" that the sawed-off shotgun was not the only firearm Bowen owned. Illinois v. Gates, 462 U. S. 213, 238 (1983) . Andit certainly would have been reasonable for an officer to assume that Bowen's sawed-off shotgun was illegal. Cf. 26 U. S. C. §§5845(a), 5861(d). Evidence of one crime is not always evidence of several, but given Bowen's possession of one illegal gun, his gang membership, his willingness to use the gun to kill someone, and his concern about the police, a reasonable officer could conclude that there would be additional illegal guns among others that Bowen owned. 3

A reasonable officer also could believe that seizure of the firearms was necessary to prevent further assaults on Kelly. California law allows a magistrate to issue a search warrant for items "in the possession of any person with the intent to use them as a means of committing a public offense," Cal. Penal Code Ann. §1524(a)(3) (West 2011), and the warrant application submitted by the officers specifically referenced this provision as a basis for the search. App. 48. Bowen had already attempted to murder Kelly once with a firearm, and had yelled "I'll kill you" as she tried to escape from him. Id., at 56–57. A reasonable officer could conclude that Bowen would make another attempt on Kelly's life and that he possessed other firearms "with the intent to use them" to that end. Cal. Penal Code Ann. §1524(a)(3).

Given the foregoing, it would not have been "entirely unreasonable" for an officer to believe, in the particular circumstances of this case, that there was probable cause to search for all firearms and firearm-related materials. Leon, supra, at 923 (internal quotation marks omitted).

With respect to the warrant's authorization to search for evidence of gang membership, the Millenders contend that "no reasonable officer could have believed that the affidavit presented to the magistrate contained a sufficient basis to conclude that the gang paraphernalia sought was contraband or evidence of a crime." Brief for Respondents 28. They argue that "the magistrate [could not] have reasonably concluded, based on the affidavit, that Bowen's gang membership had anything to do with the crime under investigation" because "[t]he affidavit described a 'spousal assault' that ensued after Kelly decided to end her 'on going dating relationship' with Bowen" and "[n]othing in that description suggests that the crime was gang-related." Ibid. (quoting App. 55).

This effort to characterize the case solely as a domes-tic dispute, however, is misleading. Cf. post, at 5 (Sotomayor, J., dissenting); post, at 2 (Kagan, J., concurring in part and dissenting in part). Messerschmidt began his affidavit in support of the warrant by explaining that he "has been investigating an assault with a deadly weapon incident" and elaborated that the crime was a "spousal assault and an assault with a deadly weapon." App. 55 (emphasis added). The affidavit also stated that Bowen was "a known Mona Park Crip gang member" "based on information provided by the victim and the cal-gang database," 4 and that he had attempted to murder Kelly after becoming enraged that she had "call[ed] the cops on [him]." Id., at 56, 58–59. A reasonable officer could certainly view Bowen's attack as motivated not by the souring of his romantic relationship with Kelly but instead by a desire to prevent her from disclosing details of his gang activity to the police. She was, after all, no longer linked with him as a girlfriend; he had assaulted her in the past; and she had indeed called the cops on him. And, as the affidavit supporting the warrant made clear,

Kelly had in fact given the police information about Bowen's gang ties. Id., at 59. 5

It would therefore not have been unreasonable—based on the facts set out in the affidavit—for an officer to believe that evidence regarding Bowen's gang affiliation would prove helpful in prosecuting him for the attack on Kelly. See Warden, Md. Penitentiary v. Hayden, 387 U. S. 294, 307 (1967) (holding that the Fourth Amendment allows a search for evidence when there is "probable cause . . . to believe that the evidence sought will aid in a particular apprehension or conviction"). Not only would such evidence help to establish motive, either apart from or in addition to any domestic dispute, it would also support the bringing of additional, related charges against Bowen for the assault. See, e.g., Cal. Penal Code Ann. §136.1(b)(1) (West 1999) (It is a crime to "attempt[ ] to prevent or dissuade another person who has been the victim of a crime or who is witness to a crime from . . . [m]aking any report of that victimization to any . . . law enforcement officer"). 6

In addition, a reasonable officer could believe that evidence demonstrating Bowen's membership in a gang might prove helpful in impeaching Bowen or rebutting various defenses he could raise at trial. For example, evidence that Bowen had ties to a gang that uses guns such as the one he used to assault Kelly would certainly be relevant to establish that he had familiarity with or access to this type of weapon.

Moreover, even if this were merely a domestic dispute, a reasonable officer could still conclude that gang paraphernalia found at the Millenders' residence would aid in the prosecution of Bowen by, for example, demonstrating Bowen's connection to other evidence found there. The warrant authorized a search for "any gang indicia that would establish the persons being sought in this warrant," and "[a]rticles of personal property tending to establish the identity of [the] person in control of the premise or premises." App. 52. Before the District Court, the Millenders "acknowledge[d] that evidence of who controlled the premises would be relevant if incriminating evidence were found and it became necessary to tie that evidence to a person, " and the District Court approved that aspect of the warrant on this basis. App. to Pet. for Cert. 158–159 (internal quotation marks omitted). Given Bowen's known gang affiliation, a reasonable officer could conclude that gang paraphernalia found at the residence would be an effective means of demonstrating Bowen's control over the premises or his connection to evidence found there. 7

Whatever the use to which evidence of Bowen's gang involvement might ultimately have been put, it would not have been "entirely unreasonable" for an officer to believe that the facts set out in the affidavit established a fair probability that such evidence would aid the prosecution of Bowen for the criminal acts at issue. Leon, 468 U. S., at 923 (internal quotation marks omitted).

B

Whether any of these facts, standing alone or taken together, actually establish probable cause is a question we need not decide. Qualified immunity "gives government officials breathing room to make reasonable but mistaken judgments." al-Kidd, 563 U. S., at ____ (slip op., at 12). The officers' judgment that the scope of the warrant was supported by probable cause may have been mistaken, but it was not "plainly incompetent." Malley, 475 U. S., at 341.

On top of all this, the fact that the officers sought and obtained approval of the warrant application from a superior and a deputy district attorney before submitting it to the magistrate provides further support for the conclusion that an officer could reasonably have believed that the scope of the warrant was supported by probable cause. Ibid. Before seeking to have the warrant issued by a magistrate, Messerschmidt conducted an extensive investigation into Bowen's background and the facts of the crime. Based on this investigation, Messerschmidt prepared a detailed warrant application that truthfully laid out the pertinent facts. The only facts omitted—the officers' knowledge of Bowen's arrest and conviction records, see supra, at 3—would only have strengthened the warrant. Messerschmidt then submitted the warrant application for review by Lawrence, another superior officer, and a deputy district attorney, all of whom approved the application without any apparent misgivings. Only after this did Messerschmidt seek the approval of a neutral magistrate, who issued the requested warrant. The officers thus "took every step that could reasonably be expected of them." Massachusetts v. Sheppard, 468 U. S. 981, 989 (1984) . In light of the foregoing, it cannot be said that "no officer of reasonable competence would have requested the warrant." Malley, 475 U. S., at 346, n. 9. Indeed, a contrary conclusion would mean not only that Messerschmidt and Lawrence were "plainly incompetent," id., at 341, but that their supervisor, the deputy district attorney, and the magistrate were as well.

The Court of Appeals, however, gave no weight to the fact that the warrant had been reviewed and approved by the officers' superiors, a deputy district attorney, and a neutral magistrate. Relying on Malley, the court held that the officers had an "independent responsibility to ensure there [was] at least a colorable argument for probable cause." 620 F. 3d, at 1034. It explained that "[t]he deputies here had a responsibility to exercise their reasonable professional judgment," and that "in circumstances such as these a neutral magistrate's approval (and, a fortiori, a non-neutral prosecutor's) cannot absolve an officer of liability." Ibid. (citation omitted).

We rejected in Malley the contention that an officer is automatically entitled to qualified immunity for seeking a warrant unsupported by probable cause, simply because a magistrate had approved the application. 475 U. S., at 345. And because the officers' superior and the deputy district attorney are part of the prosecution team, their review also cannot be regarded as dispositive. But by holding in Malley that a magistrate's approval does not automatically render an officer's conduct reasonable, we did not suggest that approval by a magistrate or review by others is irrelevant to the objective reasonableness of the officers' determination that the warrant was valid. Indeed, we expressly noted that we were not deciding "whether [the officer's] conduct in [that] case was in fact objectively reasonable." Id., at 345, n. 8. The fact that the officers secured these approvals is certainly pertinent in assessing whether they could have held a reasonable belief that the warrant was supported by probable cause.

C

In holding that the warrant in this case was so obviously defective that no reasonable officer could have believed it was valid, the court below relied heavily on our decision in Groh v. Ramirez, 540 U. S. 551 (2004) , but that precedent is far afield. There, we held that officers who carried out a warrant-approved search were not entitled to qualified immunity because the warrant in question failed to describe the items to be seized at all. Id., at 557. We explained that "[i]n the portion of the form that called for a description of the 'person or property' to be seized, [the applicant] typed a description of [the target's] two-story blue house rather than the alleged stockpile of firearms." Id., at 554. Thus, the warrant stated nonsensically that " 'there is now concealed [on the specified premises] a certain person or property, namely [a] single dwelling residence two story in height which is blue in color and has two additions attached to the east.' " Id., at 554–555, n. 2 (bracketed material in original). Because "even a cursory reading of the warrant in [that] case—

perhaps just a simple glance—would have revealed a glaring de-ficiency that any reasonable police officer would have known was constitutionally fatal," id., at 564, we held that the officer was not entitled to qualified immunity.

The instant case is not remotely similar. In contrast to Groh, any defect here would not have been obvious from the face of the warrant. Rather, any arguable defect would have become apparent only upon a close parsing of the warrant application, and a comparison of the affidavit to the terms of the warrant to determine whether the affidavit established probable cause to search for all the items listed in the warrant. This is not an error that"just a simple glance" would have revealed. Ibid. Indeed, unlike in Groh, the officers here did not merely submit their application to a magistrate. They also presented it for review by a superior officer, and a deputy district attorney, before submitting it to the magistrate. The fact that none of the officials who reviewed the application expressed concern about its validity demonstrates that any error was not obvious. Groh plainly does not control the result here.

*   *   *

The question in this case is not whether the magistrate erred in believing there was sufficient probable cause to support the scope of the warrant he issued. It is instead whether the magistrate so obviously erred that any reasonable officer would have recognized the error. The occasions on which this standard will be met may be rare, but so too are the circumstances in which it will be appropriate to impose personal liability on a lay officer in the face of judicial approval of his actions. Even if the warrant in this case were invalid, it was not so obviously lacking in probable cause that the officers can be considered "plainly incompetent" for concluding otherwise. Malley, supra, at 341. The judgment of the Court of Appeals denying the officers qualified immunity must therefore be reversed.

It is so ordered.

Albert Florence v. Board of Chosen Freeholders of the County of Burlington (April 2, 2012)

Justice Kennedy delivered the opinion of the Court, except as to Part IV. 1

Correctional officials have a legitimate interest, indeed a responsibility, to ensure that jails are not made less secure by reason of what new detainees may carry in on their bodies. Facility personnel, other inmates, and the new detainee himself or herself may be in danger if these threats are introduced into the jail population. This case presents the question of what rules, or limitations, the Constitution imposes on searches of arrested persons who are to be held in jail while their cases are being processed. The term "jail" is used here in a broad sense to include prisons and other detention facilities. The specific measures being challenged will be described in more detail; but, in broad terms, the controversy concerns whether every detainee who will be admitted to the general population may be required to undergo a close visual inspection while undressed.

The case turns in part on the extent to which this Court has sufficient expertise and information in the record to mandate, under the Constitution, the specific restrictions and limitations sought by those who challenge the visual search procedures at issue. In addressing this type of constitutional claim courts must defer to the judgment of correctional officials unless the record contains substantial evidence showing their policies are an unnecessary or unjustified response to problems of jail security. That necessary showing has not been made in this case.

I

In 1998, seven years before the incidents at issue, petitioner Albert Florence was arrested after fleeing from police officers in Essex County,

New Jersey. He was charged with obstruction of justice and use of a deadly weapon. Petitioner entered a plea of guilty to two lesser offenses and was sentenced to pay a fine in monthly installments. In 2003, after he fell behind on his payments and failed to appear at an enforcement hearing, a bench warrant was issued for his arrest. He paid the outstanding balance less than a week later; but, for some unexplained reason, the warrant remained in a statewide computer database.

Two years later, in Burlington County, New Jersey, petitioner and his wife were stopped in their automobile by a state trooper. Based on the outstanding warrant in the computer system, the officer arrested petitioner and took him to the Burlington County Detention Center. He was held there for six days and then was transferred to the Essex County Correctional Facility. It is not the arrest or confinement but the search process at each jail that gives rise to the claims before the Court.

Burlington County jail procedures required every arrestee to shower with a delousing agent. Officers would check arrestees for scars, marks, gang tattoos, and contraband as they disrobed. App. to Pet. for Cert. 53a–56a. Petitioner claims he was also instructed to open his mouth, lift his tongue, hold out his arms, turn around, and lift his genitals. (It is not clear whether this last step was part of the normal practice. See ibid.) Petitioner shared a cell with at least one other person and interacted with other inmates following his admission to the jail. Tr. of Oral Arg. 17.

The Essex County Correctional Facility, where petitioner was taken after six days, is the largest county jail in New Jersey. App. 70a. It admits more than 25,000 in-mates each year and houses about 1,000 gang members at any given time. When petitioner was transferred there, all arriving detainees passed through a metal detector and waited in a group holding cell for a more thorough search. When they left the holding cell, they were instructed to remove their clothing while an officer looked for body markings, wounds, and contraband. Apparently without touching the detainees, an officer looked at their ears, nose, mouth, hair, scalp, fingers, hands, arms, armpits, and other body openings. Id., at 57a–59a; App. to Pet.for Cert. 137a–144a. This policy applied regardless of the circumstances of the arrest, the suspected offense, or the detainee's behavior, demeanor, or criminal history. Petitioner alleges he was required to lift his genitals, turn around, and cough in a squatting position as part of the process. After a mandatory shower, during which his clothes were inspected, petitioner was admitted to the facility. App. 3a–4a, 52a, 258a. He was released the next day, when the charges against him were dismissed.

Petitioner sued the governmental entities that operated the jails, one of the wardens, and certain other defendants. The suit was commenced in the United States District Court for the District of New Jersey. Seeking relief under 42 U. S. C. §1983 for violations of his Fourth and Fourteenth Amendment rights, petitioner maintained that persons arrested for a minor offense could not be required to remove their clothing and expose the most private areas of their bodies to close visual inspection as a routine part of the intake process. Rather, he contended, officials could conduct this kind of search only if they had reason to suspect a particular inmate of concealing a weapon, drugs, or other contraband. The District Court certified a class of individuals who were charged with a nonindictable offense under New Jersey law, processed at either the Burlington County or Essex County jail, and directed to strip naked even though an officer had not articulated any reasonable suspicion they were concealing contraband.

After discovery, the court granted petitioner's motion for summary judgment on the unlawful search claim. It concluded that any policy of "strip searching" nonindictable offenders without reasonable suspicion violated the Fourth Amendment. A divided panel of the United States Court of Appeals for the Third Circuit reversed, holding that the procedures described by the District Court struck a reasonable balance between inmate privacy and the security needs of the two jails. 621 F. 3d 296 (2010). The case proceeds on the understanding that the officers searched detainees prior to their admission to the general population, as the Court of Appeals seems to have assumed. See id., at 298, 311. Petitioner has not argued this factual premise is incorrect.

The opinions in earlier proceedings, the briefs on file, and some cases of this Court refer to a "strip search." The term is imprecise. It may refer simply to the instruction to remove clothing while an officer observes from a distance of, say, five feet or more; it may mean a visual inspection from a closer, more uncomfortable distance; it may include directing detainees to shake their heads or to run their hands through their hair to dislodge what might be hidden there; or it may involve instructions to raise arms, to display foot insteps, to expose the back of the ears, to move or spread the buttocks or genital areas, or to cough in a squatting position. In the instant case, the term does not include any touching of unclothed areas by the inspecting officer. There are no allegations that the detainees here were touched in any way as part of the searches.

The Federal Courts of Appeals have come to differing conclusions as to whether the Fourth Amendment requires correctional officials to exempt some detainees who will be admitted to a jail's general population from the searches here at issue. This Court granted certiorari to address the question. 563 U. S. ___ (2011).

II

The difficulties of operating a detention center must not be underestimated by the courts.

Turner v. Safley, 482 U. S. 78–85 (1987). Jails (in the stricter sense of the term, excluding prison facilities) admit more than 13 million inmates a year. See, e.g., Dept. of Justice, Bureau of Justice Statistics, T. Minton, Jail Inmates at Midyear 2010—Statistical Tables 2 (2011). The largest facilities process hundreds of people every day; smaller jails may be crowded on weekend nights, after a large police operation, or because of detainees arriving from other jurisdictions. Maintaining safety and order at these institutions requires the expertise of correctional officials, who must have substantial discretion to devise reasonable solutions to the problems they face. The Court has confirmed the importance of deference to correctional officials and explained that a regulation impinging on an inmate's constitutional rights must be upheld "if it is reasonably related to legitimate penological interests." Turner, supra, at 89; see Overton v. Bazzetta, 539 U. S. 126–132 (2003). But see Johnson v. California, 543 U. S. 499–511 (2005) (applying strict scrutiny to racial classifications).

The Court's opinion in Bell v. Wolfish, 441 U. S. 520 (1979) , is the starting point for understanding how this framework applies to Fourth Amendment challenges. That case addressed a rule requiring pretrial detainees in any correctional facility run by the Federal Bureau of Prisons "to expose their body cavities for visual inspection as a part of a strip search conducted after every contact visit with a person from outside the institution." Id., at 558. Inmates at the federal Metropolitan Correctional Center in New York City argued there was no security justification for these searches. Officers searched guests before they entered the visiting room, and the inmates were under constant surveillance during the visit. Id., at 577–578 (Marshall, J., dissenting). There had been but one instance in which an inmate attempted to sneak contraband back into the facility. See id., at 559 (majority opinion). The Court nonetheless upheld the search policy. It deferred to the judgment of correctional officials that the inspections served not only to discover but also to deter the smuggling of weapons, drugs, and other prohibited items inside. Id., at 558. The Court explained that there is no mechanical way to determine whether intrusions on an inmate's privacy are reasonable. Id., at 559. The need for a particular search must be balanced against the resulting invasion of personal rights. Ibid.

Policies designed to keep contraband out of jails and prisons have been upheld in cases decided since Bell. In Block v. Rutherford, 468 U. S. 576 (1984), for example, the Court concluded that the Los Angeles County Jail could ban all contact visits because of the threat they posed:

"They open the institution to the introduction of drugs, weapons, and other contraband. Visitors can easily conceal guns, knives, drugs, or other contraband in countless ways and pass them to an inmate unnoticed by even the most vigilant observers. And these items can readily be slipped from the clothing of an innocent child, or transferred by other visitors permitted close contact with inmates." Id., at 586.

There were "many justifications" for imposing a general ban rather than trying to carve out exceptions for certain detainees. Id., at 587. Among other problems, it would be "a difficult if not impossible task" to identify "inmates who have propensities for violence, escape, or drug smuggling." Ibid. This was made "even more difficult by the brevity of detention and the constantly changing nature of the inmate population." Ibid.

The Court has also recognized that deterring the possession of contraband depends in part on the ability to conduct searches without predictable exceptions. In Hudson v. Palmer, 468 U. S. 517 (1984), it addressed the question of whether prison officials could perform random searches of inmate lockers and cells even without

reason to suspect a particular individual of concealing a prohibited item. Id., at 522–523. The Court upheld the constitutionality of the practice, recognizing that " '[f]or one to advocate that prison searches must be conducted only pursuant to an enunciated general policy or when suspicion is directed at a particular inmate is to ignore the realities of prison operation.' " Id., at 529 (quoting Marrero v. Commonwealth, 222 Va. 754, 757, 284 S. E. 2d 809, 811 (1981)). Inmates would adapt to any pattern or loopholes they discovered in the search protocol and then undermine the security of the institution. 468 U. S., at 529.

These cases establish that correctional officials must be permitted to devise reasonable search policies to detect and deter the possession of contraband in their facilities. See Bell, 441 U. S., at 546 ("[M]aintaining institutional security and preserving internal order and discipline are essential goals that may require limitation or retraction of retained constitutional rights of both convicted prisoners and pretrial detainees"). The task of determining whether a policy is reasonably related to legitimate security interests is "peculiarly within the province and professional expertise of corrections officials." Id., at 548. This Court has repeated the admonition that, " 'in the absence of substantial evidence in the record to indicate that the officials have exaggerated their response to these considerations courts should ordinarily defer to their expert judgment in such matters.' " Block, supra, at 584–585; Bell, supra, at 548.

In many jails officials seek to improve security by requiring some kind of strip search of everyone who is to be detained. These procedures have been used in different places throughout the country, from Cranston, Rhode Island, to Sapulpa, Oklahoma, to Idaho Falls, Idaho. See Roberts v. Rhode Island, 239 F. 3d 107, 108–109 (CA1 2001); Chapman v. Nichols, 989 F. 2d 393, 394 (CA10 1993); Giles v. Ackerman, 746 F. 2d 614, 615 (CA9

1984) (per curiam); see also, e.g., Bull v. City and Cty. of San Francisco, 595 F. 3d 964 (CA9 2010) (en banc) (San Francisco, California); Powell v. Barrett, 541 F. 3d 1298 (CA11 2008) (en banc) (Fulton Cty., Ga.); Masters v. Crouch, 872 F. 2d 1248, 1251 (CA6 1989) (Jefferson Cty., Ky.); Weber v. Dell, 804 F. 2d 796, 797–798 (CA2 1986) (Monroe Cty., N. Y.); Stewart v. Lubbock Cty., 767 F. 2d 153, 154 (CA5 1985) (Lubbock Cty., Tex.).

Persons arrested for minor offenses may be among the detainees processed at these facilities. This is, in part, a consequence of the exercise of state authority that was the subject of Atwater v. Lago Vista, 532 U. S. 318 (2001). Atwater addressed the perhaps more fundamental question of who may be deprived of liberty and taken to jail in the first place. The case involved a woman who was arrested after a police officer noticed neither she nor her children were wearing their seatbelts. The arrestee argued the Fourth Amendment prohibited her custodial arrest without a warrant when an offense could not result in jail time and there was no compelling need for immediate detention. Id., at 346. The Court held that a Fourth Amendment restriction on this power would put officers in an "almost impossible spot." Id., at 350. Their ability to arrest a suspect would depend in some cases on the precise weight of drugs in his pocket, whether he was a repeat offender, and the scope of what counted as a compelling need to detain someone. Id., at 348–349. The Court rejected the proposition that the Fourth Amendment barred custodial arrests in a set of these cases as a matter of constitutional law. It ruled, based on established principles, that officers may make an arrest based upon probable cause to believe the person has committed a criminal offense in their presence. See id., at 354. The Court stated that "a responsible Fourth Amendment balance is not well served by standards requiring sensitive, case-by-case determinations of government need, lest every discretionary judgment in the field be converted into an occasion for constitutional review." Id., at 347.

Atwater did not address whether the Constitution imposes special restrictions on the searches of offenders suspected of committing minor offenses once they are taken to jail. Some Federal Courts of Appeals have held that corrections officials may not conduct a strip search of these detainees, even if no touching is involved, absent reasonable suspicion of concealed contraband. 621 F. 3d, at 303–304, and n. 4. The Courts of Appeals to address this issue in the last decade, however, have come to the opposite conclusion. See 621 F. 3d 296 (case below); Bame v. Dillard, 637 F. 3d 380 (CADC 2011); Powell, supra; Bull, supra. The current case is set against this precedent and governed by the principles announced in Turner and Bell.

III

The question here is whether undoubted security imperatives involved in jail supervision override the assertion that some detainees must be exempt from the more invasive search procedures at issue absent reasonable suspicion of a concealed weapon or other contraband. The Court has held that deference must be given to the officials in charge of the jail unless there is "substantial evidence" demonstrating their response to the situation is exaggerated. Block, 468 U. S., at 584–585 (internal quotation marks omitted). Petitioner has not met this standard, and the record provides full justifications for the procedures used.

A

Correctional officials have a significant interest in conducting a thorough search as a standard part of the intake process. The admission of inmates creates numerous risks for facility staff, for the existing detainee population, and for a new detainee himself or herself. The danger of introducing lice or contagious infections, for example, is well documented. See, e.g., Deger &

Quick, The Enduring Menace of MRSA: Incidence, Treatment, and Prevention in a County Jail, 15 J. Correctional Health Care 174, 174–175, 177–178 (2009); Bick, Infection Control in Jails and Prisons, 45 Healthcare Epidemiology 1047, 1049 (2007). The Federal Bureau of Prisons recommends that staff screen new detainees for these conditions. See Clinical Practice Guidelines, Management of Methicillin-Resistant Staphylococcus aureus (MRSA) Infections 2 (2011); Clinical Practice Guidelines, Lice and Scabies Protocol 1 (2011). Persons just arrested may have wounds or other injuries requiring immediate medical attention. It may be difficult to identify and treat these problems until detainees remove their clothes for a visual inspection. See Prison and Jail Administration: Practice and Theory 142 (P. Carlson & G. Garrett eds., 2d ed. 2008) (hereinafter Carlson & Garrett).

Jails and prisons also face grave threats posed by the increasing number of gang members who go through the intake process. See Brief for Policemen's Benevolent As-sociation, Local 249, et al. as Amici Curiae 14 (hereinaf-ter PBA Brief); New Jersey Comm'n of Investigation, Gangland Behind Bars: How and Why Organized Criminal Street Gangs Thrive in New Jersey's Prisons . . . And What Can Be Done About It 10–11 (2009). "Gang rivalries spawn a climate of tension, violence, and coercion." Carlson & Garrett 462. The groups recruit new members by force, engage in assaults against staff, and give other inmates a reason to arm themselves. Ibid. Fights among feuding gangs can be deadly, and the officers who must maintain order are put in harm's way. PBA Brief 17. These considerations provide a reasonable basis to justify a visual inspection for certain tattoos and other signs of gang affiliation as part of the intake process. The identi-fication and isolation of gang members before they are admitted protects everyone in the facility. Cf. Fraise v. Terhune, 283 F. 3d 506, 509–510 (CA3 2002) (Alito, J.) (describing a statewide policy authorizing the identification and isolation of gang members in prison).

Detecting contraband concealed by new detainees, furthermore, is a most serious responsibility. Weapons, drugs, and alcohol all disrupt the safe operation of a jail. Cf. Hudson, 468 U. S., at 528 (recognizing "the constant fight against the proliferation of knives and guns, illicit drugs, and other contraband"). Correctional officers have had to confront arrestees concealing knives, scissors, razor blades, glass shards, and other prohibited items on their person, including in their body cavities. See Bull, 595 F. 3d, at 967, 969; Brief for New Jersey County Jail Wardens Association as Amicus Curiae 17–18 (hereinafter New Jersey Wardens Brief). They have also found crack, heroin, and marijuana. Brief for City and County of San Francisco et al. as Amici Curiae 9–11 (hereinafter San Francisco Brief). The use of drugs can embolden inmates in aggression toward officers or each other; and, even apart from their use, the trade in these substances can lead to violent confrontations. See PBA Brief 11.

There are many other kinds of contraband. The textbook definition of the term covers any unauthorized item. See Prisons: Today and Tomorrow 237 (J. Pollock ed. 1997) ("Contraband is any item that is possessed in violation of prison rules. Contraband obviously includes drugs or weapons, but it can also be money, cigarettes, or even some types of clothing"). Everyday items can undermine security if introduced into a detention facility:

"Lighters and matches are fire and arson risks or potential weapons. Cell phones are used to orchestrate violence and criminality both within and without jailhouse walls. Pills and medications enhance suicide risks. Chewing gum can block locking devices; hairpins can open handcuffs; wigs can conceal drugs and weapons." New Jersey Wardens Brief 8–9.

Something as simple as an overlooked pen can pose a significant danger. Inmates commit more than 10,000 assaults on correctional staff every year and many more among themselves. See Dept. of Justice, Bureau of Justice Statistics, J. Stephan & J. Karberg, Census of State and Federal Correctional Facilities, 2000, p. v (2003).

Contraband creates additional problems because scarce items, including currency, have value in a jail's culture and underground economy. Correctional officials inform us "[t]he competition . . . for such goods begets violence, extortion, and disorder." New Jersey Wardens Brief 2. Gangs exacerbate the problem. They "orchestrate thefts, commit assaults, and approach inmates in packs to take the contraband from the weak." Id., at 9–10. This puts the entire facility, including detainees being held for a brief term for a minor offense, at risk. Gangs do coerce inmates who have access to the outside world, such as people serving their time on the weekends, to sneak things into the jail. Id., at 10; see, e.g., Pugmire, Vegas Suspect Has Term to Serve, Los Angeles Times, Sept. 23, 2005, p. B1 ("Weekend-only jail sentences are a common punishment for people convicted of nonviolent drug crimes . . ."). These inmates, who might be thought to pose the least risk, have been caught smuggling prohibited items into jail. See New Jersey Wardens Brief 10. Concealing contraband often takes little time and effort. It might be done as an officer approaches a suspect's car or during a brief commotion in a group holding cell. Something small might be tucked or taped under an armpit, behind an ear, between the buttocks, in the instep of a foot, or inside the mouth or some other body cavity.

It is not surprising that correctional officials have sought to perform thorough searches at intake for disease, gang affiliation, and contraband. Jails are often crowded, unsanitary, and dangerous places. There is a substantial interest in preventing any new inmate, either of his own will or as a result of coercion, from putting all who live or work at these institutions at even greater risk when he is admitted to the general population.

B

Petitioner acknowledges that correctional officials must be allowed to conduct an effective search during the intake process and that this will require at least some detainees to lift their genitals or cough in a squatting position. These procedures, similar to the ones upheld in Bell, are designed to uncover contraband that can go undetected by a patdown, metal detector, and other less invasivesearches. See Brief for United States as Amicus Curiae 23 (hereinafter United States Brief); New Jersey Wardens Brief 19, n. 6. Petitioner maintains there is little benefit to conducting these more invasive steps on a new detainee who has not been arrested for a serious crime or for any offense involving a weapon or drugs. In his view these de-tainees should be exempt from this process unless they give officers a particular reason to suspect them of hiding contraband. It is reasonable, however, for correctional officials to conclude this standard would be unworkable. The record provides evidence that the seriousness of an offense is a poor predictor of who has contraband andthat it would be difficult in practice to determine whether individual detainees fall within the proposed exemption.

1

People detained for minor offenses can turn out to bethe most devious and dangerous criminals. Cf. Clements v. Logan, 454 U. S. 1304, 1305 (1981) (Rehnquist, J., in chambers) (deputy at a detention center shot by misdemeanant who had not been strip searched). Hours after the Oklahoma City bombing, Timothy McVeigh was stopped by a state trooper who noticed he was driving without a license plate. Johnston, Suspect Won't Answer Any Questions, N. Y. Times, Apr. 25,

1995, p. A1. Police stopped serial killer Joel Rifkin for the same reason. McQuiston, Confession Used to Portray Rifkin as Methodical Killer, N. Y. Times, Apr. 26, 1994, p. B6. One ofthe terrorists involved in the September 11 attacks was stopped and ticketed for speeding just two days before hijacking Flight 93. The Terrorists: Hijacker Got a Speeding Ticket, N. Y. Times, Jan. 8, 2002, p. A12. Reasonable correctional officials could conclude these uncertainties mean they must conduct the same thorough search of everyone who will be admitted to their facilities.

Experience shows that people arrested for minor of-fenses have tried to smuggle prohibited items into jail, sometimes by using their rectal cavities or genitals for the concealment. They may have some of the same incentives as a serious criminal to hide contraband. A detainee might risk carrying cash, cigarettes, or a penknife to survive in jail. Others may make a quick decision to hide unlawful substances to avoid getting in more trouble at the time of their arrest. This record has concrete examples. Officers at the Atlantic County Correctional Facility, for example, discovered that a man arrested for driving under the influence had "2 dime bags of weed, 1 pack of rolling papers, 20 matches, and 5 sleeping pills" taped under his scrotum. Brief for Atlantic County et al. as Amici Curiae 36 (internal quotation marks omitted). A person booked on a misdemeanor charge of disorderly conduct in Washington State managed to hide a lighter, tobacco, tattoo needles, and other prohibited items in his rectal cavity. See United States Brief 25, n. 15. San Francisco officials have discovered contraband hidden in body cavities of people arrested for trespassing, public nuisance, and shoplifting. San Francisco Brief 3. There have been similar incidents at jails throughout the country. See United States Brief 25, n. 15.

Even if people arrested for a minor offense do not themselves wish to introduce contraband into a jail, they may be coerced into doing so by others. See New Jersey Wardens Brief 16; cf. Block, 468 U. S., at 587 ("It is not unreasonable to assume, for instance, that low security risk detainees would be enlisted to help obtain contraband or weapons by their fellow inmates who are denied contact visits"). This could happen any time detainees are held in the same area, including in a van on the way to the station or in the holding cell of the jail. If, for example, a person arrested and detained for unpaid traffic citations is not subject to the same search as others, this will be well known to other detainees with jail experience. A hardened criminal or gang member can, in just a few minutes, approach the person and coerce him into hiding the fruits of a crime, a weapon, or some other contraband. As an expert in this case explained, "the interaction and mingling between misdemeanants and felons will only increase the amount of contraband in the facility if the jail can only conduct admission searches on felons." App. 381a. Exempting people arrested for minor offenses from a standard search protocol thus may put them at greater risk and result in more contraband being brought into the detention facility. This is a substantial reason not to mandate the exception petitioner seeks as a matter of constitutional law.

2

It also may be difficult, as a practical matter, to classify inmates by their current and prior offenses before the intake search. Jails can be even more dangerous than prisons because officials there know so little about the people they admit at the outset. See New Jersey Wardens Brief 11–14. An arrestee may be carrying a false ID or lie about his identity. The officers who conduct an initial search often do not have access to criminal history records. See, e.g., App. 235a; New Jersey Wardens Brief 13. And those records can be inaccurate or incomplete. See Department of Justice v. Reporters Comm. for Freedom of Press, 489 U. S. 749, 752 (1989) . Petitioner's rap sheet is an example. It did not reflect his previous arrest for possession of a deadly weapon. Tr. of Oral Arg. 18–19. Inthe absence of reliable information it would be illogical to require officers to assume the arrestees in front of them do not pose a risk of smuggling something into the facility.

The laborious administration of prisons would become less effective, and likely less fair and evenhanded, were the practical problems inevitable from the rules suggested by petitioner to be imposed as a constitutional mandate. Even if they had accurate information about a detainee's current and prior arrests, officers, under petitioner's proposed regime, would encounter serious implementation difficulties. They would be required, in a few minutes, to determine whether any of the underlying offenses were serious enough to authorize the more invasive search protocol. Other possible classifications based on characteristics of individual detainees also might prove to be unworkable or even give rise to charges of discriminatory application. Most officers would not be well equipped to make any of these legal determinations during the pressures of the intake process. Bull, 595 F. 3d, at 985–987 (Kozinski, C. J., concurring); see also Welsh v. Wisconsin, 466 U. S. 740–762 (1984) (White, J., dissenting) ("[T]he Court's approach will necessitate a case-by-case evaluation of the seriousness of particular crimes, a dif-ficult task for which officers and courts are poorly equipped"). To avoid liability, officers might be inclined not to conduct a thorough search in any close case, thus creating unnecessary risk for the entire jail population. Cf. Atwater, 532 U. S., at 351, and n. 22.

The Court addressed an analogous problem in Atwater. The petitioner in that case argued the Fourth Amendment prohibited a warrantless arrest when being convicted of the suspected crime "could not ultimately carry any jail time" and there was "no compelling need for immediate detention." Id., at 346. That rule "promise[d] very little in the way of administrability." Id., at 350. Officers could not be expected to draw the proposed lines on a moment's notice, and the risk of violating the Constitution would have discouraged them from arresting criminals in any questionable circumstances. Id., at 350–351 ("An officer not quite sure the drugs weighed enough to warrant jail time or not quite certain about a suspect's risk of flight would not arrest, even though it could perfectly well turn out that, in fact, the offense called for incarceration and the defendant was long gone on the day of trial"). The Fourth Amendment did not compel this result in Atwater. The Court held that officers who have probable cause to believe even a minor criminal offense has been committed in their presence may arrest the offender. See id., at 354. Individual jurisdictions can of course choose "to impose more restrictive safeguards through statutes limiting warrantless arrests for minor offenders." Id., at 352.

One of the central principles in Atwater applies with equal force here. Officers who interact with those suspected of violating the law have an "essential interest in readily administrable rules." Id., at 347; accord, New York v. Belton, 453 U. S. 454, 458 (1981) . The officials in charge of the jails in this case urge the Court to reject any complicated constitutional scheme requiring them to conduct less thorough inspections of some detainees based on their behavior, suspected offense, criminal history, and other factors. They offer significant reasons why the Constitution must not prevent them from conducting the same search on any suspected offender who will be admitted to the general population in their facilities. The restrictions suggested by petitioner would limit the intrusion on the privacy of some detainees but at the risk of increased danger to everyone in the facility, including the less serious offenders themselves.

IV

This case does not require the Court to rule on the types of searches that would be reasonable in instances where, for example, a detainee will be held without assignment to the general jail population and without substantial contact with other detainees. This describes the circumstances in Atwater. See 532 U. S., at 324 ("Officers took Atwater's 'mug shot' and placed her, alone, in a jail cell for about one hour, after which she was taken before a magistrate and released on $310 bond"). The accommodations provided in these situations may diminish the need to conduct some aspects of the searches at issue. Cf. United States Brief 30 (discussing the segregation, and less invasive searches, of individuals held by the Federal Bureau of Prisons for misdemeanors or civil contempt). The circumstances before the Court, however, do not present the opportunity to consider a narrow exception of the sort Justice Alito describes, post, at 2–3 (concurring opinion), which might restrict whether an arrestee whose detention has not yet been reviewed by a magistrate or other judicial officer, and who can be held in available facilities removed from the general population, may be subjected to the types of searches at issue here.

Petitioner's amici raise concerns about instances of officers engaging in intentional humiliation and other abusive practices. See Brief for Sister Bernie Galvin et al. as Amici Curiae; see also Hudson, 468 U. S., at 528 ("[I]ntentional harassment of even the most hardened criminals cannot be tolerated by a civilized society"); Bell, 441 U. S., at 560. There also may be legitimate concerns about the invasiveness of searches that involve the touching of detainees. These issues are not implicated on the facts of this case, however, and it is unnecessary to con-sider them here.

V

Even assuming all the facts in favor of petitioner, the search procedures at the Burlington County Detention Center and the Essex County Correctional Facility struck a reasonable balance between inmate privacy and the needs of the institutions. The Fourth and Fourteenth Amendments do not require adoption of the framework of rules petitioner proposes.

The judgment of the Court of Appeals for the Third Circuit is affirmed.

It is so ordered.

Notes

1 Justice Thomas joins all but Part IV of this opinion.

Florida v. Jardines (March 26, 2013) [Notes omitted]

Justice Scalia delivered the opinion of the Court.

We consider whether using a drug-sniffing dog on a homeowner's porch to investigate the contents of the home is a "search" within the meaning of the Fourth Amendment.

I

In 2006, Detective William Pedraja of the Miami-Dade Police Department received an unverified tip that marijuana was being grown in the home of respondent Joelis Jardines. One month later, the Department and the Drug Enforcement Administration sent a joint surveillance team to Jardines' home. Detective Pedraja was part of that team. He watched the home for fifteen minutes and saw no vehicles in the driveway or activity around the home, and could not see inside because the blinds were drawn. Detective Pedraja then approached Jardines' home accompanied by Detective Douglas Bartelt, a trained canine handler who had just arrived at the scene with his drug-sniffing dog. The dog was trained to detect the scent of marijuana, cocaine, heroin, and several other drugs, indicating the presence of any of these substances through particular behavioral changes recognizable by his handler.

Detective Bartelt had the dog on a six-foot leash, owing in part to the dog's "wild" nature, App. to Pet. for Cert. A–35, and tendency to dart around erratically while searching. As the dog approached Jardines' front porch, he apparently sensed one of the odors he had been trained to detect, and began energetically exploring the area for the strongest point source of that odor. As Detective Bartelt explained, the dog "began tracking that airborne odor by . . . tracking back and forth," engaging in what is called "bracketing," "back and forth, back and forth." Id., at A– 33 to A–34. Detective Bartelt gave the dog "the full six feet of the leash plus whatever safe distance [he could] give him" to do this—he testified that he needed to give the dog "as much distance as I can." Id., at A–35. And Detective Pedraja stood back while this was occurring, so that he would not "get knocked over" when the dog was "spinning around trying to find" the source. Id., at A–38.

After sniffing the base of the front door, the dog sat, which is the trained behavior upon discovering the odor's strongest point. Detective Bartelt then pulled the dog away from the door and returned to his vehicle. He left the scene after informing Detective Pedraja that there had been a positive alert for narcotics.

On the basis of what he had learned at the home, Detective Pedraja applied for and received a warrant to search the residence. When the warrant was executed later that day, Jardines attempted to flee and was arrested; the search revealed marijuana plants, and he was charged with trafficking in cannabis.

At trial, Jardines moved to suppress the marijuana plants on the ground that the canine investigation was an unreasonable search. The trial court granted the motion, and the Florida Third District Court of Appeal reversed. On a petition for discretionary review, the Florida Supreme Court quashed the decision of the Third District Court of Appeal and approved the trial court's decision to suppress, holding (as relevant here) that the use of the trained narcotics dog to investigate Jardines' home wasa Fourth Amendment search unsupported by probable cause, rendering invalid the warrant based upon information gathered in that search. 73 So. 3d 34 (2011).

We granted certiorari, limited to the question of whether the officers' behavior was a search within the meaning of the Fourth Amendment. 565 U. S. ____ (2012).

II

The Fourth Amendment provides in relevant part that the "right of the people to be secure in their persons, houses, papers, and effects, against unreasonable searches and seizures, shall not be violated." The Amendment establishes a simple baseline, one that for much of our history formed the exclusive basis for its protections: When "the Government obtains information by physically intruding" on persons, houses, papers, or effects, "a 'search' within the original meaning of the Fourth Amendment" has "undoubtedly occurred." United States v. Jones, 565 U. S.____, ____, n. 3 (2012) (slip op., at 6, n. 3). By reason ofour decision in Katz v. United States, 389 U. S. 347(1967), property rights "are not the sole measure of Fourth Amendment violations," Soldal v. Cook County, 506 U. S. 56, 64 (1992) —but though Katz may add to the baseline, it does not subtract anything from the Amendment's protections "when the Government does engage in [a] physical intrusion of a constitutionally protected area," United States v. Knotts, 460 U. S. 276, 286 (1983) (Brennan, J., concurring in the judgment).

That principle renders this case a straightforward one. The officers were gathering information in an area belonging to Jardines and immediately surrounding his house—in the curtilage of the house, which we have held enjoys protection as part of the home itself. And they gathered that information by physically entering and occupying the area to engage in conduct not explicitly or implicitly permitted by the homeowner.

A

The Fourth Amendment "indicates with some precision the places and things encompassed by its protections": persons, houses, papers, and effects. Oliver v. United States, 466 U. S. 170, 176 (1984). The Fourth Amendment does not, therefore, prevent all investigations conducted on private property; for example, an officer may (subject to Katz) gather information in what we have called "open fields"—even if those fields are privately owned—because such fields are not enumerated in the Amendment's text. Hester v. United States, 265 U. S. 57 (1924).

But when it comes to the Fourth Amendment, the home is first among equals. At the Amendment's "very core" stands "the right of a man to retreat into his own home and there be free from unreasonable governmental in-trusion." Silverman v. United States, 365 U. S. 505, 511 (1961). This right would be of little practical value if the State's agents could stand in a home's porch or side garden and trawl for evidence with impunity; the right to retreat would be significantly diminished if the police could enter a man's property to observe his repose from just outside the front window.

We therefore regard the area "immediately surrounding and associated with the home"—what our cases call the curtilage—as "part of the home itself for Fourth Amendment purposes." Oliver, supra, at 180. That principle has ancient and durable roots. Just as the distinction between the home and the open fields is "as old as the common law," Hester, supra, at 59, so too is the identity of home and what Blackstone called the "curtilage or homestall," for the "house protects and privileges all its branches and appurtenants." 4 W. Blackstone, Commentaries on the Laws of England

223, 225 (1769). This area around the home is "intimately linked to the home, both physically and psychologically," and is where "privacy expectations are most heightened." California v. Ciraolo, 476 U. S. 207, 213 (1986).

While the boundaries of the curtilage are generally "clearly marked," the "conception defining the curtilage" is at any rate familiar enough that it is "easily understood from our daily experience." Oliver, 466 U. S., at 182, n. 12. Here there is no doubt that the officers entered it: The front porch is the classic exemplar of an area adjacent to the home and "to which the activity of home life extends." Ibid.

B

Since the officers' investigation took place in a constitutionally protected area, we turn to the question of whether it was accomplished through an unlicensed physical in-trusion. 1 While law enforcement officers need not "shield their eyes" when passing by the home "on public thoroughfares," Ciraolo, 476 U. S., at 213, an officer's leave to gather information is sharply circumscribed when he steps off those thoroughfares and enters the Fourth Amendment's protected areas. In permitting, for example, visual observation of the home from "public navigable airspace," we were careful to note that it was done "in a physically nonintrusive manner." Ibid. Entick v. Carrington, 2 Wils. K. B. 275, 95 Eng. Rep. 807 (K. B. 1765), a case "undoubtedly familiar" to "every American statesman" at the time of the Founding, Boyd v. United States, 116 U. S. 616(1886), states the general rule clearly: "[O]ur law holds the property of every man so sacred, that no man can set his foot upon his neighbour's close without his leave." 2 Wils. K. B., at 291, 95 Eng. Rep., at 817. As it is undisputed that the detectives had all four of their feet and all four of their companion's firmly planted on the constitutionally protected extension of Jardines' home, the only question is whether he had given his leave (even implicitly) for them to do so. He had not.

"A license may be implied from the habits of the country," notwithstanding the "strict rule of the English common law as to entry upon a close." McKee v. Gratz, 260 U. S. 127, 136 (1922) (Holmes, J.). We have accordingly recognized that "the knocker on the front door is treated as an invitation or license to attempt an entry, justifying ingress to the home by solicitors, hawkers and peddlers of all kinds." Breard v. Alexandria, 341 U. S. 622, 626 (1951). This implicit license typically permits the visitor to approach the home by the front path, knock promptly, wait briefly to be received, and then (absent invitation to linger longer) leave. Complying with the terms of that traditional invitation does not require fine-grained legal knowledge; it is generally managed without incident by the Nation's Girl Scouts and trick-or-treaters. 2 Thus, a police officer not armed with a warrant may approach a home and knock, precisely because that is "no more than any private citizen might do." Kentucky v. King, 563 U. S. ____, ____ (2011) (slip op., at 16).

But introducing a trained police dog to explore the area around the home in hopes of discovering incriminating evidence is something else. There is no customary invitation to do that. An invitation to engage in canine forensic investigation assuredly does not inhere in the very act of hanging a knocker. 3 To find a visitor knocking on the door is routine (even if sometimes unwelcome); to spot that same visitor exploring the front path with a metal detector, or marching his bloodhound into the garden before saying hello and asking permission, would inspire mostof us to—well, call the police. The scope of a license—express or implied—is limited not only to a particular area but also to a specific purpose. Consent at a traffic stop to an officer's checking out an anonymous tip that there is a body in the trunk does not permit the officer to rummage through the trunk for narcotics. Here, the background

social norms that invite a visitor to the front door do not invite him there to conduct a search. 4

The State points to our decisions holding that the subjective intent of the officer is irrelevant. See Ashcroft v. al-Kidd, 563 U. S. ____ (2011); Whren v. United States, 517 U. S. 806 (1996). But those cases merely hold that a stop or search that is objectively reasonable is not vitiated by the fact that the officer's real reason for making the stop or search has nothing to do with the validating reason. Thus, the defendant will not be heard to complain that although he was speeding the officer's real reason for the stop was racial harassment. See id., at 810, 813. Here, however, the question before the court is precisely whether the officer's conduct was an objectively reasonable search. As we have described, that depends upon whether the officers had an implied license to enter the porch, which in turn depends upon the purpose for which they entered. Here, their behavior objectively reveals a purpose to conduct a search, which is not what anyone would think he had license to do.

III

The State argues that investigation by a forensic narcotics dog by definition cannot implicate any legitimate privacy interest. The State cites for authority our decisions in United States v. Place, 462 U. S. 696 (1983), United States v. Jacobsen, 466 U. S. 109 (1984), and Illinois v. Caballes, 543 U. S. 405 (2005), which held, respectively, that canine inspection of luggage in an airport, chemical testing of a substance that had fallen from a parcel in transit, and canine inspection of an automobile during a lawful traffic stop, do not violate the "reasonable expectation of privacy" described in Katz.

Just last Term, we considered an argument much like this. Jones held that tracking an automobile's where-abouts using a physically-mounted GPS receiver is a Fourth Amendment search. The Government argued that the Katz standard "show[ed] that no search occurred," as the defendant had "no 'reasonable expectation of privacy' " in his whereabouts on the public roads, Jones, 565 U. S., at ____ (slip op., at 5)—a proposition with at least as much support in our case law as the one the State marshals here. See, e.g., United States v. Knotts, 460 U. S. 276, 278 (1983). But because the GPS receiver had been physically mounted on the defendant's automobile (thus intruding on his "effects"), we held that tracking the vehicle's movements was a search: a person's " Fourth Amendment rights do not rise or fall with the Katz formulation." Jones, supra, at ____ (slip op., at 5). The Katz reasonable-expectations test "has been added to, not substituted for," the traditional property-based understanding of the Fourth Amendment, and so is unnecessary to consider when the government gains evidence by physically intruding on constitutionally protected areas. Jones, supra, at ____ (slip op., at 8).

Thus, we need not decide whether the officers' investigation of Jardines' home violated his expectation of privacy under Katz. One virtue of the Fourth Amendment's property-rights baseline is that it keeps easy cases easy. That the officers learned what they learned only by physically intruding on Jardines' property to gather evidence is enough to establish that a search occurred.

For a related reason we find irrelevant the State's argument (echoed by the dissent) that forensic dogs have been commonly used by police for centuries. This argument is apparently directed to our holding in Kyllo v. United States, 533 U. S. 27 (2001), that surveillance of the home is a search where "the Government uses a device that is not in general public use" to "explore details of the home that would previously have been unknowable without physical intrusion." Id., at 40 (emphasis added). But the implication of that statement (inclusio unius est exclusio alterius) is that when the government uses a physical intrusion to explore details of the home (including its curtilage), the antiquity of the tools that they bring along is irrelevant.

* * *

The government's use of trained police dogs to inves-tigate the home and its immediate surroundings is a "search" within the meaning of the Fourth Amendment. The judgment of the Supreme Court of Florida is therefore affirmed.

It is so ordered.

Missouri v. McNeely (April 17, 2013) [Notes omitted]

Justice Sotomayor announced the judgment of the Court and delivered the opinion of the Court with respect to Parts I, II–A, II–B, and IV, and an opinion with respect to Parts II–C and III, in which Justice Scalia, Justice Ginsburg, and Justice Kagan join.

In Schmerber v. California, 384 U. S. 757 (1966), this Court upheld a warrantless blood test of an individual arrested for driving under the influence of alcohol because the officer "might reasonably have believed that he was confronted with an emergency, in which the delay necessary to obtain a warrant, under the circumstances, threatened the destruction of evidence." Id., at 770 (internal quotation marks omitted). The question presented here is whether the natural metabolization of alcohol in the bloodstream presents a per se exigency that justifies an exception to the Fourth Amendment's warrant requirement for nonconsensual blood testing in all drunk-driving cases. We conclude that it does not, and we hold, consistent with general Fourth Amendment principles, that exigency in this context must be determined case by case based on the totality of the circumstances.

I

While on highway patrol at approximately

2:08 a.m., a Missouri police officer stopped Tyler McNeely's truck after observing it exceed the posted speed limit and repeatedly cross the centerline. The officer noticed several signs that McNeely was intoxicated, including McNeely's bloodshot eyes, his slurred speech, and the smell of alcohol on his breath. McNeely acknowledged to the officer that he had consumed "a couple of beers" at a bar, App. 20, and he appeared unsteady on his feet when he exited the truck. After McNeely performed poorly on a battery of field-sobriety tests and declined to use a portable breath-test device to measure his blood alcohol concentration (BAC), the officer placed him under arrest.

The officer began to transport McNeely to the station house. But when McNeely indicated that he would again refuse to provide a breath sample, the officer changed course and took McNeely to a nearby hospital for blood testing. The officer did not attempt to secure a warrant. Upon arrival at the hospital, the officer asked McNeely whether he would consent to a blood test. Reading froma standard implied consent form, the officer explained to McNeely that under state law refusal to submit voluntar-ily to the test would lead to the immediate revocation of his driver's license for one year and could be used against him in a future prosecution. See Mo. Ann. Stat. §§577.020.1, 577.041 (West 2011). McNeely nonetheless refused. The officer then directed a hospital lab technician to take a blood sample, and the sample was secured at approximately 2:35 a.m. Subsequent laboratory testing measured McNeely's BAC at 0.154 percent, which was well above the legal limit of 0.08 percent. See §577.012.1.

McNeely was charged with driving while intoxicated (DWI), in violation of §577.010. 1 He moved to suppress the results of the blood test, arguing in relevant part that, under the circumstances, taking his blood for chemi-cal testing without first obtaining a search warrant vio-lated his rights under the Fourth Amendment.

The trial court agreed. It concluded that the exigency exception to the warrant requirement did not apply because, apart from the fact that "[a]s in all cases involving intoxication, [McNeely's] blood alcohol was being metabolized by his liver," there were no circumstances suggesting the officer faced an emergency in which he could not practicably obtain a warrant. No. 10CG–CR01849–01 (Cir. Ct. Cape Giradeau Cty., Mo., Div. II, Mar. 3, 2011), App. to Pet.for Cert. 43a. On appeal, the Missouri Court of Appeals stated an intention to reverse but transferred the case directly to the Missouri Supreme Court. No. ED 96402 (June 21, 2011), id., at 24a.

The Missouri Supreme Court affirmed. 358 S. W. 3d 65 (2012) (per curiam). Recognizing that this Court's decision in Schmerber v. California, 384 U. S. 757, "provide[d] the backdrop" to its analysis, the Missouri Supreme Court held that "Schmerber directs lower courts to engage ina totality of the circumstances analysis when determin-ing whether exigency permits a nonconsensual, warrantless blood draw." 358 S. W. 3d, at 69, 74. The court further concluded that Schmerber "requires more than the mere dissipation of blood-alcohol evidence to support a warrantless blood draw in an alcohol-related case." 358 S. W. 3d, at 70. According to the court, exigency depends heavily on the existence of additional " 'special facts,' " such as whether an officer was delayed by the need to investigate an ac-cident and transport an injured suspect to the hospital,as had been the case in Schmerber. 358 S. W. 3d, at 70, 74. Finding that this was "unquestionably a routine DWI case" in which no factors other than the natural dissi-pation of blood-alcohol suggested that there was an emergency, the court held that the nonconsensual warrantless blood draw violated McNeely's Fourth Amendment right to be free from unreasonable searches of his person. Id., at 74–75.

We granted certiorari to resolve a split of

authority on the question whether the natural dissipation of alcohol in the bloodstream establishes a per se exigency that suffices on its own to justify an exception to the warrant requirement for nonconsensual blood testing in drunk-driving investigations. 2 See 567 U. S. ____ (2012). We now affirm.

II

A

The Fourth Amendment provides in relevant part that "[t]he right of the people to be secure in their persons, houses, papers, and effects, against unreasonable searches and seizures, shall not be violated, and no Warrants shall issue, but upon probable cause." Our cases have held that a warrantless search of the person is reasonable only if it falls within a recognized exception. See, e.g., United States v. Robinson, 414 U. S. 218, 224 (1973). That principle applies to the type of search at issue in this case, which involved a compelled physical intrusion beneath McNeely's skin and into his veins to obtain a sample of his blood for use as evidence in a criminal investigation. Such an invasion of bodily integrity implicates an individual's "most personal and deep-rooted expectations of privacy." Winston v. Lee, 470 U. S. 753, 760 (1985); see also Skinner v. Railway Labor Executives' Assn., 489 U. S. 602, 616 (1989).

We first considered the Fourth Amendment restrictions on such searches in Schmerber, where, as in this case, a blood sample was drawn from a defendant suspected of driving while under the influence of alcohol. 384 U. S., at 758. Noting that "[s]earch warrants are ordinarily required for searches of dwellings," we reasoned that "absent an emergency, no less could be required where intrusions into the human body are concerned," even when the search was conducted following a lawful arrest. Id., at 770. We explained that the importance of requiring authorization by a " 'neutral and detached magistrate' " before allowing a law enforcement officer to "invade another's body in search of evidence of guilt is indisputable and great." Ibid. (quoting Johnson v. United States, 333 U. S. 10–14 (1948)).

As noted, the warrant requirement is subject to ex-ceptions. "One well-recognized exception," and the one at issue in this case, "applies when the exigencies of the situation make the needs of law enforcement so compelling that a warrantless search is objectively reasonable under the Fourth Amendment." Kentucky v. King, 563 U. S. ____, ____ (2011) (slip op., at 6) (internal quotation marks and brackets omitted). A variety of circumstances may give rise to an exigency sufficient to justify a warrantless search, including law enforcement's need to provide emergency assistance to an occupant of a home, Michigan v. Fisher, 558 U. S. 45–48 (2009) (per curiam), engage in "hot pursuit" of a fleeing suspect, United States v. San-tana, 427 U. S. 38–43 (1976), or enter a burning building to put out a fire and investigate its cause, Michigan v. Tyler, 436 U. S. 499–510 (1978). As is relevant here, we have also recognized that in some circumstances law enforcement officers may conduct a search without a warrant to prevent the imminent destruction of evidence. See Cupp v. Murphy, 412 U. S. 291, 296 (1973); Ker v. California, 374 U. S. 23–41 (1963) (plurality opinion). While these contexts do not necessarily involve equiva-lent dangers, in each a warrantless search is potentially reasonable because "there is compelling need for official action and no time to secure a warrant." Tyler, 436 U. S., at 509.

To determine whether a law enforcement officer faced an emergency that justified acting without a warrant, this Court looks to the totality of circumstances. See Brigham City v. Stuart, 547 U. S. 398, 406 (2006) (finding officers' entry into a home to provide emergency assistance "plainly reasonable under the circumstances"); Illinois v. Mc-Arthur, 531 U. S. 326, 331 (2001) (concluding that a warrantless seizure of a person to prevent him from returning to his trailer to destroy hidden contraband was reasonable "[i]n the circumstances of the case before us" due to exigency); Cupp, 412 U. S., at 296 (holding that a limited warrantless search of a suspect's fingernails to preserve evidence that the suspect was trying to rub off was justified "[o]n the facts of this case"); see also Richards v. Wisconsin, 520 U. S. 385–396 (1997) (rejecting a per se exception to the knock-and-announce requirement for felony drug investigations based on presumed exigency, and requiring instead evaluation of police conduct "ina particular case"). We apply this "finely tuned approach" to Fourth Amendment reasonableness in this context be-cause the police action at issue lacks "the traditional justification that . . . a warrant . . . provides." Atwater v. Lago Vista, 532 U. S. 318, 347, n. 16 (2001). Absent that established justification, "the fact-specific nature of the reasonableness inquiry," Ohio v. Robinette, 519 U. S. 33, 39 (1996), demands that we evaluate each case of alleged exigency based "on its own facts and circumstances." Go-Bart Importing Co. v. United States, 282 U. S. 344(1931). 3

Our decision in Schmerber applied this totality of the circumstances approach. In that case, the petitioner had suffered injuries in an automobile accident and was taken to the hospital. 384 U. S., at 758. While he was there receiving treatment, a police officer arrested the petitioner for driving while under the influence of alcohol and ordered a blood test over his objection. Id., at 758–759. After explaining that the warrant requirement applied generally to searches that intrude into the human body, we concluded that the warrantless blood test "in the present case" was nonetheless permissible because the officer "might reasonably have believed that he was confronted with an emergency, in which the delay necessary to obtain a warrant, under the circumstances, threatened 'the destruction of evidence.' " Id., at 770 (quoting Preston v. United States, 376 U. S. 364, 367 (1964)).

In support of that conclusion, we observed that evidence could have been lost because "the percentage of alcohol in the blood begins to diminish shortly after drinking stops, as the body functions to eliminate it from the system." 384 U. S., at 770. We added that "[p]articularly in a case such as this, where time had to be taken to bring the accused to a hospital and to investigate the scene of the accident, there was no time to seek out a magistrate and secure a warrant." Id., at 770–771. "Given these special facts," we found that it was appropriate for the police to act without a warrant. Id., at 771. We further held that the blood test at issue was a reasonable way to recover the evidence because it was highly effective, "involve[d] vir-tually no risk, trauma, or pain," and was conducted in a reasonable fashion "by a physician in a hospital environment according to accepted medical practices." Ibid. And in conclusion, we noted that our judgment that there had been no Fourth Amendment violation was strictly based "on the facts of the present record." Id., at 772.

Thus, our analysis in Schmerber fits comfortably within our case law applying the exigent circumstances exception. In finding the warrantless blood test reasonable in Schmerber, we considered all of the facts and circumstances of the particular case and carefully based our holding on those specific facts.

B

The State properly recognizes that the reasonablenessof a warrantless search under the exigency exception to the warrant requirement must be evaluated based on the totality of the circumstances. Brief for Petitioner 28–29. But the State nevertheless seeks a per se rule for blood testing in drunk-driving cases. The State contends that whenever an officer has probable cause to believe an individual has been driving under the influence of alcohol, exigent circumstances will necessarily exist because BAC evidence is inherently evanescent. As a result, the State claims that so long as the officer has probable cause and the blood test is conducted in a reasonable manner, it is categorically reasonable for law enforcement to obtain the blood sample without a warrant.

It is true that as a result of the human body's natural metabolic processes, the alcohol level in a person's blood begins to dissipate once the alcohol is fully absorbed and continues to decline until the alcohol is eliminated. See Skinner, 489 U. S., at 623; Schmerber, 384 U. S., at 770–771. Testimony before the trial court in this case indicated that the percentage of alcohol in an individual's blood typically decreases by approximately 0.015 percent to 0.02 percent per hour once the alcohol has been fully absorbed. App. 47. More precise calculations of the rate at which alcohol dissipates depend on various individual characteristics (such as weight, gender, and alcohol tolerance) and the circumstances in which the alcohol was consumed. See Stripp, Forensic and Clinical Issues in Alcohol Analysis, in Forensic Chemistry Handbook 437–441 (L. Kobilinsky ed. 2012). Regardless of the exact elimination rate, it is sufficient for our purposes to note that because an individual's alcohol level gradually declines soon after he stops drinking, a significant delay in testing will negatively affect the probative value of the results. This fact was essential to our holding in Schmerber, as we recognized that, under the circumstances, further delay in order to secure a warrant after the time spent investigating the scene of the accident and transporting the injured suspect to the hospital to receive treatment would have threatened the destruction of evidence. 384 U. S., at 770–771.

But it does not follow that we should depart from careful case-by-case assessment of exigency and adopt the categorical rule proposed by the State and its amici. In those drunk-driving investigations where police officers can reasonably obtain a warrant before a blood sample can be drawn without significantly undermining the efficacy of the search, the Fourth Amendment mandates that they do so. See McDonald v. United States, 335 U. S. 451, 456 (1948) ("We cannot . . . excuse the absence of a search warrant without a showing by those who seek exemption from the constitutional mandate that the exigencies of the situation made [the search] imperative"). We do not doubt that some circumstances will make obtaining a warrant impractical such that the dissipation of alcohol from the bloodstream will support an exigency justifying a properly conducted warrantless blood test. That, however, is a reason to decide each case on its facts, as we did in Schmerber, not to accept the "considerable overgeneralization" that a per se rule would reflect. Richards, 520 U. S., at 393.

The context of blood testing is different in critical respects from other destruction-of-evidence cases in which the police are truly confronted with a " 'now or never' " situation. Roaden v. Kentucky, 413 U. S. 496, 505 (1973). In contrast to, for example, circumstances in which the suspect has control over easily disposable evidence, see Georgia v. Randolph, 547 U. S. 103, n. 6 (2006); Cupp, 412 U. S., at 296, BAC evidence from a drunk-driving suspect naturally dissipates over time in a gradual and relatively predictable manner. Moreover, because a police officer must typically transport a drunk-driving suspect to a medical facility and obtain the assistance of someone with appropriate medical training before conducting a blood test, some delay between the time of the arrest or accident and the time of the test is inevitable regardless of whether police officers are required to obtain a warrant. See State v. Shriner, 751 N. W. 2d 538, 554 (Minn. 2008) (Meyer, J., dissenting). This reality undermines the force of the State's contention, endorsed by the dissent, see post, at 3 (opinion of Thomas, J.), that we should recognize a categorical exception to the warrant requirement because BAC evidence "is actively being destroyed with every minute that passes." Brief for Petitioner 27. Consider, for example, a situation in which the warrant process will not significantly increase the delay before the blood test is conducted because an officer can take steps to secure a warrant while the suspect is being transported to a medical facility by another officer. In such a circumstance, there would be no plausible justification for an exception to the warrant requirement.

The State's proposed per se rule also fails to account for advances in the 47 years since Schmerber was decided that allow for the more expeditious processing of warrant applications, particularly in contexts like drunk-driving investigations where the evidence offered to establish probable cause is simple. The Federal Rules of Criminal Procedure were amended in 1977 to permit federal magistrate judges to issue a warrant based on sworn testimony communicated by telephone. See 91Stat. 319. As amended, the law now allows a federal magistrate judge to con-sider "information communicated by telephone or other reliable electronic means." Fed. Rule Crim. Proc. 4.1. States have also innovated. Well over a majority of States allow police officers or prosecutors to apply for search warrants remotely through various means, including telephonic or radio communication, electronic communication such as e-mail, and video conferencing. 4 And in addition to technology-based developments, jurisdictions have found other ways to streamline the warrant process, such as by using standard-form warrant applications for drunk-driving investigations. 5

We by no means claim that telecommunications innovations have, will, or should eliminate all delay from the warrant-application process. Warrants inevitably take some time for police officers or prosecutors to complete and for magistrate judges to review. Telephonic

and electronic warrants may still require officers to follow time-consuming formalities designed to create an adequate record, such as preparing a duplicate warrant before calling the magistrate judge. See Fed. Rule Crim. Proc. 4.1(b)(3). And improvements in communications technology do not guarantee that a magistrate judge will be available when an officer needs a warrant after making a late-night arrest. But technological developments that enable police officers to secure warrants more quickly, and do so without undermining the neutral magistrate judge's essential role as a check on police discretion, are relevant to an assessment of exigency. That is particularly so in this context, where BAC evidence is lost gradually and relatively predictably. 6

Of course, there are important countervailing concerns. While experts can work backwards from the BAC at the time the sample was taken to determine the BAC at the time of the alleged offense, longer intervals may raise questions about the accuracy of the calculation. For that reason, exigent circumstances justifying a warrantless blood sample may arise in the regular course of law enforcement due to delays from the warrant application process. But adopting the State's per se approach would improperly ignore the current and future technological developments in warrant procedures, and might well diminish the incentive for jurisdictions "to pursue progressive approaches to warrant acquisition that preserve the protections afforded by the warrant while meeting the legitimate interests of law enforcement." State v. Rodriguez, 2007 UT 15, ¶46, 156 P. 3d 771, 779.

In short, while the natural dissipation of alcohol in the blood may support a finding of exigency in a specific case, as it did in Schmerber, it does not do so categorically. Whether a warrantless blood test of a drunk-driving suspect is reasonable must be determined case by case based on the totality of the circumstances.

C

In an opinion concurring in part and dissenting in part, The Chief Justice agrees that the State's proposed per se rule is overbroad because "[f]or exigent circumstances to justify a warrantless search . . . there must . . . be 'no time to secure a warrant.'" Post, at 6 (quoting Tyler, 436 U. S., at 509). But The Chief Justice then goes on to suggest his own categorical rule under which a warrantless blood draw is permissible if the officer could not secure a warrant (or reasonably believed he could not secure a warrant) in the time it takes to transport the suspect to a hospital or similar facility and obtain medical assistance. Post, at 8–9. Although we agree that delay inherent to the blood-testing process is relevant to evaluating exigency, see supra, at 10, we decline to substitute The Chief Justice's modified per se rule for our traditional totality of the circumstances analysis.

For one thing, making exigency completely dependent on the window of time between an arrest and a blood test produces odd consequences. Under The Chief Justice's rule, if a police officer serendipitously stops a suspect near an emergency room, the officer may conduct a noncon-sensual warrantless blood draw even if all agree that a warrant could be obtained with very little delay under the circumstances (perhaps with far less delay than an average ride to the hospital in the jurisdiction). The rule would also distort law enforcement incentives. As with the State's per se rule, The Chief Justice's rule might discourage efforts to expedite the warrant process because it categorically authorizes warrantless blood draws so long as it takes more time to secure a warrant than to obtain medical assistance. On the flip side, making the requirement of independent judicial oversight turn exclusively on the amount of time that elapses between an arrest and BAC testing could induce police departments and individual officers to minimize testing delay to the detriment of other values. The Chief Justice correctly observes that "[t]his case involves medical personnel drawing blood at a medical facility, not police officers doing so by the side of the road." Post, at 6–7, n. 2. But The Chief Justice does not say that roadside blood draws are necessarily unreasonable, and if we accepted The Chief Justice's approach, they would become a more attractive option for the police.

III

The remaining arguments advanced in support of a per se exigency rule are unpersuasive.

The State and several of its amici, including the United States, express concern that a case-by-case approach to exigency will not provide adequate guidance to law enforcement officers deciding whether to conduct a blood test of a drunk-driving suspect without a warrant. The Chief Justice and the dissent also raise this concern. See post, at 1, 9–10 (opinion of Roberts, C. J.); post, at 5–7 (opinion of Thomas, J.). While the desire for a bright-line rule is understandable, the Fourth Amendment will not tolerate adoption of an overly broad categorical approach that would dilute the warrant requirement in a context where significant privacy interests are at stake. Moreover, a case-by-case approach is hardly unique within our Fourth Amendment jurisprudence. Numerous police actions are judged based on fact-intensive, totality of the circumstances analyses rather than according to categorical rules, including in situations that are more likely to require police officers to make difficult split-second judgments. See, e.g., Illinois v. Wardlow, 528 U. S. 119–125 (2000) (whether an officer has reasonable suspicion to make an investigative stop and to pat down a suspect for weapons under Terry v. Ohio, 392 U. S. 1 (1968)); Robinette, 519 U. S., at 39–40 (whether valid consent has been given to search); Tennessee v. Garner, 471 U. S. 1–9, 20 (1985) (whether force used to effectuate a seizure, including deadly force, is reasonable). As in those contexts, we see no valid substitute for careful case-by-case evaluation of reasonableness here. 7

Next, the State and the United States contend that the privacy interest implicated by blood draws of drunk-driving suspects is relatively minimal. That is so, they claim, both because motorists have a diminished expectation of privacy and because our cases have repeatedly indicated that blood testing is commonplace in society and typically involves "virtually no risk, trauma, or pain." Schmerber, 384 U. S., at 771. See also post, at 3, and n. 1 (opinion of Thomas, J.).

But the fact that people are "accorded less privacy in . . . automobiles because of th[e] compelling governmental need for regulation," California v. Carney, 471 U. S. 386, 392 (1985), does not diminish a motorist's privacy interest in preventing an agent of the government from piercing his skin. As to the nature of a blood test conducted in a medical setting by trained personnel, it is concededly less intrusive than other bodily invasions we have found unreasonable. See Winston, 470 U. S., at 759–766 (surgery to remove a bullet); Rochin v. California, 342 U. S. 165–174 (1952) (induced vomiting to extract narcotics capsules ingested by a suspect violated the Due Process Clause). For that reason, we have held that medically drawn blood tests are reasonable in appropriate circumstances. See Skinner, 489 U. S., at 618–633 (upholding warrantless blood testing of railroad employees involved in certain train accidents under the "special needs" doctrine); Schmerber, 384 U. S., at 770–772. We have never retreated, however, from our recognition that any compelled intrusion into the human body implicates significant, constitutionally protected privacy interests.

Finally, the State and its amici point to the compelling governmental interest in combating drunk driving and contend that prompt BAC testing, including through blood testing, is vital to pursuit of that interest. They argue that is particularly so because, in addition to laws that make it illegal to operate a motor vehicle under the influence of alcohol, all 50 States and the District of Columbia have enacted laws that make it per se unlawful to operate a motor vehicle with a BAC of over 0.08 percent. See National Highway Traffic Safety Admin. (NHTSA), Al-cohol and Highway Safety: A Review of the State of Knowledge 167 (No. 811374, Mar. 2011) (NHTSA Review). 8 To enforce these provisions, they reasonably assert, accurate BAC evidence is critical. See also post, at4–5 (opinion of Roberts, C. J.); post, at 4–5 (opinion of Thomas, J.).

"No one can seriously dispute the magnitude of the drunken driving problem or the States' interest in eradicating it." Michigan Dept. of State Police v. Sitz, 496 U. S. 444, 451 (1990). Certainly we do not. While some progress has been made, drunk driving continues to exact a terrible toll on our society. See NHTSA, Traffic Safety Facts, 2011 Data 1 (No. 811700, Dec. 2012) (reporting that 9,878 people were killed in alcohol-impaired driving crashes in 2011, an average of one fatality every 53 minutes).

But the general importance of the government's interest in this area does not justify departing from the warrant requirement without showing exigent circumstances that make securing a warrant impractical in a particular case. To the extent that the State and its amici contend that applying the traditional Fourth Amendment totality-of-the-circumstances analysis to determine whether an exigency justified a warrantless search will undermine the governmental interest in preventing and prosecuting drunk-driving offenses, we are not convinced.

As an initial matter, States have a broad range of legal tools to enforce their drunk-driving laws and to secure BAC evidence without undertaking warrantless nonconsensual blood draws. For example, all 50 States have adopted implied consent laws that require motorists, as a condition of operating a motor vehicle within the

State, to consent to BAC testing if they are arrested or otherwise detained on suspicion of a drunk-driving offense. See NHTSA Review 173; supra, at 2 (describing Missouri's implied consent law). Such laws impose significant consequences when a motorist withdraws consent; typically the motorist's driver's license is immediately suspended or revoked, and most States allow the motorist's refusal to take a BAC test to be used as evidence against him in a subsequent criminal prosecution. See NHTSA Review 173–175; see also South Dakota v. Neville, 459 U. S. 553–564 (1983) (holding that the use of such an adverse inference does not violate the Fifth Amendment right against self-incrimination).

It is also notable that a majority of States either place significant restrictions on when police officers may obtain a blood sample despite a suspect's refusal (often limiting testing to cases involving an accident resulting in death or serious bodily injury) or prohibit nonconsensual blood tests altogether. 9 Among these States, several lift restrictions on nonconsensual blood testing if law enforcement officers first obtain a search warrant or similar court order. 10 Cf. Bullcoming v. New Mexico, 564 U. S. ___, ___ (2011) (slip op., at 3) (noting that the blood test was obtained pursuant to a warrant after the petitioner refused a breath test). We are aware of no evidence indicating that restrictions on nonconsensual blood testing have compromised drunk-driving enforcement efforts in the States that have them. And in fact, field studies in States that permit nonconsensual blood testing pursuant to a warrant have suggested that, although warrants do impose administrative burdens, their use can reduce breath-test-refusal rates and improve law enforcement's ability to recover BAC evidence. See NHTSA, Use of Warrants for Breath Test Refusal: Case Studies 36–38 (No. 810852, Oct. 2007).

To be sure, "States [may] choos[e] to protect privacy beyond the level that the Fourth Amendment requires." Virginia v. Moore, 553 U. S. 164, 171 (2008). But wide-spread state restrictions on nonconsensual blood testing provide further support for our recognition that compelled blood draws implicate a significant privacy interest. They also strongly suggest that our ruling today will not "severely hamper effective law enforcement." Garner, 471 U. S., at 19.

IV

The State argued before this Court that the fact that alcohol is naturally metabolized by the human body creates an exigent circumstance in every case. The State did not argue that there were exigent circumstances in this particular case because a warrant could not have been obtained within a reasonable amount of time. In his testimony before the trial court, the arresting officer did not identify any other factors that would suggest he faced an emergency or unusual delay in securing a warrant. App. 40. He testified that he made no effort to obtain a search warrant before conducting the blood draw even though he was "sure" a prosecuting attorney was on call and even though he had no reason to believe that a magistrate judge would have been unavailable. Id., at 39, 41–42. The officer also acknowledged that he had obtained search warrants before taking blood samples in the past without difficulty. Id., at 42. He explained that he elected to forgo a warrant application in this case only because he believed it was not legally necessary to obtain a warrant. Id., at 39–40. Based on this testimony, the trial court concluded that there was no exigency and specifically found that, although the arrest took place in the middle of the night, "a prosecutor was readily available to apply for a search warrant and a judge was readily available to issue a warrant." App. to Pet. for Cert. 43a. 11

The Missouri Supreme Court in turn affirmed that judgment, holding first that the dissipation of alcohol did not establish a per se exigency, and second that the State could not otherwise satisfy its burden of establishing exigent circumstances. 358 S. W. 3d, at 70, 74–75. In petitioning for certiorari to this Court, the State challenged only the first holding; it did not separately contend that the warrantless blood test was reasonable regardless of whether the natural dissipation of alcohol in a suspect's blood categorically justifies dispensing with the warrant requirement. See Pet. for Cert. i.

Here and in its own courts the State based its case on an insistence that a driver who declines to submit to testing after being arrested for driving under the influence of alcohol is always subject to a nonconsensual blood test without any precondition for a warrant. That is incorrect.

Although the Missouri Supreme Court referred to this case as "unquestionably a routine DWI case," 358 S. W. 3d, at 74, the fact that a particular drunk-driving stop is "routine" in the sense that it does not involve " 'special facts,' " ibid., such as the need for the police to attend to a car accident, does not mean a warrant is required. Other factors present in an ordinary traffic stop, such as the procedures in place for obtaining a warrant or the availability of a magistrate judge, may affect whether the police can obtain a warrant in an expeditious way and therefore may establish an exigency that permits a warrantless search. The relevant factors in determining whether a warrantless search is reasonable, including the practical problems of obtaining a warrant within a timeframe that still preserves the opportunity to obtain reliable evidence, will no doubt vary depending upon the circumstances in the case.

Because this case was argued on the broad proposition that drunk-driving cases present a per se exigency, the arguments and the record do not provide the Court with an adequate analytic framework for a detailed discussion of all the relevant factors that can be taken into account in determining the reasonableness of acting without a warrant. It suffices to say that the metabolization

of alcohol in the bloodstream and the ensuing loss of evidence are among the factors that must be considered in deciding whether a warrant is required. No doubt, given the large number of arrests for this offense in different jurisdictions nationwide, cases will arise when anticipated delays in obtaining a warrant will justify a blood test without judicial authorization, for in every case the law must be concerned that evidence is being destroyed. But that inquiry ought not to be pursued here where the question is not properly before this Court. Having rejected the sole argument presented to us challenging the Missouri Supreme Court's decision, we affirm its judgment.

* * *

We hold that in drunk-driving investigations, the natural dissipation of alcohol in the bloodstream does not constitute an exigency in every case sufficient to justify conducting a blood test without a warrant.

The judgment of the Missouri Supreme Court is affirmed.

It is so ordered.

Maryland v. King (June 3, 2013)

Justice Kennedy delivered the opinion of the Court.

In 2003 a man concealing his face and armed with a gun broke into a woman's home in Salisbury, Maryland. He raped her. The police were unable to identify or apprehend the assailant based on any detailed description or other evidence they then had, but they did obtain from the victim a sample of the perpetrator's DNA.

In 2009 Alonzo King was arrested in Wicomico County, Maryland, and charged with first- and second-degree assault for menacing a group of people with a shotgun. As part of a routine booking procedure for serious offenses, his DNA sample was taken by applying a cotton swab or filter paper—known as a buccal swab—to the inside of his cheeks. The DNA was found to match the DNA taken from the Salisbury rape victim. King was tried and convicted for the rape. Additional DNA samples were taken from him and used in the rape trial, but there seems to be no doubt that it was the DNA from the cheek sample taken at the time he was booked in 2009 that led to his first having been linked to the rape and charged with its commission.

The Court of Appeals of Maryland, on review of King's rape conviction, ruled that the DNA taken when King was booked for the 2009 charge was an unlawful seizure because obtaining and using the cheek swab was an unreasonable search of the person. It set the rape conviction aside. This Court granted certiorari and now reverses the judgment of the Maryland court.

I

When King was arrested on April 10, 2009, for menac-ing a group of people with a shotgun and charged in state court with both first- and second-degree assault, he was processed for detention in custody at the Wicomico County Central Booking facility. Booking personnel used a cheek swab to take the DNA sample from him pursuant to provisions of the Maryland DNA Collection Act (or Act).

On July 13, 2009, King's DNA record was uploaded to the Maryland DNA database, and three weeks later, on August 4, 2009, his DNA profile was matched to the DNA sample collected in the unsolved 2003 rape case. Once the DNA was matched to King, detectives presented the forensic evidence to a grand jury, which indicted him for the rape. Detectives obtained a search warrant and took a second sample of DNA from King, which again matched the evidence from the rape. He moved to suppress the DNA match on the grounds that Maryland's DNA collection law violated the Fourth Amendment. The Circuit Court Judge upheld the statute as constitutional. King pleaded not guilty to the rape charges but was convicted and sentenced to life in prison without the possibility of parole.

In a divided opinion, the Maryland Court of Appeals struck down the portions of the Act authorizing collection of DNA from felony arrestees as unconstitutional. The majority concluded that a DNA swab was an unreasonable search in violation of the Fourth Amendment because King's "expectation of privacy is greater than the State's purported interest in using King's DNA to identify him." 425 Md. 550, 561, 42 A. 3d 549, 556 (2012). In reach-ing that conclusion the Maryland Court relied on the deci-sions of various other courts that have concluded that DNA identification of arrestees is impermissible. See, e.g., People v. Buza, 129 Cal. Rptr. 3d 753 (App. 2011) (offi-cially depublished); Mario W. v. Kaipio, 228 Ariz. 207, 265 P. 3d 389 (App. 2011).

Both federal and state courts have reached differing conclusions as to whether the Fourth Amendment prohibits the collection and analysis of a DNA sample from persons arrested, but not yet convicted, on felony charges. This Court granted certiorari, 568 U. S. ___ (2012), to address the question. King is the respondent here.

II

The advent of DNA technology is one of the most significant scientific advancements of our era. The full potential for use of genetic markers in medicine and science is still being explored, but the utility of DNA identification in the criminal justice system is already undisputed. Since the first use of forensic DNA analysis to catch a rapist and murderer in England in 1986, see J. Butler, Fundamentals of Forensic DNA Typing 5 (2009) (hereinafter Butler), law enforcement, the defense bar, and the courts have acknowledged DNA testing's "unparalleled ability both to exonerate the wrongly convicted and to identify the guilty. It has the potential to significantly improve both the criminal justice system and police investigative practices." District Attorney's Office for Third

Judicial Dist. v. Osborne, 557 U. S. 52, 55 (2009).

A

The current standard for forensic DNA testing relies on an analysis of the chromosomes located within the nucleus of all human cells. "The DNA material in chromosomes is composed of 'coding' and 'noncoding' regions. The coding regions are known as genes and contain the information necessary for a cell to make proteins. . . . Non-protein-coding regions . . . are not related directly to making proteins, [and] have been referred to as 'junk' DNA." Butler 25. The adjective "junk" may mislead the layperson, forin fact this is the DNA region used with near certainty to identify a person. The term apparently is intended to indicate that this particular noncoding region, while useful and even dispositive for purposes like identity, does not show more far-reaching and complex characteristics like genetic traits.

Many of the patterns found in DNA are shared among all people, so forensic analysis focuses on "repeated DNA sequences scattered throughout the human genome," known as "short tandem repeats" (STRs). Id., at 147–148. The alternative possibilities for the size and frequency of these STRs at any given point along a strand of DNA are known as "alleles," id., at 25; and multiple alleles are analyzed in order to ensure that a DNA profile matches only one individual. Future refinements may improve pres-ent technology, but even now STR analysis makes it "possible to determine whether a biological tissue matches a suspect with near certainty." Osborne, supra, at 62.

The Act authorizes Maryland law enforcement author-ities to collect DNA samples from "an individual who is charged with . . . a crime of violence or an attempt to commit a crime of violence; or . . . burglary or an attempt to commit burglary." Md. Pub. Saf. Code Ann. §2–504(a)(3)(i) (Lexis 2011). Maryland law defines a crime of violence to include murder, rape, first-degree assault, kidnaping, arson, sexual assault, and a variety of other serious crimes. Md. Crim. Law Code Ann. §14–101 (Lexis 2012). Once taken, a DNA sample may not be processed or placed in a database before the individual is arraigned (unless the individual consents). Md. Pub. Saf. Code Ann. §2–504(d)(1) (Lexis 2011). It is at this point that a judicial officer ensures that there is probable cause to detain the arrestee on a qualifying serious offense. If "all qualifying criminal charges are determined to be unsupported by probable cause . . . the DNA sample shall be immediately destroyed." §2–504(d)(2)(i). DNA samples are also destroyed if "a criminal action begun against the individual . . . does not result in a conviction," "the conviction is finally reversed or vacated and no new trial is permitted," or "the individual is granted an unconditional pardon." §2–511(a)(1).

The Act also limits the information added to a DNA database and how it may be used. Specifically, "[o]nly DNA records that directly relate to the identification of individuals shall be collected and stored." §2–505(b)(1). No purpose other than identification is permissible: "A person may not willfully test a DNA sample for information that does not relate to the identification of indi-viduals as specified in this subtitle." §2–512(c). Tests for familial matches are also prohibited. See §2–506(d) ("A person may not perform a search of the statewide DNA data base for the purpose of identification of an offenderin connection with a crime for which the offender may bea biological relative of the individual from whom the DNA sample was acquired"). The officers involved in taking and analyzing respondent's DNA sample complied with the Act in all respects.

Respondent's DNA was collected in this case using a common procedure known as a "buccal swab." "Buccal cell collection involves wiping a small piece of filter paper or a cotton swab similar to a Q-tip against the inside cheek of an individual's mouth to collect some skin cells."

Butler 86. The procedure is quick and painless. The swab touches inside an arrestee's mouth, but it requires no "surgical intrusio[n] beneath the skin," Winston v. Lee, 470 U. S. 753, 760 (1985) , and it poses no "threa[t] to the health or safety" of arrestees, id., at 763.

B

Respondent's identification as the rapist resulted in part through the operation of a national project to standardize collection and storage of DNA profiles. Authorized by Congress and supervised by the Federal Bureau of Investigation, the Combined DNA Index System (CODIS) connects DNA laboratories at the local, state, and national level. Since its authorization in 1994, the CODIS system has grown to include all 50 States and a number of federal agencies. CODIS collects DNA profiles provided by local laboratories taken from arrestees, convicted offenders, and forensic evidence found at crime scenes. To participatein CODIS, a local laboratory must sign a memorandum of understanding agreeing to adhere to quality standards and submit to audits to evaluate compliance with the federal standards for scientifically rigorous DNA testing. Butler 270.

One of the most significant aspects of CODIS is the standardization of the points of comparison in DNA analysis. The CODIS database is based on 13 loci at whichthe STR alleles are noted and compared. These loci make possible extreme accuracy in matching individual samples, with a "random match probability of approximately 1 in 100 trillion (assuming unrelated individuals)." Ibid. The CODIS loci are from the non-protein coding junk regions of DNA, and "are not known to have any associationwith a genetic disease or any other genetic predisposition. Thus, the information in the database is only useful for human identity testing." Id., at 279. STR informationis recorded only as a "string of numbers"; and the DNA identification is accompanied only by information denoting the

laboratory and the analyst responsible for the submission. Id., at 270. In short, CODIS sets uniform national standards for DNA matching and then facilitates connections between local law enforcement agencies who can share more specific information about matched STRprofiles.

All 50 States require the collection of DNA from felony convicts, and respondent does not dispute the validity of that practice. See Brief for Respondent 48. Twenty-eight States and the Federal Government have adopted laws similar to the Maryland Act authorizing the collection of DNA from some or all arrestees. See Brief for State of California et al. as Amici Curiae 4, n. 1 (States Brief) (collecting state statutes). Although those statutes varyin their particulars, such as what charges require a DNA sample, their similarity means that this case implicates more than the specific Maryland law. At issue is a standard, expanding technology already in widespread use throughout the Nation.

III

A

Although the DNA swab procedure used here presents a question the Court has not yet addressed, the framework for deciding the issue is well established. The Fourth Amendment, binding on the States by the Fourteenth Amendment, provides that "[t]he right of the people tobe secure in their persons, houses, papers, and effects, against unreasonable searches and seizures, shall not be violated." It can be agreed that using a buccal swab on the inner tissues of a person's cheek in order to obtain DNA samples is a search. Virtually any "intrusio[n] into the human body," Schmerber v. California, 384 U. S. 757, 770 (1966) , will work an invasion of " 'cherished personal security' that is subject to constitutional scrutiny," Cupp v. Murphy, 412 U. S. 291, 295 (1973) (quoting Terry v. Ohio, 392 U. S. 1–25 (1968)). The Court has applied the Fourth Amendment to police efforts to draw blood, see Schmerber, supra;

Missouri v. McNeely, 569 U. S. ___ (2013), scraping an arrestee's fingernails to obtain trace evidence, see Cupp, supra, and even to "a breathalyzer test, which generally requires the production of alveolaror 'deep lung' breath for chemical analysis," Skinner v. Railway Labor Executives' Assn., 489 U. S. 602, 616 (1989) .

A buccal swab is a far more gentle process than a venipuncture to draw blood. It involves but a light touch on the inside of the cheek; and although it can be deemeda search within the body of the arrestee, it requires no "surgical intrusions beneath the skin." Winston, 470 U. S., at 760. The fact than an intrusion is negligible is of central relevance to determining reasonableness, although it is still a search as the law defines that term.

B

To say that the Fourth Amendment applies here is the beginning point, not the end of the analysis. "[T]he Fourth Amendment's proper function is to constrain, not against all intrusions as such, but against intrusions which are not justified in the circumstances, or which are made in an improper manner." Schmerber, supra, at 768. "As the text of the Fourth Amendment indicates, the ultimate measure of the constitutionality of a governmental search is 'reasonableness.' " Vernonia School Dist. 47J v. Acton, 515 U. S. 646, 652 (1995) . In giving content to the inquiry whether an intrusion is reasonable, the Court has preferred "some quantum of individualized suspicion . . . [as] a prerequisite to a constitutional search or seizure. But the Fourth Amendment imposes no irreducible requirement of such suspicion." United States v. Martinez-Fuerte, 428 U. S. 543–561 (1976) (citation and footnoteomitted).

In some circumstances, such as "[w]hen faced with special law enforcement needs, diminished expectations of privacy, minimal intrusions, or the like, the Court has found that certain general, or individual, circumstances may render a warrantless search or seizure reasonable." Illinois v. McArthur, 531 U. S. 326, 330 (2001) . Those circumstances diminish the need for a warrant, either because "the public interest is such that neither a warrant nor probable cause is required," Maryland v. Buie, 494 U. S. 325, 331 (1990) , or because an individual is already on notice, for instance because of his employment, see Skinner, supra, or the conditions of his release from government custody, see Samson v. California, 547 U. S. 843 (2006) , that some reasonable police intrusion on his pri-vacy is to be expected. The need for a warrant is perhaps least when the search involves no discretion that could properly be limited by the "interpo[lation of] a neutral magistrate between the citizen and the law enforcement officer." Treasury Employees v. Von Raab, 489 U. S. 656, 667 (1989) .

The instant case can be addressed with this background. The Maryland DNA Collection Act provides that, in order to obtain a DNA sample, all arrestees charged with serious crimes must furnish the sample on a buccal swab applied, as noted, to the inside of the cheeks. The arrestee is already in valid police custody for a serious offense supported by probable cause. The DNA collection is not subject to the judgment of officers whose perspective might be "colored by their primary involvement in 'the often competitive enterprise of ferreting out crime.' " Terry, supra, at 12 (quoting Johnson v. United States, 333 U. S. 10, 14 (1948)). As noted by this Court in a differentbut still instructive context involving blood testing, "[b]oth the circumstances justifying toxicological testing and the permissible limits of such intrusions are defined nar-rowly and specifically in the regulations that authorize them . . . . Indeed, in light of the standardized nature of the tests and the minimal discretion vested in those charged with administering the program, there are virtually no facts for a neutral magistrate to evaluate." Skinner, supra, at 622. Here, the search effected by the buccal swab of respondent falls within the category of cases this Court has analyzed by reference to the proposition that the "touchstone of the Fourth Amendment is reasonableness, not individualized suspicion." Samson, supra, at 855, n. 4.

Even if a warrant is not required, a search is not beyond Fourth Amendment scrutiny; for it must be reasonable in its scope and manner of execution. Urgent government interests are not a license for indiscriminate police behavior. To say that no warrant is required is merely to acknowledge that "rather than employing a per se rule of unreasonableness, we balance the privacy-related and law enforcement-related concerns to determine if the intrusion was reasonable." McArthur, supra, at 331. This application of "traditional standards of reasonableness" requires a court to weigh "the promotion of legitimate governmen-tal interests" against "the degree to which [the search] intrudes upon an individual's privacy." Wyoming v. Houghton, 526 U. S. 295, 300 (1999) . An assessment of reasonableness to determine the lawfulness of requiring this class of arrestees to provide a DNA sample is central to the instant case.

IV

A

The legitimate government interest served by the Maryland DNA Collection Act is one that is well established: the need for law enforcement officers in a safe and accurate way to process and identify the persons and possessions they must take into custody. It is beyond dispute that "probable cause provides legal justification for arresting a person suspected of crime, and for a brief period of detention to take the administrative steps incident to arrest." Gerstein v. Pugh, 420 U. S. 103–114 (1975). Also uncontested is the "right on the part of the Government, always recognized under English and American law, to search the person of the accused when legally arrested." Weeks v. United States, 232 U. S. 383, 392 (1914) ,

overruled on other grounds, Mapp v. Ohio, 367 U. S. 643 (1961) . "The validity of the search of a person incident to a lawful arrest has been regarded as settled from its first enunciation, and has remained virtually unchallenged." United States v. Robinson, 414 U. S. 218, 224 (1973) . Even in that context, the Court has been clear that individual suspicion is not necessary, because "[t]he constitutionality of a search incident to an arrest does not depend on whether there is any indication that the person ar-rested possesses weapons or evidence. The fact of a lawful arrest, standing alone, authorizes a search." Michigan v. DeFillippo, 443 U. S. 31, 35 (1979) .

The "routine administrative procedure[s] at a police sta-tion house incident to booking and jailing the suspect" derive from different origins and have different constitutional justifications than, say, the search of a place, Illinois v. Lafayette, 462 U. S. 640, 643 (1983) ; for the search of a place not incident to an arrest depends on the "fair probability that contraband or evidence of a crime will be found in a particular place," Illinois v. Gates, 462 U. S. 213, 238 (1983) . The interests are further different when an individual is formally processed into police custody. Then "the law is in the act of subjecting the body of the accused to its physical dominion." People v. Chiagles, 237 N. Y. 193, 197, 142 N. E. 583, 584 (1923) (Cardozo, J.). When probable cause exists to remove an individual from the normal channels of society and hold him in legal custody, DNA identification plays a critical role in serving those interests.

First, "[i]n every criminal case, it is known and must be known who has been arrested and who is being tried." Hiibel v. Sixth Judicial Dist. Court of Nev., Humboldt Cty., 542 U. S. 177, 191 (2004) . An individual's identity is more than just his name or Social Security number, and the government's interest in identification goes beyond ensuring that the proper name is typed on the indictment. Identity has never been considered limited to the name on the arrestee's birth certificate. In fact, a name is of little value compared to the real interest in identification at stake when an individual is brought into custody. "It isa well recognized aspect of criminal conduct that the per-petrator will take unusual steps to conceal not only his conduct, but also his identity. Disguises used while committing a crime may be supplemented or replaced by changed names, and even changed physical features." Jones v. Murray, 962 F. 2d 302, 307 (CA4 1992). An "arrestee may be carrying a false ID or lie about his identity," and "criminal history records . . . can be inaccurate or incomplete." Florence v. Board of Chosen Freeholders of County of Burlington, 566 U. S. ____, ____ (2012) (slip op.,at 16).

A suspect's criminal history is a critical part of his identity that officers should know when processing him for detention. It is a common occurrence that "[p]eople detained for minor offenses can turn out to be the most devious and dangerous criminals. Hours after the Oklahoma City bombing, Timothy McVeigh was stopped by a state trooper who noticed he was driving without a license plate. Police stopped serial killer Joel Rifkin for the same reason. One of the terrorists involved in the September 11 attacks was stopped and ticketed for speeding just two days before hijacking Flight 93." Id., at ____ (slip op., at 14) (citations omitted). Police already seek this crucial identifying information. They use routine and accepted means as varied as comparing the suspect's booking photograph to sketch artists' depictions of persons of interest, showing his mugshot to potential witnesses, and of course making a computerized comparison of the arrestee's fingerprints against electronic databases of known criminals and unsolved crimes. In this respect the only difference between DNA analysis and the accepted use of fingerprint databases is the unparalleled accuracy DNA provides.

The task of identification necessarily entails searching public and police records based on the identifying information provided by the arrestee to see what is already known about him. The DNA collected from arrestees isan irrefutable identification of the person from whom it was taken. Like a fingerprint, the 13 CODIS loci are not themselves evidence of any particular crime, in the way that a drug test can by itself be evidence of illegal narcotics use. A DNA profile is useful to the police because it gives them a form of identification to search the records already in their valid possession. In this respect the use of DNA for identification is no different than matching an arrestee's face to a wanted poster of a previously unidentified suspect; or matching tattoos to known gang symbols to reveal a criminal affiliation; or matching the arrestee's fingerprints to those recovered from a crime scene. See Tr. of Oral Arg. 19. DNA is another metric of identification used to connect the arrestee with his or her public persona, as reflected in records of his or her actions that are available to the police. Those records may be linked to the arrestee by a variety of relevant forms of identification, including name, alias, date and time of previous convictions and the name then used, photograph, Social Security number, or CODIS profile. These data, found in official records, are checked as a routine matter to produce a more comprehensive record of the suspect's complete identity. Finding occurrences of the arrestee's CODIS profile in outstanding cases is consistent with this common practice. It uses a different form of identification than a name or fingerprint, but its function is the same.

Second, law enforcement officers bear a responsibility for ensuring that the custody of an arrestee does not create inordinate "risks for facility staff, for the existing detainee population, and for a new detainee." Florence, supra, at ____ (slip op., at 10). DNA identification can provide untainted information to those charged with de-taining suspects and detaining the property of any felon. For these purposes officers must know the type of person whom they are detaining, and DNA allows them to make critical choices about how to proceed.

"Knowledge of identity may inform an officer that a suspect is wanted for another offense, or has a record of violence or mental disorder. On the other hand, knowing identity may help clear a suspect and al-low the police to concentrate their efforts elsewhere. Identity may prove particularly important in [certain cases, such as] where the police are investigating what appears to be a domestic assault. Officers called to investigate domestic disputes need to know whom they are dealing with in order to assess the situation, the threat to their own safety, and possible danger to the potential victim." Hiibel, supra, at 186.

Recognizing that a name alone cannot address this interest in identity, the Court has approved, for example, "a visual inspection for certain tattoos and other signs of gang affiliation as part of the intake process," because "[t]he identification and isolation of gang members before they are admitted protects everyone." Florence, supra, at ____ (slip op., at 11).

Third, looking forward to future stages of criminal prosecution, "the Government has a substantial interest in ensuring that persons accused of crimes are available for trials." Bell v. Wolfish, 441 U. S. 520, 534 (1979) . A person who is arrested for one offense but knows that he has yet to answer for some past crime may be more inclined to flee the instant charges, lest continued contact with the criminal justice system expose one or more other serious offenses. For example, a defendant who had committed a prior sexual assault might be inclined to flee on a burglary charge, knowing that in every State a DNA sample would be taken from him after his conviction on the burglary charge that would tie him to the more serious charge of rape. In addition to subverting the administration of justice with respect to the crime of arrest, this ties backto the interest in safety; for a detainee who abscondsfrom custody presents a risk to law enforcement officers, other detainees, victims of previous crimes, witnesses, and society at large.

Fourth, an arrestee's past conduct is essential to an assessment of the danger he poses to the public, and this will inform a court's determination whether the individual should be released on bail. "The government's interest in preventing crime by arrestees is both legitimate and compelling." United States v. Salerno, 481 U. S. 739, 749 (1987) . DNA identification of a suspect in a violent crime provides critical information to the police and judicial officials in making a determination of the arrestee's future dangerousness. This inquiry always has entailed some scrutiny beyond the name on the defendant's driver's license. For example, Maryland law requires a judge to take into account not only "the nature and circumstances of the offense charged" but also "the defendant's family ties, employment status and history, financial resources, reputation, character and mental condition, length of res-idence in the community." 1 Md. Rules 4–216(f)(1)(A),(C) (2013). Knowing that the defendant is wanted for a previous violent crime based on DNA identification is especially probative of the court's consideration of "the danger of the defendant to the alleged victim, another person, or the community." Rule 4–216(f)(1)(G); seealso 18 U. S. C. §3142 (2006 ed. and Supp. V) (similar requirements).

This interest is not speculative. In considering laws to require collecting DNA from arrestees, government agencies around the Nation found evidence of numerouscases in which felony arrestees would have been identified as violent through DNA identification matching themto previous crimes but who later committed additional crimes because such identification was not used to detain them. See Denver's Study on

Preventable Crimes (2009) (three examples), online at http://www.denverda.org/DNA_Documents/Denver's Preventable Crimes Study.pdf (all Internet materials as visited May 31,2013, and available in Clerk of Court's case file); Chi-cago's Study on Preventable Crimes (2005) (five exam-ples), online at http://www.denverda.org/DNA_Documents/Arrestee_Database/Chicago Preventable Crimes-Final.pdf; Maryland Study on Preventable Crimes (2008) (three examples), online at http://www.denverda.org/DNA_Documents/MarylandDNAarresteestudy.pdf.

Present capabilities make it possible to complete a DNA identification that provides information essential to determining whether a detained suspect can be released pending trial. See, e.g., States Brief 18, n. 10 ("DNA identification database samples have been processed in as few as two days in California, although around 30 days has been average"). Regardless of when the initial bail decision is made, release is not appropriate until a further determination is made as to the person's identity in the sense not only of what his birth certificate states but also what other records and data disclose to give that identity more meaning in the whole context of who the person really is. And even when release is permitted, the background identity of the suspect is necessary for determining what conditions must be met before release is allowed. If release is authorized, it may take time for the conditions to be met, and so the time before actual release can be substantial. For example, in the federal system, defendants released conditionally are detained on average for 112 days; those released on unsecured bond for 37 days;on personal recognizance for 36 days; and on other financial conditions for 27 days. See Dept. of Justice, Bureau of Justice Statistics, Compendium of Federal Justice Statistics 45 (NCJ–213476, Dec. 2006) online at http://bjs.gov/content/pub/pdf/cfjs04.pdf. During this entire period, ad-ditional and supplemental data establishing more about the person's identity and background can provide critical information relevant to the conditions of release and whether to revisit an initial release determination. The facts of this case are illustrative. Though the record is not clear, if some thought were being given to releasing the respondent on bail on the gun charge, a release that would take weeks or months in any event, when the DNA report linked him to the prior rape, it would be relevant to the conditions of his release. The same would be true with a supplemental fingerprint report.

Even if an arrestee is released on bail, development of DNA identification revealing the defendant's unknown violent past can and should lead to the revocation of his conditional release. See 18 U. S. C. §3145(a) (providing for revocation of release); see also States Brief 11–12 (discussing examples where bail and diversion determinations were reversed after DNA identified the arrestee's vio-lent history). Pretrial release of a person charged with adangerous crime is a most serious responsibility. It is reason-able in all respects for the State to use an accepted database to determine if an arrestee is the object of suspicion in other serious crimes, suspicion that may provide a strong incentive for the arrestee to escape and flee.

Finally, in the interests of justice, the identification of an arrestee as the perpetrator of some heinous crime may have the salutary effect of freeing a person wrongfully imprisoned for the same offense. "[P]rompt [DNA] testing . . . would speed up apprehension of criminals before they commit additional crimes, and prevent the grotesque detention of . . . innocent people." J. Dwyer, P. Neufeld, & B. Scheck, Actual Innocence 245 (2000).

Because proper processing of arrestees is so important and has consequences for every stage of the criminal process, the Court has recognized that the "governmen-tal interests underlying a station-house search of the ar-restee's person and possessions may in some circumstancesbe even greater than those supporting a search imme-diately following arrest." Lafayette, 462 U. S., at 645. Thus, the Court has been reluctant to circumscribe the authority of the police to conduct reasonable booking searches. For example, "[t]he standards traditionally governing a search incident to lawful arrest are not . . . commuted to the stricter Terry standards." Robinson,414 U. S., at 234. Nor are these interests in identifica-tion served only by a search of the arrestee himself. "[I]nspection of an arrestee's personal property may assist the police in ascertaining or verifying his identity." Lafayette, supra, at 646. And though the Fifth Amendment's protection against self-incrimination is not, as a general rule, governed by a reasonableness standard, the Court has held that "questions . . . reasonably related to the police's administrative concerns . . . fall outside the protections of Miranda [v. Arizona, 384 U. S. 436 (1966)] and the answers thereto need not be suppressed." Pennsylvania v. Muniz, 496 U. S. 582–602 (1990).

B

DNA identification represents an important advancein the techniques used by law enforcement to serve le-gitimate police concerns for as long as there have been arrests, concerns the courts have acknowledged and approved for more than a century. Law enforcementagencies routinely have used scientific advancements in their standard procedures for the identification of arrestees. "Police had been using photography to capture the faces of criminals almost since its invention." S. Cole, Suspect Identities 20 (2001). Courts did not dispute that practice, concluding that a "sheriff in making an arrest for a felony on a warrant has the right to exercise a discretion . . . , [if] he should deem it necessary to the safe-keeping of a prisoner, and to prevent his escape, or to enable him the more readily to retake the prisoner if he should escape, to take his photograph." State ex rel. Bruns v. Clausmier, 154 Ind. 599, 601, 603, 57 N. E. 541, 542 (1900). By the time that it had become "the daily practice of the police officers and detectives of crime to use photographic pictures for the discovery and identification of criminals," the courts likewise had come to the conclusion that "it would be [a] matter of regret to have its use unduly restricted upon any fanciful theory or constitutional privilege." Shaffer v. United States, 24 App. D. C. 417, 426 (1904).

Beginning in 1887, some police adopted more exacting means to identify arrestees, using the system of precise physical measurements pioneered by the French anthropologist Alphonse Bertillon. Bertillon identification consisted of 10 measurements of the arrestee's body, along with a "scientific analysis of the features of the face and an exact anatomical localization of the various scars, marks, &c., of the body." Defense of the Bertillon System, N. Y. Times, Jan. 20, 1896, p. 3. "[W]hen a prisoner was brought in, his photograph was taken according to the Bertillon system, and his body measurements were then made. The measurements were made . . . and noted down on the back of a card or a blotter, and the photograph of the prisoner was expected to be placed on the card. This card, therefore, furnished both the likeness and description of the prisoner, and was placed in the rogues' gallery, and copies were sent to various cities where similar records were kept." People ex rel. Jones v. Diehl, 53 App. Div. 645, 646, 65 N. Y. S. 801, 802 (1900). As in the present case, the point of taking this information about each arrestee was not limited to verifying that the proper name was on the indictment. These procedures were used to "facilitate the recapture of escaped prisoners," to aid "the investigation of their past records and personal history," and "to preserve the means of identification for . . . fu-ture supervision after discharge." Hodgeman v. Olsen, 86 Wash. 615, 619, 150 P. 1122, 1124 (1915); see also McGovern v. Van Riper, 137 N. J. Eq. 24, 33–34, 43 A. 2d 514, 519 (Ch. 1945) ("[C]riminal identification is said to have two main purposes: (1) The identification of the accused as the person who committed the crime for which he is being held; and, (2) the identification of the accused as the same person who has been previously charged with, or convicted of, other offenses against the criminal law").

Perhaps the most direct historical analogue to the DNA technology used to identify respondent is the familiar practice of fingerprinting arrestees. From the advent of this technique, courts had no trouble determining that fingerprinting was a natural part of "the administrative steps incident to arrest." County of Riverside v. McLaughlin, 500 U. S. 44, 58 (1991) . In the seminal case of United States v. Kelly, 55 F. 2d 67 (CA2 1932), Judge Augustus Hand wrote that routine fingerprinting did not violate the Fourth Amendment precisely because it fit within the accepted means of processing an arrestee into custody:

"Finger printing seems to be no more than an exten-sion of methods of identification long used in dealing with persons under arrest for real or supposed vio-lations of the criminal laws. It is known to be a very certain means devised by modern science to reach the desired end, and has become especially important in a time when increased population and vast aggregations of people in urban centers have rendered the notoriety of the individual in the community no longer a ready means of identification.

.   .   .   .   .

"We find no ground in reason or authority for interfering with a method of identifying persons charged with crime which has now become widely known and frequently practiced." Id., at 69–70.

By the middle of the 20th century, it was considered "elementary that a person in lawful custody may be required to submit to photographing and fingerprinting as part of routine identification processes." Smith v. United States, 324 F. 2d 879, 882 (CADC 1963) (Burger, J.) (citations omitted).

DNA identification is an advanced technique superior to fingerprinting in many ways, so much so that to insist on fingerprints as the norm would make little sense to either the forensic expert or a layperson. The additional intrusion upon the arrestee's privacy beyond that associated with fingerprinting is not significant, see Part V, infra, and DNA is a markedly more accurate form of identifying arrestees. A suspect who has changed his facial features to evade photographic identification or even one who has undertaken the more arduous task of altering his fingerprints cannot escape the revealing power of his DNA.

The respondent's primary objection to this analogy is that DNA identification is not as fast as fingerprinting, and so it should not be considered to be the 21st-century equivalent. See Tr. of Oral Arg. 53. But rapid analysis of fingerprints is itself of recent vintage. The FBI's vaunted Integrated Automated Fingerprint Identification System (IAFIS) was only "launched on July 28, 1999. Prior to this time, the processing of . . . fingerprint submissions was largely a manual, labor-intensive process, taking weeks or months to process a single submission." Federal Bureau of Investigation, Integrated Automated Fingerprint Identification System, online at http://www.fbi.gov/about-us/cjis/fingerprints_biometrics/iafis/iafis. It was not the advent of this technology that rendered fingerprint analysis constitutional in a single moment. The question of how long it takes to process identifying information obtained from a valid search goes only to the efficacy of the search for its purpose of prompt identification, not the constitutionality of the search. Cf. Ontario v. Quon,

560 U. S. ___, ___ (2010) (slip op., at 15). Given the importance of DNA in the identification of police records pertaining to arrestees and the need to refine and confirm that identity for its important bearing on the decision to continue release on bail or to impose of new conditions, DNA serves an essential purpose despite the existence of delays such as the one that occurred in this case. Even so, the delay in processing DNA from arrestees is being reduced to a substantial degree by rapid technical advances. See, e.g., At-torney General DeWine Announces Significant Drop in DNA Turnaround Time (Jan. 4, 2013) (DNA processing time reduced from 125 days in 2010 to 20 days in 2012), online at http://ohioattorneygeneral.gov/Media/News-Releases/January-2013/Attorney-General-DeWine-Announces-Significant-Drop; Gov. Jindal Announces Elimination of DNABacklog, DNA Unit Now Operating in Real Time (Nov. 17, 2011) (average DNA report time reduced from a year or more in 2009 to 20 days in 2011), online at http://www.gov.state.la.us/index.cfm?md=newsroom&tmp=detail&articleID=3102. And the FBI has already begun testing devices that will enable police to process the DNA of arrestees within 90 minutes. See Brief for National District Attorneys Association as Amicus Curiae 20–21; Tr. of Oral Arg. 17. An assessment and understanding of the reasonableness of this minimally invasive search of a person detained for a serious crime should take account of these technical advances. Just as fingerprinting was constitutional for generations prior to the introduction of IAFIS, DNA identification of arrestees is a permissible tool of law enforcement today. New technology will only further improve its speed and therefore its effectiveness. And, as noted above, actual release of a serious offender as a routine matter takes weeks or months in any event. By identifying not only who the arrestee is but also what other available records disclose about his past to show who he is, the police can ensure that they have the proper person under arrest and that they have made the necessary arrangements for his custody; and, just as important, they can also prevent suspicion against or prosecution of the innocent.

In sum, there can be little reason to question "the legitimate interest of the government in knowing for an absolute certainty the identity of the person arrested, in knowing whether he is wanted elsewhere, and in ensuring his identification in the event he flees prosecution." 3 W. LaFave, Search and Seizure §5.3(c), p. 216 (5th ed. 2012). To that end, courts have confirmed that the Fourth Amendment allows police to take certain routine "administrative steps incident to arrest—i.e., . . . book[ing], photograph[ing], and fingerprint[ing]." McLaughlin, 500 U. S., at 58. DNA identification of arrestees, of the type approved by the Maryland statute here at issue, is "no more than an extension of methods of identification long used in dealing with persons under arrest." Kelly, 55 F. 2d, at 69. In the balance of reasonableness required by the Fourth Amendment, therefore, the Court must give great weight both to the significant government interest at stake in the identification of arrestees and to the unmatched potential of DNA identification to serve that interest.

V

A

By comparison to this substantial government interest and the unique effectiveness of DNA identification, the intrusion of a cheek swab to obtain a DNA sample is a minimal one. True, a significant government interest does not alone suffice to justify a search. The government interest must outweigh the degree to which the search in-vades an individual's legitimate expectations of privacy. In considering those expectations in this case, however, the necessary predicate of a valid arrest for a serious offense is fundamental. "Although the underlying command of the Fourth Amendment is always that searches and seizures be reasonable, what is reasonable depends on the context within which a search takes place." New Jersey v. T. L. O., 469 U. S. 325, 337 (1985) . "[T]he legitimacy of certain privacy expectations vis-à-vis the State may depend upon the individual's legal relationship with the State." Vernonia School Dist. 47J, 515 U. S., at 654.

The reasonableness of any search must be consideredin the context of the person's legitimate expectations of privacy. For example, when weighing the invasiveness of urinalysis of high school athletes, the Court noted that "[l]egitimate privacy expectations are even less with regard to student athletes. . . . Public school locker rooms, the usual sites for these activities, are not notable for the privacy they afford." Id., at 657. Likewise, the Courthas used a context-specific benchmark inapplicable to the public at large when "the expectations of privacy of covered employees are diminished by reason of their participa-tion in an industry that is regulated pervasively," Skinner, 489 U. S., at 627, or when "the 'operational realities ofthe workplace' may render entirely reasonable certain work-related intrusions by supervisors and co-workers that might be viewed as unreasonable in other contexts," Von Raab, 489 U. S., at 671.

The expectations of privacy of an individual taken into police custody "necessarily [are] of a diminished scope." Bell, 441 U. S., at 557. "[B]oth the person and the property in his immediate possession may be searched at thestation house." United States v. Edwards, 415 U. S. 800, 803 (1974). A search of the detainee's person when he is booked into custody may " 'involve a relatively extensive exploration,' " Robinson, 414 U. S., at 227, including "requir[ing] at least some detainees to lift their genitals or cough in a squatting position," Florence, 566 U. S., at _____ (slip op., at 13).

In this critical respect, the search here at issue differs from the sort of programmatic searches of either the public at large or a particular class of regulated but otherwise law-abiding citizens that the Court has previously labeled as " 'special needs' " searches. Chandler v. Miller, 520 U. S. 305, 314 (1997) . When the police stop a motorist ata checkpoint, see Indianapolis v. Edmond, 531 U. S. 32 (2000) , or test a political candidate for illegal narcotics, see Chandler, supra, they intrude upon substantial expectations of privacy. So the Court has insisted on some purpose other than "to detect evidence of ordinary criminal wrongdoing" to justify these searches in the absence of individualized suspicion. Edmond, supra, at 38. Once an individual has been arrested on probable cause for a dangerous offense that may require detention before trial, however, his or her expectations of privacy and freedom from police scrutiny are reduced. DNA identification like that at issue here thus does not require consideration of any unique needs that would be required to justify searching the average citizen. The special needs cases, thoughin full accord with the result reached here, do not have a direct bearing on the issues presented in this case, because unlike the search of a citizen who has not been suspected of a wrong, a detainee has a reduced expectation of privacy.

The reasonableness inquiry here considers two other circumstances in which the Court has held that particularized suspicion is not categorically required: "diminished expectations of privacy [and] minimal intrusions." McArthur, 531 U. S., at 330. This is not to suggest that any search is acceptable solely because a person is in custody. Some searches, such as invasive surgery, see Winston, 470 U. S. 753, or a search of the arrestee's home, see Chimel v. California, 395 U. S. 752 (1969) , involve either greater intrusions or higher expectations of privacy than are present in this case. In those situations, when the Court must "balance the privacy-related and law enforcement-related concerns to determine if the intrusion was rea-sonable," McArthur, supra, at 331, the privacy-related concerns are weighty enough that the search may require a warrant, notwithstanding the diminished expectations of privacy of the arrestee.

Here, by contrast to the approved standard procedures incident to any arrest detailed above, a buccal swab involves an even more brief and still minimal intrusion. A gentle rub along the inside of the cheek does not break the skin, and it "involves virtually no risk, trauma, or pain." Schmerber, 384 U. S., at 771. "A crucial factor in analyzing the magnitude of the intrusion . . . is the extent to which the procedure may threaten the safety or health of the individual," Winston, supra, at 761, and nothing suggests that a buccal swab poses any physical danger whatsoever. A brief intrusion of an arrestee's person is subject to the Fourth Amendment, but a swab of this nature does not increase the indignity already attendant to normal incidents of arrest.

B

In addition the processing of respondent's DNA sam-ple's 13 CODIS loci did not intrude on respondent's privacy in a way that would make his DNA identificationunconstitutional.

First, as already noted, the CODIS loci come from noncoding parts of the DNA that do not reveal the genetic traits of the arrestee. While science can always progress further, and those progressions may have Fourth Amendment consequences, alleles at the CODIS loci "are notat present revealing information beyond identification." Katsanis & Wagner, Characterization of the Standard and Recommended CODIS Markers, 58 J. Forensic Sci. S169, S171 (2013). The argument that the testing at issue in this case reveals any private medical information at all is open to dispute.

And even if non-coding alleles could provide some information, they are not in fact tested for that end. It is undisputed that law enforcement officers analyze DNA for the sole purpose of generating a unique identifying number against which future samples may be matched. This parallels a similar safeguard based on actual practice in the school drug-testing context, where the Court deemed it "significant that the tests at issue here look only for drugs, and not for whether the student is, for example, epileptic, pregnant, or diabetic." Vernonia School Dist. 47J, 515 U. S., at 658. If in the future police analyze samples to determine, for instance, an arrestee's predisposition for a particular disease or other hereditary factors not relevant to identity, that case would present additional privacy concerns not present here.

Finally, the Act provides statutory protections that guard against further invasion of privacy. As noted above, the Act requires that "[o]nly DNA records that directly relate to the identification of individuals shall be collected and stored." Md. Pub. Saf. Code Ann. §2–505(b)(1). No purpose other than identification is permissible: "A person may not willfully test a DNA sample for information that does not relate to the identification of individuals as specified in this subtitle." §2–512(c). This Court has noted often that "a 'statutory or regulatory duty to avoid unwarranted disclosures' generally allays . . . privacy concerns." NASA v. Nelson, 562 U. S. ____, ____ (2011) (slip op., at 20) (quoting Whalen v. Roe, 429 U. S. 589, 605 (1977)). The Court need not speculate about the risks posed "by a system that did not contain comparable security provisions." Id., at 606. In light of the scientific and statutory safeguards, once respondent's DNA was lawfully collected the STR analysis of respondent's DNA pursuant to CODIS procedures did not amount to a significant invasion of privacy that would render the DNA identification impermissible under the Fourth Amendment.

*   *   *

In light of the context of a valid arrest supported by probable cause respondent's expectations of privacy were not offended by the minor intrusion of a brief swab of his cheeks. By contrast, that same context of arrest gives rise to significant state interests in identifying respondent not only so that the proper name can be attached to his charges but also so that the criminal justice system can make informed decisions concerning pretrial custody. Upon these considerations the Court concludes that DNA identification of arrestees is a reasonable search that can be considered part of a routine booking procedure. When officers make an arrest supported by probable cause to hold for a serious offense and they bring the suspect to the station to be detained in custody, taking and analyzing a cheek swab of the arrestee's DNA is, like fingerprinting and photographing, a legitimate police booking procedure that is reasonable under the Fourth Amendment.

The judgment of the Court of Appeals of Maryland is reversed.

It is so ordered.

Kaley v. US (Feb 25, 2014) [Notes omitted]

Justice Kagan delivered the opinion of the Court.

A federal statute, 21 U. S. C. §853(e), authorizes a court to freeze an indicted defendant's assets prior to trial if they would be subject to forfeiture upon conviction. In United States v. Monsanto, 491 U. S. 600, 615 (1989), we approved the constitutionality of such an order so long as it is "based on a finding of probable cause to believe that the property will ultimately be proved forfeitable." And we held that standard to apply even when a defendant seeks to use the disputed property to pay for a lawyer.

In this case, two indicted defendants wishing to hire an attorney challenged a pre-trial restraint on their property. The trial court convened a hearing to consider the seizure's

legality under Monsanto. The question presented is whether criminal defendants are constitutionally entitled at such a hearing to contest a grand jury's prior determination of probable cause to believe they committed the crimes charged. We hold that they have no right to relitigate that finding.

I

A

Criminal forfeitures are imposed upon conviction to confiscate assets used in or gained from certain serious crimes. See 21 U. S. C. §853(a). Forfeitures help to ensure that crime does not pay: They at once punish wrongdoing, deter future illegality, and "lessen the economic power" of criminal enterprises. Caplin & Drysdale, Chartered v. United States, 491 U. S. 617, 630 (1989); see id., at 634 ("Forfeiture provisions are powerful weapons in the war on crime"). The Government also uses forfeited property to recompense victims of crime, improve conditions in crime-damaged communities, and support law enforcement activities like police training. See id., at 629–630. 1 Accordingly, "there is a strong governmental interest in obtaining full recovery of all forfeitable assets." Id., at 631.

In line with that interest, §853(e)(1) empowers courts to enter pre-trial restraining orders or injunctions to "preserve the availability of [forfeitable] property" while criminal proceedings are pending. Such an order, issued "[u]pon application of the United States," prevents a defendant from spending or transferring specified property, including to pay an attorney for legal services. Ibid. In Monsanto, our principal case involving this procedure, we held a pre-trial asset restraint constitutionally permissible whenever there is probable cause to believe that the property is forfeitable. See 491 U. S., at 615. That determination has two parts, reflecting the requirements for forfeit-ure under federal law: There must be probable cause to think (1) that the defendant has committed an offense permitting forfeiture, and (2) that the property at issue has the requisite connection to that crime. See §853(a). The Monsanto Court, however, declined to consider "whether the Due Process Clause requires a hearing" to establish either or both of those aspects of forfeitability. Id., at 615, n. 10. 2

Since Monsanto, the lower courts have generally pro-vided a hearing to any indicted defendant seeking to lift an asset restraint to pay for a lawyer. In that hearing, they have uniformly allowed the defendant to litigate the second issue stated above: whether probable cause exists to believe that the assets in dispute are traceable or otherwise sufficiently related to the crime charged in the indictment. 3 But the courts have divided over extending the hearing to the first issue. Some have considered, while others have barred, a defendant's attempt to challenge the probable cause underlying a criminal charge. 4 This case raises the question whether an indicted defendant has a constitutional right to contest the grand jury's prior determination of that matter.

B

The grand jury's indictment in this case charges a scheme to steal prescription medical devices and resell them for profit. The indictment accused petitioner Kerri Kaley, a sales representative for a subsidiary of Johnson & Johnson, and petitioner Brian Kaley, her husband, with transporting stolen medical devices across state lines and laundering the proceeds of that activity. 5 The Kaleys have contested those allegations throughout this litigation, arguing that the medical devices at issue were unwanted, excess hospital inventory, which they could lawfully take and market to others.

Immediately after obtaining the indictment, the Government sought a restraining order under §853(e)(1) to prevent the Kaleys from transferring any assets traceable to or involved in the alleged offenses. Included among those assets is a $500,000 certificate of deposit that the Kaleys intended to use for legal fees. The District Court entered the requested order. Later, in response to the Kaleys' motion to vacate the asset restraint, the court denied a request for an evidentiary hearing and confirmed the order, except as to $63,000 that it found (based on the parties' written submissions) was not connected to the alleged offenses.

On interlocutory appeal, the Eleventh Circuit reversed and remanded for further consideration of whether some kind of evidentiary hearing was warranted. See 579 F. 3d 1246 (2009). The District Court then concluded that it should hold a hearing, but only as to "whether the restrained assets are traceable to or involved in the alleged criminal conduct." App. to Pet. for Cert. 43, n. 5. The Kaleys informed the court that they no longer disputed that issue; they wished to show only that the "case against them is 'baseless.'" Id., at 39; see App. 107 ("We are not contesting that the assets restrained were . . . traceable to the conduct. Our quarrel is whether that conduct constitutes a crime"). Accordingly, the District Court affirmed the restraining order, and the Kaleys took another appeal. The Eleventh Circuit this time affirmed, holding that the Kaleys were not entitled at a hearing on the asset freeze "to challenge the factual foundation supporting the grand jury's probable cause determination[ ]"— that is, "the very validity of the underlying indictment." 677 F. 3d 1316, 1317 (2012).

We granted certiorari in light of the Circuit split on the question presented, 568 U. S. ____ (2013), and we now affirm the Eleventh Circuit.

II

This Court has twice considered claims, similar to the Kaleys', that the Fifth Amendment's right to due process and the Sixth Amendment's right to counsel constrain the way the federal forfeiture statute applies to assets needed to retain an attorney. See Caplin & Drysdale, 491 U. S. 617; Monsanto, 491 U. S. 600. We begin with those rulings not as mere background, but as something much more. On the single day the Court decided both those cases, it cast the die on this one too.

In Caplin & Drysdale, we considered whether the Fifth and Sixth Amendments exempt from forfeiture money that a convicted defendant has agreed to pay his attorney. See 491 U. S., at 623–635. We conceded a factual premise of the constitutional claim made in the case: Sometimes "a defendant will be unable to retain the attorney of his choice," if he cannot use forfeitable assets. Id., at 625. Still, we held, the defendant's claim was "untenable." Id., at 626. "A defendant has no Sixth Amendment right to spend another person's money" for legal fees—even if that is the only way to hire a preferred lawyer. Ibid. Consider, we submitted, the example of a "robbery suspect" who wishes to "use funds he has stolen from a bank to retain an attorney to defend him if he is apprehended." Ibid. That money is "not rightfully his." Ibid. Accordingly, we concluded, the Government does not violate the Constitution if, pursuant to the forfeiture statute, "it seizes the robbery proceeds and refuses to permit the defendant to use them" to pay for his lawyer. Ibid.

And then, we confirmed in Monsanto what our "robbery suspect" hypothetical indicated: Even prior to conviction (or trial)—when the presumption of innocence still applies—the Government could constitutionally use §853(e) to freeze assets of an indicted defendant "based on a finding of probable cause to believe that the property will ultimately be proved forfeitable." 491 U. S., at 615. In Monsanto, too, the defendant wanted to use the property at issue to pay a lawyer, and maintained that the Fifth and Sixth Amendments entitled him to do so. We dis-agreed. We first noted that the Government may sometimes "restrain persons where there is a finding of probable cause to believe that the accused has committed a serious offense." Id., at 615–616. Given that power, we could find "no

constitutional infirmity in §853(e)'s authorization of a similar restraint on [the defendant's] property" in order to protect "the community's interest" in recovering "ill-gotten gains." Id., at 616. Nor did the defendant's interest in retaining a lawyer with the disputed assets change the equation. Relying on Caplin & Drysdale, we reasoned: "[I]f the Government may, post-trial, forbid the use of forfeited assets to pay an attorney, then surely no constitutional violation occurs when, after probable cause is adequately established, the Government obtains an order barring a defendant from frustrating that end by dissipating his assets prior to trial." Ibid. So again: With probable cause, a freeze is valid.

The Kaleys little dispute that proposition; their argument is instead about who should have the last word as to probable cause. A grand jury has already found probable cause to think that the Kaleys committed the offenses charged; that is why an indictment issued. No one doubts that those crimes are serious enough to trigger forfeiture. Similarly, no one contests that the assets in question derive from, or were used in committing, the offenses. See supra, at 5. The only question is whether the Kaleys are constitutionally entitled to a judicial re-determination of the conclusion the grand jury already reached: that probable cause supports this criminal prosecution (or alternatively put, that the prosecution is not "baseless," as the Kaleys believe, supra, at 5). And that question, we think, has a ready answer, because a fundamental and historic commitment of our criminal justice system is to entrust those probable cause findings to grand juries.

This Court has often recognized the grand jury's singular role in finding the probable cause necessary to initiate a prosecution for a serious crime. See, e.g., Costello v. United States, 350 U. S. 359, 362 (1956) . "[A]n indictment 'fair upon its face,' and returned by a 'properly constituted grand jury,' " we have explained, "conclusively determines the existence of probable cause" to believe the defendant perpetrated the offense alleged. Gerstein v. Pugh, 420 U. S. 103, n. 19 (1975) (quoting Ex parte United States, 287 U. S. 241, 250 (1932)). And "conclusively" has meant, case in and case out, just that. We have found no "authority for looking into and revising the judgment of the grand jury upon the evidence, for the purpose of determining whether or not the finding was founded upon sufficient proof." Costello, 350 U. S., at 362–363 (quoting United States v. Reed, 27 F. Cas. 727, 738 (No. 16,134) (CC NDNY 1852) (Nelson, J.)). To the contrary, "the whole history of the grand jury institution" demonstrates that "a challenge to the reliability or competence of the evidence" supporting a grand jury's finding of probable cause "will not be heard." United States v. Williams, 504 U. S. 36, 54 (1992) (quoting Costello, 350 U. S., at 364, and Bank of Nova Scotia v. United States, 487 U. S. 250, 261 (1988)). The grand jury gets to say—without any review, oversight, or second-guessing—whether probable cause exists to think that a person committed a crime.

And that inviolable grand jury finding, we have decided, may do more than commence a criminal proceeding (with all the economic, reputational, and personal harm that entails); the determination may also serve the purpose of immediately depriving the accused of her freedom. If the person charged is not yet in custody, an indictment triggers "issuance of an arrest warrant without further inquiry" into the case's strength. Gerstein, 420 U. S., at 117, n. 19; see Kalina v. Fletcher, 522 U. S. 118, 129 (1997). Alternatively, if the person was arrested without a warrant, an indictment eliminates her Fourth Amendment right to a prompt judicial assessment of probable cause to support any detention. See Gerstein, 420 U. S., at 114, 117, n. 19. In either situation, this Court—relying on the grand jury's "historical role of protecting individuals from unjust persecution"—has "let [that body's] judgment substitute for that of a neutral and detached magistrate." Ibid. The grand jury, all on its own, may effect a pre-trial restraint on a person's liberty by finding probable cause to support a criminal charge. 6

The same result follows when, as here, an infringement on the defendant's property depends on a showing of probable cause that she committed a crime. If judicial review of the grand jury's probable cause determination is not warranted (as we have so often held) to put a defendant on trial or place her in custody, then neither is it needed to freeze her property. The grand jury that is good enough—reliable enough, protective enough—to inflict those other grave consequences through its probable cause findings must needs be adequate to impose this one too. Indeed, Monsanto already noted the absence of any reason to hold property seizures to different rules: As described earlier, the Court partly based its adoption of the probable cause standard on the incongruity of subjecting an asset freeze to any stricter requirements than apply to an arrest or ensuing detention. See supra, at 6; 491 U. S., at 615 ("[I]t would be odd to conclude that the Government may not restrain property" on the showing often sufficient to "restrain persons"). By similar token, the probable cause standard, once selected, should work no differently for the single purpose of freezing assets than for all others. 7 So the longstanding, unvarying rule of criminal procedure we have just described applies here as well: The grand jury's determination is conclusive.

And indeed, the alternative rule the Kaleys seek would have strange and destructive consequences. The Kaleys here demand a do-over, except with a different referee. They wish a judge to decide anew the exact question the grand jury has already answered—whether there is probable cause to think the Kaleys committed the crimes charged. But suppose the judge performed that task and came to the opposite conclusion. Two inconsistent findings would then govern different aspects of one criminal proceeding: Probable cause would exist to bring the Kaleys to trial (and, if otherwise appropriate, hold them in prison), but not to restrain their property. And assuming the prosecutor continued to press the charges, 8 the same judge who found probable cause lacking would preside over a trial premised on its presence. That legal dissonance, if sustainable at all, could not but undermine the criminal justice system's integrity—and especially the grand jury's integral, constitutionally prescribed role. For in this new world, every prosecution involving a pre-trial asset freeze would potentially pit the judge against the grand jury as to the case's foundational issue. 9

The Kaleys counter (as does the dissent, post, at 7) that apparently inconsistent findings are not really so, because the prosecutor could have presented scantier evidence to the judge than he previously offered the grand jury. Suppose, for example, that at the judicial hearing the prosecutor put on only "one witness instead of all five"; then, the Kaleys maintain, the judge's decision of no probable cause would mean only that "the Government did not satisfy its burden[ ] on that one day in time." Tr. of Oral Arg. 12, 18; see Reply Brief 11–12. But we do not think that hypothetical solves the problem. As an initial matter, it does not foreclose a different fact pattern: A judge could hear the exact same evidence as the grand jury, yet respond to it differently, thus rendering what even the Kaleys must concede is a contradictory finding. And when the Kaleys' hypothetical is true, just what does it show? Consider that the prosecutor in their example has left home some of the witnesses he took to the grand jury—presumably because, as we later discuss, he does not yet wish to reveal their identities or likely testimony. See infra, at 14–15. The judge's ruling of no probable cause therefore would not mean that the grand jury was wrong: As the Kaleys concede, the grand jury could have heard more than enough evidence to find probable cause that they committed the crimes charged. The Kaleys would win at the later hearing despite, not because of, the case's true merits. And we would then see still less reason for a judge to topple the grand jury's (better supported) finding of probable cause. 10

Our reasoning so far is straightforward. We held in Monsanto that the probable cause standard governs the pre-trial seizure of forfeitable assets, even when they are needed to hire a lawyer. And we have repeatedly affirmed a corollary of that standard: A defendant has no right to judicial review of a grand jury's determination of probable cause to think a defendant committed a crime. In combination, those settled propositions signal defeat for the Kaleys because, in contesting the seizure of their property, they seek only to relitigate such a grand jury finding.

III

The Kaleys would have us undertake a different analysis, which they contend would lead to a different conclusion. They urge us to apply the balancing test of Mathews v. Eldridge, 424 U. S. 319 (1976), to assess whether they have received a constitutionally sufficient opportunity to challenge the seizure of their assets. See Brief for Petitioners 32–64. Under that three-pronged test (reordered here for expositional purposes), a court must weigh (1) the burdens that a requested procedure would impose on the Government against (2) the private interest at stake, as viewed alongside (3) "the risk of an erroneous deprivation" of that interest without the procedure and "the probable value, if any, of [the] additional . . . procedural safeguard[ ]." Mathews, 424 U. S., at 335. Stressing the importance of their interest in retaining chosen counsel, the Kaleys argue that the Mathews balance tilts hardin their favor. It thus overrides— or so the Kaleys claim—all we have previously held about the finality of grand jury findings, entitling them to an evidentiary hearing be-fore a judge to contest the probable cause underlying the indictment.

The Government battles with the Kaleys over whether Mathews has any application to this case. This Court devised the test, the Government notes, in an administrative setting—to decide whether a Social Security recipient was entitled to a hearing before her benefits were terminated. And although the Court has since employed the approach in other contexts, the Government reads Medina v. California, 505 U. S. 437 (1992), as foreclosing its use here. In that case, we held that "the Mathews balancing test does not provide the appropriate framework for assessing the validity of state procedural rules which . . . are part of the criminal process," reasoning that because the "Bill of Rights speaks in explicit terms to many aspects of criminal procedure," the Due Process Clause "has limited operation" in the field. Id., at 443. That settles that, asserts the Government. See Brief for United States 18. But the Kaleys argue that Medina addressed a State's procedural rule and relied on federalism principles not implicated here. Further, they claim that Medina concerned a criminal proceeding proper, not a collateral action seizing property. See Reply Brief 1–5. As to that sort of action, the Kaleys contend, Mathews should govern.

We decline to address those arguments, or to define the respective reach of Mathews and Medina, because we need not do so. Even if Mathews applied here—even if, that is, its balancing inquiry were capable of trumping this Court's repeated admonitions that the grand jury's word is conclusive—the Kaleys still would not be entitled to the hearing they seek. That is because the Mathews test tips against them, and so only reinforces what we have already said. As we will explain, the problem for the Kaleys comes from Mathews' prescribed inquiry into the requested procedure's usefulness in correcting erroneous deprivations of their private interest. In light of Monsanto's holding that a seizure of the Kaleys' property is erroneous only if unsupported by probable cause, the added procedure demanded here is not sufficiently likely to make any difference.

To begin the Mathews analysis, the Government has a substantial interest in freezing potentially forfeitable assets without an evidentiary hearing about the probable cause underlying criminal charges. At the least, such an adversarial proceeding—think of it as a pre-trial mini-trial (or maybe a pre-trial not-so-mini-trial)—could consume significant prosecutorial time and resources. The hearing presumably would rehearse the case's merits, including the Government's theory and supporting evidence. And the Government also might have to litigate a range of ancillary questions relating to the conduct of the hearing itself (for example, could the Kaleys subpoena witnesses or exclude certain evidence?).

Still more seriously, requiring a proceeding of that kind could undermine the Government's ability either to obtain a conviction or to preserve forfeitable property. To ensure a favorable result at the hearing, the Government could choose to disclose all its witnesses and other evidence. But that would give the defendant knowledge of the Government's case and strategy well before the rules of criminal procedure—or principles of due process, see, e.g., Brady v. Maryland, 373 U. S. 83 (1963) —would otherwise require. See Fed. Rules Crim. Proc. 26.2(a), 16(a)(2); Weatherford v. Bursey, 429 U. S. 545–561 (1977) ("There is no general constitutional right to discovery in a criminal case"). And sometimes (particularly in organized crime and drug trafficking prosecutions, in which forfeiture questions often arise), that sneak preview might not just aid the defendant's preparations but also facilitate witness tampering or jeopardize witness safety. Alternatively, to ensure the success of its prosecution, the Government could hold back some of its evidence at the hearing or give up on the pre-trial seizure entirely. But if the Government took that tack, it would diminish the likelihood of ultimately recovering stolen assets to which the public is entitled. 11 So any defense counsel worth his salt—whatever the merits of his case—would put the prosecutor to a choice: "Protect your forfeiture by providing discovery" or "protect your conviction by surrendering the assets." 12 It is small wonder that the Government wants to avoid that lose-lose dilemma.

For their part, however, defendants like the Kaleys have a vital interest at stake: the constitutional right to retain counsel of their own choosing. See Wheat v. United States, 486 U. S. 153, 159 (1988) (describing the scope of, and various limits on, that right). This Court has recently described that right, separate and apart from the guarantee to effective representation, as "the root meaning" of the Sixth Amendment. United States v. Gonzalez-Lopez, 548 U. S. 140–148 (2006); cf. Powell v. Alabama, 287 U. S. 45, 53 (1932) ("It is hardly necessary to say that, the right to counsel being conceded, a defendant should be afforded a fair opportunity to secure counsel of his own choice"). 13 Indeed, we have held that the wrongful deprivation of choice of counsel is "structural error," immune from review for harmlessness, because it "pervades the entire trial." Gonzalez-Lopez, 548 U. S., at 150. Different lawyers do all kinds of things differently, sometimes "affect[ing] whether and on what terms the defendant . . . plea bargains, or decides instead to go to trial"—and if the latter, possibly affecting whether she gets convicted or what sentence she receives. Ibid. So for defendants like the Kaleys, having the ability to retain the "counsel [they] believe[ ] to be best"—and who might in fact be superior to any existing alternatives—matters profoundly. Id., at 146.

And yet Monsanto held, crucially for the last part of our Mathews analysis, that an asset freeze depriving a defend-ant of that interest is erroneous only when unsupported by a finding of probable cause. Recall that Monsanto considered a case just like this one, where the defendant wanted to use his property to pay his preferred lawyer. He urged the Court to hold that the Government could seize assets needed for that purpose only after conviction. But we instead decided that the Government could act "after probable cause [that the assets are forfeitable] is adequately established." 491 U. S., at 616. And that means in a case like this one—where the assets' connection to the allegedly illegal conduct is not in dispute, see supra, at 5—that a pre-trial seizure is wrongful only when there is no probable cause to believe the defendants committed the crimes charged. Or to put the same point differently, such a freeze is erroneous—notwithstanding the weighty burden it imposes on the defendants' ability to hire a chosen lawyer—only when the grand jury should never have issued the indictment.

The Mathews test's remaining prong—critical when the governmental and private interests both have weight—thus boils down to the "probable value, if any," of a judicial hearing in uncovering mistaken grand jury findings of probable cause. 424 U. S., at 335. The Kaleys (and the dissent) contend that such proceedings will serve an important remedial function because grand juries hear only a "one-sided presentation[ ]" of evidence. Brief for Petitioners 57; see post, at 16. And that argument rests on a generally sound premise: that the adversarial process leads to better, more accurate decision-making. But in this context—when the legal standard is merely probable cause and the grand jury has already made that finding—both our precedents and other courts' experience indicate that a full-dress hearing will provide little benefit.

This Court has repeatedly declined to require the use of adversarial procedures to make probable cause determinations. Probable cause, we have often told litigants, is not a high bar: It requires only the "kind of 'fair probability' on which 'reasonable and prudent [people,] not legal technicians, act.' " Florida v. Harris, 568 U. S. ___, ___ (2013) (slip op., at 5) (quoting Illinois v. Gates, 462 U. S. 213, 231, 238 (1983)); see Gerstein, 420 U. S., at 121 (contrasting probable cause to reasonable-doubt and preponderance standards). That is why a grand jury's finding of probable cause to think that a person committed a crime "can be [made] reliably without an adversary hearing," id., at 120; it is and "has always been thought sufficient to hear only the prosecutor's side," United States v. Williams, 504 U. S. 36, 51 (1992) . So, for example, we have held the "confrontation and cross-examination" of witnesses unnecessary in a grand jury proceeding. Gerstein, 420 U. S., at 121–122. Similarly, we have declined to require the presentation of exculpatory evidence, see Williams, 504 U. S., at 51, and we have allowed the introduction of hearsay alone, see Costello, 350 U. S., at 362–364. On each occasion, we relied on the same reasoning, stemming from our recognition that probable cause served only a gateway function: Given the relatively undemanding "nature of the determination," the value of requiring any additional "formalities and safeguards" would "[i]n most cases . . . be too slight." Gerstein, 420 U. S., at 121–122.

We can come out no differently here. The probable cause determinations the Kaleys contest are simply those underlying the charges in the indictment. No doubt the Kaleys could seek to poke holes in the evidence the Government offered the grand jury to support those allegations. No doubt, too, the Kaleys could present evidence of their own, which might cast the Government's in a different light. (Presumably, the Kaleys would try in those two ways to show that they did not steal, but instead lawfully obtained the medical devices they later resold. See supra, at 4.) Our criminal justice system of course relies on such contestation at trial when the question becomes whether a defendant is guilty beyond peradventure. But as we have held before, an adversarial process is far less useful to the threshold finding of probable cause, which determines only whether adequate grounds exist to proceed to trial and reach that question. The probable cause decision, by its nature, is hard to undermine, and still harder to reverse. So the likelihood that a judge holding an evidentiary hearing will repudiate the grand jury's decision strikes us, once more, as "too slight" to support a constitutional requirement. Gerstein, 420 U. S., at 122.

The evidence from other courts corroborates that view, over and over and over again. In the past two decades, the courts in several Circuits have routinely held the kind of hearing the Kaleys seek. See supra, at 3, and n. 4. Yet neither the Kaleys nor their amici (mostly lawyers' associations) have found a single case in which a judge found an absence of probable cause to believe that an indicted defendant committed the crime charged. One amicus cites 25 reported cases involving pre-trial hearings on asset freezes. See Brief for New York Council of Defense Lawyers 4, n. 2. In 24 of those, the defendant lost outright. The last involved a not-yet-indicted defendant (so no grand jury finding); there, the District Court's ruling for him was reversed on appeal. See Tr. of Oral Arg. 15, 36. To be sure, a kind of selection bias might affect those statistics: Perhaps a prosecutor with a very weak case would choose to abandon an asset freeze rather than face a difficult hearing. See id., at 16, 37. But the Kaleys and their amici have also failed to offer any anecdotes of that kind; and we suspect that the far more common reason a prosecutor relinquishes a freeze is just to avoid premature discovery. See supra, at 14–15. So experience, as far as anyone has discerned it, cuts against the Kaleys: It confirms that even under Mathews, they have no right to revisit the grand jury's finding. 14

IV

When we decided Monsanto, we effectively resolved this case too. If the question in a pre-trial forfeiture case is whether there is probable cause to think the defendant committed the crime alleged, then the answer is: whatever the grand jury decides. And even if we test that proposition by applying Mathews, we arrive at the same place: In considering such findings of probable cause, we have never thought the value of enhanced evidentiary procedures worth their costs. Congress of course may strike its own balance and give defendants like the Kaleys the kind of hearing they want. Indeed, Congress could disapprove of Monsanto itself and hold pre-trial seizures of property to a higher standard than probable cause. But the Due Process Clause, even when combined with a defendant's Sixth Amendment interests, does not command those results. Accordingly, the Kaleys cannot challenge the grand jury's conclusion that probable cause supports the charges against them. The grand jury gets the final word.

We therefore affirm the judgment of the Eleventh Circuit and remand the case for further proceedings consistent with this opinion.

It is so ordered.

Navarette v. California (April 22, 2014) [Notes omitted]

Justice THOMAS delivered the opinion of the Court.

After a 911 caller reported that a vehicle had run her off the road, a police officer located the vehicle she identified during the call and executed a traffic stop. We hold that the stop complied with the Fourth Amendment because, under the totality of the circumstances, the officer had reasonable suspicion that the driver was intoxicated.

I

On August 23, 2008, a Mendocino County 911 dispatch team for the California Highway Patrol (CHP) received a call from another CHP dispatcher in neighboring Humboldt County. The Humboldt County dispatcher relayed a tip from a 911 caller, which the Mendocino County team recorded as follows: "`Showing southbound Highway 1 at mile marker 88, Silver Ford 150 pickup. Plate of 8-David-94925.

Ran the reporting party off the roadway and was last seen approximately five [minutes] ago.'" App. 36a. The Mendocino County team then broadcast that information to CHP officers at 3:47 p.m.

A CHP officer heading northbound toward the reported vehicle responded to the broadcast. At 4:00 p.m., the officer passed the truck near mile marker 69. At about 4:05 p.m., after making a U-turn, he pulled the truck over. A second officer, who had separately responded to the broadcast, also arrived on the scene. As the two officers approached the truck, they smelled marijuana. A search of the truck bed revealed 30 pounds of marijuana. The officers arrested the driver, petitioner Lorenzo Prado Navarette, and the passenger, petitioner José Prado Navarette.

Petitioners moved to suppress the evidence, arguing that the traffic stop violated the Fourth Amendment because the officer lacked reasonable suspicion of criminal activity. Both the magistrate who presided over the suppression hearing and the Superior Court disagreed.[1] Petitioners pleaded guilty to transporting marijuana and were sentenced to 90 days in jail plus three years of probation.

The California Court of Appeal affirmed, concluding that the officer had reasonable suspicion to conduct an investigative stop. 2012 WL 4842651 (Oct. 12, 2012). The court reasoned that the content of the tip indicated that it came from an eyewitness victim of reckless driving, and that the officer's corroboration of the truck's description, location, and direction established that the tip was reliable enough to justify a traffic stop. Id., at *7. Finally, the court concluded that the caller reported driving that was sufficiently dangerous to merit an investigative stop without waiting for the officer to observe additional reckless driving himself. Id., at *9. The California Supreme Court denied review. We granted certiorari, 570 U.S. ___, 134 S.Ct. 50, 186 L.Ed.2d 963 (2013), and now affirm.

II

The Fourth Amendment permits brief investigative stops — such as the traffic stop in this case — when a law enforcement officer has "a particularized and objective basis for suspecting the particular person stopped of criminal activity." United States v. Cortez, 449 U.S. 411, 417-418, 101 S.Ct. 690, 66 L.Ed.2d 621 (1981); see also Terry v. Ohio, 392 U.S. 1, 21-22, 88 S.Ct. 1868, 20 L.Ed.2d 889 (1968). The "reasonable suspicion" necessary to justify such a stop "is dependent upon both the content of information possessed by police and its degree of reliability." Alabama v. White, 496 U.S. 325, 330, 110 S.Ct. 2412, 110 L.Ed.2d 301 (1990). The standard takes into account "the totality of the circumstances — the whole picture." Cortez, supra, at 417, 101 S.Ct. 690. Although a mere "`hunch'" does not create reasonable suspicion, Terry, supra, at 27, 88 S.Ct. 1868, the level of suspicion the standard requires is "considerably less than proof of wrongdoing by a preponderance of the evidence," and "obviously less" than is necessary for probable cause, United States v. Sokolow, 490 U.S. 1, 7, 109 S.Ct. 1581, 104 L.Ed.2d 1 (1989).

A

These principles apply with full force to investigative stops based on information from anonymous tips. We have firmly rejected the argument "that reasonable cause for a[n investigative stop] can only be based on the officer's personal observation, rather than on information supplied by another person." Adams v. Williams, 407 U.S. 143, 147, 92 S.Ct. 1921, 32

L.Ed.2d 612 (1972). Of course, "an anonymous tip alone seldom demonstrates the informant's basis of knowledge or veracity." White, 496 U.S., at 329, 110 S.Ct. 2412 (emphasis added). That is because "ordinary citizens generally do not provide extensive recitations of the basis of their everyday observations," and an anonymous tipster's veracity is "`by hypothesis largely unknown, and unknowable.'" Ibid. But under appropriate circumstances, an anonymous tip can demonstrate "sufficient indicia of reliability to provide reasonable suspicion to make [an] investigatory stop." Id., at 327, 110 S.Ct. 2412.

Our decisions in Alabama v. White, 496 U.S. 325, 110 S.Ct. 2412, 110 L.Ed.2d 301 (1990), and Florida v. J. L., 529 U.S. 266, 120 S.Ct. 1375, 146 L.Ed.2d 254 (2000), are useful guides. In White, an anonymous tipster told the police that a woman would drive from a particular apartment building to a particular motel in a brown Plymouth station wagon with a broken right tail light. The tipster further asserted that the woman would be transporting cocaine. 496 U.S., at 327, 110 S.Ct. 2412. After confirming the innocent details, officers stopped the station wagon as it neared the motel and found cocaine in the vehicle. Id., at 331, 110 S.Ct. 2412. We held that the officers' corroboration of certain details made the anonymous tip sufficiently reliable to create reasonable suspicion of criminal activity. By accurately predicting future behavior, the tipster demonstrated "a special familiarity with respondent's affairs," which in turn implied that the tipster had "access to reliable information about that individual's illegal activities." Id., at 332, 110 S.Ct. 2412. We also recognized that an informant who is proved to tell the truth about some things is more likely to tell the truth about other things, "including the claim that the object of the tip is engaged in criminal activity." Id., at 331, 110 S.Ct. 2412 (citing Illinois v. Gates, 462 U.S. 213, 244, 103 S.Ct. 2317, 76 L.Ed.2d 527 (1983)).

In J. L., by contrast, we determined that no reasonable suspicion arose from a bare-bones tip that a young black male in a plaid shirt standing at a bus stop was carrying a gun. 529 U.S., at 268, 120 S.Ct. 1375. The tipster did not explain how he knew about the gun, nor did he suggest that he had any special familiarity with the young man's affairs. Id., at 271, 120 S.Ct. 1375. As a result, police had no basis for believing "that the tipster ha[d] knowledge of concealed criminal activity." Id., at 272, 120 S.Ct. 1375. Furthermore, the tip included no predictions of future behavior that could be corroborated to assess the tipster's credibility. Id., at 271, 120 S.Ct. 1375. We accordingly concluded that the tip was insufficiently reliable to justify a stop and frisk.

B

The initial question in this case is whether the 911 call was sufficiently reliable to credit the allegation that petitioners' truck "ran the [caller] off the roadway." Even assuming for present purposes that the 911 call was anonymous, see n. 1, supra, we conclude that the call bore adequate indicia of reliability for the officer to credit the caller's account. The officer was therefore justified in proceeding from the premise that the truck had, in fact, caused the caller's car to be dangerously diverted from the highway.

By reporting that she had been run off the road by a specific vehicle — a silver Ford F-150 pickup, license plate 8D94925 — the caller necessarily claimed eyewitness knowledge of the alleged dangerous driving. That basis of knowledge lends significant support to the tip's reliability. See Gates, supra, at 234, 103 S.Ct. 2317 ("[An informant's] explicit and detailed description of alleged wrongdoing, along with a statement that the event was observed firsthand, entitles his tip to greater weight than might otherwise be the case"); Spinelli v. United States, 393 U.S. 410, 416, 89 S.Ct. 584, 21 L.Ed.2d 637 (1969) (a tip of illegal gambling is less reliable when "it is not alleged that

the informant personally observed [the defendant] at work or that he had ever placed a bet with him"). This is in contrast to J. L., where the tip provided no basis for concluding that the tipster had actually seen the gun. 529 U.S., at 271, 120 S.Ct. 1375. Even in White, where we upheld the stop, there was scant evidence that the tipster had actually observed cocaine in the station wagon. We called White a "`close case'" because "[k]nowledge about a person's future movements indicates some familiarity with that person's affairs, but having such knowledge does not necessarily imply that the informant knows, in particular, whether that person is carrying hidden contraband." 529 U.S., at 271, 120 S.Ct. 1375. A driver's claim that another vehicle ran her off the road, however, necessarily implies that the informant knows the other car was driven dangerously.

There is also reason to think that the 911 caller in this case was telling the truth. Police confirmed the truck's location near mile marker 69 (roughly 19 highway miles south of the location reported in the 911 call) at 4:00 p.m. (roughly 18 minutes after the 911 call). That timeline of events suggests that the caller reported the incident soon after she was run off the road. That sort of contemporaneous report has long been treated as especially reliable. In evidence law, we generally credit the proposition that statements about an event and made soon after perceiving that event are especially trustworthy because "substantial contemporaneity of event and statement negate the likelihood of deliberate or conscious misrepresentation." Advisory Committee's Notes on Fed. Rule Evid. 803(1), 28 U.S.C.App., p. 371 (describing the rationale for the hearsay exception for "present `sense impression[s]"). A similar rationale applies to a "statement relating to a startling event" — such as getting run off the road — "made while the declarant was under the stress of excitement that it caused." Fed. Rule Evid. 803(2) (hearsay exception for "excited utterances"). Unsurprisingly, 911 calls that would otherwise be inadmissible hearsay have often been admitted on those grounds. See D. Binder, Hearsay Handbook § 8.1, pp. 257-259 (4th ed. 2013-2014) (citing cases admitting 911 calls as present sense impressions); id., § 9.1, at 274-275 (911 calls admitted as excited utterances). There was no indication that the tip in J. L. (or even in White) was contemporaneous with the observation of criminal activity or made under the stress of excitement caused by a startling event, but those considerations weigh in favor of the caller's veracity here.

Another indicator of veracity is the caller's use of the 911 emergency system. See Brief for Respondent 40-41, 44; Brief for United States as Amicus Curiae 16-18. A 911 call has some features that allow for identifying and tracing callers, and thus provide some safeguards against making false reports with immunity. See J. L., supra, at 276, 120 S.Ct. 1375 (KENNEDY, J., concurring). As this case illustrates, see n. 1, supra, 911 calls can be recorded, which provides victims with an opportunity to identify the false tipster's voice and subject him to prosecution, see, e.g., Cal.Penal Code Ann. § 653x (West 2010) (makes "telephon[ing] the 911 emergency line with the intent to annoy or harass" punishable by imprisonment and fine); see also § 148.3 (2014 West Cum. Supp.) (prohibits falsely reporting "that an `emergency' exists"); § 148.5 (prohibits falsely reporting "that a felony or misdemeanor has been committed"). The 911 system also permits law enforcement to verify important information about the caller. In 1998, the Federal Communications Commission (FCC) began to require cellular carriers to relay the caller's phone number to 911 dispatchers. 47 CFR § 20.18(d)(1) (2013) (FCC's "Phase I enhanced 911 services" requirements). Beginning in 2001, carriers have been required to identify the caller's geographic location with increasing specificity. §§ 20.18(e)-(h) ("Phase II enhanced 911 service" requirements). And although callers may ordinarily block call recipients from obtaining their identifying information, FCC regulations exempt 911 calls from that privilege. §§ 64.1601(b), (d)(4)(ii) ("911 emergency services" exemption from rule that, when a caller so requests, "a carrier may not reveal that caller's number or name"). None of this is to suggest that tips in 911 calls are per se reliable. Given the foregoing technological and regulatory developments, however, a reasonable officer could conclude that a false tipster would think twice before using such a system. The caller's use of the 911 system is therefore one of the relevant circumstances that, taken together, justified the officer's reliance on the information reported in the 911 call.

C

Even a reliable tip will justify an investigative stop only if it creates reasonable suspicion that "criminal activity may be afoot." Terry, 392 U.S., at 30, 88 S.Ct. 1868. We must therefore determine whether the 911 caller's report of being run off the roadway created reasonable suspicion of an ongoing crime such as drunk driving as opposed to an isolated episode of past recklessness. See Cortez, 449 U.S., at 417, 101 S.Ct. 690 ("An investigatory stop must be justified by some objective manifestation that the person stopped is, or is about to be, engaged in criminal activity"). We conclude that the behavior alleged by the 911 caller, "viewed from the standpoint of an objectively reasonable police officer, amount[s] to reasonable suspicion" of drunk driving. Ornelas v. United States, 517 U.S. 690, 696, 116 S.Ct. 1657, 134 L.Ed.2d 911 (1996). The stop was therefore proper.[2]

Reasonable suspicion depends on "`"the factual and practical considerations of everyday life on which reasonable and prudent men, not legal technicians, act."'" Id., at 695, 116 S.Ct. 1657. Under that commonsense approach, we can appropriately recognize certain driving behaviors as sound indicia of drunk driving. See, e.g., People v. Wells, 38 Cal.4th 1078, 1081, 45 Cal.Rptr.3d 8, 136 P.3d 810, 811 (2006) ("'weaving all over the roadway'"); State v. Prendergast, 103 Hawai`i 451, 452-453, 83 P.3d 714, 715-716 (2004) ("cross[ing] over the center line" on a highway and "almost caus[ing] several head-on collisions"); State v. Golotta, 178 N.J. 205, 209, 837 A.2d 359, 361 (2003) (driving "'all over the road'" and "'weaving back and forth'"); State v. Walshire, 634 N.W.2d 625, 626 (Iowa 2001) ("driving in the median"). Indeed, the accumulated experience of thousands of officers suggests that these sorts of erratic behaviors are strongly correlated with drunk driving. See Nat. Highway Traffic Safety Admin., The Visual Detection of DWI Motorists 4-5 (Mar. 2010), online at http://nhtsa.gov/staticfiles/nti/pdf/808677.pdf (as visited Apr. 18, 2014, and available in Clerk of Court's case file). Of course, not all traffic infractions imply intoxication. Unconfirmed reports of driving without a seatbelt or slightly over the speed limit, for example, are so tenuously connected to drunk driving that a stop on those grounds alone would be constitutionally suspect. But a reliable tip alleging the dangerous behaviors discussed above generally would justify a traffic stop on suspicion of drunk driving.

The 911 caller in this case reported more than a minor traffic infraction and more than a conclusory allegation of drunk or reckless driving. Instead, she alleged a specific and dangerous result of the driver's conduct: running another car off the highway. That conduct bears too great a resemblance to paradigmatic manifestations of drunk driving to be dismissed as an isolated example of recklessness. Running another vehicle off the road suggests lane-positioning problems, decreased vigilance, impaired judgment, or some combination of those recognized drunk driving cues. See Visual Detection of DWI Motorists 4-5.

And the experience of many officers suggests that a driver who almost strikes a vehicle or another object — the exact scenario that ordinarily causes "running [another vehicle] off the roadway" — is likely intoxicated. See id., at 5, 8. As a result, we cannot say that the officer acted unreasonably under these circumstances in stopping a driver whose alleged conduct was a significant indicator of drunk driving.

Petitioners' attempts to second-guess the officer's reasonable suspicion of drunk driving are unavailing. It is true that the reported behavior might also be explained by, for example, a driver responding to "an unruly child or other distraction." Brief for Petitioners 21. But we have consistently recognized that reasonable suspicion "need not rule out the possibility of innocent conduct." United States v. Arvizu, 534 U.S. 266, 277, 122 S.Ct. 744, 151 L.Ed.2d 740 (2002).

Nor did the absence of additional suspicious conduct, after the vehicle was first spotted by an officer, dispel the reasonable suspicion of drunk driving. Brief for Petitioners 23-24. It is hardly surprising that the appearance of a marked police car would inspire more careful driving for a time. Cf. Arvizu, supra, at 275, 122 S.Ct. 744 ("'[s]lowing down after spotting a law enforcement vehicle'" does not dispel reasonable suspicion of criminal activity). Extended observation of an allegedly drunk driver might eventually dispel a reasonable suspicion of intoxication, but the 5-minute period in this case hardly sufficed in that regard. Of course, an officer who already has such a reasonable suspicion need not surveil a vehicle at length in order to personally observe suspicious driving. See Adams v. Williams, 407 U.S., at 147, 92 S.Ct. 1921 (repudiating the argument that "reasonable cause for a[n investigative stop] can only be based on the officer's personal observation"). Once reasonable suspicion of drunk driving arises, "[t]he reasonableness of the officer's decision to stop a suspect does not turn on the availability of less intrusive investigatory techniques." Sokolow, 490 U.S., at 11, 109 S.Ct. 1581. This would be a particularly inappropriate context to depart from that settled rule, because allowing a drunk driver a second chance for dangerous conduct could have disastrous consequences.

III

Like White, this is a "close case." 496 U.S., at 332, 110 S.Ct. 2412. As in that case, the indicia of the 911 caller's reliability here are stronger than those in J. L., where we held that a bare-bones tip was unreliable. 529 U.S., at 271, 120 S.Ct. 1375. Although the indicia present here are different from those we found sufficient in White, there is more than one way to demonstrate "a particularized and objective basis for suspecting the particular person stopped of criminal activity." Cortez, 449 U.S., at 417–418, 101 S.Ct. 690. Under the totality of the circumstances, we find the indicia of reliability in this case sufficient to provide the officer with reasonable suspicion that the driver of the reported vehicle had run another vehicle off the road. That made it reasonable under the circumstances for the officer to execute a traffic stop. We accordingly affirm.

It is so ordered.

Plumhoff v. Rickard (May 27, 2014) [Notes omitted]

Justice Alito delivered the opinion of the Court. 1 *

The courts below denied qualified immunity for police officers who shot the driver of a fleeing vehicle to put an end to a dangerous car chase. We reverse and hold that the officers did not violate the Fourth Amendment. In the alternative, we conclude that the officers were entitled to qualified immunity because they violated no clearly established law.

I

A

Because this case arises from the denial of the officers' motion for summary judgment, we view the facts in the light most favorable to the nonmoving party, the daughter of the driver who attempted to flee. Wilkie v. Robbins, 551 U. S. 537, n. 2 (2007). Near midnight on July 18, 2004, Lieutenant Joseph Forthman of the West Memphis, Arkansas, Police Department pulled over a white Honda Accord because the car had only one operating headlight. Donald Rickard was the driver of the Accord, and Kelly Allen was in the passenger seat. Forthman noticed an indentation, " 'roughly the size of a head or a basketball' " in the windshield of the car. Estate of Allen v. West Memphis, 2011 WL 197426, *1 (WD Tenn., Jan. 20, 2011). He asked Rickard if he had been drinking, and Rickard responded that he had not. Because Rickard failed to produce his driver's license upon request and appeared nervous, Forthman asked him to step out of the car. Rather than comply with Forthman's request, Rickard sped away.

Forthman gave chase and was soon joined by five other police cruisers driven by Sergeant Vance Plumhoff and Officers Jimmy Evans, Lance Ellis, Troy Galtelli, and John Gardner. The officers pursued Rickard east on Interstate 40 toward Memphis, Tennessee. While on I–40, they attempted to stop Rickard using a "rolling roadblock," id., at *2, but they were unsuccessful. The District Court described the vehicles as "swerving through traffic at high speeds," id., at *8, and respondent does not dispute that the cars attained speeds over 100 miles per hour. 2 See Memorandum of Law in Response to Defendants' Motion for Summary Judgment in No. 2:05–cv–2585 (WD Tenn.), p. 16; see also Tr. of Oral Arg. 54:23–55:6. During the chase, Rickard and the officers passed more than two dozen vehicles.

Rickard eventually exited I–40 in Memphis, and shortly afterward he made "a quick right turn," causing "contact [to] occu[r]" between his car and Evans' cruiser. 2011 WL 197426, *3. As a result of that contact, Rickard's car spun out into a parking lot and collided with Plumhoff's cruiser. Now in danger of being cornered, Rickard put his car into reverse "in an attempt to escape." Ibid. As he did so, Evans and Plumhoff got out of their cruisers and approached Rickard's car, and Evans, gun in hand, pounded on the passenger-side window. At that point, Rickard's car "made contact with" yet another police cruiser. Ibid. Rickard's tires started spinning, and his car "was rocking back and forth," ibid., indicating that Rickard was using the accelerator even though his bumper was flush against a police cruiser. At that point, Plumhoff fired three shots into Rickard's car. Rickard then "reversed in a 180 degree arc" and "maneuvered onto" another street, forcing Ellis to "step to his right to avoid the vehicle." Ibid. As Rickard continued "fleeing down" that street, ibid., Gardner and Galtelli fired 12 shots toward Rickard's car, bringing the total number of shots fired during this incident to 15. Rickard then lost control of the car and crashed into a building. Ibid. Rickard and Allen both died from some combination of gunshot wounds and injuries suffered in the crash that ended the chase. See App. 60, 76.

B

Respondent, Rickard's surviving daughter, filed this action under Rev. Stat. §1979, 42 U. S. C. §1983, against the six individual police officers and the mayor and chief of police of West Memphis. She alleged that the officers used excessive force in violation of the Fourth and Fourteenth Amendments.

The officers moved for summary judgment based on qualified immunity, but the District Court denied that motion, holding that the officers' conduct violated the Fourth Amendment and was contrary to law that was clearly established at the time in question. The officers appealed, but a Sixth Circuit motions panel initially dismissed the appeal for lack of jurisdiction based on this Court's decision in Johnson v. Jones, 515 U. S. 304, 309 (1995) . Later, however, that panel granted rehearing, vacated its dismissal order, and left the jurisdictional issue to be decided by a merits panel.

The merits panel then affirmed the District Court's decision on the merits. Estate of Allen v. West Memphis, 509 Fed. Appx. 388 (CA6 2012). On the issue of appellate jurisdiction, the merits panel began by stating that a "motion for qualified immunity denied on the basis of a district court's determination that there exists a triable issue of fact generally cannot be appealed on an interlocutory basis." Id., at 391. But the panel then noted that the Sixth Circuit had previously interpreted our decision in Scott v. Harris, 550 U. S. 372 (2007) , as creating an "exception to this rule" under which an immediate appeal may be taken to challenge " 'blatantly and demonstrably false' " factual determinations. 509 Fed. Appx., at 391 (quoting Moldowan v. Warren, 578 F. 3d 351, 370 (CA6 2009)). Concluding that none of the District Court's fac-tual determinations ran afoul of that high standard, and distinguishing the facts of this case from those in Scott, the panel held that the officers' conduct violated the Fourth Amendment. 509 Fed. Appx., at 392, and n. 3. The panel said nothing about whether the officers violated clearly established law, but since the panel affirmed the order denying the officers' summary judgment motion, 3 the panel must have decided that issue in respondent's favor.

We granted certiorari. 571 U. S. _____ (2013).

II

We start with the question whether the Court of Appeals properly exercised jurisdiction under 28 U. S. C. §1291, which gives the courts of appeals jurisdiction to hear appeals from "final decisions" of the district courts.

An order denying a motion for summary judgment is generally not a final decision within the meaning of §1291 and is thus generally not immediately appealable. Johnson, 515 U. S., at 309. But that general rule does not apply when the summary judgment motion is based on a claim of qualified immunity. Id., at 311; Mitchell v. Forsyth, 472 U. S. 511, 528 (1985) . "[Q]ualified immunity is 'an immunity from suit rather than a mere defense to liability.'" Pearson v. Callahan, 555 U. S. 223, 231 (2009) (quoting Mitchell, supra, at 526). As a result, pretrial orders denying qualified immunity generally fall within the collateral order doctrine. See Ashcroft v. Iqbal, 556 U. S. 662–672 (2009). This is so because such orders conclusively determine whether the defendant is entitled to immunity from suit; this immunity issue is both important and completely separate from the merits of the action, and this question could not be effectively reviewed on appeal from a final judgment because by that time the immunity from standing trial will have been irretrievably lost. See ibid; Johnson, supra, at 311–312 (citing Mitchell, supra, at 525–527).

Respondent argues that our decision in Johnson, forecloses appellate jurisdiction under the circumstances here, but the order from which the appeal was taken in Johnson was quite different from the order in the present case. In Johnson, the plaintiff brought suit against certain police officers who, he alleged, had beaten him. 515 U. S., at 307. These officers moved for summary judgment, asserting that they were not present at the time of the alleged beating and had nothing to do with it. Id., at 307–308. The District Court determined, however, that the evidence in the summary judgment record was sufficient to support a contrary finding, and the court therefore denied the officers' motion for summary judgment. Id., at 308. The officers then appealed, arguing that the District Court had not correctly analyzed the relevant evidence. Ibid.

This Court held that the Johnson order was not immediately appealable because it merely decided "a question of 'evidence sufficiency,' i.e., which facts a party may, or may not, be able to prove at trial." Id., at 313. The Court noted that an order denying summary judgment based on a determination of "evidence sufficiency" does not present a legal question in the sense in which the term was used in Mitchell, the decision that first held that a pretrial order rejecting a claim of qualified immunity is immediately appealable. Johnson, 515 U. S., at 314. In addition, the Court observed that a determination of evidence sufficiency is closely related to other determinations that the trial court may be required to make at later stages of the case. Id., at 317. The Court also noted that appellate courts have "no comparative expertise" over trial courts in making such determinations and that forcing appellate courts to entertain appeals from such orders would impose an undue burden. Id., at 309–310, 316.

The District Court order in this case is nothing like the order in Johnson. Petitioners do not claim that other officers were responsible for shooting Rickard; rather, they contend that their conduct did not violate the Fourth Amendment and, in any event, did not violate clearly established law. Thus, they raise legal issues; these issues are quite different from any purely factual issues that the trial court might confront if the case were tried; deciding legal issues of this sort is a core responsibility of appellate courts, and requiring appellate courts to decide such issues is not an undue burden.

The District Court order here is not materially distinguishable from the District Court order in Scott v. Harris, and in that case we expressed no doubts about the jurisdiction of the Court of Appeals under §1291. Accordingly, here, as in Scott, we hold that the Court of Appeals properly exercised jurisdiction, and we therefore turn to the merits.

III

A

Petitioners contend that the decision of the Court of Appeals is wrong for two separate reasons. They maintain that they did not violate Rickard's Fourth Amendment rights and that, in any event, their conduct did not violate any Fourth Amendment rule that was clearly established at the time of the events in question. When confronted with such arguments, we held in Saucier v. Katz, 533 U. S. 194, 200 (2001), that "the first inquiry must be whether a constitutional right would have been violated on the facts alleged." Only after deciding that question, we concluded, may an appellate court turn to the question whether the right at issue was clearly established at the relevant time. Ibid.

We subsequently altered this rigid framework in Pearson, declaring that "Saucier's procedure should not be regarded as an inflexible requirement." 555 U. S., at 227. At the same time, however, we noted that the Saucier procedure "is often beneficial" because it "promotes the development of constitutional precedent and is especially valuable with respect to questions that do not frequently arise in cases in which a qualified immunity defense is unavailable." 555 U. S., at 236. Pearson concluded that courts "have the discretion to decide whether that [Sau-cier] procedure is worthwhile in particular cases." Id., at 242.

Heeding our guidance in Pearson, we begin in this case with the question whether the officers' conduct violated the Fourth Amendment. This approach, we believe, will be "beneficial" in "develop[ing] constitutional precedent" in an area that courts typically consider in cases in which the defendant asserts a qualified immunity defense. See Pearson, supra, at 236.

B

A claim that law-enforcement officers used excessive force to effect a seizure is governed by the Fourth Amendment's "reasonableness" standard. See Graham v. Connor, 490 U. S. 386 (1989); Tennessee v. Garner, 471 U. S. 1 (1985). In Graham, we held that determining the objective reasonableness of a particular seizure under the Fourth Amendment "requires a careful balancing of the nature and quality of the intrusion on the individual's Fourth Amendment interests against the countervailing governmental interests at stake." 490 U. S., at 396 (internal quotation marks omitted). The inquiry requires analyzing the totality of the circumstances. See ibid.

We analyze this question from the perspective "of a reasonable officer on the scene, rather than with the 20/20 vision of hindsight." Ibid. We thus "allo[w] for the fact that police officers are often forced to make split-second judgments—in circumstances that are tense, uncertain, and rapidly evolving—about the amount of force that is necessary in a particular situation." Id., at 396–397.

In this case, respondent advances two main Fourth Amendment arguments. First, she contends that the Fourth Amendment did not allow petitioners to use deadly force to terminate the chase. See Brief for Respondent 24–35. Second, she argues that the "degree of force was excessive," that is, that even if the officers were permitted to fire their weapons, they went too far when they fired as many rounds as they did. See id., at 36–38. We address each issue in turn.

1

In Scott, we considered a claim that a police officer violated the Fourth Amendment when he terminated a high-speed car chase by using a technique that placed a "fleeing motorist at risk of serious injury or death." 550 U. S., at 386. The record in that case contained a videotape of the chase, and we found that the events recorded on the tape justified the officer's conduct. We wrote as follows: "Although there is no obvious way to quantify the risks on either side, it is clear from the videotape that respondent posed an actual and imminent threat to the lives of any pedestrians who might have been present, to other civilian motorists, and to the officers involved in the chase." Id., at 383–384. We also wrote:

"[R]espondent's vehicle rac[ed] down narrow, two-lane roads in the dead of night at speeds that are shock-ingly fast. We see it swerve around more than a dozen other cars, cross the double-yellow line, and force cars traveling in both directions to their respective shoulders to avoid being hit. We see it run multiple red lights and travel for considerable periods of time in the occasional center left-turn-only lane, chased by numerous police cars forced to engage in the same hazardous maneuvers just to keep up." Id., at 379–380 (footnote omitted).

In light of those facts, "we [thought] it [was] quite clear that [the police officer] did not violate the Fourth Amendment." Id., at 381. We held that a "police officer's attempt to terminate a dangerous high-speed car chase that threatens the lives of innocent bystanders does not violate the Fourth Amendment, even when it places the fleeing motorist at risk of serious injury or death." 4 Id., at 386.

We see no basis for reaching a different conclusion here. As we have explained supra, at ____, the chase in this case exceeded 100 miles per hour and lasted over five minutes. During that chase, Rickard passed more than two dozen other vehicles, several of which were forced to alter course. Rickard's outrageously reckless driving posed a grave public safety risk. And while it is true that Rickard's car eventually collided with a police car and came temporarily to a near standstill, that did not end the chase. Less than three seconds later, Rickard resumed maneuvering his car. Just before the shots were fired, when the front bumper of his car was flush with that of one of the police cruisers, Rickard was obviously pushing down on the accelerator because the car's wheels were spinning, and then Rickard threw the car into reverse "in an attempt to escape." Thus, the record conclusively disproves respondent's claim that the chase in the present case was already over when petitioners began shooting. Under the circumstances at the moment when the shots were fired, all that a reasonable police officer could have concluded was that Rickard was intent on resuming his flight and that, if he was allowed to do so, he would once again pose a deadly threat for others on the road. Rickard's conduct even after the shots were fired—as noted, he managed to drive away despite the efforts of the police to block his path—underscores the point.

In light of the circumstances we have discussed, it is beyond serious dispute that Rickard's flight posed a grave public safety risk, and here, as in Scott, the police acted reasonably in using deadly force to end that risk.

2

We now consider respondent's contention that, even if the use of deadly force was permissible, petitioners acted unreasonably in firing a total of 15 shots. We reject that argument. It stands to reason that, if police officers are justified in firing at a suspect in order to end a severe threat to public safety, the officers need not stop shooting until the threat has ended. As petitioners noted below, "if lethal force is justified, officers are taught to keep shooting until the threat is over." 509 Fed. Appx., at 392.

Here, during the 10-second span when all the shots were fired, Rickard never abandoned his attempt to flee. Indeed, even after all the shots had been fired, he managed to drive away and to continue driving until he crashed. This would be a different case if petitioners had initiated a second round of shots after an initial round had clearly incapacitated Rickard and had ended any threat of continued flight, or if Rickard had clearly given himself up. But that is not what happened.

In arguing that too many shots were fired, respondent relies in part on the presence of Kelly Allen in the front seat of the car, but we do not think that this factor changes the calculus. Our cases make it clear that "Fourth Amendment rights are personal rights which . . . may not be vicariously asserted." Alderman v. United States, 394 U. S. 165, 174 (1969) ; see also Rakas v. Illinois, 439 U. S. 128–143 (1978). Thus, the question before us is whether petitioners violated Rickard's Fourth Amendment rights, not Allen's. If a suit were brought on behalf of Allen under either §1983 or state tort law, the risk to Allen would be of central concern. 5 But Allen's presence in the car cannot enhance Rickard's Fourth Amendment rights. After all, it was Rickard who put Allen in danger by fleeing and refusing to end the chase, and it would be perverse if his disregard for Allen's safety worked to his benefit.

C

We have held that petitioners' conduct did not violate the Fourth Amendment, but even if that were not the case, petitioners would still be entitled to summary judgment based on qualified immunity.

An official sued under §1983 is entitled to qualified immunity unless it is shown that the official violated a statutory or constitutional right that was " 'clearly established' " at the time of the challenged conduct. Ashcroft v. al-Kidd, 563 U. S. ____, ____ (2011) (slip op., at 3). And a defendant cannot be said to have violated a clearly established right unless the right's contours were sufficiently definite that any reasonable official in the defendant's shoes would have understood that he was violating it. Id., at ____ (slip op., at 9). In other words, "existing precedent must have placed the statutory or constitutional question" confronted by the official "beyond debate." Ibid. In addition, "[w]e have repeatedly told courts . . . not to define clearly established law at a high level of generality," id., at ____ (slip op., at 10), since doing so avoids the crucial question whether the official acted reasonably in the particular circumstances that he or she faced. We think our decision in

Brosseau v. Haugen, 543 U. S. 194 (2004) (per curiam) squarely demonstrates that no clearly established law precluded petitioners' conduct at the time in question. In Brosseau, we held that a police officer did not violate clearly established law when she fired at a fleeing vehicle to prevent possible harm to "other officers on foot who [she] believed were in the immediate area, . . . occupied vehicles in [the driver's] path[,] and . . . any other citizens who might be in the area." Id., at 197 (quoting 339 F. 3d 857, 865 (CA9 2003); internal quotation marks omitted). After surveying lower court decisions regarding the reasonableness of lethal force as a response to vehicular flight, we observed that this is an area "in which the result depends very much on the facts of each case" and that the cases "by no means 'clearly establish[ed]' that [the officer's] conduct violated the Fourth Amendment." 543 U. S., at 201. In reaching that conclusion, we held that Garner and Graham, which are "cast at a high level of generality," did not clearly establish that the officer's decision was unreasonable. 543 U. S., at 199.

Brosseau makes plain that as of February 21, 1999—the date of the events at issue in that case—it was not clearly established that it was unconstitutional to shoot a fleeing driver to protect those whom his flight might endanger. We did not consider later decided cases because they "could not have given fair notice to [the officer]." Id., at 200, n. 4. To defeat immunity here, then, respondent must show at a minimum either (1) that the officers' conduct in this case was materially different from the conduct in Brosseau or (2) that between February 21, 1999, and July 18, 2004, there emerged either " 'controlling authority' " or a "robust 'consensus of cases of persuasive authority,' " al-Kidd, supra, at ____ (slip op., at 10) (quoting Wilsonv. Layne, 526 U. S. 603, 617 (1999) ; some internal quotation marks omitted), that would alter our analysis of the qualified immunity question. Respondent has made neither showing.

To begin, certain facts here are more favorable to the officers. In Brosseau, an officer on foot fired at a driver who had just begun to flee and who had not yet driven his car in a dangerous manner. In contrast, the officers here shot at Rickard to put an end to what had already been a lengthy, high-speed pursuit that indisputably posed a danger both to the officers involved and to any civilians who happened to be nearby. Indeed, the lone dissenting Justice in Brosseau emphasized that in that case, "there was no ongoing or prior high-speed car chase to inform the [constitutional] analysis." 543 U. S., at 206, n. 4 (opinion of Stevens, J.). Attempting to distinguish Brosseau, respondent focuses on the fact that the officer there fired only 1 shot, whereas here three officers collectively fired 15 shots. But it was certainly not clearly established at the time of the shooting in this case that the number of shots fired, under the circumstances present here, rendered the use of force excessive.

Since respondent cannot meaningfully distinguish Brosseau, her only option is to show that its analysis was out of date by 2004. Yet respondent has not pointed us to any case—let alone a controlling case or a robust consensus of cases—decided between 1999 and 2004 that could be said to have clearly established the unconstitutionality of using lethal force to end a high-speed car chase. And respondent receives no help on this front from the opinions below. The District Court cited only a single case decided between 1999 and 2004 that identified a possible constitutional violation by an officer who shot a fleeing driver, and the facts of that case—where a reasonable jury could have concluded that the suspect merely "accelerated to eighty to eighty-five miles per hour in a seventy-miles-per-hour zone" and did not "engag[e] in any evasive maneuvers," Vaughan v. Cox, 343 F. 3d 1323, 1330–1331 (CA11 2003)—bear little resemblance to those here.

* * *

Under the circumstances present in this case, we hold that the Fourth Amendment did not prohibit petitioners from using the deadly force that they employed to terminate the dangerous car chase that Rickard precipitated. In the alternative, we note that petitioners are entitled to qualified immunity for the conduct at issue because they violated no clearly established law.

The judgment of the Court of Appeals is reversed, and the case is remanded for further proceedings consistent with this opinion.

It is so ordered.

Riley v. California (June 25, 2014)

Chief Justice Roberts delivered the opinion of the Court.

These two cases raise a common question: whether the police may, without a warrant, search digital information on a cell phone seized from an individual who has been arrested.

I

A

In the first case, petitioner David Riley was stopped by a police officer for driving with expired registration tags. In the course of the stop, the officer also learned that Riley's license had been suspended. The officer impounded Riley's car, pursuant to department policy, and another officer conducted an inventory search of the car. Riley was arrested for possession of concealed and loaded firearms when that search turned up two handguns under the car's hood. See Cal. Penal Code Ann. §§12025(a)(1), 12031(a)(1) (West 2009).

An officer searched Riley incident to the arrest and found items associated with the "Bloods" street gang. He also seized a cell phone from Riley's pants pocket. According to Riley's uncontradicted assertion, the phone was a "smart phone," a cell phone with a broad range of other functions based on advanced computing capability, large storage capacity, and Internet connectivity.

The officer accessed information on the phone and noticed that some words (presumably in text messages or a contacts list) were preceded by the letters "CK"—a label that, he believed, stood for "Crip Killers," a slang term for members of the Bloods gang.

At the police station about two hours after the arrest, a detective specializing in gangs further examined the contents of the phone. The detective testified that he "went through" Riley's phone "looking for evidence, because . . . gang members will often video themselves with guns or take pictures of themselves with the guns." App. in No. 13–132, p. 20. Although there was "a lot of stuff" on the phone, particular files that "caught [the detective's] eye" included videos of young men sparring while someone yelled encouragement using the moniker "Blood." Id., at 11–13. The police also found photographs of Riley standing in front of a car they suspected had been involved in a shooting a few weeks earlier.

Riley was ultimately charged, in connection with that earlier shooting, with firing at an occupied vehicle, assault with a semiautomatic firearm, and attempted murder. The State alleged that Riley had committed those crimes for the benefit of a criminal street gang, an aggravating factor that carries an enhanced sentence. Compare Cal. Penal Code Ann. §246 (2008) with §186.22(b)(4)(B) (2014). Prior to trial, Riley moved to suppress all evidence that the police had obtained from his cell phone. He contended that the searches of his phone violated the Fourth Amendment, because they had been performed without a warrant and were not otherwise justified by exigent circumstances. The trial court rejected that argument. App. in No. 13–132, at 24, 26. At Riley's trial, police officers testified about the photographs and videos found on the phone, and some of the photographs were admitted into evidence. Riley was convicted on all three counts and received an enhanced sentence of 15 years to life in prison.

The California Court of Appeal affirmed. No. D059840 (Cal. App., Feb. 8, 2013), App. to Pet. for Cert. in No. 13–132, pp. 1a–23a. The court relied on the California Supreme Court's decision in People v. Diaz, 51 Cal. 4th 84, 244 P. 3d 501 (2011), which held that the Fourth Amendment permits a warrantless search of cell phone data incident to an arrest, so long as the cell phone was immediately associated with the arrestee's person. See id., at 93, 244 P. 3d, at 505–506.

The California Supreme Court denied Riley's petition for review, App. to Pet. for Cert. in No. 13–132, at 24a, and we granted certiorari, 571 U. S. ____ (2014).

B

In the second case, a police officer performing routine surveillance observed respondent Brima Wurie make an apparent drug sale from a car. Officers subsequently arrested Wurie and took him to the police station. At the station, the officers seized two cell phones from Wurie's person. The one at issue here was a "flip phone," a kind of phone that is flipped open for use and that generally has a smaller range of features than a smart phone. Five to ten minutes after arriving at the station, the officers noticed that the phone was repeatedly receiving calls from a source identified as "my house" on the phone's external screen. A few minutes later, they opened the phone and saw a photograph of a woman and a baby set as the phone's wallpaper. They pressed one button on the phone to access its call log, then another button to determine the phone number associated with the "my house" label. They next used an online phone directory to trace that phone number to an apartment building.

When the officers went to the building, they saw Wurie's name on a mailbox and observed through a window a woman who resembled the woman in the photograph on Wurie's phone. They secured the apartment while obtaining a search warrant and, upon later executing the warrant, found and seized 215 grams of crack cocaine, marijuana, drug paraphernalia, a firearm and ammunition, and cash.

Wurie was charged with distributing crack cocaine, possessing crack cocaine with intent to distribute, and being a felon in possession of a firearm and ammunition. See 18 U. S. C. §922(g); 21 U. S. C. §841(a). He moved to suppress the evidence obtained from the search of the apartment, arguing that it was the fruit of an unconstitutional search of his cell phone. The District Court denied the motion. 612 F. Supp. 2d 104 (Mass. 2009). Wurie was convicted on all three counts and sentenced to 262 months in prison.

A divided panel of the First Circuit reversed the denial of Wurie's motion to suppress and vacated Wurie's convictions for possession with intent to distribute and possession of a firearm as a felon. 728 F. 3d 1 (2013). The court held that cell phones are distinct from other physical possessions that may be searched incident to arrest without a warrant, because of the amount of personal data cell phones contain and the negligible threat they pose to law enforcement interests. See id., at 8–11.

We granted certiorari. 571 U. S. ____ (2014).

II

The Fourth Amendment provides:

"The right of the people to be secure in their persons, houses, papers, and effects, against unreasonable searches and seizures, shall not be violated, and no Warrants shall issue, but upon probable cause, supported by Oath or affirmation, and particularly describing the place to be searched, and the persons or things to be seized."

As the text makes clear, "the ultimate touchstone of the Fourth Amendment is 'reasonableness.' " Brigham City v. Stuart, 547 U. S. 398, 403 (2006). Our cases have determined that "[w]here a search is undertaken by law enforcement officials to discover evidence of criminal wrongdoing, . . . reasonableness generally requires the obtaining of a judicial warrant." Vernonia School Dist. 47J v. Acton, 515 U. S. 646, 653 (1995). Such a warrant ensures that the inferences to support a search are "drawn by a neutral and detached magistrate instead of being judged by the officer engaged in the often competitive enterprise of ferreting out crime." Johnson v. United States, 333 U. S. 10, 14 (1948). In the absence of a warrant, a search is reasonable only if it falls within a specific exception to the warrant requirement. See Kentucky v. King, 563 U. S. ____, ____ (2011) (slip op., at 5–6).

The two cases before us concern the reasonableness of a warrantless search incident to a lawful arrest. In 1914, this Court first acknowledged in dictum "the right on the part of the Government, always recognized under English and American law, to search the person of the accused when legally arrested to discover and seize the fruits or evidences of crime." Weeks v. United States, 232 U. S. 383. Since that time, it has been well accepted that such a search constitutes an exception to the warrant requirement. Indeed, the label "exception" is something of a misnomer in this context, as warrantless searches incident to arrest occur with far greater frequency than searches conducted pursuant to a warrant. See 3 W. LaFave, Search and Seizure §5.2(b), p. 132, and n. 15 (5th ed. 2012).

Although the existence of the exception for such searches has been recognized for a century, its scope has been de-bated for nearly as long. See Arizona v. Gant, 556 U. S. 332, 350 (2009) (noting the exception's "checkered his-tory"). That debate has focused on the extent to which officers may search property found on or near the arrestee. Three related precedents set forth the rules governing such searches:

The first, Chimel v. California, 395 U. S.

752 (1969), laid the groundwork for most of the existing search incident to arrest doctrine. Police officers in that case arrested Chimel inside his home and proceeded to search his entire three-bedroom house, including the attic and garage. In particular rooms, they also looked through the contents of drawers. Id., at 753–754.

The Court crafted the following rule for assessing the reasonableness of a search incident to arrest:

"When an arrest is made, it is reasonable for the arresting officer to search the person arrested in order to remove any weapons that the latter might seek to use in order to resist arrest or effect his escape. Otherwise, the officer's safety might well be endangered, and the arrest itself frustrated. In addition, it is entirely reasonable for the arresting officer to search for and seize any evidence on the arrestee's person in order to prevent its concealment or destruction. . . . There is ample justification, therefore, for a search of the arrestee's person and the area 'within his immediate control'—construing that phrase to mean the area from within which he might gain possession of a weapon or destructible evidence." Id., at 762–763.

The extensive warrantless search of Chimel's home did not fit within this exception, because it was not needed to protect officer safety or to preserve evidence. Id., at 763, 768.

Four years later, in United States v. Robinson, 414 U. S. 218 (1973), the Court applied the Chimel analysis in the context of a search of the arrestee's person. A police officer had arrested Robinson for driving with a revoked license. The officer conducted a patdown search and felt an object that he could not identify in Robinson's coat pocket. He removed the object, which turned out to be a crumpled cigarette package, and opened it. Inside were 14 capsules of heroin. Id., at 220, 223.

The Court of Appeals concluded that the search was unreasonable because Robinson was unlikely to have evidence of the crime of arrest on his person, and because it believed that extracting the cigarette package and opening it could not be justified as part of a protective search for weapons. This Court reversed, rejecting the notion that "case-by-case adjudication" was required to determine "whether or not there was present one of the reasons supporting the authority for a search of the person incident to a lawful arrest." Id., at 235. As the Court explained, "[t]he authority to search the person incident to a lawful custodial arrest, while based upon the need to disarm and to discover evidence, does not depend on what a court may later decide was the probability in a particular arrest situation that weapons or evidence would in fact be found upon the person of the suspect." Ibid. Instead, a "custodial arrest of a suspect based on probable cause is a reasonable intrusion under the Fourth Amendment; that intrusion being lawful, a search incident to the arrest requires no additional justification." Ibid.

The Court thus concluded that the search of Robinson was reasonable even though there was no concern about the loss of evidence, and the arresting officer had no specific concern that Robinson might be armed. Id., at 236. In doing so, the Court did not draw a line between a search of Robinson's person and a further examination of the cigarette pack found during that search. It merely noted that, "[h]aving in the course of a lawful search come upon the crumpled package of cigarettes, [the officer] was entitled to inspect it." Ibid. A few years later, the Court clarified that this exception was limited to "personal property . . . immediately associated with the person of the arrestee." United States v. Chadwick, 433 U. S. 1, 15 (1977) (200-pound, locked footlocker could not be searched incident to arrest), abrogated on other grounds by California v. Acevedo, 500 U. S. 565 (1991).

The search incident to arrest trilogy concludes with Gant, which analyzed searches of an arrestee's vehicle. Gant, like Robinson, recognized that the Chimel concerns for officer safety and evidence preservation underlie the search incident to arrest exception. See 556 U. S., at 338. As a result, the Court concluded that Chimel could authorize police to search a vehicle "only when the arrestee is unsecured and within reaching distance of the passenger compartment at the time of the search." 556 U. S., at 343. Gant added, however, an independent exception for a warrantless search of a vehicle's passenger compartment "when it is 'reasonable to believe evidence relevant to the crime of arrest might be found in the vehicle.' " Ibid. (quoting Thornton v. United States, 541 U. S. 615, 632 (2004) (Scalia, J., concurring in judgment)). That exception stems not from Chimel, the Court explained, but from "circumstances unique to the vehicle context." 556 U. S., at 343.

III

These cases require us to decide how the search incident to arrest doctrine applies to modern cell phones, which are now such a pervasive and insistent part of daily life that the proverbial visitor from Mars might conclude they were an important feature of human anatomy. A smart phone of the sort taken from Riley was unheard of ten years ago; a significant majority of American adults now own such phones. See A. Smith, Pew Research Center, Smartphone Ownership—2013 Update (June 5, 2013). Even less sophisticated phones like Wurie's, which have already faded in popularity since Wurie was arrested in 2007, have been around for less than 15 years. Both phones are based on technology nearly inconceivable just a few decades ago, when Chimel and Robinson were decided.

Absent more precise guidance from the founding era, we generally determine whether to exempt a given type of search from the warrant requirement "by assessing, on the one hand, the degree to which it intrudes upon an individual's privacy and, on the other, the degree to which it is needed for the promotion of legitimate governmental interests." Wyoming v. Houghton, 526 U. S. 295, 300 (1999). Such a balancing of interests supported the search incident to arrest exception in Robinson, and a mechanical application of Robinson might well support the warrantless searches at issue here.

But while Robinson's categorical rule strikes the appropriate balance in the context of physical objects, neither of its rationales has much force with respect to digital content on cell phones. On the government interest side, Robinson concluded that the two risks identified in Chimel—harm to officers and destruction of evidence—are present in all custodial arrests. There are no comparable risks when the search is of digital data. In addition, Robinson regarded any privacy interests retained by an individual after arrest as significantly diminished by the fact of the arrest itself. Cell phones, however, place vast quantities of personal information literally in the hands of individuals. A search of the information on a cell phone bears little resemblance to the type of brief physical search considered in Robinson.

We therefore decline to extend Robinson to searches of data on cell phones, and hold instead that officers must generally secure a warrant before conducting such a search.

A

We first consider each Chimel concern in turn. In doing so, we do not overlook Robinson's admonition that searches of a person incident to arrest, "while based upon theneed to disarm and to discover evidence," are reasonable regardless of "the probability in a particular arrest situation that weapons or evidence would in fact be found." 414 U. S., at 235. Rather than requiring the "case-by-case adjudication" that Robinson rejected, ibid., we ask instead whether application of the search incident to arrest doctrine to this particular category of effects would "untether the rule from the justifications underlying the Chimel exception," Gant, supra, at 343. See also Knowles v. Iowa, 525 U. S. 113, 119 (1998) (declining to extend Robinson to the issuance of citations, "a situation where the concern for officer safety is not present to the same extent and the concern for destruction or loss of evidence is not present at all").

1

Digital data stored on a cell phone cannot itself be used as a weapon to harm an arresting officer or to effectuate the arrestee's escape. Law enforcement officers remain free to examine the physical aspects of a phone to ensure that it will not be used as a weapon—say, to determine whether there is a razor blade hidden between the phone and its case. Once an officer has secured a phone and eliminated any potential physical threats, however, data on the phone can endanger no one.

Perhaps the same might have been said of the cigarette pack seized from Robinson's pocket. Once an officer gained control of the pack, it was unlikely that Robinson could have accessed the pack's contents. But unknown physical objects may always pose risks, no matter how slight, during the tense atmosphere of a custodial arrest. The officer in Robinson testified that he could not identify the objects in the cigarette pack but knew they were not cigarettes. See 414 U. S., at 223, 236, n. 7. Given that, a further search was a reasonable protective measure. No such unknowns exist with respect to digital data. As the First Circuit explained, the officers who searched Wurie's cell phone "knew exactly what they would find therein: data. They also knew that the data could not harm them." 728 F. 3d, at 10.

The United States and California both suggest that a search of cell phone data might help ensure officer safety in more indirect ways, for example by alerting officers that confederates of the arrestee are headed to the scene. There is undoubtedly a strong government interest in warning officers about such possibilities, but neither the United States nor California offers evidence to suggest that their concerns are based on actual experience. The proposed consideration would also represent a broadening of Chimel's concern that an arrestee himself might grab a weapon and use it against an officer "to resist arrest or effect his escape." 395 U. S., at 763. And any such threats from outside the arrest scene do not "lurk[ ] in all custodial arrests." Chadwick, 433 U. S., at 14–15. Accordingly, the interest in protecting officer safety does not justify dispensing with the warrant requirement across the board. To the extent dangers to arresting officers may be implicated in a particular way in a particular case, they are better addressed through consideration of case-specific exceptions to the warrant requirement, such as the one for exigent circumstances. See, e.g., Warden, Md. Penitentiary v. Hayden, 387 U. S. 294–299 (1967) ("The Fourth Amendment does not require police officers to delay in the course of an investigation if to do so would gravely endanger their lives or the lives of others.").

2

The United States and California focus primarily on the second Chimel rationale: preventing the destruction of evidence.

Both Riley and Wurie concede that officers could have seized and secured their cell phones to prevent destruction of evidence while seeking a warrant. See Brief for Petitioner in No. 13–132, p. 20; Brief for Respondent in No. 13–212, p. 41. That is a sensible concession. See Illinois v. McArthur, 531 U. S. 326–333 (2001); Chadwick, supra, at 13, and n. 8. And once law enforcement officers have secured a cell phone, there is no longer any risk that the arrestee himself will be able to delete incriminating data from the phone.

The United States and California argue that information on a cell phone may nevertheless be vulnerable to two types of evidence destruction unique to digital data—remote wiping and data encryption. Remote wiping occurs when a phone, connected to a wireless network, receives a signal that erases stored data. This can happen when a third party sends a remote signal or when a phone is preprogrammed to delete data upon entering or leaving certain geographic areas (so-called "geofencing"). See Dept. of Commerce, National Institute of Standards and Technology, R. Ayers, S. Brothers, & W. Jansen, Guidelines on Mobile Device Forensics (Draft) 29, 31 (SP 800–101 Rev. 1, Sept. 2013) (hereinafter Ayers). Encryption is a security feature that some modern cell phones use in addition to password protection. When such phones lock, data becomes protected by sophisticated encryption that renders a phone all but "unbreakable" unless police know the password. Brief for United States as Amicus Curiae in No. 13–132, p. 11.

As an initial matter, these broader concerns about the loss of evidence are distinct from Chimel's focus on a defendant who responds to arrest by trying to conceal or destroy evidence within his reach. See 395 U. S., at 763–764. With respect to remote wiping, the Government's primary concern turns on the actions of third parties who are not present at the scene of arrest. And data encryption is even further afield. There, the Government focuses on the ordinary operation of a phone's security features, apart from any active attempt by a defendant or his associates to conceal or destroy evidence upon arrest.

We have also been given little reason to believe that either problem is prevalent. The briefing reveals only a couple of anecdotal examples of remote wiping triggered by an arrest. See Brief for Association of State Criminal Investigative Agencies et al. as Amici Curiae in No. 13–132, pp. 9–10; see also Tr. of Oral Arg. in No. 13–132, p. 48. Similarly, the opportunities for officers to search a password-protected phone before data becomes encrypted are quite limited. Law enforcement officers are very unlikely to come upon such a phone in an unlocked state because most phones lock at the touch of a button or, as a default, after some very short period of inactivity. See, e.g., iPhone User Guide for iOS 7.1 Software 10 (2014) (default lock after about one minute). This may explain why the encryption argument was not made until the merits stage in this Court, and has never been considered by the Courts of Appeals.

Moreover, in situations in which an arrest might trigger a remote-wipe attempt or an officer discovers an unlocked phone, it is not clear that the ability to conduct a warrantless search would make much of a difference. The need to effect the arrest, secure the scene, and tend to other pressing matters means that law enforcement officers may well not be able to turn their attention to a cell phone right away. See Tr. of Oral Arg. in No. 13–132, at 50; see also Brief for United States as Amicus Curiae in No. 13–132, at 19. Cell phone data would be vulnerable to remote wiping from the time an individual anticipates arrest to the time any eventual search of the phone is completed, which might be at the station house hours later. Likewise, an officer who seizes a phone in an unlocked state might not be able to begin his search in the short time remaining before the phone locks and data becomes encrypted.

In any event, as to remote wiping, law enforcement is not without specific means to address the threat. Remote wiping can be fully prevented by disconnecting a phone from the network. There are at least two simple ways to do this: First, law enforcement officers can turn the phone off or remove its battery. Second, if they are concerned about encryption or other potential problems, they can leave a phone powered on and place it in an enclosure that isolates the phone from radio waves. See Ayers 30–31. Such devices are commonly called "Faraday bags," after the

English scientist Michael Faraday. They are essentially sandwich bags made of aluminum foil: cheap, lightweight, and easy to use. See Brief for Criminal Law Professors as Amici Curiae 9. They may not be a complete answer to the problem, see Ayers 32, but at least for now they provide a reasonable response. In fact, a number of law enforcement agencies around the country already encourage the use of Faraday bags. See, e.g., Dept. of Justice, National Institute of Justice, Electronic Crime Scene Investigation: A Guide for First Responders 14, 32 (2d ed. Apr. 2008); Brief for Criminal Law Professors as Amici Curiae 4–6.

To the extent that law enforcement still has specific concerns about the potential loss of evidence in a particular case, there remain more targeted ways to address those concerns. If "the police are truly confronted with a 'now or never' situation,"—for example, circumstances suggesting that a defendant's phone will be the target of an imminent remote-wipe attempt—they may be able to rely on exigent circumstances to search the phone immediately. Missouri v. McNeely, 569 U. S. ___, ___ (2013) (slip op., at 10) (quoting Roaden v. Kentucky, 413 U. S. 496, 505 (1973); some internal quotation marks omitted). Or, if officers happen to seize a phone in an unlocked state, they may be able to disable a phone's automatic-lock feature in order to prevent the phone from locking and encrypting data. See App. to Reply Brief in No. 13–132, p. 3a (diagramming the few necessary steps). Such a preventive measure could be analyzed under the principles set forth in our decision in McArthur, 531 U. S. 326, which approved officers' reasonable steps to secure a scene to preserve evidence while they awaited a warrant. See id., at 331–333.

B

The search incident to arrest exception rests not only on the heightened government interests at stake in a volatile arrest situation, but also on an arrestee's reduced privacy interests upon being taken into police custody. Robinson focused primarily on the first of those rationales. But it also quoted with approval then-Judge Cardozo's account of the historical basis for the search incident to arrest exception: "Search of the person becomes lawful when grounds for arrest and accusation have been discovered, and the law is in the act of subjecting the body of the accused to its physical dominion." 414 U. S., at 232 (quoting People v. Chiagles, 237 N. Y. 193, 197, 142 N. E. 583, 584 (1923)); see also 414 U. S., at 237 (Powell, J., concurring) ("an individual lawfully subjected to a custodial arrest retains no significant Fourth Amendment interest in the privacy of his person"). Put simply, a patdown of Robinson's cloth-ing and an inspection of the cigarette pack found in his pocket constituted only minor additional intrusions compared to the substantial government authority exercised in taking Robinson into custody. See Chadwick, 433 U. S., at 16, n. 10 (searches of a person are justified in part by "reduced expectations of privacy caused by the arrest").

The fact that an arrestee has diminished privacy interests does not mean that the Fourth Amendment falls out of the picture entirely. Not every search "is acceptable solely because a person is in custody." Maryland v. King, 569 U. S. ___, ___ (2013) (slip op., at 26). To the contrary, when "privacy-related concerns are weighty enough" a "search may require a warrant, notwithstanding the diminished expectations of privacy of the arrestee." Ibid. One such example, of course, is Chimel. Chimel refused to "characteriz[e] the invasion of privacy that results from a top-to-bottom search of a man's house as 'minor.' " 395 U. S., at 766–767, n. 12. Because a search of the arrestee's entire house was a substantial invasion beyond the arrest itself, the Court concluded that a warrant was required.

Robinson is the only decision from this Court applying Chimel to a search of the contents of an item found on an arrestee's person. In an earlier case, this Court had approved a search of a zipper bag carried by an arrestee, but the Court analyzed only the validity of the arrest itself. See Draper v. United States, 358 U. S. 307–311 (1959). Lower courts applying Robinson and Chimel, however, have approved searches of a variety of personal items carried by an arrestee. See, e.g., United States v. Carrion, 809 F. 2d 1120, 1123, 1128 (CA5 1987) (billfold and address book); United States v. Watson, 669 F. 2d 1374, 1383–1384 (CA11 1982) (wallet); United States v. Lee, 501 F. 2d 890, 892 (CADC 1974) (purse).

The United States asserts that a search of all data stored on a cell phone is "materially indistinguishable" from searches of these sorts of physical items. Brief for United States in No. 13–212, p. 26. That is like saying a ride on horseback is materially indistinguishable from a flight to the moon. Both are ways of getting from point A to point B, but little else justifies lumping them together. Modern cell phones, as a category, implicate privacy concerns far beyond those implicated by the search of a cigarette pack, a wallet, or a purse. A conclusion that inspecting the contents of an arrestee's pockets works no substantial additional intrusion on privacy beyond the arrest itself may make sense as applied to physical items, but any extension of that reasoning to digital data has to rest on its own bottom.

1

Cell phones differ in both a quantitative and a qualitative sense from other objects that might be kept on an arrestee's person. The term "cell phone" is itself misleading shorthand; many of these devices are in fact minicomputers that also happen to have the capacity to be used as a telephone. They could just as easily be called cameras, video players, rolodexes, calendars, tape recorders, libraries, diaries, albums, televisions, maps, or newspapers.

One of the most notable distinguishing features of modern cell phones is their immense storage capacity. Before cell phones, a search of a person was limited by physical realities and tended as a general matter to constitute only a narrow intrusion on privacy. See Kerr, Foreword: Accounting for Technological Change, 36 Harv. J. L. & Pub. Pol'y 403, 404–405 (2013). Most people cannot lug around every piece of mail they have received for the past several months, every picture they have taken, or every book or article they have read—nor would they have any reason to attempt to do so. And if they did, they would have to drag behind them a trunk of the sort held to require a search warrant in Chadwick, supra, rather than a container the size of the cigarette package in Robinson.

But the possible intrusion on privacy is not physically limited in the same way when it comes to cell phones. The current top-selling smart phone has a standard capacity of 16 gigabytes (and is available with up to 64 gigabytes). Sixteen gigabytes translates to millions of pages of text, thousands of pictures, or hundreds of videos. See Kerr, supra, at 404; Brief for Center for Democracy & Technology et al. as Amici Curiae 7–8. Cell phones couple that capacity with the ability to store many different types of information: Even the most basic phones that sell for less than $20 might hold photographs, picture messages, text messages, Internet browsing history, a calendar, a thousand-entry phone book, and so on. See id., at 30; United States v. Flores-Lopez, 670 F. 3d 803, 806 (CA7 2012). We expect that the gulf between physical practicability and digital capacity will only continue to widen in the future.

The storage capacity of cell phones has several interrelated consequences for privacy. First, a cell phone collects in one place many distinct types of information—an address, a note, a prescription, a bank statement, a video—that reveal much more in combination than any isolated record. Second, a cell phone's capacity allows even just one type of information to convey far more than previously possible. The sum of an individual's private life can be reconstructed through a thousand photographs labeled with dates, locations, and descriptions; the same cannot be said of a photograph or two of loved ones tucked into a wallet. Third, the data on a phone can date back to the purchase of the phone, or even earlier. A person might carry in his pocket a slip of paper reminding him to call Mr. Jones; he would not carry a record of all his communications with Mr. Jones for the past several months, as would routinely be kept on a phone. 1

Finally, there is an element of pervasiveness that characterizes cell phones but not physical records. Prior to the digital age, people did not typically carry a cache of sensitive personal information with them as they went about their day. Now it is the person who is not carrying a cell phone, with all that it contains, who is the exception. According to one poll, nearly three-quarters of smart phone users report being within five feet of their phones most of the time, with 12% admitting that they even use their phones in the shower. See Harris Interactive, 2013 Mobile Consumer Habits Study (June 2013). A decade ago police officers searching an arrestee might have occasionally stumbled across a highly personal item such as a diary. See, e.g., United States v. Frankenberry, 387 F. 2d 337 (CA2 1967) (per curiam). But those discoveries were likely to be few and far between. Today, by contrast, it is no exaggeration to say that many of the more than 90% of American adults who own a cell phone keep on their person a digital record of nearly every aspect of their lives—from the mundane to the intimate. See Ontario v. Quon, 560 U. S. 746, 760 (2010). Allowing the police to scrutinize such records on a routine basis is quite different from allowing them to search a personal item or two in the occasional case.

Although the data stored on a cell phone is distinguished from physical records by quantity alone, certain types of data are also qualitatively different. An Internet search and browsing history, for example, can be found on an Internet-enabled phone and could reveal an individual's private interests or concerns—perhaps a search for certain symptoms of disease, coupled with frequent visits to WebMD. Data on a cell phone can also reveal where a person has been. Historic location information is a stand-ard feature on many smart phones and can reconstruct someone's specific movements down to the minute, not only around town but also within a particular building. See United States v. Jones, 565 U. S. ___, ___ (2012) (Sotomayor, J., concurring) (slip op., at 3) ("GPS monitoring generates a precise, comprehensive record of a person's public movements that reflects a wealth of detail about her familial, political, professional, religious, and sexual associations.").

Mobile application software on a cell phone, or "apps," offer a range of tools for managing detailed information about all aspects of a person's life. There are apps for Democratic Party news and Republican Party news; apps for alcohol, drug, and gambling addictions; apps for sharing prayer requests; apps for tracking pregnancy symptoms; apps for planning your budget; apps for every conceivable hobby or pastime; apps for improving your romantic life. There are popular apps for buying or selling just about anything, and the records of such transactions may be accessible on the phone indefinitely. There are over a million apps available in each of the two major app stores; the phrase "there's an app for that" is now part of the popular lexicon. The average smart phone user has installed 33 apps, which together can form a revealing montage of the user's life. See Brief for Electronic Privacy Information Center as Amicus Curiae in No. 13–132, p. 9.

In 1926, Learned Hand observed (in an opinion later quoted in Chimel) that it is "a totally different thing to search a man's pockets and use against him what they contain, from ransacking his house for everything which may incriminate him." United States v. Kirschenblatt, 16 F. 2d 202, 203 (CA2). If his pockets contain a cell phone, however, that is no longer true. Indeed, a cell phone search would typically expose to the government far more than the most exhaustive search of a house: A phone not only contains in digital form many sensitive records previously found in the home; it also contains a broad array of private information never found in a home in any form—unless the phone is.

2

To further complicate the scope of the privacy interests at stake, the data a user views on many modern cell phones may not in fact be stored on the device itself. Treating a cell phone as a container whose contents may be searched incident to an arrest is a bit strained as an initial matter. See New York v. Belton, 453 U. S. 454, 460, n. 4 (1981) (describing a "container" as "any object capable of holding another object"). But the analogy crumbles entirely when a cell phone is used to access data located elsewhere, at the tap of a screen. That is what cell phones, with increasing frequency, are designed to do by taking advantage of "cloud computing." Cloud computing is the capacity of Internet-connected devices to display data stored on remote servers rather than on the device itself. Cell phone users often may not know whether particular information is stored on the device or in the cloud, and it generally makes little difference. See Brief for Electronic Privacy Information Center in No. 13–132, at 12–14, 20. Moreover, the same type of data may be stored locally on the device for one user and in the cloud for another.

The United States concedes that the search incident to arrest exception may not be stretched to cover a search of files accessed remotely—that is, a search of files stored in the cloud. See Brief for United States in No. 13–212, at 43–44. Such a search would be like finding a key in a suspect's pocket and arguing that it allowed law enforcement to unlock and search a house. But officers searching a phone's data would not typically know whether the information they are viewing was stored locally at the time of the arrest or has been pulled from the cloud.

Although the Government recognizes the problem, its proposed solutions are unclear. It suggests that officers could disconnect a phone from the network before searching the device—the very solution whose feasibility it contested with respect to the threat of remote wiping. Compare Tr. of Oral Arg. in No. 13–132, at 50–51, with Tr. of Oral Arg. in No. 13–212, pp. 13–14. Alternatively, the Government proposes that law enforcement agencies "develop protocols to address" concerns raised by cloud computing. Reply Brief in No. 13–212, pp. 14–15. Probably a good idea, but the Founders did not fight a revolution to gain the right to government agency protocols. The possibility that a search might extend well beyond papers and effects in the physical proximity of an arrestee is yet another reason that the privacy interests here dwarf those in Robinson.

C

Apart from their arguments for a direct extension of Robinson, the United States and California offer various fallback options for permitting warrantless cell phone searches under certain circumstances. Each of the proposals is flawed and contravenes our general preference to provide clear guidance to law enforcement through categorical rules. "[I]f police are to have workable rules, the balancing of the competing interests . . . 'must in large part be done on a categorical basis— not in an ad hoc, case-by-case fashion by individual police officers.' " Michigan v. Summers, 452 U. S. 692, 705, n. 19 (1981) (quoting Dunaway v. New York, 442 U. S. 200–220 (1979) (White, J., concurring)).

The United States first proposes that the

Gant standard be imported from the vehicle context, allowing a warrantless search of an arrestee's cell phone whenever it is reasonable to believe that the phone contains evidence of the crime of arrest. But Gant relied on "circumstances unique to the vehicle context" to endorse a search solely for the purpose of gathering evidence. 556 U. S., at 343. Justice Scalia's Thornton opinion, on which Gant was based, explained that those unique circumstances are "a reduced expectation of privacy" and "heightened law enforcement needs" when it comes to motor vehicles. 541 U. S., at 631; see also Wyoming v. Houghton, 526 U. S., at 303–304. For reasons that we have explained, cell phone searches bear neither of those characteristics.

At any rate, a Gant standard would prove no practical limit at all when it comes to cell phone searches. In the vehicle context, Gant generally protects against searches for evidence of past crimes. See 3 W. LaFave, Search and Seizure §7.1(d), at 709, and n. 191. In the cell phone context, however, it is reasonable to expect that incriminating information will be found on a phone regardless of when the crime occurred. Similarly, in the vehicle context Gant restricts broad searches resulting from minor crimes such as traffic violations. See id., §7.1(d), at 713, and n. 204. That would not necessarily be true for cell phones. It would be a particularly inexperienced or unimaginative law enforcement officer who could not come up with sev-eral reasons to suppose evidence of just about any crime could be found on a cell phone. Even an individual pulled over for something as basic as speeding might well have locational data dispositive of guilt on his phone. An individual pulled over for reckless driving might have evidence on the phone that shows whether he was texting while driving. The sources of potential pertinent information are virtually unlimited, so applying the Gant standard to cell phones would in effect give "police officers unbridled discretion to rummage at will among a person's private effects." 556 U. S., at 345.

The United States also proposes a rule that would restrict the scope of a cell phone search to those areas of the phone where an officer reasonably believes that infor-mation relevant to the crime, the arrestee's identity, or officer safety will be discovered. See Brief for United States in No. 13–212, at 51–53. This approach would again impose few meaningful constraints on officers. The proposed categories would sweep in a great deal of information, and officers would not always be able to discern in advance what information would be found where.

We also reject the United States' final suggestion that officers should always be able to search a phone's call log, as they did in Wurie's case. The Government relies on Smith v. Maryland, 442 U. S. 735 (1979), which held that no warrant was required to use a pen register at telephone company premises to identify numbers dialed by a particular caller. The Court in that case, however, concluded that the use of a pen register was not a "search" at all under the Fourth Amendment. See id., at 745–746. There is no dispute here that the officers engaged in a search of Wurie's cell phone. Moreover, call logs typically contain more than just phone numbers; they include any identifying information that an individual might add, such as the label "my house" in Wurie's case.

Finally, at oral argument California suggested a different limiting principle, under which officers could search cell phone data if they could have obtained the same information from a pre-digital counterpart. See Tr. of Oral Arg. in No. 13–132, at 38–43; see also Flores-Lopez, 670 F. 3d, at 807 ("If police are entitled to open a pocket diary to copy the owner's address, they should be entitled to turn on a cell phone to learn its number."). But the fact that a search in the pre-digital era could have turned up a photograph or two in a wallet does not justify a search of thousands of photos in a digital gallery. The fact that someone could have tucked a paper bank statement in a pocket does not justify a search of every bank statement from the last five years. And to make matters worse, such an analogue test would allow law enforcement to search a range of items contained on a phone, even though people would be unlikely to carry such a variety of information in physical form. In Riley's case, for example, it is implausible that he would have strolled around with video tapes, photo albums, and an address book all crammed into his pockets. But because each of those items has a pre-digital analogue, police under California's proposal would be able to search a phone for all of those items—a significant diminution of privacy.

In addition, an analogue test would launch courts on a difficult line-drawing expedition to determine which digital files are comparable to physical records. Is an e-mail equivalent to a letter? Is a voicemail equivalent to a phone message slip? It is not clear how officers could make these kinds of decisions before conducting a search, or how courts would apply the proposed rule after the fact. An analogue test would "keep defendants and judges guessing for years to come." Sykes v. United States, 564 U. S. 1, ____ (2011) (Scalia, J., dissenting) (slip op., at 7) (discussing the Court's analogue test under the Armed Career Criminal Act).

IV

We cannot deny that our decision today will have an impact on the ability of law enforcement to combat crime. Cell phones have become important tools in facilitating coordination and communication among members of criminal enterprises, and can provide valuable incriminating information about dangerous criminals. Privacy comes at a cost.

Our holding, of course, is not that the information on a cell phone is immune from search; it is instead that a warrant is generally required before such a search, even when a cell phone is seized incident to arrest. Our cases have historically recognized that the warrant requirement is "an important working part of our machinery of gov-ernment," not merely "an inconvenience to be somehow 'weighed' against the claims of police efficiency." Coolidge v. New Hampshire, 403 U. S. 443, 481 (1971). Recent technological advances similar to those discussed here have, in addition, made the process of obtaining a warrant itself more efficient. See McNeely, 569 U. S., at ____ (slip op., at 11–12); id., at ____ (Roberts, C. J., concurring in part and dissenting in part) (slip op., at 8) (describing jurisdiction where "police officers can e-mail warrant requests to judges' iPads [and] judges have signed such warrants and e-mailed them back to officers in less than 15 minutes").

Moreover, even though the search incident to arrest exception does not apply to cell phones, other case-specific exceptions may still justify a warrantless search of a particular phone. "One well-recognized exception applies when ' "the exigencies of the situation" make the needs of law enforcement so compelling that [a] warrantless search is objectively reasonable under the Fourth Amendment.' " Kentucky v. King, 563 U. S., at ____ (slip op., at 6) (quoting Mincey v. Arizona, 437 U. S. 385, 394 (1978)). Such exigencies could include the need to prevent the imminent destruction of evidence in individual cases, to pursue a fleeing suspect, and to assist persons who are seriously injured or are threatened with imminent injury. 563 U. S., at ____. In Chadwick, for example, the Court held that the exception for searches incident to arrest did not justify a search of the trunk at issue, but noted that "if officers have reason to believe that luggage contains some immediately dangerous instrumentality, such as explosives, it would be foolhardy to transport it to the station house without opening the luggage." 433 U. S., at 15, n. 9.

In light of the availability of the exigent circumstances exception, there is no reason to believe that law enforcement officers will not be able to address some of the more extreme hypotheticals that have been suggested: a suspect texting an accomplice who, it is feared, is preparing to detonate a bomb, or a child abductor who may have information about the child's location on his cell phone. The defendants here recognize—indeed, they stress—that such fact-specific threats may justify a warrantless search of cell phone data. See Reply Brief in No. 13–132, at 8–9; Brief for Respondent in No. 13–212, at 30, 41. The critical point is that, unlike the search incident to arrest exception, the exigent circumstances exception requires a court to examine whether an emergency justified a warrantless search in each particular case. See McNeely, supra, at ____ (slip op., at 6). 2

    *   *   *

Our cases have recognized that the Fourth Amendment was the founding generation's response to the reviled "general warrants" and "writs of assistance" of the colonial era, which allowed British officers to rummage through homes in an unrestrained search for evidence of criminal activity. Opposition to such searches was in fact one of the driving forces behind the Revolution itself. In 1761, the patriot James Otis delivered a speech in Boston denouncing the use of writs of assistance. A young John Adams was there, and he would later write that "[e]very man of a crowded audience appeared to me to go away, as I did, ready to take arms against writs of assistance." 10 Works of John Adams 247–248 (C. Adams ed. 1856). According to Adams, Otis's speech was "the first scene of the first act of opposition to the arbitrary claims of Great Britain. Then and there the child Independence was born." Id., at 248 (quoted in Boyd v. United States, 116 U. S. 616, 625 (1886)).

Modern cell phones are not just another technological convenience. With all they contain and all they may reveal, they hold for many Americans "the privacies of life," Boyd, supra, at 630. The fact that technology now allows an individual to carry such information in his hand does not make the information any less worthy of the protection for which the Founders fought. Our answer to the question of what police must do before searching a cell phone seized incident to an arrest is accordingly simple—get a warrant.

We reverse the judgment of the California Court of Appeal in No. 13–132 and remand the case for further proceedings not inconsistent with this opinion. We affirm the judgment of the First Circuit in No. 13–212.

It is so ordered.

Notes

1 Because the United States and California agree that these cases involve searches incident to arrest, these cases do not implicate the question whether the collection or inspection of aggregated digital information amounts to a search under other circumstances.

2 In Wurie's case, for example, the dissenting First Circuit judge argued that exigent circumstances could have justified a search of Wurie's phone. See 728 F. 3d 1, 17 (2013) (opinion of Howard, J.) (discussing the repeated unanswered calls from "my house," the suspected location of a drug stash). But the majority concluded that the Government had not made an exigent circumstances argument. See id., at 1. The Government acknowledges the same in this Court. See Brief for United States in No. 13–212, p. 28, n. 8.

Carroll v. Carman (Nov 10, 2014)

Per Curiam.

On July 3, 2009, the Pennsylvania State Police Department received a report that a man named Michael Zita had stolen a car and two loaded handguns. The report also said that Zita might have fled to the home of Andrew and Karen Carman. The department sent Officers Jeremy Carroll and Brian Roberts to the Carmans' home to investigate. Neither officer had been to the home before. 749 F. 3d 192, 195 (CA3 2014).

The officers arrived in separate patrol cars around 2:30 p.m. The Carmans' house sat on a corner lot—the front of the house faced a main street while the left (as viewed from the front) faced a side street. The officers initially drove to the front of the house, but after discovering that parking was not available there, turned right onto the side street. As they did so, they saw several cars parked side-by-side in a gravel parking area on the left side of the Carmans' property. The officers parked in the "first available spot," at "the far rear of the property." Ibid. (quoting Tr. 70 (Apr. 8, 2013)).

The officers exited their patrol cars. As they looked toward the house, the officers saw a small structure (either a carport or a shed) with its door open and a light on. Id., at 71. Thinking someone might be inside, Officer Carroll walked over, "poked [his] head" in, and said "Pennsylvania State Police." 749 F. 3d, at 195 (quoting Tr. 71 (Apr. 8, 2013); alteration in original). No one was there, however, so the officers continued walking toward the house. As they approached, they saw a sliding glass door that opened onto a ground-level deck. Carroll thought the sliding glass door "looked like a customary entryway," so he and Officer Roberts decided to knock on it. 749 F. 3d, at 195 (quoting Tr. 83 (Apr. 8, 2013)).

As the officers stepped onto the deck, a man came out of the house and "belligerent[ly] and aggressively approached" them. 749 F. 3d, at 195. The officers identified themselves, explained they were looking for Michael Zita, and asked the man for his name. The man refused to answer. Instead, he turned away from the officers and appeared to reach for his waist. Id., at 195–196. Carroll grabbed the man's right arm to make sure he was not reaching for a weapon. The man twisted away from Carroll, lost his balance, and fell into the yard. Id., at 196.

At that point, a woman came out of the house and asked what was happening. The officers again explained that they were looking for Zita. The woman then identified herself as Karen Carman, identified the man as her husband, Andrew Carman, and told the officers that Zita was not there. In response, the officers asked for permission to search the house for Zita. Karen Carman consented, and everyone went inside. Ibid.

The officers searched the house, but did not find Zita. They then left. The Carmans were not charged with any crimes. Ibid.

The Carmans later sued Officer Carroll in Federal District Court under 42 U. S. C. §1983. Among other things, they alleged that Carroll unlawfully entered their property in violation of the Fourth Amendment when he went into their backyard and onto their deck without a warrant. 749 F. 3d, at 196.

At trial, Carroll argued that his entry was lawful under the "knock and talk" exception to the warrant requirement. That exception, he contended, allows officers to knock on someone's door, so long as they stay "on those portions of [the] property that the general public is allowed to go on." Tr. 7 (Apr. 8, 2013). The Carmans responded that a normal visitor would have gone to their front door, rather than into their backyard or onto their deck. Thus, they argued, the "knock and talk" exception did not apply.

At the close of Carroll's case in chief, the parties each moved for judgment as a matter of law. The District Court denied both motions, and sent the case to a jury. As relevant here, the District Court instructed the jury that the "knock and talk" exception "allows officers without a warrant to knock on a resident's door or otherwise approach the residence seeking to speak to the inhabitants, just as any private citizen might." Id., at 24 (Apr. 10, 2013). The District Court further explained that "officers should restrict their movements to walkways, driveways, porches and places where visitors could be expected to go." Ibid. The jury then returned a verdict for Carroll.

The Carmans appealed, and the Court of Appeals for the Third Circuit reversed in relevant part. The court held that Officer Carroll violated the Fourth Amendment as a matter of law because the "knock and talk" exception "requires that police officers begin their encounter at the front door, where they have an implied invitation to go." 749 F. 3d, at 199. The court also held that Carroll was not entitled to qualified immunity because his actions violated clearly established law. Ibid. The court therefore reversed the District Court and held that the Carmans were entitled to judgment as a matter of law.

Carroll petitioned for certiorari. We grant the petition and reverse the Third Circuit's determination that Carroll was not entitled to qualified immunity.

A government official sued under §1983 is entitled to qualified immunity unless the official violated a statutory or constitutional right that was clearly established at the time of the challenged conduct. See Ashcroft v. al-Kidd, 563 U. S. ____, ____ (2011) (slip op., at 3). A right is clearly established only if its contours are sufficiently clear that "a reasonable official would understand that what he is doing violates that right." Anderson v. Creighton, 483 U. S. 635, 640 (1987) . In other words, "existing precedent must have placed the statutory or constitutional question beyond debate." al-Kidd, 563 U. S., at ____ (slip op., at 9). This doctrine "gives government officials breathing room to make reasonable but mistaken judgments," and "protects 'all but the plainly incompetent or those who knowingly violate the law.'" Id., at ____ (slip op., at 12) (quoting Malley

v. Briggs, 475 U. S. 335, 341 (1986)).

Here the Third Circuit cited only a single case to support its decision that Carroll was not entitled to qualified immunity—Estate of Smith v. Marasco, 318 F. 3d 497 (CA3 2003). Assuming for the sake of argument that a controlling circuit precedent could constitute clearly established federal law in these circumstances, see Reichle v. Howards, 566 U. S. ____, ____ (2012) (slip op., at 7), Marasco does not clearly establish that Carroll violated the Carmans' Fourth Amendment rights.

In Marasco, two police officers went to Robert Smith's house and knocked on the front door. When Smith did not respond, the officers went into the backyard, and at least one entered the garage. 318 F. 3d, at 519. The court acknowledged that the officers' "entry into the curtilage after not receiving an answer at the front door might be reasonable." Id., at 520. It held, however, that the District Court had not made the factual findings needed to decide that issue. Id., at 521. For example, the Third Circuit noted that the record "did not discuss the layout of the property or the position of the officers on that prop-erty," and that "there [was] no indication of whether the officers followed a path or other apparently open route that would be suggestive of reasonableness." Ibid. The court therefore remanded the case for further proceedings.

In concluding that Officer Carroll violated clearly established law in this case, the Third Circuit relied exclusively on Marasco's statement that "entry into the curtilage after not receiving an answer at the front door might be reasonable." Id., at 520; see 749 F. 3d, at 199 (quoting Marasco, supra, at 520). In the court's view, that statement clearly established that a "knock and talk" must begin at the front door. But that conclusion does not follow. Marasco held that an unsuccessful "knock and talk" at the front door does not automatically allow officers to go onto other parts of the property. It did not hold, however, that knocking on the front door is required before officers go onto other parts of the property that are open to visitors. Thus, Marasco simply did not answer the question whether a "knock and talk" must begin at the front door when visitors may also go to the back door. Indeed, the house at issue seems not to have even had a back door, let alone one that visitors could use. 318 F. 3d, at 521.

Moreover, Marasco expressly stated that "there [was] no indication of whether the officers followed a path or other apparently open route that would be suggestive of reasonableness." Ibid. That makes Marasco wholly different from this case, where the jury necessarily decided that Carroll "restrict[ed] [his] movements to walkways, driveways, porches and places where visitors could be expected to go." Tr. 24 (Apr. 10, 2013).

To the extent that Marasco says anything about this case, it arguably supports Carroll's view. In Marasco, the Third Circuit noted that "[o]fficers are allowed to knock on a residence's door or otherwise approach the residence seeking to speak to the inhabitants just as any private citizen may." 318 F. 3d, at 519. The court also said that, " 'when the police come on to private property . . . and restrict their movements to places visitors could be expected to go (e.g., walkways, driveways, porches), observations made from such vantage points are not covered by the Fourth Amendment.' " Ibid. (quoting 1 W. LaFave, Search and Seizure §2.3(f) (3d ed. 1996 and Supp. 2003) (footnotes omitted)). Had Carroll read those statements before going to the Carmans' house, he may have concluded—quite reasonably—that he was allowed to knock on any door that was open to visitors. 1 *

The Third Circuit's decision is even more perplexing in comparison to the decisions of other federal and state courts, which have rejected the rule the Third Circuit adopted here. For example, in United States v. Titemore, 437 F. 3d 251 (CA2 2006), a police officer approached a house that had two doors. The first was a traditional door that opened onto a driveway; the second was a sliding glass door that opened onto a small porch. The officer chose to knock on the latter. Id., at 253–254. On appeal, the defendant argued that the officer had unlawfully entered his property without a warrant in violation of the Fourth Amendment. Id., at 255–256. But the Second Circuit rejected that argument. As the court explained, the sliding glass door was "a primary entrance visible to and used by the public." Id., at 259. Thus, "[b]ecause [the officer] approached a principal entrance to the home using a route that other visitors could be expected to take," the court held that he did not violate the Fourth Amendment. Id., at 252.

The Seventh Circuit's decision in United States v. James, 40 F. 3d 850 (1994), vacated on other grounds, 516 U. S. 1022 (1995), provides another example. There, police officers approached a duplex with multiple entrances. Bypassing the front door, the officers "used a paved walkway along the side of the duplex leading to the rear side door." 40 F. 3d, at 862. On appeal, the defendant argued that the officers violated his Fourth Amendment rights when they went to the rear side door. The Seventh Circuit rejected that argument, explaining that the rear side door was "accessible to the general public" and "was commonly used for entering the duplex from the nearby alley." Ibid. In situations "where the back door of a residence is readily accessible to the general public," the court held, "the Fourth Amendment is not implicated when police officers approach that door in the reasonable belief that it is a principal means of access to the dwelling." Ibid. See also, e.g., United States v. Garcia, 997 F. 2d 1273, 1279–1280 (CA9 1993) ("If the front and back of a residence are readily accessible from a public place, like the driveway and parking area here, the Fourth Amendment is not implicated when officers go to the back door reasonably believing it is used as a principal entrance to the dwelling"); State v. Domicz, 188 N. J. 285, 302, 907 A. 2d 395, 405

(2006) ("when a law enforcement officer walks to a front or back door for the purpose of making contact with a resident and reasonably believes that the door is used by visitors, he is not unconstitutionally trespassing on to the property").

We do not decide today whether those cases were correctly decided or whether a police officer may conduct a "knock and talk" at any entrance that is open to visitors rather than only the front door. "But whether or not the constitutional rule applied by the court below was correct, it was not 'beyond debate.'" Stanton v. Sims, 571 U. S. ___, ___ (2013) (per curiam) (slip op., at 8) (quoting al-Kidd, 563 U. S., at ___ (slip op., at 9)). The Third Circuit therefore erred when it held that Carroll was not entitled to qualified immunity.

The petition for certiorari is granted. The judgment of the United States Court of Appeals for the Third Circuit is reversed, and the case is remanded for further proceedings consistent with this opinion.

It is so ordered.

Notes

1* In a footnote, the Court of Appeals "recognize[d] that there may be some instances in which the front door is not the entrance used by visitors," but noted that "this is not one such instance." 749 F. 3d 192, 198, n. 6 (2014) (emphasis added). This footnote still reflects the Third Circuit's view that the "knock and talk" exception is available for only one entrance to a dwelling, "which in most circumstances is the front door." Id., at 198. Cf. United States v. Perea-Rey, 680 F. 3d 1179, 1188 (CA9 2012) ("Officers conducting a knock and talk . . . need not approach only a specific door if there are multiple doors accessible to the public.").

Heien v. North Carolina (Dec 15, 2014)

Chief Justice Roberts delivered the opinion of the Court.

The Fourth Amendment prohibits "unreasonable searches and seizures." Under this standard, a search or seizure may be permissible even though the justification for the action includes a reasonable factual mistake. An officer might, for example, stop a motorist for traveling alone in a high-occupancy vehicle lane, only to discover upon approaching the car that two children are slumped over asleep in the back seat. The driver has not violated the law, but neither has the officer violated the Fourth Amendment.

But what if the police officer's reasonable mistake is not one of fact but of law? In this case, an officer stopped a vehicle because one of its two brake lights was out, but a court later determined that a single working brake light was all the law required. The question presented is whether such a mistake of law can nonetheless give rise to the reasonable suspicion necessary to uphold the seizure under the Fourth Amendment. We hold that it can. Because the officer's mistake about the brake-light law was reasonable, the stop in this case was lawful under the Fourth Amendment.

I

On the morning of April 29, 2009, Sergeant Matt Da-risse of the Surry County Sheriff's Department sat in his patrol car near Dobson, North Carolina, observing northbound traffic on Interstate 77. Shortly before 8 a.m., a Ford Escort passed by. Darisse thought the driver looked "very stiff and nervous," so he pulled onto the interstate and began following the Escort. A few miles down the road, the Escort braked as it approached a slower vehicle, but only the left brake light came on. Noting the faulty right brake light, Darisse activated his vehicle's lights and pulled the Escort over. App. 4–7, 15–16.

Two men were in the car: Maynor Javier Vasquez sat behind the wheel, and petitioner Nicholas Brady Heien lay across the rear seat.

Sergeant Darisse explained to Vasquez that as long as his license and registration checked out, he would receive only a warning ticket for the broken brake light. A records check revealed no problems with the documents, and Darisse gave Vasquez the warning ticket. But Darisse had become suspicious during the course of the stop—Vasquez appeared nervous, Heien remained lying down the entire time, and the two gave inconsistent answers about their destination. Darisse asked Vasquez if he would be willing to answer some questions. Vasquez assented, and Darisse asked whether the men were transporting various types of contraband. Told no, Darisse asked whether he could search the Escort. Vasquez said he had no objection, but told Darisse he should ask Heien, because Heien owned the car. Heien gave his consent, and Darisse, aided by a fellow officer who had since arrived, began a thorough search of the vehicle. In the side compartment of a duffle bag, Darisse found a sandwich bag containing cocaine. The officers arrested both men. 366 N. C. 271, 272–273, 737 S. E. 2d 351, 352–353 (2012); App. 5–6, 25, 37.

The State charged Heien with attempted trafficking in cocaine. Heien moved to suppress the evidence seized from the car, contending that the stop and search had violated the Fourth Amendment of the United States Constitution. After a hearing at which both officers testified and the State played a video recording of the stop, the trial court denied the suppression motion, concluding that the faulty brake light had given Sergeant Darisse reasonable suspicion to initiate the stop, and that Heien's subsequent consent to the search was valid. Heien pleaded guilty but reserved his right to appeal the suppression decision. App. 1, 7–10, 12, 29, 43–44.

The North Carolina Court of Appeals reversed. 214 N. C. App. 515, 714 S. E. 2d 827 (2011). The initial stop was not valid, the court held, because driving with only one working brake light was not actually a violation of North Carolina law. The relevant provision of the vehicle code provides that a car must be

"equipped with a stop lamp on the rear of the vehicle. The stop lamp shall display a red or amber light visible from a distance of not less than 100 feet to the rear in normal sunlight, and shall be actuated upon application of the service (foot) brake. The stop lamp may be incorporated into a unit with one or moreother rear lamps." N. C. Gen. Stat. Ann. §20–129(g) (2007).

Focusing on the statute's references to "a stop lamp" and "[t]he stop lamp" in the singular, the court concluded that a vehicle is required to have only one working brake light—which Heien's vehicle indisputably did. The justification for the stop was therefore "objectively unreason-able," and the stop violated the Fourth Amendment. 214 N. C. App., at 518–522, 714 S. E. 2d, at 829–831.

The State appealed, and the North Carolina Supreme Court reversed. 366 N. C. 271, 737 S. E. 2d 351. Noting that the State had chosen not to seek review of the Court of Appeals' interpretation of the vehicle code, the North Carolina Supreme Court assumed for purposes of its decision that the faulty brake light was not a violation. Id., at 275, 737 S. E. 2d, at 354. But the court concluded that, for several reasons, Sergeant Darisse could have reasonably, even if mistakenly, read the vehicle code to require that both brake lights be in good working order. Most notably, a nearby code provision requires that "all originally equipped rear lamps" be functional. Id., at 282–283, 737 S. E. 2d, at 358–359 (quoting N. C. Gen. Stat. Ann. §20–129(d)). Because Sergeant Darisse's mistaken understanding of the vehicle code was reasonable, the stop was valid. "An officer may make a mistake, including a mistake of law, yet still act reasonably under the circumstances. . . . [W]hen an officer acts reasonably under the circumstances, he is not violating the Fourth Amendment." Id., at 279, 737

S. E. 2d, at 356.

The North Carolina Supreme Court remanded to the Court of Appeals to address Heien's other arguments for suppression (which are not at issue here). Id., at 283, 737 S. E. 2d, at 359. The Court of Appeals rejected those arguments and affirmed the trial court's denial of his motion to suppress. ____ N. C. App. ____, 741 S. E. 2d 1 (2013). The North Carolina Supreme Court affirmed in turn. 367 N. C. 163, 749 S. E. 2d 278 (2013). We granted certiorari. 572 U. S. ____ (2014).

II

The Fourth Amendment provides:

"The right of the people to be secure in their persons, houses, papers, and effects, against unreason-able searches and seizures, shall not be violated, and no Warrants shall issue, but upon probable cause, supported by Oath or affirmation, and particularly describing the place to be searched, and the persons or things to be seized."

A traffic stop for a suspected violation of law is a "seizure" of the occupants of the vehicle and therefore must be conducted in accordance with the Fourth Amendment. Brendlin v. California, 551 U. S. 249–259 (2007). All parties agree that to justify this type of seizure, officers need only "reasonable suspicion"—that is, "a particularized and objective basis for suspecting the particular person stopped" of breaking the law. Prado Navarette v. California, 572 U. S. ____, ____ (2014) (slip op., at 3) (internal quotation marks omitted). The question here is whether reasonable suspicion can rest on a mistaken understanding of the scope of a legal prohibition. We hold that it can.

As the text indicates and we have repeatedly affirmed, "the ultimate touchstone of the Fourth Amendment is 'reasonableness.'" Riley v. California, 573 U. S. ____, ____ (2014) (slip op., at 5) (some internal quotation marks omitted). To be reasonable is not to be perfect, and so the Fourth Amendment allows for some mistakes on the part of government officials, giving them "fair leeway for enforcing the law in the community's protection." Brinegar v. United States, 338 U. S. 160, 176 (1949) . We have recognized that searches and seizures based on mistakes of fact can be reasonable. The warrantless search of a home, for instance, is reasonable if undertaken with the consent of a resident, and remains lawful when officers obtain the consent of someone who reasonably appears to be but is not in fact a resident. See Illinois v. Rodriguez, 497 U. S. 177–186 (1990). By the same token, if officers with probable cause to arrest a suspect mistakenly arrest an individual matching the suspect's description, neither the seizure nor an accompanying search of the arrestee would be unlawful. See Hill v. California, 401 U. S. 797–805 (1971). The limit is that "the mistakes must be those of reasonable men." Brinegar, supra, at 176.

But reasonable men make mistakes of law, too, and such mistakes are no less compatible with the concept of reasonable suspicion. Reasonable suspicion arises from the combination of an officer's understanding of the facts and his understanding of the relevant law. The officer may be reasonably mistaken on either ground. Whether the facts turn out to be not what was thought, or the law turns out to be not what was thought, the result is the same: the facts are outside the scope of the law. There is no reason, under the text of the Fourth Amendment or our precedents, why this same result should be acceptable when reached by way of a reasonable mistake of fact, but not when reached by way of a similarly reasonable mistake of law.

The dissent counters that our cases discussing probable cause and reasonable suspicion, most notably Ornelas v. United States, 517 U. S. 690–697 (1996), have contained "scarcely a peep" about mistakes of law. Post, at 2–3 (opinion of Sotomayor, J.). It would have been surprising, of course, if they had, since none of those cases involved a mistake of law.

Although such recent cases did not address mistakes of law, older precedents did. In fact, cases dating back two centuries support treating legal and factual errors alike in this context. Customs statutes enacted by Congress not long after the founding authorized courts to issue certificates indemnifying customs officers against damages suits premised on unlawful seizures. See, e.g., Act of Mar. 2, 1799, ch. 22, §89, 1Stat. 695–696. Courts were to issue such certificates on a showing that the officer had "reasonable cause"—a synonym for "probable cause"—for the challenged seizure. Ibid.; see Stacey v. Emery, 97 U. S. 642, 646 (1878); United States v. Riddle, 5 Cranch 311 (1809). In United States v. Riddle, a customs officer seized goods on the ground that the English shipper had violated the customs laws by preparing an invoice that undervalued the merchandise, even though the American consignee declared the true value to the customs collector. Chief Justice Marshall held that there had been no violation of the customs law because, whatever the shipper's intention, the consignee had not actually attempted to defraud the Government. Nevertheless, because "the construction of the law was liable to some question," he affirmed the issuance of a certificate of probable cause: "A doubt as to the true construction of the law is as reasonable a cause for seizure as a doubt respecting the fact." Id., at 313.

This holding—that reasonable mistakes of law, like those of fact, would justify certificates of probable cause—was reiterated in a number of 19th-century decisions. See, e.g., The Friendship, 9 F. Cas. 825, 826 (No. 5,125) (CC Mass. 1812) (Story, J.); United States v. The Reindeer, 27 F. Cas. 758, 768 (No. 16,145) (CC RI 1848); United States v. The Recorder, 27 F. Cas. 723 (No. 16,130) (CC SDNY 1849). By the Civil War, there had been "numerous cases in which [a] captured vessel was in no fault, and had not, under a true construction of the law, presented even ground of suspicion, and yet the captor was exonerated because he acted under an honest mistake of the law." The La Manche, 14 F. Cas. 965, 972 (No. 8,004) (D Mass. 1863).

Riddle and its progeny are not directly on point. Chief Justice Marshall was not construing the Fourth Amendment, and a certificate of probable cause functioned much like a modern-day finding of qualified immunity, which depends on an inquiry distinct from whether an officer has committed a constitutional violation. See, e.g., Carroll v. Carman, ante, at 7 (per curiam). But Chief Justice Marshall was nevertheless explaining the concept of probable cause, which, he noted elsewhere, "in all cases of seizure, has a fixed and well known meaning. It imports a seizure made under circumstances which warrant suspicion." Locke v. United States, 7 Cranch 339, 348 (1813). We have said the phrase "probable cause" bore this "fixed and well known meaning" in the Fourth Amendment, see Brinegar, supra, at 175, and n. 14, and Riddle illustrates that it encompassed suspicion based on reasonable mistakes of both fact and law. No decision of this Court in the two centuries since has undermined that understanding. 1

The contrary conclusion would be hard to reconcile with a much more recent precedent. In Michigan v. DeFillippo, 443 U. S. 31 (1979), we addressed the validity of an arrest made under a criminal law later declared unconstitu-tional. A Detroit ordinance that authorized police officers to stop and question individuals suspected of criminal activ-ity also made it an offense for such an individual "to refuse to identify himself and produce evidence of his identity." Id., at 33. Detroit police officers sent to investigate a report of public intoxication arrested Gary DeFillippo after he failed to identify himself. A search incident to arrest uncovered drugs, and DeFillippo was charged with possession of a controlled substance.

The Michigan Court of Appeals ordered the suppression of the drugs, concluding that the identification ordinance was unconstitutionally vague and that DeFillippo's arrest was therefore invalid. Id., at 34–35.

Accepting the unconstitutionality of the ordinance as a given, we nonetheless reversed. At the time the officers arrested DeFillippo, we explained, "there was no controlling precedent that this ordinance was or was not constitutional, and hence the conduct observed violated a presumptively valid ordinance." Id., at 37. Acknowledging that the outcome might have been different had the ordinance been "grossly and flagrantly unconstitutional," we concluded that under the circumstances "there was abundant probable cause to satisfy the constitutional prerequisite for an arrest." Id., at 37–38.

The officers were wrong in concluding that DeFillippo was guilty of a criminal offense when he declined to iden-tify himself. That a court only later declared the ordinance unconstitutional does not change the fact that DeFillippo's conduct was lawful when the officers observed it. See Danforth v. Minnesota, 552 U. S. 264, 271 (2008). But the officers' assumption that the law was valid was reason-able, and their observations gave them "abundant probable cause" to arrest DeFillippo. 443 U. S., at 37. Although DeFillippo could not be prosecuted under the identifica-tion ordinance, the search that turned up the drugs was constitutional.

Heien struggles to recast DeFillippo as a case solely about the exclusionary rule, not the Fourth Amendment itself. In his view, the officers' mistake of law resulted in a violation the Fourth Amendment, but suppression of the drugs was not the proper remedy. We did say in a footnote that suppression of the evidence found on DeFillippo would serve none of the purposes of the exclusionary rule. See id., at 38, n. 3. But that literally marginal discussion does not displace our express holding that the arrest was constitutionally valid because the officers had probable cause. See id., at 40. Nor, contrary to Heien's suggestion, did either United States v. Leon, 468 U. S. 897 (1984), or Illinois v. Gates, 462 U. S. 213 (1983), somehow erase that holding and transform DeFillippo into an exclusionary rule decision. See Brief for Petitioner 28–29. In Leon, we said DeFillippo paid "attention to the purposes underlying the exclusionary rule," but we also clarified that it did "not involv[e] the scope of the rule itself." 468 U. S., at 911–912. As for Gates, only Justice White's separate opinion (joined by no other Justice) discussed DeFillippo, and it acknowledged that "DeFillippo did not modify the exclusionary rule itself" but instead "upheld the validity of an arrest." 462 U. S., at 256, n. 12 (opinion concurring in judgment).

Heien is correct that in a number of decisions we have looked to the reasonableness of an officer's legal error in the course of considering the appropriate remedy for a constitutional violation, instead of whether there was a violation at all. See, e.g., Davis v. United States, 564 U. S. ____, ____ (2011) (slip op., at 11) (exclusionary rule); Illinois v. Krull, 480 U. S. 340–360 (1987) (exclusionary rule); Wilson v. Layne, 526 U. S. 603, 615 (1999) (qualified immunity); Anderson v. Creighton, 483 U. S. 635, 641 (1987) (qualified immunity). In those cases, however, we had already found or assumed a Fourth Amendment violation. An officer's mistaken view that the conduct at issue did not give rise to such a violation—no matter how reason-able—could not change that ultimate conclusion. See Brief for Respondent 29–31; Brief for United States as Amicus Curiae 30, n. 3. Any consideration of the reasonableness of an officer's mistake was therefore limited to the separate matter of remedy.

Here, by contrast, the mistake of law relates to the antecedent question of whether it was reasonable for an officer to suspect that the defendant's conduct was illegal. If so, there was no violation of the Fourth Amendment in the first place. None of the cases Heien or the dissent cites precludes a court from considering a reasonable mistake of law in addressing that question. Cf. Herring v. United States, 555 U. S. 135, 139 (2009) (assuming a Fourth Amendment violation while rejecting application of the exclusionary rule, but noting that "[w]hen a probable-cause determination was based on reasonable but mistaken assumptions, the person subjected to a search or seizure has not necessarily been the victim of a constitutional violation").

Heien also contends that the reasons the Fourth Amendment allows some errors of fact do not extend to errors of law. Officers in the field must make factual assessments on the fly, Heien notes, and so deserve a margin of error. In Heien's view, no such margin is appropriate for questions of law: The statute here either requires one working brake light or two, and the answer does not turn on anything "an officer might suddenly confront in the field." Brief for Petitioner 21. But Heien's point does not consider the reality that an officer may "suddenly confront" a situation in the field as to which the application of a statute is unclear—however clear it may later become. A law prohibiting "vehicles" in the park either covers Segways or not, see A. Scalia & B. Garner, Reading Law: The Interpretation of Legal Texts 36–38 (2012), but an officer will nevertheless have to make a quick decision on the law the first time one whizzes by.

Contrary to the suggestion of Heien and amici, our decision does not discourage officers from learning the law. The Fourth Amendment tolerates only reasonable mistakes, and those mistakes—whether of fact or of law—must be objectively reasonable. We do not examine the subjective understanding of the particular officer involved. Cf. Whren v. United States, 517 U. S. 806, 813 (1996) . And the inquiry is not as forgiving as the one employed in the distinct context of deciding whether an officer is entitled to qualified immunity for a constitutional or statutory violation. Thus, an officer can gain no Fourth Amendment advantage through a sloppy study of the laws he is duty-bound to enforce.

Finally, Heien and amici point to the well-known maxim, "Ignorance of the law is no excuse," and contend that it is fundamentally unfair to let police officers get away with mistakes of law when the citizenry is accorded no such leeway. Though this argument has a certain rhetorical appeal, it misconceives the implication of the maxim. The true symmetry is this: Just as an individual generally cannot escape criminal liability based on a mistaken understanding of the law, so too the government cannot impose criminal liability based on a mistaken understanding of the law. If the law required two working brake lights, Heien could not escape a ticket by claiming he reasonably thought he needed only one; if the law required only one, Sergeant Darisse could not issue a valid ticket by claiming he reasonably thought drivers needed two. But just because mistakes of law cannot justify either the imposition or the avoidance of criminal liability, it does not follow that they cannot justify an investigatory stop. And Heien is not appealing a brake-light ticket; he is appealing a cocaine-trafficking conviction as to which there is no asserted mistake of fact or law.

III

Here we have little difficulty concluding that the officer's error of law was reasonable. Although the North Carolina statute at issue refers to "a stop lamp," suggesting the need for only a single working brake light, it also provides that "[t]he stop lamp may be incorporated into a unit with one or more other rear lamps." N. C. Gen. Stat. Ann. §20–129(g) (emphasis added). The use of "other" suggests to the everyday reader of English that a "stop lamp" is a type of "rear lamp." And another subsection of the same provision requires that vehicles "have all originally equipped rear lamps or the equivalent in good working order," §20–129(d), arguably indicating that if a vehicle has multiple "stop lamp[s]," all must be functional.

The North Carolina Court of Appeals concluded that the "rear lamps" discussed in subsection (d) do not include brake lights, but, given the "other," it would at least have been reasonable to think they did. Both the majority and the dissent in the North Carolina Supreme Court so concluded, and we agree. See 366 N. C., at 282–283, 737 S. E. 2d, at 358–359; id., at 283, 737 S. E. 2d, at 359 (Hudson, J., dissenting) (calling the Court of Appeals' decision "surprising"). This "stop lamp" provision, moreover, had never been previously construed by North Carolina's appellate courts. See id., at 283, 737 S. E. 2d, at 359 (majority opinion). It was thus objectively reasonable for an officer in Sergeant Darisse's position to think that Heien's faulty right brake light was a violation of North Carolina law. And because the mistake of law was reasonable, there was reasonable suspicion justifying the stop.

The judgment of the Supreme Court of North Carolina is

Affirmed.

Notes

1 The dissent contends that "the tolerance of mistakes of law in cases like Riddle was a result of the specific customs statute that Congress had enacted." Post, at 8, n. 3 (citing The Apollon, 9 Wheat. 362, 373 (1824) (Story, J.)). The relevant portion of The Apollon, however, addressed "the effect of probable cause," not what gave rise to it. Id., at 372 (emphasis added); see id., at 376 (finding it "unnecessary" to decide whether probable cause existed because it "would not, under the circumstances of this case, constitute a valid defence"). Justice Story understandably did not cite Riddle or discuss its tolerance of mistakes of law anywhere in The Apollon.

Rodriguez v. United States (April 21, 2015)

Justice Ginsburg delivered the opinion of the Court.

In Illinois v. Caballes, 543 U. S. 405 (2005), this Court held that a dog sniff conducted during a lawful traffic stop does not violate the Fourth Amendment's proscription of unreasonable seizures. This case presents the question whether the Fourth Amendment tolerates a dog sniff conducted after completion of a traffic stop. We hold that a police stop exceeding the time needed to handle the matter for which the stop was made violates the Constitution's shield against unreasonable seizures. A seizure justified only by a police-observed traffic violation, therefore, "become[s] unlawful if it is prolonged beyond the time reasonably required to complete th[e] mission" of issuing a ticket for the violation. Id., at 407. The Court so recognized in Caballes, and we adhere to the line drawn in that decision.

I

Just after midnight on March 27, 2012, police officer Morgan Struble observed a Mercury Mountaineer veer slowly onto the shoulder of Nebraska State Highway 275 for one or two seconds and then jerk back onto the road. Nebraska law prohibits driving on highway shoulders, see Neb. Rev. Stat. §60–6,142 (2010), and on that basis, Struble pulled the Mountaineer over at 12:06 a.m. Struble is a K–9 officer with the Valley Police Department in Ne-braska, and his dog Floyd was in his patrol car that night. Two men were in the Mountaineer: the driver, Dennys Rodriguez, and a front-seat passenger, Scott Pollman.

Struble approached the Mountaineer on the passenger's side. After Rodriguez identified himself, Struble asked him why he had driven onto the shoulder. Rodriguez replied that he had swerved to avoid a pothole. Struble then gathered

Rodriguez's license, registration, and proof of insurance, and asked Rodriguez to accompany him to the patrol car. Rodriguez asked if he was required to do so, and Struble answered that he was not. Rodriguez decided to wait in his own vehicle.

After running a records check on Rodriguez, Struble returned to the Mountaineer. Struble asked passenger Pollman for his driver's license and began to question him about where the two men were coming from and where they were going. Pollman replied that they had traveled to Omaha, Nebraska, to look at a Ford Mustang that was for sale and that they were returning to Norfolk, Ne-braska. Struble returned again to his patrol car, where he completed a records check on Pollman, and called for a second officer. Struble then began writing a warning ticket for Rodriguez for driving on the shoulder of the road.

Struble returned to Rodriguez's vehicle a third time to issue the written warning. By 12:27 or 12:28 a.m., Struble had finished explaining the warning to Rodriguez, and had given back to Rodriguez and Pollman the documents obtained from them. As Struble later testified, at that point, Rodriguez and Pollman "had all their documents back and a copy of the written warning. I got all the reason[s] for the stop out of the way[,] . . . took care of all the business." App. 70.

Nevertheless, Struble did not consider Rodriguez "free to leave." Id., at 69–70. Although justification for the traffic stop was "out of the way," id., at 70, Struble asked for permission to walk his dog around Rodriguez's vehicle. Rodriguez said no. Struble then instructed Rodriguez to turn off the ignition, exit the vehicle, and stand in front of the patrol car to wait for the second officer. Rodriguez complied. At 12:33 a.m., a deputy sheriff arrived. Struble retrieved his dog and led him twice around the Mountaineer. The dog alerted to the presence of drugs halfway through Struble's second pass. All told, seven or eight minutes had elapsed from the time Struble issued the written warning until the dog indicated the presence of drugs. A search of the vehicle revealed a large bag of methamphetamine.

Rodriguez was indicted in the United States District Court for the District of Nebraska on one count of possession with intent to distribute 50 grams or more of methamphetamine, in violation of 21 U. S. C. §§841(a)(1) and (b)(1). He moved to suppress the evidence seized from his car on the ground, among others, that Struble had prolonged the traffic stop without reasonable suspicion in order to conduct the dog sniff.

After receiving evidence, a Magistrate Judge recommended that the motion be denied. The Magistrate Judge found no probable cause to search the vehicle independent of the dog alert. App. 100 (apart from "information given by the dog," "Officer Struble had [no]thing other than a rather large hunch"). He further found that no reasonable suspicion supported the detention once Struble issued the written warning. He concluded, however, that under Eighth Circuit precedent, extension of the stop by "seven to eight minutes" for the dog sniff was only a de minimis intrusion on Rodriguez's Fourth Amendment rights and was therefore permissible.

The District Court adopted the Magistrate Judge's factual findings and legal conclusions and denied Rodriguez's motion to suppress. The court noted that, in the Eighth Circuit, "dog sniffs that occur within a short time following the completion of a traffic stop are not constitutionally prohibited if they constitute only de minimis intrusions." App. 114 (quoting United States v. Alexander, 448 F. 3d 1014, 1016 (CA8 2006)). The court thus agreed with the Magistrate Judge that the "7 to 10 minutes" added to the stop by the dog sniff "was not of constitu-tional significance." App. 114. Impelled by that decision, Rodriguez entered a conditional guilty plea and was sentenced to five years in prison.

The Eighth Circuit affirmed. The "seven- or eight-minute delay" in this case, the opinion noted, resembled delays that the court had previously ranked as permissible. 741 F. 3d 905, 907 (2014). The Court of Appeals thus ruled that the delay here constituted an acceptable "de minimis intrusion on Rodriguez's personal liberty." Id., at 908. Given that ruling, the court declined to reach the question whether Struble had reasonable suspicion to continue Rodriguez's detention after issuing the written warning.

We granted certiorari to resolve a division among lower courts on the question whether police routinely may extend an otherwise-completed traffic stop, absent reason-able suspicion, in order to conduct a dog sniff. 573 U. S. ___ (2014). Compare, e.g., United States v. Morgan, 270 F. 3d 625, 632 (CA8 2001) (postcompletion delay of "well under ten minutes" permissible), with, e.g., State v. Baker, 2010 UT 18, ¶13, 229 P. 3d 650, 658 (2010) ("[W]ithout additional reasonable suspicion, the officer must allow the seized person to depart once the purpose of the stop has concluded.").

II

A seizure for a traffic violation justifies a police investigation of that violation. "[A] relatively brief encounter," a routine traffic stop is "more analogous to a so-called 'Terry stop' . . . than to a formal arrest." Knowles v. Iowa, 525 U. S. 113, 117 (1998) (quoting Berkemer v. McCarty, 468 U. S. 420, 439 (1984), in turn citing Terry v. Ohio, 392 U. S. 1 (1968)). See also Arizona v. Johnson, 555 U. S. 323, 330 (2009). Like a Terry stop, the tolerable duration of police inquiries in the traffic-stop context is determined by the seizure's "mission"—to address the traffic violation that warranted the stop, Caballes, 543 U. S., at 407, and attend to related safety concerns, infra, at 6–7. See also United States v. Sharpe, 470 U. S. 675, 685 (1985); Florida v. Royer, 460 U. S. 491, 500 (1983) (plurality opinion) ("The scope of the detention must be carefully tailored to its underlying justification."). Because addressing the infraction is the purpose of the stop, it may "last no longer than is necessary to effectuate th[at] purpose." Ibid. See also Caballes, 543 U. S., at 407. Authority for the seizure thus ends when tasks tied to the traffic infraction are—or reasonably should have been—completed. See Sharpe, 470 U. S., at 686 (in determining the reasonable duration of a stop, "it [is] appropriate to examine whether the police diligently pursued [the] investigation").

Our decisions in Caballes and Johnson heed these constraints. In both cases, we concluded that the Fourth Amendment tolerated certain unrelated investigations that did not lengthen the roadside detention. Johnson, 555 U. S., at 327–328 (questioning); Caballes, 543 U. S., at 406, 408 (dog sniff). In Caballes, however, we cautioned that a traffic stop "can become unlawful if it is prolonged beyond the time reasonably required to complete th[e] mission" of issuing a warning ticket. 543 U. S., at 407. And we repeated that admonition in Johnson: The seizure remains lawful only "so long as [unrelated] inquiries do not measurably extend the duration of the stop." 555 U. S., at 333. See also Muehler v. Mena, 544 U. S. 93, 101 (2005) (because unrelated inquiries did not "exten[d] the time [petitioner] was detained[,] . . . no additional Fourth Amendment justification . . . was required"). An officer, in other words, may conduct certain unrelated checks during an otherwise lawful traffic stop. But contrary to Justice Alito's suggestion, post, at 4, n. 2, he may not do so in a way that prolongs the stop, absent the reasonable suspicion ordinarily demanded to justify detaining an individ-ual. But see post, at 1–2 (Alito, J., dissenting) (premising opinion on the dissent's own finding of "reasonable suspicion," although the District Court reached the opposite conclusion, and the Court of Appeals declined to consider the issue).

Beyond determining whether to issue a

traffic ticket, an officer's mission includes "ordinary inquiries incident to [the traffic] stop." Caballes, 543 U. S., at 408. Typically such inquiries involve checking the driver's license, determining whether there are outstanding warrants against the driver, and inspecting the automobile's registration and proof of insurance. See Delaware v. Prouse, 440 U. S. 648–660 (1979). See also 4 W. LaFave, Search and Seizure §9.3(c), pp. 507–517 (5th ed. 2012). These checks serve the same objective as enforcement of the traffic code: ensuring that vehicles on the road are operated safely and responsibly. See Prouse, 440 U. S., at 658–659; LaFave, Search and Seizure §9.3(c), at 516 (A "warrant check makes it possible to determine whether the apparent traffic violator is wanted for one or more previous traffic offenses.").

A dog sniff, by contrast, is a measure aimed at "detect[ing] evidence of ordinary criminal wrongdoing." Indianapolis v. Edmond, 531 U. S. 32–41 (2000). See also Florida v. Jardines, 569 U. S. 1, ___–___ (2013) (slip op., at 7–8). Candidly, the Government acknowledged at oral argument that a dog sniff, unlike the routine measures just mentioned, is not an ordinary incident of a traffic stop. See Tr. of Oral Arg. 33. Lacking the same close connection to roadway safety as the ordinary inquiries, a dog sniff is not fairly characterized as part of the officer's traffic mission.

In advancing its de minimis rule, the Eighth Circuit relied heavily on our decision in Pennsylvania v. Mimms, 434 U. S. 106 (1977) (per curiam). See United States v. $404,905.00 in U. S. Currency, 182 F. 3d 643, 649 (CA8 1999). In Mimms, we reasoned that the government's "legitimate and weighty" interest in officer safety outweighs the "de minimis" additional intrusion of requiring a driver, already lawfully stopped, to exit the vehicle. 434 U. S., at 110–111. See also Maryland v. Wilson, 519 U. S. 408–415 (1997) (passengers may be required to exit vehicle stopped for traffic violation). The Eighth Circuit,

echoed in Justice Thomas's dissent, believed that the imposition here similarly could be offset by the Government's "strong interest in interdicting the flow of illegal drugs along the nation's highways." $404,905.00 in U. S. Currency, 182 F. 3d, at 649; see post, at 9.

Unlike a general interest in criminal enforcement, however, the government's officer safety interest stems from the mission of the stop itself. Traffic stops are "especially fraught with danger to police officers," Johnson, 555 U. S., at 330 (internal quotation marks omitted), so an officer may need to take certain negligibly burdensome precautions in order to complete his mission safely. Cf. United States v. Holt, 264 F. 3d 1215, 1221–1222 (CA10 2001) (en banc) (recognizing officer safety justification for criminal record and outstanding warrant checks), abrogated on other grounds as recognized in United States v. Stewart, 473 F. 3d 1265, 1269 (CA10 2007). On-scene investigation into other crimes, however, detours from that mission. See supra, at 6–7. So too do safety precautions taken in order to facilitate such detours. But cf. post, at 2–3 (Alito, J., dissenting). Thus, even assuming that the imposition here was no more intrusive than the exit order in Mimms, the dog sniff could not be justified on the same basis. Highway and officer safety are interests different in kind from the Government's endeavor to detect crime in general or drug trafficking in particular.

The Government argues that an officer may "incremental[ly]" prolong a stop to conduct a dog sniff so long as the officer is reasonably diligent in pursuing the traffic-related purpose of the stop, and the overall duration of the stop remains reasonable in relation to the duration of other traffic stops involving similar circumstances. Brief for United States 36–39. The Government's argument, in effect, is that by completing all traffic-related tasks expeditiously, an officer can earn bonus time to pursue an unrelated criminal investigation. See also post, at 2–5 (Thomas, J., dissenting) (embracing the Government's argument). The reasonableness of a seizure, however, depends on what the police in fact do. See Knowles, 525 U. S., at 115–117. In this regard, the Government acknowledges that "an officer always has to be reasonably diligent." Tr. of Oral Arg. 49. How could diligence be gauged other than by noting what the officer actually did and how he did it? If an officer can complete traffic-based inquiries expeditiously, then that is the amount of "time reasonably required to complete [the stop's] mission." Caballes, 543 U. S., at 407. As we said in Caballes and reiterate today, a traffic stop "prolonged beyond" that point is "unlawful." Ibid. The critical question, then, is not whether the dog sniff occurs before or after the officer issues a ticket, as Justice Alito supposes, post, at 2–4, but whether conducting the sniff "prolongs"—i.e., adds time to—"the stop," supra, at 6.

III

The Magistrate Judge found that detention for the dog sniff in this case was not independently supported by individualized suspicion, see App. 100, and the District Court adopted the Magistrate Judge's findings, see id., at 112–113. The Court of Appeals, however, did not review that determination. But see post, at 1, 10–12 (Thomas, J., dissenting) (resolving the issue, nevermind that the Court of Appeals left it unaddressed); post, at 1–2 (Alito, J., dissenting) (upbraiding the Court for addressing the sole issue decided by the Court of Appeals and characterizing the Court's answer as "unnecessary" because the Court, instead, should have decided an issue the Court of Appeals did not decide). The question whether reasonable suspicion of criminal activity justified detaining Rodriguez beyond completion of the traffic infraction investigation, therefore, remains open for Eighth Circuit consideration on remand.

*   *   *

For the reasons stated, the judgment of the United States Court of Appeals for the Eighth Circuit is vacated, and the case is remanded for further proceedings consistent with this opinion.

It is so ordered.

City and County of San Francisco v. Sheehan (May 18, 2015) [Notes omitted]

Justice Alito delivered the opinion of the Court.

We granted certiorari to consider two questions relating to the manner in which San Francisco police officers arrested a woman who was suffering from a mental illness and had become violent. After reviewing the parties' submissions, we dismiss the first question as improvidently granted. We decide the second question and hold that the officers are entitled to qualified immunity because they did not violate any clearly established Fourth Amendment rights.

I

Petitioners are the City and County of San Francisco, California (San Francisco), and two police officers, Sergeant Kimberly Reynolds and Officer Kathrine Holder. Respondent is Teresa Sheehan, a woman who suffers from a schizoaffective disorder. Because this case arises in a summary judgment posture, we view the facts in the light most favorable to Sheehan, the nonmoving party. See, e.g., Plumhoff v. Rickard, 572 U. S. ____, ____–____ (2014) (slip op., at 1–2).

In August 2008, Sheehan lived in a group home for people dealing with mental illness. Although she shared common areas of the building with others, she had a private room. On August 7, Heath Hodge, a social worker who supervised the counseling staff in the building, attempted to visit Sheehan to conduct a welfare check. Hodge was concerned because Sheehan had stopped taking her medication, no longer spoke with her psychiatrist, and reportedly was no longer changing her clothes or eating. See 743 F. 3d 1211,

1218 (CA9 2014); App. 23–24.

Hodge knocked on Sheehan's door but received no answer. He then used a key to enter her room and found Sheehan on her bed. Initially, she would not respond to questions. But she then sprang up, reportedly yelling, "Get out of here! You don't have a warrant! I have a knife, and I'll kill you if I have to." Hodge left without seeing whether she actually had a knife, and Sheehan slammed the door shut behind him. See 743 F. 3d, at 1218.

Sheehan, Hodge realized, required "some sort of intervention," App. 96, but he also knew that he would need help. Hodge took steps to clear the building of other people and completed an application to have Sheehan detained for temporary evaluation and treatment. See Cal. Welf. & Inst. Code Ann. §5150 (West 2015 Cum. Supp.) (authorizing temporary detention of someone who "as a result of a mental health disorder, is a danger to others, or to himself or herself, or gravely disabled"). On that application, Hodge checked off boxes indicating that Sheehan was a "threat to others" and "gravely disabled," but he did not mark that she was a danger to herself. 743 F. 3d, at 1218. He telephoned the police and asked for help to take Sheehan to a secure facility.

Officer Holder responded to police dispatch and headed toward the group home. When she arrived, Holder reviewed the temporary-detention application and spoke with Hodge. Holder then sought assistance from Sergeant Reynolds, a more experienced officer. After Reynolds arrived and was brought up to speed, Hodge spoke with a nurse at the psychiatric emergency services unit at San Francisco General Hospital who said that the hospital would be able to admit Sheehan.

Accompanied by Hodge, the officers went to Sheehan's room, knocked on her door, announced who they were, and told Sheehan that "we want to help you." App. 36. When Sheehan did not answer, the officers used Hodge's key to enter the room. Sheehan reacted violently. She grabbed a kitchen knife with an approximately 5-inch blade and began approaching the officers, yelling something along the lines of "I am going to kill you. I don't need help. Get out." Ibid. See also id., at 284 ("[Q.] Did you tell them I'll kill you if you don't get out of here? A. Yes"). The officers—who did not have their weapons drawn—"retreated and Sheehan closed the door, leaving Sheehan in her room and the officers and Hodge in the hallway." 743 F. 3d, at 1219. The officers called for backup and sent Hodge downstairs to let in reinforcements when they arrived.

The officers were concerned that the door to Sheehan's room was closed. They worried that Sheehan, out of their sight, might gather more weapons—Reynolds had already observed other knives in her room, see App. 228—or even try to flee through the back window, id., at 227. Because Sheehan's room was on the second floor, she likely would have needed a ladder to escape. Fire escapes, however, are common in San Francisco, and the officers did not know whether Sheehan's room had such an escape. (Neither officer asked Hodge about a fire escape, but if they had, it seems he "probably" would have said there was one, id., at 117). With the door closed, all that Reynolds and Holder knew for sure was that Sheehan was unstable, she had just threatened to kill three people, and she had a weapon. 1

Reynolds and Holder had to make a decision. They could wait for backup—indeed, they already heard sirens. Or they could quickly reenter the room and try to subdue Sheehan before more time elapsed. Because Reynolds believed that the situation "required [their] immediate attention," id., at 235, the officers chose reentry. In making that decision, they did not pause to consider whether Sheehan's disability should be accommodated. See 743 F. 3d, at 1219. The officers obviously knew that Sheehan was unwell, but in

Reynolds' words, that was "a secondary issue" given that they were "faced with a violent woman who had already threatened to kill her social worker" and "two uniformed police officers." App. 235.

The officers ultimately decided that Holder—the larger officer—should push the door open while Reynolds used pepper spray on Sheehan. With pistols drawn, the officers moved in. When Sheehan, knife in hand, saw them, she again yelled for them to leave. She may also have again said that she was going to kill them. Sheehan is "not sure" if she threatened death a second time, id., at 284, but "concedes that it was her intent to resist arrest and to use the knife," 743 F. 3d, at 1220. In any event, Reynolds began pepper-spraying Sheehan in the face, but Sheehan would not drop the knife. When Sheehan was only a few feet away, Holder shot her twice, but she did not collapse. Reynolds then fired multiple shots. 2 After Sheehan finally fell, a third officer (who had just arrived) kicked the knife out of her hand. Sheehan survived.

Sometime later, San Francisco prosecuted Sheehan for assault with a deadly weapon, assault on a peace officer with a deadly weapon, and making criminal threats. The jury acquitted Sheehan of making threats but was unable to reach a verdict on the assault counts, and prosecutors decided not to retry her.

Sheehan then brought suit, alleging, among other things, that San Francisco violated the Americans with Disabilities Act of 1990 (ADA), 104 Stat. 327, 42 U. S. C. §12101 et seq., by subduing her in a manner that did not reasonably accommodate her disability. She also sued Reynolds and Holder in their personal capacities under Rev. Stat. §1979, 42 U. S. C. §1983, for violating her Fourth Amendment rights. In support of her claims, she offered testimony from a former deputy police chief, Lou Reiter, who contended that Reynolds and Holder fell short of their

training by not using practices designed to minimize the risk of violence when dealing with the mentally ill.

The District Court granted summary judgment for petitioners. Relying on Hainze v. Richards, 207 F. 3d 795 (CA5 2000), the court held that officers making an arrest are not required "to first determine whether their actions would comply with the ADA before protecting themselves and others." App. to Pet. for Cert. 80. The court also held that the officers did not violate the Fourth Amendment. The court wrote that the officers "had no way of knowing whether [Sheehan] might escape through a back window or fire escape, whether she might hurt herself, or whether there was anyone else in her room whom she might hurt." Id., at 71. In addition, the court observed that Holder did not begin shooting until it was necessary for her to do so in order "to protect herself" and that "Reynolds used deadly force only after she found that pepper spray was not enough force to contain the situation." Id., at 75, 76–77.

On appeal, the Ninth Circuit vacated in part. Relevant here, the panel held that because the ADA covers public "services, programs, or activities," §12132, the ADA's accommodation requirement should be read to "to encompass 'anything a public entity does,' " 743 F. 3d, at 1232. The Ninth Circuit agreed "that exigent circumstances inform the reasonableness analysis under the ADA," ibid., but concluded that it was for a jury to decide whether San Francisco should have accommodated Sheehan by, for instance, "respect[ing] her comfort zone, engag[ing] in non-threatening communications and us[ing] the passage of time to defuse the situation rather than precipitating a deadly confrontation." Id., at 1233.

As to Reynolds and Holder, the panel held that their initial entry into Sheehan's room was lawful and that, after the officers opened the door for the second time, they reasonably used their firearms when the pepper spray failed to stop Sheehan's advance. Nonetheless, the panel also held that a jury could find that the officers "provoked" Sheehan by needlessly forcing that second confrontation. Id., at 1216, 1229. The panel further found that it was clearly established that an officer cannot "forcibly enter the home of an armed, mentally ill subject who had been acting irrationally and had threatened anyone who entered when there was no objective need for immediate entry." Id., at 1229. Dissenting in part, Judge Graber would have held that the officers were entitled to qualified immunity.

San Francisco and the officers petitioned for a writ of certiorari and asked us to review two questions. We granted the petition. 574 U. S. ____ (2014).

II

Title II of the ADA commands that "no qualified individual with a disability shall, by reason of such disability, be excluded from participation in or be denied the benefits of the services, programs, or activities of a public entity, or be subjected to discrimination by any such entity." 42 U. S. C. §12132. The first question on which we granted review asks whether this provision "requires law enforcement officers to provide accommodations to an armed, violent, and mentally ill suspect in the course of bringing the suspect into custody." Pet. for Cert. i. When we granted review, we understood this question to embody what appears to be the thrust of the argument that San Francisco made in the Ninth Circuit, namely that " 'Title II does not apply to an officer's on-the-street responses to reported disturbances or other similar incidents, whether or not those calls involve subjects with mental disabilities, prior to the officer's securing the scene and ensuring that there is no threat to human life.' " Brief for Appellees in No. 11–16401 (CA9), p. 36 (quoting Hainze, supra, at 801; emphasis added); see also Brief for Appellees in No. 11–16401, at 37

(similar).

As San Francisco explained in its reply brief at the certiorari stage, resolving its "question presented" "does not require a fact-intensive 'reasonable accommodation' inquiry," since "the only question for this Court to resolve is whether any accommodation of an armed and violent individual is reasonable or required under Title II of the ADA." Reply to Brief in Opposition 3.

Having persuaded us to grant certiorari, San Francisco chose to rely on a different argument than what it pressed below. In its brief in this Court, San Francisco focuses on the statutory phrase "qualified individual," §12132, and a regulation declaring that Title II "does not require a public entity to permit an individual to participate in or benefit from the services, programs, or activities of that public entity when that individual poses a direct threat to the health or safety of others." 28 CFR §35.139(a) (2014). Another regulation defines a "direct threat" as "a significant risk to the health or safety of others that cannot be eliminated by a modification of policies, practices or procedures, or by the provision of auxiliary aids or services." §35.104. Putting these authorities together, San Fran-cisco argues that "a person who poses a direct threat or significant risk to the safety of others is not qualified for accommodations under the ADA," Brief for Petitioners 17. Contending that Sheehan clearly posed a "direct threat," San Francisco concludes that she was therefore not "qualified" for an accommodation.

Though, to be sure, this "qualified" argument does appear in San Francisco's certiorari petition, San Francisco never hinted at it in the Ninth Circuit. The Court does not ordinarily decide questions that were not passed on below. More than that, San Francisco's new argument effectively concedes that the relevant provision of the ADA, 42 U. S. C. §12132, may "requir[e] law enforcement officers to provide accommodations to an armed, violent, and mentally ill suspect in the course of bringing the suspect into custody." Pet. for Cert. i. This is so because there may be circumstances in which any "significant risk" presented by "an armed, violent, and mentally ill suspect" can be "eliminated by a modification of policies, practices or procedures, or by the provision of auxiliary aids or services."

The argument that San Francisco now advances is predicated on the proposition that the ADA governs the manner in which a qualified individual with a disability is arrested. The relevant provision provides that a public entity may not "exclud[e]" a qualified individual with a disability from "participat[ing] in," and may not "den[y]" that individual the "benefits of[,] the services, programs, or activities of a public entity." §12132. This language would apply to an arrest if an arrest is an "activity" in which the arrestee "participat[es]" or from which the arrestee may "benefi[t]."

This same provision also commands that "no qualified individual with a disability shall be . . . subjected to discrimination by any [public] entity." Ibid. This part of the statute would apply to an arrest if the failure to arrest an individual with a mental disability in a manner that reasonably accommodates that disability constitutes "discrimination." Ibid.

Whether the statutory language quoted above applies to arrests is an important question that would benefit from briefing and an adversary presentation. But San Fran-cisco, the United States as amicus curiae, and Sheehan all argue (or at least accept) that §12132 applies to arrests. No one argues the contrary view. As a result, we do not think that it would be prudent to decide the question in this case.

Our decision not to decide whether the ADA applies to arrests is reinforced by the parties' failure to address a related question: whether a public entity can be liable for damages under Title II for an arrest made by its police officers. Only public entities are subject to Title II, see, e.g., Pennsylvania Dept. of Corrections v. Yeskey, 524 U. S. 206, 208 (1998) , and the parties agree that such an entity can be held vicariously liable for money damages for the purposeful or deliberately indifferent conduct of its employees. See Tr. of Oral Arg. 10–12, 22. But we have never decided whether that is correct, and we decline to do so here, in the absence of adversarial briefing.

Because certiorari jurisdiction exists to clarify the law, its exercise "is not a matter of right, but of judicial discretion." Supreme Court Rule 10. Exercising that discretion, we dismiss the first question presented as improvidently granted. See, e.g., Board of Trustees of Univ. of Ala. v. Garrett, 531 U. S. 356, 360, n. 1 (2001) (partial dismissal); Parker v. Dugger, 498 U. S. 308, 323 (1991) (same).

III

The second question presented is whether Reynolds and Holder can be held personally liable for the injuries that Sheehan suffered. We conclude they are entitled to qualified immunity. 3

Public officials are immune from suit under 42 U. S. C. §1983 unless they have "violated a statutory or constitutional right that was clearly established at the time of the challenged conduct." Plumhoff, 572 U. S., at ____ (slip op., at 12) (internal quotation marks omitted). An officer "cannot be said to have violated a clearly established right unless the right's contours were sufficiently definite that any reasonable official in [his] shoes would have understood that he was violating it," ibid., meaning that "existing precedent . . . placed the statutory or constitutional question beyond debate." Ashcroft v. al-Kidd, 563 U. S. ____, ____ (2011) (slip op., at 9). This exacting standard "gives government officials breathing room to make reasonable but mistaken judgments" by "protect[ing] all but the plainly incompetent or those who knowingly violate the law." Id., at ____ (slip op., at 12).

In this case, although we disagree with the Ninth Circuit's ultimate conclusion on the question of qualified immunity, we agree with its analysis in many respects. For instance, there is no doubt that the officers did not violate any federal right when they opened Sheehan's door the first time. See 743 F. 3d, at 1216, 1223. Reynolds and Holder knocked on the door, announced that they were police officers, and informed Sheehan that they wanted to help her. When Sheehan did not come to the door, they entered her room. This was not unconstitutional. "[L]aw enforcement officers may enter a home without a warrant to render emergency assistance to an injured occupant or to protect an occupant from imminent injury." Brigham City v. Stuart, 547 U. S. 398, 403 (2006) . See also Kentucky v. King, 563 U. S. ___, ___ (2011) (slip op., at 6).

Nor is there any doubt that had Sheehan not been dis-abled, the officers could have opened her door the second time without violating any constitutional rights. For one thing, "because the two entries were part of a single, continuous search or seizure, the officers [were] not required to justify the continuing emergency with respect to the second entry." 743 F. 3d, at 1224 (following Michigan v. Tyler, 436 U. S. 499, 511 (1978)). In addition, Reynolds and Holder knew that Sheehan had a weapon and had threatened to use it to kill three people. They also knew that delay could make the situation more dangerous. The Fourth Amendment standard is reasonableness, and it is reasonable for police to move quickly if delay "would gravely endanger their lives or the lives of others." Warden, Md. Penitentiary v. Hayden, 387 U. S. 294–299 (1967). This is true even when, judged with the benefit of hindsight, the officers may have made "some mistakes." Heien v. North Carolina, 574 U. S. ___, ___ (2014) (slip op., at 5). The Constitution is not blind to "the fact that police officers are often forced to make split-second judgments." Plumhoff, supra, at ___ (slip op., at 8).

We also agree with the Ninth Circuit that after the officers opened Sheehan's door the second time, their use of force was reasonable. Reynolds tried to subdue Sheehan with pepper spray, but Sheehan kept coming at the officers until she was "only a few feet from a cornered Officer Holder." 743 F. 3d, at 1229. At this point, the use of potentially deadly force was justified. See Scott v. Harris, 550 U. S. 372, 384 (2007) . Nothing in the Fourth Amendment barred Reynolds and Holder from protecting themselves, even though it meant firing multiple rounds. See Plumhoff, supra, at ___ (slip op., at 11).

The real question, then, is whether, despite these dangerous circumstances, the officers violated the Fourth Amendment when they decided to reopen Sheehan's door rather than attempting to accommodate her disability. Here we come to another problem. San Francisco, whose attorneys represent Reynolds and Holder, devotes scant briefing to this question. Instead, San Francisco argues almost exclusively that even if it is assumed that there was a Fourth Amendment violation, the right was not clearly established. This Court, of course, could decide the constitutional question anyway. See Pearson v. Callahan, 555 U. S. 223, 242 (2009) (recognizing discretion). But because this question has not been adequately briefed, we decline to do so. See id., at 239. Rather, we simply decide whether the officers' failure to accommodate Sheehan's illness violated clearly established law. It did not.

To begin, nothing in our cases suggests the constitutional rule applied by the Ninth Circuit. The Ninth Circuit focused on Graham v. Connor, 490 U. S. 386 (1989) , but Graham holds only that the " 'objective reasonableness' " test applies to excessive-force claims under the Fourth Amendment. See id., at 388. That is far too general a proposition to control this case. "We have repeatedly told courts—and the Ninth Circuit in particular—not to define clearly established law at a high level of generality." al-Kidd, supra, at ____ (citation omitted) (slip op., at 10); cf. Lopez v. Smith, 574 U. S. ____, ____ (2014) (per curiam) (slip op., at 5). Qualified immunity is no immunity at all if "clearly established" law can simply be defined as the right to be free from unreasonable searches and seizures.

Even a cursory glance at the facts of Graham confirms just how different that case is from this one. That case did not involve a dangerous, obviously unstable person making threats, much less was there a weapon involved. There is a world of difference between needlessly withholding sugar from an innocent person who is suffering from an insulin reaction, see Graham, supra, at 388–389, and responding to the perilous situation Reynolds and Holder confronted. Graham is a nonstarter.

Moving beyond Graham, the Ninth Circuit also turned to two of its own cases. But even if "a controlling circuit precedent could constitute clearly established federal law in these circumstances," Carroll v. Carman, 574 U. S. ____, ____ (2014) (per curiam) (slip op., at 4), it does not do so here.

The Ninth Circuit first pointed to Deorle v. Rutherford, 272 F. 3d 1272 (CA9 2001), but from the very first paragraph of that opinion we learn that Deorle involved an officer's use of a beanbag gun to subdue "an emotionally disturbed" person who "was unarmed, had not attacked or even touched anyone, had generally obeyed the instructions given him by various police officers, and had not committed any serious offense." Id., at 1275. The officer there, moreover, "observed Deorle at close proximity for about five to ten minutes before shooting him" in the face. See id., at 1281. Whatever the merits of the decision in Deorle, the differences between that case and the case before us leap from the page. Unlike Deorle,

Sheehan was dangerous, recalcitrant, law-breaking, and out of sight.

The Ninth Circuit also leaned on Alexander v. City and County of San Francisco, 29 F. 3d 1355 (CA9 1994), another case involving mental illness. There, officials from San Francisco attempted to enter Henry Quade's home "for the primary purpose of arresting him" even though they lacked an arrest warrant. Id., at 1361. Quade, in response, fired a handgun; police officers "shot back, and Quade died from gunshot wounds shortly thereafter." Id., at 1358. The panel concluded that a jury should decide whether the officers used excessive force. The court reasoned that the officers provoked the confrontation because there were no "exigent circumstances" excusing their entrance. Id., at 1361.

Alexander too is a poor fit. As Judge Graber observed below in her dissent, the Ninth Circuit has long read Alexander narrowly. See 743 F. 3d, at 1235 (Graber, J., concurring in part and dissenting in part) (citing Billington v. Smith, 292 F. 3d 1177 (CA9 2002)). Under Ninth Circuit law, 4 an entry that otherwise complies with the Fourth Amendment is not rendered unreasonable because it provokes a violent reaction. See id., at 1189–1190. Under this rule, qualified immunity necessarily applies here because, as explained above, competent officers could have believed that the second entry was justified under both continuous search and exigent circumstance rationales. Indeed, even if Reynolds and Holder misjudged the situation, Sheehan cannot "establish a Fourth Amendment violation based merely on bad tactics that result in a deadly confrontation that could have been avoided." Id., at 1190. Courts must not judge officers with "the 20/20 vision of hindsight.'" Ibid. (quoting Graham, 490 U. S., at 396).

When Graham, Deorle, and Alexander are viewed together, the central error in the Ninth Circuit's reasoning is apparent. The panel majority concluded that these three cases "would have placed any reasonable, competent officer on notice that it is unreasonable to forcibly enter the home of an armed, mentally ill suspect who had been acting irrationally and had threatened anyone who entered when there was no objective need for immediate entry." 743 F. 3d, at 1229. But even assuming that is true, no precedent clearly established that there was not "an objective need for immediate entry" here. No matter how carefully a reasonable officer read Graham, Deorle, and Alexander beforehand, that officer could not know that reopening Sheehan's door to prevent her from escaping or gathering more weapons would violate the Ninth Circuit's test, even if all the disputed facts are viewed in respondent's favor. Without that "fair notice," an officer is entitled to qualified immunity. See, e.g., Plumhoff, 572 U. S., at ___ (slip op., at 13).

Nor does it matter for purposes of qualified immunity that Sheehan's expert, Reiter, testified that the officers did not follow their training. According to Reiter, San Francisco trains its officers when dealing with the mentally ill to "ensure that sufficient resources are brought to the scene," "contain the subject" and "respect the suspect's "comfort zone," "use time to their advantage," and "employ non-threatening verbal communication and open-ended questions to facilitate the subject's participation in communication." Brief for Respondent 7. Likewise, San Francisco's policy is " 'to use hostage negotiators' " when dealing with " 'a suspect [who] resists arrest by barricading himself.' " Id., at 8 (quoting San Francisco Police Department General Order 8.02, §II(B) (Aug. 3, 1994), online at http://www.sf-police.org (as visited May 14, 2015, and available in Clerk of Court's case file)).

Even if an officer acts contrary to her training, however, (and here, given the generality of that training, it is not at all clear that Reynolds and Holder did so), that does not itself negate qualified immunity where it would otherwise be warranted. Rather, so long as "a reasonable officer could have believed that his conduct was justified," a plaintiff cannot "avoi[d] summary judgment by simply producing an expert's report that an officer's conduct leading up to a deadly confrontation was imprudent, inappropriate, or even reckless." Billington, supra, at 1189. Cf. Saucier v. Katz, 533 U. S. 194, 216, n. 6 (2001) (Ginsburg, J., concurring in judgment) (" '[I]n close cases, a jury does not automatically get to second-guess these life and death decisions, even though a plaintiff has an expert and a plausible claim that the situation could better have been handled differently' " (quoting Roy v. Inhabitants of Lewiston, 42 F. 3d 691, 695 (CA1 1994))). Considering the specific situation confronting Reynolds and Holder, they had sufficient reason to believe that their conduct was justified.

Finally, to the extent that a "robust consensus of cases of persuasive authority" could itself clearly establish the federal right respondent alleges, al-Kidd, 563 U. S., at ___ (slip op., at 10), no such consensus exists here. If anything, the opposite may be true. See, e.g., Bates v. Chesterfield County, 216 F. 3d 367, 372 (CA4 2000) ("Knowledge of a person's disability simply cannot foreclose officers from protecting themselves, the disabled person, and the general public"); Sanders v. Minneapolis, 474 F. 3d 523, 527 (CA8 2007) (following Bates, supra); Menuel v. Atlanta, 25 F. 3d 990 (CA11 1994) (upholding use of deadly force to try to apprehend a mentally ill man who had a knife and was hiding behind a door).

In sum, we hold that qualified immunity applies because these officers had no "fair and clear warning of what the Constitution requires." al-Kidd, supra, at ___ (Kennedy, J., concurring) (slip op., at 3). Because the qualified immunity analysis is straightforward, we need not decide whether the Constitution was violated by the officers' failure to accommodate Sheehan's illness.

*   *   *

For these reasons, the first question presented is dismissed as improvidently granted. On the second question, we reverse the judgment of the Ninth Circuit. The case is remanded for further proceedings consistent with this opinion.

It is so ordered.

Justice Breyer took no part in the consideration or decision of this case.

Los Angeles v. Patel (June 22, 2015) [Notes omitted]

Justice Sotomayor delivered the opinion of the Court.

Respondents brought a Fourth Amendment challenge to a provision of the Los Angeles Municipal Code that compels "[e]very operator of a hotel to keep a record" containing specified information concerning guests and to make this record "available to any officer of the Los Angeles Police Department for inspection" on demand. Los Angeles Municipal Code §§41.49(2), (3)(a), (4) (2015). The questions presented are whether facial challenges to statutes can be brought under the Fourth Amendment and, if so, whether this provision of the Los Angeles Municipal Code is facially invalid. We hold facial challenges can be brought under the Fourth Amendment. We further hold that the provision of the Los Angeles Municipal Code that requires hotel operators to make their registries available to the police on demand is facially unconstitutional because it penalizes them for declining to turn over their records without affording them any opportunity for precompliance review.

I

A

Los Angeles Municipal Code (LAMC) §41.49 requires hotel operators to record information about their guests, including: the guest's name and address; the number of people in each guest's party; the make, model, and license plate number of any guest's vehicle parked on hotel property; the guest's date and time of arrival and scheduled departure date; the room number assigned to the guest; the rate charged and amount collected for the room; and the method of payment. §41.49(2). Guests without reservations, those who pay for their rooms with cash, and any guests who rent a room for less than 12 hours must present photographic identification at the time of check-in, and hotel operators are required to record the number and expiration date of that document. §41.49(4). For those guests who check in using an electronic kiosk, the hotel's records must also contain the guest's credit card information. §41.49(2)(b). This information can be maintained in either electronic or paper form, but it must be "kept on the hotel premises in the guest reception or guest check-in area or in an office adjacent" thereto for a period of 90 days. §41.49(3)(a).

Section 41.49(3)(a)—the only provision at issue here—states, in pertinent part, that hotel guest records "shall be made available to any officer of the Los Angeles Police Department for inspection," provided that "[w]henever possible, the inspection shall be conducted at a time and in a manner that minimizes any interference with the operation of the business." A hotel operator's failure to make his or her guest records available for police inspection is a misdemeanor punishable by up to six months in jail and a $1,000 fine. §11.00(m) (general provision applicable to entire LAMC).

B

In 2003, respondents, a group of motel operators along with a lodging association, sued the city of Los Angeles (City or petitioner) in three consolidated cases challenging the constitutionality of §41.49(3)(a). They sought declaratory and injunctive relief. The parties "agree[d] that the sole issue in the . . . action [would be] a facial constitu-tional challenge" to §41.49(3)(a) under the Fourth Amend-ment. App. 195. They further stipulated that respondents have been subjected to mandatory record inspections under the ordinance without consent or a warrant. Id., at 194–195.

Following a bench trial, the District Court entered judgment in favor of the City, holding that respondents' facial challenge failed because they lacked a reasonable expectation of privacy in the records subject to inspection. A divided panel of the Ninth Circuit affirmed on the same grounds. 686 F. 3d 1085 (2012). On rehearing en banc, however, the Court of Appeals reversed. 738 F. 3d 1058, 1065 (2013).

The en banc court first determined that a police officer's nonconsensual inspection of hotel records under §41.49 is a Fourth Amendment "search" because "[t]he business records covered by §41.49 are the hotel's private property" and the hotel therefore "has the right to exclude others from prying into the[ir] contents." Id., at 1061. Next, the court assessed "whether the searches authorized by §41.49 are reasonable." Id., at 1063. Relying on Donovan v. Lone Steer, Inc., 464 U. S. 408 (1984), and See v. Seattle, 387 U. S. 541 (1967), the court held that §41.49 is facially unconstitutional "as it authorizes inspections" of hotel records "without affording an opportunity to 'obtain judicial review of the reasonableness of the demand prior to suffering penalties for refusing to comply.'" 738 F. 3d, at 1065 (quoting See, 387 U. S., at 545).

Two dissenting opinions were filed. The first dissent argued that facial relief should rarely be available for Fourth Amendment challenges, and was inappropriate here because the ordinance would be constitutional in those circumstances where police officers demand access to hotel records with a warrant in hand or exigent circumstances justify the search. 738 F. 3d, at 1065–1070 (opinion of Tallman, J.). The second dissent conceded that inspections under §41.49 constitute Fourth Amendment searches, but faulted the majority for assessing the reasonableness of these searches without accounting for the weakness of the hotel operators' privacy interest in the content of their guest registries. Id., at 1070–1074 (opinion of Clifton, J.).

We granted certiorari, 574 U. S. ____ (2014), and now affirm.

II

We first clarify that facial challenges under the Fourth Amendment are not categorically barred or especially disfavored.

A

A facial challenge is an attack on a statute itself as opposed to a particular application. While such challenges are "the most difficult . . . to mount successfully," United States v. Salerno, 481 U. S. 739, 745 (1987), the Court has have never held that these claims cannot be brought under any otherwise enforceable provision of the Constitution. Cf. Fallon, Fact and Fiction About Facial Chal-lenges, 99 Cal. L. Rev. 915, 918 (2011) (pointing to several Terms in which "the Court adjudicated more facial challenges on the merits than it did as-applied challenges"). Instead, the Court has allowed such challenges to proceed under a diverse array of constitutional provisions. See, e.g., Sorrell v. IMS Health Inc., 564 U. S. ____ (2011) (First Amendment); District of Columbia v. Heller, 554 U. S. 570(2008) (Second Amendment); Chicago v. Morales, 527 U. S. 41 (1999) (Due Process Clause of the Fourteenth Amendment); Kraft Gen. Foods, Inc. v. Iowa Dept. of Revenue and Finance, 505 U. S. 71 (1992) (Foreign Commerce Clause).

Fourth Amendment challenges to statutes authorizing warrantless searches are no exception. Any claim to the contrary reflects a misunderstanding of our decision in Sibron v. New

York, 392 U. S. 40 (1968). In Sibron, two criminal defendants challenged the constitutionality of a statute authorizing police to, among other things, " 'stop any person abroad in a public place whom [they] reason-ably suspec[t] is committing, has committed or is about to commit a felony." Id., at 43 (quoting then N. Y. Code Crim. Proc. §180–a). The Court held that the search of one of the defendants under the statute violated the Fourth Amendment, 392 U. S., at 59, 62, but refused to opine more broadly on the statute's validity, stating that "[t]he constitutional validity of a warrantless search is pre-eminently the sort of question which can only be decided in the concrete factual context of the individual case." Id., at 59.

This statement from Sibron—which on its face might suggest an intent to foreclose all facial challenges to statutes authorizing warrantless searches—must be understood in the broader context of that case. In the same section of the opinion, the Court emphasized that the "operative categories" of the New York law at issue were "susceptible of a wide variety of interpretations," id., at 60, and that "[the law] was passed too recently for the State's highest court to have ruled upon many of the questions involving potential intersections with federal constitutional guarantees," id., at 60, n. 20. Sibron thus stands for the simple proposition that claims for facial relief under the Fourth Amendment are unlikely to succeed when there is substantial ambiguity as to what conduct a statute authorizes: Where a statute consists of "extraordinarily elastic categories," it may be "impossible to tell" whether and to what extent it deviates from the requirements of the Fourth Amendment. Id., at 59, 61, n. 20.

This reading of Sibron is confirmed by subsequent precedents. Since Sibron, the Court has entertained facial challenges under the Fourth Amendment to statutes authorizing warrantless searches. See, e.g., Vernonia School District 47J v. Acton, 515 U. S. 646, 648 (1995) ("We granted certiorari to decide whether" petitioner's student athlete drug testing policy "violates the Fourth and Fourteenth Amendments to the United States Constitution"); Skinner v. Railway Labor Executives' Assn., 489 U. S. 602, 633, n. 10 (1989) ("[R]espondents have challenged the administrative scheme on its face. We deal therefore with whether the [drug] tests contemplated by the regulation can ever be conducted"); cf. Illinois v. Krull, 480 U. S. 340, 354 (1987) ("[A] person subject to a statute authorizing searches without a warrant or probable cause may bring an action seeking a declaration that the statute is unconstitutional and an injunction barring its implementation"). Perhaps more importantly, the Court has on numerous occasions declared statutes facially invalid under the Fourth Amendment. For instance, in Chandler v. Miller, 520 U. S. 305–309 (1997), the Court struck down a Georgia statute requiring candidates for certain state offices to take and pass a drug test, concluding that this "requirement . . . [did] not fit within the closely guarded category of constitutionally permissible suspicionless searches." Similar examples abound. See, e.g., Ferguson v. Charleston, 532 U. S. 67, 86 (2001) (holding that a hospital policy authorizing "nonconsensual, warrantless, and suspicionless searches" contravened the Fourth Amendment); Payton v. New York, 445 U. S. 573, 574, 576 (1980) (holding that a New York statute "authoriz[ing] police officers to enter a private residence without a warrant and with force, if necessary, to make a routine felony arrest" was "not consistent with the Fourth Amendment"); Torres v. Puerto Rico, 442 U. S. 465, 466, 471 (1979) (holding that a Puerto Rico statute authorizing "police to search the luggage of any person arriving in Puerto Rico from the United States" was unconstitutional because it failed to require either probable cause or a warrant).

B

Petitioner principally contends that facial challenges to statutes authorizing warrantless searches must fail because such searches will never be unconstitutional in all applications. Cf. Salerno, 481 U. S., at 745 (to obtain facial relief the party seeking it "must establish that no set of circumstances exists under which the [statute] would be valid"). In particular, the City points to situations where police are responding to an emergency, where the subject of the search consents to the intrusion, and where police are acting under a court-ordered warrant. See Brief for Petitioner 19–20. While petitioner frames this argument as an objection to respondents' challenge in this case, its logic would preclude facial relief in every Fourth Amendment challenge to a statute authorizing warrantless searches. For this reason alone, the City's argument must fail: The Court's precedents demonstrate not only that facial challenges to statutes authorizing warrantless searches can be brought, but also that they can succeed. See Part II–A, supra.

Moreover, the City's argument misunderstands how courts analyze facial challenges. Under the most exacting standard the Court has prescribed for facial challenges, a plaintiff must establish that a "law is unconstitutional in all of its applications." Washington State Grange v. Washington State Republican Party, 552 U. S. 442, 449 (2008). But when assessing whether a statute meets this standard, the Court has considered only applications of the statute in which it actually authorizes or prohibits conduct. For instance, in Planned Parenthood of Southeastern Pa. v. Casey, 505 U. S. 833 (1992), the Court struck down a provision of Pennsylvania's abortion law that required a woman to notify her husband before obtaining an abortion. Those defending the statute argued that facial relief was inappropriate because most women voluntarily notify their husbands about a planned abortion and for them the law

would not impose an undue burden. The Court rejected this argument, explaining: The "[l]egislation is measured for consistency with the Constitution by its impact on those whose conduct it affects. . . . The proper focus of the constitutional inquiry is the group for whom the law is a restriction, not the group for whom the law is irrelevant." Id., at 894.

Similarly, when addressing a facial challenge to a statute authorizing warrantless searches, the proper focus of the constitutional inquiry is searches that the law actually authorizes, not those for which it is irrelevant. If exigency or a warrant justifies an officer's search, the subject of the search must permit it to proceed irrespective of whether it is authorized by statute. Statutes authorizing warrantless searches also do no work where the subject of a search has consented. Accordingly, the constitutional "applications" that petitioner claims prevent facial relief here are irrelevant to our analysis because they do not involve actual applications of the statute. [1]

III

Turning to the merits of the particular claim before us, we hold that §41.49(3)(a) is facially unconstitutional because it fails to provide hotel operators with an opportunity for precompliance review.

A

The Fourth Amendment protects "[t]he right of the people to be secure in their persons, houses, papers, and effects, against unreasonable searches and seizures." It further provides that "no Warrants shall issue, but upon probable cause." Based on this constitutional text, the Court has repeatedly held that " 'searches conducted outside the judicial process, without prior approval by [a] judge or [a] magistrate [judge], are per se unreasonable . . . subject only to a few specifically established and well-delineated exceptions.' " Arizona v. Gant, 556 U. S. 332, 338 (2009) (quoting Katz v. United States, 389 U. S. 347, 357

(1967)). This rule "applies to commercial premises as well as to homes." Marshall v. Barlow's, Inc., 436 U. S. 307, 312 (1978).

Search regimes where no warrant is ever required may be reasonable where " 'special needs . . . make the warrant and probable-cause requirement impracticable,' " Skinner, 489 U. S., at 619 (quoting Griffin v. Wisconsin, 483 U. S. 868, 873 (1987) (some internal quotation marks omitted)), and where the "primary purpose" of the searches is "[d]istinguishable from the general interest in crime control," Indianapolis v. Edmond, 531 U. S. 32, 44 (2000). Here, we assume that the searches authorized by §41.49 serve a "special need" other than conducting criminal investigations: They ensure compliance with the recordkeeping requirement, which in turn deters criminals from operating on the hotels' premises. 2 The Court has referred to this kind of search as an "administrative searc[h]." Camara v. Municipal Court of City and County of San Francisco, 387 U. S. 523, 534 (1967). Thus, we consider whether §41.49 falls within the administrative search exception to the warrant requirement.

The Court has held that absent consent, exigent circumstances, or the like, in order for an administrative search to be constitutional, the subject of the search must be afforded an opportunity to obtain precompliance review before a neutral decisionmaker. See See, 387 U. S., at 545; Lone Steer, 464 U. S., at 415 (noting that an administrative search may proceed with only a subpoena where the subpoenaed party is sufficiently protected by the opportunity to "question the reasonableness of the subpoena, before suffering any penalties for refusing to comply with it, by raising objections in an action in district court"). And, we see no reason why this minimal requirement is inapplicable here. While the Court has never attempted to prescribe the exact form an opportunity for precompliance review must take, the City does not even attempt to argue that §41.49(3)(a) affords hotel operators any opportunity whatsoever. Section 41.49(3)(a) is, therefore, facially invalid.

A hotel owner who refuses to give an officer access to his or her registry can be arrested on the spot. The Court has held that business owners cannot reasonably be put to this kind of choice. Camara, 387 U. S., at 533 (holding that "broad statutory safeguards are no substitute for individualized review, particularly when those safeguards may only be invoked at the risk of a criminal penalty"). Absent an opportunity for precompliance review, the ordinance creates an intolerable risk that searches authorized by it will exceed statutory limits, or be used as a pretext to harass hotel operators and their guests. Even if a hotel has been searched 10 times a day, every day, for three months, without any violation being found, the operator can only refuse to comply with an officer's demand to turn over the registry at his or her own peril.

To be clear, we hold only that a hotel owner must be afforded an opportunity to have a neutral decisionmaker review an officer's demand to search the registry before he or she faces penalties for failing to comply. Actual review need only occur in those rare instances where a hotel operator objects to turning over the registry. Moreover, this opportunity can be provided without imposing onerous burdens on those charged with an administrative scheme's enforcement. For instance, respondents accept that the searches authorized by §41.49(3)(a) would be constitutional if they were performed pursuant to an administrative subpoena. Tr. of Oral Arg. 36–37. These subpoenas, which are typically a simple form, can be issued by the individual seeking the record—here, officers in the field—without probable cause that a regulation is being infringed. See See, 387 U. S., at 544 ("[T]he demand to inspect may be issued by the agency"). Issuing a subpoena will usually be the full extent of an officer's burden because "the great majority of businessmen can be expected in normal course to consent to inspection without warrant." Barlow's, Inc., 436 U. S., at 316. Indeed, the City has cited no evidence suggesting that without an ordinance authorizing on-demand searches, hotel operators would regularly refuse to cooperate with the police.

In those instances, however, where a subpoenaed hotel operator believes that an attempted search is motivated by illicit purposes, respondents suggest it would be sufficient if he or she could move to quash the subpoena before any search takes place. Tr. of Oral Arg. 38–39. A neutral decisionmaker, including an administrative law judge, would then review the subpoenaed party's objections before deciding whether the subpoena is enforceable. Given the limited grounds on which a motion to quash can be granted, such challenges will likely be rare. And, in the even rarer event that an officer reasonably suspects that a hotel operator may tamper with the registry while the motion to quash is pending, he or she can guard the registry until the required hearing can occur, which ought not take long. Riley v. California, 573 U. S. ____ (2014) (slip op., at 12) (police may seize and hold a cell phone "to prevent destruction of evidence while seeking a warrant"); Illinois v. McArthur, 531 U. S. 326, 334 (2001) (citing cases upholding the constitutionality of "temporary restraints where [they are] needed to preserve evidence until police could obtain a warrant"). Cf. Missouri v. McNeely, 569 U. S. ____ (2013) (slip op., at 12) (noting that many States have procedures in place for considering warrant applications telephonically). 3

Procedures along these lines are ubiquitous. A 2002 report by the Department of Justice "identified approximately 335 existing administrative subpoena authorities held by various [federal] executive branch entities." Office of Legal Policy, Report to Congress on the Use of Administrative Subpoena Authorities by Executive Branch Agencies and Entities 3, online at http://www.justice.gov/archive/olp/rpt_to_congr ess.htm(All Internet materials as visited June 19, 2015, and available in Clerk of Court's case file). Their prevalence confirms what common sense alone would otherwise lead us to conclude: In most contexts, business owners can be afforded at least an opportunity to contest an administrative search's propriety without unduly compromising the government's ability to achieve its regulatory aims.

Of course administrative subpoenas are only one way in which an opportunity for precompliance review can be made available. But whatever the precise form, the availability of precompliance review alters the dynamic between the officer and the hotel to be searched, and reduces the risk that officers will use these administrative searches as a pretext to harass business owners.

Finally, we underscore the narrow nature of our holding. Respondents have not challenged and nothing in our opinion calls into question those parts of §41.49 that require hotel operators to maintain guest registries containing certain information. And, even absent legislative action to create a procedure along the lines discussed above, see supra, at 11, police will not be prevented from obtaining access to these documents. As they often do, hotel operators remain free to consent to searches of their registries and police can compel them to turn them over if they have a proper administrative warrant—including one that was issued ex parte—or if some other exception to the warrant requirement applies, including exigent circumstances. 4

B

Rather than arguing that §41.49(3)(a) is constitutional under the general administrative search doctrine, the City and Justice Scalia contend that hotels are "closely regulated," and that the ordinance is facially valid under the more relaxed standard that applies to searches of this category of businesses. Brief for Petitioner 28–47; post, at 5. They are wrong on both counts.

Over the past 45 years, the Court has identified only four industries that "have such a history of government oversight that no reasonable expectation of privacy . . . could exist for a proprietor over the stock of such an enterprise," Barlow's, Inc., 436 U. S., 313. Simply listing these industries refutes petitioner's argument that hotels should be counted among them. Unlike liquor sales, Colonnade Catering Corp. v. United States, 397 U. S. 72 (1970), firearms dealing, United States v. Biswell, 406 U. S. 311–312 (1972), mining, Donovan v. Dewey, 452 U. S. 594 (1981), or running an automobile junkyard, New York v. Burger, 482 U. S. 691 (1987), nothing inherent in the operation of hotels poses a clear and significant risk to the public welfare. See, e.g., id., at 709 ("Automobile junkyards and vehicle dismantlers provide the major market for stolen vehicles and vehicle parts"); Dewey, 452 U. S., at 602 (describing the mining industry as "among the most hazardous in the country"). 5

Moreover, "[t]he clear import of our cases is that the closely regulated industry . . . is the exception." Barlow's, Inc., 436 U. S., at 313. To classify hotels as pervasively regulated would permit what has always been a narrow exception to swallow the rule. The City wisely refrains from arguing that §41.49 itself renders hotels closely regulated. Nor do any of the other regulations on which petitioner and Justice Scalia rely— regulations requiring hotels to, inter alia, maintain a license, collect taxes, conspicuously post their rates, and meet certain sanitary standards— establish a comprehensive scheme of regulation that distinguishes hotels from numerous other businesses. See Brief for Petitioner 33–34 (citing regulations); post, at 7 (same). All businesses in Los Angeles need a license to operate. LAMC §§21.03(a), 21.09(a). While some regulations apply to a smaller set of businesses, see e.g. Cal. Code Regs., tit. 25, §40 (2015) (requiring linens to be changed between rental guests), online at http://www.oal.ca.gov/ccr.htm, these can hardly be said to have created a " 'comprehensive' " scheme that puts hotel owners on notice that their " 'property will be subject to periodic inspections undertaken for specific purposes,' " Burger, 482 U. S., at 705, n. 16 (quoting Dewey, 452 U. S., at 600). Instead, they are more akin to the widely applicable minimum wage and maximum hour rules that the Court rejected as a basis for deeming "the entirety of American interstate commerce" to be closely regulated in Barlow's, Inc. 436 U. S., at 314. If such general regulations were sufficient to invoke the closely regulated industry exception, it would be hard to imagine a type of business that would not qualify. See Brief for Google Inc. as Amicus Curiae 16–17; Brief for the Chamber of Commerce of United States of America as Amicus Curiae 12–13.

Petitioner attempts to recast this hodgepodge of reg-ulations as a comprehensive scheme by referring to a "centuries-old tradition" of warrantless searches of hotels. Brief for Petitioner 34–36. History is relevant when deter- mining whether an industry is closely regulated. See, e.g., Burger, 482 U. S., at 707. The historical record here, however, is not as clear as petitioner suggests. The City and Justice Scalia principally point to evidence that hotels were treated as public accommodations. Brief for Petitioner 34–36; post, at 5–6, and n. 1. For instance, the Commonwealth of Massachusetts required innkeepers to " 'furnish[ ] . . . suitable provisions and lodging, for the refreshment and entertainment of strangers and travellers, pasturing and stable room, hay and provender . . . for their horses and cattle.' " Brief for Petitioner 35 (quoting An Act For The Due Regulation Of Licensed Houses (1786), reprinted in Acts and Laws of the Commonwealth of Massachusetts 209 (1893)). But laws obligating inns to provide suitable lodging to all paying guests are not the same as laws subjecting inns to warrantless searches. Petitioner also asserts that "[f]or a long time, [hotel] owners left their registers open to widespread inspection." Brief for Petitioner 51. Setting aside that modern hotel registries contain sensitive information, such as driver's licenses and credit card numbers for which there is no historic analog, the fact that some hotels chose to make registries accessible to the public has little bearing on whether government authorities could have viewed these documents on demand without a hotel's consent.

Even if we were to find that hotels are pervasively regulated, §41.49 would need to satisfy three additional criteria to be reasonable under the Fourth Amendment: (1) "[T]here must be a 'substantial' government interest that informs the regulatory scheme pursuant to which the inspection is made"; (2) "the warrantless inspections must be 'necessary' to further [the] regulatory scheme"; and (3) "the statute's inspection program, in terms of the certainty and regularity of its application, [must] provid[e] a constitutionally adequate substitute for a warrant." Burger, 482 U. S., at 702–703 (internal quotation marks omitted). We assume petitioner's interest in ensuring that hotels maintain accurate and complete registries might fulfill the first of these requirements, but conclude that §41.49 fails the second and third prongs of this test.

The City claims that affording hotel operators any opportunity for precompliance review would fatally undermine the scheme's efficacy by giving operators a chance to falsify their records. Brief for Petitioner 41–42. The Court has previously rejected this exact argument, which could be made regarding any recordkeeping requirement. See Barlow's, Inc., 436 U. S., at 320 ("[It is not] apparent why the advantages of surprise would be lost if, after being refused entry, procedures were available for the [Labor] Secretary

to seek an ex parte warrant to reappear at the premises without further notice to the establishment being inspected"); cf. Lone Steer, 464 U. S., at 411, 415 (affirming use of administrative subpoena which provided an opportunity for precompliance review as a means for obtaining "payroll and sales records"). We see no reason to accept it here.

As explained above, nothing in our decision today precludes an officer from conducting a surprise inspection by obtaining an ex parte warrant or, where an officer reasonably suspects the registry would be altered, from guarding the registry pending a hearing on a motion to quash. See Barlow's, Inc., 436 U. S., at 319–321; Riley, 573 U. S., at ____ (slip op., at 12). Justice Scalia's claim that these procedures will prove unworkable given the large number of hotels in Los Angeles is a red herring. See post, at 11. While there are approximately 2,000 hotels in Los Angeles, ibid., there is no basis to believe that resort to such measures will be needed to conduct spot checks in the vast majority of them. See supra, at 11.

Section 41.49 is also constitutionally deficient under the "certainty and regularity" prong of the closely regulated industries test because it fails sufficiently to constrain police officers' discretion as to which hotels to search and under what circumstances. While the Court has upheld inspection schemes of closely regulated industries that called for searches at least four times a year, Dewey, 452 U. S., at 604, or on a "regular basis," Burger, 482 U. S., at 711, §41.49 imposes no comparable standard.

* * *

For the foregoing reasons, we agree with the Ninth Circuit that §41.49(3)(a) is facially invalid insofar as it fails to provide any opportunity for precompliance review before a hotel must give its guest registry to the police for inspection. Accordingly, the judgment of the Ninth Circuit is affirmed.

It is so ordered.

Mullenix v. Luna (Nov 9, 2015)

PER CURIAM.

On the night of March 23, 2010, Sergeant Randy Baker of the Tulia, Texas Police Department followed Israel Leija, Jr., to a drive-in restaurant, with a warrant for his arrest. 773 F.3d 712, 715-716 (C.A.5 2014). When Baker approached Leija's car and informed him that he was under arrest, Leija sped off, headed for Interstate 27. 2013 WL 4017124, *1 (N.D.Tex., Aug. 7, 2013). Baker gave chase and was quickly joined by Trooper Gabriel Rodriguez of the Texas Department of Public Safety (DPS). 773 F.3d, at 716.

Leija entered the interstate and led the officers on an 18-minute chase at speeds between 85 and 110 miles per hour. Ibid. Twice during the chase, Leija called the Tulia Police dispatcher, claiming to have a gun and threatening to shoot at police officers if they did not abandon their pursuit. The dispatcher relayed Leija's threats, together with a report that Leija might be intoxicated, to all concerned officers.

As Baker and Rodriguez maintained their pursuit, other law enforcement officers set up tire spikes at three locations. Officer Troy Ducheneaux of the Canyon Police Department manned the spike strip at the first location Leija was expected to reach, beneath the overpass at Cemetery Road. Ducheneaux and the other officers had received training on the deployment of spike strips, including on how to take a defensive position so as to minimize the risk posed by the passing driver. Ibid.

DPS Trooper Chadrin Mullenix also responded. He drove to the Cemetery Road overpass, initially intending to set up a spike strip there. Upon learning of the other spike strip positions, however, Mullenix began to consider another tactic: shooting at Leija's car in order to disable it. 2013 WL 4017124, *1. Mullenix had not received training in this tactic and had not attempted it before, but he radioed the idea to Rodriguez. Rodriguez responded "10-4," gave Mullenix his position, and said that Leija had slowed to 85 miles per hour. Mullenix then asked the DPS dispatcher to inform his supervisor, Sergeant Byrd, of his plan and ask if Byrd thought it was "worth doing." 773 F.3d, at 716-717. Before receiving Byrd's response, Mullenix exited his vehicle and, armed with his service rifle, took a shooting position on the overpass, 20 feet above I-27. Respondents allege that from this position, Mullenix still could hear Byrd's response to "stand by" and "see if the spikes work first." Ibid.[*]

As Mullenix waited for Leija to arrive, he and another officer, Randall County Sheriff's Deputy Tom Shipman, discussed whether Mullenix's plan would work and how and where to shoot the vehicle to best carry it out. 2013 WL 4017124, *2. Shipman also informed Mullenix that another officer was located beneath the overpass. 773 F.3d, at 717.

Approximately three minutes after Mullenix took up his shooting position, he spotted Leija's vehicle, with Rodriguez in pursuit. As Leija approached the overpass, Mullenix fired six shots. Leija's car continued forward beneath the overpass, where it engaged the spike strip, hit the median, and rolled two and a half times. It was later determined that Leija had been killed by Mullenix's shots, four of which struck his upper body. There was no evidence that any of Mullenix's shots hit the car's radiator, hood, or engine block. Id., at 716-717; 2013 WL 4017124, *2-*3.

Respondents sued Mullenix under Rev. Stat. § 1979, 42 U.S.C. § 1983, alleging that he had violated the Fourth Amendment by using excessive force against Leija. Mullenix moved for summary judgment on the ground of qualified immunity, but the District Court denied his motion, finding that "[t]here are genuine issues of fact as to whether Trooper Mullenix acted recklessly, or acted as a reasonable, trained peace officer would have acted in the same or similar circumstances." 2013 WL 4017124, *6.

Mullenix appealed, and the Court of Appeals for the Fifth Circuit affirmed. 765 F.3d 531 (2014). The court agreed with the District Court that the "immediacy of the risk posed by Leija is a disputed fact that a reasonable jury could find either in the plaintiffs' favor or in the officer's favor, precluding us from concluding that Mullenix acted objectively reasonably as a matter of law." Id., at 538.

Judge King dissented. She described the "`fact issue' referenced by the majority" as "simply a restatement of the objective reasonableness test that applies to Fourth Amendment excessive force claims," which, she noted, the Supreme Court has held "`is a pure question of law.'" Id., at 544-545 (quoting Scott v. Harris, 550 U.S. 372, 381, n. 8, 127 S.Ct. 1769, 167 L.Ed.2d 686 (2007)). Turning to that legal question, Judge King concluded that Mullenix's actions were objectively reasonable. When Mullenix fired, she emphasized, he knew not only that Leija had threatened to shoot the officers involved in his pursuit, but also that Leija was seconds away from encountering such an officer beneath the overpass. Judge King also dismissed the notion that Mullenix should have given the spike strips a chance to work. She explained that because spike strips are often ineffective, and because officers operating them are vulnerable to gunfire from passing cars, Mullenix reasonably feared that the officers manning them faced a significant risk of harm. 765 F.3d, at 548-549.

Mullenix sought rehearing en banc before the Fifth Circuit, but the court denied his petition. Judge Jolly dissented, joined by six other members of the court. Judge King, who joined Judge Jolly's dissent, also filed a separate dissent of her own. 777 F.3d 221 (2014) (per curiam). On the same day, however, the two members forming the original panel's majority withdrew their previous opinion and substituted a new one. 773 F.3d 712. The revised opinion recognized that objective unreasonableness is a question of law that can be resolved on summary judgment — as Judge King had explained in her dissent — but reaffirmed the denial of qualified immunity. Id., at 715, 718. The majority concluded that Mullenix's actions were objectively unreasonable because several of the factors that had justified deadly force in previous cases were absent here: There were no innocent bystanders, Leija's driving was relatively controlled, Mullenix had not first given the spike strips a chance to work, and Mullenix's decision was not a split-second judgment. Id., at 720-724. The court went on to conclude that Mullenix was not entitled to qualified immunity because "the law was clearly established such that a reasonable officer would have known that the use of deadly force, absent a sufficiently substantial and immediate threat, violated the Fourth Amendment." Id., at 725.

We address only the qualified immunity question, not whether there was a Fourth Amendment violation in the first place, and now reverse.

The doctrine of qualified immunity shields officials from civil liability so long as their conduct "`does not violate clearly established statutory or constitutional rights of which a reasonable person would have known.'" Pearson v. Callahan, 555 U.S. 223, 231, 129 S.Ct. 808, 172 L.Ed.2d 565 (2009) (quoting Harlow v. Fitzgerald, 457 U.S. 800, 818, 102 S.Ct. 2727, 73 L.Ed.2d 396 (1982)). A clearly established right is one that is "sufficiently clear that every reasonable official would have understood that what he is doing violates that right." Reichle v. Howards, 566 U.S. ___, ___, 132 S.Ct. 2088, 2093, 182 L.Ed.2d 985 (2012) (internal quotation marks and alteration omitted). "We do not require a case directly on point, but existing precedent must have placed the statutory or constitutional question beyond debate." Ashcroft v. al-Kidd, 563 U.S. 731, 741, 131 S.Ct. 2074, 179 L.Ed.2d 1149 (2011). Put simply, qualified immunity protects "all but the plainly incompetent or those who knowingly violate the law." Malley v. Briggs, 475 U.S. 335, 341, 106 S.Ct. 1092, 89 L.Ed.2d 271 (1986).

"We have repeatedly told courts... not to define clearly established law at a high level of generality." al-Kidd, supra, at 742, 131 S.Ct. 2074. The dispositive question is "whether the violative nature of particular conduct is clearly established." Ibid. (emphasis added). This inquiry "`must be undertaken in light of the specific context of the case, not as a broad general proposition.'" Brosseau v. Haugen, 543 U.S. 194, 198, 125 S.Ct. 596, 160 L.Ed.2d 583 (2004) (per curiam) (quoting Saucier v. Katz, 533 U.S. 194, 201, 121 S.Ct. 2151, 150 L.Ed.2d 272 (2001)). Such specificity is especially important in the Fourth Amendment context, where the Court has recognized that "[i]t is sometimes difficult for an officer to determine how the relevant legal doctrine, here excessive force, will apply to the factual situation the officer confronts." 533 U.S., at 205, 121 S.Ct. 2151.

In this case, the Fifth Circuit held that Mullenix violated the clearly established rule that a police officer may not "`use deadly force against a fleeing felon who does not pose a sufficient threat of harm to the officer or others.'" 773 F.3d, at 725. Yet this Court has previously considered — and rejected — almost that exact formulation of the qualified immunity question in the Fourth Amendment context. In Brosseau, which also involved the shooting of a suspect fleeing by car, the Ninth Circuit denied qualified immunity on the ground that the officer had violated the clearly established rule, set forth in Tennessee v. Garner, 471 U.S. 1, 105 S.Ct. 1694, 85 L.Ed.2d 1 (1985), that "deadly force is only permissible where the officer

has probable cause to believe that the suspect poses a threat of serious physical harm, either to the officer or to others." Haugen v. Brosseau, 339 F.3d 857, 873 (C.A.9 2003) (internal quotation marks omitted). This Court summarily reversed, holding that use of Garner's "general" test for excessive force was "mistaken." Brosseau, 543 U.S., at 199, 125 S.Ct. 596. The correct inquiry, the Court explained, was whether it was clearly established that the Fourth Amendment prohibited the officer's conduct in the "`situation [she] confronted': whether to shoot a disturbed felon, set on avoiding capture through vehicular flight, when persons in the immediate area are at risk from that flight." Id., at 199-200, 125 S.Ct. 596. The Court considered three court of appeals cases discussed by the parties, noted that "this area is one in which the result depends very much on the facts of each case," and concluded that the officer was entitled to qualified immunity because "[n]one of [the cases] squarely governs the case here." Id., at 201, 125 S.Ct. 596 (emphasis added).

Anderson v. Creighton, 483 U.S. 635, 107 S.Ct. 3034, 97 L.Ed.2d 523 (1987), is also instructive on the required degree of specificity. There, the lower court had denied qualified immunity based on the clearly established "right to be free from warrantless searches of one's home unless the searching officers have probable cause and there are exigent circumstances." Id., at 640, 107 S.Ct. 3034. This Court faulted that formulation for failing to address the actual question at issue: whether "the circumstances with which Anderson was confronted... constitute[d] probable cause and exigent circumstances." Id., at 640-641, 107 S.Ct. 3034. Without answering that question, the Court explained, the conclusion that Anderson's search was objectively unreasonable did not "follow immediately" from — and thus was not clearly established by — the principle that warrantless searches not supported by probable cause and exigent circumstances violate the Fourth

Amendment. Id., at 641, 107 S.Ct. 3034.

In this case, Mullenix confronted a reportedly intoxicated fugitive, set on avoiding capture through high-speed vehicular flight, who twice during his flight had threatened to shoot police officers, and who was moments away from encountering an officer at Cemetery Road. The relevant inquiry is whether existing precedent placed the conclusion that Mullenix acted unreasonably in these circumstances "beyond debate." al-Kidd, supra, at 741, 131 S.Ct. 2074. The general principle that deadly force requires a sufficient threat hardly settles this matter. See Pasco v. Knoblauch, 566 F.3d 572, 580 (C.A.5 2009) ("[I]t would be unreasonable to expect a police officer to make the numerous legal conclusions necessary to apply Garner to a high-speed car chase ...").

Far from clarifying the issue, excessive force cases involving car chases reveal the hazy legal backdrop against which Mullenix acted. In Brosseau itself, the Court held that an officer did not violate clearly established law when she shot a fleeing suspect out of fear that he endangered "other officers on foot who [she] believed were in the immediate area," "the occupied vehicles in [his] path," and "any other citizens who might be in the area." 543 U.S., at 197, 125 S.Ct. 596 (first alteration in original; internal quotation marks omitted; emphasis added). The threat Leija posed was at least as immediate as that presented by a suspect who had just begun to drive off and was headed only in the general direction of officers and bystanders. Id., at 196-197, 125 S.Ct. 596. By the time Mullenix fired, Leija had led police on a 25-mile chase at extremely high speeds, was reportedly intoxicated, had twice threatened to shoot officers, and was racing towards an officer's location.

This Court has considered excessive force claims in connection with high-speed chases on only two occasions since Brosseau. In Scott v. Harris, 550 U.S. 372, 127 S.Ct. 1769, the Court held that an officer did not violate the Fourth Amendment by ramming the car of a fugitive whose reckless driving "posed an actual and imminent threat to the lives of any pedestrians who might have been present, to other civilian motorists, and to the officers involved in the chase." Id., at 384, 127 S.Ct. 1769. And in Plumhoff v. Rickard, 572 U.S. ___, 134 S.Ct. 2012, 188 L.Ed.2d 1056 (2014), the Court reaffirmed Scott by holding that an officer acted reasonably when he fatally shot a fugitive who was "intent on resuming" a chase that "pose[d] a deadly threat for others on the road." 572 U.S., at ___, 134 S.Ct., at 2022. The Court has thus never found the use of deadly force in connection with a dangerous car chase to violate the Fourth Amendment, let alone to be a basis for denying qualified immunity. Leija in his flight did not pass as many cars as the drivers in Scott or Plumhoff; traffic was light on I-27. At the same time, the fleeing fugitives in Scott and Plumhoff had not verbally threatened to kill any officers in their path, nor were they about to come upon such officers. In any event, none of our precedents "squarely governs" the facts here. Given Leija's conduct, we cannot say that only someone "plainly incompetent" or who "knowingly violate[s] the law" would have perceived a sufficient threat and acted as Mullenix did. Malley, 475 U.S., at 341, 106 S.Ct. 1092.

The dissent focuses on the availability of spike strips as an alternative means of terminating the chase. It argues that even if Leija posed a threat sufficient to justify deadly force in some circumstances, Mullenix nevertheless contravened clearly established law because he did not wait to see if the spike strips would work before taking action. Spike strips, however, present dangers of their own, not only to drivers who encounter them at speeds between 85 and 110 miles per hour, but also to officers manning them. See, e.g., Thompson v. Mercer, 762 F.3d 433, 440 (C.A.5 2014); Brief for National Association of Police Organizations et al. as Amici Curiae 15-16. Nor are spike strips always successful in ending the chase. See, e.g., Cordova v. Aragon, 569 F.3d 1183, 1186 (C.A.10 2009); Brief for National Association of Police Organizations et al. as Amici Curiae 16 (citing examples). The dissent can cite no case from this Court denying qualified immunity because officers entitled to terminate a high-speed chase selected one dangerous alternative over another.

Even so, the dissent argues, there was no governmental interest that justified acting before Leija's car hit the spikes. Mullenix explained, however, that he feared Leija might attempt to shoot at or run over the officers manning the spike strips. Mullenix also feared that even if Leija hit the spike strips, he might still be able to continue driving in the direction of other officers. The dissent ignores these interests by suggesting that there was no "possible marginal gain in shooting at the car over using the spike strips already in place." Post, at 315 (opinion of SOTOMAYOR, J.). In fact, Mullenix hoped his actions would stop the car in a manner that avoided the risks to other officers and other drivers that relying on spike strips would entail. The dissent disputes the merits of the options available to Mullenix, post, at 314-315, but others with more experience analyze the issues differently. See, e.g., Brief for National Association of Police Organizations et al. as Amici Curiae 15-16. Ultimately, whatever can be said of the wisdom of Mullenix's choice, this Court's precedents do not place the conclusion that he acted unreasonably in these circumstances "beyond debate." al-Kidd, 563 U.S., at 741, 131 S.Ct. 2074.

More fundamentally, the dissent repeats the Fifth Circuit's error. It defines the qualified immunity inquiry at a high level of generality — whether any governmental interest justified choosing one tactic over another — and then fails to consider that question in "the specific context of the case." Brosseau v. Haugen, 543 U.S., at 198,

125 S.Ct. 596 (internal quotation marks omitted). As in Anderson, the conclusion that Mullenix's reasons were insufficient to justify his actions simply does not "follow immediately" from the general proposition that force must be justified. 483 U.S., at 641, 107 S.Ct. 3034.

Cases decided by the lower courts since Brosseau likewise have not clearly established that deadly force is inappropriate in response to conduct like Leija's. The Fifth Circuit here principally relied on its own decision in Lytle v. Bexar County, 560 F.3d 404 (2009), denying qualified immunity to a police officer who had fired at a fleeing car and killed one of its passengers. That holding turned on the court's assumption, for purposes of summary judgment, that the car was moving away from the officer and had already traveled some distance at the moment the officer fired. See id., at 409. The court held that a reasonable jury could conclude that a receding car "did not pose a sufficient threat of harm such that the use of deadly force was reasonable." Id., at 416. But, crucially, the court also recognized that if the facts were as the officer alleged, and he fired as the car was coming towards him, "he would likely be entitled to qualified immunity" based on the "threat of immediate and severe physical harm." Id., at 412. Without implying that Lytle was either correct or incorrect, it suffices to say that Lytle does not clearly dictate the conclusion that Mullenix was unjustified in perceiving grave danger and responding accordingly, given that Leija was speeding towards a confrontation with officers he had threatened to kill.

Cases that the Fifth Circuit ignored also suggest that Mullenix's assessment of the threat Leija posed was reasonable. In Long v. Slaton, 508 F.3d 576 (2007), for example, the Eleventh Circuit held that a sheriff's deputy did not violate the Fourth Amendment by fatally shooting a mentally unstable individual who was attempting to flee in the deputy's car, even though at the time of the shooting the individual had not yet operated the cruiser dangerously. The court explained that "the law does not require officers in a tense and dangerous situation to wait until the moment a suspect uses a deadly weapon to act to stop the suspect" and concluded that the deputy had reason to believe Long was dangerous based on his unstable state of mind, theft of the cruiser, and failure to heed the deputy's warning to stop. Id., at 581-582. The court also rejected the notion that the deputy should have first tried less lethal methods, such as spike strips. "[C]onsidering the unpredictability of Long's behavior and his fleeing in a marked police cruiser," the court held, "we think the police need not have taken that chance and hoped for the best." Id., at 583 (alteration and internal quotation marks omitted). But see Smith v. Cupp, 430 F.3d 766, 774-777 (C.A.6 2005) (denying qualified immunity to an officer who shot an intoxicated suspect who had stolen the officer's cruiser where a reasonable jury could have concluded that the suspect's flight did not immediately threaten the officer or any other bystander).

Other cases cited by the Fifth Circuit and respondents are simply too factually distinct to speak clearly to the specific circumstances here. Several involve suspects who may have done little more than flee at relatively low speeds. See, e.g., Walker v. Davis, 649 F.3d 502, 503 (C.A.6 2011); Kirby v. Duva, 530 F.3d 475, 479-480 (C.A.6 2008); Adams v. Speers, 473 F.3d 989, 991 (C.A.9 2007); Vaughan v. Cox, 343 F.3d 1323, 1330-1331, and n. 7 (C.A.11 2003). These cases shed little light on whether the far greater danger of a speeding fugitive threatening to kill police officers waiting in his path could warrant deadly force. The court below noted that "no weapon was ever seen," 773 F.3d, at 723, but surely in these circumstances the police were justified in taking Leija at his word when he twice told the dispatcher he had a gun and was prepared to use it.

Finally, respondents argue that the danger Leija represented was less substantial than the threats that courts have found sufficient to justify deadly force. But the mere fact that courts have approved deadly force in more extreme circumstances says little, if anything, about whether such force was reasonable in the circumstances here. The fact is that when Mullenix fired, he reasonably understood Leija to be a fugitive fleeing arrest, at speeds over 100 miles per hour, who was armed and possibly intoxicated, who had threatened to kill any officer he saw if the police did not abandon their pursuit, and who was racing towards Officer Ducheneaux's position. Even accepting that these circumstances fall somewhere between the two sets of cases respondents discuss, qualified immunity protects actions in the "`hazy border between excessive and acceptable force.'" Brosseau, supra, at 201, 125 S.Ct. 596 (quoting Saucier, 533 U.S., at 206, 121 S.Ct. 2151; some internal quotation marks omitted).

Because the constitutional rule applied by the Fifth Circuit was not "`beyond debate,'" Stanton v. Sims, 571 U.S. ___, ___, 134 S.Ct. 3, 7, 187 L.Ed.2d 341 (2013) (per curiam) (slip op., at 8), we grant Mullenix's petition for certiorari and reverse the Fifth Circuit's determination that Mullenix is not entitled to qualified immunity.

It is so ordered.

Notes

[*] Although Mullenix disputes hearing Byrd's response, we view the facts in the light most favorable to respondents, who oppose Mullenix's motion for summary judgment. See Tolan v. Cotton, 572 U.S. ___, ___, 134 S.Ct. 1861, 1863, 188 L.Ed.2d 895 (2014) (per curiam).

Luis v. US (March 30, 2016) [Appendix omitted]

Justice Breyer announced the judgment of the Court and delivered an opinion in which The Chief Justice, Justice Ginsburg, and Justice Sotomayor join.

A federal statute provides that a court may freeze before trial certain assets belonging to a criminal defendant accused of violations of federal health care or banking laws. See 18 U. S. C. §1345. Those assets include: (1) property "obtained as a result of" the crime, (2) property "traceable" to the crime, and (3) other "property of equivalent value." §1345(a)(2). In this case, the Government has obtained a court order that freezes assets belonging to the third category of property, namely, property that is untainted by the crime, and that belongs fully to the defendant. That order, the defendant says, prevents her from paying her lawyer. She claims that insofar as it does so, it violates her Sixth Amendment "right . . . to have the Assistance of Counsel for [her] defence." We agree.

I

In October 2012, a federal grand jury charged the petitioner, Sila Luis, with paying kickbacks, conspiring to commit fraud, and engaging in other crimes all related to health care. See §1349; §371; 42 U. S. C. §1320a–7b(b)(2)(A). The Government claimed that Luis had fraudulently obtained close to $45 million, almost all of which she had already spent. Believing it would convict Luis of the crimes charged, and hoping to preserve the $2 million remaining in Luis' possession for payment of restitution and other criminal penalties (often referred to as criminal forfeitures, which can include innocent— not just tainted—assets, a point of critical importance here), the Government sought a pretrial order prohibiting Luis from dissipating her assets. See 18 U. S. C. §1345(a)(2). And the District Court ultimately issued an order prohibiting her from "dissipating, or otherwise disposing of . . . assets, real or personal . . . up to the equivalent value of the proceeds of the Federal health care fraud ($45 million)." App. to Pet. for Cert. A–6.

The Government and Luis agree that this court order will prevent Luis from using her own untainted funds, i.e., funds not connected with the crime, to hire counsel to defend her in her criminal case. See App. 161 (stipulating "that an unquantified amount of revenue not connected to the indictment [had] flowed into some of the accounts" subject to the restraining order); ibid. (similarly stipulating that Luis used "revenue not connected to the indictment" to pay for real property that she possessed). Al-though the District Court recognized that the order might prevent Luis from obtaining counsel of her choice, it held "that there is no Sixth Amendment right to use untainted, substitute assets to hire counsel." 966 F. Supp. 2d 1321, 1334 (SD Fla. 2013).

The Eleventh Circuit upheld the District Court. See 564 Fed. Appx. 493, 494 (2014) (per curiam) (referring to, e.g., Kaley v. United States, 571 U. S. ____ (2014); Caplin & Drysdale, Chartered v. United States, 491 U. S. 617, 631 (1989) ; United States v. Monsanto, 491 U. S. 600, 616 (1989)). We granted Luis' petition for certiorari.

II

The question presented is "[w]hether the pretrial restraint of a criminal defendant's legitimate, untainted assets (those not traceable to a criminal offense) needed to retain counsel of choice violates the Fifth and Sixth Amendments." Pet. for Cert. ii. We see no reasonable way to interpret the relevant statutes to avoid answering this constitutional question. Cf. Monsanto, supra, at 614. Hence, we answer it, and our answer is that the pretrial restraint of legitimate, untainted assets needed to retain counsel of choice violates the Sixth Amendment. The nature and importance of the constitutional right taken together with the nature of the assets lead us to this conclusion.

A

No one doubts the fundamental character of a criminal defendant's Sixth Amendment right to the "Assistance of Counsel." In Gideon v. Wainwright, 372 U. S. 335 (1963), the Court explained:

" 'The right to be heard would be, in many cases, of little avail if it did not comprehend the right to be heard by counsel. Even the intelligent and educated layman has small and sometimes no skill in the science of law. If charged with crime, he is incapable, generally, of determining for himself whether the indictment is good or bad. He is unfamiliar with the rules of evidence. Left without the aid of counsel he may be put on trial without a proper charge, and convicted upon incompetent evidence, or evidence irrelevant to the issue or otherwise inadmissible. He lacks both the skill and knowledge adequately to prepare his defense, even though he have a perfect one. He requires the guiding hand of counsel at every step in the proceedings against him. Without it, though he be not guilty, he faces the danger of conviction because he does not know how to establish his innocence.' " Id., at 344–345 (quoting Powell v. Alabama, 287 U. S. 45–69 (1932)).

It is consequently not surprising: first, that this Court's opinions often refer to the right to counsel as "fundamental," id., at 68; see Grosjean v. American Press Co., 297 U. S. 233–244 (1936) (similar); Johnson v. Zerbst, 304 U. S. 458–463 (1938) (similar); second, that commentators describe the right as a "great engin[e] by which an innocent man can make the truth of his innocence visible," Amar, Sixth Amendment First Principles, 84 Geo. L. J. 641, 643 (1996); see Herring v. New York, 422 U. S. 853, 862 (1975); third, that we have understood the right to require that the Government provide counsel for an indigent defendant accused of all but the least serious crimes, see Gideon, supra, at 344; and fourth, that we have considered the wrongful deprivation of the right to counsel a "structural" error that so "affec[ts] the framework within which the trial proceeds" that courts may not even ask whether the error harmed the defendant. United States v. Gonzalez-Lopez, 548 U. S. 140, 148 (2006) (internal quotation marks omitted); see id., at 150.

Given the necessarily close working relationship between lawyer and client, the need for confidence, and the critical importance of trust, neither is it surprising that the Court has held that the Sixth Amendment grants a defendant "a fair opportunity to secure counsel of his own choice." Powell, supra, at 53; see Gonzalez-Lopez, supra, at 150 (describing "these myriad aspects of representation"). This "fair opportunity" for the defendant to secure counsel of choice has limits. A defendant has no right, for example, to an attorney who is not a member of the bar, or who has a conflict of interest due to a relationship with an opposing party. See Wheat v. United States, 486 U. S. 153, 159 (1988). And an indigent defendant, while entitled to adequate representation, has no right to have the Government pay for his preferred representational choice. See Caplin & Drysdale, 491 U. S., at 624.

We nonetheless emphasize that the constitutional right at issue here is fundamental: "[T]he Sixth Amendment guarantees a defendant the right to be represented by an otherwise qualified attorney whom that defendant can afford to hire." Ibid.

B

The Government cannot, and does not, deny Luis' right to be represented by a qualified attorney whom she chooses and can afford. But the Government would undermine the value of that right by taking from Luis the ability to use the funds she needs to pay for her chosen attorney. The Government points out that, while freezing the funds may have this consequence, there are important interests on the other side of the legal equation: It wishes to guarantee that those funds will be available later to help pay for statutory penalties (including forfeiture of untainted assets) and restitution, should it secure convictions. And it points to two cases from this Court, Caplin & Drysdale, supra, at 619, and Monsanto, 491 U. S., at 615, which, in the Government's view, hold that the Sixth Amendment does not pose an obstacle to its doing so here. In our view, however, the nature of the assets at issue here differs from the assets at issue in those earlier cases. And that distinction makes a difference.

1

The relevant difference consists of the fact that the property here is untainted; i.e., it belongs to the defendant, pure and simple. In this respect it differs from a robber's loot, a drug seller's cocaine, a burglar's tools, or other property associated with the planning, implementing, or concealing of a crime. The Government may well be able to freeze, perhaps to seize, assets of the latter, "tainted" kind before trial. As a matter of property law the defendant's ownership interest is imperfect. The robber's loot belongs to the victim, not to the defendant. See Telegraph Co. v. Davenport, 97 U. S. 369, 372 (1878) ("The great principle that no one can be deprived of his property without his assent, except by the processes of the law, requires . . . that the property wrongfully transferred or stolen should be restored to its rightful owner"). The cocaine is contraband, long considered forfeitable to the Government wherever found. See, e.g., 21 U. S. C. §881(a) ("[Controlled substances] shall be subject to forfeiture to the United States and no property right shall exist in them"); Carroll v. United States, 267 U. S. 132, 159 (1925) (describing the seizure of "contraband forfeitable property"). And title to property used to commit a crime (or otherwise "traceable" to a crime) often passes to the Government at the instant the crime is planned or committed. See, e.g., §853(c) (providing that the Government's ownership interest in such property relates back to the time of the crime).

The property at issue here, however, is not loot, contraband, or otherwise "tainted." It belongs to the defendant. That fact undermines the Government's reliance upon precedent, for both Caplin & Drysdale and Monsanto relied critically upon the fact that the property at issue was "tainted," and that title to the property therefore had passed from the defendant to the Government before the court issued its order freezing (or otherwise disposing of) the assets.

In Caplin & Drysdale, the Court considered a post-conviction forfeiture that took from a convicted defendant funds he would have used to pay his lawyer. The Court held that the forfeiture was constitutional. In doing so, however, it emphasized that the forfeiture statute at issue provided that " '[a]ll right, title, and interest in property [constituting or derived from any proceeds obtained from the crime] vests in the United States upon the commission of the act giving rise to [the] forfeiture.' " 491 U. S., at 625, n. 4 (quoting §853(c)) (emphasis added). It added that the law had "long-recognized" as "lawful" the "practice of vesting title to any forfeitable asset[s] in the United State[s] at the time of the crim[e]." Id., at 627. It pointed out that the defendant did not "claim, as a general proposition, that the [vesting] provision is unconstitutional, or that Congress cannot, as a general matter, vest title to assets derived from the crime in the Government, as of the date of the criminal act in question." Id., at 627–628. And, given the vesting language, the Court explained that the defendant "did not hold good title" to the property. Id., at 627. The Court therefore concluded that "[t]here is no constitutional principle that gives one person [namely, the defendant] the right to give another's [namely, the Government's] property to a third party," namely, the lawyer. Id., at 628.

In Monsanto, the Court considered a pretrial restraining order that prevented a not-yet-convicted defendant from using certain assets to pay for his lawyer. The defendant argued that, given this difference, Caplin & Drysdale's conclusion should not apply. The Court noted, however, that the property at issue was forfeitable under the same statute that was at issue in Caplin & Drysdale. See Monsanto, supra, at 614. And, as in Caplin & Drysdale, the application of that statute to Monsanto's case concerned only the pretrial restraint of assets that were traceable to the crime, see 491 U. S., at 602–603; thus, the statute passed title to those funds at the time the crime was committed (i.e., before the trial), see §853(c). The Court said that Caplin & Drysdale had already "weigh[ed] . . . th[e] very interests" at issue. Monsanto, supra, at 616. And it "rel[ied] on" its "conclusion" in Caplin & Drysdale to dispose of, and to reject, the defendant's "similar constitutional claims." 491 U. S., at 614.

Justice Kennedy prefers to read Caplin & Drysdale and Monsanto broadly, as holding that "the Government, having established probable cause to believe that Luis' substitute [i.e., innocent] assets will be forfeitable upon conviction, should be permitted to obtain a restraining order barring her from spending those funds prior to trial." Post, at 6–7 (dissenting opinion). In other words, he believes that those cases stand for the proposition that property—whether tainted or untainted—is subject to pretrial restraint, so long as the property might someday be subject to forfeiture. But this reading asks too much of our precedents. For one thing, as discussed, Caplin & Drysdale and Monsanto involved the restraint only of tainted assets, and thus we had no occasion to opine in those cases about the constitutionality of pretrial restraints of other, untainted assets.

For another thing, Justice Kennedy's broad rule ignores the statutory background against which Caplin & Drysdale and Monsanto were decided. The Court in those cases referenced §853(c) more than a dozen times. And it

acknowledged that whether property is "forfeitable" or subject to pretrial restraint under Congress' scheme is a nuanced inquiry that very much depends on who has the superior interest in the property at issue. See Caplin & Drysdale, supra, at 626–628; Monsanto, 491 U. S., at 616. We see this in, for example, §853(e)(1), which explicitly authorizes restraining orders or injunctions against "property described in subsection (a) of this section" (i.e., tainted assets). We see this too in §853(e)(1)(B), which requires the Government—in certain circumstances—to give "notice to persons appearing to have an interest in the property and opportunity for hearing" before obtaining a restraining order against such property. We see this in §853(c), which allows "bona fide purchaser[s] for value" to keep property that would otherwise be subject to forfeiture. And we see this in §853(n)(6)(A), which exempts certain property from forfeiture when a third party can show a vested interest in the property that is "superior" to that of the Government.

The distinction that we have discussed is thus an important one, not a technicality. It is the difference between what is yours and what is mine. In Caplin & Drysdale and Monsanto, the Government wanted to impose restrictions upon (or seize) property that the Government had probable cause to believe was the proceeds of, or traceable to, a crime. See Monsanto, supra, at 615. The relevant statute said that the Government took title to those tainted assets as of the time of the crime. See §853(c). And the defendants in those cases consequently had to concede that the disputed property was in an important sense the Government's at the time the court imposed the restrictions. See Caplin & Drysdale, supra, at 619–620; Monsanto, supra, at 602–603.

This is not to say that the Government "owned" the tainted property outright (in the sense that it could take possession of the property even before obtaining a conviction). See post, at 7–10

(Kennedy, J., dissenting). Rather, it is to say that the Government even before trial had a "substantial" interest in the tainted property sufficient to justify the property's pretrial restraint. See Caplin & Drysdale, supra, at 627 ("[T]he property rights given the Government by virtue of [§853(c)'s relation-back provision] are more substantial than petitioner acknowledges"); United States v. Stowell, 133 U. S. 1, 19 (1890) ("As soon as [the possessor of the forfeitable asset committed the violation] . . . , the forfeiture . . . took effect, and (though needing judicial condemnation to perfect it) operated from that time as a statutory conveyance to the United States of all right, title and interest then remaining in the [possessor]; and was as valid and effectual, against all the world, as a recorded deed" (emphasis added)).

If we analogize to bankruptcy law, the Government, by application of §853(c)'s relation-back provision, became something like a secured creditor with a lien on the defendant's tainted assets superior to that of most any other party. See 4 Collier on Bankruptcy ¶506.03[1] (16th ed. 2015). For this reason, §853(c) has operated in our cases as a significant limitation on criminal defendants' property rights in such assets—even before conviction. See Monsanto, supra, at 613 ("Permitting a defendant to use [tainted] assets for his private purposes that, under this [relation-back] provision, will become the property of the United States if a conviction occurs cannot be sanctioned"); cf. Grupo Mexicano de Desarrollo, S. A. v. Alliance Bond Fund, Inc., 527 U. S. 308, 326 (1999) (noting that the Court had previously authorized injunctions against the further dissipation of property where, among other things, "the creditor (the Government) asserted an equitable lien on the property").

Here, by contrast, the Government seeks to impose restrictions upon Luis' untainted property without any showing of any equivalent governmental interest in that property. Again, if this were a bankruptcy case, the Government would be at most an unsecured creditor. Al-though such creditors someday might collect from a debtor's general assets, they cannot be said to have any present claim to, or interest in, the debtor's property. See id., at 330 ("[B]efore judgment . . . an unsecured creditor has no rights at law or in equity in the property of his debtor"); see also 5 Collier on Bankruptcy ¶541.05[1][b] ("[G]eneral unsecured creditor[s]" have "no specific property interest in the goods held or sold by the debtor"). The competing property interests in the tainted- and untainted-asset contexts therefore are not "exactly the same." Post, at 2 (Kagan, J., dissenting). At least regarding her untainted assets, Luis can at this point reasonably claim that the property is still "mine," free and clear.

2

This distinction between (1) what is primarily "mine" (the defendant's) and (2) what is primarily "yours" (the Government's) does not by itself answer the constitutional question posed, for the law of property sometimes allows a person without a present interest in a piece of property to impose restrictions upon a current owner, say, to prevent waste. A holder of a reversionary interest, for example, can prevent the owner of a life estate from wasting the property. See, e.g., Peterson v. Ferrell, 127 N. C. 169, 170, 37 S. E. 189, 190 (1900). Those who later may become beneficiaries of a trust are sometimes able to prevent the trustee from dissipating the trust's assets. See, e.g., Kollock v. Webb, 113 Ga. 762, 769, 39 S. E. 339, 343 (1901). And holders of a contingent, future executory interest in property (an interest that might become possessory at some point down the road) can, in limited circumstances, enjoin the activities of the current owner. See, e.g., Dees v. Cheuvronts, 240 Ill. 486, 491, 88 N. E. 1011, 1012 (1909) ("[E]quity w[ill] interfere . . . only when it is made to appear that the contingency . . . is reasonably certain to happen, and the waste is . . .

wanton and conscienceless"). The Government here seeks a somewhat analogous order, i.e., an order that will preserve Luis' untainted assets so that they will be available to cover the costs of forfeiture and restitution if she is convicted, and if the court later determines that her tainted assets are insufficient or otherwise unavailable.

The Government finds statutory authority for its request in language authorizing a court to enjoin a criminal defendant from, for example, disposing of innocent "property of equivalent value" to that of tainted property. 18 U. S. C. §1345(a)(2)(B)(i). But Luis needs some portion of those same funds to pay for the lawyer of her choice. Thus, the legal conflict arises. And, in our view, insofar as innocent (i.e., untainted) funds are needed to obtain counsel of choice, we believe that the Sixth Amendment prohibits the court order that the Government seeks.

Three basic considerations lead us to this conclusion. First, the nature of the competing interests argues against this kind of court order. On the one side we find, as we have previously explained, supra, at 3–5, a Sixth Amendment right to assistance of counsel that is a fundamental constituent of due process of law, see Powell, 287 U. S., at 68–69. And that right includes "the right to be represented by an otherwise qualified attorney whom that defendant can afford to hire." Caplin & Drysdale, 491 U. S., at 624. The order at issue in this case would seriously undermine that constitutional right.

On the other side we find interests that include the Government's contingent interest in securing its punishment of choice (namely, criminal forfeiture) as well as the victims' interest in securing restitution (notably, from funds belonging to the defendant, not the victims). While these interests are important, to deny the Government the order it requests will not inevitably undermine them, for, at least sometimes, the defendant may possess other assets—say, "tainted" property—that might be used for forfeitures and restitution. Cf. Gonzalez-Lopez, 548 U. S., at 148 ("Deprivation of the right" to counsel of the defendant's choice "is 'complete' when the defendant is erroneously prevented from being represented by the lawyer he wants"). Nor do the interests in obtaining payment of a criminal forfeiture or restitution order enjoy constitutional protection. Rather, despite their importance, compared to the right to counsel of choice, these interests would seem to lie somewhat further from the heart of a fair, effective criminal justice system.

Second, relevant legal tradition offers virtually no significant support for the Government's position. Rather, tradition argues to the contrary. Describing the 18th-century English legal world (which recognized only a limited right to counsel), Blackstone wrote that "only" those "goods and chattels" that "a man has at the time of conviction shall be forfeited." 4 W. Blackstone, Commentaries on the Laws of England 388 (1765) (emphasis added); see 1 J. Chitty, Practical Treatise on the Criminal Law 737 (1816) ("[T]he party indicted may sell any of [his property] . . . to assist him in preparing for his defense on the trial").

Describing the common law as understood in 19th-century America (which recognized a broader right to counsel), Justice Story wrote:

"It is well known, that at the common law, in many cases of felonies, the party forfeited his goods and chattels to the crown. The forfeiture . . . was a part, or at least a consequence, of the judgment of conviction. It is plain from this statement, that no right to the goods and chattels of the felon could be acquired by the crown by the mere commission of the offense; but the right attached only by the conviction of the offender. . . . In the contemplation of the common law, the offender's right was not divested until the conviction." The Palmyra, 12 Wheat. 1, 14 (1827).

See generally Powell, supra, at 60–61

(describing the scope of the right to counsel in 18th-century Britain and colonial America).

As we have explained, supra, at 6–10, cases such as Caplin & Drysdale and Monsanto permit the Government to freeze a defendant's assets pretrial, but the opinions in those cases highlight the fact that the property at issue was "tainted," i.e., it did not belong entirely to the defendant. We have found no decision of this Court authorizing unfettered, pretrial forfeiture of the defendant's own "innocent" property—property with no connection to the charged crime. Nor do we see any grounds for distinguishing the historic preference against preconviction forfeitures from the preconviction restraint at issue here. As far as Luis' Sixth Amendment right to counsel of choice is concerned, a restraining order might as well be a forfeiture; that is, the restraint itself suffices to completely deny this constitutional right. See Gonzalez-Lopez, supra, at 148.

Third, as a practical matter, to accept the Government's position could well erode the right to counsel to a considerably greater extent than we have so far indicated. To permit the Government to freeze Luis' untainted assets would unleash a principle of constitutional law that would have no obvious stopping place. The statutory provision before us authorizing the present restraining order refers only to "banking law violation[s]" and "Federal health care offense[s]." 18 U. S. C. §1345(a)(2). But, in the Government's view, Congress could write more statutes authorizing pretrial restraints in cases involving other illegal behavior—after all, a broad range of such behavior can lead to postconviction forfeiture of untainted assets. See, e.g., §1963(m) (providing for forfeiture of innocent, substitute assets for any violation of the Racketeer Influenced and Corrupt Organizations Act).

Moreover, the financial consequences of a criminal conviction are steep. Even beyond the forfeiture itself, criminal fines can be high, and restitution orders expensive. See, e.g., §1344 ($1 million fine for bank fraud); §3571 (mail and wire fraud fines of up to $250,000 for individuals and $500,000 for organizations); United States v. Gushlak, 728 F. 3d 184, 187, 203 (CA2 2013) ($17.5 million restitution award against an individual defendant in a fraud-on-the-market case); FTC v. Trudeau, 662 F. 3d 947, 949 (CA7 2011) ($37.6 million remedial sanction for fraud). How are defendants whose innocent assets are frozen in cases like these supposed to pay for a lawyer—particularly if they lack "tainted assets" because they are innocent, a class of defendants whom the right to counsel certainly seeks to protect? See Powell, 287 U. S., at 69; Amar, 84 Geo. L. J., at 643 ("[T]he Sixth Amendment is generally designed to elicit truth and protect innocence").

These defendants, rendered indigent, would fall back upon publicly paid counsel, including overworked and underpaid public defenders. As the Department of Justice explains, only 27 percent of county-based public defender offices have sufficient attorneys to meet nationally recommended caseload standards. Dept. of Justice, Bureau of Justice Statistics, D. Farole & L. Langton, Census of Public Defender Offices, 2007: County-based and Local Public Defender Offices, 2007, p. 10 (Sept. 2010). And as one amicus points out, "[m]any federal public defender organizations and lawyers appointed under the Criminal Justice Act serve numerous clients and have only limited resources." Brief for New York Council of Defense Lawyers 11. The upshot is a substantial risk that accepting the Government's views would—by increasing the government-paid-defender workload—render less effective the basic right the Sixth Amendment seeks to protect.

3

We add that the constitutional line we have drawn should prove workable. That line distinguishes between a criminal defendant's (1) tainted funds and (2) innocent funds needed to pay for counsel. We concede, as Justice Kennedy points out, post, at 12–13, that money is fungible; and sometimes it will be difficult to say whether a particular bank account contains tainted or untainted funds. But the law has tracing rules that help courts implement the kind of distinction we require in this case. With the help of those rules, the victim of a robbery, for example, will likely obtain the car that the robber used stolen money to buy. See, e.g., 1 G. Palmer, Law of Restitution §2.14, p. 175 (1978) ("tracing" permits a claim against "an asset which is traceable to or the product of" tainted funds); 4 A. Scott, Law of Trusts §518, pp. 3309–3314 (1956) (describing the tracing rules governing commingled accounts). And those rules will likely also prevent Luis from benefiting from many of the money transfers and purchases Justice Kennedy describes. See post, at 12–13.

Courts use tracing rules in cases involving fraud, pension rights, bankruptcy, trusts, etc. See, e.g., Montanile v. Board of Trustees of Nat. Elevator Industry Health Benefit Plan, 577 U. S. ___, ___–___ (2016) (slip op., at 8–9). They consequently have experience separating tainted assets from untainted assets, just as they have experience determining how much money is needed to cover the costs of a lawyer. See, e.g., 18 U. S. C. §1345(b) ("The court shall proceed as soon as practicable to the hearing and determination of [actions to freeze a defendant's tainted or untainted assets]"); 28 U. S. C. §2412(d) (courts must determine reasonable attorneys' fees under the Equal Access to Justice Act); see also Kaley, 571 U. S., at ___, and n. 3 (slip op., at 3, and n. 3) ("Since Monsanto, the lower courts have generally provided a hearing. . . . [to determine] whether probable cause exists to believe that the assets in dispute are traceable . . . to the crime charged in the indictment"). We therefore see little reason to worry, as Justice Kennedy seems to, that defendants will "be allowed to circumvent [the usual forfeiture rules] by using . . . funds to pay for a high, or even the highest, priced defense team [they] can find." Post, at 7.

*　　*　　*

For the reasons stated, we conclude that the defendant in this case has a Sixth Amendment right to use her own "innocent" property to pay a reasonable fee for the assistance of counsel. On the assumptions made here, the District Court's order prevents Luis from exercising that right. We consequently vacate the judgment of the Court of Appeals and remand the case for further proceedings.

It is so ordered.

Utah v. Strieff (June 20, 2016)

Justice Thomas delivered the opinion of the Court.

To enforce the Fourth Amendment's prohibition against "unreasonable searches and seizures," this Court has at times required courts to exclude evidence obtained by unconstitutional police conduct. But the Court has also held that, even when there is a Fourth Amendment violation, this exclusionary rule does not apply when the costs of exclusion outweigh its deterrent benefits. In some cases, for example, the link between the unconstitutional conduct and the discovery of the evidence is too attenuated to justify suppression. The question in this case is whether this attenuation doctrine applies when an officer makes an unconstitutional investigatory stop; learns during that stop that the suspect is subject to a valid arrest warrant; and proceeds to arrest the suspect and seize incriminating evidence during a search incident to that arrest. We hold that the evidence the officer seized as part of the search incident to arrest is admissible because the officer's discovery of the arrest warrant attenuated the connection between the unlawful stop and the evidence seized incident to arrest.

I

This case began with an anonymous tip. In December 2006, someone called the South Salt Lake City police's drug-tip line to report "narcotics activity" at a particular residence. App. 15. Narcotics detective Douglas Fackrell investigated the tip. Over the course of about a week, Officer Fackrell conducted intermittent surveillance of the home. He observed visitors who left a few minutes after arriving at the house. These visits were sufficiently frequent to raise his suspicion that the occupants were dealing drugs.

One of those visitors was respondent Edward Strieff. Officer Fackrell observed Strieff exit the house and walk toward a nearby convenience store. In the store's parking lot, Officer Fackrell detained Strieff, identified himself, and asked Strieff what he was doing at the residence.

As part of the stop, Officer Fackrell requested Strieff's identification, and Strieff produced his Utah identification card. Officer Fackrell relayed Strieff's information to a police dispatcher, who reported that Strieff had an outstanding arrest warrant for a traffic violation. Officer Fackrell then arrested Strieff pursuant to that warrant. When Officer Fackrell searched Strieff incident to the arrest, he discovered a baggie of methamphetamine and drug paraphernalia.

The State charged Strieff with unlawful possession of methamphetamine and drug paraphernalia. Strieff moved to suppress the evidence, arguing that the evidence was inadmissible because it was derived from an unlawful investigatory stop. At the suppression hearing, the prosecutor conceded that Officer Fackrell lacked reasonable suspicion for the stop but argued that the evidence should not be suppressed because the existence of a valid arrest warrant attenuated the connection between the unlawful stop and the discovery of the contraband.

The trial court agreed with the State and admitted the evidence. The court found that the short time between the illegal stop and the search weighed in favor of suppressing the evidence, but that two countervailing considerations made it admissible. First, the court considered the presence of a valid arrest warrant to be an " 'extraordinary intervening circumstance.' " App. to Pet. for Cert. 102 (quoting United States v. Simpson, 439 F. 3d 490, 496 (CA8 2006). Second, the court stressed the absence of flagrant misconduct by Officer Fackrell, who was conducting a legitimate investigation of a suspected drug house.

Strieff conditionally pleaded guilty to reduced charges of attempted possession of a controlled substance and possession of drug paraphernalia, but reserved his right to appeal the trial court's denial of the suppression motion. The Utah Court of Appeals affirmed. 2012 UT App 245, 286 P. 3d 317.

The Utah Supreme Court reversed. 2015 UT 2, 357 P. 3d 532. It held that the evidence was inadmissible because only "a voluntary act of a defendant's free will (as in a confession or consent to search)" sufficiently breaks the connection between an illegal search and the discovery of evidence. Id., at 536. Because Officer Fackrell's discovery of a valid arrest warrant did not fit this description, the court ordered the evidence suppressed. Ibid.

We granted certiorari to resolve disagreement about how the attenuation doctrine applies where an unconstitutional detention leads to the discovery of a valid arrest warrant. 576 U. S. ____ (2015). Compare, e.g., United States v. Green, 111 F. 3d 515, 522–523 (CA7 1997) (holding that discovery of the warrant is a dispositive intervening circumstance where police misconduct was not flagrant), with, e.g., State v. Moralez, 297 Kan. 397, 415, 300 P. 3d 1090, 1102 (2013) (assigning little significance to the discovery of the warrant). We now reverse.

II

A

The Fourth Amendment protects "[t]he right of the people to be secure in their persons, houses, papers, and effects, against unreasonable searches and seizures." Because officers who violated the Fourth Amendment were traditionally considered trespassers, individuals subject to unconstitutional searches or seizures historically enforced their rights through tort suits or self-help. Davies, Recovering the Original Fourth Amendment, 98 Mich. L. Rev. 547, 625 (1999). In the 20th century, however, the exclusionary rule—the rule that often requires trial courts to exclude unlawfully seized evidence in a criminal trial—became the principal judicial remedy to deter Fourth Amendment violations. See, e.g., Mapp v. Ohio, 367 U. S. 643, 655 (1961).

Under the Court's precedents, the exclusionary rule encompasses both the "primary evidence obtained as a direct result of an illegal search or seizure" and, relevant here, "evidence later discovered and found to be derivative of an illegality," the so-called " 'fruit of the poisonous tree.' " Segura v. United States, 468 U. S. 796, 804 (1984). But the significant costs of this rule have led us to deem it "applicable only . . . where its deterrence benefits outweigh its substantial social costs." Hudson v. Michigan, 547 U. S. 586, 591 (2006) (internal quotation marks omitted). "Suppression of evidence . . . has always been our last resort, not our first impulse." Ibid.

We have accordingly recognized several exceptions to the rule. Three of these exceptions involve the causal relationship between the unconstitutional act and the discovery of evidence. First, the independent source doctrine allows trial courts to admit evidence obtained in an unlawful search if officers independently acquired it from a separate, independent source. See Murray v. United States, 487 U. S. 533, 537 (1988). Second, the inevitable discovery doctrine allows for the admission of evidence that would have been discovered even without the unconstitutional source. See Nix v. Williams, 467 U. S. 431–444 (1984). Third, and at issue here, is the attenuation doctrine: Evidence is admissible when the connection between unconstitutional police conduct and the evidence is remote or has been interrupted by some intervening circumstance, so that "the interest protected by the constitutional guarantee that has been violated would not be served by suppression of the evidence obtained." Hudson, supra, at 593.

B

Turning to the application of the attenuation doctrine to this case, we first address a threshold question: whether this doctrine applies at all to a case like this, where the intervening circumstance that the State relies on is the discovery of a valid, pre-existing, and untainted arrest warrant. The Utah Supreme Court declined to apply the attenuation doctrine because it read our precedents as applying the doctrine only "to circumstances involving an independent act of a defendant's 'free will' in confessing to a crime or consenting to a search." 357 P. 3d, at 544. In this Court, Strieff has not defended this argument, and we disagree with it, as well. The attenuation doctrine evaluates the causal link between the government's unlawful act and the discovery of evidence, which often has nothing to do with a defendant's actions. And the logic of our prior attenuation cases is not limited to independent acts by the defendant.

It remains for us to address whether the discovery of a valid arrest warrant was a sufficient intervening event to break the causal chain between the unlawful stop and the discovery of drug-related evidence on Strieff's person. The three factors articulated in Brown v. Illinois, 422 U. S. 590 (1975), guide our analysis. First, we look to the "temporal proximity" between the unconstitutional conduct and the discovery of evidence to determine how closely the discovery of evidence followed the unconstitutional search. Id., at 603. Second, we consider "the presence of intervening circumstances." Id., at 603–604. Third, and "particularly" significant, we examine "the purpose and flagrancy of the official misconduct." Id., at 604. In evaluating these factors, we assume without deciding (because the State conceded the point) that Officer Fackrell lacked reasonable suspicion to initially stop Strieff. And, because we ultimately conclude that the warrant breaks the causal chain, we also have no need to decide whether the warrant's existence alone would make the initial stop constitutional even if Officer Fackrell was unaware of its existence.

1

The first factor, temporal proximity between the ini-tially unlawful stop and the search, favors suppressing the evidence. Our precedents have declined to find that this factor favors attenuation unless "substantial time" elapses between an unlawful act and when the evidence is obtained. Kaupp v. Texas, 538 U. S. 626, 633 (2003) (per curiam). Here, however, Officer Fackrell discovered drug contraband on Strieff's person only minutes after the illegal stop. See App. 18–19. As the Court explained in Brown, such a short time interval counsels in favor of suppression; there, we found that the confession should be suppressed, relying in part on the "less than two hours" that separated the unconstitutional arrest and the confession. 422 U. S., at 604.

In contrast, the second factor, the presence of intervening circumstances, strongly favors the State. In Segura, 468 U. S. 796, the Court addressed similar facts to those here and found sufficient intervening circumstances to allow the admission of evidence. There, agents had probable cause to believe that apartment occupants were dealing cocaine. Id., at 799–800. They sought a warrant. In the meantime, they entered the apartment, arrested an occupant, and discovered evidence of drug activity during a limited search for security reasons. Id., at 800–801. The next evening, the Magistrate Judge issued the search warrant. Ibid. This Court deemed the evidence admissible notwithstanding the illegal search because the information supporting the warrant was "wholly unconnected with the [arguably illegal] entry and was known to the agents well before the initial entry." Id., at 814.

Segura, of course, applied the independent source doctrine because the unlawful entry "did not contribute in any way to discovery of the evidence seized under the warrant." Id., at 815. But the Segura Court suggested that the existence of a valid warrant favors finding that the connection between unlawful conduct and the discovery of evidence is "sufficiently attenuated to dissipate the taint." Ibid. That principle applies here.

In this case, the warrant was valid, it predated Officer Fackrell's investigation, and it was entirely unconnected with the stop. And once Officer Fackrell discovered the warrant, he had an obligation to arrest Strieff. "A warrant is a judicial mandate to an officer to conduct a search or make an arrest, and the officer has a sworn duty to carry out its provisions." United States v. Leon, 468 U. S. 897, 920, n. 21 (1984) (internal quotation marks omitted). Officer Fackrell's arrest of Strieff thus was a ministerial act that was independently compelled by the pre-existing warrant. And once Officer Fackrell was authorized to arrest Strieff, it was undisputedly lawful to search Strieff as an incident of his arrest to protect Officer Fackrell's safety. See Arizona v. Gant, 556 U. S. 332, 339 (2009) (explaining the permissible scope of searches incident to arrest).

Finally, the third factor, "the purpose and flagrancy of the official misconduct," Brown, supra, at 604, also strongly favors the State. The exclusionary rule exists to deter police misconduct. Davis v. United States, 564 U. S. 229–237 (2011). The third factor of the attenuation doctrine reflects that rationale by favoring exclusion only when the police misconduct is most in need of deterrence— that is, when it is purposeful or flagrant.

Officer Fackrell was at most negligent. In stopping Strieff, Officer Fackrell made two good-faith mistakes. First, he had not observed what time Strieff entered the suspected drug house, so he did not know how long Strieff had been there. Officer Fackrell thus lacked a sufficient basis to conclude that Strieff was a short-term visitor who may have been consummating a drug transaction. Second, because he lacked confirmation that Strieff was a short-term visitor, Officer Fackrell should have asked Strieff whether he would speak with him, instead of demanding that Strieff do so. Officer Fackrell's stated purpose was to "find out what was going on [in] the house." App. 17. Nothing prevented him from approaching Strieff simply to ask. See Florida v. Bostick, 501 U. S. 429, 434 (1991) ("[A] seizure does not occur simply because a police officer approaches an individual and asks a few questions"). But these errors in judgment hardly rise to a purposeful or flagrant violation of Strieff's Fourth Amendment rights.

While Officer Fackrell's decision to initiate the stop was mistaken, his conduct thereafter was lawful. The officer's decision to run the warrant check was a "negligibly burdensome precautio[n]" for officer safety. Rodriguez v. United States, 575 U. S. ___, ___ (2015) (slip op., at 7). And Officer Fackrell's actual search of Strieff was a lawful search incident to arrest. See Gant, supra, at 339.

Moreover, there is no indication that this unlawful stop was part of any systemic or recurrent police misconduct. To the contrary, all the evidence suggests that the stop was an isolated instance of negligence that occurred in connection with a bona fide investigation of a suspected drug house. Officer Fackrell saw Strieff leave a suspected drug house. And his suspicion about the house was based on an anonymous tip and his personal observations.

Applying these factors, we hold that the evidence discovered on Strieff's person was admissible because the unlawful stop was sufficiently attenuated by the pre-existing arrest warrant. Although the illegal stop was close in time to Strieff's arrest, that consideration is outweighed by two factors supporting the State. The outstanding arrest warrant for Strieff's arrest is a critical intervening circumstance that is wholly independent of the illegal stop. The discovery of that warrant broke the causal chain between the unconstitutional stop and the discovery of evidence by compelling Officer Fackrell to arrest Strieff. And, it is especially significant that there is no evidence that Officer Fackrell's illegal stop reflected flagrantly unlawful police misconduct.

2

We find Strieff's counterarguments unpersuasive.

First, he argues that the attenuation doctrine should not apply because the officer's stop was purposeful and flagrant. He asserts that Officer Fackrell stopped him solely to fish for evidence of suspected wrongdoing. But Officer Fackrell sought information from Strieff to find out what was happening inside a house whose occupants were legitimately suspected of dealing drugs. This was not a suspicionless fishing expedition "in the hope that something would turn up." Taylor v. Alabama, 457 U. S. 687, 691 (1982) .

Strieff argues, moreover, that Officer Fackrell's conduct was flagrant because he detained Strieff without the necessary level of cause (here, reasonable suspicion). But that conflates the standard for an illegal stop with the standard for flagrancy. For the violation to be flagrant, more severe police misconduct is required than the mere absence of proper cause for the seizure. See, e.g., Kaupp, 538 U. S., at 628, 633 (finding flagrant violation where a warrantless arrest was made in the arrestee's home after police were denied a warrant and at least some officers knew they lacked probable cause). Neither the officer's alleged purpose nor the flagrancy of the violation rise to a level of misconduct to warrant suppression.

Second, Strieff argues that, because of the prevalence of outstanding arrest warrants in many jurisdictions, police will engage in dragnet searches if the exclusionary rule is not applied. We think that this outcome is unlikely. Such wanton conduct would expose police to civil liability. See 42 U. S. C. §1983; Monell v. New York City Dept. of Social Servs., 436 U. S. 658, 690 (1978); see also Segura, 468 U. S., at 812. And in any event, the Brown factors take account of the purpose and flagrancy of police misconduct. Were evidence of a dragnet search presented here, the application of the Brown factors could be different. But there is no evidence that the concerns that Strieff raises with the criminal justice system are present in South Salt Lake City, Utah.

*   *   *

We hold that the evidence Officer Fackrell seized as part of his search incident to arrest is admissible because his discovery of the arrest warrant attenuated the connection between the unlawful stop and the evidence seized from Strieff incident to arrest. The judgment of the Utah Supreme Court, accordingly, is reversed.

It is so ordered.

Birchfield v. North Dakota (June 23, 2016)

Justice Alito delivered the opinion of the Court.

Drunk drivers take a grisly toll on the Nation's roads, claiming thousands of lives, injuring many more victims, and inflicting billions of dollars in property damage every year. To fight this problem, all States have laws that prohibit motorists from driving with a blood alcohol concentration (BAC) that exceeds a specified level. But determining whether a driver's BAC is over the legal limit requires a test, and many drivers stopped on suspicion of drunk driving would not submit to testing if given the option. So every State also has long had what are termed "implied consent laws." These laws impose penalties on motorists who refuse to undergo testing when there is sufficient reason to believe they are violating the State's drunk-driving laws.

In the past, the typical penalty for noncompliance was suspension or revocation of the motorist's license. The cases now before us involve laws that go beyond that and make it a crime for a motorist to refuse to be tested after being lawfully arrested for driving while impaired. The question presented is whether such laws violate the Fourth Amendment's prohibition against unreasonable searches.

I

The problem of drunk driving arose almost as soon as motor vehicles came into use. See J. Jacobs, Drunk Driving: An American Dilemma 57 (1989) (Jacobs). New Jersey enacted what was perhaps the Nation's first drunk-driving law in 1906, 1906 N. J. Laws pp. 186, 196, and other States soon followed. These early laws made it illegal to drive while intoxicated but did not provide a statistical definition of intoxication. As a result, prosecutors normally had to present testimony that the defendant was showing outward signs of intoxication, like imbalance or slurred speech. R. Donigan, Chemical Tests and the Law 2 (1966) (Donigan). As one early case put it, "[t]he effects resulting from the drinking of intoxicating liquors are manifested in various ways, and before any one can be shown to be under the influence of intoxicating liquor it is necessary for some witness to prove that some one or more of these effects were perceptible to him." State v. Noble, 119 Ore. 674, 677, 250 P. 833, 834 (1926).

The 1930's saw a continued rise in the number of motor vehicles on the roads, an end to Prohibition, and not coincidentally an increased interest in combating the growing problem of drunk driving. Jones, Measuring Alcohol in Blood and Breath for Forensic Purposes—A Historical Review, 8 For. Sci. Rev. 13, 20, 33 (1996) (Jones). The American Medical Association and the National Safety Council set up committees to study the problem and ultimately concluded that a driver with a BAC of 0.15% or higher could be presumed to be inebriated. Donigan 21–22. In 1939, Indiana enacted the first law that defined presumptive intoxication based on BAC levels, using the recommended 0.15% standard. 1939 Ind. Acts p. 309; Jones 21. Other States soon followed and then, in response to updated guidance from national organizations, lowered the presumption to a BAC level of 0.10%. Donigan 22–23. Later, States moved away from mere presumptions that defendants might rebut, and adopted laws providing that driving with a 0.10% BAC or higher was per se illegal. Jacobs 69–70.

Enforcement of laws of this type obviously requires the measurement of BAC. One way of doing this is to analyze a sample of a driver's blood directly. A technician with medical training uses a syringe to draw a blood sample from the veins of the subject, who must remain still during the procedure, and then the sample is shipped to a separate laboratory for measurement of its alcohol concentration. See 2 R. Erwin, Defense of Drunk Driving Cases §§17.03–17.04 (3d ed. 2015) (Erwin). Although it is possible for a subject to be forcibly immobilized so that a sample may be drawn, many States prohibit drawing blood from a driver who resists since this practice helps "to avoid violent confrontations." South Dakota v. Neville, 459 U. S. 553, 559 (1983).

The most common and economical method of calculating BAC is by means of a machine that measures the amount of alcohol in a person's breath. National Highway Traffic Safety Admin. (NHTSA), E. Haire, W. Leaf, D. Preusser, & M. Solomon, Use of Warrants to Reduce Breath Test Refusals: Experiences from North Carolina 1 (No. 811461, Apr. 2011). One such device, called the "Drunkometer," was invented and first sold in the 1930's. Note, 30 N. C. L. Rev. 302, 303, and n. 10 (1952). The test subject would inflate a small balloon, and then the test analyst would release this captured breath into the machine, which forced it through a chemical solution that reacted to the presence of alcohol by changing color. Id., at 303. The test analyst could observe the amount of breath required to produce the color change and calculate the subject's breath alcohol concentration and by extension, BAC, from this figure. Id., at 303–304. A more practical machine, called the "Breathalyzer," came into common use beginning in the 1950's, relying on the same basic scientific principles. 3 Erwin §22.01, at 22–3; Jones 34.

Over time, improved breath test machines were developed. Today, such devices can detect the presence of alcohol more quickly and accurately than before, typically using infrared technology rather than a chemical reaction. 2 Erwin §18A.01; Jones 36. And in practice all breath testing machines used for evidentiary purposes must be approved by the National Highway Traffic Safety Administration. See 1 H. Cohen & J. Green, Apprehending and Prosecuting the Drunk Driver §7.04[7] (LexisNexis 2015). These machines are generally regarded as very reliable because the federal standards require that the devices produce accurate and reproducible test results at a variety of BAC levels, from the very low to the very high. 77 Fed. Reg. 35747 (2012); 2 Erwin §18.07; Jones 38; see also California v. Trombetta, 467 U. S. 479, 489 (1984).

Measurement of BAC based on a breath test requires the cooperation of the person being tested. The subject must take a deep breath and exhale through a mouthpiece that connects to the machine. Berger, How Does it Work? Alcohol Breath Testing, 325 British Medical J. 1403 (2002) (Berger). Typically the test subject must blow air into the device " 'for a period of several seconds' " to produce an adequate breath sample, and the process is sometimes repeated so that analysts can compare multiple samples to ensure the device's accuracy. Trombetta, supra, at 481; see also 2 Erwin §21.04[2][b](L), at 21–14 (describing the Intoxilyzer 4011 device as requiring a 12-second exhalation, although the subject may take a new breath about halfway through).

Modern breath test machines are designed to capture so-called "deep lung" or alveolar air. Trombetta, supra, at 481. Air from the alveolar region of the lungs provides the best basis for determining the test subject's BAC, for it is in that part of the lungs that alcohol vapor and other gases are exchanged between blood and breath. 2 Erwin §18.01[2][a], at 18–7.

When a standard infrared device is used, the whole process takes only a few minutes from start to finish. Berger 1403; 2 Erwin §18A.03[2], at 18A–14. Most evidentiary breath tests do not occur next to the vehicle, at the side of the road, but in a police station, where the controlled environment is especially conducive to reliable testing, or in some cases in the officer's patrol vehicle or in special mobile testing facilities. NHTSA, A. Berning et al., Refusal of Intoxication Testing: A Report to Congress 4, and n. 5 (No. 811098, Sept. 2008).

Because the cooperation of the test subject is necessary when a breath test is administered and highly preferable when a blood sample is taken, the enactment of laws defining intoxication based on BAC made it necessary for States to find a way of securing such cooperation. 1 So-called "implied consent" laws were enacted to achieve this result. They provided that cooperation with BAC testing was a condition of the privilege of driving on state roads and that the privilege would be rescinded if a suspected drunk driver refused to honor that condition. Donigan 177. The first such law was enacted by New York in 1953, and many other States followed suit not long thereafter. Id., at 177–179. In 1962, the Uniform Vehicle Code also included such a provision. Id., at 179. Today, "all 50 States have adopted implied consent laws that require motorists, as a condition of operating a motor vehicle within the State, to consent to BAC testing if they are arrested or otherwise detained on suspicion of a drunk-driving offense." Missouri v. McNeely, 569 U. S. ___, ___ (2013) (plurality opinion) (slip op., at 18). Suspension or revocation of the motorist's driver's license remains the standard legal consequence of refusal. In addition, evidence of the motorist's refusal is admitted as evidence of likely intoxication in a drunk-driving prosecution. See ibid.

In recent decades, the States and the Federal Government have toughened drunk-driving laws, and those efforts have corresponded to a dramatic decrease in alcohol-related fatalities. As of the early 1980's, the number of annual fatalities averaged 25,000; by 2014, the most recent year for which statistics are available, the number had fallen to below 10,000. Presidential Commission on Drunk Driving 1 (Nov. 1983); NHTSA, Traffic Safety Facts, 2014 Data, Alcohol-Impaired Driving 2 (No. 812231, Dec. 2015) (NHTSA, 2014 Alcohol-Impaired Driving). One legal change has been further lowering the BAC standard from 0.10% to 0.08%. See 1 Erwin, §2.01[1], at 2–3 to 2–4. In addition, many States now impose increased penalties for recidivists and for drivers with a BAC level that exceeds a higher threshold. In North Dakota, for example, the standard penalty for first-time drunk-driving offenders is license suspension and a fine. N. D. Cent. Code Ann. §39–08–01(5)(a)(1) (Supp. 2015); §39–20–04.1(1). But an offender with a BAC of 0.16% or higher must spend at least two days in jail. §39–08–01(5)(a)(2). In addition, the State imposes increased mandatory minimum sentences for drunk-driving recidivists. §§39–08–01(5)(b)–(d).

Many other States have taken a similar approach, but this new structure threatened to undermine the effectiveness of implied consent laws. If the penalty for driving with a greatly elevated BAC or for repeat violations exceeds the penalty for refusing to submit to testing, motorists who fear conviction for the more severely punished offenses have an incentive to reject testing. And in some States, the refusal rate is high. On average, over one-fifth of all drivers asked to submit to BAC testing in 2011 refused to do so. NHTSA, E. Namuswe, H. Coleman, & A. Berning, Breath Test Refusal Rates in the United States—2011 Update 1 (No. 811881, Mar. 2014). In North Dakota, the refusal rate for 2011 was a representative 21%. Id.,at 2. Minnesota's was below average, at 12%. Ibid.

To combat the problem of test refusal, some States have begun to enact laws making it a crime to refuse to undergo testing. Minnesota has taken this approach for decades. See 1989 Minn. Laws p. 1658; 1992 Minn. Laws p. 1947. And that may partly explain why its refusal rate now is below the national average. Minnesota's rate is also half the 24% rate reported for 1988, the year before its first criminal refusal law took effect. See Ross, Simon, Cleary, Lewis, & Storkamp, Causes and Consequences of Implied Consent Refusal, 11 Alcohol, Drugs and Driving 57, 69 (1995). North Dakota adopted a similar law, in 2013, after a pair of drunk-driving accidents claimed the lives of an entire young family and another family's 5- and 9-year-old boys. 2 2013 N. D. Laws pp. 1087–1088 (codified at §§39–08–01(1)–(3)). The Federal Government also encourages this approach as a means for overcoming the incentive that drunk drivers have to refuse a test. NHTSA, Refusal of Intoxication Testing, at 20.

II

A

Petitioner Danny Birchfield accidentally drove his car off a North Dakota highway on October 10, 2013. A state trooper arrived and watched as Birchfield unsuccessfully tried to drive back out of the ditch in which his car was stuck. The trooper approached, caught a strong whiff of alcohol, and saw that Birchfield's eyes were bloodshot and watery. Birchfield spoke in slurred speech and struggled to stay steady on his feet. At the trooper's request, Birchfield agreed to take several field sobriety tests and performed poorly on each. He had trouble reciting sections of the alphabet and counting backwards in compliance with the trooper's directions.

Believing that Birchfield was intoxicated, the trooper informed him of his obligation under state law to agree to a BAC test. Birchfield consented to a roadside breath test. The device used for this sort of test often differs from the machines used for breath tests administered in a police station and is intended to provide a preliminary assessment of the driver's BAC. See, e.g., Berger 1403. Because the reliability of these preliminary or screening breath tests varies, many jurisdictions do not permit their numerical results to be admitted in a drunk-driving trial as evidence of a driver's BAC. See generally 3 Erwin §24.03[1]. In North Dakota, results from this type of test are "used only for determining whether or not a further test shall be given." N. D. Cent. Code Ann. §39–20–14(3). In Birchfield's case, the screening test estimated that his BAC was 0.254%, more than three times the legal limit of 0.08%. See §39–08–01(1)(a).

The state trooper arrested Birchfield for driving while impaired, gave the usual Miranda warnings, again advised him of his obligation under North Dakota law to undergo BAC testing, and informed him, as state law requires, see §39–20–01(3)(a), that refusing to take the test would expose him to criminal penalties. In addition to mandatory addiction treatment, sentences range from a mandatory fine of $500 (for first-time offenders) to fines of at least $2,000 and imprisonment of at least one year and one day (for serial offenders). §39–08–01(5). These criminal penalties apply to blood, breath, and urine test refusals alike. See §§39–08–01(2), 39–20–01, 39–20–14.

Although faced with the prospect of prosecution under this law, Birchfield refused to let his blood be drawn. Just three months before, Birchfield had received a citation for driving under the influence, and he ultimately pleaded guilty to that offense. State v. Birchfield, Crim. No. 30–2013–CR–00720 (Dist. Ct. Morton Cty., N. D., Jan. 27, 2014). This time he also pleaded guilty—to a misde-meanor violation of the refusal statute—but his plea wasa conditional one: while Birchfield admitted refusing the blood test, he argued that the Fourth Amendment prohibited criminalizing his refusal to submit to the test. The State District Court rejected this argument and imposed a sentence that accounted for his prior conviction. Cf. §39–08–01(5)(b). The sentence included 30 days in jail (20 of which were suspended and 10 of which had already been served), 1 year of unsupervised probation, $1,750 in fine and fees, and mandatory participation in a sobriety program and in a substance abuse evaluation. App. to Pet. for Cert. in No. 14–1468, p. 20a.

On appeal, the North Dakota Supreme Court affirmed. 2015 ND 6, 858 N. W. 2d 302. The court found support for the test refusal statute in this Court's McNeely plurality opinion, which had spoken favorably about "acceptable 'legal tools' with 'significant consequences' for refusing to submit to testing." 858 N. W. 2d, at 307 (quoting McNeely, 569 U. S., at ___ (slip op., at 18)).

B

On August 5, 2012, Minnesota police received a report of a problem at a South St. Paul boat launch. Three apparently intoxicated men had gotten their truck stuck in the river while attempting to pull their boat out of the water. When police arrived, witnesses informed them that a man in underwear had been driving the truck. That man proved to be William Robert Bernard, Jr., petitioner in the second of these cases. Bernard admitted that he had been drinking but denied driving the truck (though he was holding its keys) and refused to perform any field sobriety tests. After noting that Bernard's breath smelled of alcohol and that his eyes were bloodshot and watery, officers arrested Bernard for driving while impaired.

Back at the police station, officers read Bernard Minnesota's implied consent advisory, which like North Dakota's informs motorists that it is a crime under state law to refuse to submit to a legally required BAC test. See Minn. Stat. §169A.51, subd. 2 (2014). Aside from noncriminal penalties like license revocation, §169A.52, subd. 3, test refusal in Minnesota can result in criminal penalties ranging from no more than 90 days' imprisonment and up to a $1,000 fine for a misdemeanor violation to seven years' imprisonment and a $14,000 fine for repeat offenders, §169A.03, subd. 12; §169A.20, subds. 2–3; §169A.24, subd. 2; §169A.27, subd. 2.

The officers asked Bernard to take a breath test. After he refused, prosecutors charged him with test refusal in the first degree because he had four prior impaired-driving convictions. 859 N. W. 2d 762, 765, n. 1 (Minn. 2015) (case below). First-degree refusal carries the highest maximum penalties and a mandatory minimum 3-year prison sentence. §169A.276, subd. 1.

The Minnesota District Court dismissed the charges on the ground that the warrantless breath test demanded of Bernard was not permitted under the Fourth Amendment. App. to Pet. for Cert. in No. 14–1470, pp. 48a, 59a. The Minnesota Court of Appeals reversed, id., at 46a, and the State Supreme Court affirmed that judgment. Based on the longstanding doctrine that authorizes warrantless searches incident to a lawful arrest, the high court concluded that police did not need a warrant to insist on a test of Bernard's breath. 859 N. W. 2d, at 766–772. Two justices dissented. Id., at 774–780 (opinion of Page and Stras, JJ.).

C

A police officer spotted our third petitioner, Steve Michael Beylund, driving the streets of Bowman, North Dakota, on the night of August 10, 2013. The officer saw Beylund try unsuccessfully to turn into a driveway. In the process, Beylund's car nearly hit a stop sign before coming to a stop still partly on the public road. The officer walked up to the car and saw that Beylund had an empty wine glass in the center console next to him. Noticing that Beylund also smelled of alcohol, the officer asked him to step out of the car. As Beylund did so, he struggled to keep his balance.

The officer arrested Beylund for driving while impaired and took him to a nearby hospital. There he read Beylund North Dakota's implied consent advisory, informing him that test refusal in these circumstances is itself a crime. See N. D. Cent. Code Ann. §39–20–01(3)(a). Unlike the other two petitioners in these cases, Beylund agreed to have his blood drawn and analyzed. A nurse took a blood sample, which revealed a blood alcohol concentration of 0.250%, more than three times the legal limit.

Given the test results, Beylund's driver's license was suspended for two years after an administrative hearing. Beylund appealed the hearing officer's decision to a North Dakota District Court, principally arguing that his consent to the blood test was coerced by the officer's warning that refusing to consent would itself be a crime. The District Court rejected this argument, and Beylund again appealed.

The North Dakota Supreme Court affirmed. In response to Beylund's argument that his consent was insufficiently voluntary because of the announced criminal penalties for refusal, the court relied on the fact that its then-recent Birchfield decision had upheld the constitutionality of those penalties. 2015 ND 18, ¶¶14–15, 859 N. W. 2d 403, 408–409. The court also explained that it had found consent offered by a similarly situated motorist to be voluntary, State v. Smith, 2014 ND 152, 849 N. W. 2d 599. In that case, the court emphasized that North Dakota's implied consent advisory was not misleading because it truthfully related the penalties for refusal. Id., at 606.

We granted certiorari in all three cases and consolidated them for argument, see 577 U. S. ____ (2015), in order to decide whether motorists lawfully arrested for drunk driving may be convicted of a crime or otherwise penalized for refusing to take a warrantless test measuring the alcohol in their bloodstream.

III

As our summary of the facts and proceedings in these three cases reveals, the cases differ in some respects. Petitioners Birchfield and Beylund were told that they were obligated to submit to a blood test, whereas petitioner Bernard was informed that a breath test was required. Birchfield and Bernard each refused to undergo a test and was convicted of a crime for his refusal. Beylund complied with the demand for a blood sample, and his license was then suspended in an administrative proceeding based on test results that revealed a very high blood alcohol level.

Despite these differences, success for all three petitioners depends on the proposition that the criminal law ordinarily may not compel a motorist to submit to the taking of a blood sample or to a breath test unless a warrant authorizing such testing is issued by a magistrate. If, on the other hand, such warrantless searches comport with the Fourth Amendment, it follows that a State may criminalize the refusal to comply with a demand to submit to the required testing, just as a State may make it a crime for a person to obstruct the execution of a valid search warrant. See, e.g., Conn. Gen. Stat. §54–33d (2009); Fla. Stat. §933.15 (2015); N. J. Stat. Ann. §33:1–63 (West 1994); 18 U. S. C. §1501; cf. Bumper v. North Carolina, 391 U. S. 543, 550 (1968) ("When a law enforcement officer claims authority to search a home under a warrant, he announces in effect that the occupant has no right to resist the search"). And by the same token, if such warrantless searches are constitutional, there is no obstacle under federal law to the admission of the results that they yield in either a criminal prosecution or a civil or administrative proceeding. We therefore begin by considering whether the searches demanded in these cases were consistent with the Fourth Amendment.

IV

The Fourth Amendment provides:

"The right of the people to be secure in their persons, houses, papers, and effects, against unreasonable searches and seizures, shall not be violated, and no Warrants shall issue, but upon probable cause, supported by Oath or affirmation, and particularly describing the place to be searched, and the persons or things to be seized."

The Amendment thus prohibits "unreasonable searches," and our cases establish that the taking of a blood sam-ple or the administration of a breath test is a search.See Skinner v. Railway Labor Executives' Assn., 489 U. S. 602–617 (1989); Schmerber v. California, 384 U. S. 757–768 (1966). The question, then, is whether the warrantless searches at issue here were reasonable. See Vernonia School Dist. 47J v. Acton, 515 U. S. 646, 652 (1995) ("As the text of the Fourth Amendment indicates, the ultimate measure of the constitutionality of a governmental search is 'reasonableness' ").

"[T]he text of the Fourth Amendment does not specify when a search warrant must be obtained." Kentucky v. King, 563 U. S. 452, 459 (2011) ; see also California v. Acevedo, 500 U. S. 565, 581 (1991) (Scalia, J., concur-ring in judgment) ("What [the text] explicitly states regard-ing warrants is by way of limitation upon their issuance rather than requirement of their use"). But "this Court has inferred that a warrant must [usually] be secured." King, 563 U. S., at 459. This usual requirement, however, is subject to a number of exceptions. Ibid.

We have previously had occasion to examine whether one such exception—for "exigent circumstances"—applies in drunk-driving investigations. The exigent circum-stances exception allows a warrantless search when an emergency leaves police insufficient time to seek a warrant. Michigan v. Tyler, 436 U. S. 499, 509 (1978) . It permits, for instance, the warrantless entry of private property when there is a need to provide urgent aid to those inside, when police are in hot pursuit of a fleeing suspect, and when police fear the imminent destruction of evidence. King, supra, at 460.

In Schmerber v. California, we held that drunk driving may present such an exigency. There, an officer directed hospital personnel to take a blood sample from a driver who was receiving treatment for car crash injuries. 384 U. S., at 758. The Court concluded that the officer "might reasonably have believed that he was confronted with an emergency" that left no time to seek a warrant because "the percentage of alcohol in the blood begins to diminish shortly after drinking stops." Id., at 770. On the specific facts of that case, where time had already been lost taking the driver to the hospital and investigating the accident, the Court found no Fourth Amendment violation even though the warrantless blood draw took place over the driver's objection. Id., at 770–772.

More recently, though, we have held that the natural dissipation of alcohol from the bloodstream does not always constitute an exigency justifying the warrantless taking of a blood sample. That was the holding of Missouri v. McNeely, 569 U. S. ___, where the State of Missouri was seeking a per se rule that "whenever an officer has probable cause to believe an individual has been driving under the influence of alcohol, exigent circumstances will necessarily exist because BAC evidence is inherently evanescent." Id., at ____ (opinion of the Court) (slip op., at 8). We disagreed, emphasizing that Schmerber had adopted a case-specific analysis depending on "all of the facts and circumstances of the particular case." 569 U. S., at ____ (slip op., at 8). We refused to "depart from careful case-by-case assessment of exigency and adopt the categorical rule proposed by the State." Id., at ____ (slip op., at 9).

While emphasizing that the exigent-circumstances exception must be applied on a case-by-case basis, the McNeely Court noted that other exceptions to the warrant requirement "apply categorically" rather than in a "case-specific" fashion. Id., at ____, n. 3 (slip op., at 7, n. 3). One of these, as the McNeely opinion recognized, is the long-established rule that a warrantless search may be conducted incident to a lawful arrest. See ibid. But the Court pointedly did not address any potential justification for warrantless testing of drunk-driving suspects except for the exception "at issue in th[e] case," namely, the exception for exigent circumstances. Id., at ____ (slip op., at 5). Neither did any of the Justices who wrote separately. See id., at ____– ____ (Kennedy, J., concurring in part)(slip op., at 1–2); id., at ____–____ (Roberts, C. J., concurring in part and dissenting in part) (slip op., at 1–11); id., at ____–____ (Thomas, J., dissenting) (slip op., at 1–8).

In the three cases now before us, the drivers were searched or told that they were required to submit to a search after being placed under arrest for drunk driving. We therefore consider how the search-incident-to-arrest doctrine applies to breath and blood tests incident to such arrests.

V

A

The search-incident-to-arrest doctrine has an ancient pedigree. Well before the Nation's founding, it was recognized that officers carrying out a lawful arrest had the authority to make a warrantless search of the arrestee's person. An 18th-century manual for justices of the peace provides a representative picture of usual practice shortly before the Fourth Amendment's adoption:

"[A] thorough search of the felon is of the utmost consequence to your own safety, and the benefit of the public, as by this means he will be deprived of instruments of mischief, and evidence may probably be found on him sufficient to convict him, of which, if he has either time or opportunity allowed him, he will besure [sic] to find some means to get rid of." The Conductor Generalis 117 (J. Parker ed. 1788) (reprinting S. Welch, Observations on the Office of Constable 19 (1754)).

One Fourth Amendment historian has observed that, prior to American independence, "[a]nyone arrested could expect that not only his surface clothing but his body, luggage, and saddlebags would be searched and, perhaps, his shoes, socks, and mouth as well." W. Cuddihy, The Fourth Amendment: Origins and Original Meaning: 602–1791, p. 420 (2009).

No historical evidence suggests that the Fourth Amendment altered the permissible bounds of arrestee searches. On the contrary, legal scholars agree that "the legitimacy of body searches as an adjunct to the arrest process had been thoroughly established in colonial times, so much so that their constitutionality in 1789 can not be doubted." Id., at 752; see also T. Taylor, Two Studies in Constitutional Interpretation 28–29, 39, 45 (1969); Stuntz, The Substantive Origins of

Criminal Procedure, 105 Yale L. J. 393, 401 (1995).

Few reported cases addressed the legality of such searches before the 19th century, apparently because the point was not much contested. In the 19th century, the subject came up for discussion more often, but court decisions and treatises alike confirmed the searches' broad acceptance. E.g., Holker v. Hennessey, 141 Mo. 527, 539–540, 42 S. W. 1090, 1093 (1897); Ex parte Hurn, 92 Ala. 102, 112, 9 So. 515, 519 (1891); Thatcher v. Weeks, 79 Me. 547, 548–549, 11 A. 599 (1887); Reifsnyder v. Lee, 44 Iowa 101, 103 (1876); F. Wharton, Criminal Pleading and Practice §60, p. 45 (8th ed. 1880); 1 J. Bishop, Criminal Procedure §211, p. 127 (2d ed. 1872).

When this Court first addressed the question, we too confirmed (albeit in dicta) "the right on the part of the Government, always recognized under English and American law, to search the person of the accused when legally arrested to discover and seize the fruits or evidence of crime." Weeks v. United States, 232 U. S. 383, 392 (1914) . The exception quickly became a fixture in our Fourth Amendment case law. But in the decades that followed, we grappled repeatedly with the question of the authority of arresting officers to search the area surrounding the arrestee, and our decisions reached results that were not easy to reconcile. See, e.g., United States v. Lefkowitz, 285 U. S. 452, 464 (1932) (forbidding "unrestrained" search of room where arrest was made); Harris v. United States, 331 U. S. 145, 149, 152 (1947) (permitting complete search of arrestee's four-room apartment); United States v. Rabinowitz, 339 U. S. 56–65 (1950) (permitting complete search of arrestee's office).

We attempted to clarify the law regarding searches incident to arrest in Chimel v. California, 395 U. S. 752, 754 (1969) , a case in which officers had searched the arrestee's entire three-bedroom house. Chimel endorsed a general rule that arresting officers, in order to prevent the arrestee from obtaining a weapon or destroying evidence, could search both "the person arrested" and "the area 'within his immediate control.' " Id., at 763. "[N]o comparable justification," we said, supported "routinely searching any room other than that in which an arrest occurs—or, for that matter, for searching through all the desk drawers or other closed or concealed areas in that room itself." Ibid.

Four years later, in United States v. Robinson, 414 U. S. 218 (1973) , we elaborated on Chimel's meaning. We noted that the search-incident-to-arrest rule actually comprises "two distinct propositions": "The first is that a search may be made of the person of the arrestee by virtue of the lawful arrest. The second is that a search may be made of the area within the control of the arrestee." 414 U. S., at 224. After a thorough review of the relevant common law history, we repudiated "case-by-case adjudication" of the question whether an arresting officer had the authority to carry out a search of the arrestee's person. Id., at 235. The permissibility of such searches, we held, does not depend on whether a search of a particular arrestee is likely to protect officer safety or evidence: "The authority to search the person incident to a lawful custodial arrest, while based upon the need to disarm and to discover evidence, does not depend on what a court may later decide was the probability in a particular arrest situation that weapons or evidence would in fact be found upon the person of the suspect." Ibid. Instead, the mere "fact of the lawful arrest" justifies "a full search of the person." Ibid. In Robinson itself, that meant that police had acted permissibly in searching inside a package of cigarettes found on the man they arrested. Id., at 236.

Our decision two Terms ago in Riley v. California, 573 U. S. ____ (2014), reaffirmed "Robinson's categorical rule" and explained how the rule should be applied in situations that could not have been envisioned when the Fourth Amendment was adopted. Id., at ____ (slip op., at 9). Riley concerned a search of data contained in the memory of a modern cell phone. "Absent more precise guidance from the founding era," the Court wrote, "we generally determine whether to exempt a given type of search from the warrant requirement 'by assessing, on the one hand, the degree to which it intrudes upon an individual's privacy and, on the other, the degree to which it is needed for the promotion of legitimate governmental interests.' " Ibid.

Blood and breath tests to measure blood alcohol concentration are not as new as searches of cell phones, but here, as in Riley, the founding era does not provide any definitive guidance as to whether they should be allowed incident to arrest. 3 Lacking such guidance, we engage in the same mode of analysis as in Riley: we examine "the degree to which [they] intrud[e] upon an individual's privacy and . . . the degree to which [they are] needed for the promotion of legitimate governmental interests.' " Ibid.

B

We begin by considering the impact of breath and blood tests on individual privacy interests, and we will discuss each type of test in turn.

1

Years ago we said that breath tests do not "implicat[e] significant privacy concerns." Skinner, 489 U. S., at 626. That remains so today.

First, the physical intrusion is almost negligible. Breath tests "do not require piercing the skin" and entail "a minimum of inconvenience." Id., at 625. As Minnesota describes its version of the breath test, the process requires the arrestee to blow continuously for 4 to 15 seconds into a straw-like mouthpiece that is connected by a tube to the test machine. Brief for Respondent in No. 14–1470, p. 20. Independent sources describe other breath test devices in essentially the same terms. See

supra, at 5. The effort is no more demanding than blowing up a party balloon.

Petitioner Bernard argues, however, that the process is nevertheless a significant intrusion because the arrestee must insert the mouthpiece of the machine into his or her mouth. Reply Brief in No. 14–1470, p. 9. But there is nothing painful or strange about this requirement. The use of a straw to drink beverages is a common practice and one to which few object.

Nor, contrary to Bernard, is the test a significant intrusion because it "does not capture an ordinary exhalation of the kind that routinely is exposed to the public" but instead " 'requires a sample of "alveolar" (deep lung) air.' " Brief for Petitioner in No. 14–1470, p. 24. Humans have never been known to assert a possessory interest in or any emotional attachment to any of the air in their lungs. The air that humans exhale is not part of their bodies. Exhalation is a natural process—indeed, one that is necessary for life. Humans cannot hold their breath for more than a few minutes, and all the air that is breathed into a breath analyzing machine, including deep lung air, sooner or later would be exhaled even without the test. See gener-ally J. Hall, Guyton and Hall Textbook of Medical Physiology 519–520 (13th ed. 2016).

In prior cases, we have upheld warrantless searches involving physical intrusions that were at least as significant as that entailed in the administration of a breath test. Just recently we described the process of collecting a DNA sample by rubbing a swab on the inside of a person's cheek as a "negligible" intrusion. Maryland v. King, 569 U. S. ____, ____ (2013) (slip op., at 8). We have also upheld scraping underneath a suspect's fingernails to find evidence of a crime, calling that a "very limited intrusion." Cupp v. Murphy, 412 U. S. 291, 296 (1973) . A breath test is no more intrusive than either of these procedures.

Second, breath tests are capable of

revealing only one bit of information, the amount of alcohol in the subject's breath. In this respect, they contrast sharply with the sample of cells collected by the swab in Maryland v. King. Although the DNA obtained under the law at issue in that case could lawfully be used only for identification pur-poses, 569 U. S., at ____ (slip op., at 5), the process put into the possession of law enforcement authorities a sample from which a wealth of additional, highly personal information could potentially be obtained. A breath test, by contrast, results in a BAC reading on a machine, nothing more. No sample of anything is left in the possession of the police.

Finally, participation in a breath test is not an experience that is likely to cause any great enhancement in the embarrassment that is inherent in any arrest. See Skinner, supra, at 625 (breath test involves "a minimum of . . . embarrassment"). The act of blowing into a straw is not inherently embarrassing, nor are evidentiary breath tests administered in a manner that causes embarrassment. Again, such tests are normally administered in private at a police station, in a patrol car, or in a mobile testing facility, out of public view. See supra, at 5. Moreover, once placed under arrest, the individual's expectation of privacy is necessarily diminished. Maryland v. King, supra, at ____–____ (slip op., at 24–25).

For all these reasons, we reiterate what we said in Skinner: A breath test does not "implicat[e] significant privacy concerns." 489 U. S., at 626.

2

Blood tests are a different matter. They "require piercing the skin" and extract a part of the subject's body. Skinner, supra, at 625; see also McNeely, 569 U. S., at ____ (opinion of the Court) (slip op., at 4) (blood draws are "a compelled physical intrusion beneath [the defendant's] skin and into his veins"); id., at ____ (opinion of Roberts, C. J.) (slip op., at 9) (blood draws are "significant bodily intrusions"). And while humans exhale air from their lungs many times per minute, humans do not continually shed blood. It is true, of course, that people voluntarily submit to the taking of blood samples as part of a physical examination, and the process involves little pain or risk. See id., at ____ (plurality opinion) (slip op., at 16) (citing Schmerber, 384 U. S., at 771). Nevertheless, for many, the process is not one they relish. It is significantly more intrusive than blowing into a tube. Perhaps that is why many States' implied consent laws, including Minnesota's, specifically prescribe that breath tests be administered in the usual drunk-driving case instead of blood tests or give motorists a measure of choice over which test to take. See 1 Erwin §4.06; Minn. Stat. §169A.51, subd. 3.

In addition, a blood test, unlike a breath test, places in the hands of law enforcement authorities a sample that can be preserved and from which it is possible to extract information beyond a simple BAC reading. Even if the law enforcement agency is precluded from testing the blood for any purpose other than to measure BAC, the potential remains and may result in anxiety for the person tested.

C

Having assessed the impact of breath and blood testing on privacy interests, we now look to the States' asserted need to obtain BAC readings for persons arrested for drunk driving.

1

The States and the Federal Government have a "paramount interest . . . in preserving the safety of . . . public highways." Mackey v. Montrym, 443 U. S. 1, 17 (1979) . Although the number of deaths and injuries caused by motor vehicle accidents has declined over the years, the statistics are still staggering. See, e.g., NHTSA, Traffic Safety Facts 1995—Overview 2 (No. 95F7, 1995) (47,087 fatalities, 3,416,000 injuries in 1988); NHTSA, Traffic Safety Facts, 2014 Data, Summary of Motor Vehicle Crashes 1 (No. 812263, May 2016) (Table

1) (29,989 fatalities, 1,648,000 injuries in 2014).

Alcohol consumption is a leading cause of traffic fatalities and injuries. During the past decade, annual fatalities in drunk-driving accidents ranged from 13,582 deaths in 2005 to 9,865 deaths in 2011. NHTSA, 2014 Alcohol-Impaired Driving 2. The most recent data report a total of 9,967 such fatalities in 2014—on average, one death every 53 minutes. Id., at 1. Our cases have long recognized the "carnage" and "slaughter" caused by drunk drivers. Neville, 459 U. S., at 558; Breithaupt v. Abram, 352 U. S. 432, 439 (1957) .

Justice Sotomayor's partial dissent suggests that States' interests in fighting drunk driving are satisfied once suspected drunk drivers are arrested, since such arrests take intoxicated drivers off the roads where they might do harm. See post, at 9 (opinion concurring in part and dissenting in part). But of course States are not solely concerned with neutralizing the threat posed by a drunk driver who has already gotten behind the wheel. They also have a compelling interest in creating effective "deterrent[s] to drunken driving" so such individuals make responsible decisions and do not become a threat to others in the first place. Mackey, supra, at 18.

To deter potential drunk drivers and thereby reduce alcohol-related injuries, the States and the Federal Government have taken the series of steps that we recounted earlier. See supra, at 2–8. We briefly recapitulate. After pegging inebriation to a specific level of blood alcohol, States passed implied consent laws to induce motorists to submit to BAC testing. While these laws originally provided that refusal to submit could result in the loss of the privilege of driving and the use of evidence of refusal in a drunk-driving prosecution, more recently States and the Federal Government have concluded that these consequences are insufficient. In particular, license suspension alone is unlikely to persuade the most dangerous offenders, such as those who drive with a BAC significantly above the current limit of 0.08% and recidivists, to agree to a test that would lead to severe criminal sanctions. NHTSA, Implied Consent Refusal Impact, pp. xvii, 83 (No. 807765, Sept. 1991); NHTSA, Use of Warrants for Breath Test Refusal 1 (No. 810852, Oct. 2007). The laws at issue in the present cases—which make it a crime to refuse to submit to a BAC test—are designed to provide an incentive to cooperate in such cases, and we conclude that they serve a very important function.

2

Petitioners and Justice Sotomayor contend that the States and the Federal Government could combat drunk driving in other ways that do not have the same impact on personal privacy. Their arguments are unconvincing.

The chief argument on this score is that an officer making an arrest for drunk driving should not be allowed to administer a BAC test unless the officer procures a search warrant or could not do so in time to obtain usable test results. The governmental interest in warrantless breath testing, Justice Sotomayor claims, turns on " 'whether the burden of obtaining a warrant is likely to frustrate the governmental purpose behind the search.' " Post, at 3–4 (quoting Camara v. Municipal Court of City and County of San Francisco, 387 U. S. 523, 533 (1967)).

This argument contravenes our decisions holding that the legality of a search incident to arrest must be judged on the basis of categorical rules. In Robinson, for example, no one claimed that the object of the search, a package of cigarettes, presented any danger to the arresting officer or was at risk of being destroyed in the time that it would have taken to secure a search warrant. The Court nevertheless upheld the constitutionality of a warrantless search of the package, concluding that a categorical rule was needed to give police adequate guidance: "A police officer's determination as to how and where to search the person of a suspect whom he has arrested is necessarily a quick ad hoc judgment which the Fourth Amendment does not require to be broken down in each instance into an analysis of each step in the search." 414 U. S., at 235; cf. Riley, 573 U. S., at ___ (slip op., at 22) ("If police are to have workable rules, the balancing of the competing interests must in large part be done on a categorical basis—not in an ad hoc, case-by-case fashion by individual police officers" (brackets, ellipsis, and internal quotation marks omitted)).

It is not surprising, then, that the language Justice Sotomayor quotes to justify her approach comes not from our search-incident-to-arrest case law, but a case that addressed routine home searches for possible housing code violations. See Camara, 387 U. S., at 526. Camara's express concern in the passage that the dissent quotes was "whether the public interest demands creation of a general exception to the Fourth Amendment's warrant requirement." Id., at 533 (emphasis added). Camara did not explain how to apply an existing exception, let alone the long-established exception for searches incident to a lawful arrest, whose applicability, as Robinson and Riley make plain, has never turned on case-specific variables such as how quickly the officer will be able to obtain a warrant in the particular circumstances he faces.

In advocating the case-by-case approach, petitioners and Justice Sotomayor cite language in our McNeely opinion. See Brief for Petitioner in No. 14–1468, p. 14; post, at 12. But McNeely concerned an exception to the warrant requirement—for exigent circumstances—that always requires case-by-case determinations. That was the basis for our decision in that case. 569 U. S., at ___ (slip op., at 9). Although Justice Sotomayor contends that the categorical search-incident-to-arrest doctrine and case-by-case exigent circumstances doctrine are actually parts of a single framework, post, at 6–7, and n. 3, in

McNeely the Court was careful to note that the decision did not address any other exceptions to the warrant requirement, 569 U. S., at ___, n. 3 (slip op., at 7, n. 3).

Petitioners and Justice Sotomayor next suggest that requiring a warrant for BAC testing in every case in which a motorist is arrested for drunk driving would not impose any great burden on the police or the courts. But of course the same argument could be made about searching through objects found on the arrestee's possession, which our cases permit even in the absence of a warrant. What about the cigarette package in Robinson? What if a motorist arrested for drunk driving has a flask in his pocket? What if a motorist arrested for driving while under the influence of marijuana has what appears to be a mari-juana cigarette on his person? What about an unmarked bottle of pills?

If a search warrant were required for every search incident to arrest that does not involve exigent circumstances, the courts would be swamped. And even if we arbitrarily singled out BAC tests incident to arrest for this special treatment, as it appears the dissent would do, see post, at 12–14, the impact on the courts would be considerable. The number of arrests every year for driving under the influence is enormous—more than 1.1 million in 2014. FBI, Uniform Crime Report, Crime in the United States, 2014, Arrests 2 (Fall 2015). Particularly in sparsely populated areas, it would be no small task for courts to field a large new influx of warrant applications that could come on any day of the year and at any hour. In many jurisdictions, judicial officers have the authority to issue warrants only within their own districts, see, e.g., Fed. Rule Crim. Proc. 41(b); N. D. Rule Crim. Proc. 41(a) (2016–2017), and in rural areas, some districts may have only a small number of judicial officers.

North Dakota, for instance, has only 51 state district judges spread across eight judicial districts. 4 Those judges are assisted by 31 magistrates, and there are no magistrates in 20 of the State's 53 counties. 5 At any given location in the State, then, relatively few state officials have authority to issue search warrants. 6 Yet the State, with a population of roughly 740,000, sees nearly 7,000 drunk-driving arrests each year. Office of North Dakota Attorney General, Crime in North Dakota, 2014, pp. 5, 47 (2015). With a small number of judicial officers authorized to issue warrants in some parts of the State, the burden of fielding BAC warrant applications 24 hours per day, 365 days of the year would not be the light burden that petitioners and Justice Sotomayor suggest.

In light of this burden and our prior search-incident-to-arrest precedents, petitioners would at a minimum have to show some special need for warrants for BAC testing. It is therefore appropriate to consider the benefits that such applications would provide. Search warrants protect privacy in two main ways. First, they ensure that a search is not carried out unless a neutral magistrate makes an independent determination that there is probable cause to believe that evidence will be found. See, e.g., Riley, 573 U. S., at ___ (slip op., at 5). Second, if the magistrate finds probable cause, the warrant limits the intrusion on privacy by specifying the scope of the search—that is, the area that can be searched and the items that can be sought. United States v. Chadwick, 433 U. S. 1, 9 (1977), abrogated on other grounds, Acevedo, 500 U. S. 565.

How well would these functions be performed by the warrant applications that petitioners propose? In order to persuade a magistrate that there is probable cause for a search warrant, the officer would typically recite the same facts that led the officer to find that there was probable cause for arrest, namely, that there is probable cause to believe that a BAC test will reveal that the motorist's blood alcohol level is over the limit. As these three cases suggest, see Part II,

supra, the facts that establish probable cause are largely the same from one drunk-driving stop to the next and consist largely of the officer's own characterization of his or her observations—for example, that there was a strong odor of alcohol, that the motorist wobbled when attempting to stand, that the motorist paused when reciting the alphabet or counting backwards, and so on. A magistrate would be in a poor position to challenge such characterizations.

As for the second function served by search warrants—delineating the scope of a search—the warrants in question here would not serve that function at all. In every case the scope of the warrant would simply be a BAC test of the arrestee. Cf. Skinner, 489 U. S., at 622 ("[I]n light of the standardized nature of the tests and the minimal discretion vested in those charged with administering the program, there are virtually no facts for a neutral magistrate to evaluate"). For these reasons, requiring the police to obtain a warrant in every case would impose a substantial burden but no commensurate benefit.

Petitioners advance other alternatives to warrantless BAC tests incident to arrest, but these are poor substitutes. Relying on a recent NHTSA report, petitioner Birchfield identifies 19 strategies that he claims would be at least as effective as implied consent laws, including high-visibility sobriety checkpoints, installing ignition interlocks on repeat offenders' cars that would disable their operation when the driver's breath reveals a sufficiently high alcohol concentration, and alcohol treatment programs. Brief for Petitioner in No. 14–1468, at 44–45. But Birchfield ignores the fact that the cited report describes many of these measures, such as checkpoints, as significantly more costly than test refusal penalties. NHTSA, A. Goodwin et al., Countermeasures That Work: A Highway Safety Countermeasures Guide for State Highway Safety Offices, p. 1–7 (No. 811727, 7th ed. 2013). Others, such as ignition interlocks, target only a segment of the drunk-driver population. And still others, such as treatment programs, are already in widespread use, see id., at 1–8, including in North Dakota and Minnesota. Moreover, the same NHTSA report, in line with the agency's guidance elsewhere, stresses that BAC test refusal penalties would be more effective if the consequences for refusal were made more severe, including through the addition of criminal penalties. Id., at 1–16 to 1–17.

3

Petitioner Bernard objects to the whole idea of analyzing breath and blood tests as searches incident to arrest. That doctrine, he argues, does not protect the sort of governmental interests that warrantless breath and blood tests serve. On his reading, this Court's precedents permit a search of an arrestee solely to prevent the arrestee from obtaining a weapon or taking steps to destroy evidence. See Reply Brief in No. 14–1470, at 4–6. In Chimel, for example, the Court derived its limitation for the scope of the permitted search—"the area into which an arrestee might reach"—from the principle that officers may reasonably search "the area from within which he might gain possession of a weapon or destructible evidence." 395 U. S., at 763. Stopping an arrestee from destroying evidence, Bernard argues, is critically different from preventing the loss of blood alcohol evidence as the result of the body's metabolism of alcohol, a natural process over which the arrestee has little control. Reply Brief in No. 14–1470, at 5–6.

The distinction that Bernard draws between an arrestee's active destruction of evidence and the loss of evidence due to a natural process makes little sense. In both situations the State is justifiably concerned that evidence may be lost, and Bernard does not explain why the cause of the loss should be dispositive. And in fact many of this Court's post-Chimel cases have recognized the State's concern, not just in avoiding an

arrestee's intentional destruction of evidence, but in "evidence preservation" or avoiding "the loss of evidence" more generally. Riley, 573 U. S., at ____ (slip op., at 8); see also Robinson, 414 U. S., at 234 ("the need to preserve evidence on his person"); Knowles v. Iowa, 525 U. S. 113–119 (1998) ("the need to discover and preserve evidence;" "the concern for destruction or loss of evidence" (emphasis added)); Virginia v. Moore, 553 U. S. 164, 176 (2008) (the need to "safeguard evidence"). This concern for preserving evidence or preventing its loss readily encompasses the inevitable metabolization of alcohol in the blood.

Nor is there any reason to suspect that Chimel's use of the word "destruction," 395 U. S., at 763, was a deliberate decision to rule out evidence loss that is mostly beyond the arrestee's control. The case did not involve any evidence that was subject to dissipation through natural processes, and there is no sign in the opinion that such a situation was on the Court's mind.

Bernard attempts to derive more concrete support for his position from Schmerber. In that case, the Court stated that the "destruction of evidence under the direct control of the accused" is a danger that is not present "with respect to searches involving intrusions beyond the body's surface." 384 U. S., at 769. Bernard reads this to mean that an arrestee cannot be required "to take a chemical test" incident to arrest, Brief for Petitioner in No. 14–1470, at 19, but by using the term "chemical test," Bernard obscures the fact that Schmerber's passage was addressed to the type of test at issue in that case, namely a blood test. The Court described blood tests as "searches involving intrusions beyond the body's surface," and it saw these searches as implicating important "interests in human dignity and privacy," 384 U. S., at 769–770. Al-though the Court appreciated as well that blood tests "in-volv[e] virtually no risk, trauma, or pain," id., at 771, its point was that such searches still impinge on far more sensitive interests than the typical search of the person of an arrestee. Cf. supra, at 22–23. But breath tests, unlike blood tests, "are not invasive of the body," Skinner, 489 U. S., at 626 (emphasis added), and therefore the Court's comments in Schmerber are inapposite when it comes to the type of test Bernard was asked to take. Schmerber did not involve a breath test, and on the question of breath tests' legality, Schmerber said nothing.

Finally, Bernard supports his distinction using a passage from the McNeely opinion, which distinguishes between "easily disposable evidence" over "which the suspect has control" and evidence, like blood alcohol evidence, that is lost through a natural process "in a gradual and relatively predictable manner." 569 U. S., at ____ (slip op., at 10); see Reply Brief in No. 14–1470, at 5–6. Bernard fails to note the issue that this paragraph addressed. McNeely concerned only one exception to the usual warrant requirement, the exception for exigent circumstances, and as previously discussed, that exception has always been understood to involve an evaluation of the particular facts of each case. Here, by contrast, we are concerned with the search-incident-to-arrest exception, and as we made clear in Robinson and repeated in McNeely itself, this authority is categorical. It does not depend on an evaluation of the threat to officer safety or the threat of evidence loss in a particular case. 7

Having assessed the effect of BAC tests on privacy interests and the need for such tests, we conclude that the Fourth Amendment permits warrantless breath tests incident to arrests for drunk driving. The impact of breath tests on privacy is slight, and the need for BAC testing is great.

We reach a different conclusion with respect to blood tests. Blood tests are significantly more intrusive, and their reasonableness must be judged in light of the availability of the less invasive alternative of a breath test. Respondents have offered no satisfactory justification for demanding the more intrusive alternative without a warrant.

Neither respondents nor their amici dispute the effectiveness of breath tests in measuring BAC. Breath tests have been in common use for many years. Their results are admissible in court and are widely credited by juries, and respondents do not dispute their accuracy or utility. What, then, is the justification for warrantless blood tests?

One advantage of blood tests is their ability to detect not just alcohol but also other substances that can impair a driver's ability to operate a car safely. See Brief for New Jersey et al. as Amici Curiae 9; Brief for United States as Amicus Curiae 6. A breath test cannot do this, but police have other measures at their disposal when they have reason to believe that a motorist may be under the influence of some other substance (for example, if a breath test indicates that a clearly impaired motorist has little if any alcohol in his blood). Nothing prevents the police from seeking a warrant for a blood test when there is sufficient time to do so in the particular circumstances or from relying on the exigent circumstances exception to the warrant requirement when there is not. See McNeely, 569 U. S., at ____ – ____ (slip op., at 22–23).

A blood test also requires less driver participation than a breath test. In order for a technician to take a blood sample, all that is needed is for the subject to remain still, either voluntarily or by being immobilized. Thus, it is possible to extract a blood sample from a subject who forcibly resists, but many States reasonably prefer not to take this step. See, e.g., Neville, 459 U. S., at 559–560. North Dakota, for example, tells us that it generally opposes this practice because of the risk of dangerous altercations between police officers and arrestees in rural areas where the arresting officer may not have backup. Brief for

Respondent in No. 14–1468, p. 29. Under current North Dakota law, only in cases involving an accident that results in death or serious injury may blood be taken from arrestees who resist. Compare N. D. Cent. Code Ann. §§39–20–04(1), 39–20–01, with §39–20–01.1.

It is true that a blood test, unlike a breath test, may be administered to a person who is unconscious (perhaps as a result of a crash) or who is unable to do what is needed to take a breath test due to profound intoxication or injuries. But we have no reason to believe that such situations are common in drunk-driving arrests, and when they arise, the police may apply for a warrant if need be.

A breath test may also be ineffective if an arrestee deliberately attempts to prevent an accurate reading by failing to blow into the tube for the requisite length of time or with the necessary force. But courts have held that such conduct qualifies as a refusal to undergo testing, e.g., Andrews v. Turner, 52 Ohio St. 2d 31, 36–37, 368 N. E. 2d 1253, 1256–1257 (1977); In re Kunneman, 501 P. 2d 910, 910–911 (Okla. Civ. App. 1972); see generally 1 Erwin §4.08[2] (collecting cases), and it may be prosecuted as such. And again, a warrant for a blood test may be sought.

Because breath tests are significantly less intrusive than blood tests and in most cases amply serve law enforcement interests, we conclude that a breath test, but not a blood test, may be administered as a search incident to a lawful arrest for drunk driving. As in all cases involving reasonable searches incident to arrest, a warrant is not needed in this situation. 8

VI

Having concluded that the search incident to arrest doctrine does not justify the warrantless taking of a blood sample, we must address respondents' alternative argument that such tests are justified based on the driver's legally implied consent to submit to them. It is well established that a search is reasonable when the subject consents, e.g., Schneckloth v. Bustamonte, 412 U. S. 218, 219 (1973), and that sometimes consent to a search need not be express but may be fairly inferred from context, cf. Florida v. Jardines, 569 U. S. 1, ___–___ (2013) (slip op., at 6–7); Marshall v. Barlow's, Inc., 436 U. S. 307, 313 (1978). Our prior opinions have referred approvingly to the general concept of implied-consent laws that impose civil penalties and evidentiary consequences on motorists who refuse to comply. See, e.g., McNeely, supra, at ___ (plural-ity opinion) (slip op., at 18); Neville, supra, at 560. Petitioners do not question the constitutionality of those laws, and nothing we say here should be read to cast doubt on them.

It is another matter, however, for a State not only to insist upon an intrusive blood test, but also to impose criminal penalties on the refusal to submit to such a test. There must be a limit to the consequences to which motorists may be deemed to have consented by virtue of a decision to drive on public roads.

Respondents and their amici all but concede this point. North Dakota emphasizes that its law makes refusal a misdemeanor and suggests that laws punishing refusal more severely would present a different issue. Brief for Respondent in No. 14–1468, at 33–34. Borrowing from our Fifth Amendment jurisprudence, the United States suggests that motorists could be deemed to have consented to only those conditions that are "reasonable" in that they have a "nexus" to the privilege of driving and entail penalties that are proportional to severity of the violation. Brief for United States as Amicus Curiae 21–27. But in the Fourth Amendment setting, this standard does not differ in substance from the one that we apply, since reasonableness is always the touchstone of Fourth Amendment analysis, see Brigham City v. Stuart, 547 U. S. 398, 403 (2006). And applying this standard, we conclude that motorists cannot be deemed to have consented to submit to a blood test on pain of committing a criminal offense.

VII

Our remaining task is to apply our legal conclusions to the three cases before us.

Petitioner Birchfield was criminally prosecuted for refusing a warrantless blood draw, and therefore the search he refused cannot be justified as a search incident to his arrest or on the basis of implied consent. There is no indication in the record or briefing that a breath test would have failed to satisfy the State's interests in acquiring evidence to enforce its drunk-driving laws against Birchfield. And North Dakota has not presented any case-specific information to suggest that the exigent circumstances exception would have justified a warrantless search. Cf. McNeely, 569 U. S., at ____–____ (slip op., at 20–23). Unable to see any other basis on which to justify a warrantless test of Birchfield's blood, we conclude that Birchfield was threatened with an unlawful search and that the judgment affirming his conviction must be reversed.

Bernard, on the other hand, was criminally prosecuted for refusing a warrantless breath test. That test was a permissible search incident to Bernard's arrest for drunk driving, an arrest whose legality Bernard has not con-tested. Accordingly, the Fourth Amendment did not require officers to obtain a warrant prior to demanding the test, and Bernard had no right to refuse it.

Unlike the other petitioners, Beylund was not prosecuted for refusing a test. He submitted to a blood test after police told him that the law required his submission, and his license was then suspended and he was fined in an administrative proceeding. The North Dakota Supreme Court held that Beylund's consent was voluntary on the erroneous assumption that the State could permissibly compel both blood and breath tests. Because voluntariness of consent to a search must be "determined from the totality of all the circumstances," Schneckloth, supra, at 227, we leave it to the state court on remand to reevaluate Beylund's consent given the partial inaccuracy of the officer's advisory. 9

We accordingly reverse the judgment of the North Da-kota Supreme Court in No. 14–1468 and remand the case for further proceedings not inconsistent with this opinion. We affirm the judgment of the Minnesota Supreme Court in No. 14–1470. And we vacate the judgment of the North Dakota Supreme Court in No. 14–1507 and remand the case for further proceedings not inconsistent with this opinion.

It is so ordered.

Notes

1 In addition, BAC may be determined by testing a subject's urine, which also requires the test subject's cooperation. But urine tests appear to be less common in drunk-driving cases than breath and blood tests, and none of the cases before us involves one.

2 See Smith, Moving From Grief to Action: Two Families Push for Stronger DUI Laws in N. D., Bismarck Tribune, Feb. 2, 2013, p. 1A; Haga, Some Kind of Peace: Parents of Two Young Boys Killed in Campground Accident Urge for Tougher DUI Penalties in N. D., Grand Forks Herald, Jan. 15, 2013, pp. A1–A2.

3 At most, there may be evidence that an arrestee's mouth could be searched in appropriate circumstances at the time of the founding. See W. Cuddihy, Fourth Amendment: Origins and Original Meaning: 602–1791, p. 420 (2009). Still, searching a mouth for weapons or contraband is not the same as requiring an arrestee to give up breath or blood.

4 See North Dakota Supreme Court, All District Judges, http://www.ndcourts.gov/court/districts/judges.htm (all Internet materials as last visited June 21, 2016).

5 See North Dakota Supreme Court,

Magistrates, http://www.ndcourts.gov/court/counties/magistra/members.htm.

6 North Dakota Supreme Court justices apparently also have author-ity to issue warrants statewide. See ND Op. Atty. Gen. 99–L–132, p. 2 (Dec. 30, 1999). But we highly doubt that they regularly handle search-warrant applications, much less during graveyard shifts.

7 Justice Sotomayor objects to treating warrantless breath tests as searches incident to a lawful arrest on two additional grounds.First, she maintains that "[a]ll of this Court's postarrest exceptions to the warrant requirement require a law enforcement interest separate from criminal investigation." Post, at 14. At least with respect to the search-incident-to-arrest doctrine, that is not true. As the historical authorities discussed earlier attest, see Part V–A, supra, the doctrine has always been understood as serving investigative ends, such as "discover[ing] and seiz[ing] . . . evidences of crime." Weeks v. United States, 232 U. S. 383, 392 (1914) ; see also United States v. Robinson, 414 U. S. 218, 235 (1973) (emphasizing "the need . . . to discover evidence"). Using breath tests to obtain evidence of intoxication is therefore well within the historical understanding of the doctrine's purposes. Second, Justice Sotomayor contends that the search-incident-to-arrest doctrine does not apply when "a narrower exception to the warrant requirement adequately satisfies the governmental needs asserted." Post, at 7, n. 3; see also post, at 17–19. But while this Court's cases have certainly recognized that "more targeted" exceptions to the warrant requirement may justify a warrantless search even when the search-incident-to-arrest exception would not, Riley v. California, 573 U. S. ___, ___ (2014) (slip op., at 14), Justice Sotomayor cites no authority for the proposition that an exception to the warrant requirement cannot apply simply because a "narrower" exception might apply.

8 Justice Thomas partly dissents from this holding, calling any distinction between breath and blood tests "an arbitrary line in the sand." Post, at 3 (opinion concurring in judgment in part and dissenting in part). Adhering to a position that the Court rejected in McNeely, Justice Thomas would hold that both breath and blood tests are constitutional with or without a warrant because of the natural metabolization of alcohol in the bloodstream. Post, at 3–5. Yet Justice Thomas does not dispute our conclusions that blood draws are more invasive than breath tests, that breath tests generally serve state interests in combating drunk driving as effectively as blood tests, and that our decision in Riley calls for a balancing of individual privacy interests and legitimate state interests to determine the reasonableness of the category of warrantless search that is at issue. Contrary to Justice Thomas's contention, this balancing does not leave law enforcement officers or lower courts with unpredictable rules, because it is categorical and not "case-by-case," post, at 3. Indeed, today's decision provides very clear guidance that the Fourth Amendment allows warrantless breath tests, but as a general rule does not allow warrantless blood draws, incident to a lawful drunk-driving arrest.

9 If the court on remand finds that Beylund did not voluntarily consent, it will have to address whether the evidence obtained in the search must be suppressed when the search was carried out pursuant to a state statute, see Heien v. North Carolina, 574 U. S. ___, ___–___ (2014) (slip op., at 8–10), and the evidence is offered in an administrative rather than criminal proceeding, see Pennsylvania Bd. of Probation and Parole v. Scott, 524 U. S. 357–364 (1998). And as Beylund notes, remedies may be available to him under state law. See Brief for Petitioner in No. 14–1507, pp. 13–14.

White v. Pauly (Jan 9, 2017)

Per Curiam.

This case addresses the situation of an officer who—having arrived late at an ongoing police action and having witnessed shots being fired by one of several individuals in a house surrounded by other officers—shoots and kills an armed occupant of the house without first giving a warning.

According to the District Court and the Court of Appeals, the record, when viewed in the light most favorable to respondents, shows the following. Respondent Daniel Pauly was involved in a road-rage incident on a highway near Santa Fe, New Mexico. 814 F. 3d 1060, 1064–1065 (CA10 2016). It was in the evening, and it was raining. The two women involved called 911 to report Daniel as a " 'drunk driver' " who was " 'swerving all crazy.' " Id., at 1065. The women then followed Daniel down the highway, close behind him and with their bright lights on. Daniel, feeling threatened, pulled his truck over at an off-ramp to confront them. After a brief, nonviolent encounter, Daniel drove a short distance to a secluded house where he lived with his brother, Samuel Pauly.

Sometime between 9 p.m. and 10 p.m., Officer Kevin Truesdale was dispatched to respond to the women's 911 call. Truesdale, arriving after Daniel had already left the scene, interviewed the two women at the off-ramp. The women told Truesdale that Daniel had been driving recklessly and gave his license plate number to Truesdale. The state police dispatcher identified the plate as being registered to the Pauly brothers' address.

After the women left, Officer Truesdale was joined at the off-ramp by Officers Ray White and Michael Mariscal. The three agreed there was insufficient probable cause to arrest Daniel. Still, the officers decided to speak with Daniel to (1) get his side of the story, (2) " 'make sure nothing else happened,' " and (3) find out if he was intoxicated. Id., at 1065. The officers split up. White stayed at the off-ramp in case Daniel returned. Truesdale and Mariscal drove in separate patrol cars to the Pauly brothers' address, less than a half mile away. Record 215. Neither officer turned on his flashing lights.

When Officers Mariscal and Truesdale arrived at the address they had received from the dispatcher, they found two different houses, the first with no lights on inside and a second one behind it on a hill. Id., at 217, 246. Lights were on in the second one. The officers parked their cars near the first house. They examined a vehicle parked near that house but did not find Daniel's truck. Id., at 310.

Officers Mariscal and Truesdale noticed the lights on in the second house and approached it in a covert manner to maintain officer safety. Both used their flashlights in an intermittent manner. Truesdale alone turned on his flashlight once they got close to the house's front door. Upon reaching the house, the officers found Daniel's pickup truck and spotted two men moving around inside the residence. Truesdale and Mariscal radioed White, who left the off-ramp to join them.

At approximately 11 p.m., the Pauly brothers became aware of the officers' presence and yelled out " 'Who are you?' " and " 'What do you want?' " 814 F. 3d, at 1066. In response, Officers Mariscal and Truesdale laughed and responded: " 'Hey, (expletive), we got you surrounded. Come out or we're coming in.' " Ibid. Truesdale shouted once: " 'Open the door, State Police, open the door.' " Ibid. Mariscal also yelled: " 'Open the door, open the door.' " Ibid.

The Pauly brothers heard someone yelling, " 'We're coming in. We're coming in.' " Ibid. Neither Samuel nor Daniel heard the officers identify themselves as state police. Record 81–82. The brothers armed themselves, Samuel with a handgun and Daniel with a shotgun. One of the brothers yelled at the police officers that " 'We have guns.' " 814 F. 3d, at 1066. The officers saw someone run to the back of the house, so Officer Truesdale positioned himself behind the house and shouted " 'Open the door, come outside.' " Ibid.

Officer White had parked at the first house and was walking up to its front door when he heard shouting from the second house. He half-jogged, half-walked to the Paulys' house, arriving "just as one of the brothers said: 'We have guns.' " Ibid.; see also Civ. No. 12–1311 (D NM, Feb. 5, 2014), App. to Pet. for Cert. 75–78. When White heard that statement, he drew his gun and took cover behind a stone wall 50 feet from the front of the house. Officer Mariscal took cover behind a pickup truck.

Just "a few seconds" after the "We have guns" statement, Daniel stepped part way out of the back door and fired two shotgun blasts while screaming loudly. 814 F. 3d, at 1066–1067. A few seconds after those shots, Samuel opened the front window and pointed a handgun in Officer White's direction. Officer Mariscal fired immediately at Samuel but missed. " 'Four to five seconds' " later, White shot and killed Samuel. Id., at 1067.

The District Court denied the officers' motions for summary judgment, and the facts are viewed in the light most favorable to the Paulys. Mullenix v. Luna, 577 U. S. ___, ___, n. (2015) (per curiam) (slip op., at 2, n.). Because this case concerns the defense of qualified immunity, however, the Court considers only the facts that were knowable to the defendant officers. Kingsley v. Hendrickson, 576 U. S. ___, ___ (2015) (slip op., at 9).

Samuel's estate and Daniel filed suit against, inter alia, Officers Mariscal, Truesdale, and White. One of the claims was that the officers were liable under Rev. Stat. §1979, 42 U. S. C. §1983, for violating Samuel's Fourth Amendment right to be free from excessive force. All three officers moved for summary judgment on qualified immunity grounds. White in particular argued that the Pauly brothers could not show that White's use

of force violated the Fourth Amendment and, regardless, that Samuel's Fourth Amendment right to be free from deadly force under the circumstances of this case was not clearly established.

The District Court denied qualified immunity. A di-vided panel of the Court of Appeals for the Tenth Circuit affirmed. As to Officers Mariscal and Truesdale, the court held that "[a]ccepting as true plaintiffs' version of the facts, a reasonable person in the officers' position should have understood their conduct would cause Samuel and Daniel Pauly to defend their home and could result in the commission of deadly force against Samuel Pauly by Officer White." 814 F. 3d, at 1076. The panel majority analyzed Officer White's claim separately from the other officers because "Officer White did not participate in the events leading up to the armed confrontation, nor was he there to hear the other officers ordering the brothers to 'Come out or we're coming in.' " Ibid. Despite the fact that "Officer White . . . arrived late on the scene and heard only 'We have guns' . . . before taking cover behind a stone wall," the majority held that a jury could have concluded that White's use of deadly force was not reasonable. Id., at 1077, 1082. The majority also decided that this rule—that a reasonable officer in White's position would believe that a warning was required despite the threat of serious harm—was clearly established at the time of Samuel's death. The Court of Appeals' ruling relied on general statements from this Court's case law that (1) "the reasonableness of an officer's use of force depends, in part, on whether the officer was in danger at the precise moment that he used force" and (2) "if the suspect threatens the officer with a weapon[,] deadly force may be used if necessary to prevent escape, and if[,] where feasible, some warning has been given." Id., at 1083 (citing, inter alia, Tennessee v. Garner, 471 U. S. 1 (1985), and Graham v. Connor, 490 U. S. 386 (1989) ; emphasis deleted; internal quotation marks and alterations omitted). The court concluded that a reasonable officer in White's position would have known that, since the Paulys could not have shot him unless he moved from his position behind a stone wall, he could not have used deadly force without first warning Samuel Pauly to drop his weapon.

Judge Moritz dissented, contending that the "majority impermissibly second-guesses" Officer White's quick choice to use deadly force. 814 F. 3d, at 1084. Judge Moritz explained that the majority also erred by defining the clearly established law at too high a level of generality, in contravention of this Court's precedent.

The officers petitioned for rehearing en banc, which 6 of the 12 judges on the Court of Appeals voted to grant. In a dissent from denial of rehearing, Judge Hartz noted that he was "unaware of any clearly established law that suggests . . . that an officer . . . who faces an occupant pointing a firearm in his direction must refrain from firing his weapon but, rather, must identify himself and shout a warning while pinned down, kneeling behind a rock wall." 817 F. 3d 715, 718 (CA10 2016). Judge Hartz expressed his hope that "the Supreme Court can clarify the governing law." Id., at 719.

The officers petitioned for certiorari. The petition is now granted, and the judgment is vacated: Officer White did not violate clearly established law on the record described by the Court of Appeals panel.

Qualified immunity attaches when an official's conduct " 'does not violate clearly established statutory or constitutional rights of which a reasonable person would have known.' " Mullenix v. Luna, 577 U. S., at ___–___ (slip op., at 4–5). While this Court's case law " 'do[es] not require a case directly on point' " for a right to be clearly established, " 'existing precedent must have placed the statutory or constitutional question beyond debate.' " Id., at ___ (slip op., at 5). In

other words, immunity protects " 'all but the plainly incompetent or those who knowingly violate the law.' " Ibid.

In the last five years, this Court has issued a number of opinions reversing federal courts in qualified immunity cases. See, e.g., City and County of San Francisco v. Sheehan, 575 U. S. ___, ___, n. 3 (2015) (slip op., at 10, n.3) (collecting cases). The Court has found this necessary both because qualified immunity is important to " 'society as a whole,' " ibid., and because as " 'an immunity from suit,' " qualified immunity " 'is effectively lost if a case is erroneously permitted to go to trial,' " Pearson v. Callahan, 555 U. S. 223, 231 (2009).

Today, it is again necessary to reiterate the longstanding principle that "clearly established law" should not be defined "at a high level of generality." Ashcroft v. al-Kidd, 563 U. S. 731, 742 (2011). As this Court explained decades ago, the clearly established law must be "particularized" to the facts of the case. Anderson v. Creighton, 483 U. S. 635, 640 (1987). Otherwise, "[p]laintiffs would be able to convert the rule of qualified immunity . . . into a rule of virtually unqualified liability simply by alleging violation of extremely abstract rights." Id., at 639.

The panel majority misunderstood the "clearly established" analysis: It failed to identify a case where an officer acting under similar circumstances as Officer White was held to have violated the Fourth Amendment. Instead, the majority relied on Graham, Garner, and their Court of Appeals progeny, which—as noted above—lay out excessive-force principles at only a general level. Of course, "general statements of the law are not inherently incapable of giving fair and clear warning" to officers, United States v. Lanier, 520 U. S. 259, 271 (1997), but "in the light of pre-existing law the unlawfulness must be apparent," Anderson v. Creighton, supra, at 640. For that reason, we have held that Garner and Graham do not by themselves create clearly established law outside "an obvious case." Brosseau v. Haugen, 543 U. S. 194,199 (2004) (per curiam); see also Plumhoff v. Rickard, 572 U. S. ___, ___ (2014) (slip op., at 13) (emphasizing that Garner and Graham "are 'cast at a high level of generality' ").

This is not a case where it is obvious that there was a violation of clearly established law under Garner and Graham. Of note, the majority did not conclude that White's conduct—such as his failure to shout a warning—constituted a run-of-the-mill Fourth Amendment violation. Indeed, it recognized that "this case presents a unique set of facts and circumstances" in light of White's late arrival on the scene. 814 F. 3d, at 1077. This alone should have been an important indication to the majority that White's conduct did not violate a "clearly established" right. Clearly established federal law does not prohibit a reasonable officer who arrives late to an ongoing police action in circumstances like this from assuming that proper procedures, such as officer identification, have already been followed. No settled Fourth Amendment principle requires that officer to second-guess the earlier steps already taken by his or her fellow officers in instances like the one White confronted here.

On the record described by the Court of Appeals, Officer White did not violate clearly established law. The Court notes, however, that respondents contend Officer White arrived on the scene only two minutes after Officers Truesdale and Mariscal and more than three minutes before Daniel's shots were fired. On the assumption that the conduct of Officers Truesdale and Mariscal did not adequately alert the Paulys that they were police officers, respondents suggest that a reasonable jury could infer that White witnessed the other officers' deficient performance and should have realized that corrective action was necessary before using deadly force. Brief in Opposition 11, 22, n. 5. This Court expresses no position on this potential alternative ground for affirmance, as it appears that neither the District Court nor the Court of Appeals panel addressed it. The Court also expresses no opinion on the question whether this ground was properly preserved or whether—in light of this Court's holding today—Officers Truesdale and Mariscal are entitled to qualified immunity.

For the foregoing reasons, the petition for certiorari is granted; the judgment of the Court of Appeals is vacated; and the case is remanded for further proceedings consistent with this opinion.

It is so ordered.

Honeycutt v. US (June 5, 2017)

Justice Sotomayor delivered the opinion of the Court.

A federal statute— 21 U. S. C. §853— mandates forfeiture of "any property constituting, or derived from, any proceeds the person obtained, directly or indirectly, as the result of" certain drug crimes. This case concerns how §853 operates when two or more defendants act as part of a conspiracy. Specifically, the issue is whether, under §853, a defendant may be held jointly and severally liable for property that his co-conspirator derived from the crime but that the defendant himself did not acquire. The Court holds that such liability is inconsistent with the statute's text and structure.

I

Terry Michael Honeycutt managed sales and inventory for a Tennessee hardware store owned by his brother, Tony Honeycutt. After observing several " 'edgy looking folks' " purchasing an iodine-based water-purification product known as Polar Pure, Terry Honeycutt contacted the Chattanooga Police Department to inquire whether the iodine crystals in the product could be used to manufacture methamphetamine. App. to Pet. for Cert. 2a. An officer confirmed that individuals were using Polar Pure for this purpose and advised Honeycutt to cease selling it if the sales made Honeycutt " 'uncomfortable.' " Ibid. Notwithstanding the officer's advice, the store continued to sell large quantities of Polar Pure. Although each bottle of Polar Pure contained enough iodine to purify 500 gallons of water, and despite the fact that most people have no legitimate use for the product in large quantities, the brothers sold as many as 12 bottles in a single transaction to a single customer. Over a 3-year period, the store grossed roughly $400,000 from the sale of more than 20,000 bottles of Polar Pure.

Unsurprisingly, these sales prompted an investigation by the federal Drug Enforcement Administration along with state and local law enforcement. Authorities executed a search warrant at the store in November 2010 and seized its entire inventory of Polar Pure—more than 300 bottles. A federal grand jury indicted the Honeycutt brothers for various federal crimes relating to their sale of iodine while knowing or having reason to believe it would be used to manufacture methamphetamine. Pursuant to the Comprehensive Forfeiture Act of 1984, §303, 98Stat. 2045, 21 U. S. C. §853(a)(1), which mandates forfeiture of "any proceeds the person obtained, directly or indirectly, as the result of" drug distribution, the Government sought forfeiture money judgments against each brother in the amount of $269,751.98, which represented the hardware store's profits from the sale of Polar Pure. Tony Honeycutt pleaded guilty and agreed to forfeit $200,000. Terry went to trial. A jury acquitted Terry Honeycutt of 3 charges but found him guilty of the remaining 11, including conspiring to and knowingly distributing iodine in violation of §§841(c)(2), 843(a)(6), and 846.

The District Court sentenced Terry Honeycutt to 60 months in prison. Despite conceding that Terry had no "controlling interest in the store" and "did not stand to benefit personally," the Government insisted that the District Court "hold [him] jointly liable for the profit from the illegal sales." App. to Pet. for Cert. 60a–61a. The Government thus sought a money judgment of $69,751.98, the amount of the conspiracy profits outstanding after Tony Honeycutt's forfeiture payment. The District Court declined to enter a forfeiture judgment, reasoning that Honeycutt was a salaried employee who had not person-ally received any profits from the iodine sales.

The Court of Appeals for the Sixth Circuit reversed. As co-conspirators, the court held, the brothers are " 'jointly and severally liable for any proceeds of the conspiracy.' " 816 F. 3d 362, 380 (2016). The court therefore concluded that each brother bore full responsibility for the entire forfeiture judgment. Ibid.

The Court granted certiorari to resolve disagreement among the Courts of Appeals regarding whether joint and several liability applies under §853.[1] 580 U. S. ___ (2016).

II

Criminal forfeiture statutes empower the Government to confiscate property derived from or used to facilitate criminal activity. Such statutes serve important governmental interests such as "separating a criminal from his ill-gotten gains," "returning property, in full, to those wrongfully deprived or defrauded of it," and "lessen[ing] the economic power" of criminal enterprises. Caplin & Drysdale, Chartered v. United States, 491 U. S. 617 –630 (1989). The statute at issue here—§853— mandates forfeiture with respect to persons convicted of certain serious drug crimes. The question presented is whether §853 embraces joint and several liability for forfeiture judgments.

A creature of tort law, joint and several liability "applies when there has been a judgment against multiple defendants." McDermott, Inc. v. AmClyde, 511 U. S. 202 –221 (1994). If two or more defendants jointly cause harm, each defendant is held liable for the entire amount of the harm; provided, however, that the plaintiff recover only once for the full amount. See Restatement (Second) of Torts §875 (1977). Application of that principle in the forfeiture context when two or more defendants conspire to violate the law would require that each defendant be held liable for a forfeiture judgment based not only on property that he used in or acquired because of the crime, but also on property obtained by his co-conspirator.

An example is instructive. Suppose a farmer masterminds a scheme to grow, harvest, and distribute marijuana on local college campuses. The mastermind recruits a college student to deliver packages and pays the student $300 each month from the distribution proceeds for his services. In one year, the mastermind earns $3 million. The student, meanwhile, earns $3,600. If joint and several liability applied, the student would face a forfeiture judgment for the entire amount of the conspiracy's proceeds: $3 million. The student would be bound by that judgment even though he never personally acquired any proceeds beyond the $3,600. This case requires determination whether this form of liability is permitted under §853(a)(1). The Court holds that it is not.

A

Forfeiture under §853 applies to "any person" convicted of certain serious drug crimes. Section 853(a) limits the statute's reach by defining the property subject to forfeiture in three separate provisions. An understanding of how these three provisions work to limit the operation of the statute is helpful to resolving the question in this case. First, the provision at issue here, §853(a)(1), limits forfeit-ure to "property constituting, or derived from, any proceeds the person obtained, directly or indirectly, as the result of" the crime. Second, §853(a)(2) restricts forfeiture to "property used, or intended to be

used, in any manner or part, to commit, or to facilitate the commission of," the crime. Finally, §853(a)(3) applies to persons "convicted of engaging in a continuing criminal enterprise"—a form of conspiracy—and requires forfeiture of "property described in paragraph (1) or (2)" as well as "any of [the defendant's] interest in, claims against, and property or contractual rights affording a source of control over, the continuing criminal enterprise." These provisions, by their terms, limit forfeiture under §853 to tainted property; that is, property flowing from (§853(a)(1)), or used in (§853(a)(2)), the crime itself. The limitations of §853(a) thus provide the first clue that the statute does not countenance joint and several liability, which, by its nature, would require forfeiture of untainted property.

Recall, for example, the college student from the earlier hypothetical. The $3,600 he received for his part in the marijuana distribution scheme clearly falls within §853(a)(1): It is property he "obtained . . . as the result of" the crime. But if he were held jointly and severally liable for the proceeds of the entire conspiracy, he would owe the Government $3 million. Of the $3 million, $2,996,400 would have no connection whatsoever to the student's participation in the crime and would have to be paid from the student's untainted assets. Joint and several liability would thus represent a departure from §853(a)'s restriction of forfeiture to tainted property.

In addition to limiting forfeiture to tainted property, §853(a) defines forfeitable property solely in terms of personal possession or use. This is most clear in the specific text of §853(a)(1)—the provision under which the Government sought forfeiture in this case. Section 853(a)(1) limits forfeiture to property the defendant "obtained . . . as the result of" the crime. At the time Congress enacted §853(a)(1), the verb "obtain" was defined as "to come into possession of" or to "get or acquire." Random House Dictionary of the English

Language 995 (1966); see also 7 Oxford English Dictionary 37 (1933) (defining "obtain" as "[t]o come into the possession or enjoyment of (something) by one's own effort, or by request; to procure or gain, as the result of purpose and effort"). That definition persists today. See Black's Law Dictionary 1247 (10th ed. 2014) (defining "obtain" as "[t]o bring into one's own possession; to procure, esp. through effort"); cf. Sekhar v. United States, 570 U. S. ___, ___–___ (2013) (slip op., at 4–5) ("Obtaining property requires '. . . the acquisition of property' "). Neither the dictionary definition nor the common usage of the word "obtain" supports the conclusion that an individual "obtains" property that was acquired by someone else. Yet joint and several liability would mean just that: The college student would be presumed to have "obtained" the $3 million that the mastermind acquired.

Section 853(a)(1) further provides that the forfeitable property may be "obtained, directly or indirectly." The adverbs "directly" and "indirectly" modify—but do not erase—the verb "obtain." In other words, these adverbs refer to how a defendant obtains the property; they do not negate the requirement that he obtain it at all. For instance, the marijuana mastermind might receive payments directly from drug purchasers, or he might arrange to have drug purchasers pay an intermediary such as the college student. In all instances, he ultimately "obtains" the property— whether "directly or indirectly."

The other provisions of §853(a) are in accord with the limitation of forfeiture to property the defendant himself obtained. Section 853(a)(2) mandates forfeiture of property used to facilitate the crime but limits forfeiture to "the person's property." Similarly, §853(a)(3) requires forfeiture of property related to continuing criminal enterprises, but contrary to joint and several liability principles, requires the defendant to forfeit only "his interest in" the enterprise.

Section 853(a)'s limitation of forfeiture to tainted property acquired or used by the defendant, together with the plain text of §853(a)(1), foreclose joint and several liability for co-conspirators.

B

Joint and several liability is not only contrary to §853(a), it is—for the same reasons— contrary to several other provisions of §853. Two provisions expressly incorporate the §853(a) limitations. First, §853(c) provides that "[a]ll right, title, and interest in property described in subsection (a)"—e.g., tainted property obtained as the result of or used to facilitate the crime—"vests in the United States upon the commission of the act giving rise to forfeiture." Consistent with its text, the Court has previously acknowledged that §853(c) applies to tainted property only. See Luis v. United States, 578 U. S. ___, ___ (2016) (slip op., at 8).

Second, §853(e)(1) authorizes pretrial freezes "to preserve the availability of property described in subsection (a) . . . for forfeiture." Pretrial restraints on forfeitable property are permitted only when the Government proves, at a hearing, that (1) the defendant has committed an offense triggering forfeiture, and (2) "the property at issue has the requisite connection to that crime." Kaley v. United States, 571 U. S. ___, ___ (2014) (slip op., at 3); see also id., at ___, n. 11 (slip op., at 15, n. 11) ("[F]orfeiture applies only to specific assets").

Another provision, §853(d), does not reference subsection (a) but incorporates its requirements on its own terms. Section 835(d) establishes a "rebuttable presumption" that property is subject to forfeiture only if the Government proves that "such property was acquired by [the defendant] during the period of the violation" and that "there was no likely source for such property other than" the crime. Contrary to all of these provisions, joint and several liability would mandate forfeiture of untainted property that the defendant did not acquire as a result of the crime.

It would also render futile one other provision of the statute. Section 853(p)—the sole provision of §853 that permits the Government to confiscate property untainted by the crime—lays to rest any doubt that the statute permits joint and several liability. That provision governs forfeiture of "substitute property" and applies "if any property described in subsection (a), as a result of any act or omission of the defendant" either:

"(A) cannot be located upon the exercise of due diligence;

"(B) has been transferred or sold to, or deposited with, a third party;

"(C) has been placed beyond the jurisdiction of the court;

"(D) has been substantially diminished in value; or

"(E) has been commingled with other property which cannot be divided without difficulty." §853(p)(1).

Only if the Government can prove that one of these five conditions was caused by the defendant may it seize "any other property of the defendant, up to the value of" the tainted property—rather than the tainted property itself. §853(p)(2). This provision begins from the premise that the defendant once possessed tainted property as "described in subsection (a)," and provides a means for the Government to recoup the value of the property if it has been dissipated or otherwise disposed of by "any act or omission of the defendant." §853(p)(1).

Section 853(p)(1) demonstrates that Congress contemplated situations where the tainted property itself would fall outside the Government's reach. To remedy that situation, Congress did not authorize the Government to confiscate substitute property from other defendants or co-conspirators; it authorized the Government to confiscate assets only from the defendant who initially acquired the property and who bears responsibility for its dissipation. Permitting the Government to force other co-conspirators to turn over untainted substitute property would allow the Government to circumvent Congress' carefully constructed statutory scheme, which permits forfeiture of substitute property only when the requirements of §§853(p) and (a) are satisfied. There is no basis to read such an end run into the statute.

III

Against all of this, the Government asserts the "bedrock principle of conspiracy liability" under which "conspirators are legally responsible for each other's foreseeable actions in furtherance of their common plan." Brief for United States 9; see also Pinkerton v. United States, 328 U. S. 640 (1946) . Congress, according to the Government, must be presumed to have legislated against the background principles of conspiracy liability, and thus, "when the traceable proceeds of a conspiracy are unavailable, [§]853 renders conspirators jointly and severally liable for the amount of the proceeds foreseeably obtained by the conspiracy." Brief for United States 10. Not so.

The plain text and structure of §853 leave no doubt that Congress did not incorporate those background principles. Congress provided just one way for the Government to recoup substitute property when the tainted property itself is unavailable—the procedures outlined in §853(p). And, for all the Government makes of the background principles of conspiracy liability, it fails to fully engage with the most important background principles underlying §853: those of forfeiture.

Traditionally, forfeiture was an action against the tainted property itself and thus proceeded in rem; that is, proceedings in which "[t]he thing [was] primarily considered as the offender, or rather the offence [was] attached primarily to the thing." The Palmyra, 12 Wheat. 1, 14 (1827). The forfeiture "proceeding in rem st[ood] independent of, and wholly unaffected by any criminal proceeding in personam" against the defendant. Id., at 15. Congress altered this distinction in enacting §853 by effectively merging the in rem forfeiture proceeding with the in personam criminal proceeding and by expanding forfeiture to include not just the "thing" but "property . . . derived from . . . any proceeds" of the crime. §853(a)(1). But as is clear from its text and structure, §853 maintains traditional in rem forfeiture's focus on tainted property unless one of the preconditions of §853(p) exists. For those who find it relevant, the legislative history confirms as much: Congress altered the traditional system in order to "improv[e] the procedures applicable in forfeiture cases." S. Rep. No. 98–225, p. 192 (1983). By adopting an in personam aspect to criminal forfeiture, and providing for substitute-asset forfeiture, Congress made it easier for the Government to hold the defendant who acquired the tainted property responsible. Congress did not, however, enact any "significant expansion of the scope of property subject to forfeiture." Ibid.[2]

IV

Forfeiture pursuant to §853(a)(1) is limited to property the defendant himself actually acquired as the result of the crime. In this case, the Government has conceded that Terry Honeycutt had no ownership interest in his brother's store and did not personally benefit from the Polar Pure sales. App. to Pet. for Cert. 60a. The District Court agreed. Id., at 40a. Because Honeycutt never obtained tainted property as a result of the crime, §853 does not require any forfeiture.

The judgment of the Court of Appeals for the Sixth Circuit is reversed.

It is so ordered.

Justice Gorsuch took no part in the consideration or decision of this case.

Notes

1 Compare United States v. Van Nguyen, 602 F. 3d 886, 904 (CA8 2010) (applying joint and several liability to forfeiture under §853); United States v. Pitt, 193 F. 3d 751, 765 (CA3 1999) (same); United States v. McHan, 101 F. 3d 1027 (CA4 1996) (same); and United States v. Benevento, 836 F. 2d 129, 130 (CA2 1988) (per curiam) (same), with United States v. Cano-Flores, 796 F. 3d 83, 91 (CADC 2015) (declining to apply joint and several liability under §853).

2 Section 853(o) directs that "the provisions of [§853] shall be liberally construed to effectuate its remedial purposes." The Government points to this as license to read joint and several liability into the statute. But the Court cannot construe a statute in a way that negates its plain text, and here, Congress expressly limited forfeiture to tainted property that the defendant obtained. As explained above, that limitation is incompatible with joint and several liability.

District of Columbia v. Wesby (Jan 22, 2018) [Notes omitted]

Justice Thomas delivered the opinion of the Court.

This case involves a civil suit against the District of Columbia and five of its police officers, brought by 16 individuals who were arrested for holding a raucous, late-night party in a house they did not have permission to enter. The United States Court of Appeals for the District of Columbia Circuit held that there was no probable cause to arrest the partygoers, and that the officers were not entitled to qualified immunity. We reverse on both grounds.

I

Around 1 a.m. on March 16, 2008, the District's Metropolitan Police Department received a complaint about loud music and illegal activities at a house in Northeast D. C. The caller, a former neighborhood commissioner, told police that the house had been vacant for several months. When officers arrived at the scene, several neighbors confirmed that the house should have been empty. The officers approached the house and, consistent with the complaint, heard loud music playing inside.

After the officers knocked on the front door, they saw a man look out the window and then run upstairs. One of the partygoers opened the door, and the officers entered. They immediately observed that the inside of the house " 'was in disarray' " and looked like " 'a vacant property.' " 841 F. Supp. 2d 20, 31 (DC 2012) (quoting Defs. Exh. A). The officers smelled marijuana and saw beer bottles and cups of liquor on the floor. In fact, the floor was so dirty that one of the partygoers refused to sit on it while being questioned. Although the house had working electricity and plumbing, it had no furniture downstairs other than a few padded metal chairs. The only other signs of habitation were blinds on the windows, food in the refrigerator, and toiletries in the bathroom.

In the living room, the officers found a makeshift strip club. Several women were wearing only bras and thongs, with cash tucked into their garter belts. The women were giving lap dances while other partygoers watched. Most of the onlookers were holding cash and cups of alcohol. After seeing the uniformed officers, many partygoers scattered into other parts of the house.

The officers found more debauchery upstairs. A naked woman and several men were in the bedroom. A bare mattress—the only one in the house—was on the floor, along with some lit candles and multiple open condom wrappers. A used condom was on the windowsill. The officers found one partygoer hiding in an upstairs closet, and another who had shut himself in the bathroom and refused to come out.

The officers found a total of 21 people in the house. After interviewing all 21, the officers did not get a clear or consistent story. Many partygoers said they were there for a bachelor party, but no one could identify the bachelor. Each of the partygoers claimed that someone had invited them to the house, but no one could say who. Two of the women working the party said that a woman named "Peaches" or "Tasty" was renting the house and had given them permission to be there. One of the women explained that the previous owner had recently passed away, and Peaches had just started renting the house from the grandson who inherited it. But the house had no boxes or moving supplies. She did not know Peaches' real name. And Peaches was not there.

An officer asked the woman to call Peaches on her phone so he could talk to her. Peaches answered and explained that she had just left the party to go to the store. When the officer asked her to return, Peaches refused because she was afraid of being arrested. The sergeant supervising the investigation also spoke with Peaches. At first, Peaches claimed to be renting the house from the owner, who was fixing it up for her. She also said that she had given the attendees permission to have the party. When the sergeant again asked her who had given her permission to use the house, Peaches became evasive and hung up. The sergeant called her back, and she began yelling and insisting that she had permission before hanging up a second time. The officers eventually got Peaches on the phone again, and she admitted that she did not have permission to use the house.

The officers then contacted the owner. He told them that he had been trying to negotiate a lease with Peaches, but they had not reached an agreement. He confirmed that he had not given Peaches (or anyone else) permission to be in the house—let alone permission to use it for a bachelor party. At that point, the officers arrested the 21 partygoers for unlawful entry. See D. C. Code §22–3302 (2008). The police transported the partygoers to the police station, where the lieutenant decided to charge them with disorderly conduct. See §22–1321. The partygoers were released, and the charges were eventually dropped.[1]

II

Respondents, 16 of the 21 partygoers, sued the District and five of the arresting officers. They sued the officers for false arrest under the Fourth Amendment, Rev. Stat. §1979, 42 U. S. C. §1983, and under District law. They sued the District for false arrest and negligent supervision under District law. The partygoers' claims were all "predicated upon the allegation that [they] were arrested without probable cause." 841 F. Supp. 2d, at 32.

On cross-motions for summary judgment, the District Court awarded partial summary judgment to the party- goers. Id., at 48–49. It concluded that the officers lacked probable cause to arrest the partygoers for unlawful entry.[2] Id., at 32–33. The officers were told that Peaches had invited the partygoers to the house, the District Court reasoned, and nothing the officers learned in their investigation suggested the partygoers " 'knew or should have known that [they were] entering against the [owner's] will.' " Id., at 32. The District Court also concluded that the officers were not entitled to qualified immunity under §1983.[3] It noted that, under District case law, "probable cause to arrest for unlawful entry requires evidence that the alleged intruder knew or should have known, upon entry, that such entry was against the will of the owner." Id., at 37. And in its view, the officers had no such evidence. Id., at 32–33, 37–38.

With liability resolved, the case proceeded to trial on damages. The jury awarded the partygoers a total of $680,000 in compensatory damages. After the District Court awarded attorney's fees, the total award was nearly $1 million.

On appeal, a divided panel of the D. C. Circuit affirmed. On the question of probable cause, the panel majority made Peaches' invitation "central" to its determination that the officers lacked probable cause to arrest the party- goers for unlawful entry. 765 F. 3d 13, 21 (2014). The panel majority asserted that, "in the absence of any conflicting information, Peaches' invitation vitiates the necessary element of [the partygoers'] intent to enter against the will of the lawful owner." Ibid. And the panel major- ity determined that "there is simply no evidence in the record that [the partygoers] had any reason to think the invitation was invalid." Ibid.

On the question of qualified immunity, the panel majority determined that it was "perfectly clear" that a person with "a good purpose and bona fide belief of her right to enter" lacks the necessary intent for unlawful entry. Id., at 27. In other words, the officers needed "some evidence" that the partygoers "knew or should have known they were entering against the will of the lawful owner." Ibid. And here, the panel majority asserted, the officers must "have known that uncontroverted evidence of an invitation to enter the premises would vitiate probable cause for unlawful entry." Ibid.

Judge Brown dissented. She concluded that summary judgment on the false-arrest claims was improper because, under the totality of the circumstances, a reasonable officer "could disbelieve [the partygoers'] claim of innocent entry" and infer that they knew or should have known that they did not have permission to be in the house. Id., at 34. She also disagreed with the denial of qualified immunity, contending that a reasonable officer could have found probable cause to arrest in this "unusual factual scenario, not well represented in the controlling case law." Id., at 36.

The D. C. Circuit denied rehearing en banc over the dissent of four judges. The dissenters focused on qualified immunity, contending that the panel opinion "contravene[d] . . . emphatic

Supreme Court directives" that "police officers may not be held liable for damages unless the officers were 'plainly incompetent' or 'knowingly violate[d]' clearly established law." 816 F. 3d 96, 102 (2016) (quoting Carroll v. Carman, 574 U. S. ____, ____ (2014) (per curiam) (slip op., at 4)). The panel majority— Judges Pillard and Edwards— responded in a joint concurrence. 816 F. 3d, at 96–101. They insisted that the panel opinion did not misapply the law of qualified immunity, and that their disagreement with the dissenters was a mere "case-specific assessment of the circumstantial evidence in the record." Id., at 100.

We granted certiorari to resolve two questions: whether the officers had probable cause to arrest the partygoers, and whether the officers were entitled to qualified immunity. See 580 U. S. ____ (2017). We address each question in turn.

III

The Fourth Amendment protects "[t]he right of the people to be secure in their persons, houses, papers, and effects, against unreasonable searches and seizures." Because arrests are "seizures" of "persons," they must be reasonable under the circumstances. See Payton v. New York, 445 U. S. 573, 585 (1980) . A warrantless arrest is reasonable if the officer has probable cause to believe that the suspect committed a crime in the officer's presence. Atwater v. Lago Vista, 532 U. S. 318, 354 (2001) .

To determine whether an officer had probable cause for an arrest, "we examine the events leading up to the arrest, and then decide 'whether these historical facts, viewed from the standpoint of an objectively reasonable police officer, amount to' probable cause." Maryland v. Pringle, 540 U. S. 366, 371 (2003) (quoting Ornelas v. United States, 517 U. S. 690, 696 (1996)). Because probable cause "deals with probabilities and depends on the totality of the circumstances," 540 U. S., at 371, it is "a fluid concept" that is "not readily, or even usefully, reduced to a neat set of

legal rules," Illinois v. Gates, 462 U. S. 213, 232 (1983) . It "requires only a probability or substantial chance of criminal activity, not an actual showing of such activity." Id., at 243–244, n. 13 (1983). Probable cause "is not a high bar." Kaley v. United States, 571 U. S. ____, ____ (2014) (slip op., at 18).

A

There is no dispute that the partygoers entered the house against the will of the owner. Nonetheless, the partygoers contend that the officers lacked probable cause to arrest them because the officers had no reason to believe that they "knew or should have known" their "entry was unwanted." Ortberg v. United States, 81 A. 3d 303, 308 (D. C. 2013). We disagree. Considering the totality of the circumstances, the officers made an "entirely reason- able inference" that the partygoers were knowingly taking advantage of a vacant house as a venue for their late-night party. Pringle, supra, at 372.

Consider first the condition of the house. Multiple neighbors, including a former neighborhood official, informed the officers that the house had been vacant for several months.[4] The house had no furniture, except for a few padded metal chairs and a bare mattress. The rest of the house was empty, save for some fixtures and large appliances. The house had a few signs of inhabitance—working electricity and plumbing, blinds on the windows, toiletries in the bathroom, and food in the refrigerator. But those facts are not necessarily inconsistent with the house being unoccupied. The owner could have paid the utilities and kept the blinds while he looked for a new tenant, and the partygoers could have brought the food and toiletries. Although one woman told the officers that Peaches had recently moved in, the officers had reason to doubt that was true. There were no boxes or other moving supplies in the house; nor were there other possessions, such as clothes in the closet, suggesting someone lived there.

In addition to the condition of the house, consider the partygoers' conduct. The party was still going strong when the officers arrived after 1 a.m., with music so loud that it could be heard from outside. Upon entering the house, multiple officers smelled marijuana.[5] The party-goers left beer bottles and cups of liquor on the floor, and they left the floor so dirty that one of them refused to sit on it. The living room had been converted into a makeshift strip club. Strippers in bras and thongs, with cash stuffed in their garter belts, were giving lap dances. Upstairs, the officers found a group of men with a single, naked woman on a bare mattress—the only bed in the house—along with multiple open condom wrappers and a used condom.

Taken together, the condition of the house and the conduct of the partygoers allowed the officers to make several " 'common-sense conclusions about human behavior.' " Gates, supra, at 231 (quoting United States v. Cortez, 449 U. S. 411, 418 (1981)). Most homeowners do not live in near-barren houses. And most homeowners do not invite people over to use their living room as a strip club, to have sex in their bedroom, to smoke marijuana inside, and to leave their floors filthy. The officers could thus infer that the partygoers knew their party was not authorized.

The partygoers' reaction to the officers gave them further reason to believe that the partygoers knew they lacked permission to be in the house. Many scattered at the sight of the uniformed officers. Two hid themselves, one in a closet and the other in a bathroom. "[U]nprovoked flight upon noticing the police," we have explained, "is certainly suggestive" of wrongdoing and can be treated as "suspicious behavior" that factors into the totality of the circumstances. Illinois v. Wardlow, 528 U. S. 119 –125 (2000). In fact, "deliberately furtive actions and flight at the approach of . . . law officers are strong indicia of

mens rea." Sibron v. New York, 392 U. S. 40, 66 (1968) (emphasis added). A reasonable officer could infer that the partygoers' scattering and hiding was an indication that they knew they were not supposed to be there.

The partygoers' answers to the officers' questions also suggested their guilty state of mind. When the officers asked who had given them permission to be there, the partygoers gave vague and implausible responses. They could not say who had invited them. Only two people claimed that Peaches had invited them, and they were working the party instead of attending it. If Peaches was the hostess, it was odd that none of the partygoers mentioned her name. Additionally, some of the partygoers claimed the event was a bachelor party, but no one could identify the bachelor. The officers could have disbelieved them, since people normally do not throw a bachelor party without a bachelor. Based on the vagueness and implausibility of the partygoers' stories, the officers could have reasonably inferred that they were lying and that their lies suggested a guilty mind. Cf. Devenpeck v. Alford, 543 U. S. 146 –156 (2004) (noting that the suspect's "untruthful and evasive" answers to police questioning could support probable cause).

The panel majority relied heavily on the fact that Peaches said she had invited the partygoers to the house. But when the officers spoke with Peaches, she was nervous, agitated, and evasive. Cf. Wardlow, supra, at 124 (explaining that the police can take a suspect's "nervous, evasive behavior" into account). After initially insisting that she had permission to use the house, she ultimately confessed that this was a lie—a fact that the owner confirmed. Peaches' lying and evasive behavior gave the officers reason to discredit everything she had told them. For example, the officers could have inferred that Peaches lied to them when she said she had invited the others to the house, which was consistent with the fact that hardly anyone at the party knew her name. Or the officers could have inferred that Peaches told the partygoers (like she eventually told the police) that she was not actually renting the house, which was consistent with how the party-goers were treating it.

Viewing these circumstances as a whole, a reasonable officer could conclude that there was probable cause to believe the partygoers knew they did not have permission to be in the house.

B

In concluding otherwise, the panel majority engaged in an "excessively technical dissection" of the factors supporting probable cause. Gates, 462 U. S., at 234. Indeed, the panel majority failed to follow two basic and well-established principles of law.

First, the panel majority viewed each fact "in isolation, rather than as a factor in the totality of the circumstances." Pringle, 540 U. S., at 372, n. 2. This was "mistaken in light of our precedents." Ibid. The "totality of the circumstances" requires courts to consider "the whole picture." Cortez, supra, at 417. Our precedents recognize that the whole is often greater than the sum of its parts—especially when the parts are viewed in isolation. See United States v. Arvizu, 534 U. S. 266 –278 (2002). Instead of considering the facts as a whole, the panel majority took them one by one. For example, it dismissed the fact that the partygoers "scattered or hid when the police entered the house" because that fact was "not sufficient standing alone to create probable cause." 765 F. 3d, at 23 (emphasis added). Similarly, it found "nothing in the record suggesting that the condition of the house, on its own, should have alerted the [partygoers] that they were unwelcome." Ibid. (emphasis added). The totality-of-the-circumstances test "precludes this sort of divide-and-conquer analysis." Arvizu, 534 U. S., at 274.

Second, the panel majority mistakenly believed that it could dismiss outright any circumstances that were "susceptible of innocent explanation." Id., at 277. For example, the panel majority brushed aside the drinking and the lap dances as "consistent with" the partygoers' explanation that they were having a bachelor party. 765 F. 3d, at 23. And it similarly dismissed the condition of the house as "entirely consistent with" Peaches being a "new tenant." Ibid. But probable cause does not require officers to rule out a suspect's innocent explanation for suspicious facts. As we have explained, "the relevant inquiry is not whether particular conduct is 'innocent' or 'guilty,' but the degree of suspicion that attaches to particular types of noncriminal acts." Gates, 462 U. S., at 244, n. 13. Thus, the panel majority should have asked whether a reasonable officer could conclude—considering all of the surrounding circumstances, including the plausibility of the explanation itself—that there was a "substantial chance of criminal activity." Ibid.

The circumstances here certainly suggested criminal activity. As explained, the officers found a group of people who claimed to be having a bachelor party with no bachelor, in a near-empty house, with strippers in the living room and sexual activity in the bedroom, and who fled at the first sign of police. The panel majority identified innocent explanations for most of these circumstances in isolation, but again, this kind of divide-and-conquer approach is improper. A factor viewed in isolation is often more "readily susceptible to an innocent explanation" than one viewed as part of a totality. Arvizu, supra, at 274. And here, the totality of the circumstances gave the officers plenty of reasons to doubt the partygoers' protestations of innocence.

For all of these reasons, we reverse the D. C. Circuit's holding that the officers lacked probable cause to arrest. Accordingly, the District and its officers are entitled to summary judgment on all of the partygoers' claims.[6]

IV

Our conclusion that the officers had probable cause to arrest the partygoers is sufficient to resolve this case. But where, as here, the Court of Appeals erred on both the merits of the constitutional claim and the question of qualified immunity, "we have discretion to correct its errors at each step." Ashcroft v. al-Kidd, 563 U. S. 731, 735 (2011) ; see, e.g., Plumhoff v. Rickard, 572 U. S. ___ (2014). We exercise that discretion here because the D. C. Circuit's analysis, if followed elsewhere, would "undermine the values qualified immunity seeks to promote." al-Kidd, supra, at 735.[7]

A

Under our precedents, officers are entitled to qualified immunity under §1983 unless (1) they violated a federal statutory or constitutional right, and (2) the unlawfulness of their conduct was "clearly established at the time." Reichle v. Howards, 566 U. S. 658, 664 (2012) . "Clearly established" means that, at the time of the officer's conduct, the law was " 'sufficiently clear' that every 'reason- able official would understand that what he is doing' " is unlawful. al-Kidd, supra, at 741 (quoting Anderson v. Creighton, 483 U. S. 635, 640 (1987)). In other words, existing law must have placed the constitutionality of the officer's conduct "beyond debate." al-Kidd, supra, at 741. This demanding standard protects "all but the plainly incompetent or those who knowingly violate the law." Malley v. Briggs, 475 U. S. 335, 341 (1986) .

To be clearly established, a legal principle must have a sufficiently clear foundation in then-existing precedent. The rule must be "settled law," Hunter v. Bryant, 502 U. S. 224, 228 (1991) (per curiam), which means it is dictated by "controlling authority" or "a robust 'consensus of cases of persuasive authority,' " al-Kidd, supra, at 741–742 (quoting Wilson v. Layne, 526 U. S. 603, 617 (1999)). It is not enough that the rule is suggested by then-existing precedent. The precedent must be clear enough that every reasonable official would interpret it to establish the particular rule the plaintiff seeks to apply. See Reichle, 566 U. S., at 666. Otherwise, the rule is not one that "every reasonable official" would know. Id., at 664 (internal quotation marks omitted).

The "clearly established" standard also requires that the legal principle clearly prohibit the officer's conduct in the particular circumstances before him. The rule's contours must be so well defined that it is "clear to a reasonable officer that his conduct was unlawful in the situation he confronted." Saucier v. Katz, 533 U. S. 194, 202 (2001) . This requires a high "degree of specificity." Mullenix v. Luna, 577 U. S. ___, ___ (2015) (per curiam) (slip op., at 6). We have repeatedly stressed that courts must not "define clearly established law at a high level of generality, since doing so avoids the crucial question whether the official acted reasonably in the particular circumstances that he or she faced." Plumhoff, supra, at ___–___ (slip op., at 12–13) (internal quotation marks and citation omitted). A rule is too general if the unlawfulness of the officer's conduct "does not follow immediately from the conclusion that [the rule] was firmly established." Anderson, supra, at 641. In the context of a warrantless arrest, the rule must obviously resolve "whether 'the circumstances with which [the particular officer] was confronted . . . constitute[d] probable cause.' " Mullenix, supra, at ___ (slip op., at 6) (quoting Anderson, supra, at 640–641; some alterations in original).

We have stressed that the "specificity" of the rule is "especially important in the Fourth Amendment context." Mullenix, supra, at ___ (slip op., at 5). Probable cause "turn[s] on the assessment of probabilities in particular factual contexts" and cannot be "reduced to a neat set of legal rules." Gates, 462 U. S., at 232. It is "incapable of precise definition or quantification into percentages." Pringle, 540 U. S., at 371. Given its imprecise nature, officers will often find it difficult to know how the general standard of probable cause applies in "the precise situation encountered." Ziglar v. Abbasi, 582 U. S. ___, ___ (2017) (slip op., at 28). Thus, we have stressed the need to "identify a case where an officer acting under similar circumstances . . . was held to have violated the Fourth Amendment." White v. Pauly, 580 U. S. ___, ___ (2017) (per curiam) (slip op., at 6); e.g., Plumhoff, supra, at ___. While there does not have to be "a case directly on point," existing precedent must place the lawfulness of the particular arrest "beyond debate." al-Kidd, supra, at 741. Of course, there can be the rare "obvious case," where the unlawfulness of the officer's conduct is sufficiently clear even though existing precedent does not address similar circumstances. Brosseau v. Haugen, 543 U. S. 194, 199 (2004) (per curiam). But "a body of relevant case law" is usually necessary to " 'clearly establish' the answer" with respect to probable cause. Ibid.

Under these principles, we readily conclude that the officers here were entitled to qualified immunity. We start by defining "the circumstances with which [the officers] w[ere] confronted." Anderson, 483 U. S., at 640. The officers found a group of people in a house that the neighbors had identified as vacant, that appeared to be vacant, and that the partygoers were treating as vacant. The group scattered, and some hid, at the sight of law enforcement. Their explanations for being at the house were full of holes. The source of their claimed invitation admitted that she had no right to be in the house, and the owner confirmed that fact.

Even assuming the officers lacked actual probable cause to arrest the partygoers, the officers are entitled to qualified immunity because they "reasonably but mistakenly conclude[d] that probable cause [wa]s present." Id., at 641. Tellingly, neither the panel majority nor the party-goers have identified a single precedent—much less a controlling case or robust consensus of cases—finding a Fourth Amendment violation "under similar circumstances." Pauly, supra, at ___ (slip op., at 6). And it should go without saying that this is not an "obvious case" where "a body of relevant case law" is not needed. Brosseau, supra, at 199. The officers were thus entitled to qualified immunity.

B

The panel majority did not follow this straightforward analysis. It instead reasoned that, under clearly established District law, a suspect's "good purpose and bona fide belief of her right to enter" vitiates probable cause to arrest her for unlawful entry. 765 F. 3d, at 26–27. The panel majority then concluded—in a two-sentence paragraph without any explanation—that the officers must have known that "uncontroverted evidence of an invitation to enter the premises would vitiate probable cause for unlawful entry." Id., at 27. By treating the invitation as "uncontroverted evidence," the panel majority assumed that the officers could not infer the partygoers' intent from other circumstances. And by treating the invitation as if it automatically vitiated probable cause, the panel majority assumed that the officers could not disbelieve the party-goers' story.

The rule applied by the panel majority was not clearly established because it was not "settled law." Hunter, 502 U. S., at 228. The panel majority relied on a single decision, Smith v. United States, 281 A. 2d 438 (D. C. 1971).[8] The defendant in Smith, who was found trespassing in a locked construction site near midnight, asserted that he was entitled to a jury instruction explaining that a bona fide belief of a right to enter is a complete defense to unlawful entry. Id., at 439–440. The D. C. Court of Appeals affirmed the trial court's refusal to give the instruction because the defendant had not established a "reasonable basis" for his alleged bona fide belief. Ibid. Smith does not say anything about whether the officers here could infer from all the evidence that the partygoers knew that they were trespassing.

Nor would it have been clear to every reasonable officer that, in these circumstances, the partygoers' bona fide belief that they were invited to the house was "uncontroverted." The officers knew that the partygoers had entered the home against the will of the owner. And District case law suggested that officers can infer a suspect's guilty state of mind based solely on his conduct.[9] In Tillman v. Washington Metropolitan Area Transit Authority, 695 A. 2d 94 (D. C. 1997), for example, the D. C. Court of Appeals held that officers had probable cause to believe the plaintiff knowingly entered the paid area of a subway station without paying. Id., at 96. The court rejected the argument that "the officers had no reason to believe that [the suspect] was 'knowingly' in the paid area" because the officers "reasonably could have inferred from [the suspect's] undisputed conduct that he had the intent required." Ibid. The court emphasized that officers can rely on "the ordinary and reasonable inference that people know what they are doing when they act." Ibid. The court also noted that "it would be an unusual case where the circumstances, while undoubtedly proving an unlawful act, nonetheless demonstrated so clearly that the suspect lacked the required intent that the police would not even have probable cause for an arrest." Ibid. And the fact that a case is unusual, we have held, is "an important indication . . . that [the officer's] conduct did not violate a 'clearly established' right." Pauly, 580 U. S., at ____ (slip op., at 7).

Moreover, existing precedent would have given the officers reason to doubt that they had to accept the party- goers' assertion of a bona fide belief. The D. C. Court of Appeals has held that officers are not required to take a suspect's innocent explanation at face value. See, e.g., Nichols v. Woodward & Lothrop, Inc., 322 A. 2d 283, 286 (1974) (holding that an officer was not "obliged to believe the explanation of a suspected shoplifter"). Similar precedent exists in the Federal Courts of Appeals, which have recognized that officers are free to disregard either all innocent explanations,[10] or at least innocent explanations that are inherently or circumstantially implausible.[11] These cases suggest that innocent explanations— even uncontradicted ones—do not have any automatic, probable-cause-vitiating effect.

For these reasons, a reasonable officer, looking at the entire legal landscape at the time of the arrests, could have interpreted the law as permitting the arrests here. There was no controlling case holding that a bona fide belief of a right to enter defeats probable cause, that officers cannot infer a suspect's guilty state of mind based on his conduct alone, or that officers must accept a suspect's innocent explanation at face value. Indeed, several precedents suggested the opposite. The officers were thus entitled to summary judgment based on qualified immunity.

*　　*　　*

The judgment of the D. C. Circuit is therefore reversed, and the case is remanded for further proceedings consistent with this opinion.

It is so ordered.

Kisela v. Hughes (April 2, 2018)

PER CURIAM.

Petitioner Andrew Kisela, a police officer in Tucson, Arizona, shot respondent Amy Hughes. Kisela and two other officers had arrived on the scene after hearing a police radio report that a woman was engaging in erratic behavior with a knife. They had been there but a few minutes, perhaps just a minute. When Kisela fired, Hughes was holding a large kitchen knife, had taken steps toward another woman standing nearby, and had refused to drop the knife after at least two commands to do so. The question is whether at the time of the shooting Kisela's actions violated clearly established law.

The record, viewed in the light most favorable to Hughes, shows the following. In May 2010, somebody in Hughes' neighborhood called 911 to report that a woman was hacking a tree with a kitchen knife. Kisela and another police officer, Alex Garcia, heard about the report over the radio in their patrol car and responded. A few minutes later the person who had called 911 flagged down the officers; gave them a description of the woman with the knife; and told them the woman had been acting erratically. About the same time, a third police officer, Lindsay Kunz, arrived on her bicycle.

Garcia spotted a woman, later identified as Sharon Chadwick, standing next to a car in the driveway of a nearby house. A chain-link fence with a locked gate separated Chadwick from the officers. The officers then saw another woman, Hughes, emerge from the house carrying a large knife at her side. Hughes matched the description of the woman who had been seen hacking a tree. Hughes walked toward Chadwick and stopped no more than six feet from her.

All three officers drew their guns. At least twice they told Hughes to drop the knife. Viewing the record in the light most favorable to Hughes, Chadwick said "take it easy" to both Hughes and the officers. Hughes appeared calm, but she did not acknowledge the officers' presence or drop the knife. The top bar of the chain-link fence blocked Kisela's line of fire, so he dropped to the ground and shot Hughes four times through the fence. Then the officers jumped the fence, handcuffed Hughes, and called paramedics, who transported her to a hospital. There she was treated for non-life-threatening injuries. Less than a minute had transpired from the moment the officers saw Chadwick to the moment Kisela fired shots.

All three of the officers later said that at the time of the shooting they subjectively believed Hughes to be a threat to Chadwick. After the shooting, the officers discovered that Chadwick and Hughes were roommates, that Hughes had a history of mental illness, and that Hughes had been upset with Chadwick over a $20 debt. In an affidavit produced during discovery, Chadwick said that a few minutes before the shooting her boyfriend had told her Hughes was threatening to kill Chadwick's dog, named Bunny. Chadwick "came home to find" Hughes "somewhat distressed," and Hughes was in the house holding Bunny "in one hand and a kitchen knife in the other." Hughes asked Chadwick if she "wanted [her] to use the knife on the dog." The officers knew none of this, though. Chad- wick went outside to get $20 from her car, which is when the officers first saw her. In her affidavit Chadwick said that she did not feel endangered at any time. Ibid. Based on her experience as Hughes' roommate, Chadwick stated that Hughes "occasionally has episodes in which she acts inappropriately," but "she is only seeking attention." 2 Record 108.

Hughes sued Kisela under Rev. Stat. §1979, 42 U. S. C. §1983, alleging that Kisela had used excessive force in violation of the Fourth Amendment. The District Court granted summary judgment to Kisela, but the Court of Appeals for the Ninth Circuit reversed. 862 F. 3d 775 (2016).

The Court of Appeals first held that the record, viewed in the light most favorable to Hughes, was sufficient to demonstrate that Kisela violated the Fourth Amendment. See id., at 782. The court next held that the violation was clearly established because, in its view, the constitutional violation was obvious and because of Circuit precedent that the court perceived to be analogous. Id., at 785. Kisela filed a petition for rehearing en banc. Over the dissent of seven judges, the Court of Appeals denied it. Kisela then filed a petition for certiorari in this Court. That petition is now granted.

In one of the first cases on this general subject, Tennessee v. Garner, 471 U. S. 1 (1985), the Court addressed the constitutionality of the police using force that can be deadly. There, the Court held that "[w]here the officer has probable cause to believe that the suspect poses a threat of serious physical harm, either to the officer or to others, it is not constitutionally unreasonable to prevent escape by using deadly force." Id., at 11.

In Graham v. Connor, 490 U. S. 386, 396 (1989), the Court held that the question whether an officer has used excessive force "requires careful attention to the facts and circumstances of each particular case, including the severity of the crime at issue, whether the suspect poses an immediate threat to the safety of the officers or others, and whether he is actively resisting arrest or attempting to evade arrest by flight." "The 'reasonableness' of a particular use of force must be judged from the perspective of a reasonable officer on the scene, rather than with the 20/20 vision of hindsight." Ibid. And "[t]he calculus of reasonableness must embody allowance for the fact that police officers are often forced to make split-second judgments—in circumstances that are tense, uncertain, and rapidly evolving—about the amount of force that is necessary in a particular situation." Id., at 396–397.

Here, the Court need not, and does not, decide whether Kisela violated the Fourth Amendment when he used deadly force against Hughes. For even assuming a Fourth Amendment violation occurred—a proposition that is not at all evident—on these facts Kisela was at least entitled to qualified immunity.

"Qualified immunity attaches when an official's conduct does not violate clearly established statutory or constitutional rights of which a reasonable person would have known." White v. Pauly, 580 U. S. ___, ___ (2017) (per curiam) (slip op., at 6) (alterations and internal quotation marks omitted). "Because the focus is on whether the officer had fair notice that her conduct was unlawful, reasonableness is judged against the backdrop of the law at the time of the conduct." Brosseau v. Haugen, 543 U. S. 194, 198 (2004) (per curiam).

Although "this Court's caselaw does not require a case directly on point for a right to be clearly established, existing precedent must have placed the statutory or constitutional question beyond debate." White, 580 U. S., at ___ (slip op., at 6) (internal quotation marks omitted). "In other words, immunity protects all but the plainly incompetent or those who knowingly violate the law." Ibid. (internal quotation marks omitted). This Court has "'repeatedly told courts—and the Ninth Circuit in particular—not to define clearly established law at a high level of generality.'" City and County of San Francisco v. Sheehan, 575 U. S. ___, ___ (2015) (slip op., at 13) (quoting Ashcroft v. al-Kidd, 563 U. S. 731, 742 (2011)); see also Brosseau, supra, at 198–199. "[S]pecificity is especially important in the Fourth Amendment context, where the Court has recognized that it is sometimes difficult for an officer to determine how the relevant legal doctrine, here excessive force, will apply to the factual situation the officer confronts." Mullenix v. Luna, 577 U. S. ___, ___ (2015) (per curiam) (slip op., at 5) (internal quotation marks omitted). Use of excessive force is an area of the law "in which the result depends very much on the facts of each case," and thus police officers are entitled to qualified immunity unless existing precedent "squarely governs" the specific facts at issue. Id., at ___ (slip op., at 6) (internal quotation marks omitted and emphasis deleted). Precedent involving similar facts can help move a case beyond the otherwise "hazy border between excessive and acceptable force" and thereby provide an officer notice that a specific use of force is unlawful. Id., at ___ (slip op., at 12) (internal quotation marks omitted).

"Of course, general statements of the law are not inherently incapable of giving fair and clear warning to officers." White, 580 U. S., at ____ (slip op., at 7) (internal quotation marks omitted). But the general rules set forth in "Garner and Graham do not by themselves create clearly established law outside an 'obvious case.'" Ibid. Where constitutional guidelines seem inapplicable or too remote, it does not suffice for a court simply to state that an officer may not use unreasonable and excessive force, deny qualified immunity, and then remit the case for a trial on the question of reasonableness. An officer "cannot be said to have violated a clearly established right unless the right's contours were sufficiently definite that any reasonable official in the defendant's shoes would have understood that he was violating it." Plumhoff v. Rickard, 572 U. S. ____, ____ (2014) (slip op., at 12). That is a necessary part of the qualified-immunity standard, and it is a part of the standard that the Court of Appeals here failed to implement in a correct way.

Kisela says he shot Hughes because, although the officers themselves were in no apparent danger, he believed she was a threat to Chadwick. Kisela had mere seconds to assess the potential danger to Chadwick. He was con- fronted with a woman who had just been seen hacking a tree with a large kitchen knife and whose behavior was erratic enough to cause a concerned bystander to call 911 and then flag down Kisela and Garcia. Kisela was separated from Hughes and Chadwick by a chain-link fence; Hughes had moved to within a few feet of Chadwick; and she failed to acknowledge at least two commands to drop the knife. Those commands were loud enough that Chadwick, who was standing next to Hughes, heard them. This is far from an obvious case in which any competent officer would have known that shooting Hughes to protect Chadwick would violate the Fourth Amendment.

The Court of Appeals made additional errors in concluding that its own precedent clearly established that Kisela used excessive force. To begin with, "even if a controlling circuit precedent could constitute clearly established law in these circumstances, it does not do so here." Sheehan, supra, at ____ (slip op., at 13). In fact, the most analogous Circuit precedent favors Kisela. See Blanford v. Sacramento County, 406 F. 3d 1110 (CA9 2005). In Blanford, the police responded to a report that a man was walking through a residential neighborhood carrying a sword and acting in an erratic manner. Id., at 1112. There, as here, the police shot the man after he refused their commands to drop his weapon (there, as here, the man might not have heard the commands). Id., at 1113. There, as here, the police believed (perhaps mistakenly), that the man posed an immediate threat to others. Ibid. There, the Court of Appeals determined that the use of deadly force did not violate the Fourth Amendment. Id., at 1119. Based on that decision, a reasonable officer could have believed the same thing was true in the instant case.

In contrast, not one of the decisions relied on by the Court of Appeals—Deorle v. Rutherford, 272 F. 3d 1272 (CA9 2001), Glenn v. Washington County, 673 F. 3d 864 (CA9 2011), and Harris v. Roderick, 126 F. 3d 1189 (CA9 1997)—supports denying Kisela qualified immunity. As for Deorle, this Court has already instructed the Court of Appeals not to read its decision in that case too broadly in deciding whether a new set of facts is governed by clearly established law. Sheehan, 572 U. S., at ____–____ (slip op., at 13–14). Deorle involved a police officer who shot an unarmed man in the face, without warning, even though the officer had a clear line of retreat; there were no by-standers nearby; the man had been "physically compliant and generally followed all the officers' instructions"; and he had been under police observation for roughly 40 minutes. 272 F. 3d, at 1276, 1281–1282. In this case, by contrast, Hughes was armed with a large knife; was within striking distance of Chadwick; ignored the officers' orders to drop the weapon; and the situation unfolded in less than a minute. "Whatever the merits of the decision in Deorle, the differences between that case and the case before us leap from the page." Sheehan, supra, at ___ (slip op., at 14).

Glenn, which the panel described as "[t]he most analogous Ninth Circuit case," 862 F. 3d, at 783, was decided after the shooting at issue here. Thus, Glenn "could not have given fair notice to [Kisela]" because a reasonable officer is not required to foresee judicial decisions that do not yet exist in instances where the requirements of the Fourth Amendment are far from obvious. Brosseau, 543 U. S., at 200, n. 4. Glenn was therefore "of no use in the clearly established inquiry." Brosseau, supra, at 200, n. 4. Other judges brought this mistaken or misleading citation to the panel's attention while Kisela's petition for rehearing en banc was pending before the Court of Appeals. 862 F.3d, at 795, n. 2 (Ikuta, J., dissenting from denial of rehearing en banc). The panel then amended its opinion, but nevertheless still attempted to "rely on Glenn as illustrative, not as indicative of the clearly established law in 2010." Id., at 784, n. 2 (majority opinion). The panel failed to explain the difference between "illustrative" and "indicative" precedent, and none is apparent.

The amended opinion also asserted, for the first time and without explanation, that the Court of Appeals' decision in Harris clearly established that the shooting here was unconstitutional. Id., at 785. The new mention of Harris replaced a reference in the panel's first opinion to Glenn—the case that postdated the shooting at issue here. Compare 841 F. 3d 1081, 1090 (CA9 2016) ("As indicated by Glenn and Deorle, . . . that right was clearly established"), with 862 F. 3d, at 785 ("As indicated by Deorle and Harris, . . . that right was clearly established").

The panel's reliance on Harris "does not pass the straight-face test." 862 F. 3d, at 797 (opinion of Ikuta, J.). In Harris, the Court of Appeals determined that an FBI sniper, who was positioned safely on a hilltop, used excessive force when he shot a man in the back while the man was retreating to a cabin during what has been referred to as the Ruby Ridge standoff. 126 F. 3d, at 1202–1203. Suffice it to say, a reasonable police officer could miss the connection between the situation confronting the sniper at Ruby Ridge and the situation confronting Kisela in Hughes' front yard.

For these reasons, the petition for certiorari is granted; the judgment of the Court of Appeals is reversed; and the case is remanded for further proceedings consistent with this opinion.

It is so ordered.

Byrd v. US (May 14, 2018)

Justice Kennedy delivered the opinion of the Court.

In September 2014, Pennsylvania State Troopers pulled over a car driven by petitioner Terrence Byrd. Byrd was the only person in the car. In the course of the traffic stop the troopers learned that the car was rented and that Byrd was not listed on the rental agreement as an authorized driver. For this reason, the troopers told Byrd they did not need his consent to search the car, including its trunk where he had stored personal effects. A search of the trunk uncovered body armor and 49 bricks of heroin.

The evidence was turned over to federal authorities, who charged Byrd with distribution and possession of heroin with the intent to distribute in violation of 21 U. S. C. §841(a)(1) and possession of body armor by a prohibited person in violation of 18 U. S. C. §931(a)(1). Byrd moved to suppress the evidence as the fruit of an unlawful search. The United States District Court for the Middle District of Pennsylvania denied the motion, and the Court of Appeals for the Third Circuit affirmed. Both courts concluded that, because Byrd was not listed on the rental agreement, he lacked a reasonable expectation of privacy in the car. Based on this conclusion, it appears that both the District Court and Court of Appeals deemed it unnecessary to consider whether the troopers had probable cause to search the car.

This Court granted certiorari to address the question whether a driver has a reasonable expectation of privacy in a rental car when he or she is not listed as an authorized driver on the rental agreement. The Court now holds that, as a general rule, someone in otherwise lawful possession and control of a rental car has a reasonable expectation of privacy in it even if the rental agreement does not list him or her as an authorized driver.

The Court concludes a remand is necessary to address in the first instance the Government's argument that this general rule is inapplicable because, in the circumstances here, Byrd had no greater expectation of privacy than a car thief. If that is so, our cases make clear he would lack a legitimate expectation of privacy. It is necessary to remand as well to determine whether, even if Byrd had a right to object to the search, probable cause justified it in any event.

I

On September 17, 2014, petitioner Terrence Byrd and Latasha Reed drove in Byrd's Honda Accord to a Budget car-rental facility in Wayne, New Jersey. Byrd stayed in the parking lot in the Honda while Reed went to the Budget desk and rented a Ford Fusion. The agreement Reed signed required her to certify that she had a valid driver's license and had not committed certain vehicle-related offenses within the previous three years. An addendum to the agreement, which Reed initialed, provides the following restriction on who may drive the rental car:

"I understand that the only ones permitted to drive the vehicle other than the renter are the renter's spouse, the renter's co-employee (with the renter's permission, while on company business), or a person who appears at the time of the rental and signs an Additional Driver Form. These other drivers must also be at least 25 years old and validly licensed.

"PERMITTING AN UNAUTHORIZED DRIVER TO OPERATE THE VEHICLE IS A VIOLATION OF THE RENTAL AGREEMENT. THIS MAY RESULT IN ANY AND ALL COVERAGE OTHERWISE PROVIDED BY THE RENTAL AGREEMENT BEING VOID AND MY BEING FULLY RESPONSIBLE FOR ALL LOSS OR DAMAGE, INCLUDING LIABILITY TO THIRD PARTIES." App. 19.

In filling out the paperwork for the rental agreement, Reed did not list an additional driver.

With the rental keys in hand, Reed returned to the parking lot and gave them to Byrd. The two then left the facility in separate cars—she in his Honda, he in the rental car. Byrd returned to his home in Patterson, New Jersey, and put his personal belongings in the trunk of the rental car. Later that afternoon, he departed in the car alone and headed toward Pittsburgh, Pennsylvania.

After driving nearly three hours, or roughly half the distance to Pittsburgh, Byrd passed State Trooper David Long, who was parked in the median of Interstate 81 near Harrisburg, Pennsylvania. Long was suspicious of Byrd because he was driving with his hands at the "10 and 2" position on the steering wheel, sitting far back from the steering wheel, and driving a rental car. Long knew the Ford Fusion was a rental car because one of its windows contained a barcode. Based on these observations, he decided to follow Byrd and, a short time later, stopped him for a possible traffic infraction.

When Long approached the passenger window of Byrd's car to explain the basis for the stop and to ask for identification, Byrd was "visibly nervous" and "was shaking and had a hard time obtaining his driver's license." Id., at 37. He handed an interim license and the rental agreement to Long, stating that a friend had rented the car. Long returned to his vehicle to verify Byrd's license and noticed Byrd was not listed as an additional driver on the rental agreement. Around this time another trooper, Travis Martin, arrived at the scene. While Long processed Byrd's license, Martin conversed with Byrd, who again stated that a friend had rented the vehicle. After Martin walked back to Long's patrol car, Long commented to Martin that Byrd was "not on the renter agreement," to which Martin replied, "yeah, he has no expectation of privacy." 3 App. to Brief for Appellant in No. 16–1509 (CA3), at 21:40.

A computer search based on Byrd's identification returned two different names. Further inquiry suggested the other name might be an alias and also revealed that Byrd had prior convictions for weapons and drug charges as well as an outstanding warrant in New Jersey for a probation violation. After learning that New Jersey did not want Byrd arrested for extradition, the troopers asked Byrd to step out of the vehicle and patted him down.

Long asked Byrd if he had anything illegal in the car. When Byrd said he did not, the troopers asked for his consent to search the car. At that point Byrd said he had a "blunt" in the car and offered to retrieve it for them. The officers understood "blunt" to mean a marijuana cigarette. They declined to let him retrieve it and continued to seek his consent to search the car, though they stated they did not need consent because he was not listed on the rental agreement. The troopers then opened the passenger and driver doors and began a thorough search of the passenger compartment.

Martin proceeded from there to search the car's trunk, including by opening up and taking things out of a large cardboard box, where he found a laundry bag containing body armor. At this point, the troopers decided to detain Byrd. As Martin walked toward Byrd and said he would be placing him in handcuffs, Byrd began to run away. A third trooper who had arrived on the scene joined Long and Martin in pursuit. When the troopers caught up to Byrd, he surrendered and admitted there was heroin in the car. Back at the car, the troopers resumed their search of the laundry bag and found 49 bricks of heroin.

In pretrial proceedings Byrd moved to suppress the evidence found in the trunk of the rental car, arguing that the search violated his Fourth Amendment rights. Al-though Long contended at a suppression hearing that the troopers had probable cause to search the car after Byrd stated it contained marijuana, the District Court denied Byrd's motion on the ground that Byrd lacked "standing" to contest the search as an initial matter, 2015 WL 5038455, *2 (MD Pa., Aug. 26, 2015) (citing United States v. Kennedy, 638 F. 3d 159, 165 (CA3 2011)). Byrd later entered a conditional guilty plea, reserving the right to appeal the suppression ruling.

The Court of Appeals affirmed in a brief summary opinion. 679 Fed. Appx. 146 (CA3 2017). As relevant here, the Court of Appeals recognized that a "circuit split exists as to whether the sole occupant of a rental vehicle has a Fourth Amendment expectation of privacy when that occupant is not named in the rental agreement"; but it noted that Circuit precedent already had "spoken as to this issue . . . and determined such a person has no expectation of privacy and therefore no standing to challenge a search of the vehicle." Id., at 150 (citing Kennedy, supra, at 167–168). The Court of Appeals did not reach the probable-cause question.

This Court granted Byrd's petition for a writ of certio-rari, 582 U. S. ___ (2017), to address the conflict among the Courts of Appeals over whether an unauthorized driver has a reasonable expectation of privacy in a rental car. Compare United States v. Seeley, 331 F. 3d 471, 472 (CA5 2003) (per curiam); United States v. Wellons, 32 F. 3d 117, 119 (CA4 1994); United States v. Roper, 918 F. 2d 885, 887–888 (CA10 1990), with United States v. Smith, 263 F. 3d 571, 581–587 (CA6 2001); Kennedy, supra, at 165–168, and with United States v. Thomas, 447 F. 3d 1191, 1196–1199 (CA9 2006); United States v. Best, 135 F. 3d 1223, 1225 (CA8 1998).

II

Few protections are as essential to individual liberty as the right to be free from unreasonable searches and seizures. The Framers made that right explicit in the Bill of Rights following their experience with the indignities and invasions of privacy wrought by "general warrants and warrantless searches that had so alienated the colonists and had helped speed the movement for independence." Chimel v. California, 395 U. S. 752, 761 (1969). Ever mindful of the Fourth Amendment and its history, the Court has viewed with disfavor practices that permit "police officers unbridled discretion to rummage at will among a person's private effects." Arizona v. Gant, 556 U. S. 332, 345 (2009).

This concern attends the search of an automobile. See Delaware v. Prouse, 440 U. S. 648, 662 (1979). The Court has acknowledged, however, that there is a diminished expectation of privacy in automobiles, which often permits officers to dispense with obtaining a warrant before conducting a lawful search. See, e.g., California v. Acevedo, 500 U. S. 565, 579 (1991).

Whether a warrant is required is a separate question from the one the Court addresses here, which is whether the person claiming a constitutional violation "has had his own Fourth Amendment rights infringed by the search and seizure which he seeks to challenge." Rakas v. Illinois, 439 U. S. 128, 133 (1978). Answering that question requires examination of

whether the person claiming the constitutional violation had a "legitimate expectation of privacy in the premises" searched. Id., at 143. "Expectations of privacy protected by the Fourth Amendment, of course, need not be based on a common-law interest in real or personal property, or on the invasion of such an interest." Id., at 144, n. 12. Still, "property concepts" are instructive in "determining the presence or absence of the privacy interests protected by that Amendment." Ibid.

Indeed, more recent Fourth Amendment cases have clarified that the test most often associated with legitimate expectations of privacy, which was derived from the second Justice Harlan's concurrence in Katz v. United States, 389 U. S. 347 (1967), supplements, rather than displaces, "the traditional property-based understanding of the Fourth Amendment." Florida v. Jardines, 569 U. S. 1, 11 (2013). Perhaps in light of this clarification, Byrd now argues in the alternative that he had a common-law property interest in the rental car as a second bailee that would have provided him with a cognizable Fourth Amendment interest in the vehicle. But he did not raise this argument before the District Court or Court of Appeals, and those courts did not have occasion to address whether Byrd was a second bailee or what consequences might follow from that determination. In those courts he framed the question solely in terms of the Katz test noted above. Because this is "a court of review, not of first view," Cutter v. Wilkinson, 544 U. S. 709, 718, n. 7 (2005), it is generally unwise to consider arguments in the first instance, and the Court declines to reach Byrd's contention that he was a second bailee.

Reference to property concepts, however, aids the Court in assessing the precise question here: Does a driver of a rental car have a reasonable expectation of privacy in the car when he or she is not listed as an authorized driver on the rental agreement?

III

A

One who owns and possesses a car, like one who owns and possesses a house, almost always has a reasonable expectation of privacy in it. More difficult to define and delineate are the legitimate expectations of privacy of others.

On the one hand, as noted above, it is by now well established that a person need not always have a recognized common-law property interest in the place searched to be able to claim a reasonable expectation of privacy in it. See Jones v. United States, 362 U. S. 257, 259 (1960); Katz, supra, at 352; Mancusi v. DeForte, 392 U. S. 364, 368 (1968); Minnesota v. Olson, 495 U. S. 91, 98 (1990).

On the other hand, it is also clear that legitimate presence on the premises of the place searched, standing alone, is not enough to accord a reasonable expectation of privacy, because it "creates too broad a gauge for measurement of Fourth Amendment rights." Rakas, 439 U. S., at 142; see also id., at 148 ("We would not wish to be understood as saying that legitimate presence on the premises is irrelevant to one's expectation of privacy, but it cannot be deemed controlling"); Minnesota v. Carter, 525 U. S. 83, 91 (1998).

Although the Court has not set forth a single metric or exhaustive list of considerations to resolve the circumstances in which a person can be said to have a reasonable expectation of privacy, it has explained that "[l]egitimation of expectations of privacy by law must have a source outside of the Fourth Amendment, either by reference to concepts of real or personal property law or to understandings that are recognized and permitted by society." Rakas, 439 U. S., at 144, n. 12. The two concepts in cases like this one are often linked. "One of the main rights attaching to property is the right to exclude others," and, in the main, "one who owns or lawfully possesses or controls property will in all likelihood have a legitimate expectation of privacy by virtue of the right to exclude." Ibid. (citing 2 W. Blackstone, Commentaries on the Laws of England, ch. 1). This general property-based concept guides resolution of this case.

B

Here, the Government contends that drivers who are not listed on rental agreements always lack an expectation of privacy in the automobile based on the rental company's lack of authorization alone. This per se rule rests on too restrictive a view of the Fourth Amendment's protections. Byrd, by contrast, contends that the sole occupant of a rental car always has an expectation of privacy in it based on mere possession and control. There is more to recommend Byrd's proposed rule than the Government's; but, without qualification, it would include within its ambit thieves and others who, not least because of their lack of any property-based justification, would not have a reasonable expectation of privacy.

1

Stripped to its essentials, the Government's position is that only authorized drivers of rental cars have expectations of privacy in those vehicles. This position is based on the following syllogism: Under Rakas, passengers do not have an expectation of privacy in an automobile glove compartment or like places; an unauthorized driver like Byrd would have been the passenger had the renter been driving; and the unauthorized driver cannot obtain greater protection when he takes the wheel and leaves the renter behind. The flaw in this syllogism is its major premise, for it is a misreading of Rakas.

The Court in Rakas did not hold that passengers cannot have an expectation of privacy in automobiles. To the contrary, the Court disclaimed any intent to hold "that a passenger lawfully in an automobile may not invoke the exclusionary rule and challenge a search of that vehicle unless he happens to own or have a possessory interest in it." 439 U. S., at 150, n. 17 (internal quotation marks omitted). The Court instead rejected the argument that legitimate presence alone was sufficient to assert a Fourth Amendment interest, which was fatal to the petitioners' case there because they had "claimed only that they were 'legitimately on [the] premises' and did not claim that they had any legitimate expectation of privacy in the areas of the car which were searched." Ibid.

What is more, the Government's syllogism is beside the point, because this case does not involve a passenger at all but instead the driver and sole occupant of a rental car. As Justice Powell observed in his concurring opinion in Rakas, a "distinction . . . may be made in some circumstances between the Fourth Amendment rights of passengers and the rights of an individual who has exclusive control of an automobile or of its locked compartments." Id., at 154. This situation would be similar to the defendant in Jones, supra, who, as Rakas notes, had a reasonable expectation of privacy in his friend's apartment because he "had complete dominion and control over the apartment and could exclude others from it," 439 U. S., at 149. Justice Powell's observation was also consistent with the majority's explanation that "one who owns or lawfully possesses or controls property will in all likelihood have a legitimate expectation of privacy by virtue of [the] right to exclude," id., at 144, n. 12, an explanation tied to the majority's discussion of Jones.

The Court sees no reason why the expectation of privacy that comes from lawful possession and control and the attendant right to exclude would differ depending on whether the car in question is rented or privately owned by someone other than the person in current possession of it, much as it did not seem to matter whether the friend of the defendant in Jones

owned or leased the apartment he permitted the defendant to use in his absence. Both would have the expectation of privacy that comes with the right to exclude. Indeed, the Government conceded at oral argument that an unauthorized driver in sole possession of a rental car would be permitted to exclude third parties from it, such as a carjacker. Tr. of Oral Arg. 48–49.

2

The Government further stresses that Byrd's driving the rental car violated the rental agreement that Reed signed, and it contends this violation meant Byrd could not have had any basis for claiming an expectation of privacy in the rental car at the time of the search. As anyone who has rented a car knows, car-rental agreements are filled with long lists of restrictions. Examples include prohibitions on driving the car on unpaved roads or driving while using a handheld cellphone. Few would contend that violating provisions like these has anything to do with a driver's reasonable expectation of privacy in the rental car—as even the Government agrees. Brief for United States 32.

Despite this concession, the Government argues that permitting an unauthorized driver to take the wheel of a rental car is a breach different in kind from these others, so serious that the rental company would consider the agreement "void" the moment an unauthorized driver takes the wheel. Id., at 4, 15, 16, 27. To begin with, that is not what the contract says. It states: "Permitting an unauthorized driver to operate the vehicle is a violation of the rental agreement. This may result in any and all coverage otherwise provided by the rental agreement being void and my being fully responsible for all loss or damage, including liability to third parties." App. 24 (emphasis deleted).

Putting the Government's misreading of the contract aside, there may be countless innocuous reasons why an unauthorized driver might get behind the wheel of a rental car and drive it—perhaps the renter is drowsy or inebriated and the two think it safer for the friend to drive them to their destination. True, this constitutes a breach of the rental agreement, and perhaps a serious one, but the Government fails to explain what bearing this breach of contract, standing alone, has on expectations of privacy in the car. Stated in different terms, for Fourth Amendment purposes there is no meaningful difference between the authorized-driver provision and the other provisions the Government agrees do not eliminate an expectation of privacy, all of which concern risk allocation between private parties—violators might pay additional fees, lose insurance coverage, or assume liability for damage resulting from the breach. But that risk allocation has little to do with whether one would have a reasonable expectation of privacy in the rental car if, for example, he or she other-wise has lawful possession of and control over the car.

3

The central inquiry at this point turns on the concept of lawful possession, and this is where an important qualification of Byrd's proposed rule comes into play. Rakas makes clear that " 'wrongful' presence at the scene of a search would not enable a defendant to object to the legality of the search." 439 U. S., at 141, n. 9. "A burglar plying his trade in a summer cabin during the off season," for example, "may have a thoroughly justified subjective expectation of privacy, but it is not one which the law recognizes as 'legitimate.' " Id., at 143, n. 12. Likewise, "a person present in a stolen automobile at the time of the search may [not] object to the lawfulness of the search of the automobile." Id., at 141, n. 9. No matter the degree of possession and control, the car thief would not have a reasonable expectation of privacy in a stolen car.

On this point, in its merits brief, the Government asserts that, on the facts here, Byrd should have no greater expectation of privacy than a car thief because he intentionally used a third party as a strawman in a calculated plan to mislead the rental company from the very outset, all to aid him in committing a crime. This argument is premised on the Government's inference that Byrd knew he would not have been able to rent the car on his own, because he would not have satisfied the rental company's requirements based on his criminal record, and that he used Reed, who had no intention of using the car for her own purposes, to procure the car for him to transport heroin to Pittsburgh.

It is unclear whether the Government's allegations, if true, would constitute a criminal offense in the acquisition of the rental car under applicable law. And it may be that there is no reason that the law should distinguish between one who obtains a vehicle through subterfuge of the type the Government alleges occurred here and one who steals the car outright.

The Government did not raise this argument in the District Court or the Court of Appeals, however. It relied instead on the sole fact that Byrd lacked authorization to drive the car. And it is unclear from the record whether the Government's inferences paint an accurate picture of what occurred. Because it was not addressed in the District Court or Court of Appeals, the Court declines to reach this question. The proper course is to remand for the argument and potentially further factual development to be considered in the first instance by the Court of Appeals or by the District Court.

IV

The Government argued in its brief in opposition to certiorari that, even if Byrd had a Fourth Amendment interest in the rental car, the troopers had probable cause to believe it contained evidence of a crime when they initiated their search. If that were true, the troopers may have been permitted to conduct a warrantless search of the car in line with the Court's cases concerning the automobile exception to the warrant requirement. See, e.g., Acevedo, 500 U. S., at 580. The Court of Appeals did not reach this question because it concluded, as an initial matter, that Byrd lacked a reasonable expectation of privacy in the rental car.

It is worth noting that most courts analyzing the question presented in this case, including the Court of Appeals here, have described it as one of Fourth Amendment "standing," a concept the Court has explained is not distinct from the merits and "is more properly subsumed under substantive Fourth Amendment doctrine." Rakas, supra, at 139.

The concept of standing in Fourth Amendment cases can be a useful shorthand for capturing the idea that a person must have a cognizable Fourth Amendment interest in the place searched before seeking relief for an unconstitutional search; but it should not be confused with Article III standing, which is jurisdictional and must be assessed before reaching the merits. Arizona Christian School Tuition Organization v. Winn, 563 U. S. 125, 129 (2011) ("To obtain a determination on the merits in federal court, parties seeking relief must show that they have standing under Article III of the Constitution"); see also Rakas, supra, at 138–140. Because Fourth Amendment standing is subsumed under substantive Fourth Amendment doctrine, it is not a jurisdictional question and hence need not be addressed before addressing other aspects of the merits of a Fourth Amendment claim. On remand, then, the Court of Appeals is not required to assess Byrd's reason-able expectation of privacy in the rental car before, in its discretion, first addressing whether there was probable cause for the search, if it finds the latter argument has been preserved.

V

Though new, the fact pattern here continues a well-traveled path in this Court's Fourth Amendment jurisprudence. Those cases support the proposition, and the Court now holds, that the mere fact that a driver in lawful possession or control of a rental car is not listed on the rental agreement will not defeat his or her otherwise reasonable expectation of privacy. The Court leaves for remand two of the Government's arguments: that one who intentionally uses a third party to procure a rental car by a fraudulent scheme for the purpose of committing a crime is no better situated than a car thief; and that probable cause justified the search in any event. The Court of Appeals has discretion as to the order in which these questions are best addressed.

*   *   *

The judgment of the Court of Appeals is vacated, and the case is remanded for further proceedings consistent with this opinion.

It is so ordered.

Collins v. Virginia (May 29, 2018) [Notes omitted]

Justice Sotomayor delivered the opinion of the Court.

This case presents the question whether the automobile exception to the Fourth Amendment permits a police officer, uninvited and without a warrant, to enter the curtilage of a home in order to search a vehicle parked therein. It does not.

I

Officer Matthew McCall of the Albemarle County Police Department in Virginia saw the driver of an orange and black motorcycle with an extended frame commit a traffic infraction. The driver eluded Officer McCall's attempt to stop the motorcycle. A few weeks later, Officer David Rhodes of the same department saw an orange and black motorcycle traveling well over the speed limit, but the driver got away from him, too. The officers compared notes and concluded that the two incidents involved the same motorcyclist.

Upon further investigation, the officers learned that the motorcycle likely was stolen and in the possession of petitioner Ryan Collins. After discovering photographs on Collins' Facebook profile that featured an orange and black motorcycle parked at the top of the driveway of a house, Officer Rhodes tracked down the address of the house, drove there, and parked on the street. It was later established that Collins' girlfriend lived in the house and that Collins stayed there a few nights per week. 1

From his parked position on the street, Officer Rhodes saw what appeared to be a motorcycle with an extended frame covered with a white tarp, parked at the same angle and in the same location on the driveway as in the Facebook photograph. Officer Rhodes, who did not have a warrant, exited his car and walked toward the house. He stopped to take a photograph of the covered motorcycle from the sidewalk, and then walked onto the residential property and up to the top of the driveway to where the motorcycle was parked. In order "to investigate further," App. 80, Officer Rhodes pulled off the tarp, revealing a motorcycle that looked like the one from the speeding incident. He then ran a search of the license plate and vehicle identification numbers, which confirmed that the motorcycle was stolen. After gathering this information, Officer Rhodes took a photograph of the uncovered motorcycle, put the tarp back on, left the property, and returned to his car to wait for Collins.

Shortly thereafter, Collins returned home. Officer Rhodes walked up to the front door of the house and knocked. Collins answered, agreed to speak with Officer Rhodes, and admitted that the motorcycle was his and that he had bought it without title. Officer Rhodes then arrested Collins.

Collins was indicted by a Virginia grand jury for receiving stolen property. He filed a pretrial motion to suppress the evidence that Officer Rhodes had obtained as a result of the warrantless search of the motorcycle. Collins argued that Officer Rhodes had trespassed on the curtilage of the house to conduct an investigation in violation of the Fourth Amendment. The trial court denied the motion and Collins was convicted.

The Court of Appeals of Virginia affirmed. It assumed that the motorcycle was parked in the curtilage of the home and held that Officer Rhodes had probable cause to believe that the motorcycle under the tarp was the same motorcycle that had evaded him in the past. It further concluded that Officer Rhodes' actions were lawful under the Fourth Amendment even absent a warrant because "numerous exigencies justified both his entry onto the property and his moving the tarp to view the motorcycle and record its identification number." 65 Va. App. 37, 46, 773 S. E. 2d 618, 623 (2015).

The Supreme Court of Virginia affirmed on different reasoning. It explained that the case was most properly resolved with reference to the Fourth Amendment's automobile exception. 292 Va. 486, 496–501, 790 S. E. 2d 611, 616–618 (2016). Under that framework, it held that Officer Rhodes had probable cause to believe that the motorcycle was contraband, and that the warrantless search therefore was justified. Id., at 498–499, 790 S. E. 2d, at 617.

We granted certiorari, 582 U. S. ____ (2017), and now reverse.

II

The Fourth Amendment provides in relevant part that the "right of the people to be secure in their persons, houses, papers, and effects, against unreasonable searches and seizures, shall not be violated." This case arises at the intersection of two components of the Court's Fourth Amendment jurisprudence: the automobile exception to the warrant requirement and the protection extended to the curtilage of a home.

A

1

The Court has held that the search of an automobile can be reasonable without a warrant. The Court first articulated the so-called automobile exception in Carroll v. United States, 267 U. S. 132 (1925). In that case, law enforcement officers had probable cause to believe that a car they observed traveling on the road contained illegal liquor. They stopped and searched the car, discovered and seized the illegal liquor, and arrested the occupants. Id., at 134–136. The Court upheld the warrantless search and seizure, explaining that a "necessary difference" exists between searching "a store, dwelling house or other structure" and searching "a ship, motor boat, wagon or automobile" because a "vehicle can be quickly moved out of the locality or jurisdiction in which the warrant must be sought." Id., at 153.

The "ready mobility" of vehicles served as the core justification for the automobile exception for many years. California v. Carney, 471 U. S. 386, 390 (1985) (citing, e.g., Cooper v. California, 386 U. S. 58, 59 (1967); Chambers v. Maroney, 399 U. S. 42, 51–52 (1970)). Later cases then introduced an additional rationale based on "the pervasive regulation of vehicles capable of traveling on the public highways." Carney, 471 U. S., at 392. As the Court explained in South Dakota v. Opperman, 428 U. S. 364 (1976):

"Automobiles, unlike homes, are subjected to pervasive and continuing governmental regulation and controls, including periodic inspection and licensing requirements. As an everyday occurrence, police stop and examine vehicles when license plates or inspection stickers have expired, or if other violations, such as exhaust fumes or excessive noise, are noted, or if headlights or other safety equipment are not in proper working order." Id., at 368.

In announcing each of these two justifications, the Court took care to emphasize that the rationales applied only to automobiles and not to houses, and therefore supported "treating automobiles differently from houses" as a constitutional matter. Cady v. Dombrowski, 413 U. S. 433, 441 (1973).

When these justifications for the automobile exception "come into play," officers may search an automobile without having obtained a warrant so long as they have probable cause to do so. Carney, 471 U. S., at 392–393.

2

Like the automobile exception, the Fourth Amendment's protection of curtilage has long been black letter law. "[W]hen it comes to the Fourth Amendment, the home is first among equals." Florida v. Jardines, 569 U. S. 1, 6 (2013). "At the Amendment's 'very core' stands 'the right of a man to retreat into his own home and there be free from unreasonable governmental intrusion.' " Ibid. (quoting Silverman v. United States, 365 U. S. 505, 511 (1961)). To give full practical effect to that right, the Court considers curtilage—"the area 'immediately surrounding and associated with the home' "—to be " 'part of the home itself for Fourth Amendment purposes.' " Jardines, 569 U. S., at 6 (quoting Oliver v. United States, 466 U. S. 170, 180 (1984)). "The protection afforded the curtilage is essentially a protection of families and personal privacy in an area intimately linked to the home, both physically and psychologically, where privacy expectations are most heightened." California v. Ciraolo, 476 U. S. 207, 212–213 (1986).

When a law enforcement officer physically intrudes on the curtilage to gather evidence, a search within the meaning of the Fourth Amendment has occurred. Jardines, 569 U. S., at 11. Such conduct thus is presumptively unreasonable absent a warrant.

B

1

With this background in mind, we turn to the application of these doctrines in the instant case. As an initial matter, we decide whether the part of the driveway where Collins' motorcycle was parked and subsequently searched is curtilage.

According to photographs in the record, the driveway runs alongside the front lawn and up a few yards past the front perimeter of the house. The top portion of the driveway that sits behind the front perimeter of the house is enclosed on two sides by a brick wall about the height of a car and on a third side by the house. A side door provides direct access between this partially enclosed section of the driveway and the house. A visitor endeavoring to reach the front door of the house would have to walk partway up the driveway, but would turn off before entering the enclosure and instead proceed up a set of steps leading to the front porch. When Officer Rhodes searched the motorcycle, it was parked inside this partially enclosed top portion of the driveway that abuts the house.

The " 'conception defining the curtilage' is . . . familiar enough that it is 'easily understood from our daily experience.' " Jardines, 569 U. S., at 7 (quoting Oliver, 466 U. S., at 182, n. 12). Just like the front porch, side garden, or area "outside the front window," Jardines, 569 U. S., at 6, the driveway enclosure where Officer Rhodes searched the motorcycle constitutes "an area adjacent to the home and 'to which the activity of home life extends,' " and so is properly considered curtilage, id., at 7 (quoting Oliver, 466 U. S., at 182, n. 12).

2

In physically intruding on the curtilage of Collins' home to search the motorcycle, Officer Rhodes not only invaded Collins' Fourth Amendment interest in the item searched, i.e., the motorcycle, but also invaded Collins' Fourth Amendment interest in the curtilage of his home. The question before the Court is whether the automobile exception justifies the invasion of the curtilage. 2 The answer is no.

Applying the relevant legal principles to a slightly different factual scenario confirms that this is an easy case. Imagine a motorcycle parked inside the living room of a house, visible through a window to a passerby on the street. Imagine further that an officer has probable cause to believe that the motorcycle was involved in a traffic infraction. Can the officer, acting without a warrant, enter the house to search the motorcycle and confirm whether it is the right one? Surely not.

The reason is that the scope of the automobile exception extends no further than the automobile itself. See, e.g., Pennsylvania v. Labron, 518 U. S. 938, 940 (1996) (per curiam) (explaining that the automobile exception "permits police to search the vehicle"); Wyoming v. Houghton, 526 U. S. 295, 300 (1999) ("[T]he Framers would have regarded as reasonable (if there was probable cause) the warrantless search of containers within an automobile"). Virginia asks the Court to expand the scope of the automobile exception to permit police to invade any space outside an automobile even if the Fourth Amendment protects that space. Nothing in our case law, however, suggests that the automobile exception gives an officer the right to enter a home or its curtilage to access a vehicle without a warrant. Expanding the scope of the automobile exception in this way would both undervalue the core Fourth Amendment protection afforded to the home and its curtilage and " 'untether' " the automobile exception " 'from the justifications underlying' " it. Riley v. California, 573 U. S. ___, ___ (2014) (slip op., at 10) (quoting Arizona v. Gant, 556 U. S. 332, 343 (2009)).

The Court already has declined to expand the scope of other exceptions to the warrant requirement to permit warrantless entry into the home. The reasoning behind those decisions applies equally well in this context. For instance, under the plain-view doctrine, "any valid warrantless seizure of incriminating evidence" requires that the officer "have a lawful right of access to the object itself." Horton v. California, 496 U. S. 128, 136–137 (1990); see also id., at 137, n. 7 (" [E]ven where the object is contraband, this

Court has repeatedly stated and enforced the basic rule that the police may not enter and make a warrantless seizure' "); G. M. Leasing Corp. v. United States, 429 U. S. 338, 354 (1977) ("It is one thing to seize without a warrant property resting in an open area . . . , and it is quite another thing to effect a warrantless seizure of property . . . situated on private premises to which access is not otherwise available for the seizing officer"). A plain-view seizure thus cannot be justified if it is effectuated "by unlawful trespass." Soldal v. Cook County, 506 U. S. 56, 66 (1992). Had Officer Rhodes seen illegal drugs through the window of Collins' house, for example, assuming no other warrant exception applied, he could not have entered the house to seize them without first obtaining a warrant.

Similarly, it is a "settled rule that warrantless arrests in public places are valid," but, absent another exception such as exigent circumstances, officers may not enter a home to make an arrest without a warrant, even when they have probable cause. Payton v. New York, 445 U. S. 573, 587–590 (1980). That is because being " 'arrested in the home involves not only the invasion attendant to all arrests but also an invasion of the sanctity of the home.' " Id., at 588–589 (quoting United States v. Reed, 572 F. 2d 412, 423 (CA2 1978)). Likewise, searching a vehicle parked in the curtilage involves not only the invasion of the Fourth Amendment interest in the vehicle but also an invasion of the sanctity of the curtilage.

Just as an officer must have a lawful right of access to any contraband he discovers in plain view in order to seize it without a warrant, and just as an officer must have a lawful right of access in order to arrest a person in his home, so, too, an officer must have a lawful right of access to a vehicle in order to search it pursuant to the automobile exception. The automobile exception does not afford the necessary lawful right of access to search a vehicle parked within a home or its curtilage because it does not justify an intrusion on a person's separate and substantial Fourth Amendment interest in his home and curtilage.

As noted, the rationales underlying the automobile exception are specific to the nature of a vehicle and the ways in which it is distinct from a house. See Part II–A–1, supra. The rationales thus take account only of the balance between the intrusion on an individual's Fourth Amendment interest in his vehicle and the governmental interests in an expedient search of that vehicle; they do not account for the distinct privacy interest in one's home or curtilage. To allow an officer to rely on the automobile exception to gain entry into a house or its curtilage for the purpose of conducting a vehicle search would unmoor the exception from its justifications, render hollow the core Fourth Amendment protection the Constitution extends to the house and its curtilage, and transform what was meant to be an exception into a tool with far broader application. Indeed, its name alone should make all this clear enough: It is, after all, an exception for automobiles. 3

Given the centrality of the Fourth Amendment interest in the home and its curtilage and the disconnect between that interest and the justifications behind the automobile exception, we decline Virginia's invitation to extend the automobile exception to permit a warrantless intrusion on a home or its curtilage.

III

A

Virginia argues that this Court's precedent indicates that the automobile exception is a categorical one that permits the warrantless search of a vehicle anytime, anywhere, including in a home or curtilage. Specifically, Virginia points to two decisions that it contends resolve this case in its favor. Neither is dispositive or persuasive.

First, Virginia invokes Scher v. United States, 305 U. S. 251 (1938). In that case, federal officers received a confidential tip that a particular car would be transporting bootleg liquor at a specified time and place. The officers identified and followed the car until the driver "turned into a garage a few feet back of his residence and within the curtilage." Id., at 253. As the driver exited his car, an officer approached and stated that he had been informed that the car was carrying contraband. The driver acknowledged that there was liquor in the trunk, and the officer proceeded to open the trunk, find the liquor, arrest the driver, and seize both the car and the liquor. Id., at 253–254. Although the officer did not have a search warrant, the Court upheld the officer's actions as reasonable. Id., at 255.

Scher is inapposite. Whereas Collins' motorcycle was parked and unattended when Officer Rhodes intruded on the curtilage to search it, the officers in Scher first encountered the vehicle when it was being driven on public streets, approached the curtilage of the home only when the driver turned into the garage, and searched the vehicle only after the driver admitted that it contained contraband. Scher by no means established a general rule that the automobile exception permits officers to enter a home or its curtilage absent a warrant. The Court's brief analysis referenced Carroll, but only in the context of observing that, consistent with that case, the "officers properly could have stopped" and searched the car "just before [petitioner] entered the garage," a proposition the petitioner did "not seriously controvert." Scher, 305 U. S., at 254–255. The Court then explained that the officers did not lose their ability to stop and search the car when it entered "the open garage closely followed by the observing officer" because "[n]o search was made of the garage." Id., at 255. It emphasized that "[e]xamination of the automobile accompanied an arrest, without objection and upon admission of probable guilt," and cited two search-incident-to-arrest cases. Ibid. (citing Agnello v. United States,

269 U. S. 20, 30 (1925); Wisniewski v. United States, 47 F. 2d 825, 826 (CA6 1931)). Scher's reasoning thus was both case specific and imprecise, sounding in multiple doctrines, particularly, and perhaps most appropriately, hot pursuit. The decision is best regarded as a factbound one, and it certainly does not control this case.

Second, Virginia points to Labron, 518 U. S. 938, where the Court upheld under the automobile exception the warrantless search of an individual's pickup truck that was parked in the driveway of his father-in-law's farmhouse. Id., at 939–940; Commonwealth v. Kilgore, 544 Pa. 439, 444, 677 A. 2d 311, 313 (1995). But Labron provides scant support for Virginia's position. Unlike in this case, there was no indication that the individual who owned the truck in Labron had any Fourth Amendment interest in the farmhouse or its driveway, nor was there a determination that the driveway was curtilage.

B

Alternatively, Virginia urges the Court to adopt a more limited rule regarding the intersection of the automobile exception and the protection afforded to curtilage. Virginia would prefer that the Court draw a bright line and hold that the automobile exception does not permit warrantless entry into "the physical threshold of a house or a similar fixed, enclosed structure inside the curtilage like a garage." Brief for Respondent 46. Requiring officers to make "case-by-case curtilage determinations," Virginia reasons, unnecessarily complicates matters and "raises the potential for confusion and . . . error." Id., at 46–47 (internal quotation marks omitted).

The Court, though, has long been clear that curtilage is afforded constitutional protection. See Oliver, 466 U. S., at 180. As a result, officers regularly assess whether an area is curtilage before executing a search. Virginia provides no reason to conclude that this practice has proved to be unadministrable, either generally or in this context. Moreover, creating a carveout to the general rule that curtilage receives Fourth Amendment protection, such that certain types of curtilage would receive Fourth Amendment protection only for some purposes but not for others, seems far more likely to create confusion than does uniform application of the Court's doctrine.

In addition, Virginia's proposed rule rests on a mistaken premise about the constitutional significance of visibility. The ability to observe inside curtilage from a lawful vantage point is not the same as the right to enter curtilage without a warrant for the purpose of conducting a search to obtain information not otherwise accessible. Cf. Cir-aolo, 476 U. S., at 213–214 (holding that "physically non-intrusive" warrantless aerial observation of the curtilage of a home did not violate the Fourth Amendment, and could form the basis for probable cause to support a warrant to search the curtilage). So long as it is curtilage, a parking patio or carport into which an officer can see from the street is no less entitled to protection from trespass and a warrantless search than a fully enclosed garage.

Finally, Virginia's proposed bright-line rule automatically would grant constitutional rights to those persons with the financial means to afford residences with garages in which to store their vehicles but deprive those persons without such resources of any individualized consideration as to whether the areas in which they store their vehicles qualify as curtilage. See United States v. Ross, 456 U. S. 798, 822 (1982) ("[T]he most frail cottage in the kingdom is absolutely entitled to the same guarantees of privacy as the most majestic mansion").

IV

For the foregoing reasons, we conclude that the automobile exception does not permit an officer without a warrant to enter a home or its curtilage in order to search a vehicle therein. We leave for resolution on remand whether Officer Rhodes' warrantless intrusion on the curtilage of Collins' house may have been reasonable on a different basis, such as the exigent circumstances exception to the warrant requirement. The judgment of the Supreme Court of Virginia is therefore reversed, and the case is remanded for further proceedings not inconsistent with this opinion.

It is so ordered.

Carpenter v. US (June 22, 2018) [Notes omitted]

Chief Justice Roberts delivered the opinion of the Court.

This case presents the question whether the Government conducts a search under the Fourth Amendment when it accesses historical cell phone records that provide a comprehensive chronicle of the user's past movements.

I

A

There are 396 million cell phone service accounts in the United States—for a Nation of 326 million people. Cell phones perform their wide and growing variety of functions by connecting to a set of radio antennas called "cell sites." Although cell sites are usually mounted on a tower, they can also be found on light posts, flagpoles, church steeples, or the sides of buildings. Cell sites typically have several directional antennas that divide the covered area into sectors.

Cell phones continuously scan their environment looking for the best signal, which generally comes from the closest cell site. Most modern devices, such as smartphones, tap into the wireless network several times a minute whenever their signal is on, even if the owner is not using one of the phone's features. Each time the phone connects to a cell site, it generates a time-stamped record known as cell-site location information (CSLI). The precision of this information depends on the size of the geographic area covered by the cell site. The greater the concentration of cell sites, the smaller the coverage area. As data usage from cell phones has increased, wireless carriers have installed more cell sites to handle the traffic. That has led to increasingly compact coverage areas, especially in urban areas.

Wireless carriers collect and store CSLI for their own business purposes, including finding weak spots in their network and applying "roaming" charges when another carrier routes data through their cell sites. In addition, wireless carriers often sell aggregated location records to data brokers, without individual identifying information of the sort at issue here. While carriers have long retained CSLI for the start and end of incoming calls, in recent years phone companies have also collected location information from the transmission of text messages and routine data connections. Accordingly, modern cell phones generate increasingly vast amounts of increasingly precise CSLI.

B

In 2011, police officers arrested four men suspected of robbing a series of Radio Shack and (ironically enough) T-Mobile stores in Detroit. One of the men confessed that, over the previous four months, the group (along with a rotating cast of getaway drivers and lookouts) had robbed nine different stores in Michigan and Ohio. The suspect identified 15 accomplices who had participated in the heists and gave the FBI some of their cell phone numbers; the FBI then reviewed his call records to identify additional numbers that he had called around the time of the robberies.

Based on that information, the prosecutors applied for court orders under the Stored Communications Act to obtain cell phone records for petitioner Timothy Carpenter and several other suspects. That statute, as amended in 1994,

permits the Government to compel the disclosure of certain telecommunications records when it "offers specific and articulable facts showing that there are reasonable grounds to believe" that the records sought "are relevant and material to an ongoing criminal investigation." 18 U. S. C. §2703(d). Federal Magistrate Judges issued two orders directing Carpenter's wireless carriers— MetroPCS and Sprint—to disclose "cell/site sector [information] for [Carpenter's] telephone[ ] at call origination and at call termination for incoming and outgoing calls" during the four-month period when the string of robberies occurred. App. to Pet. for Cert. 60a, 72a. The first order sought 152 days of cell-site records from MetroPCS, which produced records spanning 127 days. The second order requested seven days of CSLI from Sprint, which produced two days of records covering the period when Carpenter's phone was "roaming" in northeastern Ohio. Altogether the Government obtained 12,898 location points cataloging Carpenter's movements—an average of 101 data points per day.

Carpenter was charged with six counts of robbery and an additional six counts of carrying a firearm during a federal crime of violence. See 18 U. S. C. §§924(c), 1951(a). Prior to trial, Carpenter moved to suppress the cell-site data provided by the wireless carriers. He argued that the Government's seizure of the records violated the Fourth Amendment because they had been obtained without a warrant supported by probable cause. The District Court denied the motion. App. to Pet. for Cert. 38a–39a.

At trial, seven of Carpenter's confederates pegged him as the leader of the operation. In addition, FBI agent Christopher Hess offered expert testimony about the cell-site data. Hess explained that each time a cell phone taps into the wireless network, the carrier logs a time-stamped record of the cell site and particular sector that were used. With this information, Hess produced maps that placed Carpenter's phone near four of the charged robberies. In the Government's view, the location records clinched the case: They confirmed that Carpenter was "right where the . . . robbery was at the exact time of the robbery." App. 131 (closing argument). Carpenter was convicted on all but one of the firearm counts and sentenced to more than 100 years in prison.

The Court of Appeals for the Sixth Circuit affirmed. 819 F. 3d 880 (2016). The court held that Carpenter lacked a reasonable expectation of privacy in the location information collected by the FBI because he had shared that information with his wireless carriers. Given that cell phone users voluntarily convey cell-site data to their carriers as "a means of establishing communication," the court concluded that the resulting business records are not entitled to Fourth Amendment protection. Id., at 888 (quoting Smith v. Maryland, 442 U. S. 735, 741 (1979)).

We granted certiorari. 582 U. S. ____ (2017).

II

A

The Fourth Amendment protects "[t]he right of the people to be secure in their persons, houses, papers, and effects, against unreasonable searches and seizures." The "basic purpose of this Amendment," our cases have recognized, "is to safeguard the privacy and security of individuals against arbitrary invasions by governmental officials." Camara v. Municipal Court of City and County of San Francisco, 387 U. S. 523, 528 (1967). The Founding generation crafted the Fourth Amendment as a "response to the reviled 'general warrants' and 'writs of assistance' of the colonial era, which allowed British officers to rummage through homes in an unrestrained search for evidence of criminal activity." Riley v. California, 573 U. S. ____, ____ (2014) (slip op., at 27). In fact, as John Adams recalled, the patriot James Otis's 1761 speech condemning writs of assistance was "the first act of opposition to the arbitrary claims of Great Britain" and helped spark the Revolution itself. Id., at ____–____ (slip op., at 27–28) (quoting 10 Works of John Adams 248 (C. Adams ed. 1856)).

For much of our history, Fourth Amendment search doctrine was "tied to common-law trespass" and focused on whether the Government "obtains information by physically intruding on a constitutionally protected area." United States v. Jones, 565 U. S. 400, 405, 406, n. 3 (2012). More recently, the Court has recognized that "property rights are not the sole measure of Fourth Amendment violations." Soldal v. Cook County, 506 U. S. 56, 64 (1992). In Katz v. United States, 389 U. S. 347, 351 (1967), we established that "the Fourth Amendment protects people, not places," and expanded our conception of the Amendment to protect certain expectations of privacy as well. When an individual "seeks to preserve something as private," and his expectation of privacy is "one that society is prepared to recognize as reasonable," we have held that official intrusion into that private sphere generally qualifies as a search and requires a warrant supported by probable cause. Smith, 442 U. S., at 740 (internal quotation marks and alterations omitted).

Although no single rubric definitively resolves which expectations of privacy are entitled to protection, 1 the analysis is informed by historical understandings "of what was deemed an unreasonable search and seizure when [the Fourth Amendment] was adopted." Carroll v. United States, 267 U. S. 132, 149 (1925). On this score, our cases have recognized some basic guideposts. First, that the Amendment seeks to secure "the privacies of life" against "arbitrary power." Boyd v. United States, 116 U. S. 616, 630 (1886). Second, and relatedly, that a central aim of the Framers was "to place obstacles in the way of a too permeating police surveillance." United States v. Di Re, 332 U.

S. 581, 595 (1948).

We have kept this attention to Founding-era understandings in mind when applying the Fourth Amendment to innovations in surveillance tools. As technology has enhanced the Government's capacity to encroach upon areas normally guarded from inquisitive eyes, this Court has sought to "assure[ ] preservation of that degree of privacy against government that existed when the Fourth Amendment was adopted." Kyllo v. United States, 533 U. S. 27, 34 (2001). For that reason, we rejected in Kyllo a "mechanical interpretation" of the Fourth Amendment and held that use of a thermal imager to detect heat radiating from the side of the defendant's home was a search. Id., at 35. Because any other conclusion would leave homeowners "at the mercy of advancing technology," we determined that the Government—absent a warrant—could not capitalize on such new sense-enhancing technology to explore what was happening within the home. Ibid.

Likewise in Riley, the Court recognized the "immense storage capacity" of modern cell phones in holding that police officers must generally obtain a warrant before searching the contents of a phone. 573 U. S., at ____ (slip op., at 17). We explained that while the general rule allowing warrantless searches incident to arrest "strikes the appropriate balance in the context of physical objects, neither of its rationales has much force with respect to" the vast store of sensitive information on a cell phone. Id., at ____ (slip op., at 9).

B

The case before us involves the Government's acquisition of wireless carrier cell-site records revealing the location of Carpenter's cell phone whenever it made or received calls. This sort of digital data—personal location information maintained by a third party—does not fit neatly under existing precedents. Instead, requests for cell-site records lie at the intersection of two lines of cases, both of which inform our understanding of the privacy interests at stake.

The first set of cases addresses a person's expectation of privacy in his physical location and movements. In United States v. Knotts, 460 U. S. 276 (1983), we considered the Government's use of a "beeper" to aid in tracking a vehicle through traffic. Police officers in that case planted a beeper in a container of chloroform before it was purchased by one of Knotts's co-conspirators. The officers (with intermittent aerial assistance) then followed the automobile carrying the container from Minneapolis to Knotts's cabin in Wisconsin, relying on the beeper's signal to help keep the vehicle in view. The Court concluded that the "augment[ed]" visual surveillance did not constitute a search because "[a] person traveling in an automobile on public thoroughfares has no reasonable expectation of privacy in his movements from one place to another." Id., at 281, 282. Since the movements of the vehicle and its final destination had been "voluntarily conveyed to anyone who wanted to look," Knotts could not assert a privacy interest in the information obtained. Id., at 281.

This Court in Knotts, however, was careful to distinguish between the rudimentary tracking facilitated by the beeper and more sweeping modes of surveillance. The Court emphasized the "limited use which the government made of the signals from this particular beeper" during a discrete "automotive journey." Id., at 284, 285. Significantly, the Court reserved the question whether "different constitutional principles may be applicable" if "twenty-four hour surveillance of any citizen of this country [were] possible." Id., at 283–284.

Three decades later, the Court considered more sophisticated surveillance of the sort envisioned in Knotts and found that different principles did indeed apply. In United States v.

Jones, FBI agents installed a GPS tracking device on Jones's vehicle and remotely monitored the vehicle's movements for 28 days. The Court decided the case based on the Government's physical trespass of the vehicle. 565 U. S., at 404–405. At the same time, five Justices agreed that related privacy concerns would be raised by, for example, "surreptitiously activating a stolen vehicle detection system" in Jones's car to track Jones himself, or conducting GPS tracking of his cell phone. Id., at 426, 428 (Alito, J., concurring in judgment); id., at 415 (Sotomayor, J., concurring). Since GPS monitoring of a vehicle tracks "every movement" a person makes in that vehicle, the concurring Justices concluded that "longer term GPS monitoring in investigations of most offenses impinges on expectations of privacy"—regardless whether those movements were disclosed to the public at large. Id., at 430 (opinion of Alito, J.); id., at 415 (opinion of Sotomayor, J.). 2

In a second set of decisions, the Court has drawn a line between what a person keeps to himself and what he shares with others. We have previously held that "a person has no legitimate expectation of privacy in information he voluntarily turns over to third parties." Smith, 442 U. S., at 743–744. That remains true "even if the information is revealed on the assumption that it will be used only for a limited purpose." United States v. Miller, 425 U. S. 435, 443 (1976). As a result, the Government is typically free to obtain such information from the recipient without triggering Fourth Amendment protections.

This third-party doctrine largely traces its roots to Miller. While investigating Miller for tax evasion, the Government subpoenaed his banks, seeking several months of canceled checks, deposit slips, and monthly statements. The Court rejected a Fourth Amendment challenge to the records collection. For one, Miller could "assert neither ownership nor possession" of the documents; they were "business records of the banks." Id., at 440.

For another, the nature of those records confirmed Miller's limited expectation of privacy, because the checks were "not confidential communications but negotiable instruments to be used in commercial transactions," and the bank statements contained information "exposed to [bank] employees in the ordinary course of business." Id., at 442. The Court thus concluded that Miller had "take[n] the risk, in revealing his affairs to another, that the information [would] be conveyed by that person to the Government." Id., at 443.

Three years later, Smith applied the same principles in the context of information conveyed to a telephone company. The Court ruled that the Government's use of a pen register—a device that recorded the outgoing phone numbers dialed on a landline telephone—was not a search. Noting the pen register's "limited capabilities," the Court "doubt[ed] that people in general entertain any actual expectation of privacy in the numbers they dial." 442 U. S., at 742. Telephone subscribers know, after all, that the numbers are used by the telephone company "for a variety of legitimate business purposes," including routing calls. Id., at 743. And at any rate, the Court explained, such an expectation "is not one that society is prepared to recognize as reasonable." Ibid. (internal quotation marks omitted). When Smith placed a call, he "voluntarily conveyed" the dialed numbers to the phone company by "expos[ing] that information to its equipment in the ordinary course of business." Id., at 744 (internal quotation marks omitted). Once again, we held that the defendant "assumed the risk" that the company's records "would be divulged to police." Id., at 745.

III

The question we confront today is how to apply the Fourth Amendment to a new phenomenon: the ability to chronicle a person's past movements through the record of his cell phone signals. Such tracking partakes of many of the qualities of the GPS monitoring we considered in Jones. Much like GPS tracking of a vehicle, cell phone location information is detailed, encyclopedic, and effortlessly compiled.

At the same time, the fact that the individual continuously reveals his location to his wireless carrier implicates the third-party principle of Smith and Miller. But while the third-party doctrine applies to telephone numbers and bank records, it is not clear whether its logic extends to the qualitatively different category of cell-site records. After all, when Smith was decided in 1979, few could have imagined a society in which a phone goes wherever its owner goes, conveying to the wireless carrier not just dialed digits, but a detailed and comprehensive record of the person's movements.

We decline to extend Smith and Miller to cover these novel circumstances. Given the unique nature of cell phone location records, the fact that the information is held by a third party does not by itself overcome the user's claim to Fourth Amendment protection. Whether the Government employs its own surveillance technology as in Jones or leverages the technology of a wireless carrier, we hold that an individual maintains a legitimate expectation of privacy in the record of his physical movements as captured through CSLI. The location information obtained from Carpenter's wireless carriers was the product of a search. 3

A

A person does not surrender all Fourth Amendment protection by venturing into the public sphere. To the contrary, "what [one] seeks to preserve as private, even in an area accessible to the public, may be constitutionally protected." Katz, 389 U. S., at 351–352. A majority of this Court has already recognized that individuals have a reasonable expectation of privacy in the whole of their physical movements. Jones, 565 U. S., at 430 (Alito, J., concurring in judgment); id., at 415 (Sotomayor, J., concurring). Prior to the digital age, law enforcement might have pursued a suspect for a brief stretch, but doing so "for any extended period of time was difficult and costly and therefore rarely undertaken." Id., at 429 (opinion of Alito, J.). For that reason, "society's expectation has been that law enforcement agents and others would not—and indeed, in the main, simply could not—secretly monitor and catalogue every single movement of an individual's car for a very long period." Id., at 430.

Allowing government access to cell-site records contravenes that expectation. Although such records are generated for commercial purposes, that distinction does not negate Carpenter's anticipation of privacy in his physical location. Mapping a cell phone's location over the course of 127 days provides an all-encompassing record of the holder's whereabouts. As with GPS information, the time-stamped data provides an intimate window into a person's life, revealing not only his particular movements, but through them his "familial, political, professional, religious, and sexual associations." Id., at 415 (opinion of Sotomayor, J.). These location records "hold for many Americans the 'privacies of life.'" Riley, 573 U. S., at ___ (slip op., at 28) (quoting Boyd, 116 U. S., at 630). And like GPS monitoring, cell phone tracking is remarkably easy, cheap, and efficient compared to traditional investigative tools. With just the click of a button, the Government can access each carrier's deep repository of historical location information at practically no expense.

In fact, historical cell-site records present even greater privacy concerns than the GPS monitoring of a vehicle we considered in Jones. Unlike the bugged container in Knotts or the car in Jones, a cell phone—almost a "feature of human anatomy," Riley, 573 U. S., at ___ (slip op., at 9)—tracks nearly exactly the movements of its owner. While individuals regularly leave their vehicles, they compulsively carry cell phones with them all the time. A cell phone faithfully follows its owner beyond public thoroughfares and into private residences, doctor's offices, political headquarters, and other potentially revealing locales. See id., at ____ (slip op., at 19) (noting that "nearly three-quarters of smart phone users report being within five feet of their phones most of the time, with 12% admitting that they even use their phones in the shower"); contrast Cardwell v. Lewis, 417 U. S. 583, 590 (1974) (plurality opinion) ("A car has little capacity for escaping public scrutiny."). Accordingly, when the Government tracks the location of a cell phone it achieves near perfect surveillance, as if it had attached an ankle monitor to the phone's user.

Moreover, the retrospective quality of the data here gives police access to a category of information otherwise unknowable. In the past, attempts to reconstruct a person's movements were limited by a dearth of records and the frailties of recollection. With access to CSLI, the Government can now travel back in time to retrace a person's whereabouts, subject only to the retention polices of the wireless carriers, which currently maintain records for up to five years. Critically, because location information is continually logged for all of the 400 million devices in the United States—not just those belonging to persons who might happen to come under investigation—this newfound tracking capacity runs against everyone. Unlike with the GPS device in Jones, police need not even know in advance whether they want to follow a particular individual, or when.

Whoever the suspect turns out to be, he has effectively been tailed every moment of every day for five years, and the police may—in the Government's view—call upon the results of that surveillance without regard to the constraints of the Fourth Amendment. Only the few with-out cell phones could escape this tireless and absolute surveillance.

The Government and Justice Kennedy contend, however, that the collection of CSLI should be permitted because the data is less precise than GPS information. Not to worry, they maintain, because the location records did "not on their own suffice to place [Carpenter] at the crime scene"; they placed him within a wedge-shaped sector ranging from one-eighth to four square miles. Brief for United States 24; see post, at 18–19. Yet the Court has already rejected the proposition that "inference insulates a search." Kyllo, 533 U. S., at 36. From the 127 days of location data it received, the Government could, in combination with other information, deduce a detailed log of Carpenter's movements, including when he was at the site of the robberies. And the Government thought the CSLI accurate enough to highlight it during the closing argument of his trial. App. 131.

At any rate, the rule the Court adopts "must take account of more sophisticated systems that are already in use or in development." Kyllo, 533 U. S., at 36. While the records in this case reflect the state of technology at the start of the decade, the accuracy of CSLI is rapidly approaching GPS-level precision. As the number of cell sites has proliferated, the geographic area covered by each cell sector has shrunk, particularly in urban areas. In addition, with new technology measuring the time and angle of signals hitting their towers, wireless carriers already have the capability to pinpoint a phone's location within 50 meters. Brief for Electronic Frontier Foundation et al. as Amici Curiae 12 (describing triangulation methods that estimate a device's location inside a given cell sector).

Accordingly, when the Government accessed CSLI from the wireless carriers, it invaded Carpenter's reason-able expectation of privacy in the whole of his physical movements.

B

The Government's primary contention to the contrary is that the third-party doctrine governs this case. In its view, cell-site records are fair game because they are "business records" created and maintained by the wireless carriers. The Government (along with Justice Kennedy) recognizes that this case features new technology, but asserts that the legal question nonetheless turns on a garden-variety request for information from a third-party witness. Brief for United States 32–34; post, at 12–14.

The Government's position fails to contend with the seismic shifts in digital technology that made possible the tracking of not only Carpenter's location but also everyone else's, not for a short period but for years and years. Sprint Corporation and its competitors are not your typical witnesses. Unlike the nosy neighbor who keeps an eye on comings and goings, they are ever alert, and their memory is nearly infallible. There is a world of difference between the limited types of personal information addressed in Smith and Miller and the exhaustive chronicle of location information casually collected by wireless carriers today. The Government thus is not asking for a straightforward application of the third-party doctrine, but instead a significant extension of it to a distinct category of information.

The third-party doctrine partly stems from the notion that an individual has a reduced expectation of privacy in information knowingly shared with another. But the fact of "diminished privacy interests does not mean that the Fourth Amendment falls out of the picture entirely." Riley, 573 U. S., at ____ (slip op., at 16). Smith and Miller, after all, did not rely solely on the act of sharing. Instead, they considered "the nature of the particular documents sought" to determine whether "there is a legitimate 'expectation of privacy' concerning their contents." Miller, 425 U. S., at 442. Smith pointed out the limited capabilities of a pen register; as explained in Riley, telephone call logs reveal little in the way of "identifying information." Smith, 442 U. S., at 742;

Riley, 573 U. S., at ____ (slip op., at 24). Miller likewise noted that checks were "not confidential communications but negotiable instruments to be used in commercial transactions." 425 U. S., at 442. In mechanically applying the third-party doctrine to this case, the Government fails to appreciate that there are no comparable limitations on the revealing nature of CSLI.

The Court has in fact already shown special solicitude for location information in the third-party context. In Knotts, the Court relied on Smith to hold that an individual has no reasonable expectation of privacy in public movements that he "voluntarily conveyed to anyone who wanted to look." Knotts, 460 U. S., at 281; see id., at 283 (discussing Smith). But when confronted with more pervasive tracking, five Justices agreed that longer term GPS monitoring of even a vehicle traveling on public streets constitutes a search. Jones, 565 U. S., at 430 (Alito, J., concurring in judgment); id., at 415 (Sotomayor, J., concurring). Justice Gorsuch wonders why "someone's location when using a phone" is sensitive, post, at 3, and Justice Kennedy assumes that a person's discrete movements "are not particularly private," post, at 17. Yet this case is not about "using a phone" or a person's movement at a particular time. It is about a detailed chronicle of a person's physical presence compiled every day, every moment, over several years. Such a chronicle implicates privacy concerns far beyond those considered in Smith and Miller.

Neither does the second rationale underlying the third-party doctrine—voluntary exposure—hold up when it comes to CSLI. Cell phone location information is not truly "shared" as one normally understands the term. In the first place, cell phones and the services they provide are "such a pervasive and insistent part of daily life" that carrying one is indispensable to participation in modern society. Riley, 573 U. S., at ____ (slip op., at 9). Second, a cell phone logs a cell-site record by dint of its operation, without any affirmative act on the part of the user beyond powering up. Virtually any activity on the phone generates CSLI, including incoming calls, texts, or e-mails and countless other data connections that a phone automatically makes when checking for news, weather, or social media updates. Apart from disconnecting the phone from the network, there is no way to avoid leaving behind a trail of location data. As a result, in no meaningful sense does the user voluntarily "assume[ ] the risk" of turning over a comprehensive dossier of his physical movements. Smith, 442 U. S., at 745.

We therefore decline to extend Smith and Miller to the collection of CSLI. Given the unique nature of cell phone location information, the fact that the Government obtained the information from a third party does not overcome Carpenter's claim to Fourth Amendment protection. The Government's acquisition of the cell-site records was a search within the meaning of the Fourth Amendment.

* * *

Our decision today is a narrow one. We do not express a view on matters not before us: real-time CSLI or "tower dumps" (a download of information on all the devices that connected to a particular cell site during a particular interval). We do not disturb the application of Smith and Miller or call into question conventional surveillance techniques and tools, such as security cameras. Nor do we address other business records that might incidentally reveal location information. Further, our opinion does not consider other collection techniques involving foreign affairs or national security. As Justice Frankfurter noted when considering new innovations in airplanes and radios, the Court must tread carefully in such cases, to ensure that we do not "embarrass the future." Northwest Airlines, Inc. v. Minnesota, 322 U. S. 292, 300 (1944). 4

IV

Having found that the acquisition of

Carpenter's CSLI was a search, we also conclude that the Government must generally obtain a warrant supported by probable cause before acquiring such records. Although the "ultimate measure of the constitutionality of a governmental search is 'reasonableness,' " our cases establish that warrantless searches are typically unreasonable where "a search is undertaken by law enforcement officials to discover evidence of criminal wrongdoing." Vernonia School Dist. 47J v. Acton, 515 U. S. 646, 652–653 (1995). Thus, "[i]n the absence of a warrant, a search is reasonable only if it falls within a specific exception to the warrant requirement." Riley, 573 U. S., at ___ (slip op., at 5).

The Government acquired the cell-site records pursuant to a court order issued under the Stored Communications Act, which required the Government to show "reasonable grounds" for believing that the records were "relevant and material to an ongoing investigation." 18 U. S. C. §2703(d). That showing falls well short of the probable cause required for a warrant. The Court usually requires "some quantum of individualized suspicion" beforea search or seizure may take place. United States v.Martinez-Fuerte, 428 U. S. 543, 560–561 (1976). Under the standard in the Stored Communications Act, however, law enforcement need only show that the cell-site evidence might be pertinent to an ongoing investigation—a "gigantic" departure from the probable cause rule, as the Government explained below. App. 34. Consequently, an order issued under Section 2703(d) of the Act is not a permissible mechanism for accessing historical cell-site records. Before compelling a wireless carrier to turn over a subscriber's CSLI, the Government's obligation is a familiar one—get a warrant.

Justice Alito contends that the warrant requirement simply does not apply when the Government acquires records using compulsory process. Unlike an actual search, he says, subpoenas for documents do not involve the direct taking of evidence; they are at most a "constructive search" conducted by the target of the subpoena. Post, at 12. Given this lesser intrusion on personal privacy, Justice Alito argues that the compulsory production of records is not held to the same probable cause standard. In his view, this Court's precedents set forth a categorical rule—separate and distinct from the third-party doctrine—subjecting subpoenas to lenient scrutiny without regard to the suspect's expectation of privacy in the records. Post, at 8–19.

But this Court has never held that the Government may subpoena third parties for records in which the suspect has a reasonable expectation of privacy. Almost all of the examples Justice Alito cites, see post, at 14–15, contemplated requests for evidence implicating diminished privacy interests or for a corporation's own books. 5 The lone exception, of course, is Miller, where the Court's analysis of the third-party subpoena merged with the application of the third-party doctrine. 425 U. S., at 444 (concluding that Miller lacked the necessary privacy interest to contest the issuance of a subpoena to his bank).

Justice Alito overlooks the critical issue. At some point, the dissent should recognize that CSLI is an entirely different species of business record—something that implicates basic Fourth Amendment concerns about arbitrary government power much more directly than corporate tax or payroll ledgers. When confronting new concerns wrought by digital technology, this Court has been careful not to uncritically extend existing precedents. See Riley, 573 U. S., at ____ (slip op., at 10) ("A search of the information on a cell phone bears little resemblance to the type of brief physical search considered [in prior precedents].").

If the choice to proceed by subpoena provided a categorical limitation on Fourth Amendment protection, no type of record would ever be protected by the warrant requirement. Under Justice Alito's view, private letters, digital contents of a cell phone—any personal information reduced to document form, in fact—may be collected by subpoena for no reason other than "official curiosity." United States v. Morton Salt Co., 338 U. S. 632, 652 (1950). Justice Kennedy declines to adopt the radical implications of this theory, leaving open the question whether the warrant requirement applies "when the Government obtains the modern-day equivalents of an individual's own 'papers' or 'effects,' even when those papers or effects are held by a third party. " Post, at 13 (citing United States v. Warshak, 631 F. 3d 266, 283–288 (CA6 2010)). That would be a sensible exception, because it would prevent the subpoena doctrine from overcoming any reasonable expectation of privacy. If the third-party doctrine does not apply to the "modern-day equivalents of an individual's own 'papers' or 'effects,' " then the clear implication is that the documents should receive full Fourth Amendment protection. We simply think that such protection should extend as well to a detailed log of a person's movements over several years.

This is certainly not to say that all orders compelling the production of documents will require a showing of probable cause. The Government will be able to use subpoenas to acquire records in the overwhelming majority of investigations. We hold only that a warrant is required in the rare case where the suspect has a legitimate privacy interest in records held by a third party.

Further, even though the Government will generally need a warrant to access CSLI, case-specific exceptions may support a warrantless search of an individual's cell-site records under certain circumstances. "One well-recognized exception applies when ' "the exigencies of the situation" make the needs of law enforcement so compelling that [a] warrantless search is objectively reasonable under the Fourth Amendment.' " Kentucky v. King, 563 U. S. 452, 460 (2011) (quoting Mincey v. Arizona, 437 U. S. 385, 394 (1978)). Such exigencies include the need to pursue a fleeing suspect, protect individuals who are threatened with imminent harm, or prevent the imminent destruction of evidence. 563 U. S., at 460, and n. 3.

As a result, if law enforcement is confronted with an urgent situation, such fact-specific threats will likely justify the warrantless collection of CSLI. Lower courts, for instance, have approved warrantless searches related to bomb threats, active shootings, and child abductions. Our decision today does not call into doubt warrantless access to CSLI in such circumstances. While police must get a warrant when collecting CSLI to assist in the mine-run criminal investigation, the rule we set forth does not limit their ability to respond to an ongoing emergency.

*　　*　　*

As Justice Brandeis explained in his famous dissent, the Court is obligated—as "[s]ubtler and more far-reaching means of invading privacy have become available to the Government"—to ensure that the "progress of science" does not erode Fourth Amendment protections. Olmstead v. United States, 277 U. S. 438, 473–474 (1928). Here the progress of science has afforded law enforcement a powerful new tool to carry out its important responsibilities. At the same time, this tool risks Government encroachment of the sort the Framers, "after consulting the lessons of history," drafted the Fourth Amendment to prevent. Di Re, 332 U. S., at 595.

We decline to grant the state unrestricted access to a wireless carrier's database of physical location information. In light of the deeply revealing nature of CSLI, its depth, breadth, and comprehensive reach, and the inescapable and automatic nature of its collection, the fact that such information is gathered by a third party does not make it any less deserving of Fourth Amendment protection. The Government's acquisition of the cell-site records here was a search under that Amendment.

The judgment of the Court of Appeals is reversed, and the case is remanded for further proceedings consistent with this opinion.

It is so ordered.

Mitchell v. Wisconsin (June 27, 2019) [Notes omitted]

Justice ALITO announced the judgment of the Court and delivered an opinion, in which THE CHIEF JUSTICE, Justice BREYER, and Justice KAVANAUGH join.

In this case, we return to a topic that we have addressed twice in recent years: the circumstances under which a police officer may administer a warrantless blood alcohol concentration (BAC) test to a motorist who appears to have been driving under the influence of alcohol. We have previously addressed what officers may do in two broad categories of cases. First, an officer may conduct a BAC test if the facts of a particular case bring it within the exigent-circumstances exception to the Fourth Amendment's general requirement of a warrant. Second, if an officer has probable cause to arrest a motorist for drunk driving, the officer may conduct a breath test (but not a blood test) under the rule allowing warrantless searches of a person incident to arrest.

Today, we consider what police officers may do in a narrow but important category of cases: those in which the driver is unconscious and therefore cannot be given a breath test. In such cases, we hold, the exigent-circumstances rule almost always permits a blood test without a warrant. When a breath test is impossible, enforcement of the drunk-driving laws depends upon the administration of a blood test. And when a police officer encounters an unconscious driver, it is very likely that the driver would be taken to an emergency room and that his blood would be drawn for diagnostic purposes even if the police were not seeking BAC information. In addition, police officers most frequently come upon unconscious drivers when they report to the scene of an accident, and under those circumstances, the officers' many responsibilities —such as attending to other injured drivers or passengers and preventing further accidents—may be incompatible with the procedures that would be required to obtain a warrant. Thus, when a driver is unconscious, the general rule is that a warrant is not needed.

I

A

In Birchfield v. North Dakota, 579 U.S. ____, 136 S.Ct. 2160, 195 L.Ed.2d 560 (2016), we recounted the country's efforts over the years to address the terrible problem of drunk driving. Today, "all States have laws that prohibit motorists from driving with a [BAC] that exceeds a specified level." Id., at ____, 136 S.Ct., at 2166. And to help enforce BAC limits, every State has passed what are popularly called implied-consent laws. Ibid. As "a condition of the privilege of using the public roads, these laws require that drivers submit to BAC testing "when there is sufficient reason to believe they are violating the State's drunk-driving laws." Id., at ____, ____, 136 S.Ct., at 2166, 2169).

Wisconsin's implied-consent law is much like those of the other 49 States and the District of Columbia. It deems drivers to have consented to breath or blood tests if an officer has reason to believe they have committed one of several drug- or alcohol-related offenses.[1] See Wis. Stat. §§ 343.305(2), (3). Officers seeking to conduct a BAC test must read aloud a statement declaring their intent to administer the test and advising drivers of their options and the implications of their

choice. § 343.305(4). If a driver's BAC level proves too high, his license will be suspended; but if he refuses testing, his license will be revoked and his refusal may be used against him in court. See ibid. No test will be administered if a driver refuses —or, as the State would put it, "withdraws" his statutorily presumed consent. But "[a] person who is unconscious or otherwise not capable of withdrawing consent is presumed not to have" withdrawn it. § 343.305(3)(b). See also §§ 343.305(3)(ar)1-2. More than half the States have provisions like this one regarding unconscious drivers.

B

The sequence of events that gave rise to this case began when Officer Alexander Jaeger of the Sheboygan Police Department received a report that petitioner Gerald Mitchell, appearing to be very drunk, had climbed into a van and driven off. Jaeger soon found Mitchell wandering near a lake. Stumbling and slurring his words, Mitchell could hardly stand without the support of two officers. Jaeger judged a field sobriety test hopeless, if not dangerous, and gave Mitchell a preliminary breath test. It registered a BAC level of 0.24%, triple the legal limit for driving in Wisconsin. Jaeger arrested Mitchell for operating a vehicle while intoxicated and, as is standard practice, drove him to a police station for a more reliable breath test using better equipment.

On the way, Mitchell's condition continued to deteriorate—so much so that by the time the squad car had reached the station, he was too lethargic even for a breath test. Jaeger therefore drove Mitchell to a nearby hospital for a blood test; Mitchell lost consciousness on the ride over and had to be wheeled in. Even so, Jaeger read aloud to a slumped Mitchell the standard statement giving drivers a chance to refuse BAC testing. Hearing no response, Jaeger asked hospital staff to draw a blood sample. Mitchell remained unconscious while the sample was taken, and analysis of his blood showed that his BAC, about 90 minutes after his arrest, was 0.222%.

Mitchell was charged with violating two related drunk-driving provisions. See §§ 346.63(1)(a), (b). He moved to suppress the results of the blood test on the ground that it violated his Fourth Amendment right against "unreason-able searches" because it was conducted without a warrant. Wisconsin chose to rest its response on the notion that its implied-consent law (together with Mitchell's free choice to drive on its highways) rendered the blood test a consensual one, thus curing any Fourth Amendment problem. In the end, the trial court denied Mitchell's motion to suppress, and a jury found him guilty of the charged offenses. The intermediate appellate court certified two questions to the Wisconsin Supreme Court: first, whether compliance with the State's implied-consent law was sufficient to show that Mitchell's test was consistent with the Fourth Amendment and, second, whether a warrantless blood draw from an unconscious person violates the Fourth Amendment. See 2018 WI 84, ¶15, 383 Wis.2d 192, 202-203, 914 N.W.2d 151, 155-156 (2018). The Wisconsin Supreme Court affirmed Mitchell's convictions, and we granted certiorari, 586 U.S. ____, 139 S.Ct. 915, 202 L.Ed.2d 642 (2019), to decide "[w]hether a statute authorizing a blood draw from an unconscious motorist provides an exception to the Fourth Amendment warrant requirement," Pet. for Cert. ii.

II

In considering Wisconsin's implied-consent law, we do not write on a blank slate. "Our prior opinions have referred approvingly to the general concept of implied-consent laws that impose civil penalties and evidentiary consequences on motorists who refuse to comply." Birchfield, 579 U.S., at ____, 136 S.Ct., at 2185. But our decisions have not rested on the idea that these laws do what their popular name might seem to suggest—that is, create actual consent to all the searches they authorize. Instead, we have based our decisions on the precedent regarding the specific constitutional claims in each case, while keeping in mind the wider regulatory scheme developed over the years to combat drunk driving. That scheme is centered on legally specified BAC limits for drivers—limits enforced by the BAC tests promoted by implied-consent laws.

Over the last 50 years, we have approved many of the defining elements of this scheme. We have held that forcing drunk-driving suspects to undergo a blood test does not violate their constitutional right against self-incrimination. See Schmerber v. California, 384 U.S. 757, 765, 86 S.Ct. 1826, 16 L.Ed.2d 908 (1966). Nor does using their refusal against them in court. See South Dakota v. Neville, 459 U.S. 553, 563, 103 S.Ct. 916, 74 L.Ed.2d 748 (1983). And punishing that refusal with automatic license revocation does not violate drivers' due process rights if they have been arrested upon probable cause, Mackey v. Montrym, 443 U.S. 1, 99 S.Ct. 2612, 61 L.Ed.2d 321 (1979); on the contrary, this kind of summary penalty is "unquestionably legitimate." Neville, supra, at 560, 103 S.Ct. 916.

These cases generally concerned the Fifth and Fourteenth Amendments, but motorists charged with drunk driving have also invoked the Fourth Amendment's ban on "unreasonable searches" since BAC tests are "searches." See Birchfield, 579 U.S., at ____, 136 S.Ct., at 2173. Though our precedent normally requires a warrant for a lawful search, there are well-defined exceptions to this rule. In Birchfield, we applied precedent on the "search-incident-to-arrest" exception to BAC testing of conscious drunk-driving suspects. We held that their drunk-driving arrests, taken alone, justify warrantless breath tests but not blood tests, since breath tests are less intrusive, just as informative, and (in the case of conscious suspects) readily available. Id., at ____, 136 S.Ct., at 2184-85.

We have also reviewed BAC tests under the "exigent circumstances" exception —which, as noted, allows warrantless searches "to prevent the imminent destruction of evidence." Missouri v. McNeely, 569 U.S. 141, 149, 133 S.Ct. 1552, 185 L.Ed.2d 696 (2013). In McNeely, we were asked if this exception covers BAC testing of drunk-driving suspects in light of the fact that blood-alcohol evidence is always dissipating due to "natural metabolic processes." Id., at 152, 133 S.Ct. 1552. We answered that the fleeting quality of BAC evidence alone is not enough. Id., at 156, 133 S.Ct. 1552. But in Schmerber it did justify a blood test of a drunk driver who had gotten into a car accident that gave police other pressing duties, for then the "further delay" caused by a warrant application really "would have threatened the destruction of evidence." McNeely, supra, at 152, 133 S.Ct. 1552 (emphasis added).

Like Schmerber, this case sits much higher than McNeely on the exigency spectrum. McNeely was about the minimum degree of urgency common to all drunk-driving cases. In Schmerber, a car accident heightened that urgency. And here Mitchell's medical condition did just the same.

Mitchell's stupor and eventual unconsciousness also deprived officials of a reasonable opportunity to administer a breath test. To be sure, Officer Jaeger managed to conduct "a preliminary breath test" using a portable machine when he first encountered Mitchell at the lake. App. to Pet. for Cert. 60a. But he had no reasonable opportunity to give Mitchell a breath test using "evidence-grade breath testing machinery." Birchfield, 579 U.S., at ____, 136 S.Ct., at 2192 (SOTOMAYOR, J., concurring in part and dissenting in part). As a result, it was reasonable for Jaeger to seek a better breath test at the station; he acted with reasonable dispatch to procure one; and when Mitchell's condition got in the way, it was reasonable for Jaeger to pursue a blood test. As Justice SOTOMAYOR explained in her partial dissent in Birchfield:

"There is a common misconception that breath tests are conducted roadside, immediately after a driver is arrested. While some preliminary testing is conducted roadside, reliability concerns with roadside tests confine their use in most circumstances to establishing probable cause for an arrest.... The standard evidentiary breath test is conducted after a motorist is arrested and transported to a police station, governmental building, or mobile testing facility where officers can access reliable, evidence-grade breath testing machinery." Id., at ____, 136 S.Ct., at 2192.

Because the "standard evidentiary breath test is conducted after a motorist is arrested and transported to a police station" or another appropriate facility, ibid., the important question here is what officers may do when a driver's unconsciousness (or stupor) eliminates any reasonable opportunity for that kind of breath test.

III

The Fourth Amendment guards the "right of the people to be secure in their persons ... against unreasonable searches" and provides that "no Warrants shall issue, but upon probable cause." A blood draw is a search of the person, so we must determine if its administration here without a warrant was reasonable. See Birchfield, 579 U.S. at ____, 136 S.Ct., at 2174. Though we have held that a warrant is normally required, we have also "made it clear that there are exceptions to the warrant requirement." Illinois v. McArthur, 531 U.S. 326, 330, 121 S.Ct. 946, 148 L.Ed.2d 838 (2001). And under the exception for exigent circumstances, a warrantless search is allowed when "`there is compelling need for official action and no time to secure a warrant.'" McNeely, supra, at 149, 133 S.Ct. 1552 (quoting Michigan v. Tyler, 436 U.S. 499, 509, 98 S.Ct. 1942, 56 L.Ed.2d 486 (1978)). In McNeely, we considered how the exigent-circumstances exception applies to the broad category of cases in which a police officer has probable cause to believe that a motorist was driving under the influence of alcohol, and we do not revisit that question. Nor do we settle whether the exigent-circumstances exception covers the specific facts of this case.[2] Instead, we address how the exception bears on the category of cases encompassed by the question on which we granted certiorari—those involving unconscious drivers.[3] In those cases, the need for a blood test is compelling, and an officer's duty to attend to more pressing needs may leave no time to seek a warrant.

A

The importance of the needs served by BAC testing is hard to overstate. The bottom line is that BAC tests are needed for enforcing laws that save lives. The specifics, in short, are these: Highway safety is critical; it is served by laws that criminalize driving with a certain BAC level; and enforcing these legal BAC limits requires efficient testing to obtain BAC evidence, which naturally dissipates. So BAC tests are crucial links in a chain on which vital interests hang. And when a breath test is unavailable to advance those aims, a blood test becomes essential. Here we add a word about each of these points.

First, highway safety is a vital public interest. For decades, we have strained our vocal chords to give adequate expression to the stakes. We have called highway safety a "compelling interest," Mackey, 443 U.S., at 19, 99 S.Ct. 2612; we have called it "paramount," id., at 17, 99 S.Ct. 2612. Twice we have referred to the effects of irresponsible driving as "slaughter" comparable to the ravages of war. Breithaupt v. Abram, 352 U.S. 432, 439, 77 S.Ct. 408, 1 L.Ed.2d 448 (1957); Perez v. Campbell, 402 U.S. 637, 657, 672, 91 S.Ct. 1704, 29 L.Ed.2d 233 (1971) (Blackmun, J., concurring in result in part and dissenting in part). We have spoken of "carnage," Neville, 459 U.S., at 558-559, 103 S.Ct. 916, and even "frightful carnage," Tate v. Short, 401 U.S. 395, 401, S.Ct. 668, 28 L.Ed.2d 130 (1971) (Blackmun, J., concurring). The frequency of preventable collisions, we have said, is "tragic," Neville, supra, at 558, 103 S.Ct. 916, and "astounding," Breithaupt, supra, at 439, 77 S.Ct. 408. And behind this fervent language lie chilling figures, all captured in the fact that from 1982 to 2016, alcohol-related accidents took roughly 10,000 to 20,000 lives in this Nation every single year. See National Highway Traffic Safety Admin. (NHTSA), Traffic Safety Facts 2016, p. 40 (May 2018). In the best years, that would add up to more than one fatality per hour.

Second, when it comes to fighting these harms and promoting highway safety, federal and state lawmakers have long been convinced that specified BAC limits make a big difference. States resorted to these limits when earlier laws that included no "statistical definition of intoxication" proved ineffectual or hard to enforce. See Birchfield, 579 U.S., at ____-____, 136 S.Ct., at 2167. The maximum permissible BAC, initially set at 0.15%, was first lowered to 0.10% and then to 0.08%. Id., at ____, ____-____, 136 S.Ct., at 2167, 2168-69. Congress encouraged this process by conditioning the award of federal highway funds on the establishment of a BAC limit of 0.08%, see 23 U.S.C. § 163(a); 23 CFR § 1225.1 (2012), and every State has adopted this limit.[4] Not only that, many States, including Wisconsin, have passed laws imposing increased penalties for recidivists or for drivers with a BAC level that exceeds a higher threshold. See Wis. Stat. § 346.65(2)(am); Birchfield, 579 U.S., at ____, 136 S.Ct., at 2169.

There is good reason to think this strategy has worked. As we noted in Birchfield, these tougher measures corresponded with a dramatic drop in highway deaths and injuries: From the mid-1970's to the mid-1980's, "the number of annual fatalities averaged 25,000; by 2014 ..., the number had fallen to below 10,000." Id., at ____, 136 S.Ct., at 2169.

Third, enforcing BAC limits obviously

requires a test that is accurate enough to stand up in court, id., at ____, 136 S.Ct., at 2167-68; see also McNeely, 569 U.S., at 159-160, 133 S.Ct. 1552 (plurality opinion). And we have recognized that "[e]xtraction of blood samples for testing is a highly effective means of" measuring "the influence of alcohol." Schmerber, 384 U.S., at 771, 86 S.Ct. 1826.

Enforcement of BAC limits also requires prompt testing because it is "a biological certainty" that "[a]lcohol dissipates from the bloodstream at a rate of 0.01 percent to 0.025 percent per hour.... Evidence is literally disappearing by the minute." McNeely, 569 U.S., at 169, 133 S.Ct. 1552 (opinion of ROBERTS, C.J.). As noted, the ephemeral nature of BAC was "essential to our holding in Schmerber," which itself allowed a warrantless blood test for BAC. Id., at 152, 133 S.Ct. 1552 (opinion of the Court). And even when we later held that the exigent-circumstances exception would not permit a warrantless blood draw in every drunk-driving case, we acknowledged that delays in BAC testing can "raise questions about ... accuracy." Id., at 156, 133 S.Ct. 1552.

It is no wonder, then, that the implied-consent laws that incentivize prompt BAC testing have been with us for 65 years and now exist in all 50 States. Birchfield, supra, at ____, 136 S.Ct., at 2169. These laws and the BAC tests they require are tightly linked to a regulatory scheme that serves the most pressing of interests.

Finally, when a breath test is unavailable to promote those interests, "a blood draw becomes necessary." McNeely, 569 U.S., at 170, 133 S.Ct. 1552 (opinion of ROBERTS, C.J.). Thus, in the case of unconscious drivers, who cannot blow into a breathalyzer, blood tests are essential for achieving the compelling interests described above.

Indeed, not only is the link to pressing interests here tighter; the interests themselves are greater: Drivers who are drunk enough to pass out at the wheel or soon afterward pose a much greater risk. It would be perverse if the more wanton behavior were rewarded—if the more harrowing threat were harder to punish.

For these reasons, there clearly is a "compelling need" for a blood test of drunk-driving suspects whose condition deprives officials of a reasonable opportunity to conduct a breath test. Id., at 149, 133 S.Ct. 1552 (opinion of the Court) (internal quotation marks omitted). The only question left, under our exigency doctrine, is whether this compelling need justifies a warrantless search because there is, furthermore, "`no time to secure a warrant.'" Ibid.

B

We held that there was no time to secure a warrant before a blood test of a drunk-driving suspect in Schmerber because the officer there could "reasonably have believed that he was confronted with an emergency, in which the delay necessary to obtain a warrant, under the circumstances, threatened the destruction of evidence." 384 U.S., at 770, 86 S.Ct. 1826 (internal quotation marks omitted). So even if the constant dissipation of BAC evidence alone does not create an exigency, see McNeely, supra, at 150-151, 133 S.Ct. 1552, Schmerber shows that it does so when combined with other pressing needs:

"We are told that [1] the percentage of alcohol in the blood begins to diminish shortly after drinking stops, as the body functions to eliminate it from the system. Particularly in a case such as this, where [2] time had to be taken to bring the accused to a hospital and to investigate the scene of the accident, there was no time to seek out a magistrate and secure a warrant. Given these special facts, we conclude that the attempt to secure evidence of blood-alcohol content in this case [without a warrant] was ... appropriate ...." 384 U.S., at 770-771, 86 S.Ct. 1826.

Thus, exigency exists when (1) BAC evidence is dissipating and (2) some other factor creates pressing health, safety, or law enforcement needs that would take priority over a warrant application. Both conditions are met when a drunk-driving suspect is unconscious, so Schmerber controls: With such suspects, too, a warrantless blood draw is lawful.

1

In Schmerber, the extra factor giving rise to urgent needs that would only add to the delay caused by a warrant application was a car accident; here it is the driver's unconsciousness. Indeed, unconsciousness does not just create pressing needs; it is itself a medical emergency.[5] It means that the suspect will have to be rushed to the hospital or similar facility not just for the blood test itself but for urgent medical care.[6] Police can reasonably anticipate that such a driver might require monitoring, positioning, and support on the way to the hospital;[7] that his blood may be drawn anyway, for diagnostic purposes, immediately on arrival;[8] and that immediate medical treatment could delay (or otherwise distort the results of) a blood draw conducted later, upon receipt of a warrant, thus reducing its evidentiary value. See McNeely, supra, at 156, 133 S.Ct. 1552 (plurality opinion). All of that sets this case apart from the uncomplicated drunk-driving scenarios addressed in McNeely. Just as the ramifications of a car accident pushed Schmerber over the line into exigency, so does the condition of an unconscious driver bring his blood draw under the exception. In such a case, as in Schmerber, an officer could "reasonably have believed that he was confronted with an emergency." 384 U.S., at 770, 86 S.Ct. 1826.

Indeed, in many unconscious-driver cases, the exigency will be more acute, as elaborated in the briefing and argument in this case. A driver so drunk as to lose consciousness is quite likely to crash, especially if he passes out before managing to park. And then the accident might give officers a slew of urgent tasks beyond that of securing (and working around) medical care for the suspect.

Police may have to ensure that others who are injured receive prompt medical attention; they may have to provide first aid themselves until medical personnel arrive at the scene. In some cases, they may have to deal with fatalities. They may have to preserve evidence at the scene and block or redirect traffic to prevent further accidents. These pressing matters, too, would require responsible officers to put off applying for a warrant, and that would only exacerbate the delay —and imprecision—of any subsequent BAC test.

In sum, all these rival priorities would put officers, who must often engage in a form of triage, to a dilemma. It would force them to choose between prioritizing a warrant application, to the detriment of critical health and safety needs, and delaying the warrant application, and thus the BAC test, to the detriment of its evidentiary value and all the compelling interests served by BAC limits. This is just the kind of scenario for which the exigency rule was born—just the kind of grim dilemma it lives to dissolve.

2

Mitchell objects that a warrantless search is unnecessary in cases involving unconscious drivers because warrants these days can be obtained faster and more easily. But even in our age of rapid communication,

"[w]arrants inevitably take some time for police officers or prosecutors to complete and for magistrate judges to review. Telephonic and electronic warrants may still require officers to follow time-consuming formalities designed to create an adequate record, such as preparing a duplicate warrant before calling the magistrate judge.... And improvements in communications technology do not guarantee that a magistrate judge will be available when an officer needs a warrant after making a late-night arrest." McNeely, 569 U.S., at 155, 133 S.Ct. 1552.

In other words, with better technology, the

time required has shrunk, but it has not disappeared. In the emergency scenarios created by unconscious drivers, forcing police to put off other tasks for even a relatively short period of time may have terrible collateral costs. That is just what it means for these situations to be emergencies.

IV

When police have probable cause to believe a person has committed a drunk-driving offense and the driver's unconsciousness or stupor requires him to be taken to the hospital or similar facility before police have a reasonable opportunity to administer a standard evidentiary breath test, they may almost always order a warrantless blood test to measure the driver's BAC without offending the Fourth Amendment. We do not rule out the possibility that in an unusual case a defendant would be able to show that his blood would not have been drawn if police had not been seeking BAC information, and that police could not have reasonably judged that a warrant application would interfere with other pressing needs or duties. Because Mitchell did not have a chance to attempt to make that showing, a remand for that purpose is necessary.

* * *

The judgment of the Supreme Court of Wisconsin is vacated, and the case is remanded for further proceedings.

It is so ordered.

Kansas v. Glover (April 6, 2020) [Notes omitted]

JUSTICE THOMAS delivered the opinion of the Court.

This case presents the question whether a police officer violates the Fourth Amendment by initiating an investigative traffic stop after running a vehicle's license plate and learning that the registered owner has a revoked driver's license. We hold that when the officer lacks information negating an inference that the owner is the driver of the vehicle, the stop is reasonable.

I

Kansas charged respondent Charles Glover, Jr., with driving as a habitual violator after a traffic stop revealed that he was driving with a revoked license. See Kan. Stat. Ann. §8-285(a)(3) (2001). Glover filed a motion to suppress all evidence seized during the stop, claiming that the officer lacked reasonable suspicion. Neither Glover nor the police officer testified at the suppression hearing. Instead, the parties stipulated to the following facts:

"1. Deputy Mark Mehrer is a certified law enforcement officer employed by the Douglas County Kansas Sheriff's Office.

2. On April 28, 2016, Deputy Mehrer was on routine patrol in Douglas County when he observed a 1995 Chevrolet 1500 pickup truck with Kansas plate 295ATJ.

3. Deputy Mehrer ran Kansas plate 295ATJ through the Kansas Department of Revenue's file service. The registration came back to a 1995 Chevrolet 1500 pickup truck.

4. Kansas Department of Revenue files indicated the truck was registered to Charles Glover Jr. The files also indicated that Mr. Glover had a revoked driver's license in the State of Kansas.

5. Deputy Mehrer assumed the registered owner of the truck was also the driver, Charles Glover Jr.

6. Deputy Mehrer did not observe any traffic infractions, and did not attempt to identify the driver [of] the truck. Based solely on the information that the registered owner of the truck was revoked, Deputy Mehrer initiated a traffic stop.

7. The driver of the truck was identified as the defendant, Charles Glover Jr." App. to Pet. for Cert. 60-61.

The District Court granted Glover's motion to suppress. The Court of Appeals reversed, holding that "it was reasonable for [Deputy] Mehrer to infer that the driver was the owner of the vehicle" because "there were specific and articulable facts from which the officer's common-sense inference gave rise to a reasonable suspicion." 54 Kan. App. 2d 377, 385, 400 P. 3d 182, 188 (2017).

The Kansas Supreme Court reversed. According to the court, Deputy Mehrer did not have reasonable suspicion because his inference that Glover was behind the wheel amounted to "only a hunch" that Glover was engaging in criminal activity. 308 Kan. 590, 591, 422 P. 3d 64, 66 (2018). The court further explained that Deputy Mehrer's "hunch" involved "applying and stacking unstated assumptions that are unreasonable without further factual basis," namely, that "the registered owner was likely the primary driver of the vehicle" and that "the owner will likely disregard the suspension or revocation order and continue to drive." Id., at 595-597, 422 P. 3d, at 68-70. We granted Kansas' petition for a writ of certiorari, 587 U. S. ___ (2019), and now reverse.

II

Under this Court's precedents, the Fourth Amendment permits an officer to initiate a brief investigative traffic stop when he has "a particularized and objective basis for suspecting the particular person stopped of criminal activity." United States v. Cortez, 449 U. S. 411, 417-418 (1981); see also Terry v. Ohio, 392 U. S. 1, 21-22 (1968). "Although a mere `hunch' does not create reasonable suspicion, the level of suspicion the standard requires is considerably less than proof of wrongdoing by a preponderance of the evidence, and obviously less than is necessary for probable cause." Prado Navarette v. California, 572 U. S. 393, 397 (2014) (quotation altered); United States v. Sokolow, 490 U. S. 1, 7 (1989).

Because it is a "less demanding" standard, "reasonable suspicion can be established with information that is different in quantity or content than that required to establish probable cause." Alabama v. White, 496 U. S. 325, 330 (1990). The standard "depends on the factual and practical considerations of everyday life on which reasonable and prudent men, not legal technicians, act." Navarette, supra, at 402 (quoting Ornelas v. United States, 517 U. S. 690, 695 (1996) (emphasis added; internal quotation marks omitted)). Courts "cannot reasonably demand scientific certainty... where none exists." Illinois v. Wardlow, 528 U. S. 119, 125 (2000). Rather, they must permit officers to make "commonsense judgments and inferences about human behavior." Ibid.; see also Navarette, supra, at 403 (noting that an officer "`need not rule out the possibility of innocent conduct'").

III

We have previously recognized that States have a "vital interest in ensuring that only those qualified to do so are permitted to operate motor vehicles [and] that licensing, registration, and vehicle inspection requirements are being observed." Delaware v. Prouse, 440 U. S. 648, 658 (1979). With this in mind, we turn to whether the facts known to Deputy Mehrer at the time of the stop gave rise to reasonable suspicion. We conclude that they did.

Before initiating the stop, Deputy Mehrer observed an individual operating a 1995 Chevrolet 1500 pickup truck with Kansas plate 295ATJ. He also knew that the registered owner of the truck had a revoked license and that the model of the truck matched the observed vehicle. From these three facts, Deputy Mehrer drew the commonsense inference that Glover was likely the driver of the vehicle, which provided more than reasonable suspicion to initiate the stop.

The fact that the registered owner of a vehicle is not always the driver of the vehicle does not negate the reasonableness of Deputy Mehrer's inference. Such is the case with all reasonable inferences. The reasonable suspicion inquiry "falls considerably short" of 51% accuracy, see United States v. Arvizu, 534 U. S. 266, 274 (2002), for, as we have explained, "[t]o be reasonable is not to be perfect," Heien v. North Carolina, 574 U. S. 54, 60 (2014).

Glover's revoked license does not render Deputy Mehrer's inference unreasonable either. Empirical studies demonstrate what common experience readily reveals: Drivers with revoked licenses frequently continue to drive and therefore to pose safety risks to other motorists and pedestrians. See, e.g., 2 T. Neuman et al., National Coop. Hwy. Research Program Report 500: A Guide for Addressing Collisions Involving Unlicensed Drivers and Drivers With Suspended or Revoked Licenses, p. III-1 (2003) (noting that 75% of drivers with suspended or revoked licenses continue to drive); National Hwy. and Traffic Safety Admin., Research Note: Driver License Compliance Status in Fatal Crashes 2 (Oct. 2014) (noting that approximately 19% of motor vehicle fatalities from 2008-2012 "involved drivers with invalid licenses").

Although common sense suffices to justify this inference, Kansas law reinforces that it is reasonable to infer that an individual with a revoked license may continue driving. The State's license-revocation scheme covers drivers who have already demonstrated a disregard for the law or are categorically unfit to drive. The Division of Vehicles of the Kansas Department of Revenue (Division) "shall" revoke a driver's license upon certain convictions for involuntary manslaughter, vehicular homicide, battery, reckless driving, fleeing or attempting to elude a police officer, or conviction of a felony in which a motor vehicle is used. Kan. Stat. Ann. §§8-254(a), 8-252. Reckless driving is defined as "driv[ing] any vehicle in willful or wanton disregard for the safety of persons or property." §8-1566(a). The Division also has discretion to revoke a license if a driver "[h]as

been convicted with such frequency of serious offenses against traffic regulations governing the movement of vehicles as to indicate a disrespect for traffic laws and a disregard for the safety of other persons on the highways," "has been convicted of three or more moving traffic violations committed on separate occasions within a 12-month period," "is incompetent to drive a motor vehicle," or "has been convicted of a moving traffic violation, committed at a time when the person's driving privileges were restricted, suspended[,] or revoked." §§8-255(a)(1)-(4). Other reasons include violating license restrictions, §8-245(c), being under house arrest, §21-6609(c), and being a habitual violator, §8-286, which Kansas defines as a resident or nonresident who has been convicted three or more times within the past five years of certain enumerated driving offenses, §8-285. The concerns motivating the State's various grounds for revocation lend further credence to the inference that a registered owner with a revoked Kansas driver's license might be the one driving the vehicle.

IV

Glover and the dissent respond with two arguments as to why Deputy Mehrer lacked reasonable suspicion. Neither is persuasive.

A

First, Glover and the dissent argue that Deputy Mehrer's inference was unreasonable because it was not grounded in his law enforcement training or experience. Nothing in our Fourth Amendment precedent supports the notion that, in determining whether reasonable suspicion exists, an officer can draw inferences based on knowledge gained only through law enforcement training and experience. We have repeatedly recognized the opposite. In Navarette, we noted a number of behaviors—including driving in the median, crossing the center line on a highway, and swerving—that as a matter of common sense provide "sound indicia of drunk driving." 572 U. S., at 402. In Wardlow, we made the unremarkable observation that "[h]eadlong flight— wherever it occurs—is the consummate act of evasion" and therefore could factor into a police officer's reasonable suspicion determination. 528 U. S., at 124. And in Sokolow, we recognized that the defendant's method of payment for an airplane ticket contributed to the agents' reasonable suspicion of drug trafficking because we "fe[lt] confident" that "[m]ost business travelers . . . purchase airline tickets by credit card or check" rather than cash. 490 U. S., at 8-9. So too here. The inference that the driver of a car is its registered owner does not require any specialized training; rather, it is a reasonable inference made by ordinary people on a daily basis.

The dissent reads our cases differently, contending that they permit an officer to use only the common sense derived from his "experiences in law enforcement." Post, at 5 (opinion of SOTOMAYOR, J.). Such a standard defies the "common sense" understanding of common sense, i.e., information that is accessible to people generally, not just some specialized subset of society. More importantly, this standard appears nowhere in our precedent. In fact, we have stated that reasonable suspicion is an "abstract" concept that cannot be reduced to "a neat set of legal rules," Arvizu, 534 U. S., at 274 (internal quotation marks omitted), and we have repeatedly rejected courts' efforts to impose a rigid structure on the concept of reasonableness, ibid.; Sokolow, 490 U. S., at 7-8. This is precisely what the dissent's rule would do by insisting that officers must be treated as bifurcated persons, completely precluded from drawing factual inferences based on the commonly held knowledge they have acquired in their everyday lives.

The dissent's rule would also impose on police the burden of pointing to specific training materials or field experiences justifying reasonable suspicion for the myriad infractions in municipal criminal codes. And by removing common sense as a source of evidence, the dissent would considerably narrow the daylight between the showing required for probable cause and the "less stringent" showing required for reasonable suspicion. Prouse, 440 U. S., at 654; see White, 496 U. S., at 330. Finally, it would impermissibly tie a traffic stop's validity to the officer's length of service. See Devenpeck v. Alford, 543 U. S. 146, 154 (2004). Such requirements are inconsistent with our Fourth Amendment jurisprudence, and we decline to adopt them here.

In reaching this conclusion, we in no way minimize the significant role that specialized training and experience routinely play in law enforcement investigations. See, e.g., Arvizu, 534 U. S., at 273-274. We simply hold that such experience is not required in every instance.

B

Glover and the dissent also contend that adopting Kansas' view would eviscerate the need for officers to base reasonable suspicion on "specific and articulable facts" particularized to the individual, see Terry, 392 U. S., at 21, because police could instead rely exclusively on probabilities. Their argument carries little force.

As an initial matter, we have previously stated that officers, like jurors, may rely on probabilities in the reasonable suspicion context. See Sokolow, 490 U. S., at 8-9; Cortez, 449 U. S., at 418. Moreover, as explained above, Deputy Mehrer did not rely exclusively on probabilities. He knew that the license plate was linked to a truck matching the observed vehicle and that the registered owner of the vehicle had a revoked license. Based on these minimal facts, he used common sense to form a reasonable suspicion that a specific individual was potentially engaged in specific criminal activity—driving with a revoked license. Traffic stops of this nature do not delegate to officers "broad and unlimited discretion" to stop drivers at random. United States v. Brignoni-

Ponce, 422 U. S. 873, 882 (1975). Nor do they allow officers to stop drivers whose conduct is no different from any other driver's. See Brown v. Texas, 443 U. S. 47, 52 (1979). Accordingly, combining database information and commonsense judgments in this context is fully consonant with this Court's Fourth Amendment precedents.[1]

V

This Court's precedents have repeatedly affirmed that "`the ultimate touchstone of the Fourth Amendment is "reasonableness."'" Heien, 574 U. S., at 60 (quoting Riley v. California, 573 U. S. 373, 381 (2014)). Under the totality of the circumstances of this case, Deputy Mehrer drew an entirely reasonable inference that Glover was driving while his license was revoked.

We emphasize the narrow scope of our holding. Like all seizures, "[t]he officer's action must be `justified at its inception.'" Hiibel v. Sixth Judicial Dist. Court of Nev., Humboldt Cty., 542 U. S. 177, 185 (2004) (quoting United States v. Sharpe, 470 U. S. 675, 682 (1985)). "The standard takes into account the totality of the circumstances—the whole picture." Navarette, 572 U. S., at 397 (internal quotation marks omitted). As a result, the presence of additional facts might dispel reasonable suspicion. See Terry, supra, at 28. For example, if an officer knows that the registered owner of the vehicle is in his mid-sixties but observes that the driver is in her mid-twenties, then the totality of the circumstances would not "raise a suspicion that the particular individual being stopped is engaged in wrongdoing." Cortez, 449 U. S., at 418; Ornelas, 517 U. S., at 696 ("`[e]ach case is to be decided on its own facts and circumstances'" (quoting Ker v. California, 374 U. S. 23, 33 (1963))). Here, Deputy Mehrer possessed no exculpatory information—let alone sufficient information to rebut the reasonable inference that Glover was driving his own truck—and thus the stop was justified.[2]

* * *

For the foregoing reasons, we reverse the judgment of the Kansas Supreme Court, and we remand the case for further proceedings not inconsistent with this opinion.

It is so ordered.

Torres v. Madrid (March 25, 2021) [Note omitted]

Chief Justice Roberts delivered the opinion of the Court.

The Fourth Amendment prohibits unreasonable "seizures" to safeguard "[t]he right of the people to be secure in their persons." Under our cases, an officer seizes a person when he uses force to apprehend her. The question in this case is whether a seizure occurs when an officer shoots someone who temporarily eludes capture after the shooting. The answer is yes: The application of physical force to the body of a person with intent to restrain is a seizure, even if the force does not succeed in subduing the person.

I

At dawn on July 15, 2014, four New Mexico State Police officers arrived at an apartment complex in Albuquerque to execute an arrest warrant for a woman accused of white collar crimes, but also "suspected of having been involved in drug trafficking, murder, and other violent crimes." App. to Pet. for Cert. 11a. What happened next is hotly contested. We recount the facts in the light most favorable to petitioner Roxanne Torres because the court below granted summary judgment to Officers Janice Madrid and Richard Williamson, the two respondents here. Tolan v. Cotton, 572 U. S. 650, 655–656 (2014) (per curiam).

The officers observed Torres standing with another person near a Toyota FJ Cruiser in the parking lot of the complex. Officer Williamson concluded that neither Torres nor her companion was the target of the warrant. As the officers approached the vehicle, the companion departed, and Torres—at the time experiencing methamphetamine withdrawal—got into the driver's seat. The officers attempted to speak with her, but she did not notice their presence until one of them tried to open the door of her car.

Although the officers wore tactical vests marked with police identification, Torres saw only that they had guns. She thought the officers were carjackers trying to steal her car, and she hit the gas to escape them. Neither Officer Madrid nor Officer Williamson, according to Torres, stood in the path of the vehicle, but both fired their service pistols to stop her. All told, the two officers fired 13 shots at Torres, striking her twice in the back and temporarily paralyzing her left arm.

Steering with her right arm, Torres accelerated through the fusillade of bullets, exited the apartment complex, drove a short distance, and stopped in a parking lot. After asking a bystander to report an attempted carjacking, Torres stole a Kia Soul that happened to be idling nearby and drove 75 miles to Grants, New Mexico. The good news for Torres was that the hospital in Grants was able to airlift her to another hospital where she could receive appropriate care. The bad news was that the hospital was back in Albuquerque, where the police arrested her the next day. She pleaded no contest to aggravated fleeing from a law enforcement officer, assault on a peace officer, and unlawfully taking a motor vehicle.

Torres later sought damages from Officers Madrid and Williamson under 42 U. S. C. §1983, which provides a cause of action for the deprivation of constitutional rights by persons acting under color of state law. She claimed that the officers applied excessive force, making the shooting an unreasonable seizure under the Fourth Amendment. The District Court granted summary judgment to the officers, and the Court of Appeals for the Tenth Circuit affirmed on the ground that "a suspect's continued flight after being shot by police negates a Fourth Amendment excessive-force claim." 769 Fed. Appx. 654, 657 (2019). The court relied on Circuit precedent providing that "no seizure can occur unless there is physical touch or a show of authority," and that "such physical touch (or force) must terminate the suspect's movement" or otherwise give rise to physical control over the suspect. Brooks v. Gaenzle, 614 F. 3d 1213, 1223 (2010).

We granted certiorari. 589 U. S. ____ (2019).

II

The Fourth Amendment protects "[t]he right of the people to be secure in their persons, houses, papers, and effects, against unreasonable searches and seizures." This case concerns the "seizure" of a "person," which can take the form of "physical force" or a "show of authority" that "in some way restrain[s] the liberty" of the person. Terry v. Ohio, 392 U. S. 1, 19, n. 16 (1968). The question before us is whether the application of physical force is a seizure if the force, despite hitting its target, fails to stop the person.

We largely covered this ground in California v. Hodari D., 499 U. S. 621 (1991). There we interpreted the term "seizure" by consulting the common law of arrest, the "quintessential 'seizure of the person' under our Fourth Amendment jurisprudence." Id., at 624. As Justice Scalia explained for himself and six other Members of the Court, the common law treated "the mere grasping or application of physical force with lawful authority" as an arrest, "whether or not it succeeded in subduing the arrestee." Ibid.; see id., at 625 ("merely touching" sufficient to constitute an arrest). Put another way, an officer's application of physical force to the body of a person " 'for the purpose of arresting him' " was itself an arrest—not an attempted arrest—even if the person did not yield. Id., at 624 (quoting

Whithead v. Keyes, 85 Mass. 495, 501 (1862)).

The common law distinguished the application of force from a show of authority, such as an order for a suspect to halt. The latter does not become an arrest unless and until the arrestee complies with the demand. As the Court explained in Hodari D., "[a]n arrest requires either physical force . . . or, where that is absent, submission to the assertion of authority." 499 U. S., at 626 (emphasis in original).

Hodari D. articulates two pertinent principles. First, common law arrests are Fourth Amendment seizures. And second, the common law considered the application of force to the body of a person with intent to restrain to be an arrest, no matter whether the arrestee escaped. We need not decide whether Hodari D., which principally concerned a show of authority, controls the outcome of this case as a matter of stare decisis, because we independently reach the same conclusions.

At the adoption of the Fourth Amendment, a "seizure" was the "act of taking by warrant" or "of laying hold on suddenly"—for example, when an "officer seizes a thief." 2 N. Webster, An American Dictionary of the English Language 67 (1828) (Webster) (emphasis deleted). A seizure did not necessarily result in actual control or detention. It is true that, when speaking of property, "[f]rom the time of the founding to the present, the word 'seizure' has meant a 'taking possession.'" Hodari D., 499 U. S., at 624 (quoting 2 Webster 67). But the Framers selected a term— seizure—broad enough to apply to all the concerns of the Fourth Amendment: "persons," as well as "houses, papers, and effects." As applied to a person, "[t]he word 'seizure' readily bears the meaning of a laying on of hands or application of physical force to restrain movement, even when it is ultimately unsuccessful." 499 U. S., at 626. Then, as now, an ordinary user of the English language could remark: "She seized the purse-snatcher, but he broke out of her grasp." Ibid.

The "seizure" of a "person" plainly refers to an arrest. That linkage existed at the founding. Samuel Johnson, for example, defined an "arrest" as "[a]ny . . . seizure of the person." 1 A Dictionary of the English Language 108 (4th ed. 1773). And that linkage persists today. As we have repeatedly recognized, "the arrest of a person is quintessentially a seizure." Payton v. New York, 445 U. S. 573, 585 (1980) (internal quotation marks omitted); see Hodari D., 499 U. S., at 624.

Because arrests are seizures of a person, Hodari D. properly looked to the common law of arrest for "historical understandings 'of what was deemed an unreasonable search and seizure when the Fourth Amendment was adopted.'" Carpenter v. United States, 585 U. S. ___, ___ (2018) (slip op., at 6) (quoting Carroll v. United States, 267 U. S. 132, 149 (1925); alteration omitted). Sometimes the historical record will not yield a well-settled legal rule. See, e.g., Atwater v. Lago Vista, 532 U. S. 318, 327–328 (2001); Payton, 445 U. S., at 593– 596. We do not face that problem here. The cases and commentary speak with virtual unanimity on the question before us today.

The common law rule identified in Hodari D.—that the application of force gives rise to an arrest, even if the officer does not secure control over the arrestee—achieved recognition to such an extent that English lawyers could confidently (and accurately) proclaim that "[a]ll the authorities, from the earliest time to the present, establish that a corporal touch is sufficient to constitute an arrest, even though the defendant do not submit." Nicholl v. Darley, 2 Y. & J. 399, 400, 148 Eng. Rep. 974 (Exch. 1828) (citing Hodges v. Marks, Cro. Jac. 485, 79 Eng. Rep. 414 (K. B. 1615)). The slightest application of force could satisfy this rule. In Genner v. Sparks, 6 Mod. 173, 87 Eng. Rep. 928 (Q. B. 1704), the defendant did not submit to the authority of an arrest warrant, but the court explained that the bailiff would have made an arrest if he "had but touched the defendant even with the end of his finger." Ibid., 87 Eng. Rep., at 929. So too, if a "bailiff caught one by the hand (whom he had a warrant to arrest) as he held it out of a window," that alone would accomplish an arrest. Anonymus, 1 Vent. 306, 86 Eng. Rep. 197 (K. B. 1677). The touching of the person—frequently called a laying of hands— was enough. See Dunscomb v. Smith, Cro. Car. 164, 79 Eng. Rep. 743 (K. B. 1629). Only later did English law grow to recognize arrest without touching through a submission to a show of authority. See Horner v. Battyn, Bull. N. P. 62 (K. B. 1738), reprinted in W. Loyd, Cases on Civil Procedure 798 (1916). Even so, the traditional rule persisted that all an arrest required was "corporal seising or touching the defendant's body." 3 W. Blackstone, Commentaries on the Laws of England 288 (1768) (Blackstone).

Early American courts adopted this mere-touch rule from England, just as they embraced other common law principles of search and seizure. See Wilson v. Arkansas, 514 U. S. 927, 933 (1995). Justice Baldwin, instructing a jury in his capacity as Circuit Justice, defined an arrest to include "touching or putting hands upon [the arrestee] in the execution of process." United States v. Benner, 24 F. Cas. 1084, 1086–1087 (No. 14,568) (CC ED Pa. 1830). State courts agreed that "any touching, however slight, is enough," Butler v. Washburn, 25 N. H. 251, 258 (1852), provided the officer made his intent to arrest clear, see Jones v. Jones, 35 N. C. 448, 448–449 (1852). Courts continued to hold that an arrest required only the application of force—not control or custody— through the framing of the Fourteenth Amendment, which incorporated the protections of the Fourth Amendment against the States. See Whitehead, 85 Mass., at 501; Searls v. Viets, 2 Thomp. & C. 224, 226 (N. Y. Sup. Ct. 1873); State v. Dennis, 16 Del. 433, 436–437, 43 A. 261, 262 (1895); see also H. Voorhees, The Law of Arrest in

Civil and Criminal Actions §74, p. 44 (1904).

Stated simply, the cases "abundantly shew that the slightest touch [was] an arrest in point of law." Nicholl, 2 Y. & J., at 404, 148 Eng. Rep., at 976. Indeed, it was not even required that the officer have, at the time of such an arrest, "the power of keeping the party so arrested under restraint." Sandon v. Jervis, El. Bl. & El. 935, 940, 120 Eng. Rep. 758, 760 (Q. B. 1858). The consequences would be "pernicious," an English judge worried, if the question of control "were perpetually to be submitted to a jury." Ibid.; cf. 3 Blackstone 120 (describing how "[t]he least touching of another's person" could satisfy the common law definition of force to commit battery, "for the law cannot draw the line between different degrees of violence").

This case, of course, does not involve "laying hands," Sheriff v. Godfrey, 7 Mod. 288, 289, 87 Eng. Rep. 1247 (K. B. 1739), but instead a shooting. Neither the parties nor the United States as amicus curiae suggests that the officers' use of bullets to restrain Torres alters the analysis in any way. And we are aware of no common law authority addressing an arrest under such circumstances, or indeed any case involving an application of force from a distance.

The closest decision seems to be Countess of Rutland's Case, 6 Co. Rep. 52b, 77 Eng. Rep. 332 (Star Chamber 1605). In that case, serjeants-at-mace tracked down Isabel Holcroft, Countess of Rutland, to execute a writ for a judgment of debt. They "shewed her their mace, and touching her body with it, said to her, we arrest you, madam." Id., at 54a, 77 Eng. Rep., at 336. We think the case is best understood as an example of an arrest made by touching with an object, for the serjeants-at-mace announced the arrest at the time they touched the countess with the mace. See, e.g., Hodges, Cro. Jac., at 485, 79 Eng. Rep., at 414 (similar announcement upon laying of hands). Maybe the arrest could be viewed as a submission to a show of authority, because a mace served not only as a weapon but also as an insignia of office. See Kelly, The Great Mace, and Other Corporation Insignia of the Borough of Leicester, 3 Transactions of the Royal Hist. Soc. 295, 296–301 (1874). But that view is difficult to reconcile with the fact that English courts did not recognize arrest by submission to a show of authority until the following century. See supra, at 6.1*

However one reads Countess of Rutland, we see no basis for drawing an artificial line between grasping with a hand and other means of applying physical force to effect an arrest. The dissent (though not the officers) argues that the common law limited arrests by force to the literal placement of hands on the suspect, because no court published an opinion discussing a suspect who continued to flee after being hit with a bullet or some other weapon. See post, at 18–20 (opinion of Gorsuch, J.). This objection calls to mind the unavailing defense of the person who "persistently denied that he had laid hands upon a priest, for he had only cudgelled and kicked him." 2 S. Pufendorf, De Jure Naturae et Gentium 795 (C. Oldfather & W. Oldfather transl. 1934). The required "corporal seising or touching the defendant's body" can be as readily accomplished by a bullet as by the end of a finger. 3 Blackstone 288.

We will not carve out this greater intrusion on personal security from the mere-touch rule just because founding- era courts did not confront apprehension by firearm. While firearms have existed for a millennium and were certainly familiar at the founding, we have observed that law enforcement did not carry handguns until the latter half of the 19th century, at which point "it bec[a]me possible to use deadly force from a distance as a means of apprehension." Tennessee v. Garner, 471 U. S. 1, 14–15 (1985). So it should come as no surprise that neither we nor the dissent has located a common law case in which an officer used a gun to apprehend a suspect. Cf. post, at 20 (discussing Dickenson v. Watson, Jones, T. 205, 84 Eng. Rep. 1218, 1218–1219 (K. B. 1682), in which a tax collector accidentally discharged hailshot into a passerby's eye). But the focus of the Fourth Amendment is "the privacy and security of individuals," not the particular manner of "arbitrary invasion[ ] by governmental officials." Camara v. Municipal Court of City and County of San Francisco, 387 U. S. 523, 528 (1967). As noted, our precedent protects "that degree of privacy against government that existed when the Fourth Amendment was adopted," Kyllo v. United States, 533 U. S. 27, 34 (2001)—a protection that extends to "[s]ubtler and more far-reaching means of invading privacy" adopted only later, Olmstead v. United States, 277 U. S. 438, 473 (1928) (Brandeis, J., dissenting). There is nothing subtle about a bullet, but the Fourth Amendment preserves personal security with respect to methods of apprehension old and new.

We stress, however, that the application of the common law rule does not transform every physical contact between a government employee and a member of the public into a Fourth Amendment seizure. A seizure requires the use of force with intent to restrain. Accidental force will not qualify. See County of Sacramento v. Lewis, 523 U. S. 833, 844 (1998). Nor will force intentionally applied for some other purpose satisfy this rule. In this opinion, we consider only force used to apprehend. We do not accept the dissent's invitation to opine on matters not presented here—pepper spray, flash-bang grenades, lasers, and more. Post, at 23.

Moreover, the appropriate inquiry is whether the challenged conduct objectively manifests an intent to restrain, for we rarely probe the subjective motivations of police officers in the Fourth Amendment context. See Nieves v. Bartlett,

587 U. S. ___, ___ (2019) (slip op., at 10). Only an objective test "allows the police to determine in advance whether the conduct contemplated will implicate the Fourth Amendment." Michigan v. Chesternut, 486 U. S. 567, 574 (1988). While a mere touch can be enough for a seizure, the amount of force remains pertinent in assessing the objective intent to restrain. A tap on the shoulder to get one's attention will rarely exhibit such an intent. See INS v. Delgado, 466 U. S. 210, 220 (1984); Jones, 35 N. C., at 448–449.

Nor does the seizure depend on the subjective perceptions of the seized person. Here, for example, Torres claims to have perceived the officers' actions as an attempted carjacking. But the conduct of the officers—ordering Torres to stop and then shooting to restrain her movement— satisfies the objective test for a seizure, regardless whether Torres comprehended the governmental character of their actions.

The rule we announce today is narrow. In addition to the requirement of intent to restrain, a seizure by force—absent submission—lasts only as long as the application of force. That is to say that the Fourth Amendment does not recognize any "continuing arrest during the period of fugitivity." Hodari D., 499 U. S., at 625. The fleeting nature of some seizures by force undoubtedly may inform what damages a civil plaintiff may recover, and what evidence a criminal defendant may exclude from trial. See, e.g., Utah v. Strieff, 579 U. S. ___, ___ (2016) (slip op., at 4). But brief seizures are seizures all the same.

Applying these principles to the facts viewed in the light most favorable to Torres, the officers' shooting applied physical force to her body and objectively manifested an intent to restrain her from driving away. We therefore conclude that the officers seized Torres for the instant that the bullets struck her.

III

In place of the rule that the application of force completes an arrest even if the arrestee eludes custody, the officers would introduce a single test for all types of seizures: intentional acquisition of control. This alternative rule is inconsistent with the history of the Fourth Amendment and our cases.

A

The officers and their amici stress that common law rules are not automatically "elevated to constitutional proscriptions," Hodari D., 499 U. S., at 626, n. 2, especially if they are "distorted almost beyond recognition when literally applied," Garner, 471 U. S., at 15. In their view, the common law doctrine recognized in Hodari D. is just "a narrow legal rule intended to govern liability in civil cases involving debtors." Brief for National Association of Counties et al. as Amici Curiae 12. The dissent presses the same argument. See post, at 14–17.

But the common law did not define the arrest of a debtor any differently from the arrest of a felon. Whether the arrest was authorized by a criminal indictment or a civil writ, "there must be a corporal seizing, or touching the defendant's person; or, what is tantamount, a power of taking immediate possession of the body, and the party's submission thereto, and a declaration of the officer that he makes an arrest." 1 J. Backus, A Digest of Laws Relating to the Offices and Duties of Sheriff, Coroner and Constable 115–116 (1812). Treatises on the law governing criminal arrests cited Genner v. Sparks, 6 Mod. 173, 87 Eng. Rep. 928—the preeminent mere-touch case involving a debtor— for the proposition that, "[i]n making the arrest, the constable or party making it should actually seize or touch the offender's body, or otherwise restrain his liberty." 1 R. Burn, The Justice of the Peace 275 (28th ed. 1837). When English courts confronted arrests for criminal offenses, they too relied on precedents concerning arrests for civil offenses. See Bridgett v. Coyney, 1 Man. & Ryl. 1, 5–6 (K. B. 1827); Arrowsmith v. Le Mesurier, 2

Bos. & Pul. 211, 211–212, 127 Eng. Rep. 605, 606 (C. P. 1806). American courts likewise articulated a materially identical definition in criminal cases—that "[t]he arrest itself is the laying hands on the defendant," State v. Townsend, 5 Del. 487, 488 (Ct. Gen. Sess. 1854), or that an arrest is "the taking, seizing, or detaining of the person of another, either by touching him or putting hands on him," McAdams v. State, 30 Okla. Crim. 207, 210, 235 P. 241, 242 (1925).

This uniform definition also explains why an arrest by mere touch carried legal consequences in both the criminal and civil contexts. The point of an arrest was of course to take custody of a person to secure his appearance at a proceeding. But some arrests did not culminate in actual control of the individual, let alone a trip to the gaol or compter. See Nicholl, 2 Y. & J., at 403–404, 148 Eng. Rep., at 975–976. When an officer let an arrestee get away, the officer risked becoming a defendant himself in an action for "escape." See Perkins, The Law of Arrest, 25 Iowa L. Rev. 201, 204 (1940). The laying of hands constituted a taking custody and would expose the officer to liability for the escape of felons and debtors alike. See 1 M. Hale, Pleas of the Crown 590–591, 597, 603 (1736); 2 id., at 93 (no liability for escape "if the felon were not once in the hands of an officer"); see also Perkins, 25 Iowa L. Rev., at 206.

The tort of false imprisonment, which the dissent rightly acknowledges as the " 'closest analogy' to an arrest without probable cause," post, at 12 (quoting Wallace v. Kato, 549 U. S. 384, 388–389 (2007)), reinforces the conclusion that the common law considered touching to be a seizure. Stated generally, false imprisonment required "confinement," such as "taking a person into custody under an asserted legal authority." Restatement of Torts §§35, 41 (1934); see 3 Blackstone 127. But that element of confinement demanded no more than that the defendant "had

for one moment taken possession of the plaintiff's person"—including, "for example, if he had tapped her on the shoulder, and said, 'You are my prisoner.' " Simpson v. Hill, 1 Esp. 431, 431–432, 170 Eng. Rep. 409 (N. P. 1795); see Restatement of Torts §41, Comment h (noting that "the touching alone of the person against whom [legal authority] was asserted would be sufficient to constitute" confinement by arrest when the authority was valid). While the dissent emphasizes that "the court [in Simpson] proceeded to reject the plaintiff 's claim for false imprisonment," post, at 13, that was only because "the constable never touched the plaintiff, or took her into custody." 1 Esp., at 431, 170 Eng. Rep., at 409.

To be sure, the mere-touch rule was particularly well documented in cases involving the execution of civil process. An officer pursuing a debtor could not forcibly enter the debtor's home unless the debtor had escaped arrest, such as by fleeing after being touched. See Semayne's Case, 5 Co. Rep. 91a, 91b, 77 Eng. Rep. 194, 196 (K. B. 1604); see also Miller v. United States, 357 U. S. 301, 307 (1958). Officers seeking to execute criminal process, on the other hand, possessed greater pre-arrest authority to enter a felon's home. See Payton, 445 U. S., at 598. But the fact that the common law rules of arrest generated more litigation in the civil context proves only that creditors had ready recourse to the courts to pursue escape actions for unsatisfactory arrests. There is no reason to suspect that English jurists silently adopted a special definition of arrest only for debt collection—indeed, they told us just the opposite. See supra, at 12. Nothing specific to debt collection elevated escape from arrest into a justification for entry of the home. Whenever a person was "lawfully arrested for any Cause and afterwards escape[d], and shelter[ed] himself in a House," the officer could break open the doors of the house. 2 W. Hawkins, Pleas of the Crown 87 (1721) (emphasis added).

In any event, the officers and the dissent misapprehend the history of the Fourth Amendment by minimizing the role of practices in civil cases. "[A]rrests in civil suits were still common in America" at the founding. Long v. Ansell, 293 U. S. 76, 83 (1934). And questions regarding the legality of an arrest "typically arose in civil damages actions for trespass or false arrest." Payton, 445 U. S., at 592. Accordingly, this Court has not hesitated to rely on such decisions when interpreting the Fourth Amendment. See, e.g., United States v. Jones, 565 U. S. 400, 404–405 (2012); Boyd v. United States, 116 U. S. 616, 626 (1886). We see no reason to break with our settled approach in this case.

B

The officers and the dissent derive from our cases a different touchstone for the seizure of a person: "an intentional acquisition of physical control." Brower v. County of Inyo, 489 U. S. 593, 596 (1989). Under their alternative rule, the use of force becomes a seizure "only when there is a governmental termination of freedom of movement through means intentionally applied." Id., at 597 (emphasis deleted); see Brief for Respondents 12–15; post, at 6–7.

This approach improperly erases the distinction between seizures by control and seizures by force. In all fairness, we too have not always been attentive to this distinction when a case did not implicate the issue. See, e.g., Brendlin v. California, 551 U. S. 249, 254 (2007). But each type of seizure enjoys a separate common law pedigree that gives rise to a separate rule. See Hodari D., 499 U. S., at 624–625; A. Cornelius, The Law of Search and Seizure §47, pp. 163–164 (2d ed. 1930) (contrasting actual control with "constructive detention" by touching).

Unlike a seizure by force, a seizure by acquisition of control involves either voluntary submission to a show of authority or the termination of freedom of movement. A prime example of the latter comes from Brower, where the police seized a driver when he crashed into their roadblock. 489 U. S., at 598–599; see also, e.g., Scott v. Harris, 550 U. S. 372, 385 (2007) (ramming car off road); Williams v. Jones, Cas. t. Hard. 299, 301, 95 Eng. Rep. 193, 194 (K. B. 1736) (locking person in room). Under the common law rules of arrest, actual control is a necessary element for this type of seizure. See Wilgus, Arrest Without a Warrant, 22 Mich. L. Rev. 541, 553 (1924). Such a seizure requires that "a person be stopped by the very instrumentality set in motion or put in place in order to achieve that result." Brower, 489 U. S., at 599. But that requirement of control or submission never extended to seizures by force. See, e.g., Sandon, El. Bl. & El., at 940–941, 120 Eng. Rep., at 760.

As common law courts recognized, any such requirement of control would be difficult to apply in cases involving the application of force. See supra, at 7. At the most basic level, it will often be unclear when an officer succeeds in gaining control over a struggling suspect. Courts will puzzle over whether an officer exercises control when he grabs a suspect, when he tackles him, or only when he slaps on the cuffs. Neither the officers nor the dissent explains how long the control must be maintained—only for a moment, into the squad car, or all the way to the station house. To cite another example, counsel for the officers speculated that the shooting would have been a seizure if Torres stopped "maybe 50 feet" or "half a block" from the scene of the shooting to allow the officers to promptly acquire control. Tr. of Oral Arg. 45. None of this squares with our recognition that " '[a] seizure is a single act, and not a continuous fact.' " Hodari D., 499 U. S., at 625 (quoting Thompson v. Whitman, 18 Wall. 457, 471 (1874)). For centuries, the common law rule has avoided such line-drawing problems by clearly fixing the moment of the seizure.

IV

The dissent sees things differently. It insists that the term "seizure" has always entailed a taking of possession, whether the officer is seizing a person, a ship, or a promissory note. See post, at 6–7. But the facts of the cases and the language of the opinions confirm that the concept of possession included the "constructive detention" of persons "never actually brought within the physical control of the party making an arrest." Wilgus, 22 Mich. L. Rev., at 556 (emphasis deleted); see, e.g., Nicholl, 2 Y. & J., at 404, 148 Eng. Rep., at 976 (explaining that the "slightest touch" can constitute "custody"); Anonymus, 1 Vent., at 306, 86 Eng. Rep., at 197 (describing a touch as a "taking" of a person). Even the dissent acknowledges that a touch can establish a form of constructive possession. See post, at 20.

The dissent says that "common law courts never contemplated" that the touching itself could effect a seizure. Post, at 18. But one need only look at the many decisions adopting that definition of arrest. See supra, at 5–8, 12–13. The dissent can offer no case expressing doubt about the rule that the touching constitutes an arrest, much less refusing to apply that rule in any context—felon or debtor. And we have, as noted, definitively stated that "the arrest of a person is quintessentially a seizure." Payton, 445 U. S., at 585 (internal quotation marks omitted). The dissent's attempt to ignore arrests it appraises as "unfortunate" or "peculiar," post, at 15, 16, pays insufficient regard to the complete history underlying the Fourth Amendment.

The dissent argues that we advance a "schizophrenic reading of the word 'seizure.'" Post, at 7. But our cases demonstrate the unremarkable proposition that the nature of a seizure can depend on the nature of the object being seized. It is not surprising that the concept of constructive detention or the mere-touch rule developed in the context of seizures of a person—capable of fleeing and with an interest in doing so—rather than seizures of "houses, papers, and effects."

The dissent also criticizes us for "posit[ing] penumbras" of "privacy" and "personal security" in our analysis of the Fourth Amendment. Post, at 24. But the text of the Fourth Amendment expressly guarantees the "right of the people to be secure in their persons," and our earliest precedents recognized privacy as the "essence" of the Amendment—not some penumbral emanation. Boyd, 116 U. S., at 630. We have relied on that understanding in construing the meaning of the Amendment. See, e.g., Riley v. California, 573 U. S. 373, 403 (2014).

The dissent speculates that the real reason for today's decision is an "impulse" to provide relief to Torres, post, at 23, or maybe a desire "to make life easier for ourselves," post, at 22. It may even be, says the dissent, that the Court "at least hopes to be seen as trying" to achieve particular goals. Post, at 25. There is no call for such surmise. At the end of the day we simply agree with the analysis of the common law of arrest and its relation to the Fourth Amendment set forth thirty years ago by Justice Scalia, joined by six of his colleagues, rather than the competing view urged by the dissent today.

*　*　*

We hold that the application of physical force to the body of a person with intent to restrain is a seizure even if the person does not submit and is not subdued. Of course, a seizure is just the first step in the analysis. The Fourth Amendment does not forbid all or even most seizures—only unreasonable ones. All we decide today is that the officers seized Torres by shooting her with intent to restrain her movement. We leave open on remand any questions regarding the reasonableness of the seizure, the damages caused by the seizure, and the officers' entitlement to qualified immunity.

The judgment of the Court of Appeals is vacated, and the case is remanded for further proceedings consistent with this opinion.

It is so ordered.

Caniglia v. Strom (May 17, 2021)

Justice THOMAS, delivered the opinion of the Court.

Decades ago, this Court held that a warrantless search of an impounded vehicle for an unsecured firearm did not violate the Fourth Amendment. Cady v. Dombrowski, 413 U. S. 433 (1973). In reaching this conclusion, the Court observed that police officers who patrol the "public highways" are often called to discharge noncriminal "community caretaking functions," such as responding to disabled vehicles or investigating accidents. Id., at 441. The question today is whether Cady's acknowledgment of these "caretaking" duties creates a standalone doctrine that justifies warrantless searches and seizures in the home. It does not.

I

During an argument with his wife at their Rhode Island home, Edward Caniglia (petitioner) retrieved a handgun from the bedroom, put it on the dining room table, and asked his wife to "shoot [him] now and get it over with." She declined, and instead left to spend the night at a hotel. The next morning, when petitioner's wife discovered that she could not reach him by telephone, she called the police (respondents) to request a welfare check.

Respondents accompanied petitioner's wife to the home, where they encountered petitioner on the porch. Petitioner spoke with respondents and confirmed his wife's account of the argument, but denied that he was suicidal. Respondents, however, thought that petitioner posed a risk to himself or others. They called an ambulance, and petitioner agreed to go to the hospital for a psychiatric evaluation— but only after respondents allegedly promised not to confiscate his firearms. Once the ambulance had taken petitioner away, however, respondents seized the weapons. Guided by petitioner's wife— whom they allegedly misinformed about his wishes—respondents entered the home and took two handguns.

Petitioner sued, claiming that respondents violated the Fourth Amendment when they entered his home and seized him and his firearms without a warrant. The District Court granted summary judgment to respondents, and the First Circuit affirmed solely on the ground that the decision to remove petitioner and his firearms from the premises fell within a "community caretaking exception" to the warrant requirement. 953 F. 3d 112, 121-123, 131 and nn. 5, 9 (2020). Citing this Court's statement in Cady that police officers often have noncriminal reasons to interact with motorists on "public highways," 413 U. S. ___, at 441, the First Circuit extrapolated a freestanding community-caretaking exception that applies to both cars and homes. 953 F. 3d, at 124 ("Threats to individual and community safety are not confined to the highways"). Accordingly, the First Circuit saw no need to consider whether anyone had consented to respondents' actions; whether these actions were justified by "exigent circumstances"; or whether any state law permitted this kind of mental-health intervention. Id., at 122-123. All that mattered was that respondents' efforts to protect petitioner and those around him were "distinct from `the normal work of criminal investigation,'" fell "within the realm of reason," and generally tracked what the court viewed to be "sound police procedure." Id., at 123-128, 132-133. We granted certiorari. 592 U. S. ___ (2020).

II

The Fourth Amendment protects "[t]he right of the people to be secure in their persons, houses, papers, and effects, against unreasonable searches and seizures." The "`very core'" of this guarantee is "`the right of a man to retreat into his own home and there be free from unreasonable governmental intrusion.'" Florida v. Jardines, 569 U. S. 1, 6 (2013).

To be sure, the Fourth Amendment does not prohibit all unwelcome intrusions "on private property," ibid.—only "unreasonable" ones. We have thus recognized a few permissible invasions of the home and its curtilage. Perhaps most familiar, for example, are searches and seizures pursuant to a valid warrant. See Collins v. Virginia, 584 U. S. ___, ___-___ (2018) (slip op., at 5-6). We have also held that law enforcement officers may enter private property without a warrant when certain exigent circumstances exist, including the need to "`render emergency assistance to an injured occupant or to protect an occupant from imminent injury.'" Kentucky v. King, 563 U. S. 452, 460, 470 (2011); see also Brigham City v. Stuart, 547 U. S. 398, 403-404 (2006) (listing other examples of exigent circumstances). And, of course, officers may generally take actions that "`any private citizen might do'" without fear of liability. E.g., Jardines, 569 U. S. ___, at 8 (approaching a home and knocking on the front door).

The First Circuit's "community caretaking" rule, however, goes beyond anything this Court has recognized. The decision below assumed that respondents lacked a warrant or consent, and it expressly disclaimed the possibility that they were reacting to a crime. The court also declined to consider whether any recognized exigent circumstances were present because respondents had forfeited the point. Nor did it find that respondents' actions were akin to what a private citizen might have had authority to do if petitioner's wife had approached a neighbor for assistance instead of the police.

Neither the holding nor logic of Cady justified that approach. True, Cady also involved a warrantless search for a firearm. But the location of that search was an impounded vehicle—not a home—"`a constitutional difference'" that the opinion repeatedly stressed. 413 U. S. ___, at 439; see also id., at 440-442. In fact, Cady expressly contrasted its treatment of a vehicle already under police control with a search of a car "parked adjacent to the dwelling place of the owner." Id., at 446-448 (citing Coolidge v. New Hampshire, 403 U. S. 443 (1971)).

Cady's unmistakable distinction between vehicles and homes also places into proper context its reference to "community caretaking." This quote comes from a portion of the opinion explaining that the "frequency with which . . . vehicle[s] can become disabled or involved in . . . accident[s] on public highways" often requires police to perform noncriminal "community caretaking functions," such as providing aid to motorists. 413 U. S. ___, at 441. But, this recognition that police officers perform many civic tasks in modern society was just that—a recognition that these tasks exist, and not an open-ended license to perform them anywhere.

* * *

What is reasonable for vehicles is different from what is reasonable for homes. Cady acknowledged as much, and this Court has repeatedly "declined to expand the scope of . . . exceptions to the warrant requirement to permit warrantless entry into the home." Collins, 584 U. S. ___, at ___ (slip op., at 8). We thus vacate the judgment below and remand for further proceedings consistent with this opinion.

It is so ordered.

US v. Cooley (June 1, 2021)

Justice BREYER, delivered the opinion of the Court.

The question presented is whether an Indian tribe's police officer has authority to detain temporarily and to search a non-Indian on a public right-of-way that runs through an Indian reservation. The search and detention, we assume, took place based on a potential violation of state or federal law prior to the suspect's transport to the proper nontribal authorities for prosecution.

We have previously noted that a tribe retains inherent sovereign authority to address "conduct [that] threatens or has some direct effect on . . . the health or welfare of the tribe." Montana v. United States, 450 U. S. 544, 566 (1981); see also Strate v. A-1 Contractors, 520 U. S. 438, 456, n. 11 (1997). We believe this statement of law governs here. And we hold the tribal officer possesses the authority at issue.

I

Late at night in February 2016, Officer James Saylor of the Crow Police Department was driving east on United States Highway 212, a public right-of-way within the Crow Reservation, located within the State of Montana. Saylor saw a truck parked on the westbound side of the highway. Believing the occupants might need assistance, Saylor approached the truck and spoke to the driver, Joshua James Cooley. Saylor noticed that Cooley had "watery, bloodshot eyes" and "appeared to be non-native." App. to Pet. for Cert. 95a. Saylor also noticed two semiautomatic rifles lying on the front seat. Eventually fearing violence, Saylor ordered Cooley out of the truck and conducted a patdown search. He called tribal and county officers for assistance. While waiting for the officers to arrive, Saylor returned to the truck. He saw a glass pipe and plastic bag that contained methamphetamine. The other officers, including an officer with the federal Bureau of Indian Affairs, then arrived. They directed Saylor to seize all contraband in plain view, leading him to discover more methamphetamine. Saylor took Cooley to the Crow Police Department where federal and local officers further questioned Cooley.

In April 2016, a federal grand jury indicted Cooley on drug and gun offenses. See 21 U. S. C. §841(a)(1); 18 U. S. C. §924(c)(1)(A). The District Court granted Cooley's motion to suppress the drug evidence that Saylor had seized. It reasoned that Saylor, as a Crow Tribe police officer, lacked the authority to investigate nonapparent violations of state or federal law by a non-Indian on a public right-of-way crossing the reservation.

The Government appealed. See 18 U. S. C. §3731. The Ninth Circuit affirmed the District Court's evidencesuppression determination. The Ninth Circuit panel wrote that tribes "cannot exclude non-Indians from a state or federal highway" and "lack the ancillary power to investigate non-Indians who are using such public rights-of-way." 919 F. 3d 1135, 1141 (2019). It added that a tribal police officer nonetheless could stop (and hold for a reasonable time) a non-Indian suspect, but only if (1) the officer first tried to determine whether "the person is an Indian," and, if the person turns out to be a non-Indian, (2) it is "apparent" that the person has violated state or federal law. Id., at 1142. Non-Indian status, the panel added, can usually be determined by "ask[ing] one question." Ibid. (internal quotation marks omitted). Because Saylor had not initially tried to determine whether Cooley was an Indian, the panel held that the lower court correctly suppressed the evidence.

The Ninth Circuit denied the Government's request for rehearing en banc. We then granted the Government's petition for certiorari in order to decide whether a tribal police officer has authority to detain temporarily and to search non-Indians traveling on public rights-of-way running through a reservation for potential violations of state or federal law.

II

Long ago we described Indian tribes as "distinct, independent political communities" exercising sovereign authority. Worcester v. Georgia, 6 Pet. 515, 559 (1832). Due to their incorporation into the United States, however, the "sovereignty that the Indian tribes retain is of a unique and limited character." United States v. Wheeler, 435 U. S. 313, 323 (1978). Indian tribes may, for example, determine tribal membership, regulate domestic affairs among tribal members, and exclude others from entering tribal land. See, e.g., Plains Commerce Bank v. Long Family Land & Cattle Co., 554 U. S. 316, 327-328 (2008). On the other hand, owing to their "dependent status," tribes lack any "freedom independently to determine their external relations" and cannot, for instance, "enter into direct commercial or governmental relations with foreign nations." Wheeler, 435 U. S., at 326. Tribes also lack inherent sovereign power to exercise criminal jurisdiction over non-Indians. See Oliphant v. Suquamish Tribe, 435 U. S. 191, 212 (1978). In all cases, tribal authority remains subject to the plenary authority of Congress. See, e.g., Michigan v. Bay Mills Indian Community, 572 U. S. 782, 788 (2014).

Here, no treaty or statute has explicitly divested Indian tribes of the policing authority at issue. We turn to precedent to determine whether a tribe has retained inherent sovereign authority to exercise that power. In answering this question, our decision in Montana v. United States, 450 U. S. 544 (1981), is highly relevant. In that case we asked whether a tribe could regulate hunting and fishing by non-Indians on land that non-Indians owned in fee simple on a reservation. We held that it could not. We supported our conclusion by referring to our holding in Oliphant that a tribe could not "exercise criminal jurisdiction over non-Indians." Montana, 450 U. S., at 565. We then wrote that the "principles on which [Oliphant] relied support the general proposition that the inherent sovereign powers of an Indian tribe do not extend to the activities of nonmembers of the tribe." Ibid.

At the same time, we made clear that Montana's "general proposition" was not an absolute rule. Ibid. We set forth two important exceptions. First, we said that a "tribe may regulate, through taxation, licensing, or other means, the activities of nonmembers who enter consensual relationships with the tribe or its members, through commercial dealing, contracts, leases, or other arrangements." Ibid. Second, we said that a "tribe may also retain inherent power to exercise civil authority over the conduct of non-Indians on fee lands within its reservation when that conduct threatens or has some direct effect on the political integrity, the economic security, or the health or welfare of the tribe." Id., at 566 (emphasis added).

The second exception we have just quoted fits the present case, almost like a glove. The phrase speaks of the protection of the "health or welfare of the tribe." To deny a tribal police officer authority to search and detain for a reasonable time any person he or she believes may commit or has committed a crime would make it difficult for tribes to protect themselves against ongoing threats. Such threats may be posed by, for instance, non-Indian drunk drivers, transporters of contraband, or other criminal offenders operating on roads within the boundaries of a tribal reservation. As the Washington Supreme Court has noted, "[a]llowing a known drunk driver to get back in his or her car, careen off down the road, and possibly kill or injure Indians or non-Indians would certainly be detrimental to the health or welfare of the Tribe." State v. Schmuck, 121 Wash. 2d 373, 391, 850 P. 2d 1332, 1341, cert. denied, 510 U. S. 931 (1993).

We have subsequently repeated Montana's proposition and exceptions in several cases involving a tribe's jurisdiction over the activities of non-Indians within the reservation. See, e.g., Plains Commerce Bank, 554 U. S., at 328-330; Nevada v. Hicks, 533 U. S. 353, 358-360, and n. 3 (2001); South Dakota v. Bourland, 508 U. S. 679, 694-696 (1993); Duro v. Reina, 495 U. S. 676, 687-688 (1990); Brendale v. Confederated Tribes and Bands of Yakima Nation, 492 U. S. 408, 426-430

(1989) (plurality opinion). In doing so we have reserved a tribe's inherent sovereign authority to engage in policing of the kind before us. Most notably, in Strate v. A-1 Contractors, 520 U. S. 438, 456-459 (1997), we relied upon Montana's general jurisdiction-limiting principle to hold that tribal courts did not retain inherent authority to adjudicate personal-injury actions against nonmembers of the tribe based upon automobile accidents that took place on public rights-of-way running through a reservation. But we also said:

"We do not here question the authority of tribal police to patrol roads within a reservation, including rights-of-way made part of a state highway, and to detain and turn over to state officers nonmembers stopped on the highway for conduct violating state law. Cf. State v. Schmuck, 121 Wash. 2d 373, 390, 850 P. 2d 1332, 1341 (en banc) (recognizing that a limited tribal power `to stop and detain alleged offenders in no way confers an unlimited authority to regulate the right of the public to travel on the Reservation's roads'), cert. denied, 510 U. S. 931 (1993)." 520 U. S., at 456, n. 11.

We reiterated this point in Atkinson Trading Co. v. Shirley, 532 U. S. 645, 651 (2001), there confirming that Strate "did not question the ability of tribal police to patrol the highway."

Similarly, we recognized in Duro that "[w]here jurisdiction to try and punish an offender rests outside the tribe, tribal officers may exercise their power to detain the offender and transport him to the proper authorities." 495 U. S., at 697. The authority to search a non-Indian prior to transport is ancillary to this authority that we have already recognized. Cf. Ortiz-Barraza v. United States, 512 F. 2d 1176, 1180-1181 (CA9 1975). Indeed, several state courts and other federal courts have held that tribal officers possess the authority at issue here. See, e.g., Schmuck, 121 Wash. 2d, at 390, 850 P. 2d, at 1341; State v. Pamperien, 156 Ore. App. 153, 155-159, 967 P. 2d

503, 504-506 (1998); State v. Ryder, 98 N. M. 453, 456, 649 P. 2d 756, 759 (1982); see also United States v. Terry, 400 F. 3d 575, 579-580 (CA8 2005); Ortiz-Barraza, 512 F. 2d, at 1180-1181; see generally F. Cohen, Handbook of Federal Indian Law §9.07, p. 773 (2012). To be sure, in Duro we traced the relevant tribal authority to a tribe's right to exclude non-Indians from reservation land. See 495 U. S., at 696-697. But tribes "have inherent sovereignty independent of th[e] authority arising from their power to exclude," Brendale, 492 U. S., at 425 (plurality opinion), and here Montana's second exception recognizes that inherent authority.

We also note that our prior cases denying tribal jurisdiction over the activities of non-Indians on a reservation have rested in part upon the fact that full tribal jurisdiction would require the application of tribal laws to non-Indians who do not belong to the tribe and consequently had no say in creating the laws that would be applied to them. See Duro, 495 U. S., at 693 (noting the concern that tribal-court criminal jurisdiction over nonmembers would subject such defendants to "trial by political bodies that do not include them"); Plains Commerce Bank, 554 U. S., at 337 (noting that nonmembers "have no part in tribal government" and have "no say in the laws and regulations that govern tribal territory"). Saylor's search and detention, however, do not subsequently subject Cooley to tribal law, but rather only to state and federal laws that apply whether an individual is outside a reservation or on a state or federal highway within it. As the Solicitor General points out, an initial investigation of non-Indians'"violations of federal and state laws to which those non-Indians are indisputably subject" protects the public without raising "similar concerns" of the sort raised in our cases limiting tribal authority. Brief for United States 24-25.

Finally, we have doubts about the

workability of the standards that the Ninth Circuit set out. Those standards require tribal officers first to determine whether a suspect is non-Indian and, if so, allow temporary detention only if the violation of law is "apparent." 919 F. 3d, at 1142. The first requirement, even if limited to asking a single question, would produce an incentive to lie. The second requirement—that the violation of law be "apparent"—introduces a new standard into search and seizure law. Whether, or how, that standard would be met is not obvious. At the same time, because most of those who live on Indian reservations are non-Indians, this problem of interpretation could arise frequently. See, e.g., Brief for Former United States Attorneys as Amici Curiae 24 (noting that 3.5 million of the 4.6 million people living in American Indian areas in the 2010 census were non-Indians); Brief for National Indigenous Women's Resource Center et al. as Amici Curiae 19-20 (noting that more than 70% of residents on several reservations are non-Indian).

III

In response, Cooley cautions against "inappropriately expand[ing] the second Montana exception." Brief for Respondent 24-25 (citing Atkinson, 532 U. S., at 657, n. 12, and Strate, 520 U. S., at 457-458). We have previously warned that the Montana exceptions are "limited" and "cannot be construed in a manner that would swallow the rule." Plains Commerce Bank, 554 U. S., at 330 (internal quotation marks omitted). But we have also repeatedly acknowledged the existence of the exceptions and preserved the possibility that "certain forms of nonmember behavior" may "sufficiently affect the tribe as to justify tribal oversight." Id., at 335. Given the close fit between the second exception and the circumstances here, we do not believe the warnings can control the outcome.

Cooley adds that federal cross-deputization statutes already grant many Indian tribes a degree of authority to enforce federal law.

See Brief for Respondent 28-30; see generally 25 U. S. C. §§2803(5), (7) (Secretary of the Interior may authorize tribal officers to "make inquiries of any person" related to the "carrying out in Indian country" of federal law and to "perform any other law enforcement related duty"); §2805 (Secretary of the Interior may promulgate rules "relating to the enforcement of" federal criminal law in Indian country); 25 CFR §12.21 (2019) (Bureau of Indian Affairs may "issue law enforcement commissions" to tribal police officers "to obtain active assistance" in enforcing federal criminal law). Because Congress has specified the scope of tribal police activity through these statutes, Cooley argues, the Court must not interpret tribal sovereignty to fill any remaining gaps in policing authority. See Brief for Respondent 12.

We are not convinced by this argument. The statutory and regulatory provisions to which Cooley refers do not easily fit the present circumstances. They are overinclusive, for instance encompassing the authority to arrest. See §2803(3). And they are also underinclusive. Because these provisions do not govern violations of state law, tribes would still need to strike agreements with a variety of other authorities to ensure complete coverage. See Brief for Cayuga Nation et al. as Amici Curiae 7-8, 25-27. More broadly, cross-deputization agreements are difficult to reach, and they often require negotiation between other authorities and the tribes over such matters as training, reciprocal authority to arrest, the "geographical reach of the agreements, the jurisdiction of the parties, liability of officers performing under the agreements, and sovereign immunity." Fletcher, Fort, & Singel, Indian Country Law Enforcement and Cooperative Public Safety Agreements, 89 Mich. Bar J. 42, 44 (2010).

In short, we see nothing in these provisions that shows that Congress sought to deny tribes the authority at issue, authority that rests upon a tribe's retention of sovereignty as interpreted by Montana, and in particular its second exception. To the contrary, in our view, existing legislation and executive action appear to operate on the assumption that tribes have retained this authority. See, e.g., Brief for Current and Former Members of Congress as Amici Curiae 23-25; Brief for Former U. S. Attorneys as Amici Curiae 28-29.

* * *

For these reasons, we vacate the Ninth Circuit's judgment and remand the case for further proceedings consistent with this opinion.

It is so ordered.

Van Buren v. US (June 3, 2021) [Notes omitted]

Justice BARRETT, delivered the opinion of the Court.

Nathan Van Buren, a former police sergeant, ran a license-plate search in a law enforcement computer database in exchange for money. Van Buren's conduct plainly flouted his department's policy, which authorized him to obtain database information only for law enforcement purposes. We must decide whether Van Buren also violated the Computer Fraud and Abuse Act of 1986 (CFAA), which makes it illegal "to access a computer with authorization and to use such access to obtain or alter information in the computer that the accesser is not entitled so to obtain or alter."

He did not. This provision covers those who obtain information from particular areas in the computer—such as files, folders, or databases— to which their computer access does not extend. It does not cover those who, like Van Buren, have improper motives for obtaining information that is otherwise available to them.

I

A

Technological advances at the dawn of the 1980s brought computers to schools, offices, and homes across the Nation. But as the public and private sectors harnessed the power of computing for improvement and innovation, so-called hackers hatched ways to coopt computers for illegal ends. After a series of highly publicized hackings captured the public's attention, it became clear that traditional theft and trespass statutes were ill suited to address cybercrimes that did not deprive computer owners of property in the traditional sense. See Kerr, Cybercrime's Scope: Interpreting "Access" and "Authorization" in Computer Misuse Statutes, 78 N. Y. U. L. Rev. 1596, 1605-1613 (2003).

Congress, following the lead of several States, responded by enacting the first federal computer-crime statute as part of the Comprehensive Crime Control Act of 1984. § 2102(a), 98 Stat. 2190-2192. A few years later, Congress passed the CFAA, which included the provisions at issue in this case. The Act subjects to criminal liability anyone who "intentionally accesses a computer without authorization or exceeds authorized access," and thereby obtains computer information. 18 U. S. C. § 1030(a)(2). It defines the term "exceeds authorized access" to mean "to access a computer with authorization and to use such access to obtain or alter information in the computer that the accesser is not entitled so to obtain or alter." § 1030(e)(6).

Initially, subsection (a)(2)'s prohibition barred accessing only certain financial information. It has since expanded to cover any information from any computer "used in or affecting interstate or foreign commerce or communication." § 1030(e)(2)(B). As a result, the prohibition now applies—at a minimum—to all information from all computers that connect to the Internet. §§ 1030(a)(2)(C), (e)(2)(B).

Those who violate § 1030(a)(2) face penalties ranging from fines and misdemeanor sentences to imprisonment for up to 10 years. § 1030(c)(2). They also risk civil liability under the CFAA's private cause of action, which allows persons suffering "damage" or "loss" from CFAA violations to sue for money damages and equitable relief. § 1030(g).

B

This case stems from Van Buren's time as a police sergeant in Georgia. In the course of his duties, Van Buren crossed paths with a man named Andrew Albo. The deputy chief of Van Buren's department considered Albo to be "very volatile" and warned officers in the department to deal with him carefully. Notwithstanding that warning, Van Buren developed a friendly relationship with Albo. Or so Van Buren thought when he went to Albo to ask for a personal loan. Unbeknownst to Van Buren, Albo secretly recorded that request and took it to the local sheriff's office, where he complained that Van Buren had sought to "shake him down" for cash.

The taped conversation made its way to the Federal Bureau of Investigation (FBI), which devised an operation to see how far Van Buren would go for money. The steps were straightforward: Albo would ask Van Buren to search the state law enforcement computer database for a license plate purportedly belonging to a woman whom Albo had met at a local strip club. Albo, no stranger to legal troubles, would tell Van Buren that he wanted to ensure that the woman was not in fact an undercover officer. In return for the search, Albo would pay Van Buren around $5,000.

Things went according to plan. Van Buren used his patrol-car computer to access the law enforcement database with his valid credentials. He searched the database for the license plate that Albo had provided. After obtaining the FBI-created license-plate entry, Van Buren told Albo that he had information to share.

The Federal Government then charged Van Buren with a felony violation of the CFAA on the ground that running the license plate for Albo violated the "exceeds authorized access" clause of 18 U. S. C. § 1030(a)(2).[1] The trial evidence showed that Van Buren had been trained not to use the law enforcement database for "an improper purpose," defined as "any personal use." App. 17. Van Buren therefore knew that the search breached department policy. And according to the Government, that violation of department policy also violated the CFAA. Consistent with that position, the Government told the jury that Van Buren's access of the database "for a non[-]law[-]enforcement purpose" violated the CFAA "concept" against "using" a computer network in a way contrary to "what your job or policy prohibits." Id., at 39. The jury convicted Van Buren, and the District Court sentenced him to 18 months in prison.

Van Buren appealed to the Eleventh Circuit, arguing that the "exceeds authorized access" clause applies only to those who obtain information to which their computer access does not extend, not to those who misuse access that they otherwise have. While several Circuits see the clause Van Buren's way, the Eleventh Circuit is among those that have taken a broader view.[2] Consistent with its Circuit precedent, the panel held that Van Buren had violated the CFAA by accessing the law enforcement database for an "inappropriate reason." 940 F. 3d 1192, 1208 (2019). We granted certiorari to resolve the split in authority regarding the scope of liability under the CFAA's "exceeds authorized access" clause. 590 U. S. ___ (2020).

II

A

1

Both Van Buren and the Government raise a host of policy arguments to support their respective interpretations. But we start where we always do: with the text of the statute. Here, the most relevant text is the phrase "exceeds authorized access," which means "to access a computer with authorization and to use such access to obtain . . . information in the computer that the accesser is not entitled so to obtain." § 1030(e)(6).

The parties agree that Van Buren "access[ed] a computer with authorization" when he used his patrol-car computer and valid credentials to log into the law enforcement database. They also agree that Van Buren "obtain[ed] . . . information in the computer" when he acquired the license-plate record for Albo. The dispute is whether Van Buren was "entitled so to obtain" the record.

"Entitle" means "to give . . . a title, right, or claim to something." Random House Dictionary of the English Language 649 (2d ed. 1987). See also Black's Law Dictionary 477 (5th ed. 1979) ("to give a right or legal title to"). The parties agree that Van Buren had been given the right to acquire license-plate information—that is, he was "entitled to obtain" it—from the law enforcement computer database. But was Van Buren "entitled so to obtain" the license-plate information, as the statute requires?

Van Buren says yes. He notes that "so," as used in this statute, serves as a term of reference that recalls "the same manner as has been stated" or "the way or manner described." Black's Law Dictionary, at 1246; 15 Oxford English Dictionary 887 (2d ed. 1989). The disputed phrase "entitled so to obtain" thus asks whether one has the right, in "the same manner as has been stated," to obtain the relevant information. And the only manner of obtaining information already stated in the definitional provision is "via a computer [one] is otherwise authorized to access." Reply Brief 3. Putting that together, Van Buren contends that the disputed phrase—"is not entitled so to obtain"— plainly refers to information one is not allowed to obtain by using a computer that he is authorized to

access. On this reading, if a person has access to information stored in a computer— e.g., in "Folder Y," from which the person could permissibly pull information—then he does not violate the CFAA by obtaining such information, regardless of whether he pulled the information for a prohibited purpose. But if the information is instead located in prohibited "Folder X," to which the person lacks access, he violates the CFAA by obtaining such information.

The Government agrees that the statute uses "so" in the word's term-of-reference sense, but it argues that "so" sweeps more broadly. It reads the phrase "is not entitled so to obtain" to refer to information one was not allowed to obtain in the particular manner or circumstances in which he obtained it. The manner or circumstances in which one has a right to obtain information, the Government says, are defined by any "specifically and explicitly" communicated limits on one's right to access information. Brief for United States 19. As the Government sees it, an employee might lawfully pull information from Folder Y in the morning for a permissible purpose—say, to prepare for a business meeting—but unlawfully pull the same information from Folder Y in the afternoon for a prohibited purpose—say, to help draft a resume to submit to a competitor employer.

The Government's interpretation has surface appeal but proves to be a sleight of hand. While highlighting that "so" refers to a "manner or circumstance," the Government simultaneously ignores the definition's further instruction that such manner or circumstance already will "`ha[ve] been stated,'" "`asserted,'" or "`described.'" Id., at 18 (quoting Black's Law Dictionary, at 1246; 15 Oxford English Dictionary, at 887). Under the Government's approach, the relevant circumstance—the one rendering a person's conduct illegal—is not identified earlier in the statute. Instead, "so" captures any circumstance-based limit appearing anywhere—in the United

States Code, a state statute, a private agreement, or anywhere else. And while the Government tries to cabin its interpretation by suggesting that any such limit must be "specifically and explicitly" stated, "express," and "inherent in the authorization itself," the Government does not identify any textual basis for these guardrails. Brief for United States 19; Tr. of Oral Arg. 41.

Van Buren's account of "so"—namely, that "so" references the previously stated "manner or circumstance" in the text of § 1030(e)(6) itself—is more plausible than the Government's. "So" is not a free-floating term that provides a hook for any limitation stated anywhere. It refers to a stated, identifiable proposition from the "preceding" text; indeed, "so" typically "[r]epresent[s]" a "word or phrase already employed," thereby avoiding the need for repetition. 15 Oxford English Dictionary, at 887; see Webster's Third New International Dictionary 2160 (1986) (so "often used as a substitute . . . to express the idea of a preceding phrase"). Myriad federal statutes illustrate this ordinary usage.[3] We agree with Van Buren: The phrase "is not entitled so to obtain" is best read to refer to information that a person is not entitled to obtain by using a computer that he is authorized to access.[4]

2

The Government's primary counterargument is that Van Buren's reading renders the word "so" superfluous. Recall the definition: "to access a computer with authorization and to use such access to obtain . . . information in the computer that the accesser is not entitled so to obtain." § 1030(e)(6) (emphasis added). According to the Government, "so" adds nothing to the sentence if it refers solely to the earlier stated manner of obtaining the information through use of a computer one has accessed with authorization. What matters on Van Buren's reading, as the Government sees it, is simply that the person obtain information that he is not

entitled to obtain—and that point could be made even if "so" were deleted. By contrast, the Government insists, "so" makes a valuable contribution if it incorporates all of the circumstances that might qualify a person's right to obtain information. Because only its interpretation gives "so" work to do, the Government contends, the rule against superfluity means that its interpretation wins. See Republic of Sudan v. Harrison, 587 U. S. ___, ___ (2019) (slip op., at 10).

But the canon does not help the Government because Van Buren's reading does not render "so" superfluous. As Van Buren points out, without "so," the statute would allow individuals to use their right to obtain information in nondigital form as a defense to CFAA liability. Consider, for example, a person who downloads restricted personnel files he is not entitled to obtain by using his computer. Such a person could argue that he was "entitled to obtain" the information if he had the right to access personnel files through another method (e.g., by requesting hard copies of the files from human resources). With "so," the CFAA forecloses that theory of defense. The statute is concerned with what a person does on a computer; it does not excuse hacking into an electronic personnel file if the hacker could have walked down the hall to pick up a physical copy.

This clarification is significant because it underscores that one kind of entitlement to information counts: the right to access the information by using a computer. That can expand liability, as the above example shows. But it narrows liability too. Without the word "so," the statute could be read to incorporate all kinds of limitations on one's entitlement to information. The dissent's take on the statute illustrates why.

3

While the dissent accepts Van Buren's definition of "so," it would arrive at the Government's result by way of the word "entitled."

One is "entitled" to do something, the dissent contends, only when "`proper grounds'" are in place. Post, at 3 (opinion of THOMAS, J.) (quoting Black's Law Dictionary, at 477). Deciding whether a person was "entitled" to obtain information, the dissent continues, therefore demands a "circumstance dependent" analysis of whether access was proper. Post, at 3. This reading, like the Government's, would extend the statute's reach to any circumstance-based limit appearing anywhere.

The dissent's approach to the word "entitled" fares fine in the abstract but poorly in context. The statute does not refer to "information . . . that the accesser is not entitled to obtain." It refers to "information . . . that the accesser is not entitled so to obtain." 18 U. S. C. § 1030(e)(6) (emphasis added). The word "entitled," then, does not stand alone, inviting the reader to consider the full scope of the accesser's entitlement to information. The modifying phrase "so to obtain" directs the reader to consider a specific limitation on the accesser's entitlement: his entitlement to obtain the information "in the manner previously stated." Supra, at 7. And as already explained, the manner previously stated is using a computer one is authorized to access. Thus, while giving lipservice to Van Buren's reading of "so," the dissent, like the Government, declines to give "so" any limiting function.[5]

The dissent cannot have it both ways. The consequence of accepting Van Buren's reading of "so" is the narrowed scope of "entitled." In fact, the dissent's examples implicitly concede as much: They all omit the word "so," thereby giving "entitled" its full sweep. See post, at 3-4. An approach that must rewrite the statute to work is even less persuasive than the Government's.

4

The Government falls back on what it describes as the "common parlance" meaning of the phrase "exceeds authorized access." Brief for United States 20-21. According to the Government, any ordinary speaker of the English language would think that Van Buren "exceed[ed] his authorized access" to the law enforcement database when he obtained license-plate information for personal purposes. Id., at 21. The dissent, for its part, asserts that this point "settles" the case. Post, at 9.

If the phrase "exceeds authorized access" were all we had to go on, the Government and the dissent might have a point. But both breeze by the CFAA's explicit definition of the phrase "exceeds authorized access." When "a statute includes an explicit definition" of a term, "we must follow that definition, even if it varies from a term's ordinary meaning." Tanzin v. Tanvir, 592 U. S. ___, ___ (2020) (slip op., at 3) (internal quotation marks omitted). So the relevant question is not whether Van Buren exceeded his authorized access but whether he exceeded his authorized access as the CFAA defines that phrase. And as we have already explained, the statutory definition favors Van Buren's reading.

That reading, moreover, is perfectly consistent with the way that an "appropriately informed" speaker of the language would understand the meaning of "exceeds authorized access." Nelson, What Is Textualism? 91 Va. L. Rev. 347, 354 (2005). When interpreting statutes, courts take note of terms that carry "technical meaning[s]." A. Scalia & B. Garner, Reading Law: The Interpretation of Legal Texts 73 (2012). "Access" is one such term, long carrying a "well established" meaning in the "computational sense"— a meaning that matters when interpreting a statute about computers. American Heritage Dictionary 10 (3d ed. 1992). In the computing context, "access" references the act of entering a computer "system itself" or a particular "part of a computer system," such as files, folders, or databases.[6] It is thus consistent with that meaning to equate "exceed[ing] authorized access" with the act of entering a part of the system to which a computer user lacks access privileges.[7] The Government and the dissent's broader interpretation is neither the only possible nor even necessarily the most natural one.

B

While the statute's language "spells trouble" for the Government's position, a "wider look at the statute's structure gives us even more reason for pause." Romag Fasteners, Inc. v. Fossil Group, Inc., 590 U. S. ___, ___-___ (2020) (slip op., at 2-3).

The interplay between the "without authorization" and "exceeds authorized access" clauses of subsection (a)(2) is particularly probative. Those clauses specify two distinct ways of obtaining information unlawfully. First, an individual violates the provision when he "accesses a computer without authorization." § 1030(a)(2). Second, an individual violates the provision when he "exceeds authorized access" by accessing a computer "with authorization" and then obtaining information he is "not entitled so to obtain." §§ 1030(a)(2), (e)(6). Van Buren's reading places the provision's parts "into an harmonious whole." Roberts v. Sea-Land Services, Inc., 566 U. S. 93, 100 (2012) (internal quotation marks omitted). The Government's does not.

Start with Van Buren's view. The "without authorization" clause, Van Buren contends, protects computers themselves by targeting so-called outside hackers—those who "acces[s] a computer without any permission at all." LVRC Holdings LLC v. Brekka, 581 F. 3d 1127, 1133 (CA9 2009); see also Pulte Homes, Inc. v. Laborers' Int'l Union of North Am., 648 F. 3d 295, 304 (CA6 2011). Van Buren reads the "exceeds authorized access" clause to provide complementary protection for certain information within computers. It does so, Van Buren asserts, by targeting so-called inside hackers—those who access a computer with permission, but then "`exceed' the parameters of authorized access by

entering an area of the computer to which [that] authorization does not extend." United States v. Valle, 807 F. 3d 508, 524 (CA2 2015).

Van Buren's account of subsection (a)(2) makes sense of the statutory structure because it treats the "without authorization" and "exceeds authorized access" clauses consistently. Under Van Buren's reading, liability under both clauses stems from a gates-up-or-down inquiry—one either can or cannot access a computer system, and one either can or cannot access certain areas within the system.[8] And reading both clauses to adopt a gates-up-or-down approach aligns with the computer-context understanding of access as entry. See supra, at 11-12.[9]

By contrast, the Government's reading of the "exceeds authorized access" clause creates "inconsistenc[ies] with the design and structure" of subsection (a)(2). University of Tex. Southwestern Medical Center v. Nassar, 570 U. S. 338, 353 (2013). As discussed, the Government reads the "exceeds authorized access" clause to incorporate purposebased limits contained in contracts and workplace policies. Yet the Government does not read such limits into the threshold question whether someone uses a computer "without authorization"—even though similar purpose restrictions, like a rule against personal use, often govern one's right to access a computer in the first place. See, e.g., Royal Truck & Trailer Sales & Serv., Inc. v. Kraft, 974 F. 3d 756, 757 (CA6 2020). Thus, the Government proposes to read the first phrase "without authorization" as a gates-upor-down inquiry and the second phrase "exceeds authorized access" as one that depends on the circumstances. The Government does not explain why the statute would prohibit accessing computer information, but not the computer itself, for an improper purpose.[10]

The Government's position has another structural problem. Recall that violating § 1030(a)(2), the provision under which Van Buren was charged, also gives rise to civil liability. See § 1030(g). Provisions defining "damage" and "loss" specify what a plaintiff in a civil suit can recover. "`[D]amage,'" the statute provides, means "any impairment to the integrity or availability of data, a program, a system, or information." § 1030(e)(8). The term "loss" likewise relates to costs caused by harm to computer data, programs, systems, or information services. § 1030(e)(11). The statutory definitions of "damage" and "loss" thus focus on technological harms—such as the corruption of files—of the type unauthorized users cause to computer systems and data. Limiting "damage" and "loss" in this way makes sense in a scheme "aimed at preventing the typical consequences of hacking." Royal Truck, 974 F. 3d, at 760. The term's definitions are ill fitted, however, to remediating "misuse" of sensitive information that employees may permissibly access using their computers. Ibid. Van Buren's situation is illustrative: His run of the license plate did not impair the "integrity or availability" of data, nor did it otherwise harm the database system itself.

C

Pivoting from text and structure, the Government claims that precedent and statutory history support its interpretation. These arguments are easily dispatched.

As for precedent, the Government asserts that this Court's decision in Musacchio v. United States, 577 U. S. 237 (2016), bolsters its reading. There, in addressing a question about the standard of review for instructional error, the Court described § 1030(a)(2) as prohibiting "(1) obtaining access without authorization; and (2) obtaining access with authorization but then using that access improperly." Id., at 240. This paraphrase of the statute does not do much for the Government. As an initial matter, Musacchio did not address—much less resolve in the Government's favor—the "point now at issue," and

we thus "are not bound to follow" any dicta in the case. Central Va. Community College v. Katz, 546 U. S. 356, 363 (2006). But in any event, Van Buren's interpretation, no less than the Government's, involves "using [one's] access improperly." It is plainly "improper" for one to use the opportunity his computer access provides to obtain prohibited information from within the computer.

As for statutory history, the Government claims that the original 1984 Act supports its interpretation of the current version. In a precursor to the "exceeds authorized access" clause, the 1984 Act covered any person who, "having accessed a computer with authorization, uses the opportunity such access provides for purposes to which such authorization does not extend," and thus expressly alluded to the purpose of an insider's computer access. 18 U. S. C. § 1030(a)(2) (1982 ed. Supp. III). According to the Government, this confirms that the amended CFAA—which makes no mention of purpose in defining "exceeds authorized access"—likewise covers insiders like Van Buren who use their computer access for an unauthorized purpose.[11] The Government's argument gets things precisely backward. "When Congress amends legislation, courts must presume it intends the change to have real and substantial effect." Ross v. Blake, 578 U. S. 632, 641-642 (2016) (internal quotation marks and brackets omitted). Congress' choice to remove the statute's reference to purpose thus cuts against reading the statute "to capture that very concept." Brief for United States 22. The statutory history thus hurts rather than helps the Government's position.

III

To top it all off, the Government's interpretation of the statute would attach criminal penalties to a breathtaking amount of commonplace computer activity. Van Buren frames the far-reaching consequences of the

Government's reading as triggering the rule of lenity or constitutional avoidance. That is not how we see it: Because the text, context, and structure support Van Buren's reading, neither of these canons is in play. Still, the fallout underscores the implausibility of the Government's interpretation. It is "extra icing on a cake already frosted." Yates v. United States, 574 U. S. 528, 557 (2015) (KAGAN, J., dissenting).

If the "exceeds authorized access" clause criminalizes every violation of a computer-use policy, then millions of otherwise law-abiding citizens are criminals. Take the workplace. Employers commonly state that computers and electronic devices can be used only for business purposes. So on the Government's reading of the statute, an employee who sends a personal e-mail or reads the news using her work computer has violated the CFAA. Or consider the Internet. Many websites, services, and databases—which provide "information" from "protected computer[s]," § 1030(a)(2)(C)—authorize a user's access only upon his agreement to follow specified terms of service. If the "exceeds authorized access" clause encompasses violations of circumstance-based access restrictions on employers' computers, it is difficult to see why it would not also encompass violations of such restrictions on website providers' computers. And indeed, numerous amici explain why the Government's reading of subsection (a)(2) would do just that— criminalize everything from embellishing an online-dating profile to using a pseudonym on Facebook. See Brief for Orin Kerr as Amicus Curiae 10-11; Brief for Technology Companies as Amici Curiae 6, n. 3, 11; see also Brief for Reporters Committee for Freedom of the Press et al. as Amici Curiae 10-13 (journalism activity); Brief for Kyratso Karahalios et al. as Amici Curiae 11-17 (online civil-rights testing and research).

In response to these points, the Government posits that other terms in the statute—specifically "authorization" and "use"— "may well" serve to cabin its prosecutorial power. Brief for United States 35; see Tr. of Oral Arg. 38, 40, 58 ("instrumental" use; "individualized" and "fairly specific" authorization). Yet the Government stops far short of endorsing such limitations. Cf. Brief for United States 37 (concept of "authorization" "may not logically apply"); id., at 38 ("`use'" might be read in a more "limited" fashion, even though it "often has a broader definition"); see also, e.g., post, at 11-12 (mens rea requirement "might" preclude liability in some cases). Nor does it cite any prior instance in which it has read the statute to contain such limitations— to the contrary, Van Buren cites instances where it hasn't. See Reply Brief 14-15, 17 (collecting cases); cf. Sandvig v. Barr, 451 F. Supp. 3d 73, 81-82 (DC 2020) (discussing Department of Justice testimony indicating that the Government could "`bring a CFAA prosecution based'" on terms-of-service violations causing "`de minimis harm'"). If anything, the Government's current CFAA charging policy shows why Van Buren's concerns are far from "hypothetical," post, at 12: The policy instructs that federal prosecution "may not be warranted"—not that it would be prohibited—"if the defendant exceed[s] authorized access solely by violating an access restriction contained in a contractual agreement or term of service with an Internet service provider or website."[12] And while the Government insists that the intent requirement serves as yet another safety valve, that requirement would do nothing for those who intentionally use their computers in a way their "job or policy prohibits"—for example, by checking sports scores or paying bills at work. App. 39.

One final observation: The Government's approach would inject arbitrariness into the assessment of criminal liability. The Government concedes, as it must, that the "exceeds authorized access" clause prohibits only unlawful information "access," not downstream information "`misus[e].'" Brief in Opposition 17 (statute does not cover "`subsequen[t] misus[e of] information'"). But the line between the two can be thin on the Government's reading. Because purpose-based limits on access are often designed with an eye toward information misuse, they can be expressed as either access or use restrictions. For example, one police department might prohibit using a confidential database for a non-law-enforcement purpose (an access restriction), while another might prohibit using information from the database for a non-law-enforcement purpose (a use restriction). Conduct like Van Buren's can be characterized either way, and an employer might not see much difference between the two. On the Government's reading, however, the conduct would violate the CFAA only if the employer phrased the policy as an access restriction. An interpretation that stakes so much on a fine distinction controlled by the drafting practices of private parties is hard to sell as the most plausible.

IV

In sum, an individual "exceeds authorized access" when he accesses a computer with authorization but then obtains information located in particular areas of the computer— such as files, folders, or databases—that are off limits to him. The parties agree that Van Buren accessed the law enforcement database system with authorization. The only question is whether Van Buren could use the system to retrieve license-plate information. Both sides agree that he could. Van Buren accordingly did not "excee[d] authorized access" to the database, as the CFAA defines that phrase, even though he obtained information from the database for an improper purpose. We therefore reverse the contrary judgment of the Eleventh Circuit and remand the case for further proceedings consistent with this opinion.

It is so ordered.

Made in the USA
Las Vegas, NV
20 January 2025

16672830R00450